The Oxford Colour Russian Dictionary

compiled by
Della Thompson

D0242870

OXFORD UNIVERSITY PRESS

OXFORD
UNIVERSITY PRESS

Great Clarendon Street, Oxford OX2 6DP

Oxford University Press is a department of the University of Oxford.
It furthers the University's objective of excellence in research, scholarship,
and education by publishing worldwide in

Oxford New York

Athens Auckland Bangkok Bogotá Buenos Aires Cape Town
Chennai Dar es Salaam Delhi Florence Hong Kong Istanbul Karachi
Kolkata Kuala Lumpur Madrid Melbourne Mexico City Mumbai Nairobi
Paris São Paulo Shanghai Singapore Taipei Tokyo Toronto Warsaw

with associated companies in Berlin Ibadan

© Oxford University Press, 1998

First published 1996 as The Oxford Paperback Russian Dictionary
First published 1998 as The Oxford Colour Russian Dictionary

British Library Cataloguing in Publication Data

Data available

Library of Congress Cataloging in Publication Data

Data available

ISBN 0–19–860211–1

10 9 8 7 6 5 4 3

Printed in Spain by
Mateu Cromo Artes Graficas S.A.
Madrid

Contents

Preface

The Oxford Colour Russian Dictionary is the latest addition to the Oxford Russian Dictionary range. Colour headwords throughout make it the most useful and easy-to-use dictionary for beginners. The word games in the centre of the dictionary build knowledge of grammar and vocabulary, and provide valuable practice in using your dictionary, helping you get the best out of it.

Particular attention has been given to the provision of inflected forms where these cause difficulty, and to showing the stressed syllable of every Russian word as well as changes in stress where they occur. Perfective and imperfective aspects are distinguished and both are given wherever appropriate.

Thanks are due to Alexander and Nina Levtov for their editorial help and valuable advice on contemporary Russian usage, and to Helen McCurdy for help with proofreading.

D. J. T.

Introduction

As an aid to easy reference all main headwords, compounds, and derivatives appear in blue.

In order to save space, related words are often grouped together in paragraphs, as are cross-references and compound entries.

The swung dash (∼) and the hyphen are also used to save space. The swung dash represents the headword preceding it in bold, or the preceding Russian word, e.g. **Georgian** *n* грузи́н, ∼ка. The hyphen is mainly used, in giving grammatical forms, to stand for part of the preceding, or (less often) following, Russian word, e.g. **приходи́ть** (-ожу́, -о́дишь).

Russian headwords are followed by inflexional information where considered necessary. So-called regular inflexions for the purpose of this dictionary are listed in the Appendices.

Where a noun ending is given but not labeled in the singular, it is the genitive ending; other cases are named; in the plural, where cases are identifiable by their endings, they are not labelled, e.g. **сестра́** (*pl* сёстры, сестёр, сёстрам). The gender of Russian nouns can usually be deduced from their endings and it is indicated only in exceptional cases (e.g. for masculine nouns in **-а**, **-я**, and **-ь**, neuter nouns in **-мя**, and all indeclinable nouns).

Verbs are labeled *impf* or *pf* to show their aspect. Where a perfective verb is formed by the addition of a prefix to the imperfective, this is shown at the headword by a light vertical stroke, e.g. про|лепета́ть. When a verb requires the use of a case other than the accusative, this is indicated, e.g. **маха́ть** *impf*, **махну́ть** *pf* + *instr* wave, brandish.

Both the comma and the ampersand (&) are used to show alternatives, e.g. **хоте́ть** + *gen, acc* means that the Russian verb may govern either the genitive or accusative; **сирота́** *m* & *f* orphan means that the Russian noun is treated as masculine or feminine according to the sex of the person denoted;

Cossack *n* каза́к, -а́чка represents the masculine and feminine translations of Cossack; **dilate** *vt* & *i* расширя́ть(ся) means that the Russian verb forms cover both the transitive and intransitive English verbs.

Stress

The stress of Russian words is shown by an acute accent over the vowel of the stressed syllable. The vowel ё has no stress-mark since it is almost always stressed. The presence of two stress-marks indicates that either of the marked syllables may be stressed.

Changes of stress in inflexion are shown, e.g.

  i) **предложи́ть** (-жу́, -жишь)

The absence of a stress-mark on the second person singular indicates that the stress is on the preceding syllable and that the rest of the conjugation is stressed in this way.

  ii) **нача́ть** (............; на́чал, -а́, -о)

The final form, на́чало, takes the stress of the first of the two preceding forms when these differ from each other. Forms that are not shown, here на́чали, are stressed like the last form given.

  iii) **дождь** (-дя́)

The single form given in brackets is the genitive singular and all other forms have the same stressed syllable.

  iv) **душа́** (*acc* -у; *pl* -и)

If only one case-labeled form is given in the singular, it is an exception to the regular paradigm. If only one plural form is given (the nominative), the rest follow this. In other words, in this example, the accusative singular and all the plural forms have initial stress.

  v) **скоба́** (*pl* -ы, -а́м)

In the plural, forms that are not shown (here instrumental and prepositional) are stressed like the last form given.

Proprietary terms

This dictionary includes some words which are, or are asserted to be, proprietary names or trade marks. Their inclusion does not imply that they have acquired for legal purposes a non-proprietary or general significance, nor is any other judgement implied concerning their legal status. In cases where the editor has some evidence that a word is used as a proprietary name or trade mark this is indicated by the label *propr*, but no judgement concerning the legal status of such words is made or implied thereby.

Abbreviations

abbr	abbreviation	fig	figurative
abs	absolute	fut	future (tense)
acc	accusative		
adj, adjs	adjective(s)	gen	genitive
adv, advs	adverb(s)	geog	geography
aeron	aeronautics	geol	geology
agric	agriculture	geom	geometry
anat	anatomy	gram	grammar
approx	approximate(ly)		
archaol	archaeology	hist	historical
archit	architecture		
astron	astronomy	imper	imperative
attrib	attributive	impers	impersonal
aux	auxiliary	impf	imperfective
		indecl	indeclinable
bibl	biblical	indef	indefinite
biol	biology	indet	indeterminate
bot	botany	inf	infinitive
		instr	instrumental
chem	chemistry	int	interjection
cin	cinema(tography)	interrog	interrogative
coll	colloquial		
collect	collective(ly)	ling	linguistics
comb	combination	loc	locative
comm	commerce		
comp	comparative	m	masculine
comput	computing	math	mathematics
conj, conjs	conjunction(s)	med	medicine
cul	culinary	meteorol	meteorology
		mil	military
dat	dative	mus	music
def	definite		
derog	derogatory	n	noun
det	determinate	naut	nautical
dim	diminutive	neg	negative
		neut	neuter
eccl	ecclesiastical	nn	nouns
econ	economics	nom	nominative
electr	electricity		
electron	electronics	o.s.	oneself
emph	emphatic		
esp	especially	parl	parliamentary
etc.	etcetera	part	participle
		partl	particle
f	feminine	pers	person

pf	perfective
philos	philosophy
phon	phonetics
phot	photography
phys	physics
pl	plural
polit	political
poss	possessive
predic	predicate; predicative
pref	prefix
prep	preposition; prepositional
pres	present (tense)
pron, prons	pronoun(s)
propr	proprietary term
psych	psychology
refl	reflexive
rel	relative
relig	religion; religious
rly	railway
sb	substantive
sg	singular
sl	slang
s.o.	someone
sth	something
superl	superlative
tech	technical
tel	telephony
theat	theatre
theol	theology
univ	university
usu	usually
v	verb
v aux	auxiliary verb
vbl	verbal
vi	intransitive verb
voc	vocative
vt	transitive verb
vulg	vulgar
vv	verbs
zool	zoology

A

a¹ *conj* and, but; **a (не) то** or else, otherwise.

a² *int* oh, ah.

абажу́р lampshade.

абба́тство abbey.

аббревиату́ра abbreviation.

абза́ц indention; paragraph.

абонеме́нт subscription, season ticket. **абоне́нт** subscriber.

абориге́н aborigine.

або́рт abortion; **де́лать** *impf,* **с~** *pf* **~** have an abortion.

абрико́с apricot.

абсолю́тно *adv* absolutely. **абсолю́тный** absolute.

абстра́ктный abstract.

абсу́рд absurdity; the absurd. **абсу́рдный** absurd.

абсце́сс abscess.

аванга́рд advanced guard; vanguard; avant-garde. **аванга́рдный** avant-garde. **аванпо́ст** outpost; forward position.

ава́нс advance (*of money*); *pl* advances, overtures. **ава́нсом** *adv* in advance, on account.

авансце́на proscenium.

авантю́ра (*derog*) adventure; venture; escapade; shady enterprise. **авантюри́ст** (*derog*) adventurer. **авантюри́стка** (*derog*) adventuress. **авантю́рный** adventurous; adventure.

авари́йный breakdown; emergency. **ава́рия** accident, crash; breakdown.

а́вгуст August. **а́вгустовский** August.

а́виа *abbr* (*of* **авиапо́чтой**) by airmail.

авиа- *abbr in comb* (*of* **авиацио́нный**) air-, aero-; aviation. **авиали́ния** air-route, airway. **~но́сец (-сца)** aircraft carrier. **~по́чта** airmail.

авиацио́нный aviation; flying; aircraft. **авиа́ция** aviation; aircraft; airforce.

авока́до *neut indecl* avocado (pear).

аво́сь *adv* perhaps; **на ~** at random, on the off-chance.

австрали́ец (-и́йца), австрали́йка Australian. **австрали́йский** Australian. **Австра́лия** Australia.

австри́ец (-и́йца), австри́йка Austrian. **австри́йский** Austrian. **А́встрия** Austria.

авто- *in comb* self-; auto-; automatic; motor-. **автоба́за** motor-transport depot. **~биографи́ческий** autobiographical. **~биогра́фия** autobiography; curriculum vitae. **автобус** bus. **~вокза́л** bus-station. **авто́граф** autograph. **~запра́вочная ста́нция** petrol station. **~кра́т** autocrat. **~крати́ческий** autocratic. **~кра́тия** autocracy. **~магистра́ль** motorway. **~маши́на** motor vehicle. **~моби́ль** *m* car. **~но́мия** autonomy. **~но́мный** autonomous; self-contained. **~пило́т** automatic pilot. **~портре́т** self-portrait. **~ру́чка** fountain-pen. **~ста́нция** bus-station. **~стра́да** motorway.

автома́т slot-machine; automatic device, weapon, gun; sub-machine gun; robot; **(телефо́н-)~** public call-box. **автоматиза́ция** automation. **автоматизи́ровать** *impf & pf* automate; make automatic. **автомати́ческий** automatic.

а́втор author; composer; inventor; (*fig*) architect.

авторизо́ванный authorized.

авторите́т authority. **авторите́тный** authoritative.

а́вторск|ий author's; **~ий гонора́р** royalty; **~ое пра́во** copyright. **а́вторство** authorship.

ага́ *int* aha; yes.

аге́нт agent. **аге́нтство** agency. **агенту́ра** (network of) agents.

агита́тор agitator, propagandist; canvasser. **агитацио́нный** propaganda. **агита́ция** propaganda, agitation;

campaign. **агити́ровать** *impf* (*pf* c~) agitate, campaign; (try to) persuade, win over. **агитпу́нкт** *abbr* agitation centre.

агóния agony.

агрáрный agrarian.

агрегáт aggregate; unit.

агресси́вный aggressive. **агрéссия** aggression. **агрéссор** aggressor.

агронóм agronomist. **агронóмия** agriculture.

ад (*loc* -ý) hell.

адáптер adapter; (*mus*) pick-up.

адвокáт lawyer. **адвокату́ра** legal profession; lawyers.

администрати́вный administrative. **администрáтор** manager. **администрáция** administration; management.

адмирáл admiral.

áдрес (*pl* -á) address. **адресáт** addressee. **áдрес|ый** address; ~ая кни́га directory. **адресовáть** *impf* & *pf* address, send.

áдский infernal, hellish.

адъютáнт aide-de-camp; стáрший ~ adjutant.

ажу́рн|ый delicate, lacy; ~ая рабóта openwork; tracery.

азáрт heat; excitement; fervour, ardour, passion. **азáртн|ый** venturesome; heated; ~ая игрá game of chance.

áзбука alphabet; ABC.

Азербайджáн Azerbaijan. **азербайджáнец** (-нца), **азербайджáнка** Azerbaijani. **азербайджáнский** Azerbaijani.

азиáт, ~ка Asian. **азиáтский** Asian, Asiatic. **Áзия** Asia.

азóт nitrogen.

áист stork.

ай *int* oh; oo.

áйсберг iceberg.

акадéмик academician. **академи́ческий** academic. **акадéмия** academy.

аквалáнг aqualung.

акварéль water-colour.

аквáриум aquarium.

акведýк aqueduct.

акклиматизи́ровать *impf* & *pf* acclimatize; ~ся become acclimatized. **аккомпанемéнт** accompaniment; под ~ +*gen* to the accompaniment

of. **аккомпаниáтор** accompanist. **аккомпани́ровать** *impf* +*dat* accompany.

аккóрд chord.

аккордеóн accordion.

аккóрдн|ый by agreement; ~ая рабóта piece-work.

аккредити́в letter of credit. **аккредитовáть** *impf* & *pf* accredit.

аккумуля́тор accumulator.

аккурáтный neat, careful; punctual; exact, thorough.

акри́л acrylic. **акри́ловый** acrylic.

акробáт acrobat.

аксессуáр accessory; (stage) props.

аксиóма axiom.

акт act; deed, document; обвини́тельный ~ indictment.

актёр actor.

акти́в (*comm*) asset(s).

активизáция stirring up, making (more) active. **активизи́ровать** *impf* & *pf* make (more) active, stir up. **акти́вный** active.

акти́ровать *impf* & *pf* (*pf also* c~) register, record, presence or absence of; (*sl*) write off.

áктовый зал assembly hall.

актри́са actress.

актуáльный topical, urgent.

акýла shark.

акýстика acoustics. **акусти́ческий** acoustic.

акушéр obstetrician. **акушéрка** midwife.

акцéнт accent, stress. **акценти́ровать** *impf* & *pf* accent; accentuate.

акционéр shareholder. **акционéрный** joint-stock. **áкция**[1] share; *pl* stock. **áкция**[2] action.

áлгебра algebra.

áлиби *neut indecl* alibi.

алимéнты (*pl*; *gen* -ов) (*law*) maintenance.

алкоголи́зм alcoholism. **алкогóлик** alcoholic. **алкогóль** *m* alcohol. **алкогóльный** alcoholic.

аллегóрия allegory.

аллéргия allergy.

аллéя avenue; path, walk.

аллигáтор alligator.

аллó hello! (*on telephone*).

алмáз diamond.

алтáрь (-я́) *m* altar; chancel, sanctuary.

алфави́т alphabet. алфави́тный alphabetical.

а́лчный greedy, grasping.

а́лый scarlet.

альбо́м album; sketch-book.

альмана́х literary miscellany; almanac.

альпи́йский Alpine. альпини́зм mountaineering. альпини́ст, альпини́стка (mountain-)climber.

альт (-а́; pl -ы́) alto; viola.

альтернати́ва alternative. альтернати́вный alternative.

альтруисти́ческий altruistic.

алюми́ний aluminium.

амазо́нка Amazon; horsewoman; riding-habit.

амба́р barn; storehouse, warehouse.

амби́ция pride; arrogance.

амбулато́рия out-patients' department; surgery. амбулато́рный больно́й sb outpatient.

Аме́рика America. америка́нец (-нца), америка́нка American. америка́нский American; US.

аминокислота́ amino acid.

ами́нь m amen.

аммиа́к ammonia.

амни́стия amnesty.

амора́льный amoral; immoral.

амортиза́тор shock-absorber. амортиза́ция depreciation; shock-absorption.

ампе́р (gen pl ампе́р) ampere.

ампута́ция amputation. ампути́ровать impf & pf amputate.

амфетами́н amphetamine.

амфи́бия amphibian.

амфитеа́тр amphitheatre; circle.

ана́лиз analysis; ~ кро́ви blood test. анализи́ровать impf & pf analyse. анали́тик analyst. аналити́ческий analytic(al).

ана́лог analogue. аналоги́чный analogous. анало́гия analogy.

анана́с pineapple.

анархи́ст, ~ка anarchist. анархи́ческий anarchic. ана́рхия anarchy.

анатоми́ческий anatomical. анато́мия anatomy.

анахрони́зм anachronism. анахрони́ческий anachronistic.

анга́р hangar.

а́нгел angel. а́нгельский angelic.

анги́на sore throat.

англи́йск|ий English; ~ая була́вка safety-pin. англича́нин (pl -ча́не, -ча́н) Englishman. англича́нка Englishwoman. А́нглия England, Britain.

анекдо́т anecdote, story; funny thing.

анеми́я anaemia.

анестезио́лог anaesthetist. анестези́ровать impf & pf anaesthetize. анестези́рующее сре́дство anaesthetic. анестези́я anaesthesia.

анке́та questionnaire, form.

аннекси́ровать impf & pf annex. анне́ксия annexation.

аннули́ровать impf & pf annul; cancel, abolish.

анома́лия anomaly. анома́льный anomalous.

анони́мка anonymous letter. анони́мный anonymous.

анонси́ровать impf & pf announce.

аноре́ксия anorexia.

анса́мбль m ensemble; company, troupe.

антагони́зм antagonism.

Анта́рктика the Antarctic.

анте́нна antenna; aerial.

антибио́тик antibiotic(s).

антидепресса́нт antidepressant.

антиква́р antiquary; antique-dealer. антиквариа́т antique-shop. антиква́рный antiquarian; antique.

антило́па antelope.

антипа́тия antipathy.

антисемити́зм anti-Semitism. антисеми́тский anti-Semitic.

антисе́птик antiseptic. антисепти́ческий antiseptic.

антите́зис (philos) antithesis.

антите́ло (pl -а́) antibody.

антифри́з antifreeze.

анти́чность antiquity. анти́чный ancient, classical.

антоло́гия anthology.

антра́кт interval.

антраци́т anthracite.

антреко́т entrecôte, steak.

антрепренёр impresario.

антресо́ли (pl; gen -ей) mezzanine; shelf.

антропо́лог anthropologist. антропологи́ческий anthropological. антрополо́гия anthropology.

анфила́да suite (of rooms).

анчо́ус anchovy.

аншла́г 'house full' notice.

апартеи́д apartheid.

апати́чный apathetic. апа́тия apathy.

апелли́ровать *impf & pf* appeal. апелляцио́нный суд Court of Appeal. апелля́ция appeal.

апельси́н orange; orange-tree. апельси́нный, апельси́новый orange.

аплоди́ровать *impf +dat* applaud. аплодисме́нты *m pl* applause.

апло́мб aplomb.

Апока́липсис Revelation. апокалипти́ческий apocalyptic.

апо́стол apostle.

апостро́ф apostrophe.

аппара́т apparatus; machinery, organs. аппарату́ра apparatus, gear; (*comput*) hardware. аппара́тчик operator; apparatchik.

аппе́ндикс appendix. аппендици́т appendicitis.

аппети́т appetite; прия́тного ~а! bon appétit! аппети́тный appetizing.

апре́ль *m* April. апре́льский April.

апте́ка chemist's. апте́карь *m* chemist. апте́чка medicine chest; first-aid kit.

ара́б, ара́бка Arab. ара́бский Arab, Arabic.

арави́йский Arabian.

аранжи́ровать *impf & pf* (*mus*) arrange. аранжиро́вка (*mus*) arrangement.

ара́хис peanut.

арби́тр arbitrator. арбитра́ж arbitration.

арбу́з water-melon.

аргуме́нт argument. аргумента́ция reasoning; arguments. аргументи́ровать *impf & pf* argue, (try to) prove.

аре́на arena, ring.

аре́нда lease. аренда́тор tenant. аре́ндная пла́та rent. арендова́ть *impf & pf* rent.

аре́ст arrest. арестова́ть *pf*, аре́стовывать *impf* arrest; seize, sequestrate.

аристокра́т, ~ка aristocrat. аристократи́ческий aristocratic. аристокра́тия aristocracy.

арифме́тика arithmetic. арифмети-

ческий arithmetical.

а́рия aria.

а́рка arch.

А́рктика the Arctic. аркти́ческий arctic.

армату́ра fittings; reinforcement; armature. армату́рщик fitter.

арме́йский army.

Арме́ния Armenia.

а́рмия army.

армяни́н (*pl* -я́не, -я́н), армя́нка Armenian. армя́нский Armenian.

арома́т scent, aroma. арома́тный aromatic, fragrant.

арсена́л arsenal.

арте́ль artel.

арте́рия artery.

арти́куль *m* (*gram*) article.

артилле́рия artillery.

арти́ст, ~ка artiste, artist; expert. артисти́ческий artistic.

артри́т arthritis.

а́рфа harp.

архаи́ческий archaic.

арха́нгел archangel.

архео́лог archaeologist. археологи́ческий archaeological. археоло́гия archaeology.

архи́в archives. архиви́ст archivist. архи́вный archive, archival.

архиепи́скоп archbishop. архиере́й bishop.

архипела́г archipelago.

архите́ктор architect. архитекту́ра architecture. архитекту́рный architectural.

арши́н arshin (*71 cm.*).

асбе́ст asbestos.

асимметри́чный asymmetrical. асимметри́я asymmetry.

аске́т ascetic. аске́тизм asceticism. аскети́ческий ascetic.

асоциа́льный antisocial.

аспира́нт, ~ка post-graduate student. аспиранту́ра post-graduate course.

аспири́н aspirin.

ассамбле́я assembly.

ассигна́ция banknote.

ассимиля́ция assimilation.

ассисте́нт assistant; junior lecturer, research assistant.

ассортиме́нт assortment.

ассоциа́ция association. ассоции́ровать *impf & pf* associate.

а́стма asthma. **астмати́ческий** asthmatic.

астро́лог astrologer. **астроло́гия** astrology.

астрона́вт astronaut. **астроно́м** astronomer. **астрономи́ческий** astronomical. **астроно́мия** astronomy.

асфа́льт asphalt.

ата́ка attack. **атакова́ть** impf & pf attack.

атама́н ataman (*Cossack chieftain*); (gang-)leader.

атеи́зм atheism. **атеи́ст** atheist.

ателье́ neut indecl studio; atelier.

а́тлас[1] atlas.

атла́с[2] satin. **атла́сный** satin.

атле́т athlete; strong man. **атле́тика** athletics. **атлети́ческий** athletic.

атмосфе́ра atmosphere. **атмосфе́рный** atmospheric.

а́том atom. **а́томный** atomic.

атташе́ m indecl attaché.

аттеста́т testimonial; certificate; pedigree. **аттестова́ть** impf & pf attest; recommend.

аттракцио́н attraction; sideshow; star turn.

ау́ int hi, cooee.

аудито́рия auditorium, lecture-room.

аукцио́н auction.

ау́л aul (*Caucasian or Central Asian village*).

ауто́псия autopsy.

афе́ра speculation, trickery. **афери́ст** speculator, trickster.

афи́ша placard, poster.

афори́зм aphorism.

А́фрика Africa. **африка́нец** (-нца), **африка́нка** African. **африка́нский** African.

аффе́кт fit of passion; temporary insanity.

ах int ah, oh. **а́хать** impf (pf **а́хнуть**) sigh; exclaim; gasp.

аэро|вокза́л air terminal. **~дина́мика** aerodynamics. **~дро́м** aerodrome, air-field. **~зо́ль** m aerosol. **~по́рт** (loc -ý) airport.

Б

б partl: see **бы**

ба́ба (coll) (old) woman; **снежная ~** snowman.

ба́бочка butterfly.

ба́бушка grandmother; grandma.

бага́ж (-á) luggage. **бага́жник** carrier; luggage-rack; boot. **бага́жный ваго́н** luggage-van.

баго́р (-гра́) boat-hook.

багро́вый crimson, purple.

бадья́ (gen pl -де́й) tub.

ба́за base; depot; basis; **~ да́нных** database.

база́р market; din.

ба́зис base; basis.

байда́рка canoe.

ба́йка flannelette.

бак[1] tank, cistern.

бак[2] forecastle.

бакала́вр (univ) bachelor.

бакале́йный grocery. **бакале́я** groceries.

ба́кен buoy.

бакенба́рды (pl; gen -ба́рд) side-whiskers.

баклажа́н (gen pl -ов or -жа́н) aubergine.

бакте́рия bacterium.

бал (loc -ý; pl -ы́) dance, ball.

балага́н farce.

балала́йка balalaika.

бала́нс (econ) balance.

баланси́ровать impf (pf с~) balance; keep one's balance.

балбе́с booby.

балдахи́н canopy.

балери́на ballerina. **бале́т** ballet.

ба́лка[1] beam, girder.

ба́лка[2] gully.

балко́н balcony.

балл mark (in school); degree; force; **ве́тер в пять ~ов** wind force 5.

балла́да ballad.

балла́ст ballast.

балло́н container, carboy, cylinder; balloon tyre.

баллоти́ровать impf vote; put to the vote; **~ся** stand, be a candidate (в or на +acc for).

балова́ть impf (pf из~) spoil, pamper; **~ся** play about, get up to tricks; amuse o.s. **баловство́** spoiling; mischief.

Балти́йское мо́ре Baltic (Sea).

бальза́м balsam; balm.

балюстра́да balustrade.

бамбу́к bamboo.

ба́мпер bumper.

бана́льность banality; platitude.
  бана́льный banal.

бана́н banana.

ба́нда band, gang.

банда́ж (-á) truss; belt, band.

бандеро́ль wrapper; printed matter,
  book-post.

ба́нджо *neut indecl* banjo.

банди́т bandit; gangster.

банк bank.

ба́нка jar; tin.

банке́т banquet.

банки́р banker. **банкно́та** banknote.
  банкро́т bankrupt. **банкро́тство**
  bankruptcy.

бант bow.

ба́ня bath; bath-house.

бараба́н drum. **бараба́нить** *impf*
  drum, thump. **бараба́нная пере-
  по́нка** ear-drum. **бараба́нщик**
  drummer.

бара́к wooden barrack, hut.

бара́н ram; sheep. **бара́нина** mutton.

бара́нка ring-shaped roll; (steering-)
  wheel.

барахло́ old clothes, jumble; odds
  and ends. **барахо́лка** flea market.

бара́шек (-шка) young ram; lamb;
  wing nut; catkin. **бара́шковый**
  lambskin.

баржа́ (*gen pl* барж(е́й)) barge.

ба́рин (*pl* -ре *or* -ры, бар) landowner;
  sir.

барито́н baritone.

ба́рка barge.

ба́рмен barman.

баро́кко *neut indecl* baroque.

баро́метр barometer.

баро́н baron. **бароне́сса** baroness.

баро́чный baroque.

баррика́да barricade.

барс snow-leopard.

ба́рский lordly; grand.

барсу́к (-á) badger.

барха́н dune.

ба́рхат (-у) velvet. **ба́рхатный** velvet.

ба́рыня landowner's wife; madam.

ба́рыш (-á) profit. **бары́шник**
  dealer; (ticket) speculator.

ба́рышня (*gen pl* -шень) young lady;
  miss.

барье́р barrier; hurdle.

бас (*pl* -ы́) bass.

баскетбо́л basket-ball.

баснословный mythical, legendary;
  fabulous. **ба́сня** (*gen pl* -сен) fable;
  fabrication.

басо́вый bass.

бассе́йн (*geog*) basin; pool; reservoir.

бастова́ть *impf* be on strike.

батальо́н battalion.

батаре́йка, батаре́я battery; radiator.

бато́н long loaf; stick, bar.

ба́тька *m*, **ба́тюшка** *m* father; priest.
  ба́тюшки *int* good gracious!

бах *int* bang!

бахва́льство bragging.

бахрома́ fringe.

бац *int* bang! crack!

баци́лла bacillus. **бациллоноси́-
  тель** *m* carrier.

бачо́к (-чка́) cistern.

башка́ head.

башлы́к (-á) hood.

башма́к (-á) shoe; **под ~о́м** y+*gen*
  under the thumb of.

ба́шня (*gen pl* -шен) tower, turret.

баю́кать *impf* (*pf* ~) sing lullabies
  (to). **ба́юшки-баю́** *int* hushabye!

бая́н accordion.

бде́ние vigil. **бди́тельность** vigilance. **бди́тельный** vigilant.

бег (*loc* -ý, *pl* -á) run, running; race.
  бе́гать *indet* (*det* бежа́ть) *impf* run.

бегемо́т hippopotamus.

бегле́ц (-á), **бегля́нка** fugitive.
  бе́глость speed, fluency, dexterity.
  бе́глый rapid, fluent; fleeting, cursory; *sb* fugitive, runaway. **бегово́й**
  running; race. **бего́м** *adv* running, at
  the double. **беготня́** running about;
  bustle **бе́гство** flight; escape. **бегу́н**
  (-á), **бегу́нья** (*gen pl* -ний) runner.

беда́ (*pl* -ы) misfortune; disaster;
  trouble; **~ в том, что** the trouble is
  (that). **бедне́ть** *impf* (*pf* о~) grow
  poor. **бе́дность** poverty; the poor.
  бе́дный (-ден, -дна́, -дно) poor.
  бедня́га, бедня́жка *m* & *f* poor
  thing. **бедня́к** (-á), **бедня́чка** poor
  peasant; poor man, poor woman.

бедро́ (*pl* бёдра, -дер) thigh; hip.

бе́дственный disastrous. **бе́дствие**
  disaster. **бе́дствовать** *impf* live in
  poverty.

бежа́ть (бегу́ *det*; *indet* бе́гать) *impf*

(*pf* по~) run; flow; fly; boil over; *impf* & *pf* escape. **бе́женец** (-нца), **бе́женка** refugee.

без *prep+gen* without; ~ пяти́ (мину́т) три five (minutes) to three; ~ че́тверти a quarter to.

без-, безъ-, бес- *in comb* in-, un-; non-; -less. **без**алкого́льный non-alcoholic. ~апелляцио́нный peremptory, categorical. ~бо́жие atheism. ~бо́жный godless; shameless, outrageous. ~боле́зненный painless. ~бра́чный celibate. ~бре́жный boundless. ~ве́стный unknown; obscure. ~вку́сие lack of taste, bad taste. ~вку́сный tasteless. ~вла́стие anarchy. ~во́дный arid. ~возвра́тный irrevocable; irrecoverable. ~возме́здный free, gratis. ~во́лие lack of will. ~во́льный weak-willed. ~вре́дный harmless. ~вре́менный untimely. ~вы́ходный hopeless, desperate; uninterrupted. ~гла́зый one-eyed; eyeless. ~гра́мотный illiterate. ~грани́чный boundless, infinite. ~да́рный untalented. ~де́йственный inactive. ~де́йствие inertia, idleness; negligence. ~де́йствовать *impf* be idle, be inactive; stand idle.

безде́лица trifle. **безделу́шка** knick-knack. **безде́льник** idler; ne'er-do-well. **безде́льничать** *impf* idle, loaf.

бе́здна abyss, chasm; a huge number, a multitude.

без-. бездоказа́тельный unsubstantiated. ~до́мный homeless. ~до́нный bottomless; fathomless. ~доро́жье lack of (good) roads; season when roads are impassable. ~ду́мный unthinking. ~ду́шный heartless; inanimate; lifeless. ~жа́лостный pitiless, ruthless. ~жи́зненный lifeless. ~забо́тный carefree; careless. ~заве́тный selfless, wholehearted. ~зако́ние lawlessness; unlawful act. ~зако́нный illegal; lawless. ~засте́нчивый shameless, barefaced. ~защи́тный defenceless. ~зву́чный silent. ~зло́бный good-natured. ~ли́чный characterless; impersonal. ~лю́дный uninhabited; sparsely populated; lonely.

безме́н steelyard.

без-. безме́рный immense; excessive. ~мо́лвие silence. ~мо́лвный silent, mute. ~мяте́жный serene, placid. ~надёжный hopeless. ~надзо́рный neglected. ~нака́занно *adv* with impunity. ~нака́занный unpunished. ~но́гий legless; one-legged. ~нра́вственный immoral.

безо *prep+gen* = **без** (*used before* весь *and* всякий).

безобра́зие ugliness; disgrace, scandal. **безобра́зничать** *impf* make a nuisance of o.s. **безобра́зный** ugly; disgraceful.

без-. безоговóрочный unconditional. ~опа́сность safety; security. ~опа́сный safe; secure. ~ору́жный unarmed. ~основа́тельный groundless. ~остано́вочный unceasing; non-stop. ~отве́тный meek, unanswering; dumb. ~отве́тственный irresponsible. ~отка́зно *adv* without a hitch. ~отка́зный trouble-free, smooth-(running). ~отлага́тельный urgent. ~относи́тельно *adv+к+dat* irrespective of. ~отчётный unaccountable. ~оши́бочный unerring; correct. ~рабо́тица unemployment. ~рабо́тный unemployed. ~разли́чие indifference. ~разли́чно *adv* indifferently; it is all the same. ~разли́чный indifferent. ~рассу́дный reckless, imprudent. ~ро́дный alone in the world; without relatives. ~ро́потный uncomplaining; meek. ~рука́вка sleeveless pullover. ~ру́кий armless; one-armed. ~уда́рный unstressed. ~у́держный unrestrained; impetuous. ~укори́зненный irreproachable.

безу́мец (-мца) madman. **безу́мие** madness. **безу́мный** mad. **безу́мство** madness.

без-. безупре́чный irreproachable, faultless. ~усло́вно *adv* unconditionally; of course, undoubtedly. ~усло́вный unconditional, absolute; indisputable. ~успе́шный unsuccessful. ~уста́нный tireless. ~уте́шный inconsolable. ~уча́стие indifference, apathy. ~уча́стный indifferent, apathetic. ~ымя́нный nameless, anonymous; ~ымя́нный па́лец ring-finger. ~ыску́сный artless, ingenuous. ~ысхо́дный irreparable; interminable.

бейсбо́л baseball.

бека́р (*mus*) natural.

бека́с snipe.

беко́н bacon.

Белару́с, Belarus.

беле́ть *impf* (*pf* по~) turn white; show white.

белизна́ whiteness. **бели́ла** (*pl*; *gen* -и́л) whitewash; Tippex (*propr*). **бели́ть** (бе́лишь) *impf* (*pf* вы́~, на~, по~) whitewash; whiten; bleach.

бе́лка squirrel.

беллетри́ст writer of fiction. **беллетри́стика** fiction.

бело- *in comb* white-, leuco-. **белогварде́ец** (-е́йца) White Guard. ~кро́вие leukaemia. ~ку́рый fair, blonde. ~ру́с, ~ру́ска, ~ру́сский Belorussian. ~сне́жный snow-white.

белови́к (-а́) fair copy. **белово́й** clean, fair.

бело́к (-лка́) white (*of egg, eye*); protein.

белошве́йка seamstress. **белошве́йный** linen.

белу́га white sturgeon. **белу́ха** white whale.

бе́л|ый (бел, -а́, бе́ло́) white; clean, blank; *sb* white person; ~ая берёза silver birch; ~ое кале́ние white heat; ~ый медве́дь polar bear; ~ые но́чи white nights, midnight sun.

бельги́ец, -**ги́йка** Belgian. **бельги́йский** Belgian. **Бе́льгия** Belgium.

бельё linen; bedclothes; underclothes; washing.

бельмо́ (*pl* -а) cataract.

бельэта́ж first floor; dress circle.

бемо́ль *m* (*mus*) flat.

бенефи́с benefit (performance).

бензи́н petrol.

бензо- *in comb* petrol. **бензоба́к** petrol-tank. ~во́з petrol tanker. ~запра́вочная *sb* filling-station. ~коло́нка petrol pump. ~прово́д petrol pipe, fuel line.

бере́г *etc.*: *see* бере́чь

бе́рег (*loc* -у́; *pl* -а́) bank, shore;

coast; на ~у́ мо́ря at the seaside. **берегово́й** coast; coastal.

бережёшь *etc.*: *see* бере́чь. **бережли́вый** thrifty. **бе́режный** careful.

берёза birch. **Берёзка** hard-currency shop.

береме́нет *impf* (*pf* за~) be(come) pregnant. **бере́менная** pregnant (+*instr* with). **бере́менность** pregnancy; gestation.

бере́т beret.

бере́чь (-регу́, -режёшь; -рёг, -ла́) *impf* take care of; keep; cherish; husband; be sparing of; ~ся take care; beware (+*gen* of).

берло́га den, lair.

беру́ *etc.*: *see* брать

бес devil, demon.

бес-: *see* без-

бесе́да talk, conversation. **бесе́дка** summer-house. **бесе́довать** *impf* talk, converse.

беси́ть (бешу́, бе́сишь) *impf* (*pf* вз~) enrage; ~ся go mad; be furious.

бес-. **бесконе́чность** infinity; endlessness. ~коне́чный endless. ~коры́стие disinterestedness. ~коры́стный disinterested. ~кра́йний boundless.

бесо́вский devilish.

бес-. **беспа́мятство** unconsciousness. ~парти́йный non-party ~перспекти́вный without prospects; hopeless. ~пе́чность carelessness, unconcern. ~пла́тно *adv* free. ~пла́тный free. ~пло́дие sterility, barrenness. ~пло́дность futility. ~пло́дный sterile, barren; futile. ~поворо́тный irrevocable. ~подо́бный incomparable. ~позвоно́чный invertebrate.

беспоко́ить *impf* (*pf* o~, по~) disturb, bother; trouble; ~ся worry; trouble. **беспоко́йный** anxious; troubled; fidgety. **беспоко́йство** anxiety.

бес-. **бесполе́зный** useless. ~по́мощный helpless; feeble. ~поро́дный mongrel, not thoroughbred. ~поря́док (-дка) disorder; untidy state. ~поря́дочный disorderly; untidy. ~поса́дочный non-stop. ~по́чвенный groundless. ~по́шлинный duty-free. ~поща́дный merciless. ~пра́вный without rights. ~преде́льный boundless. ~предме́тный aimless; abstract. ~препя́тственный unhindered; unimpeded. ~преры́вный continuous. ~проста́нный continual.

беспризо́рник, -ница waif, homeless child. беспризо́рный neglected; homeless; sb waif, homeless child.

бес-. бесприме́рный unparalleled. ~принци́пный unscrupulous. ~пристра́стие impartiality. ~пристра́стный impartial. ~просве́тный pitch-dark; hopeless; unrelieved. ~пу́тный dissolute. ~свя́зный incoherent. ~серде́чный heartless. ~си́лие impotence; feebleness. ~си́льный impotent, powerless. ~сла́вный inglorious. ~сле́дно adv without trace. ~слове́сный dumb; silent, meek; (theat) walk-on. ~сме́нный permanent, continuous. ~сме́ртие immortality. ~сме́ртный immortal. ~смы́сленный senseless; foolish; meaningless. ~смы́слица nonsense. ~со́вестный unscrupulous; shameless. ~созна́тельный unconscious; involuntary. ~со́нница insomnia. ~спо́рный indisputable. ~сро́чный indefinite; without a time limit. ~стра́стный impassive. ~стра́шный fearless. ~сты́дный shameless. ~та́ктный tactless.

бестолко́вщина confusion, disorder. бестолко́вый muddle-headed, stupid; incoherent.

бес-. бесфо́рменный shapeless. ~хара́ктерный weak, spineless. ~хи́тростный artless; unsophisticated. ~хозя́йственный improvident. ~цве́тный colourless. ~це́льный aimless; pointless. ~це́нный priceless. ~це́нок: за ~це́нок very cheap, for a song. ~церемо́нный unceremonious. ~челове́чный inhuman. ~че́стить (-е́щу) impf (pf о~че́стить) dishonour. ~че́стный dishonourable. ~чи́сленный innumerable, countless.

бесчу́вственный insensible; insensitive. бесчу́вствие insensibility; insensitivity.

бес-. бесшу́мный noiseless. бето́н concrete. бето́нный concrete.

бетономеша́лка concrete-mixer. бето́нщик concrete-worker.

бечева́ tow-rope; rope. бечёвка cord, string.

бе́шенство rabies; rage. бе́шеный rabid; furious.

бешу́ etc.: see беси́ть

библе́йский biblical. библиографи́ческий bibliographical. библиогра́фия bibliography. библиоте́ка library. библиоте́карь m, -те́карша librarian. би́блия bible.

бива́к bivouac, camp.

би́вень (-вня) m tusk.

бигуди́ pl indecl curlers.

бидо́н can; churn.

бие́ние beating; beat.

бижуте́рия costume jewellery.

би́знес business. бизнесме́н businessman.

биле́т ticket; card; pass. биле́тный ticket.

биллио́н billion.

билья́рд billiards.

бино́кль m binoculars.

бинт (-á) bandage. бинтова́ть impf (pf за~) bandage. бинто́вка bandaging.

био́граф biographer. биографи́ческий biographical. биогра́фия biography. био́лог biologist. биологи́ческий biological. биоло́гия biology. биохи́мия biochemistry.

би́ржа exchange.

би́рка name-plate; label.

бирюза́ turquoise

бис int encore.

би́сер (no pl) beads.

бискви́т sponge cake.

би́та bat.

би́тва battle.

битко́м adv: ~ наби́т packed.

би́тум bitumen.

бить (бью, бьёшь) impf (pf за~, по~, про~, уда́рить) beat; hit; defeat; sound; thump, bang; smash; ~ в цель hit the target; ~ на+acc strive for; ~ отбо́й beat a retreat; ~ по+dat damage, wound; ~ся fight; beat; struggle; break; +instr knock, hit, strike; +над+instr struggle with, rack one's brains over.

бифште́кс beefsteak.

бич (-á) whip, lash; scourge; homeless person. бичева́ть (-чу́ю) impf flog; castigate.

бла́го good; blessing.

бла́го- in comb well-, good-. **Благове́щение** Annunciation. **~ви́дный** plausible, specious. **~во-ле́ние** goodwill; favour. **~воспи́-танный** well-brought-up.

благодари́ть (-рю́) impf (pf по~) thank. **благода́рность** gratitude; не сто́ит благода́рности don't mention it. **благода́рный** grateful. **бла-года́ря́** prep+dat thanks to, owing to.

благо-. благоде́тель m benefactor. **~де́тельница** benefactress. **~де́-тельный** beneficial. **~ду́шный** placid; good-humoured. **~жела́тель** m well-wisher. **~жела́тельный** well-disposed; benevolent. **~звуч-ный** melodious, harmonious. **~на-дёжный** reliable. **~наме́ренный** well-intentioned. **~полу́чие** well-being; happiness. **~полу́чно** adv all right, well; happily; safely. **~по-лу́чный** happy, successful; safe. **~прия́тный** favourable. **~при-я́тствовать** impf +dat favour. **~разу́мие** sense; prudence. **~разу́мный** sensible. **~ро́дие** ва́ше **~ро́дие** Your Honour. **~ро́дный** noble. **~ро́дство** nobility. **~скло́н-ность** favour, good graces. **~скло́нный** favourable; gracious. **~слови́ть** pf, **благословля́ть** impf bless. **~состоя́ние** prosperity. **~твори́тель** m, **-ница** philanthrop-ist. **~твори́тельный** charitable, charity. **~тво́рный** salutary; benefi-cial; wholesome. **~устро́енный** well-equipped, well-planned; with all amenities.

блаже́нный blissful; simple-minded. **блаже́нство** bliss.

бланк form.

блат (sl) string-pulling; pull, influ-ence. **блатно́й** criminal; soft, cushy.

бледне́ть (-е́ю) impf (pf по~) (grow) pale. **бле́дность** paleness, pallor. **бле́дный** (-ден, -дна́, -о) pale.

блеск brightness, brilliance, lustre; magnificence.

блесну́ть (-ну́, -нёшь) pf flash, gleam; shine. **блесте́ть** (-ещу́, -сти́шь or бле́щешь) impf shine; glitter.

блёстка sparkle; sequin. **блестя́щий** shining, bright; brilliant.

бле́ять (-е́ет) impf bleat.

ближа́йший nearest, closest; next. **бли́же** comp of бли́зкий, бли́зко. **бли́жний** near, close; neighbouring. sb neighbour. **близ** prep+gen near, by. **бли́з**|**кий** (-зок, -зка́, -о) near; close; imminent; **~кие** sb pl one's nearest and dearest, close relatives. **бли́зко** adv near (от+gen to). **близ-не́ц** (-а́) twin; pl Gemini. **близо-ру́кий** short-sighted. **бли́зость** closeness, proximity.

блик patch of light; highlight.

блин (-а́) pancake.

блинда́ж (-а́) dug-out.

блиста́ть impf shine; sparkle.

блок block, pulley, sheave.

блока́да blockade. **блоки́ровать** impf & pf blockade; **~ся** form a bloc. **блокно́т** writing-pad, note-book.

блонди́н, блонди́нка blond(e).

блоха́ (pl -и, -а́м) flea.

блуд lechery. **блудни́ца** whore. **блужда́ть** impf roam, wander.

блу́за, блу́зка blouse.

блю́дечко saucer; small dish. **блю́до** dish; course. **блю́дце** saucer.

боб (-а́) bean. **бобо́вый** bean.

бобр (-а́) beaver.

Бог (voc Бо́же) God; **дай ~** God grant; **~ его́ зна́ет** who knows? не **дай ~** God forbid; **Бо́же (мой)!** my God! good God!; **ра́ди ~а** for God's sake; **сла́ва ~у** thank God.

богате́ть impf (pf раз~) grow rich. **бога́тство** wealth. **бога́тый** rich, wealthy; sb rich man. **бога́ч** (-а́) rich man.

богаты́рь (-я́) m hero; strong man.

боги́ня goddess. **Богома́терь** Mother of God. **богомо́лец** (-льца), **богомо́лка** devout person; pilgrim. **богомо́лье** pilgrimage. **богомо́ль-ный** religious, devout. **Богоро́дица** the Virgin Mary. **богосло́в** theolo-gian. **богосло́вие** theology. **бого-служе́ние** divine service. **боготво-ри́ть** impf idolize; deify. **бого-ху́льство** blasphemy.

бодри́ть impf. stimulate, invigorate; **~ся** try to keep up one's spirits. **бо́дрость** cheerfulness, courage. **бо́дрствовать** be awake; stay awake; keep vigil. **бо́дрый** (бодр, -á, -о) cheerful, bright.

боеви́к (-á) smash hit. **боево́й** fighting, battle. **боеголо́вка** warhead. **боеприпа́сы** (*pl*; *gen* -ов) ammunition. **боеспосо́бный** battle-worthy. **бое́ц** (бойца́) soldier; fighter; warrior.

Бо́же: *see* Бог. **бо́жеский** divine; just. **боже́ственный** divine. **божество́** deity; divinity. **бо́ж|ий** God's; ~**ья коро́вка** ladybird. **божо́к** (-жка́) idol.

бой (-ю; *loc* -ю́; *pl* -и́, -ёв) battle, action, fight; fighting; slaughtering; striking; breakage(s).

бо́йкий (бо́ек, бойка́, -о) smart, sharp; glib; lively.

бойко́т boycott.

бо́йня (*gen pl* бо́ен) slaughter-house; butchery.

бок (*loc* -ý; *pl* -á) side; flank; ~ ó ~ side by side; на́ ~ to the side; на ~ý on one side; по́д ~ом near by; с ~у from the side, from the flank; с ~у на́ бок from side to side.

бока́л glass; goblet.

боково́й side; lateral. **бо́ком** *adv* sideways.

бокс boxing. **боксёр** boxer.

болва́н blockhead. **болва́нка** pig (*of iron etc.*).

болга́рин (*pl* -га́ры), **болга́рка** Bulgarian. **болга́рский** Bulgarian. **Болга́рия** Bulgaria.

бо́лее *adv* more; ~ всего́ most of all; тем ~, что especially as.

боле́зненный sickly; unhealthy; painful. **боле́знь** illness, disease; abnormality.

боле́льщик, -щица fan, supporter. **боле́ть**[1] (-е́ю) *impf* be ill, suffer. **боле́ть**[2] (-ли́т) *impf* ache, hurt. **боло́тистый** marshy. **боло́то** marsh, bog.

болта́ть[1] *impf* stir; shake; dangle; ~**ся** dangle, swing; hang about.

болта́ть[2] *impf* chat, natter. **болтли́вый** talkative; indiscreet. **болтовня́** talk; chatter; gossip. **болту́н** (-á), **болту́нья** chatterbox. **боль** pain; ache. **больни́ца** hospital. **больни́чный** hospital; ~ **листо́к** medical certificate. **бо́льно**[1] *adv* painfully, badly; *predic*+*dat* it hurts.

бо́льно[2] *adv* very, terribly. **больно́й** (-лен, -льна́) ill, sick; diseased; sore; *sb* patient, invalid. **бо́льше** *comp of* **большо́й, мно́го**; bigger, larger; greater; more; ~ не not any more, no longer; ~ того́ and what is more; *adv* for the most part. **большеви́к** Bolshevik. **бо́льш|ий** greater, larger; ~**ей ча́стью** for the most part. **большинство́** majority. **больш|о́й** big, large; great; grown-up; ~**áя бу́ква** capital letter; ~**о́й па́лец** thumb; big toe; ~**и́е** *sb pl* grown-ups.

бо́мба bomb. **бомбардирова́ть** *impf* bombard; bomb. **бомбарди́ровка** bombardment, bombing. **бомбардиро́вщик** bomber. **бомбёжка** bombing. **бомби́ть** (-блю́) bomb. **бомбоубе́жище** bomb shelter.

бор (*loc* -ý; *pl* -ы́) coniferous forest.

бордо́вый wine-red.

бордю́р border.

боре́ц (-рца́) fighter; wrestler.

бо́рзый swift.

бормаши́на (dentist's) drill.

бормота́ть (-очу́, -о́чешь) *impf* (*pf* про~) mutter, mumble.

борода́ (*acc* бо́роду, *pl* бо́роды, -ро́д, -а́м) beard. **борода́вка** wart. **борода́тый** bearded.

борозда́ (*pl* борозды, -о́зд, -а́м) furrow; fissure. **борозди́ть** (-зжу́) *impf* (*pf* вз~) furrow; plough.

борона́ (*acc* бо́рону, *pl* бо́роны, -ро́н, -а́м) harrow. **борони́ть** *impf* (*pf* вз~) harrow.

боро́ться (-рю́сь, бо́решься) *impf* wrestle; struggle, fight.

борт (*loc* -ý; *pl* -á, -о́в) side, ship's side; front; за ~, за ~ом overboard; на ~, на ~ý on board. **бортпроводни́к** (-á) air steward. **бортпроводни́ца** air hostess.

борщ (-á) borshch (*beetroot soup*).

борьба́ wrestling; struggle, fight.

босико́м *adv* barefoot.

босни́ец (-и́йца), **босни́йка** Bosnian. **босни́йский** Bosnian. **Бо́сния** Bosnia.

босо́й (бос, -á, -о) barefooted. **босоно́жка** sandal.

бот, бо́тик small boat.

бота́ник botanist. **бота́ника** botany.

ботани́ческий botanical.

боти́нок (-нка) (ankle-high) boot.

бо́цман boatswain

бо́чка barrel. бочо́нок (-нка) keg, small barrel.

боязли́вый timid, timorous. боя́знь fear, dread.

боя́рин (pl -я́ре, -я́р) boyar.

боя́рышник hawthorn.

боя́ться (бою́сь) impf +gen be afraid of, fear; dislike.

брак[1] marriage.

брак[2] defective goods; waste. бракова́ть impf (pf за~) reject.

браконье́р poacher.

бракоразво́дный divorce. бракосочета́ние wedding.

брани́ть impf (pf вы~) scold; abuse, curse; ~ся (pf по~) swear, curse; quarrel. бра́нный abusive; ~ое сло́во swear-word.

брань bad language; abuse.

брасле́т bracelet.

брасс breast stroke.

брат (pl -тья, -тьев) brother; comrade; mate; lay brother, monk. брата́ться impf (pf по~) fraternize. братоуби́йство fratricide. бра́тский brotherly, fraternal. бра́тство brotherhood, fraternity.

брать (беру́, -рёшь; брал, -а́, -о) impf (pf взять) take; obtain; seize; demand, require; surmount, clear; work; +instr succeed by means of; ~ся +за+acc touch; seize; get down to; +за+acc or inf undertake; appear, come.

бра́чный marriage; mating.

бревенча́тый log. бревно́ (pl брёвна, -вен) log, beam.

бред (loc -у́) delirium; raving(s). бре́дить (-е́жу) impf be delirious, rave; +instr rave about, be infatuated with. бредо́вый delirious; fantastic, nonsensical.

бреду́ etc.: see брести́. бре́жу etc.: see бре́дить

бре́згать impf (pf по~) +inf or instr be squeamish about. брезгли́вый squeamish.

брезе́нт tarpaulin.

бре́зжить(ся) impf dawn; gleam faintly, glimmer.

брён etc.: see брести́

брело́к charm, pendant.

бремени́ть impf (pf о~) burden. бре́мя (-мени) neut burden; load.

бренча́ть (-чу́) impf strum; jingle.

брести́ (-еду́, -едёшь; брёл, -а́) impf stroll; drag o.s. along.

брете́ль, брете́лька shoulder strap.

брешь breach; gap.

бре́ю etc.: see брить

брига́да brigade; crew, team. брига́ди́р brigadier; team-leader; foreman.

бриллиа́нт, брилья́нт diamond.

брита́нец (-нца), брита́нка Briton. брита́нск|ий British; Б~ие острова́ the British Isles.

бри́тва razor. бри́твенный shaving. бри́тый shaved; clean-shaven. брить (бре́ю) impf (pf по~) shave; ~ся shave (o.s.).

бровь (pl -и, -е́й) eyebrow; brow.

брод ford.

броди́ть (-ожу́, -о́дишь) impf wander, roam, stroll; ferment. бродя́га m & f tramp, vagrant. бродя́жничество vagrancy. бродя́чий vagrant; wandering. броже́ние ferment, fermentation.

броне- in comb armoured, armour. броневи́к (-а́) armoured car. ~во́й armoured. ~но́сец (-сца) battleship; armadillo.

бро́нза bronze; bronzes. бро́нзовый bronze; tanned.

брони́рованный armoured.

брони́ровать impf & pf (pf also за~) reserve, book.

бронхи́т bronchitis.

броня́[1] reservation; commandeering.

броня́[2] armour.

броса́ть impf, бро́сить (-о́шу) pf throw (down); leave, desert; give up, leave off; ~ся throw o.s.; rush; +inf begin; +instr squander; pelt one another with; ~ся в глаза́ be striking. бро́ский striking; garish, glaring. бросо́к (-ска́) throw; bound, spurt.

бро́шка, брошь brooch.

брошю́ра pamphlet, brochure.

брус (pl -сья, -сьев) squared beam, joist; (паралле́льные) ~ья parallel bars.

брусни́ка red whortleberry; red whortleberries.

брусо́к (-ска́) bar; ingot.

бру́тто indecl adj gross.

бры́згать (-зжу *or* -гаю) *impf*, **бры́знуть** (-ну) *pf* splash; sprinkle. **бры́зги** (брызг) *pl* spray, splashes; fragments.

брыка́ть *impf*, **брыкну́ть** (-ну́, -нёшь) *pf* kick.

брюзга́ *m & f* grumbler. **брюзгли́вый** grumbling, peevish. **брюзжа́ть** (-жу́) *impf* grumble.

брю́ква swede.

брю́ки (*pl; gen* брюк) trousers.

брюне́т dark-haired man. **брюне́тка** brunette.

брю́хо (*pl* -и) belly; stomach. **брюшно́й** abdominal; ~ тиф typhoid. **бряца́ть** *impf* rattle; clank, clang.

бу́бен (-бна) tambourine. **бубене́ц** (-нца́) small bell. **бу́бны** (*pl; gen* -бён, *dat* -бна́м) (*cards*) diamonds. **бубно́вый** diamond.

буго́р (-гра́) mound, hillock; bump, lump.

будди́зм Buddhism. **будди́йский** Buddhist. **будди́ст** Buddhist.

бу́дет that will do; +*inf* it's time to stop.

буди́льник alarm-clock. **буди́ть** (бужу́, бу́дишь) *impf* (*pf* про~, раз~) wake; arouse.

бу́дка box, booth; hut; stall.

бу́дни (*pl; gen* -ней) *pl* weekdays; working days; humdrum existence. **бу́дний**, **бу́дничный** weekday; everyday; humdrum.

бу́дто *conj* as if, as though; ~ (бы), (как) ~ apparently, ostensibly.

бу́ду *etc.: see* быть. **бу́дучи** being. **бу́дущий** future; next; ~ее *sb* future. **бу́дущность** future. **бу́дь(те)**: *see* быть

бужу́: *see* буди́ть

бузина́ (*bot*) elder.

буй (*pl* -и́, -ёв) buoy.

бу́йвол buffalo.

бу́йный (бу́ен, буйна́, -о) violent, turbulent; luxuriant, lush. **бу́йство** unruly behaviour. **бу́йствовать** *impf* create an uproar, behave violently.

бук beech.

бука́шка small insect.

бу́ква (*gen pl* букв) letter; ~ в бу́кву literally. **буква́льно** *adv* literally. **буква́льный** literal. **буква́рь** (-я́) *m* ABC. **буквое́д** pedant.

буке́т bouquet; aroma.

букини́ст second-hand bookseller.

бу́кля curl, ringlet.

бу́ковый beech.

букси́р tug-boat; tow-rope. **букси́ровать** *impf* tow.

буксова́ть *impf* spin, slip.

була́вка pin.

бу́лка roll. **бу́лочная** *sb* baker's. **бу́лочник** baker.

булы́жник cobble-stone, cobbles.

бульва́р avenue; boulevard.

бульдо́г bulldog.

бульдо́зер bulldozer.

бу́лькать *impf* gurgle.

бульо́н broth.

бум (*sport*) beam.

бума́га cotton; paper; document. **бума́жка** piece of paper; note. **бума́жник** wallet; paper-maker. **бума́жн|ый** cotton; paper; ~ змей kite.

бу́нкер bunker.

бунт (*pl* -ы́) rebellion; riot; mutiny. **бунта́рь** (-я́) *m* rebel; insurgent. **бунтова́ть(ся** *impf* (*pf* вз~) rebel; riot. **бунтовщи́к** (-а́), **-щи́ца** rebel, insurgent.

бур auger.

бура́в (-а́; *pl* -а́) auger; gimlet. **бура́вить** (-влю) *impf* (*pf* про~) bore, drill.

бура́н snowstorm.

буреве́стник stormy petrel.

буре́ние boring, drilling.

буржуа́ *m indecl* bourgeois. **буржуази́я** bourgeoisie. **буржуа́зный** bourgeois.

бури́льщик borer, driller. **бури́ть** *impf* (*pf* про~) bore, drill.

бурли́ть *impf* seethe.

бу́рный (-рен, -рна́, -о) stormy; rapid; energetic.

буров|о́й boring; ~а́я вы́шка derrick; ~а́я (сква́жина) borehole; ~о́й стано́к drilling rig.

бу́рый (бур, -а́, -о) brown.

бурья́н tall weeds.

бу́ря storm.

бу́сина bead. **бу́сы** (*pl; gen* бус) beads.

бутафо́рия (*theat*) props.

бутербро́д open sandwich.

буто́н bud.

бу́тсы (*pl; gen* -ов) *pl* football boots.

бутылка bottle. **бутыль** large bottle; carboy.

буфет snack bar; sideboard; counter. **буфетчик** barman. **буфетчица** barmaid.

бух *int* bang, plonk. **бухать** *impf* (*pf* **бухнуть**) thump, bang; bang down; thunder, thud; blurt out.

буханка loaf.

бухгалтер accountant. **бухгалтерия** accountancy; accounts department.

бухнуть (-ну) *impf* swell.

бухта bay.

бушевать (-шую) *impf* rage, storm.

буян rowdy. **буянить** *impf* create an uproar.

бы, **б** *partl* I. +*past tense or inf* indicates the conditional or subjunctive. II. (+ни) forms indef prons and conjs.

бывалый experienced; former; habitual, familiar. **бывать** *impf* be; happen; be inclined to be; **как ни в чём не бывало** as if nothing had happened; **бывало** *partl* used to, would; **мать бывало часто пела эту песню** my mother would often sing this song. **бывший** former, ex-.

бык (-а) bull, ox; pier.

былина ancient Russian epic.

было *partl* nearly, on the point of; (only) just. **былой** past, bygone; ~ое *sb* the past. **быль** true story; fact.

быстрота speed. **быстрый** (быстр, -á, -о) fast, quick.

быт (*loc* -ý) way of life. **бытие** being, existence; objective reality; **книга Бытия** Genesis. **бытовой** everyday; social.

быть (*pres 3rd sg* есть, *pl* суть; *fut* буду; *past* был, -á, -о; *imper* будь(те)) *impf* be; be situated; happen. **бытьё** way of life.

бычок (-чка) steer.

бью *etc.: see* бить

бюджет budget.

бюллетень *m* bulletin; ballot-paper; doctor's certificate.

бюро *neut indecl* bureau; office; writing-desk. **бюрократ** bureaucrat. **бюрократизм** bureaucracy. **бюрократический** bureaucratic. **бюрократия** bureaucracy; bureaucrats.

бюст bust. **бюстгальтер** bra.

В

в, **во** *prep* I. +*acc* into, to; on; at; within; through; **быть в** take after; **в два раза больше** twice as big; **в наши дни** in our day; **войти в дом** go into the house; **в понедельник** on Monday; **в четыре часа** at four o'clock **высотой в три метра** three metres high; **играть в шахматы** play chess; **поехать в Москву** go to Moscow; **сесть в вагон** get into the carriage; **смотреть в окно** look out of the window. II. +*prep* in; at; **в двадцатом веке** in the twentieth century; **в театре** at the theatre; **в трёх километрах от города** three kilometres from the town; **в этом году** this year; **в январе** in January.

вагон carriage, coach; ~-**ресторан** restaurant car. **вагонетка** truck, trolley. **вагоновожатый** *sb* tram-driver.

важничать *impf* give o.s. airs; +*instr* plume o.s., pride o.s., on. **важность** importance; pomposity. **важный** (-жен, -жна, -о) important; weighty; pompous.

ваза vase, bowl.

вазелин Vaseline (*propr*).

вакансия vacancy. **вакантный** vacant.

вакса (shoe-)polish.

вакуум vacuum.

вакцина vaccine.

вал[1] (*loc* -ý; *pl* -ы) bank; rampart; billow, roller; barrage.

вал[2] (*loc* -ý; *pl* -ы) shaft.

валенок (-нка; *gen pl* -нок) felt boot.

валет knave, Jack.

валик roller, cylinder.

валить[1] *impf* flock, throng; **вали(те)!** have a go!

валить[2] (-лю, -лишь) *impf* (*pf* по~, с~) throw down, bring down; pile up; ~ся fall, collapse.

валовой gross; wholesale.

валторна French horn.

валун (-а) boulder.

вальс waltz. **вальсировать** *impf* waltz.

валюта currency; foreign currency.

валя́ть *impf* (*pf* на~, с~) drag; roll; shape; bungle; ~ **дурака́** play the fool; **валя́й(те)!** go ahead!; ~**ся** lie, lie about; roll, wallow.

вам, ва́ми: *see* вы

вампи́р vampire.

ванда́л vandal. **вандали́зм** vandalism.

вани́ль vanilla.

ва́нна bath. **ва́нная** *sb* bathroom.

ва́рвар barbarian. **ва́рварский** barbaric. **ва́рварство** barbarity; vandalism.

ва́режка mitten.

варёный boiled. **варе́нье** jam.

вари́ть (-рю́, -ришь) *impf* (*pf* с~) boil; cook; ~**ся** boil; cook.

вариа́нт version; option; scenario.

вас: *see* вы

василёк (-лька́) cornflower.

ва́та cotton wool; wadding.

ватерли́ния water-line. **ватерпа́с** (spirit-)level.

вати́н (sheet) wadding. **ва́тник** quilted jacket. **ва́тный** quilted, wadded.

ватру́шка cheese-cake.

ватт (*gen pl* ватт) watt.

ва́учер coupon (*exchangeable for government-issued share*).

ва́фля (*gen pl* -фель) wafer; waffle.

ва́хта (*naut*) watch. **вахтёр** janitor, porter.

ваш (-его) *m*, **ва́ша** (-ей) *f*, **ва́ше** (-его) *neut*, **ва́ши** (-их) *pl*, *pron* your, yours.

вбега́ть *impf*, **вбежа́ть** (вбегу́) *pf* run in.

вберу́ *etc.*: *see* вобра́ть

вбива́ть *impf of* вбить

вбира́ть *impf of* вобра́ть

вбить (вобью́, -ьёшь) *pf* (*impf* вбива́ть) drive in, hammer in.

вблизи́ *adv* (+от+*gen*) close (to), near by.

вбок *adv* sideways, to one side.

вброд *adv:* переходи́ть ~ ford, wade.

вва́ливать *impf*, **ввали́ть** (-лю́, -лишь) *pf* throw heavily, heave, bundle; ~**ся** fall heavily; sink, become sunken; burst in.

введе́ние introduction. **введу́** *etc.*: *see* ввести́

ввезти́ (-зу́, -зёшь; ввёз, -ла́) *pf* (*impf* ввози́ть) import; bring in.

вве́рить *pf* (*impf* вверя́ть) entrust, confide; ~**ся** +*dat* trust in, put one's faith in.

ввернуть (-ну́, -нёшь) *pf*, **ввёр-тывать** *impf* screw in; insert.

вверх *adv* up, upward(s); ~**дном** upside down; ~ (по ле́стнице) upstairs. **вверху́** *adv* above, overhead.

вверя́ть(ся) *impf of* вве́рить(ся)

ввести́ (-еду́, -едёшь; ввёл, -а́) *pf* (*impf* вводи́ть) bring in; introduce.

ввиду́ *prep*+*gen* in view of.

ввинти́ть (-нчу́) *pf*, **вви́нчивать** *impf* screw in.

ввод lead-in. **вводи́ть** (-ожу́, -о́дишь) *impf of* ввести́. **вво́дный** introductory; parenthetic.

ввожу́ *see* вводи́ть, ввози́ть

ввоз importation; import(s). **ввози́ть** (-ожу́, -о́зишь) *impf of* ввезти́

вво́лю *adv* to one's heart's content.

ввысь *adv* up, upward(s).

ввяза́ть (-яжу́, -я́жешь) *pf*, **ввя́зывать** *impf* knit in; involve; ~**ся** meddle, get or be mixed up (in).

вглубь *adv & prep*+*gen* deep (into), into the depths.

вгляде́ться (-яжу́сь) *pf*, **вгля́-дываться** *impf* peer, look closely (в+*acc* at).

вгоня́ть *impf of* вогна́ть. **вда-ва́ться** (вдаю́сь, -ёшься) *impf of* вда́ться

вдави́ть (-авлю́, -а́вишь) *pf*, **вда́-вливать** *impf* press in.

вдалеке́, вдали́ *adv* in the distance, far away. **вдаль** *adv* into the distance.

вда́ться (-а́мся, -а́шься, -а́стся, -ади́мся; -а́лся, -ла́сь) *pf* (*impf* вдава́ться) jut out; penetrate, go in.

вдво́е *adv* twice; double; ~ бо́льше twice as big, as much, as many. **вдвоём** *adv* (the) two together, both. **вдвойне́** *adv* twice as much; double; doubly.

вдева́ть *impf of* вдеть

вде́лать *pf*, **вде́лывать** *impf* set in, fit in.

вдёргивать *impf*, **вдёрнуть** (-ну) *pf* в+*acc* thread through, pull through.

вдеть (-е́ну) *pf* (*impf* вдева́ть) put in, thread.

вдоба́вок *adv* in addition; besides.

вдова́ widow. вдове́ц (-вца́) widower.

вдо́воль *adv* enough; in abundance.

вдого́нку *adv* (за+*instr*) after, in pursuit (of).

вдоль *adv* lengthwise; ~ и попере́к far and wide; in detail; *prep*+*gen* or по+*dat* along.

вдох breath. вдохнове́ние inspiration, вдохнове́нный inspired. вдохнови́ть (-влю́) *pf*, вдохновля́ть *impf* inspire. вдохну́ть (-ну́, -нёшь) *pf* (*impf* вдыха́ть) breathe in.

вдре́безги *adv* to smithereens.

вдруг *adv* suddenly.

вду́маться *pf*, вду́мываться *impf* ponder, meditate; +в+*acc* think over. вду́мчивый thoughtful.

вдыха́ние inhalation. вдыха́ть *impf* of вдохну́ть

вегетариа́нец (-нца), -нка vegetarian. вегетариа́нский vegetarian.

ве́дать *impf* know; +*instr* manage, handle. ве́дение[1] authority, jurisdiction.

ве́дение[2] conducting, conduct; ~ книг book-keeping. ве́домость (*gen pl* -éй) list, register. ве́домственный departmental. ве́домство department.

ведро́ (*pl* вёдра, -дер) bucket; vedro (approx 12 litres).

веду́ *etc*.: *see* вести́. веду́щий leading.

ведь *partl* & *conj* you see, you know; isn't it? is it?

ве́дьма witch.

ве́ер (*pl* -á) fan.

ве́жливость politeness. ве́жливый polite.

везде́ *adv* everywhere.

везе́ние luck. везу́чий lucky. везти́ (-зу́, -зёшь; вёз, -ла́) *impf* (*pf* по~) convey; bring, take; *impers*+*dat* be lucky; ему́ не везло́ he had no luck.

век (*loc* -ý; *pl* -á) century; age; life, lifetime. век *adv* for ages.

ве́ко (*pl* -и, век) eyelid.

веково́й ancient, age-old.

ве́ксель (*pl* -я́, -éй) *m* promissory note, bill (of exchange).

вёл *etc*.: *see* вести́

веле́ть (-лю́) *impf* & *pf* order; не ~ forbid.

велика́н giant. вели́кий (вели́к, -а or -á) great; big, large; too big; ~ пост Lent.

велико- *in comb* great. Великобрита́ния Great Britain. великоду́шие magnanimity. ~ду́шный magnanimous. ~ле́пие splendour. ~ле́пный splendid.

велича́вый stately, majestic. велича́йший greatest, supreme. вели́чественный majestic, grand. вели́чество Majesty. вели́чие greatness, grandeur. величина́ (*pl* -и́ны, -а́м) size; quantity, magnitude; value; great figure.

велосипе́д bicycle. велосипеди́ст cyclist.

вельве́т velveteen; ~ в ру́бчик corduroy.

вельмо́жа *m* grandee.

ве́на vein.

венге́рец (-рца), венге́рка Hungarian. венге́рский Hungarian. венгр Hungarian. Ве́нгрия Hungary.

венде́тта vendetta.

венери́ческий venereal.

вене́ц (-нца́) crown; wreath.

ве́ник besom; birch twigs.

вено́к (-нка́) wreath, garland.

ве́нтиль *m* valve.

вентиля́тор ventilator; extractor (fan). вентиля́ция ventilation.

венча́ние wedding; coronation. венча́ть *impf* (*pf* об~, по~, у~) crown; marry; ~ся be married, marry. ве́нчик halo; corolla; rim; ring, bolt.

ве́ра faith, belief.

вера́нда veranda.

ве́рба willow; willow branch. ве́рбн|ый; ~ое воскресе́нье Palm Sunday.

верблю́д camel.

вербова́ть *impf* (*pf* за~) recruit; win over. вербо́вка recruitment.

верёвка rope; string; cord. верёвочный rope.

вери́ница row, file, line, string.

ве́реск heather.

веретено́ (*pl* -тёна) spindle.

вереща́ть (-щу́) *impf* squeal; chirp.

ве́рить *impf* (*pf* по~) believe, have faith; +*dat* or в+*acc* trust (in), believe in.

вермише́ль vermicelli.

вернее *adv* rather. **верно** *partl* probably, I suppose. **верность** faithfulness, loyalty.

вернуть (-ну́, -нёшь) *pf* (*impf* возвраща́ть) give back, return; ~ся return.

верный (-рен, -рна́, -о) faithful, loyal; true; correct; reliable.

верование belief. **веровать** *impf* believe. **вероисповедание** religion; denomination. **вероломный** treacherous, perfidious. **вероотступник** apostate. **веротерпимость** (religious) toleration. **вероятно** *adv* probably. **вероятность** probability. **вероятный** probable.

версия version.

верста (*pl* вёрсты) verst (*1.06 km.*).

верстак (-а́) work-bench.

вертел (*pl* -а́) spit, skewer. **вертеть** (-чу́, -тишь) *impf* turn (round); twirl; ~ся turn (round), spin. **вертлявый** fidgety; flighty.

вертикаль vertical line. **вертикальный** vertical.

вертолёт helicopter.

вертушка flirt.

верующий *sb* believer.

верфь shipyard.

верх (*loc* -ý; *pl* -и́) top; summit; height; *pl* upper crust, top brass; high notes. **верхний** upper; top. **верхо́вный** supreme. **верхово́й** riding; *sb* rider. **верхо́вье** (*gen pl* -ьев) upper reaches. **верхола́з** steeplejack. **верхо́м** *adv* on horseback; astride. **верху́шка** top, summit; apex; top brass.

верчу́ *etc.: see* **верте́ть**

вершина top, summit; peak; apex. **вершить** *impf* +*instr* manage, control.

вершо́к vershok (*4.4 cm.*); smattering.

вес (*loc* -ý; *pl* -а́) weight.

веселить *impf* (*pf* раз~) cheer, gladden; ~ся enjoy o.s.; amuse o.s. **весело** *adv* merrily. **весёлый** (весел, -а́, -о) merry; cheerful. **веселье** merriment.

весенний spring.

весить (вешу) *impf* weigh. **веский** weighty, solid.

весло (*pl* вёсла, -сел) oar.

весна (*pl* вёсны, -сен) spring.

весной *adv* in (the) spring.

веснушка freckle.

вест (*naut*) west; west wind.

вести (веду́, -дёшь; вёл, -а́) *impf* (*pf* по~) lead, take; conduct; drive; run; keep; ~ себя behave, conduct o.s.; ~сь be the custom.

вестибюль *m* (entrance) hall, lobby.

вестник herald; bulletin. **весть**[1] (*gen pl* -е́й) news; без вести without trace. **весть**[2]: Бог ~ God knows.

весы (*pl*; *gen* -о́в) scales, balance; Libra.

весь (всего́ *m*, вся, всей *f*, всё, всего́ *neut*, все, всех *pl*) *pron* all, the whole of; всего хорошего! all the best!; всё everything; без всего without anything; все everybody.

весьма *adv* very, highly.

ветвь (*gen pl* -е́й) branch; bough.

ветер (-тра, *loc* -ý) wind. **ветеро́к** (-рка́) breeze.

ветеран veteran.

ветеринар vet.

ветка branch; twig.

вето *neut indecl* veto.

ветошь old clothes, rags.

ветреный windy; frivolous. **ветров|о́й** wind; ~ое стекло́ windscreen. **ветряк** (-а́) wind turbine; windmill.

ветхий (ветх, -а́, -о) old; dilapidated; В~ завет Old Testament.

ветчина ham.

ветшать *impf* (*pf* об~) decay; become dilapidated.

веха landmark.

вечер (*pl* -а́) evening; party. **вечеринка** party. **вечерний** evening. **вечерня** (*gen pl* -рен) vespers. **вечером** *adv* in the evening.

вечно *adv* for ever, eternally. **вечнозелёный** evergreen. **вечность** eternity; ages. **вечный** eternal.

вешалка peg, rack; tab, hanger. **вешать** *impf* (*pf* взвесить, повесить, сва́шать) hang; weigh (out); ~ся hang o.s.; weigh o.s.

вешу *etc.: see* **весить**

веща́ние broadcasting. **веща́ть** *impf* broadcast.

вещево́й clothing; ~ мешо́к hold-all, kit-bag. **веще́ственный** substantial, material, real. **вещество́** substance; matter. **вещь** (*gen pl* -е́й) thing;

ве́ялка winnowing-machine. ве́яние winnowing; blowing; trend. ве́ять (ве́ю) *impf* (*pf* про~) winnow; blow; flutter.

взад *adv* backwards; ~ и вперёд back and forth.

взаи́мность reciprocity. взаи́мный mutual, reciprocal.

взаимо- *in comb* inter-. взаимоде́йствие interaction; co-operation. ~де́йствовать *impf* interact; cooperate. ~отноше́ние interrelation; *pl* relations. ~по́мощь mutual aid. ~понима́ние mutual understanding. ~связь interdependence, correlation.

взаймы́ *adv*: взять ~ borrow; дать ~ lend.

взаме́н *prep+gen* instead of; in return for.

взаперти́ *adv* under lock and key; in seclusion.

взба́лмошный unbalanced, eccentric.

взбега́ть *impf*, взбежа́ть (-егу́) *pf* run up.

взберу́сь *etc.*: *see* взобра́ться. вз|бе́сить(ся (-ешу́(сь, -е́сишь(ся) *pf*. взбива́ть *impf of* взбить.

взбира́ться *impf of* взобра́ться

взби́тый whipped, beaten. взбить (взобью́, -бьёшь) *pf* (*impf* взбива́ть) beat (up); whip; shake up.

вз|борозди́ть (-зжу́) *pf*.

вз|бунтова́ться *pf*.

взбуха́ть *impf*, взбу́хнуть (-нет; -ух) *pf* swell (out).

взва́ливать *impf*, взвали́ть (-лю́, -лишь) *pf* load; + на+*acc* saddle with.

взве́сить (-е́шу) *pf* (*impf* ве́шать, взве́шивать) weigh.

взвести́ (-еду́, -едёшь; -ёл, -á) *pf* (*impf* взводи́ть) lead up; raise; cock; + на+*acc* impute to.

взве́шивать *impf of* взве́сить

взвива́ть(ся *impf of* взви́ть(ся

взви́зг scream; yelp. взви́згивать *impf*, взви́згнуть (-ну) *pf* scream; yelp.

взвинти́ть (-нчу́) *pf*, взви́нчивать *impf* excite, work up; inflate. взви́нченный worked up; nervy; inflated.

взвить (взовью́, -ёшь; -ил, -á, -о) *pf* (*impf* взвива́ть) raise; ~ся rise, be hoisted; soar.

взвод¹ platoon, troop.

взвод² notch. взводи́ть (-ожу́, -о́дишь) *impf of* взвести́

взволно́ванный agitated; worried.

вз|волнова́ть(ся (-ну́ю(сь) *pf*.

взгляд look; glance; opinion. взгля́дывать *impf*, взгляну́ть (-яну́, -я́нешь) *pf* look, glance.

взго́рье hillock.

вздёргивать *impf*, вздёрнуть (-ну) *pf* hitch up; jerk up; turn up.

вздор nonsense. вздо́рный cantankerous; foolish.

вздорожа́ние rise in price. вз|дорожа́ть *pf*.

вздох sigh. вздохну́ть (-ну́, -нёшь) *pf* (*impf* вздыха́ть) sigh.

вздра́гивать *impf* (*pf* вздро́гнуть) shudder, quiver.

вздремну́ть *pf* have a nap, doze.

вздро́гнуть (-ну) *pf* (*impf* вздра́гивать) start; wince.

вздува́ть(ся *impf of* вздуть¹(ся

вздума́ть *pf* take it into one's head; не вздумай(те)! don't you dare!

вздутие swelling. вздутый swollen. вздуть¹ *pf* (*impf* вздува́ть) inflate; ~ся swell.

вздуть² *pf* thrash.

вздыха́ть *impf* (*pf* вздохну́ть) breathe; sigh.

взима́ть *impf* levy, collect.

взла́мывать *impf of* взлома́ть. вз|леле́ять *pf*.

взлёт flight; take-off. взлета́ть *impf*, взлете́ть (-лечу́) *pf* fly (up); take off. взлётный take-off; взлётно-поса́дочная полоса́ runway.

взлом breaking open, breaking in. взлома́ть *pf* (*impf* взла́мывать) break open; break up. взло́мщик burglar.

взлохма́ченный dishevelled.

взмах stroke, wave, flap. взма́хивать *impf*, взмахну́ть (-ну́, -нёшь) *pf* +*instr* wave, flap.

взмо́рье seaside; coastal waters.

вз|мути́ть (-учу́, -у́тишь) *pf*.

взнос payment; fee, dues.

взнузда́ть *pf*, взну́здывать *impf* bridle.

взобра́ться (взберу́сь, -ёшься; -áлся, -лáсь, -áлóсь) *pf* (*impf* взбира́ться) climb (up).

взобью́ *etc.*: *see* взбить. взовью́ *etc.*:

see взвить

взойти́ (-йду́, -йдёшь; -ошёл, -шла́) *pf* (*impf* вос-, всходи́ть) rise, go up; на+*acc* mount.

взор look, glance.

взорва́ть (-ву́, -вёшь; -а́л, -а́, -о) *pf* (*impf* взрыва́ть) blow up; exasperate; ~ся burst, explode.

взро́слый *adj & sb* adult.

взрыв explosion; outburst. взрыва́тель *m* fuse. взрыва́ть *impf*, взрыть (-ро́ю) *pf* (*pf also* взорва́ть) blow up; ~ся explode. взрывно́й explosive; blasting. взрывча́тка explosive. взры́вчатый explosive.

взъеро́шенный tousled, dishevelled. взъеро́шивать *impf*, взъеро́шить (-шу) *pf* tousle, rumple.

взыва́ть *impf of* воззва́ть

взыска́ние penalty; exaction. взыска́тельный exacting. взыска́ть (-ыщу́, -ы́щешь) *pf*, взы́скивать *impf* exact, recover; call to account.

взя́тие taking, capture. взя́тка bribe. взя́точничество bribery. взя́ть(ся (возьму́(сь, -мёшь(ся; -я́л(ся, -а́(сь, -о(сь) *pf of* брать(ся

вибра́ция vibration. вибри́ровать *impf* vibrate.

вивисе́кция vivisection.

вид[1] (*loc* -ý) look; appearance; shape, form; condition; view; prospect; sight; де́лать вид pretend; име́ть в ~ý intend; bear in mind.

вид[2] kind; species.

вида́ться *impf* (*pf* по~) meet.

виде́ние[1] sight, vision. виде́ние[2] vision, apparition.

ви́део *neut indecl* video (cassette) recorder; video film; video cassette. видеоигра́ video game. видеока́мера video camera. видеокассе́та video cassette. видеомагнитофо́н video (cassette) recorder.

ви́деть (ви́жу) *impf* (*pf* у~) see; ~ во сне dream (of); ~ся see one another; appear. ви́димо *adv* evidently. ви́димость visibility; appearance. ви́димый visible; apparent, evident. ви́дный (-ден, -дна́, -о) visible; distinguished.

видоизмене́ние modification. видоизмени́ть *pf*, видоизменя́ть *impf* modify.

видоиска́тель *m* view-finder.

ви́жу *see* ви́деть

ви́за visa.

визг squeal; yelp. визжа́ть (-жу́) *impf* squeal, yelp, squeak.

визи́т visit. визи́тка business card.

викто́рина quiz.

ви́лка fork; plug. ви́лы (*pl*; *gen* вил) pitchfork.

вильну́ть (-ну́, -нёшь) *pf*, виля́ть *impf* twist and turn; prevaricate; +*instr* wag.

вина́ (*pl* ви́ны) fault, guilt; blame.

винегре́т Russian salad; medley.

вини́тельный accusative. вини́ть *impf* accuse; ~ся (*pf* по~) confess.

ви́нный wine; winy. вино́ (*pl* -а) wine.

винова́тый guilty. вино́вник initiator; culprit. вино́вный guilty.

виногра́д vine; grapes. виногра́дник vineyard. виногра́дный grape; wine. виноку́ренный заво́д distillery.

винт (-а́) screw. винти́ть (-нчу́) *impf* screw up. винто́вка rifle. винтово́й screw; spiral.

виолонче́ль cello.

вира́ж (-а́) turn; bend.

виртуо́з virtuoso. виртуо́зный masterly.

ви́рус virus. ви́русный virus.

ви́селица gallows. висе́ть (вишу́) *impf* hang. ви́снуть (-ну; вис(нул) *impf* hang; droop.

ви́ски *neut indecl* whisky.

висо́к (-ска́) temple.

високо́сный год leap-year.

вист whist.

вися́чий hanging; ~ замо́к padlock; ~ мост suspension bridge.

витами́н vitamin.

витева́тый flowery, ornate. вито́й twisted, spiral. вито́к (-тка́) turn, coil.

витра́ж (-а́) stained-glass window. витри́на shop-window; showcase.

вить (вью, вьёшь; вил, -а́, -о) *impf* (*pf* с~) twist, wind, weave; ~ся wind, twine; curl; twist; whirl.

вихо́р (-хра́) tuft. вихра́стый shaggy. вихрь *m* whirlwind; vortex; снеж́ный ~ blizzard.

ви́це- *pref* vice-. ви́це-адмира́л vice-admiral. ~президе́нт vice-president.

вицмунди́р (dress) uniform.

ВИЧ (*abbr of* ви́рус иммуно-дефици́та челове́ка) HIV.

вишнёвый cherry. ви́шня (*gen pl* -шен) cherry, cherries; cherry-tree.

вишу́: *see* висе́ть

вишь *partl* look, just look!

вка́лывать *impf* (*sl*) work hard; *impf of* вколо́ть

вка́пывать *impf of* вкопа́ть

вкати́ть (-ачу́, -а́тишь) *pf*, вка́тывать *impf* roll in; administer.

вклад deposit; contribution. вкла́д-ка supplementary sheet. вкладно́й лист loose leaf, insert. вкла́дчик depositor.

вкла́дывать *impf of* вложи́ть

вкле́ивать *impf*, вкле́ить *pf* stick in.

вкли́нивать *impf*, вклини́ться *pf* edge one's way in.

включа́тель *m* switch. включа́ть *impf*, включи́ть (-чу́) *pf* include; switch on; plug in; ~ся в+*acc* join in, enter into. включа́я including. включе́ние inclusion, insertion; switching on. включи́тельно *adv* inclusive.

вкола́чивать *impf*, вколоти́ть (-очу́, -о́тишь) *pf* hammer in, knock in.

вколо́ть (-олю́, -о́лешь) *pf* (*impf* вка́лывать) stick (in).

вкопа́ть *pf* (*impf* вка́пывать) dig in.

вкось *adv* obliquely.

вкра́дчивый ingratiating. вкра́-дываться *impf*, вкра́сться (-аду́сь, -аде́шься) *pf* creep in; insinuate o.s.

вкра́тце *adv* briefly, succinctly.

вкривь *adv* aslant; wrongly, per-versely.

вкруг = вокру́г

вкрутую *adv* hard(-boiled).

вкус taste. вкуси́ть (-ушу́, -у́сишь) *pf*, вкуша́ть *impf* taste; partake of. вку́сный (-сен, -сна́, -о) tasty, nice.

вла́га moisture.

влага́лище vagina.

владе́лец (-льца), -лица owner. владе́ние ownership; possession; property. владе́тель *m*, -ница pos-sessor; sovereign. владе́ть (-е́ю) *impf* +*instr* own, possess; control.

влады́ка *m* master, sovereign. влады́чество dominion, sway.

вла́жность humidity; moisture.

вла́жный (-жен, -жна́, -о) damp, moist, humid.

вла́мываться *impf of* вломи́ться

вла́ствовать *impf* +(над+) *instr* rule, hold sway over. власте́лин ruler; master. вла́стный imperious, commanding; empowered, compe-tent. власть (*gen pl* -е́й) power; au-thority.

вле́во *adv* to the left (от+*gen* of).

влеза́ть *impf*, влезть (-зу; влез) *pf* climb in; get in; fit in.

влёк *etc.*: *see* влечь

влета́ть *impf*, влете́ть (-ечу́) *pf* fly in; rush in.

влече́ние attraction; inclination. влечь (-еку́, -ечёшь; влёк, -ла́) *impf* draw; attract; ~ за собо́й involve, entail.

влива́ть *impf*, влить (волью́, -ёшь; влил, -а́, -о) *pf* pour in; instil.

влия́ние influence. влия́тельный influential. влия́ть *impf* (*pf* по~) на+*acc* influence, affect.

вложе́ние enclosure; investment. вложи́ть (-ожу́, -о́жишь) *pf* (*impf* вкла́дывать) put in, insert; enclose; invest.

вломи́ться (-млю́сь, -мишься) *pf* (*impf* вла́мываться) break in.

влюби́ть (-блю́, -бишь) *pf*, влю-бля́ть *impf* make fall in love (в+*acc* with); ~ся fall in love. влю-блённый (-лён, -а́) in love; *sb* lover.

вма́зать (-а́жу) *pf*, вма́зывать *impf* cement, putty in.

вмени́ть *pf*, вменя́ть *impf* impute; impose. вменя́емый (*law*) respon-sible; sane.

вме́сте *adv* together; ~ с тем at the same time, also.

вмести́лище receptacle. вмести́-мость capacity; tonnage. вмести́-тельный capacious. вмести́ть (-ещу́) *pf* (*impf* вмеща́ть) hold, accommo-date; put; ~ся go in.

вме́сто *prep*+*gen* instead of.

вмеша́тельство interference; inter-vention. вмеша́ть *pf*, вме́шивать *impf* mix in; implicate; ~ся interfere, intervene.

вмеща́ть(ся *impf of* вмести́ть(ся

вмиг *adv* in an instant.

вмина́ть *impf*, вмять (вомну́, -нёшь) *pf* press in, dent. вмя́тина dent.

внаём, внаймы *adv* to let; for hire.

внача́ле *adv* at first.

вне *prep+gen* outside; ~ себя́ beside o.s.

вне- *pref* extra-; outside; -less. **вне-бра́чный** extra-marital; illegitimate. **~вре́менный** timeless. **~кла́ссный** extracurricular. **~очередно́й** out of turn; extraordinary. **~шта́тный** freelance, casual.

внедре́ние introduction; inculcation. **внедри́ть** *pf*, **внедря́ть** *impf* inculcate; introduce; ~ся take root.

внеза́пно *adv* suddenly. **внеза́пный** sudden.

внемлю *etc.: see* **внима́ть**

внесе́ние bringing in; deposit. **внести́** (-су́, -сёшь; внёс, -ла́) *pf* (*impf* **вноси́ть**) bring in; introduce; deposit; insert.

вне́шне *adv* outwardly. **вне́шний** outer; external; outside; foreign. **вне́шность** exterior; appearance.

вниз *adv* down(wards); ~ по+*dat* down. **внизу́** *adv* below; downstairs.

вника́ть *impf*, **вни́кнуть** (-ну; вник) *pf* в+*acc* go carefully into, investigate thoroughly.

внима́ние attention. **внима́тельный** attentive. **внима́ть** *impf* (*pf* **внять**) listen to; heed.

вничью́ *adv*: окончи́ться ~ end in a draw; сыгра́ть ~ draw.

вновь *adv* anew, again.

вноси́ть (-ошу́, -о́сишь) *impf of* **внести́**

внук grandson; *pl* grandchildren, descendants.

вну́тренний inner; internal. **вну́тренность** interior; *pl* entrails; internal organs. **внутри́** *adv & prep+gen* inside. **внутрь** *adv & prep+gen* inside, in; inwards.

внуча́та (*pl*; *gen* -ча́т) grandchildren. **внуча́тый** second, great-; ~ брат second cousin; ~ племя́нник great-nephew. **вну́чка** grand-daughter.

внуша́ть *impf*, **внуши́ть** (-шу́) *pf* instil; +*dat* inspire with. **внуше́ние** suggestion; reproof. **внуши́тельный** inspiring; imposing.

вня́тный distinct. **внять** (*no fut*; -ял, -а́, -о) *pf of* **внима́ть**

во: *see* **в**

вобра́ть (вберу́, -рёшь; -а́л, -а́, -о)

pf (*impf* **вбира́ть**) absorb; inhale.

вобью́ *etc.: see* **вбить**

вовлека́ть *impf*, **вовле́чь** (-еку́, -ечёшь; ~ёк, -екла́) *pf* draw in, involve.

во́время *adv* in time; on time.

во́все *adv* quite; ~ не not at all.

во-вторы́х *adv* secondly.

вогна́ть (вгоню́, -о́нишь; -гна́л, -а́, -о) *pf* (*impf* **вгоня́ть**) drive in.

во́гнутый concave. **вогну́ть** (-ну́, -нёшь) *pf* (*impf* **вгиба́ть**) bend or curve inwards.

вода́ (*acc* во́ду, *gen* -ы́; *pl* -ы) water; *pl* the waters; spa.

водвори́ть *pf*, **водворя́ть** *impf* settle, install; establish.

води́тель *m* driver. **води́ть** (вожу́, во́дишь) *impf* lead; conduct; take; drive; ~ся be found; associate (with); be the custom.

во́дка vodka. **во́дн|ый** water; ~ые лы́жи water-skiing; water-skis.

водо- *in comb* water-; water-; hydraulic; hydro-. **водобоя́знь** hydrophobia. **~воро́т** whirlpool; maelstrom. **~ём** reservoir. **~измеще́ние** displacement. **~ка́чка** water-tower, pumping station. **~ла́з** diver. **~ле́й** Aquarius. **~непроница́емый** waterproof. **~отво́дный** drainage. **~па́д** waterfall. **~по́й** watering-place. **~прово́д** water-pipe, water-main; water supply. **~прово́дчик** plumber. **~разде́л** watershed. **~ро́д** hydrogen. **во́доросль** water-plant; seaweed. **~снабже́ние** water supply. **~сто́к** drain, gutter. **~храни́лище** reservoir.

водружа́ть *impf*, **водрузи́ть** (-ужу́) *pf* hoist; erect.

водяни́стый watery. **водяно́й** water.

воева́ть (вою́ю) *impf* wage war. **воево́да** *m* voivode; commander.

воеди́но *adv* together.

военко́м military commissar.

военно- *in comb* military; war-. **вое́нно-возду́шный** air-, air-force. **вое́нно-морско́й** naval. **~пле́нный** *sb* prisoner of war. **вое́нно-полево́й суд** court-martial. **~слу́жащий** *sb* serviceman.

вое́нн|ый military; war; *sb* serviceman; ~ое положе́ние martial law;

вор (pl -ы, -óв) thief; criminal.

ворва́ться (-ву́сь, -вёшься; -а́лся, -ла́сь, -а́лóсь) pf (impf врыва́ться) burst in.

воркотня́ grumbling.

воробе́й sparrow.

ворова́тый thievish; furtive. воро́ва́ть impf (pf с~) steal. воро́вка woman thief. воровски́ adv furtively. воровско́й thieves'. воро́вство́ stealing; theft.

во́рон raven. воро́на crow.

воро́нка funnel; crater.

вороно́й black.

во́рот[1] collar; neckband.

во́рот[2] winch; windlass.

воро́та (pl; gen -ро́т) gate(s); gateway; goal.

вороти́ть (-очу́, -о́тишь) pf bring back, get back; turn back; ~ся return.

воротни́к (-á) collar.

во́рох (pl -á) heap, pile; heaps.

воро́чать impf turn; move; +instr have control of; ~ся move, turn.

ворочу́(сь etc.: see вороти́ть(ся

вороши́ть (-шу́) impf stir up; turn (over).

ворс nap, pile.

ворча́ть (-чу́) impf grumble; growl. ворчли́вый peevish; grumpy.

восвоя́си adv home.

восемна́дцатый eighteenth. восемна́дцать eighteen. во́семь (-сьми́, instr -сьмью́ or -семью́) eight. во́семьдесят eighty. восемьсо́т (-сьмисо́т, -ста́ми) eight hundred. во́семью adv eight times.

воск wax, beeswax.

воскли́кнуть (-ну) pf, восклица́ть impf exclaim. восклица́ние exclamation. восклица́тельный exclamatory; ~ знак exclamation mark.

восково́й wax; waxy; waxed.

воскреса́ть impf, воскре́снуть (-ну; -éс) pf rise from the dead; revive. воскресе́ние resurrection. воскресе́нье Sunday. воскреси́ть (-ешу́) pf, воскреша́ть impf resurrect; revive. воскреше́ние resurrection; revival.

воспале́ние inflammation. воспалённый (-лён, -á) inflamed. воспали́ть pf, воспаля́ть impf inflame; ~ся become inflamed.

воспита́ние upbringing, education. воспи́танник, -ница pupil. воспи́танный well-brought-up. воспита́тель m tutor; educator. воспита́тельный educational. воспита́ть pf, воспи́тывать impf bring up; foster; educate.

воспламени́ть pf, воспламеня́ть impf ignite; fire; ~ся ignite; flare up. воспламеня́емый inflammable.

вос|по́льзоваться pf.

воспомина́ние recollection, memory; pl memoirs; reminiscences.

вос|препя́тствовать pf.

воспрети́ть (-ещу́) pf, воспреща́ть impf forbid. воспреще́ние prohibition. воспрещённый (-щён, -á) prohibited.

восприи́мчивый impressionable; susceptible. воспринима́ть impf, восприня́ть (-иму́, -и́мешь; -и́нял, -á, -о) pf perceive; grasp. восприя́тие perception.

воспроизведе́ние reproduction. воспроизвести́ (-еду́, -еде́шь; -вёл, -á) pf, воспроизводи́ть (-ожу́, -о́дишь) impf reproduce. воспроизводи́тельный reproductive. воспроизво́дство reproduction.

вос|проти́виться (-влюсь) pf.

воссоедине́ние reunification. воссоедини́ть pf, воссоединя́ть impf reunite.

восстава́ть (-таю́, -таёшь) impf of восста́ть.

восста́ние insurrection.

восстанови́ть (-влю́, -вишь) pf (impf восстана́вливать) restore; reinstate; recall; ~ про́тив+gen set against. восстановле́ние restoration.

восста́ть (-а́ну) pf (impf восстава́ть) rise (up).

восто́к east.

восто́рг delight, rapture. восторга́ться+instr be delighted with, go into raptures over. восто́рженный enthusiastic.

восто́чный east, eastern; easterly; oriental.

востре́бование: до востре́бования to be called for, poste restante.

восхвали́ть (-лю́, -лишь) pf, восхваля́ть impf praise, extol.

восхити́тельный entrancing; delightful. восхити́ть (-хищу́) pf, восхища́ть impf enrapture; ~ся +instr be enraptured by. восхище́ние delight; admiration.

восхо́д rising. восходи́ть (-ожу́, -о́дишь) impf of взойти́; ~ к+dat go back to, date from. восхожде́ние ascent. восходя́щий rising.

восше́ствие accession.

восьма́я sb eighth; octave. восьме́рка eight; figure eight; No. 8; figure of eight.

восьми- in comb eight-; octo-. восьмигра́нник octahedron. ~деся́тый eightieth. ~ле́тний eight-year; eight-year-old. ~со́тый eight-hundredth. ~уго́льник octagon. ~уго́льный octagonal.

восьмо́й eighth.

вот partl here (is), there (is); this (is); ~ и всё and that's all; ~ как! no! really? ~ та́к! that's right!; ~ что! no! not really? вот-во́т just, on the point of; partl that's right!

воткну́ть (-ну́, -нёшь) pf (impf втыка́ть) stick in, drive in.

вотру́ etc.: see втере́ть

воцари́ться pf, воцаря́ться impf come to the throne; set in.

вошёл etc.: see войти́

вошь (вши; gen pl вше́й) louse.

вошью́ etc.: see вшить

во́ю etc.: see выть

воюю́ etc.: see воева́ть

впада́ть impf, впасть (-аду́) pf flow; lapse; fall in; +в+acc verge on, approximate to. впаде́ние confluence, (river-)mouth. впа́дина cavity, hollow; socket. впа́лый sunken.

впервы́е adv for the first time.

вперёд adv forward(s), ahead; in future; in advance; идти́ ~ (of clock) be fast. впереди́ adv in front, ahead; in (the) future; prep+gen in front of, before.

впечатле́ние impression. впечатли́тельный impressionable.

вписа́ть (-ишу́, -и́шешь) pf, впи́сывать impf enter, insert; ~ся be enrolled, join.

впита́ть pf, впи́тывать impf absorb, take in; ~ся soak.

впихну́ть (-ну́, -нёшь) pf, впи́хивать impf cram in; shove.

вплавь adv (by) swimming.

вплести́ (-ету́, -етёшь; -ёл, -а́) pf, вплета́ть impf plait in, intertwine; involve.

вплотну́ю adv close; in earnest.

вплоть adv; ~ до+gen (right) up to.

вполго́лоса adv under one's breath.

вполне́ adv fully, entirely; quite.

впопыха́х adv in one's haste.

впо́ру adv at the right time; just right, exactly.

впосле́дствии adv subsequently.

впотьма́х adv in the dark.

впра́ве adv: быть ~ have a right.

впра́во adv to the right (от+gen of).

впредь adv in (the) future; ~ до+gen until.

впро́голодь adv half starving.

впро́чем conj however, but; though.

впры́скивание injection. впры́скивать impf, впры́снуть (-ну) pf inject.

впряга́ть impf впрячь (-ягу́, -яжёшь; -яг, -ла́) pf harness.

впуск admittance. впуска́ть impf, впусти́ть (-ущу́, -у́стишь) pf admit, let in.

впусту́ю adv to no purpose, in vain.

впущу́ etc.: see впусти́ть

враг (-а́) enemy. вражда́ enmity. вражде́бный hostile. враждова́ть be at enmity. вра́жеский enemy.

вразбро́д adv separately, disunitedly.

вразре́з adv: идти́ ~ с+instr go against.

вразуми́тельный intelligible, clear; persuasive.

враспло́х adv unawares.

враста́ть impf, врасти́ (-тёт; врос, -ла́) pf grow in; take root.

врата́рь (-я́) m goalkeeper.

врать (вру, врёшь; -ал, -а́, -о) impf (pf на~, со~) lie, tell lies; talk nonsense.

врач (-а́) doctor. враче́бный medical.

враща́ть impf rotate, revolve; ~ся revolve, rotate. враще́ние rotation, revolution.

вред (-а́) harm; damage. вреди́тель m pest; wrecker; pl vermin. вреди́тельство wrecking, (act of) sabotage. вреди́ть (-ежу́) impf (pf по~) +dat harm; damage. вре́дный (-ден, -дна́, -о) harmful.

вре́зать (-е́жу) pf, вреза́ть impf cut

in; set in; (*sl*) +*dat* hit; ~**ся** cut (into); run (into); be engraved; fall in love.
времена́ми *adv* at times. **вре́менно** *adv* temporarily. **временно́й** temporal. **вре́менный** temporary; provisional. **вре́мя** (-мени; *pl* -мена́, -мён, -а́м) *neut* time; tense; ~ го́да season; ~ от вре́мени at times, from time to time; на ~ for a time; ско́лько вре́мени? what is the time?; тем вре́менем meanwhile.
вро́вень *adv* level, on a level.
вро́де *prep*+*gen* like; *partl* such as, like; apparently.
врождённый (-дён, -а́) innate.
врознь, врозь *adv* separately, apart.
врос *etc.*: *see* **врасти́. вру** *etc.*: *see* **врать**
врун (-а́), **вру́нья** liar.
вруча́ть *impf*, **вручи́ть** (-чу́) *pf* hand, deliver; entrust.
вручну́ю *adv* by hand.
врыва́ть(ся *impf of* **ворва́ться**
вряд (ли) *adv* it's not likely; hardly, scarcely.
вса́дить (-ажу́, -а́дишь) *pf*, **вса́живать** *impf* thrust in; sink in. **вса́дник** rider, horseman. **вса́дница** rider, horsewoman.
вса́сывать *impf of* **всоса́ть**
всё, все *pron*: *see* **весь. всё** *adv* always, all the time; ~ (ещё) still; *conj* however, nevertheless; ~ же all the same.
все- *in comb* all-, omni-. **все-возмо́жный** of every kind; all possible. ~**дозво́ленность** permissiveness. ~**ме́рный** of every kind. ~**ми́рный** world, world-wide. ~**могу́щий** omnipotent. ~**наро́дно** *adv* publicly. ~**наро́дный** national; nation-wide. ~**объе́млющий** comprehensive, all-embracing. ~**росси́йский** All-Russian. ~**си́льный** omnipotent. ~**сторо́нний** all-round; comprehensive.
всегда́ always.
всего́ *adv* in all, all told; only.
вселе́нная *sb* universe.
всели́ть *pf*, **вселя́ть** *impf* install, lodge; inspire; ~**ся** move in, install o.s.; be implanted.
всено́щная *sb* night service.
всео́бщий general, universal.
всерьёз *adv* seriously, in earnest.

всё-таки *conj* & *partl* all the same, still. **всеце́ло** *adv* completely.
вска́кивать *impf of* **вскочи́ть**
вскачь *adv* at a gallop.
вскипа́ть *impf*, **вс|кипе́ть** (-плю́) *pf* boil up; flare up.
вс|кипяти́ть(ся (-ячу́(сь) *pf*.
всколыхну́ть (-ну́, -нёшь) *pf* stir; stir up.
вско́льзь *adv* slightly; in passing.
вско́ре *adv* soon, shortly after.
вскочи́ть (-очу́, -о́чишь) *pf* (*impf* **вска́кивать**) jump up.
вскри́кивать *impf*, **вскри́кнуть** (-ну) *pf* shriek, scream. **вскрича́ть** (-чу́) *pf* exclaim.
вскрыва́ть *impf*, **вскрыть** (-ро́ю) *pf* open; reveal; dissect. **вскры́тие** opening; revelation; post-mortem.
вслед *adv* & *prep*+*dat* after; ~ за+*instr* after, following. **всле́дствие** *prep*+*gen* in consequence of.
вслепу́ю *adv* blindly; blindfold.
вслух *adv* aloud.
вслу́шаться *pf*, **вслу́шиваться** *impf* listen attentively.
всма́триваться *impf*, **всмотре́ться** (-рю́сь, -ришься) *pf* look closely.
всмя́тку *adv* soft(-boiled).
всо́вывать *impf of* **всу́нуть**
всоса́ть (-су́, -сёшь) *pf* (*impf* **вса́сывать**) suck in; absorb; imbibe.
вс|паха́ть (-ашу́, -а́шешь) *pf*, **вспа́хивать** *impf* plough up. **вспа́шка** ploughing.
вс|пе́ниться *pf*.
всплеск splash. **всплёскивать** *impf*, **всплесну́ть** (-ну́, -нёшь) *pf* splash; ~ рука́ми throw up one's hands.
всплыва́ть *impf*, **всплыть** (-ыву́, -ывёшь; -ыл, -а́, -о) *pf* rise to the surface; come to light.
вспомина́ть *impf*, **вспо́мнить** *pf* remember; ~**ся** *impers*+*dat*: мне вспо́мнилось I remembered.
вспомога́тельный auxiliary.
вс|поте́ть *pf*.
вспры́гивать *impf*, **вспры́гнуть** (-ну) *pf* jump up.
вспуха́ть *impf*, **вс|пу́хнуть** (-нет; -ух) *pf* swell up.
вспыли́ть *pf* flare up. **вспы́льчивый** hot-tempered.
вспы́хивать *impf*, **вспы́хнуть** (-ну)

pf blaze up; flare up. **вспы́шка** flash; outburst; outbreak.

встава́ть (-таю́, -таёшь) *impf of* **встать**

вста́вить (-влю) *pf*, **вставля́ть** *impf* put in, insert. **вста́вка** insertion; framing, mounting; inset. **вставн|о́й** inserted; set in; ~ы́е зу́бы false teeth.

встать (-а́ну) *pf* (*impf* **встава́ть**) get up; stand up.

встрево́женный *adj* anxious. **вс|трево́жить** (-жу) *pf*.

встрепену́ться (-ну́сь, -нёшься) *pf* rouse o.s.; start (up); beat faster.

встре́тить (-е́чу) *pf*, **встреча́ть** *impf* meet (with); ~ся meet; be found. **встре́ча** meeting. **встре́чный** coming to meet; contrary, head; counter; *sb* person met with; пе́рвый ~ the first person you meet, anybody.

встря́ска shaking; shock. **встря́хивать** *impf*, **встряхну́ть** (-ну́, -нёшь) *pf* shake (up); rouse; ~ся shake o.s.; rouse o.s.

вступа́ть *impf*, **вступи́ть** (-плю́, -пишь) *pf* +в+*acc* enter (into); join (in); +на+*acc* go up, mount; ~ся intervene; +за+*acc* stand up for. **вступи́тельный** introductory; entrance. **вступле́ние** entry, joining; introduction.

всу́нуть (-ну) *pf* (*impf* **всо́вывать**) put in, stick in.

всхли́пнуть (-ну) *pf*, **всхли́пывать** *impf* sob.

всходи́ть (-ожу́, -о́дишь) *impf of* **взойти́. всхо́ды** (*pl; gen* -ов) (corn-) shoots.

всю: *see* **весь**

всю́ду *adv* everywhere.

вся: *see* **весь**

вся́к|ий any; every, all kinds of; ~ом слу́чае in any case; на ~ий слу́чай just in case; *pron* anyone. **вся́чески** *adv* in every possible way.

вта́йне *adv* secretly.

вта́лкивать *impf of* **втолкну́ть. вта́птывать** *impf of* **втопта́ть. вта́скивать** *impf of* **втащи́ть** (-щу́, -щишь) *pf* drag in.

втере́ть (вотру́, вотрёшь; втёр) *pf* (*impf* **втира́ть**) rub in; ~ся insinuate o.s., worm o.s.

втира́ть(ся *impf of* **втере́ть(ся**

втиски́вать *impf*, **вти́снуть** (-ну) *pf* squeeze in; ~ся squeeze (o.s.) in.

втихомо́лку *adv* surreptitiously.

втолкну́ть (-ну́, -нёшь) *pf* (*impf* **вта́лкивать**) push in.

втопта́ть (-пчу́, -пчешь) *pf* (*impf* **вта́птывать**) trample (in).

вторга́ться *impf*, **вто́ргнуться** (-нусь; вто́ргся, -лась) *pf* invade; intrude. **вторже́ние** invasion; intrusion.

вто́рить *impf* play or sing second part; +*dat* repeat, echo. **втори́чный** second, secondary. **вто́рник** Tuesday. **втор|о́й** second; ~о́е *sb* second course. **второстепе́нный** secondary, minor.

второпя́х *adv* in haste.

в-тре́тьих *adv* thirdly. **втро́е** *adv* three times. **втроём** *adv* three (together). **втройне́** *adv* three times as much.

вту́лка plug.

втыка́ть *impf of* **воткну́ть**

втя́гивать *impf*, **втяну́ть** (-ну́, -нешь) *pf* draw in; ~ся +в+*acc* enter; get used to.

вуа́ль veil.

вуз *abbr* (*of* вы́сшее уче́бное заведе́ние) higher educational establishment; college.

вулка́н volcano.

вульга́рный vulgar.

вундерки́нд infant prodigy.

вход entrance; entry. **входи́ть** (-ожу́, -о́дишь) *impf of* **войти́. входно́й** entrance.

вхолосту́ю *adv* idle, free.

вцепи́ться (-плю́сь, -пишься) *pf*, **вцепля́ться** *impf* +в+*acc* clutch, catch hold of.

вчера́ *adv* yesterday. **вчера́шний** yesterday's.

вчерне́ in rough.

вче́тверо *adv* four times. **вчетверо́м** *adv* four (together).

вши *etc.: see* **вошь**

вшива́ть *impf of* **вшить**

вши́вый lousy.

вширь *adv* in breadth; widely.

вшить (вошью́, -ьёшь) *pf* (*impf* вшива́ть) sew in.

въе́дливый corrosive; caustic.

въезд entry; entrance. **въезжа́ть** *impf*, **въе́хать** (-е́ду, -е́дешь) *pf*

(+в+*acc*) ride in(to); drive in(to); crash into.

вы (вас, вам, ва́ми, вас) *pron* you.

выбега́ть *impf*, вы́бежать (-егу, -ежишь) *pf* run out.

вы́|белить *pf*.

вы́беру *etc.: see* вы́брать. выбива́ть(ся *impf of* вы́бить(ся. выбира́ть(ся *impf of* вы́брать(ся

вы́бить (-бью) *pf* (*impf* выбива́ть) knock out; dislodge; ~ся get out; break loose; come out; ~ся из сил exhaust o.s.

вы́бор choice; selection; *pl* election(s). вы́борный elective; electoral. вы́борочный selective.

вы́|бранить *pf*. выбра́сывать(ся *impf of* вы́бросить(ся

вы́брать (-беру) *pf* (*impf* выбира́ть) choose; elect; take out; ~ся get out.

выбрива́ть *impf*, вы́брить (-рею) *pf* shave.

вы́бросить (-ошу) *pf* (*impf* выбра́сывать) throw out; throw away; ~ся throw o.s. out, leap out.

выбыва́ть *impf*, вы́быть (-буду) *pf* из+*gen* leave, quit.

выва́ливать *impf*, вы́валить *impf* throw out; pour out; ~ся tumble out.

вы́везти (-зу; -ез) *pf* (*impf* вывози́ть) take, bring, out; export; rescue.

вы́верить *pf* (*impf* выверя́ть) adjust, regulate.

вы́вернуть (-ну) *pf*, вывёртывать *impf* turn inside out; unscrew; wrench.

выверя́ть *impf of* вы́верить

вы́весить (-ешу) *pf* (*impf* выве́шивать) weigh; hang out. вы́веска sign; pretext.

вы́вести (-еду; -ел) *pf* (*impf* выводи́ть) lead, bring, take, out; drive out; remove; exterminate; deduce; hatch; grow, breed; erect; depict; draw; ~сь go out of use; become extinct; come out; hatch out.

выве́тривание airing.

выве́шивать *impf of* вы́весить

вы́вих dislocation. выви́хивать *impf*, вы́вихнуть (-ну) *pf* dislocate.

вы́вод conclusion; withdrawal. вы́водить(ся (-ожу(сь, -о́дишь(ся) *impf of* вы́вести(сь. вы́водок (-дка) brood; litter.

вывожу́ *see* выводи́ть, вывози́ть

вы́воз export; removal. вывози́ть (-ожу́, -о́зишь) *impf of* вы́везти. вывозно́й export.

вы́гадать *pf*, выга́дывать *impf* gain, save.

вы́гиб curve. выгиба́ть *impf of* вы́гнуть

вы́гладить (-ажу) *pf*.

вы́глядеть (-яжу) *impf* look, look like. выгля́дывать *impf*, вы́глянуть (-ну) *pf* look out; peep out.

вы́гнать (-гоню) *pf* (*impf* выгоня́ть) drive out; distil.

вы́гнутый curved, convex. вы́гнуть (-ну) *pf* (*impf* выгиба́ть) bend, arch.

выгова́ривать *impf*, вы́говорить *pf* pronounce, speak; +*dat* reprimand; ~ся speak out. вы́говор pronunciation; reprimand.

вы́года advantage; gain. вы́годный advantageous; profitable.

вы́гон pasture; common. выгоня́ть *impf of* вы́гнать

выгора́ть *impf*, вы́гореть (-рит) *pf* burn down; fade.

вы́|гравировать *pf*.

выгружа́ть *impf*, вы́грузить (-ужу) *pf* unload; disembark. вы́грузка unloading; disembarkation.

выдава́ть (-даю́, -даёшь) *impf*, вы́дать (-ам, -ашь, -аст, -адим) *pf* give (out); issue; betray; extradite; +за+*acc* pass off as; ~ся protrude; stand out; present itself. вы́дача issue; payment; extradition. выдаю́щийся prominent.

выдвига́ть *impf*, вы́двинуть (-ну) *pf* move out; pull out; put forward, nominate; ~ся move forward, move out; come out; get on (in the world). выдвиже́ние nomination; promotion.

выделе́ние secretion; excretion; isolation; apportionment. вы́делить *pf*, выделя́ть *impf* pick out; detach; allot; secrete; betray; isolate; ~ курси́вом italicize; ~ся stand out, be noted (+*instr* for).

выдёргивать *impf of* вы́дернуть

вы́держанный consistent; self-possessed; firm; matured, seasoned. вы́держать (-жу) *pf*, выде́рживать *impf* bear; endure; contain o.s.; pass (*exam*); sustain. вы́держка[1] endurance; self-possession; exposure.

вы́держка² excerpt.

вы́дернуть *pf* (*impf* **выдёргивать**) pull out.

вы́дохнуть (-ну) *pf* (*impf* **выдыха́ть**) breathe out; **~ся** have lost fragrance or smell; be past one's best.

вы́дра otter.

вы́|драть (-деру) *pf.* **вы|дрессирова́ть** *pf.*

выдува́ть *impf of* **вы́дуть**

вы́думанный made-up, fabricated. **вы́думать** *pf*, **выду́мывать** *impf* invent; fabricate. **вы́думка** invention; device; inventiveness.

вы́|дуть *pf* (*impf also* **выдува́ть**) blow; blow out.

выдыха́ние exhalation. **выдыха́ть(ся** *impf of* **вы́дохнуть(ся**

вы́езд departure; exit. **вы́ездн|о́й** exit; **~ая се́ссия суда́** assizes. **выезжа́ть** *impf of* **вы́ехать**

вы́емка taking out; excavation; hollow.

вы́ехать (-еду) *pf* (*impf* **выезжа́ть**) go out, depart; drive out, ride out; move (house).

вы́жать (-жму, -жмешь) *pf* (*impf* **выжима́ть**) squeeze out; wring out.

вы́жечь (-жгу) *pf* (*impf* **выжига́ть**) burn out; cauterize.

выжива́ние survival. **выжива́ть** *impf of* **вы́жить**

выжига́ть *impf of* **вы́жечь**

выжида́тельный waiting; temporizing.

выжима́ть *impf of* **вы́жать**

вы́жить (-иву) *pf* (*impf* **выжива́ть**) survive; hound out; **~ из ума́** become senile.

вы́звать (-зову) *pf* (*impf* **вызыва́ть**) call (out); send for; challenge; provoke; **~ся** volunteer.

выздора́вливать *impf*, **вы́|здороветь** (-ею) *pf* recover. **выздоровле́ние** recovery; convalescence.

вы́зов call; summons; challenge.

вы́золоченный gilt.

вызубривать *impf*, **вы́|зубрить** *pf* learn by heart.

вызыва́ть(ся *impf of* **вы́звать(ся.** **вызыва́ющий** defiant; provocative.

вы́играть *pf*, **выи́грывать** *impf* win; gain. **вы́игрыш** win; gain; prize. **вы́игрышный** winning; lottery; advantageous.

вы́йти (-йду; -шел, -шла) *pf* (*impf* **выходи́ть**) go out; come out; get out; appear; turn out; be used up; have expired; **~ в свет** appear; **~ за́муж** (за+*acc*) marry; **~ из себя́** lose one's temper.

выка́лывать *impf of* **вы́колоть.** **выка́пывать** *impf of* **вы́копать**

выка́рмливать *impf of* **вы́кормить**

вы́качать *pf*, **выка́чивать** *impf* pump out.

выки́дывать *impf*, **вы́кинуть** *pf* throw out, reject; put out; miscarry, abort; **~ флаг** hoist a flag. **вы́кидыш** miscarriage, abortion.

вы́кладка laying out; lay-out; facing; kit; computation, calculation. **выкла́дывать** *impf of* **вы́ложить**

выключа́тель *m* switch. **выключа́ть** *impf*, **вы́ключить** (-чу) *pf* turn off, switch off; remove, exclude.

выкола́чивать *impf*, **вы́колотить** (-лочу) *pf* knock out, beat out; beat; extort, wring out.

вы́колоть (-лю) *pf* (*impf* **выка́лывать**) put out; gouge out; tattoo.

вы́|копать *pf* (*impf also* **выка́пывать**) dig; dig up, dig out; exhume; unearth.

вы́кормить (-млю) *pf* (*impf* **выка́рмливать**) rear, bring up.

выкорчёвывать *impf* uproot, root out; eradicate.

выкра́ивать *impf of* **вы́кроить**

вы́|красить (-ашу) *pf*, **выкра́шивать** *impf* paint; dye.

выкри́кивать *impf*, **вы́крикнуть** (-ну) *pf* cry out; yell.

вы́кроить *pf* (*impf* **выкра́ивать**) cut out; find (*time etc.*). **вы́кройка** pattern.

вы́крутить (-учу) *pf*, **выкру́чивать** *impf* unscrew; twist; **~ся** extricate o.s.

вы́куп ransom; redemption.

вы́|купать¹(ся *pf.*

выкупа́ть² *impf*, **вы́купить** (-плю) *pf* ransom, redeem.

вы́лазка sally, sortie; excursion.

выла́мывать *impf of* **вы́ломать**

вылеза́ть *impf*, **вы́лезти** (-зу; -лез) *pf* climb out; come out.

вы́|лепить (-плю) *pf.*

вы́лет flight; take-off. **вылета́ть**

impf, **вы́лететь** (-ечу) *pf* fly out; take off.

выле́чивать *impf,* **вы́лечить** (-чу) *pf* cure; ∼ся recover, be cured.

вылива́ть(ся *pf of* **вы́лить(ся** **вы|линять** *pf.*

вы́лить (-лью) *pf* (*impf* **вылива́ть**) pour out; cast, found; ∼ся flow (out); be expressed.

вы́ложить (-жу) *pf* (*impf* **выкла́дывать**) lay out.

вы́ломать *pf,* **вы́ломить** (-млю) *pf* (*impf* **выла́мывать**) break open.

вы́лупиться (-плюсь) *pf,* **вылупля́ться** *impf* hatch (out).

вы́лью *etc.: see* **вы́лить**

вы́|мазать (-мажу) *pf,* **вымазывать** *impf* smear, dirty.

выма́нивать *impf,* **вы́манить** *pf* entice, lure.

вы́мереть (-мрет; -мер) *pf* (*impf* **вымира́ть**) die out; become extinct. **вы́мерший** extinct.

вы́мести (-ету) *pf,* **выметать** *impf* sweep (out).

вымога́тельство blackmail, extortion. **вымога́ть** *impf* extort.

вымока́ть *impf,* **вы́мокнуть** (-ну; -ок) *pf* be drenched; soak; rot.

вы́молвить (-влю) *pf* say, utter.

вы́|мостить (-ощу) *pf.* **вымою** *etc.: see* **вы́мыть**

вы́мпел pennant.

вы́мрет *see* **вы́мереть. вымыва́ть(ся** *impf of* **вы́мыть(ся**

вы́мысел (-сла) invention, fabrication; fantasy.

вы́|мыть (-мою) *pf* (*impf also* **вымыва́ть**) wash; wash out, off; wash away; ∼ся wash o.s.

вы́мышленный fictitious.

вы́мя (-мени) *neut* udder.

вына́шивать *impf of* **вы́носить²**

вы́нести (-су; -нес) *pf* (*impf* **выноси́ть¹**) carry out, take out; carry away; endure.

вынима́ть(ся *impf of* **вы́нуть(ся**

вы́нос carrying out. **выноси́ть** (-ошу, -осишь) *impf of* **вы́нести. выноси́ть²** *pf* (*impf* **вына́шивать**) bear; nurture. **вы́носка** carrying out; removal; footnote. **выно́сливость** endurance; hardiness.

вы́нудить (-ужу) *pf,* **вынужда́ть** *impf* force, compel. **вы́нужденный**

forced.

вы́нуть (-ну) *pf* (*impf* **вынима́ть**) take out.

вы́пад attack; lunge. **выпада́ть** *impf of* **вы́пасть**

выпа́ливать *impf of* **вы́полоть**

выпа́ривать *impf,* **вы́парить** evaporate; steam.

выпа́рывать *impf of* **вы́пороть²**

вы́пасть (-аду; -ал) *pf* (*impf* **выпада́ть**) fall out; fall; occur, turn out; lunge.

выпека́ть *impf,* **вы́печь** (-еку; -ек) *pf* bake.

выпива́ть *impf of* **вы́пить;** enjoy a drink. **вы́пивка** drinking bout; drinks.

выпи́ливать *impf,* **вы́пилить** *pf* saw, cut out.

вы́писать (-ишу) *pf,* **выпи́сывать** *impf* copy out; write out; order; subscribe to; send for; ∼ из больни́цы discharge from hospital; ∼ся be discharged. **вы́писка** writing out; extract; ordering, subscription; discharge.

вы́|пить (-пью) *pf* (*impf also* **выпива́ть**) drink; drink up.

вы́плавить (-влю) *pf,* **выплавля́ть** *impf* smelt. **вы́плавка** smelting; smelted metal.

вы́плата payment. **вы́платить** (-ачу) *pf,* **выпла́чивать** *impf* pay (out); pay off.

выплёвывать *impf of* **вы́плюнуть**

выплыва́ть *impf,* **вы́плыть** (-ыву) *pf* swim out, sail out; emerge; crop up.

вы́плюнуть (-ну) *pf* (*impf* **выплёвывать**) spit out.

выполза́ть *impf,* **вы́ползти** (-зу; -олз) *pf* crawl out.

выполне́ние execution, carrying out; fulfilment. **вы́полнить** *pf,* **выполня́ть** *impf* execute, carry out; fulfil.

вы́|полоскать (-ощу) *pf.*

вы́|полоть (-лю) *pf* (*impf also* **выпа́ливать**) weed out; weed.

вы́|пороть¹ (-рю) *pf.*

вы́|пороть² (-рю) *pf* (*impf* **выпа́рывать**) rip out, rip up.

вы́|потрошить (-шу) *pf.*

вы́правка bearing; correction.

выпра́шивать *impf of* **вы́просить;** solicit.

выпрова́живать *impf,* **вы́прово-**

дить (-ожу) pf send packing.
вы́просить (-ошу) pf (impf вы-
пра́шивать) (ask for and) get.
выпряга́ть impf of вы́прячь
вы́прямить (-млю) pf, выпрямля́ть
impf straighten (out); rectify; ~ся
become straight; draw o.s. up.
вы́прячь (-ягу; -яг) pf (impf выпря-
га́ть) unharness.
вы́пуклый protuberant; bulging; convex.
вы́пуск output; issue; discharge; part,
instalment; final-year students; omission. выпуска́ть impf, вы́пустить
(-ущу) pf let out; issue; produce; omit.
выпускни́к (-а́), -и́ца final-year student. выпускно́й discharge; exhaust; ~о́й экза́мен finals, final examination.
вы́путать pf, вы́путывать impf disentangle; ~ся extricate o.s.
вы́пью etc.: see вы́пить
выраба́тывать impf, вы́работать
pf work out; work up; draw up; produce, make; earn. вы́работка manufacture; production; working out;
drawing up; output; make.
выра́внивать(ся impf of вы́ров-
нять(ся
выража́ть impf, вы́разить (-ажу) pf
express; ~ся express o.s. выраже́-
ние expression. вырази́тельный
expressive.
выраста́ть impf, вы́расти (-ту; -рос)
pf grow, grow up. вы́растить (-ащу)
pf, выра́щивать impf bring up;
breed; cultivate.
вы́рвать[1] (-ву) pf (impf вырыва́ть[2])
pull out, tear out; extort; ~ся break
loose, break free; escape; shoot.
вы́|рвать[2] (-ву) pf.
вы́рез cut; décolletage. вы́резать
(-ежу) pf, выреза́ть impf, вы́резы-
вать impf cut (out); engrave. вы́-
резка cutting out, excision; cutting;
fillet.
вы́ровнять pf (impf выра́внивать)
level; straighten (out); draw up; ~ся
become level; equalize; catch up.
вы́родиться pf, вырожда́ться
impf degenerate. вы́родок (-дка)
degenerate; black sheep. вырож-
де́ние degeneration.
вы́ронить pf drop.
вы́рос etc.: see вы́расти

вы́рою etc.: see вы́рыть
выруба́ть impf, вы́рубить (-блю) pf
cut down; cut (out); carve (out).
вы́рубка cutting down; hewing out.
вы́|ругать(ся pf.
выру́ливать impf, вы́|рулить pf
taxi.
выруча́ть impf, вы́ручить (-чу) pf
rescue; help out; gain; make. вы́руч-
ка rescue; gain; proceeds; earnings.
вырыва́ть[1] impf, вы́рыть (-рою) pf
dig up, unearth.
вырыва́ть[2](ся impf of вы́рвать(ся
вы́садить (-ажу) pf, выса́живать
impf set down; put ashore; transplant;
smash; ~ся alight; disembark. вы́-
садка disembarkation; landing;
transplanting.
выса́сывать impf of вы́сосать
вы́свободить (-божу) pf, высво-
божда́ть impf free; release.
высека́ть impf of вы́сечь[2]
выселе́ние eviction. вы́селить pf,
выселя́ть impf evict; evacuate,
move; ~ся move, remove.
вы́|сечь[1] (-еку; -сек) pf. вы́сечь[2]
(-еку; -сек) (impf высека́ть) cut
(out); carve.
вы́сидеть (-ижу) pf, выси́живать
impf sit out; stay; hatch.
вы́ситься impf rise, tower.
выска́бливать impf of вы́скоблить
вы́сказать (-ажу) pf, выска́зы-
вать impf express; state; ~ся speak
out. выска́зывание utterance; pronouncement.
выска́кивать impf of вы́скочить
вы́скоблить (-блю) pf (impf выска́бли-
вать) scrape out; erase; remove.
вы́скочить (-чу) pf (impf выска́ки-
вать) jump out; spring out; ~ с+instr
come out with. вы́скочка upstart.
вы́слать (вы́шлю) pf (impf
высыла́ть) send (out); exile; deport.
вы́следить (-ежу) pf, высле́жи-
вать impf trace; shadow.
выслу́живать impf, вы́служить
(-жу) pf qualify for; serve (out); ~ся
gain promotion; curry favour.
вы́слушать pf, выслу́шивать impf
hear out; sound; listen to.
высме́ивать impf, вы́смеять (-ею)
pf ridicule.
вы́|сморкать(ся pf. высо́вывать-
(ся impf of вы́сунуть(ся

высо́кий (-о́к, -а́, -о́ко́) high; tall; lofty; elevated.

высоко- in comb high-, highly. высокоблагоро́дие (your) Honour, Worship. ~во́льтный high-tension. ~го́рный mountain. ~ка́чественный high-quality. ~квалифици́рованный highly qualified. ~ме́рие haughtiness. ~ме́рный haughty. ~па́рный high-flown; bombastic. ~часто́тный high-frequency.

вы́сосать (-осу) pf (impf выса́сывать) suck out.

высота́ (pl -ы) height, altitude. высо́тный high-altitude; high-rise.

вы́сохнуть (-ну; -ох) pf (impf also высыха́ть) dry (out); dry up; wither (away).

вы́спаться (-плюсь, -пишься) pf (impf высыпа́ться²) have a good sleep.

вы́ставить (-влю) pf, выставля́ть impf display, exhibit; post; put forward; set down; take out; +instr represent as; ~ся show off. вы́ставка exhibition.

выста́ивать impf of вы́стоять

вы́|стегать (-ся. вы́|стирать pf.

вы́стоять (-ою) pf (impf выста́ивать) stand; stand one's ground.

вы́страдать pf suffer; gain through suffering.

выстра́ивать(ся impf of вы́строить(ся

вы́стрел shot; report. вы́стрелить pf shoot, fire.

вы́|строгать pf.

вы́строить pf (impf выстра́ивать) build; draw up, order, arrange; form up. ~ся form up.

вы́ступ protuberance, projection. выступа́ть impf, вы́ступить (-плю) pf come forward; come out; perform; speak; +из+gen go beyond. выступле́ние appearance, performance; speech; setting out.

вы́сунуть (-ну) pf (impf высо́вывать) put out, thrust out; ~ся show o.s., thrust o.s. forward.

вы́|сушить(ся (-шу(сь) pf.

вы́сший highest; high; higher.

высыла́ть impf of вы́слать. вы́сылка sending, dispatch; expulsion; exile.

вы́сыпать (-плю) pf, высыпа́ть impf pour out; spill; ~ся¹ pour out; spill.

высыпа́ться² impf of вы́спаться

высыха́ть impf of вы́сохнуть

высь height; summit.

выта́лкивать impf of вы́толкать, вы́толкнуть. выта́скивать impf of вы́тащить. выта́чивать impf of вы́точить

вы́|тащить (-щу) pf (impf also выта́скивать) drag out; pull out.

вы́|твердить (-ржу) pf.

вытека́ть impf (pf вы́течь); ~ из+gen flow from, out of; result from.

вы́тереть (-тру; -тер) pf (impf вытира́ть) wipe (up); dry; wear out.

вы́терпеть (-плю) pf endure.

вы́тертый threadbare.

вы́теснить pf, вытесня́ть impf force out; oust; displace.

вы́течь (-чет; -ек) pf (impf вытека́ть) flow out, run out.

вытира́ть impf of вы́тереть

вы́толкать pf, вы́толкнуть (-ну) pf (impf выта́лкивать) throw out; push out.

вы́точенный turned. вы́|точить (-чу) pf (impf also выта́чивать) turn; sharpen; gnaw through.

вы́|травить (-влю) pf, вытра́вливать impf, вытравля́ть impf exterminate, destroy; remove; etch; trample down, damage.

вытрезви́тель m detoxification centre. вы́трезвить(ся (-влю(сь) pf, вытрезвля́ть(ся impf sober up.

вы́тру etc.: see вы́тереть

вы́|трясти (-су; -яс) pf shake out.

вытря́хивать impf, вы́тряхнуть (-ну) pf shake out.

выть (во́ю) impf howl; wail.

вытя́гивать impf, вы́тянуть (-ну) pf stretch (out); extend; extract; endure; ~ся stretch, stretch out, stretch o.s.; shoot up; draw o.s. up. вы́тяжка drawing out, extraction; extract.

вы́|утюжить (-жу) pf.

выу́чивать impf, вы́|учить (-чу) pf learn; teach; ~ся +dat or inf learn.

выха́живать impf of вы́ходить²

вы́хватить (-ачу) pf, выхва́тывать impf snatch out, up, away; pull out.

вы́хлоп exhaust. выхлопно́й exhaust, discharge.

вы́ход going out; departure; way out,

exit; vent; appearance; yield; ~ замуж marriage. вы́ходец (-дца) emigrant; immigrant. выходи́ть[1] (-ожу́, -о́дишь) impf of вы́йти; +на +acc look out on.

выходи́ть[2] (-ожу) pf (impf выха́живать) nurse; rear, bring up.

вы́ходка trick; prank.

выходн|о́й exit; going-out, outgoing; discharge; ~о́й день day off; ~о́й sb person off duty; day off. выхожу́ etc.: see выходи́ть[1]. выхожу́ etc.: see выходи́ть[2]

вы́цвести (-ветет) pf, выцвета́ть impf fade. вы́цветший faded.

вычёркивать impf, вы́черкнуть (-ну) pf cross out.

вы́черпать pf, выче́рпывать impf bale out.

вы́честь (-чту; -чел, -чла) pf (impf вычита́ть) subtract. вы́чет deduction.

вычисле́ние calculation. вычисли́тель m calculator. вычисли́тельн|ый calculating, computing; ~ая маши́на computer. вы́числить pf, вычисля́ть impf calculate, compute.

вы́|чистить (-ищу) pf (impf also вычища́ть) clean, clean up.

вычита́ние subtraction. вычита́ть impf of вы́честь

вычища́ть impf of вы́чистить. вы́чту etc.: see вы́честь

вы́швырнуть (-ну) pf, вышвы́ривать impf chuck out.

вы́ше higher, taller; prep+gen beyond; over; adv above.

выше- in comb above-, afore-. вышеизло́женный foregoing. ~на́званный afore-named. ~ска́занный, ~ука́занный aforesaid. ~упомя́нутый afore-mentioned.

вы́шел etc.: see вы́йти

вышиба́ла m chucker-out. вышиба́ть impf, вы́шибить (-бу; -иб) pf knock out; chuck out.

вышива́ние embroidery, needlework. вышива́ть impf of вы́шить. вы́шивка embroidery.

вышина́ height.

вы́шить (-шью) pf (impf вышива́ть) embroider. вы́шитый embroidered. вы́шка tower; (бурова́я) ~ derrick.

вы́шлю etc.: see вы́слать. вы́шью etc.: see вы́шить

вы́явить (-влю) pf, выявля́ть impf

reveal; make known; expose; ~ся come to light, be revealed.

выясне́ние elucidation; explanation. вы́яснить pf, выясня́ть impf elucidate; explain; ~ся become clear; turn out.

Вьетна́м Vietnam. вьетна́мец, -мка Vietnamese. вьетна́мский Vietnamese.

вью etc.: see вить

вью́га snow-storm, blizzard.

вьюно́к (-нка́) bindweed.

вьючн|ый pack; ~ое живо́тное beast of burden.

вью́щийся climbing; curly.

вяжу́ etc.: see вяза́ть. вя́жущий binding; astringent.

вяз elm.

вяза́ние knitting; crocheting; binding, tying. вяза́нка[1] knitted garment. вяза́нка[2] bundle. вя́заный knitted, crocheted. вяза́нье knitting; crochet(-work). вяза́ть (вяжу́, вя́жешь) impf (pf c~) tie, bind; knit, crochet; be astringent; ~ся accord; tally. вя́зка tying; knitting, crocheting; bunch.

вя́зкий (-зок, -зка́, -о) viscous; sticky; boggy. вя́знуть (-ну; вяз(нул), -зла) impf (pf за~, у~) stick, get stuck.

вя́зовый elm.

вязь ligature; arabesque.

вя́леный dried; sun-cured.

вя́лый limp; sluggish; slack. вя́нуть (-ну; вял) impf (pf за~, у~) fade, wither; flag.

Г

г. abbr (of год) year; (of го́род) city; (of господи́н) Mr.

г abbr (of грамм) gram.

га abbr (of гекта́р) hectare.

га́вань harbour.

гага́чий пух eiderdown.

гад reptile; repulsive person; pl. vermin. гада́лка fortune-teller. гада́ние fortune-telling; guess-work. гада́ть impf (pf по~) tell fortunes; guess.

га́дина reptile; repulsive person; pl. vermin. га́дить (га́жу) impf (pf на~) +в +prep, на +acc, prep foul, dirty, defile. га́дкий (-док, -дка́, -о) nasty, vile, repulsive. га́дость filth, muck; dirty trick; pl filthy expressions.

гадю́ка adder, viper; repulsive person.

гáечный ключ spanner, wrench.

газ¹ gauze.

газ² gas; wind; **дать ~** step on the gas; **сбáвить ~** reduce speed.

газéта newspaper. **газéтчик** journalist; newspaper-seller.

газирóванный aerated. **гáзовый** gas.

газóн lawn. **газонокоси́лка** lawn-mower.

газопровóд gas pipeline; gas-main.

гáйка nut; female screw.

галáктика galaxy.

галантерéйный магази́н haberdasher's. **галантерéя** haberdashery.

галáнтный gallant.

галерéя gallery. **галёрка** gallery, gods.

галифé indecl pl riding-breeches.

гáлка jackdaw.

галлюцинáция hallucination.

галóп gallop.

гáлочка tick.

гáлстук tie; neckerchief.

галу́шка dumpling.

гáлька pebble; pebbles; shingle.

гам din, uproar.

гамáк (-á) hammock.

гáмма scale; gamut; range.

гангрéна gangrene.

гáнгстер gangster.

гантéль dumb-bell.

гарáж (-á) garage.

гаранти́ровать impf & pf guarantee. **гарáнтия** guarantee.

гардерóб wardrobe; cloakroom. **гардерóбщик, -щица** cloakroom attendant.

гарди́на curtain.

гармонизи́ровать impf & pf harmonize.

гармóника accordion, concertina.

гармони́ческий, гармони́чный harmonious. **гармóния** harmony; concord. **гармóнь** accordion, concertina.

гарнизóн garrison.

гарни́р garnish; vegetables.

гарниту́р set; suite.

гарь burning; cinders.

гаси́тель m extinguisher; suppressor. **гаси́ть (гашу́, гáсишь)** impf (pf за~, по~) extinguish; suppress. **гáснуть (-ну; гас)** impf (pf за~, по~, у~) be extinguished, go out; grow feeble.

гастрóли f pl tour; guest-appearance, performance. **гастроли́ровать** impf (be on) tour.

гастронóм gourmet; provision shop. **гастрономи́ческий** gastronomic; provision. **гастронóмия** gastronomy; provisions; delicatessen.

гауптвáхта guardroom.

гаши́ш hashish.

гвардéец (-éйца) guardsman. **гвардéйский** guards'. **гвáрдия** Guards.

гвóздик tack. **гвозди́ка** pink(s), carnation(s); cloves. **гвóздики (-ов)** pl stilettos. **гвоздь (-я́; pl -и, -éй)** m nail; tack; crux; highlight, hit.

гг. abbr (of гóды) years.

где adv where; **~ бы ни** wherever. **гдé-либо** adv anywhere. **гдé-нибудь** adv somewhere; anywhere. **гдé-то** adv somewhere.

гектáр hectare.

гéлий helium.

гемоглоби́н haemoglobin.

геморрóй haemorrhoids. **гемофили́я** haemophilia.

ген gene.

гéнезис origin, genesis.

генерáл general. **генерáльн|ый** general; **~ая репети́ция** dress rehearsal.

генерáтор generator.

генерáция generation; oscillation.

генéтика genetics. **генети́ческий** genetic.

гениáльный brilliant. **гéний** genius.

гео- in comb geo-. **геóграф** geographer. **~графи́ческий** geographical. **~грáфия** geography. **геóлог** geologist. **~логи́ческий** geological. **~лóгия** geology. **~метри́ческий** geometric. **~мéтрия** geometry.

георги́н dahlia.

геофи́зика geophysics.

гепáрд cheetah.

гепати́т hepatitis.

герáнь geranium.

герб arms, coat of arms. **гéрбов|ый** heraldic; **~ая печáть** official stamp.

геркулéс Hercules; rolled oats.

германéц (-нца) ancient German. **Гермáния** Germany. **гермáнский** Germanic.

гермафроди́т hermaphrodite.

гермети́чный hermetic; hermetically sealed; air-tight.

геройзм heroism. геройня heroine. геройческий heroic. герой hero. геройский heroic.

герц (*gen pl* герц) hertz.

герцог duke. герцогиня duchess.

г-жа *abbr* (*of* госпожа) Mrs.; Miss.

гиацинт hyacinth.

гибель death; destruction, ruin; loss; wreck; downfall. гибельный disastrous, fatal.

гибкий (-бок, -бка, -бко) flexible, adaptable, versatile; supple. гибкость flexibility; suppleness.

гибнуть (-ну; гиб(нул)) *impf* (*pf* по~) perish.

гибрид hybrid.

гигант giant. гигантский gigantic.

гигиена hygiene. гигиенический, -ичный hygienic, sanitary.

гид guide.

гидравлический hydraulic.

гидро- *pref* hydro-. ~электростанция hydro-electric power-station.

гиена hyena.

гильза cartridge-case; sleeve; (cigarette-)wrapper.

гимн hymn.

гимназия grammar school, high school.

гимнаст gymnast. гимнастика gymnastics. гимнастический gymnastic.

гинеколог gynaecologist. гинекология gynaecology.

гипербола hyperbole.

гипноз hypnosis. гипнотизёр hypnotist. гипнотизировать *impf* (*pf* за~) hypnotize. гипнотический hypnotic.

гипотеза hypothesis. гипотетический hypothetical.

гиппопотам hippopotamus.

гипс gypsum, plaster (of Paris); plaster cast. гипсовый plaster.

гирлянда garland.

гиря weight.

гистерэктомия hysterectomy.

гитара guitar.

гл. *abbr* (*of* глава) chapter.

глав- *abbr in comb* head, chief, main. глава (*pl* -ы) head; chief; chapter; cupola. главарь (-я) *m* leader, ringleader. главк central directorate. главнокомандующий *sb* commander-in-chief. главный chief, main; ~ым образом chiefly, mainly,

for the most part; ~ое *sb* the main thing; the essentials.

глагол verb.

гладить (-ажу) *impf* (*pf* вы~, по~) stroke; iron. гладкий smooth; plain. гладко *adv* smoothly. гладь smooth surface.

глаз (*loc* -у; *pl* -а, глаз) eye; в ~á to one's face; за ~á+*gen* behind the back of; смотреть во все ~á be all eyes.

глазированный glazed; glossy; iced; glacé.

глазница eye-socket. глазной eye; optic; ~ врач oculist. глазок (-зка) peephole.

глазунья fried eggs.

глазурь glaze; syrup; icing.

гланды (гланд) *pl* tonsils.

гласность publicity; glasnost, openness. гласный public; vowel; *sb* vowel.

глина clay. глинистый clayey. глиняный clay; earthenware; clayey.

глиссер speed-boat.

глист (*intestinal*) worm.

глицерин glycerine.

глобус globe.

глотать *impf* swallow. глотка gullet; throat. глоток (-тка) gulp; mouthful.

глохнуть (-ну; глох) *impf* (*pf* за~, о~) become deaf; die away, subside; grow wild.

глубина (*pl* -ы) depth; heart, interior. глубокий (-ок, -а, -око) deep; profound; late, advanced, extreme. глубокомыслие profundity. глубокоуважаемый (*in formal letters*) dear.

глумиться (-млюсь) *impf* mock, jeer (над+*instr* at). глумление mockery.

глупеть (-ею) *impf* (*pf* по~) grow stupid. глупец (-пца) fool. глупость stupidity. глупый (глуп, -á, -о) stupid.

глухарь (-я) *m* capercaillie. глух|ой (глух, -á, -о) deaf; muffled; obscure, vague; dense; wild; remote; deserted; sealed; blank; ~ой, ~яя *sb* deaf man, woman. глухонемой deaf and dumb; *sb* deaf mute. глухота deafness. глушитель *m* silencer. глушить (-шу) *impf* (*pf* за~, о~) stun; muffle; dull; jam; extinguish; stifle;

suppress. **глушь** backwoods.
глы́ба clod; lump, block.
глюко́за glucose.
гляде́ть (-жу́) *impf* (*pf* по~, гля́нуть) look, gaze, peer; ~ в о́ба be on one's guard; (того́ и) гля́ди it looks as if; I'm afraid; **гля́дя** по+*dat* depending on.
гля́нец (-нца) gloss, lustre; polish.
гля́нуть (-ну) *pf* (*impf* гляде́ть) glance.
гм *int* hm!
г-н *abbr* (*of* господи́н) Mr.
гнать (гоню́, го́нишь; гнал, -á, -o) *impf* drive; urge (on); hunt, chase; persecute; distil; ~ся за+*instr* pursue.
гнев anger, rage. **гне́ваться** *impf* (*pf* раз~) be angry. **гне́вный** angry.
гнедо́й bay.
гнездо́ (*pl* гнёзда) nest.
гнёт weight; oppression. **гнету́щий** oppressive.
гни́да nit.
гние́ние decay, putrefaction, rot.
гнило́й (-ил, -á, -o) rotten; muggy.
гнить (-ию, -иёшь; -ил, -á, -o) *impf* (*pf* с~) rot. **гное́ние** suppuration.
гно́иться *impf* (*pf* с~) suppurate, discharge matter. **гной** pus. **гно́йник** abscess; ulcer. **гно́йный** purulent.
гну́сный (-сен, -сна́, -o) vile, foul.
гнуть (гну, гнёшь) *impf* (*pf* со~) bend; aim at; ~ся bend; stoop.
гнуша́ться *impf* (*pf* по~) disdain; +*gen or instr* shun; abhor.
гобеле́н tapestry.
гобо́й oboe.
гове́ть (-е́ю) *impf* fast.
говно́ (*vulg*) shit.
говори́ть *impf* (*pf* по~, сказа́ть) speak, talk; say; tell; ~ся: как говори́тся as they say.
говя́дина beef. **говя́жий** beef.
го́гот cackle; loud laughter. **гогота́ть** (-очу́, -о́чешь) *impf* cackle; roar with laughter.
год (*loc* -ý; *pl* -ы *or* -á, *gen* -о́в *or* лет) year. **года́ми** *adv* for years (on end).
годи́ться, (-жу́сь) *impf* be fit, suitable; serve.
годи́чный a year's; annual.
го́дный (-ден, -дна́, -o, -ы *or* -ы́) fit, suitable; valid.
годова́лый one-year-old. **годово́й**

annual. **годовщи́на** anniversary.
гожу́сь *etc.*: *see* годи́ться
гол goal.
голени́ще (boot-)top. **го́лень** shin.
голла́ндец (-дца) Dutchman. **Голла́ндия** Holland. **голла́ндка** Dutchwoman; tiled stove. **голла́ндский** Dutch.
голова́ (*acc* го́лову; *pl* го́ловы, -о́в, -áм) head. **голова́стик** tadpole. **голо́вка** head; cap, nose, tip. **головно́й** head; leading; ~áя боль headache; ~о́й мозг brain, cerebrum; ~о́й убо́р headgear, headdress. **головокруже́ние** giddiness, dizziness. **головоло́мка** puzzle. **головоре́з** cut-throat; rascal.
го́лод hunger; famine; acute shortage. **голода́ние** starvation; fasting. **голода́ть** *impf* go hungry, starve; fast. **голо́дный** (го́лоден, -дна́, -o, -ы *or* -ы́) hungry. **голодо́вка** hunger-strike.
гололёд, гололе́дица (period of) black ice.
го́лос (*pl* -á) voice; part; vote. **голоси́ть** (-ошу́) *impf* sing loudly; cry; wail.
голосло́вный unsubstantiated, unfounded.
голосова́ние voting; poll. **голосова́ть** *impf* (*pf* про~) vote; vote on.
голу́бка pigeon; (my) dear, darling. **голубо́й** light blue. **голу́бчик** my dear (fellow); darling. **го́лубь** *m* pigeon, dove. **голубя́тня** (*gen pl* -тен) dovecote, pigeon-loft.
го́лый (гол, -лá, -ло) naked, bare.
гомоге́нный homogeneous.
го́мон hubbub.
гомосексуали́ст homosexual. **гомосексуа́льный** homosexual.
гондо́ла gondola.
гоне́ние persecution. **го́нка** race; dashing; haste.
гонора́р fee.
го́ночный racing.
гонча́р (-á) potter.
го́нщик racer. **гоню́** *etc.*: *see* гнать.
гоня́ть *impf* drive; send on errands; ~ся +за+*instr* chase, hunt.
гора́ (*acc* го́ру; *pl* го́ры, -áм) mountain; hill; в го́ру uphill; под го́ру downhill.
гора́здо *adv* much, far, by far.

горб (-á, *loc* -ý) hump; bulge. горбáтый hunchbacked. горбить (-блю) *impf* (*pf* с~) arch, hunch; ~ся stoop. горбýн (-á) *m*, горбýнья (*gen pl* -ний) hunchback. горбýшка (*gen pl* -шек) crust (*of loaf*).

гордиться (-ржýсь) *impf* put on airs; +*instr* be proud of. гóрдость pride. гóрдый (горд, -á, -о, гóрды) proud. гордыня arrogance.

гóре grief, sorrow; trouble. горевáть (-рю́ю) *impf* grieve.

горéлка burner. горéлый burnt. горéние burning, combustion; enthusiasm.

гóрестный mournful. гóресть sorrow; *pl* misfortunes.

горéть (-рю́) *impf* (*pf* с~) burn.

гóрец (-рца) mountain-dweller.

гóречь bitterness; bitter taste.

горизóнт horizon. горизонтáль horizontal. горизонтáльный horizontal.

гóристый mountainous, hilly. гóрка hill; hillock; steep climb.

гóрло throat; neck. горловóй throat; guttural; raucous. гóрлышко neck.

гормóн hormone.

горн[1] furnace, forge.

горн[2] bugle.

гóрничная *sb* maid, chambermaid.

горнорабóчий *sb* miner.

горностáй ermine.

гóрный mountain; mountainous; mineral; mining. горня́к (-á) miner.

гóрод (*pl* -á) town; city. городóк (-дкá) small town. городскóй urban; city; municipal. горожáнин (*pl* -áне, -áн) *m*, -жáнка town-dweller.

гороскóп horoscope.

горóх pea, peas. горóшек (-шка) spots, spotted pattern; души́стый ~ sweet peas; зелёный ~ green peas. горóшина pea.

горсовéт *abbr* (*of* городскóй совéт) city soviet, town soviet.

горсть (*gen pl* -éй) handful.

гортáнный guttural. гортáнь larynx.

горчи́ца mustard. горчи́чник mustard plaster.

горшóк (-шкá) flowerpot; pot; potty; chamber-pot.

гóрький (-рек, -рькá, -о) bitter.

горю́чий combustible; ~ee *sb* fuel. горя́чий (-ря́ч, -á) hot; passionate; ardent.

горячи́ться (-чýсь) *impf* (*pf* раз~) get excited. горя́чка fever; feverish haste. горя́чность zeal.

гос- *abbr in comb* (*of* государственный) state.

гóспиталь *m* (military) hospital.

гóсподи *int* good heavens! господи́н (*pl* -одá, -óд, -áм) master; gentleman; Mr; *pl* ladies and gentlemen. госпóдство supremacy. госпóдствовать *impf* hold sway; prevail. Госпóдь (Гóспода, *voc* Гóсподи) *m* God, the Lord. госпожá lady; Mrs.

гостеприи́мный hospitable. гостеприи́мство hospitality. гости́ная *sb* drawing-room, sitting-room. гости́ница hotel. гости́ть (гощý) *impf* stay, be on a visit. гость (*gen pl* -éй) *m*, гóстья (*gen pl* -ий) guest, visitor.

госудáрственный State, public. госудáрство State. госудáрыня, госудáрь *m* sovereign; Your Majesty.

готи́ческий Gothic.

готóвить (-влю) *impf* (*pf* с~) prepare; ~ся prepare (o.s.); be at hand. готóвность readiness, willingness. готóвый ready.

гофриро́ванный corrugated; waved; pleated.

грабёж robbery; pillage. граби́тель *m* robber. граби́тельский predatory; exorbitant. грáбить (-блю) *impf* (*pf* о~) rob, pillage.

грáбли (-бель *or* -блей) *pl* rake.

гравёр, грави́ро́вщик engraver. грáвий gravel. грави́ровáть *impf* (*pf* вы́~) engrave; etch. грави́рóвка engraving.

гравитацио́нный gravitational. гравю́ра engraving, print; etching.

град[1] city, town.

град[2] hail; volley. грáдина hailstone.

грáдус degree. грáдусник thermometer.

граждани́н (*pl* грáждане, -дан), граждáнка citizen. граждáнский civil; civic; civilian. граждáнство citizenship.

грамзáпись (gramophone) recording.

грамм gram.

граммáтика grammar. граммати́ческий grammatical.

грáмота reading and writing; official document; deed. грáмотность literacy. гра́мотный literate; competent.

грампласти́нка (gramophone) record.

грана́т pomegranate; garnet. грана́та shell, grenade.

грандио́зный grandiose.

гранёный cut, faceted; cut-glass.

грани́т granite.

грани́ца border; boundary, limit; за грани́цей, за грани́цу abroad. грани́чить impf border.

грань border, verge; side, facet.

граф count; earl.

графа́ column. гра́фик graph; chart; schedule; graphic artist. гра́фика drawing; graphics; script.

графи́н carafe; decanter.

графи́ня countess.

графи́т graphite.

графи́ческий graphic.

графлёный ruled.

гра́фство county.

грацио́зный graceful. гра́ция grace.

грач (-á) rook.

гребёнка comb. гре́бень (-бня) m comb; crest. гребе́ц (-бца́) rower, oarsman. гребно́й rowing. гребу́ etc.: see грести́

грёза day-dream, dream. гре́зить (-е́жу) impf dream.

грек Greek.

гре́лка hot-water bottle.

греме́ть impf (pf про~) thunder, roar; rattle; resound. грему́чая змея́ rattlesnake.

грести́ (-ебу́, -ебёшь; грёб, -бла́) impf row; rake.

греть (-е́ю) impf warm, heat; ~ся warm o.s., bask.

грех (-á) sin. грехо́вный sinful. грехопаде́ние the Fall; fall.

Гре́ция Greece. гре́цкий оре́х walnut. греча́нка Greek, Grecian. гре́ческий Greek, Grecian.

гречи́ха buckwheat. гре́чневый buckwheat.

греши́ть (-шу́) impf (pf по~, co~) sin. гре́шник, -ница sinner. гре́шный (-шен, -шна́, -о) sinful.

гриб (-á) mushroom. грибно́й mushroom.

гри́ва mane.

гри́венник ten-copeck piece.

грим make-up; grease-paint.

гримирова́ть impf (pf за~) make

up; +instr make up as.

грипп flu.

гриф neck (of violin etc.).

гри́фель m pencil lead.

гроб (loc -ý; pl -ы́ or -á) coffin; grave. гробни́ца tomb. гробово́й coffin; deathly. гробовщи́к (-á) coffin-maker; undertaker.

гроза́ (pl -ы) (thunder-)storm.

гроздь (pl -ди or -дья, -де́й or -дьев) cluster, bunch.

грози́ть(ся) (-ожу́(сь)) impf (pf по~, при~) threaten. гро́зный (-зен, -зна́, -о) menacing; terrible; severe.

гром (pl -ы, -о́в) thunder.

грома́да mass; bulk, pile. грома́дный huge, colossal.

громи́ть (-млю́) impf destroy; smash, rout.

гро́мкий (-мок, -мка́, -о) loud; famous; notorious; fine-sounding. гро́мко adv loud(ly); aloud. громкоговори́тель m loud-speaker. громово́й thunder; thunderous; crushing. громогла́сный loud; public.

громозди́ть (-зжу́) impf (pf на~) pile up; ~ся tower; clamber up. громо́здкий cumbersome.

гро́мче comp of гро́мкий, гро́мко

гроссме́йстер grand master.

гроте́скный grotesque.

гро́хот crash, din.

грохота́ть (-очу́, -о́чешь) impf (pf про~) crash; rumble; roar.

грош (-á) half-copeck piece; farthing. грошо́вый cheap; trifling.

грубе́ть (-е́ю) impf (pf за~, о~, по~) grow coarse. груби́ть (-блю́) impf (pf на~) be rude. грубия́н boor. гру́бость rudeness; coarseness; rude remark. гру́бый (груб, -á, -о) coarse; rude.

гру́да heap, pile.

груди́на breastbone. груди́нка brisket; breast. грудно́й breast, chest; pectoral. грудь (-á or -и, instr -ю, loc -и́; pl -и, -е́й) breast; chest.

груз load; burden.

грузи́н (gen pl -и́н), грузи́нка Georgian. грузи́нский Georgian.

грузи́ть (-ужу́, -у́зишь) impf (pf за~, на~, по~) load, lade, freight; ~ся load, take on cargo.

Гру́зия Georgia.

гру́зный (-зен, -зна́, -о) weighty;

bulky. грузови́к lorry, truck. грузово́й goods, cargo. гру́зчик stevedore; loader.

грунт ground, soil; priming. грунтова́ть *impf* (*pf* за~) prime. грунтово́й soil, earth; priming.

гру́ппа group. группирова́ть *impf* (*pf* с~) group; ~ся group, form groups. группиро́вка grouping. группово́й group; team.

грусти́ть (-ущу́) *impf* grieve, mourn; +по+*dat* pine for. гру́стный (-тен, -тна́, -о) sad. грусть sadness.

гру́ша pear.

гры́жа hernia, rupture.

грызть (-зу́, -зёшь; грыз) *impf* (*pf* раз~) gnaw; nag; ~ся fight; squabble. грызу́н (-а́) rodent.

гряда́ (*pl* -ы, -а́м) ridge; bed; row, series; bank. гря́дка (flower-)bed.

гряду́щий approaching; future.

гря́зный (-зен, -зна́, -о) muddy; dirty. грязь (*loc* -и́) mud; dirt; filth; *pl* mud-cure.

гря́нуть (-ну) *pf* ring out, crash out; strike up.

губа́ (*pl* -ы, -а́м) lip; *pl* pincers.

губерна́тор governor. губе́рния province. губе́рнский provincial.

губи́тельный ruinous; pernicious. губи́ть (-блю́, -бишь) *impf* (*pf* по~) ruin; spoil.

гу́бка sponge.

губна́я пома́да lipstick.

гу́бчатый porous, spongy.

гуверна́нтка governess. гувернёр tutor.

гуде́ть (гужу́) *impf* (*pf* про~) hum; drone; buzz; hoot. гудо́к (-дка́) hooter, siren, horn, whistle; hoot.

гудро́н tar. гудро́нный tar, tarred.

гул rumble. гу́лкий (-лок, -лка́, -о) resonant; booming.

гуля́нье (*gen pl* -ний) walk; fête; outdoor party. гуля́ть *impf* (*pf* по~) stroll; go for a walk; have a good time.

гуманита́рный of the humanities; humane. гума́нный humane.

гумно́ (*pl* -а, -мен *or* -мён, -ам) threshing-floor; barn.

гурт (-а́) herd; flock. гуртовщи́к (-а́) herdsman. гурто́м *adv* wholesale; en masse.

гуса́к (-а́) gander.

гу́сеница caterpillar; (caterpillar) track. гу́сеничный caterpillar.

гусёнок (-нка; *pl* -ся́та, -о́ят) gosling. гуси́н|ый goose; ~ая ко́жа gooseflesh.

густе́ть (-е́ет) *impf* (*pf* за~) thicken. густо́й (густ, -а́, -о) thick, dense; rich. густота́ thickness, density; richness.

гусы́ня goose. гусь (*pl* -и, -е́й) *m* goose. гусько́м *adv* in single file.

гутали́н shoe-polish.

гу́ща grounds, sediment; thicket; thick. гу́ще *comp of* густо́й.

ГЭС *abbr* (*of* гидроэлектроста́нция) hydro-electric power station.

Д

д. *abbr* (*of* дере́вня) village; (*of* дом) house.

да *conj* and; but.

да *partl* yes; really? well; +*3rd pers of v*, may, let; да здра́вствует...! long live ...!

дава́ть (даю́, -ёшь) *impf of* дать; дава́й(те) let us, let's; come on; ~ся yield; come easy.

дави́ть (-влю́, -вишь) *impf* (*pf* за~, по~, раз~, у~) press; squeeze; crush; oppress; ~ся choke; hang o.s. да́вка crushing; crush. давле́ние pressure.

да́вний ancient; of long standing. давно́ *adv* long ago; for a long time. да́вность antiquity; remoteness; long standing. давны́м-давно́ *adv* long long ago.

дади́м *etc.*: *see* дать. даю́ *etc.*: *see* дава́ть

да́же even.

да́лее *adv* further; и так ~ and so on, etc. далёкий (-ёк, -а́, -ёко́) distant, remote; far (away). далеко́ *adv* far; far off; by a long way; ~ за long after; ~ не far from. даль (*loc* -и́) distance. дальне́йший further. да́льний distant, remote; long; ~ Восто́к the Far East. дально-зо́ркий long-sighted. да́льность distance; range. да́льше *adv* further; then, next; longer.

дам *etc.*: *see* дать

да́ма lady; partner; queen.

да́мба dike; dam.

да́мский ladies'.

Да́ния Denmark.

да́нные *sb pl* data; facts. **да́нный** given, present. **дань** tribute; debt.

данти́ст dentist.

дар (*pl* -ы́) gift. **дари́ть** (-рю́, -ришь) *impf* (*pf* по~) +*dat* give, make a present.

дарова́ние talent. **дарова́ть** *impf & pf* grant, confer. **дарови́тый** gifted. **дарово́й** free (of charge). **да́ром** *adv* free, gratis; in vain.

да́та date.

да́тельный dative.

дати́ровать *impf & pf* date.

да́тский Danish. **датча́нин** (*pl* -а́не, -а́н), **датча́нка** Dane.

дать (дам, дашь, даст, дади́м; дал, -а́, да́ло) *pf* (*impf* дава́ть) give; grant; let; ~ взаймы́ lend; ~ся *pf of* дава́ться

да́ча dacha; на да́че in the country. **да́чник** (holiday) visitor.

два *m & neut*, **две** *f* (двух, -ум, -умя́, -ух) two. **двадцатиле́тний** twenty-year; twenty-year-old. **двадца́тый** twentieth; ~ые го́ды the twenties. **два́дцать** (-и, *instr* -ью) twenty. **два́жды** *adv* twice; double. **двена́дцатый** twelfth. **двена́дцать** twelve.

дверь (*loc* -и́; *pl* -и, -е́й, *instr* -я́ми or -ьми́) door.

две́сти (двухсо́т, -умста́м, -умяста́ми, -ухста́х) two hundred.

дви́гатель *m* engine, motor; motive force. **дви́гать** (-аю *or* -ижу) *impf*, **дви́нуть** (-ну) *pf* move; set in motion; advance; ~ся move; advance; get started. **движе́ние** movement; motion; exercise; traffic. **дви́жимость** chattels; personal property. **дви́жимый** movable; moved. **дви́жущий** motive.

дво́е (-и́х) two; two pairs. **двое-** *in comb* two-; double(-). **двоебо́рье** biathlon. ~**же́нец** (-нца) bigamist. ~**же́нство** bigamy. ~**то́чие** colon.

двои́ться *impf* divide in two; appear double; у него́ двои́лось в глаза́х he saw double. **дво́йка** two; figure 2; No. 2. **двойни́к** (-а́) double. **двойно́й** double,

twofold; binary. **двойня́** (*gen pl* -о́ен) twins. **дво́йственный** two-faced; dual.

двор (-а́) yard; courtyard; homestead; court. **дворе́ц** (-рца́) palace. **дво́рник** yard caretaker; windscreen-wiper. **дво́рня** servants. **дворо́вый** yard, courtyard; *sb* house-serf. **дворяни́н** (*pl* -я́не, -я́н), **дворя́нка** member of the nobility or gentry. **дворя́нство** nobility, gentry.

двою́родн|ый; ~ый брат, ~ая сестра́ (first) cousin; ~ый дя́дя, ~ая тётка first cousin once removed. **двоя́кий** double; two-fold.

дву-, двух- *in comb* two-; bi-; double. **двубо́ртный** double-breasted. ~**ли́чный** two-faced. ~**но́гий** two-legged. ~**ру́чный** two-handed; two-handed. ~**ру́шник** double-dealer. ~**смы́сленный** ambiguous. ~(х)**спа́льный** double. ~**сторо́нний** double-sided; two-way; bilateral. ~**х-годи́чный** two-year; ~**ле́тний** two-year; two-year-old; biennial. ~**хме́стный** two-seater; two-berth. ~**хмото́рный** twin-engined. ~**хсотле́тие** bicentenary. ~**хсо́тый** two-hundredth. ~**хта́ктный** two-stroke. ~**хэта́жный** two-storey. ~**язы́чный** bilingual.

деба́ты (-ов) *pl* debate.

де́бет debit. **дебетова́ть** *impf & pf* debit.

деби́т yield, output.

де́бри (-ей) *pl* jungle; thickets; the wilds.

дебю́т début.

де́ва maid, maiden; Virgo.

девальва́ция devaluation.

дева́ться *impf of* де́ться

деви́з motto; device.

деви́ца spinster; girl. **де́ви́ч|ий** girlish, maidenly; ~ья фами́лия maiden name. **де́вка** wench; lass; tart. **де́вочка** (little) girl. **де́вственник, -ица** virgin. **де́вственный** virgin; innocent. **де́вушка** girl. **девчо́нка** girl.

девяно́сто ninety. **девяно́стый** ninetieth. **девя́тка** nine; figure 9; No. 9. **девятна́дцатый** nineteenth. **девятна́дцать** nineteen. **девя́тый** ninth. **де́вять** (-и́, *instr* -ью́) nine. **девятьсо́т** (-тисо́т, -тиста́м, -тью-

ста́ми, -тиста́х) nine hundred.
дегенери́ровать *impf* & *pf* degenerate.
дёготь (-гтя) tar.
дегуста́ция tasting.
дед grandfather; grandad. де́душка grandfather; grandad.
дееприча́стие adverbial participle.
дежу́рить *impf* be on duty. дежу́рный duty; on duty; *sb* person on duty. дежу́рство (being on) duty.
дезерти́р deserter. дезерти́ровать *impf* & *pf* desert.
дезинфе́кция disinfection. дезинфици́ровать *impf* & *pf* disinfect.
дезодора́нт deodorant; air-freshener.
дезориента́ция disorientation. дезориенти́ровать *impf* & *pf* disorient; ~ся lose one's bearings.
де́йственный efficacious; effective. де́йствие action; operation; effect; act. действи́тельно *adv* really; indeed. действи́тельность reality; validity; efficacy. действи́тельный actual; valid; efficacious; active. де́йствовать *impf* (*pf* по~) affect, have an effect; act; work. де́йствующий active; in force; working; ~ее лицо́ character; ~ие ли́ца cast.
декабри́ст Decembrist. дека́брь (-я́) *m* December. дека́брьский December.
дека́да ten-day period *or* festival.
дека́н dean. декана́т office of dean.
деклама́ция recitation, declamation. деклами́ровать *impf* (*pf* про~) recite, declaim.
деклара́ция declaration.
декорати́вный decorative. декора́тор scene-painter. декора́ция scenery.
декре́т decree; maternity leave. декре́тный о́тпуск maternity leave.
де́ланный artificial, affected. де́лать *impf* (*pf* с~) make; do; ~ вид pretend; ~ся become; happen.
делега́т delegate. делега́ция delegation; group.
делёж (-а́), делёжка sharing; partition. деле́ние division; point (*on a scale*).
деле́ц (-льца́) smart operator.
делика́тный delicate.
дели́мое *sb* dividend. дели́мость divisibility. дели́тель *m* divisor.

дели́ть (-лю́, -лишь) *impf* (*pf* по~, раз~) divide; ~ шесть на три divide six by three; ~ся divide; be divisible; +*instr* share.
де́ло (*pl* -á) business: affair: matter: deed; thing; case; в са́мом де́ле really, indeed; ~ в том the point is; как (ваши) дела́? how are things?; на са́мом де́ле in actual fact; по де́лу, по дела́м on business. делови́тый business-like, efficient. делово́й business; business-like. де́льный efficient; sensible.
де́льта delta.
дельфи́н dolphin.
демаго́г demagogue.
демобилиза́ция demobilization. демобилизова́ть *impf* & *pf* demobilize.
демокра́т democrat. демократиза́ция democratization. демократизи́ровать *impf* & *pf* democratize. демократи́ческий democratic. демокра́тия democracy.
де́мон demon.
демонстра́ция demonstration. демонстри́ровать *impf* & *pf* demonstrate.
де́нежный monetary; money; ~ перево́д money order.
де́нусь *etc.*: *see* де́ться
день (дня) *m* day; afternoon; днём in the afternoon; на днях the other day; one of these days; че́рез ~ every other day.
де́ньги (-нег, -ьга́м) *pl* money.
департа́мент department.
депо́ *neut indecl* depot.
депорта́ция deportation. депорти́ровать *impf* & *pf* deport.
депута́т deputy; delegate.
дёргать *impf* (*pf* дёрнуть) pull, tug; pester; ~ся twitch; jerk.
дереве́нский village; rural. дере́вня (*pl* -и, -ве́нь, -вня́м) village; the country. де́рево (*pl* -е́вья, -ьев) tree; wood. деревя́нный wood; wooden.
держа́ва power. держа́ть (-жу́, -жишь) *impf* hold; support; keep; ~ пари́ bet; ~ себя́ behave; ~ся hold; be held up; hold o.s.; hold out; +*gen* keep to.
дерза́ние daring. дерза́ть *impf*, дерзну́ть (-ну́, -нёшь) *pf* dare.

де́рзкий impudent; daring. **де́рзость** impertinence; daring.

дёрн turf.

дёрнуть(ся (-ну(сь) *pf of* дёргать(ся

деру́ *etc.: see* драть

деса́нт landing; landing force.

де́скать *partl indicating reported speech.*

десна́ (*pl* дёсны, -сен) gum.

де́спот despot.

десятиле́тие decade; tenth anniversary. **десятиле́тка** ten-year (*secondary*) school. **десятиле́тний** ten-year; ten-year-old. **десяти́чный** decimal. **деся́тка** ten; figure 10; No. 10; tenner (*10-rouble note*). **деся́ток** (-тка) ten; decade. **деся́тый** tenth. **де́сять** (-и́, *instr* -ью) ten.

детдо́м children's home. **детса́д** kindergarten.

дета́ль detail; part, component. **дета́льный** detailed; minute.

детекти́в detective story.

детёныш young animal; *pl* young. **де́ти** (-те́й, -тям, -тьми, -тях) *pl* children. **де́тская** *sb* nursery. **де́тский** children's; childish. **де́тство** childhood.

де́ться (де́нусь) *pf* (*impf* дева́ться) get to. disappear to.

дефе́кт defect.

дефи́с hyphen.

дефици́т deficit; shortage. **дефици́тный** scarce.

дешеве́ть (-е́ет) *impf* (*pf* по~) fall in price. **деше́вле** *comp of* дёшево, дешёвый. **дёшево** *adv* cheap, cheaply. **дешёвый** (дёшев, -а́, -о) cheap; empty, worthless.

де́ятель *m*: госуда́рственный ~ statesman; обще́ственный ~ public figure. **де́ятельность** activity; work. **де́ятельный** active, energetic.

джаз jazz.

дже́мпер pullover.

джентльме́н gentleman.

джинсо́вый denim. **джи́нсы** (-ов) *pl* jeans.

джо́йстик joystick.

джу́нгли (-ей) *pl* jungle.

диабе́т diabetes.

диа́гноз diagnosis.

диагона́ль diagonal

диагра́мма diagram.

диале́кт dialect. **диале́ктика** dialectics.

диало́г dialogue.

диа́метр diameter.

диапазо́н range; band.

диапозити́в slide, transparency.

диафра́гма diaphragm.

дива́н sofa; divan.

диверса́нт saboteur. **диве́рсия** sabotage.

диви́зия division.

диви́ться (-влю́сь) *impf* (*pf* по~) marvel (at + *dat*).

ди́вный marvellous. **ди́во** wonder, marvel.

дида́ктика didactics.

дие́з (*mus*) sharp.

дие́та diet. **диети́ческий** dietetic.

ди́зель *m* diesel; diesel engine. **ди́зельный** diesel.

дизентери́я dysentery.

дика́рь (-я́) *m*, **дика́рка** savage. **ди́кий** wild; savage; queer; preposterous. **дикобра́з** porcupine. **дикорасту́щий** wild. **ди́кость** wildness, savagery; absurdity.

дикта́нт dictation. **дикта́тор** dictator. **диктату́ра** dictatorship.

диктова́ть *impf* (*pf* про~) dictate. **ди́ктор** announcer. **ди́кция** diction.

диле́мма dilemma.

дилета́нт dilettante.

дина́мика dynamics.

динами́т dynamite.

динами́ческий dynamic.

дина́стия dynasty.

диноза́вр dinosaur.

дипло́м diploma; degree; degree work. **диплома́т** diplomat. **дипломати́ческий** diplomatic.

директи́ва instructions; directives. **дире́ктор** (*pl* ~а́) director; principal. **дире́кция** management.

дирижа́бль *m* airship, dirigible.

дирижёр conductor. **дирижи́ровать** *impf* +*instr* conduct.

диск disc, disk; dial; discus.

ди́скант treble.

дискоте́ка discotheque.

дискре́тный discrete; digital.

дискримина́ция discrimination.

диску́ссия discussion, debate.

диспансе́р clinic.

диспе́тчер controller.

ди́спут public debate.

диссерта́ция dissertation, thesis.

дистанцио́нный distance, distant,

remote; remote-control. **дистанция** distance; range; region.

дисциплина discipline.

дитя (-яти; pl **дети**, -ей) neut child; baby.

дифтерит diphtheria.

дифтонг diphthong.

диффамация libel.

дичь game.

длина length. **длинный** (-нен, -нна, -о) long. **длительность** duration. **длительный** long, protracted. **длиться** impf (pf про~) last.

для prep+gen for; for the sake of; ~ того, чтобы... in order to.

дневальный sb orderly, man on duty. **дневник** (-а) diary, journal. **дневной** day; daily. **днём** adv in the day time; in the afternoon. **дни** etc.: see **день**

днище bottom.

ДНК abbr (of **дезоксирибонуклеиновая кислота**) DNA.

дно (pl **донья**, -ьев) bottom.

до prep+gen (up) to; as far as; until; before; to the point of; **до нашей эры** BC; **до сих пор** till now; **до тех пор till then**, before; **до того, как** before; **до того, что** to such an extent that, to the point where; **мне не до** I'm not in the mood for.

добавить (-влю) pf, **добавлять** impf (+acc or gen) add. **добавка** addition; second helping. **добавление** addition; supplement; extra. **добавочный** additional.

добегать impf, **добежать** (-егу) pf +**до**+gen run to, as far as; reach.

добивать impf, **добить** (-бью, -бьёшь) pf finish (off); ~**ся**+gen get, obtain; ~**ся своего** get one's way.

добираться impf of **добраться**

доблесть valour.

добраться (-берусь, -ёшься; -ался, -лась, -алóсь) pf (impf **добираться**) +**до**+gen get to, reach.

добро good; **это не к добру** it is a bad sign.

добро- in comb good-, well-. **доброволец** (-льца) volunteer. ~**вольно** adv voluntarily. ~**вольный** voluntary. ~**детель** virtue. ~**детельный** virtuous. ~**душие** good nature. ~**душный** good-natured. ~**качест-**

венный of good quality; benign. ~**совестный** conscientious.

доброта goodness, kindness. **добротный** of good quality. **добрый** (добр, -á, -о, добры) good; kind; **будьте добры**+imper please; would you be kind enough to.

добывать impf, **добыть** (-буду; добыл, -á, -о) pf get, obtain, procure; mine. **добыча** output; mining; booty.

добью etc.: see **добить**. **доведу** etc.: see **довести**

довезти (-езу, -езёшь; -вёз, -ла) pf (impf **довозить**) take (to), carry (to), drive (to).

доверенность warrant; power of attorney. **доверенный** trusted; sb agent, proxy. **доверие** trust, confidence. **доверить** pf (impf **доверять**) entrust; ~**ся** +dat trust in; confide in.

доверху adv to the top.

доверчивый trustful, credulous. **доверять** impf of **доверить**; (+dat) to trust.

довесок (-ска) makeweight.

довести (-еду, -едёшь; -вёл, -á) pf, **доводить** (-ожу, -одишь) impf lead, take (to); bring, drive (to). **довод** argument, reason.

довоенный pre-war.

довозить (-ожу, -озишь) impf of **довезти**

довольно adv enough; quite, fairly. **довольный** satisfied, pleased. **довольство** contentment. **довольствоваться** impf (pf у~) be content.

догадаться pf, **догадываться** impf guess; suspect. **догадка** surmise, conjecture. **догадливый** quick-witted.

догма dogma.

догнать (-гоню, -гонишь; -гнал, -á, -о) pf (impf **догонять**) catch up (with).

договариваться impf, **договориться** pf come to an agreement; arrange. **договор** (pl -ы or -á, -ов) agreement; contract; treaty. **договорный** contractual; agreed.

догонять impf of **догнать**

догорать impf, **догореть** (-рит) pf burn out, burn down.

доеду etc.: see **доехать**. **доезжать** impf of **доехать**

доехать (-еду) pf (impf **доезжать**)

+до+*gen* reach, arrive at.

дожда́ться (-ду́сь, -дёшься; -а́лся, -ла́сь, -а́ло́сь) *pf* +*gen* wait for, wait until.

дождеви́к (-а́) raincoat. дождево́й rain(y). дождли́вый rainy. дождь (-я́) *m* rain; ~ идёт it is raining.

дожива́ть *impf*, дожи́ть (-иву́, -ивёшь; до́жи́л, -а́, -о) *pf* live out; spend.

дожида́ться *impf* +*gen* wait for.

до́за dose.

дозво́лить *pf*, дозволя́ть *impf* permit.

дозвони́ться *pf* get through, reach by telephone.

дозо́р patrol.

дозрева́ть *impf*, дозре́ть (-е́ет) *pf* ripen.

доистори́ческий prehistoric.

дои́ть *impf* (*pf* по~) milk.

дойти́ (дойду́, -дёшь; дошёл, -шла́) *pf* (*impf* доходи́ть) +до+*gen* reach; get through to.

док dock.

доказа́тельный conclusive. доказа́тельство proof, evidence. доказа́ть (-ажу́) *pf*, дока́зывать *impf* demonstrate, prove.

докати́ться (-ачу́сь, -а́тишься) *pf*, дока́тываться *impf* roll; boom; +до+*gen* sink into.

докла́д report; lecture. докладна́я (запи́ска) report; memo. докла́дчик speaker, lecturer. докла́дывать *impf of* доложи́ть

до́красна́ *adv* to red heat; to redness.

до́ктор (*pl* -а́) doctor. до́кторский doctoral. до́кторша woman doctor; doctor's wife.

доктри́на doctrine.

докуме́нт document; deed. докумета́льный documentary. докумета́ция documentation; documents.

долби́ть (-блю́) *impf* hollow; chisel; repeat; swot up.

долг (*loc* -у́; *pl* -и́) duty; debt; взять в ~ borrow; дать в ~ lend.

до́лгий (до́лог, -лга́, -о) long. до́лго *adv* long, (for) a long time. долгове́чный lasting; durable. долгожда́нный long-awaited. долгоигра́ющая пласти́нка LP.

долголе́тие longevity. долго-

ле́тний of many years; long-standing. долгосро́чный long-term.

долгота́ (*pl* -ы) length; longitude.

долево́й lengthwise. до́лее *adv* longer.

должа́ть *impf* (*pf* за~) borrow.

до́лжен (-жна́) *predic*+*dat* in debt to; +*inf* obliged; bound; likely; must, have to, ought to; должно́ быть probably. должни́к (-а́), -ни́ца debtor. до́лжное *sb* due. должностно́й official. до́лжность (*gen pl* -е́й) post, office; duties. до́лжный due, fitting.

доли́на valley.

до́ллар dollar.

доложи́ть¹ (-ожу́, -о́жишь) *pf* (*impf* докла́дывать) add.

доложи́ть² (-ожу́, -о́жишь) *pf* (*impf* докла́дывать) +*acc or* о+*prep* report; announce.

доло́й *adv* away, off; +*acc* down with!

долото́ (*pl* -а) chisel.

до́лька segment; clove.

до́льше *adv* longer.

до́ля (*gen pl* -е́й) portion; share; lot, fate.

дом (*loc* -у́; *pl* -а́) house; home. до́ма *adv* at home. дома́шний house; home; domestic; home-made; ~яя хозя́йка housewife.

до́менн|ый blast-furnace; ~ая печь blast-furnace.

домини́ровать *impf* dominate, predominate.

домкра́т jack.

до́мна blast-furnace.

домовладе́лец (-льца), -лица houseowner; landlord. домово́дство housekeeping; domestic science. домо́вый house; household; housing.

домога́тельство solicitation; bid. домога́ться *impf* +*gen* solicit, bid for.

домо́й *adv* home, homewards. домохозя́йка housewife. домрабо́тница domestic servant, maid.

доне́льзя *adv* in the extreme.

донесе́ние dispatch, report. донести́ (-су́, -сёшь; -нёс, -сла́) *pf* (*impf* доноси́ть) report, announce; +*dat* inform; +на+*acc* inform against; ~сь be heard; +до+*gen* reach.

до́низу *adv* to the bottom; све́рху ~ from top to bottom.

до́нор donor.

доно́с denunciation, information. **доноси́ть(ся** (-ношу́(сь, -но́сишь(ся) *impf of* донести́(сь

доно́счик informer.

донско́й Don.

доны́не *adv* hitherto.

до́нья *etc.: see* дно

до н.э. *abbr* (*of* до на́шей э́ры) BC.

допла́та additional payment, excess fare. **доплати́ть** (-ачу́, -а́тишь) *pf*, **допла́чивать** *impf* pay in addition; pay the rest.

допо́длинно *adv* for certain. **допо́длинный** authentic, genuine.

дополне́ние supplement, addition; (*gram*) object. **дополни́тельно** *adv* in addition. **дополни́тельный** supplementary, additional. **допо́лнить** *pf*, **дополня́ть** *impf* supplement.

допра́шивать *impf*, **допроси́ть** (-ошу́, -о́сишь) *pf* interrogate. **допро́с** interrogation.

до́пуск right of entry, admittance. **допуска́ть** *impf*, **допусти́ть** (-ущу́, -у́стишь) *pf* admit; permit; tolerate; suppose. **допусти́мый** permissible, acceptable. **допуще́ние** assumption.

дореволюцио́нный pre-revolutionary.

доро́га road; way; journey; route: по доро́ге on the way.

до́рого *adv* dear, dearly. **дорогови́зна** high prices. **дорого́й** (до́рог, -а́, -о) dear.

доро́дный portly.

дорожа́ть *impf* (*pf* вз~, по~) rise in price, go up. **доро́же** *comp of* до́рого, дорого́й. **дорожи́ть** (-жу́) *impf* +*instr* value.

доро́жка path; track; lane; runway; strip, runner, stair-carpet. **доро́жный** road; highway; travelling.

доса́да annoyance. **досади́ть** (-ажу́) *pf*, **досажда́ть** *impf* +*dat* annoy. **доса́дный** annoying. **доса́довать** be annoyed (на+*acc* with).

доска́ (*acc* до́ску; *pl* -и, -со́к, -ска́м) board; slab; plaque.

досло́вный literal; word-for-word.

досмо́тр inspection.

доспе́хи *pl* armour.

досро́чный ahead of time, early.

достава́ть(ся (-таю́(сь, -ёшь(ся) *impf of* доста́ть(ся

доста́вить (-влю) *pf*, **доставля́ть** *impf* deliver; supply; cause, give. **доста́вка** delivery.

доста́ну *etc.: see* доста́ть

доста́ток (-тка) sufficiency; prosperity. **доста́точно** *adv* enough, sufficiently. **доста́точный** sufficient; adequate.

доста́ть (-а́ну) *pf* (*impf* достава́ть) take (out); get, obtain; +*gen or* до+*gen* touch; reach; *impers* suffice; ~ся+*dat* be inherited by; fall to the lot of: ему́ доста́нется he'll catch it.

достига́ть *impf*, **дости́гнуть**, **дости́чь** (-и́гну; -стиг) *pf* +*gen* reach, achieve; +*gen or* до+*gen* reach. **достиже́ние** achievement.

достове́рный reliable, trustworthy; authentic.

досто́инство dignity; merit; value. **досто́йный** deserved; suitable; worthy; +*gen* worthy of.

достопримеча́тельность sight, notable place.

достоя́ние property.

до́ступ access. **досту́пный** accessible; approachable; reasonable; available.

досу́г leisure, (spare) time. **досу́жий** leisure; idle.

до́сыта *adv* to satiety.

досье́ *neut indecl* dossier.

досяга́емый attainable.

дота́ция grant, subsidy.

дотла́ utterly; to the ground.

дотра́гиваться *impf*, **дотро́нуться** (-нусь) *pf* +до+*gen* touch.

дотя́гивать *impf*, **дотяну́ть** (-яну́, -я́нешь) *pf* draw, drag, stretch out; hold out; live; put off; ~ся stretch, reach; drag on.

до́хлый dead; sickly. **до́хнуть**[1] (-нет; дох) (*pf* из~, по~, с~) die; kick the bucket.

дохну́ть[2] (-ну́, -нёшь) *pf* draw a breath.

дохо́д income; revenue. **доходи́ть** (-ожу́, -о́дишь) *impf of* дойти́. **дохо́дный** profitable. **дохо́дчивый** intelligible.

доце́нт reader, senior lecturer.

до́чиста *adv* clean; completely.

до́чка daughter. **дочь** (-чери, *instr* -черью; *pl* -чери, -чере́й, *instr* -черьми́) daughter.

дошёл etc.: see **дойти́**

дошко́льник, -ница child under school age. **дошко́льный** pre-school.

доща́тый plank, board. **доще́чка** small plank, board; plaque.

дойрка milkmaid.

драгоце́нность jewel; treasure; pl jewellery; valuables. **драгоце́нный** precious.

дразни́ть (-ню́, -нишь) impf tease.

дра́ка fight.

драко́н dragon.

дра́ма drama. **драмати́ческий** dramatic. **драмату́рг** playwright. **драматурги́я** dramatic art; plays.

драп thick woollen cloth.

драпиро́вка draping; curtain; hangings. **драпиро́вщик** upholsterer.

драть (деру́, -рёшь; драл, -а́, -о) impf (pf вы́~, за~, со~) tear (up); irritate; make off; flog; ~ся fight.

дре́безги pl; в ~ to smithereens. **дребезжа́ть** (-жи́т) impf jingle, tinkle.

древеси́на wood; timber. **древе́сный** wood; ~ у́голь charcoal.

дре́вко (pl -и, -ов) pole, staff; shaft.

древнегре́ческий ancient Greek. **древнееврейский** Hebrew. **древнеру́сский** Old Russian. **дре́вний** ancient; aged. **дре́вность** antiquity.

дрейф drift; leeway. **дрейфова́ть** impf drift.

дрема́ть (-млю́, -млешь) impf doze; slumber. **дремо́та** drowsiness.

дрему́чий dense.

дрессиро́ванный trained; performing. **дрессирова́ть** impf (pf вы́~) train; school. **дрессиро́вка** training. **дрессиро́вщик** trainer.

дроби́ть (-блю́) impf (pf раз~) break up, smash; crush; ~ся break to pieces, smash. **дробови́к** (-а́) shot-gun. **дробь** (small) shot; drumming; fraction. **дро́бный** fractional.

дрова́ (дров) pl firewood.

дро́гнуть (-ну) pf, **дрожа́ть** (-жу́) impf tremble; shiver; quiver.

дро́жжи (-ей) pl yeast.

дрожь shivering, trembling.

дрозд (-а́) thrush.

дро́ссель m throttle, choke.

дро́тик javelin, dart.

друг[1] (pl -узья́, -зе́й) friend. **друг**[2]:

~ дру́га (дру́гу) each other, one another. **друго́й** other, another; different; на ~ день (the) next day. **дру́жба** friendship. **дружелю́бный, дру́жеский, дру́жественный** friendly. **дружи́ть** (-жу́, -жи́шь) impf be friends; ~ся (pf по~ся) make friends. **дру́жный** (-жен, -жна́, -о) amicable; harmonious; simultaneous, concerted.

дря́блый (дрябл, -а́, -о) flabby.

дря́зги (-зг) pl squabbles.

дрянно́й worthless; good-for-nothing. **дрянь** rubbish.

дряхле́ть (-е́ю) impf (pf о~) become decrepit. **дря́хлый** (-хл, -ла́, -о) decrepit, senile.

дуб (pl -ы́) oak; blockhead. **дуби́на** club, cudgel; blockhead. **дуби́нка** truncheon, baton.

дублёнка sheepskin coat.

дублёр understudy. **дублика́т** duplicate. **дубли́ровать** duplicate; understudy; dub.

дубо́вый oak; coarse; clumsy.

дуга́ (pl -и) arc; arch.

ду́дка pipe, fife.

ду́ло muzzle; barrel.

ду́ма thought; Duma; council. **ду́мать** impf (pf по~) think; +inf think of, intend. **ду́маться** impf (impers +dat) seem.

дунове́ние puff, breath. **ду́нуть** (-ну) pf of **дуть**

дупло́ (pl -а, -пел) hollow; hole; cavity.

ду́ра, дура́к (-а́) fool. **дура́чить** (-чу) impf (pf о~) fool, dupe; ~ся play the fool.

дуре́ть (-е́ю) impf (pf о~) grow stupid.

дурма́н narcotic; intoxicant. **дурма́нить** impf (pf о~) stupefy.

дурно́й (-рен, -рна́, -о) bad, evil; ugly; мне ду́рно I feel faint, sick. **дурнота́** faintness; nausea.

ду́тый hollow; inflated. **дуть** (ду́ю) impf (pf вы́~, по~, ду́нуть) blow; ду́ет there is a draught. **дутьё** glass-blowing. **ду́ться** (ду́юсь) impf pout; sulk.

дух spirit; spirits; heart; mind; breath; ghost; smell; в ~e in a good mood; не в моём ~e not to my taste; ни слу́ху ни ~у no news, not a word.

духи́ (-о́в) pl scent, perfume. Ду́хов день Whit Monday. духове́нство clergy. духови́дец (-дца) clairvoyant; medium. духо́вка oven. духо́вный spiritual; ecclesiastical. духово́й wind. духота́ stuffiness, closeness.

душ shower(-bath).

душа́ (acc -y, pl -и) soul; heart; feeling; spirit; inspiration; в душе́ inwardly; at heart; от всей души́ with all one's heart.

душева́я sb shower-room.

душевнобольно́й mentally ill, insane; sb mental patient; lunatic. душе́вный mental; sincere, cordial.

души́стый fragrant; ~ горо́шек sweet pea(s).

души́ть (-шу́, -шишь) impf (pf за~) strangle; stifle, smother.

души́ться (-шу́сь, -шишься) impf (pf на~) use, put on, perfume.

ду́шный (-шен, -шна́, -о) stuffy, close.

дуэ́ль duel.

дуэ́т duet.

ды́бом adv on end; у меня́ во́лосы вста́ли ~ my hair stood on end. дыбы́: станови́ться на ~ rear; resist.

дым (loc -ý, pl -ы́) smoke. дыми́ть (-млю́) impf (pf на~) smoke; ~ся smoke, steam; billow. ды́мка haze. ды́мный smoky. дымово́й smoke; ~ая труба́ flue, chimney. дымо́к (-мка́) puff of smoke. дымохо́д flue.

ды́ня melon.

дыра́ (pl -ы), ды́рка (gen pl -рок) hole; gap.

дыха́ние breathing; breath. дыха́тельн|ый respiratory; breathing; ~ое го́рло windpipe. дыша́ть (-шу́, -шишь) impf breathe.

дья́вол devil. дья́вольский devilish, diabolical.

дья́кон (pl -á) deacon.

дю́жина dozen.

дюйм inch.

дю́на dune.

дя́дя (gen pl -ей) m uncle.

дя́тел (-тла) woodpecker.

E

ева́нгелие gospel; the Gospels. евангели́ческий evangelical.

евре́й, евре́йка Jew; Hebrew. евре́йский Jewish.

Евро́па Europe. европе́ец (-е́йца) European. европе́йский European.

Еги́пет Egypt. еги́петский Egyptian. египтя́нин (pl -я́не, -я́н), египтя́нка Egyptian.

его́ see он, оно́; pron his; its.

еда́ food; meal.

едва́ adv & conj hardly; just; scarcely; ~ ли hardly; ~ (ли) не almost, all but.

еди́м etc.: see есть[1]

едине́ние unity. едини́ца (figure) one; unity; unit; individual. еди́ничный single; individual.

едино- in comb mono-, uni-; one; co-. единобра́чие monogamy. ~вла́стие autocracy. ~вре́менно adv only once; simultaneously. ~гла́сие, ~ду́шие unanimity. ~гла́сный, ~ду́шный unanimous. ~кро́вный брат half-brother. ~мы́слие likemindedness; agreement. ~мы́шленник like-minded person. ~утро́бный брат half-brother.

еди́нственно adv only, solely. еди́нственный only, sole. еди́нство unity. еди́ный one; single; united.

е́дкий (е́док, едка́, -о) caustic; pungent.

едо́к (-á) mouth, head; eater.

е́ду etc.: see е́хать

её see она́; pron her, hers; its.

ёж (ежа́) hedgehog.

еже- in comb every; -ly. ежего́дник annual, year-book. ~го́дный annual. ~дне́вный daily. ~ме́сячник, ~ме́сячный monthly. ~неде́льник, ~неде́льный weekly.

ежеви́ка (no pl; usu collect) blackberry; blackberries; blackberry bush.

е́жели conj if.

ёжиться (ёжусь) impf (pf съ~) huddle up; shrink away.

езда́ ride, riding; drive, driving; journey. е́здить (е́зжу) impf go; ride, drive; ~ верхо́м ride. ездо́к (-á) rider.

ей see она́

ей-бо́гу int really! truly!

ел etc.: see есть[1]

éле adv scarcely; only just. éле-éле emphatic variant of éле

ёлка fir-tree, spruce; Christmas tree.
ёлочка herring-bone pattern.
ёлочный Christmas-tree. ель fir-tree; spruce.
ем *etc.: see* есть[1]
ёмкий capacious. ёмкость capacity.
ему́ *see* он, оно́
епи́скоп bishop.
е́ресь heresy. ерети́к (-а́) heretic. ерети́ческий heretical.
ёрзать *impf* fidget.
еро́шить (-шу) *impf* (*pf* взъ~) ruffle, rumple.
ерунда́ nonsense.
е́сли *conj* if; ~ бы if only; ~ бы не but for, if it were not for; ~ не unless.
ест *see* есть[1]
есте́ственно *adv* naturally. есте́ственный natural. естество́ nature; essence. естествозна́ние (natural) science.
есть[1] (ем, ешь, ест, еди́м; ел) *impf* (*pf* съ~) eat; corrode, eat away.
есть[2] *see* быть; is, are; there is, there are; у меня́ ~ I have.
ефре́йтор lance-corporal.
е́хать (е́ду) *impf* (*pf* по~) go; ride, drive; travel; ~ верхо́м ride.
ехи́дный malicious, spiteful.
ешь *see* есть[1]
ещё *adv* still; yet; (some) more; any more; yet, further; again; +*comp* still, yet even; всё ~ still; ~ бы! of course! oh yes! can you ask?; ~ не, нет ~ not yet; ~ раз once more, again; пока́ ~ for the present, for the time being.
е́ю *see* она́

Ж

ж *conj: see* же
жа́ба toad.
жа́бра (*gen pl* -бр) gill.
жа́воронок (-нка) lark.
жа́дничать *impf* be greedy; be mean. жа́дность greed; meanness. жа́дный (-ден, -дна́, -о) greedy; avid; mean.
жа́жда thirst; +*gen* thirst, craving for. жа́ждать (-ду) *impf* thirst, yearn.
жаке́т, жаке́тка jacket.
жале́ть (-е́ю) *impf* (*pf* по~) pity, feel sorry for; regret; +*acc or gen* grudge.

жа́лить *impf* (*pf* у~) sting, bite.
жа́лкий (-лок, -лка́, -о) pitiful. жа́лко *predic: see* жаль
жа́ло sting.
жа́лоба complaint. жа́лобный plaintive.
жа́лованье salary. жа́ловать *impf* (*pf* по~) +*acc* or *dat of person, instr or acc of thing* grant, bestow on; ~ся complain (на+*acc* of, about).
жа́лостливый compassionate. жа́лостный piteous; compassionate. жа́лость pity. жаль, жа́лко *predic, impers* (it is) a pity; +*dat* it grieves; +*gen* grudge; как ~ what a pity! мне ~ его́ I'm sorry for him.
жалюзи́ *neut indecl* Venetian blind.
жанр genre.
жар (*loc* -у́) heat; heat of the day; fever; (high) temperature; ardour. жара́ heat; hot weather.
жарго́н slang.
жа́реный roast; grilled; fried. жа́рить *impf* (*pf* за~, из~) roast; grill; fry; scorch, burn; ~ся roast, fry. жа́ркий (-рок, -рка́, -о) hot; passionate; -ое *sb* roast (meat). жаро́вня (*gen pl* -вен) brazier. жар-пти́ца Firebird. жа́рче *comp of* жа́ркий
жа́тва harvest. жать[1] (жну, жнёшь) *impf* (*pf* с~) reap, cut.
жать[2] (жму, жмёшь) *impf* press, squeeze; pinch; oppress.
жва́чка chewing, rumination; cud; chewing-gum. жва́чн|ый ruminant; ~ое *sb* ruminant.
жгу *etc.: see* жечь
жгут (-а́) plait; tourniquet.
жгу́чий burning. жёг *etc.: see* жечь
ждать (жду, ждёшь; -ал, -а́, -о) *impf* +*gen* wait (for); expect.
же, ж *conj* but; and; however; also; *partl* giving emphasis or expressing identity; мне же ка́жется it seems to me, however; сего́дня же this very day; что же ты де́лаешь? what on earth are you doing?
жева́тельная рези́нка chewing-gum. жева́ть (жую́, жуёшь) *impf* chew; ruminate.
жезл (-а́) rod; staff.
жела́ние wish, desire. жела́нный longed-for; beloved. жела́тельный desirable; advisable. жела́ть *impf*

(*pf* по~) +*gen* wish for, desire; want.
желе́ *neut indecl* jelly.

железа́ (*pl* же́лезы, -лёз, -за́м) gland; *pl* tonsils.
железнодоро́жник railwayman. железнодоро́жный railway. желе́зн|ый iron; ~ая доро́га railway. желе́зо iron.
железобето́н reinforced concrete.
жёлоб (*pl* -а́) gutter. желобо́к (-бка́) groove, channel, flute.
желте́ть (-е́ю) *impf* (*pf* по~) turn yellow; be yellow. желто́к (-тка́) yolk. желту́ха jaundice. жёлтый (жёлт, -а́, жёлто́) yellow.
желу́док (-дка) stomach. желу́дочный stomach; gastric.
жёлудь (*gen pl* -е́й) *m* acorn.
жёлчный bilious; gall; irritable. жёлчь bile, gall.
жема́ниться *impf* mince, put on airs. жема́нный mincing, affected. жема́нство affectedness.
же́мчуг (*pl* -а́) pearl(s). жемчу́жина pearl. жемчу́жный pear(ly).
жена́ (*pl* жёны) wife. жена́тый married.
жени́ть (-ню́, -нишь) *impf* & *pf* (*pf also* по~) marry. жени́тьба marriage. жени́ться (-ню́сь, -нишься) *impf* & *pf* (+на+*prep*) marry, get married (to). жени́х (-а́) fiancé; bridegroom. же́нский woman's; feminine; female. же́нственный womanly, feminine. же́нщина woman.
жердь (*gen pl* -е́й) pole; stake.
жеребёнок (-нка; *pl* -бя́та, -бя́т) foal. жеребе́ц (-бца́) stallion.
жеребьёвка casting of lots.
жерло́ (*pl* -а) muzzle; crater.
жёрнов (*pl* -а́, -о́в) millstone.
же́ртва sacrifice; victim. же́ртвенный sacrificial. же́ртвовать *impf* (*pf* по~) present, make a donation (of); +*instr* sacrifice.
жест gesture. жестикули́ровать *impf* gesticulate.
жёсткий (-ток, -тка́, -о) hard, tough; rigid, strict.
жесто́кий (-то́к, -а́, -о) cruel; severe. жесто́кость cruelty.
жесть tin(-plate). жестяно́й tin.
жето́н medal; counter; token.
жечь (жгу, жжёшь; жёг, жгла) *impf*

(*pf* с~) burn; ~ся burn, sting; burn o.s.

живи́тельный invigorating. жи́вность poultry, fowl. жив|о́й (жив, -а́, -о) living, alive; lively; vivid; brisk; animated; poignant; bright; на ~ую ни́тку hastily, anyhow; шить на ~ую ни́тку tack. живопи́сец (-сца) painter. живопи́сный picturesque. жи́вопись painting. жи́вость liveliness.
живо́т (-а́) abdomen; stomach. животново́дство animal husbandry. живо́тное *sb* animal. живо́тный animal.
живу́ *etc.*: *see* жить. живу́чий hardy. живьём *adv* alive.
жи́дк|ий (-док, -дка́, -о) liquid; watery; weak; sparse; ~ий криста́лл liquid crystal. жи́дкость liquid, fluid; wateriness, weakness. жи́жа sludge; slush; liquid. жи́же *comp of* жи́дкий
жи́зненный life, of life; vital; living; ~ у́ровень standard of living. жизнеописа́ние biography. жизнера́достный cheerful. жизнеспосо́бный capable of living; viable. жизнь life.
жи́ла vein; tendon, sinew.
жиле́т, жиле́тка waistcoat.
жиле́ц (-льца́), жили́ца lodger; tenant; inhabitant.
жили́ще dwelling, abode. жили́щный housing; living.
жи́лка vein; fibre; streak.
жил|о́й dwelling; habitable; ~о́й дом dwelling house; block of flats; ~а́я пло́щадь, жилпло́щадь floor-space; housing, accommodation. жильё habitation; dwelling.
жир (*loc* -у́; *pl* -ы́) fat; grease. жире́ть (-ре́ю) *impf* (*pf* о~, раз~) grow fat. жи́рный (-рен, -рна́, -о) fatty; greasy; rich. жирово́й fatty; fat.
жира́ф giraffe.
жите́йский worldly; everyday. жи́тель *m* inhabitant; dweller. жи́тельство residence. жи́тница granary. жи́то corn, cereal. жить (живу́, -вёшь; жил, -а́, -о) *impf* live. житьё life; existence; habitation.
жму *etc.*: *see* жать[2]
жму́риться *impf* (*pf* за~) screw up one's eyes, frown.

жнивьё (pl -ья, -ьев) stubble (-field).

жну etc.: see жать[1]

жокéй jockey.

жонглёр juggler.

жрать (жру, жрёшь; -ал, -á, -о) guzzle.

жрéбий lot; fate, destiny; ~ брóшен the die is cast.

жрец priest. жрúца priestess.

жужжáть (-жжý) hum, buzz, drone; whiz(z).

жук (-á) beetle.

жýлик petty thief; cheat. жýльничать impf (pf c~) cheat.

журáвль (-я) m crane.

журúть impf reprove.

журнáл magazine, periodical. журналúст journalist. журналúстика journalism.

журчáние babble; murmur. журчáть (-чúт) impf babble, murmur.

жýткий (-ток, -ткá, -о) uncanny; terrible, terrifying. жýтко adv terrifyingly; terribly, awfully.

жую etc.: see жевáть

жюрú neut indecl judges.

З

за prep **I.** +acc (indicating motion or action) or instr (indicating rest or state) behind; beyond; across, the other side of; at; to; зá гóрод, зá гóродом out of town; за рубежóм abroad; сесть за роя́ль sit down at the piano; сидéть за роя́лем be at the piano; зá угол, за углóм round the corner. **II.** +acc after; over; during, in the space of; by; for; to; за вáше здорóвье! your health!; вестú зá руку lead by the hand; далекó зá полночь long after midnight; за два дня до+gen two days before; зá три киломéтра от дерéвни three kilometres from the village; платúть за билéт pay for a ticket; за послéднее врéмя lately. **III.** +instr after; for; because of; at; during; год за гóдом year after year; идтú за молокóм go for milk; за обéдом at dinner.

забáва amusement; game; fun. забавля́ть impf amuse; ~ся amuse o.s. забáвный amusing, funny.

забастовáть pf strike; go on strike. забастóвка strike. забастóвщик striker.

забвéние oblivion.

забéг heat, race. забегáть impf, забежáть (-егý) pf run up; +к+dat drop in on; ~ вперёд run ahead; anticipate.

за|берéменеть (-ею) pf become pregnant.

заберý etc.: see забрáть

забивáние jamming. забивáть(ся impf of забúть(ся[1]

забинтовáть pf, забинтóвывать impf bandage.

забирáть(ся impf of забрáть(ся

забúтый downtrodden. забúть[1] (-бью, -бьёшь) pf (impf забивáть) drive in, hammer in; score; seal, block up; obstruct; choke; jam; cram; beat up; beat; ~ся hide, take refuge; become cluttered or clogged; +в+acc get into, penetrate. за|бúть(ся[2] pf begin to beat. забия́ка m & f squabbler; bully.

заблаговрéменно adv in good time; well in advance. заблаговрéменный timely.

заблестéть (-ещý, -естúшь or -éщешь) pf begin to shine, glitter, glow.

заблудúться (-ужýсь, -ýдишься) pf get lost. заблýдший lost, stray. заблуждáться impf be mistaken. заблуждéние error; delusion.

забóй (pit-)face.

заболевáемость sickness rate. заболевáние sickness, illness; falling ill. заболевáть[1] impf, заболéть[1](-éю) pf fall ill; +instr go down with. заболевáть[2] impf, заболéть[2] (-лúт) pf (begin to) ache, hurt.

забóр[1] fence.

забóр[2] taking away; obtaining on credit.

забóта concern; care; trouble(s). забóтить (-óчу) impf (pf o~) trouble, worry; ~ся (pf по~) worry; take care of; take trouble; care. забóтливый solicitous, thoughtful.

за|браковáть pf.

забрáсывать impf of забросáть, забрóсить

забрáть (-берý, -берёшь; -ál, -á, -о)

pf (*impf* **забира́ть**) take; take away; seize; appropriate; ~**ся** climb; get to, into.

забреда́ть *impf*, **забрести́** (-еду́, -едёшь; -ёл, -а́) *pf* stray, wander; drop in.

за|брони́ровать *pf*.

заброса́ть *pf* (*impf* **забра́сывать**) fill up; bespatter; deluge. **забро́сить** (-о́шу) *pf* (*impf* **забра́сывать**) throw; abandon; neglect. **забро́шенный** neglected; deserted.

забры́згать *pf*, **забры́згивать** *impf* splash, bespatter.

забыва́ть *impf*, **забы́ть** (-бу́ду) *pf* forget; ~**ся** doze off; lose consciousness; forget o.s. **забы́вчивый** forgetful. **забытьё** oblivion; drowsiness.

забью́ *etc.*: *see* **забы́ть**

зава́ливать *impf*, **завали́ть** (-лю́, -лишь) *pf* block up; pile; cram; overload; knock down; make a mess of; ~**ся** fall; collapse; tip up.

зава́ривать *impf*, **завари́ть** (-арю́, -а́ришь) *pf* make; brew; weld. **зава́рка** brewing; brew; welding.

заведе́ние establishment. **заве́довать** *impf* +*instr* manage.

заве́домо *adv* wittingly. **заве́домый** notorious, undoubted.

заведу́ *etc.*: *see* **завести́**

заве́дующий *sb* (+*instr*) manager; head.

завезти́ (-зу́, -зёшь; -ёз, -ла́) *pf* (*impf* **завози́ть**) convey, deliver.

за|вербова́ть *pf*.

заве́ритель *m* witness. **заве́рить** *pf* (*impf* **заверя́ть**) assure; certify; witness.

заверну́ть (-ну́, -нёшь) *pf* (*impf* **завёртывать, завора́чивать**) wrap, wrap up; roll up; screw tight, screw up; turn (off); drop in, call in.

заверте́ться (-рчу́сь, -ртишься) *pf* begin to turn *or* spin; lose one's head.

завёртывать *impf of* **заверну́ть**

заверша́ть *impf*, **заверши́ть** (-шу́) *pf* complete, conclude. **заверше́ние** completion; end.

заверя́ть *impf of* **заве́рить**

заве́са veil, screen. **заве́сить** (-е́шу) *pf* (*impf* **заве́шивать**) curtain (off).

завести́ (-еду́, -ёшь; -вёл, -а́) *pf* (*impf* **заводи́ть**) take, bring; drop off; start up; acquire; introduce; wind (up), crank; ~**сь** be; appear; be established; start.

заве́т behest, bidding, ordinance; Testament. **заве́тный** cherished; secret.

заве́шивать *impf of* **заве́сить**

завеща́ние will, testament. **завеща́ть** bequeath.

завзя́тый inveterate, out-and-out.

завива́ть(ся *impf of* **зави́ть(ся. зави́вка** waving; curling; wave.

зави́дно *impers+dat*: мне ~ I feel envious. **зави́дный** enviable. **зави́довать** *impf* (*pf* по~) +*dat* envy.

завинти́ть (-нчу́) *pf*, **зави́нчивать** *impf* screw up.

зави́сеть (-и́шу) *impf* +от+*gen* depend on. **зави́симость** dependence; в зави́симости от depending on, subject to. **зави́симый** dependent.

зави́стливый envious. **за́висть** envy.

завито́й (за́вит, -а́, -о) curled, waved. **завито́к** (-тка́) curl, lock; flourish. **зави́ть** (-вью́, -вьёшь; -и́л, -а́, -о) *pf* (*impf* **завива́ть**) curl, wave; ~**ся** curl, wave, twine; have one's hair curled.

завладева́ть *impf*, **завладе́ть** (-е́ю) *pf* +*instr* take possession of; seize.

завлека́тельный alluring; fascinating. **завлека́ть** *impf*, **завле́чь** (-еку́, -ечёшь; -лёк, -ла́) *pf* lure; fascinate.

заво́д[1] factory; works; studfarm. **заво́д**[2] winding mechanism. **заводи́ть(ся** (-ожу́(сь, -о́дишь(ся) *impf of* **завести́(сь. заводно́й** clockwork; winding, cranking.

заводско́й factory; *sb* factory worker. **заво́дчик** factory owner.

за́водь backwater.

завоева́ние winning; conquest; achievement. **завоева́тель** *m* conqueror. **завоева́ть** (-о́юю) *pf*, **завоёвывать** *impf* conquer; win, gain; try to get.

завожу́ *etc.*: *see* **заводи́ть, завози́ть**

заво́з delivery; carriage. **завози́ть** (-ожу́, -о́зишь) *impf of* **завезти́**

завора́чивать *impf of* **заверну́ть. заворо́т** turn, turning; sharp bend.

завою́ *etc.*: *see* **завы́ть**

завсегда́ *adv* always. **завсегда́тай** habitué, frequenter.

за́втра tomorrow. **за́втрак** breakfast; lunch. **за́втракать** *impf* (*pf* по~) have breakfast; have lunch. **за́втрашний** tomorrow's; ~ день tomorrow.

завыва́ть *impf*, **завы́ть** (-во́ю) *pf* (begin to) howl.

завяза́ть (-яжу́, -я́жешь) *pf* (*impf* **завя́зывать**) tie, tie up; start; ~ся start; arise; (*of fruit*) set. **завя́зка** string, lace; start; opening.

за|вя́знуть (-ну; -я́з) *pf*. **завя́зывать(ся** *impf of* завяза́ть(ся **завя́нуть** (-ну; -я́л) *pf*.

загада́ть, зага́дывать *impf* think of; plan ahead; guess at the future; ~ зага́дку ask a riddle. **зага́дка** riddle; enigma. **зага́дочный** enigmatic, mysterious.

зага́р sunburn, tan.

за|гаси́ть (-ашу́, -а́сишь) *pf*. **за|га́снуть** (-ну) *pf*.

загво́здка snag; difficulty.

заги́б fold; exaggeration. **загиба́ть** *impf of* загну́ть

за|гипнотизи́ровать *pf*.

загла́вие title; heading. **загла́вный** title; ~ая бу́ква capital letter.

загла́дить (-а́жу) *pf*, **загла́живать** *impf* iron, iron out; make up for; expiate; ~ся iron out, become smooth; fade.

за|гло́хнуть (-ну; -гло́х) *pf*.

заглуша́ть *impf*, **за|глуши́ть** (-шу́) *pf* drown, muffle; jam; suppress, stifle; alleviate.

загляде́нье lovely sight. **загляде́ться** (-яжу́сь) *pf*, **загля́дываться** *impf* на+*acc* stare at; be lost in admiration of. **загля́дывать** *impf*, **загляну́ть** (-ну́, -нешь) *pf* peep; drop in.

загна́ть (-гоню́, -го́нишь; -а́л, -а́, -о) *pf* (*impf* **загоня́ть**) drive in, drive home; drive; exhaust.

загнива́ние decay; suppuration. **загнива́ть** *impf*, **загни́ть** (-ию́, -иёшь; -и́л, -а́, -о) *pf* rot; decay; fester.

загну́ть (-ну́, -нёшь) *pf* (*impf* **загиба́ть**) turn up, turn down; bend.

загова́ривать *impf*, **заговори́ть** *pf* begin to speak; tire out with talk; cast a spell over; protect with a charm (от+*gen* against). **за́говор** plot; spell. **загово́рщик** conspirator.

заголо́вок (-вка) title; heading; headline.

заго́н enclosure, pen; driving in. **загоня́ть¹** *impf of* загна́ть. **загоня́ть²** *pf* tire out; work to death.

загора́живать *impf of* загороди́ть

загора́ть *impf*, **загоре́ть** (-рю́) *pf* become sunburnt; ~ся catch fire; blaze; *impers+dat* want very much. **загоре́лый** sunburnt.

загороди́ть (-рожу́, -ро́ди́шь) *pf* (*impf* **загора́живать**) enclose, fence in; obstruct. **загоро́дка** fence, enclosure.

за́городный suburban; country.

загота́вливать *impf*, **заготовля́ть** *impf*, **загото́вить** (-влю) *pf* lay in (a stock of); store; prepare. **загото́вка** (State) procurement, purchase; laying in.

загради́ть (-ажу́) *pf*, **загражда́ть** *impf* block, obstruct; bar. **загражде́ние** obstruction; barrier.

грани́ца abroad, foreign parts. **заграни́чный** foreign.

загреба́ть *impf*, **загрести́** (-ебу́, -ебёшь; -ёб, -ла́) *pf* rake up; gather; rake in.

загри́вок (-вка) withers; nape (of the neck).

за|гримирова́ть *pf*.

загромозжда́ть *impf*, **загромозди́ть** (-зжу́) *pf* block up, encumber; cram.

загружа́ть *impf*, **за|грузи́ть** (-ужу́, -у́зишь) *pf* load; feed; ~ся +*instr* load up with, take on. **загру́зка** loading, feeding; charge, load, capacity.

за|грунтова́ть *pf*.

загрусти́ть (-ущу́) *pf* grow sad.

загрязне́ние pollution. **за|грязни́ть** *pf*, **загрязня́ть** *impf* soil; pollute; ~ся become dirty.

загс *abbr* (*of* (отде́л) за́писи а́ктов гражда́нского состоя́ния) registry office.

загуби́ть (-блю́, -бишь) *pf* ruin; squander, waste.

загуля́ть, загу́ливать *impf* take to drink.

за|густе́ть *pf*.

зад (*loc* -у́; *pl* -ы́) back; hindquarters; buttocks; ~ом наперёд back to front.

задава́ть(ся (-даю́(сь) *impf of* зада́ть(ся

задави́ть (-влю́, -вишь) *pf* crush; run over.

задади́м *etc.*, **зада́м** *etc.: see* **зада́ть**

зада́ние task, job.

зада́тки (-тков) *pl* abilities, promise.

зада́ток (-тка) deposit, advance.

зада́ть (-а́м, -а́шь, -а́ст, -ади́м; за́дал, -á, -о) *pf* (*impf* **задава́ть**) set; give; ~ вопро́с ask a question; ~ся turn out well; succeed; ~ся мы́слью, це́лью make up one's mind. **зада́ча** problem; task.

задвига́ть *impf*, **задви́нуть** (-ну) *pf* bolt; bar; push; ~ся shut; slide. **задви́жка** bolt; catch.

задво́рки (-рок) *pl* back yard; backwoods.

задева́ть *impf of* **заде́ть**

заде́лать *pf*, **заде́лывать** *impf* do up; block up, close up.

заде́ну *etc.: see* **заде́ть**. **задёрги-вать** *impf of* **задёрнуть**

задержа́ние detention. **задержа́ть** (-жу́, -жишь) *pf*, **заде́рживать** *impf* delay; withhold; arrest; ~ся stay too long; be delayed. **заде́ржка** delay.

задёрнуть (-ну) *pf* (*impf* за-дёргивать) pull; draw.

заде́ру *etc.: see* **задра́ть**

заде́ть (-е́ну) *pf* (*impf* **задева́ть**) brush (against), graze; offend; catch (against).

зади́ра *m & f* bully; trouble-maker. **задира́ть** *impf of* **задра́ть**

за́дн|ий back, rear; **дать** ~ий ход reverse; ~яя мысль ulterior motive; ~ий план background; ~ий прохо́д anus. **за́дник** back; backdrop.

задо́лго *adv* +до+*gen* long before.

за|должа́ть *pf*. **задо́лженность** debts.

задо́р fervour. **задо́рный** provocative; fervent.

задохну́ться (-ну́сь, -нёшься; -о́хся *or* -у́лся) *pf* (*impf* задыха́ться) suffocate; choke; pant.

за|дра́ть (-деру́, -дерёшь; -а́л, -á, -о) *pf* (*impf also* задира́ть) tear to pieces, kill; lift up; break; provoke, insult.

задрема́ть (-млю́, -млешь) *pf* doze off.

задрожа́ть (-жу́) *pf* begin to tremble.

задува́ть *impf of* **заду́ть**

заду́мать *pf*, **заду́мывать** *impf* plan; intend; think of; ~ся become thoughtful; meditate. **заду́мчивость** reverie. **заду́мчивый** pensive.

заду́ть (-у́ю) *pf* (*impf* задува́ть) blow out; begin to blow.

задуше́вный sincere; intimate.

за|души́ть (-ушу́, -у́шишь) *pf*.

задыха́ться *impf of* задохну́ться

заеда́ть *impf of* **зае́сть**

зае́зд calling in; lap, heat. **зае́здить** (-зжу) *pf* override; wear out. **зае-зжа́ть** *impf of* **зае́хать**. **зае́зжен-ный** hackneyed; worn out. **зае́зжий** visiting.

заём (за́йма) loan.

зае́сть (-е́м, -е́шь, -е́ст, -еди́м) *pf* (*impf* заеда́ть) torment; jam; entangle.

зае́хать (-е́ду) *pf* (*impf* заезжа́ть) call in; enter, ride in, drive in; reach; +за+*acc* go past; +за+*instr* call for, fetch.

за|жа́рить(ся *pf*.

зажа́ть (-жму́, -жмёшь) *pf* (*impf* зажима́ть) squeeze; grip; suppress.

заже́чь (-жгу́, -жжёшь; -жёг, -жгла́) *pf* (*impf* зажига́ть) set fire to; kindle; light; ~ся catch fire.

зажива́ть *impf of* зажи́ть. **за-живи́ть** (-влю́) *pf*, **заживля́ть** *impf* heal. **за́живо** *adv* alive.

зажига́лка lighter. **зажига́ние** ignition. **зажига́тельный** inflammatory; incendiary. **зажига́ть(ся** *impf of* заже́чь(ся

зажи́м clamp; terminal; suppression. **зажима́ть** *impf of* зажа́ть. **за-жи́мный** tight-fisted.

зажи́точный prosperous. **зажи́ть** (-иву́, -ивёшь; -ил, -á, -о) *pf* (*impf* зажива́ть) heal; begin to live.

зажму́ *etc.: see* зажа́ть. **за|жму́-риться** *pf*.

зазвене́ть (-и́т) *pf* begin to ring.

зазелене́ть (-е́ет) *pf* turn green.

заземле́ние earthing; earth. **за-земли́ть** *pf*, **заземля́ть** *impf* earth.

зазнава́ться (-наю́сь, -наёшься) *impf*, **зазна́ться** *pf* give o.s. airs.

зазу́брина notch.

за|зубри́ть (-рю́, -у́бри́шь) *pf*.

заи́грывать *impf* flirt.

заи́ка *m & f* stammerer. **заика́ние** stammer. **заика́ться** *impf*, **заик-ну́ться** (-ну́сь, -нёшься) *pf* stammer, stutter; +о+*prep* mention.

займствование borrowing. **займ-ствовать** *impf & pf* (*pf also* по~) borrow.

заинтересо́ванный interested. заинтересова́ть *pf*, заинтересо́вывать *impf* interest; ~ся +*instr* become interested in.

заи́скивать *impf* ingratiate o.s.

зайду́ *etc.*: *see* зайти́. займу́ *etc.*: *see* заня́ть

зайти́ (-йду́, -йдёшь; зашёл, -шла́) *pf* (*impf* заходи́ть) call; drop in; set; +в+*acc* reach; +за+*acc* go behind, turn; +за+*instr* call for, fetch.

за́йчик little hare (*esp. as endearment*); reflection of sunlight. за́йчиха doe hare.

закабали́ть *pf*, закабаля́ть *impf* enslave.

закады́чный intimate, bosom.

зака́з order; на ~ to order. заказа́ть (-ажу́, -а́жешь) *pf*, зака́зывать *impf* order; book. заказн|о́й made to order; ~о́е (письмо́) registered letter. зака́зчик customer, client.

зака́л temper; cast. зака́ливать *impf*, закали́ть (-лю́) *pf* (*impf also* закаля́ть) temper; harden. зака́лка tempering, hardening.

зака́лывать *impf of* заколо́ть. закаля́ть *impf of* закали́ть. зака́нчивать(ся *impf of* зако́нчить(ся

зака́пать *pf*, зака́пывать[1] *impf* begin to drip; rain; spot.

зака́пывать[2] *impf of* закопа́ть

зака́т sunset. закати́ть *pf*, зака́тывать[1] *impf* begin to roll; roll up; roll out. закати́ть (-ачу́, -а́тишь) *pf*, зака́тывать[2] *impf* roll; ~ся roll; set.

заква́ска ferment; leaven.

закида́ть *pf*, заки́дывать[1] *impf* shower; bespatter.

заки́дывать[2] *impf*, заки́нуть (-ну) *pf* throw (out, away).

закипа́ть *impf*, закипе́ть (-пи́т) *pf* begin to boil.

закиса́ть *impf*, заки́снуть (-ну; -ис, -ла) *pf* turn sour; become apathetic. за́кись oxide.

закла́д pawn; pledge; bet; би́ться об ~ bet; в ~е in pawn. закла́дка laying; bookmark. закладно́й pawn.

закла́дывать *impf of* заложи́ть

закле́ивать *impf*, закле́ить *pf* glue up.

за|клейми́ть (-млю́) *pf*.

заклепа́ть *pf*, заклёпывать. *impf*

rivet. заклёпка rivet; riveting.

заклина́ние incantation; spell. заклина́ть *impf* invoke; entreat.

заключа́ть *impf*, заключи́ть (-чу́) *pf* conclude; enter into; contain; confine. заключа́ться consist; lie, be. заключе́ние conclusion; decision; confinement. заключённый *sb* prisoner. заключи́тельный final, concluding.

закля́тие pledge. закля́тый sworn.

закова́ть (-кую́, -куёшь) *pf*, зако́вывать *impf* chain; shackle.

зако́лачивать *impf of* заколоти́ть

заколдо́ванный bewitched; ~ круг vicious circle. заколдова́ть *pf* bewitch; lay a spell on.

зако́лка hair-grip; hair-slide.

заколоти́ть (-лочу́, -ло́тишь) *pf* (*impf* зако́лачивать) board up; knock in; knock insensible.

заколо́ть (-олю́, -о́лешь) *pf* (*impf also* зака́лывать) stab; pin up; (*impers*) у меня́ заколо́ло в боку́ I have a stitch.

зако́н law. законнорождённый legitimate. зако́нность legality. зако́нный legal; legitimate.

законо- *in comb* law, legal. законове́дение law, jurisprudence. ~да́тельный legislative. ~да́тельство legislation. ~ме́рность regularity, normality. ~ме́рный regular, natural. ~прое́кт bill.

за|консерви́ровать . *pf*. за|конспекти́ровать *pf*.

зако́нченность completeness. зако́нченный finished; accomplished. зако́нчить (-чу) *pf* (*impf* зака́нчивать) end, finish; ~ся end, finish.

закопа́ть *pf* (*impf* зака́пывать[2]) begin to dig; bury.

закопте́лый sooty, smutty. за|копте́ть (-ти́т) *pf*. за|копти́ть (-пчу́) *pf*.

закоренелый deep-rooted; inveterate.

закосне́лый incorrigible.

закоу́лок (-лка) alley; nook.

закочене́лый numb with cold. за|коченеть (-е́ю) *pf*.

закра́дываться *impf of* закра́сться

закра́сить (-а́шу) *pf* (*impf* закра́шивать) paint over.

закра́сться (-аду́сь, -адёшься) *pf* (*impf* закра́дываться) steal in, creep in.

закра́шивать *impf of* **закра́сить**

закрепи́тель *m* fixative. **закрепи́ть** (-плю́) *pf,* **закрепля́ть** *impf* fasten; fix; consolidate; **+за** *+instr* assign to; ~ **за собо́й** secure.

закрепости́ть (-ощу́) *pf,* **закрепо-ща́ть** *impf* enslave. **закрепоще́ние** enslavement; slavery, serfdom.

закрича́ть (-чу́) *pf* cry out; begin to shout.

закро́йщик cutter.

закро́ю *etc.: see* **закры́ть**

закругле́ние rounding; curve. **за-кругли́ть** (-лю́) *pf,* **закругля́ть** *impf* make round; round off; ~ся be-come round; round off.

закружи́ться (-ужу́сь, -у́жи́шься) *pf* begin to whirl *or* go round.

за|крути́ть (-учу́, -у́тишь) *pf,* **за-кру́чивать** *impf* twist, twirl; wind round; turn; screw in; turn the head of; ~ся twist, twirl, whirl; wind round.

закрыва́ть *impf,* **закры́ть** (-ро́ю) *pf* close, shut; turn off; close down; cover; ~ся close, shut; end; close down; cover o.s.; shelter. **закры́тие** closing; shutting; closing down; shel-ter. **закры́тый** closed, shut; private.

закули́сный behind the scenes; backstage.

закупа́ть *impf,* **закупи́ть** (-плю́, -пишь) *pf* buy up; stock up with. **заку́пка** purchase.

заку́поривать *impf,* **заку́порить** *pf* cork; stop up; coop up. **заку́порка** corking; thrombosis.

заку́почный purchase. **заку́пщик** buyer.

заку́ривать *impf,* **закури́ть** (-рю́, -ришь) *pf* light up; begin to smoke.

закуси́ть (-ушу́, -у́сишь) *pf,* **за-ку́сывать** *impf* have a snack; bite. **заку́ска** hors-d'oeuvre; snack. **за-ку́сочная** *sb* snack-bar.

за|ку́тать *pf,* **заку́тывать** *impf* wrap up; ~ся wrap o.s. up.

зал hall; ~ **ожида́ния** waiting-room.

залега́ть *impf of* **зале́чь**

за|ледене́ть (-е́ю) *pf.*

залежа́лый stale, long unused. **за-лежа́ться** (-жу́сь) *pf,* **зале́жи-ваться** *impf* lie too long; find no market; become stale. **за́лежь** de-

posit, seam; stale goods.

залеза́ть *impf,* **зале́зть** (-зу; -ез) *pf* climb, climb up; get in; creep in.

за|лепи́ть (-плю́, -пишь) *pf,* **за-лепля́ть** *impf* paste over; glue up.

залета́ть *impf,* **залете́ть** (-ечу́) *pf* fly; **+в** *+acc* fly into.

зале́чивать *impf,* **залечи́ть** (-чу́, -чишь) *pf* heal, cure; ~ся heal (up).

зале́чь (-ля́гу, -ля́жешь; залёг, -ла́) *pf* (*impf* **залега́ть**) lie down; lie low; lie, be deposited.

зали́в bay; gulf. **залива́ть** *impf,* **зали́ть** (-лью́, -льёшь; за́ли́л, -а́, -о) *pf* flood, inundate; spill on; extin-guish; spread; ~ся be flooded; pour, spill; **+instr** break into.

зало́г deposit; pledge; security, mort-gage; token; voice. **заложи́ть** (-жу́, -жишь) *pf* (*impf* **закла́дывать**) lay; put; mislay; pile up; pawn, mortgage; harness; lay in. **зало́жник** hostage.

залп volley, salvo; ~**ом** without paus-ing for breath.

залью́ *etc.: see* **зали́ть**. **заля́гу** *etc.: see* **зале́чь**

зам *abbr* (*of* **замести́тель**) assistant, deputy. **зам-** *abbr in comb* (*of* **за-мести́тель**) assistant, deputy, vice-.

за|ма́зать (-а́жу) *pf,* **зама́зывать** *impf* paint over; putty; smear; soil; ~ся get dirty. **зама́зка** putty; puttying.

зама́лчивать *impf of* **замолча́ть**

зама́нивать *impf,* **замани́ть** (-ню́, -нишь) *pf* entice; decoy. **зама́н-чивый** tempting.

за|маринова́ть *pf.*

за|маскирова́ть *pf,* **замаскиро́-вывать** *impf* mask; disguise; ~ся disguise o.s.

зама́х threatening gesture. **зама́-хиваться** *impf,* **замахну́ться** (-ну́сь, -нёшься) *pf* **+instr** raise threaten-ingly.

зама́чивать *impf of* **замочи́ть**

замедле́ние slowing down, decelera-tion; delay. **заме́длить** *pf,* **за-медля́ть** *impf* slow down; slacken; delay; ~ся slow down.

замёл *etc.: see* **замести́**

заме́на substitution; substitute. **за-мени́мый** replaceable. **замени́тель** *m* (*+gen*) substitute (for). **замени́ть** (-ню́, -нишь) *pf,* **заменя́ть** *impf* replace; be a substitute for.

замере́ть (-мру́, -мрёшь; за́мер, -ла́, -о) *pf* (*impf* **замира́ть**) stand still; freeze; die away.

замерза́ние freezing. **замерза́ть** *impf*, **за|мёрзнуть** (-ну) *pf* freeze (up); freeze to death.

заме́рить *pf* (*impf* **замеря́ть**) measure, gauge.

замеси́ть (-ешу́, -е́сишь) *pf* (*impf* **заме́шивать**[2]) knead.

замести́ (-ету́, -етёшь; -мёл, -а́) *pf* (*impf* **замета́ть**) sweep up; cover.

замести́тель *m* substitute; assistant, deputy, vice-. **замести́ть** (-ещу́) *pf* (*impf* **замеща́ть**) replace; deputize for.

замета́ть *impf of* **замести́**

заме́тить (-е́чу) *pf* (*impf* **замеча́ть**) notice; note; remark. **заме́тка** mark; note. **заме́тный** noticeable; outstanding.

замеча́ние remark; reprimand. **замеча́тельный** remarkable; splendid. **замеча́ть** *impf of* **заме́тить**

замеша́тельство confusion; embarrassment. **замеша́ть** *pf*, **заме́шивать**[1] *impf* mix up, entangle. **заме́шивать**[2] *impf of* **замеси́ть**

замеща́ть *impf of* **замести́ть**. **замеще́ние** substitution; filling.

зами́нка hitch; hesitation.

замира́ть *impf of* **замере́ть**

за́мкнутый reserved; closed, exclusive. **замкну́ть** (-ну́, -нёшь) *pf* (*impf* **замыка́ть**) lock; close; ~**ся** close; shut o.s. up; become reserved.

за́мок[1] (-мка) castle.

замо́к[2] (-мка́) lock; padlock; clasp.

замолка́ть *impf*, **замо́лкнуть** (-ну; -мо́лк) *pf* fall silent; stop.

замолча́ть (-чу́) *pf* (*impf* **зама́лчивать**) fall silent; cease corresponding; hush up.

замора́живать *impf*, **заморо́зить** (-ро́жу) *pf* freeze. **заморо́женный** frozen; iced. **за́морозки** (-ов) *pl* (slight) frosts.

замо́рский overseas.

за|мочи́ть (-чу́, -чишь) *pf* (*impf also* **зама́чивать**) wet; soak; ret.

замо́чная сква́жина keyhole.

замру́ *etc.*: *see* **замере́ть**

за́муж *adv*: **вы́йти** ~ (**за**+*acc*) marry. **за́мужем** *adv* married (**за**+*instr* to).

за|му́чить (-чу) *pf* torment; wear out; bore to tears. **за|му́читься** (-чусь) *pf*.

за́мша suede.

замыка́ние locking; short circuit. **замыка́ть(ся** *impf of* **замкну́ть(ся**

за́мысел (-сла) project, plan. **замы́слить** *pf*, **замышля́ть** *impf* plan; contemplate.

за́навес, занаве́ска curtain.

занести́ (-су́, -сёшь; -ёс, -ла́) *pf* (*impf* **заноси́ть**) bring; note down; (*impers*) cover with snow etc.; (*impers*) skid.

занима́ть *impf* (*pf* **заня́ть**) occupy; interest; engage; borrow; ~**ся** +*instr* be occupied with; work at; study.

зано́за splinter. **заноза́ть** (-ожу́) *pf* get a splinter in.

зано́с snow-drift; skid. **заноси́ть** (-ошу́, -о́сишь) *impf of* **занести́**. **зано́счивый** arrogant.

заня́тие occupation; *pl* studies. **занято́й** busy. **за́нятый** (-нят, -а́, -о) occupied; taken; engaged. **заня́ть(ся** (займу́(сь, -мёшь(ся; за́нял(ся, -а́(сь, -о(сь) *pf of* **занима́ть(ся**

заодно́ *adv* in concert; at one; at the same time.

заостри́ть *pf*, **заостря́ть** *impf* sharpen; emphasize.

зао́чник, -ница student taking correspondence course; external student. **зао́чно** *adv* in one's absence; by correspondence course. **зао́чный курс** correspondence course.

за́пад west. **за́падный** west, western; westerly.

западня́ (*gen pl* -не́й) trap; pitfall, snare.

за|пакова́ть *pf*, **запако́вывать** *impf* pack; wrap up.

запа́л ignition; fuse. **запа́ливать** *impf*, **запали́ть** *pf* light, kindle; set fire to. **запа́льная свеча́** (spark-)plug.

запа́с reserve; supply; hem. **запаса́ть** *impf*, **запасти́** (-су́, -сёшь; -а́с, -ла́) *pf* stock, store; lay in a stock of; ~**ся** +*instr* provide o.s. with; stock up with. **запасно́й** *sb* reservist. **запа́сный, запа́сный** spare; reserve; ~ **вы́ход** emergency exit.

за́пах smell.

запа́хивать *impf*, **запахну́ть**[2] (-ну́, -нёшь) *pf* wrap up.

запа́хнуть[1] (-ну; -а́х) *pf* begin to smell.

за|па́чкать *pf.*

запека́ть(ся *impf of* запе́чь(ся.
запеку́ *etc.*: *see* запе́чь

за|пелена́ть *pf.*

запере́ть (-пру́, -прёшь; за́пер, -ла́,
-ло) *pf* (*impf* запира́ть) lock; lock
in; bar; ~ся lock o.s. in.

запеча́тать *pf*, запеча́тывать *impf*
seal. запечатлева́ть *impf*, запе-
чатле́ть (-е́ю) *pf* imprint, engrave.

запе́чь (-еку́, -ечёшь; -пёк, -ла́) *pf*
(*impf* запека́ть) bake; ~ся bake;
become parched; clot, coagulate.

запива́ть *impf of* запи́ть

запина́ться *impf of* запну́ться.
запи́нка hesitation.

запира́ть(ся *impf of* запере́ть(ся

записа́ть (-ишу́, -и́шешь) *pf*,
запи́сывать *impf* note; take down;
record; enter; ~ся register, enrol
(в+*acc* at, in). запи́ска note. за-
писно́й note; inveterate; ~ая
кни́жка notebook. за́пись recording; registration; record.

запи́ть (-пью́, -пьёшь; за́пил, -а́, -о)
pf (*impf* запива́ть) begin drinking;
wash down (with).

запиха́ть *pf*, запи́хивать *impf*,
запихну́ть (-ну́, -нёшь) *pf* push in,
cram in.

запишу́ *etc.*: *see* записа́ть

запла́кать (-а́чу) *pf* begin to cry.

за|плани́ровать *pf.*

запла́та patch.

за|плати́ть (-ачу́, -а́тишь) *pf* pay
(за+*acc* for).

заплачу́ *etc.*: *see* запла́кать. за-
плачу́ *see* заплати́ть

заплести́ (-ету́, -етёшь; -ёл, -а́) *pf*,
заплета́ть *impf* plait.

за|пломбирова́ть *pf.*

заплы́в heat, round. заплыва́ть
impf, заплы́ть (-ыву́, -ывёшь; -ы́л,
-а́, -о) *pf* swim in, sail in; swim out,
sail out; be bloated.

запну́ться (-ну́сь, -нёшься) *pf* (*impf*
запина́ться) hesitate; stumble.

запове́дник reserve; preserve; госу-
да́рственный ~ national park.
запове́дный prohibited. за́поведь
precept; commandment.

заподо́зривать *impf*, заподо́зрить
pf suspect (в+*prep* of).

запозда́лый belated; delayed.
запозда́ть *pf* (*impf* запа́здывать)

be late.

запо́й hard drinking.

заполза́ть *impf*, заползти́ *pf* (-зу́,
-зёшь; -о́лз, -зла́) creep, crawl.

запо́лнить *pf*, заполня́ть *impf* fill
(in, up).

запомина́ть *impf*, запо́мнить *pf* remember; memorize; ~ся stay in
one's mind.

за́понка cuff-link; stud.

запо́р bolt; lock; constipation.

за|поте́ть (-е́ет) *pf* mist over.

запою́ *etc.*: *see* запе́ть

запра́вить (-влю) *pf*, заправля́ть
impf tuck in; prepare; refuel; season;
dress; mix in; ~ся refuel. запра́вка
refuelling; seasoning, dressing.

запра́шивать *impf of* запроси́ть

запре́т prohibition, ban. запрети́ть
(-ещу́) *pf*, запреща́ть *impf* prohibit,
ban. запре́тный forbidden. запре-
ще́ние prohibition.

за|программи́ровать *pf.*

запро́с inquiry; overcharging; *pl*
needs. запроси́ть (-ошу́, -о́сишь) *pf*
(*impf* запра́шивать) inquire.

за́просто *adv* without ceremony.

запрошу́ *etc.*: *see* запроси́ть. запру́
etc.: *see* запере́ть

запру́да dam, weir; mill-pond.

запряга́ть *impf*, запря́чь (-ягу́,
-яжёшь; -яг, -ла́) *pf* harness; yoke.

запуга́ть *pf*, запу́гивать *impf* cow,
intimidate.

за́пуск launching. запуска́ть *impf*,
запусти́ть (-ущу́, -у́стишь) *pf* thrust
(in); start; launch; (+*acc or instr*)
fling; neglect. запусте́лый neglected; desolate. запусте́ние neglect; desolation.

за|пу́тать *pf*, запу́тывать *impf* tan-
gle; confuse; ~ся get tangled; get involved.

запущу́ *etc.*: *see* запусти́ть

запча́сть (*gen pl* -е́й) *abbr* (*of*
запасна́я часть) spare part.

запыха́ться *pf* be out of breath.

запью́ *etc.*: *see* запи́ть

запя́стье wrist.

запята́я *sb* comma.

за|пятна́ть *pf.*

зараба́тывать *impf*, зарабо́тать *pf*
earn; start (up). за́работн|ый: ~ая
пла́та wages; pay. за́работок (-тка)
earnings.

заража́ть *impf*, **зарази́ть** (-ажу́) *pf* infect; ~**ся** +*instr* be infected with, catch. **зара́за** infection. **зарази́тельный** infectious. **зара́зный** infectious.

зара́нее *adv* in good time; in advance.

зараста́ть *impf*, **зарасти́** (-ту́, -тёшь; -ро́с, -ла́) *pf* be overgrown; heal.

за́рево glow.

за|регистри́ровать(ся *pf*.

за|ре́зать (-е́жу) *pf* kill, knife; slaughter.

зарека́ться *impf of* **заре́чься**

зарекомендова́ть *pf*: ~ себя́ +*instr* show o.s. to be.

заре́чься (-еку́сь, -ечёшься; -ёкся, -екла́сь) *pf* (*impf* **зарека́ться**) +*inf* renounce.

за|ржа́веть (-еет) *pf*.

зарисо́вка sketching; sketch.

зароди́ть (-ожу́) *pf*, **зарожда́ть** *impf* generate; ~**ся** be born; arise. **заро́дыш** foetus; embryo. **зарожде́ние** conception; origin.

заро́к vow, pledge.

заро́с *etc.*: *see* **зарасти́**

зарою *etc.*: *see* **зары́ть**

зарпла́та *abbr* (*of* за́работная пла́та) wages; pay.

зоруба́ть *impf of* **заруби́ть**

зарубе́жный foreign.

заруби́ть (-блю́, -бишь) *pf* (*impf* **заруба́ть**) kill, cut down; notch. **зару́бка** notch.

заруча́ться *impf*, **заручи́ться** (-учу́сь) *pf* +*instr* secure.

зарыва́ть *impf*, **зары́ть** (-ро́ю) *pf* bury.

заря́ (*pl* зо́ри, зорь) dawn; sunset.

заря́д charge; supply. **заряди́ть** (-яжу́, -я́ди́шь) *pf*, **заряжа́ть** *impf* load; charge; stoke; ~**ся** be loaded; be charged. **заря́дка** loading; charging; exercises.

заса́да ambush. **засади́ть** (-ажу́, -а́дишь) *pf*, **заса́живать** *impf* plant; drive; set (за+*acc* to); ~ (в тюрьму́) put in prison. **заса́живаться** *impf of* **засе́сть**

заса́ливать *impf of* **засоли́ть**

засвети́ть (-ечу́, -е́тишь) *pf* light; ~**ся** light up.

за|свиде́тельствовать *pf*.

засе́в sowing; seed; sown area.

засева́ть *impf of* **засе́ять**

заседа́ние meeting; session. **заседа́ть** *impf* sit, be in session.

засе́ивать *impf of* **засе́ять. засе́к** *etc.*: *see* **засе́чь. засека́ть** *impf of* **засе́чь**

засекре́тить (-е́чу) *pf*, **засекре́чивать** *impf* classify as secret; clear, give access to secret material.

засеку́ *etc.*: *see* **засе́чь. засе́л** *etc.*: *see* **засе́сть**

заселе́ние settlement. **засели́ть** *pf*, **заселя́ть** *impf* settle; colonize; populate.

засе́сть (-ся́ду; -се́л) *pf* (*impf* **заса́живаться**) sit down; sit tight; settle; lodge in.

засе́чь (-еку́, -ечёшь; -ёк, -ла́) *pf* (*impf* **засека́ть**) flog to death; notch.

засе́ять (-е́ю) *pf* (*impf* **засева́ть, засе́ивать**) sow.

заси́лье dominance, sway.

заслони́ть *pf*, **заслоня́ть** *impf* cover, screen; push into the background. **засло́нка** (*furnace, oven*) door.

заслу́га merit, desert; service. **заслу́женный** deserved, merited; Honoured; time-honoured. **заслу́живать** *impf*, **заслужи́ть** (-ужу́, -у́жишь) *pf* deserve; earn; +*gen* be worthy of.

засмея́ться (-ею́сь, -еёшься) begin to laugh.

заснима́ть *impf of* **засня́ть**

засну́ть (-ну́, -нёшь) *pf* (*impf* **засыпа́ть**) fall asleep.

засня́ть (-ниму́, -и́мешь; -я́л, -а́, -о) *pf* (*impf* **заснима́ть**) photograph.

засо́в bolt, bar.

засо́вывать *impf of* **засу́нуть**

засо́л salting, pickling. **засоли́ть** (-олю́, -о́ли́шь) *pf* (*impf* **заса́ливать**) salt, pickle.

засоре́ние littering; contamination; obstruction. **засори́ть** *pf*, **засоря́ть** *impf* litter; get dirt into; clog.

за|со́хнуть (-ну, -сох) *pf* (*impf also* **засыха́ть**) dry (up); wither.

заста́ва gate; outpost.

заставать (-таю́, -таёшь) *impf of* **заста́ть**

заста́вить (-влю) *pf*, **заставля́ть** *impf* make; compel.

заста́иваться *impf of* **застоя́ться**.

заста́ну *etc*.: *see* заста́ть

заста́ть (-а́ну) *pf* (*impf* заставля́ть) find; catch.

застёгивать *impf*, застегну́ть (-ну́, -нёшь) *pf* fasten, do up. застёжка fastening; clasp, buckle; ~-мо́лния zip.

застекли́ть *pf*, застекля́ть *impf* glaze.

засте́нок (-нка) torture chamber.

засте́нчивый shy.

застига́ть *impf*, засти́гнуть, засти́чь (-и́гну; -сти́г) *pf* catch; take unawares.

засти́чь *see* засти́гнуть

засто́й stagnation. засто́йный stagnant.

за|сто́пориться *pf*.

застоя́ться (-и́тся) *pf* (*impf* заста́иваться) stagnate; stand too long.

застра́ивать *impf of* застро́ить

застрахо́ванный insured. за|страхова́ть *pf*, застрахо́вывать *impf* insure.

застрева́ть *impf of* застря́ть

застрели́ть (-елю́, -е́лишь) *pf* shoot (dead); ~ся shoot o.s.

застро́ить (-о́ю) *pf* (*impf* застра́ивать) build over, on, up. застро́йка building.

застря́ть (-я́ну) *pf* (*impf* застрева́ть) stick; get stuck.

за́ступ spade.

заступа́ться *impf*, заступи́ться (-плю́сь, -пишься) *pf* +за+*acc* stand up for. засту́пник defender. засту́пничество protection; intercession.

застыва́ть *impf*, засты́ть (-ы́ну) *pf* harden, set; become stiff; freeze; be petrified.

засу́нуть (-ну) *pf* (*impf* засо́вывать) thrust in, push in.

за́суха drought.

засы́пать¹ (-плю) *pf*, засыпа́ть *impf* fill up; strew.

засыпа́ть² *impf of* засну́ть

засыха́ть *impf of* засо́хнуть.

зася́ду *etc*.: *see* засе́сть

затаённый (-ён, -ена́) secret; repressed. зата́ивать *impf*, затаи́ть *pf* suppress; conceal; harbour; ~ дыха́ние hold one's breath.

зата́пливать *impf of* затопи́ть.

зата́птывать *impf of* затопта́ть

зата́скивать *impf*, затащи́ть (-щу́, -щишь) *pf* drag in; drag off; drag away.

затвердева́ть *impf*, за|тверде́ть (-е́ет) *pf* become hard; set. затверде́ние hardening; callus.

затво́р bolt; lock; shutter; flood-gate. затвори́ть (-рю́, -ришь) *pf*, затворя́ть *impf* shut, close; ~ся shut o.s. up, lock o.s. in. затво́рник hermit, recluse.

затева́ть *impf of* зате́ять

затёк *etc*.: *see* зате́чь. затека́ть *impf of* зате́чь

зате́м *adv* then, next; ~ что because.

затемне́ние darkening, obscuring; blacking out; black-out. затемни́ть *pf*, затемня́ть *impf* darken, obscure; black out.

зате́ривать *impf*, затеря́ть *pf* lose, mislay; ~ся be lost; be mislaid; be forgotten.

зате́чь (-ечёт, -еку́т; -тёк, -кла́) *pf* (*impf* затека́ть) pour, flow; swell up; become numb.

зате́я undertaking, venture; escapade; joke. зате́ять *pf* (*impf* затева́ть) undertake, venture.

затиха́ть *impf*, зати́хнуть (-ну; -ти́х) *pf* die down, abate; fade. зати́шье calm; lull.

заткну́ть (-ну́, -нёшь) *pf* (*impf* затыка́ть) stop up; stick, thrust.

затмева́ть *impf*, затми́ть (-ми́шь) *pf* darken; eclipse; overshadow. затме́ние eclipse.

зато́ *conj* but then, but on the other hand.

затону́ть (-о́нет) *pf* sink, be submerged.

затопи́ть¹ (-плю́, -пишь) *pf* (*impf* зата́пливать) light; turn on the heating.

затопи́ть² (-плю́, -пишь) *pf*, затопля́ть *impf* flood, submerge; sink.

затопта́ть (-пчу́, -пчешь) *pf* (*impf* зата́птывать) trample (down).

зато́р obstruction, jam; congestion.

за|тормози́ть *pf* (-ожу́) *pf*.

зато́чивать *impf*, заточи́ть (-чу́) *pf* incarcerate. заточе́ние incarceration.

затра́гивать *impf of* затро́нуть

затра́та expense; outlay. затра́тить (-а́чу) *pf*, затра́чивать *impf* spend.

затре́бовать *pf* request, require; ask for.

затро́нуть (-ну) *pf* (*impf* затра́гивать) affect; touch (on).

затрудне́ние difficulty. затрудни́тельный difficult. затрудни́ть *pf*, затрудня́ть *impf* trouble; make difficult; hamper; ~ся +*inf or instr* find difficulty in.

за|тупи́ться (-пится) *pf*.

за|туши́ть (-шу́, -шишь) *pf* extinguish; suppress.

за́тхлый musty, mouldy; stuffy.

затыка́ть *impf of* заткну́ть

заты́лок (-лка) back of the head; scrag-end.

затя́гивать *impf*, затяну́ть (-ну́, -нешь) *pf* tighten; cover; close, heal; spin out; ~ся be covered; close; be delayed; drag on; inhale. затя́жка inhaling; prolongation; delaying, putting off; lagging. затяжно́й long-drawn-out.

заурядный ordinary; mediocre.

зау́треня morning service.

зау́чивать *impf*, заучи́ть (-чу́, -чишь) *pf* learn by heart.

за|фарширова́ть *pf*. за|фикси́ровать *pf*. за|фрахтова́ть *pf*.

захва́т seizure, capture. захвати́ть (-ачу́, -а́тишь) *pf*, захва́тывать *impf* take; seize; thrill. захва́тнический aggressive. захва́тчик aggressor. захва́тывающий gripping.

захлебну́ться (-ну́сь, -нёшься) *pf*, захлёбываться *impf* choke (от+*gen* with).

захлестну́ть (-ну́, -нёшь) *pf*, захлёстывать *impf* flow over, swamp, overwhelm.

захлопнуть (-ну) *pf*, захло́пывать *impf* slam, bang; ~ся slam (to).

захо́д sunset; calling in. заходи́ть (-ожу́, -о́дишь) *impf of* зайти́

захолу́стный remote, provincial. захолу́стье backwoods.

за|хорони́ть (-ню́, -нишь) *pf*. за|хоте́ть(ся (-очу́(сь, -о́чешь(ся, -отим(ся) *pf*.

зацвести́ (-ете́т; -вёл, -а́) *pf*, зацвета́ть *impf* come into bloom.

зацепи́ть (-плю́, -пишь) *pf*, зацепля́ть *impf* hook; engage; sting; catch (за+*acc* on); ~ся за+*acc* catch on; catch hold of.

зачасту́ю *adv* often.

зача́тие conception. зача́ток (-тка) embryo; rudiment; germ. зача́точный rudimentary. зача́ть (-чну́, -чнёшь; -ча́л, -á, -o) *pf* (*impf* зачина́ть) conceive.

зачёл *etc.: see* заче́сть

заче́м *adv* why; what for. заче́м-то *adv* for some reason.

зачёркивать *impf*, зачеркну́ть (-ну́, -нёшь) *pf*, зачёрпывать *impf* scoop up; draw up.

за|черстве́ть (-е́ет) *pf*.

заче́сть (-чту́, -чтёшь; -чёл, -чла́) *pf* (*impf* зачи́тывать) take into account, reckon as credit. зачёт test; получи́ть, сдать ~ по+*dat* pass a test in; поста́вить ~ по+*dat* pass in. зачётная кни́жка (student's) record book.

зачина́ть *impf of* зача́ть. зачи́нщик instigator.

зачи́слить *pf*, зачисля́ть *impf* include; enter; enlist; ~ся join, enter.

зачи́тывать *impf of* заче́сть. зачту́ *etc.: see* заче́сть. зашёл *etc.: see* зайти́

зашива́ть *impf*, заши́ть (-шью, -шьёшь) *pf* sew up.

за|шифрова́ть *pf*, зашифро́вывать *impf* encipher, encode.

за|шнурова́ть *pf*, зашнуро́вывать *impf* lace up.

за|шпаклева́ть (-лю́ю) *pf*. за|што́пать *pf*. за|штрихова́ть *pf*. зашью́ *etc.: see* заши́ть

защи́та defence; protection. защити́ть (-ищу́) *pf*, защища́ть *impf* defend, protect. защи́тник defender. защи́тный protective.

заяви́ть (-влю́, -вишь) *pf*, заявля́ть *impf* announce, declare; ~ся turn up. зая́вка claim; demand. заявле́ние statement; application.

за́яц (за́йца) hare; stowaway; е́хать ~ем travel without a ticket.

зва́ние rank; title. зва́ный invited; ~ обе́д banquet, dinner. зва́тельный vocative. звать (зову́, -вёшь; звал, -á, -o) *impf* (*pf* по~) call; ask, invite; как вас зову́т? what is your name?; ~ся be called.

звезда́ (*pl* звёзды) star. звёздный star; starry; starlit; stellar. звёз-

дочка little star; asterisk.
звене́ть (-ню́) *impf* ring; +*instr* jingle, clink.
звено́ (*pl* **зве́нья, -ьев**) link; team, section; unit; component. **звеньево́й** *sb* section leader.
звери́нец (-нца) menagerie. **зверово́дство** fur farming. **зве́рский** brutal; terrific. **зве́рство** atrocity. **зве́рствовать** *impf* commit atrocities. **зверь** (*pl* -и, -е́й) *m* wild animal.
звон ringing (sound); peal, chink, clink. **звони́ть** *impf* (*pf* по~) ring; ring up; ~ кому́-нибудь (по телефо́ну) ring s.o. up. **зво́нкий** (-нок, -нка́, -о) ringing, clear. **звоно́к** (-нка́) bell; (*telephone*) call.
звук sound.
звуко- *in comb* sound. **звукоза́пись** (sound) recording. ~**непроница́емый** sound-proof. ~**снима́тель** *m* pick-up.
звуково́й sound; audio; acoustic. **звуча́ние** sound(ing); vibration. **звуча́ть** (-чи́т) *impf* (*pf* про~) be heard; sound. **зву́чный** (-чен, -чна́, -о) sonorous.
зда́ние building.
здесь *adv* here. **зде́шний** local; не ~ a stranger here.
здоро́ваться *impf* (*pf* по~) exchange greetings. **здо́рово** *adv* splendidly; very (much); well done!; great! **здоро́вый** healthy, strong; well; wholesome, sound. **здоро́вье** health; за ва́ше ~! your health! как ва́ше ~? how are you? **здра́вница** sanatorium.
здравомы́слящий sensible, judicious. **здравоохране́ние** public health.
здра́вствовать *impf* be healthy; prosper. **здра́вствуй(те)** how do you do?; hello! **да здра́вствует!** long live! **здра́вый** sensible; ~ смысл common sense.
зе́бра zebra.
зева́ть *impf*, **зевну́ть** (-ну́, -нёшь) *pf* yawn; gape; (*pf also* про~) miss, let slip, lose. **зево́к** (-вка́), **зево́та** yawn.
зелене́ть (-е́ет) *impf* (*pf* по~) turn green; show green. **зелёный** (зе́лен,

-á, -o) green; ~ лук spring onions. **зе́лень** green; greenery; greens.
земе́льный land.
земле- *in comb* land; earth. **землевладе́лец** (-льца) landowner. ~**де́лец** (-льца) farmer. ~**де́лие** farming, agriculture. ~**де́льческий** agricultural. ~**ко́п** navvy. ~**ро́йный** excavating. ~**трясе́ние** earthquake.
земля́ (*acc* -ю; *pl* -и, земе́ль, -ям) earth; land; soil. **земля́к** (-а́) fellow-countryman. **земляни́ка** (*no pl; usu collect*) wild strawberry; wild strawberries. **земля́нка** dug-out; mud hut. **земляно́й** earthen; earth; earthy. **земля́чка** country-woman. **земно́й** earthly; terrestrial; ground; mundane; ~ шар the globe.
зени́т zenith. **зени́тный** zenith; anti-aircraft.
зе́ркало (*pl* -á) mirror. **зерка́льный** mirror; smooth; plate-glass.
зерни́стый grainy. **зерно́** (*pl* зёрна, зёрен) grain; seed; kernel, core; ко́фе в зёрнах coffee beans. **зерново́й** grain. **зерновы́е** *sb pl* cereals. **зернохрани́лище** granary.
зигза́г zigzag.
зима́ (*acc* -у; *pl* -ы) winter. **зи́мний** winter, wintry. **зимова́ть** *impf* (*pf* пере~, про~) spend the winter; hibernate. **зимо́вка** wintering; hibernation. **зимо́вье** winter quarters. **зимо́й** *adv* in winter.
зия́ть *impf* gape, yawn.
злак grass; cereal.
злить (злю) *impf* (*pf* обо~, разо~) anger; irritate; ~ся be angry, be in a bad temper; rage. **зло** (*gen pl* зол) evil; harm; misfortune; malice.
зло- *in comb* evil, harm, malice. **злове́щий** ominous. ~**во́ние** stink. ~**во́нный** stinking. ~**ка́чественный** malignant; pernicious. ~**па́мятный** rancorous, unforgiving. ~**ра́дный** malevolent, gloating. ~**сло́вие** malicious gossip. ~**умы́шленник** malefactor; plotter. ~**язы́чный** slanderous.
зло́ба spite; anger; ~ дня topic of the day, latest news. **зло́бный** malicious. **злободне́вный** topical. **злоде́й** villain. **злоде́йский** villainous. **злоде́йство** villainy; crime, evil

deed. **злодея́ние** crime, evil deed.
злой (зол, зла) evil; wicked; malicious; vicious; bad-tempered; severe. **зло́стный** malicious; intentional. **зло́сть** malice; fury.

злоупотреби́ть (-блю́) *pf*, **злоупотребля́ть** *impf* +*instr* abuse. **злоупотребле́ние** +*instr* abuse of.

змеи́ный snake; cunning. **змей** snake; dragon; kite. **змея́** (*pl* -и) snake.

знак sign; mark; symbol.

знако́мить (-млю) *impf* (*pf* о~, по~) acquaint; introduce; ~**ся** become acquainted; get to know; +**с** +*instr* meet, make the acquaintance of. **знако́мство** acquaintance; (circle of) acquaintances. **знако́мый** familiar; **быть** ~**ым с** +*instr* be acquainted with, know; ~**ый**, ~**ая** *sb* acquaintance.

знамена́тель *m* denominator. **знамена́тельный** significant. **зна́мение** sign. **знамени́тость** celebrity. **знамени́тый** celebrated, famous. **зна́мя** (-мени; *pl* -мёна) *neut* banner; flag.

зна́ние knowledge.

зна́тный (-тен, -тна́, -о) distinguished; aristocratic; splendid. **знато́к** (-а́) expert; connoisseur. **знать** *impf* know; **дать** ~ inform, let know.

значе́ние meaning; significance; importance. **зна́чит** so then; that means. **значи́тельный** considerable; important; significant. **зна́чить** (-чу) *impf* mean; signify; be of importance; ~**ся** be; be mentioned, appear. **значо́к** (-чка́) badge; mark.

зна́ющий expert; learned.

зноби́ть *impf*, *impers* +*acc* **меня́**, *etc.*, **зноби́т** I feel shivery.

зной intense heat. **зно́йный** hot; burning.

зов call, summons. **зову́** *etc.*: *see* **звать**

зо́дчество architecture. **зо́дчий** *sb* architect.

зол *see* **зло**, **злой**

зола́ ashes, cinders.

золо́вка sister-in-law (*husband's sister*).

золоти́стый golden. **зо́лото** gold. **золото́й** gold; golden.

золочёный gilt, gilded.

зо́на zone; region.

зонд probe. **зонди́ровать** *impf* sound, probe.

зонт (-а́), **зо́нтик** umbrella.

зоо́лог zoologist. **зоологи́ческий** zoological. **зооло́гия** zoology. **зоопа́рк** zoo. **зооте́хник** livestock specialist.

зо́ри *etc.*: *see* **заря́**

зо́ркий (-рок, -рка́, -о) sharp-sighted; perspicacious.

зрачо́к (-чка́) pupil (*of the eye*).

зре́лище sight; spectacle.

зре́лость ripeness; maturity; **аттеста́т зре́лости** school-leaving certificate. **зре́лый** (зрел, -а́, -о) ripe, mature.

зре́ние (eye)sight, vision; **то́чка зре́ния** point of view.

зреть (-е́ю) *impf* (*pf* со~) ripen; mature.

зри́мый visible.

зри́тель *m* spectator, observer; *pl* audience. **зри́тельный** visual; optic; ~ **зал** hall, auditorium.

зря *adv* in vain.

зуб (*pl* -ы *or* -бья, -о́в *or* -бьев) tooth; cog. **зуби́ло** chisel. **зубно́й** dental; tooth; ~ **врач** dentist. **зубовраче́бный** dentists'; dental; ~ **кабине́т** dental surgery. **зубочи́стка** toothpick.

зубр (European) bison; die-hard.

зубри́ть (-рю́, зу́бри́шь) *impf* (*pf* вы́~, за~) cram.

зубча́тый toothed; serrated.

зуд itch. **зуде́ть** (-и́т) itch.

зы́бкий (-бок, -бка́, -о) unsteady, shaky; vacillating. **зыбь** (*gen pl* -е́й) ripple, rippling.

зюйд (*naut*) south; south wind.

зя́блик chaffinch.

зя́бнуть (-ну; зяб) *impf* suffer from cold, feel the cold.

зябь land ploughed in autumn for spring sowing.

зять (*pl* -тья́, -тьёв) son-in-law; brother-in-law (*sister's husband or husband's sister's husband*).

И, Й

и *conj* and; even; too; (*with neg*) either; **и**... **и** both ... and.

и́бо *conj* for.

и́ва willow.

игла́ (*pl* -ы) needle; thorn; spine; quill. иглоука́лывание acupuncture.

игнори́ровать *impf & pf* ignore.

и́го yoke.

иго́лка needle.

иго́рный gaming, gambling. игра́ (*pl* -ы) play, playing; game; hand; turn; ~ слов pun. игра́льн|ый playing; ~ые ко́сти dice. игра́ть *impf* (*pf* сыгра́ть) play; act; ~ в+*acc* play (*game*); ~ на+*prep* play (*an instrument*). игри́вый playful. игро́к (-а́) player; gambler. игру́шка toy.

идеа́л ideal. идеали́зм idealism. идеа́льный ideal.

иде́йный high-principled; acting on principle; ideological.

идеологи́ческий ideological. идеоло́гия ideology.

идёт *etc.: see* идти́

иде́я idea; concept.

иди́ллия idyll.

идио́т idiot.

и́дол idol.

идти́ (иду́, идёшь; шёл, шла) *impf* (*pf* пойти́) go; come; run, work; pass; go on, be in progress; be on; fall; +(к+)*dat* suit.

иере́й priest.

иждиве́нец (-нца), -ве́нка dependant. иждиве́ние maintenance; на иждиве́нии at the expense of.

из, изо *prep*+*gen* from, out of, of.

изба́ (*pl* -ы) izba (*hut*).

изба́вить (-влю) *pf*, избавля́ть *impf* save, deliver; ~ся be saved, escape; ~ся от get rid of; get out of.

избало́ванный spoilt.

избега́ть *impf*, избе́гнуть (-ну; -бе́г(нул)) *pf*, избежа́ть (-егу́) *pf* +*gen* or *inf* avoid; escape; evade.

изберу́ *etc.: see* избра́ть

избива́ть *impf of* изби́ть. избие́ние slaughter; massacre; beating, beating-up.

избира́тель *m*, ~ница elector, voter. избира́тельный electoral; election. избира́ть *impf of* избра́ть

изби́тый trite, hackneyed. изби́ть (изобью́, -бьёшь) *pf* (*impf* избива́ть) beat unmercifully, beat up; massacre. и́збранн|ый selected; select; ~ые *sb*

pl the élite. избра́ть (-беру́, -берёшь; -а́л, -а́, -о) *pf* (*impf* избира́ть) elect; choose.

избы́ток (-тка) surplus; abundance. избы́точный surplus; abundant.

и́зверг monster. изверже́ние eruption; expulsion; excretion.

изверну́ться (-ну́сь, -нёшься) *pf* (*impf* извора́чиваться) dodge, be evasive.

изве́стие news; information; *pl* proceedings. извести́ть (-ещу́) *pf* (*impf* извеща́ть) inform, notify.

изве́стка lime.

изве́стно it is (well) known; of course, certainly. изве́стность fame, reputation. изве́стный known; well-known, famous; notorious; certain.

известня́к (-á) limestone. и́звесть lime.

извеща́ть *impf of* извести́ть. извеще́ние notification; advice.

извива́ться *impf* coil; writhe; twist, wind; meander. изви́лина bend, twist. изви́листый winding; meandering.

извине́ние excuse; apology. извини́ть *pf*, извиня́ть *impf* excuse; извини́те (меня́) excuse me, (I'm) sorry; ~ся apologize; excuse o.s.

изви́ться (изовью́сь, -вьёшься; -и́лся, -а́сь, -ось) *pf* coil; writhe.

извлека́ть *impf*, извле́чь (-еку́, -ечёшь; -ёк, -ла́) *pf* extract; derive, elicit.

извне́ *adv* from outside.

изво́зчик cabman; carrier.

извора́чиваться *impf of* изверну́ться. изворо́т bend, twist; *pl* tricks, wiles. изворо́тливый resourceful; shrewd.

изврати́ть (-ащу́) *pf*, извраща́ть *impf* distort; pervert. извраще́ние perversion; distortion. извраще́нный perverted, unnatural.

изги́б bend, twist. изгиба́ть(ся *impf of* изогну́ть(ся

изгна́ние banishment; exile. изгна́нник exile. изгна́ть (-гоню́, -го́нишь; -а́н, -а́, -о) *pf* (*impf* изгоня́ть) banish; expel.

изголо́вье bed-head.

изголода́ться be famished, starve; +по+*dat* yearn for.

изгоню́ *etc.: see* изгна́ть. изгоня́ть

impf of изгна́ть

и́згородь fence, hedge.

изгота́вливать *impf*, изгото́вить (-влю) *pf*, изготовля́ть *impf* make, manufacture; ~ся get ready. изготовле́ние making, manufacture.

издава́ть (-даю́, -даёшь) *impf of* изда́ть

и́здавна *adv* from time immemorial; for a very long time.

издади́м *etc.: see* изда́ть

издалека́, и́здали *advs* from afar.

изда́ние publication; edition; promulgation. изда́тель *m* publisher. изда́тельство publishing house. изда́ть (-а́м, -а́шь, -а́ст, -ади́м; -а́л, -а́, -о) *pf* (*impf* издава́ть) publish; promulgate; produce; emit; ~ся be published.

издева́тельство mockery; taunt. издева́ться *impf* (+над+*instr*) mock (at).

изде́лие work; make; article; *pl* wares.

изде́ржки (-жек) *pl* expenses; costs; cost.

изды́хнуть *pf.*

изжа́рить(ся *pf.*

изжо́га heartburn.

из-за *prep*+*gen* from behind; because of.

излага́ть *impf of* изложи́ть

излече́ние treatment; recovery; cure. излечи́ть (-чу́, -чишь) cure; ~ся be cured; +от+*gen* rid o.s. of.

изли́шек (-шка) surplus; excess. изли́шество excess; over-indulgence. изли́шний (-шен, -шня) superfluous.

изложе́ние exposition; account. изложи́ть (-жу́, -жишь) *pf* (*impf* излага́ть) expound; set forth; word.

изло́м break; fracture; sharp bend. излома́ть *pf* break; smash; wear out; warp.

излуча́ть *impf* radiate, emit. излуче́ние radiation; emanation.

изма́зать (-а́жу) *pf* dirty, smear all over; use up; ~ся get dirty, smear o.s. all over.

изме́на betrayal; treason; infidelity.

измене́ние change, alteration; inflection. измени́ть[1] (-ню́, -нишь) *pf* (*impf* изменя́ть[1]) change, alter; ~ся change.

измени́ть[2] (-ню́, -нишь) *pf* (*impf* изменя́ть[2]) +*dat* betray; be unfaithful to. изме́нник, -ица traitor.

изменя́емый variable. изменя́ть[1,2](ся *impf of* измени́ть[1,2](ся

измере́ние measurement, measuring. изме́рить *pf*, измеря́ть *impf* measure, gauge.

измождённый (-ён, -á) worn out.

из|му́чить (-чу) *pf* torment; tire out, exhaust; ~ся be exhausted. изму́ченный worn out.

измышле́ние fabrication, invention.

измя́тый crumpled, creased; haggard, jaded. из|мя́ть(ся (изомну́(сь, -нёшь(ся *pf.*

изна́нка wrong side; seamy side.

из|наси́ловать *pf* rape, assault.

изна́шивание wear (and tear). изна́шивать(ся *impf of* износи́ть(ся

изне́женный pampered; delicate; effeminate.

изнемога́ть *impf*, изнемо́чь (-огу́, -о́жешь; -óг, -лá) *pf* be exhausted. изнеможе́ние exhaustion.

изно́с wear; wear and tear; deterioration. износи́ть (-ошу́, -о́сишь) *pf* (*impf* изна́шивать) wear out; ~ся wear out; be used up. изно́шенный worn out; threadbare.

изнуре́ние exhaustion. изнурённый (-ён, -енá) exhausted, worn out; jaded. изнури́тельный exhausting.

изнутри́ *adv* from inside, from within.

изо *see* из

изоби́лие abundance, plenty. изоби́ловать *impf* +*instr* abound in, be rich in. изоби́льный abundant.

изоблича́ть *impf*, изобличи́ть (-чу́) *pf* expose; show. изобличе́ние exposure; conviction.

изобража́ть *impf*, изобрази́ть (-ажу́) *pf* represent, depict, portray (+*instr* as); ~ из себя́+*acc* make o.s. out to be. изображе́ние image; representation; portrayal. изобрази́тель|ный graphic; decorative; ~ые иску́сства fine arts.

изобрести́ (-ету́, -етёшь; -ёл, -á) *pf*, изобрета́ть *impf* invent; devise. изобрета́тель *m* inventor. изобрета́тельный inventive. изобрете́ние invention.

изобью́ *etc.: see* изби́ть. изовью́сь *etc.: see* изви́ться

изо́гнутый bent, curved; winding.
изогну́ть(ся (-ну́(сь, -нёшь(ся) *pf*
(*impf* изгиба́ть(ся) bend, curve.
изоли́ровать *impf* & *pf* isolate; insulate. изоля́тор insulator; isolation
ward; solitary confinement cell. изоля́ция isolation; quarantine; insulation.
изомну́(сь *etc.*: *see* измя́ть
изо́рванный tattered, torn. изорва́ть (-ву́, -вёшь; -а́л, -а́, -о) *pf* tear,
tear to pieces; ~ся be in tatters.
изощрённый (-рён, -а́) refined; keen.
изощри́ться *pf*, изощря́ться *impf*
acquire refinement; excel.
из-под *prep*+*gen* from under.
Изра́иль *m* Israel. изра́ильский Израели.
из|расхо́довать(ся *pf*.
и́зредка adv now and then.
изре́зать (-е́жу) *pf* cut up.
изрече́ние dictum, saying.
изры́ть (-ро́ю) *pf* dig up, plough up.
изры́тый pitted.
изря́д adv fairly, pretty. изря́дный fair, handsome; fairly large.
изуве́чить (-чу) *pf* maim, mutilate.
изуми́тельный amazing. изуми́ть (-млю́) *pf*, изумля́ть *impf* amaze; ~ся
be amazed. изумле́ние amazement.
изумру́д emerald.
изуро́дованный maimed; disfigured.
из|уро́довать *pf*.
изуча́ть *impf*, изучи́ть (-чу́, -чишь)
pf learn, study. изуче́ние study.
изъе́здить (-зжу) *pf* travel all over;
wear out.
изъяви́ть (-влю́, -вишь) *pf*, изъявля́ть *impf* express.
изъя́н defect, flaw.
изъя́тие withdrawal; removal; exception. изъя́ть (изыму́, -мешь) *pf*
изыма́ть *impf* withdraw.
изыска́ние investigation, research;
prospecting; survey. изы́сканный
refined. изыска́ть (-ыщу́, -ыщешь)
pf, изы́скивать *impf* search out;
(try to) find.
изю́м raisins.
изя́щество elegance, grace. изя́щный elegant, graceful.
ика́ть *impf*, икну́ть (-ну́, -нёшь) *pf*
hiccup.
ико́на icon.
ико́та hiccup, hiccups.

икра́¹ (hard) roe; caviare.
икра́² (*pl* -ы) calf (*of leg*).
ил silt; sludge.
и́ли *conj* or; ~... ~ either ... or.
и́листый muddy, silty.
иллюзиони́ст illusionist. иллю́зия
illusion.
иллюмина́тор porthole. иллюмина́ция illumination.
иллюстра́ция illustration. иллюстри́ровать *impf* & *pf* illustrate.
им *see* он, они́, оно́
им. *abbr* (*of* и́мени) named after.
и́мени *etc.*: *see* и́мя
име́ние estate.
имени́ны (-и́н) *pl* name-day (party).
имени́тельный nominative. и́менно adv namely; exactly, precisely;
вот ~! exactly!
име́ть (-е́ю) *impf* have; ~ де́ло
c+*instr* have dealings with, have to
do with; ~ ме́сто take place; ~ся
be; be available.
и́ми *see* они́
имита́ция imitation. имити́ровать
impf imitate.
иммигра́нт, ~ка immigrant.
импера́тор emperor. импера́торский imperial. императри́ца empress. империали́зм imperialism.
империали́ст imperialist. империалисти́ческий imperialist(ic). импе́рия empire.
и́мпорт import. импорти́ровать
impf & *pf* import. и́мпортный
import(ed).
импровиза́ция improvisation. импровизи́ровать *impf* & *pf* improvise.
и́мпульс impulse.
иму́щество property.
и́мя (и́мени; *pl* имена́, -ён) *neut* name;
first name; noun; ~ прилага́тельное
adjective; ~ существи́тельное noun;
~ числи́тельное numeral.
и́наче adv differently, otherwise; так
и́ли ~ in any event; *conj* otherwise,
or else.
инвали́д disabled person; invalid.
инвали́дность disablement, disability.
инвента́рь (-я́) *m* stock; equipment;
inventory.
инде́ец (-е́йца) (American) Indian.
инде́йка (*gen pl* -е́ек) turkey(-hen).

инде́йский (American) Indian.
и́ндекс index; code.
индиа́нка Indian; American Indian.
инди́ец (-и́йца) Indian.
индивидуали́зм individualism. индивидуа́льность individuality. индивидуа́льный individual. индиви́дуум individual.
инди́йский Indian. И́ндия India.
инду́с, инду́ска Hindu. инду́сский Hindu.
индустриализа́ция industrialization. индустриализи́ровать impf & pf industrialize. индустриа́льный industrial. индустри́я industry.
индю́к, индю́шка turkey.
и́ней hoar-frost.
ине́ртность inertia; sluggishness. ине́рция inertia.
инжене́р engineer; ~-меха́ник mechanical engineer; ~-строи́тель m civil engineer.
инжи́р fig.
инициа́л initial.
инициати́ва initiative. инициа́тор initiator.
инквизи́ция inquisition.
инкруста́ция inlaid work, inlay.
инкуба́тор incubator.
ино- in comb other, different; hetero-. иногоро́дний of, from, another town. ~ро́дец (-дца) non-Russian. ~ро́дный foreign. ~сказа́тельный allegorical. ~стра́нец (-нца), ~стра́нка (gen pl -нок) foreigner. ~стра́нный foreign. ~язы́чный speaking, of, another language; foreign.
иногда́ adv sometimes.
ино́й different; other; some; ~ раз sometimes.
и́нок monk. и́нокиня nun.
инотде́л foreign department.
инсектици́д insecticide.
инспе́ктор inspector. инспе́кция inspection; inspectorate.
инста́нция instance.
инсти́нкт instinct. инстинкти́вный instinctive.
институ́т institute.
инстру́ктор instructor. инстру́кция instructions.
инструме́нт instrument; tool.
инсули́н insulin.
инсцениро́вка dramatization, adap-

tation; pretence.
интегра́ция integration.
интелле́кт intellect. интеллектуа́льный intellectual.
интеллиге́нт intellectual. интеллиге́нтный cultured, educated. интеллиге́нция intelligentsia.
интенси́вность intensity. интенси́вный intensive.
интерва́л interval.
интерве́нция intervention.
интервью́ neut indecl interview.
интере́с interest. интере́сный interesting. интересова́ть impf interest; ~ся be interested (+instr in).
интерна́т boarding-school.
интернациона́льный international.
интерни́ровать impf & pf intern.
интерпрета́ция interpretation. интерпрети́ровать impf & pf interpret.
интерье́р interior.
инти́мный intimate.
интона́ция intonation.
интри́га intrigue; plot. интригова́ть impf, (pf за~) intrigue.
интуи́ция intuition.
инфа́ркт infarct; coronary (thrombosis), heart attack.
инфекцио́нный infectious. инфе́кция infection.
инфля́ция inflation.
информа́ция information.
инфракра́сный infra-red.
ио́д etc.: see йод
ио́н ion.
ипохо́ндрик hypochondriac. ипохо́ндрия hypochondria.
ипподро́м racecourse.
Ира́к Iraq. ира́кец (-кца) Iraqi. ира́кский Iraqi.
Ира́н Iran. ира́нец (-нца), ира́нка Iranian. ира́нский Iranian.
ирла́ндец (-дца) Irishman. Ирла́ндия Ireland. ирла́ндка Irishwoman. ирла́ндский Irish.
ирони́ческий ironic. иро́ния irony.
иррига́ция irrigation.
иск suit, action.
искажа́ть impf, искази́ть (-ажу́) pf distort, pervert; misrepresent. искаже́ние distortion, perversion.
искале́ченный crippled, maimed. искале́чить (-чу) pf cripple, maim; break.

искáть (ищý, и́щешь) *impf* (+*acc or gen*) seek, look for.

исключáть *impf*, **исключи́ть** (-чý) *pf* exclude; eliminate; expel. **исключáя** *prep*+*gen* except. **исключéние** exception; exclusion; expulsion; elimination; **за исключéнием** +*gen* with the exception of. **исключи́тельно** *adv* exceptionally; exclusively. **исключи́тельный** exceptional; exclusive.

искóнный primordial.

ископáемое *sb* mineral; fossil. **ископáемый** fossilized, fossil.

искорени́ть *pf*, **искореня́ть** *impf* eradicate.

и́скоса *adv* askance; sidelong.

и́скра spark.

и́скренний sincere. **и́скренность** sincerity.

искривлéние bend; distortion, warping.

ис|купáть[1] **(ся** *pf*.

искупáть[2] *impf*, **искупи́ть** (-плю́, -пишь) *pf* atone for; make up for. **искуплéние** redemption, atonement.

искуси́ть (-ушý) *pf of* **искушáть**

иску́сный skilful; expert. **иску́сственный** artificial; feigned. **иску́сство** art; skill. **искусствовéд** art historian.

искушáть *impf* (*pf* **искуси́ть**) tempt; seduce. **искушéние** temptation, seduction.

испáнец (-нца) Spaniard. **Испáния** Spain. **испáнка** Spanish woman. **испáнский** Spanish.

испарéние evaporation; *pl* fumes. **испари́ться** *pf*, **испаря́ться** *impf* evaporate.

ис|пáчкать *pf*. **ис|пéчь** (-екý, -ечёшь) *pf*.

исповéдовать *impf* & *pf* confess; profess; **~ся** confess; make one's confession; +в +*prep* unburden o.s. of. **и́споведь** confession.

исподтишкá *adv* in an underhand way; on the quiet.

исполи́н giant. **исполи́нский** gigantic.

исполкóм *abbr* (*of* **исполни́тельный комитéт**) executive committee.

исполнéние fulfilment, execution. **исполни́тель** *m*, **~ница** executor; performer. **исполни́тельный** executive. **исполнить** *pf*, **исполня́ть** *impf* carry out, execute; fulfil; perform; **~ся** be fulfilled.

использование utilization. **испóльзовать** *impf* & *pf* make (good) use of, utilize.

ис|пóртить(ся (-рчу(сь)) *pf*. **испóрченный** depraved; spoiled; rotten.

исправи́тельный correctional; corrective. **испрáвить** (-влю) *pf*, **исправля́ть** *impf* rectify, correct; mend; reform; **~ся** improve, reform. **исправлéние** repairing; improvement; correction. **исправленный** improved, corrected; revised; reformed. **исправный** in good order; punctual; meticulous.

ис|прóбовать *pf*.

испýг fright. **ис|пугáть(ся** *pf*.

испускáть *impf*, **испусти́ть** (-ущý, -ýстишь) *pf* emit, let out.

испытáние test, trial; ordeal. **испытáть** *pf*, **испы́тывать** *impf* test; try; experience.

исслéдование investigation; research. **исслéдователь** *m* researcher; investigator. **исслéдовательский** research. **исслéдовать** *impf* & *pf* investigate, examine; research into.

истаскáться *pf*, **истáскиваться** *impf* wear out; be worn out.

истекáть *impf of* **истéчь**. **истéкший** past.

истéрика hysterics. **истери́ческий** hysterical. **истéри́я** hysteria.

истечéние outflow; expiry. **истéчь** (-ечёт; -тёк, -лá) *pf* (*impf* **истекáть**) elapse; expire.

и́стина truth. **и́стинный** true.

истлевáть *impf*, **истлéть** (-éю) *pf* rot, decay; be reduced to ashes.

истóк source.

истолковáть *pf*, **истолкóвывать** *impf* interpret; comment on.

ис|толóчь (-лкý, -лчёшь; -лóк, -лклá) *pf*.

истóма languor.

исторгáть *impf*, **истóргнуть** (-ну; -óрг) *pf* throw out.

истóрик historian. **истори́ческий** historical; historic. **истóрия** history; story; incident.

истóчник spring; source.

истощáть *impf*, **истощи́ть** (-щý) *pf*

exhaust; emaciate. **истоще́ние** emaciation; exhaustion.

ис|тра́тить (-а́чу) *pf.*

истреби́тель *m* destroyer; fighter. **истреби́ть** (-блю́) *pf*, **истребля́ть** *impf* destroy; exterminate.

ис|тупи́ться (-пится) *pf.*

истяза́ние torture. **истяза́ть** *impf* torture.

исхо́д outcome; end; Exodus. **исходи́ть** (-ожу́, -о́дишь) *impf* (+из *or* от+*gen*) issue (from), come (from); proceed (from); departure.

исхо́дный initial; departure.

исхуда́лый undernourished, emaciated.

исцеле́ние healing; recovery. **исцели́ть** *pf*, **исцеля́ть** *impf* heal, cure.

исчеза́ть *impf*, **исче́знуть** (-ну; -е́з) *pf* disappear, vanish. **исчезнове́ние** disappearance.

исче́рпать *pf*, **исче́рпывать** *impf* exhaust; conclude. **исче́рпывающий** exhaustive.

исчисле́ние calculation; calculus.

ита́к *conj* thus; so then.

Ита́лия Italy. **италья́нец** (-нца), **италья́нка** Italian. **италья́нский** Italian.

ИТАР-ТАСС *abbr* (*of* Информацио́нное телегра́фное аге́нтство Росси́и; *see* ТАСС) ITAR-Tass.

и т.д. *abbr* (*of* и так да́лее) etc., and so on.

ито́г sum; total; result. **итого́** *adv* in all, altogether.

и т.п. *abbr* (*of* и тому́ подо́бное) etc., and so on.

иуде́й, **иуде́йка** Jew. **иуде́йский** Judaic.

их their, theirs; *see* они́.

иша́к (-а́) donkey.

ище́йка bloodhound; police dog.

ищу́ *etc.: see* иска́ть

ию́ль *m* July. **ию́льский** July. **ию́нь** *m* June. **ию́ньский** June.

йо́га yoga.

йод iodine.

йо́та iota.

К

к, ко *prep*+*dat* to, towards; by; for;

on; on the occasion of; **к пе́рвому января́** by the first of January; **к тому́ вре́мени** by then; **к тому́ же** besides, moreover; **к чему́?** what for?

-ка *partl* modifying force of imper or expressing decision or intention; **да́йте-ка пройти́** let me pass, please; **скажи́-ка мне** do tell me.

каба́к (-а́) tavern.

кабала́ servitude.

кабан (-а́) wild boar.

кабаре́ *neut indecl* cabaret.

кабачо́к (-чка́) marrow.

ка́бель *m* cable. **ка́бельтов** cable, hawser.

каби́на cabin; booth; cockpit; cubicle; cab. **кабине́т** study; surgery; room; office; Cabinet.

каблу́к (-а́) heel.

кабота́ж coastal shipping. **кабота́жный** coastal.

кабы́ if.

кавале́р knight; partner, gentleman. **кавалери́йский** cavalry. **кавалери́ст** cavalryman. **кавале́рия** cavalry.

ка́верзный tricky.

Кавка́з the Caucasus. **кавка́зец** (-зца́), **кавка́зка** Caucasian. **кавка́зский** Caucasian.

кавы́чки (-чек) *pl* inverted commas, quotation marks.

каде́т cadet. **каде́тский ко́рпус** military school.

кадр frame, still; close-up; cadre; *pl* establishment; staff; personnel; specialists. **ка́дровый** (*mil*) regular; skilled, trained.

кады́к (-а́) Adam's apple.

каждодне́вный daily, everyday. **ка́ждый** each, every; *sb* everybody.

ка́жется *etc.: see* каза́ться

каза́к (-а́; *pl* -а́ки, -ако́в), **каза́чка** Cossack.

каза́рма barracks.

каза́ться (кажу́сь, ка́жешься) *impf* (*pf* по~) seem, appear; *impers* **ка́жется**, **каза́лось** apparently; **каза́лось бы** it would seem; +*dat* **мне ка́жется** it seems to me; I think.

Казахста́н Kazakhstan. **каза́чий** Cossack.

каземат casemate.

казённый State; government; fiscal;

public; formal; banal, conventional. **казна́** Exchequer, Treasury; public purse; the State. **казначе́й** treasurer, bursar; paymaster.

казино́ *neut indecl* casino.

казни́ть *impf & pf* execute; punish; castigate. **казнь** execution.

кайма́ (*gen pl* каём) border, edging.

как *adv* how; what; вот ~! you don't say!; ~ вы ду́маете? what do you think?; ~ его́ зову́т? what is his name?; ~ же naturally, of course; ~ же так? how is that?; ~ ни however. **как** *conj* as; like; when; since; +*neg* but, except, than; в то вре́мя ~ while, whereas; ~ мо́жно, ~ нельзя́+*comp* as ... as possible; ~ мо́жно скоре́е as soon as possible; ~ нельзя́ лу́чше as well as possible; ~ то́лько as soon as, when; ме́жду тем, ~ while, whereas. **как бу́дто** *conj* as if; *partl* apparently. **как бы** how; as if; как бы... не what if, supposing; как бы... ни however. **ка́к-либо** *adv* somehow. **ка́к-нибудь** *adv* somehow; anyhow. **как раз** *adv* just, exactly. **как-то** *adv* somehow; once.

кака́о *neut indecl* cocoa.

како́в (-á, -ó, -ы́) *pron* what, what sort (of); ~ он? what is he like?; ~ он собо́й? what does he look like?; пого́да-то какова́! what weather! **каково́** *adv* how. **како́й** *pron* what; (such) as; which; ~... ни whatever, whichever. **како́й-либо, како́й-нибудь** *prons* some; any; only. **како́й-то** *pron* some; a; a kind of.

как раз, ка́к-то *see* как

ка́ктус cactus.

кал faeces, excrement.

каламбу́р pun.

кале́ка *m & f* cripple.

календа́рь (-я́) *m* calendar.

кале́ние incandescence.

кале́чить (-чу) *impf* (*pf* ис~, по~) cripple, maim; ~ся become a cripple.

кали́бр calibre; bore; gauge.

ка́лий potassium.

кали́тка (wicket-)gate.

каллигра́фия calligraphy.

кало́рия calorie.

кало́ша galosh.

ка́лька tracing-paper; tracing.

калькуля́ция calculation.

кальсо́ны (-н) *pl* long johns.

ка́льций calcium.

ка́мбала flat-fish; plaice; flounder.

камени́стый stony, rocky. **каменноуго́льный** coal; ~ бассе́йн coalfield. **ка́менный** stone; rock; stony; hard, immovable; ~ век Stone Age; ~ у́голь coal. **каменоло́мня** (*gen pl* -мен) quarry. **ка́менщик** (stone) mason; bricklayer. **ка́мень** (-мня; *pl* -мни, -мне́й) *m* stone.

ка́мера chamber; cell; camera; inner tube, (football) bladder; ~ хране́ния cloak-room, left-luggage office. **ка́мерный** chamber. **камерто́н** tuning-fork.

ками́н fireplace; fire.

камко́рдер camcorder.

камо́рка closet, very small room.

кампа́ния campaign; cruise.

камы́ш (-á) reed, rush; cane.

кана́ва ditch; gutter.

Кана́да Canada. **кана́дец** (-дца), **кана́дка** Canadian. **кана́дский** Canadian.

кана́л canal; channel. **канализа́ция** sewerage (system).

канаре́йка canary.

кана́т rope; cable.

канва́ canvas; groundwork; outline, design.

кандалы́ (-о́в) *pl* shackles.

кандида́т candidate; ~ нау́к person with higher degree. **кандидату́ра** candidature.

кани́кулы (-ул) *pl* vacation; holidays.

кани́стра can, canister.

канони́ческий canon(ical).

кано́э *neut indecl* canoe.

кант edging; mount. **кантова́ть** *impf;* «не ~» 'this way up'.

кану́н eve.

ка́нуть (-ну) *pf* drop, sink; как в во́ду ~ vanish into thin air.

канцеля́рия office. **канцеля́рский** office; clerical. **канцеля́рщина** red-tape.

ка́нцлер chancellor.

ка́пать (-аю *or* -плю) *impf* (*pf* ка́пнуть, на~) drip, drop; trickle; +*instr* spill.

капе́лла choir; chapel.

ка́пелька small drop; a little; ~ росы́ dew-drop.

капельме́йстер conductor; bandmaster.

капилля́р capillary.

капита́л capital. капитали́зм capitalism. капитали́ст capitalist. капиталисти́ческий capitalist. капита́льный capital; main, fundamental; major.

капита́н captain; skipper.

капитули́ровать impf & pf capitulate. капитуля́ция capitulation.

капка́н trap.

ка́пля (gen pl -пель) drop; bit, scrap. ка́пнуть (-ну) pf of ка́пать

капо́т hood, cowl, cowling; bonnet; house-coat.

капри́з caprice. капри́зничать impf play up. капри́зный capricious.

капу́ста cabbage.

капюшо́н hood.

ка́ра punishment.

кара́бкаться impf (pf вс~) clamber.

карава́н caravan; convoy.

кара́кули f pl scribble.

караме́ль caramel; caramels.

каранда́ш (-á) pencil.

каранти́н quarantine.

кара́т carat.

кара́тельный punitive. кара́ть impf (pf по~) punish.

карау́л guard; watch; ~! help! карау́лить impf guard; lie in wait for. карау́льный guard; sb sentry, sentinel, guard.

карбюра́тор carburettor.

каре́та carriage, coach.

ка́рий brown; hazel.

карикату́ра caricature; cartoon.

карка́с frame; framework.

ка́ркать impf, ка́ркнуть (-ну) pf caw, croak.

ка́рлик, ка́рлица dwarf; pygmy. ка́рликовый dwarf; pygmy.

карма́н pocket. карма́нник pickpocket. карма́нный adj pocket.

карни́з cornice; ledge.

карп carp.

ка́рта map; (playing-)card.

карта́вить (-влю) impf burr.

картёжник gambler.

карте́чь case-shot, grape-shot.

карти́на picture; scene. карти́нка picture; illustration. карти́нный picturesque; picture.

карто́н cardboard. карто́нка cardboard box.

картоте́ка card-index.

карто́фель m potatoes; potato(-plant). карто́фельный potato; ~ое пюре́ mashed potatoes.

ка́рточка card; season ticket; photo. ка́рточный card.

карто́шка potatoes; potato.

карусе́ль merry-go-round.

ка́рцер cell, lock-up.

карье́р[1] full gallop.

карье́р[2] quarry; sand-pit.

карье́ра career. карьери́ст careerist.

каса́ние contact. каса́тельная sb tangent. каса́ться impf (pf косну́ться) +gen or до+gen touch; touch on; concern; что каса́ется as regards.

ка́ска helmet.

каска́д cascade.

каспи́йский Caspian.

ка́сса till; cash-box; booking-office; box-office; cash-desk; cash.

кассе́та cassette. кассе́тный магнитофо́н cassette recorder.

касси́р, касси́рша cashier.

кастра́т eunuch. кастра́ция castration. кастри́ровать impf & pf castrate, geld.

кастрю́ля saucepan.

катало́г catalogue.

ката́ние rolling; driving; ~ верхо́м riding; ~ на конька́х skating.

катапу́льта catapult. катапульти́ровать(ся impf & pf catapult.

ката́р catarrh.

катара́кта cataract.

катастро́фа catastrophe. катастрофи́ческий catastrophic.

ката́ть impf (pf вы́~, с~) roll; (take for a) drive; ~ся roll, roll about; go for a drive; ~ся верхо́м ride, go riding; ~ся на конька́х skate, go skating.

категори́ческий categorical. катего́рия category.

ка́тер (pl -á) cutter; launch.

кати́ть (-ачу́, -а́тишь) impf bowl along, rip, tear; ~ся rush, tear; flow, stream, roll; кати́сь, кати́тесь get out! clear off! като́к (-тка́) skating-rink; roller.

като́лик, католи́чка Catholic. католи́ческий Catholic.

ка́торга penal servitude, hard labour. ка́торжник convict. ка́торжн|ый

penal; ~ые рабо́ты hard labour; drudgery.
кату́шка reel, bobbin; spool; coil.
каучу́к rubber.
кафе́ *neut indecl* café.
ка́федра pulpit; rostrum; chair; department.
ка́фель *m* Dutch tile.
кача́лка rocking-chair. кача́ние rocking, swinging; pumping. кача́ть *impf* (*pf* качну́ть) +*acc or instr* rock, swing; shake; ~ся rock, swing; roll; reel. каче́ли (-ей) *pl* swing.
ка́чественный qualitative; high-quality. ка́чество quality; в ка́честве+*gen* as, in the capacity of. ка́чка rocking; tossing.
качну́ть(ся (-ну́(сь, -нёшь(ся) *pf of* кача́ть(ся. качу́ etc.: *see* кати́ть
ка́ша gruel, porridge; завари́ть ка́шу stir up trouble.
ка́шель (-шля) cough. ка́шлянуть (-ну) *pf*, ка́шлять *impf* (have a) cough.
кашта́н chestnut. кашта́новый chestnut.
каю́та cabin, stateroom.
ка́ющийся penitent. ка́яться (ка́юсь) *impf* (*pf* по~, рас~) repent; confess; ка́юсь I (must) confess.
кв. *abbr* (*of* квадра́тный) square; (*of* кварти́ра) flat.
квадра́т square; quad; в квадра́те squared; возвести́ в ~ square. квадра́тный square; quadratic.
ква́кать *impf*, ква́кнуть (-ну) *pf* croak.
квалифика́ция qualification. квалифици́рованный qualified, skilled.
квант, ква́нта quantum. ква́нтовый quantum.
кварта́л block; quarter. кварта́льный quarterly.
кварте́т quartet.
кварти́ра flat; apartment(s); quarters. квартира́нт, -ра́нтка lodger; tenant. кварти́рная пла́та, квартпла́та rent.
кварц quartz.
квас (*pl* -ы́) kvass. ква́сить (-а́шу) *impf* sour; pickle. ква́шеная капу́ста sauerkraut.
кве́рху *adv* up, upwards.
квит, кви́ты quits.

квита́нция receipt. квито́к (-тка́) ticket, check.
КГБ *abbr* (*of* Комите́т госуда́рственной безопа́сности) KGB.
ке́гля skittle.
кедр cedar.
ке́ды (-ов) *pl* trainers.
кекс (fruit-)cake.
ке́лья (*gen pl* -лий) cell.
кем *see* кто
ке́мпинг campsite.
кенгуру́ *m indecl* kangaroo.
ке́пка cloth cap.
кера́мика ceramics.
керога́з stove. кероси́н paraffin. кероси́нка paraffin stove.
ке́та Siberian salmon. ке́тов|ый: ~ая икра́ red caviare.
кефи́р kefir, yoghurt.
кибернэ́тика cybernetics.
кива́ть *impf*, кивну́ть (-ну́, -нёшь) *pf* (голово́й) nod (one's head); (+на+*acc*) motion (to). киво́к (-вка́) nod.
кида́ть *impf* (*pf* ки́нуть) throw, fling; ~ся fling o.s.; rush; +*instr* throw.
кий (-я́; *pl* -и́, -ёв) (billiard) cue.
килев|о́й keel; ~а́я ка́чка pitching.
кило́ *neut indecl* kilo. килова́тт kilowatt. килогра́мм kilogram. киломе́тр kilometre.
киль *m* keel; fin. кильва́тер wake.
ки́лька sprat.
кинжа́л dagger.
кино́ *neut indecl* cinema.
кино- *in comb* film-, cine-. киноаппара́т cinecamera. ~арти́ст, ~арти́стка film actor, actress. ~журна́л news-reel. ~за́л cinema; auditorium. ~звезда́ film-star. ~зри́тель *m* film-goer. ~карти́на film. ~опера́тор camera-man. ~плёнка film. ~режиссёр film director. ~теа́тр cinema. ~хро́ника news-reel.
ки́нуть(ся (-ну(сь) *pf of* кида́ть(ся
кио́ск kiosk, stall.
ки́па pile, stack; bale.
кипари́с cypress.
кипе́ние boiling. кипе́ть (-плю) *impf* (*pf* вс~) boil, seethe.
кипу́чий boiling, seething; ebullient.
кипяти́льник kettle, boiler. кипяти́ть (-ячу́) *impf* (*pf* вс~) boil; ~ся boil; get excited. кипято́к (-тка́)

boiling water. **кипячёный** boiled.

Кирги́зия Kirghizia.

кирка́ pick(axe).

кирпи́ч (-á) brick; bricks. **кирпи́чный** brick; brick-red.

кисе́ль *m* kissel, blancmange.

кисе́т tobacco-pouch.

кисея́ muslin.

кислоро́д oxygen. **кислота́** (*pl* -ы) acid; acidity. **кисло́тный** acid. **ки́слый** sour; acid. **ки́снуть** (-ну; кис) *impf* (*pf* **про~**) turn sour.

ки́сточка brush; tassel. **кисть** (*gen pl* -е́й) cluster; bunch; brush; tassel; hand.

кит (-á) whale.

кита́ец (-а́йца; *pl* -цы, -цев) Chinese. **Кита́й** China. **кита́йский** Chinese. **китая́нка** Chinese (woman).

китобо́й whaler. **кито́вый** whale.

кичи́ться (-чу́сь) *impf* plume o.s.; strut. **кичли́вость** conceit. **кичли́вый** conceited.

кише́ть (-ши́т) *impf* swarm, teem.

кише́чник bowels, intestines. **кише́чный** intestinal. **кишка́** gut, intestine; hose.

клавеси́н harpsichord. **клавиату́ра** keyboard. **кла́виша** key. **кла́вишный**: ~ **инструме́нт** keyboard instrument.

клад treasure.

кла́дбище cemetery, graveyard.

кла́дка laying; masonry. **кладова́я** *sb* pantry; store-room. **кладовщи́к** (-á) storeman. **кладу́** *etc.*: *see* **класть**

кла́няться *impf* (*pf* **поклони́ться**) +*dat* bow to; greet.

кла́пан valve; vent.

кларне́т clarinet.

класс class; class-room. **кла́ссик** classic. **кла́ссика** the classics. **классифици́ровать** *impf* & *pf* classify. **класси́ческий** classical. **кла́ссный** class; first-class. **кла́ссовый** class.

класть (-аду́, -адёшь; -ал) *impf* (*pf* **положи́ть**, **сложи́ть**) lay; put.

клева́ть (клюю́, клюёшь) *impf* (*pf* **клю́нуть**) peck; bite.

кле́вер (*pl* -á) clover.

клевета́ slander; libel. **клевета́ть** (-ещу́, -е́щешь) *impf* (*pf* **на~**) +**на**+*acc* slander; libel. **клеветни́к** (-á), **-ни́ца** slanderer. **клеветни́ческий** slanderous; libellous.

клеёнка oilcloth. **кле́ить** *impf* (*pf* **с~**) glue; stick; ~**ся** stick; become sticky. **клей** (*loc* -ю́; *pl* -и́) glue, adhesive. **кле́йкий** sticky.

клейми́ть (-млю́) *impf* (*pf* **за~**) brand; stamp; stigmatize. **клеймо́** (*pl* -а) brand; stamp; mark.

кле́йстер paste.

клён maple.

клепа́ть *impf* rivet.

кле́тка cage; check; cell. **кле́точка** cellule. **кле́точный** cellular. **клетча́тка** cellulose. **кле́тчатый** checked.

клёш flare.

клешня́ (*gen pl* -е́й) claw.

клещи́ (-е́й) *pl* pincers, tongs.

клие́нт client. **клиенту́ра** clientèle.

кли́зма enema.

клик cry, call. **кли́кать** (-и́чу) *impf*, **кли́кнуть** (-ну) *pf* call.

кли́макс menopause.

кли́мат climate. **климати́ческий** climatic.

клин (*pl* -нья, -ньев) wedge. **клино́к** (-нка́) blade.

кли́ника clinic. **клини́ческий** clinical.

клипс clip-on ear-ring.

клич call. **кли́чка** name; nickname. **кли́чу** *etc.*: *see* **кли́кать**

клок (-á; *pl* -о́чья, -ьев *or* -и́, -о́в) rag, shred; tuft.

кло́кот bubbling; gurgling. **клокота́ть** (-о́чет) *impf* bubble; gurgle; boil up.

клони́ть (-ню́, -нишь) *impf* bend; incline; +**к**+*dat* drive at; ~**ся** bow, bend; +**к**+*dat* near, approach.

клоп (-á) bug.

кло́ун clown.

клочо́к (-чка́) scrap, shred. **кло́чья** *etc.*: *see* **клок**

клуб¹ club.

клуб² (*pl* -ы́) puff; cloud.

клу́бень (-бня) *m* tuber.

клуби́ться *impf* swirl; curl.

клубни́ка (*no pl*; *usu collect*) strawberry; strawberries.

клубо́к (-бка́) ball; tangle.

клу́мба (flower-)bed.

клык (-á) fang; tusk; canine (*tooth*).

клюв beak.

клю́ква cranberry; cranberries.

клю́нуть (-ну) *pf of* **клева́ть**

ключ¹ (-á) key; clue; keystone; clef;

wrench, spanner.

ключ² (-á) spring; source.

ключево́й key. ключи́ца collarbone.

клю́шка (hockey) stick; (golf-)club.

клюю́ etc.: see клева́ть

кля́кса blot, smudge.

кляну́ etc.: see клясть

кля́нчить (-чу) impf (pf вы~) beg.

кляп gag.

клясть (-яну́, -янёшь; -ял, -á, -о) impf curse; ~ся (pf по~ся) swear, vow. кля́тва oath, vow. кля́твенный on oath.

кни́га book.

кни́го- in comb book, biblio-. кни́говеде́ние¹ bibliography. ~веде́ние² book-keeping. ~изда́тель m publisher. ~люб bibliophile, book-lover. ~храни́лище library; book-stack. кни́жечка booklet. кни́жка booklet; note-book; bank-book. кни́жный book; bookish.

кни́зу adv downwards.

кно́пка drawing-pin; press-stud; (push-)button, knob.

кнут (-á) whip.

княги́ня princess. кня́жество principality. княжна́ (gen pl -жо́н) princess. князь (pl -зья, -зе́й) m prince.

ко see к prep.

коали́ция coalition.

кобура́ holster.

кобы́ла mare; (vaulting-)horse.

ко́ваный forged; wrought; terse.

кова́рный insidious, crafty; perfidious. кова́рство insidiousness, craftiness; perfidy.

кова́ть (кую́, -ёшь) impf (pf под~) forge; hammer; shoe.

ковёр (-врá) carpet; rug; mat.

коверка́ть impf (pf ис~) distort, mangle, ruin.

ко́вка forging; shoeing.

коври́жка honeycake, gingerbread. ко́врик rug; mat.

ковче́г ark.

ковш (-á) scoop, ladle.

ковы́ль m feather-grass.

ковыля́ть impf hobble.

ковырну́ть (-ну́, -нёшь) pf, ковыря́ть impf dig into; tinker; +в+prep pick (at); ~ся rummage; tinker.

когда́ adv when; ~ (бы) ни whenever; conj when; while; as; if. когда́-

либо, когда́-нибудь advs some time; ever. когда́-то adv once; formerly; some tlme.

кого́ see кто

ко́готь (-гтя; pl -гти, -гтей) m claw; talon.

код code.

коде́ин codeine.

ко́декс code.

ко́е-где́ adv here and there. ко́е-ка́к adv anyhow; somehow (or other). ко́е-како́й pron some. ко́е-кто́ pron somebody; some people. ко́е-что́ (-чего́) pron something; a little.

ко́жа skin; leather; peel. ко́жанка leather jacket. ко́жаный leather. коже́венный leather; tanning. ко́жный skin. кожура́ rind, peel, skin.

коза́ (pl -ы) goat, nanny-goat. козёл (-зла́) billy-goat. козеро́г ibex; Capricorn. ко́зий goat; ~ пух angora. козлёнок (-нка; pl -ля́та, -ля́т) kid. ко́злы (-зел) pl coach driver's seat; trestle(s); saw-horse.

ко́зни (-ей) pl machinations.

козырёк (-рька́) peak.

козырно́й trump. козырну́ть (-ну́, -нёшь) pf, козыря́ть impf lead trumps; trump; play one's trump card; salute. ко́зырь (pl -и, -ей) m trump.

ко́йка (gen pl ко́ек) berth, bunk; bed.

кока́ин cocaine.

ко́ка-ко́ла Coca-Cola (propr).

коке́тка coquette. коке́тство coquetry.

коклю́ш whooping-cough.

ко́кон cocoon.

коко́с coconut.

кокс coke.

кокте́йль m cocktail.

кол (-á; pl -лья, -ьев) stake, picket.

ко́лба retort.

колбаса́ (pl -ы) sausage.

колго́тки (-ток) pl tights.

колдова́ть impf practise witchcraft. колдовство́ sorcery. колду́н (-á) sorcerer, wizard. колду́нья (gen pl -ний) witch, sorceress.

колеба́ние oscillation; variation; hesitation. колеба́ть (-éблю) impf (pf по~) shake; ~ся oscillate; fluctuate; hesitate.

коле́но (pl -и, -ей, -ям) knee; (in pl) lap. коле́нчатый crank, cranked; bent; ~ вал crankshaft.

колесни́ца chariot. **колесо́** (*pl* -ёса) wheel.

колея́ rut; track, gauge.

ко́лика (*usu pl*) colic; stitch.

коли́чественн|ый quantitative; ~ое **числи́тельное** cardinal number. **коли́чество** quantity; number.

колле́га *m* & *f* colleague. **колле́гия** board; college.

коллекти́в collective. **коллективиза́ция** collectivization. **коллекти́вный** collective. **коллекционе́р** collector. **колле́кция** collection.

колли́зия clash, conflict.

коло́да block; pack (*of cards*).

коло́дец (-дца) well.

ко́локол (*pl* -а́, -о́в) bell. **коло́кольный** bell. **колоко́льня** belltower. **колоко́льчик** small bell; bluebell.

колониали́зм colonialism. **колониа́льный** colonial. **колониза́тор** colonizer. **колониза́ция** colonization. **колонизова́ть** *impf* & *pf* colonize. **коло́ния** colony.

коло́нка geyser; (*street*) water fountain; stand-pipe; column; **бензи́новая** ~ petrol pump. **коло́нна** column.

колори́т colouring, colour. **колори́тный** colourful, graphic.

ко́лос (-о́сья, -ьев) ear. **колоси́ться** *impf* form ears.

колосса́льный huge; terrific.

колоти́ть (-очу́, -о́тишь) *impf* (*pf* по~) beat; pound; thrash; smash; ~ся pound, thump; shake.

коло́ть[1] (-лю́, -лешь) *impf* (*pf* рас~) break, chop.

коло́ть[2] (-лю́, -лешь) *impf* (*pf* за~, кольну́ть) prick; stab; sting; slaughter; ~ся prick.

колпа́к (-а́) cap; hood, cowl.

колхо́з *abbr* (*of* коллекти́вное хозя́йство) kolkhoz, collective farm. **колхо́зник**, ~ица kolkhoz member. **колхо́зный** kolkhoz.

колыбе́ль cradle.

колыха́ть (-ы́шу) *impf*, **колыхну́ть** (-ну́, -нёшь) *pf* sway, rock; ~ся sway; flutter.

кольну́ть (-ну́, -нёшь) *pf of* **коло́ть**

кольцо́ (*pl* -а, -ле́ц, -льцам) ring.

колю́ч|ий prickly; sharp; ~ая про́волока barbed wire. **колю́чка** prickle; thorn.

коля́ска carriage; pram; side-car.

ком (*pl* -мья, -мьев) lump; ball.

ком *see* **кто**

кома́нда command; order; detachment; crew; team. **команди́р** commander. **командирова́ть** *impf* & *pf* post, send on a mission. **командиро́вка** posting; mission, business trip. **командиро́вочные** *sb pl* travelling expenses. **кома́ндование** command. **кома́ндовать** *impf* (*pf* c~) give orders; be in command; +*instr* command. **кома́ндующий** *sb* commander.

кома́р (-а́) mosquito.

комба́йн combine harvester.

комбина́т industrial complex. **комбина́ция** combination; manoeuvre; slip. **комбинезо́н** overalls, boiler suit; dungarees. **комбини́ровать** *impf* (*pf* c~) combine.

коме́дия comedy.

коменда́нт commandant; manager; warden. **комендату́ра** commandant's office.

коме́та comet.

ко́мик comic actor; comedian. **ко́микс** comic, comic strip.

комисса́р commissar.

комиссионе́р (commission-)agent, broker. **комиссио́нн|ый** commission; ~ый магази́н second-hand shop; ~ые *sb pl* commission. **коми́ссия** commission; committee.

комите́т committee.

коми́ческий comic; comical. **коми́чный** comical, funny.

ко́мкать *impf* (*pf* c~) crumple.

коммента́рий commentary; *pl* comment. **коммента́тор** commentator. **комменти́ровать** *impf* & *pf* comment (on).

коммерса́нт merchant; businessman. **комме́рция** commerce. **комме́рческий** commercial.

коммивояжёр commercial traveller.

комму́на commune. **коммуна́льный** communal; municipal. **коммуни́зм** communism.

коммуника́ция communication.

коммуни́ст, ~ка communist. **коммунисти́ческий** communist.

коммута́тор switchboard.

коммюнике́ *neut indecl* communiqué.

ко́мната room. **ко́мнатный** room; indoor.

комо́д chest of drawers.

комо́к (-мка́) lump.

компа́кт-ди́ск compact disc. **компа́ктный** compact.

компа́ния company. **компаньо́н**, ~ка companion; partner.

компа́ртия Communist Party.

ко́мпас compass.

компенса́ция compensation. **компенси́ровать** *impf & pf* compensate.

ко́мплекс complex. **ко́мплексный** complex, compound, composite; combined. **компле́кт** (complete) set; complement; kit. **комплектова́ть** *impf* (*pf* с~, у~) complete; bring up to strength. **комплекция** build; constitution.

комплиме́нт compliment.

композитор composer. **компози́ция** composition.

компоне́нт component.

компо́ст compost.

компо́стер punch. **компости́ровать** *impf* (*pf* про~) punch.

компо́т stewed fruit.

компре́ссор compressor.

компромети́ровать *impf* (*pf* с~) compromise. **компроми́сс** compromise.

компью́тер computer.

комсомо́л Komsomol. **комсомо́лец** (-льца), -лка Komsomol member. **комсомо́льский** Komsomol.

кому́ *see* кто

комфо́рт comfort.

конве́йер conveyor.

конве́рт envelope; sleeve.

конво́ир escort. **конвои́ровать** *impf* escort. **конво́й** escort, convoy.

конгре́сс congress.

конденса́тор condenser.

конди́терская *sb* confectioner's, cake shop.

кондиционе́р air-conditioner. **кондицио́нный** air-conditioning.

конду́ктор (*pl* -а́), -торша conductor; guard.

конево́дство horse-breeding. **конёк** (-нька́) *dim of* конь; hobby(-horse).

коне́ц (-нца́) end; в конце́ концо́в in the end, after all. **коне́чно** *adv* of course. **коне́чность** extremity. **ко-**

не́чный final, last; ultimate; finite.

кони́ческий conic, conical.

конкре́тный concrete.

конкуре́нт competitor. **конкуре́нция** competition. **конкури́ровать** *impf* compete. **ко́нкурс** competition; contest.

ко́нница cavalry. **ко́нный** horse; mounted; equestrian; ~ заво́д stud.

конопля́ hemp.

консервати́вный conservative. **консерва́тор** Conservative.

консервато́рия conservatoire.

консерви́ровать *impf & pf* (*pf also* за~) preserve; can, bottle. **консе́рвный** preserving; ~ая ба́нка tin; ~ый нож tin-opener. **консерво-открыва́тель** *m* tin-opener. **консе́рвы** (-ов) *pl* tinned goods.

конси́лиум consultation.

конспе́кт synopsis, summary. **конспекти́ровать** *impf* (*pf* за~, про~) make an abstract of.

конспирати́вный secret, clandestine. **конспира́ция** security.

конста́тация ascertaining; establishment. **констати́ровать** *impf & pf* ascertain; establish.

конституцио́нный constitutional. **конститу́ция** constitution.

констру́ировать *impf & pf* (*pf also* с~) construct; design. **конструкти́вный** structural; constructional; constructive. **констру́ктор** designer, constructor. **констру́кция** construction; design.

ко́нсул consul.

консульта́ция consultation; advice; clinic; tutorial. **консульти́ровать** *impf* (*pf* про~) advise; +с+*instr* consult; ~ся obtain advice; +с+*instr* consult.

конта́кт contact. **конта́ктные ли́нзы** *f pl* contact lenses.

конте́йнер container.

конте́кст context.

контине́нт continent.

конто́ра office. **конто́рский** office.

контраба́нда contraband. **контрабанди́ст** smuggler.

контраба́с double-bass.

контраге́нт contractor. **контра́кт** contract.

контра́льто *neut/fem indecl* contralto (*voice/person*).

контрама́рка complimentary ticket.

контрапу́нкт counterpoint.

контра́ст contrast.

контрибу́ция indemnity.

контрнаступле́ние counter-offensive.

контролёр inspector; ticket-collector. контроли́ровать *impf* (*pf* про~) check; inspect. контро́ль *m* control; check; inspection. контро́льн|ый control; ~ая рабо́та test.

контрразве́дка counter-intelligence; security service. контрреволю́ция counter-revolution.

конту́зия bruising; shell-shock.

ко́нтур contour, outline; circuit.

конура́ kennel.

ко́нус cone.

конфедера́ция confederation.

конфере́нция conference.

конфе́та sweet.

конфискова́ть *impf & pf* confiscate.

конфли́кт conflict.

конфо́рка ring (*on stove*).

конфу́з discomfort, embarrassment. конфу́зить (-у́жу) *impf* (*pf* с~) confuse, embarrass; ~ся feel embarrassed.

концентра́т concentrate. концентрацио́нный concentration. концентра́ция concentration. концентри́ровать(ся *impf* (*pf* с~) concentrate.

конце́пция conception.

конце́рт concert; concerto. концертме́йстер leader; soloist. конце́ртный concert.

концла́герь *abbr* (*of* концентрацио́нный ла́герь) concentration camp.

конча́ть *impf*, ко́нчить *pf* finish; end; +*inf* stop; ~ся end; finish; expire. ко́нчик tip. кончи́на decease.

конь (-я́; *pl* -и, -е́й) *m* horse; knight. коньки́ (-о́в) *pl* skates; ~ на ро́ликах roller skates. конькобе́жец (-жца) skater.

конья́к (-а́) cognac.

ко́нюх groom, stable-boy. коню́шня (*gen pl* -шен) stable.

коопера́тив cooperative. коопера́тивный cooperative. коопера́ция cooperation.

координа́та coordinate. координа́ция coordination.

копа́ть *impf* (*pf* копну́ть, вы́~) dig; dig up, dig out; ~ся rummage.

копе́йка copeck.

ко́пи (-ей) *pl* mines.

копи́лка money-box.

копи́рка carbon paper. копирова́льный copying. копи́ровать *impf* (*pf* с~) copy; imitate.

копи́ть (-плю́, -пишь) *impf* (*pf* на~) save (up); accumulate; ~ся accumulate.

ко́пия copy.

копна́ (*pl* -ы, -пён) shock, stook.

копну́ть (-ну́, -нёшь) *pf of* копа́ть

ко́поть soot.

копте́ть (-пчу́) *impf* swot; vegetate. копти́ть (-пчу́) *impf* (*pf* за~, на~) smoke, cure; blacken with smoke.

копче́ние smoking; smoked foods. копчёный smoked.

копы́то hoof.

копьё (*pl* -я, -пий) spear, lance.

кора́ bark, rind; cortex; crust.

корабе́льный ship; naval. кораблевожде́ние navigation. кораблекруше́ние shipwreck. кораблестрое́ние shipbuilding. кора́бль (-я́) *m* ship, vessel; nave.

кора́лл coral.

коре́йский Korean. Коре́я Korea.

корена́стый thickset. корени́ться *impf* be rooted. коренно́й radical, fundamental; native. ко́рень (-рня; *pl* -и, -е́й) *m* root; counterfoil.

корзи́на, корзи́нка basket.

коридо́р corridor.

кори́ца cinnamon.

кори́чневый brown.

ко́рка crust; rind, peel.

корм (*loc* -у́; *pl* -а́) fodder.

корма́ stern.

корми́лец (-льца) bread-winner. корми́ть (-млю́, -мишь) *impf* (*pf* на~, по~, про~) feed; ~ся feed; +*instr* live on, make a living by. кормле́ние feeding. кормово́й[1] fodder.

кормово́й[2] stern.

корнево́й root; radical. корнепло́ды (-ов) root-crops.

коро́бить (-блю) *impf* (*pf* по~) warp; jar upon; ~ся (*pf also* с~ся) warp.

коро́бка box.

коро́ва cow.

короле́ва queen. **короле́вский** royal. **короле́вство** kingdom. **коро́ль** (-я́) *m* king.

коромы́сло yoke; beam; rocking shaft.

коро́на crown.

коронаротромбо́з coronary (thrombosis).

коро́нка crown. **коронова́ть** *impf* & *pf* crown.

коро́ткий (ко́роток, -тка́, ко́ротко́, коро́тки́) short; intimate. **ко́ротко** *adv* briefly; intimately. **коротково́лновый** short-wave. **коро́че** *comp* of **коро́ткий, ко́ротко**

корпора́ция corporation.

ко́рпус (*pl* -ы, -ов *or* -а́, -о́в) corps; services; building; hull; housing, case; body.

корректи́ровать *impf* (*pf* про~, с~) correct, edit. **корре́ктный** correct, proper. **корре́ктор** (*pl* -а́) proof-reader. **корректу́ра** proof-reading; proof.

корреспонде́нт correspondent. **корреспонде́нция** correspondence.

корро́зия corrosion.

корру́пция corruption.

корт (tennis-)court.

корте́ж cortège; motorcade.

ко́ртик dirk.

ко́рточки (-чек) *pl*; **сиде́ть на ко́рточках** squat.

корчева́ть (-чу́ю) *impf* root out.

ко́рчить (-чу) *impf* (*pf* с~) contort; *impers* convulse; ~ **из себя́** pose as; ~**ся** writhe.

ко́ршун kite.

коры́стный mercenary. **коры́сть** avarice; profit.

коры́то trough; wash-tub.

корь measles.

коса́[1] (*acc* -у; *pl* -ы) plait, tress.

коса́[2] (*acc* ко́су́, *pl* -ы) spit.

коса́[3] (*acc* ко́су́, *pl* -ы) scythe.

ко́свенный indirect.

коси́лка mowing-machine, mower. **коси́ть**[1] (кошу́, ко́сишь) *impf* (*pf* с~) cut; mow (down).

коси́ть[2] (кошу́) *impf* (*pf* по~, с~) squint; be crooked; ~**ся** slant; look sideways; look askance.

косме́тика cosmetics, make-up. **косми́ческий** cosmic; space. **космо-**

дро́м spacecraft launching-site. **космона́вт, -на́втка** cosmonaut, astronaut. **ко́смос** cosmos; (outer) space.

косноязы́чный tongue-tied.

косну́ться (-ну́сь, -нёшься) *pf of* **каса́ться**

косогла́зие squint. **косо́й** (кос, -а́, -о) slanting; oblique; sidelong; squinting, cross-eyed.

костёр (-тра́) bonfire; camp-fire.

костля́вый bony. **ко́стный** bone. **ко́сточка** (small) bone; stone.

косты́ль (-я́) *m* crutch.

кость (*loc* и́; *pl* -и, -е́й) bone; die.

костю́м clothes; suit. **костюмиро́ванный** fancy-dress.

костяно́й bone; ivory.

косы́нка (*triangular*) head-scarf, shawl.

кот (-а́) tom-cat.

котёл (-тла́) boiler; copper, cauldron. **котело́к** (-лка́) pot; mess-tin; bowler (hat). **коте́льная** *sb* boiler-room, -house.

котёнок (-нка; *pl* -тя́та, -тя́т) kitten. **ко́тик** fur-seal; sealskin.

котле́та rissole; burger; **отбивна́я ~** chop.

котлова́н foundation pit, trench.

кото́мка knapsack.

кото́рый *pron* which, what; who; that; **~ час?** what time is it?

котя́та *etc.*: *see* **котёнок**

ко́фе *m indecl* coffee. **кофева́рка** percolator. **кофеи́н** caffeine.

ко́фта, ко́фточка blouse, top.

коча́н (-а́ *or* -чна́) (cabbage-)head.

кочева́ть (-чу́ю) *impf* be a nomad; wander; migrate. **коче́вник** nomad. **кочево́й** nomadic.

кочега́р stoker, fireman. **кочега́рка** stokehold, stokehole.

кочене́ть *impf* (*pf* за~, о~) grow numb.

кочерга́ (*gen pl* -рёг) poker.

ко́чка hummock.

кошелёк (-лька́) purse.

ко́шка cat.

кошма́р nightmare. **кошма́рный** nightmarish.

кошу́ *etc.*: *see* **коси́ть**

кощу́нство blasphemy.

коэффицие́нт coefficient.

КП *abbr* (*of* Коммунисти́ческая па́ртия) Communist Party. **КПСС** *abbr* (*of* Коммунисти́ческая па́ртия

Советского Союза) Communist Party of the Soviet Union, CPSU.

краб crab.

кра́деный stolen. **краду́** *etc.*: *see* **красть**

кра́жа theft; ~ **со взло́мом** burglary.

край (*loc* -ю́; *pl* -я́, -ёв) edge; brink; land; region. **кра́йне** *adv* extremely. **кра́йний** extreme; last; outside, wing; **по кра́йней ме́ре** at least. **кра́йность** extreme; extremity.

крал *etc.*: *see* **красть**

кран tap; crane.

крапи́ва nettle.

краса́вец (-вца) handsome man. **краса́вица** beauty. **краси́вый** beautiful; handsome.

краси́тель *m* dye. **кра́сить** (-а́шу) *impf* (*pf* вы~, о~, по~) paint; colour; dye; stain; ~ся (*pf* на~) make-up. **кра́ска** paint, dye; colour.

красне́ть (-е́ю) *impf* (*pf* по~) blush; redden; show red.

красноарме́ец (-е́йца) Red Army man. **красноарме́йский** Red Army. **красноречи́вый** eloquent.

краснота́ redness. **красну́ха** German measles. **кра́сный** (-сен, -сна́, -о) red; beautiful; fine; ~**ое де́рево** mahogany; ~**ая сморо́дина** (*no pl*; *usu collect*) redcurrant; redcurrants; ~**ая строка́** (first line of) new paragraph.

красова́ться *impf* impress by one's beauty; show off. **красота́** (*pl* -ы) beauty. **кра́сочный** paint; ink; colourful.

красть (-аду́, -аде́шь; крал) *impf* (*pf* у~) steal; ~ся creep.

кра́тер crater.

кра́ткий (-ток, -тка́, -о) short; brief. **кратковре́менный** brief; transitory. **краткосро́чный** short-term.

кра́тное *sb* multiple.

кратча́йший *superl of* **кра́ткий**. **кра́тче** *comp of* **кра́ткий**, **кра́тко**

крах crash; failure.

крахма́л starch. **крахма́лить** *impf* (*pf* на~) starch.

кра́ше *comp of* **краси́вый**, **краси́во**

кра́шеный painted; coloured; dyed; made up. **кра́шу** *etc.*: *see* **кра́сить**

креве́тка shrimp; prawn.

креди́т credit. **креди́тный** credit. **кредитоспосо́бный** solvent.

кре́йсер (*pl* -á, -óв) cruiser.

крем cream.

кремато́рий crematorium.

креме́нь (-мня́) *m* flint.

кремль (-я́) *m* citadel; Kremlin.

кре́мний silicon.

кре́мовый cream.

крен list, heel; bank. **крени́ться** *impf* (*pf* на~) heel over, list; bank.

крепи́ть (-плю́) *impf* strengthen; support; make fast; constipate; ~ся hold out. **кре́пкий** (-пок, -пка́, -о) strong; firm; ~**ие напи́тки** spirits. **крепле́ние** strengthening; fastening.

кре́пнуть (-ну; -еп) *impf* (*pf* о~) get stronger.

крепостни́чество serfdom. **крепостно́й** serf; ~**о́е пра́во** serfdom; ~**о́й** *sb* serf. **кре́пость** fortress; strength. **кре́пче** *comp of* **кре́пкий**, **кре́пко**

кре́сло (*gen pl* -сел) arm-chair; stall.

крест (-á) cross. **кре́стины** (-и́н) *pl* christening. **крести́ть** (крещу́, -е́стишь) *impf* & *pf* (*pf also* о~, пере~) christen; make sign of the cross over; ~ся cross o.s.; be christened. **крест-на́крест** *adv* crosswise. **кре́стник**, **кре́стница** godchild. **крёстный**; ~**ая (мать)** godmother; ~**ый оте́ц** godfather. **крестоно́сец** (-сца) crusader. **крестовый похо́д** crusade.

крестья́нин (*pl* -я́не, -я́н), **крестья́нка** peasant. **крестья́нский** peasant. **крестья́нство** peasantry.

креще́ние christening; Epiphany. **крещё́ный** (-ён, -ена́) baptized; *sb* Christian. **крещу́** *etc.*: *see* **крести́ть**

крива́я *sb* curve. **кривизна́** crookedness; curvature. **криви́ть** (-влю́) *impf* (*pf* по~, с~) bend, distort; ~ **душо́й** go against one's conscience; ~ся become crooked or bent; make a wry face. **кривля́ться** *impf* give o.s. airs.

криво́й (крив, -á, -о) crooked; curved; one-eyed.

кри́зис crisis.

крик cry, shout.

крике́т cricket.

кри́кнуть (-ну) *pf of* **крича́ть**

кримина́льный criminal.

криста́лл crystal. **кристалли́ческий** crystal.

критерий criterion.

критик critic. **критика** criticism; critique. **критиковать** *impf* criticize. **критический** critical.

кричать (-чу) *impf* (*pf* **крикнуть**) cry, shout.

кров roof; shelter.

кровавый bloody.

кроватка, кровать bed.

кровеносный blood-; circulatory.

кровля (*gen pl* -вель) roof.

кровный blood; thoroughbred; vital, intimate.

крово- *in comb* blood. **кровожадный** bloodthirsty. ~**излияние** haemorrhage. ~**обращение** circulation. ~**пролитие** bloodshed. ~**пролитный** bloody. ~**смешение** incest. ~**течение** bleeding; haemorrhage. ~**точить** (-чит) *impf* bleed.

кровь (*loc* -и) blood. **кровяной** blood.

кроить (крою) *impf* (*pf* с~) cut (out). **кройка** cutting out.

крокодил crocodile.

кролик rabbit.

кроль *m* crawl(-stroke).

крольчиха she-rabbit, doe.

кроме *prep*+*gen* except; besides; ~ того besides, moreover.

кромка edge.

крона crown; top.

кронштейн bracket; corbel.

кропотливый painstaking; laborious.

кросс cross-country race.

кроссворд crossword (puzzle).

крот (-á) mole.

кроткий (-ток, -тка, -тко) meek, gentle. **кротость** gentleness; mildness.

крохотный, крошечный tiny. **крошка** crumb; a bit.

круг (*loc* -ý; *pl* -и) circle; circuit; sphere. **круглосуточный** round-the-clock. **круглый** (кругл, -á, -о) round; complete; ~ год all the year round. **круговой** circular; all-round. **кругозор** prospect; outlook. **кругóм** *adv* around; *prep*+*gen* round. **кругосветный** round-the-world.

кружевной lace; lacy. **кружево** (*pl* -á, -ев, -ám) lace.

кружить (-ужý, -ýжишь) *impf* whirl, spin round; ~ся whirl, spin round.

кружка mug.

кружóк (-жкá) circle, group.

круиз cruise.

крупá (*pl* -ы) groats; sleet. **крупица** grain.

крупный large, big; great; coarse; ~ый план close-up.

крутизнá steepness.

крутить (-чý, -ýтишь) *impf* (*pf* за-, с~) twist, twirl; roll; turn, wind; ~ся turn, spin; whirl.

крутой (крут, -á, -о) steep; sudden; sharp; severe; drastic. **крýча** steep slope. **крýче** *comp of* **крутой, крýто**

кручý *etc.*: *see* **крутить**

крушение crash; ruin; collapse.

крыжóвник gooseberries; gooseberry bush.

крылáтый winged. **крылó** (*pl* -лья, -льев) wing; vane.

крыльцó (*pl* -а, -лéц, -цáм) porch; (front, back) steps.

Крым the Crimea. **крымский** Crimean.

крыса rat.

крыть (крóю) *impf* cover; roof; trump; ~ся be, lie; be concealed. **крыша** roof. **крышка** lid.

крюк (-á; *pl* -ки, -кóв *or* -ючья, -чьев) hook; detour. **крючóк** (-чкá) hook.

кряду *adv* in succession.

кряж ridge.

крякать *impf*, **крякнуть** (-ну) *pf* quack.

кряхтеть (-хчý) *impf* groan.

кстáти *adv* to the point; opportunely; at the same time; by the way.

кто (когó, комý, кем, ком) *pron* who; anyone; ~ (бы) ни whoever. **кто-либо, кто-нибудь** *prons* anyone; someone. **кто-то** *pron* someone.

куб (*pl* -ы) cube; boiler; в ~е cubed. **кубик** brick, block.

кубинский Cuban.

кубический cubic; cube.

кубок (-бка) goblet; cup.

кубометр cubic metre.

кувшин jug; pitcher. **кувшинка** water-lily.

кувыркáться *impf*, **кувыркнýться** (-нýсь) *pf* turn somersaults. **кувыркóм** *adv* head over heels; topsy-turvy.

кудá *adv* where (to); what for; +*comp* much, far; ~ (бы) ни wherever. **кудá-либо, кудá-нибудь** *adv* anywhere, somewhere. куда́-то *adv* somewhere.

ку́дри (-е́й) *pl* curls. кудря́вый curly; florid.

кузне́ц (-а́) blacksmith. кузне́чик grasshopper. ку́зница forge, smithy.

ку́зов (*pl* -а́) basket; body.

ку́кла doll; puppet. ку́колка dolly; chrysalis. ку́кольный doll's; puppet.

кукуру́за maize.

куку́шка cuckoo.

кула́к (-а́) fist; kulak. кула́цкий kulak. кула́чный fist.

кулёк (-лька́) bag.

кули́к (-а́) sandpiper.

кулина́рия cookery. кулина́рный culinary.

кули́сы (-и́с) wings; за кули́сами behind the scenes.

кули́ч (-а́) Easter cake.

кулуа́ры (-ов) *pl* lobby.

кульмина́ция culmination.

культ cult. культиви́ровать *impf* cultivate.

культу́ра culture; standard; cultivation. культури́зм body-building. культу́рно *adv* in a civilized manner. культу́рный cultured; cultivated; cultural.

куми́р idol.

кумы́с koumiss (*fermented mare's milk*).

куни́ца marten.

купа́льный bathing. купа́льня bathing-place. купа́ть *impf* (*pf* вы́~, ис~) bathe; bath; ~ся bathe; take a bath.

купе́ *neut indecl* compartment.

купе́ц (-пца́) merchant. купе́ческий merchant. купи́ть (-плю́, -пишь) *pf* (*impf* покупа́ть) buy.

ку́пол (*pl* -а́) cupola, dome.

купо́н coupon.

купоро́с vitriol.

купчи́ха merchant's wife; female merchant.

кура́нты (-ов) *pl* chiming clock; chimes.

курга́н barrow; tumulus.

куре́ние smoking. кури́льщик, -щица smoker.

кури́ный hen's; chicken's.

кури́ть (-рю́, -ришь) *impf* (*pf* по~) smoke; ~ся burn; smoke.

ку́рица (*pl* ку́ры, кур) hen, chicken.

куро́к (-рка́) cocking-piece; взвести́ ~ cock a gun; спусти́ть ~ pull the trigger.

куропа́тка partridge.

куро́рт health-resort; spa.

курс course; policy; year; exchange rate. курса́нт student.

курси́в italics.

курси́ровать *impf* ply.

ку́ртка jacket.

курча́вый curly(-headed).

ку́ры *etc*.: *see* ку́рица

курьёз a funny thing. курьёзный curious.

курье́р messenger; courier. курье́рский express.

куря́тник hen-house.

куря́щий *sb* smoker.

куса́ть *impf* bite; sting; ~ся bite.

кусо́к (-ска́) piece; lump. кусо́чек (-чка) piece.

куст (-а́) bush, shrub. куста́рник bush(es), shrub(s).

куста́рн|ый hand-made; handicrafts; primitive; ~ая промы́шленность cottage industry. куста́рь (-я́) *m* craftsman.

ку́тать *impf* (*pf* за~) wrap up; ~ся muffle o.s. up.

кути́ть (кучу́, ку́тишь) *impf*, кутну́ть (-ну́, -нёшь) *pf* carouse; go on a binge.

куха́рка cook. ку́хня (*gen pl* -хонь) kitchen; cuisine. ку́хонный kitchen.

ку́ча heap; heaps.

ку́чер (*pl* -а́) coachman.

ку́чка small heap *or* group.

кучу́ *see* кути́ть

куша́к (-а́) sash; girdle.

ку́шанье food; dish. ку́шать *impf* (*pf* по~, с~) eat.

куше́тка couch.

кую́ *etc*.: *see* кова́ть

Л

лабора́нт, -а́нтка laboratory assistant. лаборато́рия laboratory.

ла́ва lava.

лави́на avalanche.

ла́вка bench; shop. ла́вочка small shop.

лавр bay tree, laurel.

ла́герный camp. ла́герь (*pl* -я́ *or* -и,

-ей or -ей) m camp; campsite.

лад (loc -ý; pl -ы́, -о́в) harmony; manner, way; stop, fret.

ла́дан incense.

ла́дить (ла́жу) impf get on, be on good terms. **ла́дно** adv all right; very well! **ла́дный** fine, excellent; harmonious.

ладо́нь palm.

ладья́ rook, castle; boat.

ла́жу etc.: see **ла́дить, ла́зить**.

лазаре́т field hospital; sick-bay.

ла́зать see **ла́зить. лазе́йка** hole; loop-hole.

ла́зер laser.

ла́зить (ла́жу), **ла́зать** impf climb, clamber.

лазу́рный sky-blue, azure. **лазу́рь** azure.

лазу́тчик scout; spy.

лай bark, barking. **ла́йка**[1] (Siberian) husky, laika.

ла́йка[2] kid. **ла́йковый** kid; kidskin.

ла́йнер liner; airliner.

лак varnish, lacquer.

лака́ть impf (pf вы~) lap.

лаке́й footman, man-servant; lackey.

лакирова́ть impf (pf от~) varnish; lacquer.

ла́кмус litmus.

ла́ковый varnished, lacquered.

ла́комиться (-млюсь) impf (pf по~) +instr treat o.s. to. **ла́комка** m & f gourmand. **ла́комство** delicacy. **ла́комый** dainty, tasty; +до fond of.

лакони́чный laconic.

ла́мпа lamp; valve, tube. **лампа́да** icon-lamp. **ла́мпочка** lamp; bulb.

ландша́фт landscape.

ла́ндыш lily of the valley.

лань fallow deer; doe.

ла́па paw; tenon.

ла́поть (-птя; pl -и, -éй) m bast shoe.

ла́почка pet, sweetie.

лапша́ noodles; noodle soup.

ларёк (-рька́) stall. **ларь** (-я́) m chest; bin.

ла́ска[1] caress.

ла́ска[2] weasel.

ласка́ть impf caress, fondle; ~ся +к+dat make up to; fawn upon. **ла́сковый** affectionate, tender.

ла́сточка swallow.

латви́ец (-ийца), -и́йка Latvian. **латви́йский** Latvian. **Ла́твия** Latvia.

лати́нский Latin.

лату́нь brass.

ла́ты (лат) pl armour.

латы́нь Latin.

латы́ш, латы́шка Latvian, Lett. **латы́шский** Latvian, Lettish.

лауреа́т prize-winner.

ла́цкан lapel.

лачу́га hovel, shack.

ла́ять (ла́ю) impf bark.

лба etc.: see **поб**

лгать (лгу, лжёшь; лгал, -á, -о) impf (pf на~, со~) lie; tell lies; +на+acc slander. **лгун** (-á), **лгу́нья** liar.

лебеди́ный swan. **лебёдка** swan, pen; winch. **ле́бедь** (pl -и, -éй) m swan, cob.

лев (льва) lion.

левобере́жный left-bank. **левша́** (gen pl -éй) m & f left-hander. **ле́вый** adj left; left-hand; left-wing.

лёг etc.: see **печь**

лега́льный legal.

леге́нда legend. **легенда́рный** legendary.

лёгк|ий (-гок, -гка́, лёгки) light; easy; slight, mild; ~ая атле́тика field and track events. **легко́** adv easily, lightly, slightly.

легко- in comb light; easy, easily. **легкове́рный** credulous. ~ве́с light-weight. ~мы́сленный thoughtless; flippant, frivolous, superficial. ~мы́слие flippancy, frivolity.

легков|о́й: ~а́я маши́на (private) car. **лёгкое** sb lung. **лёгкость** lightness; easiness. **ле́гче** comp of **лёгкий, легко́**

лёд (льда, loc -у́) ice. **леденé́ть** (-éю) impf (pf за~, о~) freeze; grow numb with cold. **леденéц** (-нца́) fruit-drop. **ледя́нящий** chilling, icy.

лéди f indecl lady.

ле́дник[1] ice-box; refrigerator van. **ледни́к**[2] (-á) glacier. **леднико́вый** glacial; ~ пери́од Ice Age. **ледо́вый** ice. **ледоко́л** ice-breaker. **ледяно́й** icy; icy.

лежа́ть (-жу́) impf lie; be, be situated. **лежа́чий** lying (down).

ле́звие (cutting) edge; razor-blade.

лезть (-зу; лез) impf (pf по~) climb; clamber, crawl; get, go; fall out.

лейбори́ст Labourite.

лейка watering-can.

лейтенант lieutenant.

лекарство medicine.

лексика vocabulary. **лексикон** lexicon; vocabulary.

лектор lecturer. **лекция** lecture.

лелеять (-ею) *impf* (*pf* вз~) cherish, foster.

лён (льна) flax.

ленивый lazy.

ленинградский (of) Leningrad. **ленинский** (of) Lenin; Leninist.

лениться (-нюсь, -нишься) *impf* (*pf* по~) be lazy; +*inf* be too lazy to.

лента ribbon; band; tape.

лентяй, -**яйка** lazy-bones. **лень** laziness.

лепесток (-тка) petal.

лепет babble; prattle. **лепетать** (-ечу, -ечешь) *impf* (*pf* про~) babble, prattle.

лепёшка scone; tablet, pastille.

лепить (-плю, -пишь) *impf* (*pf* вы~, за~, с~) model, fashion; mould; ~ся cling; crawl. **лепка** modelling. **лепной** modelled, moulded.

лес (*loc* -у́; *pl* -а) forest, wood; *pl* scaffolding.

леса (*pl* лёсы) fishing-line.

лесник (-а) forester. **лесничий** *sb* forestry officer; forest warden. **лесной** forest.

лесо- *in comb* forest, forestry; timber wood. **лесоводство** forestry. ~**заготовка** logging. ~**пилка**, ~**пильня** (*gen pl* -лен) sawmill. ~**руб** woodcutter.

лестница stairs, staircase; ladder. **лестный** flattering. **лесть** flattery.

лёт (*loc* -у́) flight, flying.

лета (лет) *pl* years; age; **сколько вам лет?** how old are you?

летательный flying. **летать** *impf*, **лететь** (лечу) *impf* (*pf* полететь) fly; rush; fall.

летний summer.

лётный flying, flight.

лето (*pl* -а) summer; *pl* years. **летом** *adv* in summer.

летопись chronicle.

летосчисление chronology.

летучий flying; passing; brief; volatile; ~**ая мышь** bat. **лётчик**, -**чица** pilot.

лечебница clinic. **лечебный** medical; medicinal. **лечение** (medical) treatment. **лечить** (-чу́, -чишь) *impf* treat (**от** for); ~ся be given, have treatment (**от** for).

лечу *etc.*: *see* **лететь**, **лечить**

лечь (ля́гу, ля́жешь; лёг, -ла́) *pf* (*impf* **ложиться**) lie, lie down; go to bed.

лещ (-а́) bream.

лжесвидетельство false witness.

лжец (-а́) liar. **лживый** lying; deceitful.

ли, ль *interrog partl* & *conj* whether, if; **ли,... ли** whether ... or; **рано ли, поздно ли** sooner or later.

либерал liberal. **либеральный** liberal.

либо *conj* or; ~... ~ either ... or.

ливень (-вня) *m* heavy shower, downpour.

ливрея livery.

лига league.

лидер leader. **лидировать** *impf* & *pf* be in the lead.

лизать (лижу́, -ешь) *impf*, **лизну́ть** (-ну́, -нёшь) *pf* lick.

ликвидация liquidation; abolition. **ликвидировать** *impf* & *pf* liquidate; abolish.

ликёр liqueur.

ликование rejoicing. **ликовать** *impf* rejoice.

лилия lily.

лиловый lilac, violet.

лиман estuary.

лимит limit.

лимон lemon. **лимонад** lemonade; squash. **лимонный** lemon.

лимфа lymph.

лингвист linguist. **лингвистика** linguistics. **лингвистический** linguistic.

линейка ruler; line. **линейный** linear; ~ **корабль** battleship.

линза lens.

линия line.

линолеум lino(leum).

линять *impf* (*pf* вы~, по~, с~) fade; moult.

липа lime tree.

липкий (-пок, -пка́, -о) sticky. **липнуть** (-ну; лип) *impf* stick.

липовый lime.

лира lyre. **лирик** lyric poet. **лирика** lyric poetry. **лирический** lyric; lyrical.

лиса́ (pl -ы), -си́ца fox.

лист (-á; pl -ы́ or -ья, -óв or -ьев) leaf; sheet; page; form; играть с ~á play at sight. листа́ть impf leaf through. листва́ foliage. ли́ственница larch ли́ственный deciduous. листо́вка leaflet. листово́й sheet, plate; leaf. листо́к (-тка́) dim of лист; leaflet; form, pro-forma.

Литва́ Lithuania.

лите́йный founding, casting.

литера́тор man of letters. литерату́ра literature. литерату́рный literary.

лито́вец (-вца), лито́вка Lithuanian. лито́вский Lithuanian.

лито́й cast.

литр litre.

лить (лью, льёшь; лил, -á, -о) impf (pf c~) pour; shed; cast, mould. литьё founding, casting, moulding; castings, mouldings. ли́ться (льётся; ли́лся, -áсь, ли́ло́сь) impf flow; pour.

лиф bodice. ли́фчик bra.

лифт lift.

лихо́й[1] (лих, -á, -о) dashing, spirited.

лихо́й[2] (лих, -á, -о, ли́хи́) evil.

лихора́дка fever. лихора́дочный feverish.

лицево́й facial; exterior; front.

лицеме́р hypocrite. лицеме́рие hypocrisy. лицеме́рный hypocritical.

лицо́ (pl -а) face; exterior; right side; person; быть к лицу́ +dat suit, befit. личи́нка larva, grub; maggot. ли́чно adv personally, in person. ли́чность personality; person. ли́чный personal; private; ~ соста́в staff, personnel.

лиша́й lichen; herpes; shingles. лиша́йник lichen.

лиша́ть(ся impf of лиши́ть(ся

лише́ние deprivation; privation. лишённый (-ён, -ена́) +gen lacking in, devoid of. лиши́ть(~шу́) pf (impf лиша́ть) +gen deprive of; ~ся +gen lose, be deprived of. ли́шний superfluous; unnecessary; spare; ~ раз once more; c ~им odd, and more.

лишь adv only; conj as soon as; ~ бы́ if only, provided that.

лоб (лба, loc лбу) forehead.

ло́бзик fret-saw.

лови́ть (-влю́, -вишь) impf (pf пойма́ть) catch, try to catch.

ло́вкий (-вок, -вка́, -о) adroit; cunning. ло́вкость adroitness; cunning.

ло́вля (gen pl -вель) catching, hunting; fishing-ground. ло́вушка trap.

ло́вче comp of ло́вкий

логари́фм logarithm.

ло́гика logic. логи́ческий, логи́чный logical.

ло́говище, ло́гово den, lair.

ло́дка boat.

лоды́рничать impf loaf, idle about. ло́дырь m loafer, idler.

ло́жа box; (masonic) lodge.

ложби́на hollow.

ло́же couch; bed.

ложи́ться (-жу́сь) impf of лечь

ло́жка spoon.

ло́жный false. ложь (лжи) lie, falsehood.

лоза́ (pl -ы) vine.

ло́зунг slogan, catchword.

лока́тор radar or sonar apparatus.

локомоти́в locomotive.

ло́кон lock, curl.

ло́коть (-ктя; pl -и, -éй) m elbow.

лом (pl -ы, -óв) crowbar; scrap, waste. ло́маный broken. лома́ть impf (pf по~, c~) break; cause to ache; ~ся break; crack; put on airs; be obstinate.

ломба́рд pawnshop.

ло́мберный стол card-table.

ломи́ть (ло́мит) impf break; break through, rush; impers cause to ache; ~ся be (near to) breaking. ло́мка breaking; pl quarry. ло́мкий (-мок, -мка́, -о) fragile, brittle.

ломо́ть (-мтя́; pl -мти́) m large slice; hunk; chunk. ло́мтик slice.

ло́но bosom, lap.

ло́пасть (pl -и, -éй) blade; fan, vane; paddle.

лопа́та spade; shovel. лопа́тка shoulder-blade; shovel; trowel.

ло́паться impf, ло́пнуть (-ну) pf burst; split; break; fail; crash.

лопу́х (-á) burdock.

лорд lord.

лоси́на elk-skin, chamois leather; elk-meat.

лоск lustre, shine.

лоску́т (-á; pl -ы́ or -ья, -óв or -ьев) rag, shred, scrap.

лосни́ться impf be glossy, shine.

ло́сось m salmon.

лось (*pl* -и, -ей) *m* elk.
лосьо́н lotion; aftershave; cream.
лот lead, plummet.
лотере́я lottery, raffle.
лото́к (-тка́) hawker's stand *or* tray; chute; gutter; trough.
лохма́тый shaggy; dishevelled.
лохмо́тья (-ьев) *pl* rags.
ло́цман pilot.
лошади́ный horse; equine. ло́шадь (*pl* -и, -ей, *instr* -дьми́ *or* -дя́ми) horse.
лощёный glossy, polished.
лощи́на hollow, depression.
лоя́льный fair, honest; loyal.
лубо́к (-бка́) splint; popular print.
луг (*loc* -у́; *pl* -а́) meadow.
лу́жа puddle.
лужа́йка lawn, glade.
лужёный tin-plated.
лук[1] onions.
лук[2] bow.
лука́вить (-влю) *impf* (*pf* с~) be cunning. лука́вство craftiness. лука́вый crafty, cunning.
лу́ковица onion; bulb.
луна́ (*pl* -ы) moon. луна́тик sleepwalker.
лу́нка hole; socket.
лу́нный moon; lunar.
лу́па magnifying-glass.
лупи́ть (-плю́, -пишь) *impf* (*pf* от~) flog.
луч (-а́) ray; beam. лучево́й ray, beam; radial; radiation. лучеза́рный radiant.
лучи́на splinter.
лу́чше better; ~ всего́, ~ всех best of all. лу́чший better; best; в ~ем слу́чае at best; всего́ ~его! all the best!
лы́жа ski. лы́жник skier. лы́жный спорт skiing. лыжня́ ski-track.
лы́ко bast.
лысе́ть (-е́ю) *impf* (*pf* об~, по~) grow bald. лы́сина bald spot; blaze. лы́сый (лыс, -а́, -о) bald.
ль *see* ли
льва *etc.*: *see* лев. льви́ный lion, lion's. льви́ца lioness.
льго́та privilege; advantage. льго́тный privileged; favourable.
льда *etc.*: *see* лёд. льди́на block of ice; ice-floe.
льна *etc.*: *see* лён. льново́дство

flax-growing.
льнуть (-ну, -нёшь) *impf* (*pf* при~) +к+*dat* cling to; have a weakness for; make up to.
льняно́й flax, flaxen; linen; linseed.
льстец (-а́) flatterer. льсти́вый flattering; smooth-tongued. льстить (льщу) *impf* (*pf* по~) +*dat* flatter.
лью *etc.*: *see* пить
любе́зность courtesy; kindness; compliment. любе́зный courteous; obliging; kind; бу́дьте ~ы be so kind (as to).
люби́мец (-мца), -мица pet, favourite. люби́мый beloved; favourite.
люби́тель *m*, -ница lover; amateur. люби́тельский amateur. люби́ть (-блю́, -бишь) *impf* love; like.
любова́ться *impf* (*pf* по~) +*instr or* на+*acc* admire.
любо́вник lover. любо́вница mistress. любо́вный love-; loving. любо́вь (-бви́, *instr* -бо́вью) love.
любозна́тельный inquisitive.
любо́й any; either; *sb* anyone.
любопы́тный curious; inquisitive. любопы́тство curiosity.
лю́бящий loving.
лю́ди (-е́й, -ям, -дьми́, -ях) *pl* people. лю́дный populous; crowded. людое́д cannibal; ogre. людско́й human.
люк hatch(way); trap; manhole.
лю́лька cradle.
люминесце́нтный luminescent. люминесце́нция luminescence.
лю́стра chandelier.
лю́тня (*gen pl* -тен) lute.
лю́тый (лют, -а́, -о) ferocious.
ляга́ть *impf*, лягну́ть (-ну́, -нёшь) *pf* kick; ~ся kick.
ля́гу *etc.*: *see* лечь
лягу́шка frog.
ля́жка thigh, haunch.
ля́згать *impf* clank; +*instr* rattle.
ля́мка strap; тяну́ть ля́мку toil.

M

мавзоле́й mausoleum.
мавр, маврита́нка Moor. маврита́нский Moorish.
магази́н shop.
маги́стр (holder of) master's degree.

магистра́ль main; main line, main road.

маги́ческий magic(al). ма́гия magic.

магнети́зм magnetism.

ма́гний magnesium.

магни́т magnet. магни́тный magnetic. магнитофо́н tape-recorder.

мада́м *f indecl* madam, madame.

мажо́р major (key); cheerful mood. мажо́рный major; cheerful.

ма́зать (ма́жу) *impf* (*pf* вы́~, за~, из~, на~, по~, про~) oil, grease; smear, spread; soil; ~ся get dirty; make up. мазо́к (-зка́) touch, dab; smear. мазу́т fuel oil. мазь ointment; grease.

маис maize.

май May. ма́йский May.

ма́йка T-shirt.

майо́р major.

мак poppy, poppy-seeds.

макаро́ны (-н) *pl* macaroni.

мака́ть *impf* (*pf* макну́ть) dip.

маке́т model; dummy.

макну́ть (-ну́, -нёшь) *pf of* мака́ть

макре́ль mackerel.

максима́льный maximum. ма́ксимум maximum; at most.

макулату́ра waste paper; pulp literature.

маку́шка top; crown.

мал *etc.*: *see* ма́лый

малахи́т malachite.

мале́йший least, slightest. ма́ленький little; small.

мали́на (*no pl*; *usu collect*) raspberry; raspberries; raspberry-bush. мали́новый raspberry.

ма́ло *adv* little, few; not enough; ~ того́ moreover; ~ того́ что... not only ....

мало- *in comb* (too) little. малова́жный of little importance. ~вероя́тный unlikely. ~гра́мотный semi-literate; crude. ~ду́шный faint-hearted. ~иму́щий needy. ~кро́вие anaemia. ~ле́тний young; juvenile; minor. ~о́пытный inexperienced. ~чи́сленный small (in number), few.

мало-ма́льски *adv* in the slightest degree; at all. мало-пома́лу *adv* little by little.

ма́л|ый (мал, -а́) little, (too) small; са́мое ~ое at the least; *sb* fellow;

lad. малы́ш (-а́) kiddy; little boy. ма́льчик boy. мальчи́шка *m* urchin, boy. мальчуга́н little boy. малю́тка *m & f* baby, little one.

маля́р (-а́) painter, decorator.

маляри́я malaria.

ма́ма mother, mummy. мама́ша mummy. ма́мин mother's.

ма́монт mammoth.

мандари́н mandarin, tangerine.

манда́т warrant; mandate.

манёвр manoeuvre; shunting. маневри́ровать *impf* (*pf* с~) manoeuvre; shunt; +*instr* make good use of.

мане́ж riding-school.

манеке́н dummy; mannequin. манеке́нщик, -щица model.

мане́ра manner; style. мане́рный affected.

манже́та cuff.

маникю́р manicure.

манипули́ровать *impf* manipulate. манипуля́ция manipulation; machination.

мани́ть (-ню́, -нишь) *impf* (*pf* по~) beckon; attract; lure.

манифе́ст manifesto. манифеста́ция demonstration.

мани́шка (false) shirt-front.

ма́ния mania; ~ вели́чия megalomania.

ма́нная ка́ша semolina.

мано́метр pressure-gauge.

ма́нтия cloak; robe, gown.

мануфакту́ра manufacture; textiles.

манья́к maniac.

марафо́нский бег marathon.

ма́рганец (-нца) manganese.

маргари́н margarine.

маргари́тка daisy.

марино́ванный pickled. марино-ва́ть *impf* (*pf* за~) pickle; put off.

марионе́тка puppet.

ма́рка stamp; counter; brand; trade-mark; grade; reputation.

ма́ркий easily soiled.

маркси́зм Marxism. маркси́ст Marxist. маркси́стский Marxist.

ма́рлевый gauze. ма́рля gauze; cheesecloth.

мармела́д fruit jellies.

ма́рочный high-quality.

Марс Mars.

март March. ма́ртовский March.

марты́шка marmoset; monkey.

марш march.
ма́ршал marshal.
марширова́ть *impf* march.
маршру́т route, itinerary.
ма́ска mask. **маскара́д** masked ball; masquerade. **маскирова́ть** *impf* (*pf* за~) disguise; camouflage. **маски-ро́вка** disguise; camouflage.
Ма́сленица Shrovetide. **маслёнка** butter-dish; oil-can. **масли́на** olive.
ма́сло (*pl* -а́, ма́сел, -сла́м) butter; oil; oil paints. **маслобо́йка** churn. **маслобо́йня** (*gen pl* -бен), **масло-заво́д** dairy. **масляни́стый** oily. **масляно́й** oil.
ма́сса mass; a lot, lots.
масса́ж massage. **масси́ровать** *impf & pf* massage.
масси́в massif; expanse, tract. **масси́вный** massive.
ма́ссовый mass.
ма́стер (*pl* -а́), **мастери́ца** foreman, forewoman; (master) craftsman; expert. **мастери́ть** *impf* (*pf* с~) make, build. **мастерска́я** *sb* workshop. **мастерско́й** masterly. **мастерство́** craft; skill.
масти́ка mastic; putty; floor-polish.
масти́тый venerable.
масть (*pl* -и, -е́й) colour; suit.
масшта́б scale.
мат[1] checkmate.
мат[2] mat.
мат[3] foul language.
матема́тик mathematician. **матема́тика** mathematics. **математи́ческий** mathematical.
материа́л material. **материали́зм** materialism. **материалисти́ческий** materialist. **материа́льный** material.
матери́к (-а́) continent; mainland. **материко́вый** continental.
матери́нский maternal, motherly. **матери́нство** maternity.
мате́рия material; pus; topic.
ма́тка womb; female.
ма́товый matt; frosted.
матра́с, **матра́ц** mattress.
матрёшка Russian doll.
ма́трица matrix; die, mould.
матро́с sailor, seaman.
матч match.
мать (ма́тери, *instr* -рью; *pl* -тери, -ре́й) mother.

ма́фия Mafia.
мах swing, stroke. **маха́ть** (машу́, ма́шешь) *impf*, **махну́ть** (-ну́, -нёшь) *pf* +*instr* wave; brandish; wag; flap; go; rush.
махина́ция machinations.
махови́к (-а́) fly-wheel.
махро́вый dyed-in-the-wool; terry.
ма́чеха stepmother.
ма́чта mast.
маши́на machine; car. **машина́ль-ный** mechanical. **машини́ст** operator; engine-driver; scene-shifter. **маши-ни́стка** typist; ~-стенографи́стка shorthand-typist. **маши́нка** machine; typewriter; sewing-machine. **машинопи́сный** typewritten. **ма́-шинопись** typing; typescript. **маши-нострое́ние** mechanical engineering.
мая́к (-а́) lighthouse; beacon.
ма́ятник pendulum. **ма́яться** *impf* toil; suffer; languish.
мгла haze; gloom.
мгнове́ние instant, moment. **мгно-ве́нный** instantaneous, momentary.
ме́бель furniture. **меблиро́ванный** furnished. **меблиро́вка** furnishing; furniture.
мегава́тт (*gen pl* -а́тт) megawatt. **ме-го́м** megohm. **мегато́нна** megaton.
меда́ль medal. **медальо́н** medallion.
медве́дица she-bear. **медве́дь** *m* bear. **медве́жий** bear('s). **медве-жо́нок** (-нка; *pl* -жа́та, -жа́т) bear cub.
ме́дик medical student; doctor. **медикаме́нты** (-ов) *pl* medicines. **медици́на** medicine. **медици́нский** medical.
ме́дленный slow. **медли́тельный** sluggish; slow. **ме́длить** *impf* linger; be slow.
ме́дный copper; brass.
медо́вый honey; ~ ме́сяц honey-moon.
медосмо́тр medical examination, check-up. **медпу́нкт** first aid post. **медсестра́** (*pl* -сёстры, -сестёр, -сёстрам) nurse.
меду́за jellyfish.
медь copper.
меж *prep* +*instr* between.

меж- *in comb* inter-.

межа́ (*pl* -и, меж, -а́м) boundary.

междоме́тие interjection.

ме́жду *prep+instr* between; among; ~ про́чим incidentally, by the way; ~ тем meanwhile; ~ тем, как while.

между- *in comb* inter-. **междуго-ро́дный** inter-city. ~наро́дный international.

межконтинента́льный intercontinental. **межплане́тный** interplanetary.

мезони́н attic (storey); mezzanine (floor).

Ме́ксика Mexico.

мел (*loc* -у́) chalk.

мён *etc.*: *see* мести́

меланхо́лия melancholy.

меле́ть (-е́ет) *impf* (*pf* об~) grow shallow.

мелиора́ция land improvement.

ме́лкий (-лок, -лка́, -о) small; shallow; fine; petty. **ме́лко** *adv* fine, small. **мелкобуржуа́зный** petty bourgeois. **мелково́дный** shallow.

мелоди́чный melodious, melodic. **мело́дия** melody.

ме́лочный petty. **ме́лочь** (*pl* -и, -е́й) small items; (small) change; *pl* trifles, trivialities.

мель (*loc* -и́) shoal; bank; на мели́ aground.

мелька́ть *impf*, **мелькну́ть** (-ну́, -нёшь) *pf* be glimpsed fleetingly. **ме́льком** *adv* in passing; fleetingly.

ме́льник miller. **ме́льница** mill.

мельча́йший *superl of* ме́лкий. **ме́льче** *comp of* ме́лкий, ме́лко. **мелюзга́** small fry.

мелю́ *etc.*: *see* моло́ть

мембра́на membrane; diaphragm.

мемора́ндум memorandum.

мемуа́ры (-ов) *pl* memoirs.

ме́на exchange, barter.

ме́неджер manager.

ме́нее *adv* less; тем не ~ none the less.

мензу́рка measuring-glass.

меново́й exchange; barter.

менуэ́т minuet.

ме́ньше smaller; less. **меньшеви́к** (-а́) Menshevik. **ме́ньший** lesser, smaller; younger. **меньшинство́** minority.

меню́ *neut indecl* menu.

меня́ *see* я *pron*

меня́ть *impf* (*pf* об~, по~) change; exchange; ~ся change; +*instr* exchange.

ме́ра measure.

мере́щиться (-щусь) *impf* (*pf* по~) seem, appear.

мерза́вец (-вца) swine, bastard. **ме́рзкий** (-зок, -зка́, -о) disgusting.

мерзлота́: ве́чная ~ permafrost. **мёрзнуть** (-ну; мёрз) *impf* (*pf* за~) freeze.

ме́рзость vileness; abomination.

меридиа́н meridian.

мери́ло standard, criterion.

ме́рин gelding.

ме́рить *impf* (*pf* по~, с~) measure; try on. **ме́рка** measure.

ме́рный measured; rhythmical. **меро-прия́тие** measure.

мертве́ть (-е́ю) *impf* (*pf* о~, по~) grow numb; be benumbed. **мертве́ц** (-а́) corpse, dead man. **мёртвый** (мёртв, -а́, мёртво) dead.

мерца́ть *impf* twinkle; flicker.

меси́ть (мешу́, ме́сишь) *impf* (*pf* с~) knead.

ме́сса Mass.

места́ми *adv* here and there. **месте́чко** (*pl* -и, -чек) small town.

мести́ (мету́, -тёшь; мёл, -а́) *impf* sweep; whirl.

ме́стность locality; area. **ме́стный** local; locative. -**ме́стный** *in comb* -berth, -seater. **ме́сто** (*pl* -а́) place; site; seat; room; job. **местожи́тель-ство** (place of) residence. **место-име́ние** pronoun. **местонахожде́-ние** location, whereabouts. **место-рожде́ние** deposit; layer.

месть vengeance, revenge.

ме́сяц month; moon. **ме́сячный** monthly; *sb pl* period.

мета́лл metal. **металли́ческий** metal, metallic. **металлу́ргия** metallurgy.

мета́н methane.

мета́ние throwing, flinging. **мета́ть**[1] (мечу́, ме́чешь) *impf* (*pf* метну́ть) throw, fling; ~ся rush about; toss (and turn).

мета́ть[2] *impf* (*pf* на~, с~) tack.

метафи́зика metaphysics.

мета́фора metaphor.

метёлка panicle.

мете́ль snow-storm.

метео́р meteor. **метеори́т** meteorite. **метеоро́лог** meteorologist. **метеорологи́ческий** meteorological. **метеороло́гия** meteorology. **метеосво́дка** weather report. **метеоста́нция** weather-station.

ме́тить¹ (ме́чу) *impf* (*pf* на~, по~) mark.

ме́тить² (ме́чу) *impf* (*pf* на~) aim; mean.

ме́тка marking, mark.

ме́ткий (-ток, -тка́, -о) well-aimed, accurate.

метла́ (*pl* мётлы, -тел) broom.

метну́ть (-ну́, -нёшь) *pf of* мета́ть¹

ме́тод method. **мето́дика** method(s); methodology. **методи́чный** methodical. **методоло́гия** methodology.

метр metre.

ме́трика birth certificate. **метри́ческ|ий**¹: ~ое свиде́тельство birth certificate.

метри́ческий² metric; metrical.

метро́ *neut indecl*, **метрополите́н** Metro; underground.

мету́ *etc.: see* мести́

мех¹ (*loc* -у́, *pl* -а́) fur.

мех² (*pl* -и́) wine-skin, water-skin; *pl* bellows.

механиза́ция mechanization. **механи́зм** mechanism; gear(ing). **меха́ник** mechanic. **меха́ника** mechanics; trick; knack. **механи́ческий** mechanical; mechanistic.

мехово́й fur.

меч (-а́) sword.

ме́ченый marked.

мече́ть mosque.

мечта́ (day-)dream. **мечта́тельный** dreamy. **мечта́ть** *impf* dream.

ме́чу *etc.: see* ме́тить. **мечу́** *etc.: see* мета́ть

меша́лка mixer.

меша́ть¹ *impf* (*pf* по~) +*dat* hinder; prevent; disturb.

меша́ть² *impf* (*pf* по~, с~) stir; mix; mix up; ~ся (в+*acc*) interfere (in), meddle (with).

мешо́к (-шка́) bag; sack. **мешкови́на** sacking, hessian.

меща́н|ин (*pl* -а́не, -а́н) petty bourgeois; Philistine. **меща́нский** bourgeois, narrow-minded; Philistine. **ме-**

ща́нство petty bourgeoisie; philistinism, narrow-mindedness.

миг moment, instant.

мига́ть *impf*, **мигну́ть** (-ну́, -нёшь) *pf* blink; wink, twinkle.

ми́гом *adv* in a flash.

мигра́ция migration.

мигре́нь migraine.

мизантро́п misanthrope.

мизи́нец (-нца) little finger; little toe.

микро́б microbe.

микроволно́вая печь microwave oven.

микро́н micron.

микрооргани́зм micro-organism.

микроско́п microscope. **микроскопи́ческий** microscopic.

микросхе́ма microchip.

микрофо́н (*gen pl* -н) microphone.

ми́ксер (*cul*) mixer, blender.

миксту́ра medicine, mixture.

ми́ленький pretty; nice; sweet; dear.

милитари́зм militarism.

милиционе́р militiaman, policeman. **мили́ция** militia, police force.

миллиа́рд billion, a thousand million. **миллиме́тр** millimetre. **миллио́н** million. **миллионе́р** millionaire.

милосе́рдие mercy, charity. **милосе́рдный** merciful, charitable.

ми́лостивый gracious, kind. **ми́лостыня** alms. **ми́лость** favour, grace.

ми́лый (мил, -а́, -о) nice; kind; sweet; dear.

ми́ля mile.

ми́мика (facial) expression; mimicry.

ми́мо *adv & prep* +*gen* by, past. **мимолётный** fleeting. **мимохо́дом** *adv* in passing.

ми́на¹ mine; bomb.

ми́на² expression, mien.

минда́ль (-я́) *m* almond(-tree); almonds.

минера́л mineral. **минерало́гия** mineralogy. **минера́льный** mineral. **миниатю́ра** miniature. **миниатю́рный** miniature; tiny.

минима́льный minimum. **ми́нимум** minimum.

министе́рство ministry. **мини́стр** minister.

минова́ть *impf & pf* pass; *impers*+*dat* escape.

миномёт mortar. **миноно́сец** (-сца)

torpedo-boat.

минóр minor (key); melancholy.

минýвш|ий past; ~ее *sb* the past.

мúнус minus.

минýта minute. минýтный minute; momentary.

минýть (-нешь; мúнýл) *pf* pass.

мир¹ (*pl* -ы́) world.

мир² peace.

мирáж mirage.

мирúть *impf* (*pf* по~, при~) reconcile; ~ся be reconciled. мúрный peace; peaceful.

мировоззрéние (world-)outlook; philosophy. мировóй world. мирозда́ние universe.

миролюбúвый peace-loving.

мúска basin, bowl.

мисс *f indecl* Miss.

миссионéр missionary.

мúссия mission.

мúстер Mr.

мúстика mysticism.

мистификáция hoax, leg-pull.

мúтинг mass meeting; rally.

митрополúт metropolitan.

миф myth. мифúческий mythical. мифологúческий mythological. мифолóгия mythology.

мúчман warrant officer.

мишéнь target.

мúшка (Teddy) bear.

младéнец (-нца) baby; infant. млáдший younger; youngest; junior.

млекопитáющее *sb pl* mammals. Млéчный Путь Milky Way.

мне *see* я *pron*

мнéние opinion.

мнúмый imaginary; sham. мнúтельный hypochondriac; mistrustful.

мнить (мню) *impf* think.

мнóгие *sb pl* many (people); ~ое *sb* much, a great deal. мнóго *adv+gen* much; many; на ~ by far.

мнóго- *in comb* many-, poly-, multi-, multiple-. мвогобóрье combined event. ~грáнный polyhedral; many-sided. ~дéтный having many children. ~жéнство polygamy. ~значúтельный significant. ~крáтный repeated; frequentative. ~лéтний lasting, living, many years; of many years' standing; perennial. ~лю́дный crowded. ~национáльный multi-national. ~обещáющий prom-

ising. ~обрáзие diversity. ~слóвный verbose. ~сторóнний multilateral; many-sided, versatile. ~тóчие dots, omission points. ~уважáемый respected; Dear. ~угóльный polygonal. ~цвéтный multi-coloured; multiflorous. ~чúсленный numerous. ~этáжный many-storeyed. ~язы́чный polyglot.

мнóжественный plural. мнóжество great number. мнóжить (-жу) *impf* (*pf* y~) multiply; increase.

мной etc.: *see* я *pron*. мну etc.: *see* мять

мобилизáция mobilization. мобилизовáть *impf* & *pf* mobilize.

мог etc.: *see* мочь

могúла grave. могúльный (of the) grave; sepulchral.

могý etc.: *see* мочь. могýчий mighty. могýщественный powerful. могýщество power, might.

мóда fashion.

моделúровать *impf* & *pf* design. модéль model; pattern. модельéр fashion designer. модéльный model; fashionable.

модернизúровать *impf* & *pf* modernize.

модúстка milliner.

модификáция modification. модифицúровать *impf* & *pf* modify.

мóдный (-ден, -днá, -о) fashionable; fashion.

мóжет *see* мочь

можжевéльник juniper.

мóжно one may, one can; it is permissible; it is possible; как ~+*comp* as ... as possible; как ~ скорéе as soon as possible.

мозáйка mosaic; jigsaw.

мозг (*loc* -ý; *pl* -ú) brain; marrow. мозговóй cerebral.

мозóль corn; callus.

мой (моегó) *m*, моя́ (моéй) *f*, моë (моегó) *neut*, мой (-úх) *pl pron* my; mine; по-мóему in my opinion; in my way.

мóйка washing.

мóкнуть (-ну; мок) *impf* get wet; soak. мокрóта phlegm. мóкрый wet, damp.

мол (*loc* -ý) mole, pier.

молвá rumour, talk.

молéбен (-бна) church service.

молекула molecule. **молекулярный** molecular.

молитва prayer. **молить** (-лю, -лишь) *impf* pray; beg; ~ся (*pf* по~ся) pray.

моллюск mollusc.

молниеносный lightning. **молния** lightning; zip(-fastener).

молодёжь youth, young people. **молодеть** (-ею) *impf* (*pf* по~) get younger, look younger. **молодец** (-дца) fine fellow *or* girl; ~! well done! **молодожёны** (-ов) *pl* newly-weds. **молодой** (молод, -а, -о) young. **молодость** youth. **моложе** *comp of* молодой

молоко milk.

молот hammer. **молотить** (-очу, -отишь) *impf* (*pf* с~) thresh; hammer. **молоток** (-тка) hammer. **молотый** ground. **молоть** (мелю, мелешь) *impf* (*pf* с~) grind, mill.

молочная *sb* dairy. **молочный** milk; dairy; milky.

молча *adv* silently, in silence. **молчаливый** silent, taciturn; tacit. **молчание** silence. **молчать** (-чу) *impf* be *or* keep silent.

моль moth.

мольба entreaty.

мольберт easel.

момент moment; feature. **моментально** *adv* instantly. **моментальный** instantaneous.

монарх monarch. **монархист** monarchist.

монастырь (-я) *m* monastery; convent. **монах** monk. **монахиня** nun.

монгол, ~ка Mongol.

монета coin.

монография monograph.

монолитный monolithic.

монолог monologue.

монополия monopoly.

монотонный monotonous.

монтаж (-а) assembling, mounting; editing. **монтажник** rigger, fitter. **монтёр** fitter, mechanic. **монтировать** *impf* (*pf* с~) mount; install, fit; edit.

монумент monument. **монументальный** monumental.

мораль moral; morals, ethics. **моральный** moral; ethical.

морг morgue.

моргать *impf*, **моргнуть** (-ну, -нёшь)

pf blink; wink.

морда snout, muzzle; (ugly) mug.

море (*pl* -я, -ей) sea.

мореплавание navigation. **мореплаватель** *m* seafarer. **мореходный** nautical.

морж (-а), **моржиха** walrus.

Морзе *indecl* Morse; азбука ~ Morse code.

морить *impf* (*pf* у~) exhaust; ~ голодом starve.

морковка carrot. **морковь** carrots.

мороженое *sb* ice-cream. **мороженый** frozen, chilled. **мороз** frost; *pl* intensely cold weather. **морозилка** freezer compartment; freezer. **морозильник** deep-freeze. **морозить** (-ожу) freeze. **морозный** frosty.

моросить *impf* drizzle.

морской sea; maritime; marine, nautical; ~ая свинка guinea-pig; ~ой флот navy, fleet.

морфий morphine.

морщина wrinkle; crease. **морщить** (-щу) *impf* (*pf* на~, по~, с~) wrinkle; pucker; ~ся knit one's brow; wince; crease, wrinkle.

моряк (-а) sailor, seaman.

москвич (-а), ~ка Muscovite. **московский** (of) Moscow.

мост (моста, *loc* -у; *pl* -ы) bridge. **мостик** bridge. **мостить** (-ощу) *impf* (*pf* вы~) pave. **мостки** (-ов) *pl* planked footway. **мостовая** *sb* roadway; pavement. **мостовой** bridge.

мотать[1] *impf* (*pf* мотнуть, на~) wind, reel.

мотать[2] *impf* (*pf* про~) squander. **мотаться** *impf* dangle; wander; rush about.

мотив motive; reason; tune; motif. **мотивировать** *impf* & *pf* give reasons for, justify. **мотивировка** reason(s); justification.

мотнуть (-ну, -нёшь) *pf of* мотать

мото- *in comb* motor-, engine-. **мотогонки** (-нок) *pl* motor-cycle races. ~**пед** moped. ~**пехота** motorized infantry. ~**роллер** (motor-)scooter. ~**цикл** motor cycle.

моток (-тка) skein, hank.

мотор motor, engine. **моторист** motor-mechanic. **моторный** motor; engine.

мотьı́га hoe, mattock.

мотылёк (-лька́) butterfly, moth.

мох (мха *or* мо́ха, *loc* мху; *pl* мхи, мхов) moss. **мохна́тый** hairy, shaggy.

моча́ urine.

моча́лка loofah.

мочево́й пузьı́рь bladder. **мочи́ть** (-чу́, -чишь) *impf* (*pf* за~, на~) wet, moisten; soak; ~ся (*pf* по~ся) urinate.

мо́чка ear lobe.

мочь (могу́, мо́жешь; мог, -ла́) *impf* (*pf* с~) be able; мо́жет (быть) perhaps.

моше́нник rogue. **моше́нничать** *impf* (*pf* с~) cheat, swindle. **моше́н-нический** rascally.

мо́шка midge. **мошкара́** (swarm of) midges.

мо́щность power; capacity. **мо́щный** (-щен, -щна́, -о) powerful.

мощу́ *etc.*: *see* **мости́ть**

мощь power.

мо́ю *etc.*: *see* **мыть**. **мо́ющий** washing; detergent.

мрак darkness, gloom. **мракобе́с** obscurantist.

мра́мор marble. **мра́морный** marble.

мра́чный dark; gloomy.

мсти́тельный vindictive. **мстить** (мщу) *impf* (*pf* ото~) take vengeance on; +за +*acc* avenge.

мудре́ц (-а́) sage, wise man. **му́д-рость** wisdom. **му́дрый** (-др, -а́, -о) wise, sage.

муж (*pl* -жья́ *or* -и́) husband. **мужа́ть** *impf* grow up; mature; ~ся take courage. **мужеподо́бный** mannish; masculine. **му́жественный** manly, steadfast. **му́жество** courage.

мужи́к (-а́) peasant; fellow. **мужско́й** masculine; male. **мужчи́на** *m* man.

му́за muse.

музе́й museum.

му́зыка music. **музыка́льный** musical. **музыка́нт** musician.

му́ка[1] torment.

мука́[2] flour.

мультиплика́ция, мультфи́льм cartoon film.

му́мия mummy.

мунди́р (full-dress) uniform.

мундшту́к (-а́) mouthpiece; cigar-ette-holder.

муниципа́льный municipal.

мураве́й (-вья́) ant. **мураве́йник** ant-hill.

мурлы́кать (-ы́чу *or* -каю) *impf* purr.

муска́т nutmeg.

му́скул muscle. **му́скульный** muscular.

му́сор refuse; rubbish. **му́сорный я́щик** dustbin.

мусульма́нин (*pl* -ма́не, -ма́н), -а́нка Muslim.

мути́ть (мучу́, му́ти́шь) *impf* (*pf* вз~) make muddy; stir up, upset. **му́тный** (-тен, -тна́, -о) turbid, troubled; dull. **муть** sediment; murk.

му́ха fly.

муче́ние torment, torture. **му́ченик, му́ченица** martyr. **мучи́тельный** agonizing. **му́чить** (-чу) *impf* (*pf* за~, из~) torment; harass; ~ся torment o.s.; suffer agonies.

мучно́й flour, meal; starchy.

мха *etc.*: *see* **мох**

мча́ть (мчу) *impf* rush along, whirl along; ~ся rush.

мщу *etc.*: *see* **мстить**

мы (нас, нам, на́ми, нас) *pron* we; мы с ва́ми you and I.

мы́лить *impf* (*pf* на~) soap; ~ся wash o.s. **мы́ло** (*pl* -а́) soap. **мы́льница** soap-dish. **мы́льный** soap, soapy.

мыс cape, promontory.

мы́сленный mental. **мы́слимый** conceivable. **мысли́тель** *m* thinker. **мы́слить** *impf* think; conceive. **мысль** thought; idea. **мы́слящий** thinking.

мыть (мо́ю) *impf* (*pf* вы́~, по~) wash; ~ся wash (o.s.).

мыча́ть (-чу́) *impf* (*pf* про~) low, moo; bellow; mumble.

мышело́вка mousetrap.

мы́шечный muscular.

мышле́ние thinking, thought.

мы́шца muscle.

мышь (*gen pl* -е́й) mouse.

мэр mayor. **мэ́рия** town hall.

мя́гкий (-гок, -гка́, -о) soft; mild; ~ знак soft sign, the letter **ь**. **мя́гче** *comp of* **мя́гкий, мя́гко**. **мя́коть** fleshy part, flesh; pulp.

мяси́стый fleshy; meaty. **мясни́к** (-а́) butcher. **мясно́й** meat. **мя́со** meat;

flesh. **мясору́бка** mincer.

мя́та mint; peppermint.

мяте́ж (-á) mutiny, revolt. **мя-
те́жник** mutineer, rebel. **мяте́жный**
rebellious; restless.

мя́тный mint, peppermint.

мять (мну, мнёшь) *impf* (*pf* из∼,
раз∼, с∼) knead; crumple;
∼ся become crumpled; crush (easily).

мяу́кать *impf* miaow.

мяч (-á), **мя́чик** ball.

Н

на[1] *prep* I. +*acc* on; on to, to, into; at;
till, until; for; by. II. +*prep* on, upon;
in; at.

на[2] *partl* here; here you are.

наба́вить (-влю) *pf*, **набавля́ть**
impf add (to), increase.

наба́т alarm-bell.

набе́г raid, foray.

набекре́нь *adv* aslant.

на|бели́ть (-е́лишь) *pf*. **на́бело** *adv*
without corrections.

на́бережная *sb* embankment, quay.

набе́ру *etc.: see* набра́ть

набива́ть(ся *impf of* наби́ть(ся.
наби́вка stuffing, padding; (textile)
printing.

набира́ть(ся *impf of* набра́ть(ся

наби́тый packed, stuffed; crowded.
наби́ть (-бью, -бьёшь) *pf* (*impf*
набива́ть) stuff, pack, fill; smash;
print; hammer, drive; ∼ся crowd in.

наблюда́тель *m* observer. **наблю-
да́тельный** observant; observation.
наблюда́ть *impf* observe,watch;
+за+*instr* look after; supervise.
наблюде́ние observation; supervision.

на́божный devout, pious.

набо́к *adv* on one side, crooked.

наболе́вший sore, painful.

набо́р recruiting; collection, set; type-
setting.

набра́сывать(ся *impf of* набро́сать,
набро́сить(ся

набра́ть (-беру́, -берёшь; -а́л, -á, -о)
pf (*impf* набира́ть) gather; enlist;
compose, set up; ∼ но́мер dial a
number; ∼ся assemble, collect; +*gen*
find, acquire, pick up; ∼ся сме́лости

pluck up courage.

набрести́ (-еду́, -дёшь; -ёл, -елá) *pf*
+на+*acc* come across.

наброса́ть *pf* (*impf* набра́сывать)
throw (down); sketch; jot down. **на-
бро́сить** (-о́шу) *pf* (*impf* набра́-
сывать) throw; ∼ся throw o.s.; ∼ся
на attack. **набро́сок** (-ска) sketch,
draft.

набуха́ть *impf*, **набу́хнуть** (-нет;
-у́х) *pf* swell.

набью́ *etc.: see* наби́ть

наважде́ние delusion.

нава́ливать *impf*, **навали́ть** (-лю́,
-лишь) *pf* heap, pile up; load; ∼ся
lean; +на+*acc* fall (up)on.

наведе́ние laying (on); placing.

наведу́ *etc.: see* навести́

наве́к, наве́ки *adv* for ever.

навёл *etc.: see* навести́

наве́рно, наве́рное *adv* probably.
наверняка́ *adv* certainly, for sure.

наверста́ть *pf*, **навёрстывать** *impf*
make up for.

наве́рх *adv* up(wards); upstairs.
наверху́ *adv* above; upstairs.

наве́с awning.

наве́сить (-е́шу) *pf* (*impf* наве́-
шивать) hang (up). **навесно́й** hanging.

навести́ (-еду́, -едёшь; -вёл, -á) *pf*
(*impf* наводи́ть) direct; aim; cover
(with); spread; introduce, bring;
make.

навести́ть (-ещу́) *pf* (*impf* наве-
ща́ть) visit.

наве́шать *pf*, **наве́шивать**[1] *impf*
hang (out); weigh out.

наве́шивать[2] *impf of* наве́сить.

навеща́ть *impf of* навести́ть

на́взничь *adv* backwards, on one's
back.

навзры́д *adv*: пла́кать ∼ sob.

навига́ция navigation.

нависа́ть *impf*, **нави́снуть** (-нет;
-ви́с) *pf* overhang, hang (over);
threaten. **нави́сший** beetling.

навлека́ть *impf*, **навле́чь** (-еку́,
-ечёшь; -ёк, -лá) *pf* bring, draw; incur.

наводи́ть (-ожу́, -о́дишь) *impf of*
навести́; **наводя́щий вопро́с** leading question. **наво́дка** aiming; applying.

наводне́ние flood. **наводни́ть** *pf*,

наводня́ть *impf* flood; inundate.

наво́з dung, manure.

на́волочка pillowcase.

на|вра́ть (-ру́, -рёшь; -а́л, -а́, -о) *pf* tell lies, romance; talk nonsense; +в +*prep* make mistake(s) in.

навреди́ть (-ежу́) *pf* +*dat* harm.

навсегда́ *adv* for ever.

навстре́чу *adv* to meet; идти́ ~ to meet; meet halfway.

навы́ворот *adv* inside out; back to front.

на́вык experience, skill.

навы́нос *adv* to take away.

навы́пуск *adv* worn outside.

навью́чивать *impf*, на|вью́чить (-чу) *pf* load.

навяза́ть (-яжу́, -я́жешь) *pf*, навя́зывать *impf* tie, fasten; thrust, foist; ~ся thrust o.s. навя́зчивый importunate; obsessive.

на|га́дить (-а́жу) *pf*.

нага́н revolver.

нагиба́ть(ся *impf of* нагну́ть(ся

нагишо́м *adv* stark naked.

нагле́ц (-а́) impudent fellow. на́глость impudence. на́глый (нагл, -а́, -о) impudent.

нагля́дный clear, graphic; visual.

нагна́ть (-гоню́, -го́нишь; -а́л, -а́, -о) *pf* (*impf* нагоня́ть) overtake, catch up (with); inspire, arouse.

нагнести́ (-ету́, -етёшь) *pf*, нагнета́ть *impf* compress; supercharge.

нагное́ние suppuration. нагнои́ться *pf* suppurate.

нагну́ть (-ну́, -нёшь) *pf* (*impf* нагиба́ть) bend; ~ся bend, stoop.

нагова́ривать *impf*, наговори́ть *pf* slander; talk a lot (of); record.

наго́й (наг, -а́, -о) naked, bare.

на́голо *adv* naked, bare.

нагоня́ть *impf of* нагна́ть

нагора́ть *impf*, нагоре́ть (-ри́т) *pf* be consumed; impers+dat be scolded.

наго́рный upland, mountain; mountainous.

нагота́ nakedness, nudity.

награ́бить (-блю) *pf* amass by dishonest means.

награ́да reward; decoration; prize. награди́ть (-ажу́) *pf*, награжда́ть *impf* reward; decorate; award prize to.

нагрева́тельный heating. нагре-

ва́ть *impf*, нагре́ть (-е́ю) *pf* warm, heat; ~ся get hot, warm up.

нагроможда́ть *impf*, на|громозди́ть (-зжу́) *pf* heap up, pile up. нагроможде́ние heaping up; conglomeration.

на|груби́ть (-блю́) *pf*.

нагружа́ть *impf*, на|грузи́ть (-ужу́, -у́зишь) *pf* load; ~ся load o.s. нагру́зка loading; load; work; commitments.

нагря́нуть (-ну) *pf* appear unexpectedly.

над, надо *prep*+*instr* over, above; on, at.

надави́ть (-влю́, -вишь) *pf*, нада́вливать *impf* press; squeeze out; crush.

надба́вка addition, increase.

надвига́ть *impf*, надви́нуть (-ну) *pf* move, pull, push; ~ся approach.

на́двое *adv* in two.

надгро́бие epitaph. надгро́бный (on or over a) grave.

надева́ть *impf of* наде́ть

наде́жда hope. наде́жность reliability. наде́жный reliable.

наде́л allotment.

наде́лать *pf* make; cause; do.

надели́ть (-лю́, -лишь) *pf*, наделя́ть *impf* endow, provide.

наде́ть (-е́ну) *pf* (*impf* надева́ть) put on.

наде́яться (-е́юсь) *impf* (*pf* по~) hope; rely.

надзира́тель *m* overseer, supervisor. надзира́ть *impf* +за +*instr* supervise, oversee. надзо́р supervision; surveillance.

надла́мывать(ся *impf of* надломи́ть(ся

надлежа́щий fitting, proper, appropriate. надлежи́т (-жа́ло) impers (+*dat*) it is necessary, required.

надло́м break; crack; breakdown. надломи́ть (-млю́, -мишь) *pf* (*impf* надла́мывать) break; crack; breakdown; ~ся break, crack, breakdown. надло́мленный broken.

надме́нный haughty, arrogant.

на́до[1] (+*dat*) it is necessary, I (*etc.*) must, ought to; I (*etc.*) need. на́добность necessity, need.

на́до[2]: see над.

надоеда́ть *impf*, надое́сть (-е́м, -е́шь,

-éст, -еди́м *pf* +*dat* bore, pester.
надое́дливый boring, tiresome.
надо́лго *adv* for a long time.
надорва́ть (-ву́, -вёшь; -áл, -á, -о) *pf* (*impf* **надрыва́ть**) tear; strain; **~ся** tear; overstrain o.s.
на́дпись inscription.
надре́з cut, incision. **надре́зать** (-éжу) *pf,* **надреза́ть** *impf,* **надре́зывать** *impf* make an incision in.
надруга́тельство outrage. **надруга́ться** *pf* +*над*+*instr* outrage, insult.
надры́в tear; strain; breakdown; outburst. **надрыва́ть(ся** *impf of* **надорва́ть(ся. надры́вный** hysterical; heartrending.
надста́вить (-влю) *pf,* **надставля́ть** *impf* lengthen.
надстра́ивать *impf,* **надстро́ить** (-о́ю) *pf* build on top; extend upwards. **надстро́йка** building upwards; superstructure.
надува́тельство swindle. **надува́ть(ся** *impf of* **надýть(ся. наду́вной** pneumatic, inflatable.
наду́манный far-fetched.
наду́тый swollen; haughty; sulky. **надýть** (-у́ю) *pf* (*impf* **надува́ть**) inflate; swindle; **~ся** swell out; sulk.
на|души́ть(ся (-шу́(сь, -шишь(ся) *pf.*
наеда́ться *impf of* **нае́сться**
наедине́ *adv* privately, alone.
нае́зд flying visit; raid. **нае́здник, -ица** rider. **наезжа́ть** *impf of* **нае́здить, нае́хать;** pay occasional visits.
наём (на́йма) hire; renting; **взять в ~** rent; **сдать в ~** let. **наёмник** hireling; mercenary. **наёмный** hired, rented.
нае́сться (-éмся, -éшься, -éстся, -еди́мся) *pf* (*impf* **наеда́ться**) eat one's fill; stuff o.s.
нае́хать (-éду) *pf* (*impf* **наезжа́ть**) arrive unexpectedly; +*на*+*acc* run into, collide with.
нажа́ть (-жму́, -жмёшь) *pf* (*impf* **нажима́ть**) press; put pressure (on).
наждáк (-á) emery. **наждáчная бумáга** emery paper.
нажи́ва profit, gain.
нажива́ть(ся *impf of* **нажи́ть(ся**
нажи́м pressure; clamp. **нажима́ть** *impf of* **нажа́ть.**
нажи́ть (-иву́, -ивёшь; на́жил, -á, -о)

pf (*impf* **нажива́ть**) acquire; contract, incur; **~ся** (-жи́лся, -áсь) get rich.

нажму́ *etc.: see* **нажа́ть**
наза́втра *adv* the next day.
наза́д *adv* back(wards); (тому́) ~ ago.
назва́ние name; title. **назва́ть** (-зову́, -зовёшь; -áл, -á, -о) *pf* (*impf* **называ́ть**) call, name; **~ся** be called.
назе́мный ground, surface.
на́зло́ *adv* out of spite; to spite.
назнача́ть *impf,* **назна́чить** (-чу) *pf* appoint; fix, set; prescribe. **назначе́ние** appointment; fixing, setting; prescription.
назову́ *etc.: see* **назва́ть**
назо́йливый importunate.
назрева́ть *impf,* **назре́ть** (-éет) *pf* ripen, mature; become imminent.
называ́емый: так ~ so-called. **называ́ть(ся** *impf of* **назва́ть(ся**
наибо́лее *adv* (the) most. **наибо́льший** greatest, biggest.
наи́вный naive.
наивы́сший highest.
наигра́ть *pf,* **наи́грывать** *impf* win; play, pick out.
наизна́нку *adv* inside out.
наизу́сть *adv* by heart.
наилу́чший best.
наименова́ние name; title.
на́искось *adv* obliquely.
найму́ *etc.: see* **наня́ть**
найти́ (-йду́, -йдёшь; нашёл, -шла́, -шло́) *pf* (*impf* **находи́ть**) find; **~сь** be found; be, be situated.
наказа́ние punishment. **наказа́ть** (-ажу́, -а́жешь) *pf,* **наказывать** *impf* punish.
нака́л incandescence. **нака́ливать** *impf,* **накали́ть** *pf,* **нака́лять** *impf* heat; make red-hot; strain, make tense; **~ся** glow, become incandescent; become strained.
нака́ливать(ся *impf of* **наколо́ть(ся**
накану́не *adv* the day before.
нака́пливать(ся *impf of* **накопи́ть(ся**
накача́ть *pf,* **нака́чивать** *impf* pump (up).
наки́дка cloak, cape; extra charge. **наки́нуть** (-ну) *pf,* **наки́дывать** *impf* throw; throw on; **~ся** throw

o.s.; ~ся на attack.

на́кипь scum; scale.

накладна́я *sb* invoice. **накладн|о́й** laid on; false; ~ые расхо́ды overheads. **накла́дывать** *impf of* наложи́ть

на|клевета́ть (-ещу́, -е́щешь) *pf*.

накле́ивать *impf*, **накле́ить** *pf* stick on. **накле́йка** sticking (on, up); label.

накло́н slope, incline. **наклоне́ние** inclination; mood. **наклони́ть** (-ню́, -нишь) *pf*, **наклоня́ть** *impf* incline, bend; ~ся stoop, bend. **накло́нный** inclined, sloping.

нако́лка pinning; (*pinned-on*) ornament for hair; tattoo. **наколо́ть**[1] (-лю́, -лешь) *pf* (*impf* нака́лывать) prick; pin; ~ся prick o.s.

наколо́ть[2] (-лю́, -лешь) *pf* (*impf* нака́лывать) chop.

наконе́ц *adv* at last. **наконе́чник** tip, point.

на|копи́ть (-плю́, -пишь) *pf*, **накопля́ть** *impf* (*impf also* нака́пливать) accumulate; ~ся accumulate. **накопле́ние** accumulation.

на|корми́ть (-млю́, -мишь) *pf*. **на|краси́ть** (-а́шу) *pf* paint; make up. **на|кра́ситься** (-а́шусь) *pf*.

на|крахма́лить *pf*.

на|крени́ть *pf*, **накрени́ться** (-нится) *pf*, **накреня́ться** *impf* tilt; list.

накрича́ть (-чу́) *pf* (+на+*acc*) shout (at).

накро́ю *etc.: see* накры́ть

накрыва́ть *impf*, **накры́ть** (-ро́ю) *pf* cover; catch; ~ (на) стол lay the table; ~ся cover o.s.

накури́ть (-рю́, -ришь) *pf* fill with smoke.

налага́ть *impf of* наложи́ть

нала́дить (-а́жу) *pf*, **нала́живать** *impf* regulate, adjust; repair; organize; ~ся come right; get going.

на|лга́ть (-лгу́, -лжёшь; -а́л, -а́, -о) *pf*.

нале́во *adv* to the left.

налёг *etc.: see* нале́чь. **налега́ть** *impf of* нале́чь

налегке́ *adv* lightly dressed; without luggage.

налёт raid; flight; thin coating. **налета́ть**[1] *pf* have flown. **налета́ть**[2] *impf*, **налете́ть** (-лечу́) *pf*

swoop down; come flying; spring up.

налега́ть (-ля́гу, -ля́жешь; -лёг, -ла́) *pf* (*impf* налега́ть) lean, apply one's weight, lie; apply o.s.

налжёшь *etc.: see* налга́ть

налива́ть(ся *impf of* нали́ть(ся.

нали́вка fruit liqueur.

нали́ть (-лью, -льёшь; на́ли́л, -а́, -о) *pf* (*impf* налива́ть) pour (out), fill; ~ся (-и́лся, -а́сь, -и́лось) pour in; ripen.

налицо́ *adv* present; available.

нали́чие presence. **нали́чн|ый** on hand; cash; ~ые (де́ньги) ready money.

нало́г tax. **налогоплате́льщик** taxpayer. **наложенн|ый**: ~ым платежо́м C.O.D. **наложи́ть** (-жу́, -жишь) *pf* (*impf* накла́дывать, налага́ть) lay (in, on), put (in, on); apply; impose.

налью́ *etc.: see* нали́ть

наля́гу *etc.: see* нале́чь

нам *etc.: see* мы

на|ма́зать (-а́жу) *pf*, **нама́зывать** *impf* oil, grease; smear, spread.

нама́тывать *impf of* намота́ть.

нама́чивать *impf of* намочи́ть

намёк hint. **намека́ть** *impf*, **намекну́ть** (-ну́, -нёшь) *pf* hint.

намерева́ться *impf* +*inf* intend to. **наме́рен** *predic*: я ~ (а)+*inf* I intend to. **наме́рение** intention. **наме́ренный** intentional.

на|мета́ть *pf*. **на|ме́тить**[1] (-е́чу) *pf*.

наме́тить[2] (-е́чу) *pf* (*impf* намеча́ть) plan; outline; nominate; ~ся be outlined, take shape.

намно́го *adv* much, far.

намока́ть *impf*, **намо́кнуть** (-ну) *pf* get wet.

намо́рдник muzzle.

на|мо́рщить(ся (-щу(сь) *pf*.

на|мота́ть *pf* (*impf also* нама́тывать) wind, reel.

на|мочи́ть (-очу́, -о́чишь) *pf* (*impf also* нама́чивать) wet; soak; splash, spill.

намы́ливать *impf*, **на|мы́лить** *pf* soap.

нанести́ (-су́, -сёшь; -ёс, -ла́) *pf* (*impf* наноси́ть) carry, bring; draw, plot; inflict.

на|низа́ть (-ижу́, -и́жешь) *pf*, **нани́зывать** *impf* string, thread.

нанима́тель *m* tenant; employer.
нанима́ть(ся *impf of* наня́ть(ся

наноси́ть (-ошу́, -о́сишь) *impf of* нанести́

наня́ть (найму́, -мёшь; на́нял, -á, -о) *pf* (*impf* нанима́ть) hire; rent; ~ся get a job.

наоборо́т *adv* on the contrary; back to front; the other, the wrong, way (round); vice versa.

наотмашь *adv* violently.

наотре́з *adv* flatly, point-blank.

напада́ть *impf of* напа́сть. напада́ющий *sb* forward. нападе́ние attack; forwards.

напа́рник co-driver, (work)mate.

напа́сть (-аду́, -адёшь; -а́л) *pf* (*impf* напада́ть) на+*acc* attack; descend on; seize; come upon. напа́сть misfortune.

напе́в tune. напева́ть *impf of* напе́ть

наперебо́й *adv* interrupting, vying with, one another.

наперёд *adv* in advance.

наперекор *adv*+*dat* in defiance of, counter to.

напёрсток (-тка) thimble.

напе́ть (-пою́, -поёшь) *pf* (*impf* напева́ть) sing; hum, croon.

на|печа́тать(ся *pf*. напива́ться *impf of* напи́ться

на|писа́ть (-ишу́, -и́шешь) *pf*.

напи́льник file.

напи́ток (-тка) drink. напи́ться (-пью́сь, -пьёшься; -и́лся, -ила́сь, -а́сь, -и́ло́сь) *pf* (*impf* напива́ться) quench one's thirst, drink; get drunk.

напиха́ть *pf*, напи́хивать *impf* cram, stuff.

на|плева́ть (-люю́, -люёшь) *pf*; ~! to hell with it! who cares?

наплы́в influx; accumulation; canker. наплюю́ *etc.*: *see* наплева́ть

напова́л outright.

наподо́бие *prep*+*gen* like, not unlike. на|по́ить (-о́ю, -о́ишь) *pf*.

напока́з *adv* for show.

наполни́тель *m* filler. напо́лнить(ся *pf*, наполня́ть(ся *impf* fill.

наполови́ну *adv* half.

напомина́ние reminder. напомина́ть *impf*, напо́мнить *pf* (+*dat*) remind.

напо́р pressure. напо́ристый energetic, pushing.

напосле́док *adv* in the end; after all.

напою́ *etc.*: *see* напе́ть, напои́ть

напр. *abbr* (*of* наприме́р) e.g., for example.

напра́вить (-влю) *pf*, направля́ть *impf* direct; send; sharpen; ~ся make (for), go (towards). направле́ние direction; trend; warrant; order. напра́вленный purposeful.

напра́во *adv* to the right.

напра́сно *adv* in vain, for nothing; unjustly, mistakenly.

напра́шиваться *impf of* напроси́ться

наприме́р for example.

на|прока́зничать *pf*.

напрока́т *adv* for, on, hire.

напролёт *adv* through, without a break.

напроло́м *adv* straight, regardless of obstacles.

напроси́ться (-ошу́сь, -о́сишься) *pf* (*impf* напра́шиваться) thrust o.s.; suggest itself; ~ на ask for, invite.

напро́тив *adv* opposite; on the contrary. напро́тив *prep*+*gen* opposite.

напряга́ть(ся *impf of* напря́чь(ся. напряже́ние tension; exertion; voltage. напряжённый tense; intense; intensive.

напрями́к *adv* straight (out).

напря́чь (-ягу́, -яжёшь; -я́г, -ла́) *pf* (*impf* напряга́ть) strain; ~ся strain o.s.

на|пуга́ть(ся *pf*. на|пу́дриться *pf*.

напуска́ть *impf*, напусти́ть (-ущу́, -у́стишь) *pf* let in; let loose; ~ся +на+*acc* fly at, go for.

напу́тать *pf* +в+*prep* make a mess of.

на|пыли́ть *pf*.

напью́сь *etc.*: *see* напи́ться

наравне́ *adv* level; equally.

нараспа́шку *adv* unbuttoned.

нараста́ние growth, accumulation. нараста́ть *impf*, нарасти́ (-тёт; -рóс, -лá) *pf* grow; increase.

нарасхва́т *adv* very quickly, like hot cakes.

нарва́ть[1] (-ру́, -рвёшь; -а́л, -á, -о) *pf* (*impf* нарыва́ть) pick; tear up.

нарва́ть[2] (-вёт; -а́л, -á, -о) *pf* (*impf* нарыва́ть) gather.

нарва́ться (-ву́сь, -вёшься; -а́лся, -ала́сь, -а́лось) *pf* (*impf* нарыва́ться) +на+*acc* run into, run up against.

наре́зать (-е́жу) *pf*, **нареза́ть** *impf* cut (up), slice, carve; thread, rifle.

наре́чие[1] dialect.

наре́чие[2] adverb.

на|рисова́ть *pf*.

нарко́з narcosis. **наркома́н, -ма́нка** drug addict. **наркома́ния** drug addiction. **нарко́тик** narcotic.

наро́д people. **наро́дность** nationality; national character. **наро́дный** national; folk; popular; people's.

наро́с *etc.*: *see* **нарасти́**

наро́чно *adv* on purpose, deliberately. **на́рочный** *sb* courier.

нару́жность exterior. **нару́жный** external, outward. **нару́жу** *adv* outside.

нару́чник handcuff. **нару́чный** wrist.

наруше́ние breach; infringement. **наруши́тель** *m* transgressor. **нару́шить** (-шу) *pf*, **наруша́ть** *impf* break; disturb, infringe, violate.

нарци́сс narcissus; daffodil.

на́ры (нар) *pl* plank-bed.

нары́в abscess, boil. **нарыва́ть(ся** *impf of* **нарва́ть(ся**

наря́д[1] order, warrant.

наря́д[2] attire; dress. **наряди́ть** (-яжу́) *pf* (*impf* **наряжа́ть**) dress (up); ~ся dress up. **наря́дный** well-dressed.

наряду́ *adv* alike, equally; side by side.

наряжа́ть(ся *impf of* **наряди́ть(ся**. **нас** *see* **мы**

насади́ть (-ажу́, -а́дишь) *pf*, **насажда́ть** *impf* (*impf also* **наса́живать**) plant; propagate; implant. **наса́дка** setting, fixing. **насажде́ние** planting; plantation; propagation. **наса́живать** *impf of* **насади́ть**

насеко́мое *sb* insect.

населе́ние population. **населённость** density of population. **населённый** populated; ~ пункт settlement; built-up area. **насели́ть** *pf*, **населя́ть** *impf* settle, people.

наси́лие violence, force. **наси́ловать** *impf* (*pf* из~) coerce; rape. **наси́лу** *adv* with difficulty. **наси́льник** aggressor; rapist; violator. **наси́льно** *adv* by force. **наси́льственный** violent, forcible.

наска́кивать *impf of* **наскочи́ть**

насквозь *adv* through, throughout.

наско́лько *adv* how much?, how far?; as far as.

на́скоро *adv* hastily.

наскочи́ть (-очу́, -о́чишь) *pf* (*impf* **наска́кивать**) +на +*acc* run into, collide with; fly at.

наску́чить (-чу) *pf* bore.

наслади́ться (-ажу́сь) *pf*, **наслажда́ться** *impf* (+*instr*) enjoy, take pleasure. **наслажде́ние** pleasure, enjoyment.

насле́дие legacy; heritage. **насле́дить** (-ежу́) *pf*. **насле́дник** heir; successor. **насле́дница** heiress. **насле́дный** next in succession. **насле́довать** *impf & pf* (*pf also* у~) inherit, succeed to. **насле́дственность** heredity. **насле́дственный** hereditary, inherited. **насле́дство** inheritance; heritage.

на́смерть *adv* to (the) death.

на|смеши́ть (-шу́) *pf* **насме́шка** mockery; gibe. **насме́шливый** mocking.

на́сморк runny nose; cold.

на|сори́ть *pf*.

насо́с pump.

на́спех *adv* hastily.

на|спле́тничать *pf*. **настава́ть** (-таёт) *impf of* **наста́ть**

наставле́ние exhortation; directions, manual.

наста́вник tutor, mentor.

настава́ть[1] *impf of* **настоя́ть**[1]. **наста́ивать**[2](ся *impf of* **настоя́ть**[2](ся

наста́ть (-а́нет) *pf* (*impf* **настава́ть**) come, begin, set in.

на́стежь *adv* wide (open).

настелю́ *etc.*: *see* **настла́ть**

настига́ть *impf*, **насти́гнуть, насти́чь** (-и́гну; -и́г) *pf* catch up with, overtake.

насти́л flooring, planking. **настила́ть** *impf of* **настла́ть**

насти́чь *see* **настига́ть**

настла́ть (-телю́, -те́лешь) *pf* (*impf* **настила́ть**) lay, spread.

насто́йка liqueur, cordial.

насто́йчивый persistent; urgent.

насто́лько *adv* so, so much.

насто́льный table, desk; reference.

настора́живать *impf*, **насторожи́ть** (-жу́) *pf* set; prick up; ~ся prick up one's ears. **насторо́жен-**

ный (-ен, -енна) guarded; alert.
настоя́тельный insistent; urgent.
настоя́ть[1] (-ою́) pf (impf наста́ивать[1]) insist.
настоя́ть[2] (-ою́) pf (impf наста́ивать[2]) brew; ~ся draw, stand.
настоя́щее sb the present. наcтоя́щий (the) present, this; real, genuine.
настра́ивать(ся impf of настро́ить(ся
настри́чь (-игу́, -ижёшь; -и́г) pf shear, clip.
настрое́ние mood. настро́ить (-о́ю) pf (impf настра́ивать) tune (in); dispose; ~ся dispose o.s. настро́йка tuning. настро́йщик tuner.
на|стро́чить (-чу́) pf.
наступа́тельный offensive. наступа́ть[1] impf of наступи́ть[1]
наступа́ть[2] impf of наступи́ть[2]. наступа́ющий[1] coming.
наступа́ющий[2] sb attacker.
наступи́ть[1] (-плю́, -пишь) pf (impf наступа́ть[1]) tread; attack; advance.
наступи́ть[2] (-у́пит) pf (impf наступа́ть[2]) come, set in. наступле́ние[1] coming.
наступле́ние[2] offensive, attack.
насу́питься (-плю́сь) pf, насу́пливаться impf frown.
на́сухо adv dry. насуши́ть (-шу́, -шишь) pf dry.
насу́щный urgent, vital; хлеб ~ daily bread.
насчёт prep+gen about, concerning; as regards. насчита́ть pf, насчи́тывать impf count; hold; ~ся +gen number.
насы́пать (-плю) pf, насыпа́ть impf pour in, on; fill; spread; heap up. на́сыпь embankment.
насы́тить (-ы́щу) pf, насыща́ть impf satiate; saturate; ~ся be full; be saturated.
ната́лкивать(ся impf of натолкну́ть(ся. **ната́пливать** impf of натопи́ть
натаска́ть pf, ната́скивать impf train; coach, cram; bring in, lay in.
натвори́ть pf do, get up to.
натере́ть (-тру́, -трёшь; -тёр) pf (impf натира́ть) rub on, in; polish; chafe; grate; ~ся rub o.s.
на́тиск onslaught.

наткну́ться (-ну́сь, -нёшься) pf (impf натыка́ться) +на+acc run into; strike, stumble on.
натолкну́ть (-ну́, -нёшь) pf (impf ната́лкивать) push; lead; ~ся run against, across.
натопи́ть (-плю́, -пишь) pf (impf ната́пливать) heat (up); stoke up; melt.
на|точи́ть (-чу́, -чишь) pf.
натоща́к adv on an empty stomach.
натрави́ть (-влю́, -вишь) pf, натра́вливать impf, натравля́ть impf set (on); stir up.
на|трениро́ва́ть(ся pf.
на́трий sodium.
нату́ра nature. натура́льный natural; genuine. нату́рщик, -щица artist's model.
натыка́ть(ся impf of наткну́ть(ся
натюрмо́рт still life.
натя́гивать impf, натяну́ть (-ну́, -нешь) pf stretch; draw; pull (on); ~ся stretch. натя́нутость tension. натя́нутый tight; strained.
науга́д adv at random.
нау́ка science; learning.
нау́тро adv (the) next morning.
на|учи́ть (-чу́, -чишь) pf.
нау́чн|ый scientific; ~ая фанта́стика science fiction.
нау́шник ear-flap; ear-phone; informer.
нафтали́н naphthalene.
наха́л, -ха́лка impudent creature. **наха́льный** impudent. наха́льство impudence.
нахвата́ть pf, нахва́тывать impf pick up, get hold of; ~ся +gen pick up.
нахле́бник hanger-on.
нахлы́нуть (-нет) pf well up; surge; gush.
на|хму́рить(ся pf.
находи́ть(ся (-ожу́(сь, -о́дишь(ся) impf of найти́(сь. нахо́дка find. нахо́дчивый resourceful, quick-witted.
наце́ливать impf, на|це́лить pf aim; ~ся (take) aim.
наце́нка extra, addition; additional charge.
наци́зм Nazism. национализа́ция nationalization. национализи́ровать impf & pf nationalize.

национали́зм nationalism. националисти́ческий nationalist(ic). национа́льность nationality; ethnic group. национа́льный national. наци́ст, -и́стка Nazi. на́ция nation. нацме́н, -ме́нка *abbr* member of national minority.

нача́ло beginning; origin; principle, basis. нача́льник head, chief; boss. нача́льный initial; primary. нача́льство the authorities; command. нача́ть (-чну́, -чнёшь; на́чал, -а́, -о) *pf* (*impf* начина́ть) begin; ~ся begin.

начерта́ть *pf* trace, inscribe. на|черти́ть (-рчу́, -ртишь) *pf*.

начина́ние undertaking. начина́ть(ся *impf* of нача́ть(ся. начина́ющий *sb* beginner.

начини́ть *pf*, начина́ть *impf* stuff, fill. начи́нка stuffing, filling.

начи́стить (-и́щу) *pf* (*impf* начища́ть) clean. на́чисто *adv* clean; flatly, decidedly; openly, frankly. начистоту́ *adv* openly, frankly.

начи́танность learning; wide reading. начи́танный well-read.

начища́ть *impf of* начи́стить

наш (-его) *m*, на́ша (-ей) *f*, на́ше (-его) *neut*, на́ши (-их) *pl*, *pron* our, ours.

нашаты́рный спирт ammonia. нашаты́рь (-я́) *m* sal-ammoniac; ammonia.

нашёл *etc.*: *see* найти́

наше́ствие invasion.

нашива́ть *impf*, наши́ть (-шью, -шьёшь) *pf* sew on. наши́вка stripe, chevron; tab.

нашлёпать *impf* slap.

нашуме́ть (-млю) *pf* make a din; cause a sensation.

нашью́ *etc.*: *see* наши́ть

нащу́пать *pf*, нащу́пывать *impf* grope for.

на|электризова́ть *pf*.

наяву́ *adv* awake; in reality.

не *partl* not.

не- *pref* un-, in-, non-, mis-, dis-; -less; not. неаккура́тный careless; untidy; unpunctual. небезразли́чный not indifferent. небезызве́стный not unknown; notorious; well-known.

небеса́ *etc.*: *see* не́бо². небе́сный heavenly; celestial.

не-. неблагода́рный ungrateful; thankless. неблагонадёжный unreliable. неблагополу́чный unsuccessful, bad, unfavourable. неблагоприя́тный unfavourable. неблагоразу́мный imprudent. неблагоро́дный ignoble, base.

не́бо¹ palate.

не́бо² (*pl* -беса́, -бе́с) sky; heaven.

не-. небога́тый of modest means, modest. небольшо́й small, not great; с небольши́м a little over.

небосво́д firmament. небоскло́н horizon. небоскрёб skyscraper.

небо́сь *adv* I dare say; probably.

не-. небре́жный careless. небыва́лый unprecedented; fantastic. небыли́ца fable, cock-and-bull story. небытие́ non-existence. небью́щийся unbreakable. нева́жно *adv* not too well, indifferently. нева́жный unimportant; indifferent. невдалеке́ *adv* not far away. неве́дение ignorance. неве́домый unknown; mysterious. неве́жа *m* & *f* boor, lout. неве́жда *m* & *f* ignoramus. неве́жественный ignorant. неве́жество ignorance. неве́жливый rude. невели́кий (-и́к, -а́, -и́ко́) small. неве́рие unbelief, atheism; scepticism. неве́рный (-рен, -рна́, -о) incorrect, wrong; inaccurate, unsteady; unfaithful. невероя́тный improbable; incredible. неве́рующий unbelieving; *sb* atheist. неве́сомый joyless, sad. невесо́мый weightless; imponderable.

неве́ста fiancée; bride. неве́стка daughter-in-law; brother's wife, sister-in-law.

не-. невзго́да adversity. невзира́я на *prep+acc* regardless of. невзнача́й *adv* by chance. невзра́чный unattractive, plain. неви́данный unprecedented, unheard-of. неви́димый invisible. неви́нность innocence. неви́нный, невино́вный innocent. невменя́емый irresponsible. невмеша́тельство non-intervention; non-interference. невмоготу́, невмо́чь *advs* unbearable, too much (for). невнима́тельный inattentive, thoughtless.

не́вод seine(-net).

не-. невозврати́мый, невозвра́тный irrevocable, irrecoverable. невозмо́жный impossible. невозмути́мый imperturbable.

нево́льник, -ница slave. нево́льный involuntary; unintentional; forced. нево́ля captivity; necessity.

не-. невообрази́мый unimaginable, inconceivable. невооружённый unarmed; ~ным гла́зом with the naked eye. невоспи́танный ill-bred, bad-mannered. невоспламеня́ющийся non-flammable. невоспри́мчивый unreceptive; immune.

невралги́я neuralgia.

невреди́мый safe, unharmed.

невро́з neurosis. неврологи́ческий neurological. невроти́ческий neurotic.

не-. невы́годный disadvantageous; unprofitable. невы́держанный lacking self-control; unmatured. невыноси́мый unbearable. невыполни́мый impracticable. невысо́кий (-со́к, -а́, -о́ко) low; short.

не́га luxury; bliss.

негати́вный negative.

не́где adv (there is) nowhere.

не-. неги́бкий (-бок, -бка́, -о) inflexible, stiff. негла́сный secret. неглубо́кий (-о́к, -а́, -о) shallow. неглу́пый (-у́п, -а́, -о) sensible, quite intelligent. него́дный (-ден, -дна́, -о) unfit, unsuitable; worthless. негодова́ние indignation. негодова́ть impf be indignant. негодя́й scoundrel. негостеприи́мный inhospitable.

негр Negro, black man.

негра́мотность illiteracy. негра́мотный illiterate.

негритя́нка Negress, black woman. негритя́нский Negro.

не-. негро́мкий (-мок, -мка́, -о) quiet. неда́вний recent. неда́вно adv recently. недалёкий (-ёк, -а́, -ёко) near; short; not bright, dull-witted. недалеко́ adv not far, near. неда́ром adv not for nothing, not without reason. недви́жимость real estate. недви́жимый immovable. недвусмы́сленный unequivocal. недействи́тельный ineffective; invalid. недели́мый indivisible.

неде́льный of a week, week's. неде́ля week.

не-. недёшево adv dear(ly).

недоброжела́тель m ill-wisher. недоброжела́тельность hostility. недоброка́чественный of poor quality. недобросо́вестный unscrupulous; careless. недо́брый (-бр, -бра́, -о) unkind; bad. недове́рие distrust. недове́рчивый distrustful недово́льный dissatisfied. недово́льство dissatisfaction. недоеда́ние malnutrition. недоеда́ть impf be undernourished.

не-. недо́лгий (-лог, -лга́, -о) short, brief. недо́лго adv not long. недолгове́чный short-lived. недомога́ние indisposition. недомога́ть impf be unwell. недомы́слие thoughtlessness. недоно́шенный premature. недооце́нивать impf, недооцени́ть (-ню, -нишь) pf underestimate; underrate. недооце́нка underestimation. недопусти́мый inadmissible, intolerable. недоразуме́ние misunderstanding. недорого́й (-до́рог, -а́, -о) inexpensive. недосмотре́ть (-рю́, -ришь) pf overlook. недоспа́ть (-плю́; -а́л, -а́, -о) pf (impf недосыпа́ть) not have enough sleep.

недостава́ть (-таёт) impf, недоста́ть (-а́нет) pf impers be missing, be lacking. недоста́ток (-тка) shortage, deficiency. недоста́точный insufficient, inadequate. недоста́ча lack, shortage.

не-. недостижи́мый unattainable. недосто́йный unworthy, недосту́пный inaccessible. недосчита́ться pf, недосчи́тываться impf miss, find missing, be short (of). недосыпа́ть impf of недоспа́ть. недосяга́емый unattainable.

недоумева́ть impf be at a loss, be bewildered. недоуме́ние bewilderment.

не-. недоу́чка m & f half-educated person. недочёт deficit; defect. не́дра (недр) pl depths, heart, bowels. не-. неду́г enemy. недружелю́бный unfriendly.

неду́г illness, disease.

недурно́й not bad; not bad-looking.

не-. неесте́ственный unnatural. нежда́нный unexpected. нежела́ние unwillingness. нежела́тельный undesirable.

не́жели than.
женáтый unmarried.
не́женка *m & f* mollycoddle.
нежило́й uninhabited; uninhabitable.
не́житься *impf* luxuriate, bask. **не́жность** tenderness; *pl* endearments. **не́жный** tender; affectionate.
не-. **незабве́нный** unforgettable. **незабу́дка** forget-me-not. **незабывáемый** unforgettable. **независимость** independence. **независимый** independent. **незадо́лго** *adv* not long. **незаконноро́ждённый** illegitimate. **незако́нный** illegal, illicit; illegitimate. **зако́нченный** unfinished. **незамени́мый** irreplaceable. **незамерзáющий** ice-free; anti-freeze. **незаме́тный** imperceptible. **незаму́жняя** unmarried. **незапáмятный** immemorial. **незаслу́женный** unmerited. **незауря́дный** uncommon, outstanding.
не́зачем *adv* there is no need.
не-. **незащищённый** unprotected. **незвáный** uninvited. **нездоро́виться** *impf, impers* +dat: мне нездоро́вится I don't feel well. **нездоро́вый** unhealthy. **нездоро́вье** ill health. **незнако́мец** (-мца), **незнако́мка** stranger. **незнако́мый** unknown, unfamiliar. **незнáние** ignorance. **незначи́тельный** insignificant. **незре́лый** unripe, immature. **незри́мый** invisible. **незыблемый** unshakable, firm. **неизбе́жность** inevitability. **неизбе́жный** inevitable. **неизве́данный** unknown.
неизве́стность uncertainty; ignorance; obscurity. **неизве́стный** unknown; *sb* stranger.
не-. **неизлечи́мый** incurable. **неизме́нный** unchanged, unchanging; devoted. **неизменя́емый** unalterable. **неизмери́мый** immeasurable, immense. **неизу́ченный** unstudied; unexplored. **неиму́щий** poor. **неинтере́сный** uninteresting. **нейскренний** insincere. **неиску́шённый** inexperienced, unsophisticated. **неисполни́мый** impracticable. **неисправи́мый** incorrigible; irreparable. **неисправный** out of order, defect-

ive; careless. **неиссле́дованный** unexplored. **неиссякáемый** inexhaustible. **не́йстовство** fury, frenzy; atrocity. **не́йстовый** furious, frenzied, uncontrolled. **неистощи́мый**, **неисчерпáемый** inexhaustible. **неисчисли́мый** innumerable.
нейло́н, **нейло́новый** nylon.
нейро́н neuron.
нейрализáция neutralization. **нейтрализовáть** *impf & pf* neutralize. **нейтралите́т** neutrality. **нейтрáльный** neutral. **нейтро́н** neutron.
неквалифици́рованный unskilled.
не́кий *pron* a certain, some.
не́когда[1] *adv* once, formerly.
не́когда[2] *adv* there is no time; мне ~ I have no time.
не́кого (**не́кому**, **не́кем**, **не́ о ком**) *pron* there is nobody.
некомпете́нтный not competent, unqualified.
не́котор|ый *pron* some; ~ые *sb pl* some (people).
некраси́вый plain, ugly; not nice. **некроло́г** obituary.
некстáти *adv* at the wrong time, out of place.
не́кто *pron* somebody; a certain.
не́куда *adv* there is nowhere.
не-. **некульту́рный** uncivilized, uncultured. **неку́ряший** *sb* non-smoker. **нелáдный** wrong. **нелегáльный** illegal. **нелёгкий** not easy; heavy. **неле́пость** absurdity, nonsense. **неле́пый** absurd. **нело́вкий** awkward. **нело́вкость** awkwardness.
нельзя́ *adv* it is impossible; it is not allowed.
не-. **нелюби́мый** unloved. **нелюди́мый** unsociable. **немáло** *adv* quite a lot (of). **немáлый** considerable. **неме́дленно** *adv* immediately. **неме́дленный** immediate.
неме́ть (-е́ю) *impf* (*pf* о~) become dumb. **не́мец** (-мца) German. **не́мецкий** German.
неминýемый inevitable.
не́мка German woman.
немно́гие *sb pl* the few. **немно́го** *adv* a little; some; a few. **немно́жко** *adv* a little.
немо́й (**нем**, -á, -о) dumb, mute, silent. **немотá** dumbness.

не́мощный feeble.

немы́слимый unthinkable.

ненави́деть (-и́жу) *impf* hate. **ненави́стный** hated; hateful. **не́нависть** hatred.

не-. ненагля́дный beloved. **ненадёжный** unreliable. **ненадо́лго** *adv* for a short time. **нена́стье** bad weather. **ненасы́тный** insatiable. **ненорма́льный** abnormal. **нену́жный** unnecessary, unneeded. **необду́манный** thoughtless, hasty. **необеспе́ченный** without means, unprovided for. **необита́емый** uninhabited. **необозри́мый** boundless, immense. **необосно́ванный** unfounded, groundless. **необрабо́танный** uncultivated; crude; unpolished. **необразо́ванный** uneducated.

необходи́мость necessity. **необходи́мый** necessary.

не-. необъясни́мый inexplicable. **необъя́тный** immense. **необыкнове́нный** unusual. **необыча́йный** extraordinary. **необы́чный** unusual. **необяза́тельный** optional. **неограни́ченный** unlimited. **неоднокра́тный** repeated. **неодобри́тельный** disapproving. **неодушевлённый** inanimate.

неожи́данность unexpectedness. **неожи́данный** unexpected, sudden.

неоклассици́зм neoclassicism.

не-. неоко́нченный unfinished. **неопла́ченный** unpaid. **неопра́вданный** unjustified. **неопределённый** indefinite; infinitive; vague. **неопроверж́имый** irrefutable. **неопублико́ванный** unpublished. **нео́пытный** inexperienced. **неоргани́ческий** inorganic. **неоспори́мый** incontestable. **неосторо́жный** careless. **неосуществи́мый** impracticable. **неотврати́мый** inevitable.

не́откуда *adv* there is nowhere.

не-. неотло́жный urgent. **неотрази́мый** irresistible. **неотсту́пный** persistent. **неотъе́млемый** inalienable. **неофициа́льный** unofficial. **неохо́та** reluctance. **неохо́тно** *adv* reluctantly. **неоцени́мый** inestimable, invaluable. **непарти́йный** nonparty; unbefitting a member of the (Communist) Party. **непереводи́мый** untranslatable. **непереход-**

-ный intransitive. **неплатёжеспосо́бный** insolvent.

не-. неплохо́ *adv* not badly, quite well. **неплохо́й** not bad, quite good. **непобеди́мый** invincible. **неповинове́ние** insubordination. **неповоро́тливый** clumsy. **неповтори́мый** inimitable, unique. **непого́да** bad weather. **непогреши́мый** infallible. **неподалёку** *adv* not far (away). **неподви́жный** motionless, immovable; fixed. **неподде́льный** genuine; sincere. **неподку́пный** incorruptible. **неподража́емый** inimitable. **неподходя́щий** unsuitable, inappropriate. **непоколеби́мый** unshakable, steadfast. **непоко́рный** recalcitrant, unruly.

не-. непола́дки (-док) *pl* defects. **неполноце́нность; ко́мплекс неполноце́нности** inferiority complex. **неполноце́нный** defective; inadequate. **непо́лный** incomplete; not (a) full. **непоме́рный** excessive. **непонима́ние** incomprehension, lack of understanding. **непоня́тный** incomprehensible. **непоправи́мый** irreparable. **непоря́док** (-дка) disorder. **непоря́дочный** dishonourable. **непосе́да** *m & f* fidget. **непоси́льный** beyond one's strength. **непосле́довательный** inconsistent. **непослуша́ние** disobedience. **непослу́шный** disobedient. **непосре́дственный** immediate; spontaneous. **непостижи́мый** incomprehensible. **непостоя́нный** inconstant, changeable. **непохо́жий** unlike; different.

не-. непра́вда untruth. **неправдоподо́бный** improbable. **непра́вильно** *adv* wrong. **непра́вильный** irregular; wrong. **непра́вый** wrong. **непракти́чный** unpractical. **непревзойдённый** unsurpassed. **непредви́денный** unforeseen. **непредубеждённый** unprejudiced. **непредусмо́тренный** unforeseen. **непредусмотри́тельный** short-sighted. **непрекло́нный** inflexible; adamant. **непрело́жный** immutable.

не-. непреме́нно *adv* without fail. **непреме́нный** indispensable. **непреодоли́мый** insuperable. **непререка́емый** unquestionable. **непре-**

ры́вно *adv* continuously. **непре-ры́вный** continuous. **непреста́нный** incessant. **неприве́тливый** unfriendly; bleak. **непривлека́тельный** unattractive. **непривы́чный** unaccustomed. **непригля́дный** unattractive. **неприго́дный** unfit, useless. **неприе́млемый** unacceptable. **неприкоснове́нность** inviolability, immunity. **неприкоснове́нный** inviolable; reserve. **неприли́чный** indecent. **непримири́мый** irreconcilable. **непринуждённый** unconstrained; relaxed. **неприспособленный** unadapted; maladjusted. **непристо́йный** obscene. **непристу́пный** inaccessible. **непритяза́тельный**, **неприхотли́вый** unpretentious, simple. **неприя́зненный** hostile, inimical. **неприя́знь** hostility. **неприя́тель** *m* enemy. **неприя́тельский** enemy. **неприя́тность** unpleasantness; trouble. **неприя́тный** unpleasant.

не-. непрове́ренный unverified. **непрогля́дный** pitch-dark. **непрое́зжий** impassable. **непрозра́чный** opaque. **непроизводи́тельный** unproductive. **непроизво́льный** involuntary. **непромока́емый** waterproof. **непроница́емый** impenetrable. **непрости́тельный** unforgivable. **непроходи́мый** impassable. **непро́чный** (-чен, -чна́, -о) fragile, flimsy.

не прочь *predic* not averse.

не-. непро́шеный uninvited, unsolicited. **нерабо́тоспосо́бный** disabled. **нерабо́чий:** ~ **день** day off. **нера́венство** inequality. **неравноме́рный** uneven. **нера́вный** unequal. **неради́вый** lackadaisical. **неразбери́ха** muddle. **неразбо́рчивый** not fastidious; illegible. **неразвито́й** (-ра́звит, -а́, -о) undeveloped; backward. **неразгово́рчивый** taciturn. **неразделённый:** ~**ая любо́вь** unrequited love. **неразличи́мый** indistinguishable. **неразлу́чный** inseparable. **неразрешённый** unsolved; forbidden. **неразреши́мый** insoluble. **неразры́вный** indissoluble. **неразу́мный** unwise; unreasonable. **нераствори́мый** insoluble. **нерв** nerve. **не́рвничать** *impf* fret,

be nervous. **нервнобольно́й** *sb* neurotic. **не́рвный** (-вен, -вна́, -о) nervous; nerve; irritable. **нерво́зный** nervy, irritable.

не-. нереа́льный unreal; unrealistic. **нере́дкий** (-док, -дка́, -о) not infrequent, not uncommon. **нереши́тельность** indecision. **нереши́тельный** indecisive, irresolute. **нержаве́ющая сталь** stainless steel. **неро́вный** (-вен, -вна́, -о) uneven, rough; irregular. **неруши́мый** inviolable.

неря́ха *m & f* sloven. **неря́шливый** slovenly.

не-. несбы́точный unrealizable. **несваре́ние желу́дка** indigestion. **несве́жий** (-е́ж, -а́) not fresh; tainted; weary. **несвоевре́менный** ill-timed; overdue. **несво́йственный** not characteristic. **несгора́емый** fireproof. **несерьёзный** not serious.

несессе́р case.

несимметри́чный asymmetrical.

нескла́дный incoherent; awkward.

несклоня́емый indeclinable.

не́сколько (-их) *pron* some, several; *adv* somewhat.

не-. несконча́емый interminable. **нескро́мный** (-мен, -мна́, -о) immodest; indiscreet. **несло́жный** simple. **неслы́ханный** unprecedented. **неслы́шный** inaudible. **несме́тный** countless, incalculable. **несмолка́емый** ceaseless.

несмотря́ на *prep+acc* in spite of.

не-. несно́сный intolerable. **несоблюде́ние** non-observance. **несовершенноле́тний** under-age; *sb* minor. **несоверше́нный** imperfect, incomplete; imperfective. **несоверше́нство** imperfection. **несовмести́мый** incompatible. **несогла́сие** disagreement. **несогласо́ванный** uncoordinated. **несозна́тельный** irresponsible. **несоизмери́мый** incommensurable. **несокруши́мый** indestructible. **несомне́нный** undoubted, unquestionable. **несообра́зный** incongruous. **несоотве́тствие** disparity. **несостоя́тельный** insolvent; of modest means; untenable. **неспе́лый** unripe. **неспоко́йный** restless; uneasy. **неспосо́бный**

not bright; incapable. **несправедли́вость** injustice. **несправедли́вый** unjust, unfair; incorrect. **несравне́нный** (-**ёнен**, -**ённа**) incomparable. **несравни́мый** incomparable. **нестерпи́мый** unbearable.

нести́ (-**су́**, -**сёшь**; **нёс**, -**ла́**) *impf* (*pf* **по~**, **с~**) carry; bear; bring, take; suffer; incur; lay; **~сь** rush, fly; float, be carried.

не-. нестойкий unstable. **несуще́ственный** immaterial, inessential.

несу́ *etc.: see* **нести́**

несхо́дный unlike, dissimilar.

несчастли́вый unfortunate, unlucky; unhappy. **несча́стный** unhappy, unfortunate; ~ **слу́чай** accident. **несча́стье** misfortune; **к несча́стью** unfortunately.

несчётный innumerable.

нет *partl* no, not; nothing. **нет, не́ту** there is not, there are not.

не-. нетакти́чный tactless. **нетвёрдый** (-**ёрд**, -**а́**, -**о**) unsteady, shaky. **нетерпели́вый** impatient. **нетерпе́ние** impatience. **нетерпи́мый** intolerable, intolerant. **неторопли́вый** leisurely. **нето́чный** (-**чен**, -**чна́**, -**о**) inaccurate, inexact. **нетре́звый** drunk. **нетро́нутый** untouched; chaste, virginal. **нетрудово́й дохо́д** unearned income. **нетрудоспосо́бность** disability.

не́тто *indecl adj & adv* net(t).

не́ту *see* **нет**

не-. неубеди́тельный unconvincing. **неуваже́ние** disrespect. **неуве́ренность** uncertainty. **неуве́ренный** uncertain. **неувяда́емый, неувяда́ющий** unfading. **неугомо́нный** indefatigable. **неуда́ча** failure. **неуда́чливый** unlucky. **неуда́чник**, -**ница** unlucky person, failure. **неуда́чный** unsuccessful, unfortunate. **неудержи́мый** irrepressible. **неудо́бный** uncomfortable; inconvenient; embarrassing. **неудо́бство** discomfort; inconvenience; embarrassment. **неудовлетворе́ние** dissatisfaction. **неудовлетворённый** dissatisfied. **неудовлетвори́тельный** unsatisfactory. **неудово́льствие** displeasure.

неуже́ли? *partl* really?

не-. неузнава́емый unrecognizable. **неукло́нный** steady; undeviating. **неуклю́жий** clumsy. **неулови́мый** elusive; subtle. **неуме́лый** inept; clumsy. **неуме́ренный** immoderate. **неуме́стный** inappropriate; irrelevant. **неумоли́мый** implacable, inexorable. **неумы́шленный** unintentional.

не-. неупла́та non-payment. **неуравнове́шенный** unbalanced. **неурожа́й** bad harvest. **неуро́чный** untimely, inopportune. **неуря́дица** disorder, mess. **неуспева́емость** poor progress. **неусто́йка** forfeit. **неусто́йчивый** unstable; unsteady. **неуступчивый** unyielding. **неутёшный** inconsolable. **неутоли́мый** unquenchable. **неутоми́мый** tireless. **не́уч** ignoramus. **неучти́вый** discourteous. **неуязви́мый** invulnerable.

нефри́т jade.

нефте- *in comb* oil, petroleum. **нефтено́сный** oil-bearing. **~перего́нный заво́д** oil refinery. **~прово́д** (oil) pipeline. **~проду́кты** (-**ов**) *pl* petroleum products.

нефть oil, petroleum. **нефтяно́й** oil, petroleum.

не-. нехва́тка shortage. **нехорошо́** *adv* badly. **нехоро́ш|ий** (-**о́ш**, -**а́**) bad; **~о́** it is bad, it is wrong. **не́хотя** *adv* unwillingly; unintentionally. **нецелесообра́зный** inexpedient; pointless. **нецензу́рный** unprintable. **неча́янный** unexpected; accidental.

не́чего (**не́чему**, -**чем**, **не́ о чем**) *pron* (*with separable pref*) (there is) nothing.

нечелове́ческий inhuman, superhuman.

нече́стный dishonest, unfair.

нечётный odd.

нечистопло́тный dirty; slovenly; unscrupulous. **нечистота́** (*pl* -**о́ты**, -**о́т**) dirtiness, filth; *pl* sewage. **нечи́стый** (-**и́ст**, -**а́**, -**о**) dirty, unclean; impure; unclear. **не́чисть** evil spirits; scum. **нечленоразде́льный** inarticulate.

не́что *pron* something.

не-. неэконо́мный uneconomical. **неэффекти́вный** ineffective; inefficient. **нея́вка** failure to appear. **не-**

я́ркий dim, faint; dull, subdued. **нея́сный** (-сен, -сна́, -о) not clear; vague.

ни *partl* not a; **ни оди́н** (одна́, одно́) not a single; (*with prons and pronominal advs*) -ever; **кто̀... ни** whoever. **ни** *conj*: **ни... ни** neither ... nor; **ни то ни сё** neither one thing nor the other.

ни́ва cornfield, field.

нивели́р level.

нигде́ *adv* nowhere.

нидерла́ндец (-дца; *gen pl* -дцев) Dutchman. **нидерла́ндка** Dutchwoman. **нидерла́ндский** Dutch. **Нидерла́нды** (-ов) *pl* the Netherlands.

ни́же *adj* lower, humbler; *adv* below; *prep*+*gen* below, beneath. **нижесле́дующий** following. **ни́жний** lower, under-; **~ее бельё** underclothes; **~ий эта́ж** ground floor. **низ** (*loc* -у́; *pl* -ы́) bottom; *pl* lower classes; low notes.

низа́ть (нижу́, ни́жешь) *impf* (*pf* на**~**) string, thread.

низверга́ть *impf*, **низве́ргнуть** (-ну; -е́рг) *pf* throw down, overthrow; **~ся** crash down; be overthrown. **низверже́ние** overthrow.

низи́на low-lying place. **ни́зкий** (-зок, -зка́, -о) low; base, mean. **низкопокло́нство** servility. **низкопро́бный** base; low-grade. **низкоро́слый** undersized. **низкосо́ртный** low-grade.

ни́зменность lowland; baseness. **ни́зменный** low-lying; base.

низо́вье (*gen pl* -ьев) the lower reaches. **ни́зость** baseness, meanness. **ни́зший** lower, lowest; **~ее образова́ние** primary education.

ника́к *adv* in no way. **никако́й** *pron* no; no ... whatever.

ни́кель *m* nickel.

нике́м *see* никто́. **никогда́** *adv* never. **никто́** (-кого́, -кому́, -ке́м, ни о ко́м) *pron* (*with separable pref*) nobody, no one. **никуда́** nowhere. **никчёмный** useless. **нима́ло** *adv* not in the least.

нимб halo, nimbus.

ни́мфа nymph; pupa.

ниотку́да *adv* from nowhere.

нипочём *adv* it is nothing; dirt cheap.

in no circumstances.

ниско́лько *adv* not at all.

ниспроверга́ть *impf*, **ниспрове́ргнуть** (-ну; -е́рг) *pf* overthrow. **ниспроверже́ние** overthrow.

нисходя́щий descending.

ни́тка thread; string; **до ни́тки** to the skin; **на живу́ю ни́тку** hastily, anyhow. **ни́точка** thread. **нить** thread; filament.

ничего́ *etc.*: *see* ничто́. **ничего́** *adv* all right; it doesn't matter, never mind; *as indecl adj* not bad, pretty good. **ниче́й** (-чья́, -чьё) *pron* nobody's; **ничья́ земля́** no man's land. **ничья́** *sb* draw; tie.

ничко́м *adv* face down, prone.

ничто́ (-чего́, -чему́, -че́м, ни о чём) *pron* (*with separable pref*) nothing. **ничто́жество** nonentity, nobody. **ничто́жный** insignificant; worthless.

ничу́ть *adv* not a bit.

ничьё *etc.*: *see* ничей.

ни́ша niche, recess.

ни́щенка beggar-woman. **ни́щенский** beggarly. **нищета́** poverty. **ни́щий** (нищ, -а́, -е) destitute; poor; *sb* beggar.

но *conj* but; still.

нова́тор innovator. **нова́торский** innovative. **нова́торство** innovation. **Но́вая Зела́ндия** New Zealand. **нове́йший** newest, latest. **нове́лла** short story. **нове́нький** brand-new. **новизна́** novelty; newness. **нови́нка** novelty. **новичо́к** (-чка́) novice.

ново- *in comb* new(ly). **новобра́нец** (-нца) new recruit. **~бра́чный** *sb* newly-wed. **~введе́ние** innovation. **~го́дний** new year's. **~зела́ндец** (-дца; *gen pl* -дцев), **~зела́ндка** New-Zealander. **~зела́ндский** New Zealand. **~лу́ние** new moon. **~прибы́вший** newly-arrived; *sb* newcomer. **~рождённый** newborn. **~сёл** new settler. **~се́лье** new home; housewarming. **новостро́йка** new building.

но́вость news; novelty. **но́вшество** innovation, novelty. **но́вый** (нов, -а́, -о) new; modern; **~ год** New Year's Day.

нога́ (*acc* но́гу; *pl* но́ги, ног, нога́м) foot, leg.

ноготь (-гтя; *pl* -и) *m* finger-nail, toe-nail.

нож (-á) knife.

ножка small foot or leg; leg; stem, stalk.

ножницы (-иц) *pl* scissors, shears.

ножны (-жен) *pl* sheath, scabbard.

ножовка saw, hacksaw.

ноздря (*pl* -и, -éй) nostril.

нокаут knock-out. **нокаутировать** *impf & pf* knock out.

нолевой, нулевой zero. **ноль** (-я), **нуль** (-я) *m* nought, zero, nil.

номенклатура nomenclature; top positions in government.

номер (*pl* -á) number; size; (hotel-)room; item; trick. **номерок** (-ркá) tag; label, ticket.

номинал face value. **номинальный** nominal.

нора (*pl* -ы) burrow, hole.

Норвегия Norway. **норвежец** (-жца), **норвежка** Norwegian. **норвежский** Norwegian.

норд (*naut*) north; north wind.

норка mink.

норма standard, norm; rate. **нормализация** standardization. **нормально** all right, OK. **нормальный** normal; standard. **нормирование, нормировка** regulation; rate-fixing; rationing. **нормировать** *impf & pf* regulate, standardize; ration.

нос (*loc* -ý; *pl* -ы) nose; beak; bow, prow. **носик** (*small*) nose; spout.

носилки (-лок) *pl* stretcher; litter. **носильщик** porter. **носитель** *m*, **~ница** (*fig*) bearer; (*med*) carrier. **носить** (-ошý, -ócишь) *impf* carry, bear; wear; **~ся** rush, tear along, fly; float, be carried; wear. **носка** carrying, wearing. **ноский** hard-wearing.

носовой nose; nasal; **~ платок** (pocket) handkerchief. **носок** (-скá) little nose; toe; sock. **носорог** rhinoceros.

нота note; *pl* music. **нотация** notation; lecture, reprimand.

нотариус notary.

ночевать (-чую) *impf* (*pf* пере~) spend the night. **ночёвка** spending the night. **ночлег** place to spend the night; passing the night. **ночлежка** doss-house. **ночник** (-á) night-light.

ночн|ой night, nocturnal; **~ая ру-** **башка** nightdress; **~ой горшок** potty; chamber-pot. **ночь** (*loc* -и; *gen pl* -éй) night. **ночью** *adv* at night.

ноша burden. **ношеный** worn; second-hand.

ною *etc.*: *see* ныть

ноябрь (-я) *m* November. **ноябрьский** November.

нрав disposition, temper; *pl* customs, ways. **нравиться** (-влюсь) *impf* (*pf* по~) +*dat* please; **мне нравится** I like. **нравственность** morality, morals. **нравственный** moral.

ну *int & partl* well, well then.

нудный tedious.

нужда (*pl* -ы) need. **нуждаться** *impf* be in need; +в+*prep* need, require. **нужн|ый** (-жен, -жнá, -о, нужны) necessary; **~о** it is necessary; +*dat* I, *etc.*, must, ought to need.

нулевой, нуль *see* нолевой, ноль

нумерация numeration; numbering. **нумеровать** *impf* (*pf* про~) number.

нутро inside, interior; instinct(s).

ныне *adv* now; today. **нынешний** present; today's. **нынче** *adv* today; now.

нырнуть (-ну, -нёшь) *pf*, **нырять** *impf* dive.

ныть (ною) *impf* ache; whine. **нытьё** whining.

н.э. *abbr* (*of* нашей эры) AD.

нюх scent; flair. **нюхать** *impf* (*pf* по~) smell, sniff.

нянчить (-чу) *impf* nurse, look after; **~ся** с+*instr* nurse; fuss over. **нянька** nanny. **няня** (*children's*) nurse, nanny.

О

о, об, обо *prep* I. +*prep* of, about, concerning. II. +*acc* against; on, upon.

о *int* oh!

оазис oasis.

об *see* о *prep*.

оба (обоих) *m & neut*, **обе** (обеих) *f* both.

обалдевать *impf*, **обалдеть** (-ею) *pf* go crazy; become dulled; be stunned.

обанкротиться (-очусь) *pf* go bankrupt.

обая́ние fascination, charm. обая́тельный fascinating, charming.

обва́л fall(ing); crumbling; collapse; caving-in; landslide; (сне́жный) ~ avalanche. обвали́ть (-лю́, -лишь) pf (impf обва́ливать) cause to fall or collapse; crumble; heap round; ~ся collapse, cave in; crumble.

обваля́ть pf (impf обва́ливать) roll. обва́ривать impf, обвари́ть (-рю́, -ришь) pf pour boiling water over; scald; ~ся scald o.s.

обведу́ etc.: see обвести́. обве́л etc.: see обвести́. об|венча́ть(ся pf.

обверну́ть (-ну́, -нёшь) pf, обвёртывать impf wrap, wrap up.

обве́с short weight. обве́сить (-ёшу) pf (impf обве́шивать) cheat in weighing.

обвести́ (-еду́, -едёшь; -ёл, -ела́) pf (impf обводи́ть) lead round, take round; encircle; surround; outline; dodge.

обве́тренный weather-beaten.

обветша́лый decrepit. об|ветша́ть pf.

обве́шивать impf of обве́сить.

обвива́ть(ся impf of обви́ть(ся

обвине́ние charge, accusation; prosecution. обвини́тель m accuser; prosecutor. обвини́тельный accusatory; ~ акт indictment; ~ пригово́р verdict of guilty. обвини́ть pf, обвиня́ть impf prosecute, indict; +в+prep accuse of, charge with. обвиня́емый sb the accused; defendant.

обви́ть (обовью́, обовьёшь; обви́л, -á, -o) pf (impf обвива́ть) wind round; ~ся wind round.

обводи́ть (-ожу́, -о́дишь) impf of обвести́

обвора́живать impf, обворожи́ть (-жу́) pf charm, enchant. обворожи́тельный charming, enchanting.

обвяза́ть (-яжу́, -я́жешь) pf, обвя́зывать impf tie round; ~ся +instr tie round o.s.

обго́н passing. обгоня́ть impf of обогна́ть

обгора́ть impf, обгоре́ть (-рю́) pf be burnt, be scorched. обгоре́лый burnt, charred, scorched.

обде́лать pf (impf обде́лывать) fin-

ish; polish, set; manage, arrange.

обдели́ть (-лю́, -лишь) pf (impf обделя́ть) +instr do out of one's (fair) share of.

обде́лывать impf of обде́лать. обделя́ть impf of обдели́ть.

обдеру́ etc.: see ободра́ть. обдира́ть impf of ободра́ть.

обду́манный deliberate, well-considered. обду́мать pf, обду́мывать impf consider, think over.

о́бе: see о́ба. обега́ть impf of обежа́ть. обегу́ etc.: see обежа́ть

обе́д dinner, lunch. обе́дать impf (pf по~) have dinner, dine. обе́денный dinner.

обедне́вший impoverished. обедне́ние impoverishment. о|бедне́ть (-е́ю) pf.

обе́дня (gen pl -ден) mass.

обежа́ть (-егу́) pf (impf обега́ть) run round; run past; outrun.

обезбо́ливание anaesthetization. обезбо́ливать impf, обезбо́лить pf anaesthetize.

обезвре́дить (-е́жу) pf, обезвре́живать impf render harmless.

обездо́ленный unfortunate, hapless.

обеззара́живающий disinfectant.

обезли́ченный depersonalized; robbed of individuality.

обезобра́живать impf, о|безобра́зить (-а́жу) pf disfigure.

обезопа́сить (-а́шу) pf secure.

обезору́живать impf, обезору́жить (-жу) pf disarm.

обезу́меть (-ею) pf lose one's senses, lose one's head.

обезья́на monkey; ape.

обели́ть pf, обеля́ть impf vindicate; clear of blame.

оберега́ть impf, обере́чь (-егу́, -ежёшь; -рёг, -ла́) pf guard; protect.

оберну́ть (-ну́, -нёшь) pf, обёртывать impf (impf also обора́чивать) twist; wrap up; turn, turn (round); turn out; +instr or в+acc turn into. обёртка wrapper; (dust-)jacket, cover. обёрточный wrapping.

оберу́ etc.: see обобра́ть

обескура́живать impf, обескура́жить (-жу) pf discourage; dishearten.

обескро́вить (-влю) pf, обескро́вливать impf drain of blood,

bleed white; render lifeless.
обеспе́чение securing, guaranteeing;
ensuring; provision; guarantee; security. обеспе́ченность security;
+instr provision of. обеспе́ченный
well-to-do; well provided for. обес-
пе́чивать impf, обеспе́чить (-чу)
pf provide for; secure; ensure; protect; +instr provide with.
о|беспоко́ить(ся pf.
обесси́леть (-ею) pf grow weak, lose
one's strength. обесси́ливать impf,
обесси́лить pf weaken.
о|бессла́вить (-влю) pf.
обессме́ртить (-рчу) pf immortalize.
обесце́нение depreciation. обесце́-
нивать impf, обесце́нить pf depreciate; cheapen; ~ся depreciate.
о|бесче́стить (-е́щу) pf.
обе́т vow, promise. обетова́нный
promised. обеща́ние promise. обе-
ща́ть impf & pf (pf also по~) promise.
обжа́лование appeal. обжа́ловать
pf appeal against.
обже́чь (обожгу́, обожжёшь; обжёг,
обожгла́) pf, обжига́ть impf burn;
scorch; bake; ~ся burn o.s.; burn
one's fingers.
обжо́ра m & f glutton. обжо́рство
gluttony.
обзавести́сь (-еду́сь, -еде́шься;
-вёлся, -ла́сь) pf, обзаводи́ться
(-ожу́сь, -о́дишься) impf +instr provide o.s. with; acquire.
обзову́ etc.: see обозва́ть
обзо́р survey, review.
обзыва́ть impf of обозва́ть
обива́ть impf of оби́ть. оби́вка up-
holstering; upholstery.
оби́да offence, insult; nuisance. оби́-
деть (-и́жу) pf, обижа́ть impf offend; hurt; wound; ~ся take offence;
feel hurt. оби́дный offensive; annoying. оби́дчивый touchy. оби́-
женный offended.
оби́лие abundance. оби́льный
abundant.
обира́ть impf of обобра́ть
обита́емый inhabited. обита́тель m
inhabitant. обита́ть impf live.
оби́ть (обобью́, -ьёшь) pf (impf
обива́ть) upholster; knock off.
обихо́д custom, (general) use, practice. обихо́дный everyday.

обкла́дывать(ся impf of об-
ложи́ть(ся
обкра́дывать impf of обокра́сть
обла́ва raid; cordon, cordoning off.
облага́емый taxable. облага́ть
impf of обложи́ть(ся: ~ся нало́гом
be liable to tax.
облада́ние possession. облада́тель
m possessor. облада́ть impf +instr
possess.
о́блако (pl -á, -óв) cloud.
обла́мывать(ся impf of обло-
ма́ть(ся, обломи́ться
областно́й regional. о́бласть (gen
pl -е́й) region; field, sphere.
о́блачность cloudiness. о́блачный
cloudy.
облёг etc.: see обле́чь. облега́ть
impf of обле́чь
облегча́ть impf, облегчи́ть (-чу́) pf
lighten; relieve; alleviate; facilitate.
облегче́ние relief.
обледене́лый ice-covered. обледе-
не́ние icing over. обледене́ть (-е́ет)
pf become covered with ice.
облёзлый shabby; mangy.
облека́ть(ся impf of обле́чь²(ся.
облеку́ etc.: see обле́чь²
облепи́ть (-плю́, -пишь) pf, обле-
пля́ть impf stick to, cling to; throng
round; plaster.
облета́ть impf, облете́ть (-лечу́) fly
(round); spread (all over); fall.
обле́чь¹ (-ля́жет; -лёг, -ла́) pf (impf
облега́ть) cover, envelop; fit tightly.
обле́чь² (-еку́, -ечёшь; -ёк, -кла́)
pf (impf облека́ть) clothe, invest; ~ся
clothe o.s.; +gen take the form of.
облива́ть(ся impf of обли́ть(ся
облига́ция bond.
облиза́ть (-ижу́, -и́жешь) pf, об-
ли́зывать impf lick (all over); ~ся
smack one's lips.
о́блик look, appearance.
обли́тый (о́бли́т, -á, -о) covered, en-
veloped. обли́ть (оболью́, -льёшь;
о́бли́л, -и́ла, -о) pf (impf облива́ть)
pour, sluice, spill; ~ся sponge down,
take a shower; pour over o.s.
облицева́ть (-цу́ю) pf, облицо́вы-
вать impf face. облицо́вка facing;
lining.
облича́ть impf, обличи́ть (-чу́) pf
expose; reveal; point to. обличе́ние
exposure, denunciation. обличи́-

тельный denunciatory.

обложе́ние taxation; assessment.

обложи́ть (-жу́, -жишь) pf (impf обкла́дывать, облага́ть) edge; face; cover; surround; assess; круго́м обложи́ло (не́бо) the sky is completely overcast; ~ нало́гом tax; ~ся +instr surround o.s. with. обло́жка (dust-) cover; folder.

облока́чиваться impf, облоко-ти́ться (-очу́сь, -о́тишься) pf на+acc lean one's elbows on.

обломать pf (impf обла́мывать) break off; ~ся break off. обло-ми́ться (-ло́мится) pf (impf обла́-мываться) break off. обло́мок (-мка) fragment.

облу́пленный chipped.

облучи́ть (-чу́) pf, облуча́ть impf irradiate. облуче́ние irradiation.

об|лысе́ть (-е́ю) pf.

обля́жет etc.: see облечь[1]

обма́зать (-а́жу) pf, обма́зывать impf coat; putty; besmear; ~ся +instr get covered with.

обма́кивать impf, обмакну́ть (-ну́, -нёшь) pf dip.

обма́н deceit; illusion; ~ зре́ния optical illusion. обма́нный deceitful. обману́ть (-ну́, -нешь) pf, обма́ны-вать impf deceive; cheat; ~ся be de-ceived. обма́нчивый deceptive. об-ма́нщик deceiver; fraud.

обма́тывать(ся impf of обмо-та́ть(ся

обма́хивать impf, обмахну́ть (-ну́, -нёшь) pf brush off; fan; ~ся fan o.s.

обмён etc.: see обмести́

обмеле́ние shallowing. об|меле́ть (-е́ет) pf become shallow.

обмён exchange; barter; в ~ за+acc in exchange for; ~ веще́ств metabol-ism. обме́нивать impf, обмени́ть (-ню́, -нишь) pf, об|меня́ть pf ex-change; ~ся +instr exchange. об-ме́нный exchange.

обме́р measurement; false measure.

обмере́ть (обомру́, -рёшь; о́бмер, -ла́, -ло) pf (impf обмира́ть) faint; ~ от у́жаса be horror-struck.

обме́ривать impf, обме́рить pf measure; cheat in measuring.

обмести́ (-ету́, -ете́шь; -мёл, -а́) pf, обмета́ть[1] impf sweep off, dust.

обмета́ть[2] (-ечу́ or -а́ю, -е́чешь or -а́ешь) pf (impf обмётывать) oversew.

обмету́ etc.: see обмести́. обмёты-вать impf of обмета́ть. обмира́ть impf of обмере́ть

обмо́лвиться (-влюсь) pf make a slip of the tongue; +instr say, utter. обмо́лвка slip of the tongue.

обморо́женный frost-bitten.

о́бморок fainting-fit, swoon.

обмота́ть pf (impf обма́тывать) wind round; ~ся +instr wrap o.s. in. обмо́тка winding; pl puttees.

обмо́ю etc.: see обмы́ть

обмундирова́ние fitting out (with uniform); uniform. обмундирова́ть pf, обмундиро́вывать impf fit out (with uniform).

обмыва́ть impf, обмы́ть (-мо́ю) pf bathe, wash; ~ся wash, bathe.

обмяка́ть impf, обмя́кнуть (-ну; -мя́к) pf become soft or flabby.

обнадёживать impf, обнадёжить (-жу) pf reassure.

обнажа́ть impf, обнажи́ть (-жу́) pf bare, uncover; reveal. обнажённый (-ён, -ена́) naked, bare; nude.

обнаро́довать impf & pf promul-gate.

обнаруже́ние revealing; discovery; detection. обнару́живать impf, обнару́жить (-жу) pf display; re-veal; discover; ~ся come to light.

обнести́ (-су́, -сёшь; -нёс, -ла́) pf (impf обноси́ть) enclose; +instr serve round; pass over, leave out.

обнима́ть(ся impf of обня́ть(ся. обниму́ etc.: see обня́ть

обнища́ние impoverishment.

обнови́ть (-влю) pf, обновля́ть impf renovate; renew. обно́вка new acquisition; new garment. обно-вле́ние renovation, renewal.

обноси́ть (-ошу́, -о́сишь) impf of обнести́; ~ся pf have worn out one's clothes.

обня́ть (-ниму́, -ни́мешь; о́бнял, -а́, -о) pf (impf обнима́ть) embrace; clasp; ~ся embrace; hug one another.

обо see o prep.

обобра́ть (оберу́, -рёшь; обобра́л, -а́, -о) pf (impf обира́ть) rob; pick.

обобща́ть impf, обобщи́ть (-щу́) pf generalize. обобще́ние generaliza-tion. обобществи́ть (-влю) pf, обобществля́ть *impf* socialize; collectivize. обобществле́ние socialization; collectivization.

обобью́ *etc.: see* обви́ть. обовью́ *etc.: see* обви́ть.

обогати́ть (-ащу́) *pf*, обогаща́ть *impf* enrich; ~ся become rich; enrich o.s. обогаще́ние enrichment.

обогна́ть (обгоню́, -о́нишь; обогна́л, -а́, -о) *pf* (*impf* обгоня́ть) pass; outstrip.

обогну́ть (-ну́, -нёшь) *pf* (*impf* огиба́ть) round, skirt; bend round.

обогрева́тель *m* heater. обогрева́ть *impf*, обогре́ть (-е́ю) *pf* heat, warm; ~ся warm up.

о́бод (*pl* -о́дья, -ьев) rim. ободо́к (-дка́) thin rim, narrow border.

обо́дранный ragged. ободра́ть (обдеру́, -рёшь; -а́л, -а́, -о) *pf* (*impf* обдира́ть) skin, flay; peel; fleece.

ободре́ние encouragement, reassurance. ободри́тельный encouraging, reassuring. ободри́ть *pf*, ободря́ть *impf* encourage, reassure; ~ся cheer up, take heart.

обожа́ть *impf* adore.

обожгу́ *etc.: see* обже́чь.

обожестви́ть (-влю́) *pf*, обожествля́ть *impf* deify.

обожжённый (-ён, -ена́) burnt, scorched.

обо́з string of vehicles; transport.

обозва́ть (обзову́, -вёшь; -а́л, -а́, -о) *pf* (*impf* обзыва́ть) call; call names.

обозлённый (-ён, -а́) angered; embittered. обо|зли́ть *pf*, о|зли́ть *pf* anger; embitter; ~ся get angry.

обозна́ться *pf* mistake s.o. for s.o. else.

обознача́ть *impf*, обозна́чить (-чу) *pf* mean; mark; ~ся appear, reveal o.s. обозначе́ние sign, symbol.

обозрева́тель *m* reviewer; columnist. обозрева́ть *impf*, обозре́ть (-рю́) *pf* survey. обозре́ние survey; review; revue. обозри́мый visible.

обо́и (-ев) *pl* wallpaper.

обо́йма (*gen pl* -о́йм) cartridge clip.

обойти́ (-йду́, -йдёшь; -ошёл, -ошла́) *pf* (*impf* обходи́ть) go round; pass; avoid; pass over; ~сь manage, make do; +*c*+*instr* treat.

обокра́сть (обкраду́, -дёшь) *pf* (*impf* обкра́дывать) rob.

оболо́чка casing; membrane; cover, envelope, jacket; shell.

обольсти́тель *m* seducer. обольсти́тельный seductive. обольсти́ть (-льщу́) *pf*, обольща́ть *impf* seduce. обольще́ние seduction; delusion.

оболью́ *etc.: see* обли́ть.

обомру́ *etc.: see* обмере́ть.

обоня́ние (sense of) smell. обоня́тельный olfactory.

обопру́ *etc.: see* опере́ть.

обора́чивать(ся *impf of* оберну́ть(ся, обороти́ть(ся

обо́рванный torn, ragged. обо|рва́ть (-ву́, -вёшь; -а́л, -а́, -о) *pf* (*impf* обрыва́ть) tear off; break; snap; cut short; ~ся break; snap; fall; stop suddenly.

обо́рка frill, flounce.

оборо́на defence. оборони́тельный defensive. оборони́ть *pf*, обороня́ть *impf* defend; ~ся defend o.s. оборо́нный defence, defensive.

оборо́т turn; revolution; circulation; turnover; back; (turn of) phrase; смотри́ на ~е P.T.O. обороти́ть (-рочу́, -ро́тишь) *pf* (*impf* обора́чивать) turn; ~ся turn (round); +*instr or* в+*acc* turn into. оборо́тный circulating; reverse; капита́л working capital.

обору́дование equipping; equipment. обору́довать *impf & pf* equip.

обоснова́ние basing; basis, ground. обосно́ванный well-founded. обоснова́ть *pf*, обосно́вывать *impf* ground, base; substantiate; ~ся settle down.

обосо́бленный isolated, solitary.

обостре́ние aggravation. обострённый keen; strained; sharp, pointed. обостри́ть *pf*, обостря́ть *impf* sharpen; strain; aggravate; ~ся become strained; be aggravated; become acute.

оботру́ *etc.: see* обтере́ть.

обо́чина verge; shoulder, edge.

обошёл *etc.: see* обойти́. обошью́ *etc.: see* обши́ть.

обою́дный mutual, reciprocal.

обраба́тывать *impf*, обрабо́тать *pf* till, cultivate; work, work up; treat, process. **обрабо́тка** working (up); processing; cultivation.

об|ра́довать(ся pf.

о́браз shape, form; image; manner; way; icon; **гла́вным ~ом** mainly; **таки́м ~ом** thus. **образе́ц** (-зца́) model; pattern; sample. **о́бразный** graphic; figurative. **образова́ние** formation; education. **образо́ванный** educated. **образова́тельный** educational. **образова́ть** impf & pf, **образо́вывать** impf form; **~ся** form; arise; turn out well.

образу́мить (-млю) pf bring to reason; **~ся** see reason.

образцо́вый model. **обра́зчик** specimen, sample.

обра́мить (-млю) pf, **обрамля́ть** impf frame.

обраста́ть impf, **обрасти́** (-ту́, -тёшь; -ро́с, -ла́) pf be overgrown.

обрати́мый reversible, convertible. **обрати́ть** (-ащу́) pf, **обраща́ть** impf turn; convert; **~ внима́ние на**+acc pay or draw attention to; **~ся** turn; appeal; apply; address; **+в**+acc turn into; **+с**+instr treat; handle. **обра́тно** adv back; backwards; conversely; **~ пропорциона́льный** inversely proportional. **обра́тный** reverse; return; opposite; inverse. **обраще́ние** appeal, address; conversion; (+с+instr) treatment (of); handling (of); use (of).

обре́з edge; sawn-off gun; **в ~**+gen only just enough. **обре́зать** (-е́жу) pf, **обреза́ть** impf cut (off); clip, trim; pare; prune: circumcise; **~ся** cut o.s. **обре́зок** (-зка) scrap; pl ends; clippings.

обрека́ть impf of **обре́чь. обреку́** etc.: see **обре́чь. обрёл** etc.: see **обрести́**

обремени́тельный onerous. **о|бремени́ть** pf, **обременя́ть** impf burden.

обрести́ (-ету́, -етёшь; -рёл, -а́) pf, **обрета́ть** impf find.

обрече́ние doom. **обречённый** doomed. **обре́чь** (-еку́, -ечёшь; -ёк, -ла́) pf (impf **обрека́ть**) doom.

обрисова́ть pf, **обрисо́вывать** impf outline, depict; **~ся** appear (in outline).

оброни́ть (-ню, -нишь) pf drop; let drop.

обро́с etc.: see **обрасти́**

обруба́ть impf, **обруби́ть** (-блю́, -бишь) pf chop off; cut off. **обру́бок** (-бка) stump.

об|руга́ть pf.

о́бруч (pl -и, -е́й) hoop. **обруча́льн|ый** engagement; **~ое кольцо́** betrothal ring, wedding ring. **обруча́ть** impf, **обручи́ть** (-чу́) betroth; **~ся** +с+instr become engaged to. **обруче́ние** engagement.

обру́шивать impf, **об|ру́шить** (-шу) pf bring down; **~ся** come down, collapse.

обры́в precipice. **обрыва́ть(ся** impf of **оборва́ть(ся. обры́вок** (-вка) scrap; snatch.

обры́згать pf, **обры́згивать** impf splash; sprinkle.

обрю́зглый flabby.

обря́д rite, ceremony.

обсервато́рия observatory.

обслу́живание service; maintenance. **обслу́живать** impf, **обслужи́ть** (-жу́, -жишь) pf serve; service; operate.

обсле́дование inspection. **обсле́дователь** m inspector. **обсле́довать** impf & pf inspect.

обсо́хнуть (-ну; -о́х) pf (impf **обсыха́ть**) dry (off).

обста́вить (-влю) pf, **обставля́ть** impf surround; furnish; arrange. **обстано́вка** furniture; situation, conditions; set.

обстоя́тельный thorough, reliable; detailed. **обстоя́тельство** circumstance. **обстоя́ть** (-ои́т) impf be; go; **как обстои́т де́ло?** how is it going?

обстре́л firing, fire; **под ~ом** under fire. **обстре́ливать** impf, **обстреля́ть** pf fire at; bombard.

обступа́ть impf, **обступи́ть** (-у́пит) pf surround.

обсуди́ть (-ужу́, -у́дишь) pf, **обсужда́ть** impf discuss. **обсужде́ние** discussion.

обсчита́ть pf, **обсчи́тывать** impf shortchange; **~ся** miscount, miscalculate.

обсы́пать (-плю) pf, **обсыпа́ть** impf strew; sprinkle.

обсыха́ть impf of **обсо́хнуть. обта́чивать** impf of **обточи́ть обтека́емый** streamlined.

обтере́ть (оботру́, -трёшь; обтёр) pf (impf обтира́ть) wipe; rub; ~ся dry o.s.; sponge down.

о(б)теса́ть (-ешу́, -е́шешь) pf, о(б)тёсывать impf rough-hew; teach good manners to; trim.

обтира́ние sponge-down. обтира́ть(ся pf of обтере́ть(ся

обточи́ть (-чу́, -чишь) pf (impf обта́чивать) grind; machine.

обтрёпанный frayed; shabby.

обтя́гивать impf, обтяну́ть (-ну́, -нешь) pf cover; fit close. обтя́жка cover; skin; в обтя́жку close-fitting.

обува́ть(ся impf of обу́ть(ся. обу́вь footwear; boots, shoes.

обу́гливать impf, обу́глить pf char; carbonize; ~ся char, become charred.

обу́за burden.

обузда́ть pf, обу́здывать impf bridle, curb.

обурева́ть impf grip; possess.

обусло́вить (-влю) pf, обусло́вливать impf cause; +instr make conditional on; ~ся +instr be conditional on; depend on.

обу́тый shod. обу́ть (-у́ю) pf (impf обува́ть) put shoes on; ~ся put on one's shoes.

обу́х butt, back.

обуча́ть impf, об|учи́ть (-чу́, -чишь) pf teach; train; ~ся +dat or inf learn. обуче́ние teaching; training.

обхва́т girth; в ~е in circumference. обхвати́ть (-ачу́, -а́тишь) pf, обхва́тывать impf embrace; clasp.

обхо́д round(s); roundabout way; by-pass. обходи́тельный courteous; pleasant. обходи́ть(ся (-ожу́(сь, -о́дишь(ся) impf of обойти́(сь. обхо́дный roundabout.

обша́ривать impf, обша́рить pf rummage through, ransack.

обшива́ть impf of обши́ть. обши́вка edging; trimming; boarding, panelling; plating.

обши́рный extensive; vast.

обши́ть (обошью́, -шьёшь) pf (impf обшива́ть) edge; trim; make outfit(s) for; plank.

обшла́г (-а́; pl -а́, -о́в) cuff.

обща́ться impf associate.

обще- in comb common(ly), general(ly). общедосту́пный mod-

erate in price; popular. ~житие hostel. ~изве́стный generally known. ~наро́дный national, public. ~образова́тельный of general education. ~при́нятый generally accepted. ~сою́зный All-Union. ~челове́ческий common to all mankind; universal.

обще́ние contact; social intercourse. обще́ственность (the) public; public opinion; community. обще́ственный social, public; voluntary. о́бщество society; company.

о́бщий general; common; в ~ем on the whole, in general. о́бщина community; commune.

об|щипа́ть (-плю́ -плешь) pf.

общи́тельный sociable. о́бщность community.

объеда́ть(ся impf of объе́сть(ся

объедине́ние unification; merger; union, association. объединённый (-ён, -а́) united. объедини́тельный unifying. объедини́ть pf, объединя́ть impf unite; join; combine; ~ся unite.

объе́дки (-ов) pl leftovers, scraps.

объе́зд riding round; detour.

объе́здить (-зжу, -здишь) pf (impf объезжа́ть) travel over; break in.

объезжа́ть impf of объе́здить, объе́хать

объе́кт object; objective; establishment, works. объекти́в lens. объекти́вность objectivity. объекти́вный objective.

объём volume; scope. объёмный by volume, volumetric.

объе́сть (-ем, -ешь, -ест, -еди́м) pf (impf объеда́ть) gnaw (round), nibble; ~ся overeat.

объе́хать (-е́ду) pf (impf объезжа́ть) drive or go round; go past; travel over.

объяви́ть (-влю́, -вишь) pf, объявля́ть impf declare, announce; ~ся turn up; +instr declare o.s. объявле́ние declaration, announcement; advertisement.

объясне́ние explanation. объясни́мый explainable. объясни́ть pf, объясня́ть impf explain; ~ся be explained; make o.s. understood; +с+instr have it out with.

объя́тие embrace.

обыва́тель *m* Philistine. обыва́тельский narrow-minded.

обыгра́ть *pf*, обы́грывать *impf* beat (*in a game*).

обы́денный ordinary; everyday.

обыкнове́ние habit. обыкнове́нно *adv* usually. обыкнове́нный usual; ordinary.

о́быск search. обыска́ть (-ыщу́, -ы́щешь) *pf*, обы́скивать *impf* search.

обы́чай custom: usage. обы́чно *adv* usually. обы́чный usual.

обя́занность duty; responsibility. обя́занный (+*inf*) obliged; +*dat* indebted to (+*instr* for). обяза́тельно *adv* without fail. обяза́тельный obligatory. обяза́тельство obligation; commitment. обяза́ть (-яжу́, -я́жешь) *pf*, обя́зывать *impf* bind; commit; oblige; ~ся pledge o.s., undertake.

ова́л oval. ова́льный oval.

ова́ция ovation.

овдове́ть (-е́ю) *pf* become a widow, widower.

овёс (овса́) oats.

ове́чка *dim of* овца́; harmless person.

овладева́ть *impf*, овладе́ть (-е́ю) *pf* +*instr* seize; capture; master.

о́вод (*pl* -ы *or* -а́) gadfly.

о́вощ (*pl* -и, -е́й) vegetable. овощно́й vegetable.

овра́г ravine, gully.

овся́нка oatmeal; porridge. овся́ный oat, oatmeal.

овца́ (*pl* -ы, ове́ц, о́вцам) sheep; ewe. овча́рка sheep-dog. овчи́на sheepskin.

ога́рок (-рка) candle-end.

огиба́ть *impf of* обогну́ть

оглавле́ние table of contents.

огласи́ть (-ашу́) *pf*, оглаша́ть *impf* announce; fill (with sound); ~ся resound. огла́ска publicity. оглаше́ние publication.

огло́бля (*gen pl* -бель) shaft.

о|гло́хнуть (-ну; -о́х) *pf*.

оглуша́ть *impf*, о|глуши́ть (-шу́) *pf* deafen; stun. оглуши́тельный deafening.

огляде́ть (-яжу́) *pf*, огля́дывать *impf*, огляну́ть (-ну́, -нешь) *pf* look round; look over; ~ся look round; look back. огля́дка looking back.

огнево́й fire; fiery. о́гненный fiery. огнеопа́сный inflammable. огнеприпа́сы (-ов) *pl* ammunition. огнесто́йкий fire-proof. огнестре́льный: ~ое ору́жие firearm(s). огнетуши́тель *m* fire-extinguisher. огнеупо́рный fire-resistant.

ого́ *int* oho!

огова́ривать *impf*, оговори́ть *pf* slander; stipulate (for); ~ся make a proviso; make a slip (of the tongue). огово́р slander. огово́рка reservation, proviso; slip of the tongue.

оголённый bare, nude. оголи́ть *pf* (*impf* оголя́ть) bare; strip; ~ся strip o.s.; become exposed.

оголя́ть(ся *impf of* оголи́ть(ся

огонёк (-нька́) (*small*) light; zest. ого́нь (огня́) *m* fire; light.

огора́живать *impf*, огороди́ть (-рожу́, -ро́дишь) *pf* fence in, enclose; ~ся fence o.s. in. огоро́д kitchen-garden. огоро́дный kitchen-garden.

огорча́ть *impf*, огорчи́ть (-чу́) *pf* grieve, pain; ~ся grieve, be distressed. огорче́ние grief; chagrin.

о|гра́бить (-блю) *pf*. ограбле́ние robbery; burglary.

огра́да fence. огради́ть (-ажу́) *pf*, огражда́ть *impf* guard, protect.

ограниче́ние limitation, restriction. ограни́ченный limited. ограни́чивать *impf*, ограни́чить (-чу) *pf* limit, restrict; ~ся +*instr* limit or confine o.s. to; be limited to.

огро́мный huge; enormous.

о|грубе́ть (-е́ю) *pf*.

огры́зок (-зка) bit, end; stub.

огуре́ц (-рца́) cucumber.

ода́лживать *impf of* одолжи́ть

одарённый gifted. ода́ривать *impf*, одари́ть *pf*, одаря́ть *impf* give presents (to); +*instr* endow with.

одева́ть(ся *impf of* оде́ть(ся

оде́жда clothes; clothing.

одеколо́н eau-de-Cologne.

одели́ть *pf*, оделя́ть *impf* (+*instr*) present (with); endow (with).

оде́ну *etc.*: *see* оде́ть. одёргивать *impf of* одёрнуть

о|деревене́ть (-е́ю) *pf*.

одержа́ть (-жу́, -жишь) *pf*, оде́рживать *impf* gain. одержи́мый possessed.

одёрнуть (-ну) *pf* (*impf* **одёргивать**) pull down, straighten.

одётый dressed; clothed. **одеть** (-éну) *pf* (*impf* **одевать**) dress; clothe; ~**ся** dress (o.s.). **одеяло** blanket. **одеяние** garb, attire.

один (одного́), **одна** (одно́й), **одно́** (одного́); *pl* **одни́** (одни́х) one; a, an; a certain; alone; only; nothing but; same; одно́ и то же the same thing; оди́н на оди́н in private; оди́н раз once; одни́м сло́вом in a word; по одному́ one by one.

одина́ковый identical, the same, equal.

одиннадцатый eleventh. **одиннадцать** eleven.

одино́кий solitary; lonely; single. **одино́чество** solitude; loneliness. **одино́чка** *m & f* (one) person alone. **одино́чный** individual; one-man; single; ~**ое заключе́ние** solitary confinement.

одича́лый wild.

одна́жды *adv* once; one day; once upon a time.

одна́ко *conj* however.

одно- *in comb* single, one; uni-, mono-, homo-. **однобо́кий** one-sided. ~**вре́менно** *adv* simultaneously, at the same time. ~**вре́менный** simultaneous. ~**зву́чный** monotonous. ~**знача́щий** synonymous. ~**зна́чный** synonymous; one-digit. ~**имён-ный** of the same name. ~**кла́ссник** classmate. ~**кле́точный** unicellular. ~**кра́тный** single. ~**ле́тний** one-year; annual. ~**ме́стный** single-seater. ~**обра́зие**, ~**обра́зность** monotony. ~**обра́зный** monotonous. ~**ро́дность** homogeneity, uniformity. ~**ро́дный** homogeneous; similar. ~**сторо́нний** one-sided; unilateral; one-way. ~**фами́лец** (-льца) person of the same surname. ~**цве́т-ный** one-colour; monochrome. ~**эта́жный** one-storeyed.

одобре́ние approval. **одобри́тель-ный** approving. **одо́брить** *pf*, **одо-бря́ть** *impf* approve (of).

одолева́ть *impf*, **одоле́ть** (-е́ю) *pf* overcome.

одолжа́ть *impf*, **одолжи́ть** (-жу́) *pf* lend; +У+*gen* borrow from. **одол-же́ние** favour.

о|дряхле́ть (-е́ю) *pf*.

одува́нчик dandelion.

оду́маться *pf*, **оду́мываться** *impf* change one's mind.

одуре́лый stupid. **о|дуре́ть** (-е́ю) *pf*.

одурма́нивать *impf*, **о|дурма́нить** *pf* stupefy. **одуря́ть** *impf* stupefy.

одухотворённый inspired; spiritual. **одухотвори́ть** *pf*, **одухотворя́ть** *impf* inspire.

одушеви́ть (-влю́) *pf*, **одушевля́ть** *impf* animate. **одушевле́ние** animation.

одышка shortness of breath.

ожере́лье necklace.

ожесточа́ть *impf*, **ожесточи́ть** (-чу́) *pf* embitter, harden. **ожесточе́ние** bitterness. **ожесточённый** bitter; hard.

ожива́ть *impf of* **ожи́ть**

оживи́ть (-влю́) *pf*, **оживля́ть** *impf* revive; enliven; ~**ся** become animated. **оживле́ние** animation; reviving; enlivening. **оживлённый** animated, lively.

ожида́ние expectation; waiting. **ожида́ть** *impf* +*gen* wait for; expect. **ожире́ние** obesity. **о|жире́ть** (-е́ю) *pf*.

ожи́ть (-иву́, -ивёшь; о́жил, -á, -о) *pf* (*impf* **ожива́ть**) come to life, revive.

ожо́г burn, scald.

озабо́ченность preoccupation; anxiety. **озабо́ченный** preoccupied; anxious.

озагла́вить (-лю) *pf*, **озагла́вли-вать** *impf* entitle; head. **озада́-чивать** *impf*, **озада́чить** (-чу) *pf* perplex, puzzle.

озари́ть *pf*, **озаря́ть** *impf* light up, illuminate; ~**ся** light up.

оздорови́тельный бег jogging. **оздоровле́ние** sanitation.

озелени́ть *pf*, **озеленя́ть** *impf* plant (*with trees etc.*).

о́зеро (*pl* озёра) lake.

ози́мые *sb* winter crops. **ози́мый** winter. **о́зимь** winter crop.

озира́ться *impf* look round; look back.

о|зли́ть(ся: *see* **обозли́ть(ся**

озло́бить (-блю) *pf*, **озлобля́ть** *impf* embitter; ~**ся** grow bitter. **озлобле́ние** bitterness, animosity.

озлобленный embittered.

о|знакомить (-млю) *pf*, ознакомлять *impf* с+*instr* acquaint with; ~ся с+*instr* familiarize o.s. with.

ознаменовать *pf*, ознаменовывать *impf* mark; celebrate.

означать *impf* mean, signify.

озноб shivering, chill.

озон ozone.

озорник (-á) mischief-maker. озорной naughty, mischievous. озорство mischief.

озябнуть (-ну; озяб) *pf* be cold, be freezing.

ой *int* oh.

оказать (-ажу, -ажешь) *pf* (*impf* оказывать) render, provide, show; ~ся turn out, prove; find o.s., be found.

оказия unexpected event, funny thing.

оказывать(ся *impf of* оказать(ся

окаменелость fossil. окаменелый fossilized; petrified. о|каменеть (-ею) *pf*.

окантовка mount.

оканчивать(ся *impf of* окончить(ся. окапывать(ся *impf of* окопать(ся

окаянный damned, cursed.

океан ocean. океанский ocean; oceanic.

окидывать *impf*, окинуть (-ну) *pf*; ~ взглядом take in at a glance, glance over.

окисел (-сла) oxide. окисление oxidation. окись oxide.

оккупант invader. оккупация occupation. оккупировать *impf & pf* occupy.

оклад salary scale; (basic) pay.

оклеветать (-ещу, -ещешь) *pf* slander.

оклеивать *impf*, оклеить *pf* cover; paste over; ~ обоями paper.

окно (*pl* óкна) window.

óко (*pl* óчи, очей) *pl* eye.

оковы (оков) *pl* fetters.

околдовать *pf*, околдовывать *impf* bewitch.

óколо *adv & prep*+*gen* by; close (to), near; around; about.

окольный roundabout.

оконный window.

окончание end; conclusion, termination; ending. окончательный

final. окончить (-чу) *pf* (*impf* оканчивать) finish, end; ~ся finish, end.

окоп trench. окопать *pf* (*impf* окапывать) dig round; ~ся entrench o.s., dig in. окопный trench.

óкорок (*pl* -á, -óв) ham, gammon.

окоченелый stiff with cold. о|коченеть (-ею) *pf*.

окошечко, окошко (*small*) window.

окраина outskirts, outlying districts.

о|красить (-ашу) *pf*, окрашивать *impf* paint, colour; dye. окраска painting; colouring; dyeing; colouration.

о|крепнуть (-ну) *pf*. о|крестить(ся (-ещу(сь, -естишь(ся) *pf*.

окрестность environs. окрестный neighbouring.

óкрик hail; shout. окрикивать *impf*, окрикнуть (-ну) *pf* hail, call, shout to.

окровавленный blood-stained.

óкруг (*pl* ~á) district. округа neighbourhood. округлить *pf*, округлять *impf* round; round off. округлый rounded. окружать *impf*, окружить (-жу) *pf* surround; encircle. окружающий surrounding; ~ее *sb* environment; ~ие *sb pl* associates. окружение encirclement; environment. окружной district. окружность circumference.

окрылить *pf*, окрылять *impf* inspire, encourage.

октава octave.

октан octane.

октябрь (-я) *m* October. октябрьский October.

окулист oculist.

окунать *impf*, окунуть (-ну, -нёшь) *pf* dip; ~ся dip; plunge; become absorbed.

óкунь (*pl* -и, -éй) *m* perch.

окупать *impf*, окупить (-плю, -пишь) *pf* compensate, repay; ~ся be repaid, pay for itself.

окурок (-рка) cigarette-end.

окутать *pf*, окутывать *impf* wrap up; shroud, cloak.

окучивать *impf*, окучить (-чу) *pf* earth up.

оладья (*gen pl* -ий) fritter; dropscone.

оледенелый frozen. о|леденеть (-ею) *pf*. .

оле́ний deer, deer's; reindeer. **оле́нина** venison. **оле́нь** *m* deer; reindeer.

оли́ва olive. **оли́вковый** olive; olive-coloured.

олига́рхия oligarchy.

олимпиа́да olympiad; Olympics. **олимпи́йск|ий** Olympic; Olympian; **~ие и́гры** Olympic games.

оли́фа drying oil (*e.g.* linseed oil).

олицетворе́ние personification; embodiment. **олицетвори́ть** *pf*, **олицетворя́ть** *impf* personify, embody.

о́лово tin. **оловя́нный** tin.

ом ohm.

ома́р lobster.

омерзе́ние loathing. **омерзи́тельный** loathsome.

омертве́лый stiff, numb; necrotic. **о|мертве́ть** (-е́ю) *pf.*

омле́т omelette.

омоложе́ние rejuvenation.

омо́ним homonym.

омо́ю *etc.: see* **омы́ть**

омрача́ть *impf*, **омрачи́ть** (-чу́) *pf* darken, cloud.

о́мут whirlpool; maelstrom.

омыва́ть *impf*, **омы́ть** (омо́ю) *pf* wash; **~ся** be washed.

он (его́, ему́, им, о нём) *pron* he. **она́** (её, ей, ей (е́ю), о ней) *pron* she.

онда́тра musk-rat.

онеме́лый numb. **о|неме́ть** (-е́ю) *pf.*

они́ (их, им, и́ми, о них) *pron* they. **оно́** (его́, ему́, им, о нём) *pron* it; this, that.

опада́ть *impf of* **опа́сть**.

опа́здывать *impf of* **опозда́ть**

опа́ла disgrace.

о|пали́ть *pf.*

опа́ловый opal.

опа́лубка casing.

опаса́ться *impf* +*gen* fear; avoid, keep off. **опасе́ние** fear; apprehension.

опа́сность danger; peril. **опа́сный** dangerous.

опа́сть (-адёт) *pf* (*impf* **опада́ть**) fall, fall off; subside.

опе́ка guardianship; trusteeship. **опека́емый** *sb* ward. **опека́ть** *impf* be guardian of; take care of. **опеку́н** (-а́), **-у́нша** guardian; tutor; trustee.

о́пера opera.

операти́вный efficient; operative,

surgical; operation(s), operational. **опера́тор** operator; cameraman. **операцио́нн|ый** operating; **~ая** *sb* operating theatre. **опера́ция** operation.

опереди́ть (-режу́) *pf*, **опережа́ть** *impf* outstrip, leave behind.

опере́ние plumage.

опере́тта, **-е́тка** operetta.

опере́ть (обопру́, -прёшь; опёр, -ла́) *pf* (*impf* **опира́ть**) +*o+acc* lean against; **~ся на** *or* +*o+acc* lean on, lean against.

опери́ровать *impf* & *pf* operate on; operate, act; +*instr* use.

о́перный opera; operatic.

о|печа́лить(ся *pf.*

опеча́тать *pf* (*impf* **опеча́тывать**) seal up.

опеча́тка misprint.

опеча́тывать *impf of* **опеча́тать**

опеши́ть (-шу) *pf* be taken aback.

опи́лки (-лок) *pl* sawdust; filings.

опира́ть(ся *impf of* **опере́ть(ся**

описа́ние description. **описа́тельный** descriptive. **описа́ть** (-ишу́, -и́шешь) *pf*, **опи́сывать** *impf* describe; **~ся** make a slip of the pen. **опи́ска** slip of the pen. **о́пись** inventory.

о́пиум opium.

опла́кать (-а́чу) *pf*, **опла́кивать** *impf* mourn for; bewail.

опла́та payment. **оплати́ть** (-ачу́, -а́тишь) *pf*, **опла́чивать** *impf* pay (for).

опла́чу *etc.: see* **опла́кать. оплачу́** *etc.: see* **оплати́ть**

оплеу́ха slap in the face.

оплодотвори́ть *pf*, **оплодотворя́ть** *impf* impregnate; fertilize.

о|пломбирова́ть *pf.*

опло́т stronghold, bulwark.

опло́шность blunder, mistake.

оповести́ть (-ещу́) *pf*, **оповеща́ть** *impf* notify. **оповеще́ние** notification.

опозда́вший *sb* late-comer. **опозда́ние** lateness; delay. **опозда́ть** *pf* (*impf* **опа́здывать**) be late; +*на+acc* miss.

опознава́тельный distinguishing; **~ знак** landmark. **опознава́ть** (-наю́, -наёшь) *impf*, **опозна́ть** *pf* identify. **опозна́ние** identification.

о|позо́рить(ся *pf*.

ополза́ть *impf*, оползти́ (-зёт; -о́лз, -ла́) *pf* slip, slide. о́ползень (-зня) *m* landslide.

ополче́ние militia.

опо́мниться *pf* come to one's senses.

опо́р: во весь ~ at full speed.

опо́ра support; pier; то́чка опо́ры fulcrum, foothold.

опора́жнивать *impf of* опорожни́ть

опо́рный support, supporting, supported; bearing.

опорожни́ть (-чу́), опорожня́ть *impf* (*impf also* опора́жнивать) empty.

о|поро́чить (-чу) *pf*.

опохмели́ться, опохмеля́ться *impf* take a hair of the dog that bit you.

опо́шлить *pf*, опошля́ть *impf* vulgarize, debase.

опоя́сать (-я́шу) *pf*, опоя́сывать *impf* gird; girdle.

оппозицио́нный opposition. оппози́ция opposition.

оппортуни́зм opportunism.

опра́ва setting, mounting; spectacle frames.

оправда́ние justification; excuse; acquittal. оправда́тельный пригово́р verdict of not guilty. оправда́ть *pf*, опра́вдывать *impf* justify; excuse; acquit; ~ся justify o.s.; be justified.

опра́вить (-влю) *pf*, оправля́ть *impf* set right, adjust; mount; ~ся put one's dress in order; recover; +*gen* get over.

опра́шивать *impf of* опроси́ть

определе́ние definition; determination; decision. определённый definite; certain. определи́мый definable. определи́ть *pf*, определя́ть *impf* define; determine; appoint; ~ся be formed; be determined; find one's position.

опроверга́ть *impf*, опрове́ргнуть (-ну; -ве́рг) *pf* refute, disprove. опроверже́ние refutation; denial.

опроки́дывать *impf*, опроки́нуть (-ну) *pf* overturn; topple; ~ся overturn; capsize.

опроме́тчивый rash, hasty.

опро́с (cross-)examination; (opinion) poll. опроси́ть (-ошу́, -о́сишь) *pf* (*impf* опра́шивать) question; (cross-) examine. опро́сный лист questionnaire.

опры́скать *pf*, опры́скивать *impf* sprinkle; spray.

опря́тный neat, tidy.

о́птик optician. о́птика optics. опти́ческий optic, optical.

оптима́льный optimal. оптими́зм optimism. оптими́ст optimist. оптимисти́ческий optimistic.

опто́вый wholesale. о́птом *adv* wholesale.

опубликова́ние publication; promulgation. о|публикова́ть *pf*, опубли́ковывать *impf* publish; promulgate.

опуска́ть(ся *impf of* опусти́ть(ся

опусте́лый deserted. о|пусте́ть (-е́ет) *pf*.

опусти́ть (-ущу́, -у́стишь) *pf* (*impf* опуска́ть) lower; let down; turn down; omit; post; ~ся lower o.s.; sink; fall; go down; go to pieces.

опустоша́ть *impf*, опустоши́ть (-шу́) *pf* devastate. опустоше́ние devastation. опустоши́тельный devastating.

опу́тать *pf*, опу́тывать *impf* entangle; ensnare.

опуха́ть *impf*, о|пу́хнуть (-ну; опу́х) *pf* swell, swell up. о́пухоль swelling, tumour.

опу́шка edge of a forest; trimming.

опу́щу *etc.: see* опусти́ть

опыле́ние pollination. опыли́ть *pf*, опыля́ть *impf* pollinate.

о́пыт experience; experiment. о́пытный experienced; experimental.

опьяне́ние intoxication. о|пьяне́ть (-е́ю) *pf*, о|пьяни́ть *pf*, опьяня́ть *impf* intoxicate, make drunk.

опя́ть *adv* again.

ора́ва crowd, horde.

ора́кул oracle.

орангута́нг orangutan.

ора́нжевый orange. оранжере́я greenhouse, conservatory.

ора́тор orator. орато́рия oratorio.

ора́ть (ору́, орёшь) *impf* yell.

орби́та orbit; (eye-)socket.

о́рган[1] organ; body. орга́н[2] (*mus*) organ. организа́тор organizer. организацио́нный organization(al). организа́ция organization. органи́зм organism. организо́ванный organized. **организова́ть** *impf & pf* (*pf also* **с~**) organize; **~ся** be organized; organize. **органи́ческий** organic.

óргия orgy.

орда́ (*pl* **-ы**) horde.

óрден (*pl* **-а́**) order.

óрдер (*pl* **-а́**) order; warrant; writ.

ордина́та ordinate.

ордина́тор house-surgeon.

орёл (**орла́**) eagle; **~ и́ли ре́шка?** heads or tails?

орео́л halo.

оре́х nut, nuts; walnut. **оре́ховый** nut; walnut. **оре́шник** hazel; hazel-thicket.

оригина́л original; eccentric. **оригина́льный** original.

ориента́ция orientation. **ориенти́р** landmark; reference point. **ориенти́роваться** *impf & pf* orient o.s.; **+на**+*acc* head for; aim at. **ориенти́ровка** orientation. **ориенти́ровочный** reference; tentative; approximate.

орке́стр orchestra.

орли́ный eagle; aquiline.

орна́мент ornament; ornamental design.

о|робе́ть (**-е́ю**) *pf*.

ороси́тельный irrigation. **ороси́ть** (**-ошу́**) *pf*, **ороша́ть** *impf* irrigate. **ороше́ние** irrigation; **поля́ ороше́ния** sewage farm.

ору́ *etc.: see* **ора́ть**

ору́дие instrument; tool; gun. **ору́дийный** gun. **ору́довать** *impf* +*instr* handle; use. **оруже́йный** arms; gun. **ору́жие** arm, arms; weapons.

орфографи́ческий orthographic(al). **орфогра́фия** orthography, spelling.

оса́ (*pl* **-ы**) wasp.

оса́да siege. **осади́ть**[1] (**-ажу́**) *pf* (*impf* **осажда́ть**) besiege.

осади́ть[2] (**-ажу́**, **-а́дишь**) *pf* (*impf* **оса́живать**) check; force back; rein in; take down a peg.

оса́дный siege.

оса́док (**-дка**) sediment; fall-out; after-taste; *pl* precipitation, fall-out. **оса́дочный** sedimentary.

осажда́ть *impf of* **осади́ть**[1]

оса́живать *impf of* **осади́ть**[2]. **осажу́** *see* **осади́ть**[1,2]

оса́нка carriage, bearing.

осва́ивать(ся *impf of* **осво́ить(ся**

осведоми́тельный informative; information. **осве́домить** (**-млю**) *pf*, **осведомля́ть** *impf* inform; **~ся** о+*prep* inquire about, ask after. **осведомле́ние** notification. **осве́домлённый** well-informed, knowledgeable.

освежа́ть *impf*, **освежи́ть** (**-жу́**) *pf* refresh; air. **освежи́тельный** refreshing.

освети́тельный illuminating. **освети́ть** (**-ещу́**) *pf*, **освеща́ть** *pf* light up; illuminate; throw light on; **~ся** light up. **освеще́ние** lighting, illumination. **освещённый** (**-ён**, **-а́**) lit.

о|свиде́тельствовать *pf*.

освиста́ть (**-ищу́**, **-и́щешь**) *pf*, **освистывать** *impf* hiss (off); boo.

освободи́тель *m* liberator. **освободи́тельный** liberation, emancipation. **освободи́ть** (**-ожу́**) *pf*, **освобожда́ть** *impf* liberate; emancipate; dismiss; vacate; empty; **~ся** free o.s.; become free. **освобожде́ние** liberation; release; emancipation; vacation. **освобождённый** (**-ён**, **-а́**) freed; free; exempt.

освое́ние mastery; opening up. **осво́ить** *pf* (*impf* **осва́ивать**) master; become familiar with; **~ся** familiarize o.s.

освящённый (**-ён**, **-ена́**) consecrated; sanctified; **~ века́ми** time-honoured.

оседа́ть *impf of* **осе́сть**

о|седла́ть *pf*, **осе́длывать** *impf* saddle.

осе́длый settled.

осека́ться *impf of* **осе́чься**

осёл (**-сла́**) donkey; ass.

осело́к (**-лка́**) touchstone; whetstone.

осени́ть *pf* (*impf* **осеня́ть**) over-shadow; dawn upon.

осе́нний autumn(al). **о́сень** autumn. **о́сенью** *adv* in autumn.

осеня́ть *impf of* **осени́ть**

осе́сть (**ося́ду**; **-се́л**) *pf* (*impf* **оседа́ть**) settle; subside.

осётр (**-а́**) sturgeon. **осетри́на** sturgeon.

осе́чка misfire. **осе́чься** (**-еку́сь**, **-ечёшься**; **-е́кся**, **-екла́сь**) *pf* (*impf* **осека́ться**) stop short.

оси́ливать *impf*, **оси́лить** *pf* overpower; master.

осина aspen.

о|си́пнуть (-ну; оси́п) get hoarse.

осироте́лый orphaned. осироте́ть (-е́ю) pf be orphaned.

оска́ливать impf, о|ска́лить pf; ~ зу́бы, ~ся bare one's teeth.

о|сканда́лить(ся pf.

оскверни́ть pf, оскверня́ть impf profane; defile.

оско́лок (-лка) splinter; fragment.

оско́мина bitter taste (in the mouth); наби́ть оско́мину set the teeth on edge.

оскорби́тельный insulting, abusive. оскорби́ть (-блю́) pf, оскорбля́ть impf insult; offend; ~ся take offence. оскорбле́ние insult. оскорблённый (-ён, -а́) insulted.

ослабева́ть impf, о|слабе́ть (-е́ю) pf weaken; slacken. осла́бить (-блю) pf, ослабля́ть impf weaken; slacken. ослабле́ние weakening; slackening; relaxation.

ослепи́тельный blinding, dazzling. ослепи́ть (-плю́) pf, ослепля́ть impf blind, dazzle. ослепле́ние blinding, dazzling; blindness. о|слепну́ть (-ну; -сле́п) pf.

осли́ный donkey; asinine. осли́ца she-ass.

осложне́ние complication. осложни́ть pf, осложня́ть impf complicate; ~ся become complicated.

ослы́шаться (-шусь) pf mishear.

осма́тривать(ся impf of осмотре́ть(ся. осме́ивать impf of осмея́ть

о|смеле́ть (-е́ю) pf. осме́ливаться impf, осме́литься pf dare; venture.

осмея́ть (-ею́, -еёшь) pf (impf осме́ивать) ridicule.

осмо́тр examination, inspection. осмотре́ть (-рю́, -ришь) pf (impf осма́тривать) examine, inspect; look round; ~ся look round. осмотри́тельный circumspect.

осмы́сленный sensible, intelligent. осмы́сливать impf, осмы́слить pf, осмысля́ть impf interpret; comprehend.

оснасти́ть (-ащу́) pf, оснаща́ть impf fit out, equip. осна́стка rigging. оснаще́ние fitting out; equipment.

осно́ва base, basis; foundation; pl fundamentals; stem (of a word).

основа́ние founding, foundation; base; basis; reason; на како́м основа́нии? on what grounds? основа́тель m founder. основа́тельный well-founded; solid; thorough. основа́ть pf, осно́вывать impf found; base; ~ся settle; be founded, be based. основно́й fundamental, basic; main; в основно́м in the main, on the whole. основополо́жник founder.

осо́ба person. осо́бенно adv especially. осо́бенность peculiarity; в осо́бенности in particular. осо́бенный special, particular, peculiar. особня́к (-а́) private residence; detached house. особняко́м adv by o.s. осо́бо adv apart; especially. осо́бый special; particular.

осознава́ть (-наю́, -наёшь) impf, осозна́ть pf realize.

осо́ка sedge.

о́спа smallpox; pock-marks.

оспа́ривать impf, оспо́рить pf dispute; contest.

о|срами́ть(ся (-млю́(сь) pf. остава́ться (-таю́сь, -таёшься) impf of оста́ться

ост (naut) east; east wind.

оста́вить (-влю) pf, оставля́ть impf leave; abandon; reserve.

остально́й the rest of; ~о́е sb the rest; ~ы́е sb pl the others.

остана́вливать(ся impf of останови́ть(ся

оста́нки (-ов) pl remains.

останови́ть (-влю́, -вишь) pf (impf остана́вливать) stop; restrain; ~ся stop, halt; stay; +на+prep dwell on; settle on. остано́вка stop.

оста́ток (-тка) remainder; rest; residue; pl remains; leftovers. оста́ться (-а́нусь) pf (impf остава́ться) remain; stay; impers it remains, it is necessary; нам не остаётся ничего́ друго́го, как we have no choice but.

остекли́ть pf, остекля́ть impf glaze.

остервене́ть pf become enraged.

остерега́ть impf, остере́чь (-регу́, -режёшь; -рёг, -ла́) pf warn; ~ся (+gen) beware (of).

о́стов frame, framework; skeleton.

о|столбене́ть (-е́ю) pf.

осторо́жно adv carefully; ~! look

out! осторóжность care, caution. осторóжный careful, cautious.

остригáть(ся impf of острúчь(ся

остриё point; spike; (cutting) edge. острúть¹ impf sharpen. острúть² impf (pf c~) be witty.

о|стрúчь (-игý, -ижёшь; -úг) pf (impf also остригáть) cut, clip; ~ся have one's hair cut.

óстров (pl -á) island. островóк (-вкá) islet; ~ безопáсности (traffic) island.

острóта¹ witticism, joke. острóта² sharpness; keenness; pungency. остроýмие wit. остроýмный witty.

óстрый (остр, -á, -о) sharp; pointed; acute; keen. острúк (-á) wit.

о|студúть (-ужý, -ýдишь) pf, остужáть impf cool.

оступáться impf, оступúться (-плюсь, -пишься) pf stumble.

остывáть impf, остыть (-ýну) pf get cold; cool down.

осудúть (-ужý, -ýдишь) pf, осуждáть impf condemn; convict. осуждéние condemnation; conviction. осуждённый (-ён, -á) condemned, convicted; sb convict.

осýнуться (-нусь) pf grow thin, become drawn.

осушáть impf, осушúть (-шý, -шишь) pf drain; dry. осушéние drainage.

осуществúмый feasible. осуществúть (-влю) pf, осуществлять impf realize, bring about; accomplish; ~ся be fulfilled, come true. осуществлéние realization; accomplishment.

осчастлúвить (-влю) pf, осчастлúвливать impf make happy.

осыпáть (-плю) pf, осыпáть impf strew; shower; ~ся crumble; fall. óсыпь scree.

ось (gen pl -éй) axis; axle.

осьминóг octopus.

осяду etc.: see осéсть

осязáемый tangible. осязáние touch. осязáтельный tactile; tangible. осязáть impf feel.

от, ото prep+gen from; of; against.

отáпливать impf of отопúть

отáра flock (of sheep).

отбáвить (-влю) pf, отбавлять impf pour off; хоть отбавляй more than enough.

отбегáть impf, отбежáть (-егý) pf

run off.

отберý etc.: see отобрáть

отбивáть(ся impf of отбúть(ся

отбивнáя котлéта cutlet, chop.

отбирáть impf of отобрáть

отбúть (отобью, -ёшь) pf (impf отбивáть) beat (off), repel; win over; break off; ~ся break off; drop behind; +от+gen defend o.s. against.

óтблеск reflection.

отбóй repelling; retreat; ringing off. бить ~ beat a retreat; дать ~ ring off.

отбóйный молотóк (-ткá) pneumatic drill.

отбóр selection. отбóрный choice, select(ed).

отбрáсывать impf, отбрóсить (-óшу) pf throw off or away; hurl back; reject; ~ тень cast a shadow. отбрóсы (-ов) pl garbage.

отбывáть impf, отбыть (-бýду; óтбыл, -á, -о) pf depart; serve (a sentence).

отвáга courage, bravery.

отвáживаться impf, отвáжиться (-жусь) pf dare. отвáжный courageous.

отвáл dump, slag-heap; casting off; до ~а to satiety. отвáливать impf, отвалúть (-лю, -лишь) pf push aside; cast off; fork out.

отвáр broth; decoction. отвáривать impf, отварúть (-рю, -ришь) pf boil. отварнóй boiled.

отвéдать pf (impf отвéдывать) taste, try.

отведý etc.: see отвестú

отвéдывать impf of отвéдать

отвезтú (-зý, -зёшь; -вёз, -лá) pf (impf отвозúть) take or cart away.

отвёл etc.: see отвестú

отвергáть impf, отвéргнуть (-ну; -вéрг) pf reject; repudiate. отвéрженный outcast.

отвернýть (-нý, -нёшь) pf (impf отвёртывать, отворáчивать) turn aside; turn down; turn on; unscrew; screw off; ~ся turn away; come unscrewed.

отвéрстие opening; hole.

отвертéть (-рчý, -ртишь) pf (impf отвёртывать) unscrew; twist off; ~ся come unscrewed; get off. отвёртка screwdriver.

отвёртывать(ся *impf of* отверну́ть(ся, отверте́ть(ся

отве́с plumb; vertical slope. отве́сить (-е́шу) *pf* (*impf* отве́шивать) weigh out. отве́сный perpendicular, sheer.

отвести́ (-еду́, -еде́шь; -вёл, -а́) *pf* (*impf* отводи́ть) lead, take; draw *or* take aside; deflect; draw off; reject; allot.

отве́т answer.

ответви́ться *pf*, ответвля́ться *impf* branch off. ответвле́ние branch, offshoot.

отве́тить (-е́чу) *pf*, отвеча́ть *impf* answer; +на+*acc* reply to; +за+*acc* answer for. отве́тный in reply, return. отве́тственность responsibility. отве́тственный responsible. отве́тчик defendant.

отве́шивать *impf of* отве́сить. отве́шу *etc.*: *see* отве́сить

отвинти́ть (-нчу́) *pf*, отви́нчивать *impf* unscrew.

отвиса́ть *impf*, отви́снуть (-нет; -и́с) *pf* hang down, sag. отви́слый hanging, baggy.

отвлека́ть *impf*, отвле́чь (-еку́, -ечёшь; -влёк, -ла́) *pf* distract, divert; ~ся be distracted. отвлечённый abstract.

отво́д taking aside; diversion; leading, taking; rejection; allotment. отводи́ть (-ожу́, -о́дишь) *impf of* отвести́

отвоева́ть (-ою́ю) *pf*, отвоёвывать *impf* win back; spend in fighting.

отвози́ть (-ожу́, -о́зишь) *impf of* отвезти́. отвора́чивать(ся *impf of* отверну́ть(ся

отвори́ть (-рю́, -ришь) *pf* (*impf* отворя́ть) open; ~ся open.

отворя́ть(ся *impf of* отвори́ть(ся. отворю́ю *etc.*: *see* отвоева́ть

отврати́тельный disgusting. отвраще́ние disgust, repugnance.

отвыка́ть *impf*, отвы́кнуть (-ну; -вы́к) *pf* +от *or* inf lose the habit of; grow out of.

отвяза́ть (-яжу́, -я́жешь) *pf*, отвя́зывать *impf* untie, unfasten; ~ся come untied, come loose; +от+*gen* get rid of; leave alone.

отгада́ть *pf*, отга́дывать *impf* guess. отга́дка answer.

отгиба́ть(ся *impf of* отогну́ть(ся

отгла́дить (-а́жу) *pf*, отгла́живать *impf* iron (out).

отгова́ривать *impf*, отговори́ть *pf* dissuade; ~ся +*instr* plead. отгово́рка excuse, pretext.

отголо́сок (-ска) echo.

отгоня́ть *impf of* отогна́ть

отгора́живать *impf*, отгороди́ть (-ожу́, -о́дишь) *pf* fence off; partition off; ~ся shut o.s. off.

отдава́ть[1](ся (-даю́(сь) *impf of* отда́ть(ся. отдава́ть[2] (-аёт) *impf impers*+*instr* taste of; smell of; smack of; от него́ отдаёт во́дкой he reeks of vodka.

отдале́ние removal; distance. отдалённый remote. отдали́ть *pf*, отдаля́ть *impf* remove; estrange; postpone; ~ся move away; digress.

отда́ть (-а́м, -а́шь, -а́ст, -ади́м; о́тдал, -а́, -о) *pf* (*impf* отдава́ть[1]) give back, return; give; give up; give away; recoil; cast off; ~ся give o.s. (up); resound. отда́ча return; payment; casting off; efficiency; output; recoil.

отде́л department; section.

отде́лать *pf* (*impf* отде́лывать) finish, put the finishing touches to; trim; ~ся +от+*gen* get rid of; +*instr* get off with.

отделе́ние separation; department; compartment; section. отдели́ть (-елю́, -е́лишь) *pf* (*impf* отделя́ть) separate; detach; ~ся separate; detach o.s.; get detached.

отде́лка finishing; finish, decoration. отде́лывать(ся *impf of* отде́лать(ся

отде́льно separately; apart. отде́льный separate. отделя́ть(ся *impf of* отдели́ть(ся

отдёргивать *impf*, отдёрнуть (-ну) *pf* draw *or* pull aside *or* back.

отдеру́ *etc.*: *see* отодра́ть. отдира́ть *impf of* отодра́ть

отдохну́ть (-ну́, -нёшь) *pf* (*impf* отдыха́ть) rest.

отду́шина air-hole, vent.

о́тдых rest. отдыха́ть *impf* (*pf* отдохну́ть) rest; be on holiday.

отдыша́ться (-шу́сь, -шишься) *pf* recover one's breath.

отека́ть *impf of* оте́чь. о|тели́ться (-е́лится) *pf*.

отéль *m* hotel.

отесáть *etc.: see* **обтесáть**

отéц (отцá) father. **отéческий** fatherly, paternal. **отéчественный** home, native. **отéчество** native land, fatherland.

отéчь (-екý, -ечёшь; отёк, -лá) *pf* (*impf* **отекáть**) swell (up).

отживáть *impf*, **отжить** (-ивý, -ивёшь; óжил, -á, -о) *pf* become obsolete *or* outmoded. **отживший** obsolete; outmoded.

óтзвук echo.

óтзыв[1] opinion; reference; review; response. **отзыв**[2] recall. **отзывáть(ся** *impf of* **отозвáть(ся. отзывчивый** responsive.

откáз refusal; repudiation; failure; natural. **отказáть** (-ажý, -áжешь) *pf*, **откáзывать** *impf* break down; (+*dat* в+*prep*) refuse, deny (*s.o. sth*); ~**ся** (+ от+*gen or* +*inf*) refuse; turn down; renounce, give up.

откáлывать(ся *impf of* **отколóть**(-(ся. **откáпывать** *impf of* **откопáть. откáрмливать** *impf of* **откормить**

откатить (-ачý, -áтишь) *pf*, **откáтывать** *impf* roll away; ~**ся** roll away *or* back; be forced back.

откачáть *pf*, **откáчивать** *impf* pump out; give artificial respiration to.

откáшливаться *impf*, **откáшляться** *pf* clear one's throat.

откиднóй folding, collapsible. **откидывать** *impf*, **откинуть** (-ну) *pf* fold back; throw aside.

отклáдывать *impf of* **отложить**

отклéивать *impf*, **отклéить** (-éю) *pf* unstick; ~**ся** come unstuck.

óтклик response; comment; echo. **откликáться** *impf*, **откликнуться** (-нусь) *pf* answer, respond.

отклонéние deviation; declining, refusal; deflection. **отклонить** (-ню, -нишь) *pf*, **отклонять** *impf* deflect; decline; ~**ся** deviate; diverge.

отключáть *impf*, **отключить** (-чý) *pf* cut off, disconnect.

откотить (-очý, -óтишь) *pf* knock off; beat up.

отколóть (-лю, -лешь) *pf* (*impf* **откáлывать**) break off; chop off; unpin; ~**ся** break off; come unpinned; break away.

откопáть *pf* (*impf* **откáпывать**) dig

up; exhume.

откормить (-млю, -мишь) *pf* (*impf* **откáрмливать**) fatten.

откóс slope.

открепить (-плю) *pf*, **откреплять** *impf* unfasten; ~**ся** become unfastened.

откровéние revelation. **откровéнный** frank; outspoken; unconcealed. **открою** *etc.: see* **открыть**

открутить (-учý, -ýтишь) *pf*, **открýчивать** *impf* untwist, unscrew.

открывáть *impf*, **открыть** (-рóю) *pf* open; reveal; discover; turn on; ~**ся** open; come to light, be revealed. **открытие** discovery; revelation; opening. **открытка** postcard; card. **открыто** openly. **открытый** open.

откýда *adv* from where; from which; how; ~ **ни возьмись** from out of nowhere. **откýда-либо, -нибудь** from somewhere or other. **откýда-то** from somewhere.

откýпоривать *impf*, **откýпорить** *pf* uncork.

откусить (-ушý, -ýсишь) *pf*, **откýсывать** *impf* bite off.

отлагáтельство delay. **отлагáть** *impf of* **отложить**

от|**лакировáть** *pf.* **отлáмывать** *impf of* **отломáть, отломить**

отлепить (-плю, -пишь) *pf* unstick, take off; ~**ся** come unstuck, come off.

отлёт flying away; departure. **отлетáть** *impf*, **отлетéть** (-лечý) *pf*, fly, fly away, fly off; rebound.

отлив ebb, ebb-tide; tint; play of colours. **отливáть** *impf*, **отлить** (отолью; óтлил, -á, -о) *pf* pour off; pump out; cast, found; (*no pf*) +*instr* be shot with. **отливка** casting; moulding.

отличáть *impf*, **отличить** (-чý) *pf* distinguish; ~**ся** distinguish *oneself*; ~**ся** differ; +*instr* be notable for. **отличие** difference; distinction; **знак отличия** order, decoration; **с отличием** with honours. **отличник** outstanding student, worker, etc. **отличительный** distinctive; distinguishing. **отличный** different; excellent.

отлóгий sloping.

отложéние sediment; deposit. **отложить** (-ожý, -óжишь) *pf* (*impf*

откла́дывать, отлага́ть) put aside; postpone; deposit.

отлома́ть, отломи́ть (-млю́, -мишь) *pf* (*impf* **отла́мывать**) break off. **от|лупи́ть** *pf.*

отлуча́ть *impf*, **отлучи́ть** (-чу́) *pf* (**от це́ркви**) excommunicate; **~ся** absent o.s. **отлу́чка** absence.

отлы́нивать *impf* +**от**+*gen* shirk.

отма́хиваться *impf*, **отмахну́ться** (-ну́сь, -нёшься) *pf* **от**+*gen* brush off; brush aside.

отмежева́ться (-жу́юсь) *pf*, **от-межёвываться** *impf* **от**+*gen* dissociate o.s. from.

о́тмель (sand-)bank.

отме́на abolition; cancellation. **отме-ни́ть** (-ню́, -нишь) *pf*, **отменя́ть** *impf* repeal; abolish; cancel.

отмере́ть (отомрёт; о́тмер, -ла́, -ло) *pf* (*impf* **отмира́ть**) die off; die out.

отме́ривать *impf*, **отме́рить** *pf*, **отмеря́ть** *impf* measure off.

отмести́ (-ету́, -етёшь; -ёл, -а́) *pf* (*impf* **отмета́ть**) sweep aside.

отмета́ть *impf of* **отмести́**

отме́тить (-е́чу) *pf*, **отмеча́ть** *impf* mark, note; celebrate; **~ся** sign one's name; sign out. **отме́тка** note; mark.

отмира́ть *impf of* **отмере́ть**

отмора́живать *impf*, **отморо́зить** (-о́жу) *pf* injure by frost-bite. **отмо-ро́жение** frost-bite. **отморо́жен-ный** frost-bitten.

отмо́ю *etc.: see* **отмы́ть**

отмыва́ть *impf*, **отмы́ть** (-мо́ю) *pf* wash clean; wash off; **~ся** wash o.s. clean; come out.

отмыка́ть *impf of* **отомкну́ть**

отмы́чка master key.

отнести́ (-су́, -ёшь; -нёс, -ла́) *pf* (*impf* **относи́ть**) take; carry away; ascribe, attribute; **~сь к**+*dat* treat; regard; apply to; concern, have to do with.

отнима́ть(ся *impf of* **отня́ть(ся**

относи́тельно *adv* relatively; *prep* +*gen* concerning. **относи́тельность** relativity. **относи́тельный** relative.

относи́ть(ся (-ошу́(сь, -о́сишь(ся) *impf of* **отнести́(сь. отноше́ние** attitude; relation; respect; ratio; **в отноше́нии**+*gen*, **по отноше́нию к**+*dat* with regard to; **в прямо́м (обра́тном) отноше́нии** in direct (in-

verse) ratio.

отны́не *adv* henceforth.

отню́дь not at all.

отня́тие taking away; amputation. **отня́ть** (-ниму́, -ни́мешь; о́тнял, -а́, -о) *pf* (*impf* **отнима́ть**) take (away); amputate; **~ от груди́** wean; **~ся** be paralysed.

ото́: *see* **от**

отобража́ть *impf*, **отобрази́ть** (-ажу́) *pf* reflect; represent. **отображе́ние** reflection; representation.

отобра́ть (отберу́, -рёшь; отобра́л, -а́, -о) *pf* (*impf* **отбира́ть**) take (away); select.

отобью́ *etc.: see* **отби́ть**

отовсю́ду *adv* from everywhere.

отогна́ть (отгоню́, -о́нишь; отогна́л, -а́, -о) *pf* (*impf* **отгоня́ть**) drive away, off.

отогну́ть (-ну́, -нёшь) *pf* (*impf* **отгиба́ть**) bend back; **~ся** bend.

отогрева́ть *impf*, **отогре́ть** (-е́ю) *pf* warm.

отодвига́ть *impf*, **отодви́нуть** (-ну) *pf* move aside; put off.

отодра́ть (отдеру́, -рёшь; отодра́л, -а́, -о) *pf* (*impf* **отдира́ть**) tear off, rip off.

отож(д)естви́ть (-влю́) *pf*, **ото-ж(д)ествля́ть** *impf* identify.

отозва́ть (отзову́, -вёшь; отозва́л, -а́, -о)*pf* (*impf* **отзыва́ть**) take aside; recall; **~ся на**+*acc* answer; на+*acc* or *prep* tell on; have an affect on.

отойти́ (-йду́, -йдёшь; отошёл, -шла́) *pf* (*impf* **отходи́ть**) move away; depart; withdraw; digress; come out; recover.

отолью́ *etc.: see* **отли́ть. отомре́т** *etc.: see* **отмере́ть. ото|моти́ть** (-мщу́) *pf.*

отомкну́ть (-ну́, -нёшь) *pf* (*impf* **отмыка́ть**) unlock, unbolt.

отопи́тельный heating. **отопи́ть** (-плю́, -пишь) *pf* (*impf* **ота́пливать**) heat. **отопле́ние** heating.

отопру́ *etc.: see* **отпере́ть. отопью́** *etc.: see* **отпи́ть**

ото́рванный cut off, isolated. **ото-рва́ть** (-ву́, -вёшь) *pf* (*impf* **отры-ва́ть**) tear off; tear away; **~ся** come off, be torn off; be cut off, lose touch; break away; tear o.s. away; **~ся от земли́** take off.

оторопе́ть (-е́ю) *pf* be struck dumb.

отосла́ть (-ошлю́, -ошлёшь) pf (impf отсыла́ть) send (off); send back; +к+dat refer to.

отоспа́ться (-сплю́сь, -а́лся, -ала́сь, -ось) pf (impf отсыпа́ться) catch up on one's sleep.

отошёл etc.: see отойти́. отошлю́ etc.: see отосла́ть

отпада́ть impf of отпа́сть.

от|пари́ровать pf. отпа́рывать impf of отпоро́ть

отпа́сть (-адёт) pf (impf отпада́ть) fall off; fall away; pass.

отпева́ние funeral service.

отпере́ть (отопру́, -прёшь; о́тпер, -ла́, -ло) pf (impf отпира́ть) unlock; ~ся open; +от+gen deny; disown.

от|печа́тать pf, отпеча́тывать impf print (off); type (out); imprint. отпеча́ток (-тка) imprint, print.

отпива́ть impf of отпи́ть

отпи́ливать impf, отпили́ть (-лю́, -лишь) pf saw off.

от|пира́тельство denial. отпира́ть(ся impf of отпере́ть(ся

отпи́ть (отопью́, -пьёшь; о́тпил, -а́, -о) pf (impf отпива́ть) take a sip of.

отпи́хивать impf, отпихну́ть (-ну́, -нёшь) pf push off; shove aside.

отплати́ть (-ачу́, -а́тишь) pf, отпла́чивать impf +dat pay back.

отплыва́ть impf, отплы́ть (-ыву́, -ывёшь; -ы́л, -а́, -о) pf (set) sail; swim off. отплы́тие sailing, departure.

о́тповедь rebuke.

отполза́ть impf, отползти́ (-зу́, -зёшь; -о́лз, -ла́) pf crawl away.

от|полирова́ть pf. от|полоска́ть (-ощу́) pf.

отпо́р repulse; rebuff.

отпоро́ть (-рю́, -решь) pf (impf отпа́рывать) rip off.

отправи́тель m sender. отпра́вить (-влю) pf, отправля́ть impf send, dispatch; ~ся set off, start. отпра́вка dispatch. отправле́ние sending; departure; performance. отправно́й: ~о́й пункт, ~а́я то́чка starting-point.

от|пра́здновать pf.

отпра́шиваться impf, отпроси́ться (-ошу́сь, -о́сишься) pf ask for leave, get leave.

отпры́гивать impf, отпры́гнуть (-ну) pf jump or spring back or aside.

о́тпрыск offshoot, scion.

отпряга́ть impf of отпря́чь

отпря́нуть (-ну) pf recoil, start back.

отпря́чь (-ягу́, -яжёшь; -я́г, -ла́) pf (impf отпряга́ть) unharness.

отпу́гивать impf, отпугну́ть (-ну́, -нёшь) pf frighten off.

о́тпуск (pl -á) leave, holiday(s). отпуска́ть impf, отпусти́ть (-ущу́, -у́стишь) pf let go, let off; set free; release; slacken; (let) grow; allot; remit. отпускни́к (-á) person on leave. отпускно́й holiday; leave. отпуще́ние remission; козёл отпуще́ния scapegoat.

отраба́тывать impf, отрабо́тать pf work off; master. отрабо́танный worked out; waste, spent, exhaust.

отра́ва poison. отрави́ть (-влю́, -вишь) pf, отравля́ть impf poison.

отра́да joy, delight. отра́дный gratifying, pleasing.

отража́тель m reflector; scanner. отража́ть impf, отрази́ть (-ажу́) pf reflect; repulse; ~ся be reflected; +на+prep affect. отраже́ние reflection; repulse.

о́трасль branch.

отраста́ть impf, отрасти́ (-тёт; отро́с, -ла́) pf grow. отрасти́ть (-ащу́) pf, отра́щивать impf (let) grow.

от|реаги́ровать pf. от|регули́ровать pf. от|редакти́ровать pf.

отре́з cut; length. отре́зать (-е́жу) pf, отреза́ть impf cut off; snap.

о|трезве́ть (-е́ю) pf. отрезви́ть (-влю́, -ви́шь) pf, отрезвля́ть impf sober; ~ся sober up.

отре́зок (-зка) piece; section; segment.

отрека́ться impf of отре́чься

от|рекомендова́ть(ся pf. отрёкся etc.: see отре́чься. от|ремонти́ровать pf. от|репети́ровать pf. отре́пье, отре́пья (-ьев) pl rags.

от|реставри́ровать pf.

отрече́ние renunciation; ~ от престо́ла abdication. отре́чься (-еку́сь, -ечёшься) pf (impf отрека́ться) renounce.

отреша́ться impf, отреши́ться (-шу́сь) pf renounce; get rid of.

отрица́ние denial; negation. отрица́тельный negative. отрица́ть impf deny.

отрóс *etc.: see* отрастú. отрóсток (-тка) shoot, sprout; appendix.
óтрочество adolescence.
отрубáть *impf of* отрубúть
óтруби (-ей) *pl* bran.
отрубúть (-блю, -бишь) *pf* (*impf* отрубáть) chop off; snap back.
от|ругáть *pf.*
отрыв tearing off; alienation, isolation; в ~е от+*gen* out of touch with; ~ (от земли) take-off. отрывáть(ся *impf of* оторвáть(ся. отрывúстый staccato; disjointed. отрывнóй tear-off. отрывок (-вка) fragment, excerpt. отрывочный fragmentary, scrappy.
отрыжка belch; throw-back.
от|рыть (-рóю) *pf.*
отряд detachment; order.
отряхивать *impf*, отряхнýть (-нý, -нёшь) *pf* shake down *or* off.
от|салютовáть *pf.*
отсáсывание suction. отсáсывать *impf of* отсосáть
отсвéчивать *impf* be reflected; +*instr* shine with.
отсéв sifting, selection; dropping out. отсевáть(ся, отсéивать(ся *impf of* отсéять(ся
отсéк compartment. отсекáть *impf*, отсéчь (-екý, -ечёшь; -сéк, -лá) *pf* chop off.
отсéять (-éю) *pf* (*impf* отсевáть, отсéивать) sift, screen; eliminate; ~ся drop out.
отсидéть (-ижу) *pf*, отсúживать *impf* make numb by sitting; sit through; serve out.
отскáкивать *impf*, отскочúть (-чý, -чишь) *pf* jump aside *or* away; rebound; come off.
отслýживать *impf*, отслужúть (-жý, -жишь) *pf* serve one's time; be worn out.
отсосáть (-осý, -осёшь) *pf* (*impf* отсáсывать) suck off, draw off.
отсóхнуть (-ну) *pf* (*impf* отсыхáть) wither.
отсрóчивать *impf*, отсрóчить *pf* postpone, defer. отсрóчка postponement, deferment.
отставáние lag; lagging behind. отставáть (-таю, -аёшь) *impf of* отстáть
отстáвить (-влю) *pf*, отставлять

impf set *or* put aside. отстáвка resignation; retirement; в отстáвке retired; вы́йти в отстáвку resign, retire. отставнóй retired.
отстáивать(ся *impf of* отстоять(ся
отстáлость backwardness. отстáлый backward. отстáть (-áну) *pf* (*impf* отставáть) fall behind; lag behind; become detached; lose touch; break (off); be slow. отстающий *sb* backward pupil.
от|стегáть *pf.*
отстёгивать *impf*, отстегнýть (-нý, -нёшь) *pf* unfasten, undo; ~ся come unfastened *or* undone.
отстоять¹ (-ою) *pf* (*impf* отстáивать) defend; stand up for.
отстоять² (-оúт) *impf* на+*acc* be ... distant (от+*gen* from). отстояться *pf* (*impf* отстáиваться) settle; become stabilized.
отстрáивать(ся *impf of* отстрóить(ся
отстранéние pushing aside; dismissal. отстранúть *pf*, отстранять *impf* push aside; remove; suspend; ~ся move away; keep aloof; ~ся от dodge.
отстрéливаться *impf*, отстреляться *pf* fire back.
отстригáть *impf*, отстрúчь (-игý, -ижёшь; -рúг) *pf* cut off.
отстрóить *pf* (*impf* отстрáивать) finish building; build up.
отступáть *impf*, отступúть (-плю, -пишь) *pf* step back; recede; retreat; back down; ~ от+*gen* give up; deviate from; ~ся от+*gen* give up; go back on. отступлéние retreat; deviation; digression. отступнóй: ~ые дéньги, ~óе *sb* indemnity, compensation. отступя *adv* (farther) off, away (от+*gen* from).
отсýтствие absence; lack. отсýтствовать *impf* be absent. отсýтствующий absent; *sb* absentee.
отсчитáть *pf*, отсчúтывать *impf* count off.
отсылáть *impf of* отослáть
отсыпáть (-плю) *pf*, отсыпáть *impf* pour out; measure off.
отсыпáться *impf of* отоспáться
отсырéлый damp. от|сырéть (-éет) *pf.*
отсыхáть *impf of* отсóхнуть

отсю́да *adv* from here; hence.

отта́ивать *impf of* отта́ять

отта́лкивать *impf of* оттолкну́ть. отта́лкивающий repulsive, repellent.

отта́чивать *impf of* отточи́ть

отта́ять (-а́ю) *pf* (*impf* отта́ивать) thaw out.

отте́нок (-нка) shade, nuance; tint.

о́ттепель thaw.

оттесни́ть *pf*, оттесня́ть *impf* drive back; push aside.

о́ттиск impression; off-print, reprint.

оттого́ *adv* that is why; ~, что because.

оттолкну́ть (-ну́, -нёшь) *pf* (*impf* отта́лкивать) push away; antagonize; ~ся push off.

оттопы́ренный protruding. оттопы́ривать *impf*, оттопы́рить *pf* stick out; ~ся protrude; bulge.

отточи́ть (-чу́, -чишь) *pf* (*impf* отта́чивать) sharpen.

отту́да *adv* from there.

оття́гивать *impf*, оттяну́ть (-ну́, -нешь) *pf* draw out; draw off; delay. оття́жка delay.

отупе́ние stupefaction. о|тупе́ть (-е́ю) *pf* sink into torpor.

от|утю́жить (-жу) *pf*

отуча́ть *impf*, отучи́ть (-чу́, -чишь) *pf* break (of); ~ся break o.s. (of).

отха́ркать *pf*, отха́ркивать *impf* expectorate.

отхвати́ть (-ачу́, -а́тишь) *pf*, отхва́тывать *impf* snip *or* chop off.

отхлебну́ть (-ну́, -нёшь) *pf*, отхлёбывать *impf* sip, take a sip of.

отхлы́нуть (-нет) *pf* flood *or* rush back.

отхо́д departure; withdrawal. отходи́ть (-ожу́, -о́дишь) *impf of* отойти́. отхо́ды (-ов) *pl* waste.

отцвести́ (-ету́, -етёшь; -ёл, -а́) *pf*, отцвета́ть *impf* finish blossoming, fade.

отцепи́ть (-плю́, -пишь) *pf*, отцепля́ть *impf* unhook; uncouple.

отцо́вский father's; paternal.

отча́иваться *impf of* отча́яться

отча́ливать *impf*, отча́лить *pf* cast off.

отча́сти *adv* partly.

отча́яние despair. отча́янный desperate. отча́яться (-а́юсь) *pf* (*impf*

отча́иваться) despair.

отчего́ *adv* why. отчего́-либо, -нибудь *adv* for some reason or other. отчего́-то *adv* for some reason.

от|чека́нить *pf*.

о́тчество patronymic.

отчёт account; отда́ть себе́ ~ в+*prep* be aware of, realize. отчётливый distinct; clear. отчётность bookkeeping; accounts. отчётный *adj*: ~ год financial year, current year; ~ докла́д report.

отчи́зна native land. о́тчий paternal. о́тчим step-father.

отчисле́ние deduction; dismissal. отчи́слить *pf*, отчисля́ть *impf* deduct; dismiss.

отчита́ть *pf*, отчи́тывать *impf* tell off; ~ся report back.

отчужде́ние alienation; estrangement.

отшатну́ться (-ну́сь, -нёшься) *pf*, отша́тываться *impf* start back, recoil; +от+*gen* give up, forsake.

отши́бривать *impf*, отшибну́ть (-ну́, -нёшь) *pf* fling away; throw off. отше́льник hermit; recluse.

отшлёпать *pf* spank.

от|шлифова́ть *pf*. от|штукату́рить *pf*.

отщепе́нец (-нца) renegade.

отъе́зд departure. отъезжа́ть *impf*, отъе́хать (-е́ду) *pf* drive off, go off.

отъя́вленный inveterate.

отыгра́ть *pf*, оты́грывать *impf* win back; ~ся win back what one has lost.

отыска́ть (-ыщу́, -ы́щешь) *pf*, оты́скивать *impf* find; look for; ~ся turn up, appear.

отяготи́ть (-ощу́) *pf*, отягоща́ть *impf* burden.

офице́р officer. офице́рский officer's, officers'.

официа́льный official.

официа́нт waiter. официа́нтка waitress.

официо́з semi-official organ. официо́зный semi-official.

оформи́тель *m* designer; stage-painter. офо́рмить (-млю) *pf*, оформля́ть *impf* design; put into shape; make official; process; ~ся take shape; go through the formalities. оформле́ние design; mounting, staging; processing.

ox *int* oh! ah!

оха́пка armful.

о|характеризова́ть *pf.*

о́хать *impf (pf* о́хнуть*)* moan; sigh.

охва́т scope; inclusion; outflanking. **охвати́ть** (-ачу́, -а́тишь) *pf,* **охва́-
тывать** *impf* envelop; seize; compre-
hend.

охладева́ть *impf,* **охладе́ть** (-е́ю)
pf grow cold. **охлади́ть** (-ажу́) *pf,*
охлажда́ть *impf* cool; ~ся become
cool, cool down. **охлажде́ние** cooling; coolness.

о|хмеле́ть (-е́ю) *pf.* о́хнуть (-ну) *pf*
of о́хать

охо́та[1] hunt, hunting; chase.

охо́та[2] wish, desire.

охо́титься (-о́чусь) *impf* hunt. **охо́т-
ник**[1] hunter.

охо́тник[2] volunteer; enthusiast.

охо́тничий hunting.

охо́тно *adv* willingly, gladly.

о́хра ochre.

охра́на guarding; protection; guard.
охрани́ть *pf,* **охраня́ть** *impf* guard,
protect.

охри́плый, охри́пший hoarse.
о|хри́пнуть (-ну; охри́п) *pf* become
hoarse.

о|цара́пать(ся *pf.*

оце́нивать *impf,* **оцени́ть** (-ню́, -нишь)
pf estimate; appraise. **оце́нка** estimation; appraisal; estimate. **оце́н-
щик** valuer.

о|цепене́ть (-е́ю) *pf.*

оцепи́ть (-плю́, -пишь) *pf,* **оцепля́ть**
impf surround; cordon off.

оча́г (-а́) hearth; centre; breeding
ground; hotbed.

очарова́ние charm, fascination. **оча-
рова́тельный** charming. **очаро-
ва́ть** *pf,* **очаро́вывать** *impf* charm,
fascinate.

очеви́дец (-дца) eye-witness. **оче-
ви́дно** *adv* obviously, evidently.
очеви́дный obvious.

о́чень *adv* very; very much.

очередно́й next in turn; usual, regular; routine. **о́чередь** (*gen pl* -е́й)
turn; queue.

о́черк essay, sketch.

о|черни́ть *pf.*

о|черстве́ть (-е́ю) *pf.*

очерта́ние outline(s), contour(s).

очерти́ть (-рчу́, -ртишь) *pf,* **очер-
чивать** *impf* outline.

о́чи *etc.: see* о́ко

очисти́тельный cleansing. о|чи́-
стить (-ищу) *pf,* **очища́ть** *impf*
clean; refine; clear; peel; ~ся clear
o.s.; become clear (от+*gen* of).
очи́стка cleaning; purification; clearance. **очи́стки** (-ов) *pl* peelings.
очище́ние cleansing; purification.

очки́ (-о́в) *pl* spectacles. **очко́** (*gen
pl* -о́в) pip; point. **очко́вая змея́** co-
bra.

очну́ться (-ну́сь, -нёшься) *pf* wake
up; regain consciousness.

о́чный: ~ое обуче́ние classroom instruction; ~ая ста́вка confrontation.

очути́ться (-у́тишься) *pf* find o.s.

оше́йник collar.

ошеломи́тельный stunning. **оше-
ломи́ть** (-млю́) *pf,* **ошеломля́ть**
impf stun.

ошиба́ться *impf,* **ошиби́ться** (-бу́сь,
-бёшься; -бся) *pf* be mistaken, make
a mistake; be wrong. **оши́бка** mistake; error. **оши́бочный** erroneous.

ошпа́ривать *impf,* о|шпа́рить *pf*
scald.

о|штрафова́ть *pf.* о|штукату́рить
pf.

ощети́ниваться *impf,* о|щети́-
ниться *pf* bristle (up).

о|щипа́ть (-плю́, -плешь) *pf,* **ощи́-
пывать** *impf* pluck.

ощу́пать *pf,* **ощу́пывать** *impf* feel;
grope about. **о́щупь:** на ~ to the
touch; by touch. **о́щупью** *adv* grop-
ingly; by touch.

ощути́мый, ощути́тельный perceptible; appreciable. **ощути́ть** (-ущу́)
pf, **ощуща́ть** *impf* feel, sense. **ощу-
ще́ние** sensation; feeling.

П

па *neut indecl* dance step.

павильо́н pavilion; film studio.

павли́н peacock.

па́водок (-дка) (sudden) flood.

па́вший fallen.

па́губный pernicious, ruinous.

па́даль carrion.

па́дать *impf (pf* пасть, упа́сть*)* fall;
~ ду́хом lose heart. **паде́ж** (-а́) case.

паде́ние fall; degradation; incidence.

па́дкий на+*acc or* до+*gen* having a weakness for.

па́дчерица step-daughter.

паёк (пайка́) ration.

па́зуха bosom; sinus; axil.

пай (*pl* -и́, -ёв) share. па́йщик shareholder.

паке́т package; packet; paper bag.

Пакиста́н Pakistan. пакиста́нец (-нца), -а́нка Pakistani. пакиста́нский Pakistani.

па́кля tow; oakum.

пакова́ть *impf* (*pf* за~, у~) pack.

па́костный dirty, mean. па́кость dirty trick; obscenity.

пакт pact.

пала́та chamber, house. пала́тка tent; stall, booth.

пала́ч (-а́) executioner.

па́лец (-льца) finger; toe.

палиса́дник (*small*) front garden.

палиса́ндр rosewood.

пали́тра palette.

пали́ть[1] *impf* (*pf* о~, с~) burn; scorch.

пали́ть[2] *impf* (*pf* вы́~, пальну́ть) fire, shoot.

па́лка stick; walking-stick.

пало́мник pilgrim. пало́мничество pilgrimage.

па́лочка stick; bacillus; wand; baton.

па́луба deck.

пальба́ fire.

па́льма palm(-tree). па́льмовый palm.

пальну́ть (-ну́, -нёшь) *pf of* пали́ть

пальто́ *neut indecl* (over)coat.

паля́щий burning, scorching.

па́мятник monument; memorial. па́мятный memorable; memorial. па́мять memory; consciousness; на ~ as a keepsake.

панаце́я panacea.

пане́ль footpath; panel(ling); wainscot(ing). пане́льный panelling.

па́ника panic. паникёр alarmist.

панихи́да requiem.

пани́ческий panic; panicky.

панно́ *neut indecl* panel.

панора́ма panorama.

пансио́н boarding-house; board and lodging. пансиона́т holiday hotel. пансионе́р boarder; guest.

пантало́ны (-о́н) *pl* knickers.

панте́ра panther.

пантоми́ма mime.

па́нцирь *m* armour, coat of mail.

па́па[1] *m* pope.

па́па[2] *m*, папа́ша *m* daddy.

папа́ха tall fur cap.

папиро́са (*Russian*) cigarette.

па́пка file; folder.

па́поротник fern.

пар[1] (*loc* -у́; *pl* -ы́) steam.

пар[2] (*loc* -у́; *pl* -ы́) fallow.

па́ра pair; couple; (two-piece) suit.

пара́граф paragraph.

пара́д parade; review. пара́дный parade; gala; main, front; ~ая фо́рма full dress (uniform).

парадо́кс paradox. парадокса́льный paradoxical.

парази́т parasite.

парализова́ть *impf & pf* paralyse. парали́ч (-а́) paralysis.

паралле́ль parallel. паралле́льный parallel.

пара́метр parameter.

парано́йя paranoia.

параш́ют parachute.

паре́ние soaring.

па́рень (-рня; *gen pl* -рне́й) *m* lad; fellow.

пари́ *neut indecl* bet; держа́ть ~ bet, lay a bet.

пари́к (-а́) wig. парикма́хер hairdresser. парикма́херская *sb* hairdresser's.

пари́ровать *impf & pf* (*pf also* от~) parry, counter.

парите́т parity.

пари́ть[1] *impf* soar, hover.

па́рить[2] *impf* steam; stew; *impers* па́рит it is sultry; ~ся (*pf* по~ся) steam, sweat; stew.

парк park; depot; stock.

парке́т parquet.

парла́мент parliament. парламента́рный parliamentarian. парламентёр envoy; bearer of flag of truce. парла́ментский parliamentary; ~ зако́н Act of Parliament.

парни́к (-а́) hotbed; seed-bed. парнико́в|ый *adj*: ~ые расте́ния hothouse plants.

парни́шка *m* boy, lad.

парно́й fresh; steamy.

па́рный (forming a) pair; twin.

паро- *in comb* steam-. парово́з

(steam-)engine, locomotive. ~образ-
ный vaporous. ~ход steamer; steamship. ~ходство steamship-line.
паровой steam; steamed.
пародия parody.
пароль *m* password.
паром ferry(-boat).
парт- *abbr in comb* Party. парт-
билет Party (membership) card.
~ком Party committee. ~органи-
зация Party organization.
парта (*school*) desk.
партер stalls; pit.
партизан (*gen pl* -ан) partisan; guer-
illa. партизанский partisan; guer-
illa; unplanned.
партийный party; Party; *sb* Party
member.
партитура (*mus*) score.
партия party; group; batch; game, set;
part.
партнёр partner.
парус (*pl* -á, -óв) sail. парусина canvas. парусник sailing vessel. парус-
ный sail; ~ спорт sailing.
парфюмерия perfumes.
парча (*gen pl* -ей) brocade. пар-
човый brocade.
пасека apiary, beehive.
пасётся *see* пастись
пасквиль *m* lampoon; libel.
пасмурный overcast; gloomy.
паспорт (*pl* -á) passport.
пассаж passage; arcade.
пассажир passenger.
пассивный passive.
паста paste.
пастбище pasture.
паства flock.
пастель pastel.
пастернак parsnip.
пасти (-сý, -сёшь; пас, -лá) *impf*
graze; tend.
пастись (-сётся; пáсся, -лáсь) *impf*
graze. пастух (-á) shepherd. пá-
стырь *m* pastor.
пасть¹ mouth; jaws.
пасть² (падý, -дёшь; пал) *pf of*
падать
Пасха Easter; Passover.
пасынок (-нка) stepson, stepchild.
пат stalemate.
патент patent.
патетический passionate.
патока treacle; syrup.

патология pathology.
патриарх patriarch.
патриот patriot. патриотизм patriotism. патриотический patriotic.
патрон cartridge; chuck; lamp-socket.
патруль (-я) *m* patrol.
пауза pause; (*also mus*) rest.
паук (-á) spider. паутина cobweb;
gossamer; web.
пафос zeal, enthusiasm.
пах (*loc* -ý) groin.
пахарь *m* ploughman. пахать (пашý,
пашешь) *impf* (*pf* вс~) plough.
пахнуть¹ (-ну; пах) *impf* smell (+*instr
of*).
пахнуть² (-нёт) *pf* puff, blow.
пахота ploughing. пахотный arable.
пахучий odorous, strong-smelling.
пациент, ~ка patient.
пацифизм pacifism. пацифист
pacifist.
пачка bundle; packet, pack; tutu.
пачкать *impf* (*pf* за~, ис~) dirty,
soil, stain.
пашý *etc.*: *see* пахать. пашня (*gen pl*
-шен) ploughed field.
паштет pâté.
паяльная лампа blow-lamp. паяль-
ник soldering iron. паять (-яю) *impf*
solder.
паяц clown, buffoon.
певец (-вцá), певица singer. певу-
чий melodious. певчий singing; *sb*
chorister.
пегий piebald.
педагог teacher; pedagogue. педа-
гогика pedagogy. педагогический
pedagogical; educational; ~ институт (teachers') training college.
педаль pedal.
педиатр paediatrician. педиатрический paediatric.
пейзаж landscape; scenery.
пёк *see* печь. пекарный baking.
пекарня (*gen pl* -рен) bakery.
пекарь (*pl* -я, -ей) *m* baker. пекло
scorching heat; hell-fire. пекý *etc.*:
see печь
пелена (*gen pl* -лён) shroud. пеле-
нать *impf* (*pf* за~) swaddle; put a
nappy on.
пеленг bearing. пеленговать *impf*
& *pf* take the bearings of.
пелёнка nappy.
пельмень *m* meat dumpling.

пе́на foam; scum; froth.

пена́л pencil-case.

пе́ние singing.

пе́нистый foamy; frothy. **пе́ниться** *impf* (*pf* вс~) foam.

пе́нка skin. **пенопла́ст** plastic foam.

пеницилли́н penicillin.

пенсионе́р, пенсионе́рка pensioner. **пенсио́нный** pensionable. **пе́нсия** pension.

пень (пня) *m* stump, stub.

пенька́ hemp.

пе́пел (-пла) ash, ashes. **пе́пельница** ashtray.

перве́йший the first; first-class. **пе́рвенец** (-нца) first-born. **пе́рвенство** first place; championship. **пе́рвенствовать** *impf* take first place; take priority. **перви́чный** primary.

перво- *in comb* first; prime. **первобы́тный** primitive; primeval. ~исто́чник source; origin. ~кла́ссный first-class. ~ку́рсник first-year student. ~нача́льный original; primary. ~со́ртный best-quality; first-class. ~степе́нный paramount.

пе́рвое *sb* first course. **пе́рвый** first; former.

перга́мент parchment.

перебега́ть *impf*, **перебежа́ть** (-бегу́) *pf* cross, run across; desert. **перебе́жчик** deserter; turncoat.

перебе́гу *etc.*: *see* перебежа́ть

перебива́ть(ся *impf of* переби́ть(ся

перебира́ть(ся *impf of* перебра́ть(ся

переби́ть (-бью́, -бьёшь) *pf* (*impf* перебива́ть) interrupt; slaughter; beat; break; re-upholster; ~ся break; make ends meet. **перебо́й** interruption; stoppage; irregularity.

перебо́рка sorting out; partition; bulkhead.

переборо́ть (-рю́, -решь) *pf* overcome.

переборщи́ть (-щу́) *pf* go too far; overdo it.

перебра́сывать(ся *impf of* перебро́сить(ся

перебра́ть (-беру́, -берёшь; -а́л, -а́, -о) *pf* (*impf* перебира́ть) sort out; look through; turn over in one's mind; finger; ~ся get over, cross; move.

перебро́сить (-о́шу) *pf* (*impf* пере-

бра́сывать) throw over; transfer; ~ся fling o.s.; spread. **перебро́ска** transfer.

перебью́ *etc.*: *see* переби́ть

перева́л crossing; pass. **перева́ливать** *impf*, **перевали́ть** (-лю́, -лишь) *pf* transfer, shift; cross, pass.

перева́ривать *impf*, **перевари́ть** (-рю́, -ришь) *pf* reheat; overcook; digest; tolerate.

переведу́ *etc.*: *see* перевести́

перевезти́ (-зу́, -зёшь; -вёз, -ла́) *pf* (*impf* перевози́ть) take across; transport; (re)move.

переверну́ть (-ну́, -нёшь) *pf*, **перевёртывать** *impf* (*impf also* перевора́чивать) turn (over); upset; turn inside out; ~ся turn (over).

переве́с preponderance; advantage. **переве́сить** (-е́шу) *pf* (*impf* переве́шивать) re-weigh; outweigh; tip the scales; hang elsewhere.

перевести́ (-веду́, -ведёшь; -вёл, -а́) *pf* (*impf* переводи́ть) take across; transfer, move, shift; translate; convert; ~сь be transferred; run out; become extinct.

переве́шивать *impf of* переве́сить.

перевира́ть *impf of* переврать

перево́д transfer, move, shift; translation; conversion; waste. **переводи́ть(ся** (-ожу́(сь, -о́дишь(ся) *impf of* перевести́(сь. **переводно́й: ~а́я бума́га** carbon paper; **~а́я карти́нка** transfer. **перево́дный** transfer; translated. **перево́дчик, ~ица** translator; interpreter.

перево́з transporting; ferry. **перевози́ть** (-ожу́, -о́зишь) *impf of* перевезти́. **перево́зка** conveyance. **перево́зчик** ferryman; removal man.

перевооружа́ть *impf*, **перевооружи́ть** (-жу́) *pf* rearm; ~ся rearm. **перевооруже́ние** rearmament.

перевоплоти́ть (-лощу́) *pf*, **перевоплоща́ть** *impf* reincarnate; ~ся be reincarnated. **перевоплоще́ние** reincarnation.

перевора́чивать(ся *impf of* переверну́ть(ся. **переворо́т** revolution; overturn; cataclysm; **госуда́рственный ~** coup d'état.

перевоспита́ние re-education. **перевоспита́ть** *pf*, **перевоспи́тывать**

impf re-educate.
перевра́ть (-ру́, -рёшь; -а́л, -á, -о) *pf* (*impf* перевира́ть) garble; misquote.
перевыполне́ние over-fulfilment.
перевы́полнить *pf*, **перевыполня́ть** *impf* over-fulfil.
перевяза́ть (-яжу́, -я́жешь) *pf*, **перевя́зывать** *impf* bandage; tie up; re-tie. **перевя́зка** dressing, bandage.
переги́б bend; excess, extreme. **перегиба́ть(ся** *impf of* перегну́ть(ся
перегля́дываться *impf*, **перегляну́ться** (-ну́сь, -не́шься) *pf* exchange glances.
перегна́ть (-гоню́, -го́нишь; -а́л, -á, -о) *pf* (*impf* перегоня́ть) outdistance; surpass; drive; distil.
перегно́й humus.
перегну́ть (-ну́, -нёшь) *pf* (*impf* перегиба́ть) bend; ~ па́лку go too far; ~ся bend; lean over.
перегова́ривать *impf*, **переговори́ть** (with). **перегово́ры** (-ов) *pl* negotiations, parley. **перегово́рный** *adj*: ~ пункт public call-boxes; trunk-call office.
перего́н driving; stage. **перего́нка** distillation. **перего́нный** distilling, distillation. **перегоню́** *etc.*: *see* перегна́ть. **перегоня́ть** *impf of* перегна́ть
перегора́живать *impf of* перегороди́ть
перегора́ть *impf*, **перегоре́ть** (-ри́т) *pf* burn out, fuse.
перегороди́ть (-рожу́, -ро́ди́шь) *pf* (*impf* перегора́живать) partition off; block. **перегоро́дка** partition.
перегре́в overheating. **перегрева́ть** *impf*, **перегре́ть** (-е́ю) *pf* overheat; ~ся overheat.
перегружа́ть *impf*, **перегрузи́ть** (-ужу́, -у́зишь) *pf* overload; transfer. **перегру́зка** overload; transfer.
перегрыза́ть *impf*, **перегры́зть** (-зу́, -зёшь; -гры́з) *pf* gnaw through.
пе́ред, **пе́редо**, **пред**, **пре́до** *prep*+*instr* before; in front of; compared to. **перёд** (пе́реда; *pl* -á) front, forepart.
передава́ть (-даю́, -даёшь) *impf*, **переда́ть** (-áм, -áшь, -áст, -ади́м; пе́редал, -á, -о) *pf* pass, hand, hand

over; transfer; hand down; make over; tell; communicate; convey; give too much; ~ся pass; be transmitted; be communicated; be inherited. **переда́тчик** transmitter. **переда́ча** passing; transmission; communication; transfer; broadcast; drive; gear, gearing.
передвига́ть *impf*, **передви́нуть** (-ну) *pf* move, shift; ~ся move, shift. **передвиже́ние** movement; transportation. **передви́жка** movement; *in comb* travelling; itinerant. **передвижно́й** movable, mobile.
переде́лать *pf*, **переде́лывать** *impf* alter; refashion. **переде́лка** alteration.
передёргивать(ся *impf of* передёрнуть(ся
передержа́ть (-жу́, -жишь) *pf*, **переде́рживать** *impf* overdo; overcook; overexpose.
передёрнуть (-ну) *pf* (*impf* передёргивать) pull aside *or* across; cheat; distort; ~ся wince.
пере́дний front; ~ план foreground. **пере́дник** apron. **пере́дняя** *sb* (entrance) hall, lobby. **пере́до**: *see* пе́ред. **передово́й** (-á) exemplary worker. **передови́ца** leading article. **передово́й** advanced; foremost; leading.
передохну́ть (-ну́, -нёшь) *pf* pause for breath.
передра́знивать *impf*, **передразни́ть** (-ню́, -нишь) *pf* mimic.
переду́мать *impf*, **переду́мывать** *impf* change one's mind.
переды́шка respite.
перее́зд crossing; move. **переезжа́ть** *impf*, **перее́хать** (-е́ду) *pf* cross; run over, knock down; move (house).
пережа́ривать *impf*, **пережа́рить** *pf* overdo, overcook.
пережда́ть (-жду́, -ждёшь; -а́л, -á, -о) *pf* (*impf* пережида́ть) wait for the end of.
пережёвывать *impf* chew; repeat over and over again.
пережива́ние experience. **пережива́ть** *impf of* пережи́ть
пережида́ть *impf of* пережда́ть
пережито́е *sb* the past. **пережи́ток** (-тка) survival; vestige. **пережи́ть**

(-иву́, -иве́шь; пе́режи́л, -а́, -о) pf
(impf пережива́ть) experience; go
through; endure; outlive.

перезаряди́ть (-яжу́, -я́ди́шь) pf,
перезаряжа́ть impf recharge; re-
load.

перезва́нивать impf, перезвони́ть
pf +dat ring back.

пере|зимова́ть pf.

перезре́лый overripe.

переигра́ть pf, переи́грывать impf
play again; overact.

переизбира́ть impf, переизбра́ть
(-беру́, -берёшь; -бра́л, -а́, -о) pf re-
elect. переизбра́ние re-election.

переизда́ть (-даю́, -даёшь) impf,
переизда́ть (-а́м, -а́шь, -а́ст, -ади́м;
-а́л, -а́, -о) pf republish, reprint.
переизда́ние republication; new
edition.

переименова́ть pf, переимено́вы-
вать impf rename.

перейму́ etc.: see переня́ть

перейти́ (-йду́, -йдёшь; перешёл,
-шла́) pf (impf переходи́ть) cross;
pass; turn (в+acc to, into).

переканта́ть pf transfer (a load).

перека́пывать impf of перекопа́ть

перекати́ть (-чу́, -тишь) pf, пере-
ка́тывать impf roll; ~ся roll.

перекача́ть pf, перека́чивать impf
pump (across).

переквалифици́роваться impf &
pf retrain.

переки́дывать impf, переки́нуть
(-ну) pf throw over; ~ся leap.

пе́рекись peroxide.

перекла́дина cross-beam; joist; horizontal bar.

перекла́дывать impf of перело-
жи́ть

перекли́чка roll-call.

переключа́тель m switch. пере-
ключа́ть impf, переключи́ть (-чу́)
pf switch (over); ~ся switch (over).

перекова́ть (-кую́, -куёшь) pf, пере-
ко́вывать impf re-shoe; re-forge.

перекопа́ть pf (impf перека́пы-
вать) dig (all of); dig again.

перекоси́ть (-ошу́, -о́сишь) pf warp;
distort; ~ся warp; become distorted.

перекочева́ть (-чу́ю) pf, переко-
чёвывать impf migrate.

переко́шенный distorted, twisted.

перекра́ивать impf of перекрои́ть

перекра́сить (-а́шу) pf, перекра́-
шивать impf (re-)paint; (re-)dye;
~ся change colour; turn one's coat.

пере|крести́ть (-ещу́, -е́стишь) pf,
перекре́щивать impf cross; ~ся
cross, intersect; cross o.s. пере-
кре́стн|ый cross; ~ый допро́с
cross-examination; ~ый ого́нь cross-
fire; ~ая ссы́лка cross-reference.
перекрёсток (-тка) cross-roads,
crossing.

перекри́кивать impf, перекрича́ть
(-чу́) pf shout down.

перекро́ить (-ою́) pf (impf пере-
кра́ивать) cut out again; reshape.

перекрыва́ть impf, перекры́ть
(-ро́ю) pf re-cover; exceed. пере-
кры́тие ceiling.

перекую́ etc.: see перекова́ть

перекупа́ть impf, перекупи́ть
(-плю́, -пишь) pf buy up; buy by out-
bidding s.o. переку́пщик second-
hand dealer.

перекуси́ть (-ушу́, -у́сишь) pf, пере-
ку́сывать impf bite through; have a
snack.

перелага́ть impf of переложи́ть

перела́мывать impf of переломи́ть

перелеза́ть impf, переле́зть (-зу;
-ез) pf climb over.

переле́сок (-ска) copse.

перелёт migration; flight. переле-
та́ть impf, перелете́ть (-лечу́) pf
fly over. перелётный migratory.

перелива́ние decanting; transfusion.
перелива́ть impf of перели́ть.
перелива́ться impf of перели́ться;
gleam; modulate.

перелиста́ть pf, перели́стывать
impf leaf through.

перели́ть (-лью́, -льёшь; -и́л, -а́, -о)
pf (impf перелива́ть) pour; decant;
let overflow; transfuse. перели́ться
(-льётся; -ли́лся, -лила́сь, -ли́ло́сь)
pf (impf перелива́ться) flow; overflow.

перелицева́ть (-цу́ю) pf, пере-
лицо́вывать impf turn; have turned.

переложе́ние arrangement. пере-
ложи́ть (-жу́, -жишь) pf (impf пере-
кла́дывать, перелага́ть) put elsewhere; shift; transfer; interlay; put in
too much; set; arrange; transpose.

перело́м breaking; fracture; turning-
point, crisis; sudden change.

переломать *pf* break; ~ся break, be broken. переломить (-млю, -мишь) *pf* (*impf* переламывать) break in two; master. переломный critical.

перелью *etc.*: *see* перелить

переманивать *impf*, переманить (-ню, -нишь) *pf* win over; entice.

перемежаться *impf* alternate.

перемена change; break. переменить (-ню, -нишь) *pf*, переменять *impf* change; ~ся change. переменный variable; ~ ток alternating current. переменчивый changeable.

переместить (-мещу) *pf* (*impf* перемещать) move; transfer; ~ся move.

перемешать *pf*, перемешивать *impf* mix; mix up; shuffle; ~ся get mixed (up).

перемещать(ся *impf of* переместить(ся. перемещение transference; displacement. перемещённ|ый displaced; ~ые лица displaced persons.

перемирие armistice, truce.

перемывать *impf*, перемыть (-мою) *pf* wash (up) again.

перенапрягать *impf*, перенапрячь (-ягу, -яжёшь: -яг, -ла) *pf* overstrain.

перенаселение overpopulation. перенаселённый (-лён, -á) overpopulated; overcrowded.

перенести (-су, -сёшь; -нёс, -ла) *pf* (*impf* переносить) carry, move, take; transfer; take over; postpone; endure, bear; ~сь be carried; be carried away.

перенимать *impf of* перенять

перенос transfer; word division; знак ~а end-of-line hyphen. переносимый endurable. переносить(ся (-ошу(сь, -осишь(ся) *impf of* перенести(сь

переносица bridge (*of the nose*).

переноска carrying over; transporting; carriage. переносный portable, figurative. переносчик carrier.

пере|ночевать (-чую) *pf.* переношу *etc.*: *see* переносить

перенять (-ейму, -еймёшь; пéрен|ял, -á, -о) *pf* (*impf* перенимать) imitate; adopt.

переоборудовать *impf & pf* re-equip.

переобуваться *impf*, переобуться (-уюсь, -уешься) *pf* change one's shoes.

переодеваться *impf*, переодеться (-éнусь) *pf* change (one's clothes).

переосвидетельствовать *impf & pf* re-examine.

переоценивать *impf*, переоценить (-ню, -нишь) *pf* overestimate; revalue. переоценка overestimation; revaluation.

перепачкать *pf* make dirty; ~ся get dirty.

перепел (*pl* -á) quail.

перепеленать *pf* change (*a baby*).

перепечатать *pf*, перепечатывать *impf* reprint. перепечатка reprint.

перепиливать *impf*, перепилить (-лю, -лишь) *pf* saw in two.

переписать (-ишу, -ишешь) *pf*, переписывать *impf* copy; re-write; make a list of. переписка copying; correspondence. переписываться *impf* correspond. перепись census.

переплавить (-влю) *pf*, переплавлять *impf* smelt.

переплатить (-ачу, -áтишь) *pf*, переплачивать *impf* overpay.

переплести (-лету, -летёшь; -лёл, -á) *pf*, переплетать *impf* bind; interlace, intertwine; re-plait; ~ся interlace, interweave; get mixed up. переплёт binding. переплётчик bookbinder.

переплывать *impf*, переплыть (-ыву, -ывёшь; -ыл, -á, -о) *pf* swim *or* sail across.

переподготовка further training; refresher course.

переползать *impf*, переползти (-зу, -зёшь; -олз, -ла) *pf* crawl *or* creep across.

переполнение overfilling; overcrowding. переполненный overcrowded; too full. переполнить *pf*, переполнять *impf* overfill; overcrowd.

переполох commotion.

перепонка membrane; web.

переправа crossing; ford.

переправить (-влю) *pf*, переправлять *impf* convey; take across; forward; ~ся cross, get across.

перепродавать (-даю, -даёшь) *impf*, перепродать (-ám, -áшь, -áст, -адим; -прóдал, -á, -о) *pf* re-sell. перепродажа re-sale.

перепроизводство overproduction.

перепры́гивать *impf*, **перепры́гнуть** (-ну) *pf* jump (over).

перепуга́ть *pf* frighten, scare; ~ся get a fright.

пере|пу́тать *pf*, **перепу́тывать** *impf* tangle; confuse, mix up.

перепу́тье cross-roads.

перераба́тывать *impf*, **перерабо́тать** *pf* convert; treat; re-make; recast; process; work overtime; overwork; ~ся overwork. **перерабо́тка** processing; reworking; overtime work.

перераспределе́ние redistribution. **перераспредели́ть** *pf*, **перераспределя́ть** *impf* redistribute.

перераста́ние outgrowing; escalation; development (into). **перераста́ть** *impf*, **перерасти́** (-ту́, -тёшь; -ро́с, -ла́) *pf* outgrow; develop.

перерасхо́д over-expenditure; overdraft. **перерасхо́довать** *impf & pf* expend too much of.

перерасчёт recalculation.

перерва́ть (-ву́, -вёшь; -а́л, -ала́, -о) *pf* (*impf* **перерыва́ть**) break, tear asunder; ~ся break, come apart.

перере́зать (-е́жу) *pf*, **перереза́ть** *impf*, **перере́зывать** *impf* cut; cut off; kill.

перероди́ть (-ожу́) *pf*, **перерожда́ть** *impf* regenerate; ~ся be reborn; be regenerated; degenerate. **перерожде́ние** regeneration; degeneration.

перерос *etc.*: *see* **перерасти́**. **перерою** *etc.*: *see* **перерыть**

переруби́ть *pf*, **переруба́ть** (-блю́, -бишь) *pf* chop in two.

переры́в break; interruption; interval.

перерыва́ть[1](ся *impf of* перерва́ть(ся

перерыва́ть[2] *impf*, **перерыть** (-ро́ю) *pf* dig up; rummage through.

пересади́ть (-ажу́, -а́дишь) *pf*, **переса́живать** *impf* transplant; seat somewhere else. **переса́дка** transplantation; grafting; change.

переса́живаться *impf of* пересе́сть.

переса́ливать *impf of* пересоли́ть

пересдава́ть (-даю́сь) *impf*, **пересда́ть** (-а́м, -а́шь, -а́ст, -ади́м; -да́л, -а́, -о) *pf* sublet; re-sit.

пересека́ть(ся *impf of* пересе́чь(ся

переселе́нец (-нца) settler; immigrant. **переселе́ние** migration; im-

migration, resettlement; moving.

пересели́ть *pf*, **переселя́ть** *impf* move; ~ся move; migrate.

пересе́сть (-ся́ду) *pf* (*impf* **переса́живаться**) change one's seat; change (*trains etc.*).

пересече́ние crossing, intersection. **пересе́чь** (-секу́, -сечёшь; -сёк, -ла́) *pf* (*impf* **пересека́ть**) cross; intersect; ~ся cross, intersect.

переси́ливать *impf*, **переси́лить** *pf* overpower.

переска́з (re)telling; exposition. **пересказа́ть** (-ажу́, -а́жешь) *pf*, **переска́зывать** *impf* retell.

переска́кивать *impf*, **перескочи́ть** (-чу́, -чишь) *pf* jump *or* skip (over).

пересла́ть (-ешлю́, -шлёшь) *pf* (*impf* **пересыла́ть**) send; forward.

пересма́тривать *impf*, **пересмотре́ть** (-трю́, -тришь) *pf* look over; reconsider. **пересмо́тр** revision; reconsideration; review.

пересоли́ть (-олю́, -о́ли́шь) *pf* (*impf* **переса́ливать**) over-salt; overdo it.

пересо́хнуть (-нет; -о́х) *pf* (*impf* **пересыха́ть**) dry up, become parched.

переспа́ть (-плю́; -а́л, -а́, -о) *pf* oversleep; spend the night.

переспе́лый overripe.

переспра́шивать *impf*, **переспроси́ть** (-ошу́, -о́сишь) *pf* ask again.

перестава́ть (-таю́, -таёшь) *impf of* переста́ть

переста́вить (-влю) *pf*, **переставля́ть** *impf* move; re-arrange; transpose. **перестано́вка** rearrangement; transposition.

переста́ть (-а́ну) *pf* (*impf* **переставать**) stop, cease.

перестрада́ть *pf* have suffered.

перестра́ивать(ся *impf of* перестро́ить(ся

перестрахо́вка re-insurance; overcautiousness.

перестре́лка exchange of fire. **перестреля́ть** *pf* shoot (down).

перестро́ить *pf* (*impf* **перестра́ивать**) rebuild; reorganize; retune; ~ся reorganize o.s.; switch over (на+*acc* to). **перестро́йка** reconstruction; reorganization; retuning; perestroika.

переступа́ть *impf*, **переступи́ть**

(-плю, -пишь) *pf* step over; cross; overstep.

пересчита́ть *pf*, пересчи́тывать *impf* (*pf also* перече́сть) re-count; count.

пересыла́ть *impf of* пересла́ть. пересы́лка sending, forwarding.

пересыпа́ть *impf*, пересы́пать (-плю, -плешь) *pf* pour; sprinkle; pour too much.

пересыха́ть *impf of* пересо́хнуть. переся́ду *etc.: see* пересе́сть. перета́пливать *impf of* перетопи́ть.

перета́скивать *impf*, перетащи́ть (-щу, -щишь) *pf* drag (over, through); move.

перетере́ть (-тру́, -трёшь; -тёр) *pf*, перетира́ть *impf* wear out, wear down; grind; wipe; ~ся wear out *or* through.

перетопи́ть (-плю, -пишь) *pf* (*impf* перета́пливать) melt.

перетру́ *etc.: see* перетере́ть

перете́ть (пру, прёшь; пёр, -ла) *impf* go; make *or* force one's way; haul; come out.

перетя́гивать *impf*, перетяну́ть (-ну́, -нешь) *pf* pull, draw; win over; outweigh.

переубеди́ть *pf*, переубежда́ть *impf* make change one's mind.

переу́лок (-лка) side street, alley, lane.

переустро́йство reconstruction, reorganization.

переутоми́ть (-млю́) *pf*, переутомля́ть *impf* overtire; ~ся overtire o.s. переутомле́ние overwork.

переучёт stock-taking.

переу́чивать *impf*, переучи́ть (-чу́, -чишь) *pf* teach again.

перефрази́ровать *impf & pf* paraphrase.

перехвати́ть (-ачу́, -а́тишь) *pf*, перехва́тывать *impf* intercept; snatch a bite (of); borrow.

перехитри́ть *pf* outwit.

перехо́д transition; crossing; conversion. переходи́ть (-ожу́, -о́дишь) *impf of* перейти́. перехо́дный transitional; transitive. переходя́щий transient; intermittent; brought forward.

пе́рец (-рца) pepper.

перечёл *etc.: see* перече́сть

пе́речень (-чня) *m* list, enumeration.

перечёркивать *impf*, перечеркну́ть (-ну́, -нёшь) *pf* cross out, cancel.

перече́сть (-чту́, -чтёшь; -чёл, -чла́) *pf: see* пересчита́ть, перечита́ть

перечисле́ние enumeration; transfer. перечи́слить *pf*, перечисля́ть *impf* enumerate; transfer.

перечита́ть *pf*, перечи́тывать *impf* (*pf also* перече́сть) re-read.

пере́чить (-чу) *impf* contradict; cross, go against.

пе́речница pepper-pot.

перечту́ *etc.: see* перече́сть. пере́чу *etc.: see* пере́чить

переша́гивать *impf*, перешагну́ть (-ну́, -нёшь) *pf* step over.

переше́ек (-е́йка) isthmus, neck.

перешёл *etc.: see* перейти́

перешива́ть *impf*, переши́ть (-шью, -шьёшь) *pf* alter; have altered.

перешлю́ *etc.: see* пересла́ть

переэкзамено́вка *pf*., переэкзамено́вывать *impf* re-examine; ~ся retake an exam.

пери́ла (-и́л) *pl* railing(s); banisters. пери́на feather-bed.

пери́од period. периоди́ка periodicals. периоди́ческий periodical; recurring.

пери́стый feathery; cirrus.

периферия́ periphery.

перламу́тр mother-of-pearl. перламу́тровый mother-of-pearl. перло́вый: ~ая крупа́ pearl barley.

перма́нент perm. перма́нентный permanent.

перна́тый feathered. перна́тые *sb pl* birds. перо́ (*pl* пе́рья, -ьев) feather; pen. перочи́нный нож, но́жик penknife.

перпендикуля́рный perpendicular.

перро́н platform.

перс Persian. перси́дский Persian.

пе́рсик peach.

персия́нка Persian woman.

персо́на person; со́бственной персо́ной in person. персона́ж character; personage. персона́л personnel, staff. персона́льный personal.

перспекти́ва perspective; vista; prospect. перспекти́вный perspective; long-term; promising.

пе́рстень (-тня) *m* ring.

перфока́рта punched card.

перхоть dandruff.

перча́тка glove.

пе́рчить (-чу) impf (pf по~) pepper.

пёс (пса) dog.

пе́сенник song-book; (choral) singer; song-writer. пе́сенный song; of songs.

песе́ц (-сца́) (polar) fox.

песнь (gen pl -ей) song; canto. пе́сня (gen pl -сен) song.

песо́к (-ска́) sand. песо́чный sand; sandy.

пессими́зм pessimism. пессими́ст pessimist. пессимисти́ческий pessimistic.

пестрота́ diversity of colours; diversity. пёстрый variegated; diverse; colourful.

песча́ник sandstone. песча́ный sandy. песчи́нка grain of sand.

петербу́ргский (of) St Petersburg.

пети́ция petition.

петли́ца buttonhole; tab. пе́тля (gen pl -тель) loop; noose; buttonhole; stitch; hinge.

петру́шка¹ parsley.

петру́шка² m Punch; f Punch-and-Judy show.

пету́х (-а́) cock. петушо́к (-шка́) cockerel.

петь (пою́, поёшь) impf (pf про~, с~) sing.

пехо́та infantry, foot. пехоти́нец (-нца) infantryman. пехо́тный infantry.

печа́лить impf (pf o~) sadden; ~ся grieve, be sad. печа́ль sorrow. печа́льный sad.

печа́тать impf (pf на~, от~) print; ~ся write, be published; be at the printer's. печа́тный printing; printer's; printed; ~ые бу́квы block capitals; ~ый стано́к printing-press. печа́ть seal, stamp; print; printing; press.

пече́ние baking.

печёнка liver.

печёный baked.

пе́чень liver.

пече́нье pastry; biscuit. пе́чка stove. печно́й stove; oven; kiln. печь (loc -и́; gen pl -е́й) stove; oven; kiln. печь (пеку́, -чёшь; пёк, -ла́) impf (pf ис~) bake; ~ся bake.

пешехо́д pedestrian. пешехо́дный pedestrian; foot-. пе́ший pedestrian; foot. пе́шка pawn. пешко́м adv on foot.

пеще́ра cave. пеще́рный cave; ~ челове́к cave-dweller.

пиани́но neut indecl (upright) piano. пиани́ст, ~ка pianist.

пивна́я sb pub. пивно́й beer. пи́во beer. пивова́р brewer.

пигме́й pygmy.

пиджа́к (-а́) jacket.

пижа́ма pyjamas.

пижо́н dandy.

пик peak; часы́ пик rush-hour.

пи́ка lance.

пика́нтный piquant; spicy.

пика́п pick-up (van).

пике́ neut indecl dive.

пике́т picket. пике́тчик picket.

пи́ки pl (cards) spades.

пики́ровать impf & pf (pf also с~) dive.

пикиро́вщик, пики́рующий бомбарди́ровщик dive-bomber.

пикни́к (-а́) picnic.

пи́кнуть (-ну) pf squeak; make a sound.

пи́ковый of spades.

пила́ (pl -ы) saw; nagger. пилёный sawed, sawn. пили́ть (-лю́, -лишь) impf saw; nag (at). пи́лка sawing; fret-saw; nail-file.

пило́т pilot.

пило́тка forage-cap.

пилоти́ровать impf pilot.

пилю́ля pill.

пина́ть impf (pf пнуть) kick. пино́к (-нка́) kick.

пингви́н penguin.

пинце́т tweezers.

пио́н peony.

пионе́р pioneer. пионе́рский pioneer.

пипе́тка pipette.

пир (loc -у́; pl -ы́) feast, banquet. пирова́ть impf feast.

пирами́да pyramid.

пира́т pirate.

пиро́г (-а́) pie. пиро́жное sb cake, pastry. пирожо́к (-жка́) pasty.

пирс pier.

пируэ́т pirouette.

пи́ршество feast; celebration.

пи́саный handwritten. пи́сарь (pl

-я) *m* clerk. писа́тель *m*, писа́тельница writer, author. писа́ть (пишу́, пи́шешь) *impf* (*pf* на~) write; paint; ~ ма́слом paint in oils; ~ся be spelt.

писк squeak, chirp. пискли́вый squeaky. пи́скнуть (-ну) *pf of* пища́ть

пистоле́т pistol; gun; ~-пулемёт sub-machine gun.

писто́н (percussion-)cap; piston.

писчебума́жный stationery. пи́счая бума́га writing paper. пи́сьменно *adv* in writing. пи́сьменность literature. пи́сьменный writing, written. письмо́ (*pl* -а, -сем) letter.

пита́ние nourishment; feeding. пита́тельный nutritious; alimentary; feed. пита́ть *impf* feed; nourish; supply; ~ся be fed, eat; +*instr* feed on.

пито́мец (-мца) charge; pupil; alumnus. пито́мник nursery.

пить (пью, пьёшь; пил, -а́, -о) *impf* (*pf* вы~) drink. питьё (*pl* -тья́, -те́й, -тья́м) drinking; drink. питьево́й drinkable; drinking.

пиха́ть *impf*, пихну́ть (-ну́, -нёшь) *pf* push, shove.

пи́хта (silver) fir.

пи́чкать *impf* (*pf* на~) stuff.

пи́шущий writing; ~ая маши́нка typewriter.

пи́ща food.

пища́ть (-щу́) *impf* (*pf* пи́скнуть) squeak; cheep.

пищеваре́ние digestion. пищево́д oesophagus, gullet. пищево́й food.

пия́вка leech.

пла́вание swimming; sailing; voyage. пла́вательный swimming; ~ бассе́йн swimming-pool. пла́вать *impf* swim; float; sail. плавба́за depot ship, factory ship.

плави́льный melting, smelting. плави́льня foundry. пла́вить (-влю) *impf* (*pf* рас~) melt, smelt; ~ся melt. пла́вка fusing; melting.

пла́вки (-вок) *pl* bathing trunks.

пла́вкий fusible; fuse. плавле́ние melting.

плавни́к (-а́) fin; flipper. пла́вный smooth, flowing; liquid. плаву́чий floating.

плагиа́т plagiarism. плагиа́тор plagiarist.

пла́зма plasma.

плака́т poster; placard.

пла́кать (-а́чу) *impf* cry, weep; ~ся complain, lament; +на+*acc* complain of; bemoan.

пла́кса cry-baby. плакси́вый whining. плаку́чий weeping.

пла́менный flaming; ardent. пла́мя (-мени) *neut* flame; blaze.

план plan.

плане́р glider. планери́зм gliding. планери́ст glider-pilot.

плане́та planet. плане́тный planetary.

плани́рование[1] planning. плани́рование[2] gliding; glide. плани́ровать[1] *impf* (*pf* за~) plan. плани́ровать[2] *impf* (*pf* с~) glide (down).

пла́нка lath, slat.

пла́новый planned, systematic; planning. планоме́рный systematic, planned.

планта́ция plantation.

пласт (-а́) layer; stratum. пласти́на plate. пласти́нка plate; (*gramophone*) record.

пласти́ческий, пласти́чный plastic. пластма́сса plastic. пластма́ссовый plastic.

пла́стырь *m* plaster.

пла́та pay; charge; fee. платёж (-а́) payment. платёжеспосо́бный solvent. платёжный pay.

пла́тина platinum. пла́тиновый platinum.

плати́ть (-ачу́, -а́тишь) *impf* (*pf* за~, у~) pay; ~ся (*pf* по~ся) за+*acc* pay for. пла́тный paid; requiring payment.

плато́к (-тка́) shawl; head-scarf; handkerchief.

платони́ческий platonic.

платфо́рма platform; truck.

пла́тье (*gen pl* -ьев) clothes, clothing; dress; gown. платяно́й clothes.

плафо́н ceiling; lamp shade.

плацда́рм bridgehead, beach-head; base; springboard.

плацка́рта reserved-seat ticket.

плач weeping. плаче́вный lamentable. пла́чу *etc.*: *see* пла́кать

плачу́ *etc.*: *see* плати́ть

плашмя́ *adv* flat, prone.

плащ (-а́) cloak; raincoat.

плебе́й plebeian.

плева́тельница spittoon. плева́ть (плюю́, плюёшь) *impf* (*pf* на~, плю́нуть) spit; *inf+dat*: мне ~ I don't give a damn (на+*acc* about); ~ся spit. плево́к (-вка́) spit, spittle.

плеври́т pleurisy.

плед rug; plaid.

плёл *etc.*: *see* плести́

племенно́й tribal; pedigree. пле́мя (-мени; *pl* -мена́, -мён) *neut* tribe.

племя́нник nephew. племя́нница niece.

плен (*loc* -у́) captivity.

плена́рный plenary.

плени́тельный captivating. плени́ть *pf* (*impf* пленя́ть) captivate; ~ся be captivated.

плёнка film; tape; pellicle.

пле́нник prisoner. пле́нный captive.

пле́нум plenary session.

пленя́ть(ся *impf of* плени́ть(ся

пле́сень mould.

плеск splash, lapping. плеска́ть (-ещу́, -е́щешь) *impf* (*pf* плесну́ть) splash; lap; ~ся splash; lap.

пле́сневеть (-еет) *impf* (*pf* за~) go mouldy, grow musty.

плесну́ть (-ну́, -нёшь) *pf of* плеска́ть

плести́ (-ету́, -етёшь; плёл, -а́) *impf* (*pf* с~) plait; weave; ~сь trudge along. плете́ние plaiting; wickerwork. плетёный wattled; wicker. плете́нь (-тня́) *m* wattle fencing. плётка, плеть (*gen pl* -е́й) lash.

плечи́ко (*pl* -и, -ов) shoulder-strap; *pl* coat-hanger. плечи́стый broad-shouldered. плечо́ (*pl* -и, -а́м) shoulder.

плеши́вый bald. плеши́на, плешь bald patch.

плещу́ *etc.*: *see* плеска́ть

пли́нтус plinth; skirting-board.

плис velveteen.

плиссиро́ва́ть *impf* pleat.

плита́ (*pl* -ы) slab; flag-(stone); stove, cooker; моги́льная ~ gravestone. пли́тка tile; (thin) slab; stove, cooker; ~ шокола́да bar of chocolate. пли́точный tiled.

плове́ц (-вца́), пловчи́ха swimmer. плову́чий floating; buoyant.

плод (-а́) fruit. плоди́ть (-ожу́) *impf* (*pf* рас~) produce, procreate; ~ся propagate.

плодо- *in comb* fruit-. плодови́тый fruitful, prolific; fertile. ~во́дство fruit-growing. ~но́сный fruit-bearing, fruitful. ~овощно́й fruit and vegetable. ~ро́дный fertile. ~тво́рный fruitful.

пло́мба seal; filling. пломбирова́ть *impf* (*pf* за~, о~) fill; seal.

пло́ский (-сок, -ска́, -о) flat; trivial. плоско- *in comb* flat. плоского́рье plateau. ~гу́бцы (-ев) *pl* pliers. ~до́нный flat-bottomed.

пло́скость (*gen pl* -е́й) flatness; plane; platitude.

плот (-а́) raft.

плоти́на dam; weir; dyke.

пло́тник carpenter.

пло́тность solidity; density. пло́тный (-тен, -тна́, -о) thick; compact; dense; solid, strong; hearty.

плотоя́дный carnivorous. плоть flesh.

плохо́й bad; poor.

площа́дка area, (sports) ground, court, playground; site; landing; platform. пло́щадь (*gen pl* -е́й) area; space; square.

плуг (*pl* -и́) plough.

плут (-а́) cheat, swindler; rogue. плутова́тый cunning. плутовско́й roguish; picaresque.

плуто́ний plutonium.

плыть (-ыву́, -ывёшь; плыл, -а́, -о) *impf* swim; float; sail.

плю́нуть (-ну) *pf of* плева́ть

плюс plus; advantage.

плюш plush.

плющ (-а́) ivy.

плюю́ *etc.*: *see* плева́ть

пляж beach.

пляса́ть (-яшу́, -я́шешь) *impf* (*pf* с~) dance. пля́ска dance; dancing.

пневмати́ческий pneumatic.

пневмони́я pneumonia.

пнуть (пну, пнёшь) *pf of* пина́ть

пня *etc.*: *see* пень

по *prep* I. +*dat* on; along; round; about; by; over; according to; in accordance with; for; in; at; by (reason of); on account of; from; по понеде́льникам on Mondays; по профе́ссии by profession; по ра́дио over the radio. II. +*dat or acc of* cardinal number, *forms distributive number*: по́ два, по́ двое in twos, two by two; **по пять рубле́й шту́ка** at five roubles each. **III.** +*acc* to, up to; for, to get; **идти́ по во́ду** go to get water; **по пе́рвое сентября́** up to (and including) 1st September. **IV.** +*prep* on, (immediately) after; **по прибы́тии** on arrival.

по- *pref* **I.** *in comb* +*dat of adjs, or with advs in* -**и**, *indicates manner, use of a named language, or accordance with the opinion or wish of:* **говори́ть по-ру́сски** speak Russian; **жить по-ста́рому** live in the old style; **по-мо́ему** in my opinion. **II.** *in comb with adjs and nn, indicates situation along or near a thing:* **помо́рье** seaboard, coastal region. **III.** *in comb with comp of adjs indicates a smaller degree of comparison:* **поме́ньше** a little less.

поба́иваться *impf* be rather afraid.
побе́г[1] flight; escape.
побе́г[2] shoot; sucker.
побегу́шки: **быть на побегу́шках** run errands.
побе́да victory. **победи́тель** *m* victor; winner. **победи́ть** *pf* (*impf* **побежда́ть**) conquer; win. **побе́дный, победоно́сный** victorious, triumphant.
по|бежа́ть *pf.*
побежда́ть *impf of* **победи́ть**
по|беле́ть (-е́ю) *pf.* **по|бели́ть** *pf.* **побе́лка** whitewashing.
побере́жный coastal. **побере́жье** (sea-)coast.
по|беспоко́ить(ся *pf.*
побира́ться *impf* beg; live by begging.
по|би́ть(ся (-бью́(сь, -бьёшь(ся) *pf.*
по|благодари́ть *pf.*
побла́жка indulgence.
по|бледне́ть (-е́ю) *pf.*
поблёскивать *impf* gleam.
побли́зости *adv* nearby.
побо́и (-ев) *pl* beating. **побо́ище** slaughter; bloody battle.
побо́рник champion, advocate. **по|боро́ть** (-рю́, -решь) *pf* overcome.
побо́чный secondary; done on the side; ~ **проду́кт** by-product.
по|брани́ться *pf.*
по|брата́ться *pf.* **побрати́м** twin town.
по|брезгать *pf.* **по|бри́ть(ся** (-бре́ю(сь) *pf.*

побуди́тельный stimulating. **побуди́ть** (-ужу́) *pf,* **побужда́ть** *impf* induce, prompt. **побужде́ние** motive; inducement.
побыва́ть *pf* have been, have visited; look in, visit. **побы́вка** leave. **побы́ть** (-бу́ду, -дешь; по́был, -á, -о) *pf* stay (for a short time).
побью́(сь *etc.: see* **побить(ся**
пова́диться (-а́жусь) *pf* get into the habit (of). **пова́дка** habit.
по|вали́ть(ся (-лю́(сь, -лишь(ся) *pf.*
пова́льно *adv* without exception. **пова́льный** general, mass.
по́вар (*pl* -á) cook, chef. **пова́ренный** culinary; cookery, cooking.
по-ва́шему *adv* in your opinion.
пове́дать *pf* disclose; relate.
поведе́ние behaviour.
поведу́ *etc.: see* **повести́.** **по|везти́** (-зу́, -зёшь; -вёз, -лá) *pf.* **повёл** *etc.: see* **повести́**
повелева́ть *impf* +*instr* rule (over); +*dat* command. **повеле́ние** command. **повели́тельный** imperious; imperative.
по|венча́ть(ся *pf.*
поверга́ть *impf,* **пове́ргнуть** (-ну; -вёрг) *pf* throw down; plunge.
пове́ренная *sb* confidante. **пове́ренный** *sb* attorney; confidant; ~ **в дела́х** chargé d'affaires. **по|ве́рить**[1].
пове́рить[2] *pf* (*impf* **поверя́ть**) check; confide. **пове́рка** check; roll-call.
поверну́ть (-ну́, -нёшь) *pf,* **повёртывать** *impf* (*impf also* **повора́чивать**) turn; ~**ся** turn.
пове́рх *prep*+*gen* over. **пове́рхностный** surface, superficial. **пове́рхность** surface.
пове́рье (*gen pl* -ий) popular belief, superstition. **поверя́ть** *impf of* **пове́рить**[2]
пове́са playboy.
по|весели́ть (-е́ю) *pf.*
повесели́ть *pf* cheer (up); amuse; ~**ся** have fun.
пове́сить(ся (-ве́шу(сь) *pf of* **ве́шать(ся**
повествова́ние narrative, narration. **повествова́тельный** narrative. **повествова́ть** *impf* +о +*prep* narrate, relate.
по|вести́ (-еду́, -едёшь; -вёл, -á) *pf*

(*impf* поводи́ть) +*instr* move.
пове́стка notice; summons; ~ (дня) agenda.
по́весть (*gen pl* -е́й) story, tale.
пове́трие epidemic; craze.
пове́шу *etc.: see* пове́сить. по|вздо́рить *pf.*
повзросле́ть (-е́ю) *pf* grow up.
по|вида́ть(ся *pf.*
по-ви́димому apparently.
пови́дло jam.
по|вини́ться *pf.*
пови́нность duty, obligation; во́инская ~ conscription. пови́нный guilty.
повинова́ться *impf* & *pf* obey. повинове́ние obedience.
повиса́ть *impf*, по|ви́снуть (-ну; -ви́с) *pf* hang (on); hang down, droop.
повле́чь (-еку́, -ечёшь; -ёк, -ла́) *pf* (за собо́й) entail, bring in its train.
по|влия́ть *pf.*
по́вод[1] occasion, cause; по ~у+*gen* as regards, concerning.
по́вод[2] (*loc* -ý, *pl* -о́дья, -ьев) rein; быть на ~ý y+*gen* be under the thumb of. поводи́ть (-ожу́, -о́дишь) *impf of* повести́. поводо́к (-дка́) leash. поводы́рь (-я́) *m* guide.
пово́зка cart; vehicle.
повора́чивать(ся *impf of* поверну́ть(ся, повороти́ть(ся; повора́чивайся, -айтесь! get a move on!
поворо́т turn, turning; bend; turning-point. повороти́ть(ся (-рочу́(сь, -ро́тишь(ся) *pf* (*impf* повора́чивать(ся) turn. пово́ротливый agile, nimble; manoeuvrable. пово́ротный turning; rotary; revolving.
по|вреди́ть (-ежу́) *pf*, поврежда́ть *impf* damage; injure; ~ся be damaged; be injured. поврежде́ние damage, injury.
повремени́ть *pf* wait a little; +*c*+*instr* delay over.
повседне́вный daily; everyday.
повсеме́стно *adv* everywhere. повсеме́стный universal, general.
повста́нец (-нца) rebel, insurgent. повста́нческий rebel; insurgent.
повсю́ду *adv* everywhere.
повторе́ние repetition. повтори́ть *pf*, повторя́ть *impf* repeat; ~ся repeat o.s.; be repeated; recur. по-

вто́рный repeated.
повы́сить (-ы́шу) *pf*, повыша́ть *impf* raise, heighten; ~ся rise. повыше́ние rise; promotion. повы́шенный heightened, high.
повяза́ть (-яжу́, -я́жешь) *pf*, повя́зывать *impf* tie. повя́зка band; bandage.
по|гада́ть *pf.*
пога́нка toadstool. пога́ный foul; unclean.
погаса́ть *impf*, по|га́снуть (-ну) *pf* go out, be extinguished. по|гаси́ть (-ашу́, -а́сишь) *pf*. погаша́ть *impf* liquidate, cancel. пога́шенный used, cancelled, cashed.
погиба́ть *impf*, по|ги́бнуть (-ну; -ги́б) *pf* perish; be lost. поги́бель ruin. поги́бший lost; ruined; killed.
по|гла́дить (-а́жу) *pf.*
поглоти́ть (-ощу́, -о́тишь) *pf*, погло́щать *impf* swallow up; absorb. поглоще́ние absorption.
по|глупе́ть (-е́ю) *pf.*
по|гляде́ть (-яжу́) *pf.* погля́дывать *impf* glance (from time to time); +*за*+*instr* keep an eye on.
погна́ть (-гоню́, -го́нишь; -гна́л, -а́, -о) *pf* drive; ~ся за+*instr* run after; start in pursuit of.
по|гну́ть(ся (-ну́(сь, -нёшь(ся) *pf.* по|гнуша́ться *pf.*
поговори́ть *pf* have a talk.
погово́рка saying, proverb.
пого́да weather.
погоди́ть (-ожу́) *pf* wait a little; немно́го погодя́ a little later.
поголо́вно *adv* one and all. поголо́вный general; capitation. поголо́вье number.
пого́н (*gen pl* -о́н) shoulder-strap.
пого́нщик driver. погоню́ *etc.: see* погна́ть. пого́ня pursuit, chase. погоня́ть *impf* urge on, drive.
погорячи́ться (-чу́сь) *pf* get worked up.
пого́ст graveyard.
пограни́чник frontier guard. погра-ни́чный frontier.
по́греб (*pl* -а́) cellar. погреба́льный funeral. погреба́ть *impf of* по-грести́. погребе́ние burial.
погрему́шка rattle.
погрести́[1] (-ебу́, -ебёшь; -рёб, -ла́) *pf* (*impf* погреба́ть) bury.

погрести² (-ебу́, -ебёшь; -рёб, -ла́) pf row for a while.

погре́ть (-е́ю) pf warm; **~ся** warm o.s.

по|греши́ть (-шу́) pf sin; err. **по-гре́шность** error, mistake.

по|грози́ть(ся (-ожу́(сь) pf. **по|гру-бе́ть** (-е́ю) pf.

погружа́ть impf, **по|грузи́ть** (-ужу́, -у́зи́шь) pf load; ship; dip, plunge, immerse; **~ся** sink, plunge; dive; be plunged, absorbed. **погруже́ние** submergence; immersion; dive. **по-гру́зка** loading; shipment.

погряза́ть impf, **по|гря́знуть** (-ну; -я́з) pf be bogged down; wallow.

по|губи́ть (-блю́, -бишь) pf. **по|гуля́ть** pf.

под, подо prep I. +acc or instr under; near, close to; **взять под ру́ку**+acc take the arm of; **~ ви́дом**+gen under the guise of; **под го́ру** downhill; **~ Москво́й** in the environs of Moscow. II. +instr occupied by, used as; (meant, implied) by; in, with; **говя́дина ~ хре́ном** beef with horse-radish. III. +acc towards; to (the accompaniment of); in imitation of; on; for, to serve as; **ему́ ~ пятьдеся́т (лет)** he is getting on for fifty.

подава́ть(ся (-даю́(сь, -даёшь(ся) impf of **пода́ть(ся**

подави́ть(ся (-влю́, -вишь) pf, **подавля́ть** impf suppress; depress; overwhelm. **по|дави́ться** (-влю́сь, -вишь-ся) pf. **подавле́ние** suppression; repression. **пода́вленность** depression. **пода́вленный** suppressed; depressed. **подавля́ющий** overwhelming.

пода́вно adv all the more.

пода́гра gout.

пода́льше adv a little further.

по|дари́ть (-рю́, -ришь) pf. **пода́рок** (-рка) present.

пода́тливый pliant, pliable. **по́дать** (gen pl -е́й) tax. **пода́ть** (-а́м, -а́шь, -а́ст, -ади́м; по́дал, -а́, -о) pf (impf **подава́ть**) serve; give; put, move, turn; put forward, present, hand in; **~ся** move; give way; yield; **+на**+acc set out for. **пода́ча** giving, presenting; serve; feed, supply. **пода́чка** handout, crumb. **подаю́** etc.: see

подава́ть. подая́ние alms.

подбега́ть impf, **подбежа́ть** (-егу́) pf come running (up).

подберу́ etc.: see **подобра́ть. под-бира́ть(ся** impf of **подобра́ть(ся**

подби́ть (-добью́, -добьёшь) pf (impf **подбива́ть**) line; re-sole; bruise; put out of action; incite.

подбодри́ть pf, **подбодря́ть** impf cheer up, encourage; **~ся** cheer up, take heart.

подбо́р selection, assortment.

подборо́док (-дка) chin.

подбоче́нившись adv with hands on hips.

подбра́сывать impf, **подбро́сить** (-ро́шу) pf throw up.

подва́л cellar; basement. **подва́ль-ный** basement, cellar.

подведу́ etc.: see **подвести́**

подвезти́ (-зу́, -зёшь; -вёз, -ла́) pf (impf **подвози́ть**) bring, take; give a lift.

подвене́чный wedding.

подверга́ть impf, **подве́ргнуть** (-ну; -ве́рг) pf subject; expose; **~ся** +dat undergo. **подве́рженный** subject, liable.

подверну́ть (-ну́, -нёшь) pf, **под-вёртывать** impf turn up; tuck under; sprain; tighten; **~ся** be sprained; be turned up; be tucked under.

подве́сить (-е́шу) pf (impf **под-ве́шивать**) hang up, suspend. **под-весно́й** hanging, suspended.

подвести́ (-еду́, -едёшь; -вёл, -а́) pf (impf **подводи́ть**) lead up, bring up; place (under); bring under, subsume; let down; **~ ито́ги** reckon up; sum up.

подве́шивать impf of **подве́сить**

по́двиг exploit, feat.

подвига́ть(ся impf of **подви́нуть(ся**

подви́жник religious ascetic; champion.

подвижно́й mobile; **~ соста́в** rolling-stock. **подви́жность** mobility. **подви́жный** mobile; lively; agile.

подвиза́ться impf (**в** or **на**+prep) work (in).

подви́нуть (-ну) pf (impf **под-вига́ть**) move; push; advance; **~ся** move; advance.

подвла́стный +dat subject to; under

the control of.

подвóда cart. подводить (-ожý, -óдишь) *impf of* подвести

подвóдн|ый submarine; underwater; ~ая скалá reef.

подвóз transport; supply. подвозить (-ожý, -óзишь) *impf of* подвезти

подворóтня (*gen pl* -тен) gateway.

подвóх trick.

подвыпивший tipsy.

подвязáть (-яжý, -яжешь) *pf*, подвязывать *impf* tie up. подвязка garter; suspender.

подгибáть *impf of* подогнуть

подглядéть (-яжý) *pf*, подглядывать *impf* peep; spy.

подговáривать *impf*, подговорить *pf* incite.

подгоню *etc.: see* подогнáть. подгонять *impf of* подогнáть

подгорáть *impf*, подгорéть (-рит) *pf* get a bit burnt. подгорéлый slightly burnt.

подготовительный preparatory. подготóвить (-влю) *pf*, подготовлять *impf* prepare; ~ся prepare, get ready. подготóвка preparation, training.

поддавáться (-даюсь, -даёшься) *impf of* поддáться

поддáкивать *impf* agree, assent.

пóдданный *sb* subject; citizen. пóдданство citizenship. поддáться (-áмся, -áшься, -áстся, -адимся, -áлся, -лáсь) *pf* (*impf* поддавáться) yield, give way.

поддéлать *pf*, поддéлывать *impf* counterfeit; forge. поддéлка falsification; forgery; imitation. поддéльный false, counterfeit.

поддержáть (-жý, -жишь) *pf*, поддéрживать *impf* support; maintain. поддéржка support.

по|дéйствовать *pf*.

поделáть *pf* do; ничегó не поделаешь it can't be helped.

по|делить(ся (-лю́(сь, -лишь(ся) *pf*.

подéлка *pl* small (hand-made) articles.

поделóм *adv*: ~ ему́ (*etc.*) it serves him (*etc.*) right.

подённый by the day. подёнщик, -ица day-labourer.

подёргиваться *impf* twitch.

подéржанный second-hand.

подёрнуть (-нет) *pf* cover.

подерý *etc.: see* подрáть. по|дешевéть (-éет) *pf*.

поджáривать(ся *impf*, поджáрить(ся *pf* fry, roast, grill; toast. поджáристый brown(ed).

поджáрый lean, wiry.

поджáть (-дожмý, -дожмёшь) *pf* (*impf* поджимáть) draw in, draw under; ~ гýбы purse one's lips.

поджéчь (-дожгý, -ожжёшь; -жёг, -дожглá) *pf*, поджигáть *impf* set fire to; burn. поджигáтель *m* arsonist; instigator.

поджидáть *impf* (+*gen*) wait (for).

поджимáть *impf of* поджáть

поджóг arson.

подзаголóвок (-вка) subtitle, subheading.

подзащитный *sb* client.

подземéлье (*gen pl* -лий) cave; dungeon. подзéмный underground.

подзовý *etc.: see* подозвáть

подзóрная трубá telescope.

подзывáть *impf of* подозвáть

по|дивиться(ся (-влюсь) *pf*.

подкáпывать(ся *impf of* подкопáть(ся

подкарáуливать *impf*, подкараýлить *pf* be on the watch (for).

подкатить (-ачý, -áтишь) *pf*, подкáтывать *impf* roll up, drive up; roll.

подкáшивать(ся *impf of* подкосить(ся

подкидывать *impf*, подкинуть (-ну) *pf* throw up. подкидыш foundling.

подклáдка lining. подклáдывать *impf of* подложить

подклéивать *impf*, подклéить *pf* glue (up); mend.

подкóва (horse-)shoe. под|ковáть (-кую́, -ёшь) *pf*, подкóвывать *impf* shoe.

подкóжный hypodermic.

подкомиссия, подкомитéт subcommittee.

подкóп undermining; underground passage. подкопáть *pf* (*impf* подкáпывать) undermine; ~ся под+*acc* undermine; burrow under.

подкосить (-ошý, -óсишь) *pf* (*impf* подкáшивать) cut down; ~ся give way.

подкра́дываться *impf of* под-
кра́сться

подкра́сить (-а́шу) *pf* (*impf* под-
кра́шивать) touch up; ~ся make up
lightly.

подкра́сться (-аду́сь, -адёшься) *pf*
(*impf* подкра́дываться) sneak up.

подкра́шивать(ся *impf of* подкра́-
сить(ся. подкра́шу *etc.: see* под-
кра́сить

подкрепи́ть (-плю́) *pf*, подкре-
пля́ть *impf* reinforce; support; corroborate; fortify; ~ся fortify o.s.
подкрепле́ние confirmation; sustenance; reinforcement.

подкрути́ть (-учу́, -у́тишь) *pf* (*impf*
подкру́чивать) tighten up.

по́дкуп bribery. подкупа́ть *impf*,
подкупи́ть (-плю́, -пишь) *pf* bribe;
win over.

подла́диться (-а́жусь) *pf*, подла́-
живаться *impf* +к+*dat* adapt o.s. to;
make up to.

подла́мываться *impf of* подломи́ться

по́дле *prep+gen* by the side of, beside.

подлежа́ть (-жу́) *impf* +*dat* be subject to; не подлежи́т сомне́нию it
is beyond doubt. подлежа́щее *sb* subject. подлежа́щий +*dat* subject to.

подлеза́ть *impf*, подле́зть (-зу; -ёз)
pf crawl (under).

подле́сок (-ска) undergrowth.

подле́ц (-а́) scoundrel.

подлива́ть *impf of* подли́ть. под-
ли́вка sauce, dressing; gravy.

подли́за *m* & *f* toady. подлиза́ться
(-ижу́сь, -и́жешься) *pf*, подли́зы-
ваться *impf* +к+*dat* suck up to.

по́длинник original. по́длинно *adv*
really. по́длинный genuine; authentic; original; real.

подли́ть (-долью́, -дольёшь; по́длил,
-а́, -о) *pf* (*impf* подлива́ть) pour;
add.

подло́г forgery.

подло́дка submarine.

подложи́ть (-жу́, -жишь) *pf* (*impf*
подкла́дывать) add; +под+*acc* lay
under; line.

подло́жный false, spurious; counterfeit, forged.

подлоко́тник arm (*of chair*).

подломи́ться (-о́мится) *pf* (*impf*

подла́мываться) break; give way.

по́длость meanness, baseness; mean
trick. по́длый (подл, -а́, -о) mean,
base.

подма́зать (-а́жу) *pf*, подма́зывать
impf grease; bribe.

подмасте́рье (*gen pl* -ьев) *m* apprentice.

подме́н, подме́на replacement.
подме́нивать *impf*, подмени́ть
(-ню́, -нишь) *pf*, подменя́ть *impf* replace.

подмести́ (-ету́, -етёшь; -мёл, -а́) *pf*,
подмета́ть[1] *impf* sweep.

подмета́ть[2] *pf* (*impf* подмётывать)
tack.

подме́тить (-е́чу) *pf* (*impf* подме-
ча́ть) notice.

подмётка sole.

подмётывать *impf of* подмета́ть[2].

подмеча́ть *impf of* подме́тить

подме́шать *impf*, подме́шивать *impf*
mix in, stir in.

подми́гивать *impf*, подмигну́ть
(-ну́, -нёшь) *pf* +*dat* wink at.

подмо́га help.

подмока́ть *impf*, подмо́кнуть (-нет;
-мо́к) *pf* get damp, get wet.

подмора́живать *impf*, подморо́-
зить *pf* freeze.

подмоско́вный (situated) near Moscow.

подмо́стки (-ов) *pl* scaffolding; stage.

подмо́ченный damp; tarnished.

подмыва́ть *impf*, подмы́ть (-бю)
pf wash; wash away; его́ так и под-
мыва́ет he feels an urge (to).

подмы́шка armpit.

поднево́льный dependent; forced.

поднести́ (-су́, -сёшь; -ёс, -ла́) *pf*
(*impf* подноси́ть) present; take,
bring.

поднима́ть(ся *impf of* подня́ть(ся

поднови́ть (-влю́) *pf*, подновля́ть
impf renew, renovate.

подного́тная *sb* ins and outs.

подно́жие foot; pedestal. подно́жка
running-board. подно́жный корм
pasture.

подно́с tray. подноси́ть (-ошу́,
-о́сишь) *impf of* поднести́. подно-
ше́ние giving; present.

подня́тие raising. подня́ть (-ниму́,
-ни́мешь; по́днял, -а́, -о) *pf* (*impf*
поднима́ть, подыма́ть) raise; lift

(up); rouse; ~ся rise; go up.

по́до *see* под

подоба́ть *impf* befit, become. подоба́ющий proper.

подо́бие likeness; similarity. подо́бн|ый like, similar; и тому́ ~oe and so on, and such like; ничего́ ~ого! nothing of the sort!

подобостра́стие servility. подобостра́стный servile.

подобра́ть (-дберу́, -дберёшь; -бра́л, -á, -о) *pf* (*impf* подбира́ть) pick up; tuck up, put up; pick; ~ся steal up.

подо́бью *etc.*: *see* подби́ть

подогна́ть (-дгоню́, -дго́нишь; -áл, -á, -о) *pf* (*impf* подгоня́ть) drive; urge on; adjust.

подогну́ть (-ну́, -нёшь) *pf* (*impf* подгиба́ть) tuck in; bend under.

подогрева́ть *impf*, подогре́ть (-éю) *pf* warm up.

пододвига́ть *impf*, пододви́нуть (-ну) *pf* move up.

подо́де́я́льник blanket cover; top sheet.

подожгу́ *etc.*: *see* подже́чь

подожда́ть (-ду́, -дёшь; -áл, -á, -о) *pf* wait (+*gen or acc* for).

подожму́ *etc.*: *see* поджа́ть

подозва́ть (-дзову́, -дзовёшь; -áл, -á, -о) *pf* (*impf* подзыва́ть) call to; beckon.

подозрева́емый suspected; suspect. подозрева́ть *impf* suspect. подозре́ние suspicion. подозри́тельный suspicious.

по|до́ить (-ою́, -о́ишь) *pf*.

подойти́ (-йду́, -йдёшь; -ошёл, -шла́) *pf* (*impf* подходи́ть) approach; come up; +*dat* suit, fit.

подоко́нник window-sill.

подо́л hem.

подо́лгу *adv* for ages; for hours (*etc.*) on end.

подолью́ *etc.*: *see* подли́ть

подо́нки (-ов) *pl* dregs; scum.

подоплёка underlying cause.

подопру́ *etc.*: *see* подпере́ть

подо́пытный experimental.

подорва́ть (-рву́, -рвёшь; -áл, -á, -о) *pf* (*impf* подрыва́ть) undermine; blow up.

по|дорожа́ть *pf*.

подоро́жник plantain. подоро́жный roadside.

подосла́ть (-ошлю́, -ошлёшь) *pf* (*impf* подсыла́ть) send (secretly).

подоспева́ть *impf*, подоспе́ть (-éю) *pf* arrive, appear (in time).

подостла́ть (-дстелю́, -дсте́лешь) *pf* (*impf* подстила́ть) lay under.

подотде́л section, subdivision.

подотру́ *etc.*: *see* подтере́ть

подотчётный accountable.

по|до́хнуть (-ну) *pf* (*impf also* по-дыха́ть).

подохо́дный нало́г income-tax.

подо́шва sole; foot.

подошёл *etc.*: *see* подойти́. подошлю́ *etc.*: *see* подосла́ть подошью́ *etc.*: *see* подши́ть.

подпада́ть *impf*, подпа́сть (-аду́, -адёшь; -áл) *pf* под+*acc* fall under.

подпева́ть *impf* (+*dat*) sing along (with).

подпере́ть (-допру́; -пёр) *pf* (*impf* подпира́ть) prop up.

подпи́ливать *impf*, подпили́ть (-лю́, -лишь) *pf* saw; saw a little off.

подпира́ть *impf of* подпере́ть

подписа́ние signing. подписа́ть (-ишу́, -и́шешь) *pf*, подпи́сывать *impf* sign; ~ся sign; subscribe. подпи́ска subscription. подписно́й subscription. подпи́счик subscriber. по́дпись signature.

подплыва́ть *impf*, подплы́ть (-ыву́, -ывёшь; -плы́л, -á, -о) *pf* к+*dat* swim or sail up to.

подполза́ть *impf*, подползти́ (-зу́, -зёшь; -по́лз, -лá) *pf* creep up (к+*dat* to); +под+*acc* crawl under.

подполко́вник lieutenant-colonel.

подпо́лье cellar; underground. подпо́льный underfloor; underground.

подпо́ра, подпо́рка prop, support.

подпо́чва subsoil.

подпра́вить (-влю) *pf*, подправля́ть *impf* touch up, adjust.

подпры́гивать *impf*, подпры́гнуть (-ну) *pf* jump up (and down).

подпуска́ть *impf*, подпусти́ть (-ущу́, -у́стишь) *pf* allow to approach.

подраба́тывать *impf*, подрабо́тать *pf* earn on the side; work up.

подра́внивать *impf of* подровня́ть

подража́ние imitation. подража́ть *impf* imitate.

подразделе́ние subdivision. подраздели́ть *pf*, подразделя́ть *impf* subdivide.

подразумева́ть *impf* imply, mean; ~ся be meant, be understood.

подраста́ть *impf*, подрасти́ (-ту́, -тёшь; -ро́с, -ла́) *pf* grow.

по|дра́ть(ся (-деру́(сь, -дерёшь(ся, -а́л(ся, -ла́(сь, -о́(сь *or* -о(сь) *pf*.

подреза́ть (-е́жу) *pf*, подреза́ть *impf* cut; clip, trim.

подро́бно *adv* in detail. подро́бность detail. подро́бный detailed.

подровня́ть *pf* (*impf* подра́внивать) level, even; trim.

подро́с *etc*.: *see* подрасти́. подро́сток (-тка) adolescent; youth.

подро́ю *etc*.: *see* подры́ть.

подруба́ть¹ *impf*, подруби́ть (-блю́, -бишь) *pf* chop down; cut short(er).

подруба́ть² *impf*, подруби́ть (-блю́, -бишь) *pf* hem.

подру́га friend. по-дру́жески *adv* in a friendly way. по|дружи́ться (-жу́сь) *pf*.

по-друго́му *adv* in a different way. подру́чный at hand; improvised; *sb* assistant.

подры́в undermining; injury.

подрыва́ть¹ *impf of* подорва́ть подрыва́ть² *impf*, подры́ть (-ро́ю) *pf* undermine, sap. подрывно́й blasting, demolition; subversive.

подря́д¹ *adv* in succession.

подря́д² contract. подря́дчик contractor.

подса́живаться *impf of* подсе́сть подса́ливать *impf of* подсоли́ть подсве́чник candlestick.

подсе́сть (-ся́ду; -се́л) *pf* (*impf* подса́живаться) sit down (к+*dat* near).

подска́зывать (-ажу́, -а́жешь) *pf*, подска́зывать *impf* prompt; suggest. подска́зка prompting.

подска́кивать *impf*, подскочи́ть (-чу́, -чишь) *pf* jump (up); soar; come running.

подсласти́ть (-ащу́) *pf*, подсла́щивать *impf* sweeten.

подсле́дственный under investigation.

подслу́шать *pf*, подслу́шивать *impf* overhear; eavesdrop, listen.

подсма́тривать *impf*, подсмотре́ть (-рю́, -ришь) *pf* spy (on).

подсне́жник snowdrop.

подсо́бный subsidiary; auxiliary.

подсо́вывать *impf of* подсу́нуть подсозна́ние subconscious (mind). подсозна́тельный subconscious.

подсоли́ть (-со́лишь) *pf* (*impf* подса́ливать) add salt to.

подсо́лнечник sunflower. подсо́лнечный sunflower.

подсо́хнуть (-ну) *pf* (*impf* подсыха́ть) dry out a little.

подспо́рье help.

подста́вить (-влю) *pf*, подставля́ть *impf* put (under); bring up; expose; ~ но́жку +*dat* trip up. подста́вка stand; support. подставно́й false.

подстака́нник glass-holder.

подстелю́ *etc*.: *see* подостла́ть подстерега́ть *impf*, подстере́чь (-егу́, -ежёшь; -рёг, -ла́) *pf* lie in wait for.

подстила́ть *impf of* подостла́ть. подсти́лка litter.

подстра́ивать *impf of* подстро́ить подстрека́тель *m* instigator. подстрека́тельство instigation. подстрека́ть *impf*, подстрекну́ть (-ну́, -нёшь) *pf* instigate, incite.

подстре́ливать *impf*, подстрели́ть (-лю́, -лишь) *pf* wound.

подстрига́ть *impf*, подстри́чь (-игу́, -ижёшь; -иг) *pf* cut; clip, trim; ~ся have a hair-cut.

подстро́ить *pf* (*impf* подстра́ивать) build on; cook up.

подстро́чн|ый literal; ~ое примеча́ние footnote.

по́дступ approach. подступа́ть *impf*, подступи́ть (-плю́, -пишь) *pf* approach; ~ся к+*dat* approach.

подсуди́мый *sb* defendant; the accused. подсу́дный+*dat* under the jurisdiction of.

подсу́нуть (-ну) *pf* (*impf* подсо́вывать) put, shove; palm off.

подсчёт calculation; count. подсчита́ть *pf*, подсчи́тывать *impf* count (up); calculate.

подсыла́ть *impf of* подосла́ть. подсыха́ть *impf of* подсо́хнуть. подся́ду *etc*.: *see* подсе́сть. подта́лкивать *impf of* подтолкну́ть подта́скивать *impf of* подтащи́ть подтасова́ть *pf*, подтасо́вывать *impf* shuffle unfairly; juggle with.

подта́чивать *impf of* подточи́ть

подтащи́ть (-щу́, -щишь) *pf* (*impf* **подта́скивать**) drag up.

подтверди́ть (-ржу́) *pf*, **подтвержда́ть** *impf* confirm; corroborate. **подтвержде́ние** confirmation, corroboration.

подтёк bruise. **подтека́ть** *impf of* **подте́чь**; leak.

подтере́ть (-дотру́, -дотрёшь; подтёр) *pf* (*impf* **подтира́ть**) wipe (up).

подте́чь (-ечёт, -тёк, -ла́) *pf* (*impf* **подтека́ть**) под+*acc* flow under.

подтира́ть *impf of* **подтере́ть**

подтолкну́ть (-ну́, -нёшь) *pf* (*impf* **подта́лкивать**) push; urge on.

подточи́ть (-чу́, -чишь) *pf* (*impf* **подта́чивать**) sharpen; eat away; undermine.

подтру́нивать *impf*, **подтруни́ть** *pf* над+*instr* tease.

подтя́гивать *impf*, **подтяну́ть** (-ну́, -нешь) *pf* tighten; pull up; move up; ~**ся** tighten one's belt *etc.*; move up; pull o.s. together. **подтя́жки** *pl* braces, suspenders. **подтя́нутый** smart.

по|ду́мать *pf* think (for a while). **поду́мывать** *impf*+*inf or* о+*prep* think about.

по|ду́ть (-у́ю) *pf.*

поду́шка pillow; cushion.

подхали́м *m* toady. **подхали́мство** grovelling.

подхвати́ть (-ачу́, -а́тишь) *pf*, **подхва́тывать** *impf* catch (up), pick up; take up.

подхлестну́ть (-ну́, -нёшь) *pf*, **подхлёстывать** *impf* whip up.

подхо́д approach. **подходи́ть** (-ожу́, -о́дишь) *impf of* **подойти́**. **подходя́щий** suitable.

подцепи́ть (-плю́, -пишь) *pf*, **подцепля́ть** *impf* hook on; pick up.

подча́с *adv* sometimes.

подчёркивать *impf*, **подчеркну́ть** (-ну́, -нёшь) *pf* underline; emphasize.

подчине́ние subordination; submission. **подчинённый** subordinate.

подчини́ть *pf*, **подчиня́ть** *impf* subordinate, subject; ~**ся** +*dat* submit to.

подшива́ть *impf of* **подши́ть**. **подши́вка** hemming; lining; soling.

подши́пник bearing.

подши́ть (-дошью́, -дошьёшь) *pf*

(*impf* **подшива́ть**) hem, line; sole.

подшути́ть (-учу́, -у́тишь) *pf*, **подшу́чивать** *impf* над+*instr* mock; play a trick on.

подъ́еду *etc.: see* **подъ́ехать**

подъ́езд entrance, doorway; approach. **подъезжа́ть** *impf of* **подъ́ехать**

подъём lifting; raising; ascent; climb; enthusiasm; instep; reveille. **подъ́ёмник** lift, elevator, hoist. **подъ́ёмный** lifting; ~ **кран** crane; ~ **мост** drawbridge.

подъ́ехать (-е́ду) *pf* (*impf* **подъезжа́ть**) drive up.

подыма́ть(ся *impf of* **подня́ть(ся**

подыска́ть (-ыщу́, -ы́щешь) *pf*, **поды́скивать** *impf* seek (out).

подыто́живать *impf*, **подыто́жить** (-жу) *pf* sum up.

подыха́ть *impf of* **подо́хнуть**

подыша́ть (-шу́, -шишь) *pf* breathe.

поеда́ть *impf of* **пое́сть**

поеди́нок (-нка) duel.

по́езд (*pl* -а́) train. **пое́здка** trip.

пое́сть (-е́м, -е́шь, -е́ст, -еди́м; -е́л) *pf* (*impf* **поеда́ть**) eat, eat up; have a bite to eat.

пое́хать (-е́ду) *pf* go; set off.

по|жале́ть (-е́ю) *pf.*

по|жа́ловать(ся *pf.* **пожа́луй** *adv* perhaps. **пожа́луйста** *partl* please; you're welcome.

пожа́р fire. **пожа́рище** scene of a fire. **пожа́рник**, **пожа́рный** *sb* fireman. **пожа́рн**|**ый** fire; ~**ая кома́нда** fire-brigade; ~**ая ле́стница** fire-escape; ~**ая маши́на** fire-engine.

пожа́тие handshake. **пожа́ть**[1] (-жму́, -жмёшь) *pf* (*impf* **пожима́ть**) press; ~ **ру́ку**+*dat* shake hands with; ~ **плеча́ми** shrug one's shoulders.

пожа́ть[2] (-жну́, -жнёшь) *pf* (*impf* **пожина́ть**) reap.

пожела́ние wish, desire. **по|жела́ть** *pf.*

по|желте́ть (-е́ю) *pf.*

по|жени́ть (-ню́, -нишь) *pf.* **пожени́ться** (-же́нимся) *pf* get married.

поже́ртвование donation. **по|же́ртвовать** *pf.*

пожива́ть *impf* live; **как (вы) пожива́ете?** how are you (getting on)? **пожи́зненный** life(long). **пожило́й** elderly.

пожима́ть *impf of* пожа́ть¹. пожина́ть *impf of* пожа́ть². пожира́ть *impf of* пожра́ть.

пожи́тки (-ов) *pl* belongings.

пожи́ть (-иву́, -ивёшь; по́жил, -á, -о) *pf.* live for a while; stay.

пожму́ *etc.*: *see* пожа́ть¹. пожну́ *etc.*: *see* пожа́ть²

пожра́ть (-ру́, -рёшь; -а́л, -á, -о) *pf* (*impf* пожира́ть) devour.

по́за pose.

по|забо́титься (-о́чусь) *pf.*

позабыва́ть *impf,* позабы́ть (-у́ду) *pf* forget all about.

по|зави́довать *pf.* по|за́втракать *pf.*

позавчера́ *adv* the day before yesterday.

позади́ *adv & prep+gen* behind.

по|займствовать *pf.*

позапро́шлый before last.

по|зва́ть (-зову́, -зовёшь; -áл, -á, -о) *pf.*

позволе́ние permission. позволи́тельный permissible. позво́лить *pf,* позволя́ть *impf +dat or acc* allow, permit; позво́ль(те) allow me; excuse me.

по|звони́ть *pf.*

позвоно́к (-нка́) vertebra. позвоно́чник spine. позвоно́чн|ый spinal; vertebrate; ~ые *sb pl* vertebrates.

поздне́е *adv* later. по́здний late; по́здно it is late.

по|здоро́ваться *pf.* поздра́вить (-влю) *pf,* поздравля́ть *impf c+instr* congratulate on. поздравле́ние congratulation.

по|зелене́ть (-éет) *pf.*

по́зже *adv* later (on).

пози́ровать *impf* pose.

пози́тив positive. позити́вный positive.

пози́ция position.

познава́тельный cognitive. познава́ть (-наю́, -наёшь) *impf of* позна́ть

по|знако́мить(ся (-млю(сь) *pf.*

позна́ние cognition. позна́ть *pf* (*impf* познава́ть) get to know.

позоло́та gilding. по|золоти́ть (-лочу́) *pf.*

позо́р shame, disgrace. позо́рить *impf* (*pf* о~) disgrace; ~ся disgrace o.s. позо́рный shameful.

позы́в urge; inclination.

по|игра́ть *pf* play (for a while).

поимённо *adv* by name.

пои́мка capture.

по|интересова́ться *pf* be curious.

поиска́ть (-ищу́, -и́щешь) *pf* look for. по́иски (-ов) *pl* search.

пои́стине *adv* indeed.

пои́ть (пою́, по́ишь) *impf* (*pf* на~) give something to drink; water.

пойду́ *etc.*: *see* пойти́

пойло swill.

пойма́ть *pf of* лови́ть. пойму́ *etc.*: *see* поня́ть

пойти́ (-йду́, -йдёшь; пошёл, -шла́) *pf of* идти́, ходи́ть; go, walk; begin to walk; +*inf* begin; пошёл! off you go! I'm off; пошёл вон! be off!

пока́ *adv* for the present; cheerio; ~ что in the meanwhile. пока́ *conj* while; ~ не until.

пока́з showing, demonstration. показа́ние testimony, evidence; reading. показа́тель *m* index. показа́тельный significant; model; demonstration. показа́ть (-ажу́, -а́жешь) *pf,* пока́зывать *impf* show. по|каза́ться (-ажу́сь, -а́жешься) *pf,* пока́зываться *impf* show o.s.; appear. показно́й for show; ostentatious. показу́ха show.

по|кале́чить(ся (-чу(сь) *pf.*

покаме́ст *adv & conj* for the present; while; meanwhile.

по|кара́ть *pf.*

покати́ть (-чу́, -тишь) *pf* start (rolling); ~ся start rolling.

пока́тый sloping; slanting.

покача́ть *pf* rock, swing; ~ голово́й shake one's head. пока́чивать rock slightly; ~ся rock; stagger. покачну́ть (-ну́, -нёшь) shake; rock; ~ся sway, totter, lurch.

пока́шливать *impf* have a slight cough.

покая́ние confession; repentance. по|ка́яться *pf.*

по|квита́ться *pf* be quits; get even.

покида́ть *impf,* поки́нуть (-ну) *pf* leave; abandon. поки́нутый deserted.

поклада́|я: не ~ рук untiringly.

покла́дистый complaisant, obliging.

покло́н bow; greeting; regards. поклоне́ние worship. поклони́ться

(-ню́сь, -ни́шься) *pf of* кла́няться.
покло́нник admirer; worshipper.
поклоня́ться *impf +dat* worship.
по|коли́ться (-яню́сь, -нёшься; -я́лся, -ла́сь) *pf.*
поко́иться *impf* rest, repose. поко́й rest, peace; room. поко́йник, -ица the deceased. поко́йный calm, quiet; late.
по|колеба́ть(ся (-éблю(сь) *pf.*
поколе́ние generation.
по|колоти́ть(ся (-очу́(сь, -о́тишь(ся) *pf.*
поко́нчить (-чу) *pf* с+*instr* finish; put an end to; ~ с собо́й commit suicide.
поконе́ние conquest. покори́ть *pf* (*impf* покоря́ть) subdue; conquer; ~ся submit.
по|корми́ть(ся (-млю́(сь, -мишь(ся) *pf.*
поко́рный humble; submissive, obedient.
по|коро́бить(ся (-блю(сь) *pf.*
покоря́ть(ся *impf of* покори́ть(ся
поко́с mowing; meadow(-land).
покоси́вшийся rickety, ramshackle.
по|коси́ть(ся (-ошу́(сь) *pf.*
по|кра́сить (-а́шу) *pf.* покра́ска painting, colouring.
по|красне́ть (-éю) *pf.* по|криви́ть(ся (-влю́(сь) *pf.*
покро́в cover. покрови́тель *m*, покрови́тельница patron; sponsor. покрови́тельственный protective; patronizing. покрови́тельство protection, patronage. покрови́тельствовать *impf +dat* protect, patronize.
покро́й cut.
покроши́ть (-шу́, -шишь) *pf* crumble; chop.
покрути́ть (-учу́, -у́тишь) *pf* twist.
покрыва́ло cover; bedspread; veil. покрыва́ть *impf*, по|кры́ть (-ро́ю) *pf* cover; ~ся cover o.s.; get covered. покры́тие covering; surfacing; payment. покры́шка cover; tyre.
покупа́тель *m* buyer; customer. по|купа́ть *impf of* купи́ть. поку́пка purchase. покупно́й bought, purchased; purchase.
по|кури́ть (-рю́, -ришь) *pf* have a smoke.
по|ку́шать *pf.*

покуше́ние +на+*acc* attempted assassination of.
пол¹ (*loc* -ý; *pl* -ы́) floor.
пол² sex.
пол- in comb with n in gen, in oblique cases usu полу-, half.
пола́ (*pl* -ы) flap; из-под полы́ on the sly.
полага́ть *impf* suppose, think. полага́ться *impf of* положи́ться; полага́ется *impers* one is supposed to; +*dat* it is due to.
по|ла́комить(ся (-млю(сь) *pf.*
полго́да (полуго́да) *m* half a year.
по́лдень (-дня *or* -лу́дня) *m* noon. полдне́вный *adj.*
по́ле (*pl* -я́, -éй) field; ground; margin; brim. полев|о́й field; ~ые цветы́ wild flowers.
полежа́ть (-жу́) *pf* lie down for a while.
поле́зн|ый useful; helpful; good, wholesome; ~ая нагру́зка payload.
по|ле́зть (-зу; -лéз) *pf.*
полемизи́ровать *impf* debate, engage in controversy. поле́мика controversy; polemics. полеми́ческий polemical.
по|лени́ться (-ню́сь, -ни́шься) *pf.*
поле́но (*pl* -éнья, -ьев) log.
полёт flight. по|лете́ть (-лечу́) *pf.*
по́лзать *indet impf*, ползти́ (-зу́, -зёшь; полз, -ла́) *det impf* crawl, creep; ooze; fray. ползу́чий creeping.
поли- in comb poly-.
полива́ть(ся *impf of* поли́ть(ся. поли́вка watering.
полига́мия polygamy.
полигло́т polyglot.
полиграфи́ческий printing. полиграфи́я printing.
полиго́н range.
поликли́ника polyclinic.
полиме́р polymer.
полиня́лый faded. по|линя́ть *pf.*
полиомиели́т poliomyelitis.
полирова́льный polishing. полирова́ть *impf* (*pf* от~) polish. полиро́вка polishing; polish. полиро́вщик polisher.
полит- *abbr in comb* (*of* полити́ческий) political. политбюро́ *neut indecl* Politburo. ~заключённый *sb* political prisoner.
политехни́ческий polytechnic.

поли́тик politician. поли́тика policy; politics.полити́ческий political.

поли́ть (-лью́, -льёшь; по́лил, -á, -о) pf (impf полива́ть) pour over; water;~ся +instr pour over o.s.

полице́йский police; sb policeman. поли́ция police.

поли́чн|ое sb:c ~ым red-handed.

полк (-á, loc -ý) regiment.

по́лка shelf; berth.

полко́вник colonel.полково́дец (-дца) commander; general. полково́й regimental.

пол-ли́тра half a litre.

полне́ть (-éю) impf (pfпо~) put on weight.

по́лно adv that's enough! stop it!

полно- in comb full; completely. полнолу́ние full moon.~метра́жный full-length. ~пра́вный enjoying full rights; competent.~це́нный of full value.

полномо́чие (usu pl) authority, power. полномо́чный plenipotentiary.

по́лностью adv in full; completely. полнота́ completeness; corpulence.

по́лночь (-л(ý)ночи) midnight.

по́лный (-лон, -лна́, по́лно́) full; complete; plump.

полови́к (-á) mat, matting.

полови́на half; два с полови́ной two and a half; ~ шесто́го half-past five. полови́нка half.

полови́ца floor-board.

полово́дье high water.

полово́й[1] floor.

полово́й[2] sexual.

поло́гий gently sloping.

положе́ние position; situation; status; regulations; thesis; provisions. поло́женный agreed; determined. поло́жим let us assume; suppose. положи́тельный positive. положи́ть (-жу́, -жишь) pf (impf класть) put; lay (down); ~ся (impf полага́ться) rely.

по́лоз (pl -о́зья, -ев) runner.

по|лома́ть(ся pf. поло́мка breakage.

полоса́ (acc по́лосу́; pl по́лосы, -ло́с, -áм) stripe; strip; band; region; belt; period. полоса́тый striped.

полоска́ть (-ощу́, -о́щешь) impf (pf

вы~, от~, про~) rinse;~ го́рло gargle;~ся paddle; flap.

по́лость[1] (gen pl -éй) cavity.

по́лость[2] (gen pl -éй) travelling rug.

полоте́нце (gen pl -нец) towel.

полотёр floor-polisher.

полоти́ще width; panel. полотно́ (pl -a, -тен) linen; canvas.полотня́ный linen.

поло́ть (-лю́, -лешь) impf (pfвы~) weed.

полощу́ etc.: seeполоска́ть

полти́нник fifty copecks.

полтора́ (-лу́тора) m & neut,полторы́ (-лу́тора) f one and a half.

полтора́ста (полу́т-) a hundred and fifty.

полу-[1] seeпол-

полу-[2] in comb half-, semi-, demi-. полуботи́нок (-нка; gen pl -нок) shoe. ~го́дие half a year. ~годи́чный six months', lasting six months. ~годова́лый six-month-old. ~годово́й half-yearly, six-monthly. ~гра́мотный semi-literate. ~защи́тник half-back.~кру́г semicircle. ~кру́глый semicircular. ~ме́сяц crescent (moon). ~мра́к semi-darkness. ~но́чный midnight. ~о́стров peninsula. ~откры́тый ajar.~проводни́к (-á) semi-conductor, transistor. ~ста́нок (-нка) halt. ~тьма́ semi-darkness. ~фабрика́т semi-finished product, convenience food. ~фина́л semi-final. ~часово́й half-hourly. ~ша́рие hemisphere. ~шу́бок (-бка) sheepskin coat.

полуде́нный midday.

получа́тель m recipient. получа́ть impf,получи́ть (-чу́, -чишь) pf get, receive, obtain; ~ся come, turn up; turn out; из э́того ничего́ не получи́лось nothing came of it. получе́ние receipt. полу́чка receipt; pay(-packet).

полу́чше adv a little better.

полчаса́ (получа́са) m half an hour.

по́лчище horde.

по́лый hollow; flood.

по|лысе́ть (-éю) pf.

по́льза use; benefit; profit; в по́льзу+gen in favour of, on behalf of. по́льзование use. по́льзоваться impf (pf вос~) +instr make use of, utilize; profit by; enjoy.

по́лька Pole; polka. **по́льский** Polish; sb polonaise.

по|льсти́ть(ся (-льщу́(сь) pf. **полью́** etc. see **поли́ть**.

По́льша Poland.

полюби́ть (-блю́, -бишь) pf come to like; fall in love with.

по|любова́ться (-бу́юсь) pf.

полюбо́вный amicable.

по|любопы́тствовать pf.

по́люс pole.

поля́к Pole.

поля́на glade, clearing.

поляриза́ция polarization. **поля́рник** polar explorer. **поля́рн|ый** polar; ~ая звезда́ pole-star.

пом- abbr in comb (of **помо́щник**) assistant. ~на́ч assistant chief, assistant head.

пома́да pomade; lipstick.

помаза́ние anointment. **по|ма́зать(ся** (-а́жу(сь) pf. **помазо́к** (-зка́) small brush.

помале́ньку adv gradually; gently; modestly; so-so.

пома́лкивать impf hold one's tongue.

по|мани́ть (-ню́, -нишь) pf.

пома́рка blot; pencil mark; correction.

по|ма́слить pf.

помаха́ть (-машу́, -ма́шешь) pf, **пома́хивать** impf +instr wave; wag.

поме́длить pf +c +instr delay.

поме́ньше a little smaller; a little less.

по|меня́ть(ся pf.

помере́ть (-мру́, -мрёшь; -мер, -ла́, -ло) pf (impf помира́ть) die.

по|мере́щиться (-щусь) pf. **по|ме́рить(ся** pf.

помертве́лый deathly pale. **по|мертве́ть** (-е́ю) pf.

помести́ть (-ещу́) pf (impf помеща́ть) accommodate; place, locate; invest; ~ся lodge; find room.

поме́стье (gen pl -тий, -тьям) estate.

по́месь cross(-breed), hybrid.

помёт dung; droppings; litter, brood.

поме́та mark. **поме́тка** mark, note. **по|ме́тить** (-е́чу) pf (impf also помеча́ть) mark; date; ~ га́лочкой tick.

помеха hindrance; obstacle; pl interference.

помеча́ть impf of **поме́тить**

поме́шанный mad; sb lunatic. **помеша́телство** madness; craze. **по|меша́ть** pf. **помеша́ться** pf go mad.

помеща́ть impf of **помести́ть**. **помеща́ться** impf of **помести́ться**; be (situated); be accommodated, find room. **помеще́ние** premises; apartment, room, lodging; location; investment. **поме́щик** landowner.

помидо́р tomato.

поми́лование forgiveness. **поми́ловать** pf forgive.

поми́мо prep+gen apart from; besides; without the knowledge of.

помина́ть impf of **помяну́ть**; не ~ ли́хом remember kindly. **поми́нки** (-нок) pl funeral repast.

помира́ть impf of **помере́ть**.

по|мири́ть(ся pf.

по́мнить impf remember.

помога́ть impf of **помо́чь**.

по-мо́ему adv in my opinion.

помо́и (-ев) pl slops. **помо́йка** (gen pl -о́ек) rubbish dump. **помо́йный** slop.

помо́л grinding.

помо́лвка betrothal.

по|моли́ться (-лю́сь, -лишься) pf. **по|молоде́ть** (-е́ю) pf.

помолча́ть (-чу́) pf be silent for a time.

помо́рье: see по- II.

по|мо́рщиться (-щусь) pf.

помо́ст dais; rostrum.

по|мочи́ться (-чу́сь, -чишься) pf.

помо́чь (-огу́, -о́жешь; -о́г, -ла́) pf (impf помога́ть) (+dat) help. **помо́щник, помо́щница** assistant. **по́мощь** help; на ~! help!

помо́ю etc.: see **помы́ть**.

по́мпа pump.

помуте́ние dimness, clouding.

помча́ться (-чу́сь) pf rush; dart off.

помыка́ть impf +instr order about.

по́мысел (-сла) intention; thought.

по|мы́ть(ся (-мо́ю(сь) pf.

помяну́ть (-ну́, -нешь) pf (impf помина́ть) mention; pray for.

помя́тый crumpled. **по|мя́ться** (-мнётся) pf.

по|наде́яться (-е́юсь) pf count, rely.

пона́добиться (-блюсь) pf be or become necessary; е́сли пона́добится if necessary.

понапрáсну *adv* in vain.

понаслы́шке *adv* by hearsay.

по-настоя́щему *adv* properly, truly.

понача́лу *adv* at first.

поневóле *adv* willynilly; against one's will.

понедéльник Monday.

понемнóгу, понемнóжку *adv* little by little.

по|нести́(сь (-сý(сь, -сёшь(ся; -нёс(ся, -ла́(сь) *pf*.

понижáть *impf*, **пони́зить** (-н́жу) *pf* lower; reduce; ~ся fall, drop, go down. **пониже́ние** fall; lowering; reduction.

поникáть *impf*, **по|ни́кнуть** (-ну; -ни́к) *pf* droop, wilt.

понимáние understanding. **понимáть** *impf of* поня́ть

по-нóвому *adv* in a new fashion.

понóс diarrhoea.

поноси́ть[1] (-ошý, -óсишь) *pf* carry; wear.

поноси́ть[2] (-ошý, -óсишь) *impf* abuse (*verbally*).

понóшенный worn; threadbare.

по|нрáвиться (-влюсь) *pf*.

понтóн pontoon.

понýдить (-ýжу) *pf*, **понуждáть** *impf* compel.

понукáть *impf* urge on.

понýрить *pf*: ~ гóлову hang one's head. **понýрый** downcast.

по|ню́хать *pf*. **поню́шка**: ~ табакý pinch of snuff.

поня́тие concept; notion, idea. **поня́тливый** bright, quick. **поня́тный** understandable, comprehensible; clear; ~о naturally; ~о? (do you) see? **поня́ть** (пойму́, -мёшь; пóнял, -á, -о) *pf* (*impf* **понимáть**) understand; realize.

по|обéдать *pf*. **по|обещáть** *pf*.

пóодаль *adv* at some distance.

поодинóчке *adv* one by one.

поочерёдно *adv* in turn.

поощре́ние encouragement. **поощри́ть** *pf*, **поощря́ть** *impf* encourage.

поп (-á) priest.

попадáние hit. **попадáть(ся** *impf of* попáсть(ся

попáдья priest's wife.

попáло: *see* попáсть. **по|пáриться** *pf*.

попáрно *adv* in pairs, two by two.

попáсть (-адý, -адёшь; -áл) *pf* (*impf* **попадáть**) +в+*acc* hit; get (in)to, find o.s. in; +на+*acc* hit upon, come on; не тудá ~ get the wrong number; ~ся be caught; find o.s.; turn up; что **попадётся** anything. **попáло** *with prons & advs*: где ~ anywhere; как ~ anyhow; что ~ the first thing to hand.

поперёк *adv & prep*+*gen* across.

попеременно *adv* in turns.

попере́чник diameter. **попере́чный** transverse, diametrical; cross; ~ый разре́з, ~ое сече́ние cross-section.

поперхну́ться (-нýсь, -нёшься) *pf* choke.

по|пéрчить (-чý) *pf*.

попече́ние care; charge; на попече́нии+*gen* in the care of. **попечи́тель** *m* guardian, trustee.

попирáть *impf* (*pf* **попрáть**) trample on; flout.

попи́ть (-пью́, -пьёшь; пóпил, -ла, пóпило) *pf* have a drink.

поплавóк (-вкá) float.

поплáкать (-áчу) *pf* cry a little.

по|плати́ться (-чýсь, -тишься) *pf*.

поплы́ть (-ывý, -ывёшь; -ы́л, -ылá, -о) *pf*. start swimming.

попóйка drinking-bout.

пополáм *adv* in two, in half; half-and-half.

поползнове́ние half a mind; pretension(s).

пополне́ние replenishment; reinforcement. **по|полне́ть** (-éю) *pf*. **пополни́ть** *pf*, **пополня́ть** *impf* replenish; re-stock; reinforce.

пополýдни *adv* in the afternoon; p.m.

попóна horse-cloth.

по|пóтчевать (-чую) *pf*.

поправи́мый rectifiable. **попрáвить** (-влю) *pf*, **поправля́ть** *impf* repair; correct, put right; set straight; ~ся correct o.s.; get better, recover; improve. **попрáвка** correction; repair; adjustment; recovery.

попрáть *pf of* попирáть

по-прéжнему *adv* as before.

попрёк reproach. **попрекáть** *impf*, **попрекнýть** (-нý, -нёшь) *pf* reproach.

пóприще field; walk of life.

по|прóбовать *pf*. **по|проси́ть(ся**

(-ошу́(сь, -о́сишь(ся) *pf*.

по́просту *adv* simply; without ceremony.

попроша́йка *m & f* cadger. попроша́йничать *impf* cadge.

попроща́ться *pf* (+с+*instr*) say goodbye (to).

попры́гать *pf* jump, hop.

попуга́й parrot.

популя́рность popularity. популя́рный popular.

попусти́тельство connivance.

по-пусто́му, по́пусту *adv* in vain.

попу́тно *adv* at the same time; in passing. попу́тный passing. попу́тчик fellow-traveller.

по|пыта́ться *pf*. попы́тка attempt.

по|пя́титься (-я́чусь) *pf*. попя́тный backward; идти́ на ~ go back on one's word.

по́ра¹ pore.

пора́² (*acc* -у; *pl* -ы, пор, -а́м) time; it is time; до каки́х пор? till when?; до сих пор till now; с каки́х пор? since when?

порабо́тать *pf* do some work.

порабо́тить (-о́щу) *pf*, порабоща́ть *impf* enslave. порабоще́ние enslavement.

поравня́ться *pf* come alongside.

по|ра́довать(ся *pf*.

пора|жа́ть *impf*, по|рази́ть (-ажу́) *pf* hit; strike; defeat; affect; astonish; ~ся be astounded. пораже́ние defeat. порази́тельный striking; astonishing.

по-ра́зному *adv* differently.

пора́нить *pf* wound; injure.

порва́ть (-ву́, -вёшь; -ва́л, -а́, -о) *pf* (*impf* порыва́ть) tear (up); break, break off; ~ся tear; break (off).

по|реде́ть (-е́ет) *pf*.

поре́з cut. поре́зать (-е́жу) *pf* cut; ~ся cut o.s.

поре́й leek.

по|рекомендова́ть *pf*. по|ржа́веть (-еет) *pf*.

по́ристый porous.

порица́ние censure; blame. порица́ть *impf* blame; censure.

по́рка flogging.

по́ровну *adv* equally.

поро́г threshold; rapids.

поро́да breed; race; species. поро́дистый thoroughbred. породи́ть

(-ожу́) *pf* (*impf* порожда́ть) give birth to; give rise to.

по|родни́ть(ся *pf*. поро́дный pedigree.

порожда́ть *impf of* породи́ть

поро́жний empty.

по́рознь *adv* separately, apart.

поро́й, поро́ю *adv* at times.

поро́к vice; defect.

поросёнок (-нка; *pl* -ся́та, -ся́т) piglet.

по́росль shoots; young wood.

поро́ть¹ (-рю́, -решь) *impf* (*pf* вы́~) thrash; whip.

поро́ть² (-рю́, -решь) *impf* (*pf* рас~) undo, unpick; ~ся come unstitched.

по́рох (*pl* ~а́) gunpowder, powder. порохово́й.

поро́чить (-чу) *impf* (*pf* о~) discredit; smear. поро́чный vicious, depraved; faulty.

пороши́ть (-ши́т) *impf* snow slightly.

порошо́к (-шка́) powder.

порт (*loc* -у́; *pl* -ы, -о́в) port.

портати́вный portable.

портве́йн port (wine).

по́ртик portico.

по́ртить (-чу) *impf* (*pf* ис~) spoil; corrupt; ~ся deteriorate; go bad.

портни́ха dressmaker. портно́вский tailor's. портно́й *sb* tailor.

порто́вый port.

портре́т portrait.

портсига́р cigarette-case.

португа́лец (-льца), -лка Portuguese. Португа́лия Portugal. португа́льский Portuguese.

портфе́ль *m* brief-case; portfolio.

портье́ра curtain(s), portière.

портя́нка foot-binding.

поруга́ние desecration; humiliation. пору́ганный desecrated; outraged.

поруга́ть *pf* scold, swear at; ~ся swear; fall out.

пору́ка bail; guarantee; surety; на пору́ки on bail.

по-ру́сски *adv* (in) Russian.

поруча́ть *impf of* поручи́ть. поруче́ние assignment; errand; message.

по́ручень (-чня) *m* handrail.

поручи́тельство guarantee; bail.

поручи́ть (-чу́, -чишь) *pf* (*impf* поруча́ть) entrust; instruct.

поручи́ться (-чу́сь, -чишься) *pf of* руча́ться

порхáть *impf*, порхнýть (-нý, -нёшь) *pf* flutter, flit.

пóрция portion; helping.

пóрча spoiling; damage; curse.

пóршень (-шня) *m* piston.

порыв[1] gust; rush; fit

порыв[2] breaking. порывáть(ся[1] *impf* of порвáть(ся

порывáться[2] *impf* make jerky movements; endeavour. порывистый gusty; jerky; impetuous; fitful.

порядковый ordinal. порядок (-дка) order; sequence; manner, way; procedure; всё в порядке everything is alright; ~ дня agenda, order of the day. порядочный decent; honest; respectable; fair, considerable.

посадить (-ажý, -áдишь) *pf of* садить, сажáть. посáдка planting; embarkation; boarding; landing. посáдочный planting; landing.

посажý *etc.: see* посадить. по|свáтать(ся *pf.* по|свежéть (-éет) *pf.* по|светить (-ечý, -éтишь) *pf.* по|светлéть (-éет) *pf.*

посвистывать *impf* whistle.

по-свóему *adv* in one's own way.

посвятить (-ящý) *pf*, посвящáть *impf* devote; dedicate; let in; ordain. посвящéние dedication; initiation; ordination.

посéв sowing; crops. посевн|óй sowing; ~áя плóщадь area under crops.

по|седéть (-éю) *pf*,

поселéнец (-нца) settler; exile. поселéние settlement; exile. посели́ть *pf*, поселя́ть *impf* settle; lodge; arouse; ~ся settle, take up residence. посёлок (-лка) settlement; housing estate.

посеребрённый (-рён, -á) silver-plated. по|серебрить *pf.*

посередине *adv & prep+gen* in the middle (of).

посетитель *m* visitor. посетить (-ещý) *pf* (*impf* посещáть) visit; attend.

по|сéтовать *pf.*

посещáемость attendance. посещáть *impf of* посети́ть. посещéние visit.

по|сéять (-éю) *pf.*

посидéть (-ижý) *pf* sit (for a while).

посильный within one's powers; feasible.

посинéлый gone blue. по|синéть (-éю) *pf.*

по|скакáть (-ачý, -áчешь) *pf.*

поскользнýться (-нýсь, -нёшься) *pf* slip.

поскóльку *conj* as far as, (in) so far as.

по|скрóмничать *pf.* по|скупиться (-плюсь) *pf.*

послáнец (-нца) messenger, envoy. послáние message; epistle. послáнник envoy, minister. послáть (-шлю, -шлёшь) *pf* (*impf* посылáть) send.

пóсле *adv & prep+gen* after; afterwards.

пóсле- *in comb* post-; after-. послевоéнный post-war. ~зáвтра *adv* the day after tomorrow. ~родовóй post-natal. ~слóвие epilogue; concluding remarks.

послéдний last; recent; latest; latter. послéдователь *m* follower. послéдовательность sequence; consistency. послéдовательный consecutive; consistent. по|слéдовать *pf.* послéдствие consequence. послéдующий subsequent; consequent.

послóвица proverb, saying.

по|служить (-жý, -жишь) *pf.* послужнóй service.

послушáние obedience. по|слýшать(ся *pf.* послýшный obedient.

по|слышаться (-шится) *pf.*

посмáтривать *impf* look from time to time.

посмéиваться *impf* chuckle.

посмéртный posthumous.

по|смéть (-éю) *pf.*

посмеяние ridicule. посмеяться (-еюсь, -еёшься) *pf* laugh at; +над+*instr* laugh at.

по|смотрéть(ся (-рю(сь, -ришь(ся) *pf.*

пособие aid; allowance, benefit; textbook. пособник accomplice.

по|совéтовать(ся *pf.* по|содéйствовать *pf.*

посóл (-слá) ambassador.

по|солить (-олю, -óлишь) *pf.*

посóльство embassy.

поспáть (-сплю, -áл, -á, -о) *pf* sleep; have a nap.

поспевáть[1] *impf*, по|спéть[1] (-éет) *pf* ripen.

поспевáть[2] *impf*, поспéть[2] (-éю) *pf*

have time; be in time (к+*dat*, на+*acc* for); +за+*instr* keep up with.

по|спешить (-шу) *pf.* поспешный hasty, hurried.

по|спорить *pf.* по|способствовать *pf.*

посрамить (-млю) *pf*, посрамлять *impf* disgrace.

посреди, посредине *adv & prep+gen* in the middle (of). посредник mediator. посредничество mediation. посредственный mediocre. посредством *prep+gen* by means of.

по|ссорить(ся *pf.*

пост[1] (-á, *loc* -ý) post.

пост[2] (-á, *loc* -ý) fast(ing).

по|ставить[1] (-влю) *pf.*

поставить[2] (-влю) *pf*, поставлять *impf* supply. поставка delivery. поставщик (-á) supplier.

постамент pedestal.

постановить (-влю, -вишь) *pf* (*impf* постановлять) decree; decide. постановка production; arrangement; putting, placing. постановление decree; decision. постановлять *impf of* постановить

постановщик producer; (film) director.

по|стараться *pf.*

по|стареть (-éю) *pf.* по-старому *adv* as before.

постель bed. постелю *etc.*: *see* постлать

постепенный gradual.

по|стесняться *pf.*

постигать *impf of* постичь. постигнуть: *see* постичь. постижение comprehension, grasp. постижимый comprehensible.

постилать *impf of* постлать

постирать *pf* do some washing.

поститься (-щусь) *impf* fast.

постичь, постигнуть (-игну, -иг(нул)) *pf* (*impf* постигать) comprehend, grasp; befall.

по|стлать (-стелю, -стелешь) *pf* (*impf also* постилать) spread; make (bed).

постный lenten; lean; glum; ~ое масло vegetable oil.

постовой on point duty.

постой billeting.

постольку: ~, поскольку *conj* to that extent, insofar as.

по|сторониться (-нюсь, -нишься) *pf.* посторонний strange; foreign; extraneous, outside; *sb* stranger, outsider.

постоянный permanent; constant; continual; ~ый ток direct current. постоянство constancy.

по|стоять (-ою) *pf* stand (for a while); +за+*acc* stand up for.

пострадавший *sb* victim. по|страдать *pf.*

постригаться *impf*, постричься (-игусь, -ижёшься; -игся) *pf* take monastic vows; get one's hair cut.

построение construction; building; formation. по|строить(ся (-рою(сь) *pf.* постройка building.

постскриптум postscript.

постулировать *impf & pf* postulate.

поступательный forward. поступать *impf*, поступить (-плю, -пишь) *pf* act; do; be received; +в *or* на+*acc* enter, join; +с+*instr* treat; ~ся +*instr* waive, forgo. поступление entering, joining; receipt. поступок (-пка) act, deed. поступь gait; step.

по|стучать(ся (-чу(сь) *pf.*

по|стыдиться (-ыжусь) *pf.* постыдный shameful.

посуда crockery; dishes. посудный china; dish.

по|сулить *pf.*

посчастливиться *pf impers* (+*dat*) be lucky; ей посчастливилось +*inf* she had the luck to.

посчитать *pf* count (up). по|считаться *pf.*

посылать *impf of* послать. посылка sending; parcel; errand; premise. посыльный *sb* messenger.

посыпать (-плю, -плешь) *pf*, посыпать *impf* strew. посыпаться (-плется) *pf* begin to fall; rain down.

посягательство encroachment; infringement. посягать *impf*, посягнуть (-ну, -нёшь) *pf* encroach, infringe.

пот (*loc* -ý; *pl* -ы) sweat.

потайной secret.

потакать *impf* +*dat* indulge.

потасовка brawl.

поташ (-á) potash.

по-твоему *adv* in your opinion.

потворствовать *impf* (+*dat*) be in-

dulgent (towards), pander (to).
потёк damp patch.
потёмки (-мок) pl darkness. **по|темнеть** (-éет) pf.
потенциа́л potential. **потенциа́льный** potential.
по|тепле́ть (-éет) pf.
потерпе́вший sb victim. **по|терпе́ть** (-плю́, -пишь) pf.
поте́ря loss; waste; pl casualties. **по|теря́ть(ся** pf.
по|тесни́ть pf. **по|тесни́ться** pf sit closer, squeeze up.
поте́ть (-éю) impf (pf вс~, за~) sweat; mist over.
поте́ха fun. **по|те́шить(ся** (-шу(сь) pf. **поте́шный** amusing.
поте́чь (-чёт, -тёк, -ла́) pf begin to flow.
потира́ть impf rub.
потихо́ньку adv softly; secretly; slowly.
по́тный (-тен, -тна́, -тно) sweaty.
пото́к stream; torrent; flood.
потоло́к (-лка́) ceiling.
по|толсте́ть (-éю) pf.
пото́м adv later (on); then. **пото́мок** (-мка) descendant. **пото́мство** posterity.
потому́ adv that is why; ~ что conj because.
по|тону́ть (-ну́, -нешь) pf. **пото́п** flood, deluge. **по|топи́ть** (-плю́, -пишь) pf, **потопля́ть** impf sink.
по|топта́ть (-пчу́, -пчешь) pf. **по|торопи́ть(ся** (-плю́(сь, -пишь(ся) pf.
пото́чный continuous; production-line.
по|тра́тить (-а́чу) pf.
потреби́тель m consumer, user. **потреби́тельский** consumer; consumers'. **потреби́ть** (-блю́) pf, **потребля́ть** impf consume. **потребле́ние** consumption. **потре́бность** need, requirement. **по|тре́бовать(ся** pf.
по|трево́жить(ся (-жу(сь) pf.
потрёпанный shabby; tattered. **по|трепа́ть(ся** (-плю́(сь, -плешь(ся) pf.
по|тре́скаться pf. **потре́скивать** impf crackle.
потро́гать pf touch, feel, finger.
потроха́ (-о́в) pl giblets. **потроши́ть** (-шу́) impf (pf вы~) disembowel, clean.

потруди́ться (-ужу́сь, -у́дишься) pf do some work; take the trouble.
потряса́ть impf, **потрясти́** (-су́, -сёшь; -я́с, -ла́) pf shake; rock; stagger; +acc or instr brandish, shake. **потряса́ющий** staggering, tremendous. **потрясе́ние** shock.
поту́ги f pl vain attempts; **родовы́е** ~ labour.
по|ту́пить (-плю) pf, **потупля́ть** impf lower; ~ся look down.
по|тускне́ть (-éет) pf.
потусторо́нний мир the next world.
потуха́ть impf, **по|ту́хнуть** (-нет, -ух) pf go out; die out. **поту́хший** extinct; lifeless.
по|туши́ть (-шу́, -шишь) pf.
по́тчевать (-чую) impf (pf по~) +instr treat to.
потя́гиваться impf, **по|тяну́ться** (-ну́сь, -нешься) pf stretch o.s. **по|тяну́ть** (-ну́, -нешь) pf.
по|у́жинать pf. **по|умне́ть** (-éю) pf.
поуча́ть impf preach at. **поучи́тельный** instructive.
поха́бный obscene.
похвала́ praise. **по|хвали́ть(ся** (-лю́(сь, -лишь(ся) pf. **похва́льный** laudable; laudatory.
по|хва́стать(ся pf.
похити́тель m kidnapper; abductor; thief. **похи́тить** (-хи́щу) pf, **похища́ть** impf kidnap; abduct; steal. **похище́ние** theft; kidnapping; abduction.
похлёбка broth, soup.
по|хло́пать pf slap; clap.
по|хлопота́ть (-очу́, -о́чешь) pf.
похме́лье hangover.
похо́д campaign; march; hike; excursion.
по|хода́тайствовать pf.
походи́ть (-ожу́, -о́дишь) impf **на** +acc resemble.
похо́дка gait, walk. **похо́дный** mobile, field; marching. **похожде́ние** adventure.
похо́жий alike;~ **на** like.
похолода́ние drop in temperature.
по|хорони́ть (-ню́, -нишь) pf. **похоро́нный** funeral. **по́хороны** (-ро́н) pl funeral.
по|хороше́ть (-éю) pf.
по́хоть lust.
по|худе́ть (-éю) pf.

по|целова́ть(ся *pf.* поцелу́й kiss.
поча́ток (-тка) ear; (corn) cob.
по́чва soil; ground; basis. по́чвенный soil; ~ подпо́чва top-soil.
почём how much; how; ~ знать? who can tell?; ~ я зна́ю? how should I know?
почему́ *adv* why. почему́-либо, -нибудь *advs* for some reason or other. почему́-то *adv* for some reason.
по́черк hand(writing).
почерне́лый blackened, darkened. по|черне́ть (-ею) *pf.*
почерпну́ть (-ну́, -нёшь) *pf* draw, scoop up; glean.
по|черстве́ть (-ею) *pf.* по|чеса́ть(ся (-ешу́сь, -е́шешь(ся) *pf.*
по́честь honour. почёт honour; respect. почётный of honour; honourable; honorary.
по́чечный renal; kidney.
почива́ть *impf of* почи́ть
почи́н initiative.
по|чини́ть (-ню́, -нишь) *pf*, починя́ть *impf* repair, mend. почи́нка repair.
по|чи́стить(ся (-и́щу(сь) *pf.*
почита́ть[1] *impf* honour; revere.
почита́ть[2] *pf* read for a while.
почи́ть (-и́ю, -и́ешь) *pf* (*impf* почива́ть) rest; pass away; ~ на ла́врах rest on one's laurels.
по́чка[1] bud.
по́чка[2] kidney.
по́чта post, mail; post-office. почтальо́н postman. почта́мт (main) post-office.
почте́ние respect. почте́нный venerable; considerable.
почти́ *adv* almost.
почти́тельный respectful. почти́ть (-чту́) *pf* honour.
почто́в|ый postal; ~ая ка́рточка postcard. ~ый перево́д postal order. ~ый я́щик letter-box.
по|чу́вствовать(ся *pf.*
по|чу́диться (-ишься) *pf.*
пошата́ть (-ну, -нёшь) *pf* shake; ~ся shake; stagger.
по|шевели́ть(ся (-елю́(сь, -е́ли́шь(ся) *pf.* пошёл *etc.: see* пойти́
поши́вочный sewing.
по́шлина duty.
по́шлость vulgarity; banality. по́шлый vulgar; banal.

пошту́чный by the piece.
по|шути́ть (-учу́, -у́тишь) *pf.*
поща́да mercy. по|щади́ть (-ажу́) *pf.*
по|щекота́ть (-очу́, -о́чешь) *pf.*
пощёчина slap in the face.
по|щу́пать *pf.*
поэ́зия poetry. поэ́ма poem. поэ́т poet. поэти́ческий poetic.
поэ́тому *adv* therefore.
пою́ *etc.: see* петь, пойть
появи́ться (-влю́сь, -вишься) *pf*, появля́ться *impf* appear. появле́ние appearance.
по́яс (*pl* -а́) belt; girdle; waist-band; waist; zone.
поясне́ние explanation. поясни́тельный explanatory. поясни́ть *pf* (*impf* поясня́ть) explain, elucidate.
поясни́ца small of the back. поясно́й waist; to the waist; zonal.
поясня́ть *impf of* поясни́ть
пра- *pref* first; great-. прабабушка great-grandmother.
пра́вда (the) truth. правди́вый true; truthful. правдоподо́бный likely; plausible. пра́ведный righteous; just.
пра́вило rule; principle.
пра́вильн|ый right, correct; regular; ~о! that's right!
прави́тель *m* ruler. прави́тельственный government(al). прави́тельство government. пра́вить[1] (-влю) +*instr* rule, govern; drive.
пра́вить[2] (-влю) *impf* correct. пра́вка correcting.
правле́ние board; administration; government.
пра́|внук, ~вну́чка great-grandson, -granddaughter.
пра́во[1] (*pl* -а́) law; right; (води́тельские) права́ driving licence; на права́х+*gen* in the capacity of, as.
пра́во[2] *adv* really.
право-[1] *in comb* law; right. правове́рный orthodox. ~ме́рный lawful, rightful. ~мо́чный competent. ~наруше́ние infringement of the law, offence. ~наруши́тель *m* offender, delinquent. ~писа́ние spelling, orthography. ~сла́вный orthodox; *sb* member of the Orthodox Church. ~су́дие justice.
право-[2] *in comb* right, right-hand. правосторо́нний right; right-hand.

правово́й legal.

правота́ rightness; innocence.

пра́вый[1] right; right-hand; right-wing.

пра́вый[2] (прав, -а́, -о) right, correct; just.

пра́вящий ruling.

пра́дед great-grandfather; pl ancestors. праде́душка m great-grandfather.

пра́здник (public) holiday. пра́здничный festive. пра́зднование celebration. пра́здновать impf (pf от~) celebrate. пра́здность idleness. пра́здный idle; useless.

пра́ктика practice; practical work. практикова́ть impf practise; ~ся (pf на~ся) be practised; +в +prep practise. практи́ческий, практи́чный practical.

пра́отец (-тца) forefather.

пра́порщик ensign.

прапра́дед great-great-grandfather. прароди́тель m forefather.

прах dust; remains.

пра́чечная sb laundry. пра́чка laundress.

пребыва́ние stay. пребыва́ть impf be; reside.

превзойти́ (-йду́, -йдёшь; -ошёл, -шла́) pf (impf превосходи́ть) surpass; excel.

превозмога́ть impf, превозмо́чь (-огу́, -о́жешь; -о́г, -ла́) pf overcome.

превознести́ (-су́, -сёшь; -ёс, -ла́) pf, превозноси́ть (-ошу́, -о́сишь) impf extol, praise.

превосходи́тельство Excellency. превосходи́ть (-ожу́, -о́дишь) impf of превзойти́. превосхо́дный superlative; superb, excellent. превосхо́дство superiority. превосходя́щий superior.

преврати́ть (-ащу́) pf, превраща́ть impf convert, turn, reduce; ~ся turn, change. превра́тный wrong; changeful. превраще́ние transformation.

превы́сить (-ы́шу) pf, превыша́ть impf exceed. превыше́ние exceeding, excess.

прегра́да obstacle; barrier. прегради́ть (-ажу́) pf, прегражда́ть impf bar, block.

пред prep+instr: see пе́ред

предава́ть(ся (-даю́(сь, -даёшь(ся)

impf of преда́ть(ся

преда́ние legend; tradition; handing over, committal. пре́данность devotion. пре́данный devoted. преда́тель m, ~ница betrayer, traitor. преда́тельский treacherous. преда́тельство treachery. преда́ть (-а́м, -а́шь, -а́ст, -ади́м; пре́дал, -а́, -о) pf (impf предава́ть) hand over, commit; betray; ~ся abandon o.s.; give way, indulge.

предаю́ etc.: see предава́ть

предвари́тельный preliminary; prior. предвари́ть pf, предваря́ть impf forestall, anticipate.

предве́стник forerunner; harbinger.

предвеща́ть impf portend; augur.

предвзя́тый preconceived; biased.

предви́деть (-и́жу) impf foresee.

предвкуси́ть (-ушу́, -у́сишь) pf, предвкуша́ть impf look forward to.

предводи́тель m leader. предводи́тельствовать impf +instr lead.

предвое́нный pre-war.

предвосхи́тить (-и́щу) pf, предвосхища́ть impf anticipate.

предвы́борный (pre-)election.

предго́рье foothills.

преддве́рие threshold.

преде́л limit; bound. преде́льный boundary; maximum; utmost.

предзнаменова́ние omen, augury.

предисло́вие preface.

предлага́ть impf of предложи́ть.

предло́г[1] pretext.

предло́г[2] preposition.

предложе́ние[1] sentence; clause.

предложе́ние[2] offer; proposition; proposal; motion; suggestion; supply. предложи́ть (-жу́, -жишь) pf (impf предлага́ть) offer; propose; suggest; order.

предло́жный prepositional.

предме́стье suburb.

предме́т object; subject.

предназнача́ть impf, предназна́чить (-чу) pf destine, intend; earmark.

преднаме́ренный premeditated.

пре́до: see пе́ред

пре́док (-дка) ancestor.

предопределе́ние predetermination. предопредели́ть pf, предопределя́ть impf predetermine, predestine.

предоста́вить (-влю) pf, предоставля́ть impf grant; leave; give.

предостерега́ть impf, предостере́чь (-егу́, -ежёшь; -ёг, -ла́) pf warn. предостереже́ние warning. предосторо́жность precaution.

предосуди́тельный reprehensible.

предотврати́ть (-ащу́) pf, предотвраща́ть impf avert, prevent.

предохране́ние protection; preservation. предохрани́тель m guard; safety device, safety-catch; fuse. предохрани́тельный preservative; preventive; safety. предохрани́ть pf, предохраня́ть impf preserve, protect.

предписа́ние order; pl directions, instructions. предписа́ть (-ишу́, -и́шешь) pf, предпи́сывать impf order, direct; prescribe.

предплечье forearm.

предполага́емый supposed. предполага́ется impers it is proposed. предполага́ть impf, предположи́ть (-жу́, -о́жишь) pf suppose, assume. предположе́ние supposition, assumption. предположи́тельный conjectural; hypothetical.

предпосле́дний penultimate, last-but-one.

предпосы́лка precondition; premise.

предпоче́сть (-чту́, -чтёшь; -чёл, -чла́) pf, предпочита́ть impf prefer. предпочте́ние preference. предпочти́тельный preferable.

предприи́мчивый enterprising. предпринима́тель m owner; entrepreneur; employer. предпринима́тельство: свобо́дное ~free enterprise. предпринима́ть impf, предприня́ть (-иму́, -и́мешь; -и́нял, -á, -о) pf undertake. предприя́тие undertaking, enterprise.

предрасположе́ние predisposition.

предрассу́док (-дка) prejudice.

предрека́ть impf, предре́чь (-еку́, -ечёшь; -рёк, -ла́) pf foretell.

предреша́ть impf, предреши́ть (-шу́) pf decide beforehand; predetermine.

председа́тель m chairman.

предсказа́ние prediction. предсказа́ть (-ажу́, -а́жешь) pf, предска́зывать impf predict; prophesy.

предсме́ртный dying.

представа́ть (-таю́, -таёшь) impf of предста́ть

представи́тель m representative. представи́тельный representative; imposing. представи́тельство representation.

предста́вить (-влю) pf, представля́ть impf present; submit; introduce; represent; ~ себе́ imagine; представля́ть собо́й represent, be; ~ся present itself, occur; seem; introduce o.s.; +instr pretend to be. представле́ние presentation; performance; idea, notion.

предста́ть (-а́ну) pf (impf представа́ть) appear.

предстоя́ть (-ои́т) impf be in prospect, lie ahead. предстоя́щий forthcoming; imminent.

предте́ча m & f forerunner, precursor.

предубежде́ние prejudice.

предугада́ть pf, предуга́дывать impf guess; foresee.

предупреди́тельный preventive; warning; courteous, obliging. предупреди́ть (-ежу́) pf, предупрежда́ть impf warn; give notice; prevent; anticipate. предупрежде́ние notice; warning; prevention.

предусма́тривать impf, предусмотре́ть (-рю́, -ришь) pf envisage, foresee; provide for. предусмотри́тельный prudent; far-sighted.

предчу́вствие presentiment; foreboding. предчу́вствовать impf have a presentiment.

предше́ственник predecessor. предше́ствовать impf +dat precede.

предъяви́тель m bearer. предъяви́ть (-влю́, -вишь) pf, предъявля́ть impf show, produce; bring (lawsuit); ~ пра́во на+acc lay claim to.

предыду́щий previous.

прее́мник successor. прее́мственность succession; continuity.

пре́жде adv first; formerly; prep+gen before; ~ всего́ first of all; first and foremost; ~ чем conj before. преждевре́менный premature. пре́жний previous, former.

презервати́в condom.

президе́нт president. президе́нтский presidential. прези́диум presidium.

презира́ть *impf* despise. презре́ние contempt. презре́нный contemptible. презри́тельный scornful.

преиму́щественно *adv* mainly, chiefly, principally. преиму́щественный main, primary; preferential. преиму́щество advantage; preference; по преиму́ществу for the most part.

преиспо́дняя *sb* the underworld.

прейскура́нт price list, catalogue.

преклоне́ние admiration. преклони́ть *pf*, преклоня́ть *impf* bow, bend; ~ся bow down; +*dat* or перед +*instr* admire, worship. прекло́нный: ~ во́зраст old age.

прекра́сный beautiful; fine; excellent.

прекрати́ть (-ащу́) *pf*, прекраща́ть *impf* stop, discontinue; ~ся cease, end. прекраще́ние halt; cessation.

преле́стный delightful. пре́лесть charm, delight.

преломи́ть (-млю́, -мишь) *pf*, преломля́ть *impf* refract. преломле́ние refraction.

прельсти́ть (-льщу́) *pf*, прельща́ть *impf* attract; entice; ~ся be attracted; fall (+*instr* for).

прелюбодея́ние adultery.

прелю́дия prelude.

премину́ть (-ну) *pf with neg* not fail.

премирова́ть *impf & pf* award a prize; give a bonus. пре́мия prize; bonus; premium.

премье́р prime minister; lead(ing actor). премье́ра premiѐre. премье́р-мини́стр prime minister. премье́рша leading lady.

пренебрега́ть *impf*, пренебре́чь (-егу́, -ежёшь; -ёг, -ла́) *pf* +*instr* scorn; neglect. пренебреже́ние scorn; neglect. пренебрежи́тельный scornful.

пре́ния (-ий) *pl* debate.

преоблада́ние predominance. преоблада́ть *impf* predominate; prevail.

преобража́ть *impf*, преобрази́ть (-ажу́) *pf* transform. преображе́ние transformation; Transfiguration. преобразова́ние transformation; reform. преобразова́ть *pf*, преобразо́вывать *impf* transform; reform, reorganize.

преодолева́ть *impf*, преодоле́ть (-е́ю) *pf* overcome.

препара́т preparation.

препина́ние: зна́ки препина́ния punctuation marks.

препира́тельство altercation, wrangling.

преподава́ние teaching. преподава́тель *m*, ~ница teacher. преподава́тельский teaching. преподава́ть (-даю́, -даёшь) *impf* teach.

преподнести́ (-су́, -сёшь; -ёс, -ла́) *pf*, преподноси́ть (-ошу́, -о́сишь) present with, give.

препроводи́ть (-вожу́, -во́дишь) *pf*, препровожда́ть *impf* send, forward.

препя́тствие obstacle; hurdle. препя́тствовать *impf* (*pf* вос~) +*dat* hinder.

прерва́ть (-ву́, -вёшь; -а́л, -а́, -о) *pf* (*impf* прерыва́ть) interrupt; break off; ~ся be interrupted; break.

препрека́ние argument. пререка́ться *impf* argue.

прерыва́ть(ся *impf of* прерва́ть(ся

пресека́ть *impf*, пресе́чь (-еку́, -ечёшь; -ёк, -екла́) *pf* stop; put an end to; ~ся stop; break.

пресле́дование pursuit; persecution; prosecution. пресле́довать *impf* pursue; haunt; persecute; prosecute.

пресло́вутый notorious.

пресмыка́ться *impf* grovel. пресмыка́ющееся *sb* reptile.

пресново́дный freshwater. пре́сный fresh; unleavened; insipid; bland.

пресс press. пре́сса the press. пресс-конфере́нция press-conference.

престаре́лый aged.

прести́ж prestige.

престо́л throne.

преступле́ние crime. престу́пник criminal. престу́пность criminality; crime, delinquency. престу́пный criminal.

пресы́титься (-ы́щусь) *pf*, пресыща́ться *impf* be satiated. пресыще́ние surfeit, satiety.

претвори́ть (-рю́) *pf*, претворя́ть *impf* (в +*acc*) turn, change, convert; ~ в жизнь realize, carry out.

претенде́нт claimant; candidate; pretender. **претендова́ть** *impf* на+*acc* lay claim to; have pretensions to. **прете́нзия** claim; pretension; **быть в прете́нзии** на+*acc* have a grudge, a grievance, against.

претерпева́ть *impf*, **претерпе́ть** (-плю́, -пишь) *pf* undergo; suffer. **преть** (пре́ет) *impf* (*pf* со~) rot.

преувеличе́ние exaggeration. **преувели́чивать** *impf*, **преувели́чить** (-чу) *pf* exaggerate.

преуменьша́ть *impf*, **преуме́ньшить** (-е́ньшу) *pf* underestimate; understate.

преуспева́ть *impf*, **преуспе́ть** (-е́ю) *pf* be successful; thrive.

преходя́щий transient.

прецеде́нт precedent.

при *prep* +*prep* by, at; in the presence of; attached to; affiliated to; with; about; on; in the time of; under; during; when, in case of; ~ **всём том** for all that.

приба́вить (-влю) *pf*, **прибавля́ть** *impf* add; increase; ~**ся** increase; rise; wax; **день приба́вился** the days are getting longer. **приба́вка** addition; increase. **прибавле́ние** addition; supplement, appendix. **приба́вочный** additional; surplus.

Приба́лтика the Baltic States.

прибау́тка humorous saying.

прибега́ть[1] *impf of* прибе́гнуть

прибега́ть[2] *impf*, **прибе́гнуть** (-ну; -бег) *pf* +к+*dat* resort to.

прибежа́ть (-егу́) *pf* (*impf* прибега́ть) come running. **прибе́жище** refuge.

приберега́ть *impf*, **прибере́чь** (-егу́, -ежёшь; -ёг, -ла́) *pf* save (up), reserve.

приберу́ *etc.: see* прибра́ть. **прибива́ть** *impf of* приби́ть. **прибира́ть** *impf of* прибра́ть

приби́ть (-бью́, -бьёшь) *pf* (*impf* прибива́ть) nail; flatten; drive.

приближа́ть *impf*, **прибли́зить** (-и́жу) *pf* bring *or* move nearer; ~**ся** approach; draw nearer. **приближе́ние** approach. **приблизи́тельный** approximate.

прибо́й surf, breakers.

прибо́р instrument, device, apparatus; set. **прибо́рная доска́** instrument panel; dashboard.

прибра́ть (-беру́, -берёшь; -а́л, -а́, -о) *pf* (*impf* прибира́ть) tidy (up); put away.

прибре́жный coastal; offshore.

прибыва́ть *impf*, **прибы́ть** (-бу́ду; при́был, -а́, -о) *pf* arrive; increase, grow; rise; wax. **при́быль** profit, gain; increase, rise. **при́быльный** profitable. **прибы́тие** arrival.

прибью́ *etc.: see* приби́ть

прива́л halt.

прива́ривать *impf*, **привари́ть** (-рю́, -ришь) *pf* weld on.

приватиза́ция privatization. **приватизи́ровать** *impf* & *pf* privatize.

приведу́ *etc.: see* привести́

привезти́ (-зу́, -зёшь; -ёз, -ла́) (*impf* привози́ть) bring.

привере́дливый pernickety.

приве́рженец (-нца) adherent. **приве́рженный** devoted.

приве́сить (-е́шу) *pf* (*impf* приве́шивать) hang up, suspend.

привести́ (-еду́, -едёшь; -ёл, -а́) *pf* (*impf* приводи́ть) bring; lead; take; reduce; cite; put in(to), set.

приве́т greeting(s); regards; hi! **приве́тливый** friendly; affable. **приве́тствие** greeting; speech of welcome. **приве́тствовать** *impf* & *pf* greet, salute; welcome.

приве́шивать *impf of* приве́сить

привива́ть(**ся** *impf of* приви́ть(ся. **приви́вка** inoculation.

привиде́ние ghost; apparition. **при|ви́деться** (-дится) *pf*.

привилегиро́ванный privileged. **привиле́гия** privilege.

привинти́ть (-нчу́) *pf*, **приви́нчивать** *impf* screw on.

приви́ть (-вью́, -вьёшь; -и́л, -а́, -о) *pf* (*impf* привива́ть) inoculate; graft; inculcate; foster; ~**ся** take; become established.

при́вкус after-taste; smack.

привлека́тельный attractive. **привлека́ть** *impf*, **привле́чь** (-еку́, -ечёшь; -ёк, -ла́) *pf* attract; draw; draw in, win over; (*law*) have up; ~ **к суду́** sue. **привлече́ние** attraction.

приво́д drive, gear. **приводи́ть** (-ожу́, -о́дишь) *impf of* привести́. **приводно́й** driving.

привожу́ *etc.: see* приводи́ть, привози́ть

приво́з bringing; importation; load. **привози́ть** (-ожу́, -о́зишь) *impf of* **привезти́. привозно́й, приво́зный** imported.

привольный free.

привстава́ть (-таю́, -таёшь) *impf*, **привста́ть** (-а́ну) *pf* half-rise; rise.

привыка́ть *impf*, **привы́кнуть** (-ну; -ык) *pf* get accustomed. **привы́чка** habit. **привы́чный** habitual, usual.

привью́ *etc.*: *see* **привить**

привя́занность attachment; affection. **привяза́ть** (-яжу́, -я́жешь) *pf*, **привя́зывать** *impf* attach; tie, bind; ~ся become attached; attach o.s.; +к+*dat* pester. **привя́зчивый** annoying; affectionate. **при́вязь** tie; lead, leash; tether.

пригиба́ть *impf of* **пригну́ть**

пригласи́ть (-ашу́) *pf*, **приглаша́ть** *impf* invite. **приглаше́ние** invitation.

пригляде́ться (-яжу́сь) *pf*, **пригля́дываться** *impf* look closely; +к+*dat* scrutinize; get used to.

пригна́ть (-гоню́, -го́нишь; -а́л, -а́, -о) *pf* (*impf* **пригоня́ть**) bring in; fit, adjust.

пригну́ть (-ну́, -нёшь) *pf* (*impf* **пригиба́ть**) bend down.

пригова́ривать[1] *impf* keep saying.

пригова́ривать[2] *impf*, **приговори́ть** *pf* sentence, condemn. **пригово́р** verdict, sentence.

пригоди́ться (-ожу́сь) *pf* prove useful. **приго́дный** fit, suitable.

пригоня́ть *impf of* **пригна́ть**

пригора́ть *impf*, **пригоре́ть** (-ри́т) *pf* be burnt.

при́город suburb. **при́городный** suburban.

приго́рок (-рка) hillock.

при́горшня (*gen pl* -ей) handful.

приготови́тельный preparatory. **пригото́вить** (-влю) *pf*, **пригото́вля́ть** *impf* prepare; ~ся prepare. **приготовле́ние** preparation.

пригрева́ть *impf*, **пригре́ть** (-е́ю) *pf* warm; cherish.

пригрози́ть (-ожу́) *pf*.

придава́ть (-даю́, -даёшь) *impf*, **прида́ть** (-а́м, -а́шь, -а́ст, -ади́м; при́дал, -а́, -о) *pf* add; give; attach. **прида́ча** adding; addition; в прида́чу into the bargain.

придави́ть (-влю́, -вишь) *pf*, **прида́вливать** *impf* press (down).

прида́ное *sb* dowry. **прида́ток** (-тка) appendage.

придвига́ть *impf*, **придви́нуть** (-ну) *pf* move up, draw up; ~ся move up, draw near.

придво́рный court.

приде́лать (-аю) *pf*, **приде́лывать** *impf* attach.

приде́рживаться *impf* hold on; hold; +*gen* keep to.

придеру́сь *etc.*: *see* **придра́ться.** **придира́ться** *impf of* **придра́ться.** **приди́рка** quibble; fault-finding. **приди́рчивый** fault-finding.

придоро́жный roadside.

придра́ться (-деру́сь, -дерёшься; -а́лся, -ась, -ало́сь) *pf* (*impf* **придира́ться**) find fault.

приду́ *etc.*: *see* **прийти́**

приду́мать *pf*, **приду́мывать** *impf* think up, invent.

прие́ду *etc.*: *see* **прие́хать. прие́зд** arrival. **приезжа́ть** *impf of* **прие́хать. прие́зжий** newly arrived; *sb* newcomer.

прие́м receiving; reception; surgery; welcome; admittance; dose; go; movement; method, way; trick. **прие́млемый** acceptable. **прие́мная** *sb* waiting-room; reception room. **прие́мник** (radio) receiver. **прие́мный** receiving; reception; entrance; foster, adopted.

прие́хать (-е́ду) *pf* (*impf* **приезжа́ть**) arrive, come.

прижа́ть (-жму́, -жмёшь) *pf* (*impf* **прижима́ть**) press; clasp; ~ся nestle up.

приже́чь (-жгу́, -жжёшь; -жёг, -жгла́) *pf* (*impf* **прижига́ть**) cauterize.

прижива́ться *impf of* **прижи́ться**

прижига́ние cauterization. **прижига́ть** *impf of* **приже́чь**

прижима́ть(ся *impf of* **прижа́ть(ся**

прижи́ться (-иву́сь, -ивёшься; -жи́лся, -а́сь) *pf* (*impf* **прижива́ться**) become acclimatized.

прижму́ *etc.*: *see* **прижа́ть**

приз (*pl* -ы́) prize.

призва́ние vocation. **призва́ть** (-зову́, -зовёшь; -а́л, -а́, -о) *pf* (*impf* **призыва́ть**) call; call upon; call up.

призе́мистый stocky, squat.

приземле́ние landing. **приземли́ться** pf, **приземля́ться** impf land.

призёр prizewinner.

при́зма prism.

признава́ть (-наю́, -наёшь) impf, **призна́ть** pf recognize; admit; ~ся confess. **при́знак** sign, symptom; indication. **призна́ние** confession, declaration; acknowledgement; recognition. **при́знанный** acknowledged, recognized. **призна́тельный** grateful.

призову́ etc.: see **призва́ть**

при́зрак spectre, ghost. **при́зрачный** ghostly; illusory, imagined.

призы́в call, appeal; slogan; call-up. **призыва́ть** impf of **призва́ть**. **призывно́й** conscription.

при́иск mine.

прийти́ (приду́, -дёшь; пришёл, -шла́) pf (impf **приходи́ть**) come; arrive; ~ в себя́ regain consciousness; ~сь +на+dat fit; suit; + на+acc fall on; impers+dat have to; happen (to), fall to the lot (of).

прика́з order, command. **приказа́ние** order, command. **приказа́ть** (-ажу́, -а́жешь) pf, **прика́зывать** impf order, command.

прика́лывать impf of **приколо́ть**. **прикаса́ться** impf of **прикосну́ться**

прика́нчивать impf of **прико́нчить**. **прикати́ть** (-ачу́, -а́тишь) pf, **прика́тывать** impf roll up.

прики́дывать impf, **прики́нуть** (-ну) pf throw in, add; weigh; estimate; ~ся+instr pretend (to be).

прикла́д[1] butt.

прикла́д[2] trimmings. **прикладно́й** applied. **прикла́дывать(ся** impf of **приложи́ть(ся**

приклеива́ть impf, **прикле́ить** pf stick; glue.

приключа́ться impf, **приключи́ться** pf happen, occur. **приключе́ние** adventure. **приключе́нческий** adventure.

прикова́ть (-кую́, -куёшь) pf, **прико́вывать** impf chain; rivet.

прикола́чивать impf, **приколоти́ть** (-очу́, -о́тишь) pf nail.

приколо́ть (-лю́, -лешь) pf (impf **прика́лывать**) pin; stab.

прикомандирова́ть pf, **прикома́ндировывать** impf attach.

прико́нчить (-чу) pf (impf **прика́нчивать**) use up; finish off.

прикоснове́ние touch; concern. **прикосну́ться** (-ну́сь, -нёшься) pf (impf **прикаса́ться**) к+dat touch.

прикрепи́ть (-плю́) pf, **прикрепля́ть** impf fasten, attach. **прикрепле́ние** fastening; registration.

прикрыва́ть impf, **прикры́ть** (-ро́ю) pf cover; screen; shelter. **прикры́тие** cover; escort.

прику́ривать impf, **прикури́ть** (-рю́, -ришь) pf get a light.

прикуси́ть (-ушу́, -у́сишь) pf, **прику́сывать** impf bite.

прила́вок (-вка) counter.

прилага́тельное sb adjective. **прилага́ть** impf of **приложи́ть**

прила́дить (-а́жу) pf, **прила́живать** impf fit, adjust.

приласка́ть pf caress, pet; ~ся snuggle up.

прилега́ть impf (pf **приле́чь**) к+dat fit; adjoin. **прилега́ющий** close-fitting; adjoining, adjacent.

приле́жный diligent.

прилепи́ть(ся (-плю́(сь, -пишь(ся) pf, **прилепля́ть(ся** impf stick.

прилёт arrival. **прилета́ть** impf, **прилете́ть** (-ечу́) pf arrive, fly in; come flying.

приле́чь (-ля́гу, -ля́жешь; -ёг, -гла́) pf (impf **прилега́ть**) lie down.

прили́в flow, flood; rising tide; surge. **прилива́ть** impf of **прили́ть**. **прили́вный** tidal.

прилипа́ть impf, **прили́пнуть** (-нет; -ли́п) pf stick.

прили́ть (-льёт; -и́л, -а́, -о) pf (impf **прилива́ть**) flow; rush.

прили́чие decency. **прили́чный** decent.

приложе́ние application; enclosure; supplement; appendix. **приложи́ть** (-жу́, -жишь) pf (impf **прикла́дывать**, **прилага́ть**) put; apply; affix; add; enclose; ~ся take aim; +instr put, apply; к+dat kiss.

прильёт etc.: see **прили́ть**. **прильну́ть** (-ну́, -нёшь) pf. **приля́гу** etc.: see **приле́чь**

прима́нивать impf, **примани́ть** (-ню́, -нишь) pf lure; entice. **прима́нка**

bait. lure.

примене́ние application; use. **примени́ть** (-ню́, -нишь) *pf*, **применя́ть** *impf* apply; use; ~**ся** adapt o.s., conform.

приме́р example.

при|ме́рить *pf* (*impf* also **примеря́ть**) try on. **приме́рка** fitting.

приме́рно *adv* approximately. **приме́рный** exemplary; approximate.

примеря́ть *impf of* **приме́рить**

при́месь admixture.

приме́та sign, token. **приме́тный** perceptible; conspicuous.

примеча́ние note, footnote; *pl* comments. **примеча́тельный** notable.

примеша́ть *pf*, **приме́шивать** *impf* add, mix in.

примина́ть *impf of* **примя́ть**

примире́ние reconciliation. **примири́тельный** conciliatory. **примири́ть** *pf*, **примиря́ть** *impf* reconcile; conciliate; ~**ся** be reconciled.

примити́вный primitive.

примкну́ть (-ну́, -нёшь) *pf* (*impf* **примыка́ть**) join; fix. attach.

примну́ *etc.: see* **примя́ть**

примо́рский seaside; maritime. **примо́рье** seaside.

примо́чка wash, lotion.

приму́ *etc.: see* **приня́ть**

примча́ться (-чу́сь) *pf* come tearing along.

примыка́ть *impf of* **примкну́ть**; +**к**+*dat* adjoin. **примыка́ющий** affiliated.

примя́ть (-мну́, -мнёшь) *pf* (*impf* **примина́ть**) crush; trample down.

принадлежа́ть (-жу́) *impf* belong. **принадле́жность** belonging; membership; *pl* accessories; equipment.

принести́ (-су́, -сёшь) *pf* (*impf* **приноси́ть**) bring: fetch.

принижа́ть *impf*, **прини́зить** (-и́жу) *pf* humiliate; belittle.

принима́ть(ся *impf of* **приня́ть(ся**

приноси́ть (-ошу́, -о́сишь) *impf of* **принести́**. **приноше́ние** gift, offering.

при́нтер (*comput*) printer.

принуди́тельный compulsory. **прину́дить** (-у́жу) *pf*, **принужда́ть** *impf* compel. **принужде́ние** compulsion, coercion. **принуждённый** constrained, forced.

принц prince. **принце́сса** princess.

при́нцип principle. **принципиа́льно** *adv* on principle; in principle. **принципиа́льный** of principle; general.

приня́тие taking; acceptance; admission. **при́нято** it is accepted, it is usual; **не** ~ it is not done. **приня́ть** (-иму́, -и́мешь; при́нял, -а́, -о) *pf* (*impf* **принима́ть**) take; accept; take over; receive; +**за**+*acc* take for; ~ **уча́стие** take part; ~**ся** begin; take; take root; ~ **за рабо́ту** set to work.

приободри́ть *pf*, **приободря́ть** *impf* cheer up; ~**ся** cheer up.

приобрести́ (-ету́, -етёшь; -рёл, -а́) *pf*, **приобрета́ть** *impf* acquire. **приобрете́ние** acquisition.

приобща́ть *impf*, **приобщи́ть** (-щу́) *pf* join, attach, unite; ~**ся к**+*dat* join in.

приорите́т priority.

приостана́вливать *impf*, **приостанови́ть** (-влю́, -вишь) *pf* stop, suspend; ~**ся** stop. **приостано́вка** halt, suspension.

приоткрыва́ть *impf*, **приоткры́ть** (-ро́ю) *pf* open slightly.

припа́док (-дка) fit; attack.

припа́сы (-ов) *pl* stores, supplies.

припе́в refrain.

приписа́ть (-ишу́, -и́шешь) *pf*, **припи́сывать** *impf* add; attribute. **припи́ска** postscript; codicil.

припло́д offspring; increase.

приплыва́ть *impf*, **приплы́ть** (-ыву́, -ывёшь; -ы́л, -а́, -о) *pf* swim up; sail up.

приплю́снуть (-ну) *pf*, **приплю́щивать** *impf* flatten.

приподнима́ть *impf*, **приподня́ть** (-ниму́, -ни́мешь; -о́днял, -а́, -о) *pf* raise (a little); ~**ся** raise o.s. (a little).

припо́й solder.

приполза́ть *impf*, **приползти́** (-зу́, -зёшь; -по́лз, -ла́) *pf* creep up, crawl up.

припомина́ть *impf*, **припо́мнить** *pf* recollect.

припра́ва seasoning, flavouring. **припра́вить** (-влю) *pf*, **приправля́ть** *impf* season, flavour.

припря́тать (-я́чу) *pf*, **припря́тывать** *impf* secrete, put by.

припу́гивать *impf*, **припугну́ть** (-ну́, -нёшь) *pf* scare.

прирабáтывать *impf*, прирабóтать *pf* earn ... extra. прúработок (-тка) additional earnings.

прирáвнивать *impf*, приравнять *pf* equate (with к+*dat*).

прираста́ть *impf*, прирасти́ (-тёт; -рóс, -лá) *pf* adhere; take; increase; accrue.

прирóда nature. прирóдный natural; by birth; innate. прирождённый innate; born.

прирóс *etc.: see* прирасти́. прирóст increase.

приручáть *impf*, приручи́ть (-чý) *pf* tame; domesticate.

присáживаться *impf of* присéсть

присвáивать *impf*, присвóить *pf* appropriate; award.

п,иседáть *impf*, присéсть (-сяду) *pf* (*impf also* присáживаться) sit down, take a seat.

прискакáть (-ачý, -áчешь) *pf* come galloping.

прискóрбный sorrowful.

присла́ть (-ишлю́, -ишлёшь) *pf* (*impf* присыла́ть) send.

прислони́ть(ся (-оню́(сь, -óни́шь(ся *pf*, прислоня́ть(ся *impf* lean, rest.

прислýга servant; crew. прислýживать *impf* (к+*dat*) wait (on), attend.

прислýшаться *pf*, прислýшиваться *impf* listen; +к+*dat* listen to; heed.

присмáтривать *impf*, присмотрéть (-рю́, -ришь) *pf* +за+*instr* look after, keep an eye on; ~ся (к+*dat*) look closely (at). присмóтр supervision.

при|сни́ться (-ышý) *pf.*

присоединéние joining; addition; annexation. присоедини́ть *pf*, присоединя́ть *impf* join; add; annex; ~ся к+*dat* join; subscribe to (an opinion).

приспосóбить (-блю) *pf*, приспособля́ть *impf* fit, adjust, adapt; ~ся adapt o.s. приспособлéние adaptation; device; appliance. приспособля́емость adaptability.

приставáть (-таю́, -таёшь) *impf of* приста́ть

приста́вить (-влю) *pf* (*impf* приставля́ть) к+*dat* place, set, *or* lean against; add; appoint to look after.

приста́вка prefix.

приставля́ть *impf of* приста́вить

при|стáльный intent.

пристáнище refuge, shelter.

при́стань (*gen pl* -éй) landing-stage; pier; wharf.

приста́ть (-áну) *pf* (*impf* пристава́ть) stick, adhere (к+*dat* to); pester.

пристёгивать *impf*, пристегнýть (-нý, -нёшь) *pf* fasten.

пристóйный decent, proper.

пристрáивать(ся *impf of* пристрóить(ся

пристрáстие predilection, passion; bias. пристрáстный biased.

пристрéливать *impf*, пристрели́ть *pf* shoot (down).

пристрóить (-óю) *pf* (*impf* пристрáивать) add, build on; fix up; ~ся be fixed up, get a place. пристрóйка annexe, extension.

при́ступ assault; fit, attack. приступáть *impf*, приступи́ть (-плю́, -пишь) *pf* к+*dat* set about, start.

при|стыди́ть (-ыжý) *pf.*

при|стыковáться *pf.*

присуди́ть (-ужý, -ýдишь) *pf*, присуждáть *impf* sentence, condemn; award; confer. присуждéние awarding; conferment.

прису́тствие presence. прису́тствовать *impf* be present, attend. прису́тствующие *sb pl* those present.

прису́щий inherent; characteristic.

присылáть *impf of* присла́ть

прися́га oath. присягáть *impf*, присягнýть (-нý, -нёшь) *pf* swear.

прися́ду *etc.: see* присéсть

прися́жный *sb* juror.

притаи́ться *pf* hide.

притáптывать *impf of* притоптáть

притáскивать *impf*, притащи́ть (-ащý, -áщишь) *pf* bring, drag, haul; ~ся drag o.s.

притвори́ться *pf*, притворя́ться *impf* +*instr* pretend to be. притвóрный pretended, feigned. притвóрство pretence, sham. притвóрщик sham; hypocrite.

притекáть *impf of* притéчь

притеснéние oppression. притесни́ть *pf*, притесня́ть *impf* oppress.

притéчь (-ечёт, -екýт; -ёк, -лá) *pf* (*impf* притекáть) pour in.

притихáть *impf*, прити́хнуть (-ну; -и́х) *pf* quiet down.

приток tributary; influx.

притолока lintel.

притом *conj* (and) besides.

притон den, haunt.

притоптать (-пчу, -пчешь) *pf* (*impf* **притаптывать**) trample down.

приторный sickly-sweet, luscious, cloying.

притрагиваться *impf*, **притронуться** (-нусь) *pf* touch.

притупить (-плю, -пишь) *pf*, **притуплять** *impf* blunt, dull; deaden; ~ся become blunt *or* dull.

притча parable.

притягательный attractive, magnetic. **притягивать** *impf of* **притянуть**

притяжательный possessive.

притяжение attraction.

притязание claim, pretension. **притязательный** demanding.

притянутый far-fetched. **притянуть** (-ну, -нешь) *pf* (*impf* **притягивать**) attract; drag (up).

приурочивать *impf*, **приурочить** (-чу) *pf* к+*dat* time for.

приусадебный: ~ участок individual plot (*in kolkhoz*).

приучать *impf*, **приучить** (-чу, -чишь) *pf* train, school.

прихлебатель *m* sponger.

приход coming, arrival; receipts; parish. **приходить(ся** (-ожу(сь, -одишь(ся) *impf of* **прийти(сь**. **приходный** receipt. **приходящий** non-resident; ~ больной outpatient. **прихожанин** (*pl* -áне, -áн), **-áнка** parishioner.

прихожая *sb* hall, lobby.

прихотливый capricious; fanciful; intricate. **прихоть** whim, caprice.

прихрамывать limp (slightly).

прицел sight; aiming. **прицеливаться** *impf*, **прицелиться** *pf* take aim.

прицениваться *impf*, **прицениться** (-нюсь, -нишься) *pf* (к+*dat*) ask the price (of).

прицеп trailer. **прицепить** (-плю, -пишь) *pf*, **прицеплять** *impf* hitch, hook on; ~ся к+*dat* stick to, cling to; quibble. **прицепка** hitching, hooking on; **прицепной**: ~ вагон trailer.

причал mooring; mooring line. **причаливать** *impf*, **причалить** *pf*

moor.

причастие[1] participle. **причастие**[2] communion. **причастить** (-ащу) *pf* (*impf* **причащать**) give communion to; ~ся receive communion.

причастный[1] participial. **причастный**[2] concerned; privy.

причащать *impf of* **причастить**

причём *conj* moreover, and.

причесать (-ешу, -ешешь) *pf*, **причёсывать** *impf* comb; do the hair (of); ~ся do one's hair, have one's hair done. **причёска** hair-do; hair-cut.

причина cause; reason. **причинить** *pf*, **причинять** *impf* cause.

причислить *pf*, **причислять** *impf* number, rank (к+*dat* among); add on.

причитание lamentation. **причитать** *impf* lament.

причитаться *impf* be due.

причмокивать *impf*, **причмокнуть** (-ну) *pf* smack one's lips.

причуда caprice, whim.

при|чудиться *pf*.

причудливый odd; fantastic; whimsical.

при|швартовать *pf*. **пришел** *etc.*: *see* **прийти**

пришелец (-ьца) newcomer.

пришествие coming; advent.

пришивать *impf*, **пришить** (-шью, -шьёшь) *pf* sew on.

пришлю *etc.*: *see* **прислать**

пришпиливать *impf*, **пришпилить** *pf* pin on.

пришпоривать *impf*, **пришпорить** *pf* spur (on).

прищемить (-млю) *pf*, **прищемлять** *impf* pinch.

прищепка clothes-peg.

прищуриваться *impf*, **прищуриться** *pf* screw up one's eyes.

приют shelter, refuge. **приютить** (-ючу) *pf* shelter; ~ся take shelter.

приятель *m*, **приятельница** friend. **приятельский** friendly. **приятный** nice, pleasant.

про *prep+acc* about; for; ~ себя to o.s.

про|анализировать *pf*.

проба trial, test; hallmark; sample.

пробег run; race. **пробегать** *impf*, **пробежать** (-егу) *pf* run; cover; run past.

пробе́л blank, gap; flaw.

пробе́ру etc.: see пробрáть. про-
бивáть(ся impf of пробить(ся.
пробирáть(ся impf of пробрáть(ся
пробирка test-tube. пробировать
impf test, assay.

про|би́ть (-бью, -бьёшь) pf (impf also
пробивáть) make a way in; pierce;
punch; ~ся force, make, one's way.

про́бка cork; stopper; fuse; (traffic)
jam, congestion. про́бковый cork.

пробле́ма problem.

про́блеск flash; gleam, ray.

про́бный trial, test; ~ кáмень touchstone. про́бовать impf (pf ис~,
по~) try; attempt.

пробо́ина hole.

пробо́р parting.

про|бормотáть (-очý, -óчешь) pf.

пробрáть (-берý, -берёшь; -áл, -á,
-о) pf (impf пробирáть) penetrate;
scold; ~ся make or force one's way.

пробу́ду etc.: see пробы́ть

про|буди́ть (-ужý, -ýдишь) pf, про-
буждáть impf wake (up); arouse;
~ся wake up. пробужде́ние awak-
ening.

про|бурáвить (-влю) pf, пробу-
рáвливать impf bore (through),
drill.

про|бури́ть pf.

пробы́ть (-бýду; про́бы́л, -á, -о) pf
stay; be.

пробью́ etc.: see пробить

провáл failure; downfall; gap. прова́-
ливать impf, провали́ть (-лю,
-лишь) pf bring down; ruin; reject,
fail; ~ся collapse; fall in; fail; disappear.

прове́дать pf, прове́дывать impf
call on; learn.

проведе́ние conducting; construction; installation.

провезти́ (-зý, -зёшь; -ёз, -лá) pf
(impf провози́ть) convey, transport.

прове́рить pf, проверя́ть impf
check; test. прове́рка checking,
check; testing.

про|вести́ (-едý, -едёшь; -ёл, -á) pf
(impf also проводить) lead, take;
build; install; carry out; conduct; pass;
draw; spend; +instr pass over.

прове́тривать impf, прове́трить pf
air.

про|ве́ять (-ею) pf.

провиде́ние Providence.

прови́зия provisions.

провини́ться pf be guilty; do wrong.

провинциáльный provincial. про-
ви́нция province; the provinces.

про́вод (pl -á) wire, lead, line. про-
води́мость conductivity. прово-
ди́ть[1] (-ожý, -óдишь) impf of про-
вести́; conduct.

проводи́ть[2] (-ожý, -óдишь) pf (impf
провожáть) accompany; see off.

прово́дка leading, taking; building;
installation; wiring, wires.

проводни́к[1] (-á) guide; conductor.

проводни́к[2] (-á) conductor; bearer;
transmitter.

про́воды (-ов) pl send-off. прово-
жáтый sb guide, escort. провожáть impf of проводи́ть

прово́з conveyance, transport.

провозгласи́ть (-ашý) pf, провоз-
глашáть impf proclaim; propose.
провозглаше́ние proclamation.

провози́ть (-ожý, -ózишь) impf of
провезти́

провокáтор agent provocateur. про-
вокáция provocation.

про́волока wire. про́волочный
wire.

прово́рный quick; agile. прово́р-
ство quickness; agility.

провоци́ровать impf & pf (pf с~)
provoke.

прогадáть pf, прогáдывать impf
miscalculate.

прогáлина glade; space.

прогибáть(ся impf of прогну́ть(ся

проглáтывать impf, проглоти́ть
(-очý, -óтишь) pf swallow.

прогляде́ть (-яжý) pf, прогля́ды-
вать[1] impf overlook; look through.

прогляну́ть (-я́нет) pf, прогля́-
дывать[2] impf show, peep through,
appear.

прогнáть (-гоню́, -гóнишь; -áл, -á, -о)
pf (impf прогоня́ть) drive away;
banish; drive; sack.

прогнивáть impf, прогни́ть (-ниёт;
-и́л, -á, -о) pf rot through.

прогно́з prognosis; (weather) forecast.

прогну́ть (-нý, -нёшь) pf (impf про-
гибáть) cause to sag; ~ся sag, bend.

проговáривать impf, проговори́ть
pf say, utter; talk; ~ся let the cat

out of the bag.

проголода́ться *pf* get hungry.

про|голосова́ть *pf*.

прого́н purlin; girder; stairwell.

прогоня́ть *impf of* прогна́ть

прогора́ть *impf*, **прогоре́ть** (-рю́) *pf* burn (through); burn out; go bankrupt.

прого́рклый rancid, rank.

програ́мма programme; syllabus. **программи́ровать** *impf* (*pf* за~) programme.

прогрева́ть *impf*, **прогре́ть** (-е́ю) *pf* heat; warm up; ~ся warm up.

про|греме́ть (-млю́) *pf*. **про|грохота́ть** (-очу́, -о́чешь) *pf*.

прогре́сс progress. **прогресси́вный** progressive. **прогресси́ровать** *impf* progress.

прогрыза́ть *impf*, **прогры́зть** (-зу́, -зёшь; -ы́з) *pf* gnaw through.

про|гуде́ть (-гужу́) *pf*.

прогу́л truancy; absenteeism. **прогу́ливать** *impf*, **прогуля́ть** *pf* play truant, be absent, (from); miss; take for a walk; ~ся take a walk. **прогу́лка** walk, stroll; outing. **прогу́льщик** absentee, truant.

продава́ть (-даю́, -даёшь) *impf*, **прода́ть** (-а́м, -а́шь, -а́ст, -ади́м; про́дал, -а́, -о) *pf* sell. **продава́ться** (-даётся) *impf* be for sale; sell. **продаве́ц** (-вца́) seller, vendor; salesman. **продавщи́ца** seller, vendor; saleswoman. **прода́жа** sale. **прода́жный** for sale; corrupt.

продвига́ть *impf*, **продви́нуть** (-ну) *pf* move on, push forward; advance; ~ся move forward; push on. **продвиже́ние** advancement.

продева́ть *impf of* продеть

про|деклами́ровать *pf*.

проде́лать *pf*, **проде́лывать** *impf* do, perform, make. **проде́лка** trick; prank.

продемонстри́ровать *pf* demonstrate, show.

продёргивать *impf of* продёрнуть

продержа́ть (-жу́, -жишь) *pf* hold; keep; ~ся hold out.

продёрнуть (-ну, -нешь) *pf* (*impf* продёргивать) pass, run; criticize severely.

проде́ть (-е́ну) *pf* (*impf* продева́ть) pass; ~ ни́тку в иго́лку thread a needle.

продешеви́ть (-влю́) *pf* sell too cheap.

про|диктова́ть *pf*.

продлева́ть *impf*, **продли́ть** *pf* prolong. **продле́ние** extension. **про|дли́ться** *pf*.

продма́г grocery. **продово́льственный** food. **продово́льствие** food; provisions.

продолгова́тый oblong.

продолжа́тель *m* continuer. **продолжа́ть** *impf*, **продо́лжить** (-жу) *pf* continue; prolong; ~ся continue, last, go on. **продолже́ние** continuation; sequel; в ~+gen in the course of. **продолжи́тельность** duration. **продолжи́тельный** long; prolonged.

продо́льный longitudinal.

продро́гнуть (-ну; -о́г) *pf* be chilled to the bone.

продто́вары (-ов) *pl* food products.

продува́ть *impf* продуть

проду́кт product; *pl* food-stuffs. **продукти́вность** productivity. **продукти́вный** productive. **проду́ктовый** food. **проду́кция** production.

проду́манный well thought-out; considered. **проду́мать** *pf*, **проду́мывать** *impf* think over; think out.

проду́ть (-у́ю, -у́ешь) *pf* (*impf* продува́ть) blow through.

продыря́вить (-влю) *pf* make a hole in.

проеда́ть *impf of* прое́сть. **прое́ду** *etc.: see* прое́хать

прое́зд passage, thoroughfare; trip. **прое́здить** (-зжу) *pf* (*impf* проезжа́ть) spend travelling. **проездно́й** travelling; ~о́й биле́т ticket; ~а́я пла́та fare; ~ы́е *sb pl* travelling expenses. **проезжа́ть** *impf of* прое́здить, прое́хать. **прое́зжий** passing (by); *sb* passer-by.

прое́кт project, plan, design; draft. **проекти́ровать** *impf* (*pf* с~) project; plan. **прое́ктный** planning; planned. **прое́ктор** projector. **проекцио́нный фона́рь** projector. **прое́кция** projection.

прое́сть (-е́м, -е́шь, -е́ст, -еди́м; -е́л) *pf* (*impf* проеда́ть) eat through, corrode; spend on food.

проéхать (-éду) pf (impf проезжáть) pass, ride, drive (by, through); cover.

прожáренный (cul) well-done.

прожевáть (-жую, -жуёшь) pf, прожёвывать impf chew well.

прожéктор (pl -ы or -á) searchlight.

прожéчь (-жгу, -жжёшь; -жёг, -жглá) pf (impf прожигáть) burn (through).

проживáть impf of прожи́ть. прожигáть impf of прожéчь

прожи́точный ми́нимум living wage. прожи́ть (-иву, -ивёшь; -óжил, -á, -о) pf (impf прожива́ть) live; spend.

прожóрливый gluttonous.

прóза prose. прозаи́ческий prose; prosaic.

прозва́ние, прóзвище nickname. прозва́ть (-зову, -зовёшь; -áл, -á, -о) pf (impf прозыва́ть) nickname, name.

про|звучáть pf.

про|зева́ть pf. про|зимова́ть pf. прозову́ etc.: see прозва́ть

прозорли́вый perspicacious.

прозра́чный transparent.

прозрева́ть impf, прозре́ть pf regain one's sight; see clearly. прозре́ние recovery of sight; insight.

прозыва́ть impf of прозва́ть

прозяба́ние vegetation. прозяба́ть impf vegetate.

проигра́ть pf, прои́грывать impf lose; play; ~ся gamble away all one's money. прои́грыватель m record-player. прои́грыш loss.

произведе́ние work: production; product. произвести́ (-еду, -едёшь; -ёл, -á) pf, производи́ть (-ожу, -óдишь) impf make; carry out; produce; +в+acc/nom pl promote to (the rank of). производи́тель m producer. производи́тельность productivity. производи́тельный productive. произво́дный derivative. произво́дственный industrial; production. произво́дство production. произво́л arbitrariness; arbitrary rule. произво́льный arbitrary.

произнести́ (-су, -сёшь; -ёс, -лá) pf, произноси́ть (-ошу, -óсишь) impf pronounce; utter. произноше́ние pronunciation.

произойти́ (-ойдёт; -ошёл, -шлá) pf (impf происходи́ть) happen, occur;

result; be descended.

произраста́ть impf, произрасти́ (-ту́; -тёшь; -рóс, -лá) pf sprout; grow.

прóиски (-ов) pl intrigues.

проистека́ть impf, происте́чь (-ечёт; -ёк, -лá) pf spring, result.

происходи́ть (-ожу, -óдишь) impf of произойти́. происхожде́ние origin; birth.

происше́ствие event, incident.

пройдóха m & f sly person.

пройти́ (-йду́, -йдёшь; -ошёл, -шлá) pf (impf проходи́ть) go; go past; cover; study; get through; ~сь (impf проха́живаться) take a stroll.

прок use, benefit.

прокажённый sb leper. прока́за[1] leprosy.

прока́за[2] mischief, prank. прока́зничать impf (pf на~) be up to mischief. прока́зник prankster.

прока́лывать impf of проколо́ть

прока́пывать impf of прокопа́ть

прока́т hire.

прокати́ться (-ачу́сь, -áтишься) pf roll; go for a drive.

прока́тный rolling; rolled.

прокипяти́ть (-ячу́) pf boil (thoroughly).

прокиса́ть impf, про|ки́снуть (-нет) pf turn (sour).

прокла́дка laying; construction; washer; packing. прокла́дывать impf of проложи́ть

прокла́мация leaflet.

проклина́ть impf, прокля́сть (-яну́, -янёшь; -óклял. -á, -о) pf curse, damn. прокля́тие curse; damnation. прокля́тый (-ят, -á, -о) damned.

проко́л puncture.

проколо́ть (-лю, -лешь) pf (impf прока́лывать) prick, pierce.

прокомменти́ровать pf comment (upon).

про|компости́ровать pf. про|конспекти́ровать pf. про|консульти́ровать(ся pf. про|контроли́ровать pf.

прокопа́ть pf (impf прока́пывать) dig, dig through.

прокóрм nourishment, sustenance. про|корми́ть(ся (-млю(сь, -мишь(ся pf.

про|корректи́ровать pf.

прокрáдываться impf, прокрáсться (-аду́сь, -аде́шься) *pf* steal in.

прокурату́ра office of public prosecutor. прокуро́р public prosecutor.

прокуси́ть (-ушу́, -у́сишь) *pf*, проку́сывать *impf* bite through.

прокути́ть (-учу́, -у́тишь) *pf*, проку́чивать *impf* squander; go on a binge.

пролага́ть *impf of* проложи́ть

пролáмывать *impf of* проломáть

пролегáть *impf* lie, run.

пролезáть *impf*, проле́зть (-зу; -ле́з) *pf* get through, climb through.

про|лепетáть (-ечу́, -е́чешь) *pf*.

пролёт span; stairwell; bay.

пролетариáт proletariat. пролетáрий proletarian. пролетáрский proletarian.

пролетáть *impf*, пролете́ть (-ечу́) *pf* fly; cover; fly by, past, through.

проли́в strait. пролива́ть *impf*, проли́ть (-лью́, -льёшь; -óлил, -á, -о) *pf* spill, shed; ~ся be spilt.

проло́г prologue.

проложи́ть (-жу́, -жишь) *pf* (*impf* прокла́дывать, пролага́ть) lay; build; interlay.

проло́м breach, break. проломáть, проломи́ть (-млю́, -мишь) *pf* (*impf* пролáмывать) break (through).

пролью́ *etc.*: *see* проли́ть

про|мáзать (-áжу) *pf*. промáтывать(ся *impf of* промотáть(ся

про́мах miss; slip, blunder. промáхиваться *impf*, промахну́ться (-ну́сь, -нёшься) *pf* miss; make a blunder.

промáчивать *impf of* промочи́ть

промедле́ние delay. проме́длить *pf* delay; procrastinate.

промежу́ток (-тка) interval; space. промежу́точный intermediate

промелькну́ть (-ну́, -нёшь) *pf* flash (past, by).

проме́нивать *impf*, променя́ть *pf* exchange.

промерзáть *impf*, промёрзнуть (-ну; -ёрз) *pf* freeze through. промёрзлый frozen.

промокáть *impf*, промо́кнуть (-ну; -мóк) *pf* get soaked; let water in.

промо́лвить (-влю) *pf* say, utter.

промолчáть (-чу́) *pf* keep silent.

про|мотáть *pf* (*impf also* промáтывать) squander.

промочи́ть (-чу́, -чишь) *pf* (*impf* промáчивать) soak, drench.

промо́ю *etc.*: *see* промы́ть

промтовáры (-ов) *pl* manufactured goods.

промчáться (-чу́сь) *pf* rush by.

промывáть *impf of* промы́ть

про́мысел (-сла) trade, business; *pl* works. промыслóвый producers'; business; game.

промы́ть (-мо́ю) *pf* (*impf* промывáть) wash (thoroughly); bathe; ~ мозги́+*dat* brain-wash.

про|мычáть (-чу́) *pf*.

промы́шленник industrialist. промы́шленность industry. промы́шленный industrial.

пронести́ (-су́, -сёшь; -ёс, -лá) *pf* (*impf* проноси́ть) carry (past, through); pass (over); ~сь rush past, through; scud (past); fly; spread.

пронзáть *impf*, пронзи́ть (-нжу́) *pf* pierce, transfix. пронзи́тельный piercing.

пронизáть (-ижу́, -и́жешь) *pf*, прони́зывать *impf* pierce; permeate.

проникáть *impf*, прони́кнуть (-ну; -и́к) *pf* penetrate; percolate; ~ся be imbued. проникнове́ние penetration; feeling. проникнове́нный heartfelt.

проницáемый permeable. проницáтельный perspicacious.

проноси́ть(ся (-ошу́(сь, -óсишь(ся) *impf of* пронести́(сь. про|нумеровáть *pf*.

пронюхать *pf*, проню́хивать *impf* smell out, get wind of.

прообраз prototype.

пропагáнда propaganda. пропагандúст propagandist.

пропадáть *impf of* пропáсть. пропáжа loss.

пропáлывать *impf of* прополóть

про́пасть precipice; abyss; lots of.

пропáсть (-аду́, -адёшь) *pf* (*impf* пропадáть) be missing; be lost; disappear; be done for, die; be wasted. пропáщий lost; hopeless.

пропекáть(ся *impf of* пропе́чь(ся. про|пе́ть (-пою́, -поёшь) *pf*.

пропе́чь (-еку́, -ечёшь; -ёк, -лá) *pf* (*impf* пропекáть) bake thoroughly; ~ся get baked through.

пропивáть *impf of* пропи́ть

прописа́ть (-ишу́, -и́шешь) pf, про|пи́сывать impf prescribe; register; ~ся register. пропи́ска registration; residence permit. прописн|о́й: ~а́я бу́ква capital letter; ~а́я и́стина truism. про́писью adv in words.

пропита́ние subsistence, sustenance. пропита́ть pf, пропи́тывать impf impregnate, saturate.

пропи́ть (-пью́, -пьёшь; -о́пи́л, -а́, -о) pf (impf пропива́ть) spend on drink.

проплыва́ть impf, проплы́ть (-ыву́, -ывёшь; -ы́л, -а́, -о) pf swim, sail, or float past or through.

пропове́дник preacher; advocate. пропове́довать impf preach; advocate. про́поведь sermon; advocacy.

пропол|за́ть impf, проползти́ (-зу́, -зёшь; -по́лз, -ла́) pf crawl, creep.

пропо́лка weeding. прополо́ть (-лю́, -лешь) pf (impf пропа́лывать) weed.

про|полоска́ть (-ощу́, -о́щешь) pf.

пропорциона́льный proportional, proportionate. пропо́рция proportion.

про́пуск (pl -á or -и, -о́в or -ов) pass, permit; password; admission; omission; non-attendance; blank, gap. пропуска́ть impf, пропусти́ть (-ущу́, -у́стишь) pf let pass; let in; pass; leave out; miss. пропускн|о́й: ~а́я спосо́бность capacity.

пропью́ etc.: see пропи́ть

прора́б works superintendent.

прораба́тывать impf, прорабо́тать pf work (through, at); study; pick holes in.

прораста́ние germination; sprouting. прораста́ть impf, прорасти́ (-тёт; -ро́с, -ла́) pf germinate, sprout.

прорва́ть (-ву́, -вёшь; -а́л, -а́, -о) pf (impf прорыва́ть) break through; ~ся burst open; break through.

про|реаги́ровать pf.

проредить (-ежу́) pf, проре́живать impf thin out.

проре́з cut; slit; notch. про|ре́зать (-е́жу) pf, прореза́ть impf (impf also проре́зывать) cut through; ~ся be cut, come through.

проре́зывать(ся impf of про|ре́зать(ся. про|репети́ровать pf.

проре́ха tear, slit; flies; deficiency.

про|рецензи́ровать pf.

проро́к prophet.

пророни́ть pf utter.

проро́с etc.: see прорасти́

проро́ческий prophetic. проро́чество prophecy.

проро́ю etc.: see проры́ть

проруба́ть impf, проруби́ть (-блю́, -бишь) pf cut or hack through. про́рубь ice-hole.

проры́в break; break-through; hitch. прорыва́ть¹(ся impf of про|рва́ть(ся

прорыва́ть² impf, проры́ть (-ро́ю) pf dig through; ~ся dig one's way through.

проса́чиваться impf of просочи́ться

просве́рливать impf, просверли́ть pf drill, bore; perforate.

просве́т (clear) space; shaft of light; ray of hope; opening. просвети́тельный educational. просвети́ть¹ (-ещу́) pf (impf просвеща́ть) enlighten.

просвети́ть² (-ечу́, -е́тишь) pf (impf просве́чивать) X-ray.

просветле́ние brightening (up); lucidity. про|светле́ть (-е́ет) pf.

просве́чивание radioscopy. просве́чивать impf of просвети́ть; be translucent; be visible.

просвеща́ть impf of просвети́ть. просвеще́ние enlightenment.

просви́ра communion bread.

про́седь streak(s) of grey.

просе́ивать impf of просе́ять

просе́ка cutting, ride.

просёлок (-лка) country road.

просе́ять (-е́ю) pf (impf просе́ивать) sift.

про|сигнализи́ровать pf.

просиде́ть (-ижу́) pf, проси́живать impf sit.

проси́тельный pleading. проси́ть (-ошу́, -о́сишь) impf (pf по~) ask; beg; invite; ~ся ask; apply.

проска́кивать impf of проскочи́ть

проска́льзывать impf, проскользну́ть (-ну́, -нёшь) pf slip, creep.

проскочи́ть (-чу́, -чишь) pf (impf проска́кивать) rush by; slip through; creep in.

просла́вить (-влю) pf, прославля́ть impf glorify; make famous; ~ся become famous. просла́вленный renowned.

проследи́ть (-ежу́) *pf*, просле́живать *impf* track (down); trace.

прослези́ться (-ежу́сь) *pf* shed a few tears.

просло́йка layer, stratum.

прослужи́ть (-жу́, -жишь) *pf* serve (for a certain time).

про|слу́шать *pf*, прослу́шивать *impf* hear; listen to; miss, not catch.

про|слы́ть (-ыву́, -ывёшь, -ы́л, -а́, -о) *pf*.

просма́тривать *impf*, просмотре́ть (-рю́, -ришь) *pf* look over; overlook. просмо́тр survey; view, viewing; examination.

просну́ться (-ну́сь, -нёшься) *pf* (*impf* просыпа́ться) wake up.

про́со millet.

просо́вывать(ся *impf of* просу́нуть(ся

про|со́хнуть (-ну, -ох) *pf* (*impf also* просыха́ть) dry out.

просочи́ться (-и́тся) *pf* (*impf* проса́чиваться) percolate; seep (out); leak (out).

проспа́ть (-плю; -а́л, -а́, -о) *pf* (*impf* просыпа́ть) sleep (through); oversleep.

проспе́кт avenue.

про|спряга́ть *pf*.

просро́ченный overdue; expired. просро́чить (-чу) *pf* allow to run out; be behind with; overstay. просро́чка delay; expiry of time limit.

проста́ивать *impf of* простоя́ть

проста́к (-а́) simpleton.

просте́нок (-нка) pier (*between windows*).

простере́ться (-трётся; -тёрся) *pf*, простира́ться *impf* extend.

прости́тельный pardonable, excusable. прости́ть (-ощу́) *pf* (*impf* проща́ть) forgive; excuse; ~ся (с+*instr*) say goodbye (to).

проститу́тка prostitute. проститу́ция prostitution.

про́сто *adv* simply.

простоволо́сый bare-headed. простоду́шный simple-hearted; ingenuous.

просто́й[1] downtime.

прост|о́й[2] simple; plain; mere; ~ым гла́зом with the naked eye; ~о́е число́ prime number.

простоква́ша thick sour milk.

про́сто-на́просто *adv* simply.

простонаро́дный of the common people.

просто́р spaciousness; space. просто́рный spacious.

просторе́чие popular speech. простосерде́чный simple-hearted.

простота́ simplicity.

простоя́ть (-ою́) *pf* (*impf* проста́ивать) stand (idle).

простра́нный extensive, vast. простра́нственный spatial. простра́нство space.

простре́л lumbago. простре́ливать *impf*, прострели́ть (-лю́, -лишь) *pf* shoot through.

про|строчи́ть (-очу́, -о́чишь) *pf*.

просту́да cold. простуди́ться (-ужу́сь, -у́дишься) *pf*, простужа́ться *impf* catch (a) cold.

проступа́ть *impf*, проступи́ть (-ит) *pf* appear.

просту́пок (-пка) misdemeanour.

простыня́ (*pl* про́стыни, -ы́нь, -ня́м) sheet.

просты́ть (-ы́ну) *pf* get cold.

просу́нуть (-ну) *pf* (*impf* просо́вывать) push, thrust.

просу́шивать *impf*, просуши́ть (-шу́, -шишь) *pf* dry out; ~ся (get) dry.

просуществова́ть *pf* exist; endure.

просчёт error. просчита́ться *pf*, просчи́тываться *impf* miscalculate. просы́пать (-плю) *pf*, просыпа́ть[1] *impf* spill; ~ся get spilt.

просыпа́ть[2] *impf of* проспа́ть. просыпа́ться *impf of* просну́ться. просыха́ть *impf of* просо́хнуть

про́сьба request.

прота́лкивать *impf of* протолкну́ть. прота́пливать *impf of* протопи́ть прота́птывать *impf of* протопта́ть прота́скивать *impf*, протащи́ть (-щу́, -щишь) *pf* drag, push (through).

проте́з artificial limb, prosthesis; зубно́й ~ denture.

проте́ин protein.

протека́ть *impf of* проте́чь

проте́кция patronage.

протере́ть (-тру́, -трёшь; -тёр) *pf* (*impf* протира́ть) wipe (over); wear (through).

проте́ст protest. протеста́нт, ~ка Protestant. протестова́ть *impf & pf* protest.

проте́чь (-ечёт; -тёк, -ла́) pf (impf протека́ть) flow; leak; seep; pass; take its course.

про́тив prep+gen against; opposite; contrary to, as against.

про́тивень (-вня) m baking-tray; meat-pan.

проти́виться (-влюсь) impf (pf вос~) +dat oppose; resist. проти́вник opponent; the enemy. проти́вный[1] opposite; contrary. проти́вный[2] nasty, disgusting.

противо- in comb anti-, contra-, counter-. противове́с counterbalance. ~возду́шный anti-aircraft. ~га́з gas-mask. ~де́йствие opposition. ~де́йствовать impf +dat oppose, counteract. ~есте́ственный unnatural. ~зако́нный illegal. ~зача́точный contraceptive. ~поло́жность opposition; contrast. ~поло́жный opposite; contrary. ~поста́вить (-влю) pf, ~поставля́ть impf oppose; contrast. ~речи́вый contradictory; conflicting. ~ре́чие contradiction. ~ре́чить (-чу) impf +dat contradict. ~стоя́ть (-ою́) impf +dat resist, withstand. ~та́нковый anti-tank. ~я́дие antidote.

протира́ть impf of протере́ть

проти́скивать impf, проти́снуть (-ну) pf force, squeeze (through, into).

проткну́ть (-ну́, -нёшь) pf (impf протыка́ть) pierce; skewer.

протоко́л minutes; report; protocol.

протолкну́ть (-ну́, -нёшь) pf (impf прота́лкивать) push through.

прото́н proton.

протопи́ть (-плю́, -пишь) pf (impf прота́пливать) heat (thoroughly).

протопта́ть (-пчу́, -пчешь) pf (impf прота́птывать) tread; wear out.

проторённый beaten, well-trodden.

прототи́п prototype.

прото́чный flowing, running.

про|тра́лить pf. протру́ etc.: see протере́ть. про|тру́бить (-блю́) pf.

протрезви́ться (-влюсь) pf, протрезвля́ться impf sober up.

протуха́ть impf, проту́хнуть (-нет; -у́х) pf become rotten; go bad.

протыка́ть impf of проткну́ть

протя́гивать impf, протяну́ть (-ну́, -нешь) pf stretch; extend; hold out;

~ся stretch out; extend; last. протяже́ние extent, stretch; period. протя́жный long-drawn-out; drawling.

проу́чивать impf, проучи́ть (-чу́, -чишь) pf study; teach a lesson.

профа́н ignoramus.

профана́ция profanation.

профессиона́л professional. профессиона́льный professional; occupational. профе́ссия profession. профе́ссор (pl -á) professor.

профила́ктика prophylaxis; preventive measures.

про́филь m profile; type.

про|фильтрова́ть pf.

профсою́з trade-union.

проха́живаться impf of пройти́сь

прохво́ст scoundrel.

прохла́да coolness. прохлади́тельный refreshing, cooling. прохла́дный cool, chilly.

прохо́д passage; gangway, aisle; duct. проходи́мец (-мца) rogue. проходи́мый passable. проходи́ть (-ожу́, -о́дишь) impf of пройти́. проходно́й entrance; communicating. проходя́щий passing. прохо́жий passing, in transit; sb passer-by.

процвета́ние prosperity. процвета́ть impf prosper, flourish.

процеди́ть (-ежу́, -е́дишь) pf (impf проце́живать) filter, strain.

процеду́ра procedure; (usu in pl) treatment.

проце́живать pf of процеди́ть

проце́нт percentage; per cent; interest.

проце́сс process; trial; legal proceedings. проце́ссия procession.

про|цити́ровать pf.

проче́ска screening; combing.

проче́сть (-чту́, -чтёшь; -чёл, -чла́) pf of чита́ть

про́чий other.

прочи́стить (-и́щу) pf (impf прочища́ть) clean; clear.

про|чита́ть pf, прочи́тывать impf read (through).

прочища́ть impf of прочи́стить

про́чность firmness, stability, durability. про́чный (-чен, -чна́, -о) firm, sound, solid; durable.

прочте́ние reading. прочту́ etc.: see проче́сть

прочу́вствовать pf feel deeply;

experience, go through.

прочь *adv* away, off; averse to.

проше́дший past; last. **прошёл** *etc.*: *see* **пройти́**

проше́ние application, petition.

прошепта́ть (-пчу́, -пчёшь) *pf* whisper.

проше́ствие: по проше́ствии +*gen* after.

прошива́ть *impf*, **проши́ть** (-шью́, -шьёшь) *pf* sew, stitch.

прошлого́дний last year's. **про́шл|ый** past; last; ~oe *sb* the past.

про|шнурова́ть *pf*. **про|штуди́ровать** *pf*. **прошью́** *etc.*: *see* **проши́ть**

проща́й(те) goodbye. **проща́льный** parting; farewell. **проща́ние** farewell; parting. **проща́ть(ся** *impf of* **прости́ть(ся**

про́ще simpler, plainer.

проще́ние forgiveness, pardon.

прощу́пать *pf*, **прощу́пывать** *impf* feel.

про|экзаменова́ть *pf*.

проя́витель *m* developer. **проя́вить** (-влю́, -вишь) *pf*, **проявля́ть** *impf* show, display; develop; ~ся reveal itself. **проявле́ние** display; manifestation; developing.

проясни́ться *pf*, **проясня́ться** *impf* clear, clear up.

пруд (-á, *loc* -ý) pond. **пруди́ть** (-ужу́, -ýдишь) *impf* (*pf* за~) dam.

пружи́на spring. **пружи́нистый** springy. **пружи́нный** spring.

пру́сский Prussian.

прут (-а *or* -á; *pl* -тья) twig.

пры́гать *impf*, **пры́гнуть** (-ну) *pf* jump, leap; bounce; ~ с шесто́м pole-vault. **прыгу́н** (-á), **пры́гунья** (*gen pl* -ний) jumper. **прыжо́к** (-жка́) jump; leap; **прыжки́** jumping; **прыжки́** в во́ду diving; ~ в высоту́ high jump; ~ в длину́ long jump.

пры́скать *impf*, **пры́снуть** (-ну) *pf* spurt; sprinkle; burst out laughing.

прыть speed; energy.

прыщ (-á), **пры́щик** pimple.

пряди́льный spinning. **пряди́льня** (*gen pl* -лен) (spinning-)mill. **пряди́льщик** spinner. **пряду́** *etc.*: *see* **прясть. прядь** lock; strand. **пря́жа** yarn, thread.

пря́жка buckle, clasp.

пря́лка distaff; spinning-wheel.

пряма́я *sb* straight line. **пря́мо** *adv* straight; straight on; frankly; really.

прямоду́шие directness, straightforwardness. ~**ду́шный** direct, straightforward.

прямо́й (-ям, -á, -о) straight; upright, erect; through; direct; straightforward; real.

прямолине́йный rectilinear; straightforward. **прямоуго́льник** rectangle. **прямоуго́льный** rectangular.

пря́ник spice cake. **пря́ность** spice. **пря́ный** spicy; heady.

прясть (-яду́, -ядёшь; -ял, -я́ла, -о) *impf* (*pf* с~) spin.

пря́тать (-я́чу) *impf* (*pf* с~) hide; ~ся hide. **пря́тки** (-ток) *pl* hide-and-seek.

пса *etc.*: *see* **пёс**

псало́м (-лма́) psalm. **псалты́рь** Psalter.

псевдони́м pseudonym.

псих madman, lunatic. **психиатри́я** psychiatry. **пси́хика** psyche; psychology. **психи́ческий** mental, psychical.

психоана́лиз psychoanalysis. **психо́з** psychosis. **психо́лог** psychologist. **психологи́ческий** psychological. **психоло́гия** psychology. **психопа́т** psychopath. **психопати́ческий** psychopathic. **психосомати́ческий** psychosomatic. **психотерапе́вт** psychotherapist. **психотерапи́я** psychotherapy. **психоти́ческий** psychotic.

птене́ц (-нца́) nestling; fledgeling. **пти́ца** bird. **птицефе́рма** poultry-farm. **пти́чий** bird, bird's, poultry. **пти́чка** bird; tick.

пу́блика public; audience. **публика́ция** publication; notice, advertisement. **публикова́ть** *impf* (*pf* o~) publish. **публици́стика** writing on current affairs. **публи́чность** publicity. **публи́чный** public; ~ дом brothel.

пу́гало scarecrow. **пуга́ть** *impf* (*pf* ис~, на~) frighten, scare; ~ся (+*gen*) be frightened (of). **пуга́ч** (-á) toy pistol. **пугли́вый** fearful.

пу́говица button.

пуд (*pl* -ы́) pood (= *16.38 kg*). **пудово́й, пудо́вый** one pood in weight.

пу́дель *m* poodle.

пу́динг blancmange.

пу́дра powder. **пу́дреница** powder compact. **пу́дреный** powdered. **пу́дриться** *impf* (*pf* на~) powder one's face.

пуза́тый pot-bellied.

пузырёк (-рька́) vial; bubble. **пузы́рь** (-я́) *m* bubble; blister; bladder.

пук (*pl* -и́) bunch, bundle; tuft.

пу́кать *impf*, **пу́кнуть** *pf* fart.

пулемёт machine-gun. **пулемётчик** machine-gunner. **пуленепробива́емый** bullet-proof.

пульвериза́тор atomizer; spray.

пульс pulse. **пульси́ровать** *impf* pulsate.

пульт desk, stand; control panel.

пу́ля bullet.

пункт point; spot; post; item. **пункти́р** dotted line. **пункти́рный** dotted, broken.

пунктуа́льный punctual.

пунктуа́ция punctuation.

пунцо́вый crimson.

пуп (-а́) navel. **пупови́на** umbilical cord. **пупо́к** (-пка́) navel; gizzard.

пурга́ blizzard.

пурита́нин (*pl* -та́не, -та́н), -**а́нка** Puritan.

пурпу́р purple, crimson. **пурпу́р|ный**, ~**о́вый** purple.

пуск starting (up). **пуска́й** *see* пусть. **пуска́ть(ся** *impf of* пусти́ть(ся. **пусково́й** starting.

пусте́ть (-е́ет) *impf* (*pf* о~) empty; become deserted.

пусти́ть (пущу́, пу́стишь) *pf* (*impf* пуска́ть) let go; let in; let; start; send; set in motion; throw; put forth; ~**ся** set out; start.

пустова́ть *impf* be *or* stand empty. **пусто́й** (-ст, -а́, -о) empty; uninhabited; idle; shallow. **пустота́** (*pl* -ы) emptiness; void; vacuum; futility. **пусто́тёлый** hollow.

пусты́нный uninhabited; deserted; desert. **пусты́ня** desert. **пусты́рь** (-я́) *m* waste land; vacant plot.

пусты́шка blank; hollow object; dummy.

пусть, пуска́й *partl* let; all right; though, even if.

пустя́к (-а́) trifle. **пустяко́вый** trivial.

пу́таница muddle, confusion. **пу́таный** muddled, confused. **пу́тать** *impf* (*pf* за~, пере~, с~) tangle; confuse; mix up; ~**ся** get confused *or* mixed up.

путёвка pass; place on a group tour.

путеводи́тель *m* guide, guide-book.

путево́й travelling; road. **путём** *prep+gen* by means of. **путеше́ственник** traveller. **путеше́ствие** journey; voyage. **путеше́ствовать** *impf* travel; voyage.

пу́ты (пут) *pl* shackles.

путь (-и́, *instr* -ём, *prep* -и́) way; track; path; course; journey; voyage; means; **в пути́** en route, on one's way.

пух (*loc* -у́) down; fluff.

пу́хлый (-хл, -а́, -о) plump. **пу́хнуть** (-ну; пух) *impf* (*pf* вс~, о~) swell.

пухови́к (-а́) feather-bed. **пухо́вка** powder-puff. **пухо́вый** downy.

пучи́на abyss; the deep.

пучо́к (-чка́) bunch, bundle.

пу́шечный gun, cannon.

пуши́нка bit of fluff. **пуши́стый** fluffy.

пу́шка gun, cannon.

пушни́на furs, pelts. **пушно́й** fur; fur-bearing.

пу́ще *adv* more; ~ **всего́** most of all.

пущу́ *etc.*: *see* пусти́ть

пчела́ (*pl* -ёлы) bee. **пчели́ный** bee, bees'. **пчелово́д** bee-keeper. **пче́льник** apiary.

пшени́ца wheat. **пшени́чный** wheat(en).

пшённый millet. **пшено́** millet.

пыл (*loc* -у́) heat, ardour. **пыла́ть** *impf* blaze; burn.

пылесо́с vacuum cleaner. **пылесо́сить** *impf* vacuum (-clean).

пыли́нка speck of dust. **пыли́ть** *impf* (*pf* за~, на~) raise a dust; cover with dust; ~**ся** get dusty.

пы́лкий ardent; fervent.

пыль (*loc* -у́) dust. **пы́льный** (-лен, -льна́, -о) dusty. **пыльца́** pollen.

пыре́й couch grass.

пырну́ть (-ну́, -нёшь) *pf* jab.

пыта́ть *impf* torture. **пыта́ться** *impf* (*pf* по~) try. **пы́тка** torture, torment. **пытли́вый** inquisitive.

пыхте́ть (-хчу́) *impf* puff, pant.

пы́шка bun.

пы́шность splendour. **пы́шный**

(-шён, -шна́, -шно) splendid; lush.
пьедеста́л pedestal.
пье́са play; piece.
пью *etc.*: *see* **пить**
пьяне́ть (**-е́ю**) *impf* (*pf* **о~**) get drunk. **пьяни́ть** *impf* (*pf* **о~**) intoxicate, make drunk. **пья́ница** *m & f* drunkard. **пья́нство** drunkenness. **пья́нствовать** *impf* drink heavily. **пья́ный** drunk.
пюпи́тр lectern; stand.
пюре́ *neut indecl* purée.
пядь (*gen pl* **-е́й**) span; **ни пя́ди** not an inch.
пя́льцы (**-лец**) *pl* embroidery frame.
пята́ (*pl* **-ы, -а́м**) heel.
пята́к (**-а́**), **пятачо́к** (**-чка́**) five-copeck piece. **пятёрка** five; figure 5; No. 5; fiver (5-rouble note).
пяти- *in comb* five; penta-. **пятибо́рье** pentathlon. **~десятиле́тие** fifty years; fiftieth anniversary, birthday. **П~деся́тница** Pentecost. **~деся́тый** fiftieth; **~деся́тые го́ды** the fifties. **~коне́чный** five-pointed. **~ле́тие** five years; fifth anniversary. **~ле́тка** five-year plan. **~со́тый** five-hundredth. **~уго́льник** pentagon. **~уго́льный** pentagonal.
пя́титься (**пя́чусь**) *impf* (*pf* **по~**) move backwards; back.
пя́тка heel.
пятна́дцатый fifteenth. **пятна́дцать** fifteen.
пятна́ть *impf* (*pf* **за~**) spot, stain. **пятна́шки** (**-шек**) *pl* tag. **пятни́стый** spotted.
пя́тница Friday.
пятно́ (*pl* **-а, -тен**) stain; spot; blot; **роди́мое ~** birth-mark.
пя́тый fifth. **пять** (**-и́, *instr* -ью́**) five. **пятьдеся́т** (**-и́десяти, *instr* -ью́десятью**) fifty. **пятьсо́т** (**-тисо́т, -тиста́м**) five hundred. **пя́тью** *adv* five times.

Р

раб (**-а́**), **раба́** slave. **рабовладе́лец** (**-льца**) slave-owner. **раболе́пие** servility. **раболе́пный** servile. **раболе́пствовать** cringe, fawn.
рабо́та work; job; functioning. **рабо́тать** *impf* work; function; be open;

~ над+*instr* work on. **рабо́тник, -ица** worker. **работоспосо́бность** capacity for work, efficiency. **работоспосо́бный** able-bodied, hardworking. **рабо́тящий** hardworking. **рабо́чий** *sb* worker. **рабо́ч|ий** worker's; -working; **~ая си́ла** manpower.
ра́бский slave; servile. **ра́бство** slavery. **рабы́ня** female slave.
равви́н rabbi.
ра́венство equality. **равне́ние** alignment. **равни́на** plain.
равно́ *adv* alike; equally; **~ как** as well as. **равно́** *predic*: *see* **ра́вный**
равно- *in comb* equi-, iso-. **равнобе́дренный** isosceles. **~ве́сие** equilibrium; balance. **~де́нствие** equinox. **~ду́шие** indifference. **~ду́шный** indifferent. **~ме́рный** even; uniform. **~пра́вие** equality of rights. **~пра́вный** having equal rights. **~си́льный** of equal strength; equal, equivalent, tantamount. **~сторо́нний** equilateral. **~це́нный** of equal value; equivalent.
ра́вный (**-вен, -вна́**) equal. **равно́** *predic* make(s), equals; **всё ~о́** (it is) all the same. **равня́ть** (*pf* **с~**) make even; treat equally; **+с+*instr*** compare with, treat as equal to; **~ся** compete, compare; be equal; be tantamount.
рад (**-а, -о**) *predic* glad.
рада́р radar.
ра́ди *prep+gen* for the sake of.
радиа́тор radiator. **радиа́ция** radiation.
ра́дий radium.
радика́льный radical.
ра́дио *neut indecl* radio.
радио- *in comb* radio-; radioactive. **радиоакти́вный** radioactive. **~веща́ние** broadcasting. **~волна́** radiowave. **~гра́мма** radio-telegram. **~дио́лог** radiologist. **~ло́гия** radiology. **~лока́тор** radar (set). **~люби́тель** *m* radio amateur, ham. **~ма́як** (**-а́**) radio beacon. **~переда́тчик** transmitter. **~переда́ча** broadcast. **~приёмник** radio (set). **~связь** radio communication. **~слу́шатель** *m* listener. **~ста́нция** radio station. **~электро́ника** radioelectronics.

радио́ла radiogram.

ради́ровать impf & pf radio. ра-
дист radio operator.

ра́диус radius.

ра́довать impf (pf об~, по~) gladden, make happy; ~ся be glad, rejoice. ра́достный joyful. ра́дость
gladness, joy.

ра́дуга rainbow. ра́дужн|ый irides-
cent; cheerful; ~ая оболо́чка iris.
раду́шие cordiality. раду́шный cordial.

ражу́ etc.: see рази́ть

раз (pl -ы́, раз) time, occasion; one;
ещё ~ (once) again; как ~ just, exactly; не ~ more than once; ни ~у
not once. раз adv once, one day. раз
conj if; since.

разба́вить (-влю) pf, разбавля́ть
impf dilute.

разба́заривать impf, разбаза́рить
pf squander.

разба́лтывать(ся impf of разбол-
та́ть(ся

разбе́г running start. разбега́ться
impf, разбежа́ться (-егу́сь) pf take
a run, run up; scatter.

разберу́ etc.: see разобра́ть

разбива́ть(ся impf of разби́ть(ся.
разби́вка laying out; spacing (out).

разбинтова́ть pf, разбинто́вывать
impf unbandage.

разбира́тельство investigation.
разбира́ть impf of разобра́ть; ~ся
impf of разобра́ться

разби́ть (-зобью́, -зобьёшь) pf (impf
разбива́ть) break; smash; divide
(up); damage; defeat; mark out; space
(out); ~ся break, get broken; hurt
o.s. разби́тый broken; jaded.

раз|богате́ть (-е́ю) pf.

разбо́й robbery. разбо́йник robber.
разбо́йничий robber.

разболе́ться¹ (-ли́тся) pf begin to
ache badly.

разболе́ться² (-е́юсь) pf become ill.
разболта́ть¹ pf (impf разба́лты-
вать) divulge, give away.

разболта́ть² pf (impf разба́лты-
вать) shake up; loosen; ~ся work
loose; get out of hand.

разбомби́ть (-блю́) pf bomb, destroy
by bombing.

разбо́р analysis; critique; discrimination; investigation. разбо́рка sorting

out; dismantling. разбо́рный collapsible. разбо́рчивый legible; dis-
criminating.

разбра́сывать impf of разброса́ть
разбреда́ться impf, разбрести́сь
(-едётся; -ёлся, -ла́сь) pf disperse;
straggle. разбро́д disorder.

разбро́санный scattered; disconnected, incoherent. разброса́ть pf
(impf разбра́сывать) throw about;
scatter.

раз|буди́ть (-ужу́, -у́дишь) pf.

разбуха́ть impf, разбу́хнуть (-нет;
-бу́х) pf swell.

разбушева́ться (-шу́юсь) pf fly into
a rage; blow up; rage.

разва́л breakdown, collapse. разва́-
ливать impf, развали́ть (-лю́, -лишь)
pf pull down; mess up; ~ся collapse;
go to pieces; tumble down; sprawl.
разва́лина ruin; wreck.

ра́зве partl really?; ~ (то́лько), ~
(что) except that, only.

развева́ться impf fly, flutter.

разве́дать pf (impf разве́дывать)
find out; reconnoitre.

разведе́ние breeding; cultivation.

разведённ|ый divorced; ~ый, ~ая
sb divorcee.

разве́дка intelligence (service); reconnaissance; prospecting. разве́-
дочный prospecting, exploratory.

разведу́ etc.: see развести́

разве́дчик intelligence officer; scout;
prospector. разве́дывать impf of
разве́дать

развезти́ (-зу́, -зёшь; -ёз, -ла́) pf
(impf развози́ть) convey, transport;
deliver.

развеива́ть(ся impf of разве́ять(ся.
развёл etc.: see развести́

развенча́ть pf, разве́нчивать impf
dethrone; debunk.

развёрнутый extensive, all-out; detailed. разверну́ть (-ну́, -нёшь) pf
(impf развёртывать, развора́чи-
вать) unfold, unwrap; unroll; unfurl;
deploy; expand; develop; turn; scan;
display; ~ся unfold, unroll, come un-
wrapped; deploy; develop; spread;
turn.

развёрстка allotment, apportionment.

развёртывать(ся impf of развер-
ну́ть(ся

раз|весели́ть pf cheer up, amuse; **~ся** cheer up.

разве́сить[1] (-е́шу) pf (impf **разве́шивать**) spread; hang (out).

разве́сить[2] (-е́шу) pf (impf **разве́шивать**) weigh out. **разве́ска** weighing. **развесно́й** sold by weight.

развести́ (-еду́, -едёшь; -ёл, -а́) pf (impf **разводи́ть**) take; separate; divorce; dilute; dissolve; start; breed; cultivate; **~сь** get divorced; breed, multiply.

разветви́ться (-ви́тся) pf, **разветвля́ться** impf branch; fork. **разветвле́ние** branching, forking; branch; fork.

разве́шать pf, **разве́шивать** impf hang.

разве́шивать impf of **разве́сить**, **разве́шать**. **разве́шу** etc.: see **разве́сить**

разве́ять (-е́ю) pf (impf **разве́ивать**) scatter, disperse; dispel; **~ся** disperse; be dispelled.

развива́ть(ся impf of **разви́ть(ся** **разви́лка** fork.

разви́нтить (-нчу́) pf, **разви́нчивать** impf unscrew.

разви́тие development. **развито́й** (ра́звит, -а́, -о) developed; mature. **разви́ть** (-зову́; -зовёшь; -и́л, -а́, -о) pf (impf **развива́ть**) develop; unwind; **~ся** develop.

развлека́ть impf, **развле́чь** (-еку́, -ечёшь; -ёк, -ла́) pf entertain, amuse; **~ся** have a good time; amuse o.s. **развлече́ние** entertainment, amusement.

разво́д divorce. **разводи́ть(ся** (-ожу́(сь, -о́дишь(ся) impf of **развести́(сь**. **разво́дка** separation. **разводно́й**: **~** ключ adjustable spanner; **~** мост drawbridge.

развози́ть (-ожу́, -о́зишь) impf of **развезти́**

разволнова́ть(ся pf get excited, be agitated.

развора́чивать(ся impf of **разверну́ть(ся**

разворова́ть pf, **разворо́вывать** impf loot; steal.

разворо́т U-turn; turn; development. **развра́т** depravity, corruption. **развра-ти́ть** (-ащу́) pf, **развраща́ть** impf corrupt; deprave. **развра-**

ничать impf lead a depraved life. **развра́тный** debauched, corrupt. **развращённый** (-ён, -а́) corrupt.

развяза́ть (-яжу́, -я́жешь) pf, **развя́зывать** impf untie; unleash; **~ся** come untied; **~ся** c+instr rid o.s. of. **развя́зка** dénouement; outcome. **развя́зный** overfamiliar.

разгада́ть pf, **разга́дывать** impf solve, guess, interpret. **разга́дка** solution.

разга́р height, climax.

разгиба́ть(ся impf of **разогну́ть(ся**

разглаго́льствовать impf hold forth.

разгла́дить (-а́жу) pf, **разгла́живать** impf smooth out: iron (out).

разгласи́ть (-ашу́) pf, **разглаша́ть** impf divulge; +o+prep trumpet. **разглаше́ние** disclosure.

разгляде́ть (-яжу́) pf, **разгля́дывать** impf make out, discern.

разгне́вать pf anger. **раз|гне́ваться** pf.

разгова́ривать impf talk, converse. **разгово́р** conversation. **разгово́рник** phrase-book. **разгово́рный** colloquial. **разгово́рчивый** talkative.

разго́н dispersal; running start; distance. **разгоня́ть(ся** impf of **разогна́ть(ся**

разгора́живать impf of **разгороди́ть**

разгора́ться impf, **разгоре́ться** (-рю́сь) pf flare up.

разгороди́ть (-ожу́, -о́дишь) pf (impf **разгора́живать**) partition off.

раз|горячи́ть(ся (-чу́(сь) pf.

разграби́ть (-блю) pf plunder, loot. **разграбле́ние** plunder, looting.

разграниче́ние demarcation; differentiation. **разграни́чивать** impf, **разграни́чить** (-чу) pf delimit; differentiate.

разгреба́ть impf, **разгрести́** (-ебу́, -ебёшь; -ёб, -ла́) pf rake or shovel (away).

разгро́м crushing defeat; devastation. havoc. **разгроми́ть** (-млю́) pf rout, defeat.

разгружа́ть impf, **разгрузи́ть** (-ужу́, -у́зишь) pf unload; relieve; **~ся** unload; be relieved. **разгру́зка** unloading; relief.

разгрыза́ть *impf*, раз|гры́зть (-зу́, -зёшь, -ы́з) *pf* crack.

разгу́л revelry; outburst. разгу́ливать *impf* stroll about. разгу́ливаться *impf*, разгуля́ться *pf* spread o.s.; become wide awake; clear up. разгу́льный wild, rakish.

раздава́ть(ся (-даю́(сь, -даёшь(ся) *impf of* разда́ть(ся

раз|дави́ть (-влю́, -вишь) *pf*. разда́вливать *impf* crush; run over.

разда́ть (-а́м, -а́шь, -а́ст, -ади́м; ро́здал *or* раздал, -а́, -о) *pf* (*impf* раздава́ть) distribute, give out; ~ся be heard; resound; ring out; make way; expand; put on weight. разда́ча distribution. раздаю́ *etc.*: *see* раздава́ть

раздва́ивать(ся *impf of* раздвои́ть(ся

раздвига́ть *impf*, раздви́нуть (-ну) *pf* move apart; ~ся move apart. раздвижно́й expanding; sliding.

раздвое́ние division; split; ~ ли́чности split personality. раздво́енный forked; cloven; split. раздвои́ть (*impf* раздва́ивать) divide into two; bisect; ~ся fork; split.

раздева́лка cloakroom. раздева́ть(ся *impf of* разде́ть(ся

разде́л division; section.

разде́латься *pf* +*c* +*instr* finish with; settle accounts with.

разделе́ние division. раздели́мый divisible. раз|дели́ть (-лю́, -лишь) *pf*, разделя́ть *impf* divide; separate; share; ~ся divide; be divided; be divisible; separate. разде́льный separate.

разде́ну *etc.*: *see* разде́ть. раздеру́ *etc.*: *see* разодра́ть

разде́ть (-де́ну) *pf* (*impf* раздева́ть) undress; ~ся undress; take off one's coat.

раздира́ть *impf of* разодра́ть

раздобыва́ть *impf*, раздобы́ть (-бу́ду) *pf* get, get hold of.

раздо́лье expanse; liberty. раздо́льный free.

раздо́р discord.

раздоса́довать *pf* vex.

раздража́ть *impf*, раздражи́ть (-жу́) *pf* irritate; annoy; ~ся get annoyed. раздраже́ние irritation. раздражи́тельный irritable.

раз|дроби́ть (-блю́) *pf*, раздробля́ть *impf* break; smash to pieces.

раздува́ть(ся *impf of* разду́ть(ся

разду́мать *pf*, разду́мывать *impf* change one's mind; ponder. разду́мье meditation; thought.

разду́ть (-у́ю) *pf* (*impf* раздува́ть) blow; fan; exaggerate; whip up; swell; ~ся swell.

разева́ть *impf of* рази́нуть

разжа́лобить (-блю) *pf* move (to pity).

разжа́ловать *pf* demote.

разжа́ть (-зожму́, -мёшь) *pf* (*impf* разжима́ть) unclasp, open; release.

разжева́ть (-жую́, -жуёшь) *pf*, разжёвывать *impf* chew.

разже́чь (-зожгу́, -зожжёшь; -жёг, -зожгла́) *pf*, разжига́ть *impf* kindle; rouse.

разжима́ть *impf of* разжа́ть. раз|жире́ть (-е́ю) *pf*.

рази́нуть (-ну) *pf* (*impf* разева́ть) open; ~ рот gape. рази́ня *m & f* scatter-brain.

рази́тельный striking. рази́ть (ражу́) *impf* (*pf* по~) strike.

разлага́ть(ся *impf of* разложи́ть(ся

разла́д discord; disorder.

разла́мывать(ся *impf of* разлома́ть(ся, разломи́ть(ся. разлёгся *etc.*: *see* разле́чься

разлеза́ться *impf*, разле́зться (-зется; -ле́зся) *pf* come to pieces; fall apart.

разлета́ться *impf*, разлете́ться (-лечу́сь) *pf* fly away; scatter; shatter; rush.

разле́чься (-ля́гусь; -лёгся, -гла́сь) *pf* stretch out.

разли́в bottling; flood; overflow. разлива́ть *impf*, разли́ть (-золью́, -зольёшь; -и́л, -а́, -о) *pf* pour out; spill; flood (with); ~ся spill; overflow; spread. разливно́й draught.

различа́ть *impf*, различи́ть (-чу́) *pf* distinguish; discern; ~ся differ. разли́чие distinction; difference. различи́тельный distinctive, distinguishing. разли́чный different.

разложе́ние decomposition; decay; disintegration. разложи́ть (-жу́, -жишь) *pf* (*impf* разлага́ть, раскла́дывать) put away; spread (out); distribute; break down; decompose;

resolve; corrupt; ~ся decompose; become demoralized; be corrupted; disintegrate, go to pieces.

разло́м breaking; break. **разлома́ть, разломи́ть** (-млю́, -мишь) pf (impf **разла́мывать**) break to pieces; pull down; ~ся break to pieces.

разлу́ка separation. **разлуча́ть** impf, **разлучи́ть** (-чу́) pf separate, part; ~ся separate, part.

разлюби́ть (-блю́, -бишь) pf stop loving or liking.

разля́гусь etc.: see **разле́чься**

разма́зать (-а́жу) pf, **разма́зывать** impf spread, smear.

разма́лывать impf of **размоло́ть**

разма́тывать impf of **размота́ть**

разма́х sweep; swing; span; scope. **разма́хивать** impf +instr swing; brandish. **разма́хиваться** impf, **размахну́ться** (-ну́сь, -нёшься) pf swing one's arm. **разма́шистый** sweeping.

размежева́ние demarcation, delimitation. **размежева́ть** (-жу́ю) pf, **размежёвывать** impf delimit.

размёл etc.: see **размести́**

размельча́ть impf, **раз**|**мельчи́ть** (-чу́) pf crush, pulverize.

размелю́ etc.: see **размоло́ть**

разме́н exchange. **разме́нивать** impf, **разменя́ть** pf change; ~ся +instr exchange; dissipate. **разме́нная моне́та** (small) change.

разме́р size; measurement; amount; scale, extent; pl proportions. **разме́ренный** measured. **разме́рить** pf, **размеря́ть** impf measure.

размести́ (-ету́, -ете́шь; -мёл, -а́) pf (impf **размета́ть**) sweep clear; sweep away.

размести́ть (-ещу́) pf (impf **размеща́ть**) place, accommodate; distribute; ~ся take one's seat.

размета́ть impf of **размести́**

разме́тить (-е́чу) pf, **размеча́ть** impf mark.

разме́шать pf, **разме́шивать** impf stir (in).

размеща́ть(ся impf of **размести́ть(ся. размеще́ние** placing; accommodation; distribution. **размещу́** etc.: see **размести́ть**

размина́ть(ся impf of **размя́ть(ся**

разми́нка limbering up.

размину́ться (-ну́сь, -нёшься) pf pass; +c+instr pass; miss.

размножа́ть impf, **размно́жить** (-жу) pf multiply, duplicate; breed; ~ся multiply; breed.

размозжи́ть (-жу́) pf smash.

размо́лвка tiff.

размоло́ть (-мелю́, -ме́лешь) pf (impf **размалывать**) grind.

размора́живать impf, **разморо́зить** (-о́жу) pf unfreeze, defrost; ~ся unfreeze; defrost.

размота́ть pf (impf **разма́тывать**) unwind.

размыва́ть impf, **размы́ть** (-о́ет) pf wash away; erode.

размыка́ть impf of **разомкну́ть**

размышле́ние reflection; meditation. **размышля́ть** impf reflect, ponder.

размягча́ть impf, **размягчи́ть** (-чу́) pf soften; ~ся soften.

размяка́ть impf, **размя́кнуть** (-ну; -мя́к) pf soften.

раз|**мя́ть** (-зомну́, -зомнёшь) pf (impf also **размина́ть**) knead; mash; ~ся stretch one's legs; limber up.

разна́шивать impf of **разноси́ть**

разнести́ (-су́, -сёшь; -ёс, -ла́) pf (impf **разноси́ть**) carry; deliver; spread; note down; smash; scold; scatter; impers make puffy, swell.

разнима́ть impf of **разня́ть**

ра́зниться impf differ. **ра́зница** difference.

разно- in comb different, vari-, hetero-. **разнобо́й** lack of co-ordination; difference. **~ви́дность** variety. **~гла́сие** disagreement; discrepancy. **~обра́зие** variety, diversity. **~обра́зный** various, diverse. **~речи́вый** contradictory. **~ро́дный** heterogeneous. **~сторо́нний** many-sided; versatile. **~цве́тный** variegated. **~шёрстный** of different colours; ill-assorted.

разноси́ть[1] (-ошу́, -о́сишь) pf (impf **разна́шивать**) wear in.

разноси́ть[2] (-ошу́, -о́сишь) impf of **разнести́. разно́ска** delivery.

ра́зность difference.

разно́счик pedlar.

разношу́ etc.: see **разноси́ть**

разну́зданный unbridled.

ра́зн|**ый** different; various; ~ое sb

various things.

разню́хать *pf*, **разню́хивать** *impf* smell out.

разня́ть (-ниму́, -ни́мешь; ро́з- *or* разня́л, -а́, -о) *pf* (*impf* **разнима́ть**) take to pieces; separate.

разоблача́ть *impf*, **разоблачи́ть** (-чу́) *pf* expose. **разоблаче́ние** exposure.

разобра́ть (-зберу́, -рёшь; -а́л, -а́, -о) *pf* (*impf* **разбира́ть**) take to pieces; buy up; sort out; investigate; analyse; understand; ~**ся** sort things out; +**в**+*prep* investigate, look into; understand.

разобща́ть *impf*, **разобщи́ть** (-щу́) *pf* separate; estrange, alienate.

разобью́ *etc.*: *see* **разби́ть. разовью́** *etc.*: *see* **развить.**

ра́зовый single.

разогна́ть (-згоню́, -о́нишь; -гна́л, -а́, -о) *pf* (*impf* **разгоня́ть**) scatter; disperse; dispel; drive fast; ~**ся** gather speed.

разогну́ть (-ну́, -нёшь) *pf* (*impf* **разги-ба́ть**) unbend, straighten; ~**ся** straighten up.

разогрева́ть *impf*, **разогре́ть** (-е́ю) *pf* warm up.

разоде́ть(ся (-е́ну(сь) *pf* dress up.

разодра́ть (-здеру́, -рёшь; -а́л, -а́, -о) *pf* (*impf* **раздира́ть**) tear (up); lacerate.

разожгу́ *etc.*: *see* **разже́чь. разожму́** *etc.*: *see* **разжа́ть**

разо|зли́ть *pf*.

разойти́сь (-йду́сь, -йдёшься; -ошёл-ся, -ошла́сь) *pf* (*impf* **расходи́ться**) disperse; diverge; radiate; differ; conflict; part; be spent; be sold out.

разолью́ *etc.*: *see* **разли́ть.**

ра́зом *adv* at once, at one go.

разомкну́ть (-ну́, -нёшь) *pf* (*impf* **размыка́ть**) open; break.

разомну́ *etc.*: *see* **размя́ть**

разорва́ть (-ву́, -вёшь; -а́л, -а́, -о) *pf* (*impf* **разрыва́ть**) tear; break (off); blow up; ~**ся** tear; break; explode.

разоре́ние ruin; destruction. **разори́тельный** ruinous; wasteful. **разори́ть** *pf* (*impf* **разоря́ть**) ruin; destroy; ~**ся** ruin o.s.

разоружи́ть (-жу́) *pf* disarm; ~**ся** disarm. **разоруже́ние** disarmament.

разоря́ть(ся *impf of* **разори́ть(ся**

разосла́ть (-ошлю́, -ошлёшь) *pf* (*impf* **рассыла́ть**) distribute, circulate.

разостла́ть, **расстели́ть** (-сстелю́, -те́лешь) *pf* (*impf* **расстила́ть**) spread (out); lay; ~**ся** spread.

разотру́ *etc.*: *see* **растере́ть**

разочарова́ние disappointment.

разочарова́ть *pf*, **разочаро́вывать** *impf* disappoint; ~**ся** be disappointed.

разочту́ *etc.*: *see* **расче́сть. разо-шёлся** *etc.*: *see* **разойти́сь. разо-шлю́** *etc.*: *see* **разосла́ть. разошью́** *etc.*: *see* **расши́ть**

разраба́тывать *impf*, **разрабо́тать** *pf* cultivate; work, exploit; work out; develop. **разрабо́тка** cultivation; exploitation; working out; mining; quarry.

разража́ться *impf*, **разрази́ться** (-ажу́сь) *pf* break out; burst out.

разраста́ться *impf*, **разрасти́сь** (-тётся; -ро́сся, -ла́сь) *pf* grow; spread.

разрежённый (-ён, -á) rarefied.

разре́з cut; section; point of view. **разре́зать** (-е́жу) *pf*, **разреза́ть** *impf* cut; slit.

разреша́ть *impf*, **разреши́ть** (-шу́) *pf* (+*dat*) allow; solve; settle; ~**ся** be allowed; be solved; be settled. **разреше́ние** permission; permit; solution; settlement. **разреши́мый** solvable.

разро́зненный uncoordinated; odd; incomplete.

разро́сся *etc.*: *see* **разрасти́сь. разро́ю** *etc.*: *see* **разры́ть**

разруба́ть *impf*, **разруби́ть** (-блю́, -бишь) *pf* cut; chop up.

разру́ха ruin, collapse. **разруша́ть** *impf*, **разру́шить** (-шу) *pf* destroy; demolish; ruin; ~**ся** go to ruin, collapse. **разруше́ние** destruction. **разруши́тельный** destructive.

разры́в break; gap; rupture; burst. **разрыва́ть**¹(**ся** *impf of* **разо-рва́ть(ся**

разрыва́ть² *impf of* **разры́ть**

разрывно́й explosive.

разрыда́ться *pf* burst into tears.

разры́ть (-ро́ю) *pf* (*impf* **разрыва́ть**) dig (up).

раз|рыхли́ть *pf*, **разрыхля́ть** *impf* loosen; hoe.

разря́д[1] category; class.

разря́д[2] discharge. разряди́ть (-яжу́, -я́дишь) *pf* (*impf* разряжа́ть) unload; discharge; space out; ~ся run down; clear, ease. разря́дка spacing (out); discharging; unloading; relieving.

разряжа́ть(ся *impf of* разряди́ть(ся

разубеди́ть (-ежу́) *pf*, разубежда́ть *impf* dissuade; ~ся change one's mind.

разува́ться *impf of* разу́ться

разуве́рить *pf*, разуверя́ть *impf* dissuade, undeceive; ~ся (в+*prep*) lose faith (in).

разузнава́ть (-наю́, -наёшь) *impf*, разузна́ть *pf* (try to) find out.

разукра́сить (-а́шу) *pf*, разукра́шивать *impf* adorn, embellish.

ра́зум reason; intellect. разуме́ться (-е́ется) *impf* be understood, be meant; (само́ собо́й) разуме́ется of course; it goes without saying. разу́мный rational, intelligent; sensible; reasonable; wise.

разу́ться (-у́юсь) *pf* (*impf* разува́ться) take off one's shoes.

разу́чивать *impf*, разучи́ть (-чу́, -чишь) *pf* learn (up). разу́чиваться *impf*, разучи́ться (-чу́сь, -чишься) *pf* forget (how to).

разъеда́ть *impf of* разъе́сть

разъедини́ть *pf*, разъединя́ть *impf* separate; disconnect.

разъе́дусь *etc.*: see разъе́хаться

разъе́зд departure; siding (track); mounted patrol; *pl* travel; journeys. разъездно́й travelling. разъезжа́ть *impf* drive *or* ride about; travel; ~ся *impf of* разъе́хаться

разъе́сть (-е́ст, -едя́т; -е́л) *pf* (*impf* разъеда́ть) eat away; corrode.

разъе́хаться (-е́дусь) *pf* (*impf* разъезжа́ться) depart; separate; pass (one another); miss one another.

разъярённый (-ён, -а́) furious. разъяри́ть *pf*, разъяря́ть *impf* infuriate; ~ся get furious.

разъясне́ние explanation; interpretation. разъясни́тельный explanatory. разъясни́ть *pf*, разъясня́ть *impf* explain; interpret; ~ся become clear, be cleared up.

разыгра́ть *pf*, разы́грывать *impf* perform; draw; raffle; play a trick on;

~ся get up; run high.

разыска́ть (-ыщу́, -ы́щешь) *pf* find. разы́скивать *impf* search for.

рай (*loc* -ю́) paradise; garden of Eden.

райко́м district committee.

райо́н region. райо́нный district.

ра́йский heavenly.

рак crayfish; cancer; Cancer.

раке́та[1], раке́тка racket.

раке́та[2] rocket; missile; flare.

ра́ковина shell; sink.

ра́ковый cancer; cancerous.

раку́шка cockle-shell, mussel.

ра́ма frame. ра́мка frame; *pl* framework.

ра́мпа footlights.

ра́на wound. ране́ние wounding; wound. ра́неный wounded; injured.

ранг rank.

ра́нец (-нца) knapsack; satchel.

ра́нить *impf & pf* wound; injure.

ра́нний early. ра́но *adv* early. ра́ньше *adv* earlier; before; formerly.

папи́ра foil.

ра́порт report. рапортова́ть *impf & pf* report.

ра́са race. раси́зм, racism. раси́стский racist.

раска́иваться *impf of* раска́яться

раскалённый (-ён, -а́) scorching; incandescent. раскали́ть *pf* (*impf* раскаля́ть) make red-hot; ~ся become red-hot. раска́лывать(ся *impf of* расколо́ть(ся. раскаля́ть(ся *impf of* раскали́ть(ся. раска́пывать *impf of* раскопа́ть

раска́т roll, peal. раската́ть *pf*, раска́тывать *impf* roll (out), smooth out, level; drive *or* ride (about). раска́тистый rolling, booming. раскати́ться (-ачу́сь, -а́тишься) *pf*, раска́тываться *impf* gather speed; roll away; peal, boom.

раскача́ть *pf*, раска́чивать *impf* swing; rock; ~ся swing, rock.

раска́яние repentance. рас|ка́яться *pf* (*impf also* раска́иваться) repent.

расквита́ться *pf* settle accounts.

раски́дывать *impf*, раски́нуть (-ну) *pf* stretch (out); spread; pitch; ~ся spread out; sprawl.

раскладно́й folding. расклад́ушка camp-bed. раскла́дывать *impf of* разложи́ть

раскла́няться pf bow; take leave.

расклеи́вать impf, **расклеи́ть** pf unstick; stick (up); **~ся** come unstuck.

раско́л split; schism. **рас|коло́ть** (-лю́, -лешь) pf (impf also **раска́лывать**) split; break; disrupt; **~ся** split. **раско́льник** dissenter.

раскопа́ть pf (impf **раска́пывать**) dig up, unearth, excavate. **раско́пки** (-пок) pl excavations.

раско́сый slanting.

раскра́ивать impf of **раскрои́ть**

раскра́сить (-а́шу) pf, impf **раскра́шивать** paint, colour.

раскрепости́ть (-ощу́) pf, **раскрепоща́ть** impf liberate. **раскрепоще́ние** emancipation.

раскритикова́ть pf criticize harshly.

раскрои́ть pf (impf **раскра́ивать**) cut out.

раскрою́ etc.: see **раскры́ть**

раскрути́ть (-учу́, -у́тишь) pf, **раскру́чивать** impf untwist; **~ся** come untwisted.

раскрыва́ть impf, **раскры́ть** (-о́ю) pf open; expose; reveal; discover; **~ся** open; uncover o.s.; come to light.

раскупа́ть impf, **раскупи́ть** (-у́пит) pf buy up.

раску́поривать impf, **раску́порить** pf uncork, open.

раскуси́ть (-ушу́, -у́сишь) pf, **раску́сывать** impf bite through; see through.

ра́совый racial.

распа́д disintegration; collapse. **распада́ться** impf of **распа́сться**

распако́вывать pf, **распако́вывать** impf unpack.

распа́рывать(ся impf of **распоро́ть(ся**

распа́сться (-аде́тся) pf (impf **распада́ться**) disintegrate, fall to pieces.

распаха́ть (-ашу́, -а́шешь) pf, **распа́хивать**[1] impf plough up.

распа́хивать[2] impf, **распахну́ть** (-ну́, -нёшь) pf throw open; **~ся** fly open, swing open.

распашо́нка baby's vest.

распева́ть impf sing.

распеча́тать pf, **распеча́тывать** impf open; unseal.

распи́ливать impf, **распили́ть** (-лю́,

-лишь) pf saw up.

распина́ть impf of **распя́ть**

расписа́ние time-table. **расписа́ть** (-ишу́, -и́шешь) pf, **распи́сывать** impf enter; assign; paint; paint; register one's marriage; +в+prep sign for; acknowledge. **распи́ска** receipt. **расписно́й** painted, decorated.

распиха́ть pf, **распи́хивать** impf push, shove, stuff.

рас|пла́вить (-влю) pf, **расплавля́ть** impf melt, fuse. **распла́вленный** molten.

распла́каться (-а́чусь) pf burst into tears.

распласта́ть pf, **распла́стывать** impf spread; flatten; split; **~ся** sprawl.

распла́та payment; retribution. **расплати́ться** (-ачу́сь, -а́тишься) pf, **распла́чиваться** impf (+с+instr) pay off; get even; +за+acc pay for.

расплеска́ть(ся (-ещу́(сь, -е́щешь(ся) pf, **расплёскивать(ся** impf spill.

расплести́ (-ету́, -етёшь; -ёл, -а́) pf, **расплета́ть** impf unplait; untwist.

рас|плоди́ть(ся (-ожу́(сь) pf.

расплыва́ться impf, **расплы́ться** (-ыве́тся; -ы́лся, -а́сь) pf run. **расплы́вчатый** indistinct; vague.

расплю́щивать impf, **расплю́щить** (-щу) pf flatten out, hammer out.

распну́ etc.: see **распя́ть**

распознава́ть (-наю́, -наёшь) impf, **распозна́ть** pf recognize, identify; diagnose.

располага́ть impf (pf **расположи́ть**) +instr have at one's disposal. **располага́ться** impf of **расположи́ться**

располза́ться impf, **расползти́сь** (-зётся; -о́лзся, -зла́сь) pf crawl (away); give at the seams.

расположе́ние disposition; arrangement; situation; tendency; liking; mood. **расположенный** disposed, inclined. **расположи́ть** (-жу́, -жишь) pf (impf **располага́ть**) dispose; set out; win over; **~ся** settle down.

распо́рка cross-bar, strut.

рас|поро́ть (-рю́, -решь) pf (impf also **распа́рывать**) unpick, rip; **~ся** rip, come undone.

распоряди́тель m manager. **распоряди́тельный** capable; efficient.

распоряди́ться (-яжу́сь) pf, распоряжа́ться impf order, give orders; see; +instr manage, deal with.

распоря́док (-дка) order; routine.

распоряже́ние order; instruction; disposal, command.

распра́ва violence; reprisal.

распра́вить (-влю) pf, расправля́ть impf straighten; smooth out; spread.

распра́виться (-влюсь) pf, расправля́ться impf с+instr deal with severely; make short work of.

распределе́ние distribution; allocation. распредели́тель m distributor. распредели́тельный distributive, distributing; ~ щит switchboard.

распредели́ть pf, распределя́ть impf distribute; allocate.

распродава́ть (-даю́, -даёшь) impf, распрода́ть (-а́м, -а́шь, -а́ст, -ади́м; -о́дал, -а́, -о) pf sell off; sell out. распрода́жа (clearance) sale.

распростёртый outstretched; prostrate.

распростране́ние spreading; dissemination. распространённый (-ён, -а́) widespread, prevalent. распространи́ть pf, распространя́ть impf spread; ~ся spread.

ра́спря (gen pl -ей) quarrel.

распряга́ть impf, распря́чь (-ягу́, -яжёшь; -яг, -ла́) pf unharness.

распрями́ться pf, распрямля́ться impf straighten up.

распуска́ть impf, распусти́ть (-ущу́, -у́стишь) pf dismiss; dissolve; let out; relax; let get out of hand; melt; spread; ~ся open; come loose; dissolve; melt; get out of hand; let o.s. go.

распу́тать pf (impf распу́тывать) untangle; unravel.

распу́тица season of bad roads.

распу́тный dissolute. распу́тство debauchery.

распу́тывать impf of распу́тать распу́тье crossroads.

распуха́ть impf, распу́хнуть (-ну; -у́х) pf swell (up).

распу́щенный undisciplined; spoilt; dissolute.

распыли́тель m spray, atomizer. распыли́ть pf, распыля́ть impf spray; pulverize; disperse.

распя́тие crucifixion; crucifix. распя́ть (-пну́, -пнёшь) pf (impf распина́ть) crucify.

расса́да seedlings. рассади́ть (-ажу́, -а́дишь) pf, расса́живать impf plant out; seat; separate, seat separately.

расса́живаться impf of рассе́сться. расса́сываться impf of рассосаться

рассвести́ (-етёт; -ело́) pf, рассвета́ть impf dawn. рассве́т dawn.

рас|свирипе́ть (-е́ю) pf.

расседла́ть pf unsaddle.

рассе́ивание dispersal, scattering. рассе́ивать(ся impf of рассе́ять(ся

рассека́ть impf of рассе́чь

расселе́ние settling, resettlement; separation.

рассе́лина cleft, fissure.

рассели́ть pf, расселя́ть impf settle, resettle; separate.

рас|серди́ть(ся (-жу́(сь, -рдишь(ся) pf.

рассе́сться (-ся́дусь) pf (impf расса́живаться) take seats; sprawl.

рассе́чь (-еку́, -ечёшь; -ёк, -ла́) pf (impf рассека́ть) cut (through); cleave.

рассе́янность absent-mindedness; dispersion. рассе́янный absent-minded; diffused; scattered. рассе́ять (-е́ю) pf (impf рассе́ивать) disperse, scatter; dispel; ~ся disperse, scatter; clear; divert o.s.

расска́з story; account. рассказа́ть (-ажу́, -а́жешь) pf, расска́зывать impf tell, recount. расска́зчик story-teller, narrator.

рассла́бить (-блю) pf, рассла́блять impf weaken.

рассла́ивать(ся impf of рассло́йться

рассле́дование investigation, examination; inquiry; произвести́ ~+gen hold an inquiry into. рассле́довать impf & pf investigate, look into, hold an inquiry into.

рассло́йть pf (impf рассла́ивать) divide into layers; ~ся become stratified; flake off.

рассл́ышать (-шу) pf catch.

рассма́тривать impf of рассмотре́ть; examine; consider.

рас|смеши́ть (-шу́) pf.

рассмея́ться (-ею́сь, -еёшься) pf

burst out laughing.

рассмотре́ние examination; consideration. **рассмотре́ть** (-рю́, -ришь) *pf* (*impf* **рассма́тривать**) examine, consider; discern, make out.

рассова́ть (-сую́, -суёшь) *pf*, **рассо́вывать** *impf* **по**+*dat* shove into.

рассо́л brine; pickle.

рассо́риться *pf* с+*instr* fall out with.

рас|сортирова́ть *pf*, **рассортиро́вывать** *impf* sort out.

рассоса́ться (-сётся) *pf* (*impf* **расса́сываться**) resolve.

рассо́хнуться (-нется, -о́хся) *pf* (*impf* **рассыха́ться**) crack.

расспра́шивать *impf*, **расспроси́ть** (-ошу́, -о́сишь) *pf* question; make inquiries of.

рассро́чить (-чу) *pf* spread (over a period). **рассро́чка** instalment.

расстава́ние parting. **расстава́ться** (-таю́сь, -таёшься) *impf* of **расста́ться**

расста́вить (-влю) *pf*, **расставля́ть** *impf* place, arrange; move apart. **расстано́вка** arrangement; pause.

расста́ться (-а́нусь) *pf* (*impf* **расстава́ться**) part, separate.

расстёгивать *impf*, **расстегну́ть** (-ну́, -нёшь) *pf* undo, unfasten; ~ся come undone; undo one's coat.

расстели́ть(ся, *etc*.: *see* **разостла́ть(ся. расстила́ть(ся**, -а́ю(сь *impf of* **разостла́ть(ся**

расстоя́ние distance.

расстра́ивать(ся *impf* of **расстро́ить(ся**

расстре́л execution by firing squad. **расстре́ливать** *impf*, **расстреля́ть** *pf* shoot.

расстро́енный disordered; upset; out of tune. **расстро́ить** *pf* (*impf* **расстра́ивать**) upset; thwart; disturb; throw into confusion; put out of tune; ~ся be upset; get out of tune; fall into confusion; fall through. **расстро́йство** upset; disarray; confusion; frustration.

расступа́ться *impf*, **расступи́ться** (-у́пится) *pf* part, make way.

рассуди́тельный reasonable; sensible. **рассуди́ть** (-ужу́, -у́дишь) *pf* judge; think; decide. **рассу́док** (-дка) *pf* reason; intellect. **рассужда́ть** *impf* reason; +о+*prep* discuss. **рассу**

жде́ние reasoning; discussion; argument.

рассую́ *etc*.: *see* **рассова́ть**

рассчи́танный deliberate; intended. **рассчита́ть** *pf*, **рассчи́тывать** *impf*, **расче́сть** (разочту́, -тёшь; расчёл, разочла́) *pf* calculate; count; depend; ~ся settle accounts.

рассыла́ть *impf of* **разосла́ть. рассы́лка** distribution. **рассы́льный** *sb* delivery man.

рассы́пать (-плю) *pf*, **рассыпа́ть** *impf* spill; scatter; ~ся spill, scatter; spread out; crumble. **рассы́пчатый** friable; crumbly.

рассыха́ться *impf of* **рассо́хнуться. рассяду́сь** *etc*.: *see* **рассе́сться. раста́лкивать** *impf of* **растолка́ть. раста́пливать(ся** *impf of* **растопи́ть(ся**

растаска́ть *pf*, **раста́скивать** *impf*, **растащи́ть** (-щу́, -щишь) *pf* pilfer, filch.

растащи́ть *see* **растаска́ть. рас|та́ять** (-а́ю) *pf*.

раство́р[2] opening, span. **раство́р**[1] solution; mortar. **раствори́мый** soluble. **раствори́тель** *m* solvent.

раствори́ть[1] *pf* (*impf* **растворя́ть**) dissolve; ~ся dissolve.

раствори́ть[2] (-рю́, -ришь) *pf* (*impf* **растворя́ть**) open; ~ся open. **растворя́ть(ся** *impf of* **раствори́ть(ся. растека́ться** *impf of* **расте́чься**

расте́ние plant.

растере́ть (разотру́, -трёшь; растёр) *pf* (*impf* **растира́ть**) grind; spread; rub; massage.

растерза́ть *pf*, **расте́рзывать** *impf* tear to pieces.

расте́рянность confusion, dismay. **расте́рянный** confused, dismayed. **растеря́ть** *pf* lose; ~ся get lost; lose one's head.

расте́чься (-ечётся, -еку́тся; -тёкся, -ла́сь) *pf* (*impf* **растека́ться**) run; spread.

расти́ (-ту́, -тёшь; рос, -ла́) *impf* grow; grow up.

растира́ние grinding; rubbing, massage. **растира́ть(ся** *impf of* **растере́ть(ся**

расти́тельность vegetation; hair. **расти́тельный** vegetable. **расти́ть**

(ращу́) *impf* bring up; train; grow.

растлева́ть *impf*, **растли́ть** *pf* seduce; corrupt.

растолка́ть *pf* (*impf* **раста́лкивать**) push apart; shake.

растолкова́ть *pf*, **растолко́вывать** *impf* explain.

рас|толо́чь (-лку́, -лчёшь; -ло́к, -лкла́) *pf*.

растолсте́ть (-е́ю) *pf* put on weight.

растопи́ть[1] (-плю́, -пишь) *pf* (*impf* **раста́пливать**) melt; thaw; ~ся melt.

растопи́ть[2] (-плю́, -пишь) *pf* (*impf* **раста́пливать**) light, kindle; ~ся begin to burn.

растопта́ть (-пчу́, -пчешь) *pf* trample, stamp on.

расторга́ть *impf*, **расто́ргнуть** (-ну; -óрг) *pf* annul, dissolve. **расторже́ние** annulment, dissolution.

расторо́пный quick; efficient.

расточа́ть *impf*, **расточи́ть** (-чу́) *pf* squander, dissipate. **расточи́тельный** extravagant, wasteful.

растрави́ть (-влю́, -вишь) *pf*, **растравля́ть** *impf* irritate.

растра́та spending; waste; embezzlement. **растра́тить** (-а́чу) *pf*, **растра́чивать** *impf* spend; waste; embezzle.

растрёпанный dishevelled; tattered. **рас|трепа́ть** (-плю́, -плешь) *pf* disarrange; tatter.

растре́скаться *pf*, **растре́скиваться** *impf* crack, chap.

растро́гать *pf* move, touch; ~ся be moved.

расту́щий growing.

растя́гивать *impf*, **растяну́ть** (-ну́, -нешь) *pf* stretch (out); strain, sprain; drag out; ~ся stretch; drag on; sprawl. **растяже́ние** tension; strain, sprain. **растяжи́мый** tensile; stretchable. **растя́нутый** stretched; long-winded.

рас|фасова́ть *pf*.

расформирова́ть *pf*, **расформиро́вывать** *impf* break up; disband.

расха́живать *impf* walk about; pace up and down.

расхва́ливать *impf*, **расхвали́ть** (-лю́, -лишь) *pf* lavish praises on.

расхвата́ть *pf*, **расхва́тывать** *impf* seize on, buy up.

расхити́тель *m* embezzler. **расхи́тить** (-и́щу) *pf*, **расхища́ть** *impf* steal, misappropriate. **расхище́ние** misappropriation.

расхля́банный loose; lax.

расхо́д expenditure; consumption; *pl* expenses, outlay. **расходи́ться** (-ожу́сь, -о́дишься) *impf of* **разойти́сь**. **расхо́дование** expense, expenditure. **расхо́довать** *impf* (*pf* из~) spend; consume. **расхожде́ние** divergence.

расхола́живать *impf*, **расхолоди́ть** (-ожу́) *pf* damp the ardour of.

расхоте́ть (-очу́, -о́чешь, -оти́м) *pf* no longer want.

расхохота́ться (-очу́сь, -о́чешься) *pf* burst out laughing.

расцара́пать *pf* scratch (all over).

расцвести́ (-ету́, -етёшь; -ёл, -а́) *pf*, **расцвета́ть** *impf* blossom; flourish. **расцве́т** blossoming (out); flowering, heyday.

расцве́тка colours; colouring.

расце́нивать *impf*, **расцени́ть** (-ню́, -нишь) *pf* estimate, value; consider. **расце́нка** valuation; price; (wage-) rate.

расцепи́ть (-плю́, -пишь) *pf*, **расцепля́ть** *impf* uncouple, unhook.

расчеса́ть (-ешу́, -е́шешь) *pf* (*impf* **расчёсывать**) comb; scratch. **расчёска** comb.

расче́сть etc.: *see* **рассчита́ть**. **расчёсывать** *impf of* **расчеса́ть**

расчёт[1] calculation; estimate; gain; settlement. **расчётливый** thrifty; careful. **расчётный** calculation; pay; accounts; calculated.

расчи́стить (-и́щу) *pf*, **расчища́ть** *impf* clear; ~ся clear. **расчи́стка** clearing.

рас|члени́ть (-ню́) *pf*, **расчленя́ть** *impf* dismember; divide.

расшата́ть *pf*, **расша́тывать** *impf* shake loose, make rickety; impair.

расшевели́ть (-лю́, -éли́шь) *pf* stir; rouse.

расшиба́ть *impf*, **расшиби́ть** (-бу́, -бёшь; -и́б) *pf* smash to pieces; hurt; stub; ~ся hurt o.s.

расшива́ть *impf of* **расши́ть**

расшире́ние widening; expansion; dilation, dilatation. **расши́рить** *pf*, **расширя́ть** *impf* widen; enlarge;

expand; ~ся broaden, widen; expand, dilate.

расши́ть (разошью́, -шьёшь) pf (impf расшива́ть) embroider; unpick.

расшифрова́ть pf, расшифро́вывать impf decipher.

расшнурова́ть pf, расшнуро́вывать impf unlace.

расще́лина crevice.

расщепи́ть (-плю́) pf, расщепля́ть impf split; ~ся split. расщепле́ние splitting; fission.

ратифици́ровать impf & pf ratify.

рать army, battle.

ра́унд round.

рафини́рованный refined.

рацио́н ration.

рационализа́ция rationalization. рационализи́ровать impf & pf rationalize. рациона́льный rational; efficient.

ра́ция walkie-talkie.

рвану́ться (-ну́сь, -нёшься) pf dart, dash.

рва́ный torn; lacerated. рвать¹ (рву, рвёшь; рвал, -á, -о) impf tear (out); pull out; pick; blow up; break off; ~ся break; tear; burst, explode; be bursting.

рвать² (рвёт; рва́ло) impf (pf вы́~) impers+acc vomit.

рвач (-á) self-seeker.

рве́ние zeal.

рво́та vomiting.

реабилита́ция rehabilitation. реабилити́ровать impf & pf rehabilitate.

реаги́ровать impf (pf от~, про~) react.

реакти́в reagent. реакти́вный reactive; jet-propelled. реа́ктор reactor.

реакционе́р reactionary. реакцио́нный reactionary. реа́кция reaction.

реализа́ция realization. реали́зм realism. реализова́ть impf & pf realize. реали́ст realist. реалисти́ческий realistic.

реа́льность reality; practicability. реа́льный real; practicable.

ребёнок (-нка; pl ребя́та, -я́т and де́ти, -е́й) child; infant.

ребро́ (pl рёбра, -бер) rib; edge.

ребя́та (-я́т) pl children; guys; lads. ребя́ческий child's; childish. ребя́чество childishness. ребя́читься

(-чусь) impf be childish.

рёв roar; howl.

рева́нш revenge; return match.

ревера́нс curtsey.

реве́ть (-ву́, -вёшь) impf roar; bellow; howl.

ревизио́нный inspection; auditing. реви́зия inspection; audit; revision. ревизо́р inspector.

ревмати́зм rheumatism.

ревни́вый jealous. ревнова́ть impf (pf при~) be jealous. ре́вностный zealous. ре́вность jealousy.

револьве́р revolver.

революционе́р revolutionary. революцио́нный revolutionary. револю́ция revolution.

рега́та regatta.

ре́гби neut indecl rugby.

ре́гент regent.

регио́н region. региона́льный regional.

регистра́тор registrar. регистра́тура registry. регистра́ция registration. регистри́ровать impf & pf (pf also за~) register, record; ~ся register; register one's marriage.

регла́мент standing orders; time-limit. регламента́ция regulation. регламенти́ровать impf & pf regulate.

регресси́ровать impf regress.

регули́ровать impf (pf от~, у~) regulate; adjust. регулиро́вщик traffic controller. регуля́рный regular. регуля́тор regulator.

редакти́ровать impf (pf от~) edit. реда́ктор editor. реда́кторский editorial. редакцио́нный editorial, editing. реда́кция editorial staff; editorial office; editing.

реде́ть (-е́ет) impf (pf по~) thin (out).

реди́с radishes. реди́ска radish.

ре́дкий (-док, -дка́, -о) thin; sparse; rare. ре́дко adv sparsely; rarely, seldom. ре́дкость rarity.

редколле́гия editorial board.

рее́стр register.

режи́м régime; routine; procedure; regimen; conditions.

режиссёр-(постано́вщик) продуцер; director.

ре́жущий cutting, sharp. ре́зать (ре́жу) impf (pf за~, про~, с~) cut;

engrave; kill, slaughter.

резви́ться (-влю́сь) *impf* gambol, play. **рéзвый** frisky, playful.

резéрв reserve. **резéрвный** reserve; back-up.

резервуáр reservoir.

резéц (-зцá) cutter; chisel; incisor.

резидéнция residence.

резúна rubber. **резúнка** rubber; elastic band. **резúновый** rubber.

рéзкий sharp; harsh; abrupt; shrill. **резнóй** carved. **резня́** carnage.

резолю́ция resolution.

резонáнс resonance; response.

результáт result.

резьбá carving, fretwork.

резюмé *neut indecl* résumé.

рейд¹ roads, roadstead.

рейд² raid.

рéйка lath, rod.

рейс trip; voyage; flight.

рейтýзы (-ýз) *pl* leggings; riding breeches.

рекá (*acc* рéку, *pl* -и, рéкам) river.

рéквием requiem.

реквизúт props.

реклáма advertising, advertisement. **рекламúровать** *impf & pf* advertise. **реклáмный** publicity.

рекомендáтельный of recommendation. **рекомендáция** recommendation; reference. **рекомендовáть** *impf & pf* (*pf also* от~, по~) recommend; ~ся introduce o.s.; be advisable.

реконструúровать *impf & pf* reconstruct. **реконстрýкция** reconstruction.

рекóрд record. **рекóрдный** record, record-breaking. **рекордсмéн, -éнка** record-holder.

рéктор principal (*of university*).

релé (*electr*) *neut indecl* relay.

религиóзный religious. **релúгия** religion.

релúквия relic.

рельéф relief. **рельéфный** relief; raised, bold.

рельс rail.

ремáрка stage direction.

ремéнь (-мня́) *m* strap; belt.

ремéсленник artisan, craftsman. **ремéсленный** handicraft; mechanical. **ремеслó** (*pl* -ёсла, -ёсел) craft; trade.

ремóнт repair(s); maintenance. **ремонтúровать** *impf & pf* (*pf also* от~) repair; recondition. **ремóнтный** repair.

рéнта rent; income. **рентáбельный** paying, profitable.

рентгéн X-rays. **рентгéновский** X-ray. **рентгенóлог** radiologist. **рентгенолóгия** radiology.

реорганизáция reorganization. **реорганизовáть** *impf & pf* reorganize.

рéпа turnip.

репатриúровать *impf & pf* repatriate.

репертуáр repertoire.

репетúровать *impf* (*pf* от~, про~, с~) rehearse; coach. **репетúтор** coach. **репетúция** rehearsal.

репортáж report; reporting. **репортёр** reporter.

репрéссия repression.

репродýктор loud-speaker. **репродýкция** reproduction.

репутáция reputation.

реснúца eyelash.

респýблика republic. **республикáнский** republican.

рессóра spring.

реставрáция restoration. **реставрúровать** *impf & pf* (*pf also* от~) restore.

ресторáн restaurant.

ресýрс resort; *pl* resources.

ретранслятор (radio-)relay.

реферáт synopsis, abstract; paper, essay.

референдум referendum.

рефлéкс reflex. **рефлéктор** reflector.

рефóрма reform. **реформúровать** *impf & pf* reform.

рефрижерáтор refrigerator.

рецензúровать *impf* (*pf* про~) review. **рецéнзия** review.

рецéпт prescription; recipe.

рецидúв relapse. **рецидивúст** recidivist.

речевóй speech; vocal.

рéчка river. **речнóй** river.

речь (*gen pl* -éй) speech.

решáть(ся *impf of* решúть(ся. **решáющий** decisive, deciding. **решéние** decision; solution.

решётка grating; grille; railing; lattice; trellis; fender, (fire)guard; (fire-)

grate; tail. **решето́** (*pl* -ёта) sieve. **решётчатый** lattice, latticed.

реши́мость resoluteness; resolve. **реши́тельно** *adv* resolutely; definitely; absolutely. **реши́тельность** determination. **реши́тельный** definite; decisive. **реши́ть** (-шу́) *pf* (*impf* **реша́ть**) decide; solve; ~**ся** make up one's mind.

ржа́веть (-еет) *impf* (*pf* за~, по~) rust. **ржа́вчина** rust. **ржа́вый** rusty. **ржано́й** rye.

ржать (ржу, ржёшь) *impf* neigh.

ри́млянин (*pl* -яне, -ян), **ри́млянка** Roman. **ри́мский** Roman.

ринг boxing ring.

ри́нуться (-нусь) *pf* rush, dart.

рис rice.

риск risk. **риско́ванный** risky; risqué. **рискова́ть** *impf* run risks; +*instr or inf* risk.

рисова́ние drawing. **рисова́ть** *impf* (*pf* на~) draw; paint; depict; ~**ся** be sllhouetted; appear; pose.

ри́совый rice.

рису́нок (-нка) drawing; figure; pattern, design.

ритм rhythm. **ритми́ческий**, **ритми́чный** rhythmic.

ритуа́л ritual.

риф reef.

ри́фма rhyme. **рифмова́ть** *impf* rhyme; ~**ся** rhyme.

робе́ть (-е́ю) *impf* (*pf* о~) be timid.

ро́бкий (-бок, -бка́, -о) timid, shy. **ро́бость** shyness.

ро́бот robot.

ров (рва, *loc* -у́) ditch.

рове́сник coeval. **ро́вно** *adv* evenly; exactly; absolutely. **ро́вный** flat; even; level; equable; exact; equal. **ровня́ть** *impf* (*pf* с~) even, level.

рог (*pl* -а́, -о́в) horn; antler. **рога́тка** catapult. **рога́тый** horned. **рого́вица** cornea. **рогово́й** horn; horny; horn-rimmed.

рого́жа bast mat(ting).

род (*loc* -у́; *pl* -ы́) family, kin, clan; birth, origin, stock; generation; genus; sort, kind. **роди́льный** maternity. **ро́дина** native land; homeland. **ро́динка** birth-mark. **роди́тели** (-ей) *pl* parents. **роди́тельный** genitive. **роди́тельский** parental. **роди́ть** (рожу́, -и́л, -ила́, -о) *impf* &

pf (*impf also* **рожа́ть**, **рожда́ть**) give birth to; ~**ся** be born.

родни́к (-а́) spring.

родни́ть (*pf* по~) make related, link; ~**ся** become related. **родн|о́й** own; native; home; ~**о́й брат** brother; ~**ые** *sb pl* relatives. **родня́** relative(s); kinsfolk. **родово́й** tribal; generic; gender. **родонача́льник** ancestor; father. **родосло́вн|ый** genealogical; ~**ая** *sb* genealogy, pedigree. **ро́дственник** relative. **ро́дственный** related. **родство́** relationship, kinship. **ро́ды** (-ов) *pl* childbirth; labour.

ро́жа (ugly) mug.

рожа́ть, **рожда́ть(ся** *impf of* **роди́ть(ся**. **рожда́емость** birthrate. **рожде́ние** birth. **рожде́ственский** Christmas. **Рождество́** Christmas.

рожь (ржи) rye.

ро́за rose.

ро́зга (*gen pl* -зог) birch.

ро́здал *etc.*: *see* **разда́ть**

розе́тка electric socket; rosette.

ро́зница retail; **в** ~**у** retail. **ро́зничный** retail. **рознь** difference; dissension.

ро́знял *etc.*: *see* **разня́ть**

ро́зовый pink.

ро́зыгрыш draw; drawn game.

ро́зыск search; inquiry.

рои́ться swarm. **рой** (*loc* -ю́; *pl* -и́, -ёв) swarm.

рок fate.

рокиро́вка castling.

рок-му́зыка rock music.

роково́й fateful; fatal.

ро́кот roar, rumble. **рокота́ть** (-о́чет) *impf* roar, rumble.

ро́лик roller; castor; *pl* roller skates. **роль** (*gen pl* -е́й) role.

ром rum.

рома́н novel; romance. **романи́ст** novelist.

рома́нс (*mus*) romance.

рома́нтик romantic. **рома́нтика** romance. **романти́ческий**, **романти́чный** romantic.

рома́шка camomile.

ромб rhombus.

роня́ть *impf* (*pf* **урони́ть**) drop.

ро́пот murmur, grumble. **ропта́ть** (-пщу́, -пщешь) *impf* murmur, grumble.

рос *etc.: see* **расти́**

роса́ (*pl* -ы) dew. **роси́стый** dewy.

роско́шный luxurious; luxuriant. **ро́скошь** luxury; luxuriance.

ро́слый strapping.

ро́спись painting(s), mural(s).

ро́спуск dismissal; disbandment.

росси́йский Russian. **Росси́я** Russia.

ро́ссыпи *f pl* deposit.

рост growth; increase; height, stature.

ро́стбиф roast beef.

ростовщи́к (-á) usurer, money-lender.

росто́к (-тка́) sprout, shoot.

ро́счерк flourish.

рот (рта, *loc* рту) mouth.

ро́та company.

рота́тор duplicator.

ро́тный company; *sb* company commander.

ротозе́й, -зе́йка gaper, rubberneck; scatter-brain.

ро́ща grove.

ро́ю *etc.: see* **рыть**

роя́ль *m* (grand) piano.

ртуть mercury.

руба́нок (-нка) plane.

руба́ха, руба́шка shirt.

рубе́ж (-á) boundary, border(line); line; **за** ~**о́м** abroad.

рубе́ц (-бца́) scar; weal; hem; tripe.

руби́н ruby. **руби́новый** ruby; ruby-coloured.

руби́ть (-блю́, -бишь) *impf* (*pf* с~) fell; hew, chop; mince; build (of logs).

ру́бище rags.

ру́бка[1] felling; chopping; mincing.

ру́бка[2] deck house; **боева́я** ~ conning-tower; **рулева́я** ~ wheelhouse.

рублёвка one-rouble note. **рублё-вый** (one-)rouble.

ру́бленый minced, chopped; of logs.

рубль (-я́) *m* rouble.

ру́брика rubric, heading.

руба́тый ribbed. **ру́бчик** scar; rib.

ру́гань abuse, swearing. **руга́тель-ный** abusive. **руга́тельство** oath, swear-word. **руга́ть** *impf* (*pf* вы́~, об~, от~) curse, swear at; abuse; ~**ся** curse, swear; swear at one another.

руда́ (*pl* -ы) ore. **рудни́к** (-á) mine, pit. **рудни́чный** mine, pit; ~ **газ** fire-damp. **рудоко́п** miner.

ружи́ный rifle, gun. **ружьё** (*pl* -ья,

-жей, -ьям) gun, rifle.

руи́на *usu pl* ruin.

рука́ (*acc* -у; *pl* -и, рук, -áм) hand; arm; **идти́ по́д руку** с+*instr* walk arm in arm with; **под руко́й** at hand; **руко́й пода́ть** a stone's throw away; **э́то мне на́ руку** that suits me.

рука́в (-á; *pl* -á, -óв) sleeve. **рука-ви́ца** mitten; gauntlet.

руководи́тель *m* leader; manager; instructor; guide. **руководи́ть** (-ожу́) *impf* +*instr* lead; guide; direct, manage. **руково́дство** leadership; guidance; direction; guide; handbook, manual; leaders. **руково́дство-ваться**+*instr* follow; be guided by.

рукоде́лие needlework.

рукомо́йник washstand.

рукопа́шный hand-to-hand.

рукопи́сный manuscript. **ру́копись** manuscript.

рукоплеска́ние applause. **руко-плеска́ть** (-ещу́, -е́щешь) *impf* +*dat* applaud.

рукопожа́тие handshake.

рукоя́тка handle.

рулево́й steering; *sb* helmsman.

руле́тка tape-measure; roulette.

рули́ть *impf* (*pf* вы́~) taxi.

руль (-я́) *m* rudder; helm; (steering-)wheel; handlebar.

румы́н (*gen pl* -ын), ~**ка** Romanian. **Румы́ния** Romania. **румы́нский** Romanian.

румя́на (-я́н) *pl* rouge. **румя́нец** (-нца) (high) colour; flush; blush. **румя́ный** rosy, ruddy.

ру́пор megaphone; mouthpiece.

руса́к (-á) hare.

руса́лка mermaid.

русифици́ровать *impf* & *pf* Russify.

ру́сло river-bed, channel; course.

ру́сский Russian; *sb* Russian.

ру́сый light brown.

Русь (*hist*) Russia.

рути́на routine.

ру́хлядь junk.

ру́хнуть (-ну) *pf* crash down.

руча́ться guarantee. **руча́ться** *impf* (*pf* поручи́ться) +за+*acc* vouch for, guarantee.

руче́й (-чья́) brook.

ру́чка handle; (door-)knob; (chair-)arm. **ручн|о́й** hand; arm; manual;

tame; ∼ые часы́ wrist-watch.

ру́шить (-у) *impf* (*pf* об∼) pull down; ∼ся collapse.

ры́ба fish. **рыба́к** (-а́) fisherman. **рыба́лка** fishing. **рыба́цкий, рыба́чий** fishing. **ры́бий** fish; fishy; ∼ жир cod-liver oil. **ры́бный** fish. **рыболо́в** fisherman. **рыболо́вный** fishing.

рыво́к (-вка́) jerk.

рыда́ние sobbing. **рыда́ть** *impf* sob.

ры́жий (рыж, -а́, -е) red, red-haired; chestnut.

ры́ло snout; mug.

ры́нок (-нка) market; market-place. **ры́ночный** market.

рыса́к (-а́) trotter.

рысь[1] (*loc* -и́) trot; ∼ю, на рыся́х at a trot.

рысь[2] lynx.

рытви́на rut, groove. **ры́ть(ся** (ро́ю(сь) *impf* (*pf* вы́∼, от∼) dig; rummage.

рыхли́ть *impf* (*pf* вз∼, раз∼) loosen. **ры́хлый** (-л, -а́, -о) friable; loose.

ры́царский chivalrous. **ры́царь** *m* knight.

рыча́г (-а́) lever.

рыча́ть (-чу́) *impf* growl, snarl.

рья́ный zealous.

рюкза́к rucksack.

рю́мка wineglass.

ряби́на[1] rowan, mountain ash. **ряби́на**[2] pit, pock. **ряби́ть** (-и́т) *impf* ripple; *impers*: у меня́ ряби́т в глаза́х I am dazzled. **рябо́й** pock-marked. **ря́бчик** hazel hen, hazel grouse. **рябь** ripples; dazzle.

ря́вкать *impf*, **ря́вкнуть** (-ну) *pf* bellow, roar.

ряд (*loc* -у́; *pl* -ы́) row; line; file, rank; series; number. **рядово́й** ordinary; common; ∼ соста́в rank and file; *sb* private. **ря́дом** *adv* alongside; close by; ∼ с+*instr* next to.

ря́са cassock.

С

с, со *prep* I. +*gen* from; since; off; for, with; on; by; с ра́дости for joy; с утра́ since morning. II. +*acc* about; the size of; с неде́лю for about a week. III. +*instr* with; and; мы с

ва́ми you and I; что с ва́ми? what is the matter?

са́бля (*gen pl* -бель) sabre.

сабота́ж sabotage. **саботи́ровать** *impf & pf* sabotage.

са́ван shroud; blanket.

с|агити́ровать *pf*.

сад (*loc* -у́; *pl* -ы́) garden. **сади́ть** (сажу́, са́дишь) *impf* (*pf* по∼) plant. **сади́ться** (сажу́сь) *impf* (*pf* сесть) sit down; sit; settle; set; be seated. **садо́вник, -ница** gardener. **садо́водство** gardening; horticulture. **садо́вый** garden; cultivated.

сади́зм sadism. **сади́ст** sadist. **сади́стский** sadistic.

са́жа soot.

сажа́ть *impf* (*pf* посади́ть) plant; seat; set, put. **са́женец** (-нца) seedling; sapling.

са́жень (*pl* -и, -жен *or* -же́ней) sazhen (2.13 metres).

сажу́ *etc.*: *see* сади́ть

са́йка roll.

с|акти́ровать *pf*.

сала́зки (-зок) *pl* toboggan.

сала́т lettuce; salad.

са́ло fat, lard; suet; tallow.

сало́н salon; saloon.

салфе́тка napkin.

са́льный greasy; tallow; obscene.

салю́т salute. **салютова́ть** *impf & pf* (*pf also* от∼) +*dat* salute.

сам (-ого́) *m*, **сама́** (-о́й, *acc* -оё) *f*, **само́** (-ого́) *neut*, **са́ми** (-их) *pl*, *pron* -self, -selves; myself, *etc.*, ourselves, *etc.*; ∼ по себе́ in itself; by o.s.; ∼ собо́й of itself, of its own accord; ∼о́ собо́й (разуме́ется) of course; it goes without saying.

са́мбо *neut indecl abbr* (*of* самозащи́та без ору́жия) unarmed combat.

саме́ц (-мца́) male. **са́мка** female.

само- *in comb* self-, auto-. **самобы́тный** original, distinctive. ∼**внуше́ние** auto-suggestion. ∼**возгора́ние** spontaneous combustion. ∼**во́льный** wilful; unauthorized. ∼**де́льный** home-made. ∼**держа́вие** autocracy. ∼**держа́вный** autocratic. ∼**де́ятельность** amateur work, amateur performance; initiative. ∼**дово́льный** self-satisfied. ∼**ду́р** petty tyrant. ∼**ду́рство** high-handedness. ∼**забве́ние** selflessness. ∼**забве́нный** selfless. ∼**защи́та**

self-defence. ~зва́нец (-нца) impostor, pretender. ~ка́т scooter. ~кри́тика self-criticism. ~люби́вый proud; touchy. ~любие pride, self-esteem. ~мне́ние conceit, self-importance. ~наде́янный presumptuous. ~облада́ние self-control. ~обма́н self-deception. ~оборо́на self-defence. ~образова́ние self-education. ~обслу́живание self-service. ~определе́ние self-determination. ~отве́рженность self-lessness. ~отве́рженный selfless. ~поже́ртвование self-sacrifice. ~ро́док (-дка) nugget; person with natural talent. ~сва́л tip-up lorry. ~созна́ние (self-)consciousness. ~сохране́ние self-preservation. ~стоя́тельность independence. ~стоя́тельный independent. ~су́д lynch law, mob law. ~тёк drift. ~тёком *adv* by gravity; of its own accord. ~убийственный suicidal. ~убийство suicide. ~убийца *m* & *f* suicide. ~уваже́ние self-respect. ~уве́ренность self-confidence. ~уве́ренный self-confident. ~униже́ние self-abasement. ~управле́ние self-government. ~управля́ющийся self-governing. ~упра́вный arbitrary. ~учи́тель *m* self-instructor, manual. ~у́чка *m* & *f* self-taught person. ~хо́дный self-propelled. ~чу́вствие general state; как ва́ше ~чу́вствие? how do you feel?

самова́р samovar.
самого́н home-made vodka.
самолёт aeroplane.
самоцве́т semi-precious stone.
са́мый *pron* (the) very, (the) right; (the) same; (the) most.
сан dignity, office.
санато́рий sanatorium.
санда́лия sandal.
са́ни (-е́й) *pl* sledge, sleigh.
санита́р medical orderly; stretcher-bearer. **санита́рия** sanitation. **сани-та́рка** nurse. **санита́рн|ый** medical; health; sanitary; ~ая маши́на ambulance; ~ый у́зел = сану́зел.
са́нки (-нок) *pl* sledge; toboggan.
санкциони́ровать *impf* & *pf* sanction. **са́нкция** sanction.
сано́вник dignitary.

санпу́нкт medical centre.
санскри́т Sanskrit.
санте́хник plumber.
сантиме́тр centimetre; tape-measure.
сану́зел (-зла́) sanitary arrangements; WC.
санча́сть (*gen pl* -е́й) medical unit.
сапёр sapper.
сапо́г(-а́; *gen pl* -о́г) boot. **сапо́жник** shoemaker; cobbler. **сапо́жный** shoe.
сапфи́р sapphire.
сара́й shed; barn.
саранча́ locust(s).
сарафа́н sarafan; pinafore dress.
сарде́лька small fat sausage.
сарди́на sardine.
сарка́зм sarcasm. **саркасти́ческий** sarcastic.
сатана́ *m* Satan. **сатани́нский** satanic.
сателли́т satellite.
сати́н sateen.
сати́ра satire. **сати́рик** satirist. **сати-ри́ческий** satirical.
Сау́довская Ара́вия Saudi Arabia.
сафья́н morocco. **сафья́новый** morocco.
са́хар sugar. **сахари́н** saccharine. **са́харистый** sugary. **са́харница** sugar-basin. **са́харн|ый** sugar; sugary; ~ый заво́д sugar-refinery; ~ый песо́к granulated sugar; ~ая пу́дра castor sugar; ~ая свёкла sugar-beet.
сачо́к (-чка́) net.
сба́вить (-влю) *pf*, **сбавля́ть** *impf* take off; reduce.
с|баланси́ровать *pf*.
сбе́гать[1] *pf* run; +за+*instr* run for. **сбега́ть**[2] *impf*, **сбежа́ть** (-егу́) *pf* run down (from); run away; disappear; ~ся come running.
сберега́тельная ка́сса savings bank. **сберега́ть** *impf*, **сбере́чь** (-егу́, -ежёшь; -ёг, -ла́) *pf* save; save up; preserve. **сбереже́ние** economy; saving; savings. **сберка́сса** savings bank.
сбива́ть *impf*, **с|бить** (собью́, -бьёшь) *pf* bring down, knock down; knock off; distract; wear down; knock together; churn; whip, whisk; ~ся be dislodged; slip; go wrong; be confused; ~ся с пути́ lose one's way; ~ся с ног be run off one's feet.
сби́вчивый confused; inconsistent.

сближа́ть *impf*, **сбли́зить** (-и́жу) *pf* bring (closer) together, draw together; **~ся** draw together; become good friends. **сближе́ние** rapprochement; closing in.

сбо́ку *adv* from one side; on one side.

сбор collection; duty; fee, toll; takings; gathering. **сбо́рище** crowd, mob. **сбо́рка** assembling, assembly; gather. **сбо́рник** collection. **сбо́рный** assembly; mixed, combined; prefabricated; detachable. **сбо́рочный** assembly. **сбо́рщик** collector; assembler.

сбра́сывать(ся *impf of* **сбро́сить(ся**

сбрива́ть *impf*, **сбрить** (сбре́ю) *pf* shave off.

сброд riff-raff.

сброс fault, break. **сбро́сить** (-о́шу) *pf* (*impf* **сбра́сывать**) throw down, drop; throw off; shed; discard.

сбру́я (*collect*) (riding) tack.

сбыва́ть *impf*, **сбыть** (сбу́ду; сбыл, -а́, -о) *pf* sell, market; get rid of; **~ся** come true, be realized. **сбыт** (*no pl*) sale; market.

св. *abbr* (*of* **свято́й**) Saint.

сзаде́бный wedding. **сва́дьба** (*gen pl* -деб) wedding.

сза́ливать *impf*, **свали́ть** (-лю́, -лишь) *pf* throw down; overthrow; pile up; **~ся** fall (down), collapse. **сва́лка** dump; scuffle.

сзваля́ть *pf*.

сва́ривать *impf*, **свари́ть** (-рю́, -ришь) *pf* boil; cook; weld. **сва́рка** welding.

сварли́вый cantankerous.

сварно́й welded. **сва́рочный** welding. **сва́рщик** welder.

сва́стика swastika.

сва́тать *impf* (*pf* **по~, со~**) propose as a husband or wife; propose to; **~ся к**+*dat or* **за**+*acc* propose to.

сва́я pile.

све́дение piece of information; knowledge; *pl* information, intelligence; knowledge. **све́дущий** knowledgeable; versed.

сведу́ *etc.*: *see* **свести́**

свежезаморо́женный fresh-frozen; chilled. **све́жесть** freshness. **свеже́ть** (-е́ет) *impf* (*pf* **по~**) become cooler; freshen. **све́жий** (-еж, -а́) fresh; new.

свезти́ (-зу́, -зёшь; свёз, -ла́) *pf* (*impf* **свози́ть**) take; bring *or* take down *or* away.

свёкла beet, beetroot.

свёкор (-кра) father-in-law. **свекро́вь** mother-in-law.

свёл *etc.*: *see* **свести́**

сверга́ть *impf*, **све́ргнуть** (-ну; сверг) *pf* throw down, overthrow. **сверже́ние** overthrow.

све́рить *pf* (*impf* **сверя́ть**) collate.

сверка́ть *impf* sparkle, twinkle; glitter; gleam. **сверкну́ть** (-ну́, -нёшь) *pf* flash.

сверли́льный drill, drilling; boring. **сверли́ть** *impf* (*pf* **про~**) drill; bore (through); nag. **сверло́** drill. **сверля́щий** gnawing, piercing.

сверну́ть (-ну́, -нёшь) *pf* (*impf* **свёртывать**, **свора́чивать**) roll (up); turn; curtail, cut down; **~ шею**+*dat* wring the neck of; **~ся** roll up, curl up; curdle, coagulate; contract.

све́рстник contemporary.

свёрток (-тка) package, bundle. **свёртывание** rolling (up); curdling, coagulation; curtailment, cuts. **свёртывать(ся** *impf of* **сверну́ть(ся**

сверх *prep*+*gen* over, above, on top of; beyond; in addition to; **~ того́** moreover.

сверх- *in comb* super-, over-, hyper-. **сверхзвуково́й** supersonic. **~пла́новый** over and above the plan. **~при́быль** excess profit. **~проводни́к** (-а́) superconductor. **~секре́тный** top secret. **~уро́чный** overtime. **~уро́чные** *sb pl* overtime. **~челове́к** superman. **~челове́ческий** superhuman. **~ъесте́ственный** supernatural.

све́рху *adv* from above; **~ до́низу** from top to bottom.

сверчо́к (-чка́) cricket.

сверше́ние achievement.

сверя́ть *impf of* **све́рить**

све́сить (-е́шу) *pf* (*impf* **све́шивать**) let down, lower; **~ся** hang over, lean over.

свести́ (-еду́, -еде́шь; -ёл, -а́) *pf* (*impf* **своди́ть**) take; take down; take away; remove; bring together; reduce, bring; cramp.

свет[1] light; daybreak.

свет[2] world; society.

светáть *impf impers* dawn. светúло luminary. светúть (-ечу́, -е́тишь) *impf (pf* по~) shine; +*dat* light; light the way for; ~ся shine, gleam. светлéть (-éет) *impf (pf* по~, про~) brighten (up); grow lighter. свéтлость brightness; Grace. свéтлый light; bright; joyous. светлячóк (-чкá) glow-worm.

свето- *in comb* light, photo-. светонепроница́емый light-proof. ~фи́льтр light filter. ~фóр traffic light(s).

световóй light; luminous; ~ день daylight hours.

светопреставлéние end of the world.

свéтский fashionable; refined; secular.

светя́щийся luminous, fluorescent. свечá (*pl* -и, -éй) candle; (spark-) plug. свечéние luminescence, fluorescence. свéчка candle. свечý *etc.: see* светúть

с|вéшать *pf.* свéшивать(ся *impf of* свéсить(ся. свивáть *impf of* свить

свидáние meeting; appointment; до свидáния! goodbye!

свидéтель *m*, -ница witness. свидéтельство evidence; testimony; certificate. свидéтельствовать *impf (pf* за~, о~) give evidence, testify; be evidence (of); witness.

свина́рник pigsty.

свинéц (-нцá) lead.

свини́на pork. сви́нка mumps. свинóй pig; pork. сви́нство despicable act; outrage; squalor.

свинцóвый lead; leaden.

свинья́ (*pl* -и, -éй, -ям) pig, swine.

свирéль (reed-)pipe.

свирепéть (-éю) *impf (pf* рас~) grow savage; become violent. свирéпствовать *impf* rage; be rife. свирéпый fierce, ferocious.

свисáть *impf*, сви́снуть (-ну; -ис) *pf* hang down, dangle; trail.

свист whistle; whistling. свистáть (-ищу́, -и́щешь) *impf* whistle. свистéть (-ищу́) *impf*, сви́стнуть (-ну *pf* whistle; hiss. свистóк (-ткá) whistle.

сви́та suite; retinue. сви́тер sweater. сви́ток (-тка) roll, scroll. с|вить

(совью́, совьёшь; -ил, -á, -о) *pf (impf also* свивáть) twist, wind; ~ся roll up.

свихну́ться (-ну́сь, -нёшься) *impf* go mad; go astray.

свищ (-á) flaw; (knot-)hole; fistula.

свищу́ *etc.: see* свистáть, свистéть

свобóда freedom. свобóдно *adv* freely; easily; fluently; loose(ly). свобóдный free; easy; vacant; spare; loose; flowing. свободолюби́вый freedom-loving. свободомы́слие free-thinking.

свод code; collection; arch, vault.

свóдить (-ожу́, -óдишь) *impf of* свести́

свóдка summary; report. свóдный composite; step-.

свóдчатый arched, vaulted.

своевóлие self-will, wilfulness. своевóльный wilful, capricious.

своевремéнно *adv* in good time; opportunely. своевремéнный timely, opportune.

своенрáвие capriciousness. своенрáвный wilful, capricious.

своеобрáзие originality; peculiarity. своеобрáзный original; peculiar.

свожу́ *etc.: see* свóдить, свози́ть. свози́ть (-ожу́, -óзишь) *impf of* свезти́

свой (своегó) *m*, своя́ (своéй) *f*, своё (своегó) *neut*, свои́ (свои́х) *pl*, *pron* one's (own); my, his, her, its; our, your, their. свóйственный peculiar, characteristic. свóйство property, attribute, characteristic.

свóлочь swine; riff-raff.

свóра leash; pack.

свора́чивать *impf of* сверну́ть, свороти́ть. с|ворова́ть *pf.*

свороти́ть (-очу́, -óтишь) *pf (impf* свора́чивать) dislodge, shift; turn; twist.

свояк brother-in-law (*husband of wife's sister*). своя́ченица sister-in-law (*wife's sister*).

свыкáться *impf*, свы́кнуться (-нусь; -ыкся) *pf* get used.

высокá *adv* haughtily. свы́ше *adv* from above. свы́ше *prep+gen* over; beyond.

свя́занный constrained; combined; bound; coupled. с|вязáть (-яжу́, -я́жешь) *pf*, свя́зывать *impf* tie, bind; connect; ~ся get in touch; get involved. свя́зист, -и́стка signaller; worker in communication services. свя́зка sheaf, bundle; ligament. свя́зный connected, coherent. связь (loc -и́) connection; link, bond; liaison; communication(s).

святи́лище sanctuary. свя́тки (-ток) pl Christmas-tide. свя́то adv piously; religiously. свят|о́й (-я́т, -á, -o) holy; ~о́й, ~а́я sb saint. святы́ня sacred object or place. свяще́нник priest. свяще́нный sacred.

сгиб bend. сгиба́ть impf of согну́ть сгла́дить (-áжу) pf, сгла́живать impf smooth out; smooth over, soften.

сгла́зить (-áжу) pf put the evil eye on.

сгнива́ть impf, с|гнить (-ию́, -иёшь; -ил, -á, -о) pf rot.

с|гно́иться pf.

сгова́риваться impf, сговори́ться pf come to an arrangement; arrange. сго́вор agreement. сгово́рчивый compliant.

сгоня́ть impf of согна́ть

сгора́ние combustion; дви́гатель вну́треннего сгора́ния internal-combustion engine. сгора́ть impf of сгоре́ть

с|го́рбить(ся) (-блю(сь) pf.

с|горе́ть (-рю́) pf (impf also сгора́ть) burn down; be burnt down; be used up; burn; burn o.s. out. сгоряча́ adv in the heat of the moment.

с|гото́вить(ся) (-влю(сь) pf.

сгреба́ть impf, сгрести́ (-ебу́, -ебёшь; -ёб, -лá) pf rake up, rake together.

сгружа́ть impf, сгрузи́ть (-ужу́, -у́зишь) pf unload.

с|группирова́ть(ся pf.

сгусти́ть (-ущу́) pf, сгуща́ть impf thicken; condense; ~ся thicken; condense; clot. сгу́сток (-тка) clot. сгуще́ние thickening, condensation; clotting.

сдава́ть (сдаю́, сдаёшь) impf of сдать; ~ экза́мен take an examination; ~ся impf of сда́ться

сда́вить (-влю, -вишь) pf, сда́вливать impf squeeze.

сдать (-ам, -ашь, -аст, -ади́м; -ал, -á, -о) pf (impf сдава́ть) hand over; pass; let, hire out; surrender; give up;

deal; ~ся surrender, yield. сда́ча handing over; hiring out; surrender; change; deal.

сдвиг displacement; fault; change, improvement. сдвига́ть impf, сдви́нуть (-ну) pf shift, move; move together; ~ся move, budge; come together.

с|де́лать(ся pf. сде́лка transaction; deal, bargain. сде́льн|ый piece-work; ~ая рабо́та piece-work. сде́льщина piece-work.

сдёргивать impf of сдёрнуть

сде́ржанный restrained, reserved. сдержа́ть (-жу́, -жишь) pf, сде́рживать impf hold back; restrain; keep.

сдёрнуть (-ну) pf (impf сдёргивать) pull off.

сдеру́ etc.: see содра́ть. сдира́ть impf of содра́ть

сдо́ба shortening; fancy bread, bun(s). сдо́бный (-бен, -бнá, -о) rich, short.

с|до́хнуть (-нет; сдох) pf die; kick the bucket.

сдружи́ться (-жу́сь) pf become friends.

сдува́ть impf, сду́нуть (-ну) pf, сдуть (-у́ю) pf blow away or off.

сеа́нс performance; showing; sitting.

себесто́имость prime cost; cost (price).

себя́ (dat & prep себе́, instr собо́й or собо́ю) refl pron oneself; myself, yourself, himself, etc.; ничего́ себе́ not bad; собо́й ~-looking, in appearance.

себялю́бие selfishness.

сев sowing.

се́вер north. се́верный north, northern; northerly. се́веро-восто́к north-east. се́веро-восто́чный north-east(ern). се́веро-за́пад north-west. се́веро-за́падный north-west(ern). северя́нин (pl -я́не, -я́н) northerner.

севооборо́т crop rotation.

сего́ see сей. сего́дня adv today. сего́дняшний of today, today's.

седе́ть (-е́ю) impf (pf по~) turn grey. седина́ (pl -ы) grey hair(s).

седла́ть impf (pf o~) saddle. седло́ (pl сёдла, -дел) saddle.

седоборо́дый grey-bearded. седоволо́сый grey-haired. седо́й (сед, -á, -о) grey(-haired).

седо́к (-á) passenger; rider.

седьмо́й seventh.

сезо́н season. сезо́нный seasonal.

сей (сего́) *m*, сия́ (сей) *f*, сие́ (сего́) *neut*, сии́ (сих) *pl*, *pron* this; these; сию́ мину́ту at once, instantly.

сейсми́ческий seismic.

сейф safe.

сейча́с *adv* (just) now; soon; immediately.

сёк *etc*.: *see* сечь

секре́т secret.

секретариа́т secretariat.

секрета́рский secretarial. секрета́рша, секрета́рь (-я́) *m* secretary.

секре́тный secret.

секс sex. сексуа́льный sexual; sexy.

сексте́т sextet.

се́кта sect. секта́нт sectarian.

се́ктор sector.

секу́ *etc*.: *see* сечь

секуляриза́ция secularization.

секу́нда second. секунда́нт second. секу́ндный second. секундоме́р stop-watch.

секцио́нный sectional. се́кция section.

селёдка herring.

селезёнка spleen.

се́лезень (-зня) *m* drake.

селе́кция breeding.

селе́ние settlement, village.

сели́тра saltpetre, nitre.

сели́ть(ся) *impf* (*pf* по~) settle. село́ (*pl* сёла) village.

сельдере́й celery.

сельдь (*pl* -и, -е́й) herring.

се́льск|ий rural; village; ~ое хозя́йство agriculture. сельскохозя́йственный agricultural.

сельсове́т village soviet.

сема́нтика semantics. семанти́ческий semantic.

семафо́р semaphore; signal.

сёмга (smoked) salmon.

семе́йный family; domestic. семе́йство family.

семе́ни *etc*.: *see* се́мя

семени́ть *impf* mince.

семени́ться *impf* seed. семенни́к (-а́) testicle; seed-vessel. семенно́й seed; seminal.

семёрка seven; figure 7; No. 7.

се́меро (-ы́х) seven.

семе́стр term, semester.

се́мечко (*pl* -и) seed; *pl* sunflower seeds.

семидесятиле́тие seventy years; seventieth anniversary, birthday. семидеся́т|ый seventieth; ~ые го́ды the seventies. семиле́тка seven-year school. семиле́тний seven-year; seven-year-old.

семина́р seminar. семина́рия seminary.

семисо́тый seven-hundredth. семна́дцатый seventeenth. семна́дцать seventeen. семь (-ми́, -мью) seven. се́мьдесят (-ми́десяти, -мью́десятью) seventy. семьсо́т (-мисо́т, *instr* -мьюста́ми) seven hundred. се́мью *adv* seven times.

семья́ (*pl* -и, -е́й, -ям) family. семьяни́н family man.

се́мя (-мени; *pl* -мена́, -мя́н, -мена́м) seed; semen, sperm.

сена́т senate. сена́тор senator.

се́ни (-е́й) *pl* (entrance-)hall.

се́но hay. сенова́л hayloft. сеноко́с haymaking; hayfield. сенокоси́лка mowing-machine.

сенсацио́нный sensational. сенса́ция sensation.

сенте́нция maxim.

сентимента́льный sentimental.

сентя́брь (-я́) *m* September. сентя́брьский September.

се́псис sepsis.

се́ра sulphur; ear-wax.

серб, ~ка Serb. Се́рбия Serbia. се́рбский Serb(ian). сербскохорва́тский Serbo-Croat(ian).

серва́нт sideboard.

серви́з service, set. сервирова́ть *impf* & *pf* serve; lay (a table). сервиро́вка laying; table lay-out.

серде́чник core. серде́чность cordiality; warmth. серде́чный heart; cardiac; cordial; warm(-hearted). серди́тый angry. серди́ть (-ржу́, -рдишь) *impf* (*pf* рас~) anger; ~ся be angry. сердобо́льный tender-hearted. се́рдце (*pl* -а́, -де́ц) heart; в сердца́х in anger; от всего́ се́рдца from the bottom of one's heart. сердцебие́ние palpitation. сердцеви́дный heart-shaped. сердцеви́на core, pith, heart.

серебрёный silver-plated. серебри́стый silvery. серебри́ть *impf* (*pf* по~) silver, silver-plate; ~ся become silvery. **серебро** silver. **серебряный** silver.

середина middle.

сережка earring; catkin.

серенада serenade.

серенький grey; dull.

сержант sergeant.

серийный serial; mass. **серия** series; part.

серный sulphur; sulphuric.

сероглазый grey-eyed.

серость uncouthness; ignorance.

серп (-á) sickle; ~ луны crescent moon.

серпантин streamer.

сертификат certificate.

серый (сер, -á, -о) grey; dull; uneducated.

серьга (pl -и, -рёг) earring.

серьёзность seriousness. **серьёзный** serious.

сессия session.

сестра (pl сёстры, сестёр, сёстрам) sister.

сесть (сяду) pf (impf садиться) sit down; land; set; shrink; +на+acc board, get on.

сетка net, netting; (luggage-)rack; string bag; grid.

сетовать impf (pf по~) complain.

сетчатка retina. **сеть** (loc -й; pl -и, -ей) net; network.

сечение section. **сечь** (секу, сечёшь; сёк) impf (pf вы~) cut to pieces; flog; ~ся split.

сеялка seed drill. **сеять** (сею) impf (pf по~) sow.

сжалиться pf take pity (над+instr on.

сжатие pressure; grasp, grip; compression. **сжатый** compressed; compact; concise.

с|жать[1] (сожну, -нёшь) pf.

сжать[2] (сожму, -мёшь) pf (impf сжимать) squeeze; compress; grip, clench; ~ся tighten, clench; shrink, contract.

с|жечь (сожгу, сожжёшь; сжёг, сожгла) pf (impf сжигать) burn (down); cremate.

сживаться impf of сжиться

сжигать impf of сжечь

сжимать(ся impf of сжать[2](ся

сжиться (-ивусь, -ивёшься; -йлся, -áсь) pf (impf сживаться) с+instr

get used to.

с|жульничать pf.

сзади adv from behind; behind. **сзади** prep+gen behind.

сзывать impf of созвать

сибирский Siberian. **Сибирь** Siberia. **сибиряк** (-á), **сибирячка** Siberian.

сигара cigar. **сигарета** cigarette.

сигнал signal. **сигнализация** signalling. **сигнализировать** impf & pf (pf also про~) signal. **сигнальный** signal. **сигнальщик** signal-man.

сиделка sick-nurse. **сидение** sitting. **сиденье** seat. **сидеть** (-ижу) impf sit; be; fit. **сидячий** sitting; sedentary.

сие etc.: see сей

сизый (сиз, -á, -о) (blue-)grey.

сий see сей

сила strength; force; power; в силу +gen on the strength of, because of; не по ~ам beyond one's powers; **силой** by force. **силач** (-á) strong man. **силиться** impf try, make efforts. **силовой** power; of force.

силок (-лка) noose, snare.

силос silo; silage.

силуэт silhouette.

сильно adv strongly, violently; very much, greatly. **сильный** (-лен or -лён, -льна, -о) strong; powerful; intense, hard.

симбиоз symbiosis.

символ symbol. **символизировать** impf symbolize. **символизм** symbolism. **символический** symbolic.

симметрия symmetry.

симпатизировать impf +dat like, sympathize with. **симпатичный** likeable, nice. **симпатия** liking; sympathy.

симпозиум symposium.

симптом symptom.

симулировать impf & pf simulate, feign. **симулянт** malingerer, sham. **симуляция** simulation, pretence.

симфония symphony.

синагога synagogue.

синева blue. **синеватый** bluish. **синеглазый** blue-eyed. **синеть** (-ею) impf (pf по~) turn blue; show blue. **синий** (синь, -ня́, -не) (dark) blue.

синица titmouse.

синод synod. **синоним** synonym. **синтаксис** syntax.

синтез synthesis. **синтезировать** *impf* & *pf* synthesize. **синтетический** synthetic.

синус sine; sinus.

синхронизировать *impf* & *pf* synchronize.

синь[1] blue. **синь**[2] *see* **синий**. **синька** blueing; blue-print. **синяк** (-á) bruise.

сионизм Zionism.

сиплый hoarse, husky. **сипнуть** (-ну; сип) *impf* (*pf* о~) become hoarse, husky.

сирена siren; hooter.

сиреневый lilac(-coloured). **сирень** lilac.

Сирия Syria.

сироп syrup.

сирота (*pl* -ы) *m* & *f* orphan. **сиротливый** lonely. **сиротский** orphan's, orphans'.

система system. **систематизировать** *impf* & *pf* systematize. **систематический, систематичный** systematic.

ситец (-тца) (printed) cotton; chintz. **сито** sieve.

ситуация situation.

ситцевый print, chintz.

сифилис syphilis.

сифон siphon.

сия *see* **сей**

сияние radiance. **сиять** *impf* shine, beam.

сказ tale. **сказание** story, legend. **сказать** (-ажу, -ажешь) *pf* (*impf* говорить) say; speak; tell. **сказаться** (-ажусь, -ажешься) *pf*, **сказываться** *impf* tell (on); declare o.s. **сказитель** *m* story-teller. **сказка** (fairy-)tale; fib. **сказочный** fairytale; fantastic. **сказуемое** *sb* predicate.

скакалка skipping-rope. **скакать** (-ачу, -ачешь) *impf* (*pf* по~) skip; jump; gallop. **скаковой** race, racing.

скала (*pl* -ы) rock face; cliff. **скалистый** rocky.

скалить *impf* (*pf* о~); ~ зубы bare one's teeth; grin; ~ся bare one's teeth.

скалка rolling-pin.

скалолаз rock-climber.

скалывать *impf of* **сколоть**

скальп scalp.

скальпель *m* scalpel.

скамеечка footstool; small bench. **скамейка** bench. **скамья** (*pl* скамьй, -ей) bench; ~ подсудимых dock.

скандал scandal; brawl, rowdy scene. **скандалист** trouble-maker. **скандалиться** *impf* (*pf* о~) disgrace o.s. **скандальный** scandalous.

скандинавский Scandinavian.

скандировать *impf* & *pf* declaim.

скапливать(ся *impf of* **скопить(ся**

скарб goods and chattels.

скаредный stingy.

скарлатина scarlet fever.

скат slope; pitch.

с|катать *pf* (*impf* **скатывать**) roll (up).

скатерть (*pl* -и, -ей) table-cloth.

скатить (-ачу, -атишь) *pf*, **скатывать**[1] *impf* roll down; ~ся roll down; slip, slide. **скатывать**[2] *impf of* **скатать**

скафандр diving-suit; space-suit.

скачка gallop, galloping. **скачки** (-чек) *pl* horse-race; races. **скачок** (-чка) jump, leap.

скашивать *impf of* **скосить**

скважина slit, chink; well.

сквер public garden.

скверно badly; bad. **сквернословить** (-влю) *impf* use foul language. **скверный** foul; bad.

сквозить *impf* be transparent; show through; **сквозит** *impers* there is a draught. **сквозной** through; transparent. **сквозняк** (-á) draught. **сквозь** *prep*+*gen* through.

скворец (-рца) starling.

скелет skeleton.

скептик sceptic. **скептицизм** scepticism. **скептический** sceptical.

скетч sketch.

скидка reduction. **скидывать** *impf*, **скинуть** (-ну) *pf* throw off *or* down; knock off.

скипетр sceptre.

скипидар turpentine.

скирд (-á; *pl* -ы), **скирда** (*pl* -ы, -ám) stack, rick.

скисать *impf*, **скиснуть** (-ну; скис) *pf* go sour.

скиталец (-льца) wanderer. **скитаться** *impf* wander.

скиф Scythian.

склад[1] depot; store.

склад[2] mould; turn; logical connection; ~ **ума́** mentality.

скла́дка fold; pleat; crease; wrinkle.

скла́дно adv smoothly.

складно́й folding, collapsible.

скла́дный (-ден, -дна, -о) well-knit, well-built; smooth, coherent.

скла́дчина: в **скла́дчину** by clubbing together. **скла́дывать(ся** impf of **сложи́ть(ся**

скле́ивать impf, **с|кле́ить** pf stick together; ~**ся** stick together.

склеп (burial) vault, crypt.

склепа́ть pf, **склёпывать** impf rivet. **склёпка** riveting.

склеро́з sclerosis.

скло́ка squabble.

склон slope; на ~е лет in one's declining years. **склоне́ние** inclination; declension. **склони́ть** (-ню́, -нишь) pf, **склоня́ть** impf incline; bow; win over; decline; ~**ся** bend; bow; yield; be declined. **скло́нность** inclination; tendency. **скло́нный** (-нен, -нна, -нно) inclined, disposed. **склоня́емый** declinable.

скля́нка phial; bottle; (naut) bell.

скоба́ (pl -ы, -а́м) cramp, clamp; staple.

ско́бка dim of **скоба́**; bracket; pl parenthesis, parentheses.

скобли́ть (-облю́, -о́бли́шь) impf scrape, plane.

ско́ванность constraint. **ско́ванный** constrained; bound. **скова́ть** (скую́, скуёшь) pf (impf **ско́вывать**) forge; chain; fetter; pin down, hold, contain.

сковорода́ (pl ско́вороды, -ро́д, -а́м), **сковоро́дка** frying-pan.

ско́вывать impf of **скова́ть**

скола́чивать impf, **сколоти́ть** (-очу́, -о́тишь) pf knock together.

сколо́ть (-лю́, -лешь) pf (impf **ска́лывать**) chop off; pin together.

скольже́ние sliding, slipping; glide. **скользи́ть** (-льжу́) impf, **скользну́ть** (-ну́, -нёшь) pf slide; slip; glide. **ско́льзкий** (-зок, -зка́, -о) slippery. **скользя́щий** sliding.

ско́лько adv how much; how many; as far as.

с|кома́ндовать pf. **с|комбини́ро-** **вать** pf. **с|ко́мкать** pf. **с|комплектова́ть** pf. **с|компромети́ровать** pf. **с|конструи́ровать** pf.

сконфу́женный embarrassed, confused, disconcerted. **с|конфу́зить-(ся** -у́жу(сь) pf.

с|концентри́ровать pf.

сконча́ться pf pass away, die.

с|копи́ровать pf.

скопи́ть (-плю́, -пишь) pf (impf **ска́пливать**) save (up); amass; ~**ся** accumulate. **скопле́ние** accumulation; crowd.

ско́пом adv in a crowd, en masse.

скорбе́ть (-блю́) impf grieve. **ско́рбный** sorrowful. **скорбь** (pl -и, -е́й) sorrow.

скоре́е, скоре́й comp of **ско́рый, ско́рый;** adv rather, sooner; как мо́жно ~ as soon as possible; ~ всего́ most likely.

скорлупа́ (pl -ы) shell.

скорня́к (-а́) furrier.

ско́ро adv quickly; soon.

скоро- in comb quick-, fast-. **скорова́рка** pressure-cooker. **~гово́рка** patter; tongue-twister. **ско́ропись** cursive; shorthand. **~по́ртящийся** perishable. **~постижи́мый** sudden. **~спе́лый** early; fast-ripening; premature; hasty. **~сшива́тель** m binder, file. **~те́чный** transient, short-lived.

скоростно́й high-speed. **ско́рость** (gen pl -е́й) speed; gear.

скорпио́н scorpion; Scorpio.

с|корректи́ровать pf. **с|ко́рчить-(ся** -чу(сь) pf.

ско́р|ый (скор, -а́, -о) quick, fast; near; forthcoming; ~**ая по́мощь** first-aid; ambulance.

с|коси́ть[1] (-ошу́, -о́сишь) pf (impf also **ска́шивать**) mow.

с|коси́ть[2] (-ошу́) pf (impf also **ска́шивать**) squint; cut on the cross.

скот (-а́), **скоти́на** cattle; livestock; beast. **ско́тный** cattle.

ското- in comb cattle. **скотобо́йня** (gen pl -о́ен) slaughter-house. **~во́д** cattle-breeder. **~во́дство** cattle-raising.

ско́тский cattle; brutish. **ско́тство** brutish condition; brutality.

с|кра́сить (-а́шу) pf, **скра́шивать** impf smooth over; relieve.

скребо́к (-бка́) scraper. **скребу́** etc.: see **скрести́**

скре́жет grating; gnashing. **скреже-та́ть** (-ещу́, -е́щешь) impf grate; +instr scrape.

скре́па clamp, brace; counter-signature.

скрепи́ть (-плю́) pf, **скрепля́ть** impf fasten (together), make fast; clamp; countersign, ratify; **скрепя́ се́рдце** reluctantly. **скре́пка** paperclip. **скрепле́ние** fastening; clamping; tie, clamp.

скрести́ (-ебу́, -ебёшь; -ёб, -ла́) impf scrape; scratch; **~сь** scratch.

скрести́ть (-ещу́) pf, **скре́щивать** impf cross; interbreed. **скреще́ние** crossing. **скре́щивание** crossing; interbreeding.

с|криви́ть(ся (-влю́(сь) pf.

скрип squeak, creak. **скрипа́ч** (-а́) violinist. **скрипе́ть** (-плю́) impf, **скри́пнуть** (-ну) pf squeak, creak; scratch. **скрипи́чный** violin; **~ ключ** treble clef. **скри́пка** violin. **скри-пу́чий** squeaky, creaking.

с|крои́ть pf.

скро́мничать impf (pf по~) be (too) modest. **скро́мность** modesty. **скро́мный** (-мен, -мна́, -о) modest. **скро́ю** etc.: see **скрыть**. **скрою́** etc.: see **скрои́ть**

скрупулёзный scrupulous.

с|крути́ть (-учу́, -у́тишь) pf, **скру́-чивать** impf twist; roll; tie up.

скрыва́ть impf, **скрыть** (-о́ю) pf hide, conceal; **~ся** hide, go into hiding, be hidden; steal away; disappear. **скры́тничать** impf be secretive. **скры́тный** secretive. **скры́тый** secret, hidden; latent.

скря́га m & f miser.

ску́дный (-ден, -дна́, -о) scanty; meagre. **ску́дость** scarcity, paucity.

ску́ка boredom.

скула́ (pl -ы) cheek-bone. **скула́-стый** with high cheek-bones.

скули́ть impf whine, whimper.

ску́льптор sculptor. **скульпту́ра** sculpture.

ску́мбрия mackerel.

скунс skunk.

скупа́ть impf of **скупи́ть**

скупе́ц (-пца́) miser.

скупи́ть (-плю́, -пишь) pf (impf ску-па́ть) buy (up).

скупи́ться (-плю́сь) impf (pf по~) be stingy; skimp; be sparing (of +на+acc).

ску́пка buying (up).

ску́по adv sparingly. **скупо́й** (-п, -а́, -о) stingy, meagre. **ску́пость** stinginess.

ску́пщик buyer(-up).

ску́тер (pl -á) outboard speed-boat.

скуча́ть impf be bored; +по+dat or prep miss, yearn for.

ску́ченность density, overcrowding. **ску́ченный** dense, overcrowded. **ску́чить** (-чу) pf crowd (together); **~ся** cluster; crowd together.

ску́чный (-чен, -чна́, -о) boring; **мне ску́чно** I'm bored.

с|ку́шать pf. **скую́** etc.: see **скова́ть**

слабе́ть (-е́ю) impf (pf о~) weaken, grow weak. **слаби́тельный** laxative; **~ое** sb laxative. **сла́бить** impf impers: **его́ сла́бит** he has diarrhoea. **слабо-** in comb weak, feeble, slight. **слабово́лие** weakness of will. **~во́льный** weak-willed. **~не́рв-ный** nervy, nervous. **~ра́звитый** under-developed. **~у́мие** feeble-mindedness. **~у́мный** feeble-minded. **сла́бость** weakness. **сла́бый** (-б, -а́, -о) weak.

сла́ва glory; fame; **на сла́ву** wonderfully well. **сла́вить** (-влю) impf celebrate, sing the praises of; **~ся** (+instr) be famous (for). **сла́вный** glorious, renowned; nice.

славяни́н (pl -я́не, -я́н), **славя́нка** Slav. **славянофи́л** Slavophil(e). **славя́нский** Slav, Slavonic.

слага́емое sb component, term, member. **слага́ть** impf of **сложи́ть**

сла́дить (-а́жу) pf с+instr cope with, handle; arrange.

сла́дкий (-док, -дка́, -о) sweet; **~ое** sb sweet course. **сладостра́стник** voluptuary. **сладостра́стный** voluptuous. **сла́дость** joy; sweetness; pl sweets.

сла́женность harmony. **сла́жен-ный** co-ordinated, harmonious.

сла́мывать impf of **сломи́ть**

сла́нец (-нца) shale, slate.

сластёна m & f person with a sweet tooth. **сласть** (pl -и, -е́й) delight; pl sweets, sweet things.

слать (шлю, шлёшь) *impf* send.

слаща́вый sugary, sickly-sweet. сла́-ще *comp of* сла́дкий

сле́ва *adv* from *or* on the left; ~ напра́во from left to right.

слёг *etc.*: *see* слечь

слегка́ *adv* slightly; lightly.

след (сле́да, *dat* -у, *loc* -ý; *pl* -ы́) track; footprint; trace. следи́ть[1] (-ежу́) *impf* +за+*instr* watch; follow; keep up with; look after; keep an eye on. следи́ть[2] (-ежу́) *impf* (*pf* на~) leave footprints. сле́дование movement. сле́дователь *m* investigator. сле́довательно *adv* consequently. сле́довать *impf* (*pf* по~) I. +*dat or* за+*instr* follow; go, be bound; II. *impers* (+*dat*) ought; be owing, be owed; вам сле́дует +*inf* you ought to; как сле́дует properly; as it should be; ско́лько с меня́ сле́дует? how much do I owe (you)? сле́дом *adv* (за+*instr*) immediately after, close behind. сле́дственный investigation, inquiry. сле́дствие[1] consequence. сле́дствие[2] investigation. сле́дующий following, next. слежка shadowing.

слеза́ (*pl* -ёзы, -ам) tear.

слеза́ть *impf of* слезть

слези́ться (-и́тся) *impf* water. слезли́вый tearful. слёзный tear; tearful. слезоточи́вый watering; ~ газ tear-gas.

слезть (-зу; слез) *pf* (*impf* слеза́ть) climb *or* get down; dismount; get off; come off.

слепе́нь (-пня́) *m* horse-fly.

слепе́ц (-пца́) blind man. слепи́ть[1] *impf* blind; dazzle.

с|лепи́ть[2] (-плю́, -пишь) *pf* stick together.

сле́пнуть (-ну; слеп) *impf* (*pf* о~) go blind. сле́по *adv* blindly. слеп|о́й (-п, -á, -о) blind; ~ы́е *sb pl* the blind.

сле́пок (-пка) cast.

слепота́ blindness.

сле́сарь (*pl* -á *or* -и) *m* metalworker; locksmith.

слёт gathering; rally. слета́ть *impf*, слете́ть (-ечу́) *pf* fly down *or* away; fall down *or* off; ~ся fly together; congregate.

слечь (сля́гу, -я́жешь; слёг, -лá) *pf*

take to one's bed.

сли́ва plum; plum-tree.

слива́ть(ся *impf of* сли́ть(ся. сли́в-ки (-вок) *pl* cream. сли́вочн|ый cream; creamy; ~ое ма́сло butter; ~ое моро́женое dairy ice-cream.

сли́зистый slimy. слизня́к (-á) slug. слизь mucus; slime.

с|линя́ть *pf*.

слипа́ться *impf*, сли́пнуться (-нет-ся; -и́пся) *pf* stick together.

сли́тно together, as one word. сли́-ток (-тка) ingot, bar. с|ли́ть (солью́, -ьёшь; -ил, -á, -о) *pf* (*impf also* слива́ть) pour, pour out *or* off; fuse, amalgamate; ~ся flow together; blend; merge.

слича́ть *impf*, сличи́ть (-чý) *pf* collate; check. сличе́ние collation, checking.

сли́шком *adv* too; too much.

слия́ние confluence; merging; merger.

слова́к, -áчка Slovak. слова́цкий Slovak.

слова́рный lexical; dictionary. сло-ва́рь (-я́) *m* dictionary; vocabulary. слове́сность literature; philology. слове́сный verbal, oral. сло́вно *conj* as if; like, as. сло́во (*pl* -á) word; одни́м ~м in a word. сло́вом *adv* in a word. словообразова́ние word-formation. словоохо́тливый talkative. словосочета́ние word combination, phrase. словоупотребле́ние usage.

слог[1] style.

слог[2] (*pl* -и, -óв) syllable.

слоёный flaky.

сложе́ние composition; addition; build, constitution. сложи́ть (-жý, -жишь) *pf* (*impf* класть, скла́-дывать, слага́ть) put *or* lay (together); pile, stack; add, add up; fold (up); compose; take off, put down; lay down; ~ся turn out; take shape; arise; club together. сло́жность complication; complexity. сло́жный (-жен, -жнá, -о) complicated; complex; compound.

слои́стый stratified; flaky. слой (*pl* -и́, -ёв) layer; stratum.

слом demolition, pulling down. с|лома́ть(ся *pf*. сломи́ть (-млю́, -мишь) *pf* (*impf* сла́мывать) break (off); overcome; сломя́ го́лову at breakneck speed; ~ся break.

слон (-а́) elephant; bishop. **слони́ха** she-elephant. **слоно́в|ый** elephant; ~ая кость ivory.

слоня́ться *impf* loiter, mooch (about).

слуга́ (*pl* -и) *m* (man)servant. **служа́нка** servant, maid. **служа́щий** *sb* employee. **слу́жба** service; work. **служе́бный** office; official; auxiliary; secondary. **служе́ние** service, serving. **служи́ть** (-жу́, -жишь) *impf* (*pf* по~) serve; work.

с|лука́вить (-влю) *pf*.

слух hearing; ear; rumour; по ~у by ear. **слухов|о́й** acoustic, auditory, aural; ~о́й аппара́т hearing aid; ~о́е окно́ dormer (window).

слу́чай incident, event; case; opportunity; chance; ни в ко́ем слу́чае in no circumstances. **случа́йно** *adv* by chance, accidentally; by any chance. **случа́йность** chance. **случа́йный** accidental; chance; incidental. **случа́ться** *impf*, **случи́ться** *pf* happen.

слу́шание listening; hearing. **слу́шатель** *m* listener; student; *pl* audience. **слу́шать** *impf* (*pf* по~, про~) listen (to); hear; attend lectures on; (я) слу́шаю! hello!; very well; ~ся +*gen* obey, listen to.

слыть (-ыву́, -ывёшь; -ыл, -á, -о) *impf* (*pf* про~) have the reputation (+*instr* за+*acc* for).

слыха́ть *impf*, **слы́шать** (-шу) *impf* (*pf* y~) hear; sense. **слы́шаться** (-шится) *impf* (*pf* по~) be heard. **слы́шимость** audibility. **слы́шимый** audible. **слы́шный** audible.

слюда́ mica.

слюна́ (*pl* -и, -éй) saliva; spit; *pl* spittle. **слюня́вый** dribbling.

сля́гу *etc.: see* слечь

сля́коть slush.

см. *abbr* (*of* смотри́) see, *vide*.

сма́зать (-а́жу) *pf*, **сма́зывать** *impf* lubricate; grease; slur over. **сма́зка** lubrication; greasing; grease. **сма́зочный** lubricating.

смак relish. **смакова́ть** *impf* relish; savour.

с|маневри́ровать *pf*.

сма́нивать *impf*, **смани́ть** (-ню́, -нишь) *pf* entice.

с|мастери́ть *pf*. **сма́тывать** *impf of* смота́ть

сма́хивать *impf*, **смахну́ть** (-ну́, -нёшь) *pf* brush away *or* off.

сма́чивать *impf of* смочи́ть

сме́жный adjacent.

смека́лка native wit.

смёл *etc.: see* смести́

смеле́ть (-éю) *impf* (*pf* о~) grow bolder. **сме́лость** boldness, courage. **сме́лый** bold, courageous. **смельча́к** (-á) daredevil.

смелю́ *etc.: see* смоло́ть

сме́на changing; change; replacement(s); relief; shift. **смени́ть** (-ню́, -нишь) *pf*, **сменя́ть**[1] *impf* change; replace; relieve; ~ся hand over; be relieved; take turns; +*instr* give place to. **сме́нный** shift; changeable. **сме́нщик** relief; *pl* new shift. **сменя́ть**[2] *pf* exchange.

с|ме́рить *pf*.

смерка́ться *impf*, **сме́ркнуться** (-нется) *pf* get dark.

смерте́льный mortal, fatal, death; extreme. **сме́ртность** mortality. **сме́ртный** mortal; deadly; deadly, extreme. **смерть** (*gen pl* -éй) death.

смерч whirlwind; waterspout; sandstorm.

смеси́тельный mixing. **с|меси́ть** (-ешу́, -éсишь) *pf*.

смести́ (-ету́, -етёшь; -ёл, -á) *pf* (*impf* смета́ть) sweep off, away.

смести́ть (-ещу́) *pf* (*impf* смеща́ть) displace; remove.

смесь mixture; medley.

сме́та estimate.

смета́на sour cream.

с|мета́ть[1] *pf* (*impf also* смётывать) tack (together).

смета́ть[2] *impf of* смести́

смётливый quick, sharp.

смету́ *etc.: see* смести́. **смётывать** *impf of* смета́ть

сметь (-éю) *impf* (*pf* по~) dare.

смех laughter; laugh. **смехотво́рный** laughable.

сме́шанный mixed; combined. **с|меша́ть** *pf*, **сме́шивать** *impf* mix, blend; confuse; ~ся mix, (inter)-blend; get mixed up. **смеше́ние** mixture; mixing up.

смеши́ть (-шу́) *impf* (*pf* на~, рас~) make laugh. **смешли́вый** given to laughing. **смешно́й** funny; ridiculous.

смешу́ *etc.*: *see* **смеси́ть, смеши́ть**

смеща́ть(ся *impf of* **смести́ть(ся. смеще́ние** displacement, removal. **смещу́** *etc.*: *see* **смести́ть**

смея́ться (-ею́сь, -еёшься) *impf* laugh (at +**над**+*instr*).

смире́ние humility, meekness. **смире́нный** humble, meek. **смири́тельн|ый**: ~**ая руба́шка** strait-jacket. **смири́ть** (-рю́). **смиря́ть** *impf* restrain, subdue; ~**ся** submit; resign o.s. **сми́рно** *adv* quietly; ~! attention! **сми́рный** quiet; submissive.

смогу́ *etc.*: *see* **смочь**

смола́ (*pl* -ы) resin; pitch, tar; rosin. **смоли́стый** resinous.

смолка́ть *impf*, **смо́лкнуть** (-ну; -олк) *pf* fall silent.

смо́лоду *adv* from one's youth.

с|молоти́ть (-очу́, -о́тишь) *pf*. **с|моло́ть** (смелю́, сме́лешь) *pf*.

смоляно́й pitch, tar, resin.

с|монти́ровать *pf*.

сморка́ть *impf* (*pf* вы́~) blow; ~**ся** blow one's nose.

сморо́дина (*no pl*; *usu collect*) currant; currants; currant-bush.

смо́рщенный wrinkled. **с|мо́рщить(ся** (-щу(сь) *pf*.

смота́ть *pf* (*impf* сма́тывать) wind, reel.

смотр (*loc* -у́; *pl* -о́тры) review, inspection. **смотре́ть** (-рю́, -ришь) *impf* (*pf* по~) look (at **на**+*acc*); see; watch; look through; examine; +**за**+*instr* look after; on +*acc*, **на**+*acc* look on to; +*instr* look (like); **смотри́(те)!** take care!; **смотря́** it depends; **смотря́ по**+*dat* depending on; ~**ся** look at o.s. **смотрово́й** observation, inspection.

смочи́ть (-чу́, -чишь) *pf* (*impf* сма́чивать) moisten.

с|мочь (-огу́, -о́жешь; смог, -ла́) *pf*.

с|моше́нничать *pf*. **смо́ю** *etc.*: *see* **смыть**

смрад stench. **смра́дный** stinking.

сму́глый (-гл, -а́, -о) dark-complexioned, swarthy.

смути́ть (-ущу́) *pf*, **смуща́ть** *impf* embarrass, confuse; ~**ся** be embarrassed, be confused. **сму́тный** vague; dim; troubled. **смуще́ние** embarrassment, confusion. **смущённый** (-ён, -а́) embarrassed, confused.

смыва́ть *impf of* **смыть**

смыка́ть(ся *impf of* **сомкну́ть(ся**

смысл sense; meaning. **смы́слить** *impf* understand. **смыслово́й** semantic.

смыть (смо́ю) *pf* (*impf* смыва́ть) wash off, away.

смычо́к (-чка́) bow.

смышлёный clever.

смягча́ть *impf*, **смягчи́ть** (-чу́) *pf* soften; alleviate; ~**ся** soften; relent; grow mild.

смяте́ние confusion; commotion. **с|мять(ся** (сомну́(сь, -нёшь(ся) *pf*.

снабди́ть (-бжу́) *pf*, **снабжа́ть** *impf* +*instr* supply with. **снабже́ние** supply, supplying.

сна́йпер sniper.

снару́жи *adv* on *or* from (the) outside.

снаря́д projectile, missile; shell; contrivance; tackle, gear. **снаряди́ть** (-яжу́) *pf*, **снаряжа́ть** *impf* equip, fit out. **снаряже́ние** equipment, outfit.

снасть (*gen pl* -е́й) tackle; *pl* rigging.

снача́ла *adv* at first; all over again.

сна́шивать *impf of* **сноси́ть**

СНГ *abbr* (*of* **Содру́жество незави́симых госуда́рств**) CIS.

снег (*loc* -у́; *pl* -а́) snow.

снеги́рь (-я́) bullfinch.

снегово́й snow. **снегопа́д** snowfall. **Снегу́рочка** Snow Maiden. **сне́жинка** snow-flake. **сне́жный** snow(y); ~**ая ба́ба** snowman. **снежо́к** (-жка́) light snow; snowball.

снести́[1] (-су́, -сёшь; -ёс, -ла́) *pf* (*impf* сноси́ть) take; bring together; bring *or* fetch down; carry away; blow off; demolish; endure; ~**сь** communicate (**с**+*instr* with).

с|нести́[2](**сь** (-су́(сь, -сёшь(ся; снёс(ся, -сла́(сь) *pf*.

снижа́ть *impf*, **сни́зить** (-и́жу) *pf* lower; bring down; reduce; ~**ся** come down; fall. **сниже́ние** lowering; loss of height.

снизойти́ (-йду́, -йдёшь; -ошёл, -шла́) *pf* (*impf* снисходи́ть) condescend.

сни́зу *adv* from below.

снима́ть(ся *impf of* **снять(ся. сни́мок** (-мка) photograph. **сниму́** *etc.*: *see* **снять**

сниска́ть (-ищу́, -и́щешь) *pf*, **сни́скивать** *impf* gain, win.

снисходи́тельность condescension; leniency. снисходи́тельный condescending; lenient. снисходи́ть (-ожу́, -о́дишь) impf of снизойти́. снисхожде́ние indulgence, leniency.

сни́ться impf (pf при~) impers+dat dream.

сноби́зм snobbery.

сно́ва adv again, anew.

снова́ть (сную, снуёшь) impf rush about.

сновиде́ние dream.

сноп (-á) sheaf.

сноро́вка knack, skill.

снос demolition; drift; wear. сноси́ть¹ (-ошу́, -о́сишь) pf (impf сна́шивать) wear out. сноси́ть²(ся (-ошу́(сь, -о́сишь(ся) impf of снести́(сь. сно́ска footnote. сно́сно adv tolerably, so-so. сно́сный tolerable; fair.

снотво́рный soporific.

сноха́ (pl -и) daughter-in-law.

сноше́ние intercourse; relations, dealings.

сношу́ etc.: see сноси́ть

сня́тие taking down; removal; making. снять (сниму́, -и́мешь; -ял, -á, -о) pf (impf снима́ть) take off; take down; gather in; remove; rent; take; make; photograph; ~ся come off; move off; be photographed.

со see с prep.

со- pref co-, joint. соа́втор co-author.

соба́ка dog. соба́чий dog's; canine. соба́чка little dog; trigger.

соберу́ etc.: see собра́ть

собе́с abbr (of социа́льное обеспе́чение) social security (department).

собесе́дник interlocutor, companion. собесе́дование conversation.

собира́тель m collector. собира́ть(ся impf of собра́ть(ся

собла́зн temptation. собла́знитель m, ~ница tempter; seducer. собла́знительный tempting; seductive. соблазни́ть pf, соблазня́ть impf tempt; seduce.

соблюда́ть impf, со|блюсти́ (-юду́, -дёшь; -юл, -á) pf observe; keep (to). соблюде́ние observance; maintenance.

собо́й, собо́ю see себя́

соболе́знование sympathy, condolence(s). соболе́зновать impf +dat sympathize or commiserate with.

со́боль (pl -и or -я́) m sable.

собо́р cathedral; council, synod. собо́рный cathedral.

собра́ние meeting; assembly; collection. собра́нный collected; concentrated.

собра́т (pl -ья, -ьев) colleague.

собра́ть (-беру́, -берёшь; -áл, -á, -о) pf (impf собира́ть) gather; collect; ~ся gather; prepare; intend, be going; +c+instr collect.

со́бственник owner, proprietor. со́бственнический proprietary; proprietorial. со́бственно adv: ~ (говоря́) strictly speaking, as a matter of fact. собственнору́чно adv personally, with one's own hand. со́бственность property; ownership. со́бственный (one's) own; proper; true; и́мя ~ое proper name; ~ой персо́ной in person.

собы́тие event.

собью́ etc.: see сбить

сова́ (pl -ы) owl.

сова́ть (сую́, -ёшь) impf (pf су́нуть) thrust, shove; ~ся push, push in; butt in.

соверша́ть impf, соверши́ть (-шу́) pf accomplish; carry out; commit; complete; ~ся happen; be accomplished. соверше́ние accomplishment; perpetration. соверше́нно adv perfectly; absolutely, completely. совершенноле́тие majority. совершенноле́тний of age. соверше́нный¹ perfect; absolute, complete. соверше́нный² perfective соверше́нство perfection. соверше́нствование perfecting; improvement. соверше́нствовать impf (pf y~) perfect; improve; ~ся в+instr perfect o.s. in; improve.

со́вестливый conscientious. со́вестно impers+dat be ashamed. со́весть conscience.

сове́т advice, counsel; opinion; council; soviet, Soviet. сове́тник adviser. сове́товать impf (pf по~) advise; ~ся c+instr consult, ask advice of. совето́лог Kremlinologist. сове́т|ский Soviet; ~ая власть the Soviet regime; ∼ий Сою́з the Soviet Union. **сове́тчик** adviser.

совеща́ние conference. **совеща́тельный** consultative, deliberative. **совеща́ться** *impf* deliberate; consult.

совлада́ть *pf* с+*instr* control, cope with.

совмести́мый compatible. **совмести́тель** *m* person holding more than one office. **совмести́ть** (-ещу́) *pf*, **совмеща́ть** *impf* combine; ∼ся coincide; be combined, combine. **совме́стно** jointly. **совме́стный** joint, combined.

сово́к (-вка́) shovel; scoop; dust-pan. **совокупи́ться** (-плю́сь) *pf*, **совокупля́ться** *impf* copulate. **совокупле́ние** copulation. **совоку́пно** *adv* jointly. **совоку́пность** aggregate, sum total.

совпада́ть *impf*, **совпа́сть** (-аде́т) *pf* coincide; agree, tally. **совпаде́ние** coincidence.

соврати́ть (-ащу́) *pf* (*impf* совраща́ть) pervert, seduce.

со|вра́ть (-вру́, -врёшь; -а́л, -а́, -о) *pf*.

совраща́ть(ся *impf of* соврати́ть(ся. **совраще́ние** perverting, seduction.

совреме́нник contemporary. **совреме́нность** the present (time); contemporaneity. **совреме́нный** contemporary; modern.

совру́ *etc.: see* совра́ть

совсе́м *adv* quite; entirely.

совхо́з State farm.

совью́ *etc.: see* свить

согла́сие consent; assent; agreement; harmony. **согласи́ться** (-ашу́сь) *pf* (*impf* соглаша́ться) consent; agree. **согла́сно** *adv* in accord, in harmony; *prep*+*dat* in accordance with. **согла́сный**[1] agreeable (to); in agreement; harmonious. **согла́сный**[2] consonant(al); *sb* consonant.

согласова́ние co-ordination; agreement. **согласо́ванность** co-ordination. **согласова́ть** *pf*, **согласо́вывать** *impf* co-ordinate; make agree; ∼ся conform; agree.

соглаша́ться *impf of* согласи́ться. **соглаше́ние** agreement. **соглашу́** *etc.: see* согласи́ть

согна́ть (сгоню́, сго́нишь; -а́л, -а́, -о)

pf (*impf* сгоня́ть) drive away; drive together.

со|гну́ть (-ну́, -нёшь) *pf* (*impf also* сгиба́ть) bend, curve; ∼ся bend (down).

согрева́ть *impf*, **согре́ть** (-е́ю) *pf* warm, heat; ∼ся get warm; warm o.s.

со|греши́ть (-шу́) *pf*.

со́да soda.

соде́йствие assistance. **соде́йствовать** *impf & pf* (*pf also* по∼) +*dat* assist; promote; contribute to.

содержа́ние maintenance, upkeep; content(s); pay. **содержа́тельный** rich in content; pithy. **содержа́ть** (-жу́, -жишь) *impf* keep; maintain; contain; ∼ся be kept; be maintained; be; be contained. **содержи́мое** *sb* contents.

со|дра́ть (сдеру́, -рёшь; -а́л, -а́, -о) *pf* (*impf also* сдира́ть) tear off, strip off; fleece.

содрога́ние shudder. **содрога́ться** *impf*, **содрогну́ться** (-ну́сь, -нёшься) *pf* shudder.

содру́жество concord; commonwealth.

соедине́ние joining, combination; joint; compound; formation. **Соединённое Короле́вство** United Kingdom. **Соединённые Шта́ты (Аме́рики)** *m pl* United States (of America). **соединённый** (-ён, -а́) united, joint. **соедини́тельный** connective, connecting. **соедини́ть** *pf*, **соединя́ть** *impf* join, unite; connect; combine; ∼ся join, unite; combine.

сожале́ние regret; pity; к сожале́нию unfortunately. **сожале́ть** (-е́ю) *impf* regret, deplore.

сожгу́ *etc.: see* сжечь. **сожже́ние** burning; cremation.

сожи́тель *m*, ∼**ница** room-mate, flat-mate; lover. **сожи́тельство** cohabitation.

сожму́ *etc.: see* сжать[2]. **сожну́** *etc.: see* сжать[1]. **созва́ниваться** *impf of* созвони́ться

созва́ть (-зову́, -зовёшь; -а́л, -а́, -о) *pf* (*impf* сзыва́ть, созыва́ть) call together; call; invite.

созве́здие constellation.

созвони́ться *pf* (*impf* созва́ниваться) ring up; speak on the telephone.

созву́чие accord; assonance. **созву́чный** harmonious; +dat in keeping with.

создава́ть (-даю́, -даёшь) impf, **созда́ть** (-а́м, -а́шь, -а́ст, -ади́м; со́здал, -а́, -о) pf create; establish; ∼ся be created; arise, spring up. **созда́ние** creation; work; creature. **созда́тель** m creator; originator.

созерца́ние contemplation. **созерца́тельный** contemplative. **созерца́ть** impf contemplate.

созида́ние creation. **созида́тельный** creative.

сознава́ть (-наю́, -наёшь) impf, **созна́ть** pf be conscious of, realize; acknowledge; ∼ся confess. **созна́ние** consciousness; acknowledgement; confession. **созна́тельность** awareness, consciousness. **созна́тельный** conscious; deliberate.

созову́ etc.: see **созва́ть**

созрева́ть impf, **со|зре́ть** (-е́ю) pf ripen, mature.

созы́в summoning, calling. **созыва́ть** impf of **созва́ть**

соизмери́мый commensurable.

соиска́ние competition. **соиска́тель** m, ∼ница competitor, candidate.

сойти́ (-йду́, -йдёшь; сошёл, -шла́) pf (impf **сходи́ть**) go or come down; get off; leave; come off; pass, go off; ∼ с ума́ go mad, go out of one's mind; ∼сь meet; gather; become friends; become intimate; agree.

сок (loc -ý) juice.

со́кол falcon.

сократи́ть (-ащу́) pf, **сокраща́ть** impf shorten; abbreviate; reduce; ∼ся grow shorter; decrease; contract. **сокраще́ние** shortening; abridgement; abbreviation; reduction.

сокрове́нный secret; innermost. **сокро́вище** treasure. **сокро́вищница** treasure-house.

сокруша́ть impf, **сокруши́ть** (-шу́) pf shatter; smash; distress; ∼ся grieve, be distressed. **сокруше́ние** smashing; grief. **сокрушённый** (-ён, -á) grief-stricken. **сокруши́тельный** shattering.

сокры́тие concealment.

со|лга́ть (-лгу́, -лжёшь; -ал, -á, -о) pf.

солда́т (gen pl -áт) soldier. **солда́т-**

ский soldier's.

соле́ние salting; pickling. **солёный** (со́лон, -á, -о) salt(y); salted; pickled. **соле́нье** salted food(s); pickles.

солида́рность solidarity. **соли́дный** solid; strong; reliable; respectable; sizeable.

соли́ст, соли́стка soloist.

соли́ть (-лю́, со́ли́шь) impf (pf по∼) salt; pickle.

со́лнечный sun; solar; sunny; ∼ свет sunlight; sunshine; ∼ уда́р sunstroke. **со́лнце** sun. **солнцепёк: на ∼е** in the sun. **солнцестоя́ние** solstice.

со́ло neut indecl solo; adv solo.

солове́й (-вья́) nightingale.

со́лод malt.

солодко́вый liquorice.

соло́ма straw; thatch. **соло́менный** straw; thatch. **соло́минка** straw.

со́лон etc.: see **солёный**. **солони́на** corned beef. **соло́нка** salt-cellar.

солонча́к (-á) saline soil; pl salt marshes. **соль** (pl -и, -е́й) salt.

со́льный solo.

солью́ etc.: see **слить**

соляно́й, соля́ный salt, saline; **соляна́я кислота́** hydrochloric acid.

со́мкнутый close. **сомкну́ть** (-ну́, -нёшь) pf (impf **смыка́ть**) close; ∼ся close.

сомнева́ться impf doubt, have doubts. **сомне́ние** doubt. **сомни́тельный** doubtful.

сомну́ etc.: see **смять**

сон (сна) sleep; dream. **сонли́вость** sleepiness; somnolence. **сонли́вый** sleepy. **со́нный** sleepy; sleeping.

сона́та sonata.

соне́т sonnet.

сообража́ть impf, **сообрази́ть** (-ажу́) pf consider, think out; weigh; understand. **соображе́ние** consideration; understanding; notion. **сообрази́тельный** quick-witted.

сообра́зный с+instr conforming to, in keeping with.

сообща́ adv together. **сообща́ть** impf, **сообщи́ть** (-щу́) pf communicate, report, announce; impart; +dat inform. **сообще́ние** communication, report; announcement. **сообще́ство** association. **сообщник** accomplice.

сооруди́ть (-ужу́) pf, **сооружа́ть** impf build, erect. **сооруже́ние**

building; structure.
соотвéтственно *adv* accordingly, corresponding; *prep+dat* according to, in accordance with. **соотвéтственный** corresponding. **соотвéтствие** accordance, correspondence. **соотвéтствовать** *impf* correspond, conform. **соотвéтствующий** corresponding; suitable.

соотéчественник fellow-countryman.

соотношéние correlation.

сопéрник rival. **сопéрничать** *impf* compete, vie. **сопéрничество** rivalry.

сопéть (-плю́) *impf* wheeze; snuffle.

со́пка hill, mound.

сопли́вый snotty.

сопостáвить (-влю) *pf*, **сопоставля́ть** *impf* compare. **сопоставлéние** comparison.

сопредéльный contiguous.

со|прéть *pf*.

соприкасáться *impf*, **соприкосну́ться** (-ну́сь, -нёшься) *pf* adjoin; come into contact. **соприкосновéние** contact.

сопроводи́тельный accompanying. **сопроводи́ть** (-ожу́) *pf*, **сопровождáть** *impf* accompany; escort. **сопровождéние** accompaniment; escort.

сопротивлéние resistance. **сопротивля́ться** *impf +dat* resist, oppose.

сопу́тствовать *impf +dat* accompany.

сопью́сь *etc.: see* **спи́ться**

соп litter, rubbish.

соразмéрить *pf*, **соразмеря́ть** *impf* balance, match. **соразмéрный** proportionate, commensurate.

сорáтник comrade-in-arms.

сорвáть (-ву́, -вёшь; -áл, -á, -о) *pf* (*impf* **срывáть**) tear off, away, down; break off; pick; get; break; ruin, spoil; vent; ~**ся** break away, break loose; fall, come down; fall through.

с|организовáть *pf*.

соревновáние competition; contest. **соревновáться** *impf* compete.

сори́ть *impf* (*pf* **на~**) *+acc or instr* litter; throw about. **со́рный** rubbish. refuse; ~**ая травá** weed(s). **сорня́к** (-á) weed.

со́рок (-á) forty.

соро́ка magpie.

сороков|о́й fortieth; ~**ые го́ды** the forties.

соро́чка shirt; blouse; shift.

сорт (*pl* -á) grade, quality; sort. **сортировáть** *impf* (*pf* **рас~**) sort, grade. **сортиро́вка** sorting. **сорти́ровочн|ый** sorting; ~**ая** *sb* marshalling-yard. **сортиро́вщик** sorter. **со́ртный** high quality.

сосáть (-су́, -сёшь) *impf* suck.

со|свáтать *pf*.

сосéд (*pl* -и), **сосéдка** neighbour. **сосéдний** neighbouring; adjacent, next. **сосéдский** neighbours'. **сосéдство** neighbourhood. **соси́ска** frankfurter, sausage.

со́ска (*baby's*) dummy.

соскáкивать *impf of* **соскочи́ть**

соскáльзывать *impf*, **соскользну́ть** (-ну́, -нёшь) *pf* slide down, slide off.

соскочи́ть (-чу́, -чишь) *pf* (*impf* **соскáкивать**) jump off *or* down; come off.

соску́читься (-чусь) *pf* get bored; ~ **по+dat** miss.

сослагáтельный subjunctive.

сослáть (сошлю́, -лёшь) *pf* (*impf* **ссылáть**) exile, deport; ~**ся на+acc** refer to; cite; plead, allege.

сосло́вие estate; class.

сослужи́вец (-вца) colleague.

соснá (*pl* -ы, -сен) pine(-tree). **сосно́вый** pine; deal.

сосо́к (-скá) nipple, teat.

сосредото́ченный concentrated. **сосредото́чивать** *impf*, **сосредото́чить** (-чу) *pf* concentrate; focus; ~**ся** concentrate.

состáв composition; structure; compound; staff; strength; train; **в ~е** *+gen* consisting of. **составитель** *m* compiler. **состáвить** (-влю) *pf*, **составля́ть** *impf* put together; make (up); draw up; compile; be, constitute; total; ~**ся** form, be formed. **составно́й** compound; component, constituent.

со|стáрить(ся *pf*.

состоя́ние state, condition; fortune. **состоя́тельный** well-to-do; well-grounded. **состоя́ть** (-ою́) *impf* be; **+из+gen** consist of; **+в+prep** consist in, be. **состоя́ться** (-ои́тся) *pf* take place.

сострада́ние compassion. **сострада́тельный** compassionate.

с|остри́ть pf. **со|стря́пать** pf.

со|стыкова́ть pf, **состыко́вывать** impf dock; **~ся** dock.

состяза́ние competition, contest. **состяза́ться** impf compete.

сосу́д vessel.

сосу́лька icicle.

сосуществова́ние co-existence.

со|счита́ть pf. **сот** see **сто**.

сотворе́ние creation. **со|твори́ть** pf.

со|тка́ть (-ку́, -кёшь; -а́л, -а́ла́, -о) pf.

со́тня (gen pl -тен) a hundred.

сотру́ etc.: see **стере́ть**

сотру́дник collaborator; colleague; employee. **сотру́дничать** impf collaborate; +в+prep contribute to. **сотру́дничество** collaboration.

сотряса́ть impf, **сотрясти́** (-су́, -сёшь; -я́с, -ла́) pf shake; **~ся** tremble. **сотрясе́ние** shaking; concussion.

со́ты (-ов) pl honeycomb.

со́тый hundredth.

соумы́шленник accomplice.

со́ус sauce; gravy; dressing.

соуча́стие participation; complicity. **соуча́стник** participant; accomplice.

софа́ (pl -ы) sofa.

соха́ (pl -и) (wooden) plough.

со́хнуть (-ну; сох) impf (pf вы-, за-, про-) (get) dry; wither.

сохране́ние preservation; conservation; (safe)keeping; retention. **со|храни́ть** pf, **сохраня́ть** impf preserve, keep; **~ся** remain (intact); last out; be well preserved. **сохра́нный** safe.

социа́л-демокра́т Social Democrat. **социа́л-демократи́ческий** Social Democratic. **социали́зм** socialism. **социали́ст** socialist. **социалисти́ческий** socialist. **социа́льный** social; **~ое обеспе́чение** social security. **социо́лог** sociologist. **социоло́гия** sociology.

соцреали́зм socialist realism.

сочета́ние combination. **сочета́ть** impf & pf combine; **~ся** combine; harmonize; match.

сочине́ние composition; work. **сочини́ть** pf, **сочиня́ть** impf compose; write; make up.

сочи́ться (-и́тся) impf ooze (out), trickle; **~ кро́вью** bleed.

со́чный (-чен, -чна́, -о) juicy; rich.

сочту́ etc.: see **счесть**

сочу́вствие sympathy. **сочу́вствовать** impf +dat sympathize with.

сошёл etc.: see **сойти́**. **сошлю́** etc.: see **сосла́ть**. **сошью́** etc.: see **сшить**

сощу́ривать impf, **со|щу́рить** pf screw up, narrow; **~ся** screw up one's eyes; narrow.

сою́з[1] union; alliance; league. **сою́з**[2] conjunction. **сою́зник** ally. **сою́зный** allied; Union.

спад recession; abatement. **спада́ть** impf of **спасть**

спазм spasm.

спа́ивать impf of **спая́ть**, **спои́ть**

спа́йка soldered joint; solidarity, unity.

с|пали́ть pf.

спа́льн|ый sleeping; **~ый ваго́н** sleeping car; **~ое ме́сто** berth. **спа́льня** (gen pl -лен) bedroom.

спа́ржа asparagus.

спартакиа́да sports meeting.

спаса́тельный rescue; **~ жиле́т** life jacket; **~ круг** lifebuoy; **~ по́яс** lifebelt. **спаса́ть(ся** impf of **спасти́(сь**. **спасе́ние** rescue, escape; salvation. **спаси́бо** thank you. **спаси́тель** m rescuer; saviour. **спаси́тельный** saving; salutary.

спасти́ (-су́, -сёшь; спас, -ла́) pf (impf **спаса́ть**) save; rescue; **~сь** escape; be saved.

спасть (-адёт) pf (impf **опада́ть**) fall (down); abate.

спать (сплю; -ал, -а́, -о) impf sleep; **лечь ~** go to bed.

спа́янность cohesion, unity. **спа́янный** united. **спая́ть** pf (impf **спа́ивать**) solder, weld; unite.

спекта́кль m performance; show.

спектр spectrum.

спекули́ровать impf speculate. **спекуля́нт** speculator, profiteer. **спекуля́ция** speculation; profiteering.

спе́лый ripe.

сперва́ adv at first; first.

спе́реди adv in front, from the front; prep+gen (from) in front of.

спёртый close, stuffy.

спеси́вый arrogant, haughty. **спесь** arrogance, haughtiness.

спеть[1] (-е́ет) impf (pf по~) ripen.

с|петь[2] (спою́, спое́шь) pf.

спец- *abbr in comb* (*of* специа́льный) special. **спецко́р** special correspondent. **~оде́жда** protective clothing; overalls.

специализа́ция specialization. **специализи́роваться** *impf & pf* specialize. **специали́ст, ~ка** specialist, expert. **специа́льность** speciality; profession. **специа́льный** special; specialist.

специ́фика specific character. **специфи́ческий** specific.

спе́ция spice.

спецо́вка protective clothing; overall(s).

спеши́ть (-шу́) *impf* (*pf* по~) hurry, be in a hurry; be fast.

спе́шка hurry, haste. **спе́шный** urgent.

спива́ться *impf of* спи́ться

СПИД *abbr* (*of* синдро́м приобретённого имму́нного дефици́та) Aids.

с|пики́ровать *pf*.

спи́ливать *impf*, **спили́ть** (-лю́, -лишь) *pf* saw down, off.

спина́ (*acc* -у; *pl* -ы) back. **спи́нка** back. **спинно́й** spinal; ~ мозг spinal cord.

спира́ль spiral.

спирт alcohol, spirit(s). **спиртно́й** alcoholic; ~о́е *sb* alcohol. **спиртовка** spirit-stove. **спиртово́й** spirit, alcoholic.

списа́ть (-ишу́, -и́шешь) *pf*, **спи́сывать** *impf* copy; ~ся exchange letters. **спи́сок** (-ска) list; record.

спи́ться (сопью́сь, -ьёшься; -и́лся, -а́сь) *pf* (*impf* спива́ться) take to drink.

спи́хивать *impf*, **спихну́ть** (-ну́, -нёшь) *pf* push aside, down.

спи́ца knitting-needle; spoke.

спи́чечн|ый match; ~ая коро́бка match-box. **спи́чка** match.

спишу́ *etc.*: *see* списа́ть

сплав[1] floating. **сплав**[2] alloy. **спла́вить**[1] (-влю) *pf*, **сплавля́ть**[1] *impf* float; raft; get rid of. **спла́вить**[2] (-влю) *pf*, **сплавля́ть**[2] *impf* alloy; ~ся fuse.

с|плани́ровать *pf*. **спла́чивать(ся** *impf of* сплоти́ть(ся. **сплёвывать** *impf of* сплю́нуть

с|плести́ (-ету́, -етёшь; -ёл, -á) *pf*,

сплета́ть *impf* weave; plait; interlace. **сплете́ние** interlacing; plexus.

спле́тник, -ница gossip, scandal-monger. **спле́тничать** *impf* (*pf* на~) gossip. **спле́тня** (*gen pl* -тен) gossip, scandal.

сплоти́ть (-очу́) *pf* (*impf* спла́чивать) join; unite, rally; ~ся unite, rally; close ranks. **сплоче́ние** uniting. **сплочённость** cohesion, unity. **сплочённый** (-ён, -á) united; firm; unbroken.

сплошно́й solid; complete; continuous; utter. **сплошь** *adv* all over; completely; ~ да ря́дом pretty often.

сплю *see* спать

сплю́нуть (-ну) *pf* (*impf* сплёвывать) spit; spit out.

сплю́щивать *impf*, **сплю́щить** (-щу) *pf* flatten; ~ся become flat.

с|пляса́ть (-яшу́, -я́шешь) *pf*.

сподви́жник comrade-in-arms.

споить (-ою́, -о́ишь) *pf* (*impf* спа́ивать) make a drunkard of.

споко́йн|ый quiet; calm; ~ой но́чи good night! **споко́йствие** quiet; calm, serenity.

споласкивать *impf of* сполосну́ть

сполза́ть *impf*, **сползти́** (-зу́, -зёшь; -олз, -лá) *pf* climb down; slip (down); fall away.

сполна́ *adv* in full.

сполосну́ть (-ну́, -нёшь) *pf* (*impf* споласкивать) rinse.

спо́нсор sponsor, backer.

спор argument; controversy; dispute. **спо́рить** *impf* (*pf* по~) argue; dispute; debate. **спо́рный** debatable, questionable; disputed; moot.

спо́ра spore.

спорт sport. **спорти́вный** sports; ~ зал gymnasium. **спортсме́н, ~ка** athlete, player.

спо́соб way, method; таки́м ~ом in this way. **спосо́бность** ability, aptitude; capacity. **спосо́бный** able; clever; capable. **спосо́бствовать** *impf* (*pf* по~) +*dat* assist; further.

споткну́ться (-ну́сь, -нёшься) *pf*, **спотыка́ться** *impf* stumble.

спохвати́ться (-ачу́сь, -а́тишься) *pf*, **спохва́тываться** *impf* remember suddenly.

спою́ *etc.*: *see* спеть, споить

спра́ва *adv* from *or* on the right.

справедли́вость justice; fairness; truth. **справедли́вый** just; fair; justified.

спра́вить (-влю) *pf*, **справля́ть** *impf* celebrate. **спра́виться**[1] (-влюсь) *pf*, **справля́ться** *impf* c+*instr* cope with, manage. **спра́виться**[2] (-влюсь) *pf*, **справля́ться** *impf* inquire; +в+*prep* consult. **спра́вка** information; reference; certificate; **наводи́ть спра́вку** make inquiries. **спра́вочник** reference-book, directory. **спра́вочный** inquiry, information.

спра́шивать(ся *impf of* **спроси́ть(ся**

спринт sprint. **спри́нтер** sprinter.

с|провоци́ровать *pf*. **с|проекти́ровать** *pf*.

спрос demand; asking; **без ~у** without permission. **спроси́ть** (-ошу́, -о́сишь) *pf* (*impf* **спра́шивать**) ask (for); inquire; **~ся** ask permission.

спрут octopus.

спры́гивать *impf*, **спры́гнуть** (-ну) *pf* jump off, jump down.

спры́скивать *impf*, **спры́снуть** (-ну) *pf* sprinkle.

спряга́ть *impf* (*pf* **про~**) conjugate. **спряже́ние** conjugation.

с|прясть (-яду́, -яде́шь; -ял, -я́лá, -о) *pf*. **с|пря́тать(ся** (-я́чу(сь) *pf*.

спу́гивать *impf*, **спугну́ть** (-ну́, -нёшь) *pf* frighten off.

спуск lowering; descent; slope. **спуска́ть** *impf*, **спусти́ть** (-ущу́, -у́стишь) *pf* let down, lower; let go, release; let out; send out; go down; forgive; squander; **~ кора́бль** launch a ship; **~ куро́к** pull the trigger; **~ пе́тлю** drop a stitch; **~ся** go down, descend. **спусково́й** trigger. **спустя́** *prep+acc* after; later.

с|пу́тать(ся *pf*.

спу́тник satellite, sputnik; (travelling) companion.

спущу́ *etc.: see* **спусти́ть**

спя́чка hibernation; sleepiness.

ср. *abbr* (*of* **сравни́**) cf.

сраба́тывать *impf*, **срабо́тать** *pf* make; work, operate.

сравне́ние comparison; simile. **сра́внивать** *impf of* **сравни́ть**, **сравня́ть**. **сравни́мый** comparable. **сравни́тельно** *adv* comparatively. **сравни́тельный** comparative. **срав-**

ни́ть *pf* (*impf* **сра́внивать**) compare; **~ся** c+*instr* compare with. **с|равня́ть** *pf* (*impf also* **сра́внивать**) make even, equal; level.

сража́ть *impf*, **срази́ть** (-ажу́) *pf* strike down; overwhelm, crush; **~ся** fight. **сраже́ние** battle.

сра́зу *adv* at once.

срам shame. **срами́ть** (-млю́) *impf* (*pf* **о~**) shame; **~ся** cover o.s. with shame. **срамота́** shame.

сраста́ние growing together. **сраста́ться** *impf*, **срасти́сь** (-тётся; сро́сся, -ла́сь) *pf* grow together; knit.

среда́[1] (*pl* -ы) environment, surroundings; medium. **среда́**[2] (*acc* -у; *pl* -ы, -а́м *or* -ам) Wednesday. **среди́** *prep+gen* among; in the middle of; **~ бе́ла дня** in broad daylight. **средиземномо́рский** Mediterranean. **сре́дне** *adv* so-so. **средневеко́вый** medieval. **средневеко́вье** the Middle Ages. **сре́дний** middle; medium; mean; average; middling; secondary; neuter; **~ее** *sb* mean, average. **средото́чие** focus. **сре́дство** means; remedy.

срез cut; section; slice. **с|ре́зать** (-е́жу) *pf*. **среза́ть** *impf* cut off; slice; fail; **~ся** fail.

с|репети́ровать *pf*.

срисова́ть *pf*, **срисо́вывать** *impf* copy.

с|ровня́ть *pf*.

сро́дство affinity.

срок date; term; time, period; **в ~, к ~у** in time, to time.

сро́сся *etc.: see* **срасти́сь**

сро́чно *adv* urgently. **сро́чность** urgency. **сро́чный** urgent; for a fixed period.

сро́ю *etc.: see* **срыть**

сруб felling; framework. **сруба́ть** *impf*, **с|руби́ть** (-блю́, -бишь) *pf* cut down; build (*of logs*).

срыв disruption; breakdown; ruining. **срыва́ть**[1]**(ся** *impf of* **сорва́ть(ся**

срыва́ть[2] *impf*, **срыть** (сро́ю) *pf* raze to the ground.

сря́ду *adv* running.

сса́дина scratch. **ссади́ть** (-ажу́, -а́дишь) *pf*, **сса́живать** *impf* set down; help down; turn off.

ссо́ра quarrel. **ссо́рить** *impf* (*pf* **по~**) cause to quarrel; **~ся** quarrel.

СССР abbr (of Союз Советских Социалистических Республик) USSR.

ссуда loan. ссудить (-ужу, -удишь) pf, ссужать impf lend, loan.

ссылать(ся impf of сослать(ся. ссылка¹ exile. ссылка² reference. ссыльный, ссыльная sb exile.

ссыпать (-плю) pf, ссыпать impf pour.

стабилизатор stabilizer; tail-plane. стабилизировать(ся impf & pf stabilize. стабильность stability. стабильный stable, firm.

ставень (-вня; gen pl -вней) m, ставня (gen pl -вен) shutter. ставить (-влю) impf (pf по~) put, place, set; stand; station; erect; install; apply; present, stage. ставка¹ rate; stake. ставка² headquarters.

ставня see ставень

стадион stadium.

стадия stage.

стадность herd instinct. стадный gregarious. стадо (pl -á) herd, flock.

стаж length of service; probation. стажёр probationer; student on a special non-degree course. стажировка period of training.

стакан glass.

сталелитейный steel-founding; ~ завод steel foundry. сталеплавильный steel-making; ~ завод steel works. сталепрокатный (steel-)rolling; ~ стан rolling-mill.

сталкивать(ся impf of столкнуть(ся

стало быть conj consequently.

сталь steel. стальной steel.

стамеска chisel.

стан¹ figure, torso.

стан² camp.

стан³ mill.

стандарт standard. стандартный standard.

станица Cossack village.

станкостроение machine-tool engineering.

становиться (-влюсь, -вишься) impf of стать¹

станок (-нка) machine tool, machine.

стану etc.: see стать²

станционный station. станция station.

стапель (pl -я) m stocks.

стаптывать(ся impf of стоптать(ся

старание effort. старательность diligence. старательный diligent.

стараться impf (pf по~) try.

стареть impf (pf по~, у~) grow old.

старец (-рца) elder, (venerable) old man. старик (-á) old man. старина antiquity, olden times; antique(s); old fellow. старинный ancient; old; antique. старить impf (pf со~) age, make old; ~ся age, grow old.

старо- in comb old. старовер Old Believer. ~жил old resident. ~модный old-fashioned. ~славянский Old Slavonic.

староста head; monitor; churchwarden. старость old age.

старт start; на ~! on your marks! стартёр starter. стартовать impf & pf start. стартовый starting.

старуха, старушка old woman. старческий old man's; senile. старше comp of старый. старший oldest, eldest; senior; head; ~ие sb pl (one's) elders; ~ий sb chief; man in charge. старшина m sergeant-major; petty officer; leader, senior representative. старый (-ар, -á, -о) old. старьё old things, junk.

стаскивать impf of стащить

с|тасовать pf.

статист extra.

статистика statistics. статистический statistical.

статный stately.

статский civil, civilian.

статус status. статус-кво neut indecl status quo.

статуэтка statuette.

статуя statue.

стать¹ (-ану) pf (impf становиться) stand; take up position; stop; cost; begin; +instr become; +c+instr become of; не ~ impers+gen cease to be; disappear; его не стало he is no more; ~ на колени kneel.

стать² physique, build.

статься (-áнется) pf happen.

статья (gen pl -ей) article; clause; item; matter.

стационар permanent establishment; hospital. стационарный stationary; permanent; ~ больной in-patient.

стачечник striker. стачка strike.

с|тащить (-щу, -щишь) pf (impf also

стаскивать) drag off, pull off.

стая flock; school, shoal; pack.

ствол (-á) trunk; barrel.

створка leaf, fold.

стебель (-бля; *gen pl* -блей) *m* stem, stalk.

стёган|ый quilted; ~ое одеяло quilt. стегать¹ *impf (pf* вы~) quilt.

стегать² *impf,* стегнуть (-ну) *pf (pf also* от~) whip, lash.

стежок (-жка) stitch.

стезя path, way.

стёк *etc.: see* стечь. стекать(ся *impf of* стечь(ся

стекло (*pl* -ёкла, -кол) glass; lens; (window)pane.

стекло- *in comb* glass. стекловолокно glass fibre. ~очиститель *m* windscreen-wiper. ~рез glass-cutter. ~ткань fibreglass.

стеклянный glass; glassy. стекольщик glazier.

стелить *see* стлать

стеллаж (-á) shelves, shelving.

стелька insole.

стелю *etc.: see* стлать

с|темнеть (-éет) *pf.*

стена (*acc* -у, *pl* -ы, -ám) wall. стенгазета wall newspaper.

стенд stand.

стенка wall; side. стенной wall.

стенограмма shorthand record. стенограф, стенографист, ~ка stenographer. стенографировать *impf* & *pf* take down in shorthand. стенографический shorthand. стенография shorthand.

стенокардия angina.

степенный staid; middle-aged.

степень (*gen pl* -éй) degree; extent; power.

степной steppe. степь (*loc* -и; *gen pl* -éй) steppe.

стервятник vulture.

стерегу *etc.: see* стеречь

стерео *indecl adj* stereo. стерео- *in comb* stereo. стереотип stereotype. стереотипный stereotype(d). стереофонический stereo(phonic). ~фония stereo(phony).

стереть (сотру, сотрёшь; стёр) *pf (impf* стирать¹) wipe off; rub out, rub sore; ~ся rub off; wear down; be effaced.

стеречь (-регу, -режёшь; -ёг, -лá)

impf guard; watch for.

стержень (-жня) *m* pivot; rod; core.

стерилизовать *impf* & *pf* sterilize. стерильный sterile.

стерлинг sterling.

стерлядь (*gen pl* -éй) sterlet.

стерпеть (-плю, -пишь) *pf* bear, endure.

стёртый worn, effaced.

стеснение constraint. стеснительный shy; inconvenient. с|теснить *pf,* стеснять *impf* constrain; hamper; inhibit. с|тесниться *pf,* стесняться *impf (pf also* по~) +inf feel too shy (to), be ashamed to.

стечение confluence; gathering; combination. стечь (-чёт; -ёк, -лá) *pf (impf* стекать) flow down; ~ся flow together; gather.

стилистический stylistic. стиль *m* style. стильный stylish; period.

стимул stimulus, incentive. стимулировать *impf* & *pf* stimulate.

стипендия grant.

стиральный washing.

стирать¹(ся *impf of* стереть(ся

стирать² *impf (pf* вы~) wash, launder; ~ся wash. стирка washing, wash, laundering.

стискивать *impf,* стиснуть (-ну) *pf* squeeze; clench; hug.

стих (-á) verse; line; *pl* poetry.

стихать *impf of* стихнуть

стихийный elemental; spontaneous. стихия element.

стихнуть (-ну; стих) *pf (impf* стихать) subside; calm down.

стихотворение poem. стихотворный in verse form.

стлать, стелить (стелю, стелешь) *impf (pf* по~) spread; ~ постель make a bed; ~ся spread; creep.

сто (*gen* ста; *gen pl* сот) a hundred.

стог (*loc* -е & -ý; *pl* -á) stack, rick.

стоимость cost; value. стоить *impf* cost; be worth(while); deserve.

стой *see* стоять

стойка counter, bar; prop; upright; strut. стойкий firm; stable; steadfast. стойкость firmness, stability; steadfastness. стойло stall. стоймя *adv* upright.

сток flow; drainage; drain, gutter; sewer.

стол (-á) table; desk; cuisine.

столб (-á) post, pole, pillar, column. **столбене́ть** (-éю) *impf* (*pf* o~) be rooted to the ground. **столбня́к** (-á) stupor; tetanus.

столе́тие century; centenary. **столе́тний** hundred-year-old; of a hundred years.

столи́ца capital; metropolis. **столи́чный** (of the) capital.

столкнове́ние collision; clash. **столкну́ть** (-ну́, -нёшь) *pf* (*impf* ста́лкивать) push off, away; cause to collide; bring together; ~ся collide, clash; +c+*instr* run into.

столо́вая *sb* dining-room; canteen. **столо́вый** table.

столп (-á) pillar.

столпи́ться *pf* crowd.

столь *adv* so. **сто́лько** *adv* so much, so many.

столя́р (-á) joiner, carpenter. **столя́рный** joiner's.

стомато́лог dentist.

стометро́вка (the) hundred metres. **стон** groan. **стона́ть** (-ну́, -нешь) *impf* groan.

стоп! *int* stop!

стопа́[1] foot.

стопа́[2] (*pl* -á) ream; pile.

сто́пка[1] pile.

сто́пка[2] small glass.

сто́пор stop, catch. **сто́помриться** *impf* (*pf* за~) come to a stop.

стопроце́нтный hundred-per-cent.

стоп-сигна́л brake-light.

стопта́ть (-пчу́, -пчешь) *pf* (*impf* ста́птывать) wear down; ~ся wear down.

с|торгова́ть(ся *pf*.

сто́рож (*pl* -á) watchman, guard. **сторожево́й** watch; patrol-. **сторожи́ть** (-жу́) *impf* guard, watch (over).

сторона́ (*acc* сто́рону, *pl* сто́роны, -ро́н, -áм) side; direction; hand; feature; part; land; **в сто́рону** aside; **с мое́й стороны́** for my part; **с одно́й стороны́** on the one hand. **сторони́ться** (-ню́сь, -ни́шься) *impf* (*pf* по~) stand aside; +*gen* avoid. **сторо́нник** supporter, advocate.

сто́чный sewage, drainage.

стоя́нка stop; parking; stopping place, parking space; stand; rank. **стоя́ть** (-ою́) *impf* (*pf* по~) stand; be; stay; stop; have stopped; +за+*acc*

stand up for; ~ **на коле́нях** kneel. **стоя́чий** standing; upright; stagnant.

сто́ящий deserving; worthwhile.

стр. *abbr* (*of* страни́ца) page.

страда́ (*pl* -ды) (hard work at) harvest time.

страда́лец (-льца) sufferer. **страда́ние** suffering. **страда́тельный** passive. **страда́ть** (-áю *or* -ра́жду) *impf* (*pf* по~) suffer; ~ **за** +*gen* feel for.

стра́жа guard, watch; **под стра́жей** under arrest, in custody; **стоя́ть на стра́же** +*gen* guard.

страна́ (*pl* -ы) country; land; ~ **све́та** cardinal point.

страни́ца page.

стра́нник, стра́нница wanderer.

стра́нно *adv* strangely. **стра́нность** strangeness; eccentricity. **стра́нн|ый** (-áнен, -áнна, -о) strange.

стра́нствие wandering. **стра́нствовать** *impf* wander.

Страстн|о́й of Holy Week; ~**áя пя́тница** Good Friday.

стра́стный (-тен, -тна́, -о) passionate. **страсть**[1] (*gen pl* -éй) passion. **страсть**[2] *adv* awfully, frightfully.

стратеги́ческий strategic(al). **страте́гия** strategy.

стратосфе́ра stratosphere.

стра́ус ostrich.

страх fear.

страхова́ние insurance; ~ **жи́зни** life insurance. **страхова́ть** *impf* (*pf* за~) insure (от+*gen* against); ~ся insure o.s. **страхо́вка** insurance.

страши́ться (-шу́сь) *impf* +*gen* be afraid of. **стра́шно** *adv* awfully. **стра́шный** (-шен, -шна́, -о) terrible, awful.

стрекоза́ (*pl* -ы) dragonfly.

стрекота́ть (-очу́, -о́чешь) *impf* chirr. **стрела́** (*pl* -ы) arrow; shaft; boom. **стреле́ц** (-льца́) Sagittarius. **стре́лка** pointer; hand; needle; arrow; spit; points. **стрелко́вый** rifle; shooting; infantry. **стрело́к** (-лка́) shot; rifleman, gunner. **стре́лочник** pointsman. **стрельба́** (*pl* -ы) shooting, firing. **стре́льчатый** lancet; arched. **стреля́ть** *impf* shoot; fire; ~ся shoot o.s.; fight a duel.

стремгла́в *adv* headlong.

стреми́тельный swift; impetuous.

стреми́ться (-млю́сь) *impf* strive.
стремле́ние striving, aspiration.
стремни́на rapid(s).
стре́мя (-мени; *pl* -мена́, -мя́н, -а́м) *neut* stirrup. стремя́нка step-ladder.
стресс stress.
стри́женый short; short-haired, cropped; shorn. стри́жка hair-cut; shearing. стричь (-игу́, -ижёшь; -иг) *impf* (*pf* о~) cut, clip; cut the hair of; shear; ~ся have one's hair cut.
строга́ть *impf* (*pf* вы́~) plane, shave. стро́гий strict; severe. стро́гость strictness.
строево́й combatant; line; drill. строе́ние building; structure; composition.
строжа́йший, стро́же *superl* & *comp of* стро́гий
строи́тель *m* builder. строи́тельный building, construction. строи́тельство building, construction; building site. стро́ить *impf* (*pf* по~) build; construct; make; base; draw up; ~ся be built, be under construction; draw up; стро́йся! fall in! строй (*loc* -ю́; *pl* -и *or* -й, -ев *or* -ёв) system; régime; structure; pitch; formation. стро́йка building; building-site. стро́йность proportion; harmony; balance, order. стро́йный (-о́ен, -ойна́, -о) harmonious, orderly, well-proportioned, shapely.
строка́ (*acc* -о́ку́; *pl* -и, -а́м) line; кра́сная ~ new paragraph.
строп, стро́па sling; shroud line.
стропи́ло rafter, beam.
стропти́вый refractory.
строфа́ (*pl* -ы, -а́м) stanza.
строчи́ть (-чу́, -о́чи́шь) *impf* (*pf* на~, про~) stitch; scribble, dash off. стро́чка stitch; line.
стро́ю *etc.*: *see* стро́ить
струга́ть *impf* (*pf* вы́~) plane. стру́жка shaving.
струи́ться *impf* stream.
структу́ра structure.
струна́ (*pl* -ы) string. стру́нный stringed.
струп (*pl* -пья, -пьев) scab.
с|тру́сить (-у́шу) *pf*.
стручо́к (-чка́) pod.
струя́ (*pl* -и, -уя́м) jet, spurt, stream.
стря́пать *impf* (*pf* со~) cook; concoct. стряпня́ cooking.

стря́хивать *impf*, стряхну́ть (-ну́, -нёшь) *pf* shake off.
студени́стый jelly-like.
студе́нт, студе́нтка student. студе́нческий student.
сту́день (-дня) *m* jelly; aspic.
студи́ть (-ужу́, -у́дишь) *impf* (*pf* о~) cool.
сту́дия studio.
сту́жа severe cold, hard frost.
стук knock; clatter. сту́кать *impf*, сту́кнуть (-ну) *pf* knock; bang; strike; ~ся knock (o.s.), bang. стука́ч (-а́) informer.
стул (*pl* -лья, -льев) chair. сту́льчак (-а́) (*lavatory*) seat. сту́льчик stool.
сту́па mortar.
ступа́ть *impf*, ступи́ть (-плю́, -пишь) *pf* step; tread. ступе́нчатый stepped, graded. ступе́нь (*gen pl* -е́ней) step, rung; stage, grade. ступе́нька step.
отупня́ foot; sole.
стуча́ть (-чу́) *impf* (*pf* по~) knock; chatter; pound; ~ся в+*acc* knock at.
стушева́ться (-шу́юсь) *pf*, стушёвываться *impf* efface o.s.
с|туши́ть (-шу́, -шишь) *pf*.
стыд (-а́) shame. стыди́ть (-ыжу́) *impf* (*pf* при~) put to shame; ~ся (*pf* по~ся) be ashamed. стыдли́вый bashful. сты́дный shameful; ~о! shame! ~о *impers*+*dat* ему́ ~о he is ashamed; как тебе́ не ~о! you ought to be ashamed of yourself!
стык joint; junction. стыкова́ть *impf* (*pf* со~) join end to end; ~ся (*pf* при~ся) dock. стыко́вка docking.
сты́нуть, стыть (-ы́ну; стыл) *impf* cool; get cold.
сты́чка skirmish; squabble.
стюарде́сса stewardess.
стя́гивать *impf*, стяну́ть (-ну́, -нешь) *pf* tighten; pull together; assemble; pull off; steal; ~ся tighten; assemble.
стяжа́тель (-я) *m* money-grubber. стяжа́ть *impf* & *pf* gain, win.
суббо́та Saturday.
субсиди́ровать *impf* & *pf* subsidize. субси́дия subsidy.
субъе́кт subject; ego; person; character, type. субъекти́вный subjective.

сувени́р souvenir.

суверените́т sovereignty. сувере́нный sovereign.

сугли́нок (-нка) loam.

сугро́б snowdrift.

сугу́бо adv especially.

суд (-á) court; trial; verdict.

суда́ etc.: see суд, су́дно¹

суда́к (-á) pike-perch.

суде́бный judicial; legal; forensic. суде́йский judge's; referee's, umpire's. суди́мость previous convictions. суди́ть (сужу́, су́дишь) impf judge; try; referee, umpire; foreordain; ~ся go to law.

су́дно¹ (pl -дá, -óв) vessel, craft.

су́дно² (gen pl -ден) bed-pan.

судово́й ship's; marine.

судомо́йка kitchen-maid; scullery.

судопроизво́дство legal proceedings.

су́дорога cramp, convulsion. су́дорожный convulsive.

судостро́ение shipbuilding. судострои́тельный shipbuilding. судохо́дный navigable; shipping.

судьба́ (pl -ы, -деб) fate, destiny.

судья́ (pl -и, -éй, -ям) m judge; referee; umpire.

суеве́рие superstition. суеве́рный superstitious.

суета́ bustle, fuss. суети́ться (-ечу́сь) impf bustle, fuss. суетли́вый fussy, bustling.

сужде́ние opinion; judgement.

суже́ние narrowing; constriction. су́живать impf, су́зить (-у́жу) pf narrow, contract; ~ся narrow; taper.

сук (-á, loc -ý; pl су́чья, -ьев or -и, -óв) bough.

су́ка bitch. су́кин adj: ~ сын son of a bitch.

сукно́ (pl -а, -кон) cloth; положи́ть под ~ shelve. суко́нный cloth; clumsy, crude.

сули́ть impf (pf по~) promise.

султа́н plume.

сумасбро́д, сумасбро́дка nutcase. сумасбро́дный wild, mad. сумасбро́дство wild behaviour. сумасше́дш|ий mad; ~ий sb, ~ая sb lunatic. сумасше́ствие madness.

сумато́ха turmoil; bustle.

сумбу́р confusion. сумбу́рный confused.

су́меречный twilight. су́мерки (-рек) pl twilight, dusk.

суме́ть (-е́ю) pf +inf be able to, manage to.

су́мка bag.

су́мма sum. сумма́рный summary; total. сумми́ровать impf & pf add up; summarize.

су́мрак twilight; murk. су́мрачный gloomy.

су́мчатый marsupial.

сунду́к (-á) trunk, chest.

су́нуть(ся (-ну(сь) pf of сова́ть(ся

суп (pl -ы́) soup.

суперма́ркет supermarket.

суперобло́жка dust-jacket.

супру́г husband, spouse; pl husband and wife, (married) couple. супру́га wife, spouse. супру́жеский conjugal. супру́жество matrimony.

сургу́ч (-á) sealing-wax.

сурди́нка mute; под сурди́нку on the sly.

суро́вость severity, sternness. суро́вый severe, stern; bleak; unbleached.

суро́к (-рка́) marmot.

суррога́т substitute.

су́слик ground-squirrel.

суста́в joint, articulation.

су́тки (-ток) pl twenty-four hours; a day.

су́толока commotion.

су́точн|ый daily; round-the-clock; ~ые sb pl per diem allowance.

суту́литься impf stoop. суту́лый round-shouldered.

суть essence, main point.

суфлёр prompter. суфли́ровать impf +dat prompt.

су́ффикс suffix.

суха́рь (-я́) m rusk; pl bread-crumbs.

су́хо adv drily; coldly.

сухожи́лие tendon.

сухо́й (сух, -á, -о) dry; cold. сухопу́тный land. су́хость dryness; coldness. сухоща́вый lean, skinny.

сучкова́тый knotty; gnarled. сучо́к (-чка́) twig; knot.

су́ша (dry) land. су́ше comp of сухо́й. сушёный dried. суши́лка dryer; drying-room. суши́ть (-шу́, -шишь) impf (pf вы́~) dry, dry out, up; ~ся (get) dry.

суще́ственный essential, vital. существи́тельное sb noun. существ-

вó being, creature; essence. существ-
овáние existence. существовáть
impf exist. сýщий absolute, downright. сýщность essence.

сую *etc.: see* совáть. с|фабрикoвáть
pf. с|фальши́вить (-влю) *pf.*
с|фантази́ровать *pf.*

сфéра sphere. сфери́ческий spherical.

сфинкс sphinx.

с|формировáть(ся *pf.* с|формо-
вáть *pf.* с|формули́ровать *pf.*
с|фотографи́ровать(ся *pf.*

схвати́ть (-ачý, -áтишь) *pf*, схвáты-
вать *impf* (*impf also* хватáть) seize;
catch; grasp; ~ся snatch, catch;
grapple. схвáтка skirmish; *pl* contrac-
tions.

схéма diagram; outline, plan; circuit.
схемати́ческий schematic; sketchy.
схемати́чный sketchy.

с|хитри́ть *pf.*

схлы́нуть (-нет) *pf* (break and) flow
back; subside.

сход coming off; descent; gathering.
сходи́ть¹(ся (-ожý(сь, -óдишь(ся)
impf of сойти́(сь. сходи́ть² (-ожý,
-óдишь) *pf* go; +за+*instr* go to fetch.
схóдка gathering, meeting. схóд-
ный (-ден, -днá, -o) similar; reasonable. схóдня (*gen pl* -ей) (*usu pl*)
gang-plank. схóдство similarity.

с|хорони́ть(ся (-ню́(сь, -нишь(ся) *pf.*
сцеди́ть (-ежý, -éдишь) *pf*, сцé-
живать *impf* strain off, decant.

сцéна stage; scene. сценáрий scenario; script. сценари́ст script-writer.
сцени́ческий stage.

сцепи́ть (-плю́, -пишь) *pf*, сцепля́ть
impf couple; ~ся be coupled; grapple. сцéпка coupling. сцеплéние
coupling; clutch.

счастли́вец (-вца), счастли́вчик
lucky man. счастли́вица lucky
woman. счастли́вый (-áст/ли́в)
happy; lucky; ~o! all the best!; ~ого
пути́ bon voyage. счáстье happiness; good fortune.

счесть (сочтý(сь, -тёшь(ся; счёл-
(ся, сочлá(сь) *pf of* счита́ть(ся. счёт
(*loc* -ý; *pl* -á) bill; account; counting,
calculation; score; expense. счётный
calculating; accounts. счетовóд bookkeeper, accountant. счётчик counter; meter. счёты (-ов) *pl* abacus.

счи́стить (-и́щу) *pf* (*impf* счищáть)
clean off; clear away.

счита́ть *impf* (*pf* со~, счесть) count;
reckon; consider; ~ся (*pf also*
по~ся) settle accounts; be considered; +с+*instr* take into consideration; reckon with.

счищáть *impf of* счи́стить

США *pl indecl abbr* (*of* Соединённые
Штáты Амéрики) USA.

сшибáть *impf*, сшиби́ть (-бý, -бёшь;
сшиб) *pf* strike, hit, knock (off); ~ с
ног knock down; ~ся collide; come
to blows.

сшивáть *impf*, с|шить (сошью́, -ьёшь)
pf sew (together).

съедáть *impf of* съесть. съедóбный edible; nice.

съéду *etc.: see* съéхать

съёживаться *impf*, съ|ёжиться
(-жусь) *pf* shrivel, shrink.

съезд congress; conference; arrival.
съéздить (-зжу) *pf* go, drive, travel.
съезжáть(ся *impf of* съéхать(ся.
съел *etc.: see* съесть

съёмка removal; survey, surveying;
shooting. съёмный detachable, re-
movable. съёмщик, съёмщица tenant; surveyor.

съестнóй food; ~óe *sb* food (sup-
plies). съ|есть (-ем, -ешь, -ест, -ед-
и́м; съел) *pf* (*impf also* съедáть).

съéхать (-éду) *pf* (*impf* съезжáть)
go down; come down; move; ~ся
meet; assemble.

съ|язви́ть (-влю) *pf.*

сы́воротка whey; serum.

сыгрáть *pf of* игрáть; ~ся play
(well) together.

сын (*pl* сыновья́, -éй *or* -ы́, -óв) son.
сынóвний filial. сынóк (-нкá) little son; sonny.

сы́пать (-плю) *impf* pour; pour forth;
~ся fall; pour out; rain down; fray.
сыпнóй тиф typhus. сыпучий friable; free-flowing; shifting. сыпь
rash, eruption.

сыр (*loc* -ý; *pl* -ы́) cheese.
сырéть (-éю) *impf* (*pf* от~) become
damp.

сырéц (-рцá) raw product.

сырóй (сыр, -á, -o) damp; raw; uncooked; unboiled; unfinished; unripe.
сы́рость dampness. сырьё raw
material(s).

сыска́ть (сыщу́, сы́щешь) *pf* find.
сы́тность (-тен, -тна́, -о) filling. сы́-
тость satiety. сы́тый (сыт, -а́, -о) full.
сыч (-а́) little owl.
сы́щик detective.
с|эконо́мить (-млю) *pf*.
сэр sir.
сюда́ *adv* here, hither.
сюже́т subject; plot; topic. сюже́т-
ный subject; having a theme.
сюи́та suite.
сюрпри́з surprise.
сюрреали́зм surrealism. сюрреали́-
сти́ческий surrealist.
сюрту́к (-а́) frock-coat.
сяк *adv*: *see* так. сям *adv*: *see* там

Т

та *see* тот
таба́к (-а́) tobacco. табаке́рка snuff-
box. таба́чный tobacco.
та́бель (-я; *pl* -и, -ей *or* -я́, -ей) *m*
table, list. та́бельный table; time.
табле́тка tablet.
табли́ца table; ~ умноже́ния multiplication table.
та́бор (gipsy) camp.
табу́н (-а́) herd.
табуре́т, табуре́тка stool.
тавро́ (*pl* -а, -а́м) brand.
тавтоло́гия tautology.
таджи́к, -и́чка Tadzhik.
Таджикиста́н Tadzhikistan.
таёжный taiga.
таз (*loc* -у́; *pl* -ы́) basin; pelvis. тазо-
бе́дренный hip. та́зовый pelvic.
таи́нственный mysterious; secret.
таи́ть *impf* hide, harbour; ~ся hide;
lurk.
Тайва́нь *m* Taiwan.
тайга́ taiga.
тайко́м *adv* secretly, surreptitiously;
~ от+*gen* behind the back of.
тайм half; period of play.
та́йна secret; mystery. тайни́к (-а́)
hiding-place; *pl* recesses. та́йный secret; privy.
тайфу́н typhoon.
так *adv* so; like this; as it should be;
just like that; и ~ even so; as it is; и
~ да́лее and so on; ~ и ся́к this
way and that; не ~ wrong; ~ же in
the same way; ~ же... как as ... as;

~ и есть I thought so!; ~ ему́ и на́до
serves him right; ~ и́ли ина́че one
way or another; ~ себе́ so-so. так
conj then; so; ~ как as, since.
такела́ж rigging.
та́кже *adv* also, too, as well.
тако́в *m* (-а́ *f*, -о́ *neut*, -ы́ *pl*) *pron*
such.
тако́й *pron* such (a); в ~о́м слу́чае
in that case; кто он ~о́й? who is he?;
~о́й же the same; ~и́м о́бразом in
this way; что э́то ~о́е? what is this?
тако́й-то *pron* so-and-so; such-and-
such.
та́кса fixed *or* statutory price; tariff.
таксёр taxi-driver. такси́ *neut indecl*
taxi. такси́ст taxi-driver. таксо-
па́рк taxi depot.
такт time; bar; beat; tact.
та́к-таки after all, really.
та́ктика tactics. такти́ческий tactical.
такти́чность tact. такти́чный tactful.
та́ктов|ый time, timing; ~ая черта́
bar-line.
тала́нт talent. тала́нтливый talented.
талисма́н talisman.
та́лия waist.
тало́н, тало́нчик coupon.
та́лый thawed, melted.
тальк talc; talcum powder.
там *adv* there; ~ и сям here and
there; ~ же in the same place; ibid.
тамада́ *m* toast-master.
та́мбур[1] tambour; lobby; platform.
та́мбур[2] chain-stitch.
тамо́женник customs official. тамо́-
женный customs. тамо́жня custom-
house.
та́мошний of that place, local.
тампо́н tampon.
та́нгенс tangent.
та́нго *neut indecl* tango.
та́нец (-нца) dance; dancing.
тани́н tannin.
танк tank. та́нкер tanker. танки́ст
member of a tank crew. та́нковый
tank, armoured.
танцева́льный dancing; ~ ве́чер
dance. танцева́ть (-цу́ю) *impf*
dance. танцо́вщик, танцо́вщица
(ballet) dancer. танцо́р, танцо́рка
dancer.
та́пка, та́почка slipper.

та́ра packing; tare.

тарака́н cockroach.

тара́н battering-ram.

тара́нтул tarantula.

таре́лка plate; cymbal; satellite dish.

тари́ф tariff.

таска́ть *impf* drag, lug; carry; pull; take; pull out; swipe; wear; ~**ся** drag; hang about.

тасова́ть *impf* (*pf* с~) shuffle.

ТАСС *abbr* (*of* Телегра́фное аге́нтство Сове́тского Сою́за) Tass (Telegraph Agency of the Soviet Union).

тата́рин, тата́рка Tatar.

татуиро́вка tattooing, tattoo.

тафта́ taffeta.

тахта́ ottoman.

та́чка wheelbarrow.

тащи́ть (-щу́, -щишь) *impf* (*pf* вы́-, с~) pull; drag, lug; carry; take; pull out; swipe; ~**ся** drag o.s. along; drag.

та́ять (та́ю) *impf* (*pf* рас~) melt; thaw; dwindle.

тварь creature(s); wretch.

тверде́ть (-е́ет) *impf* (*pf* за~) harden, become hard. **тверди́ть** (-ржу́) *impf* (*pf* вы́~) repeat, say again and again; memorize. **тве́рдо** *adv* hard; firmly, firm. **твердоло́бый** thick-skulled; diehard. **тве́рдый** hard; firm; solid; steadfast; ~ **знак** hard sign, ъ; ~**ое те́ло** solid. **тверды́ня** stronghold.

твой (-его́) *m*, **твоя́** (-е́й) *f*, **твоё** (-его́) *neut*, **твои́** (-и́х) *pl* your, yours.

творе́ние creation, work; creature. **творе́ц** (-рца́) creator. **твори́тельный** instrumental. **твори́ть** *impf* (*pf* со~) create; do; make; ~**ся** happen.

творо́г (-а́) curds; cottage cheese.

тво́рческий creative. **тво́рчество** creation; creative work; works.

те *see* **тот**

т.е. *abbr* (*of* то есть) that is, i.e.

теа́тр theatre. **театра́льный** theatre; theatrical.

тебя́ *etc.*: *see* **ты**

те́зис thesis.

тёзка *m* & *f* namesake.

тёк *see* **течь**

текст text; libretto, lyrics.

тексти́ль *m* textiles. **тексти́льный** textile.

тексту́ра texture.

теку́чий fluid; unstable. **теку́щий** current; routine.

теле- *in comb* tele-; television. **телеателье́** *neut indecl* television maintenance workshop. ~**ви́дение** television. ~**визио́нный** television. ~**ви́зор** television (set). ~**гра́мма** telegram. ~**гра́ф** telegraph (office). ~**графи́ровать** *impf* & *pf* telegraph. ~**гра́фный** telegraph(ic). ~**зри́тель** *m* (television) viewer. ~**объекти́в** telephoto lens. ~**пати́ческий** telepathic. ~**па́тия** telepathy. ~**ско́п** telescope. ~**ста́нция** television station. ~**сту́дия** television studio. ~**фо́н** telephone; (telephone) number; (по)звони́ть по ~**фо́ну** +*dat* ring up. ~**фон-автома́т** public telephone, call-box. ~**фони́ст, -и́стка** (telephone) operator. ~**фо́нный** telephone; ~**фо́нная кни́га** telephone directory; ~**фо́нная ста́нция** telephone exchange; ~**фо́нная тру́бка** receiver. ~**фон-отве́тчик** answering machine. ~**фотогра́фия** telephotography. ~**центр** television centre.

теле́га cart, wagon. **теле́жка** small cart; trolley.

телёнок (-нка; *pl* -я́та, -я́т) calf.

теле́сн|ый bodily; corporal; ~**ого цве́та** flesh-coloured.

Теле́ц (-льца́) Taurus.

тели́ться *impf* (*pf* о~) calve. **тёлка** heifer.

те́ло (*pl* -á) body. **телогре́йка** padded jacket. **телосложе́ние** build. **телохрани́тель** *m* bodyguard.

теля́та *etc.*: *see* **телёнок**. **теля́тина** veal. **теля́чий** calf; veal.

тем *conj* (so much) the; ~ лу́чше so much the better; ~ не ме́нее nevertheless.

тем *see* **тот, тьма**

те́ма subject; theme. **тема́тика** subject-matter; themes. **темати́ческий** subject; thematic.

тембр timbre.

темне́ть (-е́ет) *impf* (*pf* по~, с~) become dark. **темни́ца** dungeon. **темно́** *predic* it is dark. **темноко́жий** dark-skinned, swarthy. **тёмно-си́ний** dark blue. **темнота́** darkness. **тёмный** dark.

темп tempo; rate.

темпера́мент temperament. **темпера́ментный** temperamental.

температу́ра temperature.

те́мя (-мени) *neut* crown, top of the head.

тенде́нция tendency; bias.

теневой, тени́стый shady.

те́ннис tennis. теннисист, -и́стка tennis-player. те́нни́сн|ый tennis; ~ая площа́дка tennis-court.

те́нор (*pl* -а́) tenor.

тент awning.

тень (*loc* -и́; *pl* -и, -е́й) shade; shadow; phantom; ghost; particle, vestige, atom; suspicion; те́ни для век *pl* eyeshadow.

тео́лог theologian. теологи́ческий theological. теоло́гия theology.

теоре́ма theorem. теоре́тик theoretician. теорети́ческий theoretical. тео́рия theory.

тепе́решн|ий present. тепе́рь *adv* now; today.

тепле́ть (-е́ет) *impf* (*pf* по~) get warm. те́плиться (-ится) *impf* flicker; glimmer. тепли́ца greenhouse, conservatory. тепли́чный hothouse. тепло́ heat; warmth. тепло́ *adv* warmly; *predic* it is warm. тепло- *in comb* heat; thermal; thermo-. теплово́з diesel locomotive. ~ёмкость thermal capacity. ~кро́вный warm-blooded. ~обме́н heat exchange. ~прово́дный heat-conducting. ~сто́йкий heat-resistant. ~хо́д motor ship. ~центра́ль heat and power station.

теплово́й heat; thermal. теплота́ heat; warmth. тёплый (-пел, -пла́, тёпло́) warm.

терапе́вт therapeutist. терапи́я therapy.

тереби́ть (-блю́) *impf* pull (at); pester.

тере́ть (тру, трёшь; тёр) *impf* rub; grate; ~ся rub o.s.; ~ся о́коло+*gen* hang about, hang around; ~ся среди́ +*gen* mix with.

терза́ть *impf* tear to pieces; torment; ~ся +*instr* suffer; be a prey to.

тёрка grater.

те́рмин term. терминоло́гия terminology.

терми́ческий thermic, thermal. термо́метр thermometer. те́рмос thermos (flask). термоста́т thermostat. термоя́дерный thermonuclear.

терно́вник sloe, blackthorn. терни́стый thorny.

терпели́вый patient. терпе́ние patience. терпе́ть (-плю́, -пишь) *impf* (*pf* по~) suffer; bear, endure. терпе́ться (-пится) *impf impers*+*dat*: ему́ не те́рпится +*inf* he is impatient to. терпи́мость tolerance. терпи́мый tolerant; tolerable.

те́рпкий (-пок, -пка́, -о) astringent; tart.

терра́са terrace.

территориа́льный territorial. террито́рия territory.

терро́р terror. терроризи́ровать *impf & pf* terrorize. террори́ст terrorist.

тёртый grated; experienced.

терье́р terrier.

теря́ть *impf* (*pf* по~, y~) lose; shed; ~ся get lost; disappear; fail, decline; become flustered.

тёс boards, planks. теса́ть (тешу́, те́шешь) *impf* cut, hew.

тесёмка ribbon, braid.

тесни́ть *impf* (*pf* по~, c~) crowd; squeeze, constrict; be too tight; ~ся press through; move up; crowd, jostle. теснота́ crowded state; crush. те́сн|ый crowded; (too) tight; close; compact; ~o it is crowded.

тесо́вый board, plank.

тест test.

те́сто dough; pastry.

тесть *m* father-in-law.

тесьма́ ribbon, braid.

те́терев (*pl* -а́) black grouse. тете́рка grey hen.

тётка aunt.

тетра́дка, тетра́дь exercise book.

тётя (*gen pl* -ей) aunt.

тех- *abbr in comb* (*of* техни́ческий) technical.

те́хник technician. те́хника technical equipment; technology; technique. те́хникум technical college. техни́ческ|ий technical; ~ие усло́вия specifications. техно́лог technologist. технологи́ческий technological. техноло́гия technology. техперсона́л technical personnel.

тече́ние flow; course; current, stream; trend.

течь[1] (-чёт; тёк, -ла́) *impf* flow; stream; leak. течь[2] leak.

те́шить (-шу) *impf* (*pf* по~) amuse; gratify; ~ся (+*instr*) amuse o.s. (with).

тешу́ *etc.*: *see* **теса́ть**

тёща mother-in-law.

тигр tiger. **тигри́ца** tigress.

тик[1] tic.

тик[2] teak.

ти́на slime, mud.

тип type. **типи́чный** typical. **типово́й** standard; model. **типогра́фия** printing-house, press. **типогра́фский** typographical.

тир shooting-range, -gallery. **тира́ж** (-á) draw; circulation; edition.

тира́н tyrant. **тира́нить** *impf* tyrannize. **тирани́ческий** tyrannical. **тира́ния** tyranny.

тире́ *neut indecl* dash.

ти́скать *impf*, **ти́снуть** (-ну) *pf* press, squeeze. **тиски́** (-о́в) *pl* vice; **в тиска́х** +*gen* in the grip of. **тисне́ние** stamping; imprint; design. **тиснёный** stamped.

тита́н[1] titanian.

тита́н[2] boiler.

тита́н[3] titan.

титр title, sub-title.

ти́тул title; title-page. **ти́тульный** title.

тиф (*loc* -ý) typhus.

ти́хий (тих, -á, -о) quiet; silent; calm; slow. **тихоокеа́нский** Pacific. **ти́ше** *comp* of **ти́хий**, **ти́хо**; quiet! **тишина́** quiet; silence.

т. к. *abbr* (*of* **так как**) as, since.

тка́ный woven. **ткань** fabric, cloth; tissue. **ткать** (тку, ткёшь; -ал, -áла, -о) *impf* (*pf* со~) weave. **тка́цкий** weaving; ~ **стано́к** loom. **ткач**, **ткачи́ха** weaver.

ткну́ть(**ся** (-у(сь, -ёшь(ся) *pf of* **ты́кать**(**ся**

тле́ние decay; smouldering. **тлеть** (-éет) *impf* rot, decay; smoulder; ~ся smoulder.

тля aphis.

тмин caraway(-seeds).

то *pron* that; **а не то́** or else, otherwise; (**да**) **и то́** and even then, and that; **то́ есть** that is (to say); **то и де́ло** every now and then. **то** *conj* then; **не то́..., не то́** either... or; half ..., half; **то..., то** now ..., now; **то ли..., то ли** whether ... or.

-то *partl* just, exactly; **в то́м-то и де́ло** that's just it.

тобо́й *see* **ты**

това́р goods; commodity.

това́рищ comrade; friend; colleague. **това́рищеский** comradely; friendly. **това́рищество** comradeship; company; association.

това́рный goods; commodity.

това́ро- *in comb* commodity; goods. **товарообме́н** barter. ~**оборо́т** (sales) turnover. ~**отправи́тель** *m* consignor. ~**получа́тель** *m* consignee.

тогда́ *adv* then; ~ **как** whereas. **тогда́шний** of that time.

того́ *see* **тот**

тожде́ственный identical. **то́ждество** identity.

то́же *adv* also, too.

ток (*pl* -и) current.

тока́рный turning; ~ **стано́к** lathe. **то́карь** (*pl* -я́, -е́й *or* -и, -ей) *m* turner, lathe operator.

токси́ческий toxic.

толк sense; use; **бе́з** ~**у** senselessly; **знать** ~ **в** +*prep* know well; **сби́ть с** ~**у** confuse; **с** ~**ом** intelligently.

толка́ть *impf* (*pf* **толкну́ть**) push, shove; jog; ~ся jostle.

толки́ (-о́в) *pl* rumours, gossip.

толкну́ть(**ся** (-ну́(сь, -нёшь(ся) *pf of* **толка́ть**(**ся**

толкова́ние interpretation; *pl* commentary. **толкова́ть** *impf* interpret; explain; talk. **толко́вый** intelligent; clear; ~ **слова́рь** defining dictionary. **то́лком** *adv* plainly; seriously.

толкотня́ crush, squash.

толку́ *etc.*: *see* **толо́чь**

толку́чка crush, squash; second-hand market.

толокно́ oatmeal.

толо́чь (-лку́, -лчёшь; -ло́к, -лкла́) *impf* (*pf* ис~, рас~) pound, crush.

толпа́ (*pl* -ы) crowd. **толпи́ться** *impf* crowd; throng.

толсте́ть (-е́ю) *impf* (*pf* по~) grow fat; put on weight. **толстоко́жий** thick-skinned; pachydermatous. **то́лстый** (-á, -о) fat; thick. **толстя́к** (-á) fat man *or* boy.

толчёный crushed; ground. **толчёт** *etc.*: *see* **толо́чь**

толчея́ crush, squash.

толчо́к (-чка́) push, shove; (*sport*) put; jolt; shock, tremor.

то́лща thickness; thick. то́лще *comp of* то́лстый. толщина́ thickness; fatness.

толь *m* roofing felt.

то́лько *adv* only, merely; ~ что (only) just; *conj* only, but; (как) ~, (лишь) ~ as soon as; ~ бы if only.

том (*pl* -á) volume. то́мик small volume.

тома́т tomato. тома́тный tomato.

томи́тельный tedious, wearing; agonizing. томи́ть (-млю́) *impf* (*pf* ис~) tire; torment; ~ся languish; be tormented. томле́ние languor. то́мный (-мен, -мна́, -о) languid, languorous.

тон (*pl* -á *or* -ы, -о́в) tone; note; shade; form. тона́льность key.

то́ненький thin; slim. то́нкий (-нок, -нка́, -о) thin; slim; fine; refined; subtle; keen. то́нкость thinness; slimness; fineness; subtlety.

то́нна ton.

тонне́ль *see* тунне́ль

то́нус tone.

тону́ть (-ну́, -нешь) *impf* (*pf* по~, у~) sink; drown.

то́ньше *comp of* то́нкий

то́пать *impf* (*pf* то́пнуть) stamp.

топи́ть¹ (-плю́, -пишь) *impf* (*pf* по~, у~) sink; drown; ruin; ~ся drown o.s.

топи́ть² (-плю́, -пишь) *impf* stoke; heat; melt (down); ~ся burn; melt. то́пка stoking; heating; melting (down); furnace.

то́пкий boggy, marshy.

то́пливный fuel. то́пливо fuel.

то́пнуть (-ну) *pf of* то́пать

топографи́ческий topographical. топогра́фия topography.

то́поль (*pl* -á *or* -и) *m* poplar.

топо́р (-á) axe. топо́рик hatchet. топо́рище axe-handle. топо́рный axe; clumsy, crude.

то́пот tramp; clatter. топта́ть (-пчу́, -пчешь) *impf* (*pf* по~) trample (down); ~ся stamp; ~ся на ме́сте mark time.

топча́н (-á) trestle-bed.

топь bog, marsh.

торг (*loc* -у́; *pl* -и́) trading; bargaining; *pl* auction. торгова́ть *impf* (*pf* с~) trade; ~ся bargain, haggle. торго́вец (-вца) merchant; tradesman. торго́вка market-woman; stallholder. торго́вля trade. торго́вый trade, commercial; merchant. торг-пре́д *abbr* trade representative.

торе́ц (-рца́) butt-end; wooden paving-block.

торже́ственный solemn; ceremonial. торжество́ celebration; triumph. торжествова́ть *impf* celebrate; triumph.

торможе́ние braking. то́рмоз (*pl* -á *or* -ы) brake. тормози́ть (-ожу́) *impf* (*pf* за~) brake; hamper.

тормоши́ть (-шу́) *impf* pester; bother.

торопи́ть (-плю́, -пишь) *impf* (*pf* по~) hurry; hasten; ~ся hurry. торопли́вый hasty.

торпе́да torpedo.

торс torso.

торт cake.

торф peat. торфяно́й peat.

торча́ть (-чу́) *impf* stick out; protrude; hang about.

торше́р standard lamp.

тоска́ melancholy; boredom; nostalgia; ~ по+*dat* longing for. тоскли́вый melancholy; depressed; dreary. тоскова́ть *impf* be melancholy, depressed; long; ~ по+*dat* miss.

тост toast.

тот *m* (та *f*, то *neut*, те *pl*) *pron* that; the former; the other; the one; the same; the right; и ~ и друго́й both; к тому́ же moreover; не ~ the wrong; ни ~ ни друго́й neither; тот, кто the one who, the person who. то́тчас *adv* immediately.

тоталитари́зм totalitarianism. тоталита́рный totalitarian.

тота́льный total.

точи́лка sharpener; pencil-sharpener. точи́ло whetstone, grindstone. точи́льный grinding, sharpening; ~ ка́мень whetstone, grindstone. точи́льщик (knife-)grinder. точи́ть (-чу́, -чишь) *impf* (*pf* вы́~, на~) sharpen; hone; turn; eat away; gnaw at.

то́чка spot; dot; full stop; point; ~ зре́ния point of view; ~ с запято́й semicolon. то́чно¹ *adv* exactly, precisely; punctually. то́чно² *conj* as though, as if. **то́чность** punctuality; precision; accuracy; **в то́чности** exactly, precisely. **то́чный** (-чен, -чна́, -о) exact, precise; accurate; punctual. **то́чь-в-то́чь** adv exactly; word for word.

тошни́ть impf impers: **меня́ тошни́т** I feel sick. **тошнота́** nausea. **тошнотво́рный** sickening, nauseating.

то́щий (тощ, -а́, -е) gaunt, emaciated; skinny; empty; poor.

трава́ (pl -ы) grass; herb. **трави́нка** blade of grass.

трави́ть (-влю́, -вишь) impf (pf вы́~, за~) poison; exterminate, destroy; etch; hunt; torment; badger. **травле́ние** extermination; etching. **тра́вля** hunting; persecution; badgering.

тра́вма trauma, injury.

травоя́дный herbivorous. **травяни́стый**, **травяно́й** grass; herbaceous; grassy.

траге́дия tragedy. **тра́гик** tragedian. **траги́ческий**, **траги́чный** tragic.

традицио́нный traditional. **тради́ция** tradition.

траекто́рия trajectory.

тракта́т treatise; treaty.

тракти́р inn, tavern.

трактова́ть impf interpret; treat, discuss. **тракто́вка** treatment; interpretation.

тра́ктор tractor. **тракто́рист** tractor driver.

трал trawl. **тра́лить** impf (pf про~) trawl; sweep. **тра́льщик** trawler; mine-sweeper.

трамбова́ть impf (pf у~) ram, tamp.

трамва́й tram. **трамва́йный** tram.

трампли́н spring-board; ski-jump.

транзи́стор transistor; transistor radio.

транзи́тный transit.

транс trance.

трансатланти́ческий transatlantic.

трансли́ровать impf & pf broadcast, transmit. **трансляцио́нный** transmission; broadcasting. **трансля́ция** broadcast, transmission.

тра́нспорт transport; consignment. **транспортёр** conveyor. **транспорти́р** protractor. **транспорти́ровать** impf & pf transport. **тра́нспортный** transport.

трансформа́тор transformer.

транше́я trench.

трап ladder.

тра́пеза meal.

трапе́ция trapezium; trapeze.

тра́сса line, course, direction; route, road.

тра́та expenditure; waste. **тра́тить** (-а́чу) impf (pf ис~, по~) spend, expend; waste.

тра́улер trawler.

тра́ур mourning. **тра́урный** mourning; funeral; mournful.

трафаре́т stencil; stereotype; cliché. **трафаре́тный** stencilled; conventional, stereotyped.

тра́чу etc.: see **тра́тить**

тре́бование demand; request; requirement; requisition, order; pl needs. **тре́бовательный** demanding. **тре́бовать** impf (pf по~) summon; +gen demand, require; need; ~ся be needed, be required.

трево́га alarm; anxiety. **трево́жить** (-жу) impf (pf вс~, по~) alarm; disturb; worry; ~ся worry, be anxious; trouble o.s. **трево́жный** worried, anxious; alarming; alarm.

тре́звенник teetotaller. **трезве́ть** (-е́ю) impf (pf о~) sober up.

трезво́н peal (of bells); rumours; row.

тре́звость sobriety. **тре́звый** (-зв, -á, -о) sober; teetotal.

тре́йлер trailer.

трель trill; warble.

тре́нер trainer, coach.

тре́ние friction.

тренирова́ть impf (pf на~) train, coach; ~ся be in training. **трениро́вка** training, coaching. **трениро́вочный** training.

трепа́ть (-плю́, -плешь) impf (pf ис~, по~, рас~) blow about; dishevel; wear out; pat; ~ся fray; wear out; flutter. **тре́пет** trembling; trepidation. **трепета́ть** (-ещу́, -е́щешь) impf tremble; flicker; palpitate. **тре́петный** trembling; flickering; palpitating; timid.

треск crack; crackle; fuss.

треска́ cod.

тре́скаться[1] impf (pf по~) crack; chap.

тре́скаться[2] impf of **тре́снуться**

тре́снуть (-нет) pf snap, crackle;

crack; chap; bang; ~**ся** (*impf* тре́-скаться) +*instr* bang.

трест trust.

трет|ий (-ья, -ье) third; ~**ье** *sb* sweet (course).

трети́ровать *impf* slight.

треть (*gen pl* -е́й) third. **тре́тье** *etc.*: *see* **тре́тий**. **треуго́льник** triangle.

треуго́льный triangular.

тре́фы (треф) *pl* clubs.

трёх- *in comb* three-, tri-. **трёх-годи́чный** three-year. ~**голо́сный** three-part. ~**гра́нный** three-edged; trihedral. ~**колёсный** three-wheeled. ~**ле́тний** three-year; three-year old. ~**ме́рный** three-dimensional. ~**ме́сячный** three-month; quarterly; three-month-old. ~**по́льье** three-field system. ~**со́тый** three-hundredth. ~**сторо́нний** three-sided; trilateral; tripartite. ~**эта́жный** three-storeyed.

треща́ть (-щу́) *impf* crack; crackle; creak; chirr; crack up; chatter. **тре́щина** crack, split; fissure; chap.

три (трёх, -ём, -емя́, -ёх) three.

трибу́на platform, rostrum; stand. **трибуна́л** tribunal.

тригономе́трия trigonometry.

тридцатиле́тний thirty-year; thirty-year old. **тридца́тый** thirtieth. **три́дцать** (-и́, *instr* -ью́) thirty. **три́жды** *adv* three times; thrice.

трико́ *neut indecl* tricot; tights; knickers. **трикота́ж** knitted fabric; knit-wear. **трикота́жный** jersey, tricot; knitted.

трина́дцатый thirteenth. **трина́дцать** thirteen. **трио́ль** triplet.

три́ппер gonorrhoea.

три́ста (трёхсо́т, -ёмста́м, -емяста́ми, -ёхста́х) three hundred.

трито́н *zool* triton.

триу́мф triumph.

тро́гательный touching, moving.

тро́гать(ся *impf of* тро́нуть(ся

тро́е (-и́х) *pl* three. **троебо́рье** triathlon. **троекра́тный** thrice-re-peated. **Тро́ица** Trinity; **тро́ица** trio. **Тро́ицын день** Whit Sunday. **тро́йка** three; figure 3; troika; No. 3; three-piece suit. **тройно́й** triple, treble; three-ply. **тро́йственный** triple; tripartite.

тролле́йбус trolley-bus.

тромб blood clot.

тромбо́н trombone.

трон throne.

тро́нуть (-ну) *pf* (*impf* тро́гать) touch; disturb; affect; ~**ся** start, set out; be touched; be affected.

тропа́ path.

тро́пик tropic.

тропи́нка path.

тропи́ческий tropical.

трос rope, cable.

тростни́к (-а́) reed, rush. **тро́сточ-ка, трость** (*gen pl* ~е́й) cane, walking-stick.

тротуа́р pavement.

трофе́й trophy; *pl* spoils (*of war*), booty.

трою́родн|ый: ~**ый брат**, ~**ая сестра́** second cousin.

тру *etc.*: *see* **тере́ть**

труба́ (*pl* -ы) pipe; chimney; funnel; trumpet; tube. **труба́ч** (-а́) trum-peter; trumpet-player. **труби́ть** (-блю́) *impf* (*pf* про~) blow, sound; blare. **тру́бка** tube; pipe; (*telephone*) re-ceiver. **трубопрово́д** pipe-line; pip-ing; manifold. **тру́бочист** chimney-sweep. **тру́бочный** pipe. **тру́бча-тый** tubular.

труд (-а́) labour; work; effort; **с ~о́м** with difficulty. **труди́ться** (-ужу́сь, -у́дишься) *impf* toil, labour; work; trouble. **тру́дно** *predic* it is difficult. **тру́дность** difficulty. **тру́дный** (-ден, -дна́, -о) difficult; hard.

трудо- *in comb* labour, work. **трудо-де́нь** (-дня́) *m* work-day (*unit*). ~**ёмкий** labour-intensive. ~**люби́-вый** industrious. ~**лю́бие** industry. ~**спосо́бность** ability to work. ~**спосо́бный** able-bodied; capable of working.

трудово́й work; working; earned; hard-earned. **трудя́щ|ийся** working; ~**иеся** *sb pl* the workers. **тру́-женик, тру́женица** toiler.

труп corpse; carcass.

тру́ппа troupe, company.

трус coward.

тру́сики (-ов) *pl* shorts; trunks; pants.

труси́ть[1] (-ушу́) *impf* trot, jog along.

тру́сить[2] (-ушу) *impf* (*pf* с~) be a coward; lose one's nerve; be afraid.

труси́ха coward. **трусли́вый** cow-ardly. **тру́сость** cowardice.

трусы́ (-о́в) *pl* shorts; trunks; pants.

труха́ dust; trash.

тру́шу́ *etc.: see* **труси́ть**[1], **тру́сить**[2]

трущо́ба slum; godforsaken hole.

трюк stunt; trick.

трюм hold.

трюмо́ *neut indecl* pier-glass.

трю́фель (*gen pl* **-ле́й**) *m* truffle.

тря́пка rag; spineless creature; *pl* clothes. **тряпьё** rags; clothes.

тряси́на quagmire. **тря́ска** shaking, jolting. **трясти́** (**-су́, -сёшь; -яс, -ла́**) *impf*, **тряхну́ть** (**-ну́, -нёшь**) *pf* (*pf also* **вы́~**) shake; shake out; jolt; **~сь** shake; tremble, shiver; jolt.

тсс *int* sh! hush!

туале́т dress; toilet. **туале́тный** toilet.

туберкулёз tuberculosis.

ту́го *adv* tight(ly), taut; with difficulty. **туго́й** (**туг, -а́, -о**) tight; taut; tightly filled; difficult.

туда́ *adv* there, thither; to the right place; **ни ~ ни сюда́** neither one way nor the other; **~ и обра́тно** there and back.

ту́же *comp of* **ту́го, туго́й**

тужу́рка (double-breasted) jacket.

туз (**-а́,** *acc* **-а́**) ace; bigwig.

тузе́мец (**-мца**), **-мка** native.

ту́ловище trunk; torso.

тулу́п sheepskin coat.

тума́н fog; mist; haze. **тума́нить** *impf* (*pf* **за~**) dim, cloud, obscure; **~ся** grow misty; be befogged. **тума́нность** fog, mist; nebula; obscurity. **тума́нный** foggy; misty; hazy; obscure, vague.

ту́мба post; bollard; pedestal. **ту́мбочка** bedside table.

ту́ндра tundra.

тунея́дец (**-дца**) sponger.

туни́ка tunic.

тунне́ль *m*, **тонне́ль** *m* tunnel.

тупе́ть (**-е́ю**) *impf* (*pf* **за~**) become blunt; grow dull. **тупи́к** (**-а́**) cul-de-sac, dead end; impasse; **поста́вить в ~ stump, nonplus. тупи́ться** (**-пится**) *impf* (*pf* **за~, ис~**) become blunt. **тупи́ца** *m & f* blockhead, dimwit. **тупо́й** (**туп, -а́, -о**) blunt; obtuse; dull; vacant, stupid. **ту́пость** bluntness; vacancy; dullness, slowness.

тур turn; round.

тура́ rook, castle.

турба́за holiday village; campsite.

турби́на turbine.

туре́цкий Turkish; **~ бараба́н** bass drum.

тури́зм tourism. **тури́ст, -и́стка** tourist. **тури́ст(иче)ский** tourist.

туркме́н (*gen pl* **-ме́н**), **-ка** Turkmen. **Туркмениста́н** Turkmenistan.

турне́ *neut indecl* tour.

турне́пс swede.

турни́р tournament.

ту́рок (**-рка**) Turk. **турча́нка** Turkish woman. **Ту́рция** Turkey.

ту́склый dim, dull; lacklustre. **тускне́ть** (**-е́ет**) *impf* (*pf* **по~**) grow dim.

тут *adv* here; now; **~ же** there and then.

ту́фля shoe.

ту́хлый (**-хл, -а́, -о**) rotten, bad. **ту́хнуть**[1] (**-нет; тух**) go bad.

ту́хнуть[2] (**-нет; тух**) *impf* (*pf* **по~**) go out.

ту́ча cloud; storm-cloud.

ту́чный (**-чен, -чна́, -чно**) fat; rich, fertile.

туш flourish.

ту́ша carcass.

тушева́ть (**-шу́ю**) *impf* (*pf* **за~**) shade.

тушёный stewed. **туши́ть**[1] (**-шу́, -шишь**) *impf* (*pf* **с~**) stew.

туши́ть[2] (**-шу́, -шишь**) *impf* (*pf* **за~, по~**) extinguish.

тушу́ю *etc.: see* **тушева́ть**. **тушь** Indian ink; **~ (для ресни́ц)** mascara.

тща́тельность care. **тща́тельный** careful; painstaking.

тщеду́шный feeble, frail.

тщесла́вие vanity, vainglory. **тщесла́вный** vain. **тщета́** vanity. **тще́тный** vain, futile.

ты (**тебя́, тебе́, тобо́й, тебе́**) you; thou; **быть на ты с** *+instr* be on intimate terms with.

ты́кать (**ты́чу**) *impf* (*pf* **ткнуть**) poke; prod; stick.

ты́ква pumpkin; gourd.

тыл (*loc* **-у́;** *pl* **-ы́**) back; rear. **ты́льный** back; rear.

тын paling; palisade.

ты́сяча (*instr* **-ей** *or* **-ью**) thousand.

тысячеле́тие millennium; thousandth anniversary. **ты́сячный** thousandth; of (many) thousands.

тычи́нка stamen.

тьма[1] dark, darkness.

тьма[2] host, multitude.

тюбете́йка skull-cap.

тю́бик tube.

тюк (-á) bale, package.

тюле́нь *m* seal.

тюльпа́н tulip.

тюре́мный prison. **тюре́мщик** gaoler. **тюрьма́** (*pl* -ы, -рем) prison, gaol.

тюфя́к (-á) mattress.

тя́га traction; thrust; draught; attraction; craving. **тяга́ться** *impf* vie, contend. **тяга́ч** (-á) tractor.

тя́гостный burdensome; painful. **тя́гость** burden. **тяготе́ние** gravity, gravitation; bent, inclination. **тяготе́ть** (-е́ю) *impf* gravitate; be attracted; ~ над hang over. **тяготи́ть** (-ощу́) *impf* be a burden on; oppress. **тягу́чий** malleable, ductile; viscous; slow.

тя́жба lawsuit; competition.

тяжело́ *adv* heavily; seriously. **тяжело́** *predic* it is hard; it is painful. **тяжелоатле́т** weight-lifter. **тяжелове́с** heavyweight. **тяжелове́сный** ponderous. **тяжёлый** (-ёл, -á) heavy; hard; serious; painful. **тя́жесть** gravity; weight; heaviness; severity. **тя́жкий** heavy; severe; grave.

тяну́ть (-ну́, -нешь) *impf* (*pf* по~) pull; draw; drag; drag out; weigh; *impers* attract; be tight; ~ся stretch; extend; stretch out; drag on; crawl; drift; move along one after another; last out; reach.

тяну́чка toffee.

У

у *prep+gen* by; at; with; from, of; belonging to; у меня́ (есть) I have; у нас at our place; in our country.

уба́вить (-влю) *pf*, **убавля́ть** *impf* reduce, diminish.

у|баю́кать *pf*, **убаю́кивать** *impf* lull (to sleep).

убега́ть *impf of* **убежа́ть**

убеди́тельный convincing; earnest. **убеди́ть** (-и́шь) *pf* (*impf* **убежда́ть**) convince; persuade; ~ся be convinced; make certain.

убежа́ть (-егу́) *pf* (*impf* **убега́ть**) run away; escape; boil over.

убежда́ть(ся *impf of* **убеди́ть(ся.**

убежде́ние persuasion; conviction; belief. **убеждённость** conviction. **убеждённый** (-ён, -á) convinced; staunch.

убе́жище refuge, asylum; shelter.

уберега́ть *impf*, **убере́чь** (-регу́, -режёшь; -рёг, -гла́) *pf* protect, preserve; ~ся от+*gen* protect o.s. against.

уберу́ *etc.*: *see* **убра́ть**

убива́ть(ся *impf of* **уби́ть(ся. уби́йственный** deadly; murderous; killing. **уби́йство** murder. **уби́йца** *m* & *f* murderer.

убира́ть(ся *impf of* **убра́ть(ся; убира́йся!** clear off!

уби́тый killed; crushed; *sb* dead man. **уби́ть** (убью́, -ьёшь) *pf* (*impf* **убива́ть**) kill; murder; ~ся hurt o.s.

убо́гий wretched. **убо́жество** poverty; squalor.

убо́й slaughter.

убо́р dress, attire.

убо́рка harvesting; clearing up. **убо́рная** *sb* lavatory; dressing-room. **убо́рочный** harvesting; ~ая маши́на harvester. **убо́рщик, убо́рщица** cleaner. **убра́нство** furniture. **убра́ть** (уберу́, -рёшь; -áл, -á, -о) *pf* (*impf* **убира́ть**) remove; take away; put away; harvest; clear up; decorate; ~ посте́ль make a bed; ~ со стола́ clear the table; ~ся tidy up, clean up; clear off.

убыва́ть *impf*, **убы́ть** (убу́ду; убыл, -á, -о) *pf* diminish; subside; wane; leave. **у́быль** diminution; casualties. **убы́ток** (-тка) loss; *pl* damages. **убы́точный** unprofitable.

убью́ *etc.*: *see* **уби́ть**

уважа́емый respected; dear. **уважа́ть** *impf* respect. **уваже́ние** respect; с ~м yours sincerely. **уважи́тельный** valid; respectful.

уве́домить (-млю) *pf*, **уведомля́ть** *impf* inform. **уведомле́ние** notification.

уведу́ *etc.*: *see* **увести́**

увезти́ (-зу́, -зёшь; увёз, -лá) *pf* (*impf* **увози́ть**) take (away); steal; abduct.

увекове́чивать *impf*, **увекове́чить** (-чу) *pf* immortalize; perpetuate.

увёл *etc.*: *see* **увести́**

увеличе́ние increase; magnification; enlargement. **увели́чивать** *impf*,

увели́чить (-чу) *pf* increase; magnify; enlarge; ~ся increase, grow. **увеличи́тель** *m* enlarger. **увеличи́тельный** magnifying; enlarging; ~ое стекло́ magnifying glass.

у|венча́ть *pf*, **увенчивать** *impf* crown; ~ся be crowned.

уве́ренность confidence; certainty. **уве́ренный** confident; sure; certain. **уве́рить** *pf* (*impf* уверя́ть) assure; convince; ~ся satisfy o.s.; be convinced.

уверну́ться (-ну́сь, -нёшься) *pf*, **увёртываться** *impf* от +*gen* evade. **увёртка** dodge, evasion; subterfuge; *pl* wiles. **увёртливый** evasive, shifty.

увертю́ра overture.

уверя́ть(ся *impf* of **уве́рить(ся**

увеселе́ние amusement, entertainment. **увеселительный** entertainment; pleasure. **увеселя́ть** *impf* amuse, entertain.

уве́систый weighty.

увести́ (-еду́, -едёшь; -ёл, -а́) *pf* (*impf* уводи́ть) take (away); walk off with. **уве́чить** (-чу) *impf* maim, cripple. **уве́чный** maimed, crippled; *sb* cripple. **уве́чье** maiming; injury.

уве́шать *pf*, **увешивать** *impf* hang (+*instr* with).

увеща́ть *impf*, **увещева́ть** *impf* exhort, admonish.

у|ви́дать *pf* see. **у|ви́деть(ся** (-и́жу(сь) *pf*.

уви́ливать *impf*, **увильну́ть** (-ну́, -нёшь) *pf* от +*gen* dodge; evade.

увлажни́ть *pf*, **увлажня́ть** *impf* moisten.

увлека́тельный fascinating. **увлека́ть** *impf*, **увле́чь** (-еку́, -ечёшь; -ёк, -ла́) *pf* carry away; fascinate; ~ся be carried away; become mad (+*instr* about). **увлече́ние** animation; passion; crush.

уво́д withdrawal; stealing. **уводи́ть** (-ожу́, -о́дишь) *impf* of **увести́**

увози́ть (-ожу́, -о́зишь) *impf* of **увезти́**

уво́лить *pf*, **увольня́ть** *impf* discharge, dismiss; retire; ~ся be discharged, retire. **увольне́ние** discharge, dismissal.

увы́ *int* alas!

увяда́ть *impf* of **увя́нуть**. **увя́дший**

withered.

увяза́ть[1] *impf* of **увя́знуть**

увяза́ть[2] (-яжу́, -я́жешь) *pf* (*impf* увя́зывать) tie up; pack up; co-ordinate; ~ся pack; tag along. **увя́зка** tying up; co-ordination.

у|вя́знуть (-ну; -я́з) *pf* (*impf also* увяза́ть) get bogged down.

увя́зывать(ся *impf* of **увяза́ть(ся**

у|вя́нуть (-ну) *pf* (*impf also* увяда́ть) fade, wither.

угада́ть *pf*, **уга́дывать** *impf* guess.

уга́р carbon monoxide (poisoning); ecstasy. **уга́рный газ** carbon monoxide.

угаса́ть *impf*, **у|га́снуть** (-нет; -а́с) *pf* go out; die down.

угле- in comb coal; charcoal; carbon. **углево́д** carbohydrate. ~**водоро́д** hydrocarbon. ~**добы́ча** coal extraction. ~**кислота́** carbonic acid; carbon dioxide. ~**ки́слый** carbonate (of). ~**ро́д** carbon.

углово́й corner; angular.

углуби́ть (-блю́) *pf*, **углубля́ть** *impf* deepen; ~ся deepen; delve deeply; become absorbed. **углубле́ние** depression, dip; deepening. **углублённый** deepened; profound; absorbed.

угна́ть (угоню́, -о́нишь; -а́л, -а́, -о) *pf* (*impf* угоня́ть) drive away; despatch; steal; ~ся за +*instr* keep pace with.

угнета́тель *m* oppressor. **угнета́ть** *impf* oppress; depress. **угнете́ние** oppression; depression. **угнетённый** oppressed; depressed.

угова́ривать *impf*, **уговори́ть** *pf* persuade; ~ся arrange, agree. **угово́р** persuasion; agreement.

уго́да: в уго́ду +*dat* to please. **угоди́ть** (-ожу́) *pf*, **угожда́ть** *impf* fall; get; bang; (+*dat*) hit; +*dat* or на +*acc* please. **уго́дливый** obsequious. **уго́дно** *predic*+*dat*: как вам ~ as you wish; что вам ~? what would you like?; *partl* кто ~ anyone (you like); что ~ anything (you like).

уго́дье (*gen pl* -ий) land.

у́гол (угла́, *loc* -у́) corner; angle.

уголо́вник criminal. **уголо́вный** criminal.

уголо́к (-лка́, *loc* -у́) corner.

у́голь (у́гля; *pl* у́гли, -ей *or* -е́й) *m* coal; charcoal.

уго́льник set square.

у́гольный coal; carbon(ic).

угомони́ть pf calm down; ~ся calm down.

уго́н driving away; stealing. угоня́ть impf of угна́ть

угора́ть impf, угоре́ть (-рю́) pf get carbon monoxide poisoning; be mad. угоре́лый mad; possessed.

у́горь[1] (угря́) m eel.

у́горь[2] (угря́) m blackhead.

угости́ть (-ощу́) pf, угоща́ть impf entertain; treat. угоще́ние entertaining, treating; refreshments.

угрожа́ть impf threaten. угро́за threat, menace.

угро́зыск abbr criminal investigation department.

угрызе́ние pangs.

угрю́мый sullen, morose.

удава́ться (удаётся) impf of уда́ться

у|дави́ть(ся (-влю́(сь, -вишь(ся) pf. уда́вка running-knot, half hitch.

удале́ние removal; sending away; moving off. удали́ть pf (impf удаля́ть) remove; send away; move away; ~ся move off, away; retire.

удало́й, уда́лый (-а́л, -а́, -о) daring, bold. у́даль, удальство́ daring, boldness.

удаля́ть(ся impf of удали́ть(ся

уда́р blow; stroke; attack; kick; thrust; seizure; bolt. ударе́ние accent; stress; emphasis. уда́рить pf, ударя́ть impf (impf also бить) strike; hit; beat; ~ся strike, hit; + в+acc break into; burst into. уда́рник, -ница shock-worker. уда́рный percussion; shock; stressed; urgent.

уда́ться(-а́стся, -аду́тся; -а́лся, -ла́сь) pf (impf удава́ться) succeed, be a success; impers +dat +inf succeed, manage; мне удало́сь найти́ рабо́ту I managed to find a job. уда́ча good luck; success. уда́чный successful; felicitous.

удва́ивать impf, удво́ить (-о́ю) pf double, redouble. удвое́ние (re)doubling.

уде́л lot, destiny.

удели́ть pf (impf уделя́ть) spare, give.

уделя́ть impf of удели́ть

удержа́ть impf of уделя́ть

удержа́ние deduction; retention;

keeping. удержа́ть (-жу́, -жишь) pf, уде́рживать impf hold (on to); retain; restrain; suppress; deduct; ~ся hold out; stand firm; refrain (from).

удеру́ etc.: see удра́ть

удешеви́ть (-влю́) pf, удешевля́ть impf reduce the price of.

удиви́тельный surprising, amazing; wonderful. удиви́ть (-влю́) pf, удивля́ть impf surprise, amaze; ~ся be surprised, be amazed. удивле́ние surprise, amazement.

удила́ (-и́л) pl bit.

уди́лище fishing-rod.

удира́ть impf of удра́ть

уди́ть (ужу́, у́дишь) impf fish for; ~ ры́бу fish; ~ся bite.

удлине́ние lengthening; extension. удлини́ть pf, удлиня́ть impf lengthen; extend; ~ся become longer; be extended.

удо́бно adv comfortably; conveniently. удо́бный comfortable; convenient.

удобовари́мый digestible.

удобре́ние fertilization; fertilizer. удо́брить pf, удобря́ть impf fertilize.

удо́бство comfort; convenience.

удовлетворе́ние satisfaction; gratification. удовлетворённый (-рён, -а́) satisfied. удовлетвори́тельный satisfactory. удовлетвори́ть pf, удовлетворя́ть impf satisfy; +dat meet; +instr supply with; ~ся be satisfied.

удово́льствие pleasure. у|дово́льствоваться pf.

удо́й milk-yield; milking.

удоста́ивать(ся impf of удосто́ить(ся

удостовере́ние certification; certificate; ~ ли́чности identity card. удостове́рить pf, удостоверя́ть impf certify, witness; ~ся make sure (в+prep of), assure o.s.

удосто́ить pf (impf удоста́ивать) make an award to; +gen award; +instr favour with; ~ся +gen be awarded; be favoured with.

у́дочка(fishing-)rod.

удра́ть (удеру́, -ёшь; удра́л, -а́, -о) pf (impf удира́ть) make off.

удруча́ть impf, удручи́ть (-чу́) pf depress. удручённый (-чён, -а́) depressed.

удуша́ть *impf*, удуши́ть (-шу́, -шишь) *pf* stifle, suffocate. удуше́ние suffocation. уду́шливый stifling. уду́шье asthma; asphyxia.

уедине́ние solitude; seclusion. уедине́нный secluded; lonely. уедини́ться *pf*, уединя́ться *impf* seclude o.s.

уе́зд uyezd, District.

уезжа́ть *impf*, уе́хать (уе́ду) *pf* go away, depart.

уж¹ (-á) grass-snake.

уж²: *see* уже́²; уж³, уже́³ *partl* indeed; really.

у|жа́лить *pf*.

у́жас horror, terror; *predic* it is awful. ужаса́ть *impf*, ужасну́ть (-ну́, -нёшь) *pf* horrify; ~ся be horrified, be terrified. ужа́сно *adv* terribly; awfully. ужа́сный awful, terrible.

уже́¹ *comp of* у́зкий

уже́², уж² *adv* already; ~ не no longer. уже́³: *see* уж³

уже́ние fishing.

ужива́ться *impf of* ужи́ться. ужи́вчивый easy to get on with.

ужи́мка grimace.

у́жин supper. у́жинать *impf* (*pf* по~) have supper.

ужи́ться (-иву́сь, -ивёшься; -и́лся, -ла́сь) *pf* (*impf* ужива́ться) get on.

ужу́ *see* уди́ть

узако́нивать *impf*, узако́нить *pf* legalize.

узбе́к, -е́чка Uzbek. Узбекиста́н Uzbekistan.

узда́ (*pl* -ы) bridle.

у́зел (узла́) knot; junction; centre; node; bundle.

у́зкий (у́зок, узка́, -о) narrow; tight; narrow-minded. узкоколе́йка narrow-gauge railway.

узлова́тый knotty. узлов|о́й junction; main, key; ~а́я ста́нция junction.

узнава́ть (-наю́, -наёшь) *impf*, узна́ть *pf* recognize; get to know; find out.

у́зник, у́зница prisoner.

узо́р pattern, design. узо́рчатый patterned.

у́зость narrowness; tightness.

узурпа́тор usurper. узурпи́ровать *impf* & *pf* usurp.

у́зы (уз) *pl* bonds, ties.

уйду́ *etc.*: *see* уйти́

у́йма lots (of).

уйму́ *etc.*: *see* уня́ть

уйти́ (уйду́, -дёшь; ушёл, ушла́) *pf* (*impf* уходи́ть) go away, leave, depart; escape; retire; bury o.s.; be used up; pass away.

ука́з decree; edict. указа́ние indication; instruction. ука́занный appointed, stated. указа́тель *m* indicator; gauge; index; directory. указа́тельный indicating; demonstrative; ~ па́лец index finger. указа́ть (-ажу́, -а́жешь) *pf*, ука́зывать *impf* show; indicate; point; point out. ука́зка pointer; orders.

ука́лывать *impf of* уколо́ть

уката́ть *pf*, ука́тывать¹ *impf* roll; flatten; wear out. укати́ть (-ачу́, -а́тишь) *pf*, ука́тывать² *impf* roll away; drive off; ~ся roll away.

укача́ть *pf*, ука́чивать *impf* rock to sleep; make sick.

укла́д structure; style; organization. укла́дка packing; stacking; laying; setting. укла́дчик packer; layer. укла́дывать(ся¹ *impf of* уложи́ть(ся

укла́дываться² *impf of* уле́чься

укло́н slope; incline; gradient; bias; deviation. уклоне́ние deviation; digression. уклони́ться *pf*, уклоня́ться *impf* deviate; +от+*gen* turn (off, aside); avoid; evade. укло́нчивый evasive.

уклю́чина rowlock.

уко́л prick; injection; thrust. уколо́ть (-лю́, -лешь) *pf* (*impf* ука́лывать) prick; wound.

у|комплектова́ть *pf*, укомплекто́вывать *impf* complete; bring up to (full) strength; man; +*instr* equip with.

уко́р reproach.

укора́чивать *impf of* укороти́ть

укорени́ть *pf*, укореня́ть *impf* implant, inculcate; ~ся take root.

укори́зна reproach. укори́зненный reproachful. укори́ть *pf* (*impf* укоря́ть) reproach (в+*prep* with).

укороти́ть (-очу́) *pf* (*impf* укора́чивать) shorten.

укоря́ть *impf of* укори́ть

уко́с (hay-)crop.

укра́дкой *adv* stealthily. украду́ *etc.*: *see* укра́сть

Украина Ukraine. украинец (-нца), украинка Ukrainian. украинский Ukrainian.

украсить (-ашу) pf (impf украшать) adorn, decorate; ~ся be decorated; adorn o.s.

у|красть (-аду, -адёшь) pf.

украшать(ся impf of украсить(ся. украшение decoration; adornment.

укрепить (-плю) pf, укреплять impf strengthen; fix; fortify; ~ся become stronger; fortify one's position. укрепление strengthening; reinforcement; fortification.

укромный secluded, cosy.

укроп dill.

укротитель m (animal-)tamer. укротить (-ощу) pf, укрощать impf tame; curb; ~ся become tame; calm down. укрощение taming.

укрою etc.: see укрыть

укрупнение enlargement; amalgamation. укрупнить pf, укрупнять impf enlarge; amalgamate.

укрыватель m harbourer. укрывательство harbouring; receiving. укрывать impf, укрыть (-рою) pf cover; conceal, harbour; shelter; receive; ~ся cover o.s.; take cover. укрытие cover; shelter.

уксус vinegar.

укус bite; sting. укусить (-ушу, -усишь) pf bite; sting.

укутать pf, укутывать impf wrap up; ~ся wrap o.s. up.

укушу etc.: see укусить

ул. abbr (of улица) street, road.

улавливать impf of уловить

уладить (-ажу) pf, улаживать impf settle, arrange.

улей (улья) (bee)hive.

улетать impf, улететь (улечу) pf fly (away). улетучиваться impf, улетучиться (-чусь) pf evaporate; vanish.

улечься (улягусь, -яжешься; улёгся, -глась) pf (impf укладываться) lie down; settle; subside.

улика clue; evidence.

улитка snail.

улица street; на улице in the street; outside.

уличать impf, уличить (-чу) pf establish the guilt of.

уличный street.

улов catch. уловимый perceptible; audible. уловить (-влю, -вишь) pf (impf улавливать) catch; seize. уловка trick, ruse.

уложение code. уложить (-жу, -жишь) pf (impf укладывать) lay; pack; pile; ~ спать put to bed; ~ся pack (up); fit in.

улучать impf, улучить (-чу) pf find, seize.

улучшать impf, улучшить (-шу) pf improve; better; ~ся improve; get better. улучшение improvement.

улыбаться impf, улыбнуться (-нусь, -нёшься) pf smile. улыбка smile.

ультиматум ultimatum.

ультра- in comb ultra-. ультразвуковой supersonic. ~фиолетовый ultra-violet.

улягусь etc.: see улечься

ум (-а) mind, intellect; head; сойти с ~а go mad.

умалить pf (impf умалять) belittle. умалишённый mad; sb lunatic.

умалчивать impf of умолчать

умалять impf of умалить

умелец (-льца) skilled craftsman. умелый able, skilful. умение ability, skill.

уменьшать impf, уменьшить (-шу) pf reduce, diminish, decrease; ~ся diminish, decrease; abate. уменьшение decrease, reduction; abatement. уменьшительный diminutive.

умеренность moderation. умеренный moderate; temperate.

умереть (умру, -рёшь; умер, -ла, -о) pf (impf умирать) die.

умерить pf (impf умерять) moderate; restrain.

умертвить (-рщвлю, -ртвишь) pf, умерщвлять impf kill, destroy; mortify. умерший dead; sb the deceased. умерщвление killing, destruction; mortification.

умерять impf of умерить

уместить (-ещу) pf (impf умещать) fit in, find room for; ~ся fit in. уместный appropriate; pertinent; timely.

уметь (-ею) impf be able, know how.

умещать(ся impf of уместить(ся

умиление tenderness; emotion. умилить pf, умилять impf move,

touch; ~ся be moved.
умира́ние dying. умира́ть *impf* of умере́ть. умира́ющий dying; *sb* dying person.
умиротворе́ние pacification; appeasement. умиротвори́ть *pf*, умиротворя́ть *impf* pacify; appease.
умне́ть (-е́ю) *impf* (*pf* по~) grow wiser. у́мница good girl; *m & f* clever person.
умножа́ть *impf*, у|мно́жить (-жу) *pf* multiply; increase; ~ся increase, multiply. умноже́ние multiplication; increase. умножи́тель *m* multiplier.
у́мный (умён, умна́, у́мно́) clever, wise, intelligent. умозаключе́ние deduction; conclusion.
умоли́ть *pf* (*impf* умоля́ть) move by entreaties.
умолка́ть *impf*, умо́лкнуть (-ну; -о́лк) *pf* fall silent; stop. умолча́ть (-чу́) *pf* (*impf* ума́лчивать) fail to mention; hush up.
умоля́ть *impf* of умоли́ть; beg, entreat.
умопомеша́тельство derangement.
умори́тельный incredibly funny, killing. у|мори́ть *pf* kill; exhaust.
умею́ *etc.*: *see* умы́ть. умру́ *etc.*: *see* умере́ть
у́мственный mental, intellectual.
умудри́ть *pf*, умудря́ть *impf* make wiser; ~ся contrive.
умыва́льн *sb* wash-room. умыва́льник wash-stand, wash-basin. умыва́ть(ся *impf* of умы́ть(ся
у́мысел (-сла) design, intention.
умы́ть (умо́ю) *pf* (*impf* умыва́ть) wash; ~ся wash (o.s.).
умы́шленный intentional.
у|насле́довать *pf*.
унести́ (-су́, -сёшь; -ёс, -ла́) *pf* (*impf* уноси́ть) take away; carry off, make off with; ~сь speed away; fly by; be carried (away).
универма́г *abbr* department store.
универса́льн|ый universal; all-round; versatile; all-purpose; ~ магази́н department store; ~ое сре́дство panacea. универса́м *abbr* supermarket.
университе́т university. университе́тский university.
унижа́ть *impf*, уни́зить (-и́жу) *pf* humiliate; ~ся humble o.s.; stoop.

униже́ние humiliation. уни́женный humble. унизи́тельный humiliating.
уника́льный unique.
унима́ть(ся *impf* of уня́ть(ся
унисо́н unison.
унита́з lavatory pan.
унифици́ровать *impf* & *pf* standardize.
уничижи́тельный pejorative.
уничтожа́ть *impf*, уничто́жить (-жу) *pf* destroy, annihilate; abolish; do away with. уничтоже́ние destruction, annihilation, abolition.
уноси́ть(ся (-ошу́(сь, -о́сишь(ся *impf* of унести́(сь
у́нция ounce.
уныва́ть *impf* be dejected. уны́лый dejected; doleful, cheerless. уны́ние dejection, despondency.
уня́ть (уйму́, -мёшь; -я́л, -а́, -о) *pf* (*impf* унима́ть) calm, soothe; ~ся calm down.
упа́док (-дка) decline; decay; ~ ду́ха depression. упа́дочнический decadent. упа́дочный decadent; decadent. упаду́ *etc.*: *see* упа́сть
у|накова́ть *pf*, упако́вывать *impf* pack (up). упако́вка packing; wrapping. упако́вщик packer.
упа́сть (-аду́, -адёшь) *pf* of па́дать
упере́ть (упру́, -рёшь; -ёр) *pf*, упира́ть *impf* rest, lean; ~ на+*acc* stress; ~ся rest, lean; resist; +в+*acc* come up against.
упи́танный well-fed; fattened.
упла́та payment. у|плати́ть (-ачу́, -а́тишь) *pf*, упла́чивать *impf* pay.
уплотне́ние compression; condensation; consolidation; sealing. уплотни́ть *pf*, уплотня́ть *impf* condense; compress; pack more into.
уплыва́ть *impf*, уплы́ть (-ыву́, -ывёшь; -ы́л, -а́, -о) *pf* swim *or* sail away; pass.
упова́ть *impf* +на+*acc* put one's trust in.
уподо́биться (-блюсь) *pf*, уподобля́ться *impf* +*dat* become like.
упое́ние ecstasy, rapture. упои́тельный intoxicating, ravishing.
уполза́ть *impf*, уползти́ (-зу́, -зёшь; -о́лз, -зла́) *pf* creep away, crawl away.
уполномо́ченный *sb* (authorized)

agent, representative; proxy. **уполномачивать**, **уполномочивать** *impf*, **уполномочить** (-чу) *pf* authorize, empower.

упоминание mention. **упоминать** *impf*, **упомянуть** (-ну, -нешь) *pf* mention, refer to.

упор prop, support; в ~ point-blank; **сделать** ~ **на**+*acc* or *prep* lay stress on. **упорный** obstinate; persistent. **упорство** stubbornness; persistence. **упорствовать** *impf* be stubborn; persist (в+*prep* in).

упорядочивать *impf*, **упорядочить** (-чу) *pf* regulate, put in order.

употребительный (widely-)used; common. **употребить** (-блю) *pf*, **употреблять** *impf* use. **употребление** use; usage.

управа justice.

управдом *abbr* manager (*of block of flats*). **управиться** (-влюсь) *pf*, **управляться** *impf* cope, manage; +c+*instr* deal with. **управление** management; administration; direction; control; driving, steering; government. **управляемый снаряд** guided missile. **управлять** *impf* +*instr* manage, direct, run; govern, be in charge of; operate; drive. **управляющий** *sb* manager.

упражнение exercise. **упражнять** *impf* exercise, train; ~ся practise, train.

упразднить *pf*, **упразднять** *impf* abolish.

упрашивать *impf of* **упросить**

упрёк reproach. **упрекать** *impf*, **упрекнуть** (-ну, -нёшь) *pf* reproach.

упросить (-ошу -осишь) *pf* (*impf* **упрашивать**) entreat; prevail upon.

упростить (-ощу) *pf* (*impf* **упрощать**) (over-)simplify.

упрочивать *impf*, **упрочить** (-чу) *pf* strengthen, consolidate; ~ся be firmly established.

упрошу *etc.: see* **упросить**

упрощать *impf of* **упростить**. **упрощённый** (-щён, -á) (over-)simplified.

упру *etc.: see* **упереть**

упругий elastic; springy. **упругость** elasticity; spring. **упруже** *comp of* **упругий**

упряжка harness; team. **упряжной** draught. **упряжь** harness.

упрямиться (-млюсь) *impf* be obstinate; persist. **упрямство** obstinacy. **упрямый** obstinate; persistent.

упускать *impf*, **упустить** (-ущу, -устишь) *pf* let go, let slip; miss. **упущение** omission; slip; negligence.

ура *int* hurrah!

уравнение equalization; equation. **уравнивать** *impf*, **уравнять** *pf* equalize. **уравнительный** equalizing, levelling. **уравновесить** (-ешу) *pf*, **уравновешивать** *impf* balance; counterbalance. **уравновешенность** composure. **уравновешенный** balanced, composed.

ураган hurricane; storm.

уральский Ural.

уран uranium; Uranus. **урановый** uranium.

урвать (-ву, -вёшь; -ал, -á, -о) *pf* (*impf* **урывать**) snatch.

урегулирование regulation; settlement. **у|регулировать** *pf*.

урезать (-ежу) *pf*, **урезать**, **урезывать** *impf* cut off; shorten; reduce.

урка *m* & *f* (*sl*) lag, convict.

урна urn; litter-bin.

уровень (-вня) *m* level; standard.

урод freak, monster. **уродиться** (-ожусь) *pf* ripen; grow. **уродливость** deformity; ugliness. **уродливый** deformed; ugly; bad. **уродовать** *impf* (*pf* из~) disfigure; distort. **уродство** disfigurement; ugliness.

урожай harvest; crop; abundance. **урожайность** yield; productivity. **урожайный** productive, high-yield. **урождённый** *née*. **уроженец** (-нца), **уроженка** native. **урожусь** *see* уродиться

урок lesson.

урон losses; damage. **уронить** (-ню, -нишь) *pf of* ронять

урчать (-чу) *impf* rumble.

урывать *impf of* **урвать**. **урывками** *adv* in snatches, by fits and starts.

ус (*pl* -ы) whisker; tendril; *pl* moustache.

усадить (-ажу, -áдишь) *pf*, **уса́живать** *impf* seat, offer a seat; plant. **усадьба** (*gen pl* -деб *or* -дьб) country estate; farmstead. **уса́живаться** *impf of* усесться

усатый moustached; whiskered.

усваивать *impf,* **усвоить** *pf* master; assimilate; adopt. **усвоение** mastering; assimilation; adoption.

усердие zeal; diligence. **усердный** zealous; diligent.

усесться (усядусь; -елся) *pf* (*impf* **усаживаться**) take a seat; settle down (to).

усидеть (-ижу) *pf* remain seated; hold down a job. **усидчивый** assiduous.

усик tendril; runner; antenna; *pl* small moustache.

усиление strengthening; reinforcement; intensification; amplification. **усиленный** intensified, increased; earnest. **усиливать** *impf,* **усилить** *pf* intensify, increase; amplify; strengthen, reinforce; ~ся increase, intensify; become stronger. **усилие** effort. **усилитель** *m* amplifier; booster.

ускакать (-ачу, -ачешь) *pf* skip off; gallop off.

ускользать *impf,* **ускользнуть** (-ну, -нёшь) *pf* slip off; steal away; escape.

ускорение acceleration. **ускоренный** accelerated; rapid; crash. **ускоритель** accelerator. **ускорить** *pf,* **ускорять** *impf* quicken; accelerate; hasten; ~ся accelerate, be accelerated; quicken.

условие condition. **условиться** (-влюсь) *pf,* **условливаться, уславливаться** *impf* agree; arrange. **условленный** agreed, fixed. **условность** convention. **условный** conditional; conditioned; conventional; agreed; relative.

усложнение complication. **усложнить** *pf,* **усложнять** *impf* complicate; ~ся become complicated.

услуга service; good turn. **услужливый** obliging.

услыхать (-ышу) *pf,* **услышать** (-ышу) *pf* hear; sense; scent.

усматривать *impf of* **усмотреть**

усмехаться *impf,* **усмехнуться** (-нусь, -нёшься) *pf* smile; grin; smirk. **усмешка** smile; grin; sneer.

усмирение pacification; suppression. **усмирить** *pf,* **усмирять** *impf* pacify; calm; suppress.

усмотрение discretion, judgement. **усмотреть** (-рю, -ришь) *pf* (*impf* **усматривать**) perceive; see; regard; +за+*instr* keep an eye on.

уснуть (-ну, -нёшь) *pf* go to sleep.

усовершенствование advanced studies; improvement, refinement. **у|совершенствовать(ся** *pf.*

усомниться *pf* doubt.

успеваемость progress. **успевать** *impf,* **успеть** (-ею) *pf* have time; manage; succeed; ~ся **успех** success; progress. **успешный** successful.

успокаивать *impf,* **успокоить** *pf* calm, quiet, soothe; ~ся calm down; abate. **успокаивающий** calming, sedative. **успокоение** calming, soothing; calm; peace. **успокоительн|ый** calming; reassuring; ~ое *sb* sedative, tranquillizer.

уста (-т, -там) *pl* mouth.

устав regulations, statutes; charter.

уставать (-таю, -ёшь) *impf of* **устать; не уставая** incessantly.

уставить (-влю) *pf,* **уставлять** *impf* set, arrange; cover, fill; direct; ~ся find room, go in; stare.

усталость tiredness. **усталый** tired.

устанавливать *impf,* **установить** (-влю, -вишь) *pf* put, set up; install; set; establish; fix; ~ся dispose o.s.; be established; set in. **установка** putting, setting up; installation; setting; plant, unit; directions. **установление** establishment. **установленный** established, prescribed.

устану *etc.: see* **устать**

устаревать *impf,* **у|стареть** (-ею) *pf* become obsolete; become antiquated. **устарелый** obsolete; antiquated, out-of-date.

устать (-ану) *pf* (*impf* **уставать**) get tired.

устилать *impf,* **устлать** (-телю, -телешь) *pf* cover; pave.

устный oral, verbal.

устой abutment; foundation, support. **устойчивость** stability, steadiness. **устойчивый** stable, steady. **устоять** (-ою) *pf* keep one's balance; stand firm; ~ся settle; become fixed.

устраивать(ся *impf of* **устроить(ся**

устранение removal, elimination. **утсранить** *pf,* **устранять** *impf* remove; eliminate; ~ся resign, retire.

устрашать *impf,* **устрашить** (-шу) *pf* frighten; ~ся be frightened.

устреми́ть (-млю́) pf, **устремля́ть** impf direct, fix; ~ся rush; be directed; concentrate. **устремле́ние** rush; aspiration.

у́стрица oyster.

устро́итель m, ~ница organizer. **устро́ить** pf (impf устра́ивать) arrange, organize; make; cause; settle; put in order; place, fix up; get; suit; ~ся work out; manage; settle down; be found, get fixed up. **устро́йство** arrangement; construction; mechanism, device; system.

усту́п shelf, ledge. **уступа́ть** impf, **уступи́ть** (-плю́, -пишь) pf yield; give up; ~ доро́гу make way. **усту́пка** concession. **усту́пчивый** pliable; compliant.

устыди́ться (-ыжу́сь) pf (+gen) be ashamed (of).

у́стье (gen pl -ьев) mouth; estuary.

усугуби́ть (-у́блю́) pf, **усугубля́ть** impf increase; aggravate.

усы́ see ус

усынови́ть (-влю́) pf, **усыновля́ть** impf adopt. **усыновле́ние** adoption.

усыпа́ть (-плю) pf, **усыпа́ть** impf strew, scatter.

усыпи́тельный soporific. **усыпи́ть** (-плю́) pf, **усыпля́ть** impf put to sleep; lull; weaken.

уся́дусь etc.: see усе́сться

ута́ивать impf, **утаи́ть** pf conceal; keep secret.

ута́птывать impf of утопта́ть

ута́скивать impf, **утащи́ть** (-щу́, -щишь) pf drag off.

у́тварь utensils.

утверди́тельный affirmative. **утверди́ть** (-ржу́) pf, **утвержда́ть** impf confirm; approve; ratify; establish; assert; ~ся gain a foothold; become established; be confirmed. **утвержде́ние** approval; confirmation; ratification; assertion; establishment.

утека́ть impf of уте́чь

утёнок (-нка; pl утя́та, -я́т) duckling.

утепли́ть pf, **утепля́ть** impf warm.

утере́ть (утру́, -рёшь; утёр) pf (impf утира́ть) wipe (off, dry).

утерпе́ть (-плю́, -пишь) pf restrain o.s.

утёс cliff, crag.

уте́чка leak, leakage; escape; loss. **уте́чь** (-еку́, -ечёшь; утёк, -ла́) pf (impf утека́ть) leak, escape; pass.

утеша́ть impf, **уте́шить** (-шу) pf console; ~ся console o.s. **утеше́ние** consolation. **утеши́тельный** comforting.

утилизи́ровать impf & pf utilize.

ути́ль m, **утильсырьё** scrap.

ути́ный duck, duck's.

утира́ть(ся impf of утере́ть(ся

утиха́ть impf, **ути́хнуть** (-ну; -йх) pf abate, subside; calm down.

у́тка duck; canard.

уткну́ть (-ну́, -нёшь) pf bury; fix; ~ся bury o.s.

утоли́ть pf (impf утоля́ть) quench; satisfy; relieve.

утолще́ние thickening; bulge.

утоля́ть impf of утоли́ть

утоми́тельный tedious; tiring. **утоми́ть** (-млю́) pf, **утомля́ть** impf tire, fatigue; ~ся get tired. **утомле́ние** weariness. **утомлённый** weary.

у|тону́ть (-ну́, -нешь) pf drown, be drowned; sink.

утончённый refined.

у|топи́ть(ся (-плю́(сь, -пишь(ся) pf. **уто́пленник** drowned man.

утопи́ческий utopian. **уто́пия** Utopia.

утопта́ть (-пчу́, -пчешь) pf (impf ута́птывать) trample down.

уточне́ние more precise definition; amplification. **уточни́ть** pf, **уточня́ть** impf define more precisely; amplify.

утра́ивать impf of утро́ить

у|трамбова́ть pf, **утрамбо́вывать** impf ram, tamp; ~ся become flat.

утра́та loss. **утра́тить** (-а́чу) pf, **утра́чивать** impf lose.

у́тренний morning. **у́тренник** morning performance; early-morning frost.

утри́ровать impf & pf exaggerate.

у́тро (-а or -а́, -у or -у́; pl -а, -ам or -а́м) morning.

утро́ба womb; belly.

утро́ить pf (impf утра́ивать) triple, treble.

утру́ etc.: see утере́ть, у́тро

утружда́ть impf trouble, tire.

утю́г (-а́) iron. **утю́жить** (-жу) impf (pf вы~, от~) iron.

ух int oh, ooh, ah.

уха́ fish soup.

уха́б pot-hole. **уха́бистый** bumpy.

ухáживать *impf* за+*instr* tend; look after; court.

ухвати́ть (-ачý, -áтишь) *pf*, **ухвá-тывать** *impf* seize; grasp; ~ся за+*acc* grasp, lay hold of; set to; seize; jump at. **ухвáтка** grip; skill; trick; manner.

ухитри́ться *pf*, **ухитря́ться** *impf* manage, contrive. **ухищре́ние** device, trick.

ухмы́лка smirk. **ухмыльнýться** (-нýсь, -нёшься) *pf*, **ухмыля́ться** *impf* smirk.

ýхо (*pl* ýши, ушéй) ear; ear-flap.

ухóд[1] за+*instr* care of; tending, looking after.

ухóд[2] leaving, departure. **уходи́ть** (-ожý, -óдишь) *impf of* уйти́

ухудшáть *impf*, **ухýдшить** (-шу) *pf* make worse; ~ся get worse. **ухуд-шéние** deterioration.

уцелéть (-éю) *pf* remain intact; survive.

уце́нивать *impf*, **уцени́ть** (-ню́, -нишь) *pf* reduce the price of.

уцепи́ть (-плю́, -пишь) *pf* catch hold of, seize; ~ся за+*acc* catch hold of, seize; jump at.

учáствовать *impf* take part; hold shares. **учáствующий** *sb* participant. **учáстие** participation; share; sympathy.

участи́ть (-ащý) *pf* (*impf* учащáть) make more frequent; ~ся become more frequent, quicken.

учáстливый sympathetic. **учáстник** participant. **учáсток** (-тка) plot; part, section; sector; district; field, sphere. **ýчасть** lot, fate.

учащáть(ся *impf of* участи́ть(ся **учáщийся** *sb* student; pupil. **учёба** studies; course; training. **учéбник** text-book. **учéбный** educational; school; training. **учéние** learning; studies; apprenticeship; teaching; doctrine; exercise.

учени́к (-á), **учени́ца** pupil; apprentice; disciple. **учени́ческий** pupil('s); apprentice('s); unskilled; crude. **учё-ность** learning, erudition. **учё́н|ый** learned; scholarly; academic; scientific; ~ая стéпень (*university*) degree; ~ый *sb* scholar; scientist.

учéсть (учтý, -тёшь, *past* учёл, учлá) *pf* (*impf* учи́тывать) take stock of; take

into account; discount. **учёт** stock-taking; calculation; taking into account; registration; discount; без ~а +*gen* disregarding; взять на ~ register. **учётный** registration; discount.

учи́лище (*specialist*) school.

у|чини́ть *pf*, **учиня́ть** *impf* make; carry out; commit.

учи́тель (*pl* -я́) *m*, **учи́тельница** teacher. **учи́тельск|ий** teacher's, teachers'; ~ая *sb* staff-room.

учи́тывать *impf of* учéсть

учи́ть (учý, ýчишь) *impf* (*pf* вы́~, на~, об~) teach; be a teacher; learn; ~ся be a student; +*dat or inf* learn, study.

учреди́тельный constituent. **учре-ди́ть** (-ежý) *pf*, **учреждáть** *impf* found, establish. **учреждéние** founding; establishment; institution.

учти́вый civil, courteous.

учтý *etc.*: *see* учéсть

ушáнка hat with ear-flaps.

ушёл *etc.*: *see* уйти́. **ýши** *etc.*: *see* ýхо

уши́б injury; bruise. **ушибáть** *impf*, **ушиби́ть** (-бý, -бёшь; уши́б) *pf* injure; bruise; hurt; ~ся hurt o.s.

ушкó (*pl* -и́, -óв) eye; tab.

ушнóй ear, aural.

ущéлье ravine, gorge, canyon.

ущеми́ть (-млю́) *pf*, **ущемля́ть** *impf* pinch, jam; limit; encroach on; hurt. **ущемлéние** pinching, jamming; limitation; hurting.

ущéрб detriment; loss; damage; prejudice. **ущéрбный** waning.

ущипнýть (-нý, -нёшь) *pf of* щипáть

Уэ́льс Wales. **уэ́льский** Welsh.

ую́т cosiness, comfort. **ую́тный** cosy, comfortable.

язви́мый vulnerable. **язви́ть** (-влю́) *pf*, **язвля́ть** *impf* wound, hurt.

ясни́ть *pf*, **ясня́ть** *impf* understand, make out.

Ф

фáбрика factory. **фабрикáнт** manufacturer. **фабрикáт** finished product, manufactured product. **фабри-ковáть** *impf* (*pf* с~) fabricate, forge. **фабри́чн|ый** factory; manufacturing; factory-made; ~ая мáрка, ~ое клеймó trade-mark.

фа́була plot, story.

фаго́т bassoon.

фа́за phase; stage.

фаза́н pheasant.

фа́зис phase.

файл (*comput*) file.

фа́кел torch, flare.

факс fax.

факси́миле *neut indecl* facsimile.

факт fact; **соверши́вшийся** ~ fait accompli. **факти́чески** *adv* in fact; virtually. **факти́ческий** actual; real; virtual.

фа́ктор factor.

факту́ра texture; style, execution.

факультати́вный optional. **факульте́т** faculty, department.

фа́лда tail (*of coat*).

фальсифика́тор falsifier, forger. **фальсифика́ция** falsification; adulteration; forgery. **фальсифици́ровать** *impf & pf* falsify; forge; adulterate. **фальши́вить** (-влю) *impf* (*pf* c~) be a hypocrite; sing *or* play out of tune. **фальши́вка** forged document. **фальши́вый** false; spurious; forged; artificial; out of tune. **фальшь** deception; falseness.

фами́лия surname. **фамилья́рничать** be over-familiar. **фамилья́рность** (over-)familiarity. **фамилья́рный** (over-)familiar; unceremonious.

фанати́зм fanaticism. **фана́тик** fanatic.

фане́ра veneer; plywood.

фантазёр dreamer, visionary. **фантази́ровать** *impf* (*pf* c~) dream; make up, dream up; improvise. **фанта́зия** fantasy; fancy; imagination; whim. **фанта́стика** fiction, fantasy. **фантасти́ческий**, **фантасти́чный** fantastic.

фа́ра headlight.

фарао́н pharaoh; faro.

фарва́тер fairway, channel.

фармазо́н freemason.

фармаце́вт pharmacist.

фарс farce.

фа́ртук apron.

фарфо́р china; porcelain. **фарфо́ровый** china.

фарцо́вщик currency speculator.

фарш stuffing; minced meat. **фарширова́ть** *impf* (*pf* за~) stuff.

фаса́д façade.

фасова́ть *impf* (*pf* рас~) package.

фасо́ль kidney bean(s), French bean(s); haricot beans.

фасо́н cut; fashion; style; manner. **фасо́нный** shaped.

фата́ veil.

фатали́зм fatalism. **фата́льный** fatal.

фаши́зм Fascism. **фаши́ст** Fascist. **фаши́стский** Fascist.

фа́йнс faience, pottery.

февра́ль (-я́) *m* February. **февра́льский** February.

федера́льный federal. **федера́ция** federation.

фееρи́ческий fairy-tale.

фейерве́рк firework(s).

фе́льдшер (*pl* -á), **-шери́ца** (*partly-qualified*) medical assistant.

фельето́н feuilleton, feature.

femини́зм feminism. **феминисти́ческий**, **феминⅰи́стский** feminist.

фен (hair-)dryer.

фено́мен phenomenon. **феномена́льный** phenomenal.

феода́л feudal lord. **феодали́зм** feudalism. **феода́льный** feudal.

ферзь (-я́) *m* queen.

фе́рма[1] farm.

фе́рма[2] girder, truss.

ферма́та (*mus*) pause.

ферме́нт ferment.

фе́рмер farmer.

фестива́ль *m* festival.

фетр felt. **фе́тровый** felt.

фехтова́льщик, **-щица** fencer. **фехтова́ние** fencing. **фехтова́ть** *impf* fence.

фе́я fairy.

фиа́лка violet.

фиа́ско *neut indecl* fiasco.

фи́бра fibre.

фигля́р buffoon.

фигу́ра figure; court-card; (chess-) piece. **фигура́льный** figurative, metaphorical. **фигури́ровать** *impf* figure, appear. **фигури́ст**, **-и́стка** figure-skater. **фигу́рка** figurine, statuette; figure. **фигу́рн|ый** figured; ~ое ката́ние figure-skating.

фи́зик physicist. **фи́зика** physics. **физио́лог** physiologist. **физиологи́ческий** physiological. **физиоло́гия** physiology. **физионо́мия** physi-

ognomy; face, expression. **физио-**
терапе́вт physiotherapist. **физи́-**
ческий physical; physics. **физкульту́ра** *abbr* P.E., gymnastics. **физ-**
культу́рный *abbr* gymnastic; ath-
letic; ~ **зал** gymnasium.

фикса́ж fixer. **фикса́ция** fixing.
фикси́ровать *impf & pf* (*pf also*
за~) fix; record.

фикти́вный fictitious. ~ **брак** marriage of convenience. **фи́кция** fiction.

филантро́п philanthropist. **филан-**
тро́пия philanthropy.

филармо́ния philharmonic society;
concert hall.

филатели́ст philatelist.

филе́ *neut indecl* sirloin; fillet.

филиа́л branch.

фили́стер philistine.

фило́лог philologist. **филологи́че-**
ский philological. **филоло́гия** philology.

филосо́ф philosopher. **филосо́фия**
philosophy. **филосо́фский** philosophical.

фильм film. **фильмоско́п** projector.

фильтр filter. **фильтрова́ть** *impf*
(*pf* **про**~) filter.

фина́л finale; final. **фина́льный**
final.

финанси́ровать *impf & pf* finance.
фина́нсовый financial. **фина́нсы**
(**-ов**) *pl* finance, finances.

фи́ник date.

фи́ниш finish; finishing post.

фи́нка Finn. **Финля́ндия** Finland.
финля́ндский Finnish. **финн** Finn.
фи́нский Finnish.

фиоле́товый violet.

фи́рма firm; company. **фи́рменное**
блю́до speciality of the house.

фисгармо́ния harmonium.

фити́ль (**-я́**) *m* wick; fuse.

флаг flag. **фла́гман** flagship.

флако́н bottle, flask.

фланг flank; wing.

флане́ль flannel.

флегмати́чный phlegmatic.

фле́йта flute.

фле́ксия inflexion. **флекти́вный**
inflected.

фли́гель (*pl* **-я́**) *m* wing; annexe.

флирт flirtation. **флиртова́ть** *impf*
flirt.

флома́стер felt-tip pen.

фло́ра flora.

флот fleet. **фло́тский** naval.

флю́гер (*pl* **-а́**) weather-vane.

флюоресце́нтный fluorescent.

флюс[1] gumboil, abscess.

флюс[2] (*pl* **-ы́**) flux.

фля́га flask; churn. **фля́жка** flask.

фойе́ *neut indecl* foyer.

фо́кус[1] trick.

фо́кус[2] focus. **фокуси́ровать** *impf*
focus.

фо́кусник conjurer, juggler.

фолиа́нт folio.

фольга́ foil.

фолькло́р folklore.

фон background.

фона́рик small lamp; torch. **фона́р-**
ный lamp; ~ **столб** lamp-post. **фо-**
на́рь (**-я́**) *m* lantern; lamp; light.

фонд fund; stock; reserves.

фоне́тика phonetics. **фонети́че-**
ский phonetic.

фонта́н fountain.

форе́ль trout.

фо́рма form; shape; mould, cast; uniform. **форма́льность** formality.
форма́льный formal. **форма́т** format. **форма́ция** structure; stage; formation; mentality. **фо́рменный** uniform; proper, regular. **формирова́-**
ние forming; unit, formation. **фор-**
мирова́ть *impf* (*pf* **с**~) form; organize; ~**ся** form, develop. **формова́ть**
impf (*pf* **с**~) form, shape; mould,
cast.

фо́рмула formula. **формули́ровать**
impf & pf (*pf also* **с**~) formulate.
формулиро́вка formulation; wording; formula. **формуля́р** log-book;
library card.

форси́ровать *impf & pf* force; speed
up.

форсу́нка sprayer; injector.

фортепья́но *neut indecl* piano.

фо́рточка small hinged (window-)
pane.

форту́на fortune.

фо́рум forum.

фо́сфор phosphorus.

фо́то *neut indecl* photo(graph).

фото- *in comb* photo-, photo-electric.
     фотоаппара́т camera. ~**бума́га**
photographic paper. ~**гени́чный**
photogenic. **фото́граф** photographer.

~графи́ровать *impf* (*pf* с~) photograph. ~графи́роваться be photographed, have one's photograph taken. ~графи́ческий photographic. ~гра́фия photography; photograph; photographer's studio. ~ко́пия photocopy. ~люби́тель *m* amateur photographer. ~объекти́в (camera) lens. ~репортёр press photographer. ~хро́ника news in pictures. ~элеме́нт photoelectric cell.

фрагмéнт fragment.

фра́за sentence; phrase. фразеоло́гия phraseology.

фрак tail-coat, tails.

фракцио́нный fractional; factional. фра́кция fraction; faction.

франк franc.

франкмасо́н Freemason.

франт dandy.

Фра́нция France. францу́женка Frenchwoman. францу́з Frenchman. францу́зский French.

фрахт freight. фрахтова́ть *impf* (*pf* за~) charter.

фрега́т frigate.

фрезеро́вщик milling machine operator.

фре́ска fresco.

фронт (*pl* -ы́, -о́в) front. фронтови́к (-á) front-line soldier. фронтово́й front(-line).

фронто́н pediment.

фрукт fruit. фрукто́вый fruit; ~ сад orchard.

фтор fluorine. фто́ристый fluorine; fluoride. ~ ка́льций calcium fluoride.

фу *int* ugh! oh!

фуга́нок (-нка) smoothing-plane.

фуга́с landmine. фуга́сный high-explosive.

фунда́мент foundation. фундамента́льный solid, sound; main; basic.

функциона́льный functional. функциони́ровать *impf* function. фу́нкция function.

фунт pound.

фура́ж (-á) forage, fodder. фура́жка peaked cap, forage-cap.

фурго́н van; caravan.

фут foot; foot-rule. футбо́л football. футболи́ст footballer. футбо́лка football jersey, sports shirt. футбо́льный football; ~ мяч football.

футля́р case, container.

футури́зм futurism.

фуфа́йка jersey; sweater.

фы́ркать *impf*, фы́ркнуть (-ну) *pf* snort.

фюзеля́ж fuselage.

X

хала́т dressing-gown. хала́тный careless, negligent.

халту́ра pot-boiler; hackwork; money made on the side. халту́рщик hack.

хам boor, lout. ха́мский boorish, loutish. ха́мство boorishness, loutishness.

хамелео́н chameleon.

хан khan.

хандра́ depression. хандри́ть *impf* be depressed.

ханжа́ hypocrite. ха́нжеский sanctimonious, hypocritical.

хаос chaos. хаоти́чный chaotic.

хара́ктер character. характеризова́ть *impf* & *pf* (*pf also* о~) describe; characterize; ~ся be characterized. характери́стика reference; description. характе́рный characteristic; distinctive; character.

ха́ркать *impf*, ха́ркнуть (-ну) *pf* spit.

ха́ртия charter.

ха́та peasant hut.

хвала́ praise. хвале́бный laudatory. хвалёный highly-praised. хвали́ть (-лю́, -лишь) *impf* (*pf* по~) praise; ~ся boast.

хва́стать(ся) *impf* (*pf* по~) boast. хвастли́вый boastful. хвастовство́ boasting. хвасту́н (-á) boaster.

хвата́ть[1] *impf*, хвати́ть (-ачу́, -áтишь) *pf* (*pf also* схвати́ть) snatch, seize; grab; ~ся remember; +*gen* realize the absence of; +за+*acc* snatch at, clutch at; take up.

хвата́ть[2] *impf*, хвати́ть (-áтит) *pf*, *impers* (+*gen*) suffice, be enough; last out; врéмени не хвата́ло there was not enough time; у нас не хвата́ет дéнег we haven't enough money; хва́тит! that will do! э́того ещё не хвата́ло! that's all we needed! хва́тка grasp, grip; method; skill.

хво́йн|ый coniferous; ~ые *sb pl* conifers.

хворáть *impf* be ill.

хвóрост brushwood; (*pastry*) straws. хворости́на stick, switch.

хвост (-á) tail; tail-end. хво́стик tail. хвостово́й tail.

хвóя needle(s); (*coniferous*) branch(es).

херуви́м cherub.

хиба́р(к)а shack, hovel.

хи́жина shack, hut.

хи́лый (-л, -á, -о) sickly.

химéра chimera.

хи́мик chemist. химикáт chemical. хими́ческий chemical. хи́мия chemistry.

химчи́стка dry-cleaning; dry-cleaner's.

хи́на, хини́н quinine.

хиру́рг surgeon. хирурги́ческий surgical. хирурги́я surgery.

хитре́ц (-á) cunning person. хитри́ть *impf* (*pf* с~) use cunning, be crafty. хи́трость cunning; ruse; skill; intricacy. хи́трый cunning; skilful; intricate.

хихи́кать *impf*, хихи́кнуть (-ну) *pf* giggle, snigger.

хище́ние theft; embezzlement. хи́щник predator, bird *or* beast of prey. хи́щнический predatory. хи́щн|ый predatory; rapacious; ~ые пти́цы birds of prey.

хладнокро́вие coolness, composure. хладнокро́вный cool, composed.

хлам rubbish.

хлеб (*pl* -ы, -ов *or* -á, -óв) bread; loaf; grain. хлеба́ть *impf*, хлебну́ть (-ну́, -нёшь) *pf* gulp down. хле́бный bread; baker's; grain. хлебозаво́д bakery. хлебопека́рня (*gen pl* -рен) bakery.

хлев (*loc* -ý; *pl* -á) cow-shed.

хлеста́ть (-ещу́, -е́щешь) *impf*, хлестну́ть (-ну́, -нёшь) *pf* lash; whip.

хлоп *int* bang! хло́пать *impf* (*pf* хло́пнуть) bang; slap; ~ (в ладо́ши) clap.

хлопково́дство cotton-growing. хло́пковый cotton.

хло́пнуть (-ну) *pf of* хло́пать

хлопо́к[1] (-пка́) clap.

хло́пок[2] (-пка) cotton.

хлопота́ть (-очу́, -о́чешь) *impf* (*pf* по~) busy o.s.; bustle about; take trouble; +о+*prep* or за+*acc* petition for. хлопотли́вый troublesome; ex-

acting; busy, bustling. хло́поты (-о́т) *pl* trouble; efforts.

хлопчатобума́жный cotton.

хло́пья (-ьев) *pl* flakes.

хлор chlorine. хлори́стый, хло́рный chlorine; chloride. хло́рка bleach. хлорофи́лл chlorophyll. хлорофо́рм chloroform.

хлы́нуть (-нет) *pf* gush, pour.

хлыст (-á) whip, switch.

хмеле́ть (-éю) *impf* (*pf* за~, о~) get tipsy. хмель (*loc* -ю́) *m* hop, hops; drunkenness; во хмелю́ tipsy. хмельно́й (-лён, -льна́) drunk; intoxicating.

хму́рить *impf* (*pf* на~); ~ бро́ви knit one's brows; ~ся frown; become gloomy; be overcast. хму́рый gloomy; overcast.

хны́кать (-ы́чу *or* -аю) *impf* whimper, snivel.

хо́бби *neut indecl* hobby.

хо́бот trunk. хоботок (-тка́) proboscis.

ход (*loc* -ý; *pl* -ы, -ов *or* -ы́ *or* -á, -óв) motion; going; speed; course; operation; stroke; move; manoeuvre; entrance; passage; в ~ý in demand; дать за́дний ~ reverse; дать ~ set in motion; на ~ý in transit, on the move; in motion; in operation; по́лным ~ом at full speed; пусти́ть в ~ start, set in motion; три часá ~у three hours' journey.

хода́тайство petitioning; application. хода́тайствовать *impf* (*pf* по~) petition, apply.

ходи́ть (хожу́, хо́дишь) *impf* walk; go; run; pass; go round; lead, play; move; +в+*prep* wear; +за+*instr* look after. хо́дкий (-док, -дка́, -о) fast; marketable; popular. ходьба́ walking; walk. ходя́чий walking; able to walk; popular; current.

хозрасчёт *abbr* (*of* хозя́йственный расчёт) self-financing system.

хозя́ин (*pl* -я́ева, -я́ев) owner, proprietor; master; boss; landlord; host; хозя́ева по́ля home team. хозя́йка owner; mistress; hostess; landlady. хозя́йничать *impf* keep house; be in charge; lord it. хозя́йственник financial manager. хозя́йственный economic; household; economical. хозя́йство economy; housekeeping;

equipment; farm; **дома́шнее ~** housekeeping; **се́льское ~** agriculture.

хоккеи́ст (ice-)hockey-player. **хокке́й** hockey, ice-hockey.

холе́ра cholera.

холестери́н cholesterol.

холл hall, vestibule.

холм (-á) hill. **холми́стый** hilly.

хо́лод (*pl* -á, -óв) cold; coldness; cold weather. **холоди́льник** refrigerator. **хо́лодно** *adv* coldly. **холо́дн|ый** (хо́лоден, -дна́, -о) cold; inadequate, thin; **~ое ору́жие** cold steel.

холо́п serf.

холосто́й (хо́лост, -á) unmarried, single; bachelor; idle; blank. **холостя́к** (-á) bachelor.

холст (-á) canvas; linen.

холу́й (-луя́) *m* lackey.

хому́т (-á) (horse-)collar; burden.

хомя́к (-á) hamster.

хор (*pl* хо́ры) choir; chorus.

хорва́т, **~ка** Croat. **Хорва́тия** Croatia. **хорва́тский** Croatian.

хорёк (-рька́) polecat.

хореографи́ческий choreographic. **хореогра́фия** choreography.

хори́ст member of a choir or chorus.

хорони́ть (-ню́, -нишь) *impf* (*pf* за~, по~, с~) bury.

хоро́шенький pretty; nice. **хоро́шенько** *adv* properly, thoroughly. **хороше́ть** (-е́ю) *impf* (*pf* по~) grow prettier. **хоро́ший** (-о́ш, -á, -о́) good; nice; pretty, nice-looking; **хорошо́** *predic* it is good; it is nice. **хорошо́** *adv* well; nicely; all right! good.

хо́ры (хор *or* -о́в) *pl* gallery.

хоте́ть (хочу́, хо́чешь, хоти́м) *impf* (*pf* за~) wish; +*gen, acc* want; **~ пить** be thirsty; **~ сказа́ть** mean; **~ся** *impers* +*dat* want; **мне хоте́лось бы** I should like; **мне хо́чется** I want.

хоть *conj* although; even if; *partl* at least, if only; for example; **~ бы** if only. **хотя́** *conj* although; **~ бы** even if; if only.

хо́хот loud laugh(ter). **хохота́ть** (-очу́, -о́чешь) *impf* laugh loudly.

хочу́ *etc.: see* хоте́ть

храбре́ц (-á) brave man. **храбри́ться** make a show of bravery; pluck up courage. **хра́брость** brav-

ery. **хра́брый** brave.

храм temple, church.

хране́ние keeping; storage; **ка́мера хране́ния** cloakroom, left-luggage office. **храни́лище** storehouse, depository. **храни́тель** *m* keeper, custodian; curator. **храни́ть** *impf* keep; preserve; **~ся** be, be kept.

храпе́ть (-плю́) *impf* snore; snort.

хребе́т (-бта́) spine; (mountain) range; ridge.

хрен horseradish.

хрестома́тия reader.

хрип wheeze. **хрипе́ть** (-плю́) *impf* wheeze. **хри́плый** (-пл, -á, -о) hoarse. **хри́пнуть** (-ну; хрип) *impf* (*pf* о~) become hoarse. **хрипота́** hoarseness.

христиани́н (*pl* -áне, -áн), **христиа́нка** Christian. **христиа́нский** Christian. **христиа́нство** Christianity. **Христо́с** (-иста́) Christ.

хром chromium; chrome.

хромати́ческий chromatic.

хрома́ть *impf* limp; be poor. **хромо́й** (хром, -á, -о) lame; *sb* lame person.

хромосо́ма chromosome.

хромота́ lameness.

хро́ник chronic invalid. **хро́ника** chronicle; news items; newsreel. **хрони́ческий** chronic.

хронологи́ческий chronological. **хроноло́гия** chronology.

хру́пкий (-пок, -пка́, -о) fragile; frail. **хру́пкость** fragility; frailness.

хруст crunch; crackle.

хруста́ль (-я́) *m* cut glass; crystal. **хруста́льный** cut-glass; crystal; crystal-clear.

хрусте́ть (-ущу́) *impf*, **хру́стнуть** (-ну) *pf* crunch; crackle.

хрю́кать *impf*, **хрю́кнуть** (-ну) *pf* grunt.

хрящ (-á) cartilage, gristle. **хряще-во́й** cartilaginous, gristly.

худе́ть (-е́ю) *impf* (*pf* по~) grow thin.

ху́до harm; evil. **ху́до** *adv* ill, badly.

худоба́ thinness.

худо́жественный art, arts; artistic; **~ фильм** feature film. **худо́жник** artist.

худо́й¹ (худ, -á, -о) thin, lean.

худо́й² (худ, -á, -о) bad; full of holes; worn; **ему́ ху́до** he feels bad.

худоща́вый thin, lean.

ху́дший *superl of* худо́й, плохо́й (the) worst. ху́же *comp of* худо́й, ху́до, плохо́й, пло́хо worse.

хула́ abuse, criticism.

хулига́н hooligan. хулига́нить *impf* behave like a hooligan. хулига́нство hooliganism.

ху́нта junta.

ху́тор (*pl* -á) farm; small village.

Ц

ца́пля (*gen pl* -пель) heron.

цара́пать *impf*, цара́пнуть (-ну) *pf* (*pf also* на~, о~) scratch; scribble; ~ся scratch; scratch one another. цара́пина scratch.

цари́зм tsarism. цари́ть *impf* reign, prevail. цари́ца tsarina; queen. ца́рский tsar's; royal; tsarist; regal. ца́рство kingdom, realm; reign. ца́рствование reign. ца́рствовать *impf* reign. царь (-я́) *m* tsar; king.

цвести́ (-ету́, -ете́шь; -ёл, -á) *impf* flower, blossom; flourish.

цвет[^1] (*pl* -á) colour; ~ лица́ complexion.

цвет[^2] (*loc* -ý; *pl* -ы́) flower; prime; в цвету́ in blossom. цветни́к (-á) flower-bed, flower-garden.

цветн|о́й coloured; colour; non-ferrous; ~áя капу́ста cauliflower; ~óе стекло́ stained glass.

цветов|о́й colour; ~áя слепота́ colour-blindness.

цвето́к (-тка́; *pl* цветы́ *or* цветки́, -óв) flower. цвето́чный flower. цвету́щий flowering; prosperous.

цеди́ть (цежу́, це́дишь) *impf* strain, filter.

целе́бный curative, healing.

целево́й earmarked for a specific purpose. целенапра́вленный purposeful. целесообра́зный expedient. целеустремлённый (-ён, -ённа *or* -ена́) purposeful.

целико́м *adv* whole; entirely.

целина́ virgin lands, virgin soil. цели́нн|ый virgin; ~ые зе́мли virgin lands.

цели́тельный healing, medicinal.

це́лить(ся *impf* (*pf* на~) aim, take aim.

целлофа́н cellophane.

целова́ть *impf* (*pf* по~) kiss; ~ся kiss.

це́лое *sb* whole; integer. целому́дренный chaste. целому́дрие chastity. це́лостность integrity. це́лый (цел, -á, -о) whole; safe, intact.

цель target; aim, object, goal.

це́льный (-лен, -льна́, -о) of one piece, solid; whole; integral; single. це́льность wholeness.

цеме́нт cement. цементи́ровать *impf* & *pf* cement. цеме́нтный cement.

цена́ (*acc* -у; *pl* -ы) price, cost; worth.

ценз qualification. це́нзор censor. цензу́ра censorship.

цени́тель *m* judge, connoisseur. цени́ть (-ню́, -нишь) *impf* value; appreciate. це́нность value; price; *pl* valuables; values. це́нный valuable.

цент cent. це́нтнер centner (*100kg*).

центр centre. централиза́ция centralization. централизова́ть *impf* & *pf* centralize. центра́льный central. центробе́жный centrifugal.

цепене́ть (-е́ю) *impf* (*pf* о~) freeze; become rigid. це́пкий tenacious; prehensile; sticky; obstinate. це́пкость tenacity. цепля́ться *impf* за+*acc* clutch at; cling to.

цепо́чка chain; file. цепь (*loc* -и́; *gen pl* -е́й) chain; series; circuit.

церемо́ниться *impf* (*pf* по~) stand on ceremony. церемо́ния ceremony. церковнославя́нский Church Slavonic. церко́вный church; ecclesiastical. це́рковь (-кви; *gen pl* -е́й) church.

цех (*loc* -ý; *pl* -и *or* -á) shop; section; guild.

цивилиза́ция civilization. цивилизо́ванный civilized. цивилизова́ть *impf* & *pf* civilize.

циге́йка beaver lamb.

цикл cycle.

цико́рий chicory.

цили́ндр cylinder; top hat. цилиндри́ческий cylindrical.

цимба́лы (-ал) *pl* cymbals.

цинга́ scurvy.

цини́зм cynicism. ци́ник cynic. цини́чный cynical.

цинк zinc. ци́нковый zinc.

цино́вка mat.

[^1]:
[^2]:

цирк circus.

циркули́ровать *impf* circulate. **ци́ркуль** *m* (pair of) compasses; dividers. **циркуля́р** circular. **циркуля́ция** circulation.

цисте́рна cistern, tank.

цитаде́ль citadel.

цита́та quotation. **цити́ровать** *impf* (*pf* про~) quote.

ци́трус citrus. **ци́трусов|ый** citrous; ~ые *sb pl* citrus plants.

цифербла́т dial, face.

ци́фра figure; number, numeral. **цифрово́й** numerical, digital.

цо́коль *m* socle, plinth.

цыга́н (*pl* -е, -а́н *or* -ы, -ов), **цыга́нка** gipsy. **цыга́нский** gipsy.

цыплёнок (-нка *pl* -ля́та, -ля́т) chicken; chick.

цы́почки: на ~, на цы́почках on tip-toe.

Ч

чабан (-а́) shepherd.

чад (*loc* -у́) fumes, smoke.

чадра́ yashmak.

чай (*pl* -и́, -ёв) tea. **чаевы́е** (-ы́х) *sb pl* tip.

ча́йка (*gen pl* ча́ек) (sea-)gull.

ча́йная *sb* tea-shop. **ча́йник** teapot; kettle. **ча́йный** tea. **чайхана́** tea-house.

чалма́ turban.

чан (*loc* -у́; *pl* -ы́) vat, tub.

чарова́ть *impf* bewitch; charm.

час (*with numerals* -а́, *loc* -у́; *pl* -ы́) hour; *pl* guard-duty; кото́рый час? what's the time?; ~ one o'clock; в два ~а́ at two o'clock; стоя́ть на ~а́х stand guard; ~ы́ пик rush-hour. **часо́вня** (*gen pl* -вен) chapel. **часово́й** sentry. **часово́й** clock, watch; of one hour, hour-long. **часовщи́к** (-а́) watchmaker.

части́ца small part; particle. **части́чно** *adv* partly, partially. **части́чный** partial.

ча́стник private trader.

ча́стность detail; в ча́стности in particular. **ча́стный** private; personal; particular, individual.

ча́сто *adv* often; close, thickly. **частоко́л** paling, palisade. **частота́** (*pl* -ы)

frequency. **часто́тный** frequency.

часту́шка ditty. **ча́стый** (част, -а́, -о) frequent; close (together); dense; close-woven; rapid.

часть (*gen pl* -е́й) part; department; field; unit.

часы́ (-о́в) *pl* clock, watch.

ча́хлый stunted; sickly, puny. **чахо́тка** consumption.

ча́ша bowl; chalice; ~ весо́в scale, pan. **ча́шка** cup; scale, pan.

ча́ща thicket.

ча́ще *comp of* ча́сто, ча́стый; ~ всего́ most often, mostly.

ча́яние expectation; hope. **ча́ять** (ча́ю) *impf* hope, expect.

чва́нство conceit, arrogance.

чего́ *see* что

чей *m*, **чья** *f*, **чьё** *neut*, **чьи** *pl pron* whose. **чей-либо**, **чей-нибудь** anyone's. **чей-то** someone's.

чек cheque; bill; receipt.

чека́нить *impf* (*pf* вы~, от~) mint, coin; stamp, engrave; enunciate. **чека́нка** coinage, minting. **чека́нный** stamping, engraving; stamped, engraved; precise, expressive.

чёлка fringe; forelock.

чёлн (-а́; *pl* чёлны) dug-out (canoe); boat. **челно́к** (-а́) dug-out (canoe); shuttle.

челове́к (*pl* лю́ди; *with numerals*, *gen* -ве́к, -ам) man, person.

человеко- *in comb* man-, anthropo-. **человеколюби́вый** philanthropic. ~лю́бие philanthropy. ~ненави́стнический misanthropic. **человеко-ча́с** (*pl* -ы́) man-hour.

челове́чек (-чка) little man. **челове́ческий** human; humane. **челове́чество** mankind. **челове́чность** humaneness. **челове́чный** humane.

че́люсть jaw(-bone); dentures, false teeth.

чем, **чём** *see* что. **чем** *conj* than; ~..., тем...+*comp* the more ..., the more.

чемода́н suitcase.

чемпио́н, ~ка champion, title-holder. **чемпиона́т** championship.

чему́ *see* что

чепуха́ nonsense; trifle.

че́пчик cap; bonnet.

че́рви (-е́й), **че́рвы** (черв) *pl* hearts. **черво́нн|ый** of hearts; ~ое зо́лото pure gold.

червь (-я́; *pl* -и, -е́й) *m* worm; bug. **червя́к** (-á) worm.

черда́к (-á) attic, loft.

черёд (-á, *loc* -ý) turn; идти́ свои́м ~о́м take its course. **чередова́ние** alternation. **чередова́ть** *impf* alternate; ~ся alternate, take turns.

че́рез, **чрез** *prep+acc* across; over; through; via; in; after; every other.

черёмуха bird cherry.

черено́к (-нка́) handle; graft, cutting. **че́реп** (*pl* -á) skull.

черепа́ха tortoise; turtle; tortoiseshell. **черепа́ховый** tortoise; turtle; tortoiseshell. **черепа́ший** tortoise, turtle; very slow.

черепи́ца tile. **черепи́чный** tile; tiled.

черепо́к (-пка́) potsherd, fragment of pottery.

чересчу́р *adv* too; too much.

чере́шневый cherry. **чере́шня** (*gen pl* -шен) cherry(-tree).

черке́с, **черке́шенка** Circassian.

черкну́ть (-ну́, -нёшь) *pf* scrape; leave a mark or scribble.

черне́ть (-е́ю) *impf* (*pf* по~) turn black; show black. **черни́ка** (*no pl*; *usu collect*) bilberry; bilberries. **черни́ла** (-и́л) *pl* ink. **черни́льный** ink. **черни́ть** *impf* (*pf* о~) blacken; slander. **черно-** *in comb* black; unskilled; rough. **чёрно-бе́лый** black-and-white. **~бу́рый** dark-brown; **~бу́рая лиса́** silver fox. **~воло́сый** black-haired. **~гла́зый** black-eyed. **~зём** chernozem, black earth. **~ко́жий** black; *sb* black. **~мо́рский** Black Sea. **~рабо́чий** *sb* unskilled worker, labourer. **~сли́в** prunes. **~сморо́динный** blackcurrant.

чернови́к (-á) rough copy, draft. **черново́й** rough; draft. **чернота́** blackness; darkness. **чёрн|ый** (-рен, -рна́) black; back; unskilled; ferrous; gloomy; *sb* (*derog*) black person; **~ая сморо́дина** (*no pl*; *usu collect*) blackcurrant(s).

черпа́к (-á) scoop. **че́рпать** *impf*, **черпну́ть** (-ну́, -нёшь) *pf* draw; scoop; extract.

черстве́ть (-е́ю) *impf* (*pf* за~, о~, по~) get stale; become hardened. **чёрствый** (чёрств, -á, -о) stale; hard.

чёрт (*pl* че́рти, -е́й) devil.

черта́ line; boundary; trait, characteristic. **чертёж** (-á) drawing; blueprint, plan. **чертёжник** draughtsman. **чертёжный** drawing. **черти́ть** (-рчу́, -ртишь) *impf* (*pf* на~) draw.

чёртов *adj* devil's; devilish. **черто́вский** devilish.

чертополо́х thistle.

черто́чка line; hyphen. **черче́ние** drawing. **черчу́** *etc.*: *see* черти́ть

чеса́ть (чешу́, -шешь) *impf* (*pf* по~) scratch; comb; card; ~ся scratch o.s.; itch; comb one's hair.

чесно́к (-á) garlic.

че́ствование celebration. **че́ствовать** *impf* celebrate; honour. **че́стность** honesty. **че́стный** (-тен, -тна́, -о) honest. **честолюби́вый** ambitious. **честолю́бие** ambition. **честь** (*loc* -и́) honour; **отда́ть ~** *+dat* salute.

чета́ pair, couple.

четве́рг (-á) Thursday. **четвере́ньки**: на ~, на четвере́ньках on hands and knees. **четвёрка** four; figure 4; No. 4. **че́тверо** (-ы́х) four. **четвероно́г|ий** four-legged; **~ое** *sb* quadruped. **четверости́шие** quatrain. **четвёртый** fourth. **че́тверть** (*gen pl* -е́й) quarter; quarter of an hour; без че́тверти час a quarter to one. **че́тверть-фина́л** quarter-final.

чёткий (-ток, -тка́, -о) precise; clear-cut; clear; distinct. **чёткость** precision; clarity; distinctness.

чётный even.

четы́ре (-рёх, -рьмя́, -рёх) four. **четы́реста** (-рёхсо́т, -ьмяста́ми, -ёхста́х) four hundred.

четырёх- *in comb* four-, tetra-. **четырёхкра́тный** fourfold. **~ме́стный** four-seater. **~со́тый** four-hundredth. **~уго́льник** quadrangle. **~уго́льный** quadrangular.

четы́рнадцатый fourteenth. **четы́рнадцать** fourteen.

чех Czech.

чехо́л (-хла́) cover, case.

чечеви́ца lentil; lens.

че́шка Czech. **че́шский** Czech.

чешу́ *etc.*: *see* чеса́ть

чешу́йка scale. **чешуя́** scales.

чиж (-á) siskin.

чин (*pl* -ы́) rank.

чини́ть[1] (-ню́, -нишь) *impf* (*pf* по~) repair, mend.

чини́ть² *impf* (*pf* y~) carry out; cause; ~ препя́тствия +*dat* put obstacles in the way of.

чино́вник civil servant; official.

чип (micro)chip.

чи́псы (-ов) *pl* (potato) crisps.

чири́кать *impf*, чири́кнуть (-ну) *pf* chirp.

чи́ркать *impf*, чи́ркнуть (-ну) *pf* +*instr* strike.

чи́сленность numbers; strength. чи́сленный numerical. числи́тель *m* numerator. числи́тельное *sb* numeral. чи́слить *impf* count, reckon; ~ся be; +*instr* be reckoned. число́ (*pl* -а, -сел) number; date, day; в числе́ +*gen* among; в том числе́ including; еди́нственное ~ singular; мно́жественное ~ plural. числово́й numerical.

чисти́лище purgatory.

чи́стильщик cleaner. чи́стить (чи́щу) *impf* (*pf* вы́~, о~, по~) clean; peel; clear. чи́стка cleaning; purge. чи́сто *adv* cleanly, clean; purely; completely. чистово́й fair, clean. чистокро́вный thoroughbred. чистописа́ние calligraphy. чистопло́тный clean; neat; decent. чистосерде́чный frank, sincere. чистота́ cleanness; neatness; purity. чи́стый clean; neat; pure; complete.

чита́емый widely-read, popular. чита́льный reading. чита́тель *m* reader. чита́ть *impf* (*pf* про~, проче́сть) read; recite; ~ ле́кции lecture; ~ся be legible; be discernible. чи́тка reading.

чиха́ть *impf*, чихну́ть (-ну́, -нёшь) *pf* sneeze.

чи́ще *comp of* чи́сто, чи́стый

чи́щу *etc.: see* чи́стить

член member; limb; term; part; article. члени́ть *impf* (*pf* рас~) divide; articulate. член-корреспонде́нт corresponding member, associate. членоразде́льный articulate. чле́нский membership. чле́нство membership.

чмо́кать *impf*, чмо́кнуть (-ну) *pf* smack; squelch; kiss noisily; ~ губа́ми smack one's lips.

чо́каться *impf*, чо́кнуться (-нусь) *pf* clink glasses.

чо́порный prim; stand-offish.

чрева́тый +*instr* fraught with. чре́во belly, womb. чревовеща́тель *m* ventriloquist. чревоуго́дие gluttony.

чрез *see* че́рез. чрезвыча́й|ный extraordinary; extreme; ~ое положе́ние state of emergency. чрезме́рный excessive.

чте́ние reading. чтец (-а́) reader; reciter.

чтить (чту) *impf* honour.

что, чего́, чему́, чем, о чём *pron* what?; how?; why?; how much?; which, what, who; anything; в чём де́ло? what is the matter? для чего́? what … for? why?; ~ ему́ до э́того? what does it matter to him?; ~ с тобо́й? what's the matter (with you)?; ~ за what? what sort of?; what (a) ..!; что *conj* that. что (бы) ни *pron* whatever, no matter what.

чтоб, что́бы *conj* in order (to), so as; that; to. что́-либо, что́-нибудь *prons* anything. что́-то *pron* something. что́-то² *adv* somewhat, slightly; somehow, for some reason.

чу́вственность sensuality. чувстви́тельность sensitivity; perceptibility; sentimentality. чувстви́тельный sensitive; perceptible; sentimental. чу́вство feeling; sense; senses; прийти́ в ~ come round. чу́вствовать *impf* (*pf* по~) feel; realize; appreciate; ~ся be perceptible; make itself felt.

чугу́н (-а́) cast iron. чугу́нный cast-iron.

чуда́к (-а́), чуда́чка eccentric, crank. чуда́чество eccentricity.

чудеса́ *etc.: see* чу́до. чуде́сный miraculous; wonderful.

чу́диться (-ишься) *impf* (*pf* по~, при~) seem.

чу́дно *adv* wonderfully; wonderful! чудно́й (-дён, -дна́) odd, strange. чу́дный wonderful; magical. чу́до (*pl* -деса́) miracle; wonder. чудо́вище monster. чудо́вищный monstrous. чудоде́йственный miracle-working; miraculous. чу́дом *adv* miraculously. чудотво́рный miraculous, miracle-working.

чужби́на foreign land. чужда́ться *impf* +*gen* avoid; stand aloof from. чу́ждый (-жд, -а́, -о) alien (to); +*gen* free from, devoid of. чужезе́мец (-мца), -зе́мка foreigner. чужезе́мный foreign. **чужо́й** someone else's, others'; strange, alien; foreign.

чула́н store-room; larder.

чуло́к (-лка́; *gen pl* -ло́к) stocking.

чума́ plague.

чума́зый dirty.

чурба́н block. **чу́рка** block, lump.

чу́ткий (-ток, -тка́, -о) keen; sensitive; sympathetic; delicate. **чу́ткость** keenness; delicacy.

чу́точка: ни чу́точки not in the least; чу́точку a little (bit).

чу́тче *comp of* **чу́ткий**

чуть *adv* hardly; just; very slightly; ~ не almost; ~-чуть a tiny bit.

чутьё scent; flair.

чу́чело stuffed animal, stuffed bird; scarecrow.

чушь nonsense.

чу́ять (чу́ю) *impf* scent; sense.

чьё *etc.*: *see* чей

Ш

ша́баш sabbath.

шабло́н template; mould, stencil; cliché. **шабло́нный** stencil; trite; stereotyped.

шаг (with numerals -á, *loc* -ý; *pl* -и́) step; footstep; pace. **шага́ть** *impf*, **шагну́ть** (-ну́, -нёшь) *pf* step; stride; pace; make progress. **ша́гом** *adv* at walking pace.

ша́йба washer; puck.

ша́йка[1] tub.

ша́йка[2] gang, band.

шака́л jackal.

шала́ш (-á) cabin, hut.

шали́ть *impf* be naughty; play up. **шаловли́вый** mischievous, playful. **ша́лость** prank; *pl* mischief. **шалу́н** (-á), **шалу́нья** (*gen pl* -ний) naughty child.

шаль shawl.

шально́й mad, crazy.

ша́мкать *impf* mumble.

шампа́нское *sb* champagne.

шампиньо́н field mushroom.

шампу́нь *m* shampoo.

шанс chance.

шанта́ж (-á) blackmail. **шантажи́ровать** *impf* blackmail.

ша́пка hat; banner headline. **ша́почка** hat.

шар (with numerals -á; *pl* -ы́) sphere; ball; balloon.

шара́хать *impf*, **шара́хнуть** (-ну) hit; ~ся dash; shy.

шарж caricature.

ша́рик ball; corpuscle. **ша́риков|ый**: ~ая (авто)ру́чка ball-point pen; ~ый подши́пник ball-bearing. **шарикоподши́пник** ball-bearing. **ша́рить** *impf* grope; sweep.

ша́ркать *impf*, **ша́ркнуть** (-ну) *pf* shuffle; scrape.

шарлата́н charlatan.

шарма́нка barrel-organ. **шарма́нщик** organ-grinder.

шарни́р hinge, joint.

шарова́ры (-а́р) *pl* (wide) trousers. **шарови́дный** spherical. **шарово́й** ball; globular. **шарообра́зный** spherical.

шарф scarf.

шасси́ *neut indecl* chassis.

шата́ть *impf* rock, shake; *impers* +acc его́ шата́ет he is reeling; ~ся sway; reel, stagger; come loose, be loose; be unsteady; loaf about.

шатёр (-тра́) tent; marquee.

ша́ткий unsteady; shaky.

шату́н (-á) connecting-rod.

ша́фер (*pl* -á) best man.

шах check; ~ и мат checkmate. **шахмати́ст** chess-player. **ша́хматы** (-ат) *pl* chess; chessmen.

ша́хта mine; pit; shaft. **шахтёр** miner. **шахтёрский** miner's; mining.

ша́шка[1] draught; *pl* draughts.

ша́шка[2] sabre.

шашлы́к (-á) kebab; barbecue.

шва *etc.*: *see* шов

шва́бра mop.

шваль rubbish; riff-raff.

шварто́в mooring-line; *pl* moorings. **швартова́ть** *impf* (*pf* при~) moor; ~ся moor.

швед, ~ка Swede. **шве́дский** Swedish.

швейн|ый sewing; ~ая маши́на sewing-machine.

швейца́р porter, doorman.

швейца́рец (-рца), -ца́рка Swiss. **Швейца́рия** Switzerland. **швейца́рский** Swiss.

Шве́ция Sweden.

швея́ seamstress.

швырну́ть (-ну́, -нёшь) *pf*, **швыря́ть**

impf throw, fling; ∼ся +*instr* throw (about); treat carelessly.

шевели́ть (-елю́, -е́ли́шь) *impf*, **шевельну́ть** (-ну́, -нёшь) *pf* (*pf also* по∼) (+*instr*) move, stir; ∼ся move, stir.

шеде́вр masterpiece.

ше́йка (*gen pl* ше́ек) neck.

шёл *see* идти́

ше́лест rustle. **шелесте́ть** (-сти́шь) *impf* rustle.

шёлк (*loc* -ý, *pl* -á) silk. **шелкови́стый** silky. **шелкови́ца** mulberry (-tree). **шелкови́чный** mulberry; ∼ червь silkworm. **шелкови́вый** silk.

шелохну́ть (-ну́, -нёшь) *pf* stir, agitate; ∼ся stir, move.

шелуха́ skin; peelings; pod. **шелуши́ть** (-шу́) peel; shell; ∼ся peel (off), flake off.

шепеля́вить (-влю) *impf* lisp. **шепеля́вый** lisping.

шепну́ть (-ну́, -нёшь) *pf*, **шепта́ть** (-пчу́, -пчешь) *impf* whisper; ∼ся whisper (together). **шёпот** whisper. **шёпотом** *adv* in a whisper.

шере́нга rank; file.

шерохова́тый rough; uneven.

шерсть wool; hair, coat. **шерстяно́й** wool(len).

шерша́вый rough.

шест (-á) pole; staff.

ше́ствие procession. **ше́ствовать** process; march.

шестёрка six; figure 6; No. 6.

шестерня́ (*gen pl* -рён) gear-wheel, cogwheel.

ше́стеро (-ы́х) six.

шести- *in comb* six-, hexa-, sex(i)-. **шестигра́нник** hexahedron. ∼**дне́вка** six-day (*working*) week. ∼**деся́тый** sixtieth. ∼**ме́сячный** six-month; six-month-old. ∼**со́тый** six-hundredth. ∼**уго́льник** hexagon.

шестнадцатиле́тний sixteen-year; sixteen-year-old. **шестна́дцатый** sixteenth. **шестна́дцать** sixteen. **шесто́й** sixth. **шесть** (-и́, *instr* -ью́) six. **шестьдеся́т** (-и́десяти, *instr* -ью́десятью) sixty. **шестьсо́т** (-сот, -иста́м, -ьюста́ми, -иста́х) six hundred. **ше́стью** *adv* six times.

шеф boss, chief; patron, sponsor. **шеф-по́вар** chef. **ше́фство** patronage, adoption. **ше́фствовать** *impf*

+над+*instr* adopt; sponsor.

ше́я neck.

ши́ворот collar.

шика́рный chic, smart; splendid.

ши́ло (*pl* -ья, -ьев) awl.

шимпанзе́ *m indecl* chimpanzee.

ши́на tyre; splint.

шине́ль overcoat.

шинкова́ть *impf* shred, chop.

ши́нный tyre.

шип (-á) thorn, spike, crampon; pin; tenon.

шипе́ние hissing; sizzling. **шипе́ть** (-плю́) *impf* hiss; sizzle; fizz.

шипо́вник dog-rose.

шипу́чий sparkling; fizzy. **шипу́чка** fizzy drink. **шипя́щий** sibilant.

ши́ре *comp of* широ́кий, широ́ко. **ширина́** width; gauge. **ши́рить** *impf* extend, expand; ∼ся spread, extend.

ши́рма screen.

широ́кий (-о́к, -á, -о́ко́) wide, broad; това́ры ∼ого потребле́ния consumer goods. **широ́ко** *adv* wide, widely, broadly.

широко- *in comb* wide-, broad-. **широковеща́ние** broadcasting. ∼**веща́тельный** broadcasting. ∼**экра́нный** wide-screen.

широта́ (*pl* -ы) width, breadth; latitude. **широ́тный** of latitude; latitudinal. **широча́йший** *superl of* широ́кий. **ширпотре́б** *abbr* consumption; consumer goods. **ширь** (wide) expanse.

шить (шью, шьёшь) *impf* (*pf* с∼) sew; make; embroider. **шитьё** sewing; embroidery.

ши́фер slate.

шифр cipher, code; shelf-mark. **шифро́ванный** in cipher, coded. **шифрова́ть** *impf* (*pf* за∼) encipher. **шифро́вка** enciphering; coded communication.

ши́шка cone; bump; lump; (*sl*) big shot.

шкала́ (*pl* -ы) scale; dial.

шкату́лка box, casket, case.

шкаф (*loc* -ý; *pl* -ы́) cupboard; wardrobe. **шка́фчик** cupboard, locker.

шквал squall.

шкив (*pl* -ы́) pulley.

шко́ла school. **шко́льник** schoolboy. **шко́льница** schoolgirl. **шко́льный** school.

шку́ра skin, hide, pelt. шку́рка skin; rind; emery paper, sandpaper.

шла *see* идти́

шлагба́ум barrier.

шлак slag; dross; clinker. шлако-
бло́к breeze-block.

шланг hose.

шлейф train.

шлем helmet.

шлёпать *impf*, шлёпнуть (-ну) *pf*
smack, spank; shuffle; tramp; ~ся
fall flat, plop down.

шли *see* идти́

шлифова́льный polishing; grinding.
шлифова́ть *impf* (*pf* от~) polish;
grind. шлифо́вка polishing.

шло *see* идти́. шлю *etc.*: *see* слать

шлюз lock, sluice.

шлю́пка boat.

шля́па hat. шля́пка hat; head.

шмель (-я́) *m* bumble-bee.

шмон *sl* search, frisking.

шмы́гать *impf*, шмыгну́ть (-ы́гну́,
-ы́гнёшь) *pf* dart, rush; +*instr* rub,
brush; ~ но́сом sniff.

шни́цель *m* schnitzel.

шнур (-а́) cord; lace; flex, cable. шну-
рова́ть *impf* (*pf* за~, про~) lace up;
tie. шнуро́к (-рка́) lace.

шов (шва) seam; stitch; joint.

шовини́зм chauvinism. шовини́ст
chauvinist. шовинисти́ческий chau-
vinistic.

шок shock. шоки́ровать *impf* shock.

шокола́д chocolate. шокола́дка
chocolate, bar of chocolate. шоко-
ла́дный chocolate.

шо́рох rustle.

шо́рты (шорт) *pl* shorts.

шо́ры (шор) *pl* blinkers.

шоссе́ *neut indecl* highway.

шотла́ндец (-дца) Scotsman, Scot.
Шотла́ндия Scotland. шотла́ндка[1]
Scotswoman. шотла́ндка[2] tartan.
шотла́ндский Scottish, Scots.

шофёр driver; chauffeur. шофёр-
ский driver's; driving.

шпа́га sword.

шпага́т cord; twine; string; splits.

шпаклева́ть (-лю́ю) *impf* (*pf* за~)
caulk; fill, putty. шпаклёвка filling,
puttying; putty.

шпа́ла sleeper.

шпана́ (*sl*) hooligan(s); riff-raff.

шпарга́лка crib.

шпа́рить *impf* (*pf* о~) scald.

шпат spar.

шпиль *m* spire; capstan. шпи́лька
hairpin; hat-pin; tack; stiletto heel.

шпина́т spinach.

шпио́н spy. шпиона́ж espionage.
шпио́нить *impf* spy (за+*instr* on).
шпио́нский spy's; espionage.

шпо́ра spur.

шприц syringe.

шпро́та sprat.

шпу́лька spool, bobbin.

шрам scar.

шрапне́ль shrapnel.

шрифт (*pl* -ы́) type, print.

шт. *abbr* (*of* шту́ка) item, piece.

штаб (*pl* -ы́) staff; headquarters.

шта́бель (*pl* -я́) *m* stack.

штабно́й staff; headquarters.

штамп die, punch; stamp; cliché.
штампо́ванный punched, stamped,
pressed; trite; stock.

шта́нга bar, rod, beam; weight. штан-
ги́ст weight-lifter.

штани́шки (-шек) *pl* (*child's*) shorts.
штаны́ (-о́в) trousers.

штат[1] State.

штат[2], шта́ты (-ов) *pl* staff, establishment.

штати́в tripod, base, stand.

шта́тный staff; established.

шта́тск|ий civilian; ~ое (пла́тье) ci-
vilian clothes; ~ий *sb* civilian.

ште́мпель (*pl* -я́) *m* stamp; почто́-
вый ~ postmark.

ште́псель (*pl* -я́) *m* plug, socket.

штиль *m* calm.

штифт (-а́) pin, dowel.

што́льня (*gen pl* -лен) gallery.

што́пать *impf* (*pf* за~) darn. што́п-
ка darning; darning wool.

што́пор corkscrew; spin.

што́ра blind.

шторм gale.

штраф fine. штрафно́й penal; penalty. штрафова́ть *impf* (*pf* о~) fine.

штрих (-а́) stroke; feature. штрихо-
ва́ть *impf* (*pf* за~) shade, hatch.

штуди́ровать *impf* (*pf* про~) study.

шту́ка item, one; piece; trick.

штукату́р plasterer. штукату́рить
impf (*pf* от~, о~) plaster. штука-
ту́рка plastering; plaster.

штурва́л (steering-)wheel, helm.

штурм storm, assault.
штурман (*pl* -ы *or* -а́) navigator.
штурмова́ть *impf* storm, assault.
штурмов|о́й assault; storming; ~а́я авиа́ция ground-attack aircraft.
штурмовщи́на rushed work.
шту́чный piece, by the piece.
штык (-а́) bayonet.
штырь (-я́) *m* pintle, pin.
шу́ба fur coat.
шу́лер (*pl* -а́) card-sharper.
шум noise; uproar, racket; stir. **шуме́ть** (-млю́) *impf* make a noise; row; make a fuss. **шу́мный** (-мен, -мна́, -о) noisy; loud; sensational.
шумов|о́й sound; ~ы́е эффе́кты sound effects. **шумо́к** (-мка́) noise; под ~ on the quiet.
шу́рин brother-in-law (*wife's brother*).
шурф prospecting shaft.
шурша́ть (-шу́) *impf* rustle.
шу́стрый (-тёр, -тра́, -о) smart, bright, sharp.
шут (-а́) fool; jester. **шути́ть** (-чу́, -тишь) *impf* (*pf* по~) joke; play, trifle; +над+*instr* make fun of. **шу́тка** joke, jest. **шутли́вый** humorous; joking, light-hearted. **шу́точный** comic; joking. **шутя́** *adv* for fun, in jest; easily.
шушу́каться *impf* whisper together.
шху́на schooner.
шью *etc*.: *see* шить

Щ

щаве́ль (-я́) *m* sorrel.
щади́ть (щажу́) *impf* (*pf* по~) spare.
щебёнка, **ще́бень** (-бня) *m* crushed stone, ballast; road-metal.
ще́бет twitter, chirp. **щебета́ть** (-ечу́, -е́чешь) *impf* twitter, chirp.
щего́л (-гла́) goldfinch.
щёголь *m* dandy, fop. **щегольну́ть** (-ну́, -нёшь) *pf*, **щеголя́ть** *impf* dress fashionably; strut about; +*instr* show off, flaunt. **щегольско́й** foppish.
ще́дрость generosity. **ще́дрый** (-др, -á, -о) generous; liberal.
щека́ (*acc* щёку, *pl* щёки, -а́м) cheek.
щеко́лда latch, catch.
щекота́ть (-очу́, -о́чешь) *impf* (*pf* по~) tickle. **щеко́тка** tickling, tickle. **щекотли́вый** ticklish, delicate.

щёлкать *impf*, **щёлкнуть** (-ну) *pf* crack; flick; trill; +*instr* click, snap, pop.
щёлок bleach. **щелочно́й** alkaline. **щёлочь** (*gen pl* -е́й) alkali.
щелчо́к (-чка́) flick; slight; blow.
щель (*gen pl* -е́й) crack; chink; slit; crevice; slit trench.
щеми́ть (-млю́) *impf* constrict; ache; oppress.
щено́к (-нка́; *pl* -нки́, -о́в *or* -ня́та, -я́т) pup; cub.
щепа́ (*pl* -ы, -а́м), **ще́пка** splinter, chip; kindling.
щепети́льный punctilious.
ще́пка *see* щепа́
щепо́тка, **ще́по́ть** pinch.
щети́на bristle; stubble. **щети́нистый** bristly. **щети́ниться** *impf* (*pf* o~) bristle. **щётка** brush; fetlock.
щи (щей *or* щец, щам, ща́ми) *pl* shchi, cabbage soup.
щи́колотка ankle.
щипа́ть (-плю́, -плешь) *impf*, **щипну́ть** (-ну́, -нёшь) *pf* (*pf also* об~, о~, ущипну́ть) pinch, nip; sting, bite; burn; pluck; nibble; ~ся pinch. **щипко́м** *adv* pizzicato. **щипо́к** (-пка́) pinch, nip. **щипцы́** (-о́в) *pl* tongs, pincers, pliers; forceps.
щит (-а́) shield; screen; sluice-gate; (tortoise-)shell; board; panel. **щитови́дный** thyroid. **щито́к** (-тка́) dashboard.
щу́ка pike.
щуп probe. **щу́пальце** (*gen pl* -лец) tentacle; antenna. **щу́пать** *impf* (*pf* по~) feel, touch.
щу́плый (-пл, -á, -о) weak, puny.
щу́рить *impf* (*pf* со~) screw up, narrow; ~ся screw up one's eyes; narrow.

Э

эбе́новый ebony.
эвакуа́ция evacuation. **эвакуи́рованный** *sb* evacuee. **эвакуи́ровать** *impf* & *pf* evacuate.
эвкали́пт eucalyptus.
эволюциони́ровать *impf* & *pf* evolve. **эволюцио́нный** evolutionary. **эволю́ция** evolution.
эги́да aegis.
эгои́зм egoism, selfishness. **эгои́ст**, ~**ка** egoist. **эгоисти́ческий**, **эгои-**

сти́чный egoistic, selfish.

эй *int* hi! hey!

эйфори́я euphoria.

эква́тор equator.

эквивале́нт equivalent.

экзальта́ция exaltation.

экза́мен examination; вы́держать, сдать ~ pass an examination. экзамена́тор examiner. экзаменова́ть *impf (pf* про~) examine; ~ся take an examination.

экзеку́ция (corporal) punishment.

экзе́ма eczema.

экземпля́р specimen; copy.

экзистенциали́зм existentialism.

экзоти́ческий exotic.

э́кий what (a).

экипа́ж[1] carriage.

экипа́ж[2] crew. экипирова́ть *impf & pf* equip. экипиро́вка equipping; equipment.

эклекти́зм eclecticism.

эклер éclair.

экологи́ческий ecological. эколо́гия ecology.

эконо́мика economics; economy. эконо́мист economist. эконо́мить (-млю) *impf (pf* с~) use sparingly; save; economize. экономи́ческий economic; economical. экономи́чный economical. эконо́мия economy; saving. эконо́мка housekeeper. эконо́мный economical; thrifty.

экра́н screen. экраниза́ция filming; film version.

экскава́тор excavator.

экскурса́нт tourist. экскурсио́нный excursion. экску́рсия (conducted) tour; excursion. экскурсово́д guide.

экспанси́вный effusive.

экспатриа́нт expatriate. экспатрии́ровать *impf & pf* expatriate.

экспеди́ция expedition; dispatch; forwarding office.

экспериме́нт experiment. эксперимента́льный experimental. эксперименти́ровать *impf* experiment.

экспе́рт expert. эксперти́за (expert) examination; commission of experts.

эксплуата́тор exploiter. эксплуатацио́нный operating. эксплуата́ция exploitation; operation. эксплуати́ровать *impf* exploit; operate, run.

экспози́ция lay-out; exposition; exposure. экспона́т exhibit. экспоно́метр exposure meter.

э́кспорт export. экспорти́ровать *impf & pf* export. э́кспортный export.

экспре́сс express (*train etc.*).

экспро́мт impromptu. экспро́мтом *adv* impromptu.

экспроприа́ция expropriation. экспроприи́ровать *impf & pf* expropriate.

экста́з ecstasy.

экстравага́нтный eccentric, bizarre.

экстра́кт extract.

экстреми́ст extremist. экстреми́стский extremist.

э́кстренный urgent; emergency; special.

эксцентри́чный eccentric.

эксце́сс excess.

эласти́чный elastic; supple.

элева́тор grain elevator; hoist.

элега́нтный elegant, smart.

эле́гия elegy.

электризова́ть *impf (pf* на~) electrify. эле́ктрик electrician. электрифика́ция electrification. электрифици́ровать *impf & pf* electrify. электри́ческий electric(al). электри́чество electricity. электри́чка electric train.

электро- *in comb* electro-, electric, electrical. ~во́з electric locomotive. ~дви́гатель *m* electric motor. электро́лиз electrolysis. ~магни́тный electromagnetic. ~монтёр electrician. ~одея́ло electric blanket. ~по́езд electric train. ~прибо́р electrical appliance. ~про́вод (*pl* -а́) electric cable. ~прово́дка electric wiring. ~ста́нция power-station. ~те́хник electrical engineer. ~те́хника electrical engineering. ~шо́к electric-shock treatment. ~эне́ргия electrical energy.

электро́д electrode.

электро́н electron. электро́ника electronics.

электро́нный electron; electronic.

элеме́нт element; cell; character. элемента́рный elementary.

эли́та élite.

э́ллипс ellipse.

эма́левый enamel. эмалирова́ть

impf enamel. **эма́ль** enamel.

эмансипа́ция emancipation.

эмба́рго *neut indecl* embargo.

эмбле́ма emblem.

эмбрио́н embryo.

эмигра́нт emigrant, émigré. **эмигра́ция** emigration. **эмигри́ровать** *impf & pf* emigrate.

эмоциона́льный emotional. **эмо́ция** emotion.

эмпири́ческий empirical.

эму́льсия emulsion.

э́ндшпиль *m* end-game.

энерге́тика power engineering. **энергети́ческий** energy. **энерги́чный** energetic. **эне́ргия** energy.

энтомоло́гия entomology.

энтузиа́зм enthusiasm. **энтузиа́ст** enthusiast.

энциклопеди́ческий encyclopaedic. **энциклопе́дия** encyclopaedia.

эпигра́мма epigram. **эпи́граф** epigraph.

эпиде́мия epidemic.

эпизо́д episode. **эпизоди́ческий** episodic; sporadic.

эпиле́псия epilepsy. **эпиле́птик** epileptic.

эпило́г epilogue. **эпита́фия** epitaph. **эпи́тет** epithet. **эпице́нтр** epicentre. **эпопе́я** epic.

эпо́ха epoch, era.

э́ра era; **до на́шей э́ры** BC; **на́шей э́ры** AD.

эре́кция erection.

эро́зия erosion.

эроти́зм eroticism. **эро́тика** sensuality. **эроти́ческий, эроти́чный** erotic, sensual.

эруди́ция erudition.

эска́дра (*naut*) squadron. **эскадри́лья** (*gen pl* -лий) (*aeron*) squadron. **эскадро́н** (*mil*) squadron. **эскадро́нный** squadron.

эскала́тор escalator. **эскала́ция** escalation.

эски́з sketch; draft. **эски́зный** sketch; draft.

эскимо́с, эскимо́ска Eskimo.

эско́рт escort.

эсми́нец (-нца) *abbr* (*of* эска́дренный миноно́сец) destroyer.

эссе́нция essence.

эстака́да trestle bridge; overpass; pier, boom.

эста́мп print, engraving, plate.

эстафе́та relay race; baton.

эсте́тика aesthetics. **эстети́ческий** aesthetic.

эсто́нец (-нца), **эсто́нка** Estonian. **Эсто́ния** Estonia. **эсто́нский** Estonian.

эстра́да stage, platform; variety. **эстра́дный** stage; variety; ~ **конце́рт** variety show.

эта́ж (-а́) storey, floor. **этаже́рка** shelves.

э́так *adv* so, thus; about. **э́такий** such (a), what (a).

этало́н standard.

эта́п stage; halting-place.

э́тика ethics.

этике́т etiquette.

этике́тка label.

эти́л ethyl.

этимоло́гия etymology.

эти́ческий, эти́чный ethical.

этни́ческий ethnic. **этногра́фия** ethnography.

э́то *partl* this (is), that (is), it (is). **э́тот** *m*, **э́та** *f*, **э́то** *neut*, **э́ти** *pl pron* this, these.

этю́д study, sketch; étude.

эфеме́рный ephemeral.

эфио́п, ~ка Ethiopian. **эфио́пский** Ethiopian.

эфи́р ether; air. **эфи́рный** ethereal; ether, ester.

эффе́кт effect. **эффекти́вность** effectiveness. **эффекти́вный** effective. **эффе́ктный** effective; striking.

эх *int* eh! oh!

э́хо echo.

эшафо́т scaffold.

эшело́н echelon; special train.

Ю

юбиле́й anniversary; jubilee. **юбиле́йный** jubilee.

ю́бка skirt. **ю́бочка** short skirt.

ювели́р jeweller. **ювели́рный** jeweller's, jewellery; fine, intricate.

юг south; **на ~е** in the south. **ю́го-восто́к** south-east. **ю́го-за́пад** south-west. **югосла́в, ~ка** Yugoslav. **Югосла́вия** Yugoslavia. **югосла́вский** Yugoslav.

юдофо́б anti-Semite. **юдофо́бство**

anti-Semitism.

южа́нин (*pl* -а́не, -а́н), **южа́нка** southerner. **ю́жный** south, southern; southerly.

юла́ top; fidget. **юли́ть** *impf* fidget.

ю́мор humour. **юмори́ст** humourist. **юмористи́ческий** humorous.

ю́ность youth. **ю́ноша** (*gen pl* -шей) *m* youth. **ю́ношеский** youthful. **ю́ношество** young people. **ю́ный** (юн, -а́, -о) young; youthful.

юпи́тер floodlight.

юриди́ческий legal, juridical. **юрисконсульт** legal adviser. **юри́ст** lawyer.

ю́ркий (-рок, -рка́, -рко) quick-moving, brisk; smart.

юро́дивый crazy.

ю́рта yurt, nomad's tent.

юсти́ция justice.

юти́ться (ючу́сь) *impf* huddle (together).

Я

я (меня́, мне, мной (-о́ю), (обо) мне) *pron* I.

я́беда *m & f*, tell-tale; informer.

я́блоко (*pl* -и, -ок) apple; глазно́е ~ eyeball. **я́блоневый, я́блочный** apple. **я́блоня** apple-tree.

яви́ться (явлю́сь, я́вишься) *pf*, **явля́ться** *impf* appear; arise; +*instr* be, serve as. **я́вка** appearance, attendance; secret rendez-vous. **явле́ние** phenomenon; appearance; occurrence; scene. **я́вный** obvious; overt. **я́вственный** clear. **я́вствовать** be clear, be obvious.

ягнёнок (-нка; *pl* -ня́та, -я́т) lamb.

я́года berry; berries.

я́годица buttock(s).

ягуа́р jaguar.

яд poison; venom.

я́дерный nuclear.

ядови́тый poisonous; venomous.

ядрёный healthy; bracing; juicy.

ядро́ (*pl* -а, я́дер) kernel, core; nucleus; (cannon-)ball; shot.

я́зва ulcer, sore. **я́звенн|ый** ulcerous; ~ая боле́знь ulcers. **язви́тельный**

caustic, sarcastic. **язви́ть** (-влю́) *impf* (*pf* съ~) be sarcastic.

язы́к (-а́) tongue; clapper; language. **языкове́д** linguist. **языкове́дение, языкозна́ние** linguistics. **языково́й** linguistic. **языко́вый** tongue; lingual. **язычко́вый** reed. **язы́чник** heathen, pagan. **язычо́к** (-чка́) tongue; reed; catch.

яи́чко (*pl* -и, -чек) egg; testicle. **яи́чник** ovary. **яи́чница** fried eggs. **яйцо́** (*pl* я́йца, яи́ц) egg; ovum.

я́кобы *conj* as if; *partl* supposedly.

я́кор|ный anchor; ~ая стоя́нка anchorage. **я́корь** (*pl* -я́) *m* anchor.

я́лик skiff.

я́ма pit, hole.

ямщи́к (-а́) coachman.

янва́рский January. **янва́рь** (-я́) *m* January.

янта́рный amber. **янта́рь** (-я́) *m* amber.

япо́нец (-нца), **япо́нка** Japanese. **Япо́ния** Japan. **япо́нский** Japanese.

ярд yard.

я́ркий (я́рок, ярка́, -о) bright; colourful, striking.

ярлы́к (-а́) label; tag.

я́рмарка fair.

ярмо́ (*pl* -а) yoke.

ярово́й spring.

я́ростный furious, fierce. **я́рость** fury.

я́рус circle; tier; layer.

я́рче *comp of* я́ркий

я́рый fervent; furious; violent.

я́сень *m* ash(-tree).

я́сли (-ей) *pl* manger; crèche, day nursery.

ясне́ть (-е́ет) *impf* become clear, clear. **я́сно** *adv* clearly. **яснови́дение** clairvoyance. **яснови́дец** (-дца), **яснови́дица** clairvoyant. **я́сность** clarity; clearness. **я́сный** (я́сен, ясна́, -о) clear; bright; fine.

я́ства (яств) *pl* victuals.

я́стреб (*pl* -а́) hawk.

я́хта yacht.

яче́йка cell.

ячме́нь¹ (-я́) *m* barley.

ячме́нь² (-я́) *m* stye.

я́щерица lizard.

я́щик box; drawer.

Test yourself with word games

This section contains a number of short exercises that will help you to use the dictionary more effectively. The answers to all the exercises are given at the end of the section.

1 Identifying Russian nouns and adjectives

Here is an extract from a Russian advertisement for a restaurant. See if you can find ten different nouns and eight different adjectives and make two lists. In each case, give the form of the word as it is found in the dictionary, i.e. the nominative singular of nouns and the nominative masculine singular of adjectives.

РУ́ССКИЙ РЕСТОРА́Н

Большо́й вы́бор ру́сских, англи́йских и интернациона́льных блюд

Прия́тная и дру́жеская атмосфе́ра

Высо́кий у́ровень обслу́живания

Конце́рт популя́рной му́зыки в пя́тницу и суббо́ту

2 Checking the gender of Russian nouns

Here are some English nouns that appear in the English–Russian half of the dictionary. Find out what their Russian equivalents are and make three separate lists, masculine nouns, feminine nouns, and neuter nouns.

book	club	door	England
February	grandfather	hobby	ice
journey	kitchen	life	meat
newspaper	opinion	passport	raincoat
square	tree	wine	word

3 Pronouns

What are the English equivalents of these Russian pronouns?

personal pronouns	interrogative pronouns	demonstrative pronouns	possessive pronouns
я	кто	э́тот	мой
он	что	тот	твой
мы	како́й	э́ти	ваш

4 Recognizing Russian verbs

Underline the verb in each of the following sentences

Он рабо́тает на фа́брике.

В про́шлом году́ мы е́здили во Фра́нцию.

Она́ ду́мала об о́тпуске.

Они́ оста́вили свои́ ве́щи у меня́.

Не беспоко́йтесь!

Ско́лько сто́ит биле́т?

Она́ ничего́ не бои́тся.

5 Find the verb

Some words in English can be both nouns and verbs, e.g. race. Find the following words in the English–Russian half of the dictionary and then give the Russian for the verb only; give both the imperfective and perfective infinitives where both exist:

dance	demand	fly	force
hand	hold	hope	interest
jump	love	name	phone
plan	reply	request	respect
shout	smile	trade	wave

6 Which part of speech?

Use your dictionary to help you to arrange these words in separate lists according to their part of speech (noun, adjective, adverb, etc.):

авто́бус	бы́стрый	вы	где
да	е́сли	ждать	здра́вствуй
из	ка́к-нибудь	ле́том	ме́жду
но	она́	принима́ть	роя́ль
сра́зу	Ту́рция	у	францу́зский
хотя́	целова́ть	четы́ре	шути́ть
щётка	электри́ческий	ю́бка	я

7 Plural of nouns

Use the tables at the back of the dictionary to help you find the nominative plural of the following nouns:

авто́бус	англича́нин	ба́бушка	боти́нок
враг	го́лос	гость	день
де́рево	жена́	живо́тное	зда́ние
иде́я	и́мя	кафе́	кни́жный магази́н
лицо́	мужчи́на	неде́ля	одея́ло
плато́к	пра́здник	разгово́р	сестра́
столе́тие	толпа́	трамва́й	у́лица
учёный	фами́лия	цвето́к	я́блоко

8 Translating phrasal verbs

Use the dictionary to find the correct translation for the following English sentences:

She's given up smoking.

We went back home.

He hung the picture up.

They let him in.

He's moved away.

He put a sweater on.

She ran out of money.

We sat down.

They all stood up.

He took off his coat.

She woke up late.

9 Male or female?

Some nouns have both male and female forms in Russian. This is particularly true of words that denote a person's occupation or nationality, e.g.:

учи́тель/учи́тельница = a teacher

Find out the meaning of the following Russian words by looking them up in the Russian–English half of the dictionary. Then look up the English words in the English–Russian half in order to find out the feminine equivalent:

америка́нец	вегетариа́нец	иностра́нец
не́мец	преподава́тель	продаве́ц
перево́дчик	секрета́рь	сосе́д
студе́нт	учени́к	япо́нец

10 Which meaning?

Some words have more than one meaning and it is important to check that you have chosen the right one. We have given you one meaning of the Russian words listed below. Use your dictionary to find another one.

блю́до	• = dish	• =
ви́лка	• = fork	• =
води́ть	• = to take	• =
дере́вня	• = village	• =
заходи́ть	• = to call in	• =
ка́рта	• = map	• =
купа́ться	• = to bathe	• =
ла́мпочка	• = lamp	• =
ме́рить	• = to measure	• =
мо́лния	• = lightning	• =

ничего́	• = it doesn't matter	• =
носи́ть	• = to carry	• =
опа́здывать	• = to be late	• =
пе́ред	• = in front of	• =
ра́ковина	• = sink	• =
слеза́ть	• = to climb down	• =
сто́ить	• = to cost	• =
сыро́й	• = damp	• =
тень	• = shade	• =
я́щик	• = box	• =

11 Russian reflexive verbs

Use your dictionary to find the Russian equivalents of the following English sentences:

The concert begins at seven o'clock.

He quickly got changed.

She returned late.

It's getting colder.

We quarrel a lot.

What happened to him?

We washed and dressed.

The war's coming to an end.

12 Imperfective/perfective

Most Russian verbs have an imperfective and a perfective form. Use the dictionary to find the perfective infinitives of the following verbs:

выбира́ть	выходи́ть	гляде́ть	гото́вить
объясня́ть	писа́ть	плати́ть	покупа́ть
помога́ть	хоте́ть		

13 Indeterminate/determinate

Some Russian verbs have two imperfective forms, indeterminate and determinate. Use the English–Russian half of the dictionary to find out the two imperfective forms of the Russian equivalents of the following verbs:

to carry (*by hand*)

to carry (*by transport*)

to chase

to fly

to go (*on foot*)

to go (*by transport*)

to run

to swim

Answers

1 Nouns:
рестора́н, вы́бор, блю́до, атмосфе́ра, у́ровень, обслу́живание, конце́рт, му́зыка, пя́тница, суббо́та

Adjectives:
ру́сский, большо́й, англи́йский, интернациона́льный, прия́тный, дру́жеский, высо́кий, популя́рный

2 Masculine nouns:
клуб, февра́ль, де́душка, лёд, па́спорт, плащ

Feminine nouns:
кни́га, дверь, А́нглия, ку́хня, жизнь, газе́та, пло́щадь

Neuter nouns:
хо́бби, путеше́ствие, мя́со, мне́ние, де́рево, вино́, сло́во

3

personal pronouns	interrogative pronouns	demonstrative pronouns	possessive pronouns
I	who	this	mine
he	what	that	yours
we	which	these	yours

4 Verbs:
   рабо́тает, е́здили, ду́мала, оста́вили, беспоко́йтесь, сто́ит, бои́тся

5 Russian verbs:
   танцева́ть, тре́бовать/потре́бовать, лета́ть/лете́ть/полете́ть,
   заставля́ть/заста́вить, передава́ть/переда́ть, держа́ть, наде́яться/
   понаде́яться, интересова́ть, пры́гать/пры́гнуть, люби́ть, называ́ть/
   назва́ть, звони́ть/позвони́ть, плани́ровать/заплани́ровать,
   отвеча́ть/отве́тить, проси́ть/попроси́ть, уважа́ть, крича́ть/
   кри́кнуть, улыба́ться/улыбну́ться, торгова́ть, маха́ть/махну́ть

6 Nouns: авто́бус, роя́ль, Ту́рция, щётка, ю́бка
   Adjectives: бы́стрый, францу́зский, электри́ческий
   Verbs: ждать, принима́ть, целова́ть, шути́ть
   Adverbs: где, ка́к-нибудь, ле́том, сра́зу
   Pronouns: вы, она́, я
   Prepositions: из, ме́жду, у
   Conjunctions: е́сли, но, хотя́
   Exclamation: здра́вствуй
   Number: четы́ре
   Particle: да

7 Nominative plural of nouns:
   авто́бусы, англича́не, ба́бушки, боти́нки, враги́, голоса́, го́сти,
   дни, дере́вья, жёны, живо́тные, зда́ния, иде́и, имена́, кафе́,
   кни́жные магази́ны, ли́ца, мужчи́ны, неде́ли, одея́ла, платки́,
   пра́здники, разгово́ры, сёстры, столе́тия, то́лпы, трамва́и, у́лицы,
   учёные, фами́лии, цветы́, я́блоки

8 Она́ бро́сила кури́ть.
   Мы верну́лись домо́й.
   Он пове́сил карти́ну.
   Они́ впусти́ли его́.
   Он уе́хал.
   Он наде́л сви́тер.
   У неё ко́нчились де́ньги.
   Мы се́ли.
   Они́ все вста́ли.
   Он снял пальто́.
   Она́ просну́лась по́здно.

9 Feminine equivalents:
   америка́нка, вегетариа́нка, иностра́нка, не́мка,
   перево́дчица, преподава́тельница, продавщи́ца,
   секрета́рша, сосе́дка, студе́нтка, учени́ца, япо́нка.

10	блю́до	• = dish	• = course
ви́лка	• = fork	• = plug
води́ть	• = to take	• = to drive
дере́вня	• = village	• = the country(side)
заходи́ть	• = to call in	• = to set
ка́рта	• = map	• = (playing) card
купа́ться	• = to bathe	• = to have a bath
ла́мпочка	• = lamp	• = bulb
ме́рить	• = to measure	• = to try on
мо́лния	• = lightning	• = zip(per)
ничего́	• = it doesn't matter	• = all right
носи́ть	• = to carry	• = to wear
опа́здывать	• = to be late	• = to miss
пе́ред	• = in front of	• = before
ра́ковина	• = sink	• = shell
слеза́ть	• = to climb down	• = to climb off
сто́ить	• = to cost	• = to be worth
сыро́й	• = damp	• = raw
тень	• = shade	• = shadow
я́щик	• = box	• = drawer

11 Конце́рт начина́ется в семь часо́в.

Он бы́стро переоде́лся.

Она́ верну́лась по́здно.

Стано́вится холодне́е.

Мы мно́го ссо́римся

Что с ним случи́лось?

Мы умы́лись и оде́лись.

Война́ конча́ется.

12 Perfective infinitives:

вы́брать, вы́йти, погляде́ть, пригото́вить, объясни́ть,
написа́ть, заплати́ть, купи́ть, помо́чь, захоте́ть.

13 носи́ть/нести́

вози́ть/везти́

гоня́ться/гна́ться

лета́ть/лете́ть

ходи́ть/идти́

е́здить/е́хать

бе́гать/бежа́ть

пла́вать/плыть

A

a, an *indef article, not usu translated*; **twice a week** два ра́за в неде́лю.

aback *adv*: **take ~** озада́чивать *impf*, озада́чить *pf*.

abacus *n* счёты *m pl*.

abandon *vt* покида́ть *impf*, поки́нуть *pf*; (*give up*) отка́зываться *impf*, отказа́ться *pf* от+*gen*; **~ o.s. to** предава́ться *impf*, преда́ться *pf* +*dat*. **abandoned** *adj* поки́нутый; (*profligate*) распу́тный.

abase *vt* унижа́ть *impf*, уни́зить *pf*. **abasement** *n* униже́ние.

abate *vi* затиха́ть *impf*, зати́хнуть *pf*.

abattoir *n* скотобо́йня.

abbey *n* абба́тство.

abbreviate *vt* сокраща́ть *impf*, сократи́ть *pf*. **abbreviation** *n* сокраще́ние.

abdicate *vi* отрека́ться *impf*, отре́чься *pf* от престо́ла. **abdication** *n* отрече́ние (от престо́ла).

abdomen *n* брюшна́я по́лость. **abdominal** *adj* брюшно́й.

abduct *vt* похища́ть *impf*, похи́тить *pf*. **abduction** *n* похище́ние.

aberration *n* (*mental*) помутне́ние рассу́дка.

abet *vt* подстрека́ть *impf*, подстрекну́ть *pf* (к соверше́нию преступле́ния *etc.*).

abhor *vt* ненави́деть *impf*. **abhorrence** *n* отвраще́ние. **abhorrent** *adj* отврати́тельный.

abide *vt* (*tolerate*) выноси́ть *impf*, вы́нести *pf*; **~ by** (*rules etc.*) сле́довать *impf*, по~ *pf*.

ability *n* спосо́бность.

abject *adj* (*wretched*) жа́лкий; (*humble*) уни́женный; **~ poverty** кра́йняя нищета́.

ablaze *predic* охва́ченный огнём.

able *adj* спосо́бный, уме́лый; **be ~ to** мочь *impf*, с~ *pf*; (*know how to*) уме́ть *impf*, с~ *pf*.

abnormal *adj* ненорма́льный. **abnormality** *n* ненорма́льность.

aboard *adv* на борт(у́); (*train*) в по́езд(е).

abode *n* жили́ще; **of no fixed ~** без постоя́нного местожи́тельства.

abolish *vt* отменя́ть *impf*, отмени́ть *pf*. **abolition** *n* отме́на.

abominable *adj* отврати́тельный. **abomination** *n* ме́рзость.

aboriginal *adj* коренно́й; *n* абориге́н, коренно́й жи́тель *m*. **aborigine** *n* абориге́н, коренно́й жи́тель *m*.

abort *vi* (*med*) выки́дывать *impf*, вы́кинуть *pf*; *vt* (*terminate*) прекраща́ть *impf*, прекрати́ть *pf*. **abortion** *n* або́рт; **have an ~** де́лать *impf*, с~ *pf* або́рт. **abortive** *adj* безуспе́шный.

abound *vi* быть в изоби́лии; **~ in** изоби́ловать *impf* +*instr*.

about *adv & prep* (*approximately*) о́коло+*gen*; (*concerning*) о+*prep*; насчёт+*gen*; (*up and down*) по+*dat*; (*in the vicinity*) круго́м; **be ~ to** собира́ться *impf*, собра́ться *pf* +*inf*.

above *adv* наверху́; (*higher up*) вы́ше; **from ~** све́рху; сви́ше; *prep* над+*instr*; (*more than*) сви́ше+*gen*. **above-board** *adj* че́стный. **above-mentioned** *adj* вышеупомя́нутый.

abrasion *n* истира́ние; (*wound*) сса́дина. **abrasive** *adj* абрази́вный; (*manner*) колю́чий; *n* абрази́вный материа́л.

abreast *adv* в ряд; **keep ~ of** идти́ в но́гу с+*instr*.

abridge *vt* сокраща́ть *impf*, сократи́ть *pf*. **abridgement** *n* сокраще́ние.

abroad *adv* за грани́цей, за грани́цу; **from ~** из-за грани́цы.

abrupt *adj* (*steep*) круто́й; (*sudden*) внеза́пный; (*curt*) ре́зкий.

abscess *n* абсце́сс.

abscond *vi* скрыва́ться *impf*, скры́ться *pf*.

absence *n* отсу́тствие. **absent** *adj* отсу́тствующий; **be ~** отсу́тствовать *impf; vt:* ~ **o.s.** отлуча́ться *impf,* отлучи́ться *pf.* **absentee** *n* отсу́тствующий *sb.* **absenteeism** *n* прогу́л. **absent-minded** *adj* рассе́янный.

absolute *adj* абсолю́тный; *(complete)* по́лный, соверше́нный.

absolution *n* отпуще́ние грехо́в. **absolve** *vt* проща́ть *impf,* прости́ть *pf.*

absorb *vt* впи́тывать *impf,* впита́ть *pf.* **absorbed** *adj* поглощённый. **absorbent** *adj* вса́сывающий. **absorption** *n* впи́тывание; *(mental)* погружённость.

abstain *vi* возде́рживаться *impf,* воздержа́ться *pf* (from от+gen). **abstemious** *adj* возде́ржанный. **abstention** *n* воздержа́ние; *(person)* воздержа́вшийся *sb.* **abstinence** *n* воздержа́ние.

abstract *adj* абстра́ктный, отвлечённый; *n* рефера́т.

absurd *adj* абсу́рдный. **absurdity** *n* абсу́рд.

abundance *n* оби́лие. **abundant** *adj* оби́льный.

abuse *vt* *(insult)* руга́ть *impf,* вы́~, об~, от~ *pf; (misuse)* злоупотребля́ть *impf,* злоупотреби́ть *pf; n (curses)* руга́нь, руга́тельства *neut pl; (misuse)* злоупотребле́ние. **abusive** *adj* оскорби́тельный, руга́тельный.

abut *vi* примыка́ть *impf* (on к+dat).

abysmal *adj* *(extreme)* безграни́чный; *(bad)* ужа́сный. **abyss** *n* бе́здна.

academic *adj* академи́ческий. **academician** *n* акаде́мик. **academy** *n* акаде́мия.

accede *vi* вступа́ть *impf,* вступи́ть *pf* (to в, на+acc); *(assent)* соглаша́ться *impf,* согласи́ться *pf.*

accelerate *vt & i* ускоря́ть(ся) *impf,* уско́рить(ся) *pf; (motoring)* дава́ть *impf,* дать *pf* газ. **acceleration** *n* ускоре́ние. **accelerator** *n* ускори́тель *m; (pedal)* акселера́тор.

accent *n* акце́нт; *(stress)* ударе́ние; *vt* де́лать *impf,* с~ *pf* ударе́ние на+acc. **accentuate** *vt* акценти́ровать *impf & pf.*

accept *vt* принима́ть *impf,* приня́ть *pf.* **acceptable** *adj* прие́млемый. **acceptance** *n* приня́тие.

access *n* до́ступ. **accessible** *adj* досту́пный. **accession** *n* вступле́ние (на престо́л). **accessories** *n* принадле́жности *f pl.* **accessory** *n (accomplice)* соуча́стник, -ица.

accident *n (chance)* случа́йность; *(mishap)* несча́стный слу́чай; *(crash)* ава́рия; by ~ случа́йно. **accidental** *adj* случа́йный.

acclaim *vt (praise)* восхваля́ть *impf,* восхвали́ть *pf; n* восхвале́ние.

acclimatization *n* акклиматиза́ция. **acclimatize** *vt* акклиматизи́ровать *impf & pf.*

accommodate *vt* помеща́ть *impf,* помести́ть *pf; (hold)* вмеща́ть *impf,* вмести́ть *pf.* **accommodating** *adj* услу́жливый. **accommodation** *n (hotel)* но́мер; *(home)* жильё.

accompaniment *n* сопровожде́ние; *(mus)* аккомпанеме́нт. **accompanist** *n* аккомпаниа́тор. **accompany** *vt* сопровожда́ть *impf,* сопроводи́ть *pf; (escort)* провожа́ть *impf,* проводи́ть *pf; (mus)* аккомпани́ровать *impf* +dat.

accomplice *n* соуча́стник, -ица.

accomplish *vt* соверша́ть *impf,* соверши́ть *pf.* **accomplished** *adj* зако́нченный. **accomplishment** *n* выполне́ние; *(skill)* соверше́нство.

accord *n* согла́сие; of one's own ~ доброво́льно; of its own ~ сам собо́й, сам по себе́. **accordance** *n*: in ~ with в соотве́тствии с+instr, согла́сно+dat. **according** *adv*: ~ to по+dat, ~ to him по его́ слова́м. **accordingly** *adv* соотве́тственно.

accordion *n* аккордео́н.

accost *vt* пристава́ть *impf,* приста́ть *pf* к+dat.

account *n (comm)* счёт; *(report)* отчёт; *(description)* описа́ние; on no ~ ни в ко́ем слу́чае; on ~ в счёт причита́ющейся су́ммы; on ~ of из-за+gen, по причи́не+gen; take into ~ принима́ть *impf,* приня́ть *pf* в расчёт; *vi*: ~ for объясня́ть *impf,* объясни́ть *pf.* **accountable** *adj* отве́тственный.

accountancy *n* бухгалте́рия. **accountant** *n* бухга́лтер.

accrue *vi* нараста́ть *impf,* нарасти́ *pf.*

accumulate *vt & i* нака́пливать(ся)

impf, копи́ть(ся) *impf*, на~ *pf*. **accumulation** *n* накопле́ние. **accumulator** *n* аккумуля́тор.

accuracy *n* то́чность. **accurate** *adj* то́чный.

accusation *n* обвине́ние. **accusative** *adj* (*n*) вини́тельный (паде́ж). **accuse** *vt* обвиня́ть *impf*, обвини́ть *pf* (**of** в+*prep*); **the** ~**d** обвиня́емый *sb*.

accustom *vt* приуча́ть *impf*, приучи́ть *pf* (**to** к+*dat*). **accustomed** *adj* привы́чный; **be, get** ~ привыка́ть *impf*, привы́кнуть *pf* (**to** к+*dat*).

ace *n* туз; (*pilot*) ас.

ache *n* боль; *vi* боле́ть *impf*.

achieve *vt* достига́ть *impf*, дости́чь & дости́гнуть *pf*+*gen*. **achievement** *n* достиже́ние.

acid *n* кислота́; *adj* ки́слый; ~ **rain** кисло́тный дождь. **acidity** *n* кислота́.

acknowledge *vt* признава́ть *impf*, призна́ть *pf*; (~ *receipt of*) подтвержда́ть *impf*, подтверди́ть *pf* получе́ние+*gen*. **acknowledgement** *n* призна́ние; подтвержде́ние.

acne *n* прыщи́ *m pl*.

acorn *n* жёлудь *m*.

acoustic *adj* акусти́ческий. **acoustics** *n pl* акустика.

acquaint *vt* знако́мить *impf*, по~ *pf*. **acquaintance** *n* знако́мство; (*person*) знако́мый *sb*. **acquainted** *adj* знако́мый.

acquiesce *vi* соглаша́ться *impf*, согласи́ться *pf*. **acquiescence** *n* согла́сие.

acquire *vt* приобрета́ть *impf*, приобрести́ *pf*. **acquisition** *n* приобрете́ние. **acquisitive** *adj* стяжа́тельский.

acquit *vt* опра́вдывать *impf*, оправда́ть *pf*; ~ **o.s.** вести́ *impf* себя́. **acquittal** *n* оправда́ние.

acre *n* акр.

acrid *adj* е́дкий.

acrimonious *adj* язви́тельный.

acrobat *n* акроба́т. **acrobatic** *adj* акробати́ческий.

across *adv* & *prep* че́рез+*acc*; (*athwart*) поперёк (+*gen*); (*to, on, other side*) на ту сто́рону (+*gen*), на той стороне́ (+*gen*); (*crosswise*) крест-на́крест.

acrylic *n* акри́л; *adj* акри́ловый.

act *n* (*deed*) акт, посту́пок; (*law*)

акт, зако́н; (*of play*) де́йствие; (*item*) но́мер; *vi* поступа́ть *impf*, поступи́ть *pf*; де́йствовать *impf*, по~ *pf*; *vt* игра́ть *impf*, сыгра́ть *pf*. **acting** *n* игра́; (*profession*) актёрство; *adj* исполня́ющий обя́занности+*gen*. **action** *n* де́йствие, посту́пок; (*law*) иск, проце́сс; (*battle*) бой; ~ **replay** повто́р; **be out of** ~ не рабо́тать *impf*. **activate** *vt* приводи́ть *impf*, привести́ *pf* в де́йствие. **active** *adj* акти́вный; ~ **service** действи́тельная служба; ~ **voice** действи́тельный зало́г. **activity** *n* де́ятельность. **actor** *n* актёр. **actress** *n* актри́са.

actual *adj* действи́тельный. **actuality** *n* действи́тельность. **actually** *adv* на са́мом де́ле, факти́чески.

acumen *n* проница́тельность.

acupuncture *n* иглоука́лывание.

acute *adj* о́стрый.

AD *abbr* н.э. (на́шей э́ры).

adamant *adj* непрекло́нный.

adapt *vt* приспособля́ть *impf*, приспосо́бить *pf*; (*theat*) инсцени́ровать *impf* & *pf*; ~ **o.s.** приспособля́ться *impf*, приспосо́биться *pf*. **adaptable** *adj* приспособля́ющийся. **adaptation** *n* приспособле́ние; (*theat*) инсцениро́вка. **adapter** *n* ада́птер.

add *vt* прибавля́ть *impf*, приба́вить *pf*; (*say*) доба́вить *pf*, добавля́ть *pf*; ~ **together** скла́дывать *impf*, сложи́ть *pf*; ~ **up** сумми́ровать *impf* & *pf*; ~ **up to** составля́ть *impf*, соста́вить *pf*; (*fig*) своди́ться *impf*, свести́сь *pf* к+*dat*. **addenda** *n* приложе́ния *pl*.

adder *n* гадю́ка.

addict *n* наркома́н, ~ка. **addicted** *adj*: **be** ~ **to** быть рабо́м+*gen*; **become** ~ **to** пристрасти́ться *pf* к+*dat*. **addiction** *n* (*passion*) пристра́стие; (*to drugs*) наркома́ния. **addition** *n* прибавле́ние; дополне́ние; (*math*) сложе́ние; **in** ~ вдоба́вок, кро́ме того́. **additional** *adj* доба́вочный. **additive** *n* доба́вка.

address *n* а́дрес; (*speech*) речь; ~ **book** записна́я кни́жка; *vt* адресова́ть *impf* & *pf*; (*speak to*) обраща́ться *impf*, обрати́ться *pf* к+*dat*; ~ **a meeting** выступа́ть *impf*, вы́ступить *pf* на собра́нии. **addressee**

n адреса́т.

adept *adj* све́дущий; *n* ма́стер.

adequate *adj* доста́точный.

adhere *vi* прилипа́ть *impf*, прили́пнуть *pf* (**to** к+*dat*); (*fig*) приде́рживаться *impf* +*gen*. **adherence** *n* приве́рженность. **adherent** *n* приве́рженец. **adhesive** *adj* ли́пкий; *n* кле́йкое вещество́.

ad hoc *adj* специа́льный.

ad infinitum *adv* до бесконе́чности.

adjacent *adj* сме́жный.

adjective *n* (и́мя) прилага́тельное.

adjoin *vt* прилега́ть *impf* к+*dat*.

adjourn *vt* откла́дывать *impf*, отложи́ть *pf*; *vi* объявля́ть *impf*, объяви́ть *pf* переры́в; (*move*) переходи́ть *impf*, перейти́ *pf*.

adjudicate *vi* выноси́ть *impf*, вы́нести *pf* реше́ние (**in** по+*dat*); суди́ть *impf*.

adjust *vt & i* приспособля́ть(ся) *impf*, приспосо́бить(ся) *pf*; *vt* пригоня́ть *impf*, пригна́ть *pf*; (*regulate*) регули́ровать *impf*, от~ *pf*. **adjustable** *adj* регули́руемый. **adjustment** *n* регули́рование, подго́нка.

ad lib *vt & i* импровизи́ровать *impf*, сымпровизи́ровать *pf*.

administer *vt* (*manage*) управля́ть *impf* +*instr*; (*give*) дава́ть *impf*, дать *pf*. **administration** *n* управле́ние; (*government*) прави́тельство. **administrative** *adj* администрати́вный. **administrator** *n* администра́тор.

admirable *adj* похва́льный.

admiral *n* адмира́л.

admiration *n* восхище́ние. **admire** *vt* (*look at*) любова́ться *impf*, по~ *pf* +*instr*, на+*acc*; (*respect*) восхища́ться *impf*, восхити́ться *pf* +*instr*. **admirer** *n* покло́нник.

admissible *adj* допусти́мый. **admission** *n* (*access*) до́ступ; (*entry*) вход; (*confession*) призна́ние. **admit** *vt* (*allow in*) впуска́ть *impf*, впусти́ть *pf*; (*confess*) признава́ть *impf*, призна́ть *pf*. **admittance** *n* до́ступ. **admittedly** *adv* призна́ться.

admixture *n* при́месь.

adolescence *n* о́трочество. **adolescent** *adj* подро́стковый; *n* подро́сток.

adopt *vt* (*child*) усыновля́ть *impf*, усынови́ть *pf*; (*thing*) усва́ивать *impf*, усво́ить *pf*; (*accept*) принима́ть *impf*, приня́ть *pf*. **adoptive** *adj* приёмный. **adoption** *n* усыновле́ние; приня́тие.

adorable *adj* преле́стный. **adoration** *n* обожа́ние. **adore** *vt* обожа́ть *impf*.

adorn *vt* украша́ть *impf*, украси́ть *pf*. **adornment** *n* украше́ние.

adrenalin *n* адренали́н.

adroit *adj* ло́вкий.

adulation *n* преклоне́ние.

adult *adj & n* взро́слый (*sb*).

adulterate *vt* фальсифици́ровать *impf & pf*.

adultery *n* супру́жеская изме́на.

advance *n* (*going forward*) продвиже́ние (вперёд); (*progress*) прогре́сс; (*mil*) наступле́ние; (*of pay etc.*) ава́нс; **in** ~ зара́нее; *pl* (*overtures*) ава́нсы *m pl*; *vi* (*go forward*) продвига́ться *impf*, продви́нуться *pf* вперёд; идти́ *impf* вперёд; (*mil*) наступа́ть *impf*; *vt* продвига́ть *impf*, продви́нуть *pf*; (*put forward*) выдвига́ть *impf*, вы́двинуть *pf* +*acc*. **advanced** *adj* (*modern*) передово́й.

advancement *n* продвиже́ние.

advantage *n* преиму́щество; (*profit*) вы́года, по́льза; **take** ~ **of** по́льзоваться *impf*, вос~ *pf* +*instr*. **advantageous** *adj* вы́годный.

adventure *n* приключе́ние. **adventurer** *n* иска́тель *m* приключе́ний. **adventurous** *adj* предприи́мчивый.

adverb *n* наре́чие.

adversary *n* проти́вник. **adverse** *adj* неблагоприя́тный. **adversity** *n* несча́стье.

advertise *vt* (*publicize*) реклами́ровать *impf & pf*; *vt & i* (~ **for**) дава́ть *impf*, дать *pf* объявле́ние о+*prep*. **advertisement** *n* объявле́ние, рекла́ма.

advice *n* сове́т. **advisable** *adj* жела́тельный. **advise** *vt* сове́товать *impf*, по~ *pf* +*dat & inf*; (*notify*) уведомля́ть *impf*, уве́домить *pf*. **advisedly** *adv* наме́ренно. **adviser** *n* сове́тник. **advisory** *adj* совеща́тельный.

advocate *n* (*supporter*) сторо́нник; *vt* выступа́ть *impf*, вы́ступить *pf* за+*acc*; (*advise*) сове́товать *impf*, по~ *pf*.

aegis *n* эги́да.

aerial n анте́нна; adj возду́шный.

aerobics n аэро́бика.

aerodrome n аэродро́м. **aerodynamics** n аэродина́мика. **aeroplane** n самолёт. **aerosol** n аэрозо́ль m.

aesthetic adj эстети́ческий. **aesthetics** n pl эсте́тика.

afar adv: from ~ издалека́.

affable adj приве́тливый.

affair n (business) де́ло; (love) рома́н.

affect vt влия́ть impf, по~ pf на+acc; (touch) тро́гать impf, тро́нуть pf; (concern) затра́гивать impf, затро́нуть pf; **affectation** n жема́нство.

affected adj жема́нный. **affection** n привя́занность. **affectionate** adj не́жный.

affiliated adj свя́занный (to c+instr).

affinity n (relationship) родство́; (resemblance) схо́дство; (attraction) влече́ние.

affirm vt утвержда́ть impf. **affirmation** n утвержде́ние. **affirmative** adj утверди́тельный.

affix vt прикрепля́ть impf, прикрепи́ть pf.

afflict vt постига́ть impf, пости́чь pf; **be afflicted with** страда́ть impf +instr. **affliction** n боле́знь.

affluence n бога́тство. **affluent** adj бога́тый.

afford vt позволя́ть impf, позво́лить pf себе́; (supply) предоставля́ть impf, предоста́вить pf.

affront n оскорбле́ние; vt оскорбля́ть impf, оскорби́ть pf.

afield adv: far ~ далеко́; farther ~ да́льше.

afloat adv & predic на воде́.

afoot predic: be ~ гото́виться impf.

aforesaid adj вышеупомя́нутый.

afraid predic: be ~ боя́ться impf.

afresh adv сно́ва.

Africa n А́фрика. **African** n африка́нец, -ка́нка; adj африка́нский.

after adv пото́м; prep по́сле+gen; (time) че́рез+acc; (behind) за+acc, instr; ~ all в конце́ концо́в; conj по́сле того́, как.

aftermath n после́дствия neut pl.

afternoon n втора́я полови́на дня; in the ~ днём. **aftershave** n лосьо́н по́сле бритья́. **afterthought** n запозда́лая мысль.

afterwards adv пото́м.

again adv опя́ть; (once more) ещё раз; (anew) сно́ва.

against prep (opposing) про́тив+gen; (touching) к+dat; (hitting) о+acc.

age n во́зраст; (era) век, эпо́ха; vt ста́рить impf, со~ pf; vi старе́ть impf, по~ pf. **aged** adj преста́релый.

agency n аге́нтство. **agenda** n пове́стка дня. **agent** n аге́нт.

aggravate vt ухудша́ть impf, уху́дшить pf; (annoy) раздража́ть impf, раздражи́ть pf.

aggregate adj совоку́пный; n совоку́пность.

aggression n агре́ссия. **aggressive** adj агресси́вный. **aggressor** n агре́ссор.

aggrieved adj оби́женный.

aghast predic в у́жасе (at от+gen).

agile adj прово́рный. **agility** n прово́рство.

agitate vt волнова́ть impf, вз~ pf; vi агити́ровать impf. **agitation** n волне́ние; агита́ция.

agnostic n агно́стик. **agnosticism** n агностици́зм.

ago adv (тому́) наза́д; long ~ давно́.

agonize vi му́читься impf. **agonizing** adj мучи́тельный. **agony** n аго́ния.

agrarian adj агра́рный.

agree vi соглаша́ться impf, согласи́ться pf; (arrange) догова́риваться impf, договори́ться pf. **agreeable** adj (pleasant) прия́тный. **agreement** n согла́сие; (treaty) соглаше́ние; in ~ согла́сен (-сна).

agricultural adj сельскохозя́йственный. **agriculture** n се́льское хозя́йство.

aground predic на мели́; adv: run ~ сади́ться impf, сесть pf на мель.

ahead adv (forward) вперёд; (in front) впереди́; ~ of time досро́чно.

aid vt помога́ть impf, помо́чь pf +dat; n по́мощь; (teaching) посо́бие; in ~ of в по́льзу+gen.

Aids n СПИД.

ailing adj (ill) больно́й.

ailment n неду́г.

aim n цель, наме́рение; take ~ прице́ливаться impf, прице́литься pf (at в+acc); vi це́литься impf, на~ pf (at в+acc); (also fig) ме́тить impf, на~ *pf* (at в+*acc*); *vt* наце́ливать *impf*, наце́лить *pf*; (*also fig*) наводи́ть *impf*, навести́ *pf*. **aimless** *adj* бесце́льный.

air *n* во́здух; (*look*) вид; **by** ~ самолётом; **on the** ~ в эфи́ре; *attrib* возду́шный; *vt* (*ventilate*) прове́тривать *impf*, прове́трить *pf*; (*make known*) выставля́ть *impf*, вы́ставить *pf* напока́з. **air-conditioning** *n* кондициони́рование во́здуха. **aircraft** *n* самолёт. **aircraft-carrier** *n* авиано́сец. **airfield** *n* аэродро́м. **air force** *n* ВВС (вое́нно-возду́шные си́лы) *f pl*. **air hostess** *n* стюарде́сса. **airless** *adj* ду́шный. **airlift** *n* возду́шные перево́зки *f pl*; *vt* перевози́ть *impf*, перевезти́ *pf* по во́здуху. **airline** *n* авиали́ния. **airlock** *n* возду́шная про́бка. **airmail** *n* а́виа(по́чта). **airman** *n* лётчик. **airport** *n* аэропо́рт. **air raid** *n* возду́шный налёт. **airship** *n* дирижа́бль *m*. **airstrip** *n* взлётно-поса́дочная полоса́. **airtight** *adj* гермети́чный. **air traffic controller** *n* диспе́тчер. **airwaves** *n pl* радиово́лны *f pl*.

aisle *n* боково́й неф; (*passage*) прохо́д.

ajar *predic* приоткры́тый.

akin *predic* (*similar*) похо́жий; **be** ~ **to** быть сродни́ к+*dat*.

alabaster *n* алеба́стр.

alacrity *n* быстрота́.

alarm *n* трево́га; *vt* трево́жить *impf*, вс~ *pf*; ~ **clock** буди́льник. **alarming** *adj* трево́жный. **alarmist** *n* паникёр; *adj* паникёрский.

alas *int* увы́!

album *n* альбо́м.

alcohol *n* алкого́ль *m*, спирт; спиртны́е напи́тки *m pl*. **alcoholic** *adj* алкого́льный; *n* алкого́лик, -и́чка.

alcove *n* алько́в.

alert *adj* бди́тельный; *n* трево́га; *vt* предупрежда́ть *impf*, предупреди́ть *pf*.

algebra *n* а́лгебра.

alias *adv* ина́че (называ́емый); *n* кли́чка, вы́мышленное и́мя *neut*.

alibi *n* а́либи *neut indecl*.

alien *n* иностра́нец, -нка; *adj* иностра́нный; ~ **to** чу́ждый +*dat*. **alienate** *vt* отчужда́ть *impf*. **alienation** *n* отчужде́ние.

alight[1] *vi* сходи́ть *impf*, сойти́ *pf*; (*bird*) сади́ться *impf*, сесть *pf*.

alight[2] *predic*: **be** ~ горе́ть *impf*; (*shine*) сия́ть *impf*.

align *vt* выра́внивать *impf*, вы́ровнять *pf*. **alignment** *n* выра́внивание.

alike *predic* похо́ж; *adv* одина́ково.

alimentary *adj*: ~ **canal** пищевари́тельный кана́л.

alimony *n* алиме́нты *m pl*.

alive *predic* жив, в живы́х.

alkali *n* щёлочь. **alkaline** *adj* щелочно́й.

all *adj* весь; *n* всё, *pl* все; *adv* совсе́м, соверше́нно; ~ **along** всё вре́мя; ~ **right** хорошо́, ла́дно; (*not bad*) та́к себе; непло́хо; ~ **the same** всё равно́; **in** ~ всего́; **two** ~ по́ два; **not at** ~ ниско́лько.

allay *vt* успока́ивать *impf*, успоко́ить *pf*.

allegation *n* утвержде́ние. **allege** *vt* утвержда́ть *impf*. **allegedly** *adv* я́кобы.

allegiance *adv* ве́рность.

allegorical *adj* аллегори́ческий. **allegory** *n* аллего́рия.

allergic *adj* аллерги́ческий; **be** ~ **to** име́ть аллерги́ю к+*dat*. **allergy** *n* аллерги́я.

alleviate *vt* облегча́ть *impf*, облегчи́ть *pf*. **alleviation** *n* облегче́ние.

alley *n* переу́лок.

alliance *n* сою́з. **allied** *adj* сою́зный.

alligator *n* аллига́тор.

allocate *vt* (*distribute*) распределя́ть *impf*, распредели́ть *pf*; (*allot*) выделя́ть *impf*, вы́делить *pf*. **allocation** *n* распределе́ние; выделе́ние.

allot *vt* выделя́ть *impf*, вы́делить *pf*; (*distribute*) распределя́ть *impf*, распредели́ть *pf*. **allotment** *n* выделе́ние; (*land*) уча́сток.

allow *vt* разреша́ть *impf*, разреши́ть *pf*; (*let happen; concede*) допуска́ть *impf*, допусти́ть *pf*; ~ **for** учи́тывать *impf*, уче́сть *pf*. **allowance** *n* (*financial*) посо́бие; (*deduction, also fig*) ски́дка; **make** ~(**s**) **for** учи́тывать *impf*, уче́сть *pf*.

alloy *n* сплав.

all-round *adj* разносторо́нний.

allude *vi* ссыла́ться *impf*, сосла́ться *pf* (**to** на+*acc*).

allure *vt* зама́нивать *impf*, замани́ть

pf. **allure(ment)** *n* прима́нка. **alluring** *adj* зама́нчивый.

allusion *n* ссы́лка.

ally *n* сою́зник; *vt* соединя́ть *impf*, соедини́ть *pf*; ~ **oneself with** вступа́ть *impf*, вступи́ть *pf* в сою́з с+*instr*.

almighty *adj* всемогу́щий.

almond *n* (*tree; pl collect*) минда́ль *m*; (*nut*) минда́льный оре́х.

almost *adv* почти́, едва́ не.

alms *n pl* ми́лостыня.

aloft *adv* наве́рх(-у́).

alone *predic* оди́н; (*lonely*) одино́к; *adv* то́лько; **leave** ~ оставля́ть *impf*, оста́вить *pf* в поко́е; **let** ~ не говоря́ уже́ о+*prep*.

along *prep* по+*dat*, (*position*) вдоль +*gen*; *adv* (*onward*) да́льше; **all** ~ всё вре́мя; ~ **with** вме́сте с+*instr*. **alongside** *adv* & *prep* ря́дом (с+*instr*).

aloof *predic* & *adv* (*distant*) сде́ржанный; (*apart*) в стороне́.

aloud *adv* вслух.

alphabet *n* алфави́т. **alphabetical** *adj* алфави́тный.

alpine *adj* альпи́йский.

already *adv* уже́.

also *adv* та́кже, то́же.

altar *n* алта́рь *m*.

alter *vt* (*modify*) переде́лывать *impf*, переде́лать *pf*; *vt* & *i* (*change*) изменя́ть(ся) *impf*, измени́ть(ся) *pf*. **alteration** *n* переде́лка; измене́ние.

alternate *adj* череду́ющийся; *vt* & *i* чередова́ть(ся) *impf*; **alternating current** переме́нный ток; **on** ~ **days** че́рез день. **alternation** *n* чередова́ние. **alternative** *n* альтернати́ва; *adj* альтернати́вный.

although *conj* хотя́.

altitude *n* высота́.

alto *n* альт.

altogether *adv* (*fully*) совсе́м; (*in total*) всего́.

altruistic *adj* альтруисти́ческий.

aluminium *n* алюми́ний.

always *adv* всегда́; (*constantly*) постоя́нно.

Alzheimer's disease *n* боле́знь Альцге́ймера.

a.m. *abbr* (*morning*) утра́; (*night*) но́чи.

amalgamate *vt* & *i* слива́ть(ся) *impf*,

сли́ть(ся) *pf*; (*chem*) амальгами́ровать(ся) *impf* & *pf*. **amalgamation** *n* слия́ние; (*chem*) амальгами́рование.

amass *vt* копи́ть *impf*, на~ *pf*.

amateur *n* люби́тель *m*, ~ница; *adj* люби́тельский. **amateurish** *adj* дилета́нтский.

amaze *vt* изумля́ть *impf*, изуми́ть *pf*. **amazement** *n* изумле́ние. **amazing** *adj* изуми́тельный.

ambassador *n* посо́л.

amber *n* янта́рь *m*.

ambience *n* среда́; атмосфе́ра.

ambiguity *n* двусмы́сленность. **ambiguous** *adj* двусмы́сленный.

ambition *n* (*quality*) честолю́бие; (*aim*) мечта́. **ambitious** *adj* честолюби́вый.

amble *vi* ходи́ть *indet*, идти́ *det* нетороплйвым ша́гом.

ambulance *n* маши́на ско́рой по́мощи.

ambush *n* заса́да; *vt* напада́ть *impf*, напа́сть *pf* из заса́ды на+*acc*.

ameliorate *vt* & *i* улучша́ть(ся) *impf*, улу́чшить(ся) *pf*. **amelioration** *n* улучше́ние.

amen *int* ами́нь!

amenable *adj* сгово́рчивый (**to** +*dat*).

amend *vt* (*correct*) исправля́ть *impf*, испра́вить *pf*; (*change*) вноси́ть *impf*, внести́ *pf* попра́вки в+*acc*. **amendment** *n* попра́вка, исправле́ние. **amends** *n pl*: **make** ~ **for** загла́живать *impf*, загла́дить *pf*.

amenities *n pl* удо́бства *neut pl*.

America *n* Аме́рика. **American** *adj* америка́нский; *n* америка́нец, -нка. **Americanism** *n* американи́зм.

amiable *adj* любе́зный. **amicable** *adj* дружелю́бный.

amid(st) *prep* среди́+*gen*.

amino acid *n* аминокислота́.

amiss *adj* нела́дный; **take** ~ обижа́ться *impf*, оби́деться *pf* на+*acc*.

ammonia *n* аммиа́к; (*liquid* ~) нашаты́рный спирт.

ammunition *n* боеприпа́сы *m pl*.

amnesia *n* амнези́я.

amnesty *n* амни́стия.

among(st) *prep* (*amidst*) среди́+*gen*, (*between*) ме́жду+*instr*.

amoral *adj* амора́льный.

amorous *adj* влюбчивый.

amorphous *adj* бесфо́рменный.

amortization *n* амортиза́ция.

amount *n* коли́чество; *vi:* ~ to составля́ть *impf*, соста́вить *pf*; (*be equivalent to*) быть равноси́льным+*dat*.

ampere *n* ампе́р.

amphetamine *n* амфетами́н.

amphibian *n* амфи́бия. amphibious *adj* земново́дный; (*mil*) пла́вающий.

amphitheatre *n* амфитеа́тр.

ample *adj* доста́точный. amplification *n* усиле́ние. amplifier *n* усили́тель *m*. amplify *vt* усили́вать *impf*, уси́лить *pf*. amply *adv* доста́точно.

amputate *vt* ампути́ровать *impf* & *pf*. amputation *n* ампута́ция.

amuse *vt* забавля́ть *impf*; развлека́ть *impf*, развле́чь *pf*. amusement *n* заба́ва, развлече́ние; *pl* аттракцио́ны *m pl*. amusing *adj* заба́вный; (*funny*) смешно́й.

anachronism *n* анахрони́зм. anachronistic *adj* анахрони́чный.

anaemia *n* анеми́я. anaemic *adj* анеми́чный.

anaesthesia *n* анестези́я. anaesthetic *n* обезбо́ливающее сре́дство. anaesthetist *n* анестезио́лог. anaesthetize *vt* анестези́ровать *impf* & *pf*.

anagram *n* анагра́мма.

analogous *adj* аналоги́чный. analogue *n* ана́лог. analogy *n* анало́гия.

analyse *vt* анализи́ровать *impf* & *pf*. analysis *n* ана́лиз. analyst *n* анали́тик; психоанали́тик. analytical *adj* аналити́ческий.

anarchic *adj* анархи́ческий. anarchist *n* анархи́ст, ~ка; *adj* анархи́стский. anarchy *n* ана́рхия.

anathema *n* ана́фема.

anatomical *adj* анатоми́ческий. anatomy *n* анато́мия.

ancestor *n* пре́док. ancestry *n* происхожде́ние.

anchor *n* я́корь *m*; *vt* ста́вить *impf*, по~ *pf* на я́корь; *vi* станови́ться *impf*, стать *pf* на я́корь. anchorage *n* я́корная стоя́нка.

anchovy *n* анчо́ус.

ancient *adj* дре́вний, стари́нный.

and *conj* и, (*but*) а; с+*instr*; you ~ I

мы с ва́ми; my wife ~ I мы с жено́й.

anecdote *n* анекдо́т.

anew *adv* сно́ва.

angel *n* а́нгел. angelic *adj* а́нгельский.

anger *n* гнев; *vt* серди́ть *impf*, рас~ *pf*.

angina *n* стенокарди́я.

angle[1] *n* у́гол; (*fig*) то́чка зре́ния.

angle[2] *vi* уди́ть *impf* ры́бу. angler *n* рыболо́в.

angry *adj* серди́тый.

anguish *n* страда́ние, му́ка. anguished *adj* отча́янный.

angular *adj* углово́й; (*sharp*) углова́тый.

animal *n* живо́тное *sb*; *adj* живо́тный. animate *adj* живо́й. animated *adj* оживлённый; ~ cartoon мультфи́льм. animation *n* оживле́ние.

animosity *n* вражде́бность.

ankle *n* лоды́жка.

annals *n pl* ле́топись.

annex *vt* аннекси́ровать *impf* & *pf*. annexation *n* анне́ксия. annexe *n* пристро́йка.

annihilate *vt* уничтожа́ть *impf*, уничто́жить *pf*. annihilation *n* уничтоже́ние.

anniversary *n* годовщи́на.

annotate *vt* комменти́ровать *impf* & *pf*. annotated *adj* снабжённый коммента́риями. annotation *n* анноте́ция.

announce *vt* объявля́ть *impf*, объяви́ть *pf*; заявля́ть *impf*, заяви́ть *pf*; (*radio*) сообща́ть *impf*, сообщи́ть *pf*. announcement *n* объявле́ние; сообще́ние. announcer *n* ди́ктор.

annoy *vt* досажда́ть *impf*, досади́ть *pf*; раздража́ть *impf*, раздражи́ть *pf*. annoyance *n* доса́да. annoying *adj* доса́дный.

annual *adj* ежего́дный, (*of a given year*) годово́й; *n* (*book*) ежего́дник; (*bot*) одноле́тник. annually *adv* ежего́дно. annuity *n* (ежего́дная) ре́нта.

annul *vt* аннули́ровать *impf* & *pf*. annulment *n* аннули́рование.

anoint *vt* пома́зывать *impf*, пома́зать *pf*.

anomalous *adj* анома́льный. anomaly *n* анома́лия.

anonymous *adj* анони́мный. ano-

nymity n анонимность.
anorak n куртка.
anorexia n анорексия.
another adj, pron другой; ~ one ещё (один); in ~ ten years ещё через десять лет.
answer n ответ; vt отвечать impf, ответить pf (person) +dat, (question) на+acc; ~ the door отворять impf, отворить pf дверь; ~ the phone подходить impf, подойти pf к телефону. answerable adj ответственный. answering machine n телефон-ответчик.
ant n муравей.
antagonism n антагонизм. antagonistic adj антагонистический. antagonize vt настраивать impf, настроить pf против себя.
Antarctic n Антарктика.
antelope n антилопа.
antenna n усик; (also radio) антенна.
anthem n гимн.
anthology n антология.
anthracite n антрацит.
anthropological adj антропологический. anthropologist n антрополог. anthropology антропология.
anti-aircraft adj зенитный. antibiotic n антибиотик. antibody n антитело. anticlimax n разочарование. anticlockwise adj & adv против часовой стрелки. antidepressant n антидепрессант. antidote n противоядие. antifreeze n антифриз. antipathy n антипатия. anti-Semitic adj антисемитский. anti-Semitism n антисемитизм. antiseptic adj антисептический; n антисептик. antisocial adj асоциальный. anti-tank adj противотанковый. antithesis n противоположность; (philos) антитезис.
anticipate vt ожидать impf +gen; (with pleasure) предвкушать impf, предвкусить pf; (forestall) предупреждать impf, предупредить pf. anticipation n ожидание; предвкушение; предупреждение.
antics n выходки f pl.
antiquarian adj антикварный. antiquated adj устарелый. antique adj старинный; n антикварная вещь; ~ shop антикварный магазин. antiquity n древность.

antler n олений рог.
anus n задний проход.
anvil n наковальня.
anxiety n беспокойство. anxious adj беспокойный; be ~ беспокоиться impf; тревожиться impf.
any adj, pron (some) какой-нибудь; сколько-нибудь; (every) всякий, любой; (anybody) кто-нибудь, (anything) что-нибудь; (with neg) никакой, ни один; нисколько; никто, ничто; adv сколько-нибудь; (with neg) нисколько, ничуть. anybody, anyone pron кто-нибудь; (everybody) всякий, любой; (with neg) никто. anyhow adv как-нибудь; кое-как; (with neg) никак; conj во всяком случае; всё равно. anyone see anybody. anything pron что-нибудь; всё (что угодно); (with neg) ничего. anyway adv во всяком случае; как бы то ни было. anywhere adv где/куда угодно; (with neg, interrog) где-нибудь, куда-нибудь.
apart adv (aside) в стороне, в сторону; (separately) врозь; (distant) друг от друга; (into pieces) на части; ~ from кроме+gen.
apartheid n апартеид.
apartment n (flat) квартира.
apathetic adj апатичный. apathy n апатия.
ape n обезьяна; vt обезьянничать impf, c~ pf c+gen.
aperture n отверстие.
apex n вершина.
aphorism n афоризм.
apiece adv (per person) на каждого; (per thing) за штуку; (amount) по+dat or acc with numbers.
aplomb n апломб.
Apocalypse n Апокалипсис. apocalyptic adj апокалиптический.
apologetic adj извиняющийся; be ~ извиняться impf. apologize vi извиняться impf, извиниться pf (to перед+instr; for за+acc). apology n извинение.
apostle n апостол.
apostrophe n апостроф.
appal vi ужасать impf, ужаснуть pf. appalling adj ужасный.
apparatus аппарат; прибор; (gymnastic) гимнастические снаряды m pl.

apparel *n* одея́ние.

apparent *adj* (*seeing*) ви́димый; (*manifest*) очеви́дный. **apparently** *adv* ка́жется, по-ви́димому.

apparition *n* виде́ние.

appeal *n* (*request*) призы́в, обраще́ние; (*law*) апелля́ция, обжа́лование; (*attraction*) привлека́тельность; ~ **court** апелляцио́нный суд; *vi* (*request*) взыва́ть *impf*, воззва́ть *pf* (**to** к+*dat*; **for** o+*prep*); обраща́ться *impf*, обрати́ться *pf* (с призы́вом); (*law*) апелли́ровать *impf & pf*; ~ **to** (*attract*) привлека́ть *impf*, привле́чь *pf*.

appear *vi* появля́ться *impf*, появи́ться *pf*; (*in public*) выступа́ть *impf*, вы́ступить *pf*; (*seem*) каза́ться *impf*, по~ *pf*. **appearance** *n* появле́ние; выступле́ние; (*aspect*) вид.

appease *vt* умиротворя́ть *impf*, умиротвори́ть *pf*.

append *vt* прилага́ть *impf*, приложи́ть *pf*. **appendicitis** *n* аппендици́т. **appendix** *n* приложе́ние; (*anat*) аппе́ндикс.

appertain *vi*: ~ **to** относи́ться *impf* +*dat*.

appetite *n* аппети́т. **appetizing** *adj* аппети́тный.

applaud *vt* аплоди́ровать *impf* +*dat*. **applause** *n* аплодисме́нты *m pl*.

apple *n* я́блоко; *adj* я́блочный; ~ **tree** я́блоня.

appliance *n* прибо́р. **applicable** *adj* примени́мый. **applicant** *n* кандида́т. **application** *n* (*use*) примене́ние; (*putting on*) наложе́ние; (*request*) заявле́ние. **applied** *adj* прикладно́й. **apply** *vt* (*use*) применя́ть *impf*, примени́ть *pf*; (*put on*) накла́дывать *impf*, наложи́ть *pf*; *vi* (*request*) обраща́ться *impf*, обрати́ться *pf* (**to** к+*dat*; **for** за+*acc*); ~ **for** подава́ть *impf*, пода́ть *pf* заявле́ние на+*acc*; ~ **to** относи́ться *impf* к+*dat*.

appoint *vt* назнача́ть *impf*, назна́чить *pf*. **appointment** *n* назначе́ние; (*job*) до́лжность; (*meeting*) свида́ние.

apposite *adj* уме́стный.

appraise *vt* оце́нивать *impf*, оцени́ть *pf*.

appreciable *adj* заме́тный; (*consid-erable*) значи́тельный. **appreciate** *vt* цени́ть *impf*; (*understand*) понима́ть *impf*, поня́ть *pf*; *vi* повыша́ться *impf*, повы́ситься *pf* в цене́. **appreciation** *n* (*estimation*) оце́нка; (*gratitude*) призна́тельность; (*rise in value*) повыше́ние цены́. **appreciative** *adj* призна́тельный (**of** за+*acc*).

apprehension *n* (*fear*) опасе́ние. **apprehensive** *adj* опаса́ющийся.

apprentice *n* учени́к; *vt* отдава́ть *impf*, отда́ть *pf* в уче́ние. **apprenticeship** *n* учени́чество.

approach *vt & i* подходи́ть *impf*, подойти́ *pf* (к+*dat*); приближа́ться *impf*, прибли́зиться *pf* (к+*dat*); *vt* (*apply to*) обраща́ться *impf*, обрати́ться *pf* к+*dat*; *n* приближе́ние; подхо́д; подъе́зд; (*access*) до́ступ.

approbation *n* одобре́ние.

appropriate *adj* подходя́щий; *vt* присва́ивать *impf*, присво́ить *pf*. **appropriation** *n* присвое́ние.

approval *n* одобре́ние; **on** ~ на про́бу. **approve** *vt* утвержда́ть *impf*, утверди́ть *pf*; *vt & i* (~ **of**) одобря́ть *impf*, одо́брить *pf*.

approximate *adj* приблизи́тельный; *vi* приближа́ться *impf* (**to** к+*dat*). **approximation** *n* приближе́ние.

apricot *n* абрико́с.

April *n* апре́ль *m*; *adj* апре́льский.

apron *n* передни́к.

apropos *adv*: ~ **of** по по́воду+*gen*.

apt *adj* (*suitable*) уда́чный; (*inclined*) скло́нный. **aptitude** *n* спосо́бность.

aqualung *n* аквала́нг. **aquarium** *n* аква́риум. **Aquarius** *n* Водоле́й. **aquatic** *adj* водяно́й; (*of sport*) во́дный. **aqueduct** *n* акведу́к.

aquiline *adj* орли́ный.

Arab *n* ара́б, ~ка; *adj* ара́бский. **Arabian** *adj* арави́йский. **Arabic** *adj* ара́бский.

arable *adj* па́хотный.

arbitrary *adj* произво́льный. **arbitrate** *vi* де́йствовать *impf* в ка́честве трете́йского судьи́. **arbitration** *n* арбитра́ж, трете́йское реше́ние. **arbitrator** *n* арби́тр, трете́йский судья́ *m*.

arc *n* дуга́. **arcade** *n* арка́да, (*shops*) пасса́ж.

arch[1] *n* а́рка, свод; (*of foot*) свод стопы́; *vt & i* выгиба́ть(ся) *impf*, вы́гнуть(ся) *pf*.

arch[2] *adj* игри́вый.

archaeological *adj* археологи́ческий. **archaeologist** *n* архео́лог. **archaeology** *n* археоло́гия.

archaic *adj* архаи́ческий.

archangel *n* арха́нгел.

archbishop *n* архиепи́скоп.

arched *adj* сво́дчатый.

arch-enemy *n* закля́тый враг.

archer *n* стрело́к из лу́ка. **archery** *n* стрельба́ из лу́ка.

archipelago *n* архипела́г.

architect *n* архите́ктор. **architectural** *adj* архитекту́рный. **architecture** *n* архитекту́ра.

archive(s) *n* архи́в.

archway *n* сво́дчатый прохо́д.

Arctic *adj* аркти́ческий; *n* А́рктика.

ardent *adj* горя́чий. **ardour** *n* пыл.

arduous *adj* тру́дный.

area *n* (*extent*) пло́щадь; (*region*) райо́н; (*sphere*) о́бласть.

arena *n* аре́на.

argue *vt* (*maintain*) утвержда́ть *impf*, дока́зывать *impf*; *vi* спо́рить *impf*, по~ *pf*. **argument** *n* (*dispute*) спор; (*reason*) до́вод. **argumentative** *adj* любя́щий спо́рить.

aria *n* а́рия.

arid *adj* сухо́й.

Aries *n* Ове́н.

arise *vi* возника́ть *impf*, возни́кнуть *pf*.

aristocracy *n* аристокра́тия. **aristocrat** *n* аристокра́т, ~ка. **aristocratic** *adj* аристократи́ческий.

arithmetic *n* арифме́тика. **arithmetical** *adj* арифмети́ческий.

ark *n* (Но́ев) ковче́г.

arm[1] *n* (*of body*) рука́; (*of chair*) ру́чка; ~ in ~ под руку; at ~'s length (*fig*) на почти́тельном расстоя́нии; with open ~s с распростёртыми объя́тиями.

arm[2] *n pl* (*weapons*) ору́жие; *pl* (*coat of ~s*) герб; *vt* вооружа́ть *impf*, вооружи́ть *pf*. **armaments** *n pl* вооруже́ние.

armchair *n* кре́сло.

Armenia *n* Арме́ния. **Armenian** *n* армяни́н, армя́нка; *adj* армя́нский.

armistice *n* переми́рие.

armour *n* (*for body*) доспе́хи *m pl*; (*for vehicles*; *fig*) броня́. **armoured**

adj брониро́ванный; (*vehicles etc.*) бронета́нковый, броне-; ~ car броневи́к. **armoury** *n* арсена́л.

armpit *n* подмы́шка.

army *n* а́рмия; *adj* арме́йский.

aroma *n* арома́т. **aromatic** *adj* арома́ти́чный.

around *adv* круго́м; *prep* вокру́г+*gen*; all ~ повсю́ду.

arouse *vt* (*wake up*) буди́ть *impf*, раз~ *pf*; (*stimulate*) возбужда́ть *impf*, возбуди́ть *pf*.

arrange *vt* расставля́ть *impf*, расста́вить *pf*; (*plan*) устра́ивать *impf*, устро́ить *pf*; (*mus*) аранжи́ровать *impf* & *pf*; *vi*: ~ to догова́риваться *impf*, договори́ться *pf* +*inf*. **arrangement** *n* расположе́ние; устро́йство; (*agreement*) соглаше́ние; (*mus*) аранжиро́вка; *pl* приготовле́ния *neut pl*.

array *vt* выставля́ть *impf*, вы́ставить *pf*; *n* (*dress*) наря́д; (*display*) колле́кция.

arrears *n pl* задо́лженность.

arrest *vt* аресто́вывать *impf*, арестова́ть *pf*; *n* аре́ст.

arrival *n* прибы́тие, прие́зд; (*new ~*) вновь прибы́вший *sb*. **arrive** *vi* прибыва́ть *impf*, прибы́ть *pf*; (*by vehicle*) приезжа́ть *impf*, прие́хать *pf*.

arrogance *n* высокоме́рие. **arrogant** *adj* высокоме́рный.

arrow *n* стрела́; (*pointer*) стре́лка.

arsenal *n* арсена́л.

arsenic *n* мышья́к.

arson *n* поджо́г.

art *n* иску́сство; *pl* гуманита́рные нау́ки *f pl*; *adj* худо́жественный.

arterial *adj*: ~ road магистра́ль. **artery** *n* арте́рия.

artful *adj* хи́трый.

arthritis *n* артри́т.

article *n* (*literary*) статья́; (*clause*) пункт; (*thing*) предме́т; (*gram*) арти́кль *m*.

articulate *vt* произноси́ть *impf*, произнести́ *pf*; (*express*) выража́ть *impf*, вы́разить *pf*; *adj* (*of speech*) членоразде́льный; ~ чётко выража́ть *impf* свои́ мы́сли. **articulated lorry** *n* грузово́й автомоби́ль с прице́пом.

artifice *n* хи́трость. **artificial** *adj* иску́сственный.

artillery *n* артилле́рия.

artisan n реме́сленник.

artist n худо́жник. **artiste** n арти́ст, ~ка. **artistic** adj худо́жественный.

artless adj простоду́шный.

as adv как; conj (when) когда́; в то вре́мя как; (because) так как; (manner) как; (though, however) как ни; rel pron како́й; кото́рый; что; as ... as так (же)... как; **as for, to** относи́тельно+gen; **as if** как бу́дто; **as it were** ка́к бы; так сказа́ть; **as soon as** как то́лько; **as well** та́кже; то́же.

asbestos n асбе́ст.

ascend vt (go up) поднима́ться impf, подня́ться pf по+dat; (throne) всходи́ть impf, взойти́ pf на+acc; vi возноси́ться impf, вознести́сь pf. **ascendancy** n власть. **Ascension** n (eccl) Вознесе́ние. **ascent** n восхожде́ние (of на+acc).

ascertain vt устана́вливать impf, установи́ть pf.

ascetic adj аскети́ческий; n аске́т. **asceticism** n аскети́зм.

ascribe vt припи́сывать impf, приписа́ть pf (to +dat).

ash¹ n (tree) я́сень m.

ash², **ashes** n зола́, пе́пел; (human remains) прах. **ashtray** n пе́пельница.

ashamed predic: **he is** ~ ему́ сты́дно; **be, feel,** ~ **of** стыди́ться impf, по~ pf +gen.

ashen adj (pale) мёртвенно-бле́дный.

ashore adv на бе́рег(у́).

Asia n А́зия. **Asian, Asiatic** adj азиа́тский; n азиа́т, ~ка.

aside adv в сто́рону.

ask vt & i (enquire of) спра́шивать impf, спроси́ть pf; (request) проси́ть impf, по~ pf (for acc, gen, o+prep); (invite) приглаша́ть impf, пригласи́ть pf; (demand) тре́бовать impf +gen (of от+gen); ~ **after** осведомля́ться impf, осведомиться pf o+prep; ~ **a question** задава́ть impf, зада́ть pf вопро́с.

askance adv ко́со.

askew adv кри́во.

asleep predic & adv: **be** ~ спать impf; **fall** ~ засыпа́ть impf, засну́ть pf.

asparagus n спа́ржа.

aspect n вид; (side) сторона́.

aspersion n клевета́.

asphalt n асфа́льт.

asphyxiate vt удуша́ть impf, удуши́ть.

aspiration n стремле́ние. **aspire** vi стреми́ться impf (to к+dat).

aspirin n аспири́н; (tablet) табле́тка аспири́на.

ass n осёл.

assail vt напада́ть impf, напа́сть pf на+acc; (with questions) забра́сывать impf, заброса́ть pf вопро́сами. **assailant** n напада́ющий sb.

assassin n уби́йца m & f. **assassinate** vt убива́ть impf, уби́ть pf. **assassination** n уби́йство.

assault n нападе́ние; (mil) штурм; ~ **and battery** оскорбле́ние де́йствием; vt напада́ть impf, напа́сть pf на+acc.

assemblage n сбо́рка. **assemble** vt & i собира́ть(ся) impf, собра́ть(ся) pf. **assembly** n собра́ние; (of machine) сбо́рка.

assent vi соглаша́ться impf, согласи́ться pf (to на+acc); n согла́сие.

assert vt утвержда́ть impf; ~ **o.s.** отста́ивать impf, отстоя́ть pf свои́ права́. **assertion** n утвержде́ние. **assertive** adj насто́йчивый.

assess vt (amount) определя́ть impf, определи́ть pf; (value) оце́нивать impf, оцени́ть pf. **assessment** n определе́ние; оце́нка.

asset n це́нное ка́чество; (comm; also pl) акти́в.

assiduous adj приле́жный.

assign vt (appoint) назнача́ть impf, назна́чить pf; (allot) отводи́ть impf, отвести́ pf. **assignation** n свида́ние. **assignment** n (task) зада́ние; (mission) командиро́вка.

assimilate vt усва́ивать impf, усво́ить pf. **assimilation** n усвое́ние.

assist vt помога́ть impf, помо́чь pf +dat. **assistance** n по́мощь. **assistant** n помо́щник, ассисте́нт.

associate vt ассоции́ровать impf & pf; vi обща́ться impf (with c+instr); n колле́га m & f. **association** n о́бщество, ассоциа́ция.

assorted adj ра́зный. **assortment** n ассортиме́нт.

assuage vt (calm) успока́ивать impf,

успокоить pf; (alleviate) смягчать impf, смягчить pf.

assume vt (take on) принимать impf, принять pf; (suppose) предполагать impf, предположить pf; ~d name вымышленное имя neut; let us ~ допустим. **assumption** n (taking on) принятие на себя; (supposition) предположение.

assurance n заверение; (self-~) самоуверенность; (insurance) страхование. **assure** vt уверять impf, уверить pf.

asterisk n звёздочка.

asthma n астма. **asthmatic** adj астматический.

astonish vt удивлять impf, удивить pf. **astonishing** adj удивительный. **astonishment** n удивление.

astound vt изумлять impf, изумить pf. **astounding** adj изумительный.

astray adv: go ~ сбиваться impf, сбиться pf с пути; lead ~ сбивать impf, сбить pf с пути.

astride prep верхом на+prep.

astringent adj вяжущий; терпкий.

astrologer n астролог. **astrology** n астрология. **astronaut** n астронавт. **astronomer** n астроном. **astronomical** adj астрономический. **astronomy** n астрономия.

astute adj проницательный.

asunder adv (apart) врозь; (in pieces) на части.

asylum n сумасшедший дом; (refuge) убежище.

asymmetrical adj асимметричный. **asymmetry** n асимметрия.

at prep (position) на+prep, в+prep, у+gen: at a concert на концерте; at the cinema в кино; at the window у окна; (time) в+acc: at two o'clock в два часа; at Easter на Пасху; (price) по+dat: at 5p a pound по пяти пенсов за фунт; (speed): at 60 mph со скоростью шестьдесят миль в час; ~ first сначала, сперва; ~ home дома; ~ last наконец; ~ least по крайней мере; ~ that по том; (moreover) к тому же.

atheism n атеизм. **atheist** n атеист, ~ка.

athlete n спортсмен, ~ка. **athletic** adj атлетический. **athletics** n (лёгкая) атлетика.

atlas n атлас.

atmosphere n атмосфера. **atmospheric** adj атмосферный.

atom n атом; ~ bomb атомная бомба. **atomic** adj атомный.

atone vi искупать impf, искупить pf (for +acc). **atonement** n искупление.

atrocious adj ужасный. **atrocity** n зверство.

attach vt (fasten) прикреплять impf, прикрепить pf; (append) прилагать impf, приложить pf; (attribute) придавать impf, придать pf; **attached to** (devoted) привязанный к+dat. **attaché** n атташе m indecl. **attachment** n прикрепление; привязанность; (tech) принадлежность.

attack vt нападать impf, напасть pf на+acc; n нападение; (of illness) припадок.

attain vt достигать impf, достичь & достигнуть pf +gen. **attainment** n достижение.

attempt vt пытаться impf, по- pf +inf; n попытка.

attend vt & i (be present at) присутствовать impf (на+prep); vt (accompany) сопровождать impf, сопроводить pf; (go to regularly) посещать impf, посетить pf; ~ to заниматься impf, заняться pf. **attendance** n (presence) присутствие; (number) посещаемость. **attendant** adj сопровождающий; n дежурный sb; (escort) провожатый sb.

attention n внимание; pay ~ обращать impf, обратить pf внимание (to на+acc); int (mil) смирно! **attentive** adj внимательный; (solicitous) заботливый.

attest vt & i (also ~ to) заверять impf, заверить pf; свидетельствовать impf, за- pf (о+prep).

attic n чердак.

attire vt наряжать impf, нарядить pf; n наряд.

attitude n (posture) поза; (opinion) отношение (towards к+dat).

attorney n поверенный sb; power of ~ доверенность.

attract vt привлекать impf, привлечь pf. **attraction** n привлекательность; (entertainment) аттракцион. **attractive** adj привлекательный.

attribute vt приписывать impf, приписать pf; n (quality) свойство.
attribution n приписывание. **attributive** adj атрибутивный.
attrition n: war of ~ война на истощение.
aubergine n баклажан.
auburn adj тёмно-рыжий.
auction n аукцион; vt продавать impf, продать pf с аукциона. **auctioneer** n аукционист.
audacious adj (bold) смелый; (impudent) дерзкий. **audacity** n смелость; дерзость.
audible adj слышный. **audience** n публика, аудитория; (listeners) слушатели m pl, (viewers, spectators) зрители m pl; (interview) аудиенция. **audit** n проверка счетов, ревизия; vt проверять impf, проверить pf (счета+gen). **audition** n проба; vt устраивать impf, устроить pf пробу +gen. **auditor** n ревизор. **auditorium** n зрительный зал.
augment n увеличивать impf, увеличить pf.
augur vt & i предвещать impf.
August n август; adj августовский.
august adj величественный.
aunt n тётя, тётка.
au pair n домработница иностранного происхождения.
aura n ореол.
auspices n pl покровительство. **auspicious** adj благоприятный.
austere adj строгий. **austerity** n строгость.
Australia n Австралия. **Australian** n австралиец, -ийка; adj австралийский.
Austria n Австрия. **Austrian** n австриец, -ийка; adj австрийский.
authentic adj подлинный. **authenticate** vt устанавливать impf, установить pf подлинность+gen. **authenticity** n подлинность.
author, authoress n автор.
authoritarian adj авторитарный. **authoritative** adj авторитетный. **authority** n (power) власть, полномочие; (weight; expert) авторитет; (source) авторитетный источник.
authorization n уполномочивание; (permission) разрешение. **authorize** vt (action) разрешать impf, раз-

решить pf; (person) уполномочивать impf, уполномочить pf.
authorship n авторство.
autobiographical автобиографический. **autobiography** n автобиография. **autocracy** n автократия. **autocrat** n автократ. **autocratic** adj автократический. **autograph** n автограф. **automatic** adj автоматический. **automation** n автоматизация. **automaton** n автомат. **automobile** n автомобиль m. **autonomous** adj автономный. **autonomy** n автономия. **autopilot** n автопилот. **autopsy** n вскрытие; аутопсия.
autumn n осень. **autumn(al)** adj осенний.
auxiliary adj вспомогательный; n помощник, -ица.
avail n: to no ~ напрасно; vt: ~ o.s. of пользоваться impf, вос~ pf +instr. **available** adj доступный, наличный.
avalanche n лавина.
avant-garde n авангард; adj авангардный.
avarice n жадность. **avaricious** adj жадный.
avenge vt мстить impf, ото~ pf за+acc. **avenger** n мститель m.
avenue n (of trees) аллея; (wide street) проспект; (means) путь m.
average n среднее число, среднее sb; on ~ в среднем; adj средний; vt делать impf в среднем; vt & i: ~ (out at) составлять impf, составить pf в среднем.
averse adj: not ~ to не прочь+inf, не против+gen. **aversion** n отвращение. **avert** vt (ward off) предотвращать impf, предотвратить pf; (turn away) отводить impf, отвести pf.
aviary n птичник.
aviation n авиация.
avid adj жадный; (keen) страстный.
avocado n авокадо neut indecl.
avoid vt избегать impf, избежать pf +gen; (evade) уклоняться impf, уклониться pf от+gen. **avoidance** n избегание, уклонение.
avowal n признание. **avowed** adj признанный.
await vt ждать impf +gen.
awake predic: be ~ не спать impf.

awake(n) vt пробужда́ть impf, пробуди́ть pf; vi просыпа́ться impf, просну́ться pf.

award vt присужда́ть impf, присуди́ть pf (person dat, thing acc); награжда́ть impf, награди́ть pf (person acc, thing instr); n награ́да.

aware predic: be ~ of сознава́ть impf; знать impf. **awareness** n созна́ние.

away adv прочь; be ~ отсу́тствовать impf; far ~ (from) далеко́ (от+gen); 5 miles ~ в пяти́ ми́лях отсю́да; ~ game игра́ на чужо́м по́ле.

awe n благогове́йный страх. **awful** adj ужа́сный. **awfully** adv ужа́сно.

awhile adv не́которое вре́мя.

awkward adj нело́вкий. **awkwardness** n нело́вкость.

awning n наве́с, тент.

awry adv ко́со.

axe n топо́р; vt уре́зывать, уреза́ть impf, уре́зать pf.

axiom n аксио́ма. **axiomatic** adj аксиомати́ческий.

axis, axle n ось.

ay int да!; n (in vote) го́лос „за“.

Azerbaijan n Азербайджа́н. **Azerbaijani** n азербайджа́нец (-нца), -а́нка; adj азербайджа́нский.

azure n лазу́рь; adj лазу́рный.

B

BA abbr (univ) бакала́вр.

babble n (voices) болтовня́; (water) журча́ние; vi болта́ть impf; (water) журча́ть impf.

baboon n павиа́н.

baby n младе́нец; ~-sit присма́тривать за детьми́ в отсу́тствие роди́телей; ~-sitter приходя́щая ня́ня. **babyish** adj ребя́ческий.

bachelor n холостя́к; (univ) бакала́вр.

bacillus n баци́лла.

back n (of body) спина́; (rear) за́дняя часть; (reverse) оборо́т; (of seat) спи́нка; (sport) защи́тник; adj за́дний; vt (support) подде́рживать impf, поддержа́ть pf; (car) отодвига́ть impf, отодви́нуть pf; (horse) ста́вить impf, по~ pf на+acc; (finance) финанси́ровать impf & pf; vi ото-

дви́гаться impf, отодви́нуться pf наза́д; **backed out of the garage** вы́ехал за́дом из гаража́; ~ **down** уступа́ть impf, уступи́ть pf; ~ **out** уклоня́ться impf, уклони́ться pf (of от+gen); ~ **up** (support) подде́рживать impf, поддержа́ть pf; (confirm) подкрепля́ть impf, подкрепи́ть pf. **backbiting** n спле́тни. **backbone** n позвоно́чник; (support) гла́вная опо́ра; (firmness) твёрдость хара́ктера. **backcloth, backdrop** n за́дник; (fig) фон. **backer** n спо́нсор; (supporter) сторо́нник. **backfire** vi дава́ть impf, дать pf отсе́чку. **background** n фон, за́дний план; (person's) происхожде́ние. **backhand(er)** n уда́р сле́ва. **backhanded** adj (fig) сомни́тельный. **backhander** n (bribe) взя́тка. **backing** n подде́ржка. **backlash** n реа́кция. **backlog** n задо́лженность. **backside** n зад. **backstage** adv за кули́сами; adj закули́сный. **backstroke** n пла́вание на спине́. **backup** n подде́ржка; (copy) резе́рвная ко́пия; adj вспомога́тельный. **backward** adj отста́лый. **backward(s)** adv наза́д. **backwater** n за́водь. **back yard** n за́дний двор.

bacon n беко́н.

bacterium n бакте́рия.

bad adj плохо́й; (food etc.) испо́рченный; (language) гру́бый; ~-**mannered** невоспи́танный; ~ **taste** безвку́сица; ~-**tempered** раздражи́тельный.

badge n значо́к.

badger n барсу́к; vt трави́ть impf, за~ pf.

badly adv пло́хо; (very much) о́чень.

badminton n бадминто́н.

baffle vt оза́дачивать impf, озада́чить pf.

bag n (handbag) су́мка; (plastic ~, sack, under eyes) мешо́к; (paper ~) бума́жный паке́т; pl (luggage) бага́ж.

baggage n бага́ж.

baggy adj мешкова́тый.

bagpipe n волы́нка.

bail[1] n (security) поручи́тельство; **release on** ~ отпуска́ть impf, отпусти́ть pf на пору́ки; vt (~ **out**) брать impf, взять pf на пору́ки; (help) выруча́ть *impf*, вы́ручить *pf*.

bail[2], **bale**[2] *vt* вычёрпывать *impf*, вы́черпнуть *pf* (во́ду из+*gen*); ~ **out** *vi* выбра́сываться *impf*, вы́броситься *pf* с парашю́том.

bailiff *n* суде́бный исполни́тель.

bait *n* нажи́вка; прима́нка (*also fig*); *vt* (*torment*) трави́ть *impf*, за~ *pf*.

bake *vt* & *i* печь(ся) *impf*, ис~ *pf*. **baker** *n* пе́карь *m*, бу́лочник. **bakery** *n* пека́рня; (*shop*) бу́лочная *sb*.

balalaika *n* балала́йка.

balance *n* (*scales*) весы́ *m pl*; (*equilibrium*) равнове́сие; (*econ*) бала́нс; (*remainder*) оста́ток; ~ **sheet** бала́нс; *vt* (*make equal*) уравнове́шивать *impf*, уравнове́сить *pf*; *vt* & *i* (*econ; hold steady*) баланси́ровать *impf*, с~ *pf*.

balcony *n* балко́н.

bald *adj* лы́сый; ~ **patch** лы́сина. **balding** *adj* лысе́ющий. **baldness** *n* плеши́вость.

bale[1] *n* (*bundle*) ки́па.

bale[2] *see* **bail**[2]

balk *vi* арта́читься *impf*, за~ *pf*; **she balked at the price** цена́ её испуга́ла.

ball[1] *n* (*in games*) мяч; (*sphere; billiards*) шар; (*wool*) клубо́к; ~**-bearing** шарикоподши́пник; ~**-point (pen)** ша́риковая ру́чка.

ball[2] *n* (*dance*) бал.

ballad *n* балла́да.

ballast *n* балла́ст.

ballerina *n* балери́на.

ballet *n* бале́т. **ballet-dancer** *n* арти́ст, ~ка, бале́та.

balloon *n* возду́шный шар.

ballot *n* голосова́ние. **ballot-paper** *n* избира́тельный бюллете́нь *m*; *vt* держа́ть *impf* голосова́ние между +*instr*.

balm *n* бальза́м. **balmy** *adj* (*soft*) мя́гкий.

Baltic *n* Балти́йское мо́ре; ~ **States** прибалти́йские госуда́рства, Приба́лтика.

balustrade *n* балюстра́да.

bamboo *n* бамбу́к.

bamboozle *vt* надува́ть *impf*, наду́ть *pf*.

ban *n* запре́т; *vt* запреща́ть *impf*, запрети́ть *pf*.

banal *adj* бана́льный. **banality** *n* бана́льность.

banana *n* бана́н.

band *n* (*stripe, strip*) полоса́; (*braid, tape*) тесьма́; (*category*) катего́рия; (*of people*) гру́ппа; (*gang*) ба́нда; (*mus*) орке́стр; (*radio*) диапазо́н; *vi*: ~ **together** объединя́ться *impf*, объедини́ться *pf*.

bandage *n* бинт; *vt* бинтова́ть *impf*, за~ *pf*.

bandit *n* банди́т.

bandstand *n* эстра́да для орке́стра.

bandwagon *n*: **jump on the** ~ по́льзоваться *impf*, вос~ *pf* благоприя́тными обстоя́тельствами.

bandy-legged *adj* кривоно́гий.

bane *n* отра́ва.

bang *n* (*blow*) уда́р; (*noise*) стук; (*of gun*) вы́стрел; *vt* (*strike*) ударя́ть *impf*, уда́рить *pf*; *vi* хло́пать *impf*, хло́пнуть *pf*; (*slam shut*) захло́пываться *impf*, захло́пнуться *pf*; ~ **one's head** ударя́ться *impf*, уда́риться *pf* голово́й; ~ **the door** хло́пать *impf*, хло́пнуть *pf* две́рью.

bangle *n* брасле́т.

banish *vt* изгоня́ть *impf*, изгна́ть *pf*.

banister *n* пери́ла *neut pl*.

banjo *n* ба́нджо *neut indecl*.

bank[1] *n* (*of river*) бе́рег; (*of earth*) вал; *vt* сгреба́ть *impf*, сгрести́ *pf* в ку́чу; *vi* (*aeron*) накреня́ться *impf*, накрени́ться *pf*.

bank[2] *n* (*econ*) банк; ~ **account** счёт в ба́нке; ~ **holiday** устано́вленный пра́здник; *vi* (*keep money*) держа́ть *impf* де́ньги (в ба́нке); *vt* (*put in* ~) класть *impf*, положи́ть *pf* в банк; ~ **on** полага́ться *impf*, положи́ться *pf* на+*acc*. **banker** *n* банки́р. **banknote** *n* банкно́та.

bankrupt *n* банкро́т; *adj* обанкро́тившийся; *vt* доводи́ть *impf*, довести́ *pf* до банкро́тства. **bankruptcy** *n* банкро́тство.

banner *n* зна́мя *neut*.

banquet *n* банке́т, пир.

banter *n* подшу́чивание.

baptism *n* креще́ние. **baptize** *vt* крести́ть *impf*, о~ *pf*.

bar *n* (*beam*) брус; (*of cage*) решётка; (*of chocolate*) пли́тка; (*of soap*) кусо́к; (*barrier*) прегра́да; (*law*) адвокату́ра; (*counter*) сто́йка; (*room*) бар; (*mus*) такт; *vt* (*obstruct*) прегражда́ть *impf*, прегради́ть *pf*;

(*prohibit*) запрещáть *impf*, запретíть *pf*.

barbarian *n* вáрвар. **barbaric, barbarous** *adj* вáрварский.

barbecue *n* (*party*) шашлы́к; *vt* жáрить *impf*, за~ *pf* на вéртеле.

barbed wire *n* колю́чая прóволока.

barber *n* парикмáхер; ~'s **shop** парикмáхерская *sb*.

bar code *n* маркирóвка.

bard *n* бард.

bare *adj* (*naked*) гóлый; (*empty*) пустóй; (*small*) минимáльный; *vt* обнажáть *impf*, обнажи́ть *pf*; ~ **one's teeth** скáлить *impf*, о~ *pf* зу́бы. **barefaced** *adj* нáглый. **barefoot** *adj* босóй. **barely** *adv* едвá.

bargain *n* (*deal*) сдéлка; (*good buy*) вы́годная сдéлка; *vi* торговáться *impf*, с~ *pf*; ~ **for, on** (*expect*) ожидáть *impf* +*gen*.

barge *n* бáржа; *vi*: ~ **into** (*room etc.*) вырывáться *impf*, ворвáться *pf* в+*acc*.

baritone *n* баритóн.

bark[1] *n* (*of dog*) лай; *vi* лáять *impf*.

bark[2] *n* (*of tree*) корá.

barley *n* ячмéнь *m*.

barmaid *n* буфéтчица. **barman** *n* буфéтчик.

barmy *adj* трóнутый.

barn *n* амбáр.

barometer *n* барóметр.

baron *n* барóн. **baroness** *n* баронéсса.

baroque *n* барóкко *neut indecl*; *adj* барóчный.

barrack[1] *n* казáрма.

barrack[2] *vt* освистывать *impf*, освистáть *pf*.

barrage *n* (*in river*) запру́да; (*gunfire*) огневóй вал; (*fig*) град.

barrel *n* бóчка; (*of gun*) ду́ло.

barren *adj* беспло́дный.

barricade *n* баррикáда; *vt* баррикади́ровать *impf*, за~ *pf*.

barrier *n* барьéр.

barring *prep* исключáя.

barrister *n* адвокáт.

barrow *n* телéжка.

barter *n* товарообмéн; *vi* обмéниваться *impf*, обменя́ться *pf* товáрами.

base[1] *adj* ни́зкий; (*metal*) неблагорóдный.

base[2] *n* оснóва; (*also mil*) бáза; *vt* оснóвывать *impf*, основáть *pf*.

baseball *n* бейсбóл. **baseless** *adj* необоснóванный. **basement** *n* подвáл.

bash *vt* трéснуть *pf*; *n*: **have a** ~! попрóбуй(те)!

bashful *adj* застéнчивый.

basic *adj* основнóй. **basically** *adv* в оснóвном.

basin *n* таз; (*geog*) бассéйн.

basis *n* оснóва, бáзис.

bask *vi* грéться *impf*; (*fig*) наслаждáться *impf*, наслади́ться *pf* (**in** +*instr*).

basket *n* корзи́на. **basketball** *n* баскетбóл.

bass *n* бас; *adj* басóвый.

bassoon *n* фагóт.

bastard *n* (*sl*) негодя́й.

baste *vt* (*cul*) поливáть *impf*, поли́ть *pf* жи́ром.

bastion *n* бастиóн.

bat[1] *n* (*zool*) летýчая мышь.

bat[2] *n* (*sport*) битá; *vi* бить *impf*, по~ *pf* по мячý.

bat[3] *vt*: **he didn't** ~ **an eyelid** он и глáзом не моргнýл.

batch *n* пáчка; (*of loaves*) вы́печка.

bated *adj*: **with** ~ **breath** затаи́в дыхáние.

bath *n* (*vessel*) вáнна; *pl* плáвательный бассéйн; **have a bath** принимáть *impf*, приня́ть *pf* вáнну; *vi* купáть *impf*, вы́~, ис~ *pf*. **bathe** *vi* купáться *impf*, вы́~, ис~ *pf*; *vt* омывáть *impf*, омы́ть *pf*. **bather** *n* купáльщик, -ица. **bath-house** *n* бáня. **bathing** *n*: ~ **cap** купáльная шáпочка; ~ **costume** купáльный костю́м. **bathroom** *n* вáнная *sb*.

baton *n* (*staff of office*) жезл; (*sport*) эстафéта; (*mus*) (дирижёрская) пáлочка.

battalion *n* батальóн.

batten *n* рéйка.

batter *n* взби́тое тéсто; *vt* колоти́ть *impf*, по~ *pf*.

battery *n* батарéя.

battle *n* би́тва; (*fig*) борьбá; *vi* борóться *impf*. **battlefield** *n* пóле бóя. **battlement** *n* зубчáтая стенá. **battleship** *n* линéйный корáбль *m*.

bawdy *adj* непристóйный.

bawl *vi* орáть *impf*.

bay¹ *n* (*bot*) лавр; *adj* лавро́вый.

bay² *n* (*geog*) зали́в.

bay³ *n* (*recess*) пролёт; ~ **window** фона́рь *m*.

bay⁴ *vi* (*bark*) ла́ять *impf*; (*howl*) выть *impf*.

bay⁵ *adj* (*colour*) гнедо́й.

bayonet *n* штык.

bazaar *n* база́р.

BC *abbr* до н.э. (до на́шей э́ры).

be¹ *v* 1. быть: *usually omitted in pres*: **he is a teacher** он учи́тель. 2. (*exist*) существова́ть *impf* 3. (*frequentative*) быва́ть *impf*. 4. (~ *situated*) находи́ться *impf*; (*stand*) стоя́ть *impf*; (*lie*) лежа́ть *impf* 5. (*in general definitions*) явля́ться *impf* +*instr*: **Moscow is the capital of Russia** столи́цей Росси́и явля́ется го́род Москва́. 6.: **there is, are** име́ется, име́ются; (*emph*) есть.

be² *v aux* 1. *be*+*inf, expressing duty, plan*: до́лжен+*inf*. 2. *be*+*past participle passive, expressing passive*: быть+*past participle passive in short form*: **it was done** бы́ло сде́лано; *impers construction of 3 pl*+*acc*: **I was beaten** меня́ би́ли; *reflexive construction*: **music was heard** слы́шалась му́зыка. 3. *be*+*pres participle active, expressing continuous tenses*: *imperfective aspect*: **I am reading** я чита́ю.

beach *n* пляж.

beacon *n* мая́к, сигна́льный ого́нь *m*.

bead *n* бу́сина; (*drop*) ка́пля; *pl* бу́сы *f pl*.

beak *n* клюв.

beaker *n* (*child's*) ча́шка с но́сиком; (*chem*) мензу́рка.

beam *n* ба́лка; (*ray*) луч; *vi* (*shine*) сия́ть *impf*.

bean *n* фасо́ль, боб.

bear¹ *n* медве́дь *m*.

bear² *vt* (*carry*) носи́ть *indet*, нести́ *det*, по~ *pf*; (*endure*) терпе́ть *impf*; (*child*) роди́ть *impf & pf*; ~ **out** подтвержда́ть *impf*, подтверди́ть *pf*; ~ **up** держа́ться *impf*. **bearable** *adj* терпи́мый.

beard *n* борода́. **bearded** *adj* борода́тый.

bearer *n* носи́тель *m*; (*of cheque*) предъяви́тель *m*; (*of letter*) пода́тель *m*.

bearing *n* (*deportment*) оса́нка; (*relation*) отноше́ние; (*position*) пе́ленг; (*tech*) подши́пник; **get one's** ~**s** ориенти́роваться *impf & pf*; **lose one's** ~**s** потеря́ть *pf* ориенти́ровку.

beast *n* живо́тное *sb*; (*fig*) скоти́на *m & f*. **beastly** *adj* (*coll*) проти́вный.

beat *n* бой; (*round*) обхо́д; (*mus*) такт; *vt* бить *impf*, по~ *pf*; (*cul*) взбива́ть *impf*, взбить *pf*; *vi* би́ться *impf*, ~ **off** отбива́ть *impf*, отби́ть *pf*; ~ **up** избива́ть *impf*, изби́ть *pf*. **beating** *n* битьё; (*defeat*) пораже́ние; (*of heart*) бие́ние.

beautiful *adj* краси́вый. **beautify** *vt* украша́ть *impf* укра́сить *pf*. **beauty** *n* красота́; (*person*) краса́вица.

beaver *n* бобр.

because *conj* потому́, что; так как; *adv*: ~ **of** из-за+*gen*.

beckon *vt* мани́ть *impf*, по~ *pf* к себе́.

become *vi* станови́ться *impf*, стать *pf* +*instr*; ~ **of** ста́ться *pf* c+*instr*. **becoming** *adj* (*dress*) иду́щий к лицу́ +*dat*.

bed *n* крова́ть, посте́ль; (*garden*) гря́дка; (*sea*) дно; (*river*) ру́сло; (*geol*) пласт; **go to** ~ ложи́ться *impf*, лечь *pf* спать; **make the** ~ стели́ть *impf*, по~ *pf* посте́ль. **bed and breakfast** *n* (*hotel*) ма́ленькая гости́ница. **bedclothes** *n pl*, **bedding** *n* посте́льное бельё. **bedridden** *adj* прико́ванный к посте́ли. **bedroom** *n* спа́льня. **bedside table** *n* ту́мбочка. **bedsitter** *n* однокомна́тная кварти́ра. **bedspread** *n* покрыва́ло. **bedtime** *n* вре́мя *neut* ложи́ться спать.

bedevil *vt* му́чить *impf*, за~ *pf*.

bedlam *n* бедла́м.

bedraggled *adj* растрёпанный.

bee *n* пчела́. **beehive** *n* у́лей.

beech *n* бук.

beef *n* говя́дина. **beefburger** *n* котле́та.

beer *n* пи́во.

beetle *n* жук.

beetroot *n* свёкла.

befall *vt & i* случа́ться *impf*, случи́ться *pf* (+*dat*).

befit *vt* подходи́ть *impf*, подойти́ *pf* +*dat*.

before *adv* ра́ньше; *prep* пе́ред+*instr*;

до+*gen*; *conj* до того́ как; пре́жде чем; (*rather than*) скоре́е чем; **the day ~ yesterday** позавчера́. **beforehand** *adv* зара́нее.
befriend *vt* дружи́ть *impf*, по~ *pf* с+*instr*.
beg *vt* (*ask*) о́чень проси́ть *impf*, по~ *pf* (*person*+*acc*; *thing*+*acc or gen*); *vi* ни́щенствовать *impf*; (*of dog*) служи́ть *impf*; ~ **for** проси́ть *impf*, по~ *pf* +*acc or gen*; ~ **pardon** проси́ть *impf* проще́ния.
beggar *n* ни́щий *sb*.
begin *vt* (& *i*) начина́ть(ся) *impf*, нача́ть(ся) *pf*. **beginner** *n* начина́ющий *sb*. **beginning** *n* нача́ло.
begrudge *vt* (*give reluctantly*) жале́ть *impf*, со~ *pf* о+*prep*.
beguile *vt* (*charm*) очаро́вывать *impf*, очарова́ть *pf*; (*seduce, delude*) обольща́ть *impf*, обольсти́ть *pf*.
behalf *n*: **on ~ of** от и́мени+*gen*; (*in interest of*) в по́льзу+*gen*.
behave *vi* вести́ *impf* себя́. **behaviour** *n* поведе́ние.
behest *n* заве́т.
behind *adv*, *prep* сза́ди (+*gen*), позади́ (+*gen*), за (+*acc*, *instr*); *n* зад; **be, fall, ~** отстава́ть *impf*, отста́ть *pf*.
behold *vt* смотре́ть *impf*, по~ *pf*. **beholden** *predic*: ~ **to** обя́зан+*dat*.
beige *adj* бе́жевый.
being *n* (*existence*) бытие́; (*creature*) существо́.
Belarus *n* Белару́сь.
belated *adj* запозда́лый.
belch *vi* рыга́ть *impf*, рыгну́ть *pf*; *vt* изверга́ть *impf*, изве́ргнуть *pf*.
beleaguer *vt* осажда́ть *impf*, осади́ть *pf*.
belfry *n* колоко́льня.
Belgian *n* бельги́ец, -ги́йка; *adj* бельги́йский. **Belgium** *n* Бе́льгия.
belie *vt* противоре́чить *impf*+*dat*.
belief *n* (*faith*) ве́ра; (*confidence*) убежде́ние. **believable** *adj* правдоподо́бный. **believe** *vt* ве́рить *impf*, по~ *pf* +*dat*; ~ **in** ве́рить *impf* в+*acc*. **believer** *n* ве́рующий *sb*.
belittle *vt* умаля́ть *impf*, умали́ть *pf*.
bell *n* ко́локол; (*doorbell*) звоно́к; ~ **tower** колоко́льня.
bellicose *adj* вои́нственный. **belligerence** *n* вои́нственность. **belligerent** *adj* вою́ющий; (*aggressive*)

вои́нственный.
bellow *vt* & *i* реве́ть *impf*.
bellows *n pl* мехи́ *m pl*.
belly *n* живо́т.
belong *vi* принадлежа́ть *impf* (**to** (к)+*dat*). **belongings** *n pl* пожи́тки (-ков) *pl*.
Belorussian *n* белору́с, -ка; *adj* белору́сский.
beloved *adj* & *sb* возлю́бленный.
below *adv* (*position*) вниз, (*place*) внизу́, ни́же; *prep* ни́же+*gen*.
belt *n* (*strap*) по́яс, (*also tech*) реме́нь; (*zone*) зо́на, полоса́.
bench *n* скаме́йка; (*for work*) стано́к.
bend *n* изги́б; *vt* (& *i*, *also* ~ **down**) сгиба́ть(ся) *impf*, согну́ть(ся) *pf*; ~ **over** склоня́ться *impf*, склони́ться *pf* над+*instr*.
beneath *prep* под+*instr*.
benediction *n* благослове́ние.
benefactor *n* благоде́тель *m*. **benefactress** *n* благоде́тельница
beneficial *adj* поле́зный. **beneficiary** *n* получа́тель *m*; (*law*) насле́дник.
benefit *n* по́льза; (*allowance*) посо́бие; (*theat*) бенефи́с; *vt* приноси́ть *impf*, принести́ *pf* по́льзу +*dat*; *vi* извлека́ть *impf*, извле́чь *pf* вы́году.
benevolence *n* благожела́тельность. **benevolent** *adj* благожела́тельный.
benign *adj* до́брый, мя́гкий; (*tumour*) доброка́чественный.
bent *n* скло́нность.
bequeath *vt* завеща́ть *impf* & *pf* (**to**+*dat*). **bequest** *n* посме́ртный дар.
berate *vt* руга́ть *impf*, вы́~ *pf*.
bereave *vt* лиша́ть *impf*, лиши́ть *pf* (**of** +*gen*). **bereavement** *n* тяжёлая утра́та.
berry *n* я́года.
berserk *adj*: **go ~** взбеси́ться *pf*.
berth *n* (*bunk*) ко́йка; (*naut*) стоя́нка; *vi* прича́ливать *impf*, прича́лить *pf*.
beseech *vt* умоля́ть *impf*, умоли́ть *pf*.
beset *vt* осажда́ть *impf*, осади́ть *pf*.
beside *prep* о́коло+*gen*, ря́дом с+*instr*; ~ **the point** некста́ти; ~ **o.s.** вне себя́. **besides** *adv* кро́ме того́; *prep* кро́ме+*gen*.

besiege vt осажда́ть impf, осади́ть pf.

besotted adj одурма́ненный.

bespoke adj сде́ланный на зака́з.

best adj лу́чший, са́мый лу́чший; adv лу́чше всего́, бо́льше всего́; all the ~! всего́ наилу́чшего! at ~ в лу́чшем слу́чае; do one's ~ де́лать impf, c~ pf всё возмо́жное; ~ man ша́фер.

bestial adj зве́рский. **bestiality** n зве́рство.

bestow vt дарова́ть impf & pf.

bestseller n бестсе́ллер.

bet n пари́ neut indecl; (stake) ста́вка; vi держа́ть impf пари́ (on на+acc); vt (stake) ста́вить impf, по~ pf; he bet me £5 он поспо́рил со мной 5 фу́нтов.

betray vt изменя́ть impf, измени́ть pf+dat. **betrayal** n изме́на.

better adj лу́чший; adv лу́чше; (more) бо́льше; vt улучша́ть impf, улу́чшить pf; all the ~ тем лу́чше; ~ off бо́лее состоя́тельный; ~ o.s. выдвига́ться impf, вы́двинуться pf; get ~ (health) поправля́ться impf, попра́виться pf; get the ~ of брать impf, взять pf верх над+instr; had ~: you had ~ go вам (dat) лу́чше бы пойти́; think ~ of переду́мывать impf, переду́мать pf. **betterment** n улучше́ние.

between prep ме́жду+instr.

bevel vt ска́шивать impf, скоси́ть pf.

beverage n напи́ток.

bevy n ста́йка.

beware vi остерега́ться impf, остере́чься pf (of +gen).

bewilder vt сбива́ть impf, сбить pf с то́лку. **bewildered** adj озада́ченный. **bewilderment** n замеша́тельство.

bewitch vt заколдо́вывать impf, заколдова́ть pf; (fig) очаро́вывать impf, очарова́ть pf. **bewitching** adj очарова́тельный.

beyond prep за+acc & instr; по ту сто́рону+gen; (above) сверх+gen; (outside) вне+gen; the back of ~ край све́та.

bias n (inclination) укло́н; (prejudice) предубежде́ние. **biased** adj предубеждённый.

bib n нагру́дник.

Bible n Би́блия. **biblical** adj библе́йский.

bibliographical n библиографи́ческий. **bibliography** n библиогра́фия.

bicarbonate (of soda) n питьева́я со́да.

biceps n би́цепс.

bicker vi перека́ться impf.

bicycle n велосипе́д.

bid n предложе́ние цены́; (attempt) попы́тка; vt & i предлага́ть impf, предложи́ть pf (це́ну) (for за+acc); vt (command) прика́зывать impf, приказа́ть pf+dat. **bidding** n предложе́ние цены́; (command) приказа́ние.

bide vt: ~ one's time ожида́ть impf благоприя́тного слу́чая.

biennial adj двухле́тний; n двухле́тник.

bier n катафа́лк.

bifocals n pl бифока́льные очки́ pl.

big adj большо́й; (also important) кру́пный.

bigamist n (man) двоеже́нец; (woman) двуму́жница. **bigamy** n двубра́чие.

bigwig n ши́шка.

bike n велосипе́д. **biker** n мотоцикли́ст.

bikini n бики́ни neut indecl.

bilateral adj двусторо́нний.

bilberry n черни́ка (no pl; usu collect).

bile n жёлчь. **bilious** adj жёлчный.

bilingual adj двуязы́чный.

bill[1] n счёт; (parl) законопрое́кт; (~ of exchange) ве́ксель; (poster) афи́ша; vt (announce) объявля́ть impf, объяви́ть pf в афи́шах; (charge) присыла́ть impf, присла́ть pf счёт +dat.

bill[2] n (beak) клюв.

billet vt расквартиро́вывать impf, расквартирова́ть pf.

billiards n билья́рд.

billion n биллио́н.

billow n вал; vi вздыма́ться impf.

bin n му́сорное ведро́; (corn) за́кром.

bind vt (tie) свя́зывать impf, связа́ть pf; (oblige) обя́зывать impf, обяза́ть pf; (book) переплета́ть impf, переплести́ pf. **binder** n (person) переплётчик; *(agric)* вязáльщик; *(for papers)* пáпка. **binding** *n* переплёт.

binge *n* кутёж.

binoculars *n pl* бинóкль *m*.

biochemistry *n* биохúмия. **biographer** *n* биóграф. **biographical** *adj* биографúческий. **biography** *n* биогрáфия. **biological** *adj* биологúческий. **biologist** *n* биóлог. **biology** *n* биолóгия.

bipartisan *adj* двухпартúйный.

birch *n* берёза; *(rod)* рóзга.

bird *n* птúца; ~ **of prey** хúщная птúца.

birth *n* рождéние; *(descent)* происхождéние; ~ **certificate** метрúка; ~ **control** противозачáточные мéры *f pl*. **birthday** *n* день *m* рождéния; **fourth** ~ четырёхлéтие. **birthplace** *n* мéсто рождéния. **birthright** *n* прáво по рождéнию.

biscuit *n* печéнье.

bisect *vt* разрезáть *impf*, разрéзать *pf* пополáм.

bisexual *adj* бисексуáльный.

bishop *n* епúскоп; *(chess)* слон.

bit[1] *n (piece)* кусóчек; **a** ~ немнóго; **not a** ~ ничýть.

bit[2] *n (tech)* сверлó; *(bridle)* удилá (-л) *pl*.

bitch *n (coll)* стéрва. **bitchy** *adj* стервóзный.

bite *n* укýс; *(snack)* закýска; *(fishing)* клёв; *vt* кусáть *impf*, укусúть *pf*; *vi (fish)* клевáть *impf*, клюнуть *pf*. **biting** *adj* éдкий.

bitter *adj* гóрький. **bitterness** *n* гóречь.

bitumen *n* битýм.

bivouac *n* бивáк.

bizarre *adj* стрáнный.

black *adj* чёрный; ~ **eye** подбúтый глаз; ~ **market** чёрный рынок, *v*: ~ **out** *(vt)* затемнять *impf*, затемнúть *pf*; *(vi)* терять *impf*, по~ *pf* сознáние; *n (colour)* чёрный цвет; *(~ person)* негр, ~итянка; *(mourning)* трáур. **blackberry** *n* ежевúка *(no pl; usu collect)*. **blackbird** *n* чёрный дрозд. **blackboard** *n* доскá. **blackcurrant** *n* чёрная сморóдина *(no pl; usu collect)*. **blacken** *vt (fig)* чернúть *impf*, о~ *pf*. **blackleg** *n* штрейкбрéхер. **blacklist** *n* вносúть

impf, внестú *pf* в чёрный спúсок. **blackmail** *n* шантáж; *vt* шантажúровать *impf*. **blackout** *n* затемнéние; *(faint)* потéря сознáния. **blacksmith** *n* кузнéц.

bladder *n* пузýрь *m*.

blade *n (knife)* лéзвие; *(oar)* лóпасть; *(grass)* былúнка.

blame *n* винá, порицáние; *vt* винúть *impf (for* в+*prep)*; **be to** ~ быть виновáтым. **blameless** *adj* безупрéчный.

blanch *vt (vegetables)* ошпáривать *impf*, ошпáрить *pf*; *vi* бледнéть *impf*, по~ *pf*.

bland *adj* мягкий; *(dull)* прéсный.

blandishments *n pl* лесть.

blank *adj (look)* отсýтствующий; *(paper)* чúстый; *n (space)* прóпуск; *(form)* бланк; *(cartridge)* холостóй патрóн; ~ **cheque** незапóлненный чек.

blanket *n* одеяло.

blare *vi* трубúть *impf*, про~ *pf*.

blasé *adj* пресýщенный.

blasphemous *adj* богохýльный. **blasphemy** *n* богохýльство.

blast *n (wind)* порыв вéтра; *(explosion)* взрыв; *vt* взрывáть *impf*, взорвáть *pf*; ~ **off** стартовáть *impf* & *pf*. **blast-furnace** *n* дóмна.

blatant *adj* явный.

blaze *n (flame)* плáмя *neut*; *(fire)* пожáр; *vi* пылáть *impf*.

blazer *n* лёгкий пиджáк.

bleach *n* хлóрка, отбéливатель *m*; *vt* отбéливать *impf*, отбелúть *pf*.

bleak *adj* пустынный; *(dreary)* унылый.

bleary-eyed *adj* с затумáненными глазáми.

bleat *vi* блéять *impf*.

bleed *vi* кровоточúть *impf*.

bleeper *n* персонáльный сигнализáтор.

blemish *n* пятнó.

blend *n* смесь; *vt* смéшивать *impf*, смешáть *pf*; *vi* гармонúровать *impf*. **blender** *n* мúксер.

bless *vt* благословлять *impf*, благословúть *pf*. **blessed** *adj* благословéнный. **blessing** *n (action)* благословéние; *(object)* блáго.

blight *vt* губúть *impf*, по~ *pf*.

blind *adj* слепóй; ~ **alley** тупúк; *n*

што́ра; vt ослепля́ть impf, ослепи́ть pf. **blindfold** vt завя́зывать impf, завяза́ть pf глаза́+dat. **blindness** n слепота́.

blink vi мига́ть impf, мигну́ть pf. **blinkers** n pl шо́ры (-р) pl.

bliss n блаже́нство. **blissful** adj блаже́нный.

blister n пузы́рь m, волды́рь m.

blithe adj весёлый; (carefree) беспе́чный.

blitz n бомбёжка.

blizzard n мете́ль.

bloated adj взду́тый.

blob n (liquid) ка́пля; (colour) кля́кса. **bloc** n блок.

block n (wood) чурба́н; (stone) глы́ба; (flats) жило́й дом; vt прегражда́ть impf, прегради́ть pf; ~ up забива́ть impf, заби́ть pf. **blockade** n блока́да; vt блоки́ровать impf & pf. **blockage** n зато́р.

bloke n па́рень m.

blond n блонди́н, ~ка; adj белоку́рый.

blood n кровь; ~ **donor** до́нор; ~ **poisoning** n зараже́ние кро́ви; ~ **pressure** кровяно́е давле́ние; ~ **relation** бли́зкий ро́дственник, -ая ро́дственница; ~ **transfusion** перелива́ние кро́ви. **bloodhound** n ище́йка. **bloodshed** n кровопроли́тие. **bloodshot** adj нали́тый кро́вью. **bloodthirsty** adj кровожа́дный. **bloody** adj крова́вый.

bloom n расцве́т; vi цвести́ pf.

blossom n цвет; **in** ~ в цвету́.

blot n кля́кса; пятно́; vt (dry) промока́ть impf, промокну́ть pf; (smudge) па́чкать impf, за~ pf.

blotch n пятно́.

blotting-paper n промока́тельная бума́га.

blouse n ко́фточка, блу́зка.

blow¹ n уда́р.

blow² vt & i дуть impf; ~ **away** сноси́ть impf, снести́ pf; ~ **down** вали́ть impf, по~ pf; ~ **one's nose** сморка́ться impf, сморкну́ться pf; ~ **out** задува́ть impf, заду́ть pf; ~ **over** (fig) проходи́ть impf, пройти́ pf; ~ **up** взрыва́ть impf, взорва́ть pf; (inflate) надува́ть impf, наду́ть pf. **blow-lamp** n пая́льная ла́мпа.

blubber¹ n во́рвань.

blubber² vi реве́ть impf.

bludgeon n дуби́нка; vt (compel) вынужда́ть impf, вы́нудить pf.

blue adj (dark) си́ний; (light) голубо́й; n си́ний, голубо́й, цвет. **bluebell** n колоко́льчик. **bluebottle** n си́няя му́ха. **blueprint** n си́нька, светокопия; (fig) прое́кт.

bluff n блеф; vi блефова́ть impf.

blunder n опло́шность; vi оплоша́ть pf.

blunt adj тупо́й; (person) прямо́й; vt тупи́ть impf, за~, ис~ pf.

blur vt затума́нивать impf, затума́нить pf. **blurred** adj расплы́вчатый.

blurt vt: ~ **out** выба́лтывать impf, вы́болтать pf.

blush vi красне́ть impf, по~ pf.

bluster vi бушева́ть impf; n пусты́е слова́ neut pl.

boar n бо́ров; (wild) каба́н.

board n доска́; (committee) правле́ние, сове́т; **on** ~ на борт(у́) pf; vt сади́ться impf, сесть pf (на кора́бль, в по́езд и т.д.); ~ **up** забива́ть impf, заби́ть pf. **boarder** n пансионе́р. **boarding-house** n пансио́н. **boarding-school** n интерна́т.

boast vi хва́статься impf, по~ pf; vt горди́ться impf +instr. **boaster** n хвасту́н. **boastful** adj хвастли́вый.

boat n (small) ло́дка; (large) кора́бль m.

bob vi подпры́гивать impf, подпры́гнуть pf.

bobbin n кату́шка.

bobsleigh n бо́бслей.

bode vt: ~**well/ill** предвеща́ть impf хоро́шее/недо́брое.

bodice n лиф, корса́ж.

bodily adv целико́м; adj теле́сный.

body n те́ло, ту́ловище; (corpse) труп; (group) о́рган; (main part) основна́я часть. **bodyguard** n телохрани́тель m. **bodywork** n ку́зов.

bog n боло́та; **get** ~**ged down** увяза́ть impf, увя́знуть pf. **boggy** adj боло́тистый.

bogus adj подде́льный.

boil¹ n (med) фуру́нкул.

boil² vi кипе́ть impf, вс~ pf; vt кипяти́ть impf, с~ pf; (cook) вари́ть *impf*, c~ *pf*; ~ **down** to сходи́ться *impf*, сойти́сь *pf* к тому́, что; ~**over** выкипа́ть *impf*, вы́кипеть *pf*; *n* кипе́ние; **bring to the** ~ доводи́ть *impf*, довести́ *pf* до кипе́ния. **boiled** *adj* варёный. **boiler** *n* котёл; ~ **suit** комбинезо́н. **boiling** *adj* кипя́щий; ~ **point** то́чка кипе́ния; ~ **water** кипято́к.

boisterous *adj* шумли́вый.

bold *adj* сме́лый; (*type*) жи́рный.

bollard *n* (*in road*) столб; (*on quay*) пал.

bolster *n* ва́лик; *vt*: ~ **up** подпира́ть *impf*, подпере́ть *pf*.

bolt *n* засо́в; (*tech*) болт; *vt* запира́ть *impf*, запере́ть *pf* на засо́в; скрепля́ть *impf*, скрепи́ть *pf* болта́ми; *vi* (*flee*) удира́ть *impf*, удра́ть *pf*; (*horse*) понести́ *pf*.

bomb *n* бо́мба; *vt* бомби́ть *impf*. **bombard** *vt* бомбарди́ровать *impf*. **bombardment** *n* бомбарди́ровка. **bomber** *n* бомбардиро́вщик.

bombastic *adj* напы́щенный.

bond *n* (*econ*) облига́ция; (*link*) связь; *pl* око́вы (-в) *pl*, (*fig*) у́зы (уз) *pl*.

bone *n* кость.

bonfire *n* костёр.

bonnet *n* ка́пор; (*car*) капо́т.

bonus *n* пре́мия.

bony *adj* кости́стый.

boo *vt* освисты́вать *impf*, освиста́ть *pf*; *vi* улюлю́кать *impf*.

booby trap *n* лову́шка.

book *n* кни́га; *vt* (*order*) зака́зывать *impf*, заказа́ть *pf*; (*reserve*) брони́ровать *impf*, за~ *pf*. **bookbinder** *n* переплётчик. **bookcase** *n* кни́жный шкаф. **booking** *n* зака́з; ~ **office** ка́сса. **bookkeeper** *n* бухга́лтер. **bookmaker** *n* букме́кер. **bookshop** *n* кни́жный магази́н.

boom[1] *n* (*barrier*) бон.

boom[2] *n* (*sound*) гул; (*econ*) бум; *vi* гуде́ть *impf*; (*fig*) процвета́ть *impf*.

boon *n* бла́го.

boor *n* хам. **boorish** *adj* ха́мский.

boost *n* соде́йствие; *vt* увели́чивать *impf*, увели́чить *pf*.

boot *n* боти́нок; (*high*) сапо́г; (*football*) бу́тса; (*car*) бага́жник.

booth *n* кио́ск, бу́дка; (*polling*) каби́на.

booty *n* добы́ча.

booze *n* вы́пивка; *vi* выпива́ть *impf*.

border *n* (*frontier*) грани́ца; (*trim*) кайма́; (*gardening*) бордю́р; *vi* грани́чить *impf* (**on** c+*instr*). **borderline** *n* грани́ца.

bore[1] *n* (*calibre*) кана́л (ствола́); *vt* сверли́ть *impf*, про~ *pf*.

bore[2] *n* (*thing*) ску́ка; (*person*) ску́чный челове́к; *vt* надоеда́ть *impf*, надое́сть *pf*. **boredom** *n* ску́ка. **boring** *adj* ску́чный.

born *adj* прирождённый; **be** ~ роди́ться *impf* & *pf*.

borough *n* райо́н.

borrow *vt* одолжа́ть *impf*, одолжи́ть *pf* (**from** y+*gen*).

Bosnia *n* Бо́сния. **Bosnian** *n* босни́ец, -и́йка; *adj* босни́йский.

bosom *n* грудь.

boss *n* нача́льник; *v* кома́ндовать *impf*, c~ *pf* +*instr*. **bossy** *adj* команди́рский.

botanical *adj* ботани́ческий. **botanist** *n* бота́ник. **botany** *n* бота́ника.

botch *vt* зала́тывать *impf*, залата́ть *pf*.

both *adj* & *pron* о́ба *m* & *neut*, о́бе *f*; ~ ... **and** и... и.

bother *n* доса́да; *vt* беспоко́ить *impf*.

bottle *n* буты́лка; ~**neck** суже́ние; *vt* разлива́ть *impf*, разли́ть *pf* по буты́лкам; ~ **up** сде́рживать *impf*, сдержа́ть *pf*.

bottom *n* ни́жняя часть; (*of river etc.*) дно; (*buttocks*) зад; **at the** ~ **of** (*stairs*) внизу́+gen; **get to the** ~ **of** добира́ться *impf*, добра́ться *pf* до су́ти +gen; *adj* са́мый ни́жний. **bottomless** *adj* бездо́нный.

bough *n* сук.

boulder *n* валу́н.

bounce *vi* подпры́гивать *impf*, подпры́гнуть *pf*; (*cheque*) верну́ться *pf*.

bound[1] *n* (*limit*) преде́л; *vt* ограни́чивать *impf*, ограни́чить *pf*.

bound[2] *n* (*spring*) прыжо́к; *vi* пры́гать *impf*, пры́гнуть *pf*.

bound[3] *adj*: **he is** ~ **to be there** он обяза́тельно там бу́дет.

bound[4] *adj*: **to be** ~ **for** направля́ться *impf*, напра́виться *pf* в+*acc*.

boundary *n* грани́ца.

boundless *adj* безграни́чный.

bountiful *adj* (*generous*) ще́дрый;

(*ample*) оби́льный. **bounty** *n* щед-
рость; (*reward*) пре́мия.

bouquet *n* буке́т.

bourgeois *adj* буржуа́зный. **bourgeoisie** *n* буржуази́я.

bout *n* (*med*) при́ступ; (*sport*) схва́т-
ка.

bow[1] *n* (*weapon*) лук; (*knot*) бант;
(*mus*) смычо́к.

bow[2] *n* (*obeisance*) покло́н; *vi* кла́-
няться *impf*, поклони́ться *pf*; *vt*
склоня́ть *impf*, склони́ть *pf*.

bow[3] *n* (*naut*) нос.

bowel *n* кишка́; (*depths*) не́дра (-р)
pl.

bowl[1] *n* ми́ска.

bowl[2] *n* (*ball*) шар; *vi* подава́ть *impf*,
пода́ть *pf* мяч. **bowler** *n* подаю́щий
sb мяч; (*hat*) котело́к. **bowling-al-
ley** *n* кегельба́н. **bowls** *n* игра́ в
шары́.

box[1] *n* коро́бка, я́щик; (*theat*) ло́жа;
~ **office** ка́сса.

box[2] *vi* бокси́ровать *impf*. **boxer** *n*
боксёр. **boxing** *n* бокс. **Boxing Day**
n второ́й день Рождества́.

boy *n* ма́льчик. **boyfriend** *n* моло-
до́й челове́к. **boyhood** *n* о́тро-
чество. **boyish** *adj* мальчи́шеский.

boycott *n* бойко́т; *vt* бойкоти́ровать
impf & pf.

bra *n* ли́фчик.

brace *n* (*clamp*) скре́па; *pl* подтя́жки
f pl; (*dental*) ши́на; *vt* скрепля́ть
impf, скрепи́ть *pf*; ~ **o.s.** соби-
ра́ться *impf*, собра́ться *pf* с си́лами.

bracelet *n* брасле́т.

bracing *adj* бодря́щий.

bracket *n* (*support*) кронште́йн; *pl*
ско́бки *f pl*; (*category*) катего́рия.

brag *vi* хва́статься *impf*, по~ *pf*.

braid *n* тесьма́.

braille *n* шрифт Бра́йля.

brain *n* мозг. **brainstorm** *n* припа́док
безу́мия. **brainwash** *vt* промыва́ть
impf, промы́ть *pf* мозги́+*dat*. **brain-
wave** *n* блестя́щая иде́я.

braise *vt* туши́ть *impf*, с~ *pf*.

brake *n* то́рмоз; *vt* тормози́ть *impf*,
за~ *pf*.

bramble *n* ежеви́ка.

bran *n* о́труби (-бе́й) *pl*.

branch *n* ве́тка; (*fig*) о́трасль;
(*comm*) филиа́л; *vi* разветвля́ться
impf, разветви́ться *pf*; ~ **out** (*fig*)

расширя́ть *impf*, расши́рить *pf*
де́ятельность.

brand *n* (*mark*) клеймо́; (*make*) ма́р-
ка; (*sort*) сорт; *vt* клейми́ть *impf*,
за~ *pf*.

brandish *vt* разма́хивать *impf*+*instr*.

brandy *n* конья́к.

brash *adj* наха́льный.

brass *n* лату́нь, жёлтая медь; (*mus*)
ме́дные инструме́нты *m pl*; *adj*
лату́нный, ме́дный; ~ **band** ме́дный
духово́й орке́стр; **top** ~ вы́сшее на-
ча́льство.

brassière *n* бюстга́льтер.

brat *n* чертёнок.

bravado *n* брава́да.

brave *adj* хра́брый; *vt* покоря́ть
impf, покори́ть *pf*. **bravery** *n* хра́б-
рость.

bravo *int* бра́во.

brawl *n* сканда́л; *vi* дра́ться *impf*,
по~ *pf*.

brawny *adj* му́скулистый.

bray *n* крик осла́; *vi* крича́ть *impf*.

brazen *adj* бессты́дный.

brazier *n* жаро́вня.

breach *n* наруше́ние; (*break*) про-
ло́м; (*mil*) брешь; *vt* прорыва́ть
impf, прорва́ть *pf*; (*rule*) наруша́ть
impf, нару́шить *pf*.

bread *n* хлеб; (*white*) бу́лка. **bread-
crumb** *n* кро́шка. **breadwinner** *n*
корми́лец.

breadth *n* ширина́; (*fig*) широта́.

break *n* проло́м, разры́в; (*pause*)
переры́в, па́уза; *vt* (& *i*) лома́ть(ся)
impf, с~ *pf*; разбива́ть(ся) *impf*,
разби́ть(ся) *pf*; *vt* (*violate*) на-
руша́ть *impf*, нару́шить *pf*; ~ **away**
вырыва́ться *impf*, вы́рваться *pf*; ~
down (*vi*) (*tech*) лома́ться *impf*, с~
pf; (*talks*) срыва́ться *impf*, со-
рва́ться *pf*; (*vt*) (*door*) выла́мывать
impf, вы́ломать *pf*; ~ **in(to)** вла́-
мываться *impf*, вломи́ться *pf* в+*acc*;
~ **off** (*vt & i*) отла́мывать(ся) *impf*,
отломи́ть(ся) *pf*; (*vi*) (*speaking*) за-
молча́ть *pf*; (*vt*) (*relations*) порыва́ть
impf, порва́ть *pf*; ~ **out** вырыва́-
ться *impf*, вы́рваться *pf*; (*fire*,
war) вспы́хнуть *pf*; ~ **through** проби-
ва́ться *impf*, проби́ться *pf*; ~ **up**
(*vi*) (*marriage*) распада́ться *impf*,
распа́сться *pf*; (*meeting*) прерыва́-
ться *impf*, прерва́ться *pf*; (*vt*)

(*disperse*) разгоня́ть *impf*, разо-
гна́ть *pf*; (*vt & i*) разбива́ть(ся)
impf, разби́ть(ся) *pf*; ~ **with** поры-
ва́ть *impf*, порва́ть *pf* c+*instr.* **break-
age** *n* поло́мка. **breakdown** *n* по-
ло́мка; (*med*) не́рвный срыв. **breaker** *n* буру́н. **breakfast** *n* за́втрак; *vi*
за́втракать *impf*, по~ *pf*. **breakneck**
adj: **at ~ speed** сломя́ го́лову. **breakthrough** *n* проры́в. **break-
water** *n* волноре́з.

breast *n* грудь; ~**feeding** *n* кор-
мле́ние гру́дью; ~ **stroke** *n* брасс.
breath *n* дыха́ние; **be out of ~**
запыха́ться *impf & pf*. **breathe** *vi*
дыша́ть *impf*; ~ **in** вдыха́ть *impf*,
вдохну́ть *pf*; ~ **out** выдыха́ть *impf*,
вы́дохнуть *pf*. **breather** *n* переды́ш-
ка. **breathless** *adj* запыха́вшийся.

breeches *n pl* бри́джи (-жей) *pl*.
breed *n* поро́да; *vi* размножа́ться
impf, размно́житься *pf*; *vt* разво-
ди́ть *impf*, развести́ *pf*. **breeder** *n*
n -во́д: **cattle ~** скотово́д. **breeding**
n разведе́ние, -во́дство; (*upbringing*) воспи́танность.

breeze *n* ветеро́к; (*naut*) бриз.
breezy *adj* све́жий.

brevity *n* кра́ткость.

brew *vt* (*beer*) вари́ть *impf*, с~ *pf*;
(*tea*) зава́ривать *impf*, завари́ть *pf*;
(*beer*) ва́рка; (*tea*) зава́рка. **brewer**
n пивова́р. **brewery** *n* пивова́рен-
ный заво́д.

bribe *n* взя́тка; *vt* подкупа́ть *impf*,
подкупи́ть *pf*. **bribery** *n* по́дкуп.

brick *n* кирпи́ч; *adj* кирпи́чный.
bricklayer *n* ка́меньщик.

bridal *adj* сва́дебный. **bride** *n* не-
ве́ста. **bridegroom** *n* жени́х. **brides-
maid** *n* подру́жка неве́сты.

bridge[1] *n* мост; (*of nose*) пере-
но́сица; *vt* (*gap*) заполня́ть *impf*,
запо́лнить *pf*; (*overcome*) преодо-
лева́ть *impf*, преодоле́ть *pf*.

bridge[2] *n* (*game*) бридж.

bridle *n* узда́; *vi* возмуща́ться *impf*,
возмути́ться *pf*.

brief *adj* недо́лгий; (*concise*) кра́т-
кий; *n* инстру́кция; *vt* инструкти́-
ровать *impf & pf*. **briefcase** *n*
портфе́ль *m*. **briefing** *n* инструк-
та́ж. **briefly** *adv* кра́тко. **briefs** *n pl*
трусы́ (-со́в) *pl*.

brigade *n* брига́да. **brigadier** *n*

генера́л-майо́р.

bright *adj* я́ркий. **brighten** (*also* ~
up) *vi* проясня́ться *impf*, проясни́ться *pf*; *vt* оживля́ть *impf*, ожи-
ви́ть *pf*. **brightness** *n* я́ркость.

brilliant *adj* блестя́щий.

brim *n* край; (*hat*) поля́ (-ле́й) *pl*.

brine *n* рассо́л.

bring *vt* (*carry*) приноси́ть *impf*,
принести́ *pf*; (*lead*) приводи́ть *impf*,
привести́ *pf*; (*transport*) привози́ть
impf, привезти́ *pf*; ~ **back**
возвраща́ть *impf*, возврати́ть *pf*; ~
down сва́ливать *impf*, свали́ть *pf*;
~ **round** (*unconscious person*) при-
води́ть *impf*, привести́ *pf* в себя́;
(*deliver*) привози́ть *impf*, привезти́
pf; ~ **up** (*educate*) воспи́тывать
impf, воспита́ть *pf*; (*question*) под-
нима́ть *impf*, подня́ть *pf*.

brink *n* край.

brisk *adj* (*lively*) оживлённый; (*air
etc.*) све́жий; (*quick*) бы́стрый.

bristle *n* щети́на; *vi* щети́ниться
impf, о~ *pf*.

Britain *n* Великобрита́ния, А́нглия.
British *adj* брита́нский, англи́й-
ский; ~ **Isles** Брита́нские острова́
m pl. **Briton** *n* брита́нец, -нка;
англича́нин, -а́нка.

brittle *adj* хру́пкий.

broach *vt* затра́гивать *impf*, за-
тро́нуть *pf*.

broad *adj* широ́кий; **in ~ daylight**
средь бе́ла дня; **in ~ outline** в
о́бщих черта́х. **broad-minded** *adj* с
широ́кими взгля́дами. **broadly** *adv*:
~ **speaking** вообще́ говоря́.

broadcast *n* переда́ча; *vt* передава́ть
impf, переда́ть *pf* по ра́дио, по
телеви́дению; (*seed*) се́ять *impf*,
по~ *pf* вразбро́с. **broadcaster** *n*
ди́ктор. **broadcasting** *n* радио-,
теле-, веща́ние.

brocade *n* парча́.

broccoli *n* бро́кколи *neut indecl*.

brochure *n* брошю́ра.

broke *predic* без гроша́. **broken** *adj*
сло́манный; ~**hearted** с разби́тым
се́рдцем.

broker *n* комиссионе́р.

bronchitis *n* бронхи́т.

bronze *n* бро́нза; *adj* бро́нзовый.

brooch *n* брошь, бро́шка.

brood *n* вы́водок; *vi* мра́чно размышля́ть *impf*.

brook[1] *n* ручёй.

brook[2] *vt* терпе́ть *impf*.

broom *n* метла́. **broomstick** *n* (*witches'*) помело́.

broth *n* бульо́н.

brothel *n* публи́чный дом.

brother *n* брат; ~-**in-law** (*sister's husband*) зять; (*husband's brother*) де́верь *m*; (*wife's brother*) шу́рин; (*wife's sister's husband*) своя́к. **brotherhood** *n* бра́тство. **brotherly** *adj* бра́тский.

brow *n* (*eyebrow*) бровь; (*forehead*) лоб; (*of hill*) гре́бень *m*. **browbeaten** *adj* запу́ганный.

brown *adj* кори́чневый; (*eyes*) ка́рий; *n* кори́чневый цвет; *vt* (*cul*) подрумя́нивать *impf*, подрумя́нить *pf*.

browse *vi* (*look around*) осма́триваться *impf*, осмотре́ться *pf*; (*in book*) просма́тривать *impf* просмотре́ть *pf* кни́гу.

bruise *n* синя́к; *vt* ушиба́ть *impf*, ушиби́ть *pf*.

brunette *n* брюне́тка.

brunt *n* основна́я тя́жесть.

brush *n* щётка; (*paint*) кисть; *vt* (*clean*) чи́стить *impf*, вы́~, по~ *pf* (щёткой); (*touch*) легко́ каса́ться *impf*, косну́ться *pf* +*gen*; (*hair*) расчёсывать *impf*, расчеса́ть *pf* щёткой; ~ **aside, off** отма́хиваться *impf*, отмахну́ться *pf* от+*gen*; ~ **up** смета́ть *impf*, смести́ *pf*; (*renew*) чи́щать *impf*, подчи́стить *pf*.

brushwood *n* хво́рост.

Brussels sprouts *n pl* брюссе́льская капу́ста.

brutal *adj* жесто́кий. **brutality** *n* жесто́кость. **brutalize** *vt* ожесточа́ть *impf*, ожесточи́ть *pf*. **brute** *n* живо́тное *sb*; (*person*) скоти́на. **brutish** *adj* ха́мский.

B.Sc. *abbr* бакала́вр нау́к.

bubble *n* пузы́рь *m*; *vi* пузы́риться *impf*; кипе́ть *impf*, вс~ *pf*.

buck *n* саме́ц оле́ня, кро́лика *etc.*; *vi* брыка́ться *impf*.

bucket *n* ведро́.

buckle *n* пря́жка; *vt* застёгивать *impf*, застегну́ть *pf* (пря́жкой); *vi* (*warp*) коро́биться *impf*, по~, с~ *pf*.

bud *n* по́чка.

Buddhism *n* будди́зм. **Buddhist** *n* будди́ст; *adj* будди́йский.

budge *vt* & *i* шевели́ть(ся) *impf*, по~ *pf*.

budget *n* бюдже́т; *vi:* ~ **for** предусма́тривать *impf*, предусмотре́ть *pf* в бюдже́те.

buff *adj* светло-кори́чневый.

buffalo *n* бу́йвол.

buffet[1] *n* буфе́т.

buffet[2] *vt* броса́ть *impf* (*impers*).

buffoon *n* шут.

bug *n* (*insect*) бука́шка; (*germ*) инфе́кция; (*in computer*) оши́бка в програ́мме; (*microphone*) потайно́й микрофо́н; *vt* (*install* ~) устана́вливать *impf*, установи́ть *pf* аппарату́ру для подслу́шивания в+*prep*; (*listen*) подслу́шивать *impf*.

bugle *n* горн.

build *n* (*of person*) телосложе́ние; *vt* стро́ить *impf*, по~ *pf*; ~ **on** пристра́ивать *impf*, пристро́ить *pf* (**to** к+*dat*); ~ **up** (*vt*) создава́ть *impf*, созда́ть *pf*; (*vi*) накопля́ться *impf*, накопи́ться *pf*. **builder** *n* строи́тель *m*. **building** *n* (*edifice*) зда́ние; (*action*) строи́тельство; ~ **site** стро́йка; ~ **society** жили́щно-строи́тельный кооперати́в.

built-up area *n* застро́енный райо́н.

bulb *n* (*of plant*) лу́ковица; (*electric*) ла́мпочка. **bulbous** *adj* лу́ковичный.

Bulgaria *n* Болга́рия. **Bulgarian** *n* болга́рин, -га́рка; *adj* болга́рский.

bulge *n* вы́пуклость; *vi* выпя́чиваться *impf*, вы́пятиться *impf*. **bulging** *adj* разбу́хший, оттопы́ривающийся.

bulk *n* (*size*) объём; (*greater part*) бо́льшая часть; **in** ~ гурто́м. **bulky** *adj* громо́здкий.

bull *n* бык; (*male*) саме́ц. **bulldog** *n* бульдо́г. **bulldoze** *vt* расчища́ть *impf*, расчи́стить *pf* бульдо́зером. **bulldozer** *n* бульдо́зер. **bullfinch** *n* снеги́рь *m*. **bullock** *n* вол. **bull's-eye** *n* я́блоко.

bullet *n* пу́ля. **bullet-proof** *adj* пулесто́йкий.

bulletin *n* бюллете́нь *m*.

bullion *n:* **gold** ~ зо́лото в сли́тках.

bully *n* задира *m* & *f*; *vt* запу́гивать *impf*, запуга́ть *pf*.

bum n зад.

bumble-bee n шмель m.

bump n (blow) уда́р, толчо́к; (swelling) ши́шка; (in road) уха́б; vi ударя́ться impf, уда́риться pf; ~ **into** ната́лкиваться impf, натолкну́ться pf на+acc. **bumper** n ба́мпер.

bumpkin n дереве́нщина m & f.

bumptious adj самоуве́ренный.

bumpy adj уха́бистый.

bun n сдо́бная бу́лка; (hair) пучо́к.

bunch n (of flowers) буке́т; (grapes) гроздь; (keys) свя́зка.

bundle n у́зел; vt свя́зывать impf, связа́ть pf в у́зел; ~ **off** спрова́живать impf, спрова́дить pf.

bungalow n бу́нгало neut indecl.

bungle vt по́ртить impf, ис~ pf.

bunk n ко́йка.

bunker n бу́нкер.

buoy n буй. **buoyancy** n плаву́честь; (fig) бо́дрость. **buoyant** adj плаву́чий; (fig) бо́дрый.

burden n бре́мя neut; vt обременя́ть impf, обремени́ть pf.

bureau n бюро́ neut indecl. **bureaucracy** n бюрокра́тия. **bureaucrat** n бюрокра́т. **bureaucratic** adj бюрократи́ческий.

burger n котле́та.

burglar n взло́мщик. **burglary** n кра́жа со взло́мом. **burgle** vt гра́бить impf, о~ pf.

burial n погребе́ние.

burlesque n бурле́ск.

burly adj здорове́нный.

burn n жечь impf, с~ pf; vt & i (injure) обжига́ть(ся) impf, обже́чь(ся) pf; vi горе́ть impf, с~ pf; (by sun) загора́ть impf, загоре́ть pf; n ожо́г. **burner** n горе́лка.

burnish vt полирова́ть impf, от~ pf.

burp vi рыга́ть impf, рыгну́ть pf.

burrow n нора́; vi рыть impf, вы~ pf нору́; (fig) ры́ться impf.

bursar n казначе́й. **bursary** n стипе́ндия.

burst n разры́в, вспы́шка; vi разрыва́ться impf, разорва́ться pf; (bubble) ло́паться impf, ло́пнуть pf; vt разрыва́ть impf, разорва́ть pf; ~ **into tears** распла́каться pf.

bury vt (dead) хорони́ть impf, по~ pf; (hide) зарыва́ть impf, зары́ть pf.

bus n авто́бус.

bush n куст. **bushy** adj густо́й.

busily adv энерги́чно.

business n (affair, dealings) де́ло; (firm) предприя́тие; **mind your own** ~ не ва́ше де́ло; **on** ~ по де́лу. **businesslike** adj делово́й. **businessman** n бизнесме́н.

busker n у́личный музыка́нт.

bust n бюст; (bosom) грудь.

bustle n суета́; vi суети́ться impf.

busy adj за́нятой; vt: ~ **o.s.** занима́ться impf, заня́ться pf (with +instr). **busybody** n назо́йливый челове́к.

but conj но, а; ~ **then** зато́; prep кро́ме+gen.

butcher n мясни́к; vt ре́зать impf, за~ pf; ~'s **shop** мясна́я sb.

butler n дворе́цкий sb.

butt[1] n (cask) бо́чка.

butt[2] n (of gun) прикла́д; (cigarette) оку́рок.

butt[3] n (target) мише́нь.

butt[4] vt бода́ть impf, за~ pf; ~ **in** вме́шиваться impf, вмеша́ться pf.

butter n (сли́вочное) ма́сло; vt нама́зывать impf, нама́зать pf ма́слом; ~ **up** льсти́ть impf, по~ pf. **buttercup** n лю́тик. **butterfly** n ба́бочка.

buttock n я́годица.

button n пу́говица; (knob) кно́пка; vt застёгивать impf, застегну́ть pf. **buttonhole** n пе́тля.

buttress n контрфо́рс; vt подпира́ть impf, подпере́ть pf.

buxom adj полногру́дая.

buy n поку́пка; vt покупа́ть impf, купи́ть pf. **buyer** n покупа́тель m.

buzz n жужжа́ние; vi жужжа́ть impf. **buzzard** n каню́к.

buzzer n зу́ммер.

by adv ми́мо; prep (near) о́коло+gen, y+gen; (beside) ря́дом c+instr; (past) ми́мо+gen; (time) к+dat; (means) instr without prep; ~ **and large** в це́лом.

bye int пока́!

by-election n дополни́тельные вы́боры m pl.

Byelorussian see **Belorussian**

bygone adj мину́вший; let ~s be ~s что прошло́, то прошло́. **by-law** n постановле́ние. **bypass** n обхо́д; vt обходи́ть impf, обойти́ pf. **by-product** n побо́чный проду́кт. **byroad** n

небольша́я доро́га. **bystander** n свиде́тель m. **byway** n просёлочная доро́га. **byword** n олицетворе́ние (for+gen).
Byzantineadj византи́йский.

C

cab n (taxi) такси́ neut indecl; (of lorry) каби́на.
cabaretn кабаре́ neut indecl.
cabbagen капу́ста.
cabin n (hut) хи́жина; (aeron) каби́на; (naut) каю́та.
cabinet n шкаф; (Cabinet) кабине́т; ~**maker**краснодере́вец; ~**minister** мини́стр-член кабине́та.
cable n (rope) кана́т; (electric) ка́бель m; (cablegram) телегра́мма; vt & i телеграфи́ровать impf & pf.
cachen потайно́й склад.
cackle vi гогота́ть impf.
cactus n ка́ктус.
caddyn (box) ча́йница.
cadetn новобра́нец.
cadge vt стреля́ть impf, стрельну́ть pf.
cadres n pl ка́дры m pl.
Caesarean (section) n ке́сарево-сече́ние.
cafe n кафе́ neut indecl. **cafeteria** n кафете́рий.
caffeinen кофеи́н.
cagen кле́тка.
cajole vt заба́бривать impf, задо́брить pf.
cake n (large) торт, (small) пиро́жное sb; (fruit~) кекс; vt: ~d обле́пленный (in+instr).
calamitousadj бе́дственный. **calamity**n бе́дствие.
calciumn ка́льций.
calculate vt вычисля́ть impf, вы́числить pf; vi рассчи́тывать impf, рассчита́ть pf (onна+acc). **calculation** n вычисле́ние, расчёт. **calculator**n калькуля́тор.
calendarn календа́рь m.
calf[1] n (cow) телёнок.
calf[2] n (leg) икра́.
calibrate vt калиброва́ть impf. **calibre**n кали́бр.
call v звать impf, по~ pf; (name) называ́ть impf, назва́ть pf; (cry)

крича́ть impf, кри́кнуть pf; (wake) буди́ть impf, раз~ pf; (visit) заходи́ть impf, зайти́ pf (on к+dat; at в+acc); (stop at) остана́вливаться impf, останови́ться pf (at в, на, +prep); (summon) вызыва́ть impf, вы́звать pf; (ring up) звони́ть impf, по~ pf +dat; ~ for (require) тре́бовать impf, по~ pf +gen; (fetch) заходи́ть impf, зайти́ pf за+instr; ~ off отменя́ть impf, отмени́ть pf; ~ up призыва́ть impf, призва́ть pf; n (cry) крик; (summons) зов, призы́в; (telephone) (телефо́нный) вы́зов, разгово́р; (visit) визи́т; (signal) сигна́л; ~box телефо́н-автома́т; ~up призы́в. **caller** n посети́тель m, ~ница; (tel) позвони́вший sb. **calling**n (vocation) призва́ние.
callousadj (person) чёрствый.
callusn мозо́ль.
calmadj споко́йный; n споко́йствие; vt & i (~ down) успока́ивать(ся) impf, успоко́ить(ся) pf.
calorien кало́рия.
cambern скат.
camcordern камко́рдер.
cameln верблю́д.
cameran фотоаппара́т. **cameraman** n кинооперато́р.
camouflage n камуфля́ж; vt маскирова́ть impf, за~ pf.
camp n ла́герь m; vi (set up ~) располага́ться impf, расположи́ться pf ла́герем; (go camping) жить impf в пала́тках; ~bed раскладу́шка; ~firecостёр.
campaignn кампа́ния; vi проводи́ть impf, провести́ pf кампа́нию.
campsiten ла́герь m, ке́мпинг.
campusn университе́тский городо́к.
can[1] n ба́нка; vt консерви́ровать impf, за~ pf.
can[2] v aux (be able) мочь impf, c~ pf +inf; (know how) уме́ть impf, c~ pf +inf.
Canadan Кана́да. **Canadian**n кана́дец, -дка; adj кана́дский.
canaln кана́л.
canaryn канаре́йка.
cancel vt (make void) аннули́ровать impf & pf; (call off) отменя́ть impf, отмени́ть pf; (stamp) гаси́ть impf, по~ pf. **cancellation**n аннули́рова-

ние; отмéна.

cancer *n* рак; (C~) Рак. **cancerous** *adj* ра́ковый.

candelabrum *n* канделя́бр.

candid *adj* открове́нный.

candidate *n* кандида́т.

candied *adj* заса́харенный.

candle *n* свеча́. **candlestick** *n* подсве́чник.

candour *n* открове́нность.

candy *n* сла́дости *f pl*.

cane *n* (*plant*) тростни́к; (*stick*) трость, па́лка; *vt* бить *impf*, по~ *pf* па́лкой.

canine *adj* соба́чий; *n* (*tooth*) клык.

canister *n* ба́нка, коро́бка.

canker *n* рак.

cannabis *n* гаши́ш.

cannibal *n* людое́д. **cannibalism** *n* людое́дство.

cannon *n* пу́шка; ~-ball пу́шечное ядро́.

canoe *n* кано́э *neut indecl*; *vi* пла́вать *indet*, плыть *det* на кано́э.

canon *n* кано́н; (*person*) кано́ник. **canonize** *vt* канонизова́ть *impf* & *pf*.

canopy *n* балдахи́н.

cant *n* (*hypocrisy*) ха́нжество; (*jargon*) жарго́н.

cantankerous *adj* сварли́вый.

cantata *n* канта́та.

canteen *n* столо́вая *sb*.

canter *n* лёгкий гало́п; *vi* (*rider*) е́здить *indet*, е́хать *det* лёгким гало́пом; (*horse*) ходи́ть *indet*, идти́ *det* лёгким гало́пом.

canvas *n* (*art*) холст; (*naut*) паруси́на; (*tent material*) брезе́нт.

canvass *vi* агити́ровать *impf*, с~ *pf* (**for** за+*acc*); *n* собира́ние голосо́в; агита́ция. **canvasser** *n* собира́тель *m* голосо́в.

canyon *n* канью́н.

cap *n* (*of uniform*) фура́жка; (*cloth*) ке́пка; (*woman's*) чепе́ц; (*lid*) кры́шка; *vt* превосходи́ть *impf*, превзойти́ *pf*.

capability *n* спосо́бность. **capable** *adj* спосо́бный (**of** на+*acc*).

capacious *adj* вмести́тельный. **capacity** *n* ёмкость; (*ability*) спосо́бность; **in the ~ of** в ка́честве +*gen*.

cape[1] *n* (*geog*) мыс.

cape[2] *n* (*cloak*) наки́дка.

caper *vi* скака́ть *impf*.

capers[1] *n pl* (*cul*) ка́персы *m pl*.

capillary *adj* капилля́рный.

capital *adj* (*letter*) прописно́й; ~ **punishment** сме́ртная казнь; *n* (*town*) столи́ца; (*letter*) прописна́я бу́ква; (*econ*) капита́л. **capitalism** *n* капитали́зм. **capitalist** *n* капитали́ст; *adj* капиталисти́ческий. **capitalize** *vt* извлека́ть *impf*, извле́чь *pf* вы́году (**on** из+*gen*).

capitulate *vi* капитули́ровать *impf* & *pf*. **capitulation** *n* капитуля́ция.

caprice *n* капри́з. **capricious** *adj* капри́зный.

Capricorn *n* Козеро́г.

capsize *vt* & *i* опроки́дывать(ся) *impf*, опроки́нуть(ся) *pf*.

capsule *n* ка́псула.

captain *n* капита́н; *vt* быть капита́ном +*gen*.

caption *n* по́дпись; (*cin*) титр.

captious *adj* приди́рчивый.

captivate *vt* пленя́ть *impf*, плени́ть *pf*. **captivating** *adj* плени́тельный.

captive *adj* & *n* пле́нный. **captivity** *n* нево́ля; (*esp mil*) плен. **capture** *n* взя́тие, захва́т, пои́мка; *vt* (*person*) брать *impf*, взять *pf* в плен; (*seize*) захва́тывать *impf*, захвати́ть *pf*.

car *n* маши́на; автомоби́ль *m*; ~ **park** стоя́нка.

carafe *n* графи́н.

caramel(s) *n* караме́ль.

carat *n* кара́т.

caravan *n* фурго́н; (*convoy*) карава́н.

caraway (seeds) *n* тмин.

carbohydrate *n* углево́д. **carbon** *n* углеро́д; ~ **copy** ко́пия; ~ **dioxide** углекислота́; ~ **monoxide** о́кись углеро́да; ~ **paper** копирова́льная бума́га.

carburettor *n* карбюра́тор.

carcass *n* ту́ша.

card *n* (*stiff paper*) карто́н; (*visiting* ~) ка́рточка; (*playing* ~) ка́рта; (*greetings* ~) откры́тка; (*ticket*) биле́т. **cardboard** *n* карто́н; *adj* карто́нный.

cardiac *adj* серде́чный.

cardigan *n* кардига́н.

cardinal *adj* кардина́льный; ~ **number** коли́чественное числи́тельное *sb*; *n* кардина́л.

care n (trouble) забо́та; (caution) осторо́жность; (tending) ухо́д; **in the ~ of** на попече́нии +gen; **take ~** осторо́жно!; смотри́(те)!; **take ~ of** забо́титься impf, по~ pf o+prep; vi: **I don't ~** мне всё равно́; **~ for** (look after) уха́живать impf за+instr; (like) нра́виться impf, по~ pf impers +dat.

career n карье́ра.

carefree adj беззабо́тный. **careful** adj (cautious) осторо́жный; (thorough) тща́тельный. **careless** adj (negligent) небре́жный; (incautious) неосторо́жный.

caress n ла́ска; vt ласка́ть impf.

caretaker n смотри́тель m, ~ница; attrib вре́менный.

cargo n груз.

caricature n карикату́ра; vt изобража́ть impf, изобрази́ть pf в карикату́рном ви́де.

carnage n резня́.

carnal adj пло́тский.

carnation n гвозди́ка.

carnival n карнава́л.

carnivorous adj плотоя́дный.

carol n (рожде́ственский) гимн.

carouse vi кути́ть impf, кутну́ть pf.

carp¹ n карп.

carp² vi придира́ться impf, придра́ться pf (**at** k+dat).

carpenter n пло́тник. **carpentry** n пло́тничество.

carpet n ковёр; vt покрыва́ть impf, покры́ть pf ковро́м.

carping adj приди́рчивый.

carriage n (vehicle) каре́та; (rly) ваго́н; (conveyance) перево́зка; (bearing) оса́нка. **carriageway** n прое́зжая часть доро́ги. **carrier** n (on bike) бага́жник; (firm) тра́нспортная кампа́ния; (med) бацилло-носи́тель m.

carrot n морко́вка; pl морко́вь (collect).

carry vt (by hand) носи́ть indet, нести́ det; (transport) переноси́ть impf, перенести́ pf; (in vehicle) вози́ть indet, везти́ det; (sound) передава́ть impf, переда́ть pf; vi (sound) быть слы́шен; **be carried away** увлека́ться impf, увле́чься pf; **~ on** (continue) продолжа́ть impf; **~ out** выполня́ть impf, вы́полнить pf; **~ over** пере-

cart n теле́га; vt (lug) тащи́ть impf.

cartilage n хрящ.

carton n карто́нка.

cartoon n карикату́ра; (cin) мультфи́льм. **cartoonist** n карикатури́ст, ~ка.

cartridge n патро́н; (of record player) звукоснима́тель m.

carve vt ре́зать impf по+dat; (in wood) выреза́ть impf, вы́резать pf; (in stone) высека́ть impf, вы́сечь pf; (slice) нареза́ть impf, наре́зать pf. **carving** n резьба́; **~ knife** нож для нареза́ния мя́са.

cascade n каска́д; vi па́дать impf.

case¹ n (instance) слу́чай; (law) де́ло; (med) больно́й sb; (gram) паде́ж; **in ~** (в слу́чае) е́сли; **in any ~** во вся́ком слу́чае; **in no ~** не в ко́ем слу́чае; **just in ~** на вся́кий слу́чай.

case² n (box) я́щик; (suitcase) чемода́н; (small box) футля́р; (cover) чехо́л; (display) витри́на.

cash n нали́чные sb; (money) де́ньги pl; **~ on delivery** нало́женным платежо́м; **~ desk, register** ка́сса; vt: **~ a cheque** получа́ть impf, получи́ть pf де́ньги по че́ку. **cashier** n касси́р.

casing n (tech) кожу́х.

casino n казино́ neut indecl.

cask n бо́чка.

casket n шкату́лка.

casserole n (pot) ла́тка; (stew) рагу́ neut indecl.

cassette n кассе́та; **~ recorder** кассе́тный магнитофо́н.

cassock n ря́са.

cast vt (throw) броса́ть impf, бро́сить pf; (shed) сбра́сывать impf, сбро́сить pf; (theat) распределя́ть impf, распредели́ть pf ро́ли +dat; (found) лить impf, с~ pf; **~ off** (knitting) спуска́ть impf, спусти́ть pf пе́тли; (naut) отплыва́ть impf, отплы́ть pf; **~ on** (knitting) набира́ть impf, набра́ть pf пе́тли; n (of mind etc.) склад; (mould) фо́рма; (moulded object) слепо́к; (med) ги́псовая повя́зка; (theat) де́йствующие ли́ца (-ц) pl. **castaway** n потерпе́вший sb кораблекруше́ние. **cast iron** n чугу́н. **cast-iron** adj чугу́нный. **cast-offs** n pl но́шеное пла́тье.

castanet n кастанье́та.

caste n ка́ста.

castigate vt бичева́ть impf.

castle n за́мок; (chess) ладья́.

castor n (wheel) ро́лик; ~ **sugar** са́харная пу́дра.

castrate vt кастри́ровать impf & pf. **castration** n кастра́ция.

casual adj (chance) случа́йный; (offhand) небре́жный; (clothes) обы́денный; (unofficial) неофициа́льный; (informal) лёгкий; (labour) подённый; ~ **labourer** подёнщик, -ица.

casualty n (wounded) ра́неный sb; (killed) уби́тый sb; pl поте́ри (-рь) pl; ~ **ward** пала́та ско́рой по́мощи.

cat n ко́шка; (tom) кот; ~**'s-eye** (on road) (доро́жный) рефле́ктор.

catalogue n катало́г; (price list) прейскура́нт; vt каталогизи́ровать impf & pf.

catalyst n катализа́тор. **catalytic** adj каталити́ческий.

catapult n (toy) рога́тка; (hist, aeron) катапу́льта; vt & i катапульти́ровать(ся) impf & pf.

cataract n (med) катара́кта.

catarrh n ката́рр.

catastrophe n катастро́фа. **catastrophic** adj катастрофи́ческий.

catch vt (ball, fish, thief) лови́ть impf, пойма́ть pf; (surprise) застава́ть impf, заста́ть pf; (disease) заража́ться impf, зарази́ться pf +instr; (be in time for) успева́ть impf, успе́ть pf на+acc; vt & i (snag) зацепля́ть(ся) impf, зацепи́ть(ся) pf (on за+acc); ~ **on** (become popular) привива́ться impf, приви́ться pf; ~ **up with** догоня́ть impf, догна́ть pf; n (of fish) уло́в; (trick) уло́вка; (on door etc.) щеколда. **catching** adj зара́зный. **catchword** n мо́дное слове́чко. **catchy** adj привли́чивый.

categorical adj категори́ческий. **category** n катего́рия.

cater vi: ~ **for** поставля́ть impf, поста́вить pf прови́зию для+gen; (satisfy) удовлетворя́ть impf, удовлетвори́ть pf. **caterer** n поставщи́к (прови́зии).

caterpillar n гу́сеница.

cathedral n собо́р.

catheter n кате́тер.

Catholic adj католи́ческий; n като-

лик, -и́чка. **Catholicism** n католи́чество.

cattle n скот.

Caucasus n Кавка́з.

cauldron n котёл.

cauliflower n цветна́я капу́ста.

cause n причи́на, по́вод; (law etc.) де́ло; vt причиня́ть impf, причини́ть pf; вызыва́ть impf, вы́звать pf; (induce) заставля́ть impf, заста́вить pf.

caustic adj е́дкий.

cauterize vt прижига́ть impf, прижёчь pf.

caution n осторо́жность; (warning) предостереже́ние; vt предостерега́ть impf, предостере́чь pf. **cautious** adj осторо́жный. **cautionary** adj предостерега́ющий.

cavalcade n кавалька́да. **cavalier** adj бесцеремо́нный. **cavalry** n кавале́рия.

cave n пеще́ра; vi: ~ **in** обва́ливаться impf, обвали́ться pf; (yield) сдава́ться impf, сда́ться pf. **caveman** n пеще́рный челове́к. **cavern** n пеще́ра. **cavernous** adj пеще́ристый.

caviare n икра́.

cavity n впа́дина, по́лость; (in tooth) дупло́.

cavort vi скака́ть impf.

caw vi ка́ркать impf, ка́ркнуть pf.

CD abbr (of compact disc) компа́кт-ди́ск; ~ **player** прои́грыватель m компа́кт-ди́сков.

cease vt & i прекраща́ть(ся) impf, прекрати́ть(ся) pf; vt перестава́ть impf, переста́ть pf (+inf); ~**-fire** прекраще́ние огня́. **ceaseless** adj непреста́нный.

cedar n кедр.

cede vt уступа́ть impf, уступи́ть pf.

ceiling n потоло́к; (fig) макси́ма́льный у́ровень m.

celebrate vt & i пра́здновать impf, от~ pf; (extol) прославля́ть impf, просла́вить pf. **celebrated** adj знамени́тый. **celebration** n пра́зднование. **celebrity** n знамени́тость.

celery n сельдере́й.

celestial adj небе́сный.

celibacy n безбра́чие. **celibate** adj холосто́й; n холостя́к.

cell n (prison) ка́мера; (biol) кле́тка.

cellar n подва́л.

cello n виолончéль.
cellophane n целлофáн. **cellular** adj клéточный. **celluloid** n целлулóид.
Celt n кельт. **Celtic** adj кéльтский.
cement n цемéнт; vt цементи́ровать impf, за~ pf.
cemetery n клáдбище.
censor n цéнзор; vt подвергáть impf, подвéргнуть pf цензýре. **censorious** adj сверхкрити́ческий. **censorship** n цензýра. **censure** n порицáние; vt порицáть impf.
census n пéрепись.
cent n цент; **per ~** процéнт.
centenary n столéтие. **centennial** adj столéтний. **centigrade** adj: **10° ~** 10° по Цéльсию. **centimetre** n сантимéтр. **centipede** n сороконóжка.
central adj центрáльный; **~ heating** центрáльное отоплéние. **centralization** n централизáция. **centralize** vt централизовáть impf & pf. **centre** n центр; середи́на; **~ forward** центр нападéния; vi & i: **~ on** сосредотóчивать(ся) impf, сосредотóчить(ся) pf на+prep. **centrifugal** adj центробéжный.
century n столéтие, век.
ceramic adj керами́ческий. **ceramics** n pl керáмика.
cereals n pl хлéбные злáки m pl; **breakfast ~** зерновы́е хлóпья (-ев) pl.
cerebral adj мозговóй.
ceremonial adj церемониáльный; n церемониáл. **ceremonious** adj церемóнный. **ceremony** n церемóния.
certain adj (confident) увéрен (-нна); (undoubted) несомнéнный; (unspecified) извéстный; (inevitable) вéрный; **for ~** навернякá. **certainly** adv (of course) конéчно; безуслóвно; (without doubt) несомнéнно; **~ not!** ни в кóем слýчае. **certainty** n (conviction) увéренность; (fact) несомнéнный факт.
certificate n свидéтельство; сертификáт. **certify** vt удостоверя́ть impf, удостовéрить pf.
cervical adj шéйный. **cervix** n шéйка мáтки.
cessation n прекращéние.
cf. abbr ср., сравни́.
CFCs abbr (of **chlorofluorocarbons**)

хлори́рованные фтороуглерóды m pl.
chafe vt (rub) терéть impf; (rub sore) натирáть impf, натерéть pf.
chaff n (husks) мяки́на; (straw) сéчка.
chaffinch n зя́блик.
chagrin n огорчéние.
chain n цепь; **~ reaction** цепнáя реáкция; **~ smoker** зая́длый кури́льщик.
chair n стул, (armchair) крéсло; (univ) кáфедра; vt (preside) председáтельствовать impf на+prep. **chairman, -woman** n председáтель m, -ница.
chalice n чáша.
chalk n мел. **chalky** adj меловóй.
challenge n (summons, fig) вы́зов; (sentry's) óклик; (law) отвóд; vt вызывáть impf, вы́звать pf; (sentry) оклика́ть impf, окли́кнуть pf; (law) отводи́ть impf, отвести́ pf. **challenger** n претендéнт. **challenging** adj интригýющий.
chamber n (cavity) кáмера; (hall) зал; (polit) палáта; (law) адвокáтская контóра, (judge's) кабинéт (судьи́); **~ music** кáмерная мýзыка; **~ pot** ночнóй горшóк. **chambermaid** n гóрничная sb.
chameleon n хамелеóн.
chamois n (animal) сéрна; (~ leather) зáмша.
champagne n шампáнское sb.
champion n чемпиóн, ~ка; (upholder) побóрник, -ица; vt борóться impf за +acc. **championship** n пéрвенство, чемпионáт.
chance n случáйность; (opportunity) возмóжность, (favourable) случáй; (likelihood) шанс (usu pl); **by ~** случáйно; adj случáйный; vi: **~ it** рискнýть pf.
chancellery n канцеля́рия. **chancellor** n кáнцлер; (univ) рéктор; **C~ of the Exchequer** кáнцлер казначéйства.
chancy adj рискóванный.
chandelier n лю́стра.
change n перемéна; измéнение; (of clothes etc.) смéна; (money) сдáча; (of trains etc.) пересáдка; **for a ~** для разнообрáзия; vt & i меня́ть(ся) impf; изменя́ть(ся) impf, изме-

ни́ть(ся) *pf*; *vi* (*one's clothes*) переодева́ться *impf*, переоде́ться *pf*; (*trains etc.*) переса́живаться *impf*, пересе́сть *pf*; *vt* (*a baby*) перепелёнывать *impf*, перепелена́ть *pf*; (*money*) обме́нивать *impf*, обменя́ть *pf*; (*give ~ for*) разме́нивать *impf*, разменя́ть *pf*; ~ **into** превраща́ться *impf*, преврати́ться *pf* в+*acc*; ~ **over to** переходи́ть *impf*, перейти́ *pf* на+*acc*. **changeable** *adj* изме́нчивый.

channel *n* (*water*) проли́в; (*also TV*) кана́л; (*fig*) путь *m*; **the** (English C~ Ла-Ма́нш; *vt* (*fig*) направля́ть *impf*.

chant *n* (*eccl*) песнопе́ние; *vt & i* петь *impf*; (*slogans*) сканди́ровать *impf & pf*.

chaos *n* ха́ос. **chaotic** *adj* хаоти́чный.

chap *n* (*person*) па́рень *m*.

chapel *n* часо́вня; (*Catholic*) капе́лла.

chaperone *n* компаньо́нка.

chaplain *n* капелла́н.

chapped *adj* потреска́вшийся.

chapter *n* глава́.

char *vt & i* обу́гливать(ся) *impf*, обу́глить(ся) *pf*.

character *n* хара́ктер; (*theat*) де́йствующее лицо́; (*letter*) (*Chinese etc.*) иеро́глиф. **characteristic** *adj* характе́рный; *n* сво́йство; (*of person*) черта́ хара́ктера. **characterize** *vt* характеризова́ть *impf & pf*.

charade *n* шара́да.

charcoal *n* древе́сный у́голь *m*.

charge *n* (*for gun*; *electr*) заря́д; (*fee*) пла́та; (*person*) пито́мец, -мица; (*accusation*) обвине́ние; (*mil*) ата́ка; **be in ~ of** заве́довать *impf* +*instr*; **in the ~ of** на попече́нии +*gen*; *vt* (*gun*; *electr*) заряжа́ть *impf*, заряди́ть *pf*; (*accuse*) обвиня́ть *impf*, обвини́ть *pf* (**with** в+*prep*); (*mil*) атакова́ть *impf & pf*; *vi* броса́ться *impf*, бро́ситься *pf* в ата́ку; ~ (**for**) брать *impf*, взять *pf* (за+*acc*); ~ **to** (**the account of**) запи́сывать *impf*, записа́ть *pf* на счёт+*gen*.

chariot *n* колесни́ца.

charisma *n* обая́ние. **charismatic** *adj* обая́тельный.

charitable *adj* благотвори́тельный; (*kind*, *merciful*) милосе́рдный. **char-**

-ity *n* (*kindness*) милосе́рдие; (*organization*) благотвори́тельная организа́ция.

charlatan *n* шарлата́н.

charm *n* очарова́ние; пре́лесть; (*spell*) за́говор; *pl* ча́ры (чар) *pl*; (*amulet*) талисма́н; (*trinket*) брело́к; *vt* очаро́вывать *impf*, очарова́ть *pf*. **charming** *adj* очарова́тельный, преле́стный.

chart *n* (*naut*) морска́я ка́рта; (*table*) гра́фик; *vt* наноси́ть *impf*, нанести́ *pf* на гра́фик. **charter** *n* (*document*) ха́ртия; (*statutes*) уста́в; *vt* нанима́ть *impf*, наня́ть *pf*.

charwoman *n* приходя́щая убо́рщица.

chase *vt* гоня́ться *indet*, гна́ться *det* за+*instr*; *n* пого́ня; (*hunting*) охо́та.

chasm *n* (*abyss*) бе́здна.

chassis *n* шасси́ *neut indecl*.

chaste *adj* целому́дренный.

chastise *vt* кара́ть *impf*, по~ *pf*.

chastity *n* целому́дрие.

chat *n* бесе́да; *vi* бесе́довать *impf*; ~ **show** телевизио́нная бесе́да-интервью́ *f*.

chatter *n* болтовня́; *vi* болта́ть *impf*; (*teeth*) стуча́ть *impf*. **chatterbox** *n* болту́н. **chatty** *adj* разгово́рчивый.

chauffeur *n* шофёр.

chauvinism *n* шовини́зм. **chauvinist** *n* шовини́ст; *adj* шовинисти́ческий.

cheap *adj* дешёвый. **cheapen** *vt* (*fig*) опошля́ть *impf*, опошли́ть *pf*. **cheaply** *adv* дёшево.

cheat *vt* обма́нывать *impf*, обману́ть *pf*; *vi* плутова́ть *impf*, на~, с~ *pf*; *n* (*person*) обма́нщик, -ица; плут; (*act*) обма́н.

check[1] *n* контро́ль *m*, прове́рка; (*chess*) шах; ~**mate** шах и мат; *vt* (*examine*) проверя́ть *impf*, прове́рить *pf*; контроли́ровать *impf*, про~; (*restrain*) сде́рживать *impf*, сдержа́ть *pf*; ~ **in** регистри́роваться *impf*, за~ *pf*; ~ **out** выпи́сываться *impf*, вы́писаться *pf*; ~**out** ка́сса; ~**up** осмо́тр.

check[2] *n* (*pattern*) кле́тка. **check(ed)** *adj* кле́тчатый.

cheek *n* щека́; (*impertinence*) на́глость. **cheeky** *adj* на́глый.

cheep *vi* пища́ть *impf*, пи́скнуть *pf*.

cheer n ободря́ющий во́зглас; ~s! за (ва́ше) здоро́вье!; vt (applaud) приве́тствовать impf & pf; ~ up ободря́ть(ся) impf, ободри́ть(ся) pf.
cheerful adj весёлый. **cheerio** int пока́. **cheerless** adj уны́лый.
cheese n сыр; ~-cake ватру́шка.
cheetah n гепа́рд.
chef n (шеф-)по́вар.
chemical adj хими́ческий; n химика́т. **chemist** n хи́мик; (druggist) апте́карь m; ~'s (shop) апте́ка. **chemistry** n хи́мия.
cheque n чек; ~-book че́ковая кни́жка.
cherish vt (foster) леле́ять impf; (hold dear) дорожи́ть impf +instr; (love) не́жно люби́ть impf.
cherry n ви́шня; adj вишнёвый.
cherub n херуви́м.
chess n ша́хматы (-т) pl; ~-board ша́хматная доска́; ~-men n ша́хматы (-т) pl.
chest n сунду́к; (anat) грудь; ~ of drawers комо́д.
chestnut n кашта́н; (horse) гнеда́я sb.
chew vt & i жева́ть impf. **chewing-gum** n жева́тельная рези́нка.
chic adj элега́нтный.
chick n цыплёнок. **chicken** n ку́рица; цыплёнок; adj трусли́вый; ~ out тру́сить impf, с~ pf. **chicken-pox** n ветря́нка.
chicory n цико́рий.
chief n глава́ m & f; (boss) нача́льник; (of tribe) вождь m; adj гла́вный. **chiefly** adv гла́вным о́бразом. **chieftain** n вождь m.
chiffon n шифо́н.
child n ребёнок; ~-birth ро́ды (-дов) pl. **childhood** n де́тство. **childish** adj де́тский. **childless** adj безде́тный. **childlike** adj де́тский. **childrens'** adj де́тский.
chili n стручко́вый пе́рец.
chill n хо́лод; (ailment) просту́да; vt охлажда́ть impf, охлади́ть pf. **chilly** adj прохла́дный.
chime n (set of bells) набо́р колоко́лов; pl (sound) перезво́н; (of clock) бой; vt & i (clock) бить impf, про~ pf; vi (bell) звони́ть impf, по~ pf.
chimney n труба́; ~-sweep трубочи́ст.

chimpanzee n шимпанзе́ m indecl.
chin n подборо́док.
china n фарфо́р.
China n Кита́й. **Chinese** n кита́ец, -а́янка; adj кита́йский.
chink[1] n (sound) звон; vi звене́ть impf, про~ pf.
chink[2] n (crack) щель.
chintz n си́тец.
chip vt & i отка́лывать(ся) impf, отколо́ть(ся) pf. n (of wood) ще́пка; (in cup) щерби́на; (in games) фи́шка; pl карто́фель-соло́мка (collect); (electron) чип, микросхе́ма.
chiropodist n челове́к, занима́ющийся педикю́ром. **chiropody** n педикю́р.
chirp vi чири́кать impf.
chisel n (wood) стаме́ска; (masonry) зуби́ло; vt высека́ть impf, вы́сечь pf.
chit n (note) запи́ска.
chivalrous adj ры́царский. **chivalry** n ры́царство.
chlorine n хлор. **chloroform** n хлорофо́рм. **chlorophyll** n хлорофи́лл.
chock-full adj битко́м наби́тый.
chocolate n шокола́д; (sweet) шокола́дка.
choice n вы́бор; adj отбо́рный.
choir n хор m; ~-boy пе́вчий sb.
choke n (valve) дро́ссель m; vi дави́ться impf, по~ pf; (with anger etc.) задыха́ться impf, задохну́ться pf (with от+gen); vt (suffocate) души́ть impf, за~ pf; (of plants) заглуша́ть, глуши́ть impf, заглуши́ть pf.
cholera n холе́ра.
cholesterol n холестери́н.
choose vt (select) выбира́ть impf, вы́брать pf; (decide) реша́ть impf, реши́ть pf. **choosy** adj разбо́рчивый.
chop vt (also ~ down) руби́ть impf, рубну́ть, рубану́ть pf; ~ off отруба́ть impf, отруби́ть pf; n (cul) отбивна́я котле́та.
chopper n топо́р. **choppy** adj бурли́вый.
chop-sticks n па́лочки f pl для еды́.
choral adj хорово́й. **chorale** n хора́л.
chord n (mus) акко́рд.
chore n обя́занность.
choreographer n хорео́граф. **chore-**

ography *n* хореогра́фия.

chorister *n* пе́вчий *sb*.

chortle *vi* фы́ркать *impf*, фы́ркнуть *pf*.

chorus *n* хор; (*refrain*) припе́в.

christen *vt* крести́ть *impf* & *pf*. **Christian** *n* христиани́н, -а́нка; *adj* христиа́нский; ~ **name** и́мя *neut*. **Christianity** *n* христиа́нство. **Christmas** *n* Рождество́; ~ **Day** пе́рвый день Рождества́; ~ **Eve** соче́льник; ~ **tree** ёлка.

chromatic *adj* хромати́ческий. **chrome** *n* хром. **chromium** *n* хром. **chromosome** *n* хромосо́ма.

chronic *adj* хрони́ческий.

chronicle *n* хро́ника, ле́топись.

chronological *adj* хронологи́ческий.

chrysalis *n* ку́колка.

chrysanthemum *n* хризанте́ма.

chubby *adj* пу́хлый.

chuck *vt* броса́ть *impf*, бро́сить *pf*; ~ **out** вышиба́ть *impf*, вы́шибить *pf*.

chuckle *vi* посме́иваться *impf*.

chum *n* това́рищ.

chunk *n* ломо́ть *m*.

church *n* це́рковь. **churchyard** *n* кла́дбище.

churlish *adj* гру́бый.

churn *n* маслобо́йка; *vt* сбива́ть *impf*, сбить *pf*; *vi* (*foam*) пе́ниться *impf*, вс~ *pf*; (*stomach*) крути́ть *impf*; ~ **out** выпека́ть *impf*, вы́печь *pf*; ~ **up** взбить *pf*.

chute *n* жёлоб.

cider *n* сидр.

cigar *n* сига́ра. **cigarette** *n* сигаре́та; папиро́са; ~ **lighter** зажига́лка.

cinder *n* шлак; *pl* зола́.

cine-camera *n* киноаппара́т. **cinema** *n* кино́ *neut indecl*.

cinnamon *n* кори́ца.

cipher *n* нуль *m*; (*code*) шифр.

circle *n* круг; (*theatre*) я́рус; *vi* кружи́ться *impf*; *vt* (*walking*) обходи́ть *impf*, обойти́ *pf*; (*flying*) облета́ть *impf*, облете́ть *pf*. **circuit** *n* кругооборо́т; объе́зд, обхо́д; (*electron*) схе́ма; (*electr*) цепь. **circuitous** *adj* окру́жный. **circular** *adj* кру́глый; (*moving in a circle*) кругово́й; *n* циркуля́р. **circulate** *vi* циркули́ровать *impf*; *vt* распространя́ть *impf*, распространи́ть *pf*. **circulation** *n* (*air*)

циркуля́ция; (*distribution*) распростране́ние; (*of newspaper*) тира́ж; (*med*) кровообраще́ние.

circumcise *vt* обреза́ть *impf*, обре́зать *pf*. **circumcision** *n* обреза́ние.

circumference *n* окру́жность.

circumspect *adj* осмотри́тельный.

circumstance *n* обстоя́тельство; under the ~s при да́нных обстоя́тельствах, в тако́м слу́чае; under no ~s ни при каки́х обстоя́тельствах, ни в ко́ем слу́чае.

circumvent *vt* обходи́ть *impf*, обойти́ *pf*.

circus *n* цирк.

cirrhosis *n* цирро́з.

CIS *abbr* (*of* Commonwealth of Independent States) СНГ.

cistern *n* бачо́к.

citadel *n* цитаде́ль.

cite *vt* ссыла́ться *impf*, сосла́ться *pf* на+*acc*.

citizen *n* граждани́н, -а́нка. **citizenship** *n* гражда́нство.

citrus *n* ци́трус; *adj* ци́трусовый.

city *n* го́род.

civic *adj* гражда́нский. **civil** *adj* гражда́нский; (*polite*) ве́жливый; ~ **engineer** гражда́нский инжене́р; ~ **engineering** гражда́нское строи́тельство; C~ **Servant** госуда́рственный слу́жащий *sb*; чино́вник; C~ **Service** госуда́рственная слу́жба. **civilian** *n* шта́тский *sb*; *adj* шта́тский. **civility** *n* ве́жливость. **civilization** *n* цивилиза́ция. **civilize** *vt* цивилизова́ть *impf* & *pf*. **civilized** *adj* цивилизо́ванный.

clad *adj* оде́тый.

claim *n* (*demand*) тре́бование, притяза́ние; (*assertion*) утвержде́ние; *vt* (*demand*) тре́бовать *impf* +*gen*; (*assert*) утвержда́ть *impf*, утверди́ть *pf*. **claimant** *n* претенде́нт.

clairvoyant *n* яснови́дец, -дица; *adj* яснови́дящий.

clam *n* моллю́ск; *vi*: ~ **up** отка́зываться *impf*, отказа́ться *pf* разгова́ривать.

clamber *vi* кара́бкаться *impf*, вс~ *pf*.

clammy *adj* вла́жный.

clamour *n* шум; *vi*: ~ **for** шу́мно тре́бовать *impf*, по~ *pf* +*gen*.

clamp *n* зажи́м; *vt* скрепля́ть *impf*, скрепи́ть *pf*; ~ **down on** прижа́ть *pf*.

clan *n* клан.

clandestine *adj* тайный.

clang, clank *n* лязг; *vt & i* лязгать *impf*, лязгнуть *pf* (+*instr*).

clap *vt & i* хлопать *impf*, хлопнуть *pf* +*dat*; *n* хлопок; (*thunder*) удар.

claret *n* бордо *neut indecl*.

clarification *n* (*explanation*) разъяснение. **clarify** *vt* разъяснять *impf*, разъяснить *pf*.

clarinet *n* кларнет.

clarity *n* ясность.

clash *n* (*conflict*) столкновение; (*disharmony*) дисгармония; *vi* сталкиваться *impf*, столкнуться *pf*; (*coincide*) совпадать *impf*, совпасть *pf*; не гармонировать *impf*.

clasp *n* застёжка; (*embrace*) объятие; *vt* обхватывать *impf*, обхватить *pf*; ~ one's hands сплести *pf* пальцы рук.

class *n* класс; ~-room класс; *vt* классифицировать *impf & pf*. **classic** *adj* классический; *n* классик; *pl* (*literature*) классика; (*Latin and Greek*) классические языки *m pl*. **classical** *adj* классический.

classification *n* классификация. **classified** *adj* засекреченный. **classify** *vt* классифицировать *impf & pf*.

classy *adj* классный.

clatter *n* стук; *vi* стучать *impf*, по~ *pf*.

clause *n* статья; (*gram*) предложение.

claustrophobia *n* клаустрофобия.

claw *n* коготь; *vt* царапать *impf* когтями.

clay *n* глина; *adj* глиняный.

clean *adj* чистый; *adv* (*fully*) совершенно; ~-shaven гладко выбритый; *vt* чистить *impf*, вы~, по~ *pf*. **cleaner** *n* уборщик, -ица. **cleaner's** *n* химчистка. **clean(li)ness** *n* чистота. **cleanse** *vt* очищать *impf*, очистить *pf*.

clear *adj* ясный; (*transparent*) прозрачный; (*distinct*) отчётливый; (*free*) свободный (of от+*gen*); (*pure*) чистый; *vt & i* очищать(ся) *impf*, очистить(ся) *pf*; *vt* (*jump over*) перепрыгивать *impf*, перепрыгнуть *pf*; (*acquit*) оправдывать *impf*, оправдать *pf*; ~ away убирать

убрать *pf* со стола́; ~ off (*go away*) убираться *impf*, убраться *pf*; ~ out (*vt*) вычищать *impf*, вычистить *pf*; (*vi*) (*make off*) убираться *impf*, убраться *pf*; ~ up (*tidy away*) убирать *impf*, убрать *pf*; (*weather*) проясняться *impf*, проясниться *pf*; (*explain*) выяснять *impf*, выяснить *pf*. **clearance** *n* расчистка; (*permission*) разрешение. **clearing** *n* (*glade*) поляна. **clearly** *adv* ясно.

cleavage *n* разрез груди.

clef *n* (*mus*) ключ.

cleft *n* трещина.

clemency *n* милосердие.

clench *vt* (*fist*) сжимать *impf*, сжать *pf*; (*teeth*) стискивать *impf*, стиснуть *pf*.

clergy *n* духовенство. **clergyman** *n* священник. **clerical** *adj* (*eccl*) духовный; (*of clerk*) канцелярский. **clerk** *n* конторский служащий *sb*.

clever *adj* умный. **cleverness** *n* умение.

cliche *n* клише *neut indecl*.

click *vt* щёлкать *impf*, щёлкнуть *pf* +*instr*.

client *n* клиент. **clientele** *n* клиентура.

cliff *n* утёс.

climate *n* климат. **climatic** *adj* климатический.

climax *n* кульминация.

climb *vt & i* лазить *indet*, лезть *det* на+*acc*; влезать *impf*, влезть *pf* на+*acc*; подниматься *impf*, подняться *pf* на+*acc*; ~ down (*tree*) слезать *impf*, слезть *pf* (c+*gen*); (*mountain*) спускаться *impf*, спуститься *pf* (c+*gen*); (*give in*) отступать *impf*, отступить *pf*; *n* подъём. **climber** *n* альпинист, ~ка; (*plant*) вьющееся растение. **climbing** *n* альпинизм.

clinch *vt*: ~ a deal закрепить *pf* сделку.

cling *vi* (*stick*) прилипать *impf*, прилипнуть *pf* (to к+*dat*); (*grasp*) цепляться *impf*, цепиться *pf* (to за+*acc*).

clinic *n* клиника. **clinical** *adj* клинический.

clink *vt & i* звенеть *impf*, про~ *pf* (+*instr*); ~ glasses чокаться *impf*, чокнуться *pf*; *n* звон.

clip[1] *n* скрепка; зажим; *vt* скреплять

impf, скрепить *pf*.

clip[2] *vt* (*cut*) подстригать *impf*, подстричь *pf*. **clippers** *n pl* ножницы *f pl*. **clipping** *n* (*extract*) вырезка.

clique *n* клика.

cloak *n* плащ. **cloakroom** *n* гардероб; (*lavatory*) уборная *sb*.

clock *n* часы *m pl*; ~**wise** по часовой стрелке; *vi*: ~ **in, out** отмечаться *impf*, отметиться *pf* приходя на работу/ уходя с работы.

clod *n* ком.

clog *vt*: ~ **up** засорять *impf*, засорить *pf*.

cloister *n* аркада.

close *adj* (*near*) близкий; (*stuffy*) душный; *vt & i* (*also* ~ **down**) закрывать(ся) *impf*, закрыть(ся) *pf*; (*conclude*) заканчивать *impf*, закончить *pf*; *adv* близко (**to** от+*gen*).

closed *adj* закрытый. **closeted** *adj*: **be** ~ **together** совещаться *impf* наедине. **close-up** *n* фотография снятая крупным планом. **closing** *n* закрытие; *adj* заключительный. **closure** *n* закрытие.

clot *n* сгусток; *vi* сгущаться *impf*, сгуститься *pf*.

cloth *n* ткань; (*duster*) тряпка; (*table*-~) скатерть.

clothe *vt* одевать *impf*, одеть (**in** +*instr*, **в**+*acc*) *pf*. **clothes** *n pl* одежда, платье.

cloud *n* облако; (*rain*-~) туча; *vt* затемнять *impf*, затемнить *pf*; омрачать *impf*, омрачить *pf*; ~ **over** покрываться *impf*, покрыться *pf* облаками, тучами. **cloudy** *adj* облачный; (*liquid*) мутный.

clout *vt* ударять *impf*, ударить *pf*; *n* затрещина; (*fig*) влияние.

clove *n* гвоздика; (*of garlic*) зубок.

cloven *adj* раздвоенный.

clover *n* клевер.

clown *n* клоун.

club *n* (*stick*) дубинка; *pl* (*cards*) трефы (треф) *pl*; (*association*) клуб; *vt* колотить *impf*, по~ *pf* дубинкой; *vi*: ~ **together** складываться *impf*, сложиться *pf*.

cluck *vi* кудахтать *impf*.

clue *n* (*evidence*) улика; (*to puzzle*) ключ; (*hint*) намёк.

clump *n* группа.

clumsiness *n* неуклюжесть. **clumsy** *adj* неуклюжий.

cluster *n* группа; *vi* собираться *impf*, собраться *pf* группами.

clutch *n* (*grasp*) хватка; когти *m pl*; (*tech*) сцепление; *vt* зажимать *impf*, зажать *pf*; *vi*: ~ **at** хвататься *impf*, хватиться *pf* за+*acc*.

clutter *n* беспорядок; *vt* загромождать *impf*, загромоздить *pf*.

c/o *abbr* (*of care of*) по адресу +*gen*; через+*acc*.

coach *n* (*horse-drawn*) карета; (*rly*) вагон; (*bus*) автобус; (*tutor*) репетитор; (*sport*) тренер; *vt* репетировать *impf*; тренировать *impf*, на~ *pf*.

coagulate *vi* сгущаться *impf*, сгуститься *pf*.

coal *n* уголь *m*; ~**mine** угольная шахта.

coalition *n* коалиция.

coarse *adj* грубый.

coast *n* побережье, берег; ~ **guard** береговая охрана; *vi* (*move without power*) двигаться *impf*, двинуться *pf* по инерции. **coastal** *adj* береговой, прибрежный.

coat *n* пальто *neut indecl*; (*layer*) слой; (*animal*) шерсть, мех; ~ **of arms** герб; *vt* покрывать *impf*, покрыть *pf*.

coax *vt* уговаривать *impf*, уговорить *pf*.

cob *n* (*corn*-~) початок кукурузы.

cobble *n* булыжник (*also collect*). **cobbled** *adj* булыжный.

cobbler *n* сапожник.

cobweb *n* паутина.

Coca-Cola *n* (*propr*) кока-кола.

cocaine *n* кокаин.

cock *n* (*bird*) петух; (*tap*) кран; (*of gun*) курок; *vt* (*gun*) взводить *impf*, взвести *pf* курок+*gen*.

cockerel *n* петушок.

cockle *n* сердцевидка.

cockpit *n* (*aeron*) кабина.

cockroach *n* таракан.

cocktail *n* коктейль *m*.

cocky *adj* чванный.

cocoa *n* какао *neut indecl*.

coco(a)nut *n* кокос.

cocoon *n* кокон.

cod *n* треска.

code *n* (*of laws*) кодекс; (*cipher*) код;

vt шифрова́ть *impf*, за~ *pf*. **codify** *vt* кодифици́ровать *impf* & *pf*.

co-education *n* совме́стное обуче́ние.

coefficient *n* коэффицие́нт.

coerce *vt* принужда́ть *impf*, прину́дить *pf*. **coercion** *n* принужде́ние.

coexist *vi* сосуществова́ть *impf*. **coexistence** *n* сосуществова́ние.

coffee *n* ко́фе *m indecl*; ~-**mill** *n* кофе́йница; ~-**pot** *n* кофе́йник.

coffer *n pl* казна́.

coffin *n* гроб.

cog *n* зубе́ц. **cogwheel** *n* зубча́тое колесо́.

cogent *adj* убеди́тельный.

cohabit *vi* сожи́тельствовать *impf*.

coherent *adj* свя́зный. **cohesion** *n* сплочённость. **cohesive** *adj* сплочённый.

coil *vt* & *i* свёртывать(ся) *impf*, сверну́ть(ся) *pf* кольцо́м; *n* кольцо́; (*electr*) кату́шка.

coin *n* моне́та; *vt* чека́нить *impf*, от~ *pf*.

coincide *vi* совпада́ть *impf*, совпа́сть *pf*. **coincidence** *n* совпаде́ние. **coincidental** *adj* случа́йный.

coke *n* кокс.

colander *n* дуршла́г.

cold *n* хо́лод; (*med*) просту́да, на́сморк; *adj* холо́дный; ~-**blooded** *adj* жесто́кий; (*zool*) холоднокро́вный.

colic *n* ко́лики *f pl*.

collaborate *vi* сотру́дничать *impf*. **collaboration** *n* сотру́дничество. **collaborator** *n* сотру́дник, -ица; (*traitor*) коллаборациони́ст, -и́стка.

collapse *vi* ру́хнуть *pf*; *n* паде́ние; круше́ние.

collar *n* воротни́к; (*dog's*) оше́йник; ~-**bone** ключи́ца.

colleague *n* колле́га *m* & *f*.

collect *vt* собира́ть *impf*, собра́ть *pf*; (*as hobby*) коллекциони́ровать *impf*; (*fetch*) забира́ть *impf*, забра́ть *pf*. **collected** *adj* (*calm*) собранный; ~ **works** собра́ние сочине́ний. **collection** *n* (*stamps etc.*) колле́кция; (*church etc.*) сбор; (*post*) вы́емка. **collective** *n* коллекти́в; *adj* колле́кти́вный; ~ **farm** колхо́з; ~ **noun** собира́тельное существи́тельное *sb*. **collectivization** *n* коллективиза-

ция. **collector** *n* сбо́рщик; коллекционе́р.

college *n* колле́дж, учи́лище.

collide *vi* ста́лкиваться *impf*, столкну́ться *pf*. **collision** *n* столкнове́ние.

colliery *n* каменноуго́льная ша́хта.

colloquial *adj* разгово́рный. **colloquialism** *n* разгово́рное выраже́ние.

collusion *n* та́йный сго́вор.

colon[1] *n* (*anat*) то́лстая кишка́.

colon[2] *n* (*gram*) двоето́чие.

colonel *n* полко́вник.

colonial *adj* колониа́льный. **colonialism** *n* колониали́зм. **colonize** *vt* колонизова́ть *impf* & *pf*. **colony** *n* коло́ния.

colossal *adj* колосса́льный.

colour *n* цвет, кра́ска; (*pl*) (*flag*) знамя *neut*; ~-**blind** страда́ющий дальтони́змом; ~ **film** цветна́я плёнка; *vt* раскра́шивать *impf*, раскра́сить *pf*; *vi* красне́ть *impf*, по~ *pf*. **coloured** *adj* цветно́й. **colourful** *adj* я́ркий. **colourless** *adj* бесцве́тный.

colt *n* жеребёнок.

column *n* (*archit, mil*) коло́нна; (*of smoke etc.*) столб; (*of print*) столбе́ц. **columnist** *n* журнали́ст.

coma *n* ко́ма.

comb *n* гребёнка; *vt* причёсывать *impf*, причеса́ть *pf*.

combat *n* бой; *vt* боро́ться *impf* с+*instr*, про́тив+*gen*.

combination *n* сочета́ние; комбина́ция. **combine** *n* комбина́т; (~-*harvester*) комба́йн; *vt* & *i* совмеща́ть(ся) *impf*, совмести́ть(ся) *pf*. **combined** *adj* совме́стный.

combustion *n* горе́ние.

come *vi* (*on foot*) приходи́ть *impf*, прийти́ *pf*; (*by transport*) приезжа́ть *impf*, прие́хать *pf*; ~ **about** случа́ться *impf*, случи́ться *pf*; ~ **across** случа́йно ната́лкиваться *impf*, натолкну́ться *pf* на+*acc*; ~ **back** возвраща́ться *impf*, возврати́ться *pf*; ~ **in** входи́ть *impf*, войти́ *pf*; ~ **out** выходи́ть *impf*, вы́йти *pf*; ~ **round** (*revive*) приходи́ть *impf*, прийти́ *pf* в себя́; (*visit*) заходи́ть *impf*, зайти́ *pf*; (*agree*) соглаша́ться *impf*, согласи́ться *pf*; ~ **up to** (*approach*) подходи́ть *impf*, подойти́ *pf* к+*dat*;

(*reach*) доходи́ть *impf*, дойти́ *pf* до+*gen*. **come-back** *n* возвраще́ние. **come-down** *n* униже́ние.

comedian *n* комедиа́нт. **comedy** *n* коме́дия.

comet *n* коме́та.

comfort *n* комфо́рт; (*convenience*) удо́бство; (*consolation*) утеше́ние; *vt* утеша́ть *impf*, уте́шить *pf*. **comfortable** *adj* удо́бный.

comic *adj* коми́ческий; *n* ко́мик. (*magazine*) ко́микс. **comical** *adj* смешно́й.

coming *adj* сле́дующий.

comma *n* запята́я *sb*.

command *n* (*order*) прика́з; (*order, authority*) кома́нда; **have ~ of** (*master*) владе́ть *impf* +*instr*; *vt* прика́зывать *impf*, приказа́ть *pf* +*dat*; (*mil*) кома́ндовать *impf*, с~ *pf* +*instr*. **commandant** *n* комендант. **commandeer** *vt* реквизи́ровать *impf* & *pf*. **commander** *n* команди́р; **~-in-chief** главнокома́ндующий *sb*. **commandment** *n* за́поведь. **commando** *n* деса́нтник.

commemorate *vt* ознамено́вывать *impf*, ознаменова́ть *pf*. **commemoration** *n* ознаменова́ние. **commemorative** *adj* па́мятный.

commence *vt* & *i* начина́ть(ся) *impf*, нача́ть(ся) *pf*. **commencement** *n* нача́ло.

commend *vt* хвали́ть *impf*, по~ *pf*; (*recommend*) рекомендова́ть *impf* & *pf*. **commendable** *adj* похва́льный. **commendation** *n* похвала́.

commensurate *adj* соразме́рный.

comment *n* замеча́ние; *vi* де́лать *impf*, с~ *pf* замеча́ния; **~ on** комменти́ровать *impf* & *pf*, про~ *pf*. **commentary** *n* коммента́рий. **commentator** *n* коммента́тор.

commerce *n* комме́рция. **commercial** *adj* торго́вый; *n* рекла́ма.

commiserate *vi*: **~ with** соболе́зновать *impf* +*dat*. **commiseration** *n* соболе́знование.

commission *n* (*order for work*) зака́з; (*agent's fee*) комиссио́нные *sb*; (*of inquiry etc.*) коми́ссия; (*mil*) офице́рское зва́ние; *vt* зака́зывать *impf*, заказа́ть *pf*. **commissionaire** *n* швейца́р. **commissioner** *n* комисса́р.

commit *vt* соверша́ть *impf*, соверши́ть *pf*; **~ o.s.** обя́зываться *impf*, обяза́ться *pf*. **commitment** *n* обяза́тельство.

committee *n* комите́т.

commodity *n* това́р.

commodore *n* (*officer*) коммодо́р.

common *adj* о́бщий; (*ordinary*) просто́й; *n* общи́нная земля́; **~ sense** здра́вый смысл. **commonly** *adv* обы́чно. **commonplace** *adj* бана́льный. **commonwealth** *n* содру́жество.

commotion *n* сумато́ха.

communal *adj* общи́нный, коммуна́льный. **commune** *n* комму́на; *vi* обща́ться *impf*.

communicate *vt* передава́ть *impf*, переда́ть *pf*; сообща́ть *impf*, сообщи́ть *pf*. **communication** *n* сообще́ние; связь. **communicative** *adj* разгово́рчивый.

communion *n* (*eccl*) прича́стие.

communiqué *n* коммюнике́ *neut indecl*.

Communism *n* коммуни́зм. **Communist** *n* коммуни́ст, **~ка**; *adj* коммунисти́ческий.

community *n* общи́на.

commute *vi* заменя́ть *impf*, замени́ть *pf*; (*travel*) добира́ться *impf*, добра́ться *pf* тра́нспортом. **commuter** *n* регуля́рный пассажи́р.

compact[1] *n* (*agreement*) соглаше́ние.

compact[2] *adj* компа́ктный; **~ disc** компа́кт-ди́ск; *n* пу́дреница.

companion *n* това́рищ; (*handbook*) спра́вочник. **companionable** *adj* общи́тельный. **companionship** *n* дру́жеское обще́ние. **company** *n* о́бщество, (*also firm*) компа́ния; (*theat*) тру́ппа; (*mil*) ро́та.

comparable *adj* сравни́мый. **comparative** *adj* сравни́тельный; *n* сравни́тельная сте́пень. **compare** *vt* & *i* сра́внивать(ся) *impf*, сравни́ть(ся) *pf* (**to, with** с+*instr*). **comparison** *n* сравне́ние.

compartment *n* отделе́ние; (*rly*) купе́ *neut indecl*.

compass *n* ко́мпас; *pl* ци́ркуль *m*.

compassion *n* сострада́ние. **compassionate** *adj* сострада́тельный.

compatibility *n* совмести́мость. **compatible** *adj* совмести́мый.

compatriot *n* соотéчественник, -ица.

compel *vt* заставля́ть *impf*, заста́-
вить *pf*.

compensate *vt* компенси́ровать
impf & *pf* (for за+*acc*). **compensation** *n* компенса́ция.

compete *vi* конкури́ровать *impf*;
соревнова́ться *impf*.

competence *n* компете́нтность. **competent** *adj* компете́нтный.

competition *n* (*contest*) соревно-
ва́ние, состяза́ние; (*rivalry*) конку-
ре́нция. **competitive** *adj* (*comm*)
конкурентоспосо́бный. **competitor**
n конкуре́нт, ~ка.

compilation *n* (*result*) компиля́ция;
(*act*) составле́ние. **compile** *vt* соста-
вля́ть *impf*, соста́вить *pf*. **compiler**
n состави́тель *m*, ~ница.

complacency *n* самодово́льство.
complacent *adj* самодово́льный.

complain *vi* жа́ловаться *impf*, по-
pf. **complaint** *n* жа́лоба.

complement *n* дополне́ние; (*full
number*) (ли́чный) соста́в; *vt* допол-
ня́ть *impf*, допо́лнить *pf*. **comple-
mentary** *adj* дополни́тельный.

complete *vt* заверша́ть *impf*, за-
верши́ть *pf*; *adj* (*entire, thorough*)
по́лный; (*finished*) зако́нченный.
completion *n* заверше́ние.

complex *adj* сло́жный; *n* ко́мплекс.
complexity *n* сло́жность.

complexion *n* цвет лица́.

compliance *n* усту́пчивость. **compliant** *adj* усту́пчивый.

complicate *vt* осложня́ть *impf*, осло-
жни́ть *pf*. **complicated** *adj* сло́ж-
ный. **complication** *n* осложне́ние.

complicity *n* соуча́стие.

compliment *n* комплиме́нт; *pl* при-
ве́т; *vt* говори́ть *impf*, сказа́ть ком-
пли-ме́нт(ы) +*dat*; хвали́ть *impf*, по~ *pf*.
complimentary *adj* ле́стный; (*free*)
беспла́тный.

comply *vi*: ~ **with** (*fulfil*) исполня́ть
impf, испо́лнить *pf*; (*submit to*)
подчиня́ться *impf*, подчини́ться *pf*
+*dat*.

component *n* дета́ль; *adj* составно́й.

compose *vt* (*music etc.*) сочиня́ть
impf, сочини́ть *pf*; (*draft; constitute*)
составля́ть *impf*, соста́вить *pf*.
composed *adj* споко́йный; **be** ~ **of**
состоя́ть *impf* из+*gen*. **composer** *n*
компози́тор. **composition** *n* сочи-

не́ние; (*make-up*) соста́в.

compost *n* компо́ст.

composure *n* самооблада́ние.

compound[1] *n* (*chem*) соедине́ние;
adj сло́жный.

compound[2] *n* (*enclosure*) огоро́жен-
ное ме́сто.

comprehend *vt* понима́ть *impf*, по-
ня́ть *pf*. **comprehensible** *adj* поня́т-
ный. **comprehension** *n* понима́ние.
comprehensive *adj* всеобъе́млю-
щий; ~ **school** общеобразова́тель-
ная шко́ла.

compress *vt* сжима́ть *impf*, сжать
pf. **compressed** *adj* сжа́тый. **compression** *n* сжа́тие. **compressor** *n*
компре́ссор.

comprise *vt* состоя́ть *impf* из+*gen*.

compromise *n* компроми́сс; *vt* ком-
проме-ти́ровать *impf*, с~ *pf*; *vi* идти́
impf, пойти́ *pf* на компроми́сс.

compulsion *n* принужде́ние. **compulsory** *adj* обяза́тельный.

compunction *n* угрызе́ние со́вести.

computer *n* компью́тер.

comrade *n* това́рищ. **comradeship**
n това́рищество.

con[1] *see* **pro**[1]

con[2] *vt* надува́ть *impf*, наду́ть *pf*.

concave *adj* во́гнутый.

conceal *vt* скрыва́ть *impf*, скрыть *pf*.

concede *vt* уступа́ть *impf*, уступи́ть
pf; (*admit*) признава́ть *impf*, при-
зна́ть *pf*; (*goal*) пропуска́ть *impf*,
пропусти́ть *pf*.

conceit *n* самомне́ние. **conceited**
adj самовлюблённый.

conceivable *adj* мы́слимый. **conceive** *vt* (*plan, imagine*) заду́мывать
impf, заду́мать *pf*; (*biol*) зачина́ть
impf зача́ть *pf*; *vi* зача́ть (*also chem*)
концепти́ровать *impf*, с~ *pf*. **concentration** *n* сосредото́ченность,
концентра́ция.

concentrate *vt* & *i* сосредото́чи-
вать(ся) *impf*, сосредото́чить(ся) *pf*
(**on** на+*prep*); *vt* (*also chem*)
концентри́ровать *impf*, с~ *pf*. **concentration** *n* сосредото́ченность,
концентра́ция.

concept *n* поня́тие. **conception** *n*
поня́тие; (*biol*) зача́тие.

concern *n* (*worry*) забо́та; (*comm*)
предприя́тие; *vt* каса́ться *impf* +*gen*;
~ **o.s. with** занима́ться *impf*, за-
ня́ться *pf* +*instr*. **concerned** *adj*
озабо́ченный; **as far as I'm** ~ что
каса́ется меня́. **concerning** *prep*

относи́тельно+*gen*.

concert *n* конце́рт. **concerted** *adj* согласо́ванный.

concertina *n* гармо́ника.

concession *n* усту́пка; (*econ*) конце́ссия. **concessionary** *adj* концессио́нный.

conciliation *n* примире́ние. **conciliatory** *adj* примири́тельный.

concise *adj* кра́ткий. **conciseness** *n* сжа́тость, кра́ткость.

conclude *vt* заключа́ть *impf*, заключи́ть *pf*. **concluding** *adj* заключи́тельный. **conclusion** *n* заключе́ние; (*deduction*) вы́вод. **conclusive** *adj* реша́ющий.

concoct *vt* стря́пать *impf*, со~ *pf*. **concoction** *n* стряпня́.

concourse *n* зал.

concrete *n* бето́н; *adj* бето́нный; (*fig*) конкре́тный.

concur *vi* соглаша́ться *impf*, согласи́ться *pf*. **concurrent** *adj* одновреме́нный.

concussion *n* сотрясе́ние.

condemn *vt* осужда́ть *impf*, осуди́ть *pf*; (*as unfit for use*) бракова́ть *impf*, за~ *pf*. **condemnation** *n* осужде́ние.

condensation *n* конденса́ция. **condense** *vt* (*liquid etc.*) конденси́ровать *impf* & *pf*; (*text etc.*) сокраща́ть *impf*, сократи́ть *pf*. **condensed** *adj* сжа́тый; (*milk*) сгущённый. **condenser** *n* конденса́тор.

condescend *vi* снисходи́ть *impf*, снизойти́ *pf*. **condescending** *adj* снисходи́тельный. **condescension** *n* снисхожде́ние.

condiment *n* припра́ва.

condition *n* усло́вие; (*state*) состоя́ние; *vt* (*determine*) обусло́вливать *impf*, обусло́вить *pf*; (*psych*) приуча́ть *impf*, приучи́ть *pf*. **conditional** *adj* усло́вный.

condolence *n*: *pl* соболе́знование.

condom *n* презервати́в.

condone *vt* закрыва́ть *impf*, закры́ть *pf* глаза́ на+*acc*.

conducive *adj* спосо́бствующий (**to** +*dat*).

conduct *n* (*behaviour*) поведе́ние; *vt* вести́ *impf*, по~, про~ *pf*; (*mus*) дирижи́ровать *impf* +*instr*; (*phys*) проводи́ть *impf*. **conduction** *n* про-

води́мость. **conductor** *n* (*bus*) конду́ктор; (*phys*) проводни́к; (*mus*) дирижёр.

conduit *n* трубопрово́д.

cone *n* ко́нус; (*bot*) ши́шка.

confectioner *n* конди́тер; ~'s (*shop*) конди́терская *sb*. **confectionery** *n* конди́терские изде́лия *neut pl*.

confederation *n* конфедера́ция.

confer *vt* присужда́ть *impf*, присуди́ть (**on** +*dat*) *pf*; *vi* совеща́ться *impf*. **conference** *n* совеща́ние; конфере́нция.

confess *vt* & *i* (*acknowledge*) признава́ть(ся) *impf*, призна́ть(ся) *pf* (**to** в+*prep*); (*eccl*) испове́довать(ся) *impf* & *pf*. **confession** *n* призна́ние; и́споведь. **confessor** *n* духовни́к.

confidant(e) *n* бли́жняя собесе́дник.

confide *vt* доверя́ть *impf*, дове́рить *pf*; ~ **in** дели́ться *impf*, по~ *pf* c+*instr*. **confidence** *n* (*trust*) дове́рие; (*certainty*) уве́ренность; (*self-*~) самоуве́ренность. **confident** *adj* уве́ренный. **confidential** *adj* секре́тный.

confine *vt* ограни́чивать *impf*, ограни́чить *pf*; (*shut in*) заключа́ть *impf*, заключи́ть *pf*. **confinement** *n* заключе́ние. **confines** *n pl* преде́лы *m pl*.

confirm *vt* подтвержда́ть *impf*, подтверди́ть *pf*. **confirmation** *n* подтвержде́ние; (*eccl*) конфирма́ция. **confirmed** *adj* закоренѐлый.

confiscate *vt* конфискова́ть *impf* & *pf*. **confiscation** *n* конфиска́ция.

conflict *n* конфли́кт; противоре́чие; *vi*: ~ **with** противоре́чить *impf* +*dat*. **conflicting** *adj* противоречи́вый.

conform *vi*: ~ **to** подчиня́ться *impf*, подчини́ться *pf* +*dat*. **conformity** *n* соотве́тствие; (*compliance*) подчине́ние.

confound *vt* сбива́ть *impf*, сбить *pf* с то́лку. **confounded** *adj* прокля́тый.

confront *vt* стоя́ть *impf* лицо́м к лицу́ c+*instr*; (*person*) with ста́вить *impf*, по~ *pf* лицо́м к лицу́ c+*instr*. **confrontation** *n* конфронта́ция.

confuse *vt* смуща́ть *impf*, смути́ть *pf*; (*also mix up*) пу́тать *impf*, за~, c~ *pf*. **confusion** *n* смуще́ние;

пу́таница.

congeal vt густе́ть impf, за~ pf; (blood) свёртываться impf, свернуться pf.

congenial adj прия́тный.

congenital adj врождённый.

congested adj перепо́лненный. **congestion** n (traffic) зато́р.

congratulate vt поздравля́ть impf, поздра́вить pf (on c+instr). **congratulation** n поздравле́ние; ~s! поздравля́ю!

congregate vi собира́ться impf, собра́ться pf. **congregation** n (eccl) прихожа́не (-н) pl.

congress n съезд. **Congressman** n конгрессме́н.

conic(al) adj кони́ческий.

conifer n хво́йное де́рево. **coniferous** adj хво́йный.

conjecture n дога́дка; vt гада́ть impf.

conjugal adj супру́жеский.

conjugate vt спряга́ть impf, про~ pf. **conjugation** n спряже́ние.

conjunction n (gram) сою́з; in ~ with совме́стно c+instr.

conjure vi: ~ up (in mind) вызыва́ть impf, вы́звать pf в воображе́нии. **conjurer** n фо́кусник. **conjuring trick** n фо́кус.

connect vt & i свя́зывать(ся) impf, связа́ть(ся) pf; соединя́ть(ся) impf, соедини́ть(ся) pf. **connected** adj свя́занный. **connection, -exion** n связь; (rly etc.) переса́дка.

connivance n попусти́тельство. **connive** vi: ~ at попусти́тельствовать impf+dat.

connoisseur n знато́к.

conquer vt (country) завоёвывать impf, завоева́ть pf; (enemy) побежда́ть impf, победи́ть pf; (habit) преодолева́ть impf, преодоле́ть pf. **conqueror** n завоева́тель m. **conquest** n завоева́ние.

conscience n со́весть. **conscientious** adj добросо́вестный. **conscious** adj созна́тельный; predic в созна́нии; be ~ of сознава́ть impf +acc. **consciousness** n созна́ние.

conscript vt призыва́ть impf, призва́ть pf на вое́нную слу́жбу; n призывни́к. **conscription** n во́инская пови́нность.

consecrate vt освяща́ть impf, освя-

ти́ть pf. **consecration** n освяще́ние.

consecutive adj после́довательный.

consensus n согла́сие.

consent vi соглаша́ться impf, согласи́ться pf (to +inf, на+acc); n согла́сие.

consequence n после́дствие; of great ~ большо́го значе́ния; of some ~ дово́льно ва́жный. **consequent** adj вытека́ющий. **consequential** adj ва́жный. **consequently** adv сле́довательно.

conservation n сохране́ние; (of nature) охра́на приро́ды. **conservative** adj консервати́вный; n консерва́тор. **conservatory** n оранжере́я. **conserve** vt сохраня́ть impf, сохрани́ть pf.

consider vt (think over) обду́мывать impf, обду́мать pf; (examine) рассма́тривать impf, рассмотре́ть pf; (regard as, be of opinion that) счита́ть impf, счесть pf +instr, за+acc, что; (take into account) счита́ться impf c+instr. **considerable** adj значи́тельный. **considerate** adj внима́тельный. **consideration** n рассмотре́ние; внима́ние; (factor) фа́ктор; take into ~ принима́ть impf, приня́ть pf во внима́ние. **considering** prep принима́я +acc во внима́ние.

consign vt передава́ть impf, переда́ть pf. **consignment** n (goods) па́ртия; (consigning) отпра́вка това́ров.

consist vi: ~ of состоя́ть impf из +gen. **consistency** n после́довательность; (density) консисте́нция. **consistent** adj после́довательный; ~ with совмести́мый c+instr.

consolation n утеше́ние. **console**[1] vt утеша́ть impf, уте́шить pf.

console[2] n (control panel) пульт управле́ния.

consolidate vt укрепля́ть impf, укрепи́ть pf. **consolidation** n укрепле́ние.

consonant n согла́сный sb.

consort n супру́г, -а.

conspicuous adj заме́тный.

conspiracy n за́говор. **conspirator** n заговорщик, -ица. **conspiratorial** adj заговорщицкий. **conspire** vi устра́ивать impf, устро́ить pf за́говор.

constable *n* полицейский *sb*.

constancy *n* постоянство. **constant** *adj* постоянный. **constantly** *adv* постоянно.

constellation *n* созвездие.

consternation *n* тревога.

constipation *n* запор.

constituency *n* избирательный округ. **constituent** *n* (*component*) составная часть; (*voter*) избиратель *m*; *adj* составной. **constitute** *vt* составлять *impf*, составить *pf*. **constitution** *n* (*polit, med*) конституция; (*composition*) составление. **constitutional** *adj* (*polit*) конституцио́нный.

constrain *vt* принуждать *impf*, принудить *pf*. **constrained** *adj* (*inhibited*) стеснённый. **constraint** *n* принуждение; (*inhibition*) стеснение.

constrict *vt* (*compress*) сжимать *impf*, сжать *pf*; (*narrow*) суживать *impf*, сузить *pf*. **constriction** *n* сжатие; сужение.

construct *vt* строить *impf*, по~ *pf*. **construction** *n* строительство; (*also gram*) конструкция; (*interpretation*) истолкование; ~ **site** стройка. **constructive** *adj* конструктивный.

construe *vt* истолковывать *impf*, истолковать *pf*.

consul *n* консул. **consulate** *n* консульство.

consult *vt* советоваться *impf*, по~ *pf* c+*instr*. **consultant** *n* консультант. **consultation** *n* консультация.

consume *vt* потреблять *impf*, потребить *pf*; (*eat or drink*) съедать *impf*, съесть *pf*. **consumer** *n* потребитель *m*; ~ **goods** товары *m pl* широкого потребления.

consummate *vt* завершать *impf*, завершить *pf*; ~ **a marriage** осуществлять *impf*, осуществить *pf* брачные отношения. **consummation** *n* завершение; (*of marriage*) осуществление.

consumption *n* потребление.

contact *n* контакт; (*person*) связь; ~ **lens** контактная линза; *vt* связываться *impf*, связаться *pf* c+*instr*.

contagious *adj* заразный.

contain *vt* содержать *impf*; (*restrain*) сдерживать *impf*, сдержать *pf*. **con-**

tainer *n* (*vessel*) сосуд; (*transport*) контейнер.

contaminate *vt* загрязнять *impf*, загрязнить *pf*. **contamination** *n* загрязнение.

contemplate *vt* (*gaze*) созерцать *impf*; размышлять *impf*; (*consider*) предполагать *impf*, предположить *pf*. **contemplation** *n* созерцание; размышление. **contemplative** *adj* созерцательный.

contemporary *n* современник; *adj* современный.

contempt *n* презрение; ~ **of court** неуважение к суду; **hold in** ~ презирать *impf*. **contemptible** *adj* презренный. **contemptuous** *adj* презрительный.

contend *vi* (*compete*) состязаться *impf*; ~ **for** оспаривать *impf*; ~ **with** справляться *impf*, справиться *pf* c+*instr*; *vt* утверждать *impf*. **contender** *n* претендент.

content[1] *n* содержание; *pl* содержимое *sb*; (*table of*) ~**s** содержание.

content[2] *predic* доволен (-льна); *vt*: ~ **o.s. with** довольствоваться *impf*, у~ *pf* +*instr*. **contented** *adj* довольный.

contention *n* (*claim*) утверждение. **contentious** *adj* спорный.

contest *n* состязание; *vt* (*dispute*) оспаривать *impf*, оспорить *pf*. **contestant** *n* участник, -ица, состязания.

context *n* контекст.

continent *n* материк. **continental** *adj* материковый.

contingency *n* возможный случай; ~ **plan** вариант плана. **contingent** *adj* случайный; *n* контингент.

continual *adj* непрестанный. **continuation** *n* продолжение. **continue** *vt & i* продолжать(ся) *impf*, продолжить(ся) *pf*. **continuous** *adj* непрерывный.

contort *vt* искажать *impf*, исказить *pf*. **contortion** *n* искажение.

contour *n* контур; ~ **line** горизонталь.

contraband *n* контрабанда.

contraception *n* предупреждение зачатия. **contraceptive** *n* противозачаточное средство; *adj* противозачаточный.

contract n контра́кт, догово́р; vi (make a ~) заключа́ть impf, заключи́ть pf контра́кт; vt & i (shorten, reduce) сокраща́ть(ся) impf, сократи́ть(ся) pf; vt (illness) заболева́ть impf, заболе́ть pf +instr. **contraction** n сокраще́ние; pl (med) схва́тки f pl. **contractor** n подря́дчик.

contradict vt противоре́чить impf +dat. **contradiction** n противоре́чие. **contradictory** adj противоречи́вый.

contraflow n встре́чное движе́ние.

contralto n контра́льто (voice) neut & (person) f indecl.

contraption n приспособле́ние.

contrary adj (opposite) противополо́жный; (perverse) капри́зный; ~ to вопреки́+dat; n: on the ~ наоборо́т.

contrast n контра́ст, противоположность; vt противопоставля́ть impf, противопоста́вить pf (with +dat); vi контрасти́ровать impf.

contravene vt наруша́ть impf, нару́шить pf. **contravention** n наруше́ние.

contribute vt (to fund etc.) же́ртвовать impf, по~ pf (to в+acc); ~ to (further) соде́йствовать impf & pf, по~ pf +dat; (write for) сотру́дничать impf в+prep. **contribution** n (money) поже́ртвование; (fig) вклад. **contributor** n (donor) же́ртвователь m; (writer) сотру́дник.

contrite adj ка́ющийся.

contrivance n приспособле́ние. **contrive** vt ухитря́ться impf, ухитри́ться pf +inf.

control n (mastery) контро́ль m; (operation) управле́ние; pl управле́ния pl; vt (dominate, verify) контроли́ровать impf, про~ pf; (regulate) управля́ть impf +instr; ~ o.s. сде́рживаться impf, сдержа́ться pf.

controversial adj спо́рный. **controversy** n спор.

convalesce vi выздора́вливать impf. **convalescence** n выздоровле́ние.

convection n конве́кция. **convector** n конве́ктор.

convene vt созыва́ть impf, созва́ть pf.

convenience n удо́бство; (public ~)

убо́рная sb. **convenient** adj удо́бный.

convent n же́нский монасты́рь m.

convention n (assembly) съезд; (agreement) конве́нция; (custom) обы́чай; (conventionality) усло́вность. **conventional** adj общепри́нятый; (also mil) обы́чный.

converge vi сходи́ться impf, сойти́сь pf. **convergence** n сходи́мость.

conversant predic: ~ with знако́м c+instr.

conversation n разгово́р. **conversational** adj разгово́рный. **converse¹** vi разгова́ривать impf.

converse² n обра́тное sb. **conversely** adv наоборо́т. **conversion** n (change) превраще́ние; (of faith) обраще́ние; (of building) перестро́йка. **convert** vt (change) превраща́ть impf, преврати́ть pf (into в+acc); (to faith) обраща́ть impf, обрати́ть pf (to в+acc); (a building) перестра́ивать impf, перестро́ить pf. **convertible** adj обрати́мый; n автомоби́ль m со снима́ющейся кры́шей.

convex adj вы́пуклый.

convey vt (transport) перевози́ть impf, перевезти́ pf; (communicate) передава́ть impf, переда́ть pf. **conveyance** n перево́зка; переда́ча. **conveyancing** n нотариа́льная переда́ча. **conveyor belt** n транспортёрная ле́нта.

convict n осуждённый sb; vt осужда́ть impf, осуди́ть pf. **conviction** n (law) осужде́ние; (belief) убежде́ние. **convince** vt убежда́ть impf, убеди́ть pf. **convincing** adj убеди́тельный.

convivial adj весёлый.

convoluted adj изви́листый; (fig) запу́танный.

convoy n конво́й.

convulse vt: be ~d with содрога́ться impf, содрогну́ться pf от+gen. **convulsion** n (med) конву́льсия.

cook n куха́рка, по́вар; vt гото́вить impf; vi вари́ться impf; c~ pf. **cooker** n плита́, печь. **cookery** n кулина́рия.

cool adj прохла́дный; (calm) хладнокро́вный; (unfriendly) холо́дный; vt охлажда́ть impf, охлади́ть pf; ~

down, off остыва́ть *impf*, осты́-(ну)ть *pf*. **coolness** *n* прохла́да; (*calm*) хладнокро́вие; (*manner*) хо́лод*ók*.

coop *n* куря́тник; *vt*: ~ **up** держа́ть *impf* взаперти́.

cooperate *vi* сотру́дничать *impf*. **co-operation** *n* сотру́дничество. **co-operative** *n* кооперати́в; *adj* кооперати́вный; (*helpful*) услу́жливый.

co-opt *vt* коопти́ровать *impf* & *pf*.

coordinate *vt* координи́ровать *impf* & *pf*; *n* координа́та. **coordination** *n* координа́ция.

cope *vi*: ~ **with** справля́ться *impf*, спра́виться *pf* c+*instr*.

copious *adj* оби́льный.

copper *n* (*metal*) медь; *adj* ме́дный.

coppice, copse *n* ро́щица.

copulate *vi* совокупля́ться *impf*, совокупи́ться *pf*.

copy *n* ко́пия; (*book*) экземпля́р; *vt* (*reproduce*) копи́ровать *impf*, c~ *pf*; (*transcribe*) перепи́сывать *impf*, переписа́ть *pf*; (*imitate*) подража́ть *impf* +*dat*. **copyright** *n* а́вторское пра́во.

coral *n* кора́лл.

cord *n* (*string*) верёвка; (*electr*) шнур.

cordial *adj* серде́чный.

corduroy *n* ру́бчатый вельве́т.

core *n* сердцеви́на; (*fig*) суть.

cork *n* (*material; stopper*) про́бка; (*float*) поплаво́к. **corkscrew** *n* што́пор.

corn[1] *n* зерно́; (*wheat*) пшени́ца; (*maize*) кукуру́за. **cornflakes** *n pl* кукуру́зные хло́пья (-пьев) *pl*. **cornflour** *n* кукуру́зная мука́. **corny** *adj* (*coll*) бана́льный.

corn[2] *n* (*med*) мозо́ль.

cornea *n* рогова́я оболо́чка.

corner *n* у́гол; ~**stone** *n* краеуго́льный ка́мень *m*; *vt* загоня́ть *impf*, загна́ть *pf* в у́гол.

cornet *n* (*mus*) корне́т; (*ice-cream*) рожо́к.

cornice *n* карни́з.

coronary (thrombosis) *n* коронаро-тромбо́з. **coronation** *n* корона́ция.

coroner *n* ме́дик суде́бной эксперти́зы.

corporal[1] *n* капра́л.

corporal[2] *adj* теле́сный; ~ **punishment** теле́сное наказа́ние.

corporate *adj* корпорати́вный. **corporation** *n* корпора́ция.

corps *n* ко́рпус.

corpse *n* труп.

corpulent *adj* ту́чный.

corpuscle *n* кровяно́й ша́рик.

correct *adj* пра́вильный; (*conduct*) корре́ктный; *vt* исправля́ть *impf*, испра́вить *pf*. **correction** *n* исправле́ние.

correlation *n* соотноше́ние.

correspond *vi* соотве́тствовать *impf* (**to, with** +*dat*); (*by letter*) перепи́сываться *impf*. **correspondence** *n* соотве́тствие; (*letters*) корреспонде́нция. **correspondent** *n* корреспонде́нт. **corresponding** *adj* соотве́тствующий (**to** +*dat*).

corridor *n* коридо́р.

corroborate *vt* подтвержда́ть *impf*, подтверди́ть *pf*.

corrode *vt* разъеда́ть *impf*, разъе́сть *pf*. **corrosion** *n* корро́зия. **corrosive** *adj* е́дкий.

corrugated iron *n* рифлёное желе́зо.

corrupt *adj* (*person*) развращённый; (*government*) прода́жный; *vt* развраща́ть *impf*, разврати́ть *pf*. **corruption** *n* развраще́ние; корру́пция.

corset *n* корсе́т.

cortège *n* корте́ж.

cortex *n* кора́.

corundum *n* кору́нд.

cosmetic *adj* космети́ческий. **cosmetics** *n pl* косме́тика.

cosmic *adj* косми́ческий. **cosmonaut** *n* космона́вт.

cosmopolitan *adj* космополити́ческий.

cosmos *n* ко́смос.

Cossack *n* каза́к, -ачка.

cosset *vt* не́жить *impf*.

cost *n* сто́имость, цена́; *vt* сто́ить *impf*.

costly *adj* дорого́й.

costume *n* костю́м.

cosy *adj* ую́тный.

cot *n* де́тская крова́тка.

cottage *n* котте́дж; ~ **cheese** творо́г.

cotton *n* хло́пок; (*cloth*) хлопчатобума́жная ткань; (*thread*) ни́тка; ~ **wool** ва́та; *adj* хло́пковый; хлопчатобума́жный.

couch *n* дива́н.

couchette n спа́льное ме́сто.

cough n ка́шель m; vi ка́шлять impf.

council n сове́т; ~ **tax** ме́стный нало́г; ~ **house** жильё из обще́ственного фо́нда. **councillor** n член сове́та.

counsel n (advice) сове́т; (lawyer) адвока́т; vt сове́товать impf, по~ pf +dat.

count[1] vt счита́ть impf, со~, счесть pf; ~ **on** рассчи́тывать impf на+acc; n счёт. **countdown** n отсчёт вре́мени.

count[2] n (title) граф.

countenance n лицо́; vt одобря́ть impf, одо́брить pf.

counter n прила́вок; (token) фи́шка; adv: **run** ~ **to** идти́ impf вразре́з c+instr; vt пари́ровать impf, от~ pf. **counteract** vt противоде́йствовать impf +dat. **counterbalance** n противове́с; vt уравнове́шивать impf, уравнове́сить pf. **counterfeit** adj подде́льный. **counterpart** n соотве́тственная часть. **counterpoint** n контрапу́нкт. **counter-revolutionary** n контрреволюционе́р; adj контрреволюцио́нный. **countersign** vt ста́вить impf, по~ pf втору́ю по́дпись на+prep.

countess n графи́ня.

countless adj бесчи́сленный.

country n (nation) страна́; (native land) ро́дина; (rural areas) дере́вня; adj дереве́нский, се́льский. **countryman** n (compatriot) соотéчественник; се́льский жи́тель m. **countryside** n приро́дный ландша́фт.

county n гра́фство.

coup n (polit) переворо́т.

couple n па́ра; (a few) не́сколько +gen; vt сцепля́ть impf, сцепи́ть pf.

coupon n купо́н; тало́н; ва́учер.

courage n хра́брость. **courageous** adj хра́брый.

courier n (messenger) курье́р; (guide) гид.

course n курс; (process) ход, тече́ние; (of meal) блю́до; **of** ~ коне́чно.

court n двор; (sport) корт, площа́дка; (law) суд; ~ **martial** вое́нный суд; vt уха́живать impf за+instr.

courteous adj ве́жливый. **courtesy** n ве́жливость. **courtier** n придво́рный sb. **courtyard** n двор.

cousin n двою́родный брат, -ная сестра́.

cove n бу́хточка.

covenant n догово́р.

cover n (covering; lid) покры́шка; (shelter) укры́тие; (chair ~; soft case) чехо́л; (bed) покрыва́ло; (book) переплёт, обло́жка; **under separate** ~ в отде́льном конве́рте; vt покрыва́ть impf, покры́ть pf; (hide, protect) закрыва́ть impf, закры́ть pf. **coverage** n освеще́ние. **covert** adj скры́тый.

covet vt пожела́ть pf +gen.

cow[1] n коро́ва. **cowboy** n ковбо́й. **cowshed** n хлев.

cow[2] vt запу́гивать impf, запуга́ть pf.

coward n трус. **cowardice** n тру́сость. **cowardly** adj трусли́вый.

cower vi съёживаться impf, съёжиться pf.

cox(swain) n рулево́й m.

coy adj жема́нно стыдли́вый.

crab n краб.

crack n (in cup, ice) тре́щина; (in wall) щель; (noise) треск; adj первокла́ссный; vt (break) коло́ть impf, рас~ pf; (china) щёлкать impf, с~ pf тре́щину в+acc; vi тре́снуть pf. **crackle** vi потре́скивать impf.

cradle n колыбе́ль.

craft n (trade) ремесло́; (boat) су́дно. **craftiness** n хи́трость. **craftsman** n реме́сленник. **crafty** adj хи́трый.

crag n утёс. **craggy** adj скали́стый.

cram vt (fill) набива́ть impf, наби́ть pf; (stuff in) впи́хивать impf, впихну́ть pf; vi (study) зубри́ть impf.

cramp[1] n (med) су́дорога.

cramp[2] vt стесня́ть impf, стесни́ть pf. **cramped** adj те́сный.

cranberry n клю́ква.

crane n (bird) жура́вль m; (machine) кран; vt (one's neck) вытя́гивать impf, вы́тянуть pf (ше́ю).

crank[1] n заводна́я ру́чка; ~-**shaft** коле́нчатый вал; vt заводи́ть impf, завести́ pf.

crank[2] n (eccentric) чуда́к. **cranky** adj чуда́ческий.

cranny n щель.

crash n (noise) гро́хот, треск; (accident) ава́рия; (financial) крах; ~ **course** ускоренный курс; ~ **helmet**

защи́тный шлем; ~ **landing** авари́йная поса́дка; *vi* (~ *into*) вреза́ться *impf*, вре́заться *pf* в+*acc*; (*aeron*) разбива́ться *impf*, разби́ться *pf*; (*fall with* ~) гро́хнуться *pf*; *vt* (*bang down*) гро́хнуть *pf*.

crass *adj* гру́бый.

crate *n* я́щик.

crater *n* кра́тер.

crave *vi*: ~ **for** жа́ждать *impf* +*gen*. **craving** *n* стра́стное жела́ние.

crawl *vi* по́лзать *indet*, ползти́ *det*; ~ **with** кише́ть+*instr*; *n* (*sport*) кроль *m*.

crayon *n* цветно́й каранда́ш.

craze *n* ма́ния. **crazy** *adj* поме́шанный (*about* на+*prep*).

creak *n* скрип; *vi* скрипе́ть *impf*.

cream *n* сли́вки (-вок) *pl*; (*cosmetic*; *cul*) крем; ~ **cheese** сли́вочный сыр; **soured** ~ смета́на; *vt* сбива́ть *impf*, сбить *pf*; *adj* (*of cream*) сли́вочный; (*colour*) кре́мовый. **creamy** *adj* сли́вочный, кре́мовый.

crease *n* скла́дка; *vt* мять *impf*, из~, с~ *pf*. **creased** *adj* мя́тый.

create *vt* создава́ть *impf*, созда́ть *pf*. **creation** *n* созда́ние. **creative** *adj* тво́рческий. **creator** *n* созда́тель *m*. **creature** *n* созда́ние.

crèche *n* (де́тские) я́сли (-лей) *pl*.

credence *n* ве́ра; **give** ~ ве́рить *impf* (**to** +*dat*). **credentials** *n* pl удостовере́ние; (*diplomacy*) вери́тельные гра́моты *f pl*. **credibility** *n* правдоподо́бие; (*of person*) спосо́бность вызыва́ть дове́рие. **credible** *adj* (*of thing*) правдоподо́бный; (*of person*) заслу́живающий дове́рия.

credit *n* дове́рие; (*comm*) креди́т; (*honour*) честь; **give** ~ кредитова́ть *impf* & *pf* +*acc*; отдава́ть *impf*, отда́ть *pf* до́лжное+*dat*; ~ **card** креди́тная ка́рточка; *vt*: ~ **with** припи́сывать *impf*, приписа́ть *pf* +*dat*. **creditable** *adj* похва́льный. **creditor** *n* кредито́р.

credulity *n* легкове́рие. **credulous** *adj* легкове́рный.

creed *n* убежде́ния *neut pl*; (*eccl*) вероисповеда́ние.

creep *vi* по́лзать *indet*, ползти́ *det*. **creeper** *n* (*plant*) ползу́чее расте́ние.

cremate *vt* креми́ровать *impf* & *pf*.

cremation *n* крема́ция. **crematorium** *n* кремато́рий.

crêpe *n* креп.

crescendo *adv*, *adj*, & *n* креще́ндо *indecl*.

crescent *n* полуме́сяц.

crest *n* гре́бень *m*; (*heraldry*) герб.

crevasse, **crevice** *n* расще́лина, рассе́лина.

crew *n* брига́да; (*of ship*, *plane*) экипа́ж.

crib *n* (*bed*) де́тская крова́тка; *vi* спи́сывать *impf*, списа́ть *pf*.

crick *n* растяже́ние мышц.

cricket[1] *n* (*insect*) сверчо́к.

cricket[2] *n* (*sport*) кри́кет; ~ **bat** бита́.

crime *n* преступле́ние.

Crimea *n* Крым. **Crimean** *adj* кры́мский.

criminal *n* престу́пник; *adj* престу́пный; (*of crime*) уголо́вный.

crimson *adj* мали́новый.

cringe *vi* (*cower*) съёживаться *impf*, съёжиться *pf*.

crinkle *n* морщи́на; *vt* & *i* мо́рщить(ся) *impf*, на~, с~ *pf*.

cripple *n* кале́ка *m* & *f*; *vt* кале́чить *impf*, ис~ *pf*; (*fig*) расша́тывать *impf*, расша́тать *pf*.

crisis *n* кри́зис.

crisp *adj* (*brittle*) хрустя́щий; (*fresh*) све́жий. **crisps** *n* pl хрустя́щий карто́фель *m*.

criss-cross *adv* крест-на́крест.

criterion *n* крите́рий.

critic *n* кри́тик. **critical** *adj* крити́ческий. **critically** *adv* (*ill*) тяжело́. **criticism** *n* кри́тика. **criticize** *vt* критикова́ть *impf*. **critique** *n* кри́тика.

croak *vi* ква́кать *impf*, ква́кнуть *pf*; хрипе́ть *impf*.

Croat *n* хорва́т, ~ка. **Croatia** *n* Хорва́тия. **Croatian** *adj* хорва́тский.

crochet *n* вяза́ние крючко́м; *vt* вяза́ть *impf*, с~ *pf* (крючко́м).

crockery *n* посу́да.

crocodile *n* крокоди́л.

crocus *n* кро́кус.

crony *n* закады́чный друг.

crook *n* (*staff*) по́сох; (*swindler*) моше́нник. **crooked** *adj* криво́й; (*dishonest*) нече́стный.

crop *n* (*yield*) урожа́й; *pl* культу́ры

f pl; (bird's) зоб; vt (cut) подстригáть impf, подстрúчь pf; ~ up возникáть impf, вознúкнуть pf.

croquet n крокéт.

cross n крест; (biol) пóмесь; adj (angry) злой; vt пересекáть impf, пересéчь pf; (biol) скрéщивать impf, скрестúть pf; ~ off, out вычёркивать impf, вычеркнуть pf; ~ o.s. креститься impf, пере~ pf; ~ over переходúть impf, перейтú pf (чéрез) +acc. ~bar поперéчина. ~breed пóмесь; ~-country race кросс; ~-examination перекрéстный допрóс; ~-examine, ~-question подвергáть impf, подвéргнуть pf перекрёстному допрóсу; ~-eyed косоглáзый; ~-legged: sit ~ сидéть impf по-турéцки; ~-reference перекрёстная ссылка; ~road(s) перекрёсток; (fig) распýтье; ~-section перекрёстное сечéние; ~wise adv крест-нáкрест; ~word (puzzle) кроссвóрд. crossing n (intersection) перекрёсток; (foot) перехóд; (transport; rly) переéзд.

crotch n (anat) промéжность.

crotchet n (mus) четвертнáя нóта.

crotchety adj раздражúтельный.

crouch vi приседáть impf, присéсть pf.

crow n ворóна; as the ~ flies по прямóй лúнии; vi кукарéкать impf.

crowbar n лом.

crowd n толпá; vi тесниться impf, с~ pf; ~ into втúскиваться impf, втúснуться pf. crowded adj перепóлненный.

crown n корóна; (tooth) корóнка; (head) тéмя; (hat) тулья; vt коронóвать impf & pf.

crucial adj (important) óчень вáжный; (decisive) решáющий; (critical) критúческий.

crucifix, crucifixion n распятие. crucify vt распинáть impf, распять pf.

crude adj (rude) грýбый; (raw) сырóй. crudeness, crudity n грýбость.

cruel adj жестóкий. cruelty n жестóкость.

cruise n круúз; vi крейсúровать impf. cruiser n крéйсер.

crumb n крóшка.

crumble vt крошúть impf, рас~ pf; vi обвáливаться impf, обвалúться pf. crumbly adj рассыпчатый.

crumple vt мять impf, с~ pf; (intentionally) кóмкать impf, с~ pf.

crunch n (fig) решáющий момéнт; vt грызть impf, раз~ pf; vi хрустéть impf, хрýстнуть pf.

crusade n крестóвый похóд; (fig) кампáния. crusader n крестонóсец; (fig) борéц (for за+acc).

crush n дáвка; (infatuation) сúльное увлечéние; vt давúть impf, за~, раз~ pf; (crease) мять impf, с~ pf; (fig) подавлять impf, подавúть pf.

crust n (of earth) корá; (bread etc.) кóрка.

crutch n костыль m.

crux n: ~ of the matter суть дéла.

cry n крик; a far ~ from далекó от+gen; vi (weep) плáкать impf; (shout) кричáть impf.

crypt n склеп. cryptic adj загáдочный.

crystal n кристáлл; (glass) хрустáль m. crystallize vt & i кристаллизовáть(ся) impf & pf.

cub n детёныш; bear ~ медвежóнок; fox ~ лисёнок; lion ~ львёнок; wolf ~ волчóнок.

cube n куб. cubic adj кубúческий.

cubicle n кабúна.

cuckoo n кукýшка.

cucumber n огурéц.

cuddle vt обнимáть impf, обнять pf; vi обнимáться impf, обняться pf; ~ up прижимáться impf, прижáться pf (to к+dat).

cudgel n дубúнка.

cue¹ n (theat) рéплика.

cue² n (billiards) кий.

cuff¹ n манжéта; off the ~ экспрóмтом; ~-link зáпонка.

cuff² vt (hit) шлёпать impf, шлёпнуть pf.

cul-de-sac n тупúк.

culinary adj кулинáрный.

cull vt (select) отбирáть impf, отобрáть pf; (slaughter) убивáть impf.

culminate vi кончáться impf, кóнчиться pf (in +instr). culmination n кульминациóнный пункт.

culpability n винóвность. culpable adj винóвный. culprit n винóвник.

cult n культ.

cultivate vt (land) обрабáтывать impf, обрабóтать pf; (crops) вырáщивать

impf; вы́растить *impf*; (*develop*) развива́ть *impf*, разви́ть *pf*.
cultural *adj* культу́рный. **culture** *n* культу́ра. **cultured** *adj* культу́рный.
cumbersome *adj* громо́здкий.
cumulative *adj* кумуляти́вный.
cunning *n* хи́трость; *adj* хи́трый.
cup *n* ча́шка; (*prize*) ку́бок.
cupboard *n* шкаф.
cupola *n* ку́пол.
curable *adj* излечи́мый.
curative *adj* целе́бный.
curator храни́тель *m*.
curb *vt* обу́здывать *impf*, обузда́ть *pf*.
curd (*cheese*) *n* творо́г. **curdle** *vt & i* свёртывать(ся) *impf*, сверну́ть(ся) *pf*.
cure *n* сре́дство (**for** про́тив+*gen*); *vt* выле́чивать *impf*, вы́лечить *pf*; (*smoke*) копти́ть *impf*, за~ *pf*; (*salt*) соли́ть *impf*, по~ *pf*.
curfew *n* коменда́нтский час.
curiosity *n* любопы́тство. **curious** *adj* любопы́тный.
curl *n* ло́кон; *vt* завива́ть *impf*, зави́ть *pf*; ~ **up** свёртываться *impf*, сверну́ться *pf*. **curly** *adj* кудря́вый.
currants *n pl* (*dried*) изю́м (*collect*)
currency *n* валю́та; (*prevalence*) хожде́ние. **current** *adj* теку́щий; *n* тече́ние; (*air*) струя́; (*water*; *electr*) ток.
curriculum *n* курс обуче́ния; ~ **vitae** автобиогра́фия.
curry[1] *n* кэ́рри *neut indecl.*
curry[2] *vt*: ~ **favour with** заи́скивать *impf* пе́ред+*instr*, у+*gen*.
curse *n* прокля́тие; (*oath*) руга́тельство; *vt* проклина́ть *impf*, прокля́сть *pf*; *vi* руга́ться *impf*, по~ *pf*.
cursory *adj* бе́глый.
curt *adj* ре́зкий.
curtail *vt* сокраща́ть *impf*, сократи́ть *pf*.
curtain *n* занаве́ска.
curts(e)y *n* ревера́нс; *vi* де́лать *impf*, с~ *pf* ревера́нс.
curve *n* изги́б; (*line*) крива́я *sb*; *vi* изгиба́ться *impf*, изогну́ться *pf*.
cushion *n* поду́шка; *vt* смягча́ть *impf*, смягчи́ть *pf*.
custard *n* сла́дкий заварно́й крем.
custodian *n* храни́тель *m*. **custody** *n* опе́ка; (*of police*) аре́ст; **to take**

into ~ аресто́вать *pf*.
custom *n* обы́чай; (*comm*) клиенту́ра; *pl* (*duty*) тамо́женные по́шлины *f pl*; **go through** ~**s** проходи́ть *impf*, пройти́ *pf* тамо́женный осмо́тр; ~**-house** тамо́жня; ~ **officer** тамо́женник. **customary** *adj* обы́чный. **customer** *n* клие́нт; покупа́тель *m*.
cut *vt* ре́зать *impf*, по~ *pf*; (*hair*) стричь *impf*, о~ *pf*; (*mow*) коси́ть *impf*, с~ *pf*; (*price*) снижа́ть *impf*, сни́зить *pf*; (*cards*) снима́ть *impf*, снять *pf* коло́ду; ~ **back** (*prune*) подреза́ть *impf*, подре́зать *pf*; (*reduce*) сокраща́ть *impf*, сократи́ть *pf*; ~ **down** сруба́ть *impf*, сруби́ть *pf*; ~ **off** отреза́ть *impf*, отре́зать *pf*; (*interrupt*) прерыва́ть *impf*, прерва́ть *pf*; (*disconnect*) отключа́ть *impf*, отключи́ть *pf*; ~ **out** выре́зывать *impf*, вы́резать *pf*; ~ **out for** со́зданный для+*gen*; ~ **up** разреза́ть *impf*, разре́зать *pf*; *n* (*gash*) поре́з; (*clothes*) покро́й; (*reduction*) сниже́ние; ~ **glass** хруста́ль *m*.
cute *adj* симпати́чный.
cutlery *n* ножи́, ви́лки и ло́жки *pl*.
cutlet *n* отбивна́я котле́та.
cutting *n* (*press*) вы́резка; (*plant*) черено́к; *adj* ре́зкий.
CV *abbr* (*of* **curriculum vitae**) автобиогра́фия.
cycle *n* цикл; (*bicycle*) велосипе́д; *vi* е́здить *impf* на велосипе́де. **cyclic(al)** *adj* цикли́ческий. **cyclist** *n* велосипеди́ст.
cylinder *n* цили́ндр. **cylindrical** *adj* цилиндри́ческий.
cymbals *n pl* таре́лки *f pl*.
cynic *n* ци́ник. **cynical** *adj* цини́чный. **cynicism** *n* цини́зм.
cypress *n* кипари́с.
Cyrillic *n* кири́ллица.
cyst *n* киста́.
Czech *n* чех, че́шка; *adj* че́шский; ~ **Republic** Че́шская Респу́блика.

D

dab *n* мазо́к; *vt* (*eyes etc.*) прикла́дывать *impf* плато́к к+*dat*; ~ **on** накла́дывать *impf*, наложи́ть *pf* мазка́ми.

dabble vi: ~ **in** поверхностно заниматься impf, заняться pf +instr.

dachshund n такса.

dad, daddy n папа; **~-long-legs** n долгоножка.

daffodil n жёлтый нарцисс.

daft adj глупый.

dagger n кинжал.

dahlia n георгин.

daily adv ежедневно; adj ежедневный; n (charwoman) приходящая уборщица; (newspaper) ежедневная газета.

dainty adj изящный.

dairy n маслобойня; (shop) молочная sb; adj молочный.

dais n помост.

daisy n маргаритка.

dale n долина.

dally vi (dawdle) мешкать impf; (toy) играть impf +instr; (flirt) флиртовать impf pf.

dam n (barrier) плотина; vt запруживать impf, запрудить pf.

damage n повреждение; pl убытки m pl; vt повреждать impf, повредить pf.

damn vt (curse) проклинать impf, проклясть pf; (censure) осуждать impf, осудить pf; int чёрт возьми!; **I don't give a ~** мне наплевать. **damnation** n проклятие. **damned** adj проклятый.

damp n сырость; adj сырой; vt (also dampen) смачивать impf, смочить pf; (fig) охлаждать impf, охладить pf.

dance vi танцевать impf; n танец; (party) танцевальный вечер. **dancer** n танцор, ~ка; (ballet) танцовщик, -ица; балерина.

dandelion n одуванчик.

dandruff n перхоть.

Dane n датчанин, -анка; **Great ~** дог. **Danish** adj датский.

danger n опасность. **dangerous** adj опасный.

dangle vt &i покачивать(ся) impf.

dank adj промозглый.

dapper adj выхоленный.

dare vi (have courage) осмеливаться impf, осмелиться pf; (have impudence) сметь impf, по~ pf; vt вызывать impf, вызвать pf; n вызов. **daredevil** n лихач; adj отчаянный.

daring n отвага; adj отчаянный.

dark adj тёмный; **~ blue** тёмносиний; n темнота. **darken** vt затемнять impf, затемнить pf; vi темнеть impf, по~ pf. **darkly** adv мрачно. **darkness** n темнота.

darling n дорогой sb, милый sb; adj дорогой.

darn vt штопать impf, за~ pf.

dart n стрела; (for game) метательная стрела; (tuck) вытачка; vi броситься pf.

dash n (hyphen) тире neut indecl; (admixture) примесь; vt вышрять impf, швырнуть pf; vi бросаться impf, броситься pf. **dashboard** n приборная доска. **dashing** adj лихой.

data n pl данные sb pl. **database** n база данных.

date[1] n (fruit) финик.

date[2] n число, дата; (engagement) свидание; **out of ~** устарелый; **up to ~** современный; **be in ~** в курсе дела; vt датировать impf & pf; (go out with) встречаться impf c+instr; vi (originate) относиться impf (from к+instr).

dative adj (n) дательный (падеж).

daub vt мазать impf, на~ pf (with +instr).

daughter n дочь; **~-in-law** невестка (in relation to mother), сноха (in relation to father).

daunting adj угрожающий.

dawdle vi мешкать impf.

dawn n рассвет; (also fig) заря; vi (day) рассветать impf, рассвести pf impers; **~ (up)on** осенять impf, осенить pf; **it ~ed on me** меня осенило.

day n день m; (24 hours) сутки pl; pl (period) период, время neut; **~ after ~** изо дня в день; **the ~ after tomorrow** послезавтра; **the ~ before** накануне; **the ~ before yesterday** позавчера; **the other ~** на днях; **by ~** днём; **every other ~** через день; **~ off** выходной день m; **one ~** однажды; **these ~s** в наши дни. **daybreak** n рассвет. **day-dreams** n pl мечты f pl. **daylight** n дневной свет; **in broad ~** средь бела дня. **daytime** n: **in the ~** днём.

daze n: **in a ~, dazed** adj оглушён (-ена).

dazzle vt ослепля́ть impf, ослепи́ть pf.

deacon n дья́кон.

dead adj мёртвый; (animals) до́хлый; (plants) увя́дший; (numb) онеме́вший; n: the ~ мёртвые sb pl; at ~ of night глубо́кой но́чью; adv соверше́нно; ~ end тупи́к; ~ heat одновреме́нный фи́ниш; ~line преде́льный срок; ~lock тупи́к.

deaden vt заглуша́ть impf, заглуши́ть pf.

deadly adj смерте́льный.

deaf adj глухо́й; ~ and dumb глухонемо́й. **deafen** vt оглуша́ть impf, оглуши́ть pf. **deafness** n глухота́.

deal[1] n: a great, good, ~ мно́го (+gen); (with comp) гора́здо.

deal[2] n (bargain; cards) сда́ча; vt (cards) сдава́ть impf, сдать pf; (blow) наноси́ть impf, нанести́ pf; ~ in торгова́ть impf +instr; ~ out распределя́ть impf, распредели́ть pf; ~ with (take care of) занима́ться impf, заня́ться pf +instr; (handle a person) поступа́ть impf, поступи́ть pf c+instr; (treat a subject) рассма́тривать impf, рассмотре́ть pf; (cope with) справля́ться impf, спра́виться pf c+instr. **dealer** n торго́вец (in +instr).

dean n дека́н.

dear adj дорого́й; (also n) ми́лый (sb).

dearth n недоста́ток.

death n смерть; put to ~ казни́ть impf & pf; ~bed n сме́ртное ло́же; ~ certificate свиде́тельство о сме́рти; ~ penalty сме́ртная казнь. **deathly** adj смерте́льный.

debar vt: ~ from не допуска́ть impf до+gen.

debase vt унижа́ть impf, уни́зить pf; (coinage) понижа́ть impf, пони́зить pf ка́чество +gen.

debatable adj спо́рный. **debate** n пре́ния (-ий) pl; vt обсужда́ть impf, обсуди́ть pf.

debauched adj развращённый. **debauchery** n разврат.

debilitate vt ослабля́ть impf, осла́бить pf. **debility** n сла́бость.

debit n де́бет; vt дебетова́ть impf & pf.

debris n обло́мки m pl.

debt n долг. **debtor** n должни́к.

début n дебю́т; make one's ~ дебюти́ровать impf & pf.

decade n десятиле́тие.

decadence n декаде́нтство. **decadent** adj декаде́нтский.

decaffeinated adj без кофеи́на.

decant vt перелива́ть impf, перели́ть pf. **decanter** n графи́н.

decapitate vt обезгла́вливать impf, обезгла́вить pf.

decay vi гнить impf, c~ pf; (tooth) разруша́ться impf, разру́шиться pf; n гние́ние; (tooth) разруше́ние.

decease n кончи́на. **deceased** adj поко́йный; n поко́йник, -ица.

deceit n обма́н. **deceitful** adj лжи́вый. **deceive** vt обма́нывать impf, обману́ть pf.

deceleration n замедле́ние.

December n дека́брь m; adj дека́брьский.

decency n прили́чие. **decent** adj прили́чный.

decentralization n децентрализа́ция. **decentralize** vt децентрализова́ть impf & pf.

deception n обма́н. **deceptive** adj обма́нчивый.

decibel n дециби́л.

decide vt реша́ть impf, реши́ть pf. **decided** adj реши́тельный.

deciduous adj листопа́дный.

decimal n десяти́чная дробь; adj десяти́чный; ~ point запята́я sb.

decimate vt (fig) коси́ть impf, c~ pf.

decipher vt расшифро́вывать impf, расшифрова́ть pf.

decision n реше́ние. **decisive** adj (firm) реши́тельный, (deciding) реша́ющий.

deck n па́луба; (bus etc.) эта́ж; ~chair n шезло́нг; vt: ~ out украша́ть impf, укра́сить pf.

declaim vt деклами́ровать impf, про~ pf.

declaration n объявле́ние; (document) деклара́ция. **declare** vt (proclaim) объявля́ть impf, объяви́ть pf; (assert) заявля́ть impf, заяви́ть pf.

declension n склоне́ние. **decline** n упа́док; vi приходи́ть impf, прийти́ pf в упа́док; vt отклоня́ть impf, отклони́ть pf; (gram) склоня́ть impf, про~ pf.

decode vt расшифро́вывать impf, расшифрова́ть pf.

decompose vi разлага́ться impf, разложи́ться pf.

décor n эстети́ческое оформле́ние.

decorate vt украша́ть impf, укра́сить pf; (room) ремонти́ровать impf, от~ pf; (with medal etc.) награжда́ть impf, награди́ть pf. **decoration** n украше́ние; (medal) о́рден. **decorative** adj декорати́вный. **decorator** n маля́р.

decorous adj прили́чный. **decorum** n прили́чие.

decoy n (bait) прима́нка; vt зама́нивать impf, замани́ть pf.

decrease vt & i уменьша́ть(ся) impf, уме́ньшить(ся) pf; n уменьше́ние.

decree n ука́з; vt постановля́ть impf, постанови́ть pf.

decrepit adj дря́хлый.

dedicate vt посвяща́ть impf, посвяти́ть pf. **dedication** n посвяще́ние.

deduce vt заключа́ть impf, заключи́ть pf.

deduct vt вычита́ть impf, вы́честь pf. **deduction** n (subtraction) вы́чет; (inference) вы́вод.

deed n посту́пок; (heroic) по́двиг; (law) акт.

deem vt счита́ть impf, счесть pf +acc & instr.

deep adj глубо́кий; (colour) тёмный; (sound) ни́зкий; ~ freeze морози́льник. **deepen** vt & i углубля́ть(ся) impf, углуби́ть(ся) pf.

deer n оле́нь m.

deface vt обезобра́живать impf, обезобра́зить pf.

defamation n диффама́ция. **defamatory** adj клеветни́ческий.

default n (failure to pay) неупла́та; (failure to appear) нея́вка; (comput) автомати́ческий вы́бор; vi не выполня́ть impf обяза́тельств.

defeat n пораже́ние; vt побежда́ть impf, победи́ть pf. **defeatism** n пораже́нчество. **defeatist** n пораже́нец; adj пораже́нческий.

defecate vi испражня́ться impf, испражни́ться pf.

defect n дефе́кт; vi перебега́ть impf, перебежа́ть pf. **defective** adj неиспра́вный. **defector** n перебе́жчик.

defence n защи́та. **defenceless** adj беззащи́тный. **defend** vt защища́ть impf, защити́ть pf. **defendant** n подсуди́мый sb. **defender** n защи́тник.

defensive adj оборони́тельный.

defer¹ vt (postpone) отсро́чивать impf, отсро́чить pf.

defer² vi: ~ to подчиня́ться impf +dat. **deference** n уваже́ние. **deferential** adj почти́тельный.

defiance n неповинове́ние; in ~ of вопреки́+dat. **defiant** adj вызыва́ющий.

deficiency n недоста́ток. **deficient** adj недоста́точный. **deficit** n дефици́т.

defile vt оскверня́ть impf, оскверни́ть pf.

define vt определя́ть impf, определи́ть pf. **definite** adj определённый. **definitely** adv несомне́нно. **definition** n определе́ние. **definitive** adj оконча́тельный.

deflate vt & i спуска́ть impf, спусти́ть pf; vt (person) сбива́ть impf, сбить pf спесь с+gen. **deflation** n дефля́ция.

deflect vt отклоня́ть impf, отклони́ть pf.

deforestation n обезле́сение.

deformed adj уро́дливый. **deformity** n уро́дство.

defraud vt обма́нывать impf, обману́ть pf; ~ of выма́нивать impf, вы́манить pf +acc & у+gen (of person).

defray vt опла́чивать impf, оплати́ть pf.

defrost vt размора́живать impf, разморо́зить pf.

deft adj ло́вкий.

defunct adj бо́льше не существу́ющий.

defy vt (challenge) вызыва́ть impf, вы́звать pf; (disobey) идти́ impf, по~ pf про́тив+acc; (fig) не поддава́ться impf +dat.

degenerate vi вырожда́ться impf, вы́родиться pf; adj вы́родившийся.

degradation n униже́ние. **degrade** vt унижа́ть impf, уни́зить pf. **degrading** adj унизи́тельный.

degree n сте́пень; (math etc.) гра́дус; (univ) учёная сте́пень.

dehydrate vt обезво́живать impf,

обезво́дить *pf.* **dehydration** *n* обез-
во́живание.
deign *vi* снисходи́ть *impf,* снизойти́
pf.
deity *n* божество́.
dejected *adj* удручённый.
delay *n* заде́ржка; without ~ неме́д-
ленно; *vt* заде́рживать *impf,* задер-
жа́ть *pf.*
delegate *n* делега́т; *vt* делеги́ровать
impf & pf. **delegation** *n* делега́ция.
delete *vt* вычёркивать *impf,* вы́-
черкнуть *pf.*
deliberate *adj* (*intentional*) предна-
ме́ренный; (*careful*) осторо́жный;
vt & i размышля́ть *impf,* раз-
мы́слить *pf* (o+*prep*); (*discuss*) сове-
ща́ться *impf* (o+*prep*). **deliberation**
n размышле́ние; (*discussion*) сове-
ща́ние.
delicacy *n* (*tact*) делика́тность;
(*dainty*) ла́комство. **delicate** *adj*
то́нкий; (*tactful, needing tact*) дели-
ка́тный; (*health*) боле́зненный.
delicatessen *n* гастроно́м.
delicious *adj* о́чень вку́сный.
delight *n* наслажде́ние; (*delightful
thing*) пре́лесть. **delightful** *adj* пре-
ле́стный.
delinquency *n* престу́пность. **delinquent** *n* правонаруши́тель *m,*
~ница; *adj* вино́вный.
delirious *adj*: be ~ бре́дить *impf.* **delirium** *n* бред.
deliver *vt* (*goods*) доставля́ть *impf,*
доста́вить *pf;* (*save*) избавля́ть *impf,*
изба́вить *pf* (from от+*gen*); (*lecture*)
прочита́ть *impf,* проче́сть *pf;* (*letters*) разноси́ть *impf,* разнести́ *pf;*
(*speech*) произноси́ть *impf,* произ-
нести́ *pf;* (*blow*) наноси́ть *impf,*
нанести́ *pf.* **deliverance** *n* изба-
вле́ние. **delivery** *n* доста́вка.
delta *n* де́льта.
delude *vt* вводи́ть *impf,* ввести́ *pf* в
заблужде́ние.
deluge *n* (*flood*) пото́п; (*rain*) ли́-
вень *m;* (*fig*) пото́к.
delusion *n* заблужде́ние; ~s of grandeur ма́ния вели́чия.
de luxe *adj* -люкс (*added to noun*).
delve *vi* углубля́ться *impf,* углу-
би́ться *pf* (into в+*acc*).
demand *n* тре́бование; (*econ*) спрос
(for на+*acc*); *vt* тре́бовать *impf,* по~

pf +*gen.* **demanding** *adj* тре́бова-
тельный.
demarcation *n* демарка́ция.
demean *vt*: ~ o.s. унижа́ться *impf,*
уни́зиться *pf.*
demeanour *n* мане́ра вести́ себя́.
demented *adj* сумасше́дший. **de-
mentia** *n* слабоу́мие.
demise *n* кончи́на.
demobilize *vt* демобилизова́ть *impf
& pf.*
democracy *n* демокра́тия. **democrat**
n демокра́т. **democratic** *adj* демо-
крати́ческий. **democratization** *n*
демократиза́ция.
demolish *vt* (*destroy*) разруша́ть
impf, разру́шить *pf;* (*building*) сно-
си́ть *impf,* снести́ *pf;* (*refute*)
опроверга́ть *impf,* опрове́ргнуть *pf.*
demolition *n* разруше́ние; снос.
demon *n* де́мон.
demonstrable *adj* доказу́емый. **de-
monstrably** *adv* нагля́дно. **demonstrate** *vt* демонстри́ровать *impf &
pf; vi* уча́ствовать *impf* в демон-
стра́ции. **demonstration** *n* демон-
стра́ция. **demonstrative** *adj* экспан-
си́вный; (*gram*) указа́тельный. **dem-
onstrator** *n* демонстра́тор; (*polit*)
демонстра́нт.
demoralize *vt* дем18рализова́ть *impf
& pf.*
demote *vt* понижа́ть *impf,* пони́зить
pf в до́лжности.
demure *adj* скро́мный.
den *n* берло́га.
denial *n* отрица́ние; (*refusal*) отка́з.
denigrate *vt* черни́ть *impf,* o~ *pf.*
denim *adj* джинсо́вый; *n* джинсо́вая
ткань.
Denmark *n* Да́ния.
denomination *n* (*money*) досто́ин-
ство; (*relig*) вероисповеда́ние. **denominator** *n* знамена́тель *m.*
denote *vt* означа́ть *impf,* озна́чить
pf.
denounce *vt* (*condemn*) осужда́ть
impf, осуди́ть *pf;* (*inform on*) до-
носи́ть *impf,* донести́ *pf* на+*acc.*
dense *adj* густо́й; (*stupid*) тупо́й.
density *n* пло́тность.
dent *n* вмя́тина; *vt* де́лать *impf,* с~
pf вмя́тину в+*prep.*
dental *adj* зубно́й. **dentist** *n* зубно́й
врач. **dentures** *n pl* зубно́й проте́з.

denunciation n (*condemnation*) осуждéние; (*informing*) донóс.

deny vt отрицáть *impf*; (*refuse*) откáзывать *impf*, отказáть *pf* +*dat* (*person*) в+*prep*.

deodorant n дезодорáнт.

depart vi отбывáть *impf*, отбы́ть *pf*; (*deviate*) отклоня́ться *impf*, отклони́ться *pf* (**from** от+*gen*).

department n отдéл; (*univ*) кáфедра; **~ store** универмáг.

departure n отбы́тие; (*deviation*) отклонéние.

depend vi зави́сеть *impf* (**on** от+*gen*); (*rely*) полагáться *impf*, положи́ться *pf* (**on** на+*acc*). **dependable** adj надёжный. **dependant** n иждивéнец. **dependence** n зави́симость. **dependent** adj зави́симый.

depict vt изображáть *impf*, изобрази́ть *pf*.

deplete vt истощáть *impf*, истощи́ть *pf*. **depleted** adj истощённый. **depletion** n истощéние.

deplorable adj плачéвный. **deplore** vt сожалéть *impf* о+*prep*.

deploy vt развёртывать *impf*, разверну́ть *pf*. **deployment** n развёртывание.

deport vt депорти́ровать *impf* & *pf*; высылáть *impf*, вы́слать *pf*. **deportation** n депортáция; вы́сылка.

deportment n осáнка.

depose vt сверѓáть *impf*, свéргнуть *pf*. **deposit** n (*econ*) вклад; (*advance*) задáток; (*sediment*) осáдок; (*coal etc.*) месторождéние; vt (*econ*) вноси́ть *impf*, внести́ *pf*.

depot n (*transport*) депó *neut indecl*; (*store*) склад.

deprave vt развращáть *impf*, развати́ть *pf*. **depraved** adj развращённый. **depravity** n разврáт.

deprecate vt осуждáть *impf*, осуди́ть *pf*.

depreciate vt & i (*econ*) обесцéнивать(ся) *impf*, обесцéнить(ся) *pf*. **depreciation** n обесцéнение.

depress vt (*dispirit*) удручáть *impf*, удручи́ть *pf*. **depressed** adj удручённый. **depressing** adj угнетáющий. **depression** n (*hollow*) впáдина; (*econ, med, meteorol, etc.*) депрéссия.

deprivation n лишéние. **deprive** vt

лишáть *impf*, лиши́ть *pf* (**of** +*gen*).

depth n глубинá; **in the ~ of winter** в разгáре зимы́.

deputation n депутáция. **deputize** vi замещáть *impf*, замести́ть *pf* (**for** +*acc*). **deputy** n замести́тель m; (*parl*) депутáт.

derail vt: **be derailed** сходи́ть *impf*, сойти́ *pf* с рéльсов. **derailment** n сход с рéльсов.

deranged adj сумасшéдший.

derelict adj забрóшенный.

deride vt высмéивать *impf*, вы́смеять *pf*. **derision** n высмéивание. **derisive** adj (*mocking*) насмéшливый. **derisory** adj (*ridiculous*) смехотвóрный.

derivation n происхождéние. **derivative** n произвóдное sb; adj произвóдный. **derive** vt извлекáть *impf*, извлéчь *pf*; vi: **~ from** происходи́ть *impf*, произойти́ *pf* от+*gen*.

derogatory adj отрицáтельный.

descend vi (& t) (*go down*) спускáться *impf*, спусти́ться *pf* (c+*gen*); **be descended from** происходи́ть *impf*, произойти́ *pf* из, от, +*gen*. **descendant** n потóмок. **descent** n спуск; (*lineage*) происхождéние.

describe vt опи́сывать *impf*, описáть *pf*. **description** n описáние. **descriptive** adj описáтельный.

desecrate vt осквернять *impf*, оскверни́ть *pf*. **desecration** n осквернéние.

desert[1] n (*waste*) пусты́ня.

desert[2] vt покидáть *impf*, поки́нуть *pf*; (*mil*) дезерти́ровать *impf* & *pf*. **deserter** n дезерти́р. **desertion** n дезерти́рство.

deserts n pl заслýги f pl. **deserve** vt заслýживать *impf*, заслужи́ть *pf*. **deserving** adj достóйный (**of** +*gen*).

design n (*pattern*) узóр; (*of car etc.*) констрýкция, проéкт; (*industrial*) дизáйн; (*aim*) ýмысел; vt проекти́ровать *impf*, c~ *pf*; (*intend*) предназначáть *impf*, предназнáчить *pf*. **designate** vt (*indicate*) обозначáть *impf*, обознáчить *pf*; (*appoint*) назначáть *impf*, назнáчить *pf*. **designer** n (*tech*) констрýктор; (*industrial*) дизáйнер; (*of clothes*) модельéр.

desirable adj желáтельный. **desire**

n жела́ние; *vt* жела́ть *impf*, по~ *pf* +*gen*.

desist *vi* (*refrain*) возде́рживаться *impf*, воздержа́ться *pf* (from от+*gen*).

desk *n* пи́сьменный стол; (*school*) па́рта.

desolate *adj* забро́шенный. **desolation** *n* забро́шенность.

despair *n* отча́яние; *vi* отча́иваться *impf*, отча́яться *pf*. **desperate** *adj* отча́янный. **desperation** *n* отча́яние.

despicable *adj* презре́нный. **despise** *vt* презира́ть *impf*, презре́ть *pf*.

despite *prep* несмотря́ на+*acc*.

despondency *n* уны́ние. **despondent** *adj* уны́лый.

despot *n* де́спот.

dessert *n* десе́рт.

destination *n* (*of goods*) ме́сто назначе́ния; (*of journey*) цель. **destiny** *n* судьба́.

destitute *adj* без вся́ких средств.

destroy *vt* разруша́ть *impf*, разру́шить *pf*. **destroyer** *n* (*naut*) эсми́нец. **destruction** *n* разруше́ние. **destructive** *adj* разруши́тельный.

detach *vt* отделя́ть *impf*, отдели́ть *pf*. **detached** *adj* отде́льный; (*objective*) беспристра́стный; ~ **house** особня́к. **detachment** *n* (*objectivity*) беспристра́стие; (*mil*) отря́д.

detail *n* дета́ль, подро́бность; **in detail** подро́бно; *vt* подро́бно расска́зывать *impf*, рассказа́ть *pf*. **detailed** *adj* подро́бный.

detain *vt* заде́рживать *impf*, задержа́ть *pf*. **detainee** *n* заде́ржанный *sb*.

detect *vt* обнару́живать *impf*, обнару́жить *pf*. **detection** *n* обнаруже́ние; (*crime*) рассле́дование. **detective** *n* детекти́в; ~ **film, story**, *etc*. детекти́в. **detector** *n* дете́ктор.

detention *n* задержа́ние; (*school*) заде́ржка в наказа́ние.

deter *vt* уде́рживать *impf*, удержа́ть *pf* (from от+*gen*).

detergent *n* мо́ющее сре́дство.

deteriorate *vi* ухудша́ться *impf*, уху́дшиться *pf*. **deterioration** *n* ухудше́ние.

determination *n* реши́мость. **determine** *vt* (*ascertain*) устана́вливать *impf*, установи́ть *pf*; (*be decisive fac-*

tor) определя́ть *impf*, определи́ть *pf*; (*decide*) реша́ть *impf*, реши́ть *pf*. **determined** *adj* реши́тельный.

deterrent *n* сре́дство устраше́ния.

detest *vt* ненави́деть *impf*. **detestable** *adj* отврати́тельный.

detonate *vt & i* взрыва́ть(ся) *impf*, взорва́ть(ся) *pf*. **detonator** *n* детона́тор.

detour *n* объе́зд.

detract *vi*: ~ **from** умаля́ть *impf*, умали́ть *pf* +*acc*.

detriment *n* уще́рб. **detrimental** *adj* вре́дный.

deuce *n* (*tennis*) ра́вный счёт.

devaluation *n* девальва́ция. **devalue** *vt* девальви́ровать *impf & pf*.

devastate *vt* опустоша́ть *impf*, опустоши́ть *pf*. **devastated** *adj* потрясённый. **devastating** *adj* уничтожа́ющий. **devastation** *n* опустоше́ние.

develop *vt & i* развива́ть(ся) *impf*, разви́ть(ся) *pf*; *vt* (*phot*) проявля́ть *impf*, прояви́ть *pf*. **developer** *n* (*of land etc.*) застро́йщик. **development** *n* разви́тие.

deviant *adj* ненорма́льный. **deviate** *vi* отклоня́ться *impf*, отклони́ться *pf* (from от+*gen*). **deviation** *n* отклоне́ние.

device *n* прибо́р.

devil *n* чёрт. **devilish** *adj* черто́вский.

devious *adj* (*circuitous*) окружно́й; (*person*) непоря́дочный.

devise *vt* приду́мывать *impf*, приду́мать *pf*.

devoid *adj* лишённый (**of** +*gen*).

devolution *n* переда́ча (вла́сти).

devote *vt* посвяща́ть *impf*, посвяти́ть *pf*. **devoted** *adj* пре́данный. **devotee** *n* покло́нник. **devotion** *n* пре́данность.

devour *vt* пожира́ть *impf*, пожра́ть *pf*.

devout *adj* на́божный.

dew *n* роса́.

dexterity *n* ло́вкость. **dext(e)rous** *adj* ло́вкий.

diabetes *n* диабе́т. **diabetic** *n* диабе́тик; *adj* диабети́ческий.

diabolic(al) *adj* дья́вольский.

diagnose *vt* диагности́ровать *impf & pf*. **diagnosis** *n* диа́гноз.

diagonal n диагона́ль; adj диагона́льный. **diagonally** adv по диагона́ли.

diagram n диагра́мма.

dial n (clock) цифербла́т; (tech) шкала́; vt набира́ть impf, набра́ть pf.

dialect n диале́кт.

dialogue n диало́г.

diameter n диа́метр. **diametric(al)** adj диаметра́льный; ~ly opposed диаметра́льно противополо́жный.

diamond n алма́з; (shape) ромб; pl (cards) бу́бны (-бён, -бна́м) pl.

diaper n пелёнка.

diaphragm n диафра́гма.

diarrhoea n понос.

diary n дневни́к.

dice see **die**¹

dicey adj риско́ванный.

dictate vt дикто́вать impf, про~ pf. **dictation** n дикто́вка. **dictator** n дикта́тор. **dictatorial** adj дикта́торский. **dictatorship** n диктату́ра.

diction n ди́кция.

dictionary n слова́рь m.

didactic adj дидакти́ческий.

die¹ n (pl **dice**) игра́льная кость; (pl **dies**) (stamp) штамп.

die² vi (person) умира́ть impf, умере́ть pf; (animal) до́хнуть impf, из~, по~ pf; (plant) вя́нуть impf, за~ pf; be dying to о́чень хоте́ть impf; ~ down (fire, sound) угаса́ть impf, уга́снуть pf; ~ out вымира́ть impf, вы́мереть pf.

diesel n (engine) ди́зель m; attrib ди́зельный.

diet n дие́та; (habitual food) пи́ща; vi быть на дие́те. **dietary** adj диети́ческий.

differ vi отлича́ться impf; различа́ться impf; (disagree) расходи́ться impf, разойти́сь pf. **difference** n ра́зница; (disagreement) разногла́сие. **different** adj разли́чный; ра́зный. **differential** n (math, tech) дифференциа́л; (difference) ра́зница. **differentiate** vt различа́ть impf, различи́ть pf.

difficult adj тру́дный. **difficulty** n тру́дность; (difficult situation) затрудне́ние; without ~ без труда́.

diffidence n неуве́ренность в себе́. **diffident** n неуве́ренный в себе́.

diffused adj рассе́янный.

dig n (archaeol) раско́пки f pl; (poke) тычо́к; (gibe) шпи́лька; pl (lodgings) кварти́ра; give a ~ in the ribs ткнуть pf ло́ктем под ребро́; vt копа́ть impf, вы́~ pf; рыть impf, вы́~ pf; ~ up (bone) выка́пывать impf, вы́копать pf; (land) вска́пывать impf, вскопа́ть pf.

digest vt перева́ривать impf, перевари́ть pf. **digestible** adj удобовари́мый. **digestion** n пищеваре́ние.

digger n (tech) экскава́тор.

digit n (math) знак.

dignified adj велича́вый. **dignitary** n сано́вник. **dignity** n досто́инство.

digress vi отклоня́ться impf, отклони́ться pf. **digression** n отклоне́ние.

dike n да́мба; (ditch) ров.

dilapidated adj ве́тхий.

dilate vt & i расширя́ть(ся) impf, расши́рить(ся) pf.

dilemma n диле́мма.

dilettante n дилета́нт.

diligence n прилежа́ние. **diligent** adj приле́жный.

dilute vt разбавля́ть impf, разба́вить pf.

dim adj (not bright) ту́склый; (vague) сму́тный; (stupid) тупо́й.

dimension n (pl) разме́ры m pl; (math) измере́ние. **-dimensional** in comb -ме́рный; **three-~** трёхме́рный.

diminish vt & i уменьша́ть(ся) impf, уме́ньшить(ся) pf. **diminutive** adj ма́ленький; n уменьши́тельное sb.

dimness n ту́склость.

dimple n я́мочка.

din n гро́хот; (voices) гам.

dine vi обе́дать impf, по~ pf. **diner** n обе́дающий sb.

dinghy n шлю́пка; (rubber ~) надувна́я ло́дка.

dingy adj (drab) ту́склый; (dirty) гря́зный.

dining-car n ваго́н-рестора́н. **dining-room** n столо́вая sb. **dinner** n обе́д; ~-jacket смо́кинг.

dinosaur n диноза́вр.

diocese n епа́рхия.

dip vt (immerse) окуна́ть impf, окуну́ть pf; (partially) обма́кивать impf, обмакну́ть pf; vi (slope) понижа́ться impf, пони́зиться pf; n (depres-

sion) впа́дина; (*slope*) укло́н; have a ~ (*bathe*) купа́ться *impf*, вы́~ *pf*.

diphtheria *n* дифтери́я.

diphthong *n* дифто́нг.

diploma *n* дипло́м. **diplomacy** *n* диплома́тия. **diplomat** *n* диплома́т. **diplomatic** *adj* дипломати́ческий.

dire *adj* стра́шный; (*ominous*) злове́щий.

direct *adj* прямо́й; ~ current постоя́нный ток; *vt* направля́ть *impf*, напра́вить *pf*; (*guide, manage*) руководи́ть *impf* +*instr*; (*film*) режисси́ровать *impf*. **direction** *n* направле́ние; (*guidance*) руково́дство; (*instruction*) указа́ние; (*film*) режиссу́ра; *stage* ~ рема́рка. **directive** *n* директи́ва. **directly** *adv* пря́мо; (*at once*) сра́зу. **director** *n* дире́ктор; (*film etc.*) режиссёр(-постано́вщик). **directory** *n* спра́вочник, указа́тель *m*; (*tel*) телефо́нная кни́га.

dirt *n* грязь. **dirty** *adj* гря́зный; *vt* па́чкать *impf*, за~ *pf*.

disability *n* физи́ческий/психи́ческий недоста́ток; (*disablement*) инвали́дность. **disabled** *adj*: he is ~ он инвали́д.

disadvantage *n* невы́годное положе́ние; (*defect*) недоста́ток. **disadvantageous** *adj* невы́годный.

disaffected *adj* недово́льный.

disagree *vi* не соглаша́ться *impf*, согласи́ться *pf*; (*not correspond*) не соотве́тствовать *impf* +*dat*. **disagreeable** *adj* неприя́тный. **disagreement** *n* разногла́сие; (*quarrel*) ссо́ра.

disappear *vi* исчеза́ть *impf*, исче́знуть *pf*. **disappearance** *n* исчезнове́ние.

disappoint *vt* разочаро́вывать *impf*, разочарова́ть *pf*. **disappointed** *adj* разочаро́ванный. **disappointing** *adj* разочаро́вывающий. **disappointment** *n* разочарова́ние.

disapproval *n* неодобре́ние. **disapprove** *vt* & *i* не одобря́ть *impf*.

disarm *vt* (*mil*) разоружа́ть *impf*, разоружи́ть *pf*; (*criminal; also fig*) обезору́живать *impf*, обезору́жить *pf*. **disarmament** *n* разоруже́ние.

disarray *n* беспоря́док.

disaster *n* бе́дствие. **disastrous** *adj* катастрофи́ческий.

disband *vt* распуска́ть *impf*, распусти́ть *pf*; *vi* расходи́ться *impf*, разойти́сь *pf*.

disbelief *n* неве́рие.

disc, disk *n* диск; ~ jockey веду́щий *sb* переда́чу.

discard *vt* отбра́сывать *impf*, отбро́сить *pf*.

discern *vt* различа́ть *impf*, различи́ть *pf*. **discernible** *adj* различи́мый. **discerning** *adj* проница́тельный.

discharge *vt* (*ship etc.*) разгружа́ть *impf*, разгрузи́ть *pf* (*gun; electr*) разряжа́ть *impf*, разряди́ть *pf*; (*dismiss*) увольня́ть *impf*, уво́лить *pf*; (*prisoner*) освобожда́ть *impf*, освободи́ть *pf*; (*debt; duty*) выполня́ть *impf*, вы́полнить *pf*; (*from hospital*) выпи́сывать *impf*, вы́писать *pf*; *n* разгру́зка; (*electr*) разря́д; увольне́ние; освобожде́ние; выполне́ние; (*matter discharged*) выделе́ния *neut pl*.

disciple *n* учени́к.

disciplinarian *n* сторо́нник дисципли́ны. **disciplinary** *adj* дисциплина́рный. **discipline** *n* дисципли́на; *vt* дисциплини́ровать *impf* & *pf*.

disclaim *vt* (*deny*) отрица́ть *impf*; ~ responsibility слага́ть *impf*, сложи́ть *pf* с себя́ отве́тственность.

disclose *vt* обнару́живать *impf*, обнару́жить *pf*. **disclosure** *n* обнаруже́ние.

discoloured *adj* обесцве́ченный.

discomfit *vt* смуща́ть *impf*, смути́ть *pf*. **discomfiture** *n* смуще́ние.

discomfort *n* неудо́бство.

disconcert *vt* смуща́ть *impf*, смути́ть *pf*.

disconnect *vt* разъединя́ть *impf*, разъедини́ть *pf*; (*switch off*) выключа́ть *impf*, вы́ключить *pf*. **disconnected** *adj* (*incoherent*) бессвя́зный.

disconsolate *adj* неуте́шный.

discontent *n* недово́льство. **discontented** *adj* недово́льный.

discontinue *vt* прекраща́ть *impf*, прекрати́ть *pf*.

discord *n* разногла́сие; (*mus*) диссона́нс. **discordant** *adj* несогласу́ющийся; диссони́рующий.

discotheque *n* дискоте́ка.

discount n ски́дка; vt (disregard) не принима́ть impf, приня́ть pf в расчёт.

discourage vt обескура́живать impf, обескура́жить pf; (dissuade) отгова́ривать impf, отговори́ть pf.

discourse n речь.

discourteous adj неве́жливый.

discover vt открыва́ть impf, откры́ть pf; (find out) обнару́живать impf, обнару́жить pf. **discovery** n откры́тие.

discredit n позо́р; vt дискредити́ровать impf & pf.

discreet adj такти́чный. **discretion** n (judgement) усмотре́ние; (prudence) благоразу́мие; at one's ~ по своему́ усмотре́нию.

discrepancy n несоотве́тствие.

discriminate vi различа́ть impf, различи́ть pf; ~ against дискримини́ровать impf & pf. **discrimination** n (taste) разбо́рчивость; (bias) дискримина́ция.

discus n диск.

discuss vt обсужда́ть impf, обсуди́ть pf. **discussion** n обсужде́ние.

disdain n презре́ние. **disdainful** adj презри́тельный.

disease n боле́знь. **diseased** adj больно́й.

disembark vi выса́живаться impf, вы́садиться pf.

disenchantment n разочарова́ние.

disengage vt освобожда́ть impf, освободи́ть pf; (clutch) отпуска́ть impf, отпусти́ть pf.

disentangle vt распу́тывать impf, распу́тать pf.

disfavour n неми́лость.

disfigure vt уро́довать impf, из~ pf.

disgrace n позо́р; (disfavour) неми́лость; vt позо́рить impf, о~ pf. **disgraceful** adj позо́рный.

disgruntled adj недово́льный.

disguise n маскиро́вка; vt маскирова́ть impf, за~ pf; (conceal) скрыва́ть impf, скрыть pf. **disguised** adj замаскиро́ванный.

disgust n отвраще́ние; vt внуша́ть impf, внуши́ть pf. отвраще́ние +dat. **disgusting** adj отврати́тельный.

dish n блю́до; pl посу́да collect; ~washer (посу́до)мо́ечная маши́на; vt: ~ up подава́ть impf, пода́ть pf.

dishearten vt обескура́живать impf, обескура́жить pf.

dishevelled adj растрёпанный.

dishonest adj нече́стный. **dishonesty** n нече́стность. **dishonour** n бесче́стье; vt бесче́стить impf, о~ pf. **dishonourable** adj бесче́стный.

disillusion vt разочаро́вывать impf, разочарова́ть pf. **disillusionment** n разочаро́ванность.

disinclination n нескло́нность, неохо́та. **disinclined** adj be ~ не хоте́ться impers+dat.

disinfect vt дезинфици́ровать impf & pf. **disinfectant** n дезинфици́рующее сре́дство.

disingenuous adj неи́скренний.

disinherit vt лиша́ть impf, лиши́ть pf насле́дства.

disintegrate vi распада́ться impf, распа́сться pf. **disintegration** n распа́д.

disinterested adj бескоры́стный.

disjointed adj бессвя́зный.

disk see **disc**

dislike n нелюбо́вь (for к+dat); vt не люби́ть impf.

dislocate vt (med) вы́вихнуть pf.

dislodge vt смеща́ть impf, смести́ть pf.

disloyal adj нелоя́льный. **disloyalty** n нелоя́льность.

dismal adj мра́чный.

dismantle vt разбира́ть impf, разобра́ть pf.

dismay vt смуща́ть impf, смути́ть pf; n смуще́ние.

dismiss vt (sack) увольня́ть impf, уво́лить pf; (disband) распуска́ть impf, распусти́ть pf. **dismissal** n увольне́ние; ро́спуск.

dismount vi спе́шиваться impf, спе́шиться pf.

disobedience n непослуша́ние. **disobedient** adj непослу́шный. **disobey** vt не слу́шаться impf +gen.

disorder n беспоря́док. **disorderly** adj (untidy) беспоря́дочный; (unruly) бу́йный.

disorganized adj неорганизо́ванный.

disorientation n дезориента́ция. **disoriented** adj: I am/was ~ я потеря́л(а) направле́ние.

disown vt отка́зываться impf, отказа́ться pf от+gen.

disparaging *adj* оскорби́тельный.
disparity *n* нера́венство.
dispassionate *adj* беспристра́стный.
dispatch *vt* (*send*) отправля́ть *impf*, отпра́вить *pf*; (*deal with*) распра́вля́ться *impf*, распра́виться *pf* с+*instr*; *n* отпра́вка; (*message*) донесе́ние; (*rapidity*) быстрота́; ~ **rider** мотоцикли́ст свя́зи.
dispel *vt* рассе́ивать *impf*, рассе́ять *pf*.
dispensable *adj* необяза́тельный.
dispensary *n* апте́ка.
dispensation *n* (*exemption*) освобожде́ние (от обяза́тельства). **dispense** *vt* (*distribute*) раздава́ть *impf*, разда́ть *pf*; ~ **with** обходи́ться *impf*, обойти́сь *pf* без+*gen*.
dispersal *n* распростране́ние. **disperse** *vt* (*drive away*) разгоня́ть *impf*, разогна́ть *pf*; (*scatter*) рассе́ивать *impf*, рассе́ять *pf*; *vi* расходи́ться *impf*, разойти́сь *pf*.
dispirited *adj* удручённый.
displaced *adj*: ~ **persons** перемещённые ли́ца *neut pl*.
display *n* пока́з; *vt* пока́зывать *impf*, показа́ть *pf*.
displeased *predic* недово́лен (-льна).
displeasure *n* недово́льство.
disposable *adj* однора́зовый. **disposal** *n* удале́ние; **at your** ~ **in** ва́шем распоряже́нии. **dispose** *vi*: ~ **of** избавля́ться *impf*, изба́виться *pf* от+*gen*. **disposed** *predic*: ~ **to** располо́жен (-ена) к+*dat or* +*inf*. **disposition** *n* расположе́ние; (*temperament*) нрав.
disproportionate *adj* непропорциона́льный.
disprove *vt* опроверга́ть *impf*, опрове́ргнуть *pf*.
dispute *n* (*debate*) спор; (*quarrel*) ссо́ра; *vt* оспа́ривать *impf*, оспо́рить *pf*.
disqualification *n* дисквалифика́ция. **disqualify** *vt* дисквалифици́ровать *impf & pf*.
disquieting *adj* трево́жный.
disregard *n* пренебреже́ние +*instr*; *vt* игнори́ровать *impf & pf*; пренебрега́ть *impf*, пренебре́чь *pf* +*instr*.
disrepair *n* неиспра́вность.
disreputable *adj* по́льзующийся дурно́й сла́вой. **disrepute** *n* дурна́я сла́ва.

disrespect *n* неуваже́ние. **disrespectful** *adj* непочти́тельный.
disrupt *vt* срыва́ть *impf*, сорва́ть *pf*. **disruptive** *adj* подрывно́й.
dissatisfaction *n* недово́льство. **dissatisfied** *adj* недово́льный.
dissect *vt* разреза́ть *impf*, разре́зать *pf*; (*med*) вскрыва́ть *impf*, вскрыть *pf*.
disseminate *vt* распространя́ть *impf*, распространи́ть *pf*; **dissemination** *n* распростране́ние.
dissension *n* раздо́р. **dissent** *n* расхожде́ние; (*eccl*) раско́л.
dissertation *n* диссерта́ция.
disservice *n* плоха́я услу́га.
dissident *n* дисси́дент.
dissimilar *adj* несхо́дный.
dissipate *vt* (*dispel*) рассе́ивать *impf*, рассе́ять *pf*; (*squander*) прома́тывать *impf*, промота́ть *pf*. **dissipated** *adj* распу́тный.
dissociate *vt*: ~ **o.s.** отмежёвываться *impf*, отмежева́ться *pf* (*from* от+*gen*).
dissolute *adj* распу́тный. **dissolution** *n* расторже́ние; (*parl*) ро́спуск. **dissolve** *vt & i* (*in liquid*) растворя́ть(ся) *impf*, раствори́ть(ся) *pf*; *vt* (*annul*) расторга́ть *impf*, расто́ргнуть *pf*; (*parl*) распуска́ть *impf*, распусти́ть *pf*.
dissonance *n* диссона́нс. **dissonant** *adj* диссони́рующий.
dissuade *vt* отгова́ривать *impf*, отгова́ривать *pf*.
distance *n* расстоя́ние; **from a** ~ и́здали; **in the** ~ вдалеке́. **distant** *adj* далёкий, (*also of relative*) да́льний; (*reserved*) сде́ржанный.
distaste *n* отвраще́ние. **distasteful** *adj* проти́вный.
distended *adj* наду́тый.
distil *vt* (*whisky*) перегоня́ть *impf*, перегна́ть *pf*; (*water*) дистилли́ровать *impf & pf*. **distillation** *n* перего́нка; дистилля́ция. **distillery** *n* перего́нный заво́д.
distinct *adj* (*different*) отли́чный; (*clear*) отчётливый; (*evident*) заме́тный. **distinction** *n* (*difference; excellence*) отли́чие; (*discrimination*) разли́чие. **distinctive** *adj* отличи́тельный. **distinctly** *adv* я́сно.
distinguish *vt* различа́ть *impf*,

различи́ть pf; ~ **o.s.** отлича́ться impf, отличи́ться pf. **distinguished** adj выдаю́щийся.

distort vt искажа́ть impf, искази́ть pf; (misrepresent) извраща́ть impf, изврати́ть pf. **distortion** n искаже́ние; извраще́ние.

distract vt отвлека́ть impf, отвле́чь pf. **distraction** n (amusement) развлече́ние; (madness) безу́мие.

distraught adj обезу́мевший.

distress n (suffering) огорче́ние; (danger) бе́дствие; vt огорча́ть impf, огорчи́ть pf.

distribute vt распределя́ть impf, распредели́ть pf. **distribution** n распределе́ние. **distributor** n распредели́тель m.

district n райо́н.

distrust n недове́рие; vt не доверя́ть impf. **distrustful** adj недове́рчивый.

disturb vt беспоко́ить impf, o~ pf. **disturbance** n наруше́ние поко́я; pl (polit etc.) беспоря́дки m pl.

disuse n неупотребле́ние; **fall into** ~ выходи́ть impf, вы́йти pf из употребле́ния. **disused** adj вы́шедший из употребле́ния.

ditch n кана́ва, ров.

dither vi колеба́ться impf.

ditto n то же са́мое; adv так же.

divan n дива́н.

dive vi ныря́ть impf, нырну́ть pf; (aeron) пики́ровать impf & pf; n ныро́к, прыжо́к в во́ду. **diver** n водола́з.

diverge vi расходи́ться impf, разойти́сь pf. **divergent** adj расходя́щийся.

diverse adj разнообра́зный. **diversification** n расшире́ние ассорти-ме́нта. **diversify** vt разнообра́зить impf. **diversion** n (detour) объе́зд; (amusement) развлече́ние. **diversity** n разнообра́зие. **divert** vt отклоня́ть impf, отклони́ть pf; (amuse) развлека́ть impf, развле́чь pf. **diverting** adj заба́вный.

divest vt (deprive) лиша́ть impf, лиши́ть pf (of +gen); ~ **o.s.** отка́зываться impf, отказа́ться pf (of от+gen).

divide vt (share; math) дели́ть impf, по~ pf; (separate) разделя́ть impf, раздели́ть pf. **dividend** n дивиде́нд.

divine adj боже́ственный.

diving n ныря́ние; ~-**board** трампли́н.

divinity n (quality) боже́ственность; (deity) божество́; (theology) богосло́вие.

divisible adj дели́мый. **division** n (dividing) деле́ние, разделе́ние; (section) отде́л; (mil) диви́зия.

divorce n разво́д; vi разводи́ться impf, развести́сь pf. **divorced** adj разведённый.

divulge vt разглаша́ть impf, разгласи́ть pf.

DIY abbr (of do-it-yourself): **he is good at** ~ у него́ золоты́е ру́ки; ~ **shop** магази́н «сде́лай сам».

dizziness n головокруже́ние. **dizzy** adj (causing dizziness) головокружи́тельный; **I am** ~ у меня́ кру́жится голова́.

DNA abbr (of deoxyribonucleic acid) ДНК.

do vt де́лать impf, c~ pf; vi (be suitable) годи́ться impf; (suffice) быть доста́точным; ~**it-yourself** see **DIY**; **that will** ~ хва́тит!; **how** ~ **you** ~? здра́вствуйте!; как вы пожива́ете?; ~ **away with** (abolish) уничтожа́ть impf, уничто́жить pf; ~ **in** (kill) убива́ть impf, уби́ть pf; ~ **up** (restore) ремонти́ровать impf, от~ pf; (wrap up) завёртывать impf, заверну́ть pf; (fasten) застёгивать impf, застегну́ть pf; ~ **without** обходи́ться impf, обойти́сь pf без+gen.

docile adj поко́рный. **docility** n поко́рность.

dock¹ n (naut) док; vt ста́вить impf, по~ pf в док; vi входи́ть impf, войти́ pf в док; vi (spacecraft) стыкова́ться impf, со~ pf. **docker** n до́кер. **dockyard** n верфь.

dock² n (law) скамья́ подсуди́мых.

docket n квита́нция; (label) ярлы́к.

doctor n врач; (also univ) до́ктор; vt (castrate) кастри́ровать impf & pf; (spay) удаля́ть impf, удали́ть pf яи́чники y+gen; (falsify) фальсифици́ровать impf & pf. **doctorate** n сте́пень до́ктора.

doctrine n доктри́на.

document n докуме́нт; vt документи́ровать impf & pf. **documentary** n документа́льный фильм. **docu-**

mentation n документа́ция.

doddery adj дря́хлый.

dodge n уве́ртка; vt уклоня́ться impf, уклони́ться pf от+gen; (jump to avoid) отска́кивать impf, отскочи́ть pf (от+gen). **dodgy** adj ка́верзный.

doe n са́мка.

dog n соба́ка, пёс; (fig) пресле́довать impf. **dog-eared** adj захва́танный.

dogged adj упо́рный.

dogma n до́гма. **dogmatic** adj догмати́ческий.

doings n pl дела́ neut pl.

doldrums n: be in the ~ хандри́ть impf.

dole n посо́бие по безрабо́тице; vt (~ out) выдава́ть impf, вы́дать pf.

doleful adj ско́рбный.

doll n ку́кла.

dollar n до́ллар.

dollop n соли́дная по́рция.

dolphin n дельфи́н.

domain n (estate) владе́ние; (field) о́бласть.

dome n ку́пол.

domestic adj (of household; animals) дома́шний; (of family) семе́йный; (polit) вну́тренний; n прислу́га. **domesticate** vt прируча́ть impf, приручи́ть pf. **domesticity** n дома́шняя, семе́йная, жизнь.

domicile n местожи́тельство.

dominance n госпо́дство. **dominant** adj преоблада́ющий; госпо́дствующий. **dominate** vt госпо́дствовать impf над+instr. **domineering** adj вла́стный.

dominion n влады́чество; (realm) владе́ние.

domino n кость домино́; pl (game) домино́ neut indecl.

don vt надева́ть impf, наде́ть pf.

donate vt же́ртвовать impf, по~ pf. **donation** n поже́ртвование.

donkey n осёл.

donor n же́ртвователь m; (med) до́нор.

doom n (ruin) ги́бель; vt обрека́ть impf, обре́чь pf.

door n дверь. **doorbell** n (дверно́й) звоно́к. **doorman** n швейца́р. **doormat** n поло́вик. **doorstep** n поро́г. **doorway** n дверно́й проём.

dope n (drug) нарко́тик; vt дурма́нить impf, о~ pf.

dormant adj (sleeping) спя́щий; (inactive) безде́йствующий.

dormer window n слухово́е окно́.

dormitory n о́бщая спа́льня.

dormouse n со́ня.

dorsal adj спинно́й.

dosage n дозиро́вка. **dose** n до́за.

dossier n досье́ neut indecl.

dot n то́чка; vt ста́вить impf, по~ pf то́чки на+acc; (scatter) усе́ивать impf, усе́ять pf (with +instr); ~ted line пункти́р.

dote vi: ~ on обожа́ть impf.

double adj двойно́й; (doubled) удво́енный; ~-bass контраба́с; ~ bed двуспа́льная крова́ть; ~-breasted двубо́ртный; ~-cross обма́нывать impf, обману́ть pf; ~-dealer двуру́шник; ~-dealing двуру́шничество; ~-decker двухэта́жный авто́бус; ~-edged обоюдоо́стрый; ~ glazing двойны́е ра́мы f pl; ~ room ко́мната на двои́х; adv вдво́е; (two together) вдвоём; n двойно́е коли́чество; (person's) двойни́к; pl (sport) па́рная игра́; vt & i удва́ивать(ся) impf, удво́ить(ся) pf; ~ back возвраща́ться impf, верну́ться pf наза́д; ~ up (in pain) скрю́чиваться impf, скрю́читься pf; (share a room) помеща́ться impf, помести́ться pf вдвоём в одно́й ко́мнате; (~ up as) рабо́тать impf + instr по совмести́тельству.

doubt n сомне́ние; vt сомнева́ться impf в+prep. **doubtful** adj сомни́тельный. **doubtless** adv несомне́нно.

dough n те́сто. **doughnut** n по́нчик.

douse vt (drench) залива́ть impf, зали́ть pf.

dove n го́лубь m. **dovetail** n ла́сточкин хвост.

dowdy adj неэлега́нтный.

down[1] n (fluff) пух.

down[2] adv (motion) вниз; (position) внизу́; be ~ with (ill) боле́ть impf +instr; prep вниз с+gen, по+dat; (along) (вдоль) по+dat; vt: (gulp) опроки́дывать impf, опроки́нуть pf; ~-and-out n бродя́га m; ~-cast, ~-hearted уны́лый. **downfall** n ги́бель. **downhill** adv под го́ру. **downpour**

n ли́вень *m*. **downright** *adj* я́вный; *adv* соверше́нно. **downstairs** *adv* (*motion*) вниз; (*position*) внизу́. **downstream** *adv* вниз по тече́нию. **down-to-earth** *adj* реалисти́ческий. **downtrodden** *adj* угнетённый.

dowry *n* прида́ное *sb*.

doze *vi* дрема́ть *impf*.

dozen *n* дю́жина.

drab *adj* бесцве́тный; (*boring*) ску́чный.

draft *n* (*outline, rough copy*) набро́сок; (*document*) прое́кт; (*econ*) тра́тта; *see also* **draught**; *vt* составля́ть *impf*, соста́вить *pf* план, прое́кт, +*gen*.

drag *vt* тащи́ть *impf*; (*river etc.*) драги́ровать *impf & pf*; ~ **on** (*vi*) затя́гиваться *impf*, затяну́ться *pf*; *n* (*burden*) обу́за; (*on cigarette*) затя́жка; **in** ~ в же́нской оде́жде.

dragon *n* драко́н. **dragonfly** *n* стрекоза́.

drain *n* водосто́к; (*leakage; fig*) уте́чка; *vt* осуша́ть *impf*, осуши́ть *pf*; *vi* спуска́ться *impf*, спусти́ться *pf*. **drainage** *n* дрена́ж; (*system*) канализа́ция.

drake *n* се́лезень *m*.

drama *n* дра́ма; (*quality*) драмати́зм. **dramatic** *adj* драмати́ческий. **dramatist** *n* драмату́рг. **dramatize** *vt* драматизи́ровать *impf & pf*.

drape *vt* драпирова́ть *impf*, за~ *pf*; *n* драпиро́вка.

drastic *adj* радика́льный.

draught *n* (*air*) сквозня́к; (*traction*) тя́га; *pl* (*game*) ша́шки *f pl*; *see also* **draft**; **there is a** ~ сквози́т; ~ **beer** пи́во из бо́чки. **draughtsman** *n* чертёжник. **draughty** *adj*: **it is** ~ **here** здесь дует.

draw *n* (*in lottery*) ро́зыгрыш; (*attraction*) прима́нка; (*drawn game*) ничья́; *vt* (*pull*) тяну́ть *impf*, по~ *pf*; таска́ть *indet*, тащи́ть *det*; (*curtains*) задёргивать *impf*, задёрнуть *pf* (*занаве́ски*); (*attract*) привлека́ть *impf*, привле́чь *pf*; (*pull out*) выта́скивать *impf*, вы́тащить *pf*; (*sword*) обнажа́ть *impf*, обнажи́ть *pf*; (*lots*) броса́ть *impf*, бро́сить *pf* (*жре́бий*); (*water; inspiration*) че́рпать *impf*, черпну́ть *pf*; (*evoke*) вызыва́ть *impf*, вы́звать *pf*; (*conclusion*) выводи́ть

impf, вы́вести *pf* (*заключе́ние*); (*diagram*) черти́ть *impf*, на~ *pf*; (*picture*) рисова́ть *impf*, на~ *pf*; *vi* (*sport*) сыгра́ть *pf* вничью́; ~ **aside** отводи́ть *impf*, отвести́ *pf* в сто́рону; ~ **back** (*withdraw*) отступа́ть *impf*, отступи́ть *pf*; ~ **in** втя́гивать *impf*, втяну́ть *pf*; (*train*) входи́ть *impf*, войти́ в ста́нцию; (*car*) подходи́ть *impf*, подойти́ *pf* (**to** к + *dat*); (*days*) станови́ться *impf* коро́че; ~ **out** выта́гивать *impf*, вы́тянуть *pf*; (*money*) выпи́сывать *impf*, вы́писать *pf*; (*train/car*) выходи́ть *impf*, вы́йти *pf* (*со ста́нции/на доро́гу*); ~ **up** (*car*) подходи́ть *impf*, подойти́ *pf* (**to** к + *dat*); (*document*) составля́ть *impf*, соста́вить *pf*. **drawback** *n* недоста́ток. **drawbridge** *n* подъёмный мост. **drawer** *n* я́щик. **drawing** *n* (*action*) рисова́ние, черче́ние; (*object*) рису́нок, чертёж; ~**board** чертёжная доска́; ~**pin** кно́пка; ~**room** гости́ная *sb*.

drawl *n* протя́жное произноше́ние.

dread *n* страх; *vt* боя́ться *impf* +*gen*. **dreadful** *adj* ужа́сный.

dream *n* сон; (*fantasy*) мечта́; *vi* ви́деть *impf*, у~ *pf* сон; ~ **of** ви́деть *impf*, у~ *pf* во сне́; (*fig*) мечта́ть *impf* о+*prep*.

dreary *adj* (*weather*) па́смурный; (*boring*) ску́чный.

dredge *vt* (*river etc.*) драги́ровать *impf & pf*. **dredger** *n* дра́га.

dregs *n pl* оса́дки (-ков) *pl*.

drench *vt* прома́чивать *impf*, промочи́ть *pf*; **get** ~**ed** промока́ть *impf*, промо́кнуть *pf*.

dress *n* пла́тье; (*apparel*) оде́жда; ~ **circle** бельэта́ж; ~**maker** портни́ха; ~ **rehearsal** генера́льная репети́ция; *vt & i* одева́ть(ся) *impf*, оде́ть(ся) *pf*; *vt* (*cul*) приправля́ть *impf*, припра́вить *pf*; (*med*) перевя́зывать *impf*, перевяза́ть *pf*; ~ **up** наряжа́ться *impf*, наряди́ться *pf* (**as** + *instr*).

dresser *n* ку́хонный шкаф.

dressing *n* (*cul*) припра́ва; (*med*) перевя́зка; ~**gown** хала́т; ~**room** убо́рная *sb*; ~**table** туале́тный сто́лик.

dribble *vi* (*person*) пуска́ть *impf*, пусти́ть *pf* слю́ни; (*sport*) вести́ *impf* мяч.

dried adj сушёный. **drier** n сушилка.

drift n (*meaning*) смысл; (*snow*) сугроб; vi плыть impf по течению; (*naut*) дрейфовать impf; (*snow etc.*) скопляться impf, скопиться pf; ~ **apart** расходиться impf, разойтись pf.

drill¹ n сверло; (*dentist's*) бур; vt сверлить impf, про~ pf.

drill² vt (*mil*) обучать impf, обучить pf строю; vi проходить impf, пройти pf строевую подготовку; n строевая подготовка.

drink n напиток; vt пить impf, вы~ pf; ~**-driving** вождение в нетрёзвом состоянии. **drinking-water** n питьевая вода.

drip n (*action*) капанье; (*drop*) капля; vi капать impf, капнуть pf.

drive n (*journey*) езда; (*excursion*) прогулка; (*campaign*) поход, кампания; (*energy*) энергия; (*tech*) привод; (*driveway*) подъездная дорога; vt (*urge*, *chase*) гонять indet, гнать det; (*vehicle*) водить indet, вести det; управлять impf +instr; (*convey*) возить indet, везти det, по~ pf; vi (*travel*) ездить indet, ехать det, по~ pf; vt доводить impf, довести pf (**to** до+gen); (*nail etc.*) вбивать impf, вбить pf (**into** в+acc); ~ **away** vt прогонять impf, прогнать pf; vi уезжать impf, уехать pf; ~ **up** подъезжать impf, подъехать pf (**to** к+dat).

driver n (*of vehicle*) водитель m, шофёр. **driving** adj (*force*) движущий; (*rain*) проливной; ~**-licence** водительские права neut pl; ~**-test** экзамен на получение водительских прав; ~**-wheel** ведущее колесо.

drizzle n мелкий дождь m; vi моросить impf.

drone n (*bee*, *idler*) трутень m; (*of voice*) жужжание; (*of engine*) гул; vi (*buzz*) жужжать impf; (~ **on**) бубнить impf.

drool vi пускать impf, пустить pf слюни.

droop vi поникать impf, поникнуть pf.

drop n (*of liquid*) капля; (*fall*) падение, понижение; vt & i (*price*) снижать(ся) impf, снизить(ся) pf; vi (*fall*) падать impf, упасть pf; vt (*let fall*) ронять impf, уронить pf; (*aban-*

don) бросать impf, бросить pf; ~ **behind** отставать impf, отстать pf; ~ **in** заходить impf, зайти pf (**on** к+dat); ~ **off** (*fall asleep*) засыпать impf, заснуть pf; (*from car*) высаживать impf, высадить pf; ~ **out** выбывать impf, выбыть pf (**of** из+gen). **droppings** n pl помёт.

drought n засуха.

droves n pl: **in** ~ толпами.

drown vt топить impf, у~ pf; (*sound*) заглушать impf, заглушить pf; vi тонуть impf, у~ pf.

drowsy adj сонливый.

drudgery n нудная работа.

drug n медикамент; (*narcotic*) наркотик; ~ **addict** наркоман, ~ка; vt давать impf, дать pf наркотик+dat.

drum n барабан; vi бить impf в барабан; барабанить impf; ~ **sth into s.o.** вдалбливать impf, вдолбить pf + dat of person в голову. **drummer** n барабанщик.

drunk adj пьяный. **drunkard** n пьяница m & f. **drunken** adj пьяный; ~ **driving** вождение в нетрёзвом состоянии. **drunkenness** n пьянство.

dry adj сухой; ~ **land** суша; vt сушить impf, вы~ pf; (*wipe dry*) вытирать impf, вытереть pf; vi сохнуть impf, вы~, про~ pf. **dry-cleaning** n химчистка. **dryness** n сухость.

dual adj двойной; (*joint*) совместный; ~**-purpose** двойного назначения.

dub¹ vt (*nickname*) прозывать impf, прозвать pf.

dub² vt (*cin*) дублировать impf & pf.

dubious adj сомнительный.

duchess n герцогиня. **duchy** n герцогство.

duck¹ n (*bird*) утка.

duck² vt (*immerse*) окунать impf, окунуть pf; (*one's head*) нагнуть pf; (*evade*) увёртываться impf, увернуться pf от+gen; vi (~ *down*) наклоняться impf, наклониться pf.

duckling n утёнок.

duct n проход; (*anat*) проток.

dud n (*forgery*) подделка; (*shell*) неразорвавшийся снаряд; adj поддельный; (*worthless*) негодный.

due n (*credit*) должное sb; pl взносы m pl; adj (*proper*) должный, надлежащий; *predic* (*expected*) должен

(-жна́); in ~ course со вре́менем; ~ south пря́мо на юг; ~ to благодаря́ +dat.

duel n дуэ́ль.

duet n дуэ́т.

duke n ге́рцог.

dull adj (tedious) ску́чный; (colour) ту́склый, (weather) па́смурный; (not sharp; stupid) тупо́й; vt притупля́ть impf, притупи́ть pf.

duly adv надлежа́щим о́бразом; (punctually) своевре́менно.

dumb adj немо́й. **dumbfounded** adj ошара́шенный.

dummy n (tailor's) манеке́н; (baby's) со́ска; ~ run испыта́тельный рейс.

dump n сва́лка; vt сва́ливать impf, свали́ть pf.

dumpling n клёцка.

dumpy adj призе́мистый.

dune n дю́на.

dung n наво́з.

dungarees n pl комбинезо́н.

dungeon n темни́ца.

dunk vt мака́ть impf, макну́ть pf.

duo n па́ра; (mus) дуэ́т.

dupe n надува́ть impf, наду́ть pf; n простофи́ля m & f.

duplicate n ко́пия; in ~ в двух экземпля́рах; adj (double) двойно́й; (identical) иденти́чный; vt размножа́ть impf, размно́жить pf **duplicity** n двули́чность.

durability n про́чность. **durable** adj про́чный. **duration** n продолжи́тельность.

duress n принужде́ние; under ~ под давле́нием.

during prep во вре́мя +gen; (throughout) в тече́ние +gen.

dusk n су́мерки (-рек) pl.

dust n пыль; ~bin мусорный я́щик; ~-jacket суперобло́жка; ~man му́сорщик; ~pan сово́к; vt & i (clean) стира́ть impf, стере́ть pf пыль (c+gen); (sprinkle) посыпа́ть impf, посы́пать pf sth +acc, with +instr. **duster** n пыльная тря́пка. **dusty** adj пыльный.

Dutch adj голла́ндский; n: the ~ голла́ндцы m pl. **Dutchman** n голла́ндец. **Dutchwoman** n голла́ндка.

dutiful adj послу́шный. **duty** n (obligation) долг; обя́занность; (office) дежу́рство; (tax) по́шлина; be on ~

дежу́рить impf; ~-free adj беспо́шлинный.

dwarf n ка́рлик; vt (tower above) возвыша́ться impf, возвы́ситься pf над +instr.

dwell vi обита́ть impf; ~ upon остана́вливаться impf на+prep. **dweller** n жи́тель m. **dwelling** n жили́ще.

dwindle vi убыва́ть impf, убы́ть pf.

dye n краси́тель m; vt окра́шивать impf, окра́сить pf.

dynamic adj динами́ческий. **dynamics** n pl дина́мика.

dynamite n динами́т.

dynamo n дина́мо neut indecl.

dynasty n дина́стия.

dysentery n дизентери́я.

dyslexia n дисле́ксия. **dyslexic** adj: he is ~ он дисле́ктик.

E

each adj & pron ка́ждый; ~ other друг дру́га (dat -гу, etc.).

eager adj (pupil) усе́рдный; I am ~ to мне не те́рпится +inf; о́чень жела́ю +inf. **eagerly** adv с нетерпе́нием; жа́дно. **eagerness** n си́льное жела́ние.

eagle n орёл.

ear[1] n (corn) ко́лос.

ear[2] n (anat) у́хо; (sense) слух; ~ache боль в у́хе; ~drum бараба́нная перепо́нка; ~mark (assign) предназнача́ть impf, предназна́чить pf; ~phone нау́шник; ~ring серьга́; ~shot (clip-on) клипс; ~shot: within ~ в преде́лах слы́шимости; out of ~ вне преде́лов слы́шимости.

earl n граф.

early adj ра́нний; adv ра́но.

earn vt зараба́тывать impf, зарабо́тать pf; (deserve) заслу́живать impf, заслужи́ть pf. **earnings** n pl за́работок.

earnest adj серьёзный; n: in ~ всерьёз.

earth n земля́; (soil) по́чва; vt заземля́ть impf, заземли́ть pf. **earthenware** n гли́няный. **earthly** adj земно́й. **earthquake** n землетрясе́ние. **earthy** adj земли́стый; (coarse) гру́бый.

earwig n уховёртка.

ease n (facility) лёгкость; (unconstraint) непринуждённость; **with ~** легко; vt облегчáть impf, облегчи́ть pf; vi успокáиваться impf, успоко́иться pf.
easel n мольбéрт.
east n востóк; (naut) ост; adj востóчный. **easterly** adj востóчный. **eastern** adj востóчный. **eastward(s)** adv на востóк, к востóку.
Easter n Пáсха.
easy adj лёгкий; (unconstrained) непринуждённый; **~-going** уживчивый.
eat vt есть impf, c~ pf; кýшать impf, по~, c~ pf; **~ away** разъедáть impf, разъéсть pf; **~ into** въедáться impf, въéсться pf в+acc; **~ up** доедáть impf, доéсть pf. **eatable** adj съедóбный.
eaves n pl стрехá. **eavesdrop** vi подслýшивать impf.
ebb n (tide) отли́в; (fig) упáдок.
ebony n чёрное дéрево.
ebullient adj кипýчий.
EC abbr (of European Community) Европéйское сообщество.
eccentric n чудáк; adj эксцентри́чный.
ecclesiastical adj церкóвный.
echo n э́хо; vi (resound) отражáться impf, отрази́ться pf; vt (repeat) повторя́ть impf, повтори́ть pf.
eclipse n затмéние; vt затмевáть impf, затми́ть pf.
ecological adj экологи́ческий. **ecology** n эколóгия.
economic adj экономи́ческий. **economical** adj экономный. **economist** n экономи́ст. **economize** vt & i эконо́мить impf, c~ pf. **economy** n экономика; (saving) эконо́мия.
ecstasy n экстáз. **ecstatic** adj экстати́ческий.
eddy n водоворóт.
edge n край; (blade) лéзвие; **on ~** в нéрвном состоя́нии; **have the ~ on** имéть impf преимýщество над+instr; vt (border) окаймля́ть impf, окайми́ть pf; vi пробирáться impf, пробрáться pf. **edging** n каймá. **edgy** adj раздражи́тельный.
edible adj съедóбный.
edict n укáз.
edifice n здáние. **edifying** adj назидáтельный.

edit vt редакти́ровать impf, от~ pf; (cin) монти́ровать impf, c~ pf. **edition** n издáние; (number of copies) тирáж. **editor** n редáктор. **editorial** n передовáя статья́; adj редáкторский, редакцио́нный.
educate vt давáть impf, дать pf образовáние +dat; **where was he educated?** где он получи́л образовáние? **educated** adj образóванный. **education** n образовáние. **educational** adj образовáтельный; (instructive) учéбный.
eel n ýгорь m.
eerie adj жýткий.
effect n (result) слéдствие; (validity; influence) дéйствие; (impression; theat) эффéкт; **in ~** факти́чески; **take ~** вступáть impf, вступи́ть pf в си́лу; (medicine) начинáть impf, начáть pf дéйствовать; vt производи́ть impf, произвести́ pf. **effective** adj эффекти́вный; (striking) эффéктный; (actual) факти́ческий. **effectiveness** n эффекти́вность.
effeminate adj женоподóбный.
effervesce vi пузы́риться impf. **effervescent** adj (fig) и́скря́щийся.
efficiency n эффекти́вность. **efficient** adj эффекти́вный; (person) организо́ванный.
effigy n изображéние.
effort n уси́лие.
effrontery n нáглость.
effusive adj экспанси́вный.
e.g. abbr напр.
egalitarian adj эгалитáрный.
egg[1] n яйцó; **~cup** рю́мка для яйцá; **~shell** яи́чная скорлупá.
egg[2] vt: **~ on** подстрекáть impf, подстрекнýть pf.
ego n «Я». **egocentric** adj эгоцентри́ческий. **egoism** n эгои́зм. **ego(t)ist** n эгои́ст, **~ка**. **ego(t)istical** adj эгоцентри́ческий. **egotism** n эготи́зм.
Egypt n Еги́пет. **Egyptian** n египтя́нин, **-я́нка**; adj еги́петский.
eiderdown n пухóвое одея́ло.
eight adj & n вóсемь; (number 8) восьмёрка. **eighteen** adj & n восемнáдцать. **eighteenth** adj & n восемнáдцатый. **eighth** adj & n восьмóй; (fraction) восьмáя sb. **eightieth** adj & n восьмидеся́тый.

eighty adj & n во́семьдесят; pl (decade) восьмидеся́тые го́ды (-до́в) m pl.

either adj & pron (one of two) оди́н из двух, тот и́ли друго́й; (both) и тот, и друго́й; (one or other) любо́й; adv & conj: ~ ... or и́ли... и́ли, ли́бо... ли́бо.

eject vt выбра́сывать impf, вы́бросить pf; vi (pilot) катапульти́роваться impf & pf.

eke vt: ~ out a living перебива́ться impf, переби́ться pf ко́е-как.

elaborate adj (ornate) витиева́тый; (detailed) подро́бный; vt разраба́тывать impf, разрабо́тать pf; (detail) уточня́ть impf, уточни́ть pf.

elapse vi проходи́ть impf, пройти́ pf; (expire) истека́ть impf, исте́чь pf.

elastic n рези́нка; adj эласти́чный; ~ band рези́нка. **elasticity** n эласти́чность.

elated adj в восто́рге. **elation** n восто́рг.

elbow n ло́коть m; vt: ~ (one's way) through прота́лкиваться impf, протолкну́ться pf че́рез+acc.

elder[1] n (tree) бузина́.

elder[2] n (person) ста́рец; pl ста́ршие sb; adj ста́рший. **elderly** adj пожило́й. **eldest** adj ста́рший.

elect adj и́збранный; vt избира́ть impf, избра́ть pf. **election** n вы́боры m pl. **elector** n избира́тель m. **electoral** adj избира́тельный. **electorate** n избира́тели m pl.

electric(al) adj электри́ческий; ~ shock уда́р электри́ческим то́ком. **electrician** n эле́ктрик. **electricity** n электри́чество. **electrify** vt (convert to electricity) электрифици́ровать impf & pf; (charge with electricity; fig) электризова́ть impf, на~ pf. **electrode** n электро́д. **electron** n электро́н. **electronic** adj электро́нный. **electronics** n электро́ника.

electrocute vt убива́ть impf, уби́ть pf электри́ческим то́ком; (execute) казни́ть impf & pf на электри́ческом сту́ле. **electrolysis** n электро́лиз.

elegance n эле́гантность. **elegant** adj элега́нтный.

elegy n эле́гия.

element n элеме́нт; (earth, wind, etc.) стихи́я; be in one's ~ быть в свое́й стихи́и. **elemental** adj стихи́йный. **elementary** adj элемента́рный; (school etc.) нача́льный.

elephant n слон.

elevate vt поднима́ть impf, подня́ть pf. **elevated** adj возвы́шенный. **elevation** n (height) высота́. **elevator** n (lift) лифт.

eleven adj & n оди́ннадцать. **eleventh** adj & n оди́ннадцатый; at the ~ hour в после́днюю мину́ту.

elf n эльф.

elicit vt (obtain) выявля́ть impf, вы́явить pf; (evoke) вызыва́ть impf, вы́звать pf.

eligible adj име́ющий пра́во (for на+acc); (bachelor) подходя́щий.

eliminate vt (do away with) устраня́ть impf, устрани́ть pf; (rule out) исключа́ть impf, исключи́ть pf.

élite n эли́та.

ellipse n э́ллипс. **elliptic(al)** adj эллипти́ческий.

elm n вяз.

elocution n ора́торское иску́сство.

elongate vt удлиня́ть impf, удлини́ть pf.

elope vi бежа́ть det (с возлюблен́ным).

eloquence n красноре́чие. **eloquent** adj красноречи́вый.

else adv (besides) ещё; (instead) друго́й; (with neg) бо́льше; nobody ~ никто́ бо́льше; or ~ и́на́че; a (не) то; и́ли же; s.o. ~ кто-нибу́дь друго́й; something ~? ещё что́-нибудь? **elsewhere** adv (place) в друго́м ме́сте; (direction) в друго́е ме́сто.

elucidate vt разъясня́ть impf, разъясни́ть pf.

elude vt избега́ть impf +gen. **elusive** adj неулови́мый.

emaciated adj истощённый.

emanate vi исходи́ть impf (from из, от, +gen).

emancipate vt эмансипи́ровать impf & pf. **emancipation** n эмансипа́ция.

embankment n (river) на́бережная sb; (rly) на́сыпь.

embargo n эмба́рго neut indecl.

embark vi сади́ться impf, сесть pf на кора́бль; ~ upon предпринима́ть impf, предприня́ть pf. **embarkation**

n посáдка (на корáбль).

embarrass *vt* смущáть *impf*, смутúть *pf*; be ~ed чýвствовать *impf* себя́ неудóбно. **embarrassing** *adj* неудóбный. **embarrassment** *n* смущéние.

embassy *n* посóльство.

embedded *adj* врéзанный.

embellish *vt* (*adorn*) украшáть *impf*, укрáсить *pf*; (*story*) прикрашивать *impf*, прикрáсить *pf*. **embellishment** *n* украшéние.

embers *n pl* тлéющие уголькú *m pl*.

embezzle *vt* растрáчивать *impf*, растрáтить *pf*. **embezzlement** *n* растрáта.

embitter *vt* ожесточáть *impf*, ожесточúть *pf*.

emblem *n* эмблéма.

embodiment *n* воплощéние. **embody** *vt* воплощáть *impf*, воплотúть *pf*.

emboss *vt* чекáнить *impf*, вы́~, от~ *pf*.

embrace *vt* объя́тие; *vi* обнимáться *impf*, обня́ться *pf*; обнимáть *impf*, обня́ть *pf*; (*accept*) принимáть *impf*, приня́ть *pf*; (*include*) охвáтывать *impf*, охватúть *pf*.

embroider *vt* вышивáть *impf*, вы́шить *pf*; (*story*) прикрашивать *impf*, прикрáсить *pf*. **embroidery** *n* вышивка.

embroil *vt* впýтывать *impf*, впýтать *pf*.

embryo *n* эмбриóн.

emerald *n* изумрýд.

emerge *vi* появля́ться *impf*, появúться *pf*. **emergence** *n* появлéние. **emergency** *n* крáйняя необходúмость; **state of** ~ чрезвычáйное положéние; ~ **exit** запаснóй вы́ход.

emery paper *n* наждáчная бумáга.

emigrant *n* эмигрáнт, ~ка. **emigrate** *vi* эмигрúровать *impf & pf*. **emigration** *n* эмигрáция.

eminence *n* (*fame*) знаменúтость. **eminent** *adj* выдаю́щийся. **eminently** *adv* чрезвычáйно.

emission *n* испускáние. **emit** *vt* испускáть *impf*, испустúть *pf*; (*light*) излучáть *impf*, излучúть *pf*; (*sound*) издавáть *impf*, издáть *pf*.

emotion *n* эмóция, чýвство. **emotional** *adj* эмоционáльный.

empathize *vt* сопереживáть *impf*, сопережúть *pf*. **empathy** *n* эмпáтия.

emperor *n* импарáтор.

emphasis *n* ударéние. **emphasize** *vt* подчёркивать *impf*, подчеркнýть *pf*. **emphatic** *adj* вырази́тельный; категорúческий.

empire *n* импéрия.

empirical *adj* эмпири́ческий.

employ *vt* (*use*) пóльзоваться *impf* +*instr*; (*person*) нанимáть *impf*, наня́ть *pf*. **employee** *n* сотрýдник, рабóчий *sb*. **employer** *n* работодáтель *m*. **employment** *n* рабóта, служба; (*use*) использование.

empower *vt* уполномóчивать *impf*, уполномóчить *pf* (**to** на+*acc*).

empress *n* императрúца.

emptiness *n* пустотá. **empty** *adj* пустóй; ~**-headed** пустоголóвый; *vt* (*container*) опорожня́ть *impf*, опорóжнúть *pf*; (*solid*) высыпáть *impf*, вы́сыпать *pf*; (*liquid*) выливáть *impf*, вы́лить *pf*; *vi* пустéть *impf*, o~ *pf*.

emulate *vt* достигáть *impf*, достúгнуть, достúчь *pf* +*gen*; (*copy*) подражáть *impf* +*dat*.

emulsion *n* эмýльсия.

enable *vt* давáть *impf*, дать *pf* возмóжность +*dat & inf*.

enact *vt* (*law*) принимáть *impf*, приня́ть *pf*; (*theat*) разы́грывать *impf*, разыгрáть *pf*. **enactment** *n* (*law*) постановлéние; (*theat*) игрá.

enamel *n* эмáль; *adj* эмáлевый; *vt* эмалировáть *impf & pf*.

encampment *n* лáгерь *m*.

enchant *vt* очарóвывать *impf*, очаровáть *pf*. **enchanting** *adj* очаровáтельный. **enchantment** *n* очаровáние.

encircle *vt* окружáть *impf*, окружúть *pf*.

enclave *n* анклáв.

enclose *vt* огорáживать *impf*, огородúть *pf*; (*in letter*) приклáдывать *impf*, приложúть *pf*; **please find ~d** прилагáется (-áются) +*nom*. **enclosure** *n* огорóженное мéсто; (*in letter*) приложéние.

encode *vt* шифровáть *impf*, за~ *pf*.

encompass *vt* (*encircle*) окружáть *impf*, окружúть *pf*; (*contain*) заключáть *impf*, заключúть *pf*.

encore *int* бис!; *n* вы́зов на бис.

encounter *n* встре́ча; (*in combat*) столкнове́ние; *vt* встреча́ть *impf*, встре́тить *pf*; (*fig*) ста́лкиваться *impf*, столкну́ться *pf* с+*instr*.

encourage *vt* ободря́ть *impf*, ободри́ть *pf*. **encouragement** *n* ободре́ние. **encouraging** *adj* ободри́тельный.

encroach *vt* вторга́ться *impf*, вто́ргнуться *pf* (**on** в+*acc*). **encroachment** *n* вторже́ние.

encumber *vt* обременя́ть *impf*, обремени́ть *pf*. **encumbrance** *n* обу́за.

encyclopaedia *n* энциклопе́дия. **encyclopaedic** *adj* энциклопеди́ческий.

end *n* коне́ц; (*death*) смерть; (*purpose*) цель; **an ~ in itself** самоце́ль; **in the ~** в конце́ концо́в; **make ~s meet** своди́ть *impf*, свести́ *pf* концы́ с конца́ми; **no ~ of** ма́сса+*gen*; **on ~** (*upright*) стоймя́, дыбо́м; (*continuously*) подря́д; **put an ~to** класть *impf*, положи́ть *pf* коне́ц +*dat*; *vt* конча́ть *impf*, ко́нчить *pf*; (*halt*) прекраща́ть *impf*, прекрати́ть *pf*; *vi* конча́ться *impf*, ко́нчиться *pf*.

endanger *vt* подверга́ть *impf*, подве́ргнуть *pf* опа́сности.

endearing *adj* привлека́тельный. **endearment** *n* ла́ска.

endeavour *n* попы́тка; (*exertion*) уси́лие; (*undertaking*) де́ло; *vi* стара́ться *impf*, по~ *pf*.

endemic *adj* эндеми́ческий.

ending *n* оконча́ние. **endless** *adj* бесконе́чный.

endorse *vt* (*document*) подпи́сывать *impf*, подписа́ть *pf*; (*support*) подде́рживать *impf*, поддержа́ть *pf*. **endorsement** *n* по́дпись; подде́ржка; (*on driving licence*) проко́л.

endow *vt* обеспе́чивать *impf*, обеспе́чить *pf* посто́янным дохо́дом; (*fig*) одаря́ть *impf*, одари́ть *pf*. **endowment** *n* поже́ртвование; (*talent*) дарова́ние.

endurance *n* (*of person*) выно́сливость; (*of object*) про́чность. **endure** *vt* выноси́ть *impf*, вы́нести *pf*; терпе́ть *impf*, по~ *pf*; *vi* продолжа́ться *impf*, продо́лжиться *pf*.

enemy *n* враг; *adj* вра́жеский.

energetic *adj* энерги́чный. **energy** *n*

эне́ргия; *pl* си́лы *f pl*.

enforce *vt* (*law etc.*) следи́ть *impf* за выполне́нием +*gen*. **enforcement** *n* наблюде́ние за выполне́нием +*gen*.

engage *vt* (*hire*) нанима́ть *impf*, наня́ть *pf*; (*tech*) зацепля́ть *impf*, зацепи́ть *pf*. **engaged** *adj* (*occupied*) за́нятый; **be ~** in занима́ться *impf*, заня́ться *pf* +*instr*; **become ~** обруча́ться *impf*, обручи́ться *pf* (**to** с+*instr*). **engagement** *n* (*appointment*) свида́ние; (*betrothal*) обруче́ние; (*battle*) бой; **~ ring** обруча́льное кольцо́. **engaging** *adj* привлека́тельный.

engender *vt* порожда́ть *impf*, породи́ть *pf*.

engine *n* дви́гатель *m*; (*rly*) локомоти́в; **~-driver** (*rly*) машини́ст. **engineer** *n* инжене́р; *vt* (*fig*) организова́ть *impf* & *pf*. **engineering** *n* инжене́рное де́ло, те́хника.

England *n* А́нглия. **English** *adj* англи́йский; *n*: **the ~** *pl* англича́не (-н) *pl*. **Englishman, -woman** *n* англича́нин, -а́нка.

engrave *vt* гравирова́ть *impf*, вы́~ *pf*; (*fig*) вреза́ть *impf*, вре́зать *pf*. **engraver** *n* гравёр. **engraving** *n* гравю́ра.

engross *vt* поглоща́ть *impf*, поглоти́ть *pf*; **be ~ed** in быть погло́щённым +*instr*.

engulf *vt* поглоща́ть *impf*, поглоти́ть *pf*.

enhance *vt* увели́чивать *impf*, увели́чить *pf*.

enigma *n* зага́дка. **enigmatic** *adj* зага́дочный.

enjoy *vt* получа́ть *impf*, получи́ть *pf* удово́льствие от+*gen*; наслажда́ться *impf*, наслади́ться *pf* +*instr*; (*health etc.*) облада́ть *impf* +*instr*; **~ o.s.** хорошо́ проводи́ть *impf*, провести́ *pf* вре́мя. **enjoyable** *adj* прия́тный. **enjoyment** *n* удово́льствие.

enlarge *vt* увели́чивать *impf*, увели́чить *pf*; **~ upon** распространя́ться *impf*, распространи́ться *pf* о+*prep*. **enlargement** *n* увеличе́ние.

enlighten *vt* просвеща́ть *impf*, просвети́ть *pf*. **enlightenment** *n* просвеще́ние.

enlist *vi* поступа́ть *impf*, поступи́ть *pf* на вое́нную слу́жбу; *vt* (*mil*) вербова́ть *impf*, за~ *pf*; (*support etc.*) заруча́ться *impf*, заручи́ться *pf* +*instr*.

enliven *vt* оживля́ть *impf*, оживи́ть *pf*.

enmity *n* вражда́.

ennoble *vt* облагора́живать *impf*, облагоро́дить *pf*.

ennui *n* тоска́.

enormity *n* чудо́вищность. **enormous** *adj* огро́мный. **enormously** *adv* чрезвыча́йно.

enough *adj* доста́точно +*gen*; *adv* доста́точно, дово́льно; **be ~** хвата́ть *impf*, хвати́ть *pf impers*+*gen*.

enquire, enquiry *see* inquire, inquiry

enrage *vt* беси́ть *impf*, вз~ *pf*.

enrapture *vt* восхища́ть *impf*, восхити́ть *pf*.

enrich *vt* обогаща́ть *impf*, обогати́ть *pf*.

enrol *vt & i* запи́сывать(ся) *impf*, записа́ть(ся) *pf*. **enrolment** *n* за́пись.

en route *adv* по пути́ (**to, for** в+*acc*).

ensconce *vt*: **~ o.s.** заса́живаться *impf*, засе́сть *pf* (**with** за+*acc*).

ensemble *n* (*mus*) анса́мбль *m*.

enshrine *vt* (*fig*) охраня́ть *impf*, охрани́ть *pf*.

ensign *n* (*flag*) флаг.

enslave *vt* порабоща́ть *impf*, поработи́ть *pf*.

ensue *vi* сле́довать *impf*. **ensuing** *adj* после́дующий.

ensure *vt* обеспе́чивать *impf*, обеспе́чить *pf*.

entail *vt* (*necessitate*) влечь *impf* за собо́й.

entangle *vt* запу́тывать *impf*, запу́тать *pf*.

enter *vt & i* входи́ть *impf*, войти́ *pf* в+*acc*; (*by transport*) въезжа́ть *impf*, въе́хать *pf* в+*acc*; *vt* (*join*) поступа́ть *impf*, поступи́ть *pf* в, на, +*acc*; (*competition*) вступа́ть *impf*, вступи́ть *pf* в+*acc*; (*in list*) вноси́ть *impf*, внести́ *pf* в+*acc*.

enterprise *n* (*undertaking*) предприя́тие; (*initiative*) предприи́мчивость. **enterprising** *adj* предприи́мчивый.

entertain *vt* (*amuse*) развлека́ть *impf*, развле́чь *pf*; (*guests*) принима́ть *impf*, приня́ть *pf*; угоща́ть *impf*, угости́ть *pf* (**to** +*instr*); (*hopes*) пита́ть *impf*. **entertaining** *adj* зани-

ма́тельный. **entertainment** *n* развлече́ние; (*show*) представле́ние.

enthral *vt* порабоща́ть *impf*, поработи́ть *pf*.

enthusiasm *n* энтузиа́зм. **enthusiast** *n* энтузиа́ст, ~ка. **enthusiastic** *adj* восто́рженный; по́лный энтузиа́зма.

entice *vt* зама́нивать *impf*, замани́ть *pf*. **enticement** *n* прима́нка. **enticing** *adj* зама́нчивый.

entire *adj* по́лный, це́лый, весь. **entirely** *adv* вполне́, соверше́нно; (*solely*) исключи́тельно. **entirety** *n*: **in its ~** по́лностью.

entitle *vt* (*authorize*) дава́ть *impf*, дать *pf* пра́во+*dat* (**to** на+*acc*); **be ~d** (*book*) называ́ться *impf*; **be ~d to** име́ть *impf* пра́во на+*acc*.

entity *n* объе́кт; фено́мен.

entomology *n* энтомоло́гия.

entourage *n* сви́та.

entrails *n pl* вну́тренности (-тей) *pl*.

entrance[1] *n* вход, въезд; (*theat*) вы́ход; **~ exam** вступи́тельный экза́мен; **~ hall** вестибю́ль *m*.

entrance[2] *vt* (*charm*) очаро́вывать *impf*, очарова́ть *pf*. **entrancing** *adj* очарова́тельный.

entrant *n* уча́стник (**for** +*gen*).

entreat *vt* умоля́ть *impf*, умоли́ть *pf*. **entreaty** *n* мольба́.

entrench *vt* **be, become ~ed** (*fig*) укореня́ться *impf*, укорени́ться *pf*.

entrepreneur *n* предпринима́тель *m*.

entrust *vt* (*secret*) вверя́ть *impf*, вве́рить *pf* (**to** +*dat*); (*object; person*) поруча́ть *impf*, поручи́ть *pf* (**to** +*dat*).

entry *n* вход, въезд; вступле́ние; (*theat*) вы́ход; (*note*) за́пись; (*in reference book*) статья́.

entwine *vt* (*interweave*) сплета́ть *impf*, сплести́ *pf*; (*wreathe*) обвива́ть *impf*, обви́ть *pf*.

enumerate *vt* перечисля́ть *impf*, перечи́слить *pf*.

enunciate *vt* (*express*) излага́ть *impf*, изложи́ть *pf*; (*pronounce*) произноси́ть *impf*, произнести́ *pf*. **enunciation** *n* изложе́ние; произноше́ние.

envelop *vt* оку́тывать *impf*, оку́тать *pf*. **envelope** *n* конве́рт.

enviable *adj* зави́дный. **envious** *adj* зави́стливый.

environment n среда́; (the ~) окружа́ющая среда́. **environs** n pl окре́стности f pl.

envisage vt предусма́тривать impf, предусмотре́ть pf.

envoy n посла́нник, аге́нт.

envy n за́висть; vt зави́довать impf, по~ pf +dat.

enzyme n энзи́м.

ephemeral adj эфеме́рный.

epic n эпопе́я; adj эпи́ческий.

epidemic n эпиде́мия.

epilepsy n эпиле́псия. **epileptic** n эпиле́птик; adj эпилепти́ческий.

epilogue n эпило́г.

episode n эпизо́д. **episodic** adj эпизоди́ческий.

epistle n посла́ние.

epitaph n эпита́фия.

epithet n эпи́тет.

epitome n воплоще́ние. **epitomize** vt воплоща́ть impf, воплоти́ть pf.

epoch n эпо́ха.

equal adj ра́вный, одина́ковый; (capable of) спосо́бный (to на+acc, +inf); n ра́вный sb; vt равня́ться impf +dat. **equality** n ра́венство.

equalize vt ура́внивать impf, уравня́ть pf; vi (sport) равня́ть impf, с~ pf счёт. **equally** adv равно́, ра́вным о́бразом.

equanimity n хладнокро́вие.

equate vt прира́внивать impf, приравня́ть pf (with к+dat).

equation n (math) уравне́ние.

equator n эква́тор **equatorial** adj экваториа́льный.

equestrian adj ко́нный.

equidistant adj равностоя́щий. **equilibrium** n равнове́сие.

equip vt обору́довать impf & pf; (person) снаряжа́ть impf, снаряди́ть pf; (fig) вооружа́ть impf, вооружи́ть pf. **equipment** n обору́дование, снаряже́ние.

equitable adj справедли́вый. **equity** n справедли́вость; pl (econ) обыкнове́нные а́кции f pl.

equivalent adj эквивале́нтный; n эквивале́нт.

equivocal adj двусмы́сленный.

era n э́ра.

eradicate vt искореня́ть impf, искорени́ть pf.

erase vt стира́ть impf, стере́ть pf;

(from memory) вычёркивать impf, вы́черкнуть pf (из па́мяти). **eraser** n ла́стик.

erect adj прямо́й; vt сооружа́ть impf, сооруди́ть pf. **erection** n сооруже́ние; (biol) эре́кция.

erode vt разруша́ть impf, разру́шить pf. **erosion** n эро́зия; (fig) разруше́ние.

erotic adj эроти́ческий.

err vi ошиба́ться impf, ошиби́ться pf; (sin) греши́ть impf, со~ pf.

errand n поруче́ние; run ~s быть на посы́лках (for y+gen).

erratic adj нерóвный.

erroneous adj оши́бочный. **error** n оши́бка.

erudite adj учёный. **erudition** n эруди́ция.

erupt vi взрыва́ться impf, взорва́ться pf; (volcano) изверга́ться impf, изве́ргнуться pf. **eruption** n изверже́ние.

escalate vi возраста́ть impf, возрасти́ pf; vt интенсифици́ровать impf & pf.

escalator n эскала́тор.

escapade n вы́ходка. **escape** n (from prison) побе́г; (from danger) спасе́ние; (leak) уте́чка; have a narrow ~ едва́ спасти́сь; vi (flee) бежа́ть impf & pf; убега́ть impf, убежа́ть pf; (save o.s.) спаса́ться impf, спасти́сь pf; (leak) утека́ть impf, уте́чь pf; vt избега́ть impf, избежа́ть pf +gen; (groan) вырыва́ться impf, вы́рваться pf из, у, +gen.

escort n (mil) эско́рт; (of lady) кавале́р; vt сопровожда́ть impf, сопроводи́ть pf; (mil) эскорти́ровать impf & pf.

Eskimo n эскимо́с, ~ка.

esoteric adj эзотери́ческий.

especially adv особе́нно.

espionage n шпиона́ж.

espousal n подде́ржка. **espouse** vt (fig) подде́рживать impf, поддержа́ть pf.

essay n о́черк.

essence n (philos) су́щность; (gist) суть; (extract) эссе́нция. **essential** adj (fundamental) суще́ственный; (necessary) необходи́мый; n pl (necessities) необходи́мое sb; (crux) суть; (fundamentals) осно́вы f pl.

essentially adv по существу́.

establish vt (set up) учрежда́ть impf, учреди́ть pf; (fact etc.) устана́вливать impf, установи́ть pf. **establishment** n (action) учрежде́ние, установле́ние; (institution) учрежде́ние.

estate n (property) име́ние; (after death) насле́дство; (housing ~) жило́й масси́в; ~ **agent** аге́нт по прода́же недви́жимости; ~ **car** автомоби́ль m с ку́зовом «универса́л».

esteem n уваже́ние; vt уважа́ть impf. **estimate** n (of quality) оце́нка; (of cost) сме́та; vt оце́нивать impf, оцени́ть pf. **estimation** n оце́нка, мне́ние.

Estonia n Эсто́ния. **Estonian** n эсто́нец, -нка; adj эсто́нский.

estranged adj отчуждённый. **estrangement** n отчужде́ние.

estuary n у́стье.

etc. abbr и т.д. **etcetera** и так да́лее.

etch vt трави́ть impf, вы́~ pf. **etching** n (action) травле́ние; (object) офо́рт.

eternal adj ве́чный. **eternity** n ве́чность.

ether n эфи́р. **ethereal** adj эфи́рный.

ethical adj эти́ческий, эти́чный. **ethics** n э́тика.

ethnic adj этни́ческий.

etiquette n этике́т.

etymology n этимоло́гия.

EU abbr (of European Union) ЕС.

eucalyptus n эвкали́пт.

Eucharist n Прича́стие.

eulogy n похвала́.

euphemism n эвфеми́зм. **euphemistic** adj эвфемисти́ческий.

Europe n Евро́па. **European** n европе́ец; adj европе́йский; ~ **Community** Европе́йское соо́бщество; ~ **Union** Европе́йский сою́з.

evacuate vt (person, place) эваку́ировать impf & pf. **evacuation** n эвакуа́ция.

evade vt уклоня́ться impf, уклони́ться pf от+gen.

evaluate vt оце́нивать impf, оцени́ть pf. **evaluation** n оце́нка.

evangelical adj ева́нгельский. **evangelist** n ева́нгелист.

evaporate vt & i испаря́ть(ся) impf, испари́ть(ся) pf. **evaporation** n испаре́ние.

evasion n уклоне́ние (of от+gen). **evasive** adj укло́нчивый.

eve n кану́н; on the ~ накану́не.

even adj ро́вный; (number) чётный; get ~ расквита́ться pf (with c+instr); adv да́же; (just) ещё; ~ **if** да́же е́сли; ~ **though** хотя́; ~ **so** всё-таки; not ~ да́же не; vt выра́внивать impf, вы́ровнять pf.

evening n ве́чер; adj вече́рний; ~ **class** вече́рние ку́рсы m pl.

evenly adv по́ровну, ро́вно. **evenness** n ро́вность.

event n собы́тие, происше́ствие; in the ~ of в слу́чае+gen; in any ~ во вся́ком слу́чае; in the ~ в коне́чном счёте. **eventful** adj по́лный собы́тий. **eventual** adj коне́чный. **eventuality** n возмо́жность. **eventually** adv в конце́ концо́в.

ever adv (at any time) когда́-либо, когда́-нибудь; (always) всегда́; (emph) же; ~ **since** с тех пор (как); ~ **so** о́чень; for ~ навсегда́; hardly ~ почти́ никогда́. **evergreen** adj вечнозелёный; n вечнозелёное расте́ние. **everlasting** adj ве́чный. **evermore** adv: **for** ~ навсегда́.

every adj ка́ждый, вся́кий, все (pl); ~ **now and then** вре́мя от вре́мени; ~ **other** ка́ждый второ́й; ~ **other day** че́рез день. **everybody**, **everyone** pron ка́ждый, все (pl). **everyday** adj (daily) ежедне́вный; (commonplace) повседне́вный. **everything** pron всё. **everywhere** adv всю́ду, везде́.

evict vt выселя́ть impf, вы́селить pf. **eviction** n выселе́ние.

evidence n свиде́тельство, доказа́тельство; give ~ свиде́тельствовать impf (о+prep; +acc; +что). **evident** adj очеви́дный.

evil n зло; adj злой.

evoke vt вызыва́ть impf, вы́звать pf.

evolution n эволю́ция. **evolutionary** adj эволюцио́нный. **evolve** vt & i развива́ть(ся) impf, разви́ть(ся) pf.

ewe n овца́.

ex- in comb бы́вший.

exacerbate vt обостря́ть impf, обостри́ть pf.

exact adj то́чный; vt взы́скивать

impf, взыска́ть *pf* (**from, of** c+*gen*).
exacting *adj* тре́бовательный. **ex-actitude, exactness** *n* то́чность.
exactly *adv* то́чно; (*just*) как раз; (*precisely*) и́менно.
exaggerate *vt* преувели́чивать *impf*, преувели́чить *pf*. **exaggeration** *n* преувеличе́ние.
exalt *vt* возвыша́ть *impf*, возвы́сить *pf*; (*extol*) превозноси́ть *impf*, превознести́ *pf*.
examination *n* (*inspection*) осмо́тр; (*exam*) экза́мен; (*law*) допро́с. **ex-amine** *vt* (*inspect*) осма́тривать *impf*, осмотре́ть *pf*; (*test*) экзамено́вать *impf*, про~ *pf*; (*law*) допра́шивать *impf*, допроси́ть *pf*. **exam-iner** *n* экзамена́тор.
example *n* приме́р; **for ~** наприме́р.
exasperate *vt* раздража́ть *impf*, раздражи́ть *pf*. **exasperation** *n* раздраже́ние.
excavate *vt* раска́пывать *impf*, раскопа́ть *pf*. **excavations** *n pl* раско́пки *f pl*. **excavator** *n* экскава́тор.
exceed *vt* превыша́ть *impf*, превы́сить *pf*. **exceedingly** *adv* чрезвыча́йно.
excel *vt* превосходи́ть *impf*, превзойти́ *pf*; *vi* отлича́ться *impf*, отличи́ться *pf* (**at, in** в+*prep*). **ex-cellence** *n* превосхо́дство. **excel-lency** *n* превосходи́тельство. **excel-lent** *adj* отли́чный.
except *vt* исключа́ть *impf*, исключи́ть *pf*; *prep* кро́ме+*gen*. **exception** *n* исключе́ние; **take ~ to** возража́ть *impf*, возрази́ть *pf* про́тив+*gen*. **ex-ceptional** *adj* исключи́тельный.
excerpt *n* отры́вок.
excess *n* изби́ток. **excessive** *adj* чрезме́рный.
exchange *n* обме́н (**of** +*instr*); (*of currency*) разме́н; (*building*) би́ржа; (*telephone*) центра́льная телефо́нная ста́нция; **~ rate** курс; *vt* обме́нивать *impf*, обменя́ть *pf* (**for** на+*acc*); обме́ниваться *impf*, обменя́ться *pf* +*instr*.
Exchequer *n* казначе́йство.
excise¹ *n* (*duty*) акци́з(ный сбор).
excise² *vt* (*cut out*) выреза́ть *impf*, вы́резать *pf*.
excitable *adj* возбуди́мый. **excite** *vt* (*cause, arouse*) возбужда́ть *impf*,

возбуди́ть *pf*; (*thrill, agitate*) волнова́ть *impf*, вз~ *pf*. **excitement** *n* возбужде́ние; волне́ние.
exclaim *vi* воскли́цать *impf*, воскли́кнуть *pf*. **exclamation** *n* восклица́ние; **~ mark** восклица́тельный знак.
exclude *vt* исключа́ть *impf*, исключи́ть *pf*. **exclusion** *n* исключе́ние. **exclusive** *adj* исключи́тельный.
excommunicate *vt* отлуча́ть *impf*, отлучи́ть *pf* (**от** це́ркви).
excrement *n* экскреме́нты (-тов) *pl*.
excrete *vt* выделя́ть *impf*, вы́делить *pf*. **excretion** *n* выделе́ние.
excruciating *adj* мучи́тельный.
excursion *n* экску́рсия.
excusable *adj* прости́тельный. **ex-cuse** *n* оправда́ние; (*pretext*) отгово́рка; *vt* (*forgive*) извиня́ть *impf*, извини́ть *pf*; (*justify*) опра́вдывать *impf*, оправда́ть *pf*; (*release*) освобожда́ть *impf*, освободи́ть *pf* (**from** от+*gen*); **~ me!** извини́те!; прости́те!
execute *vt* исполня́ть *impf*, испо́лнить *pf*; (*criminal*) казни́ть *impf* & *pf*. **execution** *n* исполне́ние; казнь. **executioner** *n* пала́ч. **executive** *n* исполни́тельный о́рган; (*person*) руководи́тель *m*; *adj* исполни́тельный.
exemplary *adj* приме́рный. **exem-plify** *vt* (*illustrate by example*) приводи́ть *impf*, привести́ *pf* приме́р +*gen*; (*serve as example*) служи́ть *impf*, по~ *pf* приме́ром +*gen*.
exempt *adj* освобождённый; *vt* освобожда́ть *impf*, освободи́ть *pf* (**from** от+*gen*). **exemption** *n* освобожде́ние.
exercise *n* (*use*) примене́ние; (*physical ~; task*) упражне́ние; **take ~** упражня́ться *impf*; **~ book** тетра́дь; *vt* (*use*) применя́ть *impf*, примени́ть *pf*; (*dog*) прогу́ливать *impf*; (*train*) упражня́ть *impf*.
exert *vt* ока́зывать *impf*, оказа́ть *pf*; **~ o.s.** стара́ться *impf*, по~ *pf*. **ex-ertion** *n* напряже́ние.
exhale *vt* выдыха́ть *impf*, вы́дохнуть *pf*.
exhaust *n* вы́хлоп; **~ fumes** выхлопны́е га́зы *m pl*; **~ pipe** выхлопна́я труба́; *vt* (*use up*) истоща́ть *impf*,

exhibit 323 export

истощи́ть *pf*; (*person*) изнуря́ть *impf*, изнури́ть *pf*; (*subject*) исчёрпывать *impf*, исчёрпать *pf*. **exhausted** *adj*: be ~ (*person*) быть измождённым. **exhausting** *adj* изнури́тельный. **exhaustion** *n* изнуре́ние; (*depletion*) истоще́ние. **exhaustive** *adj* исчёрпывающий.

exhibit *n* экспона́т; (*law*) веще́ственное доказа́тельство; *vt* (*manifest*) проявля́ть *impf*, прояви́ть *pf*; (*publicly*) выставля́ть *impf*, вы́ставить *pf*. **exhibition** *n* проявле́ние; (*public* ~) вы́ставка. **exhibitor** *n* экспоне́нт.

exhilarated *adj* в припо́днятом настрое́нии. **exhilarating** *adj* возбужда́ющий. **exhilaration** *n* возбужде́ние.

exhort *vt* увещева́ть *impf*. **exhortation** *n* увещева́ние.

exhume *vt* выка́пывать *impf*, вы́копать *pf*.

exile *n* изгна́ние; (*person*) изгна́нник; *vt* изгоня́ть *impf*, изгна́ть *pf*.

exist *vi* существова́ть *impf*. **existence** *n* существова́ние. **existing** *adj* существу́ющий.

exit *n* вы́ход; (*theat*) ухо́д (со сце́ны); ~ **visa** выездна́я ви́за; *vi* уходи́ть *impf*, уйти́ *pf*.

exonerate *vt* опра́вдывать *impf*, оправда́ть *pf*.

exorbitant *adj* непоме́рный.

exorcize *vt* (*spirits*) изгоня́ть *impf*, изгна́ть *pf*.

exotic *adj* экзоти́ческий.

expand *vt & i* расширя́ть(ся) *impf*, расши́рить(ся) *pf*; ~ **on** распространя́ться *impf*, распространи́ться *pf* о+*prep*. **expanse** *n* простра́нство. **expansion** *n* расшире́ние. **expansive** *adj* экспанси́вный.

expatriate *n* экспатриа́нт, ~ка.

expect *vt* (*await*) ожида́ть *impf*+*gen*; ждать *impf* +*gen*, что; (*suppose*) полага́ть *impf*; (*require*) тре́бовать *impf* +*gen*, что́бы. **expectant** *adj* выжида́тельный; ~ **mother** бере́менная же́нщина. **expectation** *n* ожида́ние.

expediency *n* целесообра́зность. **expedient** *n* приём; *adj* целесообра́зный. **expedite** *vt* ускоря́ть *impf*, уско́рить *pf*. **expedition** *n* экспеди́ция. **expeditionary** *adj* экспедицио́нный.

expel *vt* (*drive out*) выгоня́ть *impf*, вы́гнать *pf*; (*from school etc.*) исключа́ть *impf*, исключи́ть *pf*; (*from country etc.*) изгоня́ть *impf*, изгна́ть *pf*.

expend *vt* тра́тить *impf*, ис~, по~ *pf*. **expendable** *adj* необяза́тельный. **expenditure** *n* расхо́д. **expense** *n* расхо́д; *pl* расхо́ды *m pl*, at the ~ of за счёт+*gen*; (*fig*) цено́ю+*gen*. **expensive** *adj* дорого́й.

experience *n* о́пыт; (*incident*) пережива́ние; *vt* испы́тывать *impf*, испыта́ть *pf*; (*undergo*) пережива́ть *impf*, пережи́ть *pf*. **experienced** *adj* о́пытный.

experiment *n* экспериме́нт; *vi* эксперименти́ровать *impf* (on, with над, с+*instr*). **experimental** эксперимента́льный.

expert *n* экспе́рт; *adj* о́пытный. **expertise** *n* специа́льные зна́ния *neut pl*.

expire *vi* (*period*) истека́ть *impf*, исте́чь *pf*. **expiry** *n* истече́ние.

explain *vt* объясня́ть *impf*, объясни́ть *pf*. **explanation** *n* объясне́ние. **explanatory** *adj* объясни́тельный.

expletive *n* (*oath*) бра́нное сло́во.

explicit *adj* я́вный; (*of person*) прямо́й.

explode *vt & i* взрыва́ть(ся) *impf*, взорва́ть(ся) *pf*; *vt* (*discredit*) опроверга́ть *impf*, опрове́ргнуть *pf*; *vi* (*with anger etc.*) разража́ться *impf*, разрази́ться *pf*.

exploit *n* по́двиг; *vt* эксплуати́ровать *impf*; (*use to advantage*) испо́льзовать *impf & pf*. **exploitation** *n* эксплуата́ция. **exploiter** *n* эксплуата́тор.

exploration *n* иссле́дование. **exploratory** *adj* иссле́довательский. **explore** *vt* иссле́довать *impf & pf*. **explorer** *n* иссле́дователь *m*.

explosion *n* взрыв. **explosive** *n* взры́вчатое вещество́; *adj* взры́вчатый; (*fig*) взрывно́й.

exponent *n* (*interpreter*) истолкова́тель *m*; (*advocate*) сторо́нник.

export *n* вы́воз, э́кспорт; *vt* вывози́ть *impf*, вы́везти *pf*; экспорти́ровать *impf & pf*. **exporter** *n* экспортёр.

expose vt (bare) раскрыва́ть impf, раскры́ть pf; (subject) подверга́ть impf, подве́ргнуть pf (to +dat); (discredit) разоблача́ть impf, разоблачи́ть pf; (phot) экспони́ровать impf & pf.

exposition n изложе́ние.

exposure n подверга́ние (to +dat); (phot) вы́держка; (unmasking) разоблаче́ние; (med) хо́лод.

expound vt излага́ть impf, изложи́ть pf.

express n (train) экспре́сс; adj (clear) то́чный; (purpose) специа́льный; (urgent) сро́чный; vt выража́ть impf, вы́разить pf. **expression** n выраже́ние; (expressiveness) вырази́тельность. **expressive** adj вырази́тельный. **expressly** adv (clearly) я́сно; (specifically) специа́льно.

expropriate vt экспроприи́ровать impf & pf. **expropriation** n экспроприа́ция.

expulsion n (from school etc.) исключе́ние; (from country etc.) изгна́ние.

exquisite adj утончённый.

extant adj сохрани́вшийся.

extempore adv экспро́мптом. **extemporize** vt & i импровизи́ровать impf, сымпровизи́ровать pf.

extend vt (stretch out) протя́гивать impf, протяну́ть pf; (enlarge) расширя́ть impf, расши́рить pf; (prolong) продлева́ть impf, продли́ть pf; vi простира́ться impf, простере́ться pf. **extension** n (enlarging) расшире́ние; (time) продле́ние; (to house) пристро́йка; (tel) доба́вочный. **extensive** adj обши́рный. **extent** n (degree) сте́пень.

extenuating adj: ~ circumstances смягча́ющие вину́ обстоя́тельства neut pl.

exterior n вне́шность; adj вне́шний.

exterminate vt истребля́ть impf, истреби́ть pf. **extermination** n истребле́ние.

external adj вне́шний.

extinct adj (volcano) поту́хший; (species) вы́мерший; **become** ~ вымира́ть impf, вы́мереть pf. **extinction** n вымира́ние.

extinguish vt гаси́ть impf, по~ pf. **extinguisher** n огнетуши́тель m.

extol vt превозноси́ть impf, превознести́ pf.

extort vt вымога́ть impf (from у+gen). **extortion** n вымога́тельство. **extortionate** adj вымога́тельский.

extra n (theat) стати́ст, ~ка; (payment) припла́та; adj дополни́тельный; (special) осо́бый; adv осо́бенно.

extract n экстра́кт; (from book etc.) вы́держка; vt извлека́ть impf, извле́чь pf. **extraction** n извлече́ние; (origin) происхожде́ние. **extradite** vt выдава́ть impf, вы́дать pf. **extradition** n вы́дача.

extramarital adj внебра́чный.

extraneous adj посторо́нний.

extraordinary adj чрезвыча́йный.

extrapolate vt & i экстраполи́ровать impf & pf.

extravagance n расточи́тельность. **extravagant** adj расточи́тельный; (fantastic) сумасбро́дный.

extreme n кра́йность; adj кра́йний. **extremity** n (end) край; (adversity) кра́йность; pl (hands & feet) коне́чности f pl.

extricate vt выпу́тывать impf, вы́путать pf.

exuberance n жизнера́достность. **exuberant** adj жизнера́достный.

exude vt & i выделя́ть(ся) impf, вы́делить(ся) pf; (fig) излуча́ть(ся) impf, излучи́ть(ся) pf.

exult vi ликова́ть impf. **exultant** adj лику́ющий. **exultation** n ликова́ние.

eye n глаз; (needle etc.) ушко́; vt разгля́дывать impf, разгляде́ть pf. **eyeball** n глазно́е я́блоко. **eyebrow** n бровь. **eyelash** n ресни́ца. **eyelid** n ве́ко. **eyeshadow** n те́ни f pl для век. **eyesight** n зре́ние. **eyewitness** n очеви́дец.

F

fable n ба́сня.

fabric n (structure) структу́ра; (cloth) ткань. **fabricate** vt (invent) выду́мывать impf, вы́думать pf. **fabrication** n вы́думка.

fabulous adj ска́зочный.

façade n фаса́д.

face n лицо́; (expression) выраже́ние;

(*grimace*) гримáса; (*side*) сторонá; (*surface*) повéрхность; (*clock etc.*) циферблáт; make ~s кóрчить *impf* рóжи; ~ down лицóм вниз; ~ to ~ лицóм к лицý; in the ~ of пéред лицóм+*gen*, вопреки́+*dat*; on the ~ of it на пéрвый взгляд; *vt* (*be turned towards*) быть обращённым к+*dat*; (*of person*) стоя́ть *impf* лицóм к+*dat*; (*meet firmly*) смотрéть *impf* в лицó+*dat*; (*cover*) облицóвывать *impf*, облицевáть *pf*; I can't ~ я дáже дýмать об э́том не могý. faceless *adj* безли́чный.

facet *n* грань; (*fig*) аспéкт.

facetious *adj* шутли́вый.

facial *adj* лицевóй.

facile *adj* повéрхностный. **facilitate** *vt* облегчáть *impf*, облегчи́ть *pf*. **facility** *n* (*ease*) лёгкость; (*ability*) спосóбность; *pl* (*conveniences*) удóбства *neut pl*, (*opportunities*) возмóжности *f pl*.

facing *n* облицóвка; (*of garment*) отдéлка.

facsimile *n* факси́миле *neut indecl*.

fact *n* факт; the ~ is that ... дéло в том, что...; as a matter of ~ сóбственно говоря́; in ~ на сáмом дéле.

faction *n* фрáкция.

factor *n* фáктор.

factory *n* фáбрика, завóд.

factual *adj* факти́ческий.

faculty *n* спосóбность; (*univ*) факультéт.

fade *vi* (*wither*) вя́нуть *impf*, за~ *pf*; (*colour*) выцветáть *impf*, вы́цветить *pf*; (*sound*) замирáть *impf*, замерéть *pf*.

faeces *n pl* кал.

fag *n* (*cigarette*) сигарéтка.

fail *n*: without ~ обязáтельно; *vi* (*weaken*) слабéть *impf*; (*break down*) отка́зывать *impf*, отказáть *pf*; (*not succeed*) терпéть *impf*, по~ *pf* неудáчу; не удавáться *impf*, удáться *pf impers*+*dat*; *vt* & *i* (*exam*) провáливать(ся) *impf*, провали́ть(ся) *pf.*; *vt* (*disappoint*) подводи́ть *impf*, подвести́ *pf.* **failing** *n* недостáток; *prep* за неимéнием +*gen*. **failure** *n* неудáча; (*person*) неудáчник, -ица.

faint *n* обмóрок; *adj* (*weak*) слáбый; (*pale*) блéдный; I feel ~ мне дýрно;

~-hearted малодýшный; *vi* пáдать *impf*, упáсть *pf* в обмóрок

fair[1] *n* я́рмарка.

fair[2] *adj* (*hair, skin*) свéтлый; (*weather*) я́сный; (*just*) справедли́вый; (*average*) снóсный; a ~ amount довóльно мнóго +*gen*. **fairly** *adv* довóльно.

fairy *n* фéя; ~-tale скáзка.

faith *n* вéра; (*trust*) довéрие. **faithful** *adj* вéрный; yours ~ly с уважéнием.

fake *n* поддéлка; *vt* поддéлывать *impf*, поддéлать *pf*.

falcon *n* сóкол.

fall *n* падéние; *vi* пáдать *impf*, (у)пáсть *pf*; ~ apart распадáться *impf*, распáсться *pf*; ~ asleep засыпáть *impf*, заснýть *pf*; ~ back on прибегáть *impf*, прибéгнуть *pf* к+*dat*; ~ down упáсть *pf*; (*building*) развáливаться *impf*, развали́ться *pf*; ~ in рýхнуть *pf*; ~ in love with влюбля́ться *impf*, влюби́ться *pf* в+*acc*; ~ off отпадáть *impf*, отпáсть *pf*; ~ out выпадáть *impf*, вы́пасть *pf*; (*quarrel*) поссóриться *pf*; ~ over опроки́дываться *impf*, опроки́нуться *pf*; ~ through провáливаться *impf*, провали́ться *pf*; ~-out радиоакти́вные осáдки (-ков) *pl*.

fallacy *n* оши́бка.

fallible *adj* подвéрженный оши́бкам.

fallow *n*: lie ~ лежáть *impf* под пáром.

false *adj* лóжный; (*teeth*) искýсственный; ~ start невéрный старт.

falsehood *n* ложь. **falsification** *n* фальсификáция. **falsify** *vt* фальсифици́ровать *impf* & *pf*. **falsity** *n* лóжность.

falter *vi* спотыкáться *impf*, споткнýться *pf*; (*stammer*) запинáться *impf*, запнýться *pf*.

fame *n* слáва. **famed** *adj* извéстный.

familiar *adj* (*well known*) знакóмый; (*usual*) обы́чный; (*informal*) фамилья́рный. **familiarity** *n* знакóмство; фамилья́рность. **familiarize** *vt* ознакомля́ть *impf*, ознакóмить *pf* (with c+*instr*).

family *n* семья́; *attrib* семéйный; ~ tree родослóвная *sb.*

famine *n* гóлод. **famished** *adj*: be ~ голодáть *impf*.

famous *adj* знамени́тый.

fan[1] *n* вéер; (*ventilator*) вентиля́тор;

~-belt реме́нь *m* вентиля́тора; *vt* обма́хивать *impf*, обмахну́ть *pf*; (*flame*) раздува́ть *impf*, разду́ть *pf*.
fan² *n* покло́нник, -ица; (*sport*) боле́льщик. fanatic *n* фана́тик. fanatical *adj* фанати́ческий.
fanciful *adj* причу́дливый. fancy *n* фанта́зия; (*whim*) причу́да; take a ~ to увлека́ться *impf*, увле́чься *pf* +*instr*; *adj* витиева́тый; *vt* (*imagine*) представля́ть *impf*, предста́вить *pf* себе́; (*suppose*) полага́ть *impf*; (*like*) нра́виться *impf*, по~ *pf impers*+*dat*; ~ dress маскара́дный костю́м; ~-dress костюми́рованный.
fanfare *n* фанфа́ра.
fang *n* клык; (*serpent's*) ядови́тый зуб.
fantasize *vi* фантази́ровать *impf*.
fantastic *adj* фантасти́ческий. fantasy *n* фанта́зия.
far *adj* да́льний; Russia is ~ away Росси́я о́чень далеко́; *adv* далеко́; (*fig*) намно́го; as ~ as (*prep*) до +*gen*; (*conj*) поско́льку; by ~ намно́го; (in) so ~ as поско́льку; so ~ до сих пор; ~-fetched притя́нутый за́ волосы; ~-reaching далеко́ иду́щий; ~-sighted дальнови́дный.
farce *n* фарс. farcical *adj* смехотво́рный.
fare *n* (*price*) проездна́я пла́та; (*food*) пи́ща; *vi* пожива́ть *impf*.
farewell *int* проща́й(те)!; *n* проща́ние; *attrib* проща́льный; bid ~ проща́ться *impf*, прости́ться *pf* (to c+*instr*).
farm *n* фе́рма. farmer *n* фе́рмер. farming *n* се́льское хозя́йство.
fart (*vulg*) *n* пу́кание; *vi* пу́кать *impf*, пу́кнуть *pf*.
farther *see* further. farthest *see* farthest.
fascinate *vt* очаро́вывать *impf*, очарова́ть *pf*. fascinating *adj* очарова́тельный. fascination *n* очарова́ние.
Fascism *n* фаши́зм. Fascist *n* фаши́ст, -ка; *adj* фаши́стский.
fashion *n* мо́да; (*manner*) мане́ра; after a ~ не́которым о́бразом; *vt* придава́ть *impf*, прида́ть *pf* фо́рму +*dat*. fashionable *adj* мо́дный.
fast¹ *n* пост; *vi* пости́ться *impf*.
fast² *adj* (*rapid*) ско́рый, бы́стрый;

(*colour*) сто́йкий; (*shut*) пло́тно закры́тый; be ~ (*timepiece*) спеши́ть *impf*.
fasten *vt* (*attach*) прикрепля́ть *impf*, прикрепи́ть *pf* (to к+*dat*); (*tie*) привя́зывать *impf*, привяза́ть *pf* (to к+*dat*); (*garment*) застёгивать *impf*, застегну́ть *pf*. fastener, fastening *n* запо́р, задви́жка; (*on garment*) застёжка.
fastidious *adj* брезгли́вый.
fat *n* жир; *adj* (*greasy*) жи́рный; (*plump*) то́лстый; get ~ толсте́ть *impf*, по~ *pf*.
fatal *adj* роково́й; (*deadly*) смерте́льный. fatalism *n* фатали́зм. fatality *n* (*death*) смерте́льный слу́чай. fate *n* судьба́. fateful *adj* роково́й.
father *n* оте́ц; ~-in-law (*husband's* ~) свёкор; (*wife's* ~) тесть *m*. fatherhood *n* отцо́вство. fatherland *n* оте́чество. fatherly *adj* оте́ческий.
fathom *n* морска́я са́жень; *vt* (*fig*) понима́ть *impf*, поня́ть *pf*.
fatigue *n* утомле́ние; *vt* утомля́ть *impf*, утоми́ть *pf*.
fatten *vt* отка́рмливать *impf*, отко́рми́ть *pf*; *vi* толсте́ть *impf*, по~ *pf*. fatty *adj* жи́рный.
fatuous *adj* глу́пый.
fault *n* недоста́ток; (*blame*) вина́; (*geol*) сброс. faultless *adj* безупре́чный. faulty *adj* дефе́ктный.
fauna *n* фа́уна.
favour *n* (*kind act*) любе́зность; (*goodwill*) благоскло́нность; in (s.o.'s) ~ в по́льзу +*gen*; be in ~ of быть за+*acc*; *vt* (*support*) благоприя́тствовать *impf*+*dat*; (*treat with partiality*) ока́зывать *impf*, оказа́ть *pf* предпочте́ние +*dat*. favourable *adj* (*propitious*) благоприя́тный; (*approving*) благоскло́нный. favourite *n* люби́мец, -мица; (*also sport*) фавори́т, ~ка; *adj* люби́мый.
fawn¹ *n* оленёнок; *adj* желтова́то-кори́чневый.
fawn² *vi* подли́зываться *impf*, подли́заться *pf* (on к+*dat*).
fax *n* факс; *vt* посыла́ть *impf*, посла́ть *pf* по фа́ксу.
fear *n* страх, боя́знь, опасе́ние; *vt* & *i* боя́ться *impf* +*gen*; опаса́ться *impf* +*gen*. fearful *adj* (*terrible*) стра́ш-

ный; (*timid*) пугли́вый. **fearless** *adj* бесстра́шный. **fearsome** *adj* гро́зный.

feasibility *n* осуществи́мость. **feasible** *adj* осуществи́мый.

feast *n* (*meal*) пир; (*festival*) пра́здник; *vi* пирова́ть *impf*.

feat *n* по́двиг.

feather *n* перо́.

feature *n* черта́; (*newspaper*) (тема́тическая) статья́; ~ **film** худо́жественный фильм; *vt* помеща́ть *impf*, помести́ть *pf* на ви́дном ме́сте; (*in film*) пока́зывать *impf*, показа́ть *pf*; *vi* игра́ть *impf* сыгра́ть *pf* роль.

February *n* февра́ль *m*; *adj* февра́льский.

feckless *adj* безала́берный.

federal *adj* федера́льный. **federation** *n* федера́ция.

fee *n* гонора́р; (*entrance* ~ *etc.*) взнос; *pl* (*regular payment, school, etc.*) пла́та.

feeble *adj* сла́бый.

feed *n* корм; *vt* корми́ть *impf*, на~, по~ *pf*; *vi* корми́ться *impf*, по~ *pf*; ~ **up** отка́рмливать *impf*, откорми́ть *pf*; **I am fed up with** мне надое́л (-а, -о; -и) +*nom*. **feedback** *n* обра́тная связь.

feel *vt* чу́вствовать *impf*, по~ *pf*; (*think*) счита́ть *impf*, счесть *pf*; *vi* (~ *bad etc.*) чу́вствовать *impf*, по~ *pf* себя́ +*adv*, +*instr*; ~ **like** хоте́ться *impf impers*+*dat*. **feeling** *n* (*sense*) ощуще́ние; (*emotion*) чу́вство; (*impression*) впечатле́ние; (*mood*) настрое́ние.

feign *vt* притворя́ться *impf*, притвори́ться *pf* +*instr*. **feigned** *adj* притво́рный.

feline *adj* коша́чий.

fell *vt* (*tree*) сруба́ть *impf*, сруби́ть *pf*; (*person*) сбива́ть *impf*, сбить *pf* с ног.

fellow *n* па́рень *m*; (*of society etc.*) член; ~ **countryman** соотече́ственник. **fellowship** *n* това́рищество.

felt *n* фетр; *adj* фе́тровый; ~-**tip pen** флома́стер.

female *n* (*animal*) са́мка; (*person*) же́нщина; *adj* же́нский. **feminine** *adj* же́нский, же́нственный; (*gram*) же́нского ро́да. **femininity** *n* же́нст-

венность. **feminism** *n* femини́зм. **feminist** *n* feminíст, ~ка; *adj* feminíстский.

fence *n* забо́р; *vt*: ~ **in** огора́живать *impf*, огороди́ть *pf*; ~ **off** отгора́живать *impf*, отгороди́ть *pf*; *vi* (*sport*) фехтова́ть *impf*. **fencer** *n* фехтова́льщик, -и́ца. **fencing** *n* (*enclosure*) забо́р; (*sport*) фехтова́ние.

fend *vt*: ~ **off** отража́ть *impf*, отрази́ть *pf*; *vi*: ~ **for o.s.** забо́титься *impf*, по~ *pf* о себе́. **fender** *n* решётка.

fennel *n* фе́нхель *m*.

ferment *n* броже́ние; *vi* броди́ть *impf*; *vt* ква́сить *impf*, за~ *pf*; (*excite*) возбужда́ть *impf*, возбуди́ть *pf*. **fermentation** *n* броже́ние; (*excitement*) возбужде́ние.

fern *n* па́поротник.

ferocious *adj* свире́пый. **ferocity** *n* свире́пость.

ferret *n* хорёк; *vt*: ~ **out** (*search out*) разню́хивать *impf*, разню́хать *pf*; *vi*: ~ **about** (*rummage*) ры́ться *impf*.

ferry *n* паро́м; *vt* перевози́ть *impf*, перевезти́ *pf*.

fertile *adj* плодоро́дный. **fertility** *n* плодоро́дие. **fertilize** *vt* (*soil*) удобря́ть *impf*, удо́брить *pf*; (*egg*) оплодотворя́ть *impf*, оплодотвори́ть *pf*. **fertilizer** *n* удобре́ние.

fervent *adj* горя́чий. **fervour** *n* жар.

fester *vi* гнои́ться *impf*.

festival *n* пра́здник, (*music etc.*) фестива́ль *m*. **festive** *adj* пра́здничный. **festivities** *n pl* торжества́ *neut pl*.

festoon *vt* украша́ть *impf*, укра́сить *pf*.

fetch *vt* (*carrying*) приноси́ть *impf*, принести́ *pf*; (*leading*) приводи́ть *impf*, привести́ *pf*; (*go and come back with*) (*on foot*) идти́ *impf*, по~ *pf* за+*instr*; (*by vehicle*) заезжа́ть *impf*, зае́хать *pf* за+*instr*; (*price*) выруча́ть *impf*, вы́ручить *pf*. **fetching** *adj* привлека́тельный.

fetid *adj* злово́нный.

fetish *n* фети́ш.

fetter *vt* ско́вывать *impf*, скова́ть *pf*; *n*: *pl* кандалы́ (-ло́в) *pl*; (*fig*) око́вы (-в) *pl*.

fettle *n* состоя́ние.

feud *n* кро́вная месть.

feudal *adj* феода́льный. **feudalism** *n* феодали́зм.

fever *n* лихора́дка. **feverish** *adj* лихора́дочный.

few *adj* & *pron* немно́гие *pl*; ма́ло +*gen*; **a ~** не́сколько +*gen*; **quite a ~** нема́ло +*gen*.

fiancé *n* жени́х. **fiancée** *n* неве́ста.

fiasco *n* прова́л.

fib *n* враньё; *vi* привира́ть *impf*, привра́ть *pf*.

fibre *n* волокно́. **fibreglass** *n* стекловолокно́. **fibrous** *adj* волокни́стый.

fickle *adj* непостоя́нный.

fiction *n* худо́жественная литерату́ра; (*invention*) вы́думка. **fictional** *adj* беллетристи́ческий. **fictitious** *adj* вы́мышленный.

fiddle *n* (*violin*) скри́пка; (*swindle*) обма́н; *vi*: **~ about** безде́льничать *impf*; **~ with** верте́ть *impf*; *vt* (*falsify*) подде́лывать *impf*, подде́лать *pf*; (*cheat*) жи́лить *impf*, у~ *pf*.

fidelity *n* ве́рность.

fidget *n* непосе́да *m* & *f*; *vi* ёрзать *impf*; не́рвничать *impf*. **fidgety** *adj* непосе́дливый.

field *n* по́ле; (*sport*) площа́дка; (*sphere*) о́бласть; **~-glasses** полево́й бино́кль *m*. **~work** полевы́е рабо́ты *f pl*.

fiend *n* дья́вол. **fiendish** *adj* дья́вольский.

fierce *adj* свире́пый; (*strong*) си́льный.

fiery *adj* о́гненный.

fifteen *adj* & *n* пятна́дцать. **fifteenth** *adj* & *n* пятна́дцатый. **fifth** *adj* & *n* пя́тый; (*fraction*) пя́тая *sb*. **fiftieth** *adj* & *n* пятидеся́тый. **fifty** *adj* & *n* пятьдеся́т; *pl* (*decade*) пятидеся́тые го́ды (-до́в) *m pl*.

fig *n* инжи́р.

fight *n* дра́ка; (*battle*) бой; (*fig*) борьба́; *vt* боро́ться *impf* c+*instr*; *vi* дра́ться *impf*; *vt* & *i* (*wage war*) воева́ть *impf* c+*instr*. **fighter** *n* бое́ц; (*aeron*) истреби́тель *m*. **fighting** *n* бой *m pl*.

figment *n* плод воображе́ния.

figurative *adj* перено́сный. **figure** *n* (*form, body, person*) фигу́ра; (*number*) ци́фра; (*diagram*) рису́нок; (*image*) изображе́ние; (*of speech*)

оборо́т ре́чи; **~-head** (*naut*) носово́е украше́ние; (*person*) номина́льная глава́; *vt* (*think*) полага́ть *impf*; *vi* фигури́ровать *impf*; **~ out** вычисля́ть *impf*, вы́числить *pf*.

filament *n* волокно́; (*electr*) нить.

file[1] *n* (*tool*) напи́льник; *vt* подпи́ливать *impf*, подпили́ть *pf*.

file[2] *n* (*folder*) па́пка; (*comput*) файл; *vt* подшива́ть *impf*, подши́ть *pf*; (*complaint*) подава́ть *impf*, пода́ть *pf*.

file[3] *n* (*row*) ряд; **in** (**single**) **~** гусько́м.

filigree *n* филигра́нь; *adj* филигра́нный.

fill *vt* & *i* (*also* **~ up**) наполня́ть(ся) *impf*, напо́лнить(ся) *pf*; *vt* заполня́ть *impf*, запо́лнить *pf*; (*tooth*) пломбирова́ть *impf*, за~ *pf*; (*occupy*) занима́ть *impf*, заня́ть *pf*; (*satiate*) насыща́ть *impf*, насы́тить *pf*; **~ in** (*vt*) заполня́ть *impf*, запо́лнить *pf*; (*vi*) замеща́ть *impf*, замести́ть *pf*.

fillet *n* (*cul*) филе́ *neut indecl*.

filling *n* (*tooth*) пло́мба; (*cul*) начи́нка.

filly *n* кобы́лка.

film *n* (*layer*; *phot*) плёнка; (*cin*) фильм; **~ star** кинозвезда́; *vt* снима́ть *impf*, снять *pf*.

filter *n* фильтр; *vt* фильтрова́ть *impf*, про~ *pf*; **~ through, out** проса́чиваться *impf*, просочи́ться *pf*.

filth *n* грязь. **filthy** *adj* гря́зный.

fin *n* плавни́к.

final *n* фина́л; *pl* выпускны́е экза́мены *m pl*; *adj* после́дний; (*decisive*) оконча́тельный. **finale** *n* фина́л. **finalist** *n* финали́ст. **finality** *n* зако́нченность. **finalize** *vt* (*complete*) заверша́ть *impf*, заверши́ть *pf*; (*settle*) ула́живать *impf*, ула́дить *pf*. **finally** *adv* наконе́ц.

finance *n* фина́нсы (-сов) *pl*; *vt* финанси́ровать *impf* & *pf*. **financial** *adj* фина́нсовый. **financier** *n* финанси́ст.

finch *n see comb, e.g.* **bullfinch**

find *n* нахо́дка; *vt* находи́ть *impf*, найти́ *pf*; (*person*) застава́ть *impf*, заста́ть *pf*; **~ out** узнава́ть *impf*, узна́ть *pf*; **~ fault with** придира́ться *impf*, придра́ться *pf* к+*dat*. **finding**

n pl (*of inquiry*) вы́воды *m pl*.

fine¹ *n* (*penalty*) штраф; *vt* штрафова́ть *impf*, o~ *pf*.

fine² *adj* (*weather*) я́сный; (*excellent*) прекра́сный; (*delicate*) то́нкий; (*of sand etc.*) ме́лкий; ~ **arts** изобрази́тельные иску́сства *neut pl*; **I am** ~ мне хорошо́. **finery** *n* наря́д. **finesse** *n* то́нкость.

finger *n* па́лец; ~-**nail** но́готь; ~-**print** отпеча́ток па́льца; ~-**tip** ко́нчик па́льца; **have at** (**one's**) ~**s** знать *impf* как свои́ пять па́льцев; *vt* щу́пать *impf*, по~ *pf*.

finish *n* коне́ц (*polish*) отде́лка; (*sport*) фи́ниш; *vt* & *i* конча́ть(ся) *impf*, ко́нчить(ся) *pf*; *vi* ока́нчивать *impf*, око́нчить *pf*.

finite *adj* коне́чный.

Finland *n* Финля́ндия. **Finn** *n* финн, фи́нка. **Finnish** *adj* фи́нский.

fir *n* ель, пи́хта.

fire *vt* (*bake*) обжига́ть *impf*, обжечь *pf*; (*excite*) воспламеня́ть *impf*, воспламени́ть *pf*; (*gun*) стреля́ть *impf* из+*gen* (**at** в+*acc*, по+*dat*); (*dismiss*) увольня́ть *impf*, уво́лить *pf*; *n* ого́нь *m*; (*grate*) ками́н; (*conflagration*) пожа́р; (*bonfire*) костёр; (*fervour*) пыл; **be on** ~ горе́ть *impf*; **catch** ~ загора́ться *impf*, загоре́ться *pf*; **set** ~ **to, set on** ~ поджига́ть *impf*, подже́чь *pf*; ~-**alarm** пожа́рная трево́га; ~-**arm(s)** огнестре́льное ору́жие; ~ **brigade** пожа́рная кома́нда; ~-**engine** пожа́рная маши́на; ~-**escape** пожа́рная ле́стница; ~ **extinguisher** огнетуши́тель *m*; ~-**guard** ками́нная решётка; ~-**man** пожа́рный *sb*; ~ **place** ками́н; ~-**side** ме́сто у ками́на; ~ **station** пожа́рное депо́ *neut indecl*; ~-**wood** дрова́ (-) *pl*; ~-**work** фейерве́рк. **firing** *n* (*shooting*) стрельба́.

firm¹ *n* (*business*) фи́рма.

firm² *adj* твёрдый. **firmness** *n* твёрдость.

first *adj* пе́рвый; *n* пе́рвый *sb*; *adv* сперва́, снача́ла; (*for the* ~ *time*) впервы́е; **in the** ~ **place** во-пе́рвых; ~ **of all** пре́жде всего́; **at** ~ **sight** на пе́рвый взгляд; ~ **aid** пе́рвая по́мощь; ~-**class** первокла́ссный; ~-**hand** из пе́рвых рук; ~-**rate** первокла́ссный.

fiscal *adj* фина́нсовый.

fish *n* ры́ба; *adj* ры́бный; *vi* лови́ть *impf* ры́бу; ~ **for** (*compliments etc.*) напра́шиваться *impf*, напроси́ться *pf* на+*acc*; ~ **out** выта́скивать *impf*, вы́таскать *pf*. **fisherman** *n* рыба́к. **fishery** *n* ры́бный про́мысел. **fishing** *n* ры́бная ло́вля; ~ **boat** рыболо́вное су́дно; ~ **line** леса́; ~ **rod** у́дочка. **fishmonger** *n* торго́вец ры́бой. **fishy** *adj* ры́бный; (*dubious*) подозри́тельный.

fissure *n* тре́щина.

fist *n* кула́к.

fit¹ *n*: **be a good** ~ хорошо́ сиде́ть *impf*; *adj* (*suitable*) подходя́щий, го́дный; (*healthy*) здоро́вый; *vt* (*be suitable*) годи́ться *impf*, на+*acc*, для+*gen*; *vt* & *i* (*be the right size for*) подходи́ть *impf*, подойти́ *pf* (+*dat*); (*adjust*) прила́живать *impf*, прила́дить *pf* (**to** к+*dat*); (*be small enough for*) входи́ть *impf*, войти́ *pf* в+*acc*; ~ **out** снабжа́ть *impf*, снабди́ть *pf*.

fit² *n* (*attack*) припа́док; (*fig*) поры́в. **fitful** *adj* поры́вистый.

fitter *n* монтёр. **fitting** *n* (*of clothes*) приме́рка; *pl* армату́ра; *adj* подходя́щий.

five *adj* & *n* пять; (*number 5*) пятёрка; ~-**year plan** пятиле́тка.

fix *n* (*dilemma*) переде́лка; (*drugs*) уко́л; *vt* (*repair*) чини́ть *impf*, по~ *pf*; (*settle*) назнача́ть *impf*, назна́чить *pf*; (*fasten*) укрепля́ть *impf*, укрепи́ть *pf*; ~ **up** (*organize*) организова́ть *impf* & *pf*; (*install*) устана́вливать *impf*, установи́ть *pf*. **fixation** *n* фикса́ция. **fixed** *adj* устано́вленный. **fixture** *n* (*sport*) предсто́ящее спорти́вное мероприя́тие; (*fitting*) приспособле́ние.

fizz, fizzle *vi* шипе́ть *impf*; **fizzle out** выдыха́ться *impf*, вы́дохнуться *pf*. **fizzy** *adj* шипу́чий.

flabbergasted *adj* ошеломлённый.

flabby *adj* дря́блый.

flag¹ *n* флаг, зна́мя *neut*; *vt*: ~ **down** остана́вливать *impf*, останови́ть *pf*.

flag² *vi* (*weaken*) ослабева́ть *impf*, ослабе́ть *pf*.

flagon *n* кувши́н.

flagrant *adj* вопию́щий.

flagship *n* фла́гман.

flagstone n плита́.

flair n чутьё.

flake n слой; pl хло́пья (-ьев) pl; vi шелуши́ться impf. **flaky** adj слои́стый.

flamboyant adj цвети́стый.

flame n пла́мя neut, ого́нь m; vi пыла́ть impf.

flange n фла́нец.

flank n (of body) бок; (mil) фланг; vt быть сбо́ку +gen.

flannel n флане́ль; (for face) моча́лка для лица́.

flap n (board) откидна́я доска́; (pocket, tent ~) кла́пан; (panic) па́ника; vt взма́хивать impf, взмахну́ть pf +instr; vi развева́ться impf.

flare n вспы́шка; (signal) сигна́льная раке́та; vi вспы́хивать impf, вспы́хнуть pf; ~ **up** (fire) возгора́ться impf, возгоре́ться pf; (fig) вспыли́ть pf.

flash n вспы́шка; **in a** ~ ми́гом; vi сверка́ть impf, сверкну́ть pf. **flashback** n ретроспе́кция. **flashy** adj показно́й.

flask n фля́жка.

flat[1] n (dwelling) кварти́ра.

flat[2] n (mus) бемо́ль m; (tyre) спу́щенная ши́на; **on the** ~ на пло́скости; adj пло́ский; ~-**fish** камба́ла. **flatly** adv наотре́з. **flatten** vt & i выра́внивать(ся) impf, вы́ровнять(ся) pf.

flatmate n сосе́д, ~ка по кварти́ре.

flatter vt льстить impf, по~ pf +dat. **flattering** adj льсти́вый. **flattery** n лесть.

flaunt vt щеголя́ть impf, щегольну́ть pf +instr.

flautist n флейти́ст.

flavour n вкус; (fig) при́вкус; vt приправля́ть impf, припра́вить pf.

flaw n изъя́н.

flax n лён. **flaxen** adj (colour) соло́менный.

flea n блоха́; ~ **market** барахо́лка.

fleck n кра́пинка.

flee vi бежа́ть impf & pf (**from** от+gen); vt бежа́ть impf из+gen.

fleece n руно́; vt (fig) обдира́ть impf, ободра́ть pf. **fleecy** adj шерсти́стый.

fleet n флот; (vehicles) парк.

fleeting adj мимолётный.

flesh n (as opposed to mind) плоть; (meat) мя́со; **in the** ~ во плоти́. **fleshy** adj мяси́стый.

flex n шнур; vt сгиба́ть impf, согну́ть pf. **flexibility** adj ги́бкость. **flexible** adj ги́бкий.

flick vt & i щёлкать impf, щёлкнуть pf (+instr); ~ **through** пролиста́ть pf.

flicker n мерца́ние; vi мерца́ть impf.

flier see **flyer**

flight[1] n (fleeing) бе́гство; **put (take) to** ~ обраща́ть(ся) impf, обрати́ть(ся) pf в бе́гство.

flight[2] n (flying) полёт; (trip) рейс; ~ **of stairs** ле́стничный марш. **flighty** adj ве́треный.

flimsy adj (fragile) непро́чный; (dress) лёгкий; (excuse) сла́бый.

flinch vi (recoil) отпря́дывать impf, отпря́нуть pf; (fig) уклоня́ться impf, уклони́ться pf (**from** от+gen).

fling vt швыря́ть impf, швырну́ть pf; vi (also ~ o.s.) броса́ться impf, бро́ситься pf.

flint n креме́нь m.

flip vt щёлкать impf, щёлкнуть pf +instr.

flippant adj легкомы́сленный.

flipper n ласт.

flirt n коке́тка; vi флиртова́ть impf (**with** c+instr). **flirtation** n флирт.

flit vi порха́ть impf, порхну́ть pf.

float n поплаво́к; vi пла́вать indet, плыть det; vt (company) пуска́ть impf, пусти́ть в ход.

flock n (animals) ста́до; (birds) ста́я; vi стека́ться impf, сте́чься pf.

flog vt сечь impf, вы́~ pf.

flood n наводне́ние; (bibl) пото́п; (fig) пото́к; vi (river etc.) выступа́ть impf, вы́ступить pf из берего́в; vt затопля́ть impf, затопи́ть pf. **floodgate** n шлюз. **floodlight** n прожёктор.

floor n пол; (storey) эта́ж; ~**board** полови́ца; vt (confound) ста́вить impf, по~ pf в тупи́к.

flop vi (fall) плю́хаться impf, плю́хнуться pf; (fail) прова́ливаться impf, провали́ться pf.

flora n фло́ра. **floral** adj цвето́чный.

florid adj цвети́стый; (ruddy) румя́ный. **florist** n торго́вец цвета́ми.

flounce[1] vi броса́ться impf, бро́ситься pf.

flounce² *n* (*of skirt*) обо́рка.

flounder¹ *n* (*fish*) ка́мбала.

flounder² *vi* бара́хтаться *impf*.

flour *n* мука́.

flourish *n* (*movement*) разма́хивание (+*instr*); (*of pen*) ро́счерк; *vi* (*thrive*) процвета́ть *impf*; *vt* (*wave*) разма́хивать *impf*, размахну́ть *pf* +*instr*.

flout *vt* попира́ть *impf*, попра́ть *pf*.

flow *vi* течь *impf*, ли́ться *impf*; *n* тече́ние.

flower *n* цвето́к; ~-bed клу́мба; ~-pot цвето́чный горшо́к; *vi* цвести́ *impf*. **flowery** *adj* цвети́стый.

fluctuate *vi* колеба́ться *impf*, по~ *pf*. **fluctuation** *n* колеба́ние.

flue *n* дымохо́д.

fluent *adj* бе́глый. **fluently** *adv* свобо́дно.

fluff *n* пух. **fluffy** *adj* пуши́стый.

fluid *n* жи́дкость; *adj* жи́дкий.

fluke *n* случа́йная уда́ча.

fluorescent *adj* флюоресце́нтный.

fluoride *n* фтори́д.

flurry *n* (*squall*) шквал; (*fig*) волна́.

flush *n* (*redness*) румя́нец; *vi* (*redden*) красне́ть *impf*, по~ *pf*; *vt* спуска́ть *impf*, спусти́ть *pf* во́ду в+*acc*.

flustered *adj* сконфу́женный.

flute *n* фле́йта.

flutter *vi* (*flit*) порха́ть *impf*, порхну́ть *pf*; (*wave*) развева́ться *impf*.

flux *n*: **in a state of** ~ в состоя́нии измене́ния.

fly¹ *n* (*insect*) му́ха.

fly² *vi* лета́ть *indet*, лете́ть *det*, по~ *pf*; (*flag*) развева́ться *impf*; (*hasten*) нести́сь *impf*, по~ *pf*; *vt* (*aircraft*) управля́ть *impf* +*instr*; (*transport*) перевози́ть *impf*, перевезти́ *pf* (*самолётом*); (*flag*) поднима́ть *impf*, подня́ть *pf*. **flyer, flier** *n* лётчик. **flying** *n* полёт.

foal *n* (*horse*) жеребёнок.

foam *n* пе́на; ~ **plastic** пенопла́ст; ~ **rubber** пенорези́на; *vi* пе́ниться *impf*, вс~ *pf*. **foamy** *adj* пе́нистый.

focal *adj* фо́кусный. **focus** *n* фо́кус; (*fig*) центр; *vt* фокуси́ровать *impf*, с~ *pf*; (*concentrate*) сосредото́чивать *impf*, сосредото́чить *pf*.

fodder *n* корм.

foe *n* враг.

foetus *n* заро́дыш.

fog *n* тума́н. **foggy** *adj* тума́нный.

foible *n* сла́бость.

foil¹ *n* (*metal*) фольга́; (*contrast*) контра́ст.

foil² *vt* (*thwart*) расстра́ивать *impf*, расстро́ить *pf*.

foil³ *n* (*sword*) рапи́ра.

foist *vt* навя́зывать *impf*, навяза́ть *pf* (**on** +*dat*).

fold¹ *n* (*sheep-*~) овча́рня.

fold² *n* скла́дка, сгиб; *vt* скла́дывать *impf*, сложи́ть *pf*. **folder** *n* па́пка. **folding** *adj* складно́й.

foliage *n* листва́.

folk *n* наро́д, лю́ди *pl*; *pl* (*relatives*) родня́ *collect*; *attrib* наро́дный. **folklore** *n* фолькло́р.

follow *vt* сле́довать *impf*, по~ *pf* +*dat*, за+*instr*; (*walk behind*) идти́ *det* за+*instr*; (*fig*) следи́ть *impf* за+*instr*. **follower** *n* после́дователь *m*. **following** *adj* сле́дующий.

folly *n* глу́пость.

fond *adj* не́жный; **be** ~ **of** люби́ть *impf* +*acc*.

fondle *vt* ласка́ть *impf*.

fondness *n* любо́вь.

font *n* (*eccl*) купе́ль.

food *n* пи́ща, еда́. **foodstuff** *n* пищево́й проду́кт.

fool *n* дура́к; *vt* дура́чить *impf*, о~ *pf*; *vi*: ~ **about** дура́читься *impf*. **foolhardy** *adj* безрассу́дно хра́брый. **foolish** *adj* глу́пый. **foolishness** *n* глу́пость. **foolproof** *adj* абсолю́тно надёжный.

foot *n* нога́; (*measure*) фут; (*of hill etc.*) подно́жие; **on** ~ пешко́м; **put one's** ~ **in it** сесть в лу́жу. **football** *n* футбо́л; *attrib* футбо́льный. **footballer** *n* футболи́ст. **foothills** *n pl* предго́рье. **footing** *n* (*fig*) ба́зис; **lose one's** ~ оступи́ться *pf*; **on an equal** ~ на ра́вной ноге́. **footlights** *n pl* ра́мпа. **footman** *n* лаке́й. **footnote** *n* сно́ска. **footpath** *n* тропи́нка; (*pavement*) тротуа́р. **footprint** *n* след. **footstep** *n* (*sound*) шаг; (*footprint*) след. **footwear** *n* о́бувь.

for *prep* (*of time*) в тече́ние +*gen*, на +*acc*; (*of purpose*) для+*gen*, за+*acc*, +*instr*; (*price*) за+*acc*; (*on account of*) из-за +*gen*; (*in place of*) вме́сто+*gen*; ~ **the sake of** ра́ди+*gen*; **as** ~ что каса́ется+*gen*; *conj* так как.

forage n фура́ж; vi: ~ **for** разы́-
скивать impf.
foray n набе́г.
forbearance n возде́ржанность.
forbid vt запреща́ть impf, запрети́ть
pf (+dat (person) & acc (thing)). **for-
bidding** adj гро́зный.
force n (strength, validity) си́ла;
(meaning) смысл; pl (armed ~) во-
оружённые си́лы f pl; **by** ~ си́лой;
vt (compel) заставля́ть impf, за-
ста́вить pf; (lock etc.) взла́мывать
impf, взлома́ть pf. **forceful** adj
си́льный; (speech) убеди́тельный.
forcible adj наси́льственный.
forceps n щипцы́ (-цо́в) pl.
ford n брод; vt переходи́ть impf,
перейти́ pf вброд+acc.
fore n: **come to the** ~ выдвига́ться
impf, вы́двинуться pf на пере́дний
план.
forearm n предпле́чье. **foreboding**
n предчу́вствие. **forecast** n пред-
сказа́ние; (of weather) прогно́з; vt
предска́зывать impf, предсказа́ть
pf. **forecourt** n пере́дний двор. **forefather** n пре́док. **forefinger** n указа́-
тельный па́лец. **forefront** n (foreground) пере́дний план; (leading
position) аванга́рд. **foregone** adj: ~
conclusion предрешённый исхо́д.
foreground n пере́дний план. **forehead** n лоб.
foreign adj (from abroad) иностра́н-
ный; (alien) чу́ждый; (external)
вне́шний; ~ **body** иноро́дное те́ло;
~ **currency** валю́та. **foreigner** n
иностра́нец, -нка.
foreman n ма́стер.
foremost adj выдаю́щийся; **first and**
~ пре́жде всего́.
forename n и́мя.
forensic adj суде́бный.
forerunner n предве́стник. **foresee**
vt предви́деть impf. **foreshadow** vt
предвеща́ть impf. **foresight** n пред-
ви́дение; (caution) предусмотри́-
тельность.
forest n лес.
forestall vt предупрежда́ть impf,
предупреди́ть pf.
forester n лесни́чий sb. **forestry** n
лесово́дство.
foretaste n предвкуше́ние; vt пред-
вкуша́ть impf, предвкуси́ть pf. **fore-**

tell vt предска́зывать impf, пред-
сказа́ть pf. **forethought** n преду-
смотри́тельность. **forewarn** vt пре-
достерега́ть impf, предостере́чь pf.
foreword n предисло́вие.
forfeit n (in game) фант; vt лиша́ться
impf, лиши́ться pf+gen.
forge¹ n (smithy) ку́зница; (furnace)
горн; vt кова́ть impf, вы́~ pf; (fabricate) подде́лывать impf, подде́-
лать pf.
forge² vi: ~ **ahead** продвига́ться
impf, продви́нуться pf вперёд.
forger n фальшивомоне́тчик. **forgery** n подде́лка.
forget vt забыва́ть impf, забы́ть pf.
forgetful adj забы́вчивый.
forgive vt проща́ть impf, прости́ть
pf. **forgiveness** n проще́ние.
forgo vt возде́рживаться impf, воз-
держа́ться pf от+gen.
fork n (eating) ви́лка; (digging) ви́лы
(-л) pl; (in road) разветвле́ние; vi
(road) разветвля́ться impf, развет-
ви́ться pf.
forlorn adj жа́лкий.
form n (shape; kind) фо́рма; (class)
класс; (document) анке́та; vt (make,
create) образо́вывать impf, образо-
ва́ть pf; (develop; make up) состав-
ля́ть impf, соста́вить pf; vi обра-
зо́вываться impf, образова́ться pf.
formal adj форма́льный; (official)
официа́льный. **formality** n фор-
ма́льность. **format** n форма́т. **formation** n образова́ние. **formative**
adj: ~ **years** молоды́е го́ды (-до́в)
m pl.
former adj (earlier) пре́жний; (ex)
бы́вший; **the** ~ (of two) пе́рвый.
formerly adv пре́жде.
formidable adj (dread) гро́зный; (arduous) тру́дный.
formless adj бесфо́рменный.
formula n фо́рмула. **formulate** vt
формули́ровать impf, с~ pf. **formulation** n формулиро́вка.
forsake vt (desert) покида́ть impf,
поки́нуть pf; (renounce) отка́зы-
ваться impf, отказа́ться pf от+gen.
fort n форт.
forth adv вперёд, да́льше; **back and**
~ взад и вперёд; **and so** ~ и так
да́лее. **forthcoming** adj предстоя́-
щий; **be** ~ (available) поступа́ть

impf, поступить *pf*. **forthwith** *adv* немедленно.

fortieth *adj* & *n* сороковой.

fortification *n* укрепление. **fortify** *vt* укреплять *impf*, укрепить *pf*; (*fig*) подкреплять *impf*, подкрепить *pf*. **fortitude** *n* стойкость.

fortnight *n* две недели *f pl*. **fortnightly** *adj* двухнедельный; *adv* раз в две недели.

fortress *n* крепость.

fortuitous *adj* случайный.

fortunate *adj* счастливый. **fortunately** *adv* к счастью. **fortune** *n* (*destiny*) судьба; (*good* ~) счастье; (*wealth*) состояние.

forty *adj* & *n* сорок; *pl* (*decade*) сороковые годы (-дов) *m pl*.

forward *adj* передний; (*presumptuous*) развязный; *n* (*sport*) нападающий *sb*; *adv* вперёд; *vt* (*letter*) пересылать *impf*, переслать *pf*.

fossil *n* ископаемое *sb*; *adj* ископаемый. **fossilized** *adj* ископаемый.

foster *vt* (*child*) приютить *pf*; (*idea*) вынашивать *impf*, выносить *pf*; (*create*) создавать *impf*, создать *pf*; (*cherish*) лелеять *impf*; ~-**child** приёмыш.

foul *adj* (*dirty*) грязный; (*repulsive*) отвратительный; (*obscene*) непристойный; *n* (*sport*) нарушение правил; *vt* (*dirty*) пачкать *impf*, за~, ис~ *pf*; (*entangle*) запутывать *impf*, запутать *pf*.

found *vt* основывать *impf*, основать *pf*.

foundation *n* (*of building*) фундамент; (*basis*) основа; (*institution*) учреждение; (*fund*) фонд. **founder**[1] *n* основатель *m*.

founder[2] *vi* (*naut*, *fig*) тонуть *impf*, по~ *pf*.

foundry *n* литейная *sb*.

fountain *n* фонтан; ~-**pen** авторучка.

four *adj* & *n* четыре; (*number 4*) четвёрка; on all ~s на четвереньках. **fourteen** *adj* & *n* четырнадцать. **fourteenth** *adj* & *n* четырнадцатый. **fourth** *adj* & *n* четвёртый; (*quarter*) четверть.

fowl *n* (*domestic*) домашняя птица; (*wild*) дичь *collect*.

fox *n* лиса, лисица; *vt* озадачивать

impf, озадачить *pf*.

foyer *n* фойе *neut indecl*.

fraction *n* (*math*) дробь; (*portion*) частица.

fractious *adj* раздражительный.

fracture *n* перелом; *vt* & *i* ломать(ся) *impf*, с~ *pf*.

fragile *adj* ломкий.

fragment *n* обломок; (*of conversation*) отрывок; (*of writing*) фрагмент. **fragmentary** *adj* отрывочный.

fragrance *n* аромат. **fragrant** *adj* ароматный, душистый.

frail *adj* хрупкий.

frame *n* остов; (*build*) телосложение; (*picture*) рама; (*cin*) кадр; ~ **of mind** настроение; *vt* (*devise*) создавать *impf*, создать *pf*; (*formulate*) формулировать *impf*, с~ *pf*; (*picture*) вставлять *impf*, вставить *pf* в раму; (*incriminate*) фабриковать *impf*, с~ *pf* обвинение против+*gen*. **framework** *n* остов; (*fig*) рамки *f pl*.

franc *n* франк.

France *n* Франция.

franchise *n* (*comm*) привилегия; (*polit*) право голоса.

frank[1] *adj* откровенный.

frank[2] *vt* (*letter*) франкировать *impf* & *pf*.

frantic *adj* неистовый.

fraternal *adj* братский. **fraternity** *n* братство.

fraud *n* обман; (*person*) обманщик. **fraudulent** *adj* обманный.

fraught *adj*: ~ **with** чреватый +*instr*.

fray[1] *vt* & *i* обтрёпывать(ся) *impf*, обтрепать(ся) *pf*.

fray[2] *n* бой.

freak *n* урод; *attrib* необычный.

freckle *n* веснушка. **freckled** *adj* веснушчатый.

free *adj* свободный; (*gratis*) бесплатный; ~ **kick** штрафной удар; ~ **speech** свобода слова; *vt* освобождать *impf*, освободить *pf*. **freedom** *n* свобода. **freehold** *n* неограниченное право собственности на недвижимость. **freelance** *adj* внештатный. **Freemason** *n* франкмасон.

freeze *vi* замерзать *impf*, мёрзнуть *impf*, замёрзнуть *pf*; *vt* замораживать *impf*, заморозить *pf*. **freezer** *n* морози́льник; (*compartment*) моро́зилка. **freezing** *adj* моро́зный; **below ~** ни́же нуля́.

freight *n* фрахт. **freighter** *n* (*ship*) грузово́е су́дно.

French *adj* францу́зский; **~ bean** фасо́ль; **~ horn** валто́рна; **~ windows** двуство́рчатое окно́ до по́ла. **Frenchman** *n* францу́з. **Frenchwoman** *n* францу́женка.

frenetic *adj* неи́стовый.

frenzied *adj* неи́стовый. **frenzy** *n* неи́стовство.

frequency *n* частота́. **frequent** *adj* ча́стый; *vt* ча́сто посеща́ть *impf*.

fresco *n* фре́ска.

fresh *adj* све́жий; (*new*) но́вый; **~ water** пре́сная вода́. **freshen** *vt* освежа́ть *impf*, освежи́ть *pf*; *vi* свеже́ть *impf*, по~ *pf*. **freshly** *adv* свежо́; (*recently*) неда́вно. **freshness** *n* све́жесть. **freshwater** *adj* пресново́дный.

fret[1] *vi* му́читься *impf*. **fretful** *adj* раздражи́тельный.

fret[2] *n* (*mus*) лад.

fretsaw *n* ло́бзик.

friar *n* мона́х.

friction *n* тре́ние; (*fig*) тре́ния *neut pl*.

Friday *n* пя́тница.

fridge *n* холоди́льник.

fried *adj*: **~ egg** яи́чница.

friend *n* друг, подру́га; прия́тель *m*, ~ница. **friendly** *adj* дру́жеский. **friendship** *n* дру́жба.

frieze *n* фриз.

frigate *n* фрега́т.

fright *n* испу́г. **frighten** *vt* пуга́ть *impf*, ис~, на~ *pf*. **frightful** *adj* стра́шный.

frigid *adj* холо́дный.

frill *n* обо́рка.

fringe *n* бахрома́; (*of hair*) чёлка; (*edge*) край.

frisk *vi* (*frolic*) резви́ться *impf*; *vt* (*search*) шмона́ть *impf*. **frisky** *adj* резвый.

fritter *vt*: **~ away** растра́чивать *impf*, растра́тить *pf*.

frivolity *n* легкомы́сленность. **frivolous** *adj* легкомы́сленный.

fro *adv*: **to and ~** взад и вперёд.

frock *n* пла́тье.

frog *n* лягу́шка.

frolic *vi* резви́ться *impf*.

from *prep* от+*gen*; (*~ off, down ~; in time*) с+*gen*; (*out of*) из+*gen*; (*according to*) по+*dat*; (*because of*) из-за+*gen*; **~ above** све́рху; **~ abroad** из-за грани́цы; **~ afar** и́здали; **~ among** из числа́+*gen*; **~ behind** из-за+*gen*; **~ day to day** изо дня́ в день; **~ everywhere** отовсю́ду; **~ here** отсю́да; **~ memory** по па́мяти; **~ now on** отны́не; **~ there** отту́да; **~ time to time** вре́мя от вре́мени; **~ under** из-под+*gen*.

front *n* фаса́д, пере́дняя сторона́; (*mil*) фронт; **in ~ of** впереди́+*gen*, пе́ред+*instr*; *adj* пере́дний; (*first*) пе́рвый.

frontier *n* грани́ца.

frost *n* моро́з; **~-bite** отмороже́ние; **~-bitten** отморо́женный. **frosted** *adj*: **~ glass** ма́товое стекло́. **frosty** *adj* моро́зный; (*fig*) ледяно́й.

froth *n* пе́на; *vi* пе́ниться *impf*, вс~ *pf*. **frothy** *adj* пе́нистый.

frown *n* хму́рый взгляд; *vi* хму́риться *impf*, на~ *pf*.

frugal *adj* (*careful*) бережли́вый; (*scanty*) ску́дный.

fruit *n* плод; *collect* фру́кты *m pl*; *adj* фрукто́вый. **fruitful** *adj* плодотво́рный. **fruition** *n*: **come to ~** осуществи́ться *pf*. **fruitless** *adj* беспло́дный.

frustrate *vt* фрустри́ровать *impf* & *pf*. **frustrating** *adj* фрустри́рующий. **frustration** *n* фрустра́ция.

fry[1] *n*: **small ~** мелюзга́.

fry[2] *vt* & *i* жа́рить(ся) *impf*, за~, из~ *pf*. **frying-pan** *n* сковорода́.

fuel *n* то́пливо.

fugitive *n* бегле́ц.

fulcrum *n* то́чка опо́ры.

fulfil *vt* (*perform*) выполня́ть *impf*, вы́полнить *pf*; (*dreams*) осуществля́ть *impf*, осуществи́ть *pf*. **fulfilling** *adj* удовлетворя́ющий. **fulfilment** *n* выполне́ние; осуществле́ние; удовлетворе́ние.

full *adj* по́лный (*of* +*gen, instr*); (*replete*) сы́тый; **~ stop** то́чка; **~ time: I work ~ time** я рабо́таю на по́лную ста́вку; *n*: **in ~** по́лностью; **to the ~** в по́лной ме́ре. **fullness** *n* полнота́. **fully** *adv* вполне́.

fulsome *adj* чрезме́рный.

fumble *vi*: ~ **for** нащу́пывать *impf* +*acc*; ~ **with** вози́ться *impf* c+*instr*.

fume *vi* (*with anger*) кипе́ть *impf*, вс~ *pf* гне́вом. **fumes** *n pl* испаре́ния *neut pl*. **fumigate** *vt* оку́ривать *impf*, окури́ть *pf*.

fun *n* заба́ва; **it was** ~ **было** забá́вно; **have** ~ забавля́ться *impf*; **make** ~ **of** смея́ться *impf*, по~ *pf* над+*instr*.

function *n* фу́нкция; (*event*) ве́чер; *vi* функциони́ровать *impf*; де́йствовать *impf*. **functional** *adj* функциона́льный. **functionary** *n* чино́вник.

fund *n* фонд; (*store*) запа́с.

fundamental *adj* основно́й; *n*: *pl* осно́вы *f pl*.

funeral *n* по́хороны (-о́н, -она́м) *pl*.

fungus *n* гриб.

funnel *n* воро́нка; (*chimney*) дымова́я труба́.

funny *adj* смешно́й; (*odd*) стра́нный.

fur *n* мех; ~ **coat** шу́ба.

furious *adj* бе́шеный.

furnace *n* горн, печь.

furnish *vt* (*provide*) снабжа́ть *impf*, снабди́ть *pf* (**with** c+*instr*); (*house*) обставля́ть *impf*, обста́вить *pf*. **furniture** *n* ме́бель.

furrow *n* борозда́.

furry *adj* пуши́стый.

further, farther *comp adj* дальне́йший; *adv* да́льше; *vt* продвига́ть *impf*, продви́нуть *pf*. **furthermore** *adv* к тому́ же. **furthest, farthest** *superl adj* са́мый да́льний.

furtive *adj* скры́тый, та́йный.

fury *n* я́рость.

fuse¹ *vt & i* (*of metal*) сплавля́ть(ся) *impf*, спла́вить(ся) *pf*.

fuse² *n* (*in bomb*) запа́л; (*detonating device*) взрыва́тель *m*.

fuse³ *n* (*electr*) про́бка; *vi* перегора́ть *impf*, перегоре́ть *pf*.

fuselage *n* фюзеля́ж.

fusion *n* пла́вка, слия́ние.

fuss *n* суета́; *vi* суети́ться *impf*. **fussy** *adj* суетли́вый; (*fastidious*) разбо́рчивый.

futile *adj* тще́тный. **futility** *n* тще́тность.

future *n* бу́дущее *sb*; (*gram*) бу́дущее вре́мя *neut*; *adj* бу́дущий. **futuristic** *adj* футуристи́ческий.

fuzzy *adj* (*hair*) пуши́стый; (*blurred*) расплы́вчатый.

G

gabble *vi* тарато́рить *impf*.

gable *n* щипе́ц.

gad *vi*: ~ **about** шата́ться *impf*.

gadget *n* приспособле́ние.

gaffe *n* опло́шность.

gag *n* кляп; *vt* засо́вывать *impf*, засу́нуть *pf* кляп в рот+*dat*.

gaiety *n* весёлость. **gaily** *adv* ве́село.

gain *n* при́быль; *pl* дохо́ды *m pl*; (*increase*) приро́ст; *vt* (*acquire*) получа́ть *impf*, получи́ть *pf*; ~ **on** нагоня́ть *impf*, нагна́ть *pf*.

gait *n* похо́дка.

gala *n* пра́зднество; *adj* пра́здничный.

galaxy *n* гала́ктика; (*fig*) плея́да.

gale *n* бу́ря, шторм.

gall¹ *n* (*bile*) жёлчь; (*cheek*) на́глость; ~-**bladder** жёлчный пузы́рь *m*.

gall² *vt* (*vex*) раздража́ть *impf*, раздражи́ть *pf*.

gallant *adj* (*brave*) хра́брый; (*courtly*) гала́нтный. **gallantry** *n* хра́брость; гала́нтность.

gallery *n* галере́я.

galley *n* (*ship*) гале́ра; (*kitchen*) ка́мбуз.

gallon *n* галло́н.

gallop *n* гало́п; *vi* галопи́ровать *impf*.

gallows *n pl* ви́селица.

gallstone *n* жёлчный ка́мень *m*.

galore *adj* в изоби́лии.

galvanize *vt* гальванизи́ровать *impf* & *pf*.

gambit *n* гамби́т.

gamble *n* (*undertaking*) риско́ванное предприя́тие; *vi* игра́ть *impf* в аза́ртные и́гры; (*fig*) рискова́ть *impf* (**with** +*instr*); ~ **away** прои́грывать *impf*, проигра́ть *pf*. **gambler** *n* игро́к. **gambling** *n* аза́ртные и́гры *f pl*.

game *n* игра́; (*single* ~) па́ртия; (*collect, animals*) дичь; *adj* (*ready*) гото́вый. **gamekeeper** *n* лесни́к.

gammon *n* о́корок.

gamut *n* га́мма.

gang *n* ба́нда; (*workmen*) брига́да.

gangrene *n* гангре́на.

gangster *n* га́нгстер.

gangway *n* (*passage*) прохо́д; (*naut*) схо́дни (-ней) *pl*.

gaol n тюрьма́; vt заключа́ть impf, заключи́ть pf в тюрьму́. **gaoler** n тюре́мщик.

gap n (empty space; deficiency) пробе́л; (in wall etc.) брешь; (fig) разры́в.

gape vi (person) зева́ть impf (at на +acc); (chasm) зия́ть impf.

garage n гара́ж.

garb n одея́ние.

garbage n му́сор.

garbled adj искажённый.

garden n сад; attrib садо́вый. **gardener** n садо́вник. **gardening** n садово́дство.

gargle vi полоска́ть impf, про~ pf го́рло.

gargoyle n горгу́лья.

garish adj крича́щий.

garland n гирля́нда.

garlic n чесно́к.

garment n предме́т оде́жды.

garnish n гарни́р; vt гарни́ровать impf & pf.

garret n манса́рда.

garrison n гарнизо́н.

garrulous adj болтли́вый.

gas n газ; attrib га́зовый; vt отравля́ть impf, отрави́ть pf га́зом. **gaseous** adj газообра́зный.

gash n поре́з; vt поре́зать pf.

gasket n прокла́дка.

gasp vi задыха́ться impf, задохну́ться pf.

gastric adj желу́дочный.

gate n (large) воро́та (-т) pl; (small) кали́тка. **gateway** n (gate) воро́та (-т) pl; (entrance) вход.

gather vt & i собира́ть(ся) impf, собра́ть(ся) pf; vt заключа́ть impf, заключи́ть pf. **gathering** n (assembly) собра́ние.

gaudy adj крича́щий.

gauge n (measure) ме́ра; (instrument) кали́бр, измери́тельный прибо́р; (rly) колея́; (criterion) крите́рий; vt измеря́ть impf, изме́рить pf; (estimate) оце́нивать impf, оцени́ть pf.

gaunt adj то́щий.

gauntlet n рукави́ца.

gauze n ма́рля.

gay adj весёлый; (bright) пёстрый; (homosexual) гомосексуа́льный.

gaze n при́стальный взгляд; vi при́стально гляде́ть impf (at на+acc).

gazelle n газе́ль.

GCSE abbr (of General Certificate of Secondary Education) аттеста́т о сре́днем образова́нии.

gear n (equipment) принадле́жности f pl; (in car) ско́рость; ~ lever рыча́г; vt приспособля́ть impf, приспосо́бить pf (to к+dat). **gearbox** n коро́бка переда́ч.

gel n космети́ческое желе́ neut indecl. **gelatine** n желати́н.

gelding n ме́рин.

gelignite n гелигни́т.

gem n драгоце́нный ка́мень m.

Gemini n Близнецы́ m pl.

gender n род.

gene n ген.

genealogy n генеало́гия.

general n генера́л; adj о́бщий; (nationwide) всео́бщий; in ~ вообще́. **generalization** n обобще́ние. **generalize** vi обобща́ть impf, обобщи́ть pf. **generally** adv (usually) обы́чно; (in general) вообще́. **generate** vt порожда́ть impf, породи́ть pf. **generation** n (in descent) поколе́ние. **generator** n генера́тор.

generic adj родово́й; (general) о́бщий.

generosity n (magnanimity) великоду́шие; (munificence) ще́дрость. **generous** adj великоду́шный; ще́дрый.

genesis n происхожде́ние; (G~) Кни́га Бытия́.

genetic adj генети́ческий. **genetics** n гене́тика.

genial adj (of person) доброду́шный.

genital adj полово́й. **genitals** n pl половы́е о́рганы m pl.

genitive adj (n) роди́тельный (паде́ж).

genius n (person) ге́ний; (ability) гениа́льность.

genocide n геноци́д.

genre n жанр.

genteel adj благовоспи́танный.

gentile adj неевре́йский; n нееврей, ~ка.

gentility n благовоспи́танность.

gentle adj (mild) мя́гкий; (quiet) ти́хий; (light) лёгкий. **gentleman** n джентльме́н. **gentleness** n мя́гкость. **gents** n pl мужска́я убо́рная sb.

genuine adj (authentic) по́длинный;

(*sincere*) и́скренний.

genus n род.

geographical adj географи́ческий. **geography** n геогра́фия. **geological** adj геологи́ческий. **geologist** n гео́лог. **geology** n геоло́гия. **geometric(al)** adj геометри́ческий. **geometry** n геоме́трия.

Georgia n Гру́зия. **Georgian** n грузи́н, ~ка; adj грузи́нский.

geranium n гера́нь.

geriatric adj гериатри́ческий.

germ m микро́б.

German n не́мец, не́мка; adj неме́цкий; ~ **measles** красну́ха.

germane adj уме́стный.

Germanic adj герма́нский.

Germany n Герма́ния.

germinate vi прораста́ть impf, прорасти́ pf.

gesticulate vi жестикули́ровать impf. **gesture** n жест.

get vt (*obtain*) достава́ть impf, доста́ть pf; (*receive*) получа́ть impf, получи́ть pf; (*understand*) понима́ть impf, поня́ть pf; (*disease*) заража́ться impf, зарази́ться pf +instr; (*induce*) угова́ривать impf, уговори́ть pf (*to do* +inf); (*fetch*) приноси́ть impf, принести́ pf; vi (*become*) станови́ться impf, стать pf +instr; **have got** (*have*) име́ть impf; **have got to** быть до́лжен (-жна́) +inf; ~ **about** (*spread*) распространя́ться impf, распространи́ться pf; (*move around*) передвига́ться impf; (*travel*) разъезжа́ть impf; ~ **at** (*mean*) хоте́ть impf сказа́ть; ~ **away** (*slip off*) ускольза́ть impf, ускользну́ть pf; (*escape*) убега́ть impf, убежа́ть pf; (*leave*) уезжа́ть impf, уе́хать pf; ~ **away with** убега́ть impf, избежа́ть pf отве́тственности за+acc; ~ **back** (*recover*) получа́ть impf, получи́ть pf обра́тно; (*return*) возвраща́ться impf, верну́ться pf; ~ **by** (*manage*) справля́ться impf, спра́виться pf; ~ **down** сходи́ть impf, сойти́ pf; ~ **down to** принима́ться impf, приня́ться pf за+acc; ~ **off** слеза́ть impf, слезть pf c+gen; ~ **on** сади́ться impf, сесть pf в, на, +acc; (*prosper*) преуспева́ть impf, преуспе́ть pf; ~ **on with** (*person*) ужи-

ва́ться impf, ужи́ться pf c+instr; ~ **out of** (*avoid*) избавля́ться impf, изба́виться pf от+gen; (*car*) выходи́ть impf, вы́йти pf из+gen; ~ **round to** (*reach*) достига́ть impf, дости́гнуть & дости́чь pf +gen; ~ **up** (*from bed*) встава́ть impf, встать pf.

geyser n (*spring*) ге́йзер; (*water-heater*) коло́нка.

ghastly adj ужа́сный.

gherkin n огуре́ц.

ghetto n ге́тто neut indecl.

ghost n привиде́ние. **ghostly** adj при́зрачный.

giant n гига́нт; adj гига́нтский.

gibberish n тараба́рщина.

gibbet n ви́селица.

gibe n насме́шка; vi насмеха́ться impf (**at** над+instr).

giblets n pl потроха́ (-хо́в) pl.

giddiness n головокруже́ние. **giddy** predic: **I feel** ~ у меня́ кру́жится голова́.

gift n (*present*) пода́рок; (*donation*; *ability*) дар. **gifted** adj одарённый.

gig n (*theat*) выступле́ние.

gigantic adj гига́нтский.

giggle n хихи́канье; vi хихи́кать impf, хихи́кнуть pf.

gild vt золоти́ть impf, вы́~, по~ pf.

gill n (*of fish*) жа́бра.

gilt n позоло́та; adj золочёный.

gimmick n трюк.

gin n (*spirit*) джин.

ginger n имби́рь m; adj (*colour*) ры́жий.

gingerly adv осторо́жно.

gipsy n цыга́н, ~ка.

giraffe n жира́ф.

girder n ба́лка. **girdle** n по́яс.

girl n (*child*) де́вочка; (*young woman*) де́вушка. **girlfriend** n подру́га. **girlish** adj де́вичий.

girth n обхва́т; (*on saddle*) подпру́га.

gist n суть.

give vt дава́ть impf, дать pf; ~ **away** выдава́ть impf, вы́дать pf; ~ **back** возвраща́ть impf, возврати́ть pf; ~ **in** (*yield, vi*) уступа́ть impf, уступи́ть pf (**to** +dat); (*hand in, vt*) вруча́ть impf, вручи́ть pf; ~ **out** (*emit*) издава́ть impf, изда́ть pf; (*distribute*) раздава́ть impf, разда́ть pf; ~ **up** отка́зываться impf, отказа́ться *pf* от+*gen*; (*habit etc.*) броса́ть *impf*, бро́сить *pf*; ~ **o.s. up** сдава́ться *impf*, сда́ться *pf*. **given** *predic* (*inclined*) скло́нен (-онна́, -о́нно) (**to** к+*dat*).

glacier *n* ледни́к.

glad *adj* ра́достный; *predic* рад. **gladden** *vt* ра́довать *impf*, об~ *pf*.

glade *n* поля́на.

gladly *adv* охо́тно.

glamorous *adj* я́ркий; (*attractive*) привлека́тельный.

glamour *n* я́ркость; привлека́тельность.

glance *n* (*look*) бе́глый взгляд; *vi*: ~ **at** взгля́дывать *impf*, взгляну́ть *pf* на+*acc*.

gland *n* железа́. **glandular** *adj* желе́зистый.

glare *n* (*light*) ослепи́тельный блеск; (*look*) свире́пый взгляд; *vi* свире́по смотре́ть *impf* (**at** на+*acc*). **glaring** *adj* (*dazzling*) ослепи́тельный; (*mistake*) гру́бый.

glasnost *n* гла́сность.

glass *n* (*substance*) стекло́; (*drinking vessel*) стака́н; (*wine* ~) рю́мка; (*mirror*) зе́ркало; *pl* (*spectacles*) очки́ (-ко́в) *pl*; *attrib* стекля́нный. **glassy** *adj* (*look*) ту́склый.

glaze *n* глазу́рь; *vt* (*with glass*) застекля́ть *impf*, застекли́ть *pf*; (*pottery*) глазурова́ть *impf* & *pf*; (*cul*) глази́ровать *impf* & *pf*. **glazier** *n* стеко́льщик.

gleam *n* про́блеск; *vi* свети́ться *impf*.

glean *vt* собира́ть *impf*, собра́ть *pf* по крупи́цам.

glee *n* весе́лье. **gleeful** *adj* лику́ющий.

glib *adj* бо́йкий.

glide *vi* скользи́ть *impf*; (*aeron*) плани́ровать *impf*, с~ *pf*. **glider** *n* планёр.

glimmer *n* мерца́ние; *vi* мерца́ть *impf*.

glimpse *vt* мелько́м ви́деть *impf*, у~ *pf*.

glint *n* блеск; *vi* блесте́ть *impf*.

glisten, **glitter** *vi* блесте́ть *impf*.

gloat *vi* злора́дствовать *impf*.

global *adj* (*world-wide*) мирово́й; (*total*) всео́бщий. **globe** *n* (*sphere*) шар; (*the earth*) земно́й шар; (*chart*) гло́бус. **globule** *n* ша́рик.

gloom *n* мрак. **gloomy** *adj* мра́чный.

glorify *vt* прославля́ть *impf*, просла́вить *pf*. **glorious** *adj* сла́вный; (*splendid*) великоле́пный. **glory** *n* сла́ва; *vi* торжествова́ть *impf*.

gloss *n* лоск; *vt*: ~ **over** зама́зывать *impf*, зама́зать *pf*.

glossary *n* глосса́рий.

glove *n* перча́тка.

glow *n* за́рево; (*of cheeks*) румя́нец; *vi* (*incandesce*) накаля́ться *impf*, накали́ться *pf*; (*shine*) сия́ть *impf*.

glucose *n* глюко́за.

glue *n* клей; *vt* прикле́ивать *impf*, прикле́ить *pf* (**to** к+*dat*).

glum *adj* угрю́мый.

glut *n* избы́ток.

glutton *n* обжо́ра *m* & *f*. **gluttonous** *adj* обжо́рливый. **gluttony** *n* обжо́рство.

gnarled *adj* (*hands*) шишкова́тый; (*tree*) сучкова́тый.

gnash *vt* скрежета́ть *impf* +*instr*.

gnat *n* кома́р.

gnaw *vt* грызть *impf*.

gnome *n* гном.

go *n* (*energy*) эне́ргия; (*attempt*) попы́тка; **be on the** ~ быть в движе́нии; **have a** ~ пыта́ться *impf*, по~ *pf*; *vi* (*on foot*) ходи́ть *indet*, идти́ *det*, пойти́ *pf*; (*by transport*) е́здить *indet*, е́хать *det*, по~ *pf*; (*work*) рабо́тать *impf*; (*become*) станови́ться *impf*, стать *pf* +*instr*; (*belong*) идти́ *impf*; **be** ~**ing** (**to** *do*) собира́ться *impf*, собра́ться *pf* (+*inf*); ~ **about** (*set to work at*) бра́ться *impf*, взя́ться *pf* за+*acc*; (*wander*) броди́ть *indet*; ~ **away** (*on foot*) уходи́ть *impf*, уйти́ *pf*; (*by transport*) уезжа́ть *impf*, уе́хать *pf*; ~ **down** спуска́ться *impf*, спусти́ться *pf* (c+*gen*); ~ **in(to)** (*enter*) входи́ть *impf*, войти́ *pf* (в+*acc*); (*investigate*) рассле́довать *impf* & *pf*; ~ **off** (*go away*) уходи́ть *impf*, уйти́ *pf*; (*deteriorate*) по́ртиться *impf*, ис~ *pf*; ~ **on** (*continue*) продолжа́ть(ся) *impf*, продо́лжить(ся) *pf*; ~ **out** выходи́ть *impf*, вы́йти *pf*; (*flame etc.*) га́снуть *impf*, по~ *pf*; ~ **over** (*inspect*) пересма́тривать *impf*, пересмотре́ть *pf*; (*rehearse*) повторя́ть *impf*, повтори́ть *pf*; (*change allegiance etc.*) переходи́ть *impf*, перейти́ *pf* (**to** в, на, +*acc*, к+*dat*);

~ **through** (*scrutinize*) разбира́ть *impf*, разобра́ть *pf*; ~ **through with** доводи́ть *impf*, довести́ *pf* до конца́; ~ **without** обходи́ться *impf*, обойти́сь *pf* без+*gen*;~**ahead** предприи́мчивый;~**between** посре́дник.

goad *vt* (*instigate*) подстрека́ть *impf*, подстрекну́ть *pf* (**into** к+*dat*); (*taunt*) раздража́ть *impf*.

goal *n* (*aim*) цель; (*sport*) воро́та (-т) *pl*; (*point won*) гол. **goalkeeper** *n* врата́рь *m*.

goat *n* коза́; (*male*) козёл.

gobble *vt* (*eat*) жрать *impf*; ~ **up** пожира́ть *impf*, пожра́ть *pf*.

goblet *n* бока́л, ку́бок.

god *n* бог; (**G**~) Бог. **godchild** *n* кре́стник, -ица. **god-daughter** *n* кре́стница. **goddess** *n* боги́ня. **godfather** *n* кре́стный *sb*. **God-fearing** *adj* богобоя́зненный. **godless** *adj* безбо́жный. **godly** *adj* на́божный. **godmother** *n* кре́стная *sb*. **godparent** *n* кре́стный *sb*. **godsend** *n* бо́жий дар. **godson** *n* кре́стник.

goggle *vi* тара́щить *impf* глаза́ (**at** на+*acc*); *n*: *pl* защи́тные очки́ (-ко́в) *pl*.

going *adj* де́йствующий. **goings-on** *n pl* дела́ *neut pl*.

gold *n* зо́лото; *adj* золото́й;~**plated** накладно́го зо́лота; ~**smith** *n* золоты́х дел ма́стер. **golden** *adj* золото́й; ~ **eagle** бе́ркут. **goldfish** *n* золота́я ры́бка.

golf *n* гольф; ~ **club** (*implement*) клю́шка; ~ **course** площа́дка для го́льфа. **golfer** *n* игро́к в гольф.

gondola *n* гондо́ла.

gong *n* гонг.

gonorrhoea *n* три́ппер.

good *n* добро́; *pl* (*wares*) това́р(ы); **do** ~ (*benefit*) идти́ *impf*, пойти́ *pf* на по́льзу +*dat*; *adj* хоро́ший, до́брый; ~**humoured** доброду́шный; ~**looking** краси́вый; ~ **morning** до́брое у́тро!; ~ **night** споко́йной но́чи! **goodbye** *int* проща́й(те)!; до свида́ния! **goodness** *n* доброта́.

goose *n* гусь *m*; ~**flesh** гуси́ная ко́жа.

gooseberry *n* крыжо́вник.

gore[1] *n* (*blood*) запёкшаяся кровь.

gore[2] *vt* (*pierce*) бода́ть *impf*, за~ *pf*.

gorge *n* (*geog*) уще́лье; *vi* & *t* объ-

еда́ться *impf*, объе́сться *pf* (**on** +*instr*).

gorgeous *adj* великоле́пный.

gorilla *n* гори́лла.

gorse *n* утёсник.

gory *adj* крова́вый.

gosh *int* бо́же мой!

Gospel *n* Ева́нгелие.

gossip *n* спле́тня; (*person*) спле́тник, -ица; *vi* спле́тничать *impf*, на~ *pf*.

Gothic готи́ческий.

gouge *vt*:~ **out** выда́лбливать *impf*, вы́долбить *pf*; (*eyes*) выка́лывать *impf*, вы́колоть *pf*.

goulash *n* гуля́ш.

gourmet *n* гурма́н.

gout *n* пода́гра.

govern *vt* пра́вить *impf* +*instr*; (*determine*) определя́ть *impf*, определи́ть *pf* **governess** *n* гувернантка.

government *n* прави́тельство. **governmental** *adj* прави́тельственный. **governor** *n* губерна́тор; (*of school etc.*) член правле́ния.

gown *n* пла́тье; (*official's*) ма́нтия.

grab *vt* захва́тывать *impf*, захвати́ть *pf*.

grace *n* (*gracefulness*) гра́ция; (*refinement*) изя́щество; (*favour*) ми́лость; (*at meal*) моли́тва; **have the** ~ **to** быть насто́лько такти́чен, что; **with bad** ~ нелюбе́зно; **with good** ~ с досто́инством; *vt* (*adorn*) украша́ть *impf*, укра́сить *pf*; (*favour*) удоста́ивать *impf*, удосто́ить *pf* (**with** +*gen*). **graceful** *adj* грацио́зный.

gracious *adj* ми́лостивый.

gradation *n* града́ция.

grade *n* (*level*) сте́пень; (*quality*) сорт; *vt* сортирова́ть *impf*, рас~ *pf*.

gradient *n* укло́н.

gradual *adj* постепе́нный.

graduate *n* око́нчивший *sb* университе́т, вуз; *vi* кончать *impf*, око́нчить *pf* (университе́т, вуз); *vt* градуи́ровать *impf* & *pf*.

graffiti *n* на́дписи *f pl*.

graft *n* (*bot*) черено́к; (*med*) переса́дка (живо́й тка́ни); *vt* (*bot*) привива́ть *impf*, приви́ть *pf* (**to** +*dat*); (*med*) переса́живать *impf*, переса́дить *pf*.

grain *n* (*seed; collect*) зерно́; (*particle*)

крупи́нка; (of sand) песчи́нка; (of wood) (древе́сное) волокно́; **against the ~** не по нутру́.

gram(me) n грамм.

grammar n грамма́тика; **~ school** гимна́зия. **grammatical** adj граммати́ческий.

gramophone n прои́грыватель m; **~ record** грампласти́нка.

granary n амба́р.

grand adj великоле́пный; **~ piano** роя́ль m. **grandchild** n внук, вну́чка. **granddaughter** n вну́чка. **grandfather** n де́душка m. **grandmother** n ба́бушка. **grandparents** n ба́бушка и де́душка m. **grandson** n внук. **grandstand** n трибу́на.

grandeur n вели́чие.

grandiose adj грандио́зный.

granite n грани́т.

granny n ба́бушка.

grant n (financial) дота́ция; (univ) стипе́ндия; vt дарова́ть impf & pf; (concede) допуска́ть impf, допусти́ть pf; **take for ~ed** (assume) счита́ть impf, счесть pf само́ собо́й разуме́ющимся; (not appreciate) принима́ть impf как до́лжное.

granular adj зерни́стый.

granulated adj: **~ sugar** са́харный песо́к.

granule n зёрнышко.

grape n виногра́д. **grapefruit** n гре́йпфру́т.

graph n гра́фик.

graphic adj графи́ческий; (vivid) я́ркий.

graphite n графи́т.

grapple vi (struggle) боро́ться impf (with c+instr).

grasp n (grip) хва́тка; (comprehension) понима́ние; vt (clutch) хвата́ть impf, схвати́ть pf; (comprehend) понима́ть impf, поня́ть pf. **grasping** adj жа́дный.

grass n трава́. **grasshopper** n кузне́чик. **grassy** adj травяни́стый.

grate[1] n (in fireplace) решётка.

grate[2] vt (rub) тере́ть impf, на~ pf; vi (sound) скрипе́ть impf; **~ (up)on** (irritate) раздража́ть impf, раздражи́ть pf.

grateful adj благода́рный.

grater n тёрка.

gratify vt удовлетворя́ть impf, удо-

влетвори́ть pf.

grating n решётка.

gratis adv беспла́тно.

gratitude n благода́рность.

gratuitous adj (free) даровой; (motiveless) беспричи́нный.

gratuity n (tip) чаевы́е sb pl.

grave[1] n моги́ла. **gravedigger** n моги́льщик. **gravestone** n надгро́бный ка́мень m. **graveyard** n кла́дбище.

grave[2] adj серьёзный.

gravel n гра́вий.

gravitate vi тяготе́ть impf (towards к+dat). **gravitational** adj гравитацио́нный. **gravity** n (seriousness) серьёзность; (force) тя́жесть.

gravy n (мясна́я) подли́вка.

graze[1] vi (feed) пасти́сь impf.

graze[2] n (abrasion) цара́пина; vt (touch) задева́ть impf, заде́ть pf; (abrade) цара́пать impf, о~ pf.

grease n жир; (lubricant) сма́зка; **~paint** грим; vt сма́зывать impf, сма́зать pf. **greasy** adj жи́рный.

great adj (large) большо́й; (eminent) вели́кий; (splendid) великоле́пный; **to a ~ extent** в большо́й сте́пени; **a ~ deal** мно́го (+gen); **a ~ many** мно́гие; **~-aunt** двою́родная ба́бушка; **~-granddaughter** пра́внучка; **~-grandfather** пра́дед; **~-grandmother** праба́бка; **~-grandson** пра́внук; **~-uncle** двою́родный де́душка m. **Great Britain** n Великобрита́ния.

Greece n Гре́ция.

greed n жа́дность (for к+dat). **greedy** adj жа́дный (for к+dat).

Greek n грек, греча́нка; adj гре́ческий.

green n (colour) зелёный цвет; (piece of land) лужо́к; pl зе́лень collect; adj зелёный; (inexperienced) нео́пытный. **greenery** n зе́лень. **greenfly** n тля. **greengrocer** n зеленщи́к. **greenhouse** n тепли́ца; **~ effect** парнико́вый эффе́кт.

greet vt здоро́ваться impf, по~ pf с +instr; (meet) встреча́ть impf, встре́тить pf. **greeting** n приве́т(ствие).

gregarious adj общи́тельный.

grenade n грана́та.

grey adj се́рый; (hair) седо́й.

greyhound n борза́я sb.

grid n (grating) решётка; (electr) сеть; (map) координа́тная се́тка.

grief n го́ре; **come to ~** терпе́ть impf, по~ pf неуда́чу.

grievance n жа́лоба, оби́да.

grieve vt огорча́ть impf, огорчи́ть pf; vi горева́ть impf (**for** о+prep).

grievous adj тя́жкий.

grill n ра́шпер; vt (cook) жа́рить impf, за~, из~ pf (на ра́шпере); (question) допра́шивать impf, допроси́ть pf.

grille n (grating) решётка.

grim adj (stern) суро́вый; (unpleasant) неприя́тный.

grimace n грима́са; vi грима́сничать impf.

grime n грязь. **grimy** adj гря́зный.

grin n усме́шка; vi усмеха́ться impf, усмехну́ться pf.

grind vt (flour etc.) моло́ть impf, с~ pf; (axe) точи́ть impf, на~ pf; **~ one's teeth** скрежета́ть impf зуба́ми.

grip n хва́тка; vt схва́тывать impf, схвати́ть pf.

gripe vi ворча́ть impf.

gripping adj захва́тывающий.

grisly adj жу́ткий.

gristle n хрящ.

grit n песо́к; (for building) гра́вий; (firmness) вы́держка.

grizzle vi хны́кать impf.

groan n стон; vi стона́ть impf.

grocer n бакале́йщик; **~'s (shop)** бакале́йная ла́вка, гастроно́м. **groceries** n pl бакале́я collect.

groggy adj разби́тый.

groin n (anat) пах.

groom n ко́нюх; (bridegroom) жени́х; vt (horse) чи́стить impf, по~ pf; (prepare) гото́вить impf, под~ pf (**for** к+dat); **well-groomed** хорошо́ вы́глядящий.

groove n желобо́к.

grope vi нащу́пывать impf (**for, after** +acc).

gross¹ n (12 dozen) гросс.

gross² adj (fat) ту́чный; (coarse) гру́бый; (total) валово́й; **~ weight** вес бру́тто.

grotesque adj гроте́скный.

grotto n грот.

ground n земля́; (earth) по́чва; pl (dregs) гу́ща; (sport) площа́дка; pl (of house) парк; (reason) основа́ние;

~ floor пе́рвый эта́ж; vt (instruct) обуча́ть impf, обучи́ть pf осно́вам (**in** +gen); (aeron) запреща́ть impf, запрети́ть pf полёты +gen; vi (naut) сади́ться impf, сесть pf на мель.

groundless adj необосно́ванный.

groundwork n фунда́мент.

group n гру́ппа; vt & i группирова́ть(ся) impf, с~ pf.

grouse¹ n шотла́ндская куропа́тка.

grouse² vi (grumble) ворча́ть impf.

grove n ро́ща.

grovel vi пресмыка́ться impf (**before** пе́ред+instr).

grow vi расти́ impf; (become) станови́ться impf, стать pf +instr; vt (cultivate) выра́щивать impf, вы́растить pf; (hair) отра́щивать impf, отрасти́ть pf; **~ up** (person) выраста́ть impf, вы́расти pf; (custom) возника́ть impf, возни́кнуть pf.

growl n ворча́ние; vi ворча́ть impf (**at** на+acc).

grown-up adj взро́слый sb.

growth n рост; (med) о́пухоль.

grub n (larva) личи́нка; (food) жратва́; vi: **~ about** ры́ться impf. **grubby** adj запа́чканный.

grudge n зло́ба; **have a ~ against** име́ть impf зуб про́тив+gen; vt жале́ть impf, по~ pf +acc, +gen. **grudgingly** adv неохо́тно.

gruelling adj изнури́тельный.

gruesome adj жу́ткий.

gruff adj (surly) грубова́тый; (voice) хри́плый.

grumble vi ворча́ть impf (**at** на+acc).

grumpy adj брюзгли́вый.

grunt n хрю́канье; vi хрю́кать impf, хрю́кнуть pf.

guarantee n гара́нтия; vt гаранти́ровать impf & pf (**against** от+gen). **guarantor** n поручи́тель m.

guard n (device) предохрани́тель; (watch; soldiers) карау́л; (sentry) часово́й sb; (watchman) сто́рож; (rly) конду́ктор; (of prison) надзира́тель m; vt охраня́ть impf, охрани́ть pf; vi: **~ against** остерега́ться impf, остере́чься pf +gen, inf.

guardian n храни́тель m; (law) опеку́н.

guer(r)illa n партиза́н; **~ warfare** партиза́нская война́.

guess n дога́дка; vt & i дога́дываться

impf, догада́ться *pf* (o+*prep*); *vt* (~ *correctly*) уга́дывать *impf*, угада́ть *pf*. **guesswork** *n* дога́дки *f pl*.

guest *n* гость *m*; ~ **house** ма́ленькая гости́ница.

guffaw *n* хо́хот; *vi* хохота́ть *impf*.

guidance *n* руково́дство. **guide** *n* проводни́к, гид; (*guidebook*) путеводи́тель *m*; *vt* води́ть *indet*, вести́ *det*; (*direct*) руководи́ть *impf* +*instr*; ~**ed missile** управля́емая раке́та.

guidelines *n pl* инстру́кции *f pl*; (*advice*) сове́т.

guild *n* ги́льдия, цех.

guile *n* кова́рство. **guileless** *adj* простоду́шный.

guillotine *n* гильоти́на.

guilt *n* вина́; (*guiltiness*) вино́вность. **guilty** *adj* (*of crime*) вино́вный (of в+*prep*); (*of wrong*) винова́тый.

guinea-pig *n* морска́я сви́нка; (*fig*) подо́пытный кро́лик.

guise *n*: under the ~ of под ви́дом +*gen*.

guitar *n* гита́ра. **guitarist** *n* гитари́ст.

gulf *n* (*geog*) зали́в; (*chasm*) про́пасть.

gull *n* ча́йка.

gullet *n* (*oesophagus*) пищево́д; (*throat*) го́рло.

gullible *adj* легкове́рный.

gully *n* (*ravine*) овра́г.

gulp *n* глото́к; *vt* жа́дно глота́ть *impf*.

gum[1] *n* (*anat*) десна́.

gum[2] *n* каме́дь; (*glue*) клей; *vt* скле́ивать *impf*, скле́ить *pf*.

gumption *n* инициати́ва.

gun *n* (*piece of ordnance*) ору́дие, пу́шка; (*rifle etc.*) ружьё; (*pistol*) пистоле́т; *vt*: ~ **down** расстре́ливать *impf*, расстреля́ть *pf*. **gunner** *n* артиллери́ст. **gunpowder** *n* по́рох.

gurgle *vi* бу́лькать *impf*.

gush *vi* хлы́нуть *pf*.

gusset *n* клин.

gust *n* поры́в. **gusty** *adj* поры́вистый.

gusto *n* смак.

gut *n* кишка́; *pl* (*entrails*) кишки́ *f pl*; *pl* (*bravery*) му́жество; *vt* потроши́ть *impf*, вы́~ *pf*; (*devastate*) опустоша́ть *impf*, опустоши́ть *pf*.

gutter *n* (*of roof*) (водосто́чный) жёлоб; (*of road*) сто́чная кана́ва.

guttural *adj* горта́нный.

guy[1] *n* (*rope*) отта́жка.

guy[2] *n* (*fellow*) па́рень *m*.

guzzle *vt* (*food*) пожира́ть *impf*, пожра́ть *pf*; (*liquid*) хлеба́ть *impf*, хлебну́ть *pf*.

gym *n* (*gymnasium*) гимнасти́ческий зал; (*gymnastics*) гимна́стика. **gymnasium** *n* гимнасти́ческий зал. **gymnast** *n* гимна́ст. **gymnastic** *adj* гимнасти́ческий. **gymnastics** *n* гимна́стика.

gynaecologist *n* гинеко́лог. **gynaecology** *n* гинеколо́гия.

gyrate *vi* враща́ться *impf*.

H

haberdashery *n* галантере́я; (*shop*) галантере́йный магази́н.

habit *n* привы́чка; (*monk's*) ря́са.

habitable *adj* приго́дный для жилья́. **habitat** *n* есте́ственная среда́. **habitation** *n*: unfit for ~ неприго́дный для жилья́.

habitual *adj* привы́чный.

hack[1] *vt* руби́ть *impf*; ~**saw** ножо́вка.

hack[2] *n* (*hired horse*) наёмная ло́шадь; (*writer*) халту́рщик. **hackneyed** *adj* изби́тый.

haddock *n* пи́кша.

haemophilia *n* гемофили́я. **haemorrhage** *n* кровотече́ние. **haemorrhoids** *n pl* геморро́й *collect*.

hag *n* карга́.

haggard *adj* измождённый.

haggle *vi* торгова́ться *impf*, с~ *pf*.

hail[1] *n* град; *vt* it is ~**ing** идёт град. **hailstone** *n* гра́дина.

hail[2] *vt* (*greet*) приве́тствовать *impf* (& *pf in past*); (*taxi*) подзыва́ть *impf*, подозва́ть *pf*.

hair *n* (*single* ~) во́лос; *collect* (*human*) во́лосы (-о́с, -оса́м) *pl*; (*animal*) шерсть. **hairbrush** *n* щётка для воло́с. **haircut** *n* стри́жка; have a ~ постри́чься *pf*. **hair-do** *n* причёска. **hairdresser** *n* парикма́хер. **hairdresser's** *n* парикма́херская *sb*. **hair-dryer** *n* фен. **hairstyle** *n* причёска. **hairy** *adj* волоса́тый.

hale *adj*: ~ and hearty здоро́вый и бо́дрый.

half *n* полови́на; (*sport*) тайм; *adj*

половинный; in ~ пополам; one and a ~ полтора; ~ past (one etc.) половина (второго и т.д.); ~-hearted равнодушный; ~ an hour полчаса; ~-time перерыв между таймами; ~-way на полпути; ~-witted слабоумный.

hall n (large room) зал; (entrance ~) холл, вестибюль m; (~ of residence) общежитие. **hallmark** n пробирное клеймо; (fig) признак.

hallo int здрасте, привет; (on telephone) алло.

hallucination n галлюцинация.

halo n (around Saint) нимб; (fig) ореол.

halt n остановка; vt & i останавливать(ся) impf, остановить(ся) pf; int (mil) стой(те)! **halting** adj запинающий.

halve vt делить impf, раз~ pf пополам.

ham n (cul) ветчина.

hamlet n деревушка.

hammer n молоток; vt бить impf молотком.

hammock n гамак.

hamper[1] n (basket) корзина с крышкой.

hamper[2] vt (hinder) мешать impf, по~ pf +dat.

hamster n хомяк.

hand n рука; (worker) рабочий sb; (writing) почерк; (clock ~) стрелка; at ~ под рукой; on ~s and knees на четвереньках; vt передавать impf, передать pf; ~ in подавать impf, подать pf; ~ out раздавать impf, раздать pf. **handbag** n сумка. **handbook** n руководство. **handcuffs** n pl наручники m pl. **handful** n горсть.

handicap n (sport) гандикап; (hindrance) помеха. **handicapped** adj: ~ person инвалид.

handicraft n ремесло.

handiwork n ручная работа.

handkerchief n носовой платок.

handle n ручка, рукоятка; vt (people) обращаться impf с+instr; (situations) справляться impf, справиться pf с+instr; (touch) трогать impf, тронуть pf рукой, руками. **handlebar(s)** n руль m.

handmade adj ручной работы.

handout n подачка; (document) лифлет.

handrail n перила (-л) pl.

handshake n рукопожатие.

handsome adj красивый; (generous) щедрый.

handwriting n почерк.

handy adj (convenient) удобный; (skilful) ловкий; come in ~ пригодиться pf.

hang n vt вешать impf, повесить pf; vi висеть impf; ~ about слоняться impf; ~ on (cling) держаться impf; (tel) не вешать impf трубку; (persist) упорствовать impf; ~ out вывешивать impf, вывесить pf; (spend time) болтаться impf; ~ up вешать impf, повесить pf; (tel) вешать impf, повесить pf трубку. **hanger** n вешалка. **hanger-on** n прилипала m & f. **hangman** n палач.

hangar n ангар.

hangover n похмелье.

hang-up n комплекс.

hanker vi: ~ after мечтать impf о+prep.

haphazard adj случайный.

happen vi (occur) случаться impf, случиться pf; происходить impf, произойти pf; (~ to be somewhere) оказываться impf, оказаться pf; ~ upon натыкаться impf, натолкнуться pf на+acc.

happiness n счастье. **happy** adj счастливый; ~-go-lucky беззаботный.

harass vt (pester) дёргать impf; (persecute) преследовать impf. **harassment** n травля; преследование.

harbinger n предвестник.

harbour n гавань, порт; vt (person) укрывать impf, укрыть pf; (thoughts) затаивать impf, затаить pf.

hard adj твёрдый; (difficult) трудный; (difficult to bear) тяжёлый; (severe) суровый; ~-boiled egg яйцо вкрутую; ~-headed практичный; ~-hearted жестокосердный; ~-up стеснённый в средствах; ~-working трудолюбивый. **hardboard** n строительный картон.

harden vi затвердевать impf, затвердеть pf; (fig) ожесточаться impf, ожесточиться pf.

hardly adv едва (ли).

hardship n (*privation*) нужда.

hardware n скобяные изделия *neut pl*; (*comput*) аппаратура.

hardy adj (*robust*) выносливый; (*plant*) морозостойкий.

hare n заяц.

hark vi: ~ **back to** возвращаться *impf*, вернуться *pf* k+*dat*; *int* слушай(те)!

harm n вред; vt вредить *impf*, по~ *pf* +*dat*. **harmful** adj вредный. **harmless** adj безвредный.

harmonic adj гармонический. **harmonica** n губная гармоника. **harmonious** adj гармоничный. **harmonize** vi гармонировать *impf* (**with** c+*instr*). **harmony** n гармония.

harness n упряжь; vt запрягать *impf*, запрячь *pf*; (*fig*) использовать *impf* & *pf*.

harp n арфа; vi: ~ **on** твердить *impf* o+*prep*.

harpoon n гарпун.

harpsichord n клавесин.

harrow n борона. **harrowing** adj душераздирающий.

harsh adj (*sound, colour*) резкий; (*cruel*) суровый.

harvest n жатва, сбор (плодов); (*yield*) урожай; (*fig*) плоды m pl; vt & abs собирать *impf*, собрать *pf* (урожай).

hash n: **make a** ~ **of** напутать *pf* +*acc*, в+*prep*.

hashish n гашиш.

hassle n беспокойство.

hassock n подушечка.

haste n спешка. **hasten** vi спешить *impf*, по~ *pf*; vt & i торопить(ся) *impf*, по~ *pf*; vt ускорять *impf*, ускорить *pf*. **hasty** adj (*hurried*) поспешный; (*quick-tempered*) вспыльчивый.

hat n шапка; (*stylish*) шляпа.

hatch[1] n люк; ~**back** машина-пикап.

hatch[2] vi вылупливаться, вылупляться *impf*, вылупиться *pf*.

hatchet n топорик.

hate n ненависть; vt ненавидеть *impf*. **hateful** adj ненавистный. **hatred** n ненависть.

haughty adj надменный.

haul n (*fish*) улов; (*loot*) добыча; (*distance*) езда; vt (*drag*) тянуть *impf*; таскать *indet*, тащить *det*. **haulage** n перевозка.

haunt n любимое место; vt (*ghost*) обитать *impf*; (*memory*) преследовать *impf*. **haunted** adj: ~ **house** дом с привидениями. **haunting** adj навязчивый.

have vt иметь *impf*; **I** ~ (*possess*) у меня (есть; был, -á, -o) +*nom*; **I** ~ **not** у меня нет (*past* не было) +*gen*; **I** ~ **(got) to** я должен +*inf*; **you had better** вам лучше бы +*inf*; ~ **on** (*wear*) быть одетым в +*prep*; (*be engaged in*) быть занятым +*instr*.

haven n (*refuge*) убежище.

haversack n рюкзак.

havoc n (*devastation*) опустошение; (*disorder*) беспорядок.

hawk[1] n (*bird*) ястреб.

hawk[2] vt (*trade*) торговать *impf* вразнос+*instr*. **hawker** n разносчик.

hawser n трос.

hawthorn n боярышник.

hay n сено; **make** ~ косить *impf*, с~ *pf* сено; ~ **fever** сенная лихорадка. **haystack** n стог.

hazard n риск; vt рисковать *impf* +*instr*. **hazardous** adj рискованный.

haze n дымка.

hazel n лещина. **hazelnut** n лесной орех.

hazy adj туманный; (*vague*) смутный.

he *pron* он.

head n голова; (*mind*) ум; (~ *of coin*) лицевая сторона монеты; ~**s or tails?** орёл или решка?; (*chief*) глава m, начальник; *attrib* главный; vt (*lead*) возглавлять *impf*, возглавить *pf*; (*ball*) забивать *impf*, забить *pf* головой; vi: ~ **for** направляться *impf*, направиться *pf* в, на, +*acc*, к+*dat*. **headache** n головная боль. **head-dress** n головной убор. **header** n удар головой. **heading** n (*title*) заголовок. **headland** n мыс. **headlight** n фара. **headline** n заголовок. **headlong** adv стремглав. **headmaster, -mistress** n директор школы. **head-on** adj головой; adv в бок. **headphone** n наушник. **headquarters** n штаб-квартира. **headscarf** n косынка. **headstone** n надгробный камень m. **headstrong** adj своевольный. **headway** n движение вперёд. **heady** adj опьяняющий.

heal vt излечивать *impf*, излечить

pf; *vi* заживать *impf*, зажить *pf*.
healing *n* целебный.
health *n* здоровье; ~ **care** здравоохранение. **healthy** *adj* здоровый; (*beneficial*) полезный.
heap *n* куча; *vt* нагромождать *impf*, нагромоздить *pf*.
hear *vt* слышать *impf*, y~ *pf*; (*listen to*) слушать *impf*, по~ *pf*; ~ **out** выслушивать *impf*, выслушать *pf*.
hearing *n* слух; (*law*) слушание.
hearsay *n* слух.
hearse *n* катафалк.
heart *n* сердце; (*essence*) суть; *pl* (*cards*) черви (-вей) *pl*; **by** ~ наизусть; ~ **attack** сердечный приступ. **heartburn** *n* изжога. **hearten** *vt* ободрять *impf*, ободрить *pf*. **heartfelt** *adj* сердечный. **heartless** *adj* бессердечный. **heart-rending** *adj* душераздирающий. **hearty** *adj* (*cordial*) сердечный; (*vigorous*) здоровый.
hearth *n* очаг.
heat *n* жара; (*phys*) теплота; (*of feeling*) пыл; (*sport*) забег, заезд; *vt & i* (*heat up*) нагревать(ся) *impf*, нагреть(ся) *pf*; *vt* (*house*) топить *impf*. **heater** *n* нагреватель *m*. **heating** *n* отопление.
heath *n* пустошь.
heathen *n* язычник; *adj* языческий.
heather *n* вереск.
heave *vt* (*lift*) поднимать *impf*, поднять *pf*; (*pull*) тянуть *impf*, по~ *pf*.
heaven *n* (*sky*) небо; (*paradise*) рай; *pl* небеса *neut pl*. **heavenly** *adj* небесный; (*divine*) божественный.
heavy *adj* тяжёлый; (*strong, intense*) сильный. **heavyweight** *n* тяжеловес.
Hebrew *adj* (древне)еврейский.
heckle *vt* перекаться *impf* с+*instr*.
hectic *adj* лихорадочный.
hedge *n* живая изгородь. **hedgerow** *n* шпалера.
hedgehog *n* ёж.
heed *vt* обращать *impf*, обратить *pf* внимание на+*acc*. **heedless** *adj* небрежный.
heel¹ *n* (*of foot*) пята; (*of foot, sock*) пятка; (*of shoe*) каблук.
heel² *vi* крениться *impf*, на~ *pf*.
hefty *adj* дюжий.
heifer *n* тёлка.

height *n* высота; (*of person*) рост. **heighten** *vt* (*strengthen*) усиливать *impf*, усилить *pf*.
heinous *adj* гнусный.
heir *n* наследник. **heiress** *n* наследница. **heirloom** *n* фамильная вещь.
helicopter *n* вертолёт.
helium *n* гелий.
hell *n* ад. **hellish** *adj* адский.
hello see **hallo**
helm *n* руль.
helmet *n* шлем.
help *n* помощь; *vt* помогать *impf*, помочь *pf* +*dat*; (*can't* ~) не мочь *impf* не +*inf*; ~ **o.s.** брать *impf*, взять *pf* себе; ~ **yourself!** берите! **helpful** *adj* полезный; (*obliging*) услужливый. **helping** *n* (*of food*) порция. **helpless** *adj* беспомощный.
helter-skelter *adv* как попало.
hem *n* рубец; *vt* подрубать *impf*, подрубить *pf*; ~ **in** окружать *impf*, окружить *pf*.
hemisphere *n* полушарие.
hemp *n* (*plant*) коппля; (*fibre*) пенька.
hen *n* (*female bird*) самка; (*domestic fowl*) курица.
hence *adv* (*from here*) отсюда; (*as a result*) следовательно; **3 years** ~ через три года. **henceforth** *adv* отныне.
henchman *n* приспешник.
henna *n* хна.
hepatitis *n* гепатит.
her *poss pron* её; *pron* свой.
herald *n* вестник; *vt* возвещать *impf*, возвестить *pf*.
herb *n* трава. **herbaceous** *adj* травяной; ~ **border** цветочный бордюр. **herbal** *adj* травяной.
herd *n* стадо; (*people*) толпиться *impf*, с~ *pf*; *vt* (*tend*) пасти *impf*; (*drive*) загонять *impf*, загнать *pf* в стадо.
here *adv* (*position*) здесь, тут; (*direction*) сюда; ~ **is ...** вот (+*nom*); ~ **and there** там и сям; ~ **you are!** пожалуйста. **hereabout(s)** *adv* поблизости. **hereafter** *adv* в будущем. **hereby** *adv* этим. **hereupon** *adv* (*in consequence*) вследствие этого; (*after*) после этого. **herewith** *adv* при сём.

hereditary *adj* наследственный. **heredity** *n* наследственность.

heresy *n* ересь. **heretic** *n* еретик. **heretical** *adj* еретический.

heritage *n* наследие.

hermetic *adj* герметический.

hermit *n* отшельник.

hernia *n* грыжа.

hero *n* герой. **heroic** *adj* героический. **heroin** *n* героин.

heroine *n* героиня. **heroism** *n* героизм.

heron *n* цапля.

herpes *n* лишай.

herring *n* сельдь; (*food*) селёдка.

hers *poss pron* её; свой.

herself *pron* (*emph*) (она) сама; (*refl*) себя.

hertz *n* герц.

hesitant *adj* нерешительный. **hesitate** *vi* колебаться *impf*, по~ *pf*; (*in speech*) запинаться *impf*, запнуться *pf*. **hesitation** *n* колебание.

hessian *n* мешковина.

heterogeneous *adj* разнородный.

heterosexual *adj* гетеросексуальный.

hew *vt* рубить *impf*.

hexagon *n* шестиугольник.

hey *int* эй!

heyday *n* расцвет.

hi *int* привет!

hiatus *n* пробел.

hibernate *vi* быть *impf* в спячке; впадать *impf*, впасть *pf* в спячку. **hibernation** *n* спячка.

hiccup *vi* икать *impf*, икнуть *pf*; *n*: *pl* икота.

hide[1] *n* (*skin*) шкура.

hide[2] *vt* & *i* (*conceal*) прятать(ся) *impf*, с~ *pf*; скрывать(ся) *impf*, скрыть(ся) *pf*.

hideous *adj* отвратительный.

hideout *n* укрытие.

hiding *n* (*flogging*) порка.

hierarchy *n* иерархия.

hieroglyphics *pl* иероглифы *m pl*.

hi-fi *n* проигрыватель *m* с высококачественным воспроизведением звука записи.

higgledy-piggledy *adv* как придётся.

high *adj* высокий; (*wind*) сильный; (*on drugs*) в наркотическом дурмане; ~er education высшее образование; ~-handed своевольный;

~-heeled на высоких каблуках; ~ jump прыжок в высоту; ~-minded благородный; идейный; ~-pitched высокий; ~-rise высотный. high-brow *adj* интеллектуальный. highland(s) *n* горная страна. highlight *n* (*fig*) высшая точка; *vt* обращать *impf*, обратить *pf* внимание на+*acc*. highly *adv* весьма; ~-strung легко возбуждаемый. highness *n* (*title*) высочество. highstreet *n* главная улица. highway *n* магистраль.

hijack *vt* похищать *impf*, похитить *pf*. **hijacker** *n* похититель *m*.

hike *n* поход.

hilarious *adj* уморительный. **hilarity** *n* веселье.

hill *n* холм. **hillock** *n* холмик. **hillside** *n* склон холма. **hilly** *adj* холмистый.

hilt *n* рукоятка.

himself *pron* (*emph*) (он) сам; (*refl*) себя.

hind *adj* (*rear*) задний.

hinder *vt* мешать *impf*, по~ *pf* +*dat*. **hindrance** *n* помеха.

Hindu *n* индус; *adj* индусский.

hinge *n* шарнир; *vi* (*fig*) зависеть *impf* от+*gen*.

hint *n* намёк; *vi* намекать *impf*, намекнуть *pf* (at на+*acc*)

hip *n* (*anat*) бедро.

hippie *n* хиппи *neut indecl*.

hippopotamus *n* гиппопотам.

hire *n* наём, прокат; ~-purchase покупка в рассрочку; *vt* нанимать *impf*, нанять *pf*, ~ out сдавать *impf*, сдать *pf* напрокат.

his *poss pron* его; свой.

hiss *n* шипение; *vi* шипеть *impf*; *vt* (*performer*) освистывать *impf*, освистать *pf*.

historian *n* историк. **historic(al)** *adj* исторический. **history** *n* история.

histrionic *adj* театральный.

hit *n* (*blow*) удар; (*on target*) попадание (в цель); (*success*) успех; *vt* (*strike*) ударять *impf*, ударить *pf*; (*target*) попадать *impf*, попасть *pf* (в цель). ~ (up)on находить *impf*, найти *pf*.

hitch *n* (*stoppage*) задержка; *vt* (*fasten*) привязывать *impf*, привязать *pf*; ~ up подтягивать *impf*, подтянуть *pf*; ~-hike ездить *indet*, ехать det, по~ pf автостóпом.

hither adv сюдá. **hitherto** adv до сих пор.

HIV abbr (of **human immunodeficiency virus**) ВИЧ.

hive n ýлей.

hoard n запáс; vt скáпливать impf, скопи́ть pf.

hoarding n рекла́мный щит.

hoarse adj хри́плый.

hoax n надувáтельство.

hobble vi ковыля́ть impf.

hobby n хóбби neut indecl.

hock n (wine) рейнвéйн.

hockey n хоккéй.

hoe n моты́га; vt моты́жить impf.

hog n бóров.

hoist n подъёмник; vt поднимáть impf, подня́ть pf.

hold¹ n (naut) трюм.

hold² n (grasp) захвáт; (influence) влия́ние (**on** на+acc); **catch ~ of** ухвати́ться pf за+acc; vt (grasp) держáть impf; (contain) вмещáть impf, вмести́ть pf; (possess) владéть impf +instr; (conduct) проводи́ть impf, провести́ pf; (consider) считáть impf, счесть pf (+acc & instr, за+acc); vi держáться impf; (weather) продéрживаться impf, продержáться pf; ~ **back** сдéрживать(ся) impf, сдержáть(ся) pf; ~ **forth** разглагóльствовать impf; ~ **on** (wait) подождáть pf; (tel) не вéшать impf трýбку; (grip) держáться impf (**to** за+acc); ~ **out** (stretch out) протя́гивать impf, протяну́ть pf; (resist) не сдавáться impf; ~ **up** (support) поддéрживать impf, поддержáть pf; (impede) задéрживать impf, задержáть pf. **holdall** n сýмка. **hold-up** n (robbery) налёт; (delay) задéржка.

hole n дырá; (animal's) норá; (golf) лýнка.

holiday n (day off) выходнóй день; (festival) прáздник; (annual leave) óтпуск; pl (school) каникулы (-л) pl; ~**maker** тури́ст; **on ~** в óтпуске.

holiness n свя́тость.

Holland n Голлáндия.

hollow n впáдина; (valley) лощи́на; adj пустóй; (sunken) впáлый; (sound) глухóй; vt (~ out) выдáлбливать impf, вы́долбить pf.

holly n остроли́ст.

holocaust n мáссовое уничтожéние.

holster n кобурá.

holy adj святóй, свящéнный.

homage n почтéние; **pay ~ to** преклоня́ться impf, преклони́ться pf пéред+instr.

home n дом; (native land) рóдина; **at ~** дóма; **feel at ~** чýвствовать impf себя́ как дóма; adj домáшний; (native) роднóй; **H~ Affairs** внýтренние делá neut pl; adv (direction) домóй; (position) дóма. **homeland** n рóдина. **homeless** adj бездóмный. **home-made** adj (food) домáшний; (object) самодéльный. **homesick** adj: **be ~** скучáть impf по дóму. **homewards** adv домóй, восвоя́си.

homely adj простóй.

homicide n (action) уби́йство.

homogeneous adj однорóдный.

homosexual n гомосексуали́ст; adj гомосексуáльный.

honest n чéстный. **honesty** n чéстность.

honey n мёд. **honeymoon** n медóвый мéсяц. **honeysuckle** n жи́молость.

honk vi гудéть impf.

honorary adj почётный.

honour n честь; vt (respect) почитáть impf; (confer) удостáивать impf, удостóить pf (**with** +gen); (fulfil) выполня́ть impf, вы́полнить pf. **honourable** adj чéстный.

hood n капюшóн; (tech) капóт.

hoodwink vt обмáнывать impf, обманýть pf.

hoof n копы́то.

hook n крючóк; vt (hitch) зацепля́ть impf, зацепи́ть pf; (fasten) застёгивать impf, застегнýть pf.

hooligan n хулигáн.

hoop n óбруч.

hoot vi (owl) ýхать impf, ýхнуть pf; (horn) гудéть impf. **hooter** n гудóк.

hop¹ n (plant; collect) хмель m.

hop² n (jump) прыжóк; vi пры́гать impf, пры́гнуть pf (на одной ногé).

hope n надéжда; vi надéяться impf, по~ pf (**for** на+acc). **hopeful** adj (promising) обнадёживающий; **I am ~** я надéюсь. **hopefully** adv с надéждой; (it is hoped) надо надéяться. **hopeless** adj безнадёжный.

horde n (hist; fig) ордá.

horizon n горизо́нт. **horizontal** adj горизонта́льный.

hormone n гормо́н.

horn n рог; (French horn) валто́рна; (car) гудо́к.

hornet n ше́ршень m.

horny adj (calloused) мозо́листый.

horoscope n гороско́п.

horrible, horrid adj ужа́сный. **horrify** vt ужаса́ть impf, ужасну́ть pf. **horror** n у́жас.

hors-d'oeuvre n заку́ска.

horse n ло́шадь. **horse-chestnut** n ко́нский кашта́н. **horseman, -woman** n вса́дник, -ица. **horseplay** n возня́. **horsepower** n лошади́ная си́ла. **horse-racing** n ска́чки (-чек) pl. **horse-radish** n хрен. **horseshoe** n подко́ва.

horticulture n садово́дство.

hose n (~-pipe) шланг.

hosiery n чуло́чные изде́лия neut pl.

hospitable adj гостеприи́мный.

hospital n больни́ца.

hospitality n гостеприи́мство.

host[1] n (multitude) мно́жество.

host[2] n (entertaining) хозя́ин.

hostage n зало́жник.

hostel n общежи́тие.

hostess n хозя́йка; (air ~) стюарде́сса.

hostile adj вражде́бный. **hostility** n вражде́бность; pl вое́нные де́йствия neut pl.

hot adj горя́чий, жа́ркий; (pungent) о́стрый; ~-headed вспы́льчивый; ~-water bottle гре́лка. **hotbed** n (fig) оча́г. **hothouse** n тепли́ца. **hotplate** n пли́тка.

hotel n гости́ница.

hound n охо́тничья соба́ка; vt трави́ть impf, за~ pf.

hour n час. **hourly** adj ежеча́сный.

house n дом; (parl) пала́та; attrib дома́шний; vt помеща́ть impf, помести́ть pf. **household** n семья́; adj хозя́йственный; дома́шний. **housekeeper** n эконо́мка. **house-warming** n новосе́лье. **housewife** n хозя́йка. **housework** n дома́шняя рабо́та. **housing** n (accommodation) жильё; (casing) кожу́х; ~ **estate** жило́й масси́в.

hovel n лачу́га.

hover vi (bird) пари́ть impf; (heli-copter) висе́ть impf; (person) ма́ячить impf. **hovercraft** n су́дно на возду́шной поду́шке, СВП.

how adv как, каки́м о́бразом; ~ **do you do?** здра́вствуйте!; ~ **many, much** ско́лько (+gen). **however** adv как бы ни (+past); conj одна́ко, тем не ме́нее; ~ **much** ско́лько бы ни (+gen & past).

howl n вой; vi выть impf. **howler** n грубе́йшая оши́бка.

hub n (of wheel) ступи́ца; (fig) центр, средото́чие.

hubbub n шум, гам.

huddle vi: ~ **together** прижима́ться impf, прижа́ться pf друг к дру́гу.

hue n (tint) отте́нок.

huff n: in a ~ оскорблённый.

hug n объя́тие; vt (embrace) обнима́ть impf, обня́ть pf.

huge adj огро́мный.

hulk n ко́рпус (корабля́). **hulking** adj (bulky) грома́дный; (clumsy) неуклю́жий.

hull n (of ship) ко́рпус.

hum n жужжа́ние; vi (buzz) жужжа́ть impf; vt & i (person) напева́ть impf.

human adj челове́ческий, людско́й; n челове́к. **humane, humanitarian** adj челове́чный. **humanity** n (human race) челове́чество; (humaneness) гума́нность; **the Humanities** гуманита́рные нау́ки f pl.

humble adj (person) смире́нный; (abode) скро́мный; vt унижа́ть impf, уни́зить pf.

humdrum adj однообра́зный.

humid adj вла́жный. **humidity** n вла́жность.

humiliate vt унижа́ть impf, уни́зить pf. **humiliation** n униже́ние.

humility n смире́ние.

humorous adj юмористи́ческий. **humour** n ю́мор; (mood) настрое́ние; vt потака́ть impf +dat.

hump n горб; (of earth) буго́р.

humus n перегно́й.

hunch n (idea) предчу́вствие; vt го́рбить impf, с~ pf. **hunchback** n (person) горбу́н, ~ья. **hunchbacked** adj горба́тый.

hundred adj & n сто; ~s **of** со́тни f pl +gen; **two** ~ две́сти; **three** ~ три́ста; **four** ~ четы́реста; **five** ~ пятьсо́т. **hundredth** adj & n со́тый.

Hungarian *n* венгр, венге́рка; *adj* венге́рский. **Hungary** *n* Ве́нгрия.
hunger *n* го́лод; (*fig*) жа́жда (for +*gen*); ~ **strike** голодо́вка; *vi* голода́ть *impf*; ~ *pf* жа́ждать *impf* +*gen*.
hungry *adj* голо́дный.
hunk *n* ломо́ть *m*.
hunt *n* охо́та; (*fig*) по́иски *m pl* (for +*gen*); *vt* охо́титься *impf* на+*acc*, за+*instr*; (*persecute*) трави́ть *impf*, за~ *pf*; ~ **down** вы́следить *pf*; ~ **for** иска́ть *impf* +*acc or gen*; ~ **out** отыска́ть *pf*. **hunter** *n* охо́тник.
hunting *n* охо́та.
hurdle *n* (*sport*; *fig*) барье́р. **hurdler** *n* барьери́ст. **hurdles** *n pl* (*sport*) барье́рный бег.
hurl *vt* швыря́ть *impf*, швырну́ть *pf*.
hurly-burly *n* сумато́ха.
hurrah, hurray *int* ура́!
hurricane *n* урага́н.
hurried *adj* торопли́вый. **hurry** *n* спе́шка; **be in a** ~ спеши́ть *impf*; *vt & i* торопи́ть(ся) *impf*, по~ *pf*; *vi* спеши́ть *impf*, по~ *pf*.
hurt *n* уще́рб; *vi* боле́ть *impf*; *vt* поврежда́ть *impf*, повреди́ть *pf*; (*offend*) обижа́ть *impf*, оби́деть *pf*.
hurtle *vi* нести́сь *impf*, по~ *pf*.
husband *n* муж.
hush *n* тишина́; *vt*: ~ **up** замина́ть *impf*, замя́ть *pf*; *int* ти́ше!
husk *n* шелуха́.
husky *adj* (*voice*) хри́плый.
hustle *n* толкотня́; *vt* (*push*) затолка́ть *impf*, затолкну́ть *pf*; (*herd people*) загоня́ть *impf*, загна́ть *pf*; *vt & i* (*hurry*) торопи́ть(ся) *impf*, по~ *pf*.
hut *n* хи́жина.
hutch *n* кле́тка.
hyacinth *n* гиаци́нт.
hybrid *n* гибри́д; *adj* гибри́дный.
hydrangea *n* горте́нзия.
hydrant *n* гидра́нт.
hydraulic *adj* гидравли́ческий.
hydrochloric acid *n* соля́ная кислота́. **hydroelectric** *adj* гидроэлектри́ческий; ~ **power station** гидроэлектроста́нция, ГЭС *f indecl*. **hydrofoil** *n* су́дно на подво́дных кры́льях, СПК.
hydrogen *n* водоро́д.
hyena *n* гие́на.
hygiene *n* гигие́на. **hygienic** *adj* гиги-

ени́ческий.
hymn *n* гимн.
hyperbole *n* гипе́рбола.
hyphen *n* дефи́с. **hyphen(ate)** *vt* писа́ть *impf*, на~ *pf* че́рез дефи́с.
hypnosis *n* гипно́з. **hypnotic** *adj* гипноти́ческий. **hypnotism** *n* гипноти́зм. **hypnotist** *n* гипнотизёр. **hypnotize** *vt* гипнотизи́ровать *impf*, за~ *pf*.
hypochondria *n* ипохо́ндрия. **hypochondriac** *n* ипохо́ндрик.
hypocrisy *n* лицеме́рие. **hypocrite** *n* лицеме́р. **hypocritical** *adj* лицеме́рный.
hypodermic *adj* подко́жный.
hypothesis *n* гипо́теза. **hypothesize** *vi* стро́ить *impf*, по~ *pf* гипо́тезу. **hypothetical** *adj* гипотети́ческий.
hysterectomy *n* гистерэктоми́я, удале́ние ма́тки.
hysteria *n* истери́я. **hysterical** *adj* истери́ческий. **hysterics** *n pl* исте́рика.

I

I *pron* я.
ibid(em) *adv* там же.
ice *n* лёд; ~**age** леднико́вый пери́од; ~**axe** ледору́б; ~**cream** моро́женое *sb*; ~ **hockey** хокке́й (с ша́йбой); ~ **rink** като́к; ~ **skate** конёк; *vi* ката́ться *impf* на конька́х; *vt* (*chill*) замора́живать *impf*, заморо́зить *pf*; (*cul*) глазирова́ть *impf & pf*; *vi*: ~ **over, up** обледенева́ть *impf*, обледене́ть *pf*. **iceberg** *n* а́йсберг. **icicle** *n* сосу́лька. **icing** *n* (*cul*) глазу́рь. **icy** *adj* ледяно́й.
icon *n* ико́на.
ID *abbr* (*of* **identification**) удостовере́ние ли́чности.
idea *n* иде́я, мысль; (*conception*) поня́тие.
ideal *n* идеа́л; *adj* идеа́льный. **idealism** *n* идеали́зм. **idealist** *n* идеали́ст. **idealize** *vt* идеализи́ровать *impf & pf*.
identical *adj* тожде́ственный, одина́ковый. **identification** *n* (*recognition*) опозна́ние; (*of person*) установле́ние ли́чности. **identify** *vt* опознава́ть *impf*, опозна́ть *pf*. **identity** *n*

(*of person*) ли́чность; ~ **card** удостовере́ние ли́чности.

ideological *adj* идеологи́ческий. **ideology** *n* идеоло́гия.

idiom *n* идио́ма. **idiomatic** *adj* идиомати́ческий.

idiosyncrasy *n* идиосинкрази́я.

idiot *n* идио́т. **idiotic** *adj* идио́тский. **idle** *adj* (*unoccupied; lazy; purposeless*) пра́здный; (*vain*) тще́тный; (*empty*) пусто́й; (*machine*) неде́йствующий; *vi* безде́льничать *impf*; (*engine*) рабо́тать *impf* вхолосту́ю; *vt*: ~ **away** пра́здно проводи́ть *impf*, провести́ *pf*. **idleness** *n* пра́здность.

idol *n* и́дол. **idolatry** *n* идолопокло́нство; (*fig*) обожа́ние. **idolize** *vt* боготвори́ть *impf*.

idyll *n* иди́ллия. **idyllic** *adj* идилли́ческий.

i.e. *abbr* т.е., то есть.

if *conj* е́сли, е́сли бы; (*whether*) ли; **as** ~ как бу́дто; **even** ~ да́же е́сли; ~ **only** е́сли бы то́лько.

ignite *vt* зажига́ть *impf*, заже́чь *pf*; *vi* загора́ться *impf*, загоре́ться *pf*. **ignition** *n* зажига́ние.

ignoble *adj* ни́зкий.

ignominious *adj* позо́рный.

ignoramus *n* неве́жда *m*. **ignorance** *n* неве́жество, (*of certain facts*) неве́дение. **ignorant** *adj* неве́жественный; (*uninformed*) несве́дущий (**of** в+*prep*).

ignore *vt* не обраща́ть *impf* внима́ния на+*acc*; игнори́ровать *impf* & *pf*.

ilk *n*: **of that** ~ тако́го ро́да.

ill *n* (*evil*) зло; (*harm*) вред; *pl* (*misfortunes*) несча́стья (-тий) *pl*; *adj* (*sick*) больно́й; (*bad*) дурно́й; *adv* пло́хо, ду́рно; **fall** ~ заболева́ть *impf*, заболе́ть *pf*; ~**-advised** неблагоразу́мный; ~**-mannered** неве́жливый; ~**-treat** *vt* пло́хо обраща́ться *impf* с+*instr*.

illegal *adj* нелега́льный. **illegality** *n* незако́нность, нелега́льность.

illegible *adj* неразбо́рчивый.

illegitimacy *n* незако́нность; (*of child*) незаконнорождённость. **illegitimate** *adj* незако́нный; незаконнорождённый.

illicit *adj* незако́нный, недозво́ленный.

illiteracy *n* негра́мотность. **illiterate** *adj* негра́мотный.

illness *n* боле́знь.

illogical *adj* нелоги́чный.

illuminate *vt* освеща́ть *impf*, освети́ть *pf*. **illumination** *n* освеще́ние.

illusion *n* иллю́зия. **illusory** *adj* иллюзо́рный.

illustrate *vt* иллюстри́ровать *impf* & *pf*, про— *pf*. **illustration** *n* иллюстра́ция. **illustrative** *adj* иллюстрати́вный.

illustrious *adj* знамени́тый.

image *n* (*phys; statue etc.*) изображе́ние; (*optical* ~) отраже́ние; (*likeness*) ко́пия; (*metaphor; conception*) о́браз; (*reputation*) репута́ция. **imagery** *n* о́бразность.

imaginable *adj* вообрази́мый. **imaginary** *adj* вообража́емый. **imagination** *n* воображе́ние. **imagine** *vt* вообража́ть *impf*, вообрази́ть *pf*; (*conceive*) представля́ть *impf*, предста́вить *pf* себе́.

imbecile *n* слабоу́мный *sb*; (*fool*) глупе́ц.

imbibe *vt* (*absorb*) впи́тывать *impf*, впита́ть *pf*.

imbue *vt* внуша́ть *impf*, внуши́ть *pf* +*dat* (**with** +*acc*).

imitate *vt* подража́ть *impf* +*dat*. **imitation** *n* подража́ние (**of** +*dat*); *attrib* иску́сственный. **imitative** *adj* подража́тельный.

immaculate *adj* безупре́чный.

immaterial *adj* (*unimportant*) несуще́ственный.

immature *adj* незре́лый.

immeasurable *adj* неизмери́мый.

immediate *adj* (*direct*) непосре́дственный; (*swift*) неме́дленный. **immediately** *adv* то́тчас, сра́зу.

immemorial *adj*: **from time** ~ с незапа́мятных времён.

immense *adj* огро́мный.

immerse *vt* погружа́ть *impf*, погрузи́ть *pf*. **immersion** *n* погруже́ние.

immigrant *n* иммигра́нт, ~ка. **immigration** *n* иммигра́ция.

imminent *adj* надвига́ющийся; (*danger*) грозя́щий.

immobile *adj* неподви́жный. **immobilize** *vt* парализова́ть *impf* & *pf*.

immoderate *adj* неуме́ренный.

immodest *adj* нескро́мный.

immoral *adj* безнра́вственный. **immorality** *n* безнра́вственность.

immortal *adj* бессме́ртный. **immortality** *n* бессме́ртие. **immortalize** *vt* обессме́ртить *pf*.

immovable *adj* неподви́жный; *(fig)* непоколеби́мый.

immune *adj* (*to illness*) невосприи́мчивый (**to** к+*dat*); (*free from*) свобо́дный (**from** от+*gen*). **immunity** *n* иммуните́т (**from** к+*dat*); освобожде́ние (**from** от+*gen*). **immunize** *vt* иммунизи́ровать *impf* & *pf*.

immutable *adj* неизме́нный.

imp *n* бесёнок.

impact *n* уда́р; (*fig*) влия́ние.

impair *vt* вреди́ть *impf*, по~ *pf*.

impale *vt* протыка́ть *impf*, проткну́ть *pf*.

impart *vt* дели́ться *impf*, по~ *pf* +*instr* (**to** с+*instr*).

impartial *adj* беспристра́стный.

impassable *adj* непроходи́мый; (*for vehicles*) непроезжий.

impasse *n* тупи́к.

impassioned *adj* стра́стный.

impassive *adj* бесстра́стный.

impatience *n* нетерпе́ние. **impatient** *adj* нетерпели́вый.

impeach *vt* обвиня́ть *impf*, обвини́ть *pf* (**for** в+*prep*).

impeccable *adj* безупре́чный.

impecunious *adj* безде́нежный.

impedance *n* по́лное сопротивле́ние. **impede** *vt* препя́тствовать *impf*, вос~ *pf* +*dat*. **impediment** *n* препя́тствие; (*in speech*) заика́ние.

impel *vt* побужда́ть *impf*, побуди́ть *pf* (**to** +*inf*, к+*dat*).

impending *adj* предстоя́щий.

impenetrable *adj* непроница́емый.

imperative *adj* необходи́мый; *n* (*gram*) повели́тельное наклоне́ние.

imperceptible *adj* незаме́тный.

imperfect *adj* имперфе́кт; *adj* несоверше́нный. **imperfection** *n* несоверше́нство; (*fault*) недоста́ток. **imperfective** *adj* (*n*) несоверше́нный (вид).

imperial *adj* импе́рский. **imperialism** *n* империали́зм. **imperialist** *n* империали́ст; *attrib* империалисти́ческий.

imperil *vt* подверга́ть *impf*, подве́ргнуть *pf* опа́сности.

imperious *adj* вла́стный.

impersonal *adj* безли́чный.

impersonate *vt* (*imitate*) подража́ть *impf*; (*pretend to be*) выдава́ть *impf*, вы́дать *pf* себя́ за+*acc*. **impersonation** *n* подража́ние.

impertinence *n* де́рзость. **impertinent** *adj* де́рзкий.

imperturbable *adj* невозмути́мый.

impervious *adj* (*fig*) глухо́й (**to** к +*dat*).

impetuous *adj* стреми́тельный.

impetus *n* дви́жущая си́ла.

impinge *vi*: ~ (**up**)**on** ока́зывать *impf*, оказа́ть *pf* (отрица́тельный) эффе́кт на+*acc*.

implacable *adj* неумоли́мый.

implant *vt* вводи́ть *impf*, ввести́ *pf*; (*fig*) се́ять *impf*, по~ *pf*.

implement[1] *n* ору́дие, инструме́нт.

implement[2] *vt* (*fulfil*) выполня́ть *impf*, вы́полнить *pf*.

implicate *vt* впу́тывать *impf*, впу́тать *pf*. **implication** *n* (*inference*) намёк; *pl* значе́ние.

implicit *adj* подразумева́емый; (*absolute*) безогово́рочный.

implore *vt* умоля́ть *impf*.

imply *vt* подразумева́ть *impf*.

impolite *adj* неве́жливый.

imponderable *adj* неопределённый.

import *n* (*meaning*) значе́ние; (*of goods*) и́мпорт; *vt* импорти́ровать *impf* & *pf*. **importer** *n* импортёр.

importance *n* ва́жность. **important** *adj* ва́жный.

impose *vt* (*tax*) облага́ть *impf*, обложи́ть *pf* +*instr* (**on** +*acc*); (*obligation*) налага́ть *impf*, наложи́ть *pf* (**on** на+*acc*); ~ (**o.s.**) **on** налега́ть *impf* на+*acc*. **imposing** *adj* внуши́тельный. **imposition** *n* обложе́ние, наложе́ние.

impossibility *n* невозмо́жность. **impossible** *adj* невозмо́жный.

impostor *n* самозва́нец.

impotence *n* бесси́лие; (*med*) импоте́нция. **impotent** *adj* бесси́льный; (*med*) импоте́нтный.

impound *vt* (*confiscate*) конфискова́ть *impf* & *pf*.

impoverished *adj* обедне́вший.

impracticable *adj* невыполни́мый.

imprecise *n* нето́чный.

impregnable *adj* непристу́пный.

impregnate vt (fertilize) оплодотворя́ть impf, оплодотвори́ть pf; (saturate) пропи́тывать impf, пропита́ть pf.

impresario n аге́нт.

impress vt производи́ть impf, произвести́ pf (како́е-либо) впечатле́ние на+acc; ~ **upon** (s.o.) внуша́ть impf, внуши́ть pf (+dat). **impression** n впечатле́ние; (imprint) отпеча́ток; (reprint) (стереоти́пное) изда́ние.

impressionism n импрессиони́зм. **impressionist** n импрессиони́ст.

impressive adj впечатля́ющий.

imprint n отпеча́ток; vt отпеча́тывать impf, отпеча́тать pf; (on memory) запечатлева́ть impf, запечатле́ть pf.

imprison vt заключа́ть impf, заключи́ть pf (в тюрьму́). **imprisonment** n тюре́мное заключе́ние.

improbable adj невероя́тный.

impromptu adj импровизи́рованный; adv без подгото́вки, экспро́мтом.

improper adj (incorrect) непра́вильный; (indecent) неприли́чный. **impropriety** n неуме́стность.

improve vt & i улучша́ть(ся) impf, улу́чшить(ся) pf. **improvement** n улучше́ние.

improvisation n импровиза́ция. **improvise** vt импровизи́ровать impf, сымпровизи́ровать pf.

imprudent adj неосторо́жный.

impudence n на́глость. **impudent** adj на́глый.

impulse n толчо́к, и́мпульс; (sudden tendency) поры́в. **impulsive** adj импульси́вный.

impunity n: **with** ~ безнака́занно.

impure adj нечи́стый.

impute vt припи́сывать impf, приписа́ть pf (**to** +dat).

in prep (place) в+prep, на+prep; (into) в+acc, на+acc; (point in time) в+prep, на+prep; **in the morning** (etc.) у́тром (instr); **in spring** (etc.) весно́й (instr); (at some stage in; throughout) во вре́мя +gen; (duration) за+acc; (after interval of) че́рез+acc; (during course of) в тече́ние+gen; (circumstance) в+prep, при+prep; adv (place) внутри́; (motion) внутрь; (at home) до́ма; (in

fashion) в мо́де; **in here, there** (place) здесь, там; (motion) сюда́, туда́; adj вну́тренний; (fashionable) мо́дный; n: **the ins and outs** все хо́ды и вы́ходы.

inability n неспосо́бность.

inaccessible adj недосту́пный.

inaccurate adj нето́чный.

inaction n безде́йствие. **inactive** adj безде́йственный. **inactivity** n безде́йственность.

inadequate adj недоста́точный.

inadmissible adj недопусти́мый.

inadvertent adj неча́янный.

inalienable adj неотъе́млемый.

inane adj глу́пый.

inanimate adj неодушевлённый.

inappropriate adj неуме́стный.

inarticulate adj (person) косноязы́чный; (indistinct) невня́тный.

inasmuch adv: ~ **as** так как; ввиду́ того́, что.

inattentive adj невнима́тельный.

inaudible adj неслы́шный.

inaugural adj вступи́тельный. **inaugurate** vt (admit to office) торже́ственно вводи́ть impf, ввести́ pf в до́лжность; (open) открыва́ть impf, откры́ть pf; (introduce) вводи́ть impf, ввести́ pf. **inauguration** n введе́ние в до́лжность; откры́тие; нача́ло.

inauspicious adj неблагоприя́тный.

inborn, inbred adj врождённый.

incalculable adj неисчисли́мый.

incandescent adj накалённый.

incantation n заклина́ние.

incapability n неспосо́бность. **incapable** adj неспосо́бный (**of** к+dat, на+acc).

incapacitate vt де́лать impf, с~ pf неспосо́бным **incapacity** n неспосо́бность.

incarcerate vt заключа́ть impf, заключи́ть pf (в тюрьму́). **incarceration** n заключе́ние (в тюрьму́).

incarnate adj воплощённый. **incarnation** n воплоще́ние.

incendiary adj зажига́тельный.

incense[1] n фимиа́м, ла́дан.

incense[2] vt разгнева́ть pf.

incentive n побужде́ние.

inception n нача́ло.

incessant adj непреста́нный.

incest n кровосмеше́ние.

inch n дюйм; ~ by ~ ма́ло-пома́лу; vi ползти́ impf.

incidence n (phys) паде́ние; (prevalence) распростране́ние. incident n слу́чай, инциде́нт. incidental adj (casual) случа́йный; (inessential) несуще́ственный. incidentally adv ме́жду про́чим.

incinerate vt испепеля́ть impf, испепели́ть pf. incinerator n мусоросжига́тельная печь.

incipient adj начина́ющийся.

incision n надре́з (на+acc). incisive adj (fig) о́стрый. incisor n резе́ц.

incite vt подстрека́ть impf, подстрекну́ть pf (to к+dat). incitement n подстрека́тельство.

inclement adj суро́вый.

inclination n (slope) накло́н; (propensity) скло́нность (for, to к+dat). incline n накло́н; vt & i склоня́ть(ся) impf, склони́ть(ся) pf. inclined predic (disposed) скло́нен (-онна́, -о́нно) (to к+dat).

include vt включа́ть impf, включи́ть pf (in в+acc); (contain) заключа́ть impf, заключи́ть pf в себе́. including prep включа́я+acc. inclusion n включе́ние. inclusive adj включа́ющий (в себя́); adv включи́тельно.

incognito adv инко́гнито.

incoherent adj бессвя́зный.

income n дохо́д; ~ tax подохо́дный нало́г.

incommensurate adj несоразме́рный.

incomparable adj несравни́мый (to, with с+instr); (matchless) несравне́нный.

incompatible adj несовмести́мый.

incompetence n некомпете́нтность. incompetent adj некомпете́нтный.

incomplete adj непо́лный, незако́нченный.

incomprehensible adj непоня́тный.

inconceivable adj невообрази́мый.

inconclusive adj (evidence) недоста́точный; (results) неопределённый.

incongruity n несоотве́тствие. incongruous adj несоотве́тствующий.

inconsequential adj незначи́тельный.

inconsiderable adj незначи́тельный.

inconsiderate adj невнима́тельный.

inconsistency n непосле́довательность. inconsistent adj непосле́довательный.

inconsolable adj безуте́шный.

inconspicuous adj незаме́тный.

incontinence n (med) недержа́ние. incontinent adj: be ~ страда́ть impf недержа́нием.

incontrovertible adj неопровержи́мый.

inconvenience n неудо́бство; vt затрудня́ть impf, затрудни́ть pf. inconvenient adj неудо́бный.

incorporate vt (include) включа́ть impf, включи́ть pf; (unite) объединя́ть impf, объедини́ть pf.

incorrect adj непра́вильный.

incorrigible adj неисправи́мый.

incorruptible adj неподку́пный.

increase n рост, увеличе́ние; (in pay etc.) приба́вка; vt & i увеличи́вать(ся) impf, увели́чить(ся) pf.

incredible adj невероя́тный.

incredulous adj недове́рчивый.

increment n приба́вка.

incriminate vt изоблича́ть impf, изобличи́ть pf.

incubate vt (eggs) выводи́ть impf, вы́вести pf (в инкуба́торе). incubator n инкуба́тор.

inculcate vt внедря́ть impf, внедри́ть pf.

incumbent adj (in office) стоя́щий у вла́сти; it is ~ (up)on you вы обя́заны.

incur vt навлека́ть impf, навле́чь pf на себя́.

incurable adj неизлечи́мый.

incursion n (invasion) вторже́ние; (attack) набе́г.

indebted predic в долгу́ (to y+gen).

indecency n неприли́чие. indecent adj неприли́чный.

indecision n нереши́тельность. indecisive adj нереши́тельный.

indeclinable adj несклоня́емый.

indeed adv в са́мом де́ле, действи́тельно; (interrog) неуже́ли?

indefatigable adj неутоми́мый.

indefensible adj не име́ющий оправда́ния.

indefinable adj неопредели́мый. indefinite adj неопределённый.

indelible adj несмыва́емый.

indemnify vt: ~ against страхова́ть

impf, за~ *pf* от+*gen*; ~ **for** (*compensate*) компенсировать *impf* & *pf*.

indemnity *n* (*against loss*) гарантия от убытков; (*compensation*) компенсация.

indent *vt* (*printing*) писать *impf*, с~ *pf* с отступом. **indentation** *n* (*notch*) зубец; (*printing*) отступ.

independence *n* независимость, самостоятельность. **independent** *adj* независимый, самостоятельный.

indescribable *adj* неописуемый.

indestructible *adj* неразрушимый.

indeterminate *adj* неопределённый.

index *n* (*alphabetical*) указатель *m*; (*econ*) индекс; (*pointer*) стрелка; ~ **finger** указательный палец.

India *n* Индия. **Indian** *n* индиец, индианка; (*American*) индеец, индианка; *adj* индийский; (*American*) индейский; ~ **summer** бабье лето.

indicate *vt* указывать *impf*, указать *pf*; (*be a sign of*) свидетельствовать *impf* о+*prep*. **indication** *n* указание; (*sign*) признак. **indicative** *adj* указывающий; (*gram*) изъявительный; *n* изъявительное наклонение. **indicator** *n* указатель *m*.

indict *vt* обвинять *impf*, обвинить *pf* (**for** в+*prep*).

indifference *n* равнодушие. **indifferent** *adj* равнодушный; (*mediocre*) посредственный.

indigenous *adj* туземный.

indigestible *adj* неудобоваримый. **indigestion** *n* несварение желудка.

indignant *adj* негодующий; **be** ~ негодовать *impf* (**with** на+*acc*). **indignation** *n* негодование.

indignity *n* оскорбление.

indirect *adj* непрямой; (*econ; gram*) косвенный.

indiscreet *adj* нескромный. **indiscretion** *n* нескромность.

indiscriminate *adj* неразборчивый. **indiscriminately** *adv* без разбора.

indispensible *adj* необходимый.

indisposed *predic* (*unwell*) нездоров.

indisputable *adj* бесспорный.

indistinct *adj* неясный.

indistinguishable *adj* неразличимый.

individual *n* личность; *adj* индивидуальный. **individualism** *n* индивидуализм. **individualist** *n* индивидуалист. **individualistic** *adj* индивиду-

алистический. **individuality** *n* индивидуальность.

indivisible *adj* неделимый.

indoctrinate *vt* внушать *impf*, внушить *pf* +*dat* (**with** +*acc*).

indolence *n* леность. **indolent** *adj* ленивый.

indomitable *adj* неукротимый.

Indonesia *n* Индонезия.

indoor *adj* комнатный. **indoors** *adv* (*position*) в доме; (*motion*) в дом.

induce *vt* (*prevail on*) убеждать *impf*, убедить *pf*; (*bring about*) вызывать *impf*, вызвать *pf*. **inducement** *n* побуждение.

induction *n* (*logic, electr*) индукция; (*in post*) введение в должность.

indulge *vt* потворствовать *impf* +*dat*; *vi* предаваться *impf*, предаться *pf* (**in** +*dat*). **indulgence** *n* потворство; (*tolerance*) снисходительность. **indulgent** *adj* снисходительный.

industrial *adj* промышленный. **industrialist** *n* промышленник. **industrious** *adj* трудолюбивый. **industry** *n* промышленность; (*zeal*) трудолюбие.

inebriated *adj* пьяный.

inedible *adj* несъедобный.

ineffective, ineffectual *adj* безрезультатный; (*person*) неспособный.

inefficiency *n* неэффективность. **inefficient** *adj* неэффективный.

ineligible *adj* не имеющий право (**for** на+*acc*).

inept *adj* неумелый.

inequality *n* неравенство.

inert *adj* инертный. **inertia** *n* (*phys*) инерция; (*sluggishness*) инертность.

inescapable *adj* неизбежный.

inevitability *n* неизбежность. **inevitable** *adj* неизбежный.

inexact *adj* неточный.

inexcusable *adj* непростительный.

inexhaustible *adj* неистощимый.

inexorable *adj* неумолимый.

inexpensive *adj* недорогой.

inexperience *n* неопытность. **inexperienced** *adj* неопытный.

inexplicable *adj* необъяснимый.

infallible *adj* непогрешимый.

infamous *adj* позорный. **infamy** *n* позор.

infancy *n* младенчество. **infant** *n* младенец. **infantile** *adj* детский.

infantry *n* пехо́та.

infatuate *vt* вскружи́ть *pf* го́лову +*dat*. **infatuation** *n* увлече́ние.

infect *vt* заража́ть *impf*, зарази́ть *pf* (**with**+*instr*). **infection** *n* зара́за, инфе́кция. **infectious** *adj* зара́зный; (*fig*) заразительный.

infer *vt* заключа́ть *impf*, заключи́ть *pf*. **inference** *n* заключе́ние.

inferior *adj* (*in rank*) ни́зший; (*in quality*) ху́дший, плохо́й; *n* подчинённый *sb*. **inferiority** *n* бо́лее ни́зкое ка́чество; ~ **complex** ко́мплекс неполноце́нности.

infernal *adj* а́дский. **inferno** *n* ад.

infertile *adj* неплодоро́дный.

infested *adj*: **be** ~ **with** кише́ть *impf* +*instr*.

infidelity *n* неве́рность.

infiltrate *vt* постепе́нно проника́ть *impf*, прони́кнуть *pf* в+*acc*.

infinite *adj* бесконе́чный. **infinitesimal** *adj* бесконе́чно ма́лый. **infinitive** *n* инфинити́в. **infinity** *n* бесконе́чность.

infirm *adj* не́мощный. **infirmary** *n* больни́ца. **infirmity** *n* не́мощь.

inflame *vt* & *i* (*excite*) возбужда́ть(ся) *impf*, возбуди́ть(ся) *pf*; (*med*) воспаля́ть(ся) *impf*, воспали́ть(ся) *pf*. **inflammable** *adj* огнеопа́сный. **inflammation** *n* воспале́ние. **inflammatory** *adj* подстрека́тельский.

inflate *vt* надува́ть *impf*, наду́ть *pf*. **inflation** *n* (*econ*) инфля́ция.

inflection *n* (*gram*) фле́ксия.

inflexible *adj* неги́бкий; (*fig*) непрекло́нный.

inflict *vt* (*blow*) наноси́ть *impf*, нанести́ *pf* (**(up)on** +*dat*); (*suffering*) причиня́ть *impf*, причини́ть *pf* (**(up)on** +*dat*); (*penalty*) налага́ть *impf*, наложи́ть *pf* (**(up)on** на+*acc*); ~ **o.s. (up)on** навя́зываться *impf*, навяза́ться *pf* +*dat*.

inflow *n* втека́ние, прито́к.

influence *n* влия́ние; *vt* влия́ть *impf*, по~ *pf* на+*acc*. **influential** *adj* влия́тельный.

influenza *n* грипп.

influx *n* (*fig*) наплы́в.

inform *vt* сообща́ть *impf*, сообщи́ть *pf* +*dat* (**of**, **about** +*acc*, о+*prep*); *vi* доноси́ть *impf*, донести́ *pf* (**against** на+*acc*).

informal *adj* (*unofficial*) неофициа́льный; (*casual*) обыде́нный.

informant *n* осведоми́тель *m*. **information** *n* информа́ция. **informative** *adj* поучи́тельный. **informer** *n* доно́счик.

infra-red *adj* инфракра́сный.

infrequent *adj* ре́дкий.

infringe *vt* (*violate*) наруша́ть *impf*, нару́шить *pf*; *vi*: ~ **(up)on** посяга́ть *impf*, посягну́ть *pf* на+*acc*. **infringement** *n* наруше́ние; посяга́тельство.

infuriate *vt* разъяря́ть *impf*, разъяри́ть *pf*.

infuse *vt* (*fig*) внуша́ть *impf*, внуши́ть *pf* (**into** +*dat*). **infusion** *n* (*fig*) внуше́ние; (*herbs etc*) насто́й.

ingenious *adj* изобрета́тельный. **ingenuity** *n* изобрета́тельность.

ingenuous *adj* бесхи́тростный.

ingot *n* сли́ток.

ingrained *adj* закорене́лый.

ingratiate *vt* ~ **o.s.** вкра́дываться *impf*, вкра́сться *pf* в ми́лость (**with** +*dat*).

ingratitude *n* неблагода́рность.

ingredient *n* ингредие́нт, составля́ющее *sb*.

inhabit *vt* жить *impf* в, на, +*prep*; обита́ть *impf* в, на, +*prep*. **inhabitant** *n* жи́тель *m*, ~ница.

inhalation *n* вдыха́ние. **inhale** *vt* вдыха́ть *impf*, вдохну́ть *pf*.

inherent *adj* прису́щий (**in** +*dat*).

inherit *vt* насле́довать *impf* & *pf*, у~ *pf*. **inheritance** *n* насле́дство.

inhibit *vt* стесня́ть *impf*, стесни́ть *pf*. **inhibited** *adj* стесни́тельный. **inhibition** *n* стесне́ние.

inhospitable *adj* негостеприи́мный; (*fig*) недружелю́бный.

inhuman(e) *adj* бесчелове́чный.

inimical *adj* вражде́бный; (*harmful*) вре́дный.

inimitable *adj* неподража́емый.

iniquity *n* несправедли́вость.

initial *adj* (*perso*) нача́льный; *n* нача́льная бу́ква; *pl* инициа́лы *m pl*; *vt* ста́вить *impf*, по~ *pf* инициа́лы на+*acc*. **initially** *adv* в нача́ле.

initiate *vt* вводи́ть *impf*, ввести́ *pf* (**into** в+*acc*). **initiation** *n* введе́ние.

initiative *n* инициати́ва.

inject *vt* вводи́ть *impf*, ввести́ *pf* (*person* +*dat*, *substance* +*acc*). **injection** *n* укóл; (fig) инъéкция.

injunction n (law) судéбный запрéт.

injure vt поврежда́ть impf, повреди́ть pf. injury n ра́на.

injustice n несправедли́вость.

ink n черни́ла (-л).

inkling n представле́ние.

inland adj вну́тренний; adv (motion) внутрь страны́; (place) внутри́ страны́; I~ Revenue управле́ние нало́говых сбо́ров.

in-laws n pl ро́дственники m pl супру́га, -ги.

inlay n инкруста́ция; vt инкрусти́ровать impf & pf.

inlet n (of sea) у́зкий зали́в.

inmate n (prison) заключённый sb; (hospital) больно́й sb.

inn n гости́ница.

innate adj врождённый.

inner adj вну́тренний. innermost adj глубоча́йший; (fig) сокрове́ннейший.

innocence n неви́нность; (guiltlessness) невино́вность. innocent adj неви́нный; (not guilty) невино́вный (of в+prep).

innocuous adj безвре́дный.

innovate vi вводи́ть impf, ввести́ pf но́вшества. innovation n нововведе́ние. innovative adj нова́торский. innovator n нова́тор.

innuendo n намёк, инсину́ация.

innumerable adj бесчи́сленный.

inoculate vt привива́ть impf, приви́ть pf +dat (against +acc). inoculation n приви́вка.

inoffensive adj безоби́дный.

inopportune adj несвоевре́менный.

inordinate adj чрезме́рный.

inorganic adj неоргани́ческий.

in-patient n стациона́рный больно́й sb.

input n ввод.

inquest n судéбное сле́дствие, дозна́ние.

inquire vt спра́шивать impf, спроси́ть pf; vi справля́ться impf, спра́виться pf (about о+prep); рассле́довать impf & pf (into +acc). inquiry n вопро́с, спра́вка; (investigation) рассле́дование.

inquisition n инквизи́ция. inquisitive adj пытли́вый, любозна́тельный.

inroad n (attack) набе́г; (fig) посяга́тельство (on, into на+acc).

insane adj безу́мный. insanity n безу́мие.

insatiable adj ненасы́тный.

inscribe vt надпи́сывать impf, надписа́ть pf; (engrave) выреза́ть impf, вы́резать pf. inscription n на́дпись.

inscrutable adj непостижи́мый, непроница́емый.

insect n насеко́мое sb. insecticide n инсектици́д.

insecure adj (unsafe) небезопа́сный; (not confident) неуве́ренный (в себе́).

insemination n оплодотворе́ние.

insensible adj (unconscious) потеря́вший созна́ние.

insensitive adj нечувстви́тельный.

inseparable adj неотдели́мый; (people) неразлу́чный.

insert vt вставля́ть impf, вста́вить pf; вкла́дывать impf, вложи́ть pf; (coin) опуска́ть impf, опусти́ть pf. insertion n (inserting) вставле́ние, вкла́дывание; (thing inserted) вста́вка.

inshore adj прибре́жный; adv бли́зко к бе́регу.

inside n вну́тренняя часть; pl (anat) вну́тренности f pl; turn ~ out вывёртывать impf, вы́вернуть pf наизна́нку; adj вну́тренний; adv (place) внутри́; (motion) внутрь; prep (place) внутри́+gen, в+prep; (motion) внутрь+gen, в+acc.

insidious adj кова́рный.

insight n проница́тельность.

insignia n зна́ки m pl разли́чия.

insignificant adj незначи́тельный.

insincere adj неи́скренний.

insinuate vt (hint) намека́ть impf, намекну́ть pf на+acc. insinuation n инсину́ация.

insipid adj пре́сный.

insist vt & i наста́ивать impf, настоя́ть pf (on на+prep). insistence n насто́йчивость. insistent adj насто́йчивый.

insolence n на́глость. insolent adj на́глый.

insoluble adj (problem) неразреши́мый; (in liquid) нераствори́мый.

insolvent adj несостоя́тельный.

insomnia n бессо́нница.

inspect vt инспекти́ровать impf,

про~ *pf.* **inspection** *n* инспе́кция.
inspector *n* инспе́ктор; (*ticket ~*) контролёр.
inspiration *n* вдохнове́ние. **inspire** *vt* вдохновля́ть *impf*, вдохнови́ть *pf*; внуша́ть *impf*, внуши́ть *pf* +*dat* (**with** +*acc*).
instability *n* неусто́йчивость; (*of character*) неуравнове́шенность.
install *vt* (*person in office*) вводи́ть *impf*, ввести́ *pf* в до́лжность; (*apparatus*) устана́вливать *impf*, установи́ть *pf.* **installation** *n* введе́ние в до́лжность; установ́ка; *pl* сооруже́ния *neut pl.*
instalment *n* (*comm*) взнос; (*publication*) вы́пуск; часть; **by ~s** в рассро́чку.
instance *n* (*example*) приме́р; (*case*) слу́чай; **for ~** наприме́р.
instant *n* мгнове́ние, моме́нт; *adj* неме́дленный; (*coffee etc.*) раствори́мый. **instantaneous** *adj* мгнове́нный. **instantly** *adv* неме́дленно, то́тчас.
instead *adv* вме́сто (**of** +*gen*); **~ of going** вме́сто того́, что́бы пойти́.
instep *n* подъём.
instigate *vt* подстрека́ть *impf*, подстрекну́ть *pf* (**to** к+*dat*). **instigation** *n* подстрека́тельство. **instigator** *n* подстрека́тель *m*, ~ница.
instil *vt* (*ideas etc.*) внуша́ть *impf*, внуши́ть *pf* (**into** +*dat*).
instinct *n* инсти́нкт. **instinctive** *adj* инстинкти́вный.
institute *n* институ́т; *vt* (*establish*) устана́вливать *impf*, установи́ть *pf*; (*introduce*) вводи́ть *impf*, ввести́ *pf*; (*reforms*) проводи́ть *impf*, провести́ *pf*. **institution** *n* учрежде́ние.
instruct *vt* (*teach*) обуча́ть *impf*, обучи́ть *pf* (**in** +*dat*); (*inform*) сообща́ть *impf*, сообщи́ть *pf* +*dat*; (*command*) прика́зывать *impf*, приказа́ть *pf* +*dat*. **instruction** *n* (*in pl*) инстру́кция; (*teaching*) обуче́ние. **instructive** *adj* поучи́тельный. **instructor** *n* инстру́ктор.
instrument *n* ору́дие, инструме́нт. **instrumental** *adj* (*mus*) инструмента́льный; (*gram*) твори́тельный; **be ~ in** спосо́бствовать *impf*, по~ *pf* +*dat*; *n* (*gram*) твори́тельный паде́ж. **instrumentation** *n*

(*mus*) инструменто́вка.
insubordinate *adj* неподчиня́ющийся.
insufferable *adj* невыноси́мый.
insular *adj* (*fig*) ограни́ченный.
insulate *vt* изоли́ровать *impf* & *pf.* **insulation** *n* изоля́ция. **insulator** *n* изоля́тор.
insulin *n* инсули́н.
insult *n* оскорбле́ние; *vt* оскорбля́ть *impf*, оскорби́ть *pf.* **insulting** *adj* оскорби́тельный.
insuperable *adj* непреодоли́мый.
insurance *n* страхова́ние; *attrib* страхово́й. **insure** *vt* страхова́ть *impf*, за~ *pf* (**against** от+*gen*).
insurgent *n* повста́нец.
insurmountable *adj* непреодоли́мый.
insurrection *n* восста́ние.
intact *adj* це́лый.
intake *n* (*of persons*) набо́р; (*consumption*) потребле́ние.
intangible *adj* неосяза́емый.
integral *adj* неотъе́млемый. **integrate** *vt* & *i* интегри́роваться *impf* & *pf.* **integration** *n* интегра́ция.
integrity *n* (*honesty*) че́стность.
intellect *n* интелле́кт. **intellectual** *n* интеллиге́нт; *adj* интеллектуа́льный.
intelligence *n* (*intellect*) ум; (*information*) све́дения *neut pl*; (*service*) разве́дка. **intelligent** *adj* у́мный. **intelligentsia** *n* интеллиге́нция. **intelligible** *adj* поня́тный.
intemperate *adj* невозде́ржанный.
intend *vt* собира́ться *impf*, собра́ться *pf*; (*design*) предназнача́ть *impf*, предназна́чить *pf* (**for** для +*gen*, на+*acc*).
intense *adj* си́льный. **intensify** *vt* & *i* уси́ливать(ся) *impf*, уси́лить(ся) *pf.* **intensity** *n* интенси́вность, си́ла. **intensive** *adj* интенси́вный.
intent *n* наме́рение; *adj* (*resolved*) стремя́щийся (**on** к+*dat*); (*occupied*) погружённый (**on** в+*acc*); (*earnest*) внима́тельный. **intention** *n* наме́рение. **intentional** *adj* наме́ренный.
inter *vt* хорони́ть *impf*, по~ *pf.*
interact *vi* взаимоде́йствовать *impf.* **interaction** *n* взаимоде́йствие.
intercede *vi* хода́тайствовать *impf*, по~ *pf* (**for** за+*acc*; **with** пе́ред+*instr*).
intercept *vt* перехва́тывать *impf*,

interchange перехвати́ть pf. **interception** n перехва́т.

interchange n обме́н (of +instr); (junction) тра́нспортная развя́зка; vt обме́ниваться impf, обменя́ться pf +instr. **interchangeable** adj взаимозаменя́емый.

inter-city adj междугоро́дный.

intercom n вну́тренняя телефо́нная связь.

interconnected adj взаимосвя́занный. **interconnection** n взаимосвя́зь.

intercourse n (social) обще́ние; (trade; sexual) сноше́ния neut pl.

interdisciplinary adj межотраслево́й.

interest n интере́с (in к+dat); (econ) проце́нты m pl; vt интересова́ть impf; (~ person in) заинтересо́вывать impf, заинтересова́ть pf (in +instr); be ~ed in интересова́ться impf +instr. **interesting** adj интере́сный.

interfere vi вме́шиваться impf, вмеша́ться pf (in в+acc). **interference** n вмеша́тельство; (radio) поме́хи f pl.

interim n: in the ~ тем вре́менем; adj промежу́точный; (temporary) вре́менный.

interior n вну́тренность; adj вну́тренний.

interjection n восклица́ние; (gram) междоме́тие.

interlock vt & i сцепля́ть(ся) impf, сцепи́ть(ся) pf.

interloper n незва́ный гость m.

interlude n (theat) антра́кт; (mus, fig) интерлю́дия.

intermediary n посре́дник.

intermediate adj промежу́точный.

interminable adj бесконе́чный.

intermission n переры́в; (theat) антра́кт.

intermittent adj преры́вистый.

intern vt интерни́ровать impf & pf.

internal adj вну́тренний; ~ **combustion engine** дви́гатель m вну́треннего сгора́ния.

international adj междунаро́дный; n (contest) междунаро́дные состяза́ния neut pl.

internment n интерни́рование.

interplay n взаимоде́йствие.

interpret vt (explain) толкова́ть impf; (understand) истолко́вывать impf, истолкова́ть pf, vi переводи́ть impf, перевести́ pf. **interpretation** n толкова́ние. **interpreter** n перево́дчик, -ица.

interrelated adj взаимосвя́занный. **interrelationship** n взаи́мная связь.

interrogate vt допра́шивать impf, допроси́ть pf. **interrogation** n допро́с. **interrogative** adj вопроси́тельный.

interrupt vt прерыва́ть impf, прерва́ть pf. **interruption** n переры́в.

intersect vt & i пересека́ть(ся) impf, пересе́чь(ся) pf. **intersection** n пересече́ние.

intersperse vt (scatter) рассыпа́ть impf, рассы́пать pf (between, among ме́жду+instr, среди́+gen).

intertwine vt & i переплета́ть(ся) impf, переплести́(сь) pf.

interval n интерва́л; (theat) антра́кт.

intervene vi (occur) происходи́ть impf, произойти́ pf; ~ in вме́шиваться impf, вмеша́ться pf в+acc. **intervention** n вмеша́тельство; (polit) интерве́нция.

interview n интервью́ neut indecl; vt интервью́и́ровать impf & pf, про~ pf. **interviewer** n интервью́е́р.

interweave vt votка́ть pf.

intestate adj без завеща́ния.

intestine n кишка́; pl кише́чник.

intimacy n инти́мность. **intimate**[1] adj инти́мный.

intimate[2] vt (hint) намека́ть impf, намекну́ть pf на+acc. **intimation** n намёк.

intimidate vt запу́гивать impf, запуга́ть pf.

into prep в, во+acc, на+acc.

intolerable adj невыноси́мый. **intolerance** n нетерпи́мость. **intolerant** adj нетерпи́мый.

intonation n интона́ция.

intoxicated adj пья́ный. **intoxication** n опьяне́ние.

intractable adj непода́тливый.

intransigent adj н-примири́мый.

intransitive adj непереxо́дный.

intrepid adj неустраши́мый.

intricacy n запу́танность. **intricate** adj запу́танный.

intrigue n интри́га; vi интригова́ть impf; vt интригова́ть impf, за~ pf.

intrinsic adj прису́щий; (value) вну́тренний.

introduce vt вводи́ть impf, ввести́ pf; (person) представля́ть impf, предста́вить pf. **introduction** n введе́ние; представле́ние; (to book) предисло́вие. **introductory** adj вступи́тельный.

introspection n интроспе́кция.

intrude vi вторга́ться impf, вто́ргнуться pf (into в+acc); (disturb) меша́ть impf, по~ pf. **intruder** n (burglar) граби́тель m. **intrusion** n вторже́ние.

intuition n интуи́ция. **intuitive** adj интуити́вный.

inundate vt наводня́ть impf, наводни́ть pf. **inundation** n наводне́ние.

invade vt вторга́ться impf, вто́ргнуться pf в+acc. **invader** n захва́тчик.

invalid[1] n (person) инвали́д.

invalid[2] adj недействи́тельный. **invalidate** vt де́лать impf, с~ pf недействи́тельным.

invaluable adj неоцени́мый.

invariable adj неизме́нный.

invasion n вторже́ние.

invective n брань.

invent vt изобрета́ть impf, изобрести́ pf; (think up) выду́мывать impf, вы́думать pf. **invention** n изобрете́ние; вы́думка. **inventive** adj изобрета́тельный. **inventor** n изобрета́тель m.

inventory n инвента́рь m.

inverse adj обра́тный; n противополо́жность. **invert** vt перевора́чивать impf, переверну́ть pf. **inverted commas** n pl кавы́чки f pl.

invest vt & i (econ) вкла́дывать impf, вложи́ть pf (де́ньги) (in в+acc).

investigate vt иссле́довать impf & pf; (law) рассле́довать impf & pf. **investigation** n иссле́дование; рассле́дование.

investment n (econ) вклад. **investor** n вкла́дчик.

inveterate adj закорене́лый.

invidious adj оскорби́тельный.

invigorate vt оживля́ть impf, оживи́ть pf.

invincible adj непобеди́мый.

inviolable adj неруши́мый.

invisible adj неви́димый.

invitation n приглаше́ние. **invite** vt приглаша́ть impf, пригласи́ть pf. **inviting** adj привлека́тельный.

invoice n факту́ра.

invoke vt обраща́ться impf, обрати́ться pf к+dat.

involuntary adj нево́льный.

involve vt (entangle) вовлека́ть impf, вовле́чь pf; (entail) влечь impf за собо́й. **involved** adj сло́жный.

invulnerable adj неуязви́мый.

inward adj вну́тренний. **inwardly** adv внутри́. **inwards** adv внутрь.

iodine n йод.

iota n: not an ~ ни на йо́ту.

IOU n долгова́я распи́ска.

Iran n Ира́н. **Iranian** n ира́нец, -нка; adj ира́нский.

Iraq n Ира́к. **Iraqi** n ира́кец; жи́тель m, ~ница Ира́ка; adj ира́кский.

irascible adj раздражи́тельный.

irate adj гне́вный.

Ireland n Ирла́ндия.

iris n (anat) ра́дужная оболо́чка; (bot) каса́тик.

Irish adj ирла́ндский. **Irishman** n ирла́ндец. **Irishwoman** n ирла́ндка.

irk vt раздража́ть impf, раздражи́ть pf +dat. **irksome** adj раздражи́тельный.

iron n желе́зо; (for clothes) утю́г; adj желе́зный; vt гла́дить impf, вы́~ pf. **ironic(al)** adj ирони́ческий. **irony** n иро́ния.

irradiate vt (subject to radiation) облуча́ть impf, облучи́ть pf. **irradiation** n облуче́ние.

irrational adj неразу́мный.

irreconcilable adj непримири́мый.

irrefutable adj неопроверж́имый.

irregular adj нерегуля́рный; (gram) непра́вильный; (not even) неро́вный.

irrelevant adj неуме́стный.

irreparable adj непоправи́мый.

irreplaceable adj незамени́мый.

irrepressible adj неудержи́мый.

irreproachable adj безупре́чный.

irresistible adj неотрази́мый.

irresolute adj нереши́тельный.

irrespective adj: ~ of несмотря́ на +acc.

irresponsible adj безотве́тственный.

irretrievable adj непоправи́мый.

irreverent adj непочти́тельный.

irreversible *adj* необрати́мый.
irrevocable *adj* неотменя́емый.
irrigate *vt* ороша́ть *impf*, ороси́ть *pf*. **irrigation** *n* ороше́ние.
irritable *adj* раздражи́тельный. **irritate** *vt* раздража́ть *impf*, раздражи́ть *pf*. **irritation** *n* раздраже́ние.
Islam *n* исла́м. **Islamic** *adj* мусульма́нский.
island, isle *n* о́стров. **islander** *n* островитя́нин, -я́нка.
isolate *vt* изоли́ровать *impf & pf*. **isolation** *n* изоля́ция.
Israel *n* Изра́иль *m*. **Israeli** *n* израильтя́нин, -я́нка; *adj* изра́ильский.
issue *n* (*question*) (спо́рный) вопро́с; (*of bonds etc.*) вы́пуск; (*of magazine*) но́мер; *vi* выходи́ть *impf*, вы́йти *pf*; (*flow*) вытека́ть *impf*, вы́течь *pf*; *vt* выпуска́ть *impf*, вы́пустить *pf*; (*give out*) выдава́ть *impf*, вы́дать *pf*.
isthmus *n* переше́ек.
it *pron* он, она́, оно́; *demonstrative* э́то.
Italian *n* италья́нец, -нка; *adj* италья́нский.
italics *n pl* курси́в; **in ~** курси́вом. **italicize** *vt* выделя́ть *impf*, вы́делить *pf* курси́вом.
Italy *n* Ита́лия.
ITAR-Tass *abbr* ИТА́Р-ТА́СС.
itch *n* зуд; *vi* чеса́ться *impf*.
item *n* (*on list*) предме́т; (*in account*) статья́; (*on agenda*) пункт; (*in programme*) но́мер. **itemize** *vt* перечисля́ть *impf*, перечи́слить *pf*.
itinerant *adj* стра́нствующий. **itinerary** *n* маршру́т.
its *poss pron* его́, её; свой.
itself *pron* (*emph*) (он(о́)) сам(о́), (она́) сама́; (*refl*) себя́; -ся (*suffixed to vt*).
ivory *n* слоно́вая кость.
ivy *n* плющ.

J

jab *n* толчо́к; (*injection*) уко́л; *vt* ты́кать *impf*, ткнуть *pf*.
jabber *vi* тарато́рить *impf*.
jack *n* (*cards*) вале́т; (*lifting device*) домкра́т; *vt* (*~ up*) поднима́ть *impf*, подня́ть *pf* домкра́том.

jackdaw *n* га́лка.
jacket *n* (*tailored*) пиджа́к; (*anorak*) ку́ртка; (*on book*) (су́пер)обло́жка.
jackpot *n* банк.
jade *n* (*mineral*) нефри́т.
jaded *adj* утомлённый.
jagged *adj* зазу́бренный.
jaguar *n* ягуа́р.
jail *see* gaol
jam¹ *n* (*crush*) да́вка; (*in traffic*) про́бка; *vt* (*thrust*) впи́хивать *impf*, впихну́ть *pf* (**into** в+*acc*); (*wedge open*; *block*) закли́нивать *impf*, закли́нить *pf*; (*radio*) заглуша́ть *impf*, заглуши́ть *pf*; *vi* (*machine*) закли́нивать *impf*, закли́нить *pf impers*+*acc*.
jam² *n* (*conserve*) варе́нье, джем.
jangle *vi* (& *t*) звя́кать *impf* (+*instr*).
janitor *n* привра́тник.
January *n* янва́рь; *adj* янва́рский.
Japan *n* Япо́ния. **Japanese** *n* япо́нец, -нка; *adj* япо́нский.
jar¹ *n* (*container*) ба́нка.
jar² *vi* (*irritate*) раздража́ть *impf*, раздражи́ть *pf* (**upon** +*acc*).
jargon *n* жарго́н.
jasmin(e) *n* жасми́н.
jaundice *n* желту́ха. **jaundiced** *adj* (*fig*) цини́чный.
jaunt *n* прогу́лка.
jaunty *adj* бо́дрый.
javelin *n* копьё.
jaw *n* че́люсть; *pl* пасть, рот.
jay *n* со́йка.
jazz *n* джаз; *adj* джа́зовый.
jealous *adj* ревни́вый; (*envious*) зави́стливый; **be ~ of** (*person*) ревнова́ть *impf*; (*thing*) зави́довать *impf*, по~ *pf* +*dat*; (*rights*) ревни́во обере́гать *impf*, обере́чь *pf*. **jealousy** *n* ре́вность; за́висть.
jeans *n pl* джи́нсы (-сов) *pl*.
jeer *n* насме́шка; *vt & i* насмеха́ться *impf* (**at** над+*instr*).
jelly *n* (*sweet*) желе́ *neut indecl*; (*aspic*) сту́день *m*. **jellyfish** *n* меду́за.
jeopardize *vt* подверга́ть *impf*, подве́ргнуть *pf* опа́сности. **jeopardy** *n* опа́сность.
jerk *n* рыво́к; *vt* дёргать *impf* +*instr*; *vi* (*twitch*) дёргаться *impf*, дёрнуться *pf*. **jerky** *adj* неро́вный.
jersey *n* (*garment*) джéмпер; (*fabric*) джéрси *neut indecl*.
jest *n* шу́тка; **in ~** в шу́тку; *vi* шути́ть

impf, по~ *pf*. **jester** *n* шут.

jet¹ *n* (*stream*) струя́; (*nozzle*) со́пло; ~ **engine** реакти́вный дви́гатель *m*; ~ **plane** реакти́вный самолёт.

jet² *n* (*mineralogy*) гага́т; ~-**black** чёрный как смоль.

jettison *vt* выбра́сывать *impf*, вы́бросить *pf* за́ борт.

jetty *n* при́стань.

Jew *n* евре́й, евре́йка. **Jewish** *adj* евре́йский.

jewel *n* драгоце́нность, драгоце́нный ка́мень *m*. **jeweller** *n* ювели́р. **jewellery** *n* драгоце́нности *f pl*.

jib *n* (*naut*) кли́вер; *vi*: ~ **at** уклоня́ться *impf* от+*gen*.

jigsaw *n* (*puzzle*) моза́ика.

jingle *n* зво́нканье; *vi* (& *t*) звя́кать *impf*, звя́кнуть *pf* (+*instr*).

job *n* (*work*) рабо́та; (*task*) зада́ние; (*position*) ме́сто. **jobless** *adj* безрабо́тный.

jockey *n* жоке́й; *vi* оттира́ть *impf* друг дру́га.

jocular *adj* шутли́вый.

jog *n* (*push*) толчо́к; *vt* подта́лкивать *impf*, подтолкну́ть *pf*; *vi* бе́гать *impf* трусцо́й. **jogger** *n* занима́ющийся оздорови́тельным бе́гом. **jogging** *n* оздорови́тельный бег.

join *vt & i* соединя́ть(ся) *impf*, соедини́ть(ся) *pf*; *vt* (*a group of people*) присоединя́ться *impf*, присоедини́ться *pf* к+*dat*; (*as member*) вступа́ть *impf*, вступи́ть *pf* в+*acc*; *vi*: ~ **in** принима́ть *impf*, приня́ть *pf* уча́стие (в+*prep*); ~ **up** вступа́ть *impf*, вступи́ть *pf* в а́рмию.

joiner *n* столя́р.

joint *n* соедине́ние; (*anat*) суста́в; (*meat*) кусо́к; *adj* совме́стный; (*common*) о́бщий.

joist *n* перекла́дина.

joke *n* шу́тка; *vi* шути́ть *impf*, по~ *pf*. **joker** *n* шутни́к; (*cards*) джо́кер.

jollity *n* весе́лье. **jolly** *adj* весёлый; *adv* о́чень.

jolt *n* толчо́к; *vt & i* трясти́(сь) *impf*.

jostle *vt & i* толка́ть(ся) *impf*, толкну́ть(ся) *pf*.

jot *n* йо́та; **not a** ~ ни на йо́ту; *vt* (~ *down*) запи́сывать *impf*, записа́ть *pf*.

journal *n* журна́л; (*diary*) дневни́к.

journalese *n* газе́тный язы́к. **journalism** *n* журнали́стика. **journalist** *n* журнали́ст.

journey *n* путеше́ствие; *vi* путеше́ствовать *impf*.

jovial *adj* весёлый.

joy *n* ра́дость. **joyful, joyous** *adj* ра́достный. **joyless** *adj* безра́достный. **joystick** *n* рыча́г управле́ния; (*comput*) джо́йстик.

jubilant *adj* лику́ющий; **be** ~ ликова́ть *impf*. **jubilation** *n* ликова́ние.

jubilee *n* юбиле́й.

Judaism *n* юдаи́зм.

judge *n* судья́ *m*; (*connoisseur*) цени́тель *m*; *vt & i* суди́ть *impf*. **judgement** *n* (*legal decision*) реше́ние; (*opinion*) мне́ние; (*discernment*) рассуди́тельность.

judicial *adj* суде́бный. **judiciary** *n* судьи́ *m pl*. **judicious** *adj* здравомы́слящий.

judo *n* дзюдо́ *neut indecl*.

jug *n* кувши́н.

juggernaut *n* (*lorry*) многото́нный грузови́к; (*fig*) неумоли́мая си́ла.

juggle *vi* жонгли́ровать *impf*. **juggler** *n* жонглёр.

jugular *n* яре́мная ве́на.

juice *n* сок. **juicy** *adj* со́чный.

July *n* ию́ль *m*; *adj* ию́льский.

jumble *n* (*disorder*) беспоря́док; (*articles*) барахло́; *vt* перепу́тывать *impf*, перепу́тать *pf*.

jump *n* прыжо́к, скачо́к; *vi* пры́гать *impf*, пры́гнуть *pf*; скака́ть *impf*; (*from shock*) вздра́гивать *impf*, вздро́гнуть *pf*; *vt* (~ *over*) перепры́гивать *impf*, перепры́гнуть *pf*; ~ **at** (*offer*) ухва́тываться *impf*, ухвати́ться *pf* за+*acc*; ~ **up** вска́кивать *impf*, вскочи́ть *pf*.

jumper *n* дже́мпер.

jumpy *adj* не́рвный.

junction *n* (*rly*) у́зел; (*roads*) перекрёсток.

juncture *n*: **at this** ~ в э́тот моме́нт.

June *n* ию́нь *m*; *adj* ию́ньский.

jungle *n* джу́нгли (-лей) *pl*.

junior *adj* мла́дший; ~ **school** нача́льная шко́ла.

juniper *n* можжеве́льник.

junk *n* (*rubbish*) барахло́.

jurisdiction *n* юрисди́кция.

jurisprudence *n* юриспруде́нция.

juror *n* прися́жный *sb.* **jury** *n* прися́жные *sb*; (*in competition*) жюри́ *neut indecl.*

just *adj* (*fair*) справедли́вый; (*deserved*) заслу́женный; *adv* (*exactly*) как раз, и́менно; (*simply*) про́сто; (*barely*) едва́; (*very recently*) то́лько что;~ **in case** на вся́кий слу́чай.

justice *n* (*proceedings*) правосу́дие; (*fairness*) справедли́вость; **do ~ to** отдава́ть *impf*, отда́ть *pf* до́лжное +*dat.*

justify *vt* опра́вдывать *impf*, оправда́ть *pf.* **justification** *n* оправда́ние.

jut *vi* (~ *out*) выдава́ться *impf*; выступа́ть *impf.*

juvenile *n & adj* несовершенноле́тний *sb & adj.*

juxtapose *vt* помеща́ть *impf*, помести́ть *pf* ря́дом; (*for comparison*) сопоставля́ть *impf*, сопоста́вить *pf* (*with* с+*instr*).

K

kaleidoscope *n* калейдоско́п.

kangaroo *n* кенгуру́ *m indecl.*

Kazakhstan *n* Казахста́н.

keel *n* киль *m*; *vi*: ~ **over** опроки́дываться *impf*, опроки́нуться *pf.*

keen *adj* (*enthusiastic*) по́лный энтузиа́зма; (*sharp*) о́стрый; (*strong*) си́льный; **be ~ on** увлека́ться *impf*, увле́чься *pf* +*instr*; (*want to do*) о́чень хоте́ть *impf* +*inf.*

keep[1] *n* (*tower*) гла́вная ба́шня; (*maintenance*) содержа́ние.

keep[2] *vt* (*possess, maintain*) держа́ть *impf*, храни́ть *impf*; (*observe*) соблюда́ть *impf*, соблюсти́ *pf* (*the law*); сде́рживать *impf*, сдержа́ть *pf* (*one's word*); (*family*) содержа́ть *impf*; (*diary*) вести́ *impf*; (*detain*) заде́рживать *impf*, задержа́ть *pf*; (*retain, reserve*) сохраня́ть *impf*, сохрани́ть *pf*; *vi* (*remain*) остава́ться *impf*, оста́ться *pf*; (*of food*) не по́ртиться *impf*; ~ **back** (*vt*) (*hold back*) уде́рживать *impf*, удержа́ть *pf*; (*vi*) держа́ться *impf* сза́ди; ~ **doing sth** всё +*verb*: **she ~s giggling** она́ всё хихи́кает; ~ **from** уде́рживаться *impf*, удержа́ться *pf* от+*gen*; ~ **on** продолжа́ть *impf*, продол-

жить *pf* (+*inf*); ~ **up** (**with**) (*vi*) не отстава́ть *impf* (от+*gen*).

keepsake *n* пода́рок на па́мять.

keg *n* бочо́нок.

kennel *n* конура́.

kerb *n* край тротуа́ра.

kernel *n* (*nut*) ядро́; (*grain*) зерно́; (*fig*) суть.

kerosene *n* кероси́н.

kettle *n* ча́йник.

key *n* ключ; (*piano, typewriter*) кла́виш(а); (*mus*) тона́льность; *attrib* веду́щий, ключево́й. **keyboard** *n* клавиату́ра. **keyhole** *n* замо́чная сква́жина.

KGB *abbr* КГБ.

khaki *n & adj* ха́ки *neut, adj indecl.*

kick *n* уда́р ного́й, пино́к; *vt* ударя́ть *impf*, уда́рить *pf* ного́й; пина́ть *impf*, пнуть *pf*; *vi* (*of horse etc.*) ляга́ться *impf.* **kick-off** *n* нача́ло (игры́).

kid[1] *n* (*goat*) козлёнок; (*child*) малы́ш.

kid[2] *vt* (*deceive*) обма́нывать *impf*, обману́ть *pf*; *vi* (*joke*) шути́ть *impf*, по~ *pf.*

kidnap *vt* похища́ть *impf*, похи́тить *pf.*

kidney *n* по́чка.

kill *vt* убива́ть *impf*, уби́ть *pf.* **killer** *n* уби́йца *m & f.* **killing** *n* уби́йство; *adj* (*murderous, fig*) уби́йственный; (*amusing*) умори́тельный.

kiln *n* обжи́говая печь.

kilo *n* кило́ *neut indecl.* **kilohertz** *n* килоге́рц. **kilogram(me)** *n* килогра́мм. **kilometre** *n* киломе́тр. **kilowatt** *n* килова́тт.

kilt *n* шотла́ндская ю́бка.

kimono *n* кимоно́ *neut indecl.*

kin *n* (*family*) семья́; (*collect, relatives*) родня́.

kind[1] *n* сорт, род; **a ~ of** что́-то вро́де+*gen*; **this ~ of** тако́й; **what ~ of** что (э́то, он, *etc.*) за +*nom*; ~ **of** (*adv*) как бу́дто, ка́к-то.

kind[2] *adj* до́брый.

kindergarten *n* де́тский сад.

kindle *vt* зажига́ть *impf*, заже́чь *pf.* **kindling** *n* расто́пка.

kindly *adj* до́брый; *adv* любе́зно; (*with imper*) (*request*) бу́дьте добры́, +*imper.* **kindness** *n* доброта́.

kindred *adj*: ~ **spirit** родна́я душа́.

kinetic adj кинети́ческий.

king n коро́ль m (also chess, cards, fig); (draughts) да́мка. **kingdom** n короле́вство; (fig) ца́рство. **king-fisher** n зиморо́док.

kink n переги́б.

kinship n родство́; (similarity) схо́дство. **kinsman, -woman** n ро́дственник, -ица.

kiosk n кио́ск; (telephone) бу́дка.

kip n сон; vi дры́хнуть impf.

kipper n копчёная селёдка.

Kirghizia n Кирги́зия.

kiss n поцелу́й; vt & i целова́ть(ся) impf, по~ pf.

kit n (clothing) снаряже́ние; (tools) набо́р, компле́кт; vt: ~ out снаряжа́ть impf, снаряди́ть pf. **kitbag** n веще́вой мешо́к.

kitchen n ку́хня; attrib ку́хонный; ~ **garden** огоро́д.

kite n (toy) змей.

kitsch n дешёвка.

kitten n котёнок.

knack n сноро́вка.

knapsack n рюкза́к.

knead vt меси́ть impf, с~ pf.

knee n коле́но. **kneecap** n коле́нная ча́шка.

kneel vi стоя́ть impf на коле́нях; (~ down) станови́ться impf, стать pf на коле́ни.

knickers n pl тру́сики (-ов) pl.

knick-knack n безделу́шка.

knife n нож; vt коло́ть impf, за~ pf ножо́м.

knight n (hist) ры́царь m; (holder of order) кавале́р; (chess) конь m. **knighthood** n ры́царское зва́ние.

knit vt (garment) вяза́ть impf, с~ pf; vi (bones) сраста́ться impf, срасти́сь pf; ~ one's brows хму́рить impf, на~ pf бро́ви. **knitting** n (action) вяза́ние; (object) вяза́нье; ~-needle спи́ца. **knitwear** n трикота́ж.

knob n ши́шка, кно́пка; (door handle) ру́чка. **knobb(l)y** adj шишкова́тый.

knock n (noise) стук; (blow) уда́р; vt & i (strike) ударя́ть impf, уда́рить pf; (strike door etc.) стуча́ть impf, по~ pf (at в+acc); ~ about (treat roughly) колоти́ть impf, по~ pf; (wander) шата́ться impf; ~ down (person) сбива́ть impf, сбить pf с

ног; (building) сноси́ть impf, снести́ pf; ~ off сбива́ть impf, сбить pf; (stop work) шаба́шить impf (рабо́ту); (deduct) сбавля́ть impf, сба́вить pf; ~ out выбива́ть impf, вы́бить pf; (sport) нокаути́ровать impf & pf; ~-out нока́ут; ~ over опроки́дывать impf, опроки́нуть impf. **knocker** n дверно́й молото́к.

knoll n буго́р.

knot n у́зел; vt завя́зывать impf, завяза́ть pf узло́м. **knotty** adj (fig) запу́танный.

know vt знать impf; (~ how to) уме́ть impf, с~ pf +inf; ~-how уме́ние. **knowing** adj многозначи́тельный. **knowingly** adv созна́тельно. **knowledge** n зна́ние; to my ~ наско́лько мне изве́стно.

knuckle n суста́в па́льца; vi: ~ down to впряга́ться impf, впря́чься pf в+acc; ~ under уступа́ть impf, уступи́ть pf (to +dat).

Korea n Коре́я.

ko(w)tow vi (fig) раболе́пствовать impf (to пе́ред+instr).

Kremlin n Кремль m.

kudos n сла́ва.

L

label n этике́тка, ярлы́к; vt прикле́ивать impf, прикле́ить pf ярлы́к к+dat.

laboratory n лаборато́рия.

laborious adj кропотли́вый.

labour n труд; (med) ро́ды (-дов) pl; attrib трудово́й; ~ force рабо́чая си́ла; ~-intensive трудоёмкий; L~ Party лейбори́стская па́ртия; vi труди́ться impf; vt: ~ a point входи́ть impf, войти́ pf в изли́шние подро́бности. **laboured** adj затруднённый; (style) вы́мученный. **labourer** n чернорабо́чий sb. **labourite** n лейбори́ст.

labyrinth n лабири́нт.

lace n (fabric) кру́жево; (cord) шнуро́к; vt (~ up) шнурова́ть impf, за~ pf.

lacerate vt (also fig) терза́ть impf, ис~ pf. **laceration** n (wound) рва́ная ра́на.

lack n недоста́ток (of +gen, в+prep),

отсу́тствие; *vt & i* не хвата́ть *impf*, хвати́ть *pf impers +dat* (*person*), *+gen* (*object*).

lackadaisical *adj* то́мный.

laconic *adj* лакони́чный.

lacquer *n* лак; *vt* лакирова́ть *impf*, от~ *pf*.

lad *n* па́рень *m*.

ladder *n* ле́стница.

laden *adj* нагру́женный.

ladle *n* (*spoon*) полóвник; *vt* че́рпать *impf*, черпну́ть *pf*.

lady *n* да́ма, ле́ди *f indecl*. **ladybird** *n* бóжья корóвка.

lag¹ *vi*: ~ **behind** отстава́ть *impf*, отста́ть *pf* (от+*gen*).

lag² *vt* (*insulate*) изоли́ровать *impf & pf*.

lagoon *n* лагу́на.

lair *n* лóговище.

laity *n* (*in religion*) миря́не (-н) *pl*.

lake *n* о́зеро.

lamb *n* ягнёнок.

lame *adj* хромóй; **be** ~ хрома́ть *impf*; **go** ~ хроме́ть *impf*, о~ *pf*; *vt* кале́чить *impf*, о~ *pf*.

lament *n* плач; *vt* сожале́ть *impf* о+*prep*. **lamentable** *adj* приско́рбный.

laminated *adj* слóистый.

lamp *n* ла́мпа; (*in street*) фона́рь *m*. **lamp-post** *n* фона́рный столб. **lamp-shade** *n* абажу́р.

lance *n* пи́ка; *vt* (*med*) вскрыва́ть *impf*, вскрыть *pf* (ланце́том).

land *n* земля́; (*dry* ~) су́ша; (*country*) страна́; *vi* (*naut*) прича́ливать *impf*, прича́лить *pf*; *vt & i* (*aeron*) приземля́ть(ся) *impf*, приземли́ть(ся) *pf*; (*find o.s.*) попада́ть *impf*, попа́сть *pf*. **landing** *n* (*aeron*) поса́дка; (*on stairs*) площа́дка; ~**stage** при́стань. **landlady** *n* хозя́йка. **landlord** *n* хозя́ин. **landmark** *n* (*conspicuous object*) ориенти́р; (*fig*) ве́ха. **landowner** *n* землевладе́лец. **landscape** *n* ландша́фт; (*also picture*) пейза́ж. **landslide** *n* óползень *m*.

lane *n* (*in country*) доро́жка; (*street*) переу́лок; (*passage*) прохóд; (*on road*) ряд; (*in race*) доро́жка.

language *n* язы́к; (*style, speech*) речь.

languid *adj* то́мный.

languish *vi* томи́ться *impf*.

languor *n* тóмность.

lank *adj* (*hair*) гла́дкий. **lanky** *adj* долговя́зый.

lantern *n* фона́рь *m*.

lap¹ *n* (*of person*) колéни (-ней) *pl*; (*sport*) круг.

lap² *vt* (*drink*) лака́ть *impf*, вы́~ *pf*; *vi* (*water*) плеска́ться *impf*.

lapel *n* отворóт.

lapse *n* (*mistake*) оши́бка; (*interval*) промежу́ток; (*expiry*) истечéние; *vi* впада́ть *impf*, впасть *pf* (**into** в+*acc*); (*expire*) истека́ть *impf*, истéчь *pf*.

lapwing *n* чи́бис.

larch *n* ли́ственница.

lard *n* свинóе са́ло.

larder *n* кладова́я *sb*.

large *adj* большóй; *n*: **at** ~ (*free*) на свобóде; **by and** ~ вообщé говоря́. **largely** *adj* в значи́тельной стéпени.

largesse *n* щéдрость.

lark¹ *n* (*bird*) жа́воронок.

lark² *n* прока́за; *vi* (~ **about**) резви́ться *impf*.

larva *n* личи́нка.

laryngitis *n* ларинги́т. **larynx** *n* гортáнь.

lascivious *adj* похотли́вый.

laser *n* ла́зер.

lash *n* (*blow*) уда́р плéтью; (*eyelash*) ресни́ца; *vt* (*beat*) хлеста́ть *impf*, хлестну́ть *pf*; (*tie*) привя́зывать *impf*, привяза́ть *pf* (**to** к+*dat*).

last¹ *n* (*cobbler's*) колóдка.

last² *adj* (*final*) послéдний; (*most recent*) прóшлый; **the year** (*etc.*) **before** ~ позапрóшлый год (и т.д.); ~ **but one** предпослéдний; ~ **night** вчерá вéчером; **at** ~ наконéц; *adv* (*after all others*) пóсле всех; (*on the last occasion*) в послéдний раз; (*lastly*) наконéц.

last³ *vi* (*go on*) продолжа́ться *impf*, продóлжиться *pf*; дли́ться *impf*, про~ *pf*; (*be preserved*) сохраня́ться *impf*, сохрани́ться *pf*; (*suffice*) хвата́ть *impf*, хвати́ть *pf*. **lasting** *adj* (*permanent*) постоя́нный; (*durable*) прóчный.

lastly *adv* в заключéние; наконéц.

latch *n* щекóлда.

late *adj* пóздний; (*recent*) неда́вний; (*dead*) покóйный; **be** ~ **for** опа́здывать *impf*, опозда́ть *pf* на+*acc*; *adv* пóздно; *n*: **of** ~ за послéднее врéмя.

lately *adv* за послéднее врéмя.

latent *adj* скры́тый.

lateral *adj* боково́й.

lath *n* ре́йка, дра́нка (*also collect*).

lathe *n* тока́рный стано́к.

lather *n* (мы́льная) пе́на; *vt & i* мы́лить(ся) *impf*, на~ *pf*.

Latin *adj* лати́нский; *n* лати́нский язы́к; **~-American** латиноамерика́нский.

latitude *n* свобо́да; (*geog*) широта́.

latter *adj* после́дний; **~-day** совреме́нный. **latterly** *adv* за после́днее вре́мя.

lattice *n* решётка.

Latvia *n* Ла́твия. **Latvian** *n* латви́ец, -и́йка; латы́ш, ~ка; *adj* латви́йский, латы́шский.

laud *vt* хвали́ть *impf*, по~ *pf*. **laudable** *adj* похва́льный.

laugh *n* смех; *vi* смея́ться *impf* (at над+*instr*); **~ it off** отшу́чиваться *impf*, отшути́ться *pf*; **~ing-stock** посме́шище. **laughable** *adj* смешно́й. **laughter** *n* смех.

launch[1] *vt* (*ship*) спуска́ть *impf*, спусти́ть *pf* на́ воду; (*rocket*) запуска́ть *impf*, запусти́ть *pf*; (*undertake*) начина́ть *impf*, нача́ть *pf*; *n* спуск на́ воду; за́пуск. **launcher** *n* (*for rocket*) пускова́я устано́вка. **launching pad** *n* пускова́я площа́дка.

launch[2] *n* (*naut*) ка́тер.

launder *vt* стира́ть *impf*, вы́~ *pf*. **laund(e)rette** *n* пра́чечная *sb* самообслу́живания. **laundry** *n* (*place*) пра́чечная *sb*; (*articles*) бельё.

laurel *n* ла́вр(овое де́рево).

lava *n* ла́ва.

lavatory *n* убо́рная *sb*.

lavender *n* лава́нда.

lavish *adj* ще́дрый; (*abundant*) оби́льный; *vt* расточа́ть *impf* (upon +*dat*).

law *n* зако́н; (*system*) пра́во; **~ and order** правопоря́док. **law-court** *n* суд. **lawful** *adj* зако́нный. **lawless** *adj* беззако́нный.

lawn *n* газо́н; **~-mower** газонокоси́лка.

lawsuit *n* проце́сс.

lawyer *n* адвока́т, юри́ст.

lax *adj* сла́бый. **laxative** *n* слаби́тельное *sb*. **laxity** *n* сла́бость.

lay[1] *adj* (*non-clerical*) све́тский.

lay[2] *vt* (*place*) класть *impf*, положи́ть *pf*; (*cable, pipes*) прокла́ды-

вать *impf*, проложи́ть *pf*; (*carpet*) стлать *impf*, по~ *pf*; (*trap etc.*) устра́ивать *impf*, устро́ить *pf*; (*eggs*) класть *impf*, положи́ть *pf*; *v abs* (*lay eggs*) нести́сь *impf*, с~ *pf*, **~ aside** откла́дывать *impf*, отложи́ть *pf*; **~ bare** раскрыва́ть *impf*, раскры́ть *pf*; **~ a bet** держа́ть *impf* пари́ (on на+*acc*); **~ down** (*relinquish*) отка́зываться *impf*, отказа́ться *pf* от +*gen*; (*rule etc.*) устана́вливать *impf*, установи́ть *pf*; **~ off** (*workmen*) увольня́ть *impf*, уво́лить *pf*; **~ out** (*spread*) выкла́дывать *impf*, вы́ложить *pf*; (*garden*) разбива́ть *impf*, разби́ть *pf*; **~ the table** накрыва́ть *impf*, накры́ть *pf* стол (for (*meal*) к+*dat*); **~ up** (*store*) запаса́ть *impf*, запасти́ *pf* +*acc*, +*gen*; **be laid up** быть прико́ванным к посте́ли. **layabout** *n* безде́льник.

layer *n* слой, пласт.

layman *n* миря́нин; (*non-expert*) неспециали́ст.

laze *vi* безде́льничать *impf*. **laziness** *n* лень. **lazy** *adj* лени́вый; **~-bones** лентя́й, ~ка.

lead[1] *n* (*example*) приме́р; (*leadership*) руково́дство; (*position*) пе́рвое ме́сто; (*theat*) гла́вная роль; (*electr*) про́вод; (*dog's*) поводо́к; *vt* води́ть *indet*, вести́ *det*; (*be in charge of*) руководи́ть *impf* +*instr*; (*induce*) побужда́ть *impf*, побуди́ть *pf*; *vt & i* (*cards*) ходи́ть *impf* (c+*gen*); *vi* (*sport*) занима́ть *impf*, заня́ть *pf* пе́рвое ме́сто; **~ away** уводи́ть *impf*, увести́ *pf*; **~ to** (*result in*) приводи́ть *impf*, привести́ *pf* к+*dat*.

lead[2] *n* (*metal*) свине́ц. **leaden** *adj* свинцо́вый.

leader *n* руководи́тель *m*, ~ница, ли́дер; (*mus*) пе́рвая скри́пка; (*editorial*) передова́я статья́. **leadership** *n* руково́дство.

leading *adj* веду́щий, выдаю́щийся; **~ article** передова́я статья́.

leaf *n* лист; (*of table*) откидна́я доска́; *vi*: **~ through** перели́стывать *impf*, перелиста́ть *pf*. **leaflet** *n* листо́вка.

league *n* ли́га; **in ~ with** в сою́зе с +*instr*.

leak *n* течь, уте́чка; *vi* (*escape*) течь *impf*; (*allow water to ~*) пропуска́ть *impf* во́ду; ~ **out** проса́чиваться *impf*, просочи́ться *pf*.

lean¹ *adj* (*thin*) худо́й; (*meat*) по́стный.

lean² *vt & i* прислоня́ть(ся) *impf*, прислони́ть(ся) *pf* (**against** к+*dat*); *vi* (~ **on**, rely on) опира́ться *impf*, опере́ться *pf* (**on** на+*acc*); (*be inclined*) быть скло́нным (**to**(**wards**) к+*dat*); ~ **back** отки́дываться *impf*, отки́нуться *pf*; ~ **out of** высо́вываться *impf*, вы́сунуться *pf* в +*acc*. **leaning** *n* скло́нность.

leap *n* прыжо́к, скачо́к; *vi* пры́гать *impf*, пры́гнуть *pf*; скака́ть *impf*; ~ **year** високо́сный год.

learn *vt* учи́ться *impf*, об~ *pf* +*dat*; (*find out*) узнава́ть *impf*, узна́ть *pf*. **learned** *adj* учёный. **learner** *n* учени́к, -и́ца. **learning** *n* (*studies*) уче́ние; (*erudition*) учёность.

lease *n* аре́нда; *vt* (*of owner*) сдава́ть *impf*, сдать *pf* в аре́нду; (*of tenant*) брать *impf*, взять *pf* в аре́нду. **leaseholder** *n* аренда́тор.

leash *n* при́вязь.

least *adj* наиме́ньший, мале́йший; *adv* ме́нее всего́; **at** ~ по кра́йней ме́ре; **not in the** ~ ничу́ть.

leather *n* ко́жа; *attrib* ко́жаный.

leave¹ *n* (*permission*) разреше́ние; (*holiday*) о́тпуск; **on** ~ в о́тпуске; **take (one's)** ~ проща́ться *impf*, прости́ться *pf* (**of** с+*instr*).

leave² *vt & i* оставля́ть *impf*, оста́вить *pf*; (*abandon*) покида́ть *impf*, поки́нуть *pf*; (*go away*) уходи́ть *impf*, уйти́ *pf* (**from** от+*gen*); уезжа́ть *impf*, уе́хать *pf* (**from** от+*gen*); (*go out of*) выходи́ть *impf*, вы́йти *pf* из+*gen*; (*entrust*) предоставля́ть *impf*, предоста́вить *pf* (**to** +*dat*); ~ **out** пропуска́ть *impf*, пропусти́ть *pf*.

lecherous *adj* развра́тный.

lectern *n* анало́й; (*in lecture room*) пюпи́тр.

lecture *n* (*discourse*) ле́кция; (*reproof*) нота́ция; *vi* (*deliver* ~(*s*)) чита́ть *impf*, про~ *pf* ле́кцию (-ии) (**on** по+*dat*); *vt* (*admonish*) чита́ть *impf*, про~ *pf* нота́цию+*dat*; ~ **room** аудито́рия. **lecturer** *n* ле́ктор; (*univ*) преподава́тель *m*, -ница.

ledge *n* вы́ступ; (*shelf*) по́лочка.

ledger *n* гла́вная кни́га.

lee *n* защи́та; *adj* подве́тренный.

leech *n* (*worm*) пия́вка.

leek *n* лук-поре́й.

leer *vi* криви́ться *impf*, с~ *pf*.

leeward *n* подве́тренная сторона́; *adj* подве́тренный.

leeway *n* (*fig*) свобо́да де́йствий.

left *n* ле́вая сторона́; (**the L**~; *polit*) ле́вые *sb pl*; *adj* ле́вый; *adv* нале́во, сле́ва (**of** от+*gen*); ~-**hander** левша́ *m & f*; ~**wing** ле́вый.

left-luggage office *n* ка́мера хране́ния.

leftovers *n pl* оста́тки *m pl*; (*food*) объе́дки (-ков) *pl*.

leg *n* нога́; (*of furniture etc.*) но́жка; (*of journey etc.*) эта́п.

legacy *n* насле́дство.

legal *adj* (*of the law*) правово́й; (*lawful*) лега́льный. **legality** *n* лега́льность. **legalize** *vt* легализи́ровать *impf & pf*.

legend *n* леге́нда. **legendary** *adj* легенда́рный.

leggings *n pl* вя́заные рейту́зы (-з) *pl*.

legible *adj* разбо́рчивый.

legion *n* легио́н.

legislate *vi* издава́ть *impf*, изда́ть *pf* зако́ны. **legislation** *n* законода́тельство. **legislative** *adj* законода́тельный. **legislator** *n* законода́тель *m*. **legislature** *n* законода́тельные учрежде́ния *neut pl*.

legitimacy *n* зако́нность; (*of child*) законнорожде́нность. **legitimate** *adj* зако́нный; (*child*) законнорожде́нный. **legitimize** *vt* узако́нивать *impf*, узако́нить *pf*.

leisure *n* свобо́дное вре́мя, досу́г; **at** ~ на досу́ге. **leisurely** *adj* нетороли́вый.

lemon *n* лимо́н. **lemonade** *n* лимона́д.

lend *vt* дава́ть *impf*, дать *pf* взаймы́ (**to** +*dat*); ода́лживать *impf*, одолжи́ть *pf* (**to** +*dat*).

length *n* длина́; (*of time*) продолжи́тельность; (*of cloth*) отре́з; **at** ~ подро́бно. **lengthen** *vt & i* удлиня́ть(ся) *impf*, удлини́ть(ся) *pf*. **lengthways** *adv* в длину́, вдоль. **lengthy** *adj* дли́нный.

leniency *n* снисходи́тельность. **lenient** *adj* снисходи́тельный.

lens n ли́нза; (phot) объекти́в; (anat) хруста́лик.

Lent n вели́кий пост.

lentil n чечеви́ца.

Leo n Лев.

leopard n леопа́рд.

leotard n трико́ neut indecl.

leper n прокажённый sb. **leprosy** n прока́за.

lesbian n лесбия́нка; adj лесби́йский.

lesion n поврежде́ние.

less adj ме́ньший; adv ме́ньше, ме́нее; prep за вы́четом +gen.

lessee n аренда́тор.

lessen vt & i уменьша́ть(ся) impf, уме́ньшить(ся) pf.

lesser adj ме́ньший.

lesson n уро́к.

lest conj (in order that not) что́бы не; (that) как бы не.

let n (lease) сда́ча в наём; vt (allow) позволя́ть impf, позво́лить pf +dat; разреша́ть impf, разреши́ть pf +dat; (rent out) сдава́ть impf, сдать pf внаём (to +dat); v aux (imperative) (1st person) дава́й(те); (3rd person) пусть; ~ **alone** не говоря́ уже́ о+prep; ~ **down** (lower) опуска́ть impf, опусти́ть pf; (fail) подводи́ть impf, подвести́ pf; (disappoint) разочаро́вывать impf, разочарова́ть pf; ~ **go** выпуска́ть impf, вы́пустить pf; **~'s go** пойдёмте!; пошли́!; пое́хали!; ~ **in(to)** (admit) впуска́ть impf, впусти́ть pf в+acc; (into secret) посвяща́ть impf, посвяти́ть pf в+acc; ~ **know** дава́ть impf, дать pf знать +dat; ~ **off** (gun) выстрелить pf из+gen; (not punish) отпуска́ть impf, отпусти́ть pf без наказа́ния; ~ **out** (release, loosen) выпуска́ть impf, вы́пустить pf; ~ **through** пропуска́ть impf, пропусти́ть pf; ~ **up** затиха́ть impf, зати́хнуть pf.

lethal adj (fatal) смерте́льный; (weapon) смертоно́сный.

lethargic adj летарги́ческий. **lethargy** n летарги́я.

letter n письмо́; (symbol) бу́ква; (printing) ли́тера; ~-**box** почто́вый я́щик. **lettering** n шрифт.

lettuce n сала́т.

leukaemia n лейкеми́я.

level n у́ровень; adj ро́вный; ~ **crossing** (железнодоро́жный) перее́зд; ~-**headed** уравнове́шенный; vt (make ~) выра́внивать impf, вы́ровнять pf; (sport) сра́внивать impf, сравня́ть pf; (gun) наводи́ть impf, навести́ pf (at в, на, +acc); (criticism) направля́ть impf, напра́вить pf (at про́тив+gen).

lever n рыча́г. **leverage** n де́йствие рычага́; (influence) влия́ние.

levity n легкомы́слие.

levy n (tax) сбор; vt (tax) взима́ть impf (from c+gen).

lewd adj (lascivious) похотли́вый; (indecent) са́льный.

lexicon n слова́рь m.

liability n (responsibility) отве́тственность (for за+acc); (burden) обу́за. **liable** adj отве́тственный (for за+acc); (susceptible) подве́рженный (to +dat).

liaise vi подде́рживать impf связь (c+instr). **liaison** n связь; (affair) любо́вная связь.

liar n лгун, ~ья.

libel n клевета́; vt клевета́ть impf, на~ pf на+acc. **libellous** adj клевети́ческий.

liberal n либера́л; adj либера́льный; (generous) ще́дрый.

liberate vt освобожда́ть impf, освободи́ть pf. **liberation** n освобожде́ние. **liberator** n освободи́тель m.

libertine n распу́тник.

liberty n свобо́да; at ~ на свобо́де.

Libra n Весы́ (-со́в) pl.

librarian n библиоте́карь m. **library** n библиоте́ка.

libretto n либре́тто neut indecl.

licence[1] n (permission, permit) разреше́ние, лице́нзия; (liberty) (изли́шняя) во́льность. **license, -ce**[2] vt (allow) разреша́ть impf, разреши́ть pf +dat; дава́ть impf, дать pf пра́во +dat.

licentious adj распу́щенный.

lichen n лиша́йник.

lick n лиза́ние; vt лиза́ть impf, лизну́ть pf.

lid n кры́шка; (eyelid) ве́ко.

lie[1] n (untruth) ложь; vi лгать impf, со~ pf.

lie[2] n: ~ **of the land** (fig) положе́ние веще́й; vi лежа́ть impf; (be situated) находи́ться *impf*; ~ **down** ложи́ться *impf*, лечь *pf*; ~ **in** оставáться *impf* в посте́ли.

lieu *n*: **in** ~ **of** вмéсто+*gen*.

lieutenant *n* лейтенáнт.

life *n* жизнь; (*way of* ~) óбраз жи́зни; (*energy*) жи́вость. **lifebelt** *n* спасáтельный пóяс. **lifeboat** *n* спасáтельная лóдка. **lifebuoy** *n* спасáтельный круг. **lifeguard** *n* спасáтель *m*, -ница. **life-jacket** *n* спасáтельный жилéт. **lifeless** *adj* безжи́зненный. **lifelike** *adj* реалисти́чный. **lifeline** *n* спасáтельный конéц. **lifelong** *adj* пожи́зненный. **life-size(d)** *adj* в натурáльную величину́. **lifetime** *n* жизнь.

lift *n* (*machine*) лифт, подъёмник; (*force*) подъёмная сúла; **give s.o. a** ~ подвози́ть *impf*, подвезти́ *pf*; *vt & i* поднимáть(ся) *impf*, подня́ть(ся) *pf*.

ligament *n* свя́зка.

light¹ *n* свет, освещéние; (*source of* ~) огóнь *m*, лáмпа, фонáрь *m*; *pl* (*traffic*) светофóр; **can I have a** ~? мóжно прикури́ть?; **~-bulb** лáмпочка; *adj* (*bright*) свéтлый; (*pale*) блéдный; *vt & i* (*ignite*) зажигáть(ся) *impf*, зажéчь(ся) *pf*; *vt* (*illuminate*) освещáть *impf*, освети́ть *pf*; ~ **up** освещáть(ся) *impf*, освети́ть(ся) *pf*; (*begin to smoke*) закури́ть *pf*.

light² *adj* (*not heavy*) лёгкий; ~-**hearted** беззабóтный.

lighten¹ *vt* (*make lighter*) облегчáть *impf*, облегчи́ть *pf*; (*mitigate*) смягчáть *impf*, смягчи́ть *pf*.

lighten² *vt* (*illuminate*) освещáть *impf*, освети́ть *pf*; *vi* (*grow bright*) светлéть *impf*, по~ *pf*.

lighter *n* зажигáлка.

lighthouse *n* мая́к.

lighting *n* освещéние.

lightning *n* мóлния.

lightweight *n* (*sport*) легковéс; *adj* легковéсный.

like¹ *adj* (*similar*) похóжий (на+*acc*); **what is he** ~? что он за человéк?

like² *vt* нрáвиться *impf*, по~ *pf impers*+*dat*: **I** ~ **him** он мне нрáвится; люби́ть *impf*; *vi* (*wish*) хотéть *impf*; **if you** ~ éсли хоти́те; **I should** ~ я хотéл бы; мне хотéлось

бы. **likeable** *adj* симпати́чный.

likelihood *n* вероя́тность. **likely** *adj* (*probable*) вероя́тный; (*suitable*) подходя́щий.

liken *vt* уподоблять *impf*, уподóбить *pf* (**to**+*dat*).

likeness *n* (*resemblance*) схóдство; (*portrait*) портрéт.

likewise *adv* (*similarly*) подóбно; (*also*) тóже, тáкже.

liking *n* вкус; (**for** к+*dat*).

lilac *n* сирéнь; *adj* сирéневый.

lily *n* ли́лия; ~ **of the valley** лáндыш.

limb *n* член.

limber *vi*: ~ **up** разминáться *impf*, размя́ться *pf*.

limbo *n* (*fig*) состоя́ние неопределённости.

lime¹ *n* (*mineralogy*) и́звесть. **limelight** *n*: **in the** ~ (*fig*) в цéнтре внимáния. **limestone** *n* известня́к.

lime² *n* (*fruit*) лайм.

lime³ *n* (~-*tree*) ли́па.

limit *n* грани́ца, предéл; *vt* ограни́чивать *impf*, ограни́чить *pf*. **limitation** *n* ограничéние. **limitless** *adj* безграни́чный.

limousine *n* лимузи́н.

limp¹ *n* хромотá; *vi* хромáть *impf*.

limp² *adj* мя́гкий; (*fig*) вя́лый.

limpid *adj* прозрáчный.

linchpin *n* чекá.

line¹ *n* (*long mark*) ли́ния, чертá; (*transport, tel*) ли́ния; (*cord*) верёвка; (*wrinkle*) морщи́на; (*limit*) грани́ца; (*row*) ряд; (*of words*) строкá; (*of verse*) стих; *vt* (*paper*) линовáть *impf*, раз~ *pf*; *vt & i* (~ **up**) выстрáивать(ся) *impf*, вы́строить(ся) *pf* в ряд.

line² *vt* (*clothes*) класть *impf*, положи́ть *pf* на подклáдку.

lineage *n* происхождéние.

linear *adj* линéйный.

lined¹ *adj* (*paper*) линóванный; (*face*) морщи́нистый.

lined² *adj* (*garment*) на подклáдке.

linen *n* полотнó; *collect* бельё.

liner *n* лáйнер.

linesman *n* боковóй судья́ *m*.

linger *vi* задéрживаться *impf*, задержáться *pf*.

lingerie *n* дáмское бельё.

lingering *adj* (*illness*) затяжнóй.

lingo *n* жаргóн.

linguist *n* лингви́ст. **linguistic** *adj* лингвисти́ческий. **linguistics** *n* лингви́стика.

lining *n* (*clothing etc.*) подкла́дка; (*tech*) облицо́вка.

link *n* (*of chain*) звено́; (*connection*) связь; *vt* соединя́ть *impf*, соедини́ть *pf*; свя́зывать *impf*, связа́ть *pf*.

lino(leum) *n* лино́леум.

lintel *n* перемы́чка.

lion *n* лев. **lioness** *n* льви́ца.

lip *n* губа́; (*of vessel*) край. **lipstick** *n* губна́я пома́да.

liquefy *vt & i* превраща́ть(ся) *impf*, преврати́ть(ся) *pf* в жи́дкое состоя́ние.

liqueur *n* ликёр.

liquid *n* жи́дкость; *adj* жи́дкий.

liquidate *vt* ликвиди́ровать *impf & pf*. **liquidation** *n* ликвида́ция; go into ~ ликвиди́роваться *impf & pf*.

liquor *n* (спиртно́й) напи́ток.

liquorice *n* лакри́ца.

list[1] *n* спи́сок; *vt* составля́ть *impf*, соста́вить *pf* спи́сок +*gen*; (*enumerate*) перечисля́ть *impf*, перечи́слить *pf*.

list[2] *vi* (*naut*) накреня́ться *impf*, крени́ться *impf*, накрени́ться *pf*.

listen *vi* слу́шать *impf*, по~ *pf* (to +*acc*). **listener** *n* слу́шатель *m*.

listless *adj* апати́чный.

litany *n* лита́ния.

literacy *n* гра́мотность.

literal *adj* буква́льный.

literary *adj* литерату́рный.

literate *adj* гра́мотный.

literature *n* литерату́ра.

lithe *adj* ги́бкий.

lithograph *n* литогра́фия.

Lithuania *n* Литва́. **Lithuanian** *n* лито́вец, -вка; *adj* лито́вский.

litigation *n* тя́жба.

litre *n* литр.

litter *n* (*rubbish*) сор; (*brood*) помёт; *vt* (*make untidy*) сори́ть *impf*, на~ *pf* (with +*instr*).

little *n* немно́гое; ~ by ~ ма́ло-пома́лу; a ~ немно́го +*gen*; *adj* ма́ленький, небольшо́й; (*in height*) небольшо́го ро́ста; (*in distance, time*) коро́ткий; *adv* ма́ло, немно́го.

liturgy *n* литурги́я.

live[1] *adj* живо́й; (*coals*) горя́щий; (*mil*) боево́й; (*electr*) под напряже́нием; (*broadcast*) прямо́й.

live[2] *vi* жить *impf*; ~ down загла́живать *impf*, загла́дить *pf*; ~ on (*feed on*) пита́ться *impf* +*instr*; ~ through пережива́ть *impf*, пережи́ть *pf*; ~ until, to see дожива́ть *impf*, дожи́ть *pf* до+*gen*; ~ up to жить *impf* согла́сно +*dat*.

livelihood *n* сре́дства *neut pl* к жи́зни.

lively *adj* живо́й.

liven (up) *vt & i* оживля́ть(ся) *impf*, ожив́ить(ся) *pf*.

liver *n* пе́чень; (*cul*) печёнка.

livery *n* ливре́я.

livestock *n* скот.

livid *adj* (*angry*) взбешённый.

living *n* сре́дства *neut pl* к жи́зни; earn a ~ зараба́тывать *impf*, зарабо́тать *pf* на жизнь; *adj* живо́й; ~-room гости́ная *sb*.

lizard *n* я́щерица.

load *n* груз; (*also fig*) бре́мя *neut*; (*electr*) нагру́зка; *pl* (*lots*) ку́ча; *vt* (*goods*) грузи́ть *impf*, на~ *pf*; (*vehicle*) грузи́ть *impf*, на~ *pf*; (*fig*) обременя́ть *impf*, обремени́ть *pf*; (*gun, camera*) заряжа́ть *impf*, заряди́ть *pf*.

loaf[1] *n* буха́нка.

loaf[2] *vi* безде́льничать *impf*. **loafer** *n* безде́льник.

loan *n* заём; *vt* дава́ть *impf*, дать *pf* взаймы́.

loath, loth *predic*: be ~ to не хоте́ть *impf* +*inf*.

loathe *vt* ненави́деть *impf*. **loathing** *n* отвраще́ние. **loathsome** *adj* отврати́тельный.

lob *vt* высоко́ подбра́сывать *impf*, подбро́сить *pf*.

lobby *n* вестибю́ль *m*; (*parl*) кулуа́ры (-ров) *pl*.

lobe *n* (*of ear*) мо́чка.

lobster *n* ома́р.

local *adj* ме́стный.

locality *n* ме́стность.

localized *adj* локализо́ванный.

locate *vt* (*place*) помеща́ть *impf*, помести́ть *pf*; (*find*) находи́ть *impf*, найти́ *pf*; be ~d находи́ться *impf*.

location *n* (*position*) местонахожде́ние; on ~ (*cin*) на нату́ре.

locative *adj* (*n*) ме́стный (паде́ж).

lock[1] *n* (*of hair*) ло́кон; *pl* во́лосы (-о́с, -оса́м) *pl*.

lock[2] n замóк; (canal) шлюз; vt & i запирáть(ся) impf, заперéть(ся) pf; ~ **out** не впускáть impf; ~ **up** (imprison) сажáть impf, посадúть pf; (close) закрывáть(ся) impf, закры́ть(ся) pf.

locker n шкáфчик.

locket n медальóн.

locksmith n слéсарь m.

locomotion n передвижéние. **locomotive** n локомотúв.

lodge n (hunting) (охóтничий) дóмик; (porter's) сторóжка; (Masonic) лóжа; vt (accommodate) помещáть impf, поместúть pf; (complaint) подавáть impf, подáть pf; vi (reside) жить impf (with y+gen); (stick) засáживать impf, засéсть pf. **lodger** n жилéц, жилúца. **lodging** n (also pl) квартúра, (снимáемая) кóмната.

loft n (attic) чердáк.

lofty adj óчень высóкий; (elevated) возвы́шенный.

log n бревнó; (for fire) полéно; ~-**book** (naut) вáхтенный журнáл.

logarithm n логарúфм.

loggerhead n: be at ~s быть в ссóре.

logic n лóгика. **logical** adj (of logic) логúческий; (consistent) логúчный.

logistics n pl материáльно-технúческое обеспéчение; (fig) проблéмы f pl организáции.

logo n эмблéма.

loin n (pl) пояснúца; (cul) филéйная часть.

loiter vi слоня́ться impf.

lone, lonely adj одинóкий. **loneliness** n одинóчество.

long[1] vi (want) стрáстно желáть impf, по~ pf (for +gen); (miss) тосковáть impf (for по+dat).

long[2] adj (space) длúнный; (time) дóлгий; (in measurements) длинóй в+acc; **in the** ~ **run** в конéчном счёте; ~-**sighted** дальнозóркий; ~-**suffering** долготерпелúвый; ~-**term** долгосрóчный; ~-**winded** многоречúвый; adv дóлго; ~ **ago** (ужé) давнó; as ~ as покá; ~ **before** задóлго до+gen.

longevity n долговéчность.

longing n стрáстное желáние (for +gen); тоскá (for по+dat); adj тоскýющий.

longitude n долготá.

longways adv в длинý.

look n (glance) взгляд; (appearance) вид; (expression) выражéние; vi смотрéть impf, по~ pf (at на, в, +acc); (appear) вы́глядеть impf +instr; (face) выходúть impf (towards, onto на+acc); ~ **about** осмáтриваться impf, осмотрéться pf; ~ **after** (attend to) присмáтривать impf, присмотрéть pf за+instr; ~ **down on** презирáть impf; ~ **for** искáть impf +acc, +gen; ~ **forward to** предвкушáть impf, предвкусúть pf; ~ **in on** заглáдывать impf, заглянýть impf к+dat; ~ **into** (investigate) рассмáтривать impf, рассмотрéть pf; ~ **like** быть похóжим на+acc; **it** ~**s like rain** похóже на (то, что бýдет) дождь; ~ **on** (as regard) считáть impf, счесть pf (as +instr, за+instr); ~ **out** выгля́дывать impf, вы́глянуть pf (в окнó); быть насторожé; imper осторóжно!; ~ **over, through** просмáтривать impf, просмотрéть pf; ~ **round** (inspect) осмáтривать impf, осмотрéть pf; ~ **up** (raise eyes) поднимáть impf, подня́ть pf глазá; (in dictionary etc.) искáть impf; (improve) улучшáться impf, улýчшиться pf; ~ **up to** уважáть impf.

loom[1] n ткáцкий станóк.

loom[2] vi вырисóвываться impf, вы́рисоваться pf; (fig) надвигáться impf.

loop n пéтля; vi образóвывать impf, образовáть pf пéтлю; (fasten with loop) закрепля́ть impf, закрепúть pf пéтлей; (wind) обмáтывать impf, обмотáть pf (**around** вокрýг+gen).

loophole n бойнúца; (fig) лазéйка.

loose adj (free; not tight) свобóдный; (not fixed) неприкреплённый; (connection, screw) слáбый; (lax) распýщенный; **at a** ~ **end** без дéла.

loosen vt & i ослабля́ть(ся) impf, ослáбить(ся) pf.

loot n добы́ча; vt грáбить impf, о~ pf.

lop vt (tree) подрезáть impf, подрéзать pf; (~ **off**) отрубáть impf, отрубúть pf.

lope vi бéгать indet, бежáть det вприпры́жку.

lopsided adj кривобóкий.

loquacious adj болтлúвый.

lord n (master) господи́н; (eccl) Госпо́дь; (peer; title) лорд; vt: ~ **it over** помыка́ть impf +instr. **lordship** n (title) све́тлость.

lore n зна́ния neut pl.

lorry n грузови́к.

lose vt теря́ть impf, по~ pf; vt & i (game etc.) прои́грывать impf, проигра́ть pf; vi (clock) отстава́ть impf, отста́ть pf. **loss** n поте́ря; (monetary) убы́ток; (in game) про́игрыш.

lot n жре́бий; (destiny) у́часть; (of goods) па́ртия; **a** ~, ~**s** мно́го; **the** ~ всё, все pl.

loth see **loath**

lotion n лосьо́н.

lottery n лотере́я.

loud adj (sound) гро́мкий; (noisy) шу́мный; (colour) крича́щий; **out** ~ вслух. **loudspeaker** n громкогово́ри́тель m.

lounge n гости́ная sb; vi сиде́ть impf развали́сь; (idle) безде́льничать impf.

louse n вошь. **lousy** adj (coll) парши́вый.

lout n балбе́с, у́валень m.

lovable adj ми́лый. **love** n любо́вь (of, for к+dat); **in** ~ **with** влюблённый в+acc; vt люби́ть impf. **lovely** adj прекра́сный; (delightful) преле́стный. **lover** n любо́вник, -ица.

low adj ни́зкий, невысо́кий; (quiet) ти́хий.

lower[1] vt опуска́ть impf, опусти́ть pf; (price, voice, standard) понижа́ть impf, пони́зить pf.

lower[2] adj ни́жний.

lowland n ни́зменность.

lowly adj скро́мный.

loyal adj ве́рный. **loyalty** n ве́рность. **LP** abbr (of **long-playing record**) долгоигра́ющая пласти́нка.

Ltd. abbr (of **Limited**) с ограни́ченной отве́тственностью.

lubricant n сма́зка. **lubricate** vt сма́зывать impf, сма́зать pf. **lubrication** n сма́зка.

lucid adj я́сный. **lucidity** n я́сность.

luck n (chance) слу́чай; (good ~) сча́стье, уда́ча; (bad ~) неуда́ча. **luckily** adv к сча́стью. **lucky** adj счастли́вый; **be** ~ везти́ imp, по~ pf impers +dat: **I was** ~ мне повезло́.

lucrative adj при́быльный.

ludicrous adj смехотво́рный.

lug vt (drag) таска́ть indet, тащи́ть det.

luggage n бага́ж.

lugubrious adj печа́льный.

lukewarm adj теплова́тый; (fig) прохла́дный.

lull n (in storm) зати́шье; (interval) переры́в; vt (to sleep) убаю́кивать impf, убаю́кать pf; (suspicions) усыпля́ть impf, усыпи́ть pf. **lullaby** n колыбе́льная пе́сня.

lumbar adj поясни́чный.

lumber[1] vi (move) брести́ impf.

lumber[2] n (domestic) ру́хлядь; vt обременя́ть impf, обремени́ть pf. **lumberjack** n лесору́б.

luminary n свети́ло.

luminous adj светя́щийся.

lump n ком; (swelling) о́пухоль; vt: ~ **together** сме́шивать impf, сме́ша́ть pf (в одно́).

lunacy n безу́мие.

lunar adj лу́нный.

lunatic adj (n) сумасше́дший (sb).

lunch n обе́д; ~-**hour**, ~-**time** обе́денный переры́в; vi обе́дать impf, по~ pf.

lung n лёгкое sb.

lunge n де́лать impf, с~ pf вы́пад (at про́тив+gen).

lurch[1] n: **leave in the** ~ покида́ть impf, поки́нуть pf в беде́.

lurch[2] vi (stagger) ходи́ть indet, идти́ det шата́ясь.

lure n прима́нка; vt прима́нивать impf, примани́ть pf.

lurid adj (gaudy) крича́щий; (details) жу́ткий.

lurk vi зата́иваться impf, затаи́ться pf.

luscious adj со́чный.

lush adj пы́шный, со́чный.

lust n по́хоть (of, for к+dat); vi стра́стно жела́ть impf, по~ pf (for +gen). **lustful** adj похотли́вый.

lustre n гля́нец. **lustrous** adj гля́нцеви́тый.

lusty adj (healthy) здоро́вый; (lively) живо́й.

lute n (mus) лю́тня.

luxuriant adj пы́шный.

luxuriate vi наслажда́ться impf, наслади́ться pf (in+instr).

luxurious adj роско́шный. **luxury** n ро́скошь.

lymph *attrib* лимфати́ческий.
lynch *vt* линчева́ть *impf & pf*.
lyric *n* ли́рика; *pl* слова́ *neut pl* пе́сни. **lyrical** *adj* лири́ческий.

M

MA *abbr* (*of Master of Arts*) маги́стр гуманита́рных нау́к.
macabre *adj* жу́ткий.
macaroni *n* макаро́ны (-н) *pl*.
mace *n* (*of office*) жезл.
machination *n* махина́ция.
machine *n* маши́на; (*state ~*) аппара́т; *attrib* маши́нный; **~-gun** пулемёт; **~ tool** стано́к; *vt* обраба́тывать *impf*, обрабо́тать *pf* на станке́; (*sew*) шить *impf*, с~ *pf* (на маши́не). **machinery** *n* (*machines*) маши́ны *f pl*; (*of state*) аппара́т. **machinist** *n* машини́ст; (*sewing*) шве́йник, -ица, швея́.
mackerel *n* ску́мбрия, макре́ль.
mackintosh *n* плащ.
mad *adj* сумасше́дший. **madden** *vt* беси́ть *impf*, вз~ *pf*. **madhouse** *n* сумасше́дший дом. **madly** *adv* безу́мно. **madman** *n* сумасше́дший *sb*. **madness** *n* сумасше́ствие. **madwoman** *n* сумасше́дшая *sb*.
madrigal *n* мадрига́л.
maestro *n* маэ́стро *m indecl*.
Mafia *n* ма́фия.
magazine *n* журна́л; (*of gun*) магази́н.
maggot *n* личи́нка.
magic *n* ма́гия, волшебство́; *adj* (*also magical*) волше́бный. **magician** *n* волше́бник; (*conjurer*) фо́кусник.
magisterial *adj* авторите́тный.
magistrate *n* судья́ *m*.
magnanimity *n* великоду́шие. **magnanimous** *adj* великоду́шный.
magnate *n* магна́т.
magnesium *n* ма́гний.
magnet *n* магни́т. **magnetic** *adj* магни́тный; (*attractive*) притяга́тельный. **magnetism** *n* магнети́зм; притяга́тельность. **magnetize** *vt* намагни́чивать *impf*, намагни́тить *pf*.
magnification *n* увеличе́ние.
magnificence *n* великоле́пие. **magnificent** *adj* великоле́пный.

magnify *vt* увели́чивать *impf*, увели́чить *pf*; (*exaggerate*) преувели́чивать *impf*, преувели́чить *pf*. **magnifying glass** *n* увеличи́тельное стекло́.
magnitude *n* величина́; (*importance*) ва́жность.
magpie *n* соро́ка.
mahogany *n* кра́сное де́рево.
maid *n* прислу́га; **maiden** *adj* (*aunt etc.*) незаму́жняя; (*first*) пе́рвый; **~ name** де́вичья фами́лия.
mail *n* (*letters*) по́чта; **~ order** почто́вый зака́з; *vt* посыла́ть *impf*, посла́ть *pf* по по́чте.
maim *vt* кале́чить *impf*, ис~ *pf*.
main *n* (*gas ~; pl*) магистра́ль; **in the ~** в основно́м; *adj* основно́й, гла́вный; (*road*) магистра́льный. **mainland** *n* матери́к. **mainly** *adv* в основно́м. **mainstay** *n* (*fig*) гла́вная опо́ра.
maintain *vt* (*keep up*) подде́рживать *impf*, поддержа́ть *pf*; (*family*) содержа́ть *impf*; (*machine*) обслу́живать *impf*, обслужи́ть *pf*; (*assert*) утвержда́ть *impf*. **maintenance** *n* подде́ржка; содержа́ние; обслу́живание.
maize *n* кукуру́за.
majestic *adj* вели́чественный. **majesty** *n* вели́чественность; (*title*) вели́чество.
major[1] *n* (*mil*) майо́р.
major[2] *adj* (*greater*) бо́льший; (*more important*) бо́лее ва́жный; (*main*) гла́вный; (*mus*) мажо́рный; *n* (*mus*) мажо́р. **majority** *n* большинство́; (*full age*) совершенноле́тие.
make *vt* де́лать *impf*, с~ *pf*; (*produce*) производи́ть *impf*, произвести́ *pf*; (*prepare*) гото́вить *impf*, при~ *pf*; (*amount to*) равня́ться *impf* +*dat*; (*earn*) зараба́тывать *impf*, зарабо́тать *pf*; (*compel*) заставля́ть *impf*, заста́вить *pf*; (*reach*) добира́ться *impf*, добра́ться *pf* до+*gen*; (*be in time for*) успева́ть *impf*, успе́ть *pf* на+*acc*; **be made of** состоя́ть *impf* из+*gen*; **~ as if, though** де́лать *impf*, с~ *pf* вид, что; **~ a bed** стели́ть *impf*, по~ *pf* посте́ль; **~ believe** притворя́ться *impf*, притвори́ться *pf*; **~-believe** притво́рство; **~ do with** дово́льство-

ваться *impf*, у~ *pf* +*instr*; ~ off
удира́ть *impf*, удра́ть *pf*; ~ out
(*cheque*) выпи́сывать *impf*, вы́пи-
сать *pf*; (*assert*) утвержда́ть *impf*,
утверди́ть *pf*; (*understand*) разби-
ра́ть *impf*, разобра́ть *pf*; ~ over
передава́ть *impf*, переда́ть *pf*; ~ up
(*form*, *compose*, *complete*) состав-
ля́ть *impf*, соста́вить *pf*; (*invent*)
выду́мывать *impf*, вы́думать *pf*;
(*theat*) гримирова́ть(ся) *impf*, за-
pf; ~-up (*theat*) грим; (*cosmetics*)
косме́тика; (*composition*) соста́в; ~
it up мири́ться *impf*, по~ *pf* (with
с+*instr*); ~ up for возмеща́ть *impf*,
возмести́ть *pf*; ~ up one's mind
реша́ться *impf*, реши́ться *pf*. make
n ма́рка. makeshift*adj* вре́менный.
malady*n* боле́знь.
malaise*n* (*fig*) беспоко́йство.
malaria*n* маляри́я.
male *n* (*animal*) саме́ц; (*person*)
мужчи́на *m*; *adj* мужско́й.
malevolence *n* недоброжела́тель-
ность. malevolent *adj* недоброже-
ла́тельный.
malice*n* зло́ба. malicious*adj* зло́б-
ный.
malign *vt* клевета́ть *impf*, на~ *pf*
на+*acc*. malignant *adj* (*harmful*)
зловре́дный; (*malicious*) зло́бный;
(*med*) злока́чественный.
malinger*vi* притворя́ться *impf*, при-
твори́ться *pf* больны́м. malingerer
n симуля́нт.
mallard*n* кря́ква.
malleable *adj* ко́вкий; (*fig*) пода́т-
ливый.
mallet*n* (деревя́нный) молото́к.
malnutrition*n* недоеда́ние.
malpractice *n* престу́пная небре́ж-
ность.
malt*n* со́лод.
maltreat *vt* пло́хо обраща́ться *impf*
с+*instr*.
mammal*n* млекопита́ющее *sb*.
mammoth*adj* грома́дный.
man *n* (*human*, *person*) челове́к;
(*human race*) челове́чество; (*male*)
мужчи́на *m*; (*labourer*) рабо́чий *sb*;
pl (*soldiers*) солда́ты *m pl*; *vt* (*furnish with men*) укомплекто́вывать
impf, укомплектова́ть *pf* ли́чным
соста́вом; ста́вить *impf*, по~ *pf*
люде́й к+*dat*; (*stall etc.*) обслужи-

вать *impf*, обслужи́ть *pf*; (*gate*,
checkpoint) стоя́ть *impf* на+*prep*.
manacle *n* нару́чник; *vt* надева́ть
impf, наде́ть *pf* нару́чники на+*acc*.
manage *vt* (*control*) управля́ть *impf*
+*instr*; *vi*(&*t*) (*cope*) справля́ться
impf, спра́виться *pf* (с+*instr*); (*succeed*) суме́ть *pf*. management *n*
управле́ние (of +*instr*); (the ~) ад-
министра́ция. manager *n* управля́-
ющий *sb* (of +*instr*); ме́неджер.
managerial*adj* администрати́вный.
managing director*n* дире́ктор-рас-
поряди́тель *m*.
mandarin*n* мандари́н.
mandate *n* манда́т. mandated *adj*
подманда́тный. mandatory*adj* обя-
за́тельный.
mane*n* гри́ва.
manful*adj* му́жественный.
manganese*n* ма́рганец.
manger *n* я́сли (-лей) *pl*; dog in the
~ соба́ка на се́не.
mangle*vt* (*mutilate*) кале́чить *impf*,
ис~ *pf*.
mango*n* ма́нго *neut indecl*.
manhandle *vt* гру́бо обраща́ться
impf с+*instr*.
manhole*n* смотрово́й коло́дец.
manhood*n* возмужа́лость.
mania*n* ма́ния. maniac*n* манья́к,
-я́чка. manic*adj* маниака́льный.
manicure *n* маникю́р; *vt* де́лать
impf, с~ *pf* маникю́р +*dat*. mani-
curist*n* маникю́рша.
manifest*adj* очеви́дный; *vt* (*display*)
проявля́ть *impf*, прояви́ть *pf*; *n*
манифе́ст. manifestation *n* прояв-
ле́ние. manifesto*n* манифе́ст.
manifold*adj* разнообра́зный.
manipulate*vt* манипули́ровать *impf*
+*instr*. manipulation*n* манипуля́ция.
manly*adj* му́жественный.
mankind*n* челове́чество.
manner *n* (*way*) о́браз; (*behaviour*)
мане́ра; *pl* мане́ры *f pl*. mannerism
n мане́ра.
mannish*adj* мужеподо́бный.
manoeuvrable *adj* мане́вренный.
manoeuvre*n* манёвр; *vt* & *i* манев-
ри́ровать *impf*.
manor*n* поме́стье; (*house*) поме́щи-
чий дом.
manpower*n* челове́ческие ресу́рсы
m pl.

manservant n слуга́ m.

mansion n особня́к.

manslaughter n непредумы́шленное уби́йство.

mantelpiece n ками́нная доска́.

manual adj ручно́й; n руково́дство. **manually** adv вручну́ю.

manufacture n произво́дство; vt производи́ть impf, произвести́ pf. **manufacturer** n фабрика́нт.

manure n наво́з.

manuscript n ру́копись.

many adj & n мно́го +gen, мно́гие pl; **how ~** ско́лько +gen.

map n ка́рта; (of town) план; vt: **~ out** намеча́ть impf, наме́тить pf.

maple n клён.

mar n по́ртить impf, ис~ pf.

marathon n марафо́н.

marauder n мароде́р. **marauding** adj мароде́рский.

marble n мра́мор; (toy) ша́рик; attrib мра́морный.

March n март; adj ма́ртовский.

march vi марширова́ть impf, про~ pf; n марш.

mare n кобы́ла.

margarine n маргари́н.

margin n (on page) по́ле; (edge) край; **profit ~** при́быль; **safety ~** запа́с про́чности.

marigold n ноготки́ (-ко́в) pl.

marijuana n марихуа́на.

marina n мари́на.

marinade n марина́д; vt маринова́ть impf, за~ pf.

marine adj морско́й; n (soldier) солда́т морско́й пехо́ты; pl морска́я пехо́та. **mariner** n моря́к.

marionette n марионе́тка.

marital adj супру́жеский, бра́чный.

maritime adj морско́й; (near sea) примо́рский.

mark[1] n (coin) ма́рка.

mark[2] n (for distinguishing) ме́тка; (sign) знак; (school) отме́тка; (trace) след; **on your ~s** на старт!; vt (indicate; celebrate) отмеча́ть impf, отме́тить pf; (school etc.) проверя́ть impf, прове́рить pf; (stain) па́чкать impf, за~ pf; (sport) закрыва́ть impf, закры́ть pf; **~ my words** попо́мни(те) мои́ слова́!; **~ out** размеча́ть impf, разме́тить pf. **marker** n знак; (in book) закла́дка.

market n ры́нок; **~ garden** огоро́д; **~place** база́рная пло́щадь; vt продава́ть impf, прода́ть pf.

marksman n стрело́к.

marmalade n апельси́новый джем.

maroon[1] adj (n) (colour) тёмно-бордо́вый (цвет).

maroon[2] vt (put ashore) выса́живать impf, вы́садить pf (на необита́емом о́строве); (cut off) отреза́ть impf, отре́зать pf.

marquee n тэнт.

marquis n марки́з.

marriage n брак; (wedding) сва́дьба; attrib бра́чный. **marriageable** adj: **~ age** бра́чный во́зраст. **married** adj (man) жена́тый; (woman) заму́жняя, за́мужем; (to each other) жена́ты; (of ~ persons) супру́жеский.

marrow n ко́стный мозг; (vegetable) кабачо́к.

marry vt (of man) жени́ться impf & pf на +prep; (of woman) выходи́ть impf, вы́йти pf за́муж за +acc; vi (of couple) пожени́ться pf.

marsh n боло́то. **marshy** adj боло́тистый.

marshal n ма́ршал; vt выстра́ивать impf, вы́строить pf; (fig) собира́ть impf, собра́ть pf.

marsupial n су́мчатое живо́тное sb.

martial adj вое́нный; **~ law** вое́нное положе́ние.

martyr n му́ченик, -ица; vt му́чить impf, за~ pf. **martyrdom** n му́ченичество.

marvel n чу́до; vi изумля́ться impf, изуми́ться pf. **marvellous** adj чуде́сный.

Marxist n маркси́ст; adj маркси́стский. **Marxism** n маркси́зм.

marzipan n марципа́н.

mascara n тушь.

mascot n талисма́н.

masculine adj мужско́й; (gram) мужско́го ро́да; (of woman) мужеподо́бный.

mash n карто́фельное пюре́ neut indecl; vt размина́ть impf, размя́ть pf.

mask n ма́ска; vt маскирова́ть impf, за~ pf.

masochism n мазохи́зм. **masochist** n мазохи́ст. **masochistic** adj мазохи́стский.

mason n ка́менщик; (M~) масо́н.
Masonic adj масо́нский. **masonry**
n ка́менная кла́дка.

masquerade n маскара́д; vi: ~ **as**
выдава́ть impf, вы́дать pf себя́ за
+acc.

Mass n (eccl) ме́сса.

mass n ма́сса; (majority) большинство́; attrib ма́ссовый; ~ **media**
сре́дства neut pl ма́ссовой информа́ции; ~**-produced** ма́ссового произво́дства; ~ **production** ма́ссовое
произво́дство; vt масси́ровать impf
& pf.

massacre n резня́; vt выреза́ть impf,
вы́резать pf.

massage n масса́ж; vt масси́ровать
impf & pf. **masseur, -euse** n масса́жи́ст, ~ка.

massive adj масси́вный.

mast n ма́чта.

master n (owner) хозя́ин; (of ship)
капита́н; (teacher) учи́тель m; (M~,
univ) маги́стр; (workman; artist)
ма́стер; (original) по́длинник, оригина́л; **be** ~ **of** владе́ть impf +instr;
~**-key** отмы́чка; vt (overcome) преодолева́ть impf, преодоле́ть pf;
справля́ться impf, спра́виться pf
c+instr; (a subject) овладева́ть impf,
овладе́ть pf +instr. **masterful** adj
вла́стный. **masterly** adj ма́стерско́й. **masterpiece** n шеде́вр. **mastery** n (of a subject) владе́ние (of
+instr).

masturbate vi мастурби́ровать impf.

mat n ко́врик, (at door) полови́к; (on
table) подста́вка.

match[1] n спи́чка. **matchbox** n спи́чечная коро́бка.

match[2] n (equal) ро́вня m & f; (contest) матч, состяза́ние; (marriage)
па́ртия; vi & t (go well (with)) гармони́ровать impf (c+instr); подходи́ть impf, подойти́ pf (к+dat).

mate[1] n (chess) мат.

mate[2] n (one of pair) саме́ц, са́мка;
(fellow worker) това́рищ; (naut) помо́щник капита́на; vi (of animals)
спа́риваться impf, спа́риться pf.

material n материа́л; (cloth) мате́рия;
pl (necessary articles) принадле́жности f pl. **materialism** n материали́зм. **materialistic** adj материалисти́ческий. **materialize** vi осуществ-

ля́ться impf, осуществи́ться pf.

maternal adj матери́нский; ~ **grandfather** де́душка с матери́нской стороны́. **maternity** n матери́нство; ~
leave декре́тный о́тпуск; ~ **ward**
роди́льное отделе́ние.

mathematical adj математи́ческий.
mathematician n математик. **mathematics, maths** n матема́тика.

matinée n дневно́й спекта́кль m.

matriarchal adj матриарха́льный.
matriarchy n матриарха́т.

matriculate vi быть при́нятым в вуз.
matriculation n зачисле́ние в вуз.

matrimonial adj супру́жеский. **matrimony** n брак.

matrix n ма́трица.

matron n (hospital) ста́ршая сестра́.

matt adj ма́товый.

matted adj спу́танный.

matter n (affair) де́ло; (question) вопро́с; (substance) вещество́; (philos;
med) мате́рия; (printed) материа́л;
a ~ **of life and death** вопро́с жи́зни
и сме́рти; **a** ~ **of opinion** спо́рное
де́ло; **a** ~ **of taste** де́ло вку́са; **as a**
~ **of fact** факти́чески; со́бственно
говоря́; **what's the** ~? в чём де́ло?;
what's the ~ **with him?** что с ним?;
~**-of-fact** проза́ичный; vi име́ть
impf значе́ние; **it doesn't** ~ э́то не
име́ет значе́ния; **it** ~**s a lot to me**
для меня́ э́то о́чень ва́жно.

matting n рого́жа.

mattress n матра́с.

mature adj зре́лый; vi зреть impf,
co~ pf. **maturity** n зре́лость.

maul vt терза́ть impf.

mausoleum n мавзоле́й.

mauve adj (n) ро́зовато-лило́вый
(цвет).

maxim n сенте́нция.

maximum n ма́ксимум; adj максима́льный.

may v aux (possibility, permission)
мочь impf, c~ pf; (possibility)
возмо́жно, что +indicative; (wish)
пусть +indicative.

May n (month) май; adj ма́йский ~
Day Пе́рвое sb ма́я.

maybe adv мо́жет быть.

mayonnaise n майоне́з.

mayor n мэр. **mayoress** n жена́ мэ́ра;
же́нщина-мэр.

maze n лабири́нт.

meadow *n* луг.

meagre *adj* скудный.

meal[1] *n* еда; **at ~times** во время еды.

meal[2] *n* (*grain*) мука. **mealy** *adj*: **~mouthed** сладкоречивый.

mean[1] *adj* (*average*) средний; *n* (*middle point*) середина; *pl* (*method*) средство, способ; *pl* (*resources*) средства *neut pl*; **by all ~s** конечно, пожалуйста; **by ~s of** при помощи +*gen*, посредством +*gen*; **by no ~s** совсем не; **~s test** проверка нуждаемости.

mean[2] *adj* (*ignoble*) подлый; (*miserly*) скупой; (*poor*) убогий.

mean[3] *vt* (*have in mind*) иметь *impf* в виду; (*intend*) намереваться *impf* +*inf*; (*signify*) значить *impf*.

meander *vi* (*stream*) извиваться *impf*; (*person*) бродить *impf*. **meandering** *adj* извилистый.

meaning *n* значение. **meaningful** *adj* (много)значительный. **meaningless** *adj* бессмысленный.

meantime, **meanwhile** *adv* между тем.

measles *n* корь. **measly** *adj* ничтожный.

measurable *adj* измеримый. **measure** *n* мера; **made to ~** сшитый по мерке; сделанный на заказ; *vt* измерять *impf*, измерить *pf*; (*for clothes*) снимать *impf*, снять *pf* мерку с+*gen*; *vi* иметь *impf* +*acc*: **the room ~s 30 feet in length** комната имеет тридцать футов в длину; **~ off** отмерять *impf*, отмерить *pf*; **~ up to** соответствовать *impf* +*dat*. **measured** *adj* (*rhythmical*) мерный. **measurement** *n* (*action*) измерение; *pl* (*dimensions*) размеры *m pl*.

meat *n* мясо. **meatball** *n* котлета. **meaty** *adj* мясистый; (*fig*) содержательный.

mechanic *n* механик. **mechanical** *adj* механический; (*fig*; *automatic*) машинальный; **~ engineer** инженер-механик; **~ engineering** машиностроение. **mechanics** *n* механика. **mechanism** *n* механизм. **mechanization** *n* механизация. **mechanize** *vt* механизировать *impf* & *pf*.

medal *n* медаль. **medallion** *n* медальон. **medallist** *n* медалист.

meddle *vi* вмешиваться *impf*, вме-

шаться *pf* (**in**, **with** в+*acc*).

media *pl of* **medium**

mediate *vi* посредничать *impf*. **mediation** *n* посредничество. **mediator** *n* посредник.

medical *adj* медицинский; **~ student** медик, -ичка. **medicated** *adj* (*impregnated*) пропитанный лекарством. **medicinal** *adj* (*of medicine*) лекарственный; (*healing*) целебный. **medicine** *n* медицина; (*substance*) лекарство.

medieval *adj* средневековый.

mediocre *adj* посредственный. **mediocrity** *n* посредственность.

meditate *vi* размышлять *impf*. **meditation** *n* размышление. **meditative** *adj* задумчивый.

Mediterranean *adj* средиземноморский; *n* Средиземное море.

medium *n* (*means*) средство; (*phys*) среда; (*person*) медиум; *pl* (*mass media*) средства *neut pl* массовой информации; *adj* средний; **happy ~** золотая середина.

medley *n* смесь; (*mus*) попурри *neut indecl*.

meek *adj* кроткий.

meet *vt* & *i* встречать(ся) *impf*, встретить(ся) *pf*; *vt* (*make acquaintance*) знакомиться *impf*, по~ *pf* с+*instr*; *vi* (*assemble*) собираться *impf*, собраться *pf*. **meeting** *n* встреча; (*of committee*) заседание, митинг.

megalomania *n* мегаломания.

megaphone *n* мегафон.

melancholic *adj* меланхолический. **melancholy** *n* грусть; *adj* унылый, грустный.

mellow *adj* (*colour*, *sound*) сочный; (*person*) добродушный; *vi* смягчаться *impf*, смягчиться *pf*.

melodic *adj* мелодический. **melodious** *adj* мелодичный. **melody** *n* мелодия.

melodrama *n* мелодрама. **melodramatic** *adj* мелодраматический.

melon *n* дыня; (*water-~*) арбуз.

melt *vt* & *i* расталивать(ся) *impf*, растопить(ся) *pf*; (*smelt*) плавить(ся) *impf*, рас~ *pf*; (*dissolve*) растворять(ся) *impf*, растворить(ся) *pf*; *vi* (*thaw*) таять *impf*, рас~ *pf*; **~ing point** точка плавления.

member n член. **membership** n членство; (number of ~) количество членов; attrib членский.

membrane n перепонка.

memento n сувенир. **memoir** n pl мемуары (-ров) pl; воспоминания neut pl. **memorable** adj достопамятный. **memorandum** n записка. **memorial** adj мемориальный; n памятник. **memorize** vt запоминать impf, запомнить pf. **memory** n память; (recollection) воспоминание.

menace n угроза; vt угрожать impf +dat. **menacing** adj угрожающий.

menagerie n зверинец.

mend vt чинить impf, по~ pf; (clothes) штопать impf, за~ pf; ~ one's ways исправляться impf, исправиться pf.

menial adj низкий, чёрный.

meningitis n менингит.

menopause n климакс.

menstrual adj менструальный. **menstruation** n менструация.

mental adj умственный; (of ~ illness) психический; ~ **arithmetic** счёт в уме. **mentality** n ум; (character) склад ума.

mention vt упоминать impf, упомянуть pf; **don't** ~ **it** не за что!; **not to** ~ не говоря уже о+prep.

menu n меню neut indecl.

mercantile adj торговый.

mercenary adj корыстный; (hired) наёмный; n наёмник.

merchandise n товары m pl. **merchant** n купец; торговец; ~ **navy** торговый флот.

merciful adj милосердный. **mercifully** adv к счастью. **merciless** adj беспощадный.

mercurial adj (person) изменчивый. **mercury** n ртуть.

mercy n милосердие; **at the** ~ **of** во власти +gen.

mere adj простой; **a** ~ **£40** всего лишь сорок фунтов. **merely** adv только, просто.

merge vt & i сливать(ся) impf, слить(ся) pf. **merger** n объединение.

meridian n меридиан.

meringue n меренга.

merit n заслуга, достоинство; vt за-

служивать impf, заслужить pf +gen.

mermaid n русалка.

merrily adv весело. **merriment** n веселье. **merry** adj весёлый; ~-**go-round** карусель; ~-**making** веселье.

mesh n сеть; vi сцепляться impf, сцепиться pf.

mesmerize vt гипнотизировать impf, за~ pf.

mess n (disorder) беспорядок; (trouble) беда; (eating-place) столовая sb; vi: ~ **about** возиться impf; ~ **up** портить impf, ис~ pf.

message n сообщение. **messenger** n курьер.

Messiah n мессия m. **Messianic** adj мессианский.

Messrs abbr господа (gen -д) m pl.

messy adj (untidy) беспорядочный; (dirty) грязный.

metabolism n обмен веществ.

metal n металл; adj металлический. **metallic** adj металлический. **metallurgy** n металлургия.

metamorphosis n метаморфоза.

metaphor n метафора. **metaphorical** adj метафорический.

metaphysical adj метафизический. **metaphysics** n метафизика.

meteor n метеор. **meteoric** adj метеорический. **meteorite** n метеорит. **meteorological** adj метеорологический. **meteorology** n метеорология.

meter n счётчик; vt измерять impf, измерить pf.

methane n метан.

method n метод. **methodical** adj методичный.

Methodist n методист; adj методистский.

methodology n методология.

methylated adj: ~ **spirit(s)** денатурат.

meticulous adj тщательный.

metre n метр. **metric(al)** adj метрический.

metronome n метроном.

metropolis n столица. **metropolitan** adj столичный; n (eccl) митрополит.

mettle n характер.

Mexican adj мексиканский; n мексиканец, -анка. **Mexico** n Мексика.

mezzanine n антресоли f pl.

miaow *int* мя́у; *n* мя́уканье; *vi* мяу́кать *impf*, мяу́кнуть *pf*.

mica *n* слюда́.

microbe *n* микро́б. **microchip** *n* чип, микросхе́ма. **microcomputer** *n* микрокомпью́тер. **microcosm** *n* микроко́см. **microfilm** *n* микрофи́льм. **micro-organism** *n* микрооргани́зм. **microphone** *n* микрофо́н. **microscope** *n* микроско́п. **microscopic** *adj* микроскопи́ческий. **microwave** *n* микроволна́; ~ **oven** микроволно́вая печь.

mid *adj*: ~ **May** середи́на ма́я. **mid-day** *n* по́лдень *m*; *attrib* полу́денный. **middle** *n* середи́на; *adj* сре́дний; ~**-aged** сре́дних лет; **M~ Ages** сре́дние века́ *m pl*; ~**-class** буржуа́зный; ~**man** посре́дник; ~**-sized** сре́днего разме́ра. **middleweight** *n* сре́дний вес.

midge *n* мо́шка.

midget *n* ка́рлик, -ица.

midnight *n* по́лночь; *attrib* полу́ночный. **midriff** *n* диафра́гма. **midst** *n* середи́на. **midsummer** *n* середи́на ле́та. **midway** *adv* на полпути́. **midweek** *n* середи́на неде́ли. **midwinter** *n* середи́на зимы́.

midwife *n* акуше́рка. **midwifery** *n* акуше́рство.

might *n* мощь; **with all one's** ~ изо всех сил. **mighty** *adj* мо́щный.

migraine *n* мигре́нь.

migrant *adj* кочу́ющий; (*bird*) перелётный; *n* (*person*) пересе́ленец; (*bird*) перелётная пти́ца. **migrate** *vi* мигри́ровать *impf & pf*. **migration** *n* мигра́ция. **migratory** *adj* кочу́ющий; (*bird*) перелётный.

mike *n* микрофо́н.

mild *adj* мя́гкий.

mildew *n* пле́сень.

mile *n* ми́ля. **mileage** *n* расстоя́ние в ми́лях; (*of car*) пробе́г. **milestone** *n* верстово́й столб; (*fig*) ве́ха.

militancy *n* вои́нственность. **militant** *adj* вои́нствующий; *n* активи́ст. **military** *adj* вое́нный; *n* вое́нные *sb pl*. **militate** *vi*: ~ **against** говори́ть *impf* про́тив+*gen*. **militia** *n* мили́ция. **militiaman** *n* милиционе́р.

milk *n* молоко́; *attrib* моло́чный; *vt* дои́ть *impf*, по~ *pf*. **milkman** *n* продаве́ц молока́. **milky** *adj* моло́чный;

M~ Way Мле́чный Путь *m*.

mill *n* ме́льница; (*factory*) фа́брика; *vt* (*grain etc.*) моло́ть *impf*, с~ *pf*; (*metal*) фрезерова́ть *impf*, от~ *pf*; (*coin*) гурти́ть *impf*; *vi*: ~ **around** толпи́ться *impf*. **miller** *n* ме́льник.

millennium *n* тысячеле́тие.

millet *n* (*plant*) про́со; (*grain*) пшено́.

milligram(me) *n* миллигра́мм. **millimetre** *n* миллиме́тр.

million *n* миллио́н. **millionaire** *n* миллионе́р. **millionth** *adj* миллио́нный.

millstone *n* жёрнов; (*fig*) ка́мень *m* на ше́е.

mime *n* мим; (*dumb-show*) пантоми́ма; *vt* изобража́ть *impf*, изобрази́ть *pf* мими́чески. **mimic** *n* ми́мист; *vt* передра́знивать *impf*, передразни́ть *pf*. **mimicry** *n* имита́ция.

minaret *n* минаре́т.

mince *n* (*meat*) фарш; *vt* руби́ть *impf*; (*in machine*) пропуска́ть *impf*, пропусти́ть *pf* че́рез мясору́бку; *vi* (*walk*) семени́ть *impf*; **not** ~ **matters** говори́ть *impf* без обиняко́в. **mincemeat** *n* начи́нка из изю́ма, миндаля́ и т.п.

mind *n* ум; **bear in** ~ име́ть *impf* в виду́; **change one's** ~ переду́мывать *impf*, переду́мать *pf*; **make up one's** ~ реша́ться *impf*, реши́ться *pf*; **you're out of your** ~ вы с ума́ сошли́; *vt* (*give heed to*) обраща́ть *impf*, обрати́ть *pf* внима́ние на+*acc*; (*look after*) присма́тривать *impf*, присмотре́ть *pf* за+*instr*; **I don't** ~ я ничего́ не име́ю про́тив; **don't** ~ **me** не обраща́й(те) внима́ния на меня́!; ~ **you don't forget** смотри́ не забу́дь!; ~ **your own business** не вме́шивайтесь в чужи́е дела́!; **never** ~ ничего́! **mindful** *adj* по́мнящий. **mindless** *adj* бессмы́сленный.

mine[1] *poss pron* мой, свой.

mine[2] *n* ша́хта, рудни́к; (*fig*) исто́чник; (*mil*) ми́на; *vt* (*obtain from* ~) добыва́ть *impf*, добы́ть *pf*; (*mil*) мини́ровать *impf & pf*. **minefield** *n* ми́нное по́ле. **miner** *n* шахтёр.

mineral *n* минера́л; *adj* минера́льный; ~ **water** минера́льная вода́. **mineralogy** *n* минерало́гия.

mingle *vt & i* сме́шивать(ся) *impf*, смеша́ть(ся) *pf*.

miniature n миниатю́ра; adj миниатю́рный.

minibus n микроавто́бус.

minim n (mus) полови́нная но́та.

minimal adj минима́льный. **minimize** vt (reduce) доводи́ть impf, довести́ pf до ми́нимума. **minimum** n ми́нимум; adj минима́льный.

mining n го́рное де́ло.

minister n мини́стр; (eccl) свяще́нник. **ministerial** adj министе́рский. **ministration** n по́мощь. **ministry** n (polit) министе́рство; (eccl) духове́нство.

mink n но́рка; attrib но́рковый.

minor adj (unimportant) незначи́тельный; (less important) второстепе́нный; (mus) мино́рный; n (person under age) несовершенноле́тний n; (mus) мино́р. **minority** n меньшинство́; (age) несовершенноле́тие.

minstrel n менестре́ль m.

mint[1] n (plant) мя́та; (peppermint) пе́речная мя́та.

mint[2] n (econ) моне́тный двор; in ~ condition но́венький; vt чека́нить impf, от~, вы́~ pf.

minuet n менуэ́т.

minus prep ми́нус+acc; без+gen; n ми́нус.

minuscule adj малю́сенький.

minute[1] n мину́та; pl протоко́л.

minute[2] adj ме́лкий. **minutiae** n pl ме́лочи (-че́й) f pl.

miracle n чу́до. **miraculous** adj чуде́сный.

mirage n мира́ж.

mire n (mud) грязь; (swamp) боло́то.

mirror n зе́ркало; vt отража́ть impf, отрази́ть pf.

mirth n весе́лье.

misadventure n несча́стный слу́чай.

misapprehension n недопонима́ние. **misappropriate** vt незако́нно присва́ивать impf, присво́ить pf. **misbehave** vi ду́рно вести́ impf себя́. **misbehaviour** n ду́рное поведе́ние. **miscalculate** vt непра́вильно рассчи́тывать impf, рассчита́ть pf; (fig, abs) просчи́тываться impf, просчита́ться pf. **miscalculation** n просчёт. **miscarriage** n (med) вы́кидыш; ~ of justice суде́бная оши́бка. **miscarry** vi (med) име́ть impf вы́кидыш.

miscellaneous adj ра́зный, разнообра́зный. **miscellany** n смесь.

mischief n (harm) вред; (naughtiness) озорство́. **mischievous** adj озорно́й. **misconception** n непра́вильное представле́ние. **misconduct** n дурно́е поведе́ние. **misconstrue** vt непра́вильно истолко́вывать impf, истолкова́ть pf.

misdeed, misdemeanour n просту́пок. **misdirect** vt непра́вильно направля́ть impf, напра́вить pf; (letter) непра́вильно адресова́ть impf & pf.

miser n скупе́ц. **miserable** adj (unhappy, wretched) несча́стный, жа́лкий; (weather) скве́рный. **miserly** adj скупо́й. **misery** n страда́ние.

misfire vi дава́ть impf, дать pf осе́чку. **misfit** n (person) неуда́чник. **misfortune** n несча́стье. **misgiving** n опасе́ние. **misguided** adj обма́нутый.

mishap n неприя́тность. **misinform** vt непра́вильно информи́ровать impf & pf. **misinterpret** vt неве́рно истолко́вывать impf, истолкова́ть pf. **misjudge** vt неве́рно оце́нивать impf, оцени́ть pf. **misjudgement** n неве́рная оце́нка. **mislay** vt затеря́ть pf. **mislead** vt вводи́ть impf, ввести́ pf в заблужде́ние. **mismanage** vt пло́хо управля́ть impf +instr. **mismanagement** n пло́хое управле́ние. **misnomer** n непра́вильное назва́ние.

misogynist n женоненави́стник. **misogyny** n женоненави́стничество.

misplaced adj неуме́стный. **misprint** n опеча́тка. **misquote** vt непра́вильно цити́ровать impf, про~ pf. **misread** vt (fig) непра́вильно истолко́вывать impf, истолкова́ть pf. **misrepresent** vt искажа́ть impf, искази́ть pf. **misrepresentation** n искаже́ние.

Miss n (title) мисс.

miss n про́мах; vi прома́хиваться impf, промахну́ться pf; vt (fail to hit, see, hear) пропуска́ть impf, пропусти́ть pf; (train) опа́здывать impf, опозда́ть pf на+acc; (regret absence of) скуча́ть impf по+dat; ~ out пропуска́ть impf, пропусти́ть pf; ~ the point не понима́ть impf, поня́ть pf су́ти.

misshapen adj уро́дливый.

missile n снаря́д, раке́та.

missing adj отсу́тствующий, недо-ста́ющий; (person) пропа́вший без ве́сти.

mission n ми́ссия; командиро́вка. **missionary** n миссионе́р. **missive** n посла́ние.

misspell vt непра́вильно писа́ть impf, на~ pf. **misspelling** n непра́вильное написа́ние.

mist n тума́н; vt & i затума́ни-вать(ся) impf, затума́нить(ся) pf.

mistake n непра́вильно понима́ть impf, поня́ть pf; ~ for принима́ть impf, приня́ть pf за+acc; n оши́бка; **make a** ~ ошиба́ться impf, оши-би́ться pf. **mistaken** adj оши́боч-ный; **be** ~ ошиба́ться impf, оши-би́ться pf.

mister n ми́стер, господи́н.

mistletoe n оме́ла.

mistress n хозя́йка; (teacher) учи́-тельница; (lover) любо́вница.

mistrust n не доверя́ть impf +dat; n недове́рие. **mistrustful** adj недове́р-чивый.

misty adj тума́нный.

misunderstand vt непра́вильно по-нима́ть impf, поня́ть pf. **misunder-standing** n недоразуме́ние.

misuse vt непра́вильно употребля́ть impf, употреби́ть pf; (ill treat) ду́рно обраща́ться impf с+instr; n непра́-вильное употребле́ние.

mite n (insect) клещ; (child) кро́шка; **widow's** ~ ле́пта вдови́цы; **not a** ~ ничу́ть.

mitigate vt смягча́ть impf, смягчи́ть pf. **mitigation** n смягче́ние.

mitre n ми́тра.

mitten n рукави́ца.

mix vt меша́ть impf, с~ pf; vi сме́-шиваться impf, смеша́ться pf; (as-sociate) обща́ться impf; ~ **up** (con-fuse) пу́тать impf, с~ pf; **get** ~**ed up in** заме́шиваться impf, заме-ша́ться pf в+acc; n смесь. **mixer** n смеси́тель m; (cul) ми́ксер. **mixture** n смесь; (medicine) миксту́ра.

moan n стон; vi стона́ть impf, про~ pf.

moat n (крепостно́й) ров.

mob n толпа́; vt (attack) напада́ть impf, напа́сть pf толпо́й на+acc.

mobster n банди́т.

mobile adj подвижно́й, передвиж-но́й. **mobility** n подви́жность. **mo-bilization** n мобилиза́ция. **mobilize** vt & i мобилизова́ть(ся) impf & pf.

moccasin n мокаси́н (gen pl -н).

mock vt & i насмеха́ться impf над +instr; adj (sham) подде́льный; (pre-tended) мни́мый; ~**up** n маке́т. **mockery** n издева́тельство; (trav-esty) паро́дия.

mode n (manner) о́браз; (method) ме́тод.

model n (representation) моде́ль; (pattern, ideal) образе́ц; (artist's) нату́рщик, -ица; (fashion) манеке́н-щик, -ица; (make) моде́ль; adj образцо́вый; vt лепи́ть impf, вы́~, с~ pf; (clothes) демонстри́ровать impf & pf; vi (act as ~) быть нату́р-щиком, -ицей; быть манеке́нщи-ком, -ицей; ~ **after, on** создава́ть impf, созда́ть pf по образцу́ +gen.

moderate adj (various senses; polit) уме́ренный; (medium) сре́дний; vt умеря́ть impf, уме́рить pf; vi сти-ха́ть impf, сти́хнуть pf. **moderation** n уме́ренность; **in** ~ уме́ренно.

modern adj совреме́нный; (language, history) но́вый. **modernization** n модерниза́ция. **modernize** vt мо-дернизи́ровать impf & pf.

modest adj скро́мный. **modesty** n скро́мность.

modification n модифика́ция. **modify** vt модифици́ровать impf & pf.

modish adj мо́дный.

modular adj мо́дульный. **modulate** vt модули́ровать impf. **modulation** n модуля́ция. **module** n мо́дуль m.

mohair n мохе́р.

moist adj вла́жный. **moisten** vt & i увлажня́ть(ся) impf, увлажни́ть(ся) pf. **moisture** n вла́га.

molar n (tooth) коренно́й зуб.

mole[1] n (on skin) ро́динка.

mole[2] n (animal; agent) крот.

molecular adj молекуля́рный. **mol-ecule** n моле́кула.

molest vt пристава́ть impf, приста́ть pf к+dat.

mollify vt смягча́ть impf, смягчи́ть pf.

mollusc n моллю́ск.

molten adj распла́вленный.

moment n моме́нт, миг; **at the** ~

сейча́с; **at the last** ~ в после́днюю мину́ту; **just a** ~ сейча́с! **momentarily** adv на мгнове́ние. **momentary** adj мгнове́нный. **momentous** adj ва́жный. **momentum** n коли́чество движе́ния; (impetus) дви́жущая си́ла; **gather** ~ набира́ть impf, набра́ть pf ско́рость.

monarch n мона́рх. **monarchy** n мона́рхия.

monastery n монасты́рь m. **monastic** adj мона́шеский.

Monday n понеде́льник.

monetary adj де́нежный. **money** n де́ньги (-нег, -ньга́м) pl; **~-lender** ростовщи́к.

mongrel n дворня́жка.

monitor n (naut; TV) монито́р; vt проверя́ть impf, прове́рить pf.

monk n мона́х.

monkey n обезья́на.

mono n мо́но neut indecl. **monochrome** adj одноцве́тный. **monogamous** adj единобра́чный. **monogamy** n единобра́чие. **monogram** n моногра́мма. **monograph** n моногра́фия. **monolith** n моноли́т. **monolithic** adj моноли́тный. **monologue** n моноло́г. **monopolize** vt монополизи́ровать impf & pf. **monopoly** n монопо́лия. **monosyllabic** adj односло́жный. **monosyllable** n односло́жное сло́во. **monotone** n моното́нность; **in a** ~ моното́нно. **monotonous** adj моното́нный. **monotony** n моното́нность.

monsoon n (wind) муссо́н; (rainy season) дождли́вый сезо́н.

monster n чудо́вище. **monstrosity** n чудо́вище. **monstrous** adj чудо́вищный; (huge) грома́дный.

montage n монта́ж.

month n ме́сяц. **monthly** adj ме́сячный; n ежеме́сячник; adv ежеме́сячно.

monument n па́мятник. **monumental** adj монумента́льный.

moo vi мыча́ть impf.

mood[1] n (gram) наклоне́ние.

mood[2] n настрое́ние. **moody** adj капри́зный.

moon n луна́. **moonlight** n лу́нный свет; vi халту́рить impf. **moonlit** adj лу́нный.

moor[1] n ме́стность, поро́сшая ве́ре-

ском. **moorland** n ве́ресковая пу́стошь.

moor[2] vt & i швартова́ть(ся) impf, при~ pf. **mooring** n (place) прича́л; pl (cables) швартовы m pl.

Moorish adj маврита́нский.

moose n америка́нский лось m.

moot adj спо́рный.

mop n шва́бра; vt протира́ть impf, протере́ть pf (шва́брой); ~ **one's brow** вытира́ть impf, вы́тереть pf лоб; ~ **up** вытира́ть impf, вы́тереть pf.

mope vi хандри́ть impf.

moped n мопе́д.

moraine n море́на.

moral adj мора́льный; n мора́ль; pl нра́вы m pl. **morale** n мора́льное состоя́ние. **morality** n нра́вственность, мора́ль. **moralize** vi морализи́ровать impf.

morass n боло́то.

moratorium n морато́рий.

morbid adj боле́зненный.

more adj (greater quantity) бо́льше +gen; (additional) ещё бо́льше; (forming comp) бо́лее; **and what is** ~ и бо́льше того́; ~ **or less** бо́лее и́ли ме́нее; **once** ~ ещё раз. **moreover** adv сверх того́; кро́ме того́.

morgue n морг.

moribund adj умира́ющий.

morning n у́тро; **in the** ~ у́тром; **in the ~s** по утра́м; attrib у́тренний.

moron n слабоу́мный sb.

morose adj угрю́мый.

morphine n мо́рфий.

Morse (code) n а́збука Мо́рзе.

morsel n кусо́чек.

mortal adj сме́ртный; (fatal) смерте́льный; n сме́ртный sb. **mortality** n сме́ртность.

mortar n (vessel) сту́п(к)а; (cannon) миноме́т; (cement) (известко́вый) раство́р.

mortgage n ссу́да на поку́пку до́ма; vt закла́дывать impf, заложи́ть pf.

mortify vt унижа́ть impf, уни́зить pf.

mortuary n морг.

mosaic n моза́ика; adj моза́ичный.

mosque n мече́ть.

mosquito n кома́р.

moss n мох. **mossy** adj мши́стый.

most adj наибо́льший; n наибо́льшее коли́чество; adj & n (majority) большинство́ +gen; бо́льшая часть +gen; adv бо́льше всего́, наибо́лее; (forming superl) са́мый. **mostly** adv гла́вным о́бразом.

MOT (test) n техосмо́тр.

motel n моте́ль m.

moth n мотылёк; (clothes-~) моль.

mother n мать; vt относи́ться impf по-матери́нски к +dat; ~-**in-law** (wife's ~) тёща; (husband's ~) свекро́вь; ~-**of-pearl** перламу́тр; adj перламу́тровый: ~ **tongue** родно́й язы́к. **motherhood** n матери́нство. **motherland** n ро́дина. **motherly** adj матери́нский.

motif n моти́в.

motion n движе́ние; (gesture) жест; (proposal) предложе́ние; vt пока́зывать impf, показа́ть pf +dat жестом, что́бы +past. **motionless** adj неподви́жный. **motivate** vt побужда́ть impf, побуди́ть pf. **motivation** n побужде́ние. **motive** n моти́в; adj дви́жущий.

motley adj пёстрый.

motor n дви́гатель m, мото́р; ~ **bike** мотоци́кл; ~ **boat** мото́рная ло́дка; ~ **car** автомоби́ль m; ~ **cycle** мотоци́кл; ~**cyclist** мотоцикли́ст; ~ **racing** автомоби́льные го́нки f pl; ~ **scooter** моторо́ллер; ~ **vehicle** автомаши́на. **motoring** n автомобили́зм. **motorist** n автомобили́ст, ~ка. **motorize** vt моторизова́ть impf & pf. **motorway** n автостра́да.

mottled adj кра́пчатый.

motto n деви́з.

mould[1] n (shape) фо́рма, фо́рмочка; vt формова́ть impf, с~ pf. **moulding** n (archit) лепно́е украше́ние.

mould[2] n (fungi) пле́сень. **mouldy** adj заплесневе́лый.

moulder vi разлага́ться impf, разложи́ться pf.

moult vi линя́ть impf, вы́~ pf.

mound n холм; (heap) на́сыпь.

Mount n (in names) гора́.

mount n (ascend) поднима́ться impf, подня́ться pf на+acc; (~ a horse etc.) сади́ться impf, сесть pf на+acc; (picture) накле́ивать impf, накле́ить pf на карто́н; (gun) устана́вливать impf, установи́ть pf; ~ **up** (accumulate) нака́пливаться impf, накопи́ться pf; n (for picture) карто́н;

(horse) верхова́я ло́шадь.

mountain n гора́; attrib го́рный. **mountaineer** n альпини́ст, ~ка. **mountaineering** n альпини́зм. **mountainous** adj гори́стый.

mourn vt опла́кивать impf, опла́кать pf; vi скорбе́ть impf (**over** о+prep). **mournful** adj ско́рбный. **mourning** n тра́ур.

mouse n мышь.

mousse n мусс.

moustache n усы́ (усо́в) pl.

mousy adj мыши́ный; (timid) ро́бкий.

mouth n рот; (poetical) уста́ (-т) pl; (entrance) вход; (of river) у́стье; vt говори́ть impf, сказа́ть pf одними́ губа́ми. **mouthful** n глото́к. **mouthorgan** n губна́я гармо́ника. **mouthpiece** n мундшту́к; (person) ру́пор.

movable adj подви́жно́й.

move n (in game) ход; (change of residence) перее́зд; (movement) движе́ние; (step) шаг; vt & i (affect) тро́гать impf, тро́нуть pf; (propose) вноси́ть impf, внести́ pf; vi (develop) развива́ться impf, разви́ться pf; (~ house) переезжа́ть impf, перее́хать pf; ~ **away** (vt & i) удаля́ть(ся) impf, удали́ть(ся) pf; (vi) уезжа́ть impf, уе́хать pf; ~ **in** въезжа́ть impf, въе́хать pf; ~ **on** идти́ impf, пойти́ pf да́льше; ~ **out** съезжа́ть impf, съе́хать pf (**of** c+gen). **movement** n движе́ние; (mus) часть. **moving** adj дви́жущийся; (touching) тро́гательный.

mow vt (also ~ **down**) коси́ть impf, с~ pf. **mower** n коси́лка.

MP abbr (of Member of Parliament) член парла́мента.

Mr abbr ми́стер, господи́н. **Mrs** abbr ми́ссис f indecl, госпожа́.

Ms n миз, госпожа́.

much adj & n мно́го +gen; мно́гое sb; adv о́чень; (with comp adj) гора́здо.

muck n (dung) наво́з; (dirt) грязь; ~ **about** вози́ться impf; ~ **out** чи́стить impf, вы́~ pf; ~ **up** изга́живать impf, изга́дить pf.

mucous adj сли́зистый. **mucus** n слизь.

mud n грязь. **mudguard** n крыло́.

muddle vt пу́тать impf, с~ pf; vi: ~ **through** ко́е-ка́к справля́ться impf, спра́виться pf; n беспоря́док.

muddy adj гря́зный; vt обры́згивать impf, обры́згать pf гря́зью.

muff n му́фта.

muffle vt (for warmth) заку́тывать impf, заку́тать pf; (sound) глуши́ть impf, за~ pf.

mug n (vessel) кру́жка; (face) мо́рда.

muggy adj сыро́й и тёплый.

mulch n му́льча; vt мульчи́ровать impf & pf.

mule n мул.

mull vt: ~ **over** обду́мывать impf, обду́мать pf. **mulled** adj: ~ **wine** глинтве́йн.

mullet n (grey ~) кефа́ль; (red ~) бараба́лька.

multicoloured adj многокра́сочный.

multifarious adj разнообра́зный.

multilateral adj многосторо́нний.

multimillionaire n мультимиллионе́р. **multinational** adj многонациона́льный.

multiple adj составно́й; (numerous) многочи́сленный; ~ **sclerosis** рассе́янный склеро́з; n кра́тное число́; **least common** ~ о́бщее наиме́ньшее кра́тное sb. **multiplication** n умноже́ние. **multiplicity** n многочи́сленность. **multiply** vt (math) умножа́ть impf, умно́жить pf; vi размножа́ться impf, размно́житься pf.

multi-storey adj многоэта́жный.

multitude n мно́жество; (crowd) толпа́.

mum[1] adj: **keep** ~ молча́ть impf.

mum[2] n (mother) ма́ма.

mumble vt & i бормота́ть impf, про~ pf.

mummy[1] n (archaeol) му́мия.

mummy[2] n (mother) ма́ма, ма́мочка.

mumps n сви́нка.

munch vt жева́ть impf.

mundane adj земно́й.

municipal adj муниципа́льный. **municipality** n муниципалите́т.

munitions n pl вое́нное иму́щество.

mural n стенна́я ро́спись.

murder n уби́йство; vt убива́ть impf, уби́ть pf; (language) кове́ркать impf, ис~ pf. **murderer, murderess** n уби́йца m & f. **murderous** adj уби́йственный.

murky adj тёмный, мра́чный.

murmur n шёпот; vt & i шепта́ть impf, шепну́ть pf.

muscle n му́скул. **muscular** adj мы́шечный; (person) му́скулистый.

Muscovite n москви́ч, ~ка.

muse vi размышля́ть impf.

museum n музе́й.

mush n ка́ша.

mushroom n гриб.

music n му́зыка; (sheet ~) но́ты f pl; ~**-hall** мю́зик-хо́лл; ~ **stand** пюпи́тр. **musical** adj музыка́льный; n опере́тта. **musician** n музыка́нт.

musk n му́скус.

musket n мушке́т.

Muslim n мусульма́нин, -а́нка; adj мусульма́нский.

muslin n мусли́н.

mussel n ми́дия.

must v aux (obligation) до́лжен (-жна́) predic+inf; на́до impers+dat & inf; (necessity) ну́жно impers+dat & inf; ~ **not** (prohibition) нельзя́ impers +dat & inf.

mustard n горчи́ца.

muster vt собира́ть impf, собра́ть pf; (courage etc.) собира́ться impf, собра́ться pf c+instr.

musty adj за́тхлый.

mutation n мута́ция.

mute adj немо́й; n немо́й sb; (mus) сурди́нка. **muted** adj приглушённый.

mutilate vt уве́чить impf, из~ pf. **mutilation** n уве́чье.

mutineer n мяте́жник. **mutinous** adj мяте́жный. **mutiny** n мяте́ж; vi бунтова́ть impf, взбунтова́ться pf.

mutter vi бормота́ть impf; impf; n бормота́ние.

mutton n бара́нина.

mutual adj взаи́мный; (common) о́бщий.

muzzle n (animal's) мо́рда; (on animal) намо́рдник; (of gun) ду́ло; vt надева́ть impf, наде́ть pf намо́рдник на+acc; (fig) заставля́ть impf, заста́вить pf молча́ть.

my poss pron мой; свой.

myopia n близору́кость. **myopic** adj близору́кий.

myriad n мириа́ды (-д) pl; adj бесчи́сленный.

myrtle n мирт; attrib ми́ртовый.

myself pron (emph) (я) сам, сама́; (refl) себя́; -ся (suffixed to vt).

mysterious adj таи́нственный. **mystery** n та́йна.

mystic(al) adj мисти́ческий; n ми́стик. **mysticism** n мистици́зм. **mystification** n озада́ченность. **mystify** vt озада́чивать impf, озада́чить pf.

myth n миф. **mythical** adj мифи́ческий. **mythological** adj мифологи́ческий. **mythology** n мифоло́гия.

N

nag[1] n (horse) ло́шадь.

nag[2] vt (also ~ at) пили́ть impf +acc; vi (of pain) ныть impf.

nail n (finger-, toe-~) но́готь m; (metal spike) гвоздь m; ~ **varnish** лак для ногте́й; vt прибива́ть impf, приби́ть pf (гвоздя́ми).

naive adj наи́вный. **naivety** n наи́вность.

naked adj го́лый; ~ **eye** невооружённый глаз. **nakedness** n нагота́.

name n назва́ние; (forename) и́мя neut; (surname) фами́лия; (reputation) репута́ция: **what is his** ~? как его́ зову́т?; ~-**plate** доще́чка с фами́лией; ~**sake** тёзка m & f; vt называ́ть impf, назва́ть pf; (appoint) назнача́ть impf, назна́чить pf. **nameless** adj безымя́нный. **namely** adv (а) и́менно; то есть.

nanny n ня́ня.

nap n коро́ткий сон; vi вздремну́ть pf.

nape n загри́вок.

napkin n салфе́тка.

nappy n пелёнка.

narcissus n нарци́сс.

narcotic adj наркоти́ческий; n нарко́тик.

narrate vt расска́зывать impf, рассказа́ть pf. **narration** n расска́з. **narrative** n расска́з; adj повествова́тельный. **narrator** n расска́зчик.

narrow adj у́зкий; vt & i су́живать(ся) impf, су́зить(ся) pf. **narrowly** adv (hardly) чуть, чуть; **he** ~ **escaped drowning** он чуть не утону́л. **narrow-minded** adj ограни́ченный. **narrowness** n у́зость.

nasal adj носово́й; (voice) гнуса́вый.

nasturtium n насту́рция.

nasty adj неприя́тный, проти́вный; (person) злой.

nation n (people) наро́д; (country) страна́. **national** adj национа́льный, наро́дный; (of the state) госуда́рственный; n по́дданный sb. **nationalism** n национали́зм. **nationalist** n национали́ст, ~ка. **nationalistic** adj националисти́ческий. **nationality** n национа́льность; (citizenship) гражда́нство, по́дданство. **nationalization** n национализа́ция. **nationalize** vt национализи́ровать impf & pf.

native n (~ of) уроже́нец, -нка (+gen); (aborigine) тузе́мец, -мка; adj (innate) приро́дный; (of one's birth) родно́й; (indigenous) тузе́мный; ~ **land** ро́дина; ~ **language** родно́й язы́к; ~ **speaker** носи́тель m языка́.

nativity n Рождество́ (Христо́во).

natter vi болта́ть impf.

natural adj есте́ственный, приро́дный; ~ **resources** приро́дные бога́тства neut pl; ~ **selection** есте́ственный отбо́р; n (mus) бека́р. **naturalism** n натурали́зм. **naturalist** n натурали́ст. **naturalistic** adj натуралисти́ческий. **naturalization** n натурализа́ция. **naturalize** vt натурализи́ровать impf & pf. **naturally** adv есте́ственно. **nature** n приро́да; (character) хара́ктер; **by** ~ по приро́де.

naught n: **come to** ~ своди́ться impf, свести́сь pf к нулю́.

naughty adj шаловли́вый.

nausea n тошнота́. **nauseate** vt тошни́ть impf impers от +gen. **nauseating** adj тошнотво́рный. **nauseous** adj: **I feel** ~ меня́ тошни́т.

nautical adj морско́й.

naval adj (вое́нно-)морско́й.

nave n неф.

navel n пупо́к.

navigable adj судохо́дный. **navigate** vt (ship) вести́ impf; (sea) пла́вать impf по+dat. **navigation** n навига́ция. **navigator** n шту́рман.

navvy n землеко́п.

navy n вое́нно-морско́й флот; ~ **blue** тёмно-си́ний.

Nazi n наци́ст, ~ка; adj наци́стский. **Nazism** n наци́зм.

NB *abbr* нотабе́не.

near *adv* бли́зко; ~ **at hand** под руко́й; ~ **by** ря́дом; *prep* во́зле+*gen*, о́коло+*gen*, у+*gen*; *adj* бли́зкий; ~**sighted** близору́кий; *vt* & *i* приближа́ться *impf*, прибли́зиться *pf* к +*dat*. **nearly** *adv* почти́.

neat *adj* (*tidy*) опря́тный, аккура́тный; (*clear*) чёткий; (*undiluted*) неразба́вленный.

nebulous *adj* нея́сный.

necessarily *adv* обяза́тельно. **necessary** *adj* необходи́мый; (*inevitable*) неизбе́жный. **necessitate** *vt* де́лать *impf*, с~ *pf* необходи́мым. **necessity** *n* необходи́мость; неизбе́жность; (*object*) предме́т пе́рвой необходи́мости.

neck *n* ше́я; (*of garment*) вы́рез; ~ **and** ~ голова́ в го́лову. **necklace** *n* ожере́лье. **neckline** *n* вы́рез.

nectar *n* некта́р.

née adj урождённая.

need *n* нужда́; *vt* нужда́ться *impf* в+*prep*; **I** (*etc.*) ~ мне (*dat*) ну́жен (-жна́, -жно, -жны́) +*nom*; **I** ~ **five roubles** мне нужно пять рубле́й.

needle *n* игла́, иго́лка; (*knitting*) спи́ца; (*pointer*) стре́лка; *vt* придира́ться *impf*, придра́ться *pf* к+*dat*.

needless *adj* нену́жный; ~ **to say** разуме́ется. **needy** *adj* нужда́ющийся.

negation *n* отрица́ние. **negative** *adj* отрица́тельный; *n* отрица́ние; (*phot*) негати́в.

neglect *vt* пренебрега́ть *impf*, пренебре́чь *pf* +*instr*; не забо́титься *impf* о+*prep*; *n* пренебреже́ние; (*condition*) забро́шенность. **neglectful** *adj* небре́жный, невнима́тельный (*of* к+*dat*). **negligence** *n* небре́жность. **negligent** *adj* небре́жный. **negligible** *adj* незначи́тельный.

negotiate *vi* вести́ *impf* перегово́ры; *vt* (*arrange*) заключа́ть *impf*, заключи́ть *pf*; (*overcome*) преодолева́ть *impf*, преодоле́ть *pf*. **negotiation** *n* (*discussion*) перегово́ры *m pl*.

Negro *n* негр; *adj* негритя́нский.

neigh *n* рж́ание; *vi* ржать *impf*.

neighbour *n* сосе́д, ~ка. **neighbourhood** *n* ме́стность; **in the** ~ **of**

о́коло+*gen*. **neighbouring** *adj* сосе́дний. **neighbourly** *adj* доброcосе́дский.

neither *adv* та́кже не, то́же не; *pron* ни тот, ни друго́й; ~ ... **nor** ни... ни.

neon *n* нео́н; *attrib* нео́новый.

nephew *n* племя́нник.

nepotism *n* кумовство́.

nerve *n* нерв; (*courage*) сме́лость; (*impudence*) на́глость; **get on the** ~**s of** де́йствовать *impf*, по~ *pf* +*dat* на не́рвы. **nervous** *adj* не́рвный; ~ **breakdown** не́рвное расстро́йство. **nervy** *adj* нерво́зный.

nest *n* гнездо́; ~ **egg** сбереже́ния *neut pl*; *vi* гнезди́ться *impf*. **nestle** *vi* льнуть *impf*, при~ *pf*.

net[1] *n* сеть, се́тка; *vt* (*catch*) лови́ть *impf*, пойма́ть *pf* сетя́ми.

net[2], **nett** *adj* чи́стый; *vt* получа́ть *impf*, получи́ть *pf* ... чи́стого дохо́да.

Netherlands *n* Нидерла́нды (-ов) *pl*.

nettle *n* крапи́ва.

network *n* сеть.

neurologist *n* невро́лог. **neurology** *n* невроло́гия. **neurosis** *n* невро́з. **neurotic** *adj* невроти́ческий.

neuter *adj* сре́дний, сре́днего ро́да; *n* сре́дний род; *vt* кастри́ровать *impf* & *pf*. **neutral** *adj* нейтра́льный; *n* (*gear*) нейтра́льная ско́рость. **neutrality** *n* нейтралите́т. **neutralize** *vt* нейтрализова́ть *impf* & *pf*. **neutron** *n* нейтро́н.

never *adv* никогда́; ~ **again** никогда́ бо́льше; ~ **mind** ничего́!; всё равно́!; ~ **once** ни ра́зу. **nevertheless** *conj* всё же тем не ме́нее.

new *adj* но́вый; (*moon, potatoes*) молодо́й. **new-born** *adj* новорождённый. **newcomer** *n* прише́лец. **newfangled** *adj* новомо́дный. **newly** *adv* то́лько что, неда́вно. **newness** *n* новизна́.

news *n* но́вость, -ти *pl*, изве́стие, -ия *pl*. **newsagent** *n* продаве́ц газе́т. **newsletter** *n* информацио́нный бюллете́нь *m*. **newspaper** *n* газе́та. **newsprint** *n* газе́тная бума́га. **newsreel** *n* кинохро́ника.

newt *n* трито́н.

New Zealand *n* Но́вая Зела́ндия; *adj* новозела́ндский.

next *adj* сле́дующий, бу́дущий; *adv*

(~ *time*) в сле́дующий раз; (*then*) пото́м, зате́м; ~ **door** (*house*) в сосе́днем до́ме; (*flat*) в сосе́дней кварти́ре; ~ **of kin** ближа́йший ро́дственник; ~ **to** ря́дом с+*instr*; (*fig*) почти́. **next-door** *adj* сосе́дний; ~ **neighbour** ближа́йший сосе́д.

nib *n* перо́.

nibble *vt & i* грызть *impf*; *vt* обгрыза́ть *impf*, обгры́зть *pf*; (*grass*) щипа́ть *impf*; (*fish*) клева́ть *impf*.

nice *adj* (*pleasant*) прия́тный, хоро́ший; (*person*) ми́лый. **nicety** *n* то́нкость.

niche *n* ни́ша; (*fig*) своё ме́сто.

nick *n* (*scratch*) цара́пина; (*notch*) зару́бка; **in the ~ of time** в са́мый после́дний моме́нт; *vt* (*scratch*) цара́пать *impf*, о~ *pf*; (*steal*) сти́брить *pf*.

nickel *n* ни́кель *m*.

nickname *n* про́звище; *vt* прозыва́ть *impf*, прозва́ть *pf*.

nicotine *n* никоти́н.

niece *n* племя́нница.

niggardly *adj* скупо́й.

niggling *adj* ме́лочный.

night *n* ночь; (*evening*) ве́чер; **at ~** но́чью; **last ~** вчера́ ве́чером; *attrib* ночно́й; ~-**club** ночно́й клуб. **night-cap** *n* ночно́й колпа́к; (*drink*) стака́нчик спиртно́го на́ ночь. **night-dress** *n* ночна́я руба́шка. **nightfall** *n* наступле́ние но́чи. **nightingale** *n* солове́й. **nightly** *adj* ежено́щный; *adv* ежено́щно. **nightmare** *n* кошма́р. **nightmarish** *adj* кошма́рный.

nil *n* нуль *m*.

nimble *adj* прово́рный.

nine *adj & n* де́вять; (*number 9*) девя́тка. **nineteen** *adj & n* девятна́дцать. **nineteenth** *adj & n* девятна́дцатый. **ninetieth** *adj & n* девяно́стый. **ninety** *adj & n* девяно́сто; *pl* (*decade*) девяно́стые го́ды (-до́в) *m pl*. **ninth** *adj & n* девя́тый.

nip *vt* (*pinch*) щипа́ть *impf*, щипну́ть *pf*; (*bite*) куса́ть *impf*, укуси́ть *pf*; ~ **in the bud** пресека́ть *impf*, пресе́чь *pf* в заро́дыше; *n* щипо́к; уку́с; **there's a ~ in the air** во́здух па́хнет моро́зцем.

nipple *n* сосо́к.

nirvana *n* нирва́на.

nit *n* гни́да.

nitrate *n* нитра́т. **nitrogen** *n* азо́т.

no *adj* (*not any*) никако́й, не оди́н; (*not a* (*fool etc.*)) (совсе́м) не; *adv* нет; (*нисколько*) не+*comp*; *n* отрица́ние, отка́з; (*in vote*) го́лос „про́тив"; ~ **doubt** коне́чно, несомне́нно; ~ **longer** уже́ не, бо́льше не; **no one** никто́; ~ **wonder** не удиви́тельно.

Noah's ark *n* Но́ев ковче́г.

nobility *n* (*class*) дворя́нство; (*quality*) благоро́дство. **noble** *adj* дворя́нский; благоро́дный. **nobleman** *n* дворяни́н.

nobody *pron* никто́; *n* ничто́жество.

nocturnal *adj* ночно́й.

nod *vi* кива́ть *impf*, кивну́ть *pf* голово́й; *n* киво́к.

nodule *n* узело́к.

noise *n* шум. **noiseless** *adj* бесшу́мный. **noisy** *adj* шу́мный.

nomad *n* коче́вник. **nomadic** *adj* кочево́й.

nomenclature *n* номенклату́ра. **nominal** *adj* номина́льный. **nominate** *vt* (*propose*) выдвига́ть *impf*, вы́двинуть *pf*; (*appoint*) назнача́ть *impf*, назна́чить *pf*. **nomination** *n* выдвиже́ние; назначе́ние. **nominative** *adj* (*n*) имени́тельный (паде́ж). **nominee** *n* кандида́т.

non-alcoholic *adj* безалкого́льный. **non-aligned** *adj* неприсоедини́вшийся.

nonchalance *n* беззабо́тность. **nonchalant** *n* беззабо́тный.

non-commissioned *adj*: ~ **officer** у́нтер-офице́р. **non-committal** *adj* укло́нчивый.

non-conformist *n* нонконформи́ст; *adj* нонконформи́стский.

nondescript *adj* неопределённый.

none *pron* (*no one*) никто́; (*nothing*) ничто́; (*not one*) не оди́н; *adv* ниско́лько не; ~ **the less** тем не ме́нее.

nonentity *n* ничто́жество.

non-existent *adj* несуществу́ющий. **non-fiction** *n* документа́льный. **non-intervention** *n* невмеша́тельство. **non-party** *adj* беспарти́йный. **non-payment** *n* неплатёж.

nonplus *vt* ста́вить *impf*, по~ *pf* в тупи́к.

non-productive *adj* непроизводи́тельный. **non-resident** *adj* не про-

живающий (где-нибудь).
nonsense n ерунда́. **nonsensical** adj бессмы́сленный.
non-smoker n (person) некуря́щий sb; (compartment) купе́ neut indecl, для некуря́щих. **non-stop** adj безостано́вочный; (flight) беспоса́дочный; adv без остано́вок; без поса́док. **non-violent** adj ненаси́льственный.
noodles n pl лапша́.
nook n уголо́к.
noon n по́лдень m.
no one see **no**
noose n пе́тля.
nor conj и не; то́же; **neither ... ~** ни... ни.
norm n но́рма. **normal** adj норма́льный. **normality** n норма́льность. **normalize** vt нормализова́ть impf & pf.
north n се́вер; (naut) норд; adj се́верный; adv к се́веру, на се́вер; **~-east** се́веро-восто́к; **~-easterly, -eastern** се́веро-восто́чный; **~-west** се́веро-за́пад; **~-westerly, -western** се́веро-за́падный. **northerly** adj се́верный. **northern** adj се́верный. **northerner** n северя́нин, -я́нка. **northward(s)** adv на се́вер, к се́веру.
Norway n Норве́гия. **Norwegian** adj норве́жский; n норве́жец, -жка.
nose n нос; vi: **~ about, out** разню́хивать impf, разню́хать pf. **nosebleed** n кровотече́ние и́з носу. **nosedive** n пике́ neut indecl.
nostalgia n ностальги́я. **nostalgic** adj ностальги́ческий.
nostril n ноздря́.
not adv не; нет; ни; **~ at all** ниско́лько, ничу́ть; (reply to thanks) не сто́ит (благода́рности); **~ once** ни ра́зу; **~ that** не то, что́бы; **~ too** дово́льно +neg; **~ to say** что́бы не сказа́ть; **~ to speak of** не говоря́ уже́ о+prep.
notable adj заме́тный; (remarkable) замеча́тельный. **notably** adv (especially) осо́бенно; (perceptibly) заме́тно.
notary (public) n нота́риус.
notation n нота́ция; (mus) но́тное письмо́.
notch n зару́бка; vt: **~ up** выи́гры-

вать impf, вы́играть pf.
note n (record) заме́тка, за́пись; (annotation) примеча́ние; (letter) запи́ска; (banknote) банкно́т; (mus) но́та; (tone) тон; (attention) внима́ние; vt отмеча́ть impf, отме́тить pf; **~ down** запи́сывать impf, записа́ть pf. **notebook** n записна́я кни́жка. **noted** adj знамени́тый; изве́стный (for +instr). **notepaper** n почто́вая бума́га. **noteworthy** adj досто́йный внима́ния.
nothing n ничто́, ничего́; **~ but** ничего́ кро́ме+gen, то́лько; **~ of the kind** ничего́ подо́бного; **come to ~** конча́ться impf, ко́нчиться pf ниче́м; **for ~** (free) да́ром; (in vain) зря, напра́сно; **have ~ to do with** не име́ть impf никако́го отноше́ния к+dat; **there is (was) ~ for it (but) to** ничего́ друго́го не остаётся (оста́валось) (как); **to say ~ of** не говоря́ уже́ о+prep.
notice n (sign) объявле́ние; (warning) предупрежде́ние; (attention) внима́ние; (review) о́тзыв; **give (in) one's ~** подава́ть impf, пода́ть pf заявле́ние об ухо́де с рабо́ты; **give s.o. ~** предупрежда́ть impf, предупреди́ть pf об увольне́нии; **take ~ of** обраща́ть impf, обрати́ть pf внима́ния на+acc; **~-board** доска́ для объявле́ний; vt замеча́ть impf, заме́тить pf. **noticeable** adj заме́тный. **notification** n извеще́ние. **notify** vt извеща́ть impf, извести́ть pf (of о+prep).
notion n поня́тие.
notoriety n дурна́я сла́ва. **notorious** adj пресловутый.
notwithstanding prep несмотря́ на+acc; adv тем не ме́нее.
nought n (nothing) see **naught**; (zero) нуль m; (figure 0) ноль m.
noun n (им́я neut) существи́тельное sb.
nourish vt пита́ть impf, на~ pf. **nourishing** adj пита́тельный. **nourishment** n пита́ние.
novel adj но́вый; (unusual) необыкнове́нный; n рома́н. **novelist** n романи́ст. **novelty** n (newness) новизна́; (new thing) нови́нка.
November n ноя́брь m; adj ноя́брьский.

novice n (*eccl*) послушник, -ица; (*beginner*) новичо́к.

now adv тепе́рь, сейча́с; (*immediately*) то́тчас же; (*next*) тогда́; *conj*: ~ (*that*) раз, когда́; (*every*) ~ and **again, then** вре́мя от вре́мени; **by** ~ уже́; **from** ~ **on** впредь. **nowadays** adv в на́ше вре́мя.

nowhere adv (*place*) нигде́; (*direction*) никуда́; *pron*: **I have** ~ **to go** мне не́куда пойти́.

noxious adj вре́дный.

nozzle n сопло́.

nuance n нюа́нс.

nuclear adj я́дерный. **nucleus** n ядро́.

nude adj обнажённый, наго́й; n обнажённая фигу́ра.

nudge vt подта́лкивать *impf*, подтолкну́ть *pf* ло́ктем; n толчо́к ло́ктем.

nudity n нагота́.

nugget n саморо́док.

nuisance n доса́да; (*person*) раздража́ющий челове́к.

null adj: ~ **and void** недействи́тельный. **nullify** vt аннули́ровать *impf* & *pf* **nullity** n недействи́тельность.

numb adj онеме́лый; (*from cold*) окочене́лый; **go** ~ онеме́ть *pf*; (*from cold*) окочене́ть *pf*.

number n (*total*) коли́чество; (*total*; *symbol*; *math*; *gram*) число́; (*identifying numeral*; *item*) но́мер; **~plate** номерна́я доще́чка; vt (*assign* ~ *to*) нумерова́ть *impf*, за~, про~ *pf*; (*contain*) насчи́тывать *impf*: ~ **among** причи́слить *impf*, причи́слить *pf* к+*dat*; **his days are** ~ed его́ дни сочтены́.

numeral n ци́фра; (*gram*) (и́мя *neut*) числи́тельное *sb*. **numerical** adj числово́й. **numerous** adj многочи́сленный; (*many*) мно́го +*gen pl*.

nun n мона́хиня. **nunnery** n (*же́нский*) монасты́рь *m*.

nuptial adj сва́дебный; n: *pl* сва́дьба.

nurse n (*child's*) ня́ня; (*medical*) сестра́; vt (*suckle*) корми́ть *impf*, на~, по~ *pf*; (*tend sick*) уха́живать *impf* за+*instr*; **nursing home** санато́рий; дом престаре́лых. **nursery** n (*room*) де́тская *sb*; (*day* ~) я́сли (-лей) *pl*; (*for plants*) пито́мник; ~ **rhyme** де́тские прибау́тки *f pl*; ~ **school** де́тский сад.

nut n оре́х; (*for bolt etc.*) га́йка. **nutshell** n: **in a** ~ в двух слова́х.

nutmeg n муска́тный оре́х.

nutrient n пита́тельное вещество́. **nutrition** n пита́ние. **nutritious** adj пита́тельный.

nylon n нейло́н; *pl* нейло́новые чулки́ (-ло́к) *pl*.

nymph n ни́мфа.

O

O int o!; ах!

oaf n неуклю́жий челове́к.

oak n дуб; *attrib* дубо́вый.

oar n весло́. **oarsman** n гребе́ц.

oasis n оа́зис.

oath n прися́га; (*expletive*) руга́тельство.

oatmeal n овся́нка. **oats** n *pl* овёс (овса́) *collect*.

obdurate adj упря́мый.

obedience n послуша́ние. **obedient** adj послу́шный.

obese adj ту́чный. **obesity** n ту́чность.

obey vt слу́шаться *impf*, по~ *pf* +*gen*; (*law*, *order*) подчиня́ться *impf*, подчини́ться *pf* +*dat*.

obituary n некроло́г.

object n (*thing*) предме́т; (*aim*) цель; (*gram*) дополне́ние; vi возража́ть *impf*, возрази́ть *pf* (**to** про́тив+*gen*); **I don't** ~ я не про́тив. **objection** n возраже́ние; **I have no** ~ я не возража́ю. **objectionable** adj неприя́тный. **objective** adj объекти́вный; n цель. **objectivity** n объекти́вность. **objector** n возража́ющий *sb*.

obligation n обяза́тельство; **I am under an** ~ я обя́зан(а). **obligatory** adj обяза́тельный. **oblige** vt обя́зывать *impf*, обяза́ть *pf*; **be** ~d **to** (*grateful*) быть обя́занным+*dat*. **obliging** adj услу́жливый.

oblique adj косо́й; (*fig*; *gram*) ко́свенный.

obliterate vt (*efface*) стира́ть *impf*, стере́ть *pf*; (*destroy*) уничтожа́ть *impf*, уничто́жить *pf*. **obliteration** n стира́ние; уничтоже́ние.

oblivion n забве́ние. **oblivious** adj (*forgetful*) забы́вчивый; **to be** ~ **of** не замеча́ть *impf* +*gen*.

oblong adj продолгова́тый.

obnoxious *adj* проти́вный.

oboe *n* гобо́й.

obscene *adj* непристо́йный. **obscenity** *n* непристо́йность.

obscure *adj* (*unclear*) нея́сный; (*little known*) малоизве́стный; *vt* затемня́ть *impf*, затемни́ть *pf*; де́лать *impf*, с~ *pf* нея́сным. **obscurity** *n* нея́сность; неизве́стность.

obsequious *adj* подобостра́стный.

observance *n* соблюде́ние; (*rite*) обря́д. **observant** *adj* наблюда́тельный. **observation** *n* наблюде́ние; (*remark*) замеча́ние. **observatory** *n* обсервато́рия. **observe** *vt* (*law etc.*) соблюда́ть *impf*, соблюсти́ *pf*; (*watch*) наблюда́ть *impf*; замеча́ть *impf*, заме́тить *pf*. **observer** *n* наблюда́тель *m*.

obsess *vt* пресле́довать *impf*; **obsessed by** одержи́мый +*instr*. **obsession** *n* одержи́мость; (*idea*) навя́зчивая иде́я. **obsessive** *adj* навя́зчивый.

obsolete *adj* устаре́лый, вы́шедший из употребле́ния.

obstacle *n* препя́тствие.

obstetrician *n* акуше́р. **obstetrics** *n* акуше́рство.

obstinacy *n* упря́мство. **obstinate** *adj* упря́мый.

obstreperous *adj* бу́йный.

obstruct *vt* загражда́ть *impf*, загради́ть *pf*; (*hinder*) препя́тствовать *impf*, вос~ *pf* +*dat*. **obstruction** *n* загражде́ние; (*obstacle*) препя́тствие. **obstructive** *adj* загражда́ющий; препя́тствующий.

obtain *vt* получа́ть *impf*, получи́ть *pf*; доста́вать *impf*, доста́ть *pf*.

obtrusive *adj* навя́зчивый; (*thing*) броса́ющийся в глаза́.

obtuse *adj* тупо́й.

obviate *vt* устраня́ть *impf*, устрани́ть *pf*.

obvious *adj* очеви́дный.

occasion *n* слу́чай; (*cause*) по́вод; (*occurrence*) собы́тие; *vt* причиня́ть *impf*, причини́ть *pf*. **occasional** *adj* ре́дкий. **occasionally** *adv* иногда́, вре́мя от вре́мени.

occult *adj* окку́льтный; *n*: **the ~** окку́льт.

occupancy *n* заня́тие. **occupant** *n* жи́тель *m*, ~ница. **occupation** *n* заня́тие; (*military ~*) оккупа́ция; (*profession*) профе́ссия. **occupational** *adj* профессиона́льный; **~ therapy** трудотерапи́я. **occupy** *vt* занима́ть *impf*, заня́ть *pf*; (*mil*) оккупи́ровать *impf & pf*.

occur *vi* (*happen*) случа́ться *impf*, случи́ться *pf*; (*be found*) встреча́ться *impf*; **~ to** приходи́ть *impf*, прийти́ *pf* в го́лову+*dat*. **occurrence** *n* слу́чай, происше́ствие.

ocean *n* океа́н. **oceanic** *adj* океа́нский.

o'clock *adv*: (**at**) **six ~** (в) шесть часо́в.

octagonal *adj* восьмиуго́льный.

octave *n* (*mus*) окта́ва.

October *n* октя́брь *m*; *adj* октя́брьский.

octopus *n* осьмино́г.

odd *adj* (*strange*) стра́нный; (*not in a set*) разро́зненный; (*number*) нечётный; (*not paired*) непа́рный; (*casual*) случа́йный; **five hundred ~** пятьсо́т с ли́шним; **~ job** случа́йная рабо́та. **oddity** *n* стра́нность; (*person*) чуда́к, -а́чка. **oddly** *adv* стра́нно; **~ enough** как э́то ни стра́нно. **oddment** *n* оста́ток. **odds** *n pl* ша́нсы *m pl*; **be at ~ with** (*person*) не ла́дить с+*instr*; (*things*) не соотве́тствовать *impf* +*dat*; **long** (**short**) **~** нера́вные (почти́ ра́вные) ша́нсы *m pl*; **the ~ are that** вероя́тнее всего́, что; **~ and ends** обры́вки *m pl*.

ode *n* о́да.

odious *adj* ненави́стный.

odour *n* за́пах.

oesophagus *n* пищево́д.

of *prep expressing* **1**. *origin*: из+*gen*: **he comes ~ a working-class family** он из рабо́чей семьи́; **2**. *cause*: от +*gen*: **he died ~ hunger** он у́мер от го́лода; **3**. *authorship*: gen: **the works ~ Pushkin** сочине́ния Пу́шкина; **4**. *material*: из+*gen*: **made ~ wood** сде́ланный из де́рева; **5**. *reference*: о+*prep*: **he talked ~ Lenin** он говори́л о Ле́нине; **6**. *partition*: gen (*often in* -у́(-ю)): **a glass ~ milk, tea** стака́н молока́, ча́ю; из+*gen*: **one ~ them** оди́н из них; **7**. *belonging*: gen: **the capital ~ England** столи́ца А́нглии.

off adv: in phrasal vv, see v, e.g. **clear ~** убира́ться; prep (from surface of) c+gen; (away from) от+gen; **~ and on** вре́мя от вре́мени; **~-white** не совсе́м бе́лый.

offal n требуха́.

offence n (insult) оби́да; (against law) просту́пок, преступле́ние; **take ~** обижа́ться impf, оби́деться pf (at на+acc). **offend** vt обижа́ть impf, оби́деть pf; **~ against** наруша́ть impf, нару́шить pf. **offender** n правонаруши́тель m, ~ница. **offensive** adj (attacking) наступа́тельный; (insulting) оскорби́тельный; (repulsive) проти́вный; n наступле́ние.

offer vt предлага́ть impf, предложи́ть pf; n предложе́ние; **on ~** в прода́же.

offhand adj бесцеремо́нный.

office n (position) до́лжность; (place, room etc.) бюро́ neut indecl, конто́ра, канцеля́рия. **officer** n до́лжностно́е лицо́; (mil) офице́р. **official** adj служе́бный; (authorized) официа́льный; n до́лжностно́е лицо́. **officiate** vi (eccl) соверша́ть impf, соверши́ть pf богослуже́ние. **officious** adj (intrusive) навя́зчивый.

offing n: **be in the ~** предстоя́ть impf.

off-licence n ви́нный магази́н. **off-load** vt разгружа́ть impf, разгрузи́ть pf. **off-putting** adj отта́лкивающий. **offset** vt возмеща́ть impf, возмести́ть pf. **offshoot** n о́тпрыск. **offshore** adj прибре́жный. **offside** adv вне игры́. **offspring** n пото́мок; (collect) пото́мки m pl.

often adv ча́сто.

ogle vt & i смотре́ть impf с вожделе́нием с+acc.

ogre n велика́н-людое́д.

oh int o!; ах!

ohm n ом.

oil n ма́сло; (petroleum) нефть; (paint) ма́сло, ма́сляные кра́ски f pl; vt сма́зывать impf, сма́зать pf; **~-painting** карти́на, напи́санная ма́сляными кра́сками; **~ rig** нефтяна́я вы́шка; **~-tanker** та́нкер; **~-well** нефтяна́я сква́жина. **oilfield** n месторожде́ние не́фти. **oilskin** n клеёнка; pl непромока́емый костю́м.

oily adj масляни́стый.

ointment n мазь.

OK adv & adj хорошо́, норма́льно; int ла́дно!; vt одобря́ть impf, одо́брить pf.

old adj ста́рый; (ancient; of long standing) стари́нный; (former) бы́вший; **how ~ are you?** ско́лько тебе́, вам, (dat) лет?; **~ age** ста́рость; **~-age pension** пе́нсия по ста́рости; **old-fashioned** старомо́дный; **~ maid** ста́рая де́ва; **~ man** (also father, husband) стари́к; **~-time** стари́нный; **~ woman** стару́ха; (coll) стару́шка.

olive n (fruit) оли́вка; (colour) оли́вковый цвет; adj оли́вковый; **~ oil** оли́вковое ма́сло.

Olympic adj олимпи́йский; **~ games** Олимпи́йские и́гры f pl.

omelette n омле́т.

omen n предзнаменова́ние. **ominous** adj злове́щий.

omission n про́пуск; (neglect) упуще́ние. **omit** vt (leave out) пропуска́ть impf, пропусти́ть pf; (neglect) упуска́ть impf, упусти́ть pf.

omnibus n (bus) авто́бус; (collection) колле́кция.

omnipotence n всемогу́щество. **omnipotent** adj всемогу́щий. **omnipresent** adj вездесу́щий. **omniscient** adj всеве́дущий.

on prep (position) на+prep; (direction) на+acc; (time) в+acc; **~ the next day** на сле́дующий день; **~ Mondays** (repeated action) по понеде́льникам (dat pl); **~ the first of June** пе́рвого ию́ня (gen); (concerning) по+prep, о+prep, на+acc; adv да́льше, вперёд; in phrasal vv, see vv, e.g. **move ~** идти́ да́льше; **and so ~** и так да́лее, и т.д.; **be ~** (film etc.) идти́ impf; **further ~** да́льше; **later ~** по́зже.

oncoming adj: **~ traffic** встре́чное движе́ние.

one adj оди́н (одна́, -но́); (only, sin-

gle) еди́нственный; *n* оди́н; *pron: not usu translated; v translated in 2nd pers sg or by impers construction:* ~ **never knows** никогда́ не зна́ешь; **where can** ~ **buy this book?** где мо́жно купи́ть э́ту кни́гу?; ~ **after another** оди́н за други́м; ~ **and all** все до одного́; все как оди́н; ~ **and only** еди́нственный; ~ **and the same** оди́н и тот же; ~ **another** друг дру́га *(dat* -гу, *etc.)*; ~ **fine day** в оди́н прекра́сный день; ~ **o'clock** час; ~-**parent family** семья́ с одни́м роди́телем; ~-**sided, -track, -way** односторо́нний; ~-**time** бы́вший; ~-**way street** у́лица односторо́ннего движе́ния.

onerous *adj* тя́гостный.

oneself *pron* себя́; -ся *(suffixed to vt)*.

onion *n (plant; pl collect)* лук; *(single* ~*)* лу́ковица.

onlooker *n* наблюда́тель *m*.

only *adj* еди́нственный; *adv* то́лько; **if** ~ е́сли бы то́лько; ~ **just** то́лько что; *conj* но.

onset *n* нача́ло.

onslaught *n* на́тиск.

onus *n* отве́тственность.

onward(s) *adv* вперёд.

ooze *vt & i* сочи́ться *impf*.

opal *n* опа́л.

opaque *adj* непрозра́чный.

open *adj* откры́тый; *(frank)* открове́нный; **in the** ~ **air** на откры́том во́здухе; ~-**minded** *adj* непредупреждённый; *vt & i* открыва́ть(ся) *impf*, откры́ть(ся) *pf*; *vi (begin)* начина́ться *impf*, нача́ться *pf*; *(flowers)* распуска́ться *impf*, распусти́ться *pf*. **opening** *n* откры́тие; *(aperture)* отве́рстие; *(beginning)* нача́ло; *adj* нача́льный, пе́рвый; *(introductory)* вступи́тельный.

opera *n* о́пера; *attrib* о́перный; ~-**house** о́перный теа́тр.

operatic *adj* о́перный.

operate *vi* де́йствовать *impf* **(upon** на+*acc)*; *(med)* опери́ровать *impf & pf* **(on** +*acc)*; *vt* управля́ть *impf* +*instr*.

operatic *adj* о́перный.

operating-theatre *n* операцио́нная *sb*. **operation** *n* де́йствие; *(med; mil)* опера́ция. **operational** *adj (in use)* де́йствующий; *(mil)* операти́вный. **operative** *adj* де́йствующий. **oper-**

ator *n* опера́тор; *(telephone* ~*)* телефони́ст, ~ка.

operetta *n* опере́тта.

ophthalmic *adj* глазно́й.

opinion *n* мне́ние; **in my** ~ по-мо́ему; ~ **poll** опро́с обще́ственного мне́ния. **opinionated** *adj* догмати́чный.

opium *n* о́пиум.

opponent *n* проти́вник.

opportune *adj* своевре́менный. **opportunism** *n* оппортуни́зм. **opportunist** *n* оппортуни́ст. **opportunistic** *n* оппортунисти́ческий. **opportunity** *n* слу́чай, возмо́жность.

oppose *vt (resist)* сопротивля́ться *impf*, вос~ *pf* +*dat*; *(speak etc. against)* выступа́ть *impf*, вы́ступить *pf* про́тив+*gen*. **opposed** *adj* про́тив **(to** +*gen)*; **as** ~ **to** в противополо́жность+*dat*. **opposing** *adj* проти́вный; *(opposite)* противополо́жный. **opposite** *adj* противополо́жный; *(reverse)* обра́тный; *n* противополо́жность; **just the** ~ как раз наоборо́т; *adv* напро́тив; *prep (на)*про́тив+*gen*. **opposition** *n (resistance)* сопротивле́ние; *(polit)* оппози́ция.

oppress *vt* угнета́ть *impf*. **oppression** *n* угнете́ние. **oppressive** *adj* угнета́ющий. **oppressor** *n* угнета́тель *m*.

opt *vi* выбира́ть *impf*, вы́брать *pf* **(for** +*acc)*; ~ **out** не принима́ть *impf* уча́стия **(of** в+*prep)*.

optic *adj* зри́тельный. **optical** *adj* опти́ческий. **optician** *n* о́птик. **optics** *n* о́птика.

optimism *n* оптими́зм. **optimist** *n* оптими́ст. **optimistic** *adj* оптимисти́ческий. **optimum** *adj* оптима́льный.

option *n* вы́бор. **optional** *adj* необяза́тельный.

opulence *n* бога́тство. **opulent** *adj* бога́тый.

opus *n* о́пус.

or *conj* и́ли; ~ **else** ина́че; ~ **so** прибли́зительно.

oracle *n* ора́кул.

oral *adj* у́стный; *n* у́стный экза́мен.

orange *n (fruit)* апельси́н; *(colour)* ора́нжевый цвет; *attrib* апельси́новый; *adj* ора́нжевый.

oration n речь. **orator** n орáтор.

oratorio n оратóрия.

oratory n (*speech*) красноréчие.

orbit n орбúта; vt вращáться impf по орбúте вокрýг+gen. **orbital** adj орбитáльный.

orchard n фрукто́вый сад.

orchestra n оркéстр. **orchestral** adj оркестро́вый. **orchestrate** vt оркестровáть impf & pf. **orchestration** n оркестро́вка.

orchid n орхидéя.

ordain vt предпúсывать impf, предписáть pf; (eccl) посвящáть impf, посвятúть pf (в духóвный сан).

ordeal n тяжёлое испытáние.

order n поря́док; (command) прикáз; (for goods) закáз; (insignia, medal, fraternity) óрден; (archit) óрдер; pl (holy ~) духо́вный сан; **in ~ to** (для того́) что́бы +inf; (command) прикáзывать impf, приказáть pf +dat; (goods etc.) закáзывать impf, заказáть pf. **orderly** adj аккурáтный; (quiet) тúхий; n (med) санитáр; (mil) ординáрец.

ordinance n декрéт.

ordinary adj обыкновéнный, обы́чный.

ordination n посвящéние.

ore n рудá.

organ n óрган; (mus) оргáн. **organic** adj органúческий. **organism** n органúзм. **organist** n органúст. **organization** n организáция. **organize** vt организо́вывать impf (pres not used), организовáть (in pres) & pf; устрáивать impf, устрóить pf. **organizer** n организáтор.

orgy n óргия.

Orient n Востóк. **oriental** adj востóчный.

orient, orientate vt ориентúровать impf &pf (o.s. -ся). **orientation** n ориентáция.

orifice n отвéрстие.

origin n происхождéние, начáло. **original** adj оригинáльный; (initial) первоначáльный; (genuine) пóдлинный; n оригинáл. **originality** n оригинáльность. **originate** vt порождáть impf, породúть pf; vi брать impf, взять pf начáло (from, in в+prep, от+gen); (arise) возникáть impf, вознúкнуть pf. **originator** n

áвтор, инициáтор.

ornament n украшéние; vt украшáть impf, укрáсить pf. **ornamental** adj декоратúвный.

ornate adj витиевáтый.

ornithologist n орнитóлог. **ornithology** n орнитолóгия.

orphan n сиротá m & f; vt: **be ~ed** сиротéть impf, o~ pf. **orphanage** n сиро́тский дом. **orphaned** adj осиротéлый.

orthodox adj ортодоксáльный; (eccl, O~) правослáвный. **orthodoxy** n ортодóксия; (O~) правослáвие.

orthopaedic adj ортопедúческий.

oscillate vi колебáться impf, по~ pf. **oscillation** n колебáние.

osmosis n óсмос.

ostensible adj мнúмый. **ostensibly** adv я́кобы.

ostentation n выставлéние напокáз. **ostentatious** adj показнóй.

osteopath n остеопáт. **osteopathy** n остеопáтия.

ostracize vt подвергáть impf, подвéргнуть pf остракúзму.

ostrich n стрáус.

other adj другóй, инóй; тот; **every ~** кáждый вторóй; **every ~ day** чéрез день; **on the ~ hand** с другóй стороны́; **on the ~ side** на той сторонé, по ту стóрону; **one or the ~** тот úли инóй; **the ~ day** на дня́х, недáвно; **the ~ way round** наоборóт; **the ~s** остальны́е sb pl. **otherwise** adv & conj инáче, а то.

otter n вы́дра.

ouch int ой!, ай!

ought v aux дóлжен (-жнá) (бы) +inf.

ounce n ýнция.

our, ours poss pron наш; свой. **ourselves** pron (emph) (мы) сáми; (refl) себя́; -ся (suffixed to vt).

oust vt вытесня́ть impf, вы́теснить pf.

out adv **1.** in phrasal vv often rendered by pref вы-; **2.: to be ~** in various senses: **he is ~** (not at home) егó нет дóма; (not in office etc.) он вы́шел; (sport) выходúть impf, вы́йти pf из игры́; (of fashion) вы́йти pf из мóды; (be published) вы́йти pf из печáти; (of candle etc.) потýхнуть pf; (of flower) распустúться pf; (be unconscious) потеря́ть pf созна́ние; **3.**: ~-and-~ отъя́вленный; **4.**: ~ of из+gen, вне+gen; ~ of date устаре́лый, старомо́дный; ~ of doors на откры́том во́здухе; ~ of work безрабо́тный.

outbid vt предлага́ть impf, предложи́ть pf бо́лее высо́кую це́ну, чем+nom. **outboard** adj: ~ motor подвесно́й мото́р m. **outbreak** n (of anger, disease) вспы́шка; (of war) нача́ло. **outbuilding** n надво́рная постро́йка. **outburst** n взрыв. **outcast** n изгна́нник. **outcome** n результа́т. **outcry** n (шу́мные) проте́сты m pl. **outdated** adj устаре́лый. **outdo** vt превосходи́ть impf, превзойти́ pf.

outdoor adj, **outdoors** adv на откры́том во́здухе, на у́лице.

outer adj (external) вне́шний, нару́жный; (far from centre) да́льний. **outermost** adj са́мый да́льний.

outfit n (equipment) снаряже́ние; (set of things) набо́р; (clothes) наря́д. **outgoing** adj уходя́щий; (sociable) общи́тельный. **outgoings** n pl изде́ржки f pl. **outgrow** vt выраста́ть impf, вы́расти pf из+gen. **outhouse** n надво́рная постро́йка.

outing n прогу́лка, экску́рсия.

outlandish adj дико́винный. **outlaw** n лицо́ вне зако́на; банди́т; vt объявля́ть impf, объяви́ть pf вне зако́на. **outlay** n изде́ржки f pl. **outlet** n выходно́е отве́рстие; (fig) вы́ход; (market) ры́нок; (shop) торго́вая то́чка. **outline** n очерта́ние, ко́нтур; (sketch, summary) набро́сок; vt оче́рчивать impf, очерти́ть pf; (plans etc.) набра́сывать impf, наброса́ть pf. **outlive** vt пережи́ть pf. **outlook** n перспекти́вы f pl; (attitude) кругозо́р. **outlying** adj перифери́йный. **outmoded** adj старомо́дно. **outnumber** vt чи́сленно превосходи́ть impf, превзойти́ pf. **out-patient** n амбулато́рный больно́й sb. **outpost** n форпо́ст. **output** n вы́пуск, проду́кция.

outrage n безобра́зие; (indignation) возмуще́ние; vt оскорбля́ть impf, оскорби́ть pf. **outrageous** adj возмути́тельный.

outright adv (entirely) вполне́; (once for all) раз (и) навсегда́; (openly)

откры́то; adj прямо́й. **outset** n нача́ло; at the ~ внача́ле; from the ~ с са́мого нача́ла.

outside n нару́жная сторона́; at the ~ са́мое бо́льшее; from the ~ извне́; on the ~ снару́жи; adj нару́жный, вне́шний; (sport) кра́йний; adv (on the ~) снару́жи; (to the ~) нару́жу; (out of doors) на откры́том во́здухе, на у́лице; prep вне+gen; за преде́лами+gen. **outsider** n посторо́нний sb; (sport) аутса́йдер.

outsize adj бо́льше станда́ртного разме́ра. **outskirts** n pl окра́ина. **outspoken** adj прямо́й. **outstanding** adj (remarkable) выдаю́щийся; (unpaid) неупла́ченный. **outstay** vt: ~ one's welcome заси́живаться impf, засиде́ться pf. **outstretched** adj распростёртый. **outstrip** vt обгоня́ть impf, обогна́ть pf.

outward adj (external) вне́шний, нару́жный. **outwardly** adv вне́шне, на вид. **outwards** adv нару́жу.

outweigh vt переве́шивать impf, переве́сить pf. **outwit** vt перехитри́ть pf.

oval adj ова́льный; n ова́л.

ovary n я́ичник.

ovation n ова́ция.

oven n (industrial) печь; (domestic) духо́вка.

over adv & prep with vv: see vv; prep (above) над+instr; (through; covering) по+dat; (concerning) о+prep; (across) че́рез+acc; (on the other side of) по ту сто́рону+gen; (more than) свы́ше+gen; бо́лее+gen; (with age) за+acc; all ~ (finished) всё ко́нчено; (everywhere) повсю́ду; all ~ the country по всей стране́; ~ again ещё раз; ~ against по сравне́нию с+instr; ~ and above не говоря́ уже́ о+prep; ~ the telephone по телефо́ну; ~ there вон там.

overall n (entirely) вполне́; (once for all) раз (и) навсегда́; adj о́бщий. **overawe** vt внуша́ть impf, внуши́ть pf благогове́йный страх +dat. **overbalance** vi теря́ть impf, по~ pf равнове́сие. **overbearing** adj вла́стный. **overboard** adv (motion) за́ борт; (position) за бо́ртом. **overcast** adj о́блачный. **overcoat** n пальто́ neut indecl. **overcome** vt преодолева́ть impf, преодоле́ть pf;

adj охва́ченный. **overcrowded** *adj* перепо́лненный. **overcrowding** *n* переполне́ние. **overdo** *vt* (*cook*) пережа́ривать *impf*, пережа́рить *pf*; ~ **it, things** (*work too hard*) переутомля́ться *impf*, переутоми́ться *pf*; (*go too far*) перебра́рщивать *impf*, переборщи́ть *pf*.

overdose *n* чрезме́рная до́за. **overdraft** *n* превыше́ние креди́та; (*amount*) долг ба́нку. **overdraw** *vi* превыша́ть *impf*, превы́сить *pf* креди́т (в ба́нке). **overdue** *adj* просро́ченный; **be** ~ (*late*) запа́здывать *impf*, запозда́ть *pf*. **overestimate** *vt* переоце́нивать *impf*, переоцени́ть *pf*. **overflow** *vi* перелива́ться *impf*, перели́ться *pf*; (*river etc.*) разлива́ться *impf*, разли́ться *pf*; *n* (*outlet*) перели́в. **overgrown** *adj* заро́сший. **overhang** *vt* & *i* выступа́ть *impf* над+*instr*; *n* свес, вы́ступ.

overhaul *vt* ремонти́ровать *impf* & *pf*; *n*: ремо́нт. **overhead** *adv* наверху́, над голово́й; *adj* возду́шный, подвесно́й; *n*: *pl* накладны́е расхо́ды *m pl.* **overhear** *vt* неча́янно слы́шать *impf*, у~ *pf*. **overheat** *vt* & *i* перегрева́ть(ся) *impf*, перегре́ть(ся) *pf*. **overjoyed** *adj* в восто́рге (**at** от+*gen*). **overland** *adj* сухопу́тный; *adv* по су́ше. **overlap** *vt* части́чно покрыва́ть *impf*, покры́ть *pf*; *vi* части́чно совпада́ть *impf*, совпа́сть *pf*.

overleaf *adv* на оборо́те. **overload** *vt* перегружа́ть *impf*, перегрузи́ть *pf*. **overlook** *vt* (*look down on*) смотре́ть *impf* све́рху на+*acc*; (*of window*) выходи́ть *impf* на, в, +*acc*; (*not notice*) не замеча́ть *impf*, заме́тить *pf* +*gen*; (~ *offence etc.*) проща́ть *impf*, прости́ть *pf*.

overly *adv* сли́шком.

overnight *adv* (*during the night*) за́ ночь; (*suddenly*) неожи́данно; **stay** ~ ночева́ть *impf*, пере~ *pf*; *adj* ночно́й. **overpay** *vt* перепла́чивать *impf*, переплати́ть *pf*.

over-populated *adj* перенаселённый. **over-population** *n* перенаселённость *n*. **overpower** *vt* одолева́ть *impf*, одоле́ть *pf*. **overpriced** *adj* завы́шенный в цене́. **over-production** *n* перепроизво́дство. **overrate**

vt переоце́нивать *impf*, переоцени́ть *pf*. **override** *vt* (*fig*) отверга́ть *impf*, отве́ргнуть *pf*. **overriding** *adj* гла́вный, реша́ющий. **overrule** *vt* отверга́ть *impf*, отве́ргнуть *pf*. **overrun** *vt* (*conquer*) завоёвывать *impf*, завоева́ть *pf*; **be** ~ **with** кише́ть *impf* +*instr*.

overseas *adv* за мо́рем, че́рез мо́ре; *adj* замо́рский. **oversee** *vt* надзира́ть *impf* за+*instr*. **overseer** *n* надзира́тель *m*, ~ница. **overshadow** *vt* затмева́ть *impf*, затми́ть *pf*. **overshoot** *vi* переходи́ть *impf*, перейти́ *pf* грани́цу. **oversight** *n* случа́йный недосмо́тр. **oversleep** *vi* проспа́ть *impf*, проспа́ть *pf*. **overspend** *vi* тра́тить *impf* сли́шком мно́го. **overstate** *vt* преувели́чивать *impf*, преувели́чить *pf*. **overstep** *vt* переступа́ть *impf*, переступи́ть *pf* +*acc*, че́рез+*acc*.

overt *adj* я́вный, откры́тый.

overtake *vt* обгоня́ть *impf*, обогна́ть *pf*. **overthrow** *vt* сверга́ть *impf*, све́ргнуть *pf*. **overtime** *n* (*work*) сверхуро́чная рабо́та; (*payment*) сверхуро́чное *sb*; *adv* сверхуро́чно. **overtone** *n* скры́тый намёк. **overture** *n* предложе́ние; (*mus*) увертю́ра.

overturn *vt* & *i* опроки́дывать(ся) *impf*, опроки́нуть(ся) *pf*. **overwhelm** *vt* подавля́ть *impf*, подави́ть *pf*. **overwhelming** *adj* подавля́ющий. **overwork** *vt* & *i* переутомля́ть(ся) *impf*, переутоми́ть(ся) *pf*; *n* переутомле́ние.

owe *vt* (~ *money*) быть до́лжным +*acc* & *dat*; (*be indebted*) быть обя́занным +*instr* & *dat*; **he, she,** ~**s me three roubles** он до́лжен, она́ должна́, мне три рубля́; **she** ~**s him her life** она́ обя́зана ему́ жи́знью.

owing *adj*: **be** ~ причита́ться *impf* (**to** +*dat*); (*be indebted*) ~ **to** из-за+*gen*, по причи́не+*gen*.

owl *n* сова́.

own *adj* свой; (*свой*) со́бственный; **on one's** ~ самостоя́тельно; (*alone*) оди́н; *vt* (*possess*) владе́ть *impf* +*instr*; (*admit*) признава́ть *impf*, призна́ть *pf*; ~ **up** признава́ться *impf*, призна́ться *pf*. **owner** *n* владе́лец. **ownership** *n* владе́ние

(of+instr), собственность.
ox n вол.
oxidation n окисление. **oxide** n окись.
oxidize vt & i окислять(ся) impf, окислить(ся) pf. **oxygen** n кислород.
oyster n устрица.
ozone n озон.

P

pace n шаг; (fig) темп; **keep ~ with** идти impf в ногу c+instr; **set the ~** задавать impf, задать pf темп; vi: **~ up and down** ходить indet взад и вперёд. **pacemaker** n (med) электронный стимулятор.
pacifism n пацифизм. **pacifist** n пацифист. **pacify** vt усмирять impf, усмирить pf.
pack n узел, вьюк; (soldier's) ранец; (hounds) свора; (wolves) стая; (cards) колода; vt & i упаковывать(ся) impf, упаковать(ся) pf; (cram) набивать impf, набить pf. **package** n посылка, пакет; **~ holiday** организованная туристическая поездка. **packaging** n упаковка. **packet** n пакет; пачка; (large sum of money) куча денег. **packing-case** n ящик.
pact n пакт.
pad n (cushion) подушечка; (shin ~ etc.) щиток; (of paper) блокнот; vt подбивать impf, подбить pf. **padding** n набивка.
paddle[1] n (oar) весло; vi (row) грести impf.
paddle[2] vi (wade) ходить indet, идти det, пойти pf босиком по воде.
paddock n выгон.
padlock n висячий замок; vt запирать impf, запереть pf на висячий замок.
paediatric adj педиатрический. **paediatrician** n педиатр.
pagan n язычник, -ица; adj языческий. **paganism** n язычество.
page[1] n (~-boy) паж; vt (summon) вызывать impf, вызвать pf.
page[2] n (of book) страница.
pageant n пышная процессия. **pageantry** n пышность.
pail n ведро.
pain n боль; pl (efforts) усилия neut

pl; **~-killer** болеутоляющее средство; vt (fig) огорчать impf, огорчить pf. **painful** adj болезненный; **be ~** (part of body) болеть impf. **painless** adj безболезненный. **painstaking** adj старательный.
paint n краска; vt красить impf, по~ pf; (portray) писать impf, на~ pf красками. **paintbrush** n кисть. **painter** n (artist) художник, -ица; (decorator) маляр. **painting** n (art) живопись; (picture) картина.
pair n пара; often not translated with nn denoting a single object, e.g. **a ~ of scissors** ножницы (-ц) pl; **a ~ of trousers** пара брюк; vt спаривать impf, спарить pf; **~ off** разделяться impf, разделиться pf по парам.
Pakistan n Пакистан. **Pakistani** n пакистанец, -анка; adj пакистанский.
pal n приятель m, ~ница.
palace n дворец.
palatable adj вкусный; (fig) приятный. **palate** n нёбо; (fig) вкус.
palatial adj великолепный.
palaver n (trouble) беспокойство; (nonsense) чепуха.
pale[1] n (stake) кол; **beyond the ~** невообразимый.
pale[2] adj бледный; vi бледнеть impf, по~ pf.
palette n палитра.
pall[1] n покров.
pall[2] vi: **~ on** надоедать impf, надоесть pf +dat.
palliative adj паллиативный; n паллиатив.
pallid adj бледный. **pallor** n бледность.
palm[1] n (tree) пальма; **P~ Sunday** Вербное воскресенье.
palm[2] n (of hand) ладонь; vt: **~ off** всучивать impf, всучить pf (on +dat).
palpable adj осязаемый.
palpitations n pl сердцебиение.
paltry adj ничтожный.
pamper vt баловать impf, из~ pf.
pamphlet n брошюра.
pan[1] n (saucepan) кастрюля; (frying-~) сковорода; (of scales) чашка; vt: **~ out** промывать impf, промыть pf; (fig) выходить impf, выйти pf.
pan[2] vi (cin) панорамировать impf & pf.

panacea n панацéя.

panache n рисóвка.

pancake n блин.

pancreas n поджелýдочная железá.

panda n пáнда.

pandemonium n гвалт.

pander vi: ~ to потвóрствовать impf +dat.

pane n окóнное стеклó.

panel n панéль; (control-~) щит управлéния; (of experts) грýппа специалúстов; (of judges) жюрú neut indecl. **panelling** n панéльная обшúвка.

pang n pl мýки (-к) pl.

panic n пáника; ~-stricken охвáченный пáникой; vi впадáть impf, впасть pf в пáнику. **panicky** adj панúческий.

pannier n корзúнка.

panorama n панорáма. **panoramic** adj панорáмный.

pansy n анютины глáзки (-зок) pl.

pant vi дышáть impf с одышкой.

panther n пантéра.

panties n pl трусúки (-ков) pl.

pantomime n рождéственское представлéние; (dumb show) пантомúма.

pantry n кладовáя sb.

pants n pl трусы́ (-сóв) pl; (trousers) брюки (-к) pl.

papal adj пáпский.

paper n бумáга; pl докумéнты m pl; (newspaper) газéта; (wallpaper) обóи (-óев) pl; (treatise) доклáд; adj бумáжный; vt оклéивать impf, оклéить pf обóями. **paperback** n кнúга в бумáжной облóжке. **paperclip** n скрéпка. **paperwork** n канцелярская рабóта.

par n: feel below ~ чýвствовать impf себя невáжно; on a ~ with наравнé с+instr.

parable n прúтча.

parabola n парáбола.

parachute n парашют; vi спускáться impf, спустúться pf с парашютом. **parachutist** n парашютúст.

parade n парáд; vi шествовать impf, vt (show off) выставлять impf, выставить pf напокáз.

paradigm n парадúгма.

paradise n рай.

paradox n парадóкс. **paradoxical** adj парадоксáльный.

paraffin n (~ oil) керосúн.

paragon n образéц.

paragraph n абзáц.

parallel adj параллéльный; n параллéль; vt соотвéтствовать impf +dat.

paralyse vt парализовáть impf & pf. **paralysis** n паралúч.

parameter n парáметр.

paramilitary adj полувоéнный.

paramount adj первостепéнный.

paranoia n паранóйя **paranoid** adj: he is ~ он паранóик.

parapet n (mil) брýствер.

paraphernalia n принадлéжности f pl.

paraphrase n перескáз; vt перескáзывать impf, пересказáть pf.

parasite n паразúт. **parasitic** adj паразитúческий.

parasol n зóнтик.

paratrooper n парашютúст-десáнтник.

parcel n пакéт, посы́лка.

parch vt иссушáть impf, иссушúть pf: become ~ed пересыхáть impf, пересóхнуть pf.

parchment n пергáмент.

pardon n прощéние; (law) помúлование; vt прощáть impf, простúть pf; (law) помúловать pf.

pare vt (fruit) чúстить impf, о~ pf; ~ away, down урéзывать impf, урéзать pf.

parent n родúтель m, ~ница. **parentage** n происхождéние. **parental** adj родúтельский.

parentheses n pl (brackets) скóбки f pl.

parish n прихóд. **parishioner** n прихожáнин, -áнка.

parity n рáвенство.

park n парк; (for cars etc.) стоáнка; vt & abs стáвить impf, по~ pf (машúну). **parking** n стоáнка.

parliament n парлáмент. **parliamentarian** n парламентáрий. **parliamentary** adj парлáментский.

parlour n гостúная sb.

parochial adj прихóдский; (fig) огранúченный. **parochialism** n огранúченность.

parody n парóдия; vt пародúровать impf & pf.

parole n чéстное слóво; on ~ освобождённый под чéстное слóво.

paroxysm *n* парокси́зм.
parquet *n* парке́т; *attrib* парке́тный.
parrot *n* попуга́й.
parry *vt* пари́ровать *impf & pf*, от~ *pf*.
parsimonious *adj* скупо́й.
parsley *n* петру́шка.
parsnip *n* пастерна́к.
parson *n* свяще́нник.
part *n* часть; (*in play*) роль; (*mus*) па́ртия; **for the most ~** бо́льшей ча́стью; **in ~** ча́стью; **for my ~** что каса́ется меня́; **take ~ in** уча́ствовать *impf* в+*prep*; ~**-time** (за́нятый) непо́лный рабо́чий день; *vt & i* (*divide*) разделя́ть(ся) *impf*, раздели́ть(ся) *pf*; *vi* (*leave*) расстава́ться *impf*, расста́ться *pf* (**from, with** с+*instr*); ~ **one's hair** де́лать *impf*, с~ *pf* себе́ пробо́р.
partake *vi* принима́ть *impf*, приня́ть *pf* уча́стие (**in, of** в+*prep*); (*eat*) есть *impf*, съ~ *pf* (**of** +*acc*).
partial *adj* части́чный; (*biased*) пристра́стный; ~ **to** неравноду́шный к+*dat*. **partiality** *n* (*bias*) пристра́стность. **partially** *adv* части́чно.
participant *n* уча́стник, -ица (**in** +*gen*). **participate** *vi* уча́ствовать *impf* (**in** в+*prep*). **participation** *n* уча́стие.
participle *n* прича́стие.
particle *n* части́ца.
particular *adj* осо́бый, осо́бенный; (*fussy*) разбо́рчивый; *n* подро́бность; **in ~** в ча́стности.
parting *n* (*leave-taking*) проща́ние; (*of hair*) пробо́р.
partisan *n* (*adherent*) сторо́нник; (*mil*) партиза́н; *attrib* (*biased*) пристра́стный; партиза́нский.
partition *n* (*wall*) перегоро́дка; (*polit*) разде́л; *vt* разделя́ть *impf*, раздели́ть *pf*; ~ **off** отгора́живать *impf*, отгороди́ть *pf*.
partly *adv* части́чно.
partner *n* (*in business*) компаньо́н; (*in dance, game*) партнёр, ~ша. **partnership** *n* това́рищество.
partridge *n* куропа́тка.
party *n* (*polit*) па́ртия; (*group*) гру́ппа; (*social gathering*) вечери́нка; (*law*) сторона́; **be a ~ to** принима́ть *impf*, приня́ть *pf* уча́стие в+*prep*; *attrib* парти́йный; ~ **line** (*polit*)

ли́ния па́ртии; (*telephone*) о́бщий телефо́нный про́вод; ~ **wall** о́бщая стена́.
pass *vt & i* (*go past; of time*) проходи́ть *impf*, пройти́ *pf* (**by** ми́мо +*gen*); (*travel past*) проезжа́ть *impf*, прое́хать *pf* (**by** ми́мо+*gen*); (~ *examination*) сдава́ть *impf*, сдать *pf* (экза́мен); *vt* (*sport*) пасова́ть *impf*, пасну́ть *pf*; (*overtake*) обгоня́ть *impf*, обогна́ть *pf*; (*time*) проводи́ть *impf*, провести́ *pf*; (*hand on*) передава́ть *impf*, переда́ть *pf*; (*law, resolution*) утвержда́ть *impf*, утверди́ть *pf*; (*sentence*) выноси́ть *impf*, вы́нести *pf* (**upon** +*dat*); ~, **as for** слыть *impf*, про~ *pf* +*instr*, за+*acc*; ~ **away** (*die*) сконча́ться *pf*; ~ **o.s. off as** выдава́ть *impf*, вы́дать *pf* себя́ за+*acc*; ~ **out** теря́ть *impf*, по~ *pf* созна́ние; ~ **over** (*in silence*) обходи́ть *impf*, обойти́ *pf* молча́нием; ~ **round** передава́ть *impf*, переда́ть *pf*; ~ **up** подава́ть *impf*, пода́ть *pf*; (*miss*) пропуска́ть *impf*, пропусти́ть *pf*; *n* (*permit*) про́пуск; (*sport*) пас; (*geog*) перева́л; **come to ~** случа́ться *impf*, случи́ться *pf*; **make a ~ at** пристава́ть *impf*, приста́ть *pf* к+*dat*.
passable *adj* проходи́мый, прое́зжий; (*not bad*) неплохо́й.
passage *n* прохо́д; (*of time*) тече́ние; (*sea trip*) рейс; (*in house*) коридо́р; (*in book*) отры́вок; (*mus*) пасса́ж.
passenger *n* пассажи́р.
passer-by *n* прохо́жий *sb*.
passing *adj* (*transient*) мимолётный; *n*: **in ~** мимохо́дом.
passion *n* страсть (**for** к+*dat*) **passionate** *adj* стра́стный.
passive *adj* пасси́вный; (*gram*) страда́тельный; *n* страда́тельный зало́г. **passivity** *n* пасси́вность.
Passover *n* евре́йская Па́сха.
passport *n* па́спорт.
password *n* паро́ль *m*.
past *adj* про́шлый; (*gram*) проше́дший; *n* про́шлое *sb*; (*gram*) проше́дшее вре́мя *neut*; *prep* ми́мо +*gen*; (*beyond*) за+*instr*; *adv* ми́мо.
pasta *n* макаро́нные изде́лия *neut pl*.
paste *n* (*of flour*) те́сто; (*creamy mixture*) па́ста; (*glue*) клей; (*jewellery*)

страз; *vt* накле́ивать *impf*, накле́ить *pf*.

pastel *n* (*crayon*) пасте́ль; (*drawing*) рису́нок пасте́лью; *attrib* пасте́льный.

pasteurize *vt* пастеризова́ть *impf* & *pf*.

pastime *n* времяпрепровожде́ние.

pastor *n* па́стор. **pastoral** *adj* (*bucolic*) пастора́льный; (*of pastor*) па́сторский.

pastry *n* (*dough*) те́сто; (*cake*) пиро́жное *sb*.

pasture *n* (*land*) па́стбище.

pasty[1] *n* пирожо́к.

pasty[2] *adj* (~-*faced*) бле́дный.

pat *n* шлепо́к; (*of butter etc.*) кусо́к; *vt* хло́пать *impf*, по~ *pf*.

patch *n* запла́та; (*over eye*) повя́зка (на глазу́); (*spot*) пятно́; (*of land*) уча́сток земли́; *vt* ста́вить *impf*, по~ *pf* запла́ту на+*acc*; ~ **up** (*fig*) ула́живать *impf*, ула́дить *pf*. **patchwork** *n* лоску́тная рабо́та; *attrib* лоску́тный **patchy** *adj* неро́вный.

pâté *n* паште́т.

patent *adj* я́вный; ~ **leather** лакиро́ванная ко́жа; *n* пате́нт; *vt* патентова́ть *impf*, за~ *pf*.

paternal *adj* отцо́вский. **paternity** *n* отцо́вство.

path *n* тропи́нка, тропа́; (*way*) путь *m*.

pathetic *adj* жа́лкий.

pathological *adj* патологи́ческий. **pathologist** *n* пато́лог.

pathos *n* па́фос.

pathway *n* тропи́нка, тропа́.

patience *n* терпе́ние; (*cards*) пасья́нс. **patient** *adj* терпели́вый; *n* больно́й *sb*, пацие́нт, ~ка.

patio *n* терра́са.

patriarch *n* патриа́рх. **patriarchal** *adj* патриарха́льный.

patriot *n* патрио́т, ~ка. **patriotic** *adj* патриоти́ческий. **patriotism** *n* патриоти́зм.

patrol *n* патру́ль *m*; **on** ~ на дозо́ре; *vt* & *i* патрули́ровать *impf*.

patron *n* покрови́тель *m*; (*of shop*) клие́нт **patronage** *n* покрови́тельство. **patroness** *n* покрови́тельница. **patronize** *vt* (*treat condescendingly*) снисходи́тельно относи́ться *impf*, к+*dat*. **patronizing** *adj* покро-

ви́тельственный.

patronymic *n* о́тчество.

patter[1] *vi* (*sound*) бараба́нить *impf*; *n* посту́кивание.

patter[2] *n* (*speech*) скорогово́рка.

pattern *n* (*design*) узо́р; (*model*) образе́ц; (*sewing*) вы́кройка.

paunch *n* брюшко́.

pauper *n* бедня́к.

pause *n* па́уза, переры́в; (*mus*) ферма́та; *vi* остана́вливаться *impf*, останови́ться *pf*.

pave *vt* мости́ть *impf*, вы́~ *pf*; ~ **the way** подготовля́ть *impf*, подгото́вить *pf* по́чву (**for** для+*gen*). **pavement** *n* тротуа́р.

pavilion *n* павильо́н.

paw *n* ла́па; *vt* тро́гать *impf* ла́пой; (*horse*) бить *impf* копы́том.

pawn[1] *n* (*chess*) пе́шка.

pawn[2] *n*: **in** ~ в закла́де; *vt* закла́дывать *impf*, заложи́ть *pf*. **pawnbroker** *n* ростовщи́к. **pawnshop** *n* ломба́рд.

pay *vt* плати́ть *impf*, за~, у~ *pf* (**for** за+*acc*); (*bill etc.*) опла́чивать *impf*, оплати́ть *pf*; *vi* (*be profitable*) окупа́ться *impf*, окупи́ться *pf*; *n* жа́лованье, зарпла́та; ~ **packet** получка; ~**-roll** платёжная ве́домость. **payable** *adj* подлежа́щий упла́те. **payee** *n* получа́тель *m*. **payload** *n* поле́зная нагру́зка. **payment** *n* упла́та, платёж.

pea *n* (*also pl, collect*) горо́х.

peace *n* мир; **in** ~ в поко́е; ~ **and quiet** мир и тишина́. **peaceable**, **peaceful** *adj* ми́рный.

peach *n* пе́рсик.

peacock *n* павли́н.

peak *n* (*of cap*) козырёк; (*summit*; *fig*) верши́на; ~ **hour** часы́ *m pl* пик.

peal *n* (*sound*) звон, трезво́н; (*of laughter*) взрыв.

peanut *n* ара́хис.

pear *n* гру́ша.

pearl *n* (*also fig*) жемчу́жина; *pl* (*collect*) же́мчуг.

peasant *n* крестья́нин, -я́нка; *attrib* крестья́нский.

peat *n* торф.

pebble *n* га́лька.

peck *vt* & *i* клева́ть *impf*, клю́нуть *pf*; *n* клево́к.

pectoral *adj* грудно́й.

peculiar adj (distinctive) своеобра́зный; (strange) стра́нный; ~ **to** сво́йственный +dat. **peculiarity** n осо́бенность; стра́нность.

pecuniary adj де́нежный.

pedagogical adj педагоги́ческий.

pedal n педа́ль; vi нажима́ть impf, нажа́ть pf педа́ль; (ride bicycle) éхать impf, по~ pf на велосипе́де.

pedant n педа́нт. **pedantic** adj педанти́чный.

peddle vt торгова́ть impf вразно́с +instr.

pedestal n пьедеста́л.

pedestrian adj пешехо́дный; (prosaic) прозаи́ческий; n пешехо́д; ~ **crossing** перехо́д.

pedigree n родосло́вная sb; adj поро́дистый.

pedlar n разно́счик.

pee n пи-пи́ neut indecl; vi мочи́ться impf, по~ pf.

peek vi (~ **in**) загля́дывать impf, загляну́ть pf; (~ **out**) выгля́дывать impf, вы́глянуть pf.

peel n кожура́; vt очища́ть impf, очи́стить pf; vi (skin) шелуши́ться impf; (paint, ~ **off**) сходи́ть impf, сойти́ pf. **peelings** n pl очи́стки (-ков) pl.

peep vi (~ **in**) загля́дывать impf, загляну́ть pf; (~ **out**) выгля́дывать impf, вы́глянуть pf; n (glance) бы́стрый взгляд; ~-**hole** глазо́к.

peer[1] n всма́триваться impf, всмотре́ться pf (**at** в+acc).

peer[2] n (noble) пэр; (person one's age) све́рстник.

peeved adj раздражённый. **peevish** adj раздражи́тельный.

peg n ко́лышек; (clothes ~) крючо́к; (for hat etc.) ве́шалка; **off the** ~ гото́вый; vt прикрепля́ть impf, прикрепи́ть pf ко́лышком, -ками.

pejorative adj уничижи́тельный.

pelican n пелика́н.

pellet n ша́рик; (shot) дроби́на.

pelt[1] n (skin) шку́ра.

pelt[2] vt забра́сывать impf, заброса́ть pf; vi (rain) бараба́нить impf.

pelvis n таз.

pen[1] n (for writing) ру́чка; ~-**friend** друг по перепи́ске.

pen[2] n (enclosure) заго́н.

penal adj уголо́вный. **penalize** vt

штрафова́ть impf, o~ pf. **penalty** n наказа́ние; (sport) штраф; ~ **area** штрафна́я площа́дка; ~ **kick** штрафно́й уда́р. **penance** n епитимья́.

penchant n скло́нность (**for** к+dat).

pencil n каранда́ш; ~-**sharpener** точи́лка.

pendant n подве́ска.

pending adj (awaiting decision) ожида́ющий реше́ния; prep (until) в ожида́нии +gen, до+gen.

pendulum n ма́ятник.

penetrate vt проника́ть impf, прони́кнуть pf в+acc. **penetrating** adj проница́тельный; (sound) пронзи́тельный. **penetration** n проникнове́ние; (insight) проница́тельность.

penguin n пингви́н.

penicillin n пеницилли́н.

peninsula n полуо́стров.

penis n пе́нис.

penitence n раска́яние. **penitent** adj раска́ивающийся; n ка́ющийся гре́шник.

penknife n перочи́нный нож.

pennant n вы́мпел.

penniless adj без гроша́.

penny n пе́нни neut indecl, пенс.

pension n пе́нсия; vt: ~ **off** увольня́ть impf, уво́лить pf на пе́нсию. **pensionable** adj (age) пенсио́нный. **pensioner** n пенсионе́р, ~ка.

pensive adj заду́мчивый.

pentagon n пятиуго́льник; **the P~** Пентаго́н.

Pentecost n Пятидеся́тница.

penthouse n шика́рная кварти́ра на ве́рхнем этаже́.

pent-up adj (anger etc.) сде́рживаемый.

penultimate adj предпосле́дний.

penury n нужда́.

peony n пио́н.

people n pl (persons) лю́ди pl; sg (nation) наро́д; vt населя́ть impf, насели́ть pf.

pepper n пе́рец; vt пе́рчить impf, на~, по~ pf. **peppercorn** n перчи́нка. **peppermint** n пе́речная мя́та; (sweet) мя́тная конфе́та.

per prep (for each) (person) на+acc; **as** ~ согла́сно+dat; ~ **annum** в год; ~ **capita** на челове́ка; ~ **hour** в час; ~ **se** сам по себе́.

perceive *vt* воспринимáть *impf*, восприня́ть *pf*.

per cent *adv & n* процéнт. **percentage** *n* процéнт; (*part*) часть.

perceptible *adj* замéтный. **perception** *n* восприя́тие; (*quality*) понимáние. **perceptive** *adj* тóнкий.

perch¹ *n* (*fish*) óкунь *m*.

perch² *n* (*roost*) насéст; *vi* сади́ться *impf*, сесть *pf*. **perched** *adj* высокó сидя́щий, располóженный.

percussion *n* (~ *instruments*) удáрные инструмéнты *m pl*.

peremptory *adj* повели́тельный.

perennial *adj* (*enduring*) вéчный; *n* (*bot*) многолéтнее растéние.

perestroika *n* перестрóйка.

perfect *adj* совершéнный; (*gram*) перфéктный; *n* перфéкт; *vt* совершéнствовать *impf*, у~ *pf*. **perfection** *n* совершéнство. **perfective** *adj* (*n*) совершéнный (вид).

perforate *vt* перфори́ровать *impf & pf*. **perforation** *n* перфорáция.

perform *vt* (*carry out*) исполня́ть *impf*, испóлнить *pf*; (*theat, mus*) игрáть *impf*, сыгрáть *pf*; *vi* выступáть *impf*, вы́ступить *pf*; (*function*) рабóтать *impf*. **performance** *n* исполнéние; (*of person, device*) дéйствие; (*of play etc.*) представлéние, спектáкль *m*; (*of engine etc.*) эксплуатациóнные кáчества *neut pl*. **performer** *n* исполни́тель *m*.

perfume *n* духи́ (-хóв) *pl*; (*smell*) арома́т.

perfunctory *adj* повéрхностный.

perhaps *adv* мóжет быть.

peril *n* опáсность, риск. **perilous** *adj* опáсный, рискóванный.

perimeter *n* внéшняя грани́ца; (*geom*) пери́метр.

period *n* пери́од; (*epoch*) эпóха; (*menstrual*) мéсячные *sb pl*. **periodic** *adj* периоди́ческий. **periodical** *adj* периоди́ческий; *n* периоди́ческое издáние.

peripheral *adj* перифери́йный. **periphery** *n* перифери́я.

periscope *n* перискóп.

perish *vi* погибáть *impf*, поги́бнуть *pf*; (*spoil*) пóртиться *impf*, ис~ *pf*. **perishable** *adj* скоропóртящийся.

perjure *v*: ~ **o.s.** нарушáть *impf*, нару́шить *pf* кля́тву. **perjury** *n* лже-

свидéтельство.

perk¹ *n* льгóта.

perk² *vi*: ~ **up** оживля́ться *impf*, оживи́ться *pf*. **perky** *adj* бóйкий.

perm *n* перманéнт. **permanence** *n* постоя́нство. **permanent** *adj* постоя́нный.

permeable *adj* проницáемый. **permeate** *vt* проникáть *impf*, прони́кнуть *pf* в+*acc*.

permissible *adj* допусти́мый. **permission** *n* разрешéние. **permissive** *adj* (сли́шком) либерáльный; ~ **society** óбщество вседозвóленности. **permissiveness** *n* вседозвóленность. **permit** *vt* разрешáть *impf*, разреши́ть *pf* +*dat*; *n* прóпуск.

permutation *n* перестанóвка.

pernicious *adj* пáгубный.

perpendicular *adj* перпендикуля́рный; *n* перпендикуля́р.

perpetrate *vt* совершáть *impf*, соверши́ть *pf*. **perpetrator** *n* винóвник.

perpetual *adj* вéчный. **perpetuate** *vt* увековéчивать *impf*, увековéчить *pf*. **perpetuity** *n* вéчность; **in** ~ навсегдá, навéчно.

perplex *vt* озадáчивать *impf*, озадáчить *pf*. **perplexity** *n* озадáченность.

persecute *vt* преслéдовать *impf*. **persecution** *n* преслéдование.

perseverance *n* настóйчивость. **persevere** *vi* настóйчиво, продолжáть *impf* (**in**, **at** etc. +*acc*, *inf*).

Persian *n* перс, ~и́нка; *adj* перси́дский.

persist *vi* упóрствовать *impf* (**in** в+*prep*); настóйчиво продолжáть *impf* (**in** +*acc*, *inf*). **persistence** *n* упóрство. **persistent** *adj* упóрный.

person *n* человéк; (*in play; gram*) лицó; **in** ~ ли́чно. **personable** *adj* привлекáтельный. **personage** *n* ли́чность. **personal** *adj* ли́чный. **personality** *n* ли́чность. **personally** *adv* ли́чно. **personification** *n* олицетворéние. **personify** *vt* олицетворя́ть *impf*, олицетвори́ть *pf*.

personnel *n* кáдры (-ров) *pl*, персонáл; ~ **department** отдéл кáдров.

perspective *n* перспекти́ва.

perspiration *n* пот. **perspire** *vi* потéть *impf*, вс~ *pf*.

persuade *vt* (*convince*) убеждáть *impf*, убеди́ть *pf* (**of** в+*prep*); (*in-*

duce) угова́ривать _impf_, уговори́ть _pf_. **persuasion** _n_ убежде́ние. **persuasive** _adj_ убеди́тельный.

pertain _vi_: ~ **to** относи́ться _impf_ отнести́сь _pf_ к+_dat_.

pertinent _adj_ уме́стный.

perturb _vt_ трево́жить _impf_, вс~ _pf_.

peruse _vt_ (_read_) внима́тельно чита́ть _impf_, про~ _pf_; (_fig_) рассма́тривать _impf_, рассмотре́ть _pf_.

pervade _vt_ наполня́ть _impf_. **pervasive** _adj_ распространённый.

perverse _adj_ капри́зный. **perversion** _n_ извраще́ние. **pervert** _vt_ извраща́ть _impf_, изврати́ть _pf_; _n_ извращённый челове́к.

pessimism _n_ пессими́зм. **pessimist** _n_ пессими́ст. **pessimistic** _adj_ пессимисти́ческий.

pest _n_ вреди́тель _m_; (_fig_) зану́да. **pester** _vt_ пристава́ть _impf_, приста́ть _pf_ к+_dat_. **pesticide** _n_ пестици́д.

pet _n_ (_animal_) дома́шнее живо́тное _sb_; (_favourite_) люби́мец, -мица; ~ **shop** зоомагази́н; _vt_ ласка́ть _impf_.

petal _n_ лепесто́к.

peter _vi_: ~ **out** (_road_) исчеза́ть _impf_, исче́знуть _pf_; (_stream; enthusiasm_) иссяка́ть _impf_, исся́кнуть _pf_.

petite _adj_ ма́ленькая.

petition _n_ пети́ция; _vt_ подава́ть _impf_, пода́ть _pf_ проше́ние +_dat_. **petitioner** _n_ проси́тель _m_.

petrified _adj_ окамене́лый; **be** ~ (_fig_) оцепене́ть _pf_ (**with** от+_gen_).

petrol _n_ бензи́н; ~ **pump** бензоколо́нка; ~ **station** бензозапра́вочная ста́нция; ~ **tank** бензоба́к. **petroleum** _n_ нефть.

petticoat _n_ ни́жняя ю́бка.

petty _adj_ ме́лкий; ~ **cash** де́ньги (де́нег, -ньга́м) _pl_ на ме́лкие расхо́ды. **petulant** _adj_ раздражи́тельный.

pew _n_ (церко́вная) скамья́.

phallic _adj_ фалли́ческий. **phallus** _n_ фа́ллос.

phantom _n_ фанто́м.

pharmaceutical _adj_ фармацевти́ческий. **pharmacist** _n_ фармаце́вт. **pharmacy** _n_ фармаци́я; (_shop_) апте́ка.

phase _n_ фа́за; _vt_: ~ **in, out** постепе́нно вводи́ть _impf_, упраздня́ть _impf_.

Ph.D. _abbr_ (_of_ **Doctor of Philosophy**)

кандида́т нау́к.

pheasant _n_ фаза́н.

phenomenal _adj_ феномена́льный. **phenomenon** _n_ феноме́н.

phial _n_ пузырёк.

philanderer _n_ волоки́та _m_.

philanthropic _adj_ филантропи́ческий. **philanthropist** _n_ филантро́п. **philanthropy** _n_ филантро́пия.

philately _n_ филатели́я.

philharmonic _adj_ филармони́ческий.

Philistine _n_ (_fig_) фили́стер.

philosopher _n_ фило́соф. **philosophical** _adj_ филосо́фский. **philosophize** _vi_ филосо́фствовать _impf_. **philosophy** _n_ филосо́фия.

phlegm _n_ мокрота́. **phlegmatic** _adj_ флегмати́ческий.

phobia _n_ фо́бия.

phone _n_ телефо́н; _vt_ & _i_ звони́ть _impf_, по~ _pf_ +_dat. See also_ **telephone**

phonetic _adj_ фонети́ческий. **phonetics** _n_ фоне́тика.

phoney _n_ подде́льный.

phosphorus _n_ фо́сфор.

photo _n_ фо́то _neut indecl_. **photocopier** _n_ копирова́льная маши́на. **photocopy** _n_ фотоко́пия; _vt_ де́лать _impf_, с~ _pf_ фотоко́пию +_gen_. **photogenic** _adj_ фотогени́чный. **photograph** _n_ фотогра́фия; _vt_ фотографи́ровать _impf_, с~ _pf_. **photographer** _n_ фото́граф. **photographic** _adj_ фотографи́ческий. **photography** _n_ фотогра́фия.

phrase _n_ фра́за; _vt_ формули́ровать _impf_, с~ _pf_.

physical _adj_ физи́ческий; ~ **education** физкульту́ра; ~ **exercises** заря́дка. **physician** _n_ врач. **physicist** _n_ фи́зик. **physics** _n_ фи́зика.

physiological _n_ физиологи́ческий. **physiologist** _n_ физио́лог. **physiology** _n_ физиоло́гия. **physiotherapist** _n_ физиотерапе́вт. **physiotherapy** _n_ физиотерапи́я.

physique _n_ телосложе́ние.

pianist _n_ пиани́ст, ~ка. **piano** _n_ фортепья́но _neut indecl_; (_grand_) роя́ль _m_; (_upright_) пиани́но _neut indecl_.

pick[1] _vt_ (_flower_) срыва́ть _impf_, сорва́ть _pf_; (_gather_) собира́ть _impf_, собра́ть _pf_; (_select_) выбира́ть _impf_, вы́брать _pf_; ~ **one's nose, teeth** ковыря́ть _impf_, ковырну́ть _pf_ в носу́, в зуба́х; ~ a quarrel иска́ть *impf* ссо́ры (with c+*instr*); выбира́ть *impf*, вы́брать *pf* доро́гу; ~ on (nag) придира́ться *impf* к+*dat*; ~ out отбира́ть *impf*, отобра́ть *pf*; ~ up (lift) поднима́ть *impf*, подня́ть *pf*; (acquire) приобрета́ть *impf*, приобрести́ *pf*; (fetch) (on foot) заходи́ть *impf*, зайти́ *pf* за+*instr*; (in vehicle) заезжа́ть *impf*, зае́хать *pf* за+*instr*; (a cold; a girl) подцепля́ть *impf*, подцепи́ть *pf*; ~ o.s. up поднима́ться *impf*, подня́ться *pf*; ~-up (truck) пика́п; (electron) звукосни-ма́тель *m*.

pick² *n* вы́бор; (best part) лу́чшая часть; take your ~ выбира́й(те)!

pick³, pickaxe *n* кирка́.

picket *n* (person) пике́тчик, -ица; (collect) пике́т; *vt* пикети́ровать *impf*.

pickle *n* соле́нье; *vt* соли́ть *impf*, по-~ *pf*. **pickled** *adj* солёный.

pickpocket *n* карма́нник.

picnic *n* пикни́к.

pictorial *adj* изобрази́тельный; (illustrated) иллюстри́рованный. **picture** *n* карти́на; (of health etc.) воплоще́ние; (film) фильм; the ~s кино́ *neut indecl*; *vt* (to o.s.) представля́ть *impf*, предста́вить *pf* себе́. **picturesque** *adj* живопи́сный.

pie *n* пиро́г.

piece *n* кусо́к, часть; (one of set) шту́ка; (of paper) листо́к; (mus, literature) произведе́ние; (chess) фигу́ра; (coin) моне́та; take to ~s разбира́ть *impf*, разобра́ть *pf* (на ча́сти); ~ of advice сове́т; ~ of information све́дение; ~ of news но́вость; ~work сде́льщина; ~worker сде́льщик; *vt*: ~ together воссоздава́ть *impf*, воссозда́ть *pf* карти́ну +*gen*. **piecemeal** *adv* по частя́м.

pier *n* (mole) мол; (projecting into sea) пирс; (of bridge) бык; (between windows etc.) просте́нок.

pierce *vt* пронза́ть *impf*, пронзи́ть *pf*; (ears) прока́лывать *impf*, проколо́ть *pf*. **piercing** *adj* пронзи́тельный.

piety *n* на́божность.

pig *n* свинья́. **pigheaded** *adj* упря́мый. **piglet** *n* поросёнок. **pigsty** *n* свина́рник. **pigtail** *n* коси́чка.

pigeon *n* го́лубь; ~-hole отделе́ние для бума́г.

pigment *n* пигме́нт. **pigmentation** *n* пигмента́ция.

pike *n* (fish) щу́ка.

pilchard *n* сарди́н(к)а.

pile¹ *n* (heap) ку́ча, ки́па; *vt*: ~ up сва́ливать *impf*, свали́ть *pf* в ку́чу; (load) нагружа́ть *impf*, нагрузи́ть *pf* (with +*instr*); *vi*: ~ in(to), on забира́ться *impf*, забра́ться *pf* в+*acc*; ~ up накопля́ться, нака́пливаться *impf*, накопи́ться *pf*. **pile²** *n* (on cloth etc.) ворс.

piles *n pl* геморро́й *collect*.

pilfer *vt* ворова́ть *impf*.

pilgrim *n* пилигри́м. **pilgrimage** *n* пало́мничество.

pill *n* пилю́ля; the ~ противозача́точная пилю́ля.

pillage *n* грабёж *impf*, о-~ *pf*; *v abs* мародёрствовать *impf*.

pillar *n* столб; ~-box стоя́чий почто́вый я́щик.

pillion *n* за́днее сиде́нье (мотоци́кла).

pillory *n* позо́рный столб; *vt* (fig) пригвожда́ть *impf*, пригвозди́ть *pf* к позо́рному столбу́.

pillow *n* поду́шка. **pillowcase** *n* на́волочка.

pilot *n* (naut) ло́цман; (aeron) пило́т; *adj* о́пытный, про́бный; *vt* пилоти́ровать *impf*.

pimp *n* сво́дник.

pimple *n* прыщ.

pin *n* була́вка; (peg) па́лец; ~-point то́чно определя́ть *impf*, определи́ть *pf*; ~-stripe то́нкая поло́ска; *vt* прика́лывать *impf*, приколо́ть *pf*; (press) прижима́ть *impf*, прижа́ть *pf* (against к+*dat*).

pinafore *n* пере́дник.

pincers *n pl* (tool) кле́щи (-ще́й) *pl*, пинце́т; (claw) клешни́ *f pl*.

pinch *vt* щипа́ть *impf*, (y)щипну́ть *pf*; (finger in door etc.) прищемля́ть *impf*, прищеми́ть *pf*; (of shoe) жать *impf*; (steal) стяну́ть *pf*; *n* щипо́к; (of salt) щепо́тка; at a ~ в кра́йнем слу́чае.

pine¹ *vi* томи́ться *impf*; ~ for тоскова́ть *impf* по+*dat*, *prep*.

pine² *n* (tree) сосна́.

pineapple *n* анана́с.

ping-pong n пинг-по́нг.

pink n (colour) ро́зовый цвет; adj ро́зовый.

pinnacle n верши́на.

pint n пи́нта.

pioneer n пионе́р, ~ка; vt прокла́-дывать impf, проложи́ть pf путь к+dat.

pious adj на́божный.

pip[1] n (seed) зёрнышко.

pip[2] n (sound) бип.

pipe n труба́; (mus) ду́дка; (for smoking) тру́бка; ~-dream пуста́я мечта́; vt пуска́ть impf, пусти́ть pf по труба́м; vi ~ down затиха́ть impf, зати́хнуть pf. **pipeline** n трубопро-во́д; (oil ~) нефтепрово́д. **piper** n волы́нщик. **piping** adj: ~ hot с пы́лу.

piquant adj пика́нтный.

pique n: in a fit of ~ в поры́ве раз-дражёния.

pirate n пира́т.

pirouette n пируэ́т; vi де́лать impf, с~ pf пируэ́т(ы).

Pisces n Ры́бы f pl.

pistol n пистоле́т.

piston n по́ршень m.

pit n я́ма; (mine) ша́хта; (orchestra ~) орке́стр; (motor-racing) запра́вочно-ремо́нтный пункт; vt: ~ against выставля́ть impf, вы́ставить pf про́тив +gen.

pitch[1] n (resin) смола́; ~-black чёр-ный как смоль; ~-dark о́чень тём-ный.

pitch[2] vt (camp, tent) разбива́ть impf, разби́ть pf; (throw) броса́ть impf, бро́сить pf; vi (fall) па́дать impf, (у)па́сть pf; (ship) кача́ть impf, n (football ~ etc.) площа́дка; (degree) у́ровень m; (mus) высота́; (slope) укло́н.

pitcher n (vessel) кувши́н.

pitchfork n ви́лы (-л) pl.

piteous adj жа́лкий.

pitfall n западня́.

pith n серцеви́на; (essence) суть. **pithy** adj (fig) содержа́тельный.

pitiful adj жа́лкий. **pitiless** adj без-жа́лостный.

pittance n жа́лкие гроши́ (-ше́й) pl.

pity n жа́лость; it's a ~ жа́лко, жаль; take ~ on сжа́литься pf над+instr; what a ~ как жа́лко!; vt жале́ть impf, по~ pf; I ~ you мне жаль тебя́.

pivot n сте́ржень m; (fig) центр; vi враща́ться impf.

pixie n эльф.

pizza n пи́цца.

placard n афи́ша, плака́т.

placate vt умиротворя́ть impf, уми-ротвори́ть pf.

place n ме́сто; in ~ of вме́сто+gen; in the first, second, ~ во-пе́рвых, во-вторы́х; out of ~ не на ме́сте; (unsuitable) неуме́стный; take ~ случа́ться impf, случи́ться pf; (pre-arranged event) состоя́ться pf; take the ~ of заменя́ть impf, замени́ть pf; vt (stand) ста́вить impf, по~ pf; (lay) класть impf, положи́ть pf; (an order etc.) помеща́ть impf, помес-ти́ть pf.

placenta n плаце́нта.

placid adj споко́йный.

plagiarism n плагиа́т. **plagiarize** vt заи́мствовать impf & pf.

plague n чума́; vt му́чить impf, за~, из~ pf.

plaice n ка́мбала.

plain n равни́на; adj (clear) я́сный; (simple) просто́й; (ugly) некраси́-вый; ~-clothes policeman переоде́-тый полице́йский sb.

plaintiff n исте́ц, истица́.

plaintive adj жа́лобный.

plait n коса́; vt плести́ impf, с~ pf.

plan n план; vt плани́ровать impf, за~, с~ pf; (intend) намерева́ться impf +inf.

plane[1] n (tree) плата́н.

plane[2] n (tool) руба́нок; vt строга́ть impf, вы́~ pf.

plane[3] n (surface) пло́скость; (level) у́ровень m; (aeroplane) самолёт.

planet n плане́та.

plank n доска́.

plant n (of trees) расте́ние; (factory) заво́д; vt сажа́ть impf, посади́ть pf; (fix firmly) про́чно ста́вить impf, по~ pf; (garden etc.) заса́живать impf, засади́ть pf (with +instr).

plantation n (of trees) (лесо)насаж-де́ние; (of cotton etc.) планта́ция.

plaque n доще́чка.

plasma n пла́зма.

plaster n пла́стырь m; (for walls etc.) штукату́рка; (of Paris) гипс; vt (wall) штукату́рить impf, от~, о~ pf; (cover) облепля́ть impf, облепи́ть *pf.* **plasterboard** *n* сухáя штукатýрка. **plasterer** *n* штукатýр.

plastic *n* пластмáсса; *adj* (*malleable*) пласти́чный; (*made of* ~) пластмáссовый; ~ **surgery** пласти́ческая хирурги́я.

plate *n* тарéлка; (*metal sheet*) лист; (*in book*) (вкладнáя) иллюстрáция; (*name* ~ *etc.*) дощéчка.

plateau *n* платó *neut indecl.*

platform *n* платфóрма; (*rly*) перрóн.

platinum *n* плáтина.

platitude *n* банáльность.

platoon *n* взвод.

plausible *adj* правдоподóбный.

play *vt & i* игрáть *impf*, сыгрáть *pf* (*game*) в+*acc*, (*instrument*) на+*prep*, (*record*) стáвить *impf*, по~ *pf*; ~ **down** преуменьшáть *impf*, преумéньшить *pf*; ~ **a joke, trick, on** подшýчивать *impf*, подшути́ть *pf* над +*instr*; ~ **off** игрáть *impf*, сыгрáть *pf* реша́ющую па́ртию; ~**off** реша́ющая встрéча; ~ **safe** дéйствовать *impf* навернякá; *n* игрá; (*theat*) пьéса. **player** *n* игрóк; (*actor*) актёр, актри́са; (*musician*) музыкáнт. **playful** *adj* игри́вый. **playground** *n* площáдка для игр. **playgroup, playschool** *n* дéтский сад. **playing** *n*: ~**card** игрáльная кáрта; ~**field** игровáя площáдка. **playmate** *n* друг дéтства. **plaything** *n* игрýшка. **playwright** *n* драматýрг.

plea *n* (*entreaty*) мольбá; (*law*) заявлéние. **plead** *vi* умоля́ть *impf* (**with** +*acc*; **for** о+*prep*); *vt* (*offer as excuse*) ссылáться *impf*, сослáться *pf* на+*acc*; ~ (**not**) **guilty** (не) признавáть *impf*, призна́ть *pf* себя́ вино́вным.

pleasant *adj* прия́тный. **pleasantry** *n* любéзность. **please** *vt* нрáвиться *impf*, по~ *pf* +*dat*; *imper* пожáлуйста; бýдьте добры́. **pleased** *adj* довóльный; *predic* рад. **pleasing, pleasurable** *adj* прия́тный. **pleasure** *n* удовóльствие.

pleat *n* склáдка; *vt* плиссировáть *impf.*

plebiscite *n* плебисци́т.

plectrum *n* плектр.

pledge *n* (*security*) залóг; (*promise*) зарóк, обещáние; *vt* отдавáть *impf*, отдáть *pf* в залóг; ~ **o.s.** обя́зываться *impf*, обязáться *pf*; ~ **one's**

word давáть *impf*, дать *pf* слóво.

plentiful *adj* оби́льный. **plenty** *n* изоби́лие; ~ **of** мнóго+*gen.*

plethora *n* (*fig*) изоби́лие.

pleurisy *n* плеври́т.

pliable *adj* ги́бкий.

pliers *n pl* плоскогýбцы (-цев) *pl.*

plight *n* незави́дное положéние.

plimsolls *n pl* спорти́вные тáпочки *f pl.*

plinth *n* плин́тус.

plod *vi* тащи́ться *impf.*

plonk *vt* плю́хнуть *pf.*

plot *n* (*of land*) учáсток; (*of book etc.*) фáбула; (*conspiracy*) зáговор; *vt* (*on graph, map, etc.*) наноси́ть *impf*, нанести́ на грáфик, на кáрту; *v* ~ (*conspire*) составля́ть *impf*, состáвить *pf* зáговор.

plough *n* плуг; *vt* пахáть *impf*, вс~ *pf*; *vi*: ~ **through** пробивáться *impf*, проби́ться *pf* сквозь+*acc.*

ploy *n* улóвка.

pluck *n* (*courage*) смéлость; *vt* (*chicken*) щипáть *impf*, об~ *pf*; (*mus*) щипáть *impf*; (*flower*) срывáть *impf*, сорвáть *pf*; ~ **up courage** собирáться *impf*, собрáться *pf* с дýхом; *vi*: ~ **at** дёргать *impf*, дёрнуть *pf.* **plucky** *adj* смéлый.

plug *n* (*stopper*) прóбка; (*electr*) ви́лка; (*electr socket*) розéтка; *vt* (~ **up**) затыкáть *impf*, заткнýть *pf*; ~ **in** включáть *impf*, включи́ть *pf.*

plum *n* сли́ва.

plumage *n* оперéние.

plumb *n* лот; *adv* вертикáльно; (*fig*) тóчно; *vt* измеря́ть *impf*, измéрить *pf* глубинý+*gen*; (*fig*) проникáть *impf*, прони́кнуть *pf* в+*acc*; ~ **in** подключáть *impf*, подключи́ть *pf.* **plumber** *n* водопровóдчик. **plumbing** *n* водопровóд.

plume *n* (*feather*) перó; (*on hat etc.*) султáн.

plummet *vi* пáдать *impf*, (у)пáсть *pf.*

plump¹ *adj* пýхлый.

plump² *vi*: ~ **for** выбирáть *impf*, вы́брать *pf.*

plunder *vt* грáбить *impf*, о~ *pf*; *n* добы́ча.

plunge *vt & i* (*immerse*) погружáть(ся) *impf*, погрузи́ть(ся) *pf* (**into** в+*acc*); *vi* (*dive*) ныря́ть *impf*, нырнýть *pf*; (*rush*) бросáться *impf*, броситься pf. **plunger** n плу́нжер.

pluperfect n давнопрошéдшее врéмя neut.

plural n мнóжественное числó.
pluralism n плюрали́зм. **pluralistic** adj плюралисти́ческий.

plus prep плюс+acc; n (знак) плюс.

plushy adj шика́рный.

plutonium n плутóний.

ply n (tool) рабóтать impf +instr; (task) занима́ться impf +instr; (keep supplied) пóтчевать impf (with +instr); ~ with questions засыпа́ть impf, засыпа́ть pf вопрóсами.

plywood n фанéра.

p.m. adv пóсле полу́дня.

pneumatic adj пневмати́ческий; ~ drill отбóйный молотóк.

pneumonia n воспалéние лёгких.

poach[1] vt (cook) вари́ть impf; ~ed egg яйцó-пашóт.

poach[2] vi браконьéрствовать impf.
poacher n браконьéр.

pocket n карма́н; out of ~в убы́тке; ~ money карма́нные дéньги (-нег, -ньга́м) pl; vt класть impf, положи́ть pf в карма́н.

pock-marked adj рябóй.

pod n стручóк.

podgy adj тóлстенький.

podium n трибу́на; (conductor's) пульт.

poem n стихотворéние; (longer ~) поэ́ма. **poet** n поэ́т. **poetess** n поэтéсса. **poetic(al)** adj поэти́ческий. **poetry** n поэ́зия, стихи́ m pl.

pogrom n погрóм.

poignancy n острота́. **poignant** adj óстрый.

point[1] n тóчка; (place; in list) пункт; (in score) очкó; (in time) момéнт; (in space) мéсто; (essence) суть; (sense) смысл; (sharp) острие́; (tip) кóнчик; (power ~) штéпсель m; pl (rly) стрéлка; be on the ~ of (doing) собира́ться impf, собра́ться pf +inf; beside, off, the ~нектста́ти; that is the ~в э́том и дéло; the ~ is thatдéло в том, что; there is no ~ (in doing) не имéет смы́сла (+inf); to the ~кста́ти; ~blankпрямóй; ~ of viewтóчка зрéния.

point[2] vt (wall) расши́вать impf, расши́ть pf швы+gen; (gun etc.) наводи́ть impf, навести́ pf (at на+acc);

vi по-, у-, ка́зывать impf, по-, у-каза́ть pf (at, to на+acc). **pointed** adj (sharp) óстрый. **pointer** n указа́тель m, стрéлка. **pointless** adj бессмы́сленный.

poise n уравновéшенность. **poised** adj (composed) уравновéшенный; (ready) готóвый (to к+dat).

poison n-яд; vt отравля́ть impf, отрави́ть pf. **poisonous** adj ядови́тый.

poke vt (prod) ты́кать impf, ткнуть pf; ~ fun at подшу́чивать impf, подшути́ть pf над+instr; (thrust) сова́ть impf, су́нуть pf; ~ the fire меша́ть impf, по~ pf у́гли в ками́не; n тычóк. **poker**[1] n (rod) кочерга́.

poker[2] n (cards) пóкер.

poky adj тéсный.

Poland n Пóльша.

polar adj поля́рный; ~ bear бéлый медвéдь m. **polarity** n поля́рность.
polarize vt поляризова́ть impf & pf.

pole[1] n (geog; phys) пóлюс; ~star Поля́рная звезда́.

pole[2] n (rod) столб, шест; ~vaulting прыжóк с шестóм.

Pole n поля́к, пóлька.

polecat n хорёк.

polemic adj полеми́ческий; n полéмика.

police n поли́ция; (as pl) полицéйские sb; (in Russia) мили́ция; ~ station полицéйский уча́сток. **policeman** n полицéйский sb, полисмéн; (in Russia) милиционéр. **policewoman** n жéнщина-полицéйский sb; (in Russia) жéнщина-милиционéр.

policy[1] n поли́тика.

policy[2] n (insurance) пóлис.

polio n полиомиели́т.

Polish adj пóльский.

polish n (gloss, process) полирóвка; (substance) политу́ра; (fig) лоск; vt полирова́ть impf, от~ pf; ~ offрасправля́ться impf, распра́виться pf c+instr. **polished** adj отто́ченный.

polite adj вéжливый. **politeness** n вéжливость.

politic adj полити́чный. **political** adj полити́ческий; ~ economy полит-экóномика; ~ prisoner политзаключённый sb. **politician** n поли́тик. **politics** n поли́тика.

poll n (voting) голосова́ние; (opinion ~) опрóс; **go to the ~s**голосова́ть *impf*, про~ *pf*; *vt* получа́ть *impf*, получи́ть *pf*.

pollen *n* пыльца́. **pollinate** *vt* опыля́ть *impf*, опыли́ть *pf*.

polling *attrib*: ~ **booth** каби́на для голосова́ния; ~ **station** избира́тельный уча́сток.

pollutant *n* загрязни́тель *m*. **pollute** *vt* загрязня́ть *impf*, загрязни́ть *pf*. **pollution** *n* загрязне́ние.

polo *n* по́ло *neut indecl*; ~**neck sweater** водола́зка.

polyester *n* полиэфи́р. **polyethylene** *n* полиэтиле́н. **polyglot** *n* полигло́т; *adj* многоязы́чный. **polygon** *n* многоуго́льник. **polymer** *n* полиме́р. **polystyrene** *n* полистиро́л. **polytechnic** *n* техни́ческий вуз. **polythene** *n* полиэтиле́н. **polyunsaturated** *adj*: ~ **fats** полиненасы́щенные жиры́ *m pl*. **polyurethane** *n* полиурета́н.

pomp *n* пы́шность. **pomposity** *n* напы́щенность. **pompous** *adj* напы́щенный.

pond *n* пруд.

ponder *vt* обду́мывать *impf*, обду́мать *pf*; *vi* размышля́ть *impf*, размы́слить *pf*.

ponderous *adj* тяжелове́сный.

pony *n* по́ни *m indecl*.

poodle *n* пу́дель *m*.

pool¹ *n* (*of water*) прудо́к; (*puddle*) лу́жа; (*swimming* ~) бассе́йн.

pool² *n* (*collective stakes*) совоку́пность ста́вок; (*common fund*) о́бщий фонд; *vt* объединя́ть *impf*, объедини́ть *pf*.

poor *adj* бе́дный; (*bad*) плохо́й; *n*: **the** ~ бедняки́ *m pl*. **poorly** *predic* нездоро́в.

pop¹ *vi* хло́пать *impf*, хло́пнуть *pf*; *vt* (*put*) бы́стро всу́нуть *pf* (**into** в+*acc*); ~ **in on** забега́ть *impf*, забежа́ть *pf* к+*dat*; *n* хлопо́к.

pop² *adj* поп-; ~ **concert** поп-конце́рт; ~ **music** поп-му́зыка.

pope *n* Па́па *m*.

poplar *n* то́поль *m*.

poppy *n* мак.

populace *n* просто́й наро́д. **popular** *adj* наро́дный; (*liked*) популя́рный. **popularity** *n* популя́рность. **popularize** *vt* популяризи́ровать *impf* & *pf*. **populate** *vt* населя́ть *impf*, насе-

ли́ть *pf*. **population** *n* населе́ние. **populous** *adj* (мно́го)лю́дный.

porcelain *n* фарфо́р.

porch *n* крыльцо́.

porcupine *n* дикобра́з.

pore¹ *n* по́ра.

pore² *vi*: ~ **over** погружа́ться *impf*, погрузи́ться *pf* в+*acc*.

pork *n* свини́на.

pornographic *adj* порнографи́ческий. **pornography** *n* порногра́фия.

porous *adj* по́ристый.

porpoise *n* морска́я свинья́.

porridge *n* овся́ная ка́ша.

port¹ *n* (*harbour*) порт; (*town*) порто́вый го́род.

port² *n* (*naut*) ле́вый борт.

port³ *n* (*wine*) портве́йн.

portable *adj* порта́тивный.

portend *vt* предвеща́ть *impf*. **portent** *n* предзнаменова́ние. **portentous** *adj* злове́щий.

porter¹ *n* (*at door*) швейца́р.

porter² *n* (*carrier*) носи́льщик.

portfolio *n* портфе́ль *m*; (*artist's*) па́пка.

porthole *n* иллюмина́тор.

portion *n* часть, до́ля; (*of food*) по́рция.

portly *adj* доро́дный.

portrait *n* портре́т. **portray** *vt* изобража́ть *impf*, изобрази́ть *pf*. **portrayal** *n* изображе́ние.

Portugal *n* Португа́лия. **Portuguese** *n* португа́лец, -лка; *adj* португа́льский.

pose *n* по́за; *vt* (*question*) ста́вить *impf*, по~ *pf*; (*a problem*) представля́ть *impf*, предста́вить *pf*; *vi* пози́ровать *impf*; ~ **as** выдава́ть *impf*, вы́дать *pf* себя́ за+*acc*.

posh *adj* шика́рный.

posit *vt* постули́ровать *impf* & *pf*.

position *n* положе́ние, пози́ция; **in a** ~ **to** в состоя́нии +*inf*; *vt* ста́вить *impf*, по~ *pf*.

positive *adj* положи́тельный; (*convinced*) уве́ренный; (*proof*) несомне́нный; *n* (*phot*) позити́в.

possess *vt* облада́ть *impf* +*instr*; владе́ть *impf* +*instr*; (*of feeling etc.*) овладева́ть *impf*, овладе́ть *pf* +*instr*. **possessed** *adj* одержи́мый. **possession** *n* владе́ние, (**of** +*instr*); *pl* со́бственность. **possessive** *adj* со́бственнический. **possessor** n облада́тель m.

possibility n возмо́жность. **possible** adj возмо́жный; **as much as ~** ско́лько возмо́жно; **as soon as ~** как мо́жно скоре́е. **possibly** adv возмо́жно, мо́жет (быть).

post[1] n (pole) столб; vt (~ up) выве́шивать impf, вы́весить pf.

post[2] n (station) пост; (job) до́лжность; vt (station) расставля́ть impf, расста́вить pf; (appoint) назнача́ть impf, назна́чить pf.

post[3] n (letters; ~ office) по́чта; **by ~** по́чтой; attrib почто́вый; **~-box** почто́вый я́щик; **~-code** почто́вый и́ндекс; **~ office** по́чта; vt (send by ~) отправля́ть impf, отпра́вить pf по по́чте; (put in ~-box) опуска́ть impf, опусти́ть pf в почто́вый я́щик.

postage n почто́вый сбор, почто́вые расхо́ды m pl; **~ stamp** почто́вая ма́рка. **postal** adj почто́вый; **~-order** почто́вый перево́д. **postcard** n откры́тка.

poster n афи́ша, плака́т.

poste restante n до востре́бования.

posterior adj за́дний; n зад.

posterity n пото́мство.

post-graduate n аспира́нт.

posthumous adj посме́ртный.

postman n почтальо́н. **postmark** n почто́вый ште́мпель m.

post-mortem n вскры́тие тру́па.

postpone vt отсро́чивать impf, отсро́чить pf. **postponement** n отсро́чка.

postscript n постскри́птум.

postulate vt постули́ровать impf & pf.

posture n по́за, положе́ние.

post-war adj послевое́нный.

posy n буке́тик.

pot n горшо́к; (cooking ~) кастрю́ля; **~-shot** вы́стрел науга́д; vt (food) консерви́ровать impf, за~ pf; (plant) сажа́ть impf, посади́ть pf в горшо́к; (billiards) загоня́ть impf, загна́ть pf в лу́зу.

potash n пота́ш. **potassium** n ка́лий.

potato n (also collect) карто́шка (no pl); (plant; also collect) карто́фель m (no pl).

potency n си́ла. **potent** adj си́льный.

potential adj потенциа́льный; n потенциа́л. **potentiality** n потенци-

а́льность.

pot-hole n (in road) вы́боина.

potion n зе́лье.

potter[1] vi: **~ about** вози́ться impf.

potter[2] n гонча́р. **pottery** n (goods) гонча́рные изде́лия neut pl; (place) гонча́рная sb.

potty[1] adj (crazy) поме́шанный (about на+prep).

potty[2] n ночно́й горшо́к.

pouch n су́мка.

poultry n дома́шняя пти́ца.

pounce vi: **~ (up)on** набра́сываться impf, набро́ситься pf на+acc.

pound[1] n (measure) фунт; **~ sterling** фунт сте́рлингов.

pound[2] vt (strike) колоти́ть impf, по~ pf по+dat, в+acc; vi (heart) колоти́ться impf; **~ along** (run) мча́ться impf с гро́хотом.

pour vt лить impf; **~ out** налива́ть impf, нали́ть pf; vi ли́ться impf; it is **~ing (with rain)** дождь льёт как из ведра́.

pout vi ду́ть(ся) impf, на~ pf.

poverty n бе́дность; **~-stricken** убо́гий.

POW abbr военнопле́нный sb.

powder n порошо́к; (cosmetic) пу́дра; vt пу́дрить impf, на~ pf. **powdery** adj порошкообра́зный.

power n (vigour) си́ла; (might) могу́щество; (ability) спосо́бность; (control) власть; (authorization) полномо́чие; (State) держа́ва; **~ cut** переры́в электропита́ния; **~ point** розе́тка; **~ station** электроста́нция. **powerful** adj си́льный. **powerless** adj бесси́льный.

practicable adj осуществи́мый. **practical** adj практи́ческий. **practically** adv практи́чески. **practice** n пра́ктика; (custom) обы́чай; (mus) заня́тия neut pl; **in ~** на пра́ктике; **put into ~** осуществля́ть impf, осуществи́ть pf. **practise** vt (also abs of doctor etc.) практикова́ть impf; упражня́ться impf в+prep; (mus) держа́ва; ~ занима́ться impf, заня́ться pf на+prep.

practised adj о́пытный. **practitioner** n (doctor) практику́ющий врач; **general ~** врач о́бщей пра́ктики.

pragmatic adj прагмати́ческий. **pragmatism** n прагмати́зм. **pragmatist** n прагма́тик.

prairie *n* пре́рия.

praise *vt* хвали́ть *impf*, по~ *pf*; *n* похвала́. **praiseworthy** *adj* похва́льный.

pram *n* де́тская коля́ска.

prance *vi* (*horse*) гарцева́ть *impf*; (*fig*) задава́ться *impf*.

prank *n* вы́ходка.

prattle *vi* лепета́ть; *n* ле́пет.

prawn *n* креве́тка.

pray *vi* моли́ться *impf*, по~ *pf* (to +*dat*; for о+*prep*). **prayer** *n* моли́тва.

preach *vt & i* пропове́дывать *impf*. **preacher** *n* пропове́дник.

preamble *n* преа́мбула.

pre-arrange *vt* зара́нее организо́-вывать *impf*, организова́ть *pf*.

precarious *adj* ненадёжный; опа́сный.

precaution *n* предосторо́жность. **precautionary** *adj*: ~ **measures** ме́ры предосторо́жности.

precede *vt* предше́ствовать *impf* +*dat*. **precedence** *n* предпочте́ние. **precedent** *n* прецеде́нт. **preceding** *adj* предыду́щий.

precept *n* наставле́ние.

precinct *n* двор; *pl* окре́стности *f pl*. **pedestrian** ~ уча́сток для пешехо́дов; **shopping** ~ торго́вый пасса́ж.

precious *adj* драгоце́нный; (*style*) мане́рный; *adv* о́чень.

precipice *n* обры́в. **precipitate** *adj* (*person*) опроме́тчивый; *vt* (*throw down*) низверга́ть *impf*, низве́ргнуть *pf*; (*hurry*) ускоря́ть *impf*, уско́рить *pf*. **precipitation** *n* (*meteorol*) оса́дки *m pl*. **precipitous** *adj* обры́вистый.

précis *n* конспе́кт.

precise *adj* то́чный. **precisely** *adv* то́чно; (*in answer*) и́менно. **precision** *n* то́чность.

preclude *vt* предотвраща́ть *impf*, предотврати́ть *pf*.

precocious *adj* ра́но разви́вшийся.

preconceived *adj* предвзя́тый. **preconception** *n* предвзя́тое мне́ние.

pre-condition *n* предпосы́лка.

precursor *n* предше́ственник.

predator *n* хи́щник. **predatory** *adj* хи́щный.

predecessor *n* предше́ственник.

predestination *n* предопределе́ние.

predetermine *vt* предреша́ть *impf*, предреши́ть *pf*.

predicament *n* затрудни́тельное положе́ние.

predicate *n* (*gram*) сказу́емое *sb*. **predicative** *adj* предикати́вный.

predict *vt* предска́зывать *impf*, предсказа́ть *pf*. **predictable** *adj* предсказу́емый. **prediction** *n* предсказа́ние.

predilection *n* пристра́стие (for к +*dat*).

predispose *vt* предрасполага́ть *impf*, предрасположи́ть *pf* (to к+*dat*). **predisposition** *n* предрасположе́ние (to к+*dat*).

predominance *n* преоблада́ние. **predominant** *adj* преоблада́ющий. **predominate** *vi* преоблада́ть *impf*.

pre-eminence *n* превосхо́дство. **pre-eminent** *adj* выдаю́щийся.

pre-empt *vt* (*fig*) завладева́ть *impf*, завладе́ть *pf* +*instr* пре́жде други́х. **pre-emptive** *adj* (*mil*) упрежда́ющий.

preen *vt* (*of bird*) чи́стить *impf*, по~ *pf* клю́вом; ~ **o.s.** (*be proud*) горди́ться *impf* собо́й.

pre-fab *n* сбо́рный дом. **pre-fabricated** *adj* сбо́рный.

preface *n* предисло́вие.

prefect *n* префе́кт; (*school*) ста́роста *m*.

prefer *vt* предпочита́ть *impf*, предпоче́сть *pf*. **preferable** *adj* предпочти́тельный. **preference** *n* предпочте́ние. **preferential** *adj* предпочти́тельный.

prefix *n* приста́вка.

pregnancy *n* бере́менность. **pregnant** *adj* бере́менная.

prehistoric *adj* доистори́ческий.

prejudice *n* предубежде́ние; (*detriment*) уще́рб; *vt* наноси́ть *impf*, нанести́ *pf* уще́рб+*dat*; ~ **against** предубежда́ть *impf*, предубеди́ть *pf* про́тив+*gen*; **be** ~**d against** име́ть *impf* предубежде́ние про́тив +*gen*.

preliminary *adj* предвари́тельный.

prelude *n* прелю́дия.

premarital *adj* добра́чный.

premature *adj* преждевре́менный.

premeditated *adj* преднаме́ренный.

premier *adj* пе́рвый; *n* премье́р-мини́стр. **première** *n* премье́ра.

premise, premiss n (*logic*) (пред)-
посы́лка. **premises** n pl помеще́-
ние.

premium n пре́мия.

premonition n предчу́вствие.

preoccupation n озабо́ченность;
(*absorbing subject*) забо́та. **preoccupied** adj озабо́ченный. **preoc-
cupy** vt поглоща́ть impf, поглоти́ть
pf.

preparation n приготовле́ние; pl
подгото́вка (**for** к+dat); (*substance*)
препара́т. **preparatory** adj подго-
тови́тельный. **prepare** vt & i при-,
под-, гота́вливать(ся) impf, при-,
под-, гото́вить(ся) pf (**for** к+dat).
prepared adj гото́вый.

preponderance n переве́с.

preposition n предло́г.

prepossessing adj привлека́тель-
ный.

preposterous adj неле́пый.

prerequisite n предпосы́лка.

prerogative n прерогати́ва.

presage vt предвеща́ть impf.

Presbyterian n пресвитериа́нин,
-а́нка; adj пресвитериа́нский.

prescribe vt предпи́сывать impf,
предписа́ть pf; (*med*) прописа́ть
impf, прописа́ть pf. **prescription** n
(*med*) реце́пт.

presence n прису́тствие; ~ **of mind**
прису́тствие ду́ха. **present** adj при-
су́тствующий; (*being dealt with*)
да́нный; (*existing now*) ны́нешний;
(*also gram*) настоя́щий; *predic* на-
лицо́; **be** ~ прису́тствовать impf (**at**
на+prep); ~**day** ны́нешний; n: **the**
~ настоя́щее sb; (*gram*) настоя́щее
вре́мя neut; (*gift*) пода́рок; **at** ~ в
настоя́щее вре́мя neut; **for the** ~
пока́; vt предоставля́ть impf, пред-
ста́вить pf (**to** +dat);
(*award*) вруча́ть impf, вручи́ть
pf; (*a play*) ста́вить impf, по~ pf;
(*a gift*) преподноси́ть impf, препод-
нести́ pf +dat (**with** +acc); ~ **o.s.**
явля́ться impf, яви́ться pf. **present-
able** adj прили́чный. **presentation**
n (*introducing*) представле́ние;
(*awarding*) подноше́ние.

presentiment n предчу́вствие.

presently adv вско́ре.

preservation n сохране́ние. **preservative** n консерва́нт. **preserve** vt

(*keep safe*) сохраня́ть impf, со-
храни́ть pf; (*maintain*) храни́ть
impf; (*food*) консерви́ровать impf,
за~ pf; n (*for game etc*) запове́дник;
(*jam*) варе́нье.

preside vi председа́тельствовать
impf (**at** на+prep). **presidency** n
президе́нтство. **president** n прези-
де́нт. **presidential** adj президе́нт-
ский. **presidium** n прези́диум.

press n (*machine*) пресс; (*printing
firm*) типогра́фия; (*publishing house*)
изда́тельство; (*the* ~) пре́сса, пе-
ча́ть; ~ **conference** пресс-конфе-
ре́нция; vt (*button etc*) нажима́ть
impf, нажа́ть pf; (*clasp*) прижима́ть
impf, прижа́ть pf (**to** к+dat); (*iron*)
гла́дить impf, вы́~ pf; (*insist on*)
наста́ивать impf, настоя́ть pf на
+prep; (*urge*) угова́ривать impf; ~
on (*make haste*) потора́пливаться
impf.

pressing adj неотло́жный. **pressure**
n давле́ние; ~**cooker** скорова́рка;
~ **group** инициати́вная гру́ппа.
pressurize vt (*fig*) ока́зывать impf,
оказа́ть pf давле́ние на+acc. **pres-
surized** adj гермети́ческий.

prestige n прести́ж. **prestigious** adj
прести́жный.

presumably adv предположи́тельно.
presume vt полага́ть impf; (*venture*)
позволя́ть impf, позво́лить pf себе́.
presumption n предположе́ние;
(*arrogance*) самонаде́янность. **presumptuous** adj самонаде́янный.

presuppose vt предполага́ть impf.

pretence n притво́рство. **pretend** vt
притворя́ться impf, притвори́ться
pf (**to be** +instr); де́лать impf, с~ pf
вид (что); vi: ~ **to** претендова́ть
impf на+acc. **pretender** n претен-
де́нт. **pretension** n прете́нзия. **pre-
tentious** adj претенцио́зный.

pretext n предло́г.

prettiness n миловидность. **pretty**
adj хоро́шенький; adv дово́льно.

prevail vi (*predominate*) преобла-
да́ть impf; ~ (**up**)**on** угова́ривать
impf, уговори́ть pf. **prevalence** n
распростране́ние. **prevalent** adj
распространённый.

prevaricate vi уви́ливать impf увиль-
ну́ть pf.

prevent vt (*stop from happening*)

предупрежда́ть *impf*, предупреди́ть *pf*; (*stop from doing*) меша́ть *impf*, по~ *pf* +*dat*. **prevention** *n* предупрежде́ние. **preventive** *adj* предупреди́тельный.

preview *n* предвари́тельный просмо́тр.

previous *adj* предыду́щий; *adv*: ~ **to** до+*gen*; пре́жде чем +*inf*. **previously** *adv* ра́ньше.

pre-war *adj* довое́нный.

prey *n* (*animal*) добы́ча; (*victim*) же́ртва (**to** +*gen*); **bird of** ~ хи́щная пти́ца; *vi*: ~ **(up)on** (*emotion etc.*) му́чить *impf*.

price *n* цена́; ~**list** прейскура́нт; *vt* назнача́ть *impf*, назна́чить *pf* це́ну +*gen*. **priceless** *adj* бесце́нный.

prick *vt* коло́ть *impf*, у~ *pf*; (*conscience*) му́чить *impf*; ~ **up one's ears** навостри́ть *pf* у́ши; *n* уко́л. **prickle** *n* (*thorn*) колю́чка; (*spine*) игла́. **prickly** *adj* колю́чий.

pride *n* го́рдость; ~ **o.s. on** горди́ться *impf* +*instr*.

priest *n* свяще́нник; (*non-Christian*) жрец.

prig *n* педа́нт.

prim *adj* чо́порный.

primarily *adv* первонача́льно; (*above all*) пре́жде всего́. **primary** *adj* основно́й; ~ **school** нача́льная шко́ла. **prime** *n*: **in one's** ~ в расцве́те сил; *adj* (*chief*) гла́вный; ~ **minister** премье́р-мини́стр; *vt* (*engine*) заправля́ть *impf*, запра́вить *pf*; (*bomb*) активизи́ровать *impf* & *pf*; (*with facts*) инструкти́ровать *impf* & *pf*; (*with paint etc.*) грунтова́ть *impf*, за~ *pf*. **primer** *n* (*paint etc.*) грунт. **prim(a)eval** *adj* первобы́тный. **primitive** *adj* первобы́тный; (*crude*) примити́вный. **primordial** *adj* иско́нный.

primrose *n* первоцве́т; (*colour*) бле́дно-жёлтый цвет.

prince *n* принц; (*in Russia*) князь. **princely** *adj* кня́жеский; (*sum*) огро́мный. **princess** *n* принце́сса; (*wife*) княги́ня; (*daughter*) княжна́.

principal *n* гла́вный; *n* дире́ктор. **principality** *n* кня́жество. **principally** *adv* гла́вным о́бразом.

principle *n* при́нцип; **in** ~ в при́нципе; **on** ~ принципиа́льно. **prin-**

cipled *adj* принципиа́льный.

print *n* (*mark*) след; (*also phot*) отпеча́ток; (*printing*) печа́ть; (*picture*) о́ттиск; **in** ~ в прода́же; **out of** ~ распро́данный; *vt* (*impress*) запечатлева́ть *impf*, запечатле́ть *pf*; (*book etc.*) печа́тать *impf*, на~ *pf*; (*write*) писа́ть *impf*, на~ *pf* печа́тными бу́квами; (*phot*; ~ **out, off**) отпеча́тывать *impf*, отпеча́тать *pf*; ~ **out** (*of computer etc.*) распеча́тывать *impf*, распеча́тать *pf*; ~**out** распеча́тка. **printer** *n* (*person*) печа́тник, типо́граф; (*of computer*) при́нтер. **printing** *n* печа́тание; ~**press** печа́тный стано́к.

prior *adj* пре́жний; *adv*: ~ **to** до+*gen*. **priority** *n* приорите́т. **priory** *n* монасты́рь *m*.

prise *vt*: ~ **open** взла́мывать *impf*, взлома́ть *pf*.

prism *n* при́зма.

prison *n* тюрьма́; *attrib* тюре́мный; ~ **camp** ла́герь *m*. **prisoner** *n* заключённый *sb*; (~ **of war**) (вое́нно)плéнный *sb*.

pristine *adj* нетро́нутый.

privacy *n* уедине́ние; (*private life*) ча́стная жизнь. **private** *adj* (*personal*) ча́стный, ли́чный; (*confidential*) конфиденциа́льный; **in** ~ наедине́; в ча́стной жи́зни; *n* рядово́й *sb*.

privation *n* лише́ние.

privilege *n* привиле́гия. **privileged** *adj* привилегиро́ванный.

privy *adj*: ~ **to** посвящённый в+*acc*.

prize *n* пре́мия, приз; ~**winner** призёр; *vt* высоко́ цени́ть *impf*.

pro[1] *n*: ~**s and cons** до́воды *m pl* за и про́тив.

pro[2] *n* (*professional*) профессиона́л.

probability *n* вероя́тность. **probable** *adj* вероя́тный. **probably** *adv* вероя́тно.

probate *n* утвержде́ние завеща́ния.

probation *n* испыта́тельный срок; (*law*) усло́вный пригово́р; **got two years** ~ получи́л два го́да усло́вно. **probationary** *adj* испыта́тельный.

probe *n* (*med*) зонд; (*fig*) рассле́дование; *vt* зонди́ровать *impf*; (*fig*) рассле́довать *impf* & *pf*.

probity *n* че́стность.

problem *n* пробле́ма, вопро́с; (*math*)

задáча. **problematic** *adj* проблемати́чный.

procedural *adj* процеду́рный. **procedure** *n* процеду́ра. **proceed** *vi* (*go further*) идти́ *impf*, пойти́ *pf* да́льше; (*act*) поступа́ть *impf*, поступи́ть *pf*; (*abs*, ~ *to say*; *continue*) продолжа́ть *impf*, продо́лжить *pf*; (*of action*) продолжа́ться *impf*, продо́лжиться *pf*; ~ **from** исходи́ть *impf* из, от+*gen*; ~ **to** (*begin to*) принима́ться *impf*, приня́ться *pf* +*inf*. **proceedings** *n pl* (*activity*) де́ятельность; (*legal* ~) судопроизво́дство; (*published report*) труды́ *m pl*, запи́ски *f pl*. **proceeds** *n pl* вы́ручка. **process** *n* проце́сс; *vt* обраба́тывать *impf*, обрабо́тать *pf*. **procession** *n* проце́ссия, ше́ствие.

proclaim *vt* провозглаша́ть *impf*, провозгласи́ть *pf*. **proclamation** *n* провозглаше́ние.

procure *vt* достава́ть *impf*, доста́ть *pf*.

prod *vt* ты́кать *impf*, ткнуть *pf*; *n* тычо́к.

prodigal *adj* расточи́тельный.

prodigious *adj* огро́мный. **prodigy** *n*: **child** ~ вундерки́нд.

produce *vt* (*evidence etc.*) представля́ть *impf*, предста́вить *pf*; (*ticket etc.*) предъявля́ть *impf*, предъяви́ть *pf*; (*play etc.*) ста́вить *impf*, по~ *pf*; (*manufacture*, *cause*) производи́ть *impf*, произвести́ *pf*; *n* (*collect*) проду́кты *m pl*. **producer** *n* (*econ*) производи́тель *m*; (*of play etc.*) режиссёр. **product** *n* проду́кт; (*result*) результа́т. **production** *n* произво́дство; (*of play etc.*) постано́вка. **productive** *adj* продукти́вный; (*fruitful*) плодотво́рный. **productivity** *n* производи́тельность.

profane *adj* све́тский; (*blasphemous*) богоху́льный. **profanity** *n* богоху́льство.

profess *vt* (*pretend*) притворя́ться *impf*, притвори́ться *pf* (**to be** +*instr*); (*declare*) заявля́ть *impf*, заяви́ть *pf*; (*faith*) испове́довать *impf*. **profession** *n* (*job*) профе́ссия. **professional** *adj* профессиона́льный; *n* профессиона́л. **professor** *n* профе́ссор.

proffer *vt* предлага́ть *impf*, предложи́ть *pf*.

proficiency *n* уме́ние. **proficient** *adj* уме́лый.

profile *n* про́филь *m*.

profit *n* (*benefit*) по́льза; (*monetary*) при́быль; *vt* приноси́ть *impf*, принести́ *pf* по́льзу +*dat*; *vi*: ~ **from** по́льзоваться *impf*, вос~ *pf* +*instr*; (*financially*) получа́ть *impf*, получи́ть *pf* при́быль на+*prep*. **profitable** *adj* (*lucrative*) при́быльный; (*beneficial*) поле́зный. **profiteering** *n* спекуля́ция.

profligate *adj* распу́тный.

profound *adj* глубо́кий.

profuse *adj* оби́льный. **profusion** *n* изоби́лие.

progeny *n* пото́мство.

prognosis *n* прогно́з.

program(m)e *n* програ́мма; *vt* программи́ровать *impf*, за~ *pf*. **programmer** *n* программи́ст.

progress *n* прогре́сс; (*success*) успе́хи *m pl*; **make** ~ де́лать *impf*, с~ *pf* успе́хи; *vi* продвига́ться *impf*, продви́нуться *pf* вперёд. **progression** *n* продвиже́ние. **progressive** *adj* прогресси́вный.

prohibit *vt* запреща́ть *impf*, запрети́ть *pf*. **prohibition** *n* запреще́ние; (*on alcohol*) сухо́й зако́н. **prohibitive** *adj* запрети́тельный; (*price*) недосту́пный.

project *vt* (*plan*) проекти́ровать *impf*, с~ *pf*; (*a film*) демонстри́ровать *impf*, про~ *pf*; *vi* (*jut out*) выступа́ть *impf*; *n* прое́кт. **projectile** *n* снаря́д. **projection** *n* (*cin*) прое́кция; (*protrusion*) вы́ступ; (*forecast*) прогно́з. **projector** *n* прое́ктор.

proletarian *adj* пролета́рский. **proletariat** *n* пролетариа́т.

proliferate *vi* распространя́ться *impf*, распространи́ться *pf*. **proliferation** *n* распростране́ние.

prolific *adj* плодови́тый.

prologue *n* проло́г.

prolong *vt* продлева́ть *impf*, продли́ть *pf*.

promenade *n* ме́сто для гуля́нья; (*at seaside*) на́бережная *sb*; *vi* прогу́ливаться *impf*, прогуля́ться *pf*.

prominence *n* изве́стность. **prominent** *adj* выступа́ющий; (*distinguished*) выдаю́щийся.

promiscuity *n* лёгкое поведе́ние.

promiscuous adj лёгкого поведе́ния.

promise n обеща́ние; vt обеща́ть impf & pf. **promising** adj многообеща́ющий.

promontory n мыс.

promote vt (in rank) продвига́ть impf, продви́нуть pf; (assist) спосо́бствовать impf & pf +dat; (publicize) реклами́ровать impf. **promoter** n (of event etc.) аге́нт. **promotion** n (in rank) продвиже́ние; (comm) рекла́ма.

prompt adj бы́стрый, неме́дленный; adv ро́вно; vt (incite) побужда́ть impf, побуди́ть pf (to к+dat; +inf); (speaker; also fig) подска́зывать impf, подсказа́ть pf +dat; (theat) суфли́ровать impf +dat; ~ n подска́зка. **prompter** n суфлёр.

prone adj (лежа́щий) ничко́м; predic: ~ to скло́нен (-онна́, -о́нно) к+dat.

prong n зубе́ц.

pronoun n местоиме́ние.

pronounce vt (declare) объявля́ть impf, объяви́ть pf; (articulate) произноси́ть impf, произнести́ pf. **pronounced** adj я́вный; заме́тный. **pronouncement** n заявле́ние. **pronunciation** n произноше́ние.

proof n доказа́тельство; (printing) корректу́ра; ~-reader корре́ктор; adj (impenetrable) непроница́емый (against +gen); (not yielding) неподдаю́щийся (against +dat).

prop[1] n (support) подпо́рка; (fig) опо́ра; vt (~ open, up) подпира́ть impf, подпере́ть pf; (fig) подде́рживать impf, поддержа́ть pf.

prop[2] n (theat) see props

propaganda n пропага́нда.

propagate vt & i размножа́ть(ся) impf, размно́жить(ся) pf; (disseminate) распространя́ть(ся) impf, распространи́ть(ся) pf. **propagation** n размноже́ние; распростране́ние.

propel vt приводи́ть impf, привести́ pf в движе́ние. **propeller** n винт.

propensity n накло́нность (to к+dat; +inf).

proper adj (correct) пра́вильный; (suitable) подходя́щий; (decent) присто́йный; ~ noun и́мя со́бственное. **properly** adv как сле́дует.

property n (possessions) со́бственность, иму́щество; (attribute) сво́йство; pl (theat) реквизи́т.

prophecy n проро́чество. **prophesy** vt проро́чить impf, на~ pf. **prophet** n проро́к. **prophetic** adj проро́ческий.

propitious adj благоприя́тный.

proponent n сторо́нник.

proportion n пропо́рция; (due relation) соразме́рность; pl разме́ры m pl. **proportional** adj пропорциона́льный. **proportionate** adj соразме́рный (to +dat; c+instr).

proposal n предложе́ние. **propose** vt предлага́ть impf, предложи́ть pf; (intend) предполага́ть impf; vi (~ marriage) де́лать impf, c~ pf предложе́ние (to +dat). **proposition** n предложе́ние.

propound vt предлага́ть impf, предложи́ть pf на обсужде́ние.

proprietor n со́бственник, хозя́ин.

propriety n прили́чие.

props n pl (theat) реквизи́т.

propulsion n движе́ние вперёд.

prosaic adj прозаи́ческий.

proscribe vt (forbid) запреща́ть impf, запрети́ть pf.

prose n про́за.

prosecute vt пресле́довать impf. **prosecution** n суде́бное пресле́дование; (prosecuting party) обвине́ние. **prosecutor** n обвини́тель m.

prospect n вид; (fig) перспекти́ва; vi: ~ for иска́ть impf. **prospective** adj бу́дущий. **prospector** n разве́дчик. **prospectus** n проспе́кт.

prosper vi процвета́ть impf. **prosperity** n процвета́ние. **prosperous** adj процвета́ющий; (wealthy) зажи́точный.

prostate (gland) n проста́та.

prostitute n проститу́тка. **prostitution** n проститу́ция.

prostrate adj распростёртый, (лежа́щий) ничко́м; (exhausted) обесси́ленный; (with grief) уби́тый (with +instr).

protagonist n гла́вный геро́й; (in contest) протагони́ст.

protect vt защища́ть impf, защити́ть pf. **protection** n защи́та. **protective** adj защи́тный. **protector** n защи́тник.

protégé(e) n протеже́ m & f indecl.

protein n бело́к.

protest n проте́ст; vi протестова́ть impf & pf; vt (affirm) утвержда́ть impf.

Protestant n протеста́нт, ~ка; adj протеста́нтский.

protestation n (торже́ственное) заявле́ние (o+prep; что); (protest) проте́ст.

protocol n протоко́л.

proton n прото́н.

prototype n прототи́п.

protract vt тяну́ть impf. **protracted** adj дли́тельный.

protrude vi выдава́ться impf, вы́даться pf.

proud adj го́рдый; be ~ of горди́ться impf +instr.

prove vt дока́зывать impf, доказа́ть pf; vi ока́зываться impf, оказа́ться pf (to be +instr). **proven** adj дока́занный.

provenance n происхожде́ние.

proverb n посло́вица. **proverbial** adj воше́дший в погово́рку; (well-known) общеизве́стный.

provide vt (supply person) снабжа́ть impf, снабди́ть pf (with +instr); (supply thing) предоставля́ть impf, предоста́вить pf (to, for +dat); дава́ть impf, дать pf (to, for +dat); vi: ~ for предусма́тривать impf, предусмотре́ть pf +acc; (~ for family etc.) содержа́ть impf +acc. **provided (that)** conj при усло́вии, что; е́сли то́лько.

providence n провиде́ние; (foresight) предусмотри́тельность. **provident** adj предусмотри́тельный. **providential** adj счастли́вый. **providing** see provided (that)

province n о́бласть; pl (the ~) прови́нция. **provincial** adj провинциа́льный.

provision n снабже́ние; pl (food) прови́зия; (in agreement etc.) положе́ние; make ~ against принима́ть impf, приня́ть pf ме́ры про́тив+gen. **provisional** adj вре́менный. **proviso** n усло́вие.

provocation n провока́ция. **provocative** adj провокацио́нный. **provoke** vt провоци́ровать impf, c~ pf; (call forth, cause) вызыва́ть impf, вы́звать pf.

prow n нос.

prowess n уме́ние.

prowl vi ры́скать impf.

proximity n бли́зость.

proxy n полномо́чие; (person) уполномо́ченный sb, замести́тель m; by ~ по дове́ренности; stand ~ for быть impf замести́телем +gen.

prudence n благоразу́мие. **prudent** adj благоразу́мный.

prudery n притво́рная стыдли́вость. **prudish** adj ни в ме́ру стыдли́вый.

prune¹ n (plum) черносли́в.

prune² vt (trim) об-, под-, реза́ть impf, об-, под-, ре́зать pf.

pry vi сова́ть impf нос (into в+acc).

PS abbr (of postscript) постскри́птум.

psalm n псало́м.

pseudonym n псевдони́м.

psyche n пси́хика. **psychiatric** adj психиатри́ческий. **psychiatrist** n психиа́тр. **psychiatry** n психиатри́я. **psychic** adj ясновидя́щий. **psychoanalysis** n психоана́лиз. **psychoanalyst** n психоанали́тик. **psychoanalytic(al)** adj психоаналити́ческий. **psychological** adj психологи́ческий. **psychologist** n психо́лог. **psychology** n психоло́гия. **psychopath** n психопа́т. **psychopathic** adj психопати́ческий. **psychosis** n психо́з. **psychotherapy** n психотерапи́я.

PTO abbr (of please turn over) см. на об., смотри́ на оборо́те.

pub n пивна́я sb.

puberty n полова́я зре́лость.

public adj обще́ственный; (open) публи́чный, откры́тый; ~ school ча́стная сре́дняя шко́ла; n пу́блика, обще́ственность; in ~ откры́то, публи́чно. **publication** n изда́ние. **publicity** n рекла́ма. **publicize** vt реклами́ровать impf & pf. **publicly** adv публи́чно, откры́то. **publish** vt публикова́ть impf, o~ pf; (book) издава́ть impf, изда́ть pf. **publisher** n изда́тель m. **publishing** n (business) изда́тельское де́ло; ~ house изда́тельство.

pucker vt & i мо́рщить(ся) impf, c~ pf.

pudding n пу́динг, запека́нка; (dessert) сла́дкое sb.

puddle n лужа.

puff n (of wind) порыв; (of smoke) дымок; ~ **pastry** слоёное тесто; vi пыхтеть impf; ~ **at** (pipe etc.) попыхивать impf +instr; vt: ~ **up, out** (inflate) надувать impf, надуть pf.

pugnacious adj драчливый.

puke vi рвать impf, вы~ pf impers +acc.

pull vt тянуть impf, по~ pf; таскать indet, тащить det, по~ pf; (a muscle) растягивать impf, растянуть pf; vt & i дёргать impf, дёрнуть pf (at (за)+acc); ~ **s.o.'s leg** разыгрывать impf, разыграть pf; ~ **the trigger** спускать impf, спустить pf курок; ~ **apart, to pieces** разрывать impf, разорвать pf; (fig) раскритиковать pf; ~ **down** (demolish) сносить impf, снести pf; ~ **in** (of train) прибывать impf, прибыть pf; (of vehicle) подъезжать impf, подъехать pf к обочине (дороги); ~ **off** (garment) стаскивать impf, стянуть pf; (achieve) успешно завершать impf, завершить pf; ~ **on** (garment) натягивать impf, натянуть pf; ~ **out** (vt) (remove) вытаскивать impf, вытащить pf; (vi) (withdraw) отказываться impf, отказаться pf от участия (of в+prep); (of vehicle) отъезжать impf, отъехать pf от обочины (дороги); (of train) отходить impf, отойти pf (от станции); ~ **through** выживать impf, выжить pf; ~ **o.s. together** брать impf, взять pf себя в руки; ~ **up** (vt) подтягивать impf, подтянуть pf; (vt & i) (stop) останавливать(ся) impf, остановить(ся) pf; n тяга; (fig) блат.

pulley n блок.

pullover n пуловер.

pulp n пульпа.

pulpit n кафедра.

pulsate vi пульсировать impf. **pulse** n пульс.

pulses n pl (food) бобовые sb.

pulverize vt размельчать impf, размельчить pf.

pummel vt колотить impf, по~ pf.

pump n насос; vt качать impf; ~ **in(to)** вкачивать impf, вкачать pf; ~ **out** выкачивать impf, выкачать pf; ~ **up** накачивать impf, накачать pf.

pumpkin n тыква.

pun n каламбур.

punch[1] vt (with fist) ударять impf, ударить pf кулаком; (hole) пробивать impf, пробить pf; (a ticket) компостировать impf, про~ pf; ~ **up** драка; n (blow) удар кулаком; (for tickets) компостер; (for piercing) перфоратор.

punch[2] n (drink) пунш.

punctilious adj щепетильный.

punctual adj пунктуальный. **punctuality** n пунктуальность.

punctuate vt ставить impf, по~ pf знаки препинания в+acc; (fig) прерывать impf, прервать pf. **punctuation** n пунктуация; ~ **marks** знаки m pl препинания.

puncture n прокол; vt прокалывать impf, проколоть pf.

pundit n (fig) знаток.

pungent adj едкий.

punish vt наказывать impf, наказать pf. **punishable** adj наказуемый. **punishment** n наказание.

punitive adj карательный.

punter n (gambler) игрок; (client) клиент.

puny adj хилый.

pupil n ученик, -ица; (of eye) зрачок.

puppet n марионетка, кукла.

puppy n щенок.

purchase n покупка; (leverage) точка опоры; vt покупать impf, купить pf. **purchaser** n покупатель m.

pure adj чистый.

purée n пюре neut indecl.

purely adv чисто.

purgatory n чистилище; (fig) ад. **purge** vt очищать impf, очистить pf; n очищение; (polit) чистка.

purification n очистка. **purify** vt очищать impf, очистить pf.

purist n пурист.

puritan, P., n пуританин, -анка. **puritanical** adj пуританский.

purity n чистота.

purple adj (n) пурпурный, фиолетовый (цвет).

purport vt претендовать impf.

purpose n цель, намерение; **on** ~ нарочно; **to no** ~ напрасно. **purposeful** adj целеустремлённый. **purposeless** adj бесцельный. **purposely** adv нарочно.

purr vi мурлы́кать impf.

purse n кошелёк; vt поджима́ть impf, поджа́ть pf.

pursue vt пресле́довать impf. **pursuit** n пресле́дование; (pastime) заня́тие.

purveyor n поставщи́к.

pus n гной.

push vt толка́ть impf, толкну́ть pf; (press) нажима́ть impf, нажа́ть pf; (urge) подта́лкивать impf, подтолкну́ть pf; vi толка́ться impf; be ~ed for име́ть impf ма́ло+gen; he is ~ing fifty ему́ ско́ро сту́кнет пятьдеся́т; ~ one's way проти́скиваться impf, проти́снуться pf; ~ around (person) помыка́ть impf +instr; ~ aside (also fig) отстраня́ть impf, отстрани́ть pf; ~ away отта́лкивать impf, оттолкну́ть pf; ~ off (vi) (in boat) отта́лкиваться impf, оттолкну́ться pf (от бе́рега); (go away) убира́ться impf, убра́ться pf; ~ on (vi) продолжа́ть impf путь; ~ through (tel) n толчо́к; (energy) эне́ргия. **pushchair** n коля́ска. **pusher** n (drugs) продаве́ц нарко́тиков. **pushy** adj напо́ристый.

puss, pussy(-cat) n ки́ска.

put vt класть impf, положи́ть pf; (upright) ста́вить impf, по~ pf; (into specified state) приводи́ть impf, привести́ pf; (express) выража́ть impf, вы́разить pf; (a question) задава́ть impf, зада́ть pf; ~ an end, a stop, to класть impf, положи́ть pf коне́ц +dat; ~ o.s. in another's place ста́вить impf, по~ pf себя́ на ме́сто +gen; ~ about (rumour etc.) распространя́ть impf, распространи́ть pf; ~ away (tidy) убира́ть impf, убра́ть pf; (save) откла́дывать impf, отложи́ть pf; ~ back (in place) ста́вить impf, по~ pf на ме́сто; (clock) переводи́ть impf, перевести́ pf наза́д; ~ by (money) откла́дывать impf, отложи́ть pf; ~ down класть impf, положи́ть pf; (suppress) подавля́ть impf, подави́ть pf; (write down) запи́сывать impf, записа́ть pf; (passengers) выса́живать impf, вы́садить pf; (attribute) припи́сывать impf, приписа́ть pf (to +dat); ~ forward (proposal) предлага́ть impf, предложи́ть pf; (clock) переводи́ть

impf, перевести́ pf вперёд; ~ in (install) устана́вливать impf, установи́ть pf; (a claim) предъявля́ть impf, предъяви́ть pf; (interpose) вставля́ть impf, вста́вить pf; ~ in an appearance появля́ться impf, появи́ться pf; ~ off (postpone) откла́дывать impf, отложи́ть pf; (repel) отта́лкивать impf, оттолкну́ть pf; (dissuade) отгова́ривать impf, отговори́ть pf от+gen, +inf; ~ on (clothes) надева́ть impf, наде́ть pf; (kettle, a record, a play) ста́вить impf, по~ pf; (turn on) включа́ть impf, включи́ть pf; (add to) прибавля́ть impf, приба́вить pf; ~ on airs ва́жничать impf; ~ on weight толсте́ть impf, по~ pf; ~ out (vex) обижа́ть impf, оби́деть pf; (inconvenience) затрудня́ть impf, затрудни́ть pf; (a fire etc.) туши́ть impf, по~ pf; ~ through (tel) соединя́ть impf, соедини́ть pf по телефо́ну; ~ up (building) стро́ить impf, по~ pf; (hang up) ве́шать impf, пове́сить pf; (price) повыша́ть impf, повы́сить pf; (a guest) дава́ть impf, дать pf ночле́г +dat; (as guest) ночева́ть impf, пере~ pf; ~ up to (instigate) подбива́ть impf, подби́ть pf на+acc; ~ up with терпе́ть impf.

putative adj предполага́емый.

putrefy vi гнить impf, с~ pf. **putrid** adj гнило́й.

putty n зама́зка.

puzzle n (enigma) зага́дка; (toy etc.) головоло́мка; (jigsaw) моза́ика; vt озада́чивать impf, озада́чить pf; ~ out разгада́ть pf; vi: ~ over лома́ть impf себе́ го́лову над+instr.

pygmy n пигме́й.

pyjamas n pl пижа́ма.

pylon n пило́н.

pyramid n пирами́да.

pyre n погреба́льный костёр.

python n пито́н.

Q

quack[1] n (sound) кря́канье; vi кря́кать impf, кря́кнуть pf.

quack[2] n шарлата́н.

quad n (court) четырёхуго́льный двор; pl (quadruplets) че́тверо близнецо́в. **quadrangle** n (figure) четырёхуго́льник; (*court*) четырёхуго́льный двор. **quadrant** *n* квадра́нт.

quadruped *n* четвероно́гое живо́тное *sb*. **quadruple** *adj* четверно́й; *vt & i* учетверя́ть(ся) *impf*, учетве́ри́ть(ся) *pf*. **quadruplets** *n pl* четверо близнецо́в.

quagmire *n* боло́то.

quail *n* (*bird*) пе́репел.

quaint *adj* причу́дливый.

quake *vi* дрожа́ть *impf* (**with** от +*gen*).

Quaker *n* ква́кер, ∼ка.

qualification *n* (*for post etc.*) квалифика́ция; (*reservation*) огово́рка. **qualified** *adj* компете́нтный; (*limited*) ограни́ченный. **qualify** *vt & i* (*prepare for job*) гото́вить(ся) *impf* (**for** к+*dat*; +*inf*); *vt* (*render fit*) де́лать *impf*, с∼ *pf* приго́дным; (*entitle*) дава́ть *impf*, дать *pf* пра́во +*dat* (**to** на+*acc*); (*limit*); ∼ **what one says** сде́лать *pf* огово́рку; *vi* получа́ть *impf*, получи́ть *pf* дипло́м; ∼ **for** (*be entitled to*) име́ть *impf* пра́во на+*acc*.

qualitative *adj* ка́чественный. **quality** *n* ка́чество.

qualm *n* сомне́ние; (*of conscience*) угрызе́ние со́вести.

quandary *n* затрудни́тельное положе́ние.

quantify *vt* определя́ть *impf*, определи́ть *pf* коли́чество +*gen*. **quantitative** *adj* коли́чественный. **quantity** *n* коли́чество.

quarantine *n* каранти́н.

quarrel *n* ссо́ра; *vi* ссо́риться *impf*, по∼ *pf* (**with** с+*instr*; **about, for** из-за+*gen*). **quarrelsome** *adj* вздо́рный.

quarry[1] *n* (*for stone etc.*) каменоло́мня; *vt* добыва́ть *impf*, добы́ть *pf*.

quarry[2] *n* (*prey*) добы́ча.

quart *n* ква́рта. **quarter** *n* че́тверть; (*of year; of town*) кварта́л; *pl* кварти́ры *f pl*; **a** ∼ **to one** без че́тверти час; ∼**-final** че́тверть-фина́л; *vt* (*divide*) дели́ть *impf*, раз∼ *pf* на четы́ре ча́сти; (*lodge*) расквартиро́вывать *impf*, расквартирова́ть *pf*. **quarterly** *adj* кварта́льный; *adv* раз в кварта́л. **quartet** *n* кварте́т.

quartz *n* кварц.

quash *vt* (*annul*) аннули́ровать *impf & pf*; (*crush*) подавля́ть *impf*, подави́ть *pf*.

quasi- *in comb* квази-.

quaver *vi* дрожа́ть *impf*; *n* (*mus*) восьма́я *sb* но́ты.

quay *n* на́бережная *sb*.

queasy *adj*: **I feel** ∼ меня́ тошни́т.

queen *n* короле́ва; (*cards*) да́ма; (*chess*) ферзь *m*.

queer *adj* стра́нный.

quell *vt* подавля́ть *impf*, подави́ть *pf*.

quench *vt* (*thirst*) утоля́ть *impf*, утоли́ть *pf*; (*fire, desire*) туши́ть *impf*, по∼ *pf*.

query *n* вопро́с; *vt* (*express doubt*) выража́ть *impf* вы́разить *pf* сомне́ние в+*prep*. **quest** *n* по́иски *m pl*; **in** ∼ **of** в по́исках+*gen*. **question** *n* вопро́с; **beyond** ∼ вне сомне́ния; **it is a** ∼ **of** э́то вопро́с+*gen*; **it is out of the** ∼ об э́том не мо́жет быть и ре́чи; **the person in** ∼ челове́к, о кото́ром идёт речь; **the** ∼ **is this** де́ло в э́том; ∼ **mark** вопроси́тельный знак; *vt* расспра́шивать *impf*, расспроси́ть *pf*; (*interrogate*) допра́шивать *impf* допроси́ть *pf*; (*doubt*) сомнева́ться *impf* в+*prep*. **questionable** *adj* сомни́тельный. **questionnaire** *n* вопро́сник.

queue *n* о́чередь; *vi* стоя́ть *impf* в о́череди.

quibble *n* софи́зм; (*minor criticism*) приди́рка; *vi* придира́ться *impf*; (*argue*) спо́рить *impf*.

quick *adj* ско́рый, бы́стрый; ∼**-tempered** вспы́льчивый; ∼**-witted** нахо́дчивый; *n*: **to the** ∼ за живо́е; *adv* ско́ро, бы́стро; **as** *imper* скоре́е! **quicken** *vt & i* ускоря́ть(ся) *impf*, уско́рить(ся) *pf*. **quickness** *n* быстрота́. **quicksand** *n* зыбу́чий песо́к. **quicksilver** *n* ртуть.

quid *n* фунт.

quiet *n* (*silence*) тишина́; (*calm*) споко́йствие; *adj* ти́хий; споко́йный; *int* ти́ше!; *vt & i* успока́ивать(ся) *impf*, успоко́ить(ся) *pf*.

quill *n* перо́; (*spine*) игла́.

quilt *n* (стёганое) одея́ло; *vt* стега́ть *impf*, вы́∼ *pf*. **quilted** *adj* стёганый.

quintessential *adj* наибо́лее суще́ственный.

quintet *n* квинте́т. **quins, quintuplets**

n pl пять близнецо́в.

quip *n* острота́; остри́ть *impf*, c~ *pf*.

quirk *n* причу́да. **quirky** *adj* с причу́дами.

quit *vt* (*leave*) покида́ть *impf*, поки́нуть *pf*; (*stop*) перестава́ть *impf*, переста́ть *pf*; (*give up*) броса́ть *impf*, бро́сить *pf*; (*resign*) уходи́ть *impf*, уйти́ *pf* c+*gen*.

quite *adv* (*wholly*) совсе́м; (*rather*) дово́льно; ~ **a few** дово́льно мно́го.

quits *predic*: **we are** ~ мы с тобо́й кви́ты; **I am** ~ **with him** я расквита́лся (*past*) с ним.

quiver *vi* (*tremble*) трепета́ть *impf*; *n* тре́пет.

quiz *n* виктори́на. **quizzical** *adj* насме́шливый.

quorum *n* кво́рум.

quota *n* но́рма.

quotation *n* цита́та; (*of price*) цена́; ~ **marks** кавы́чки (-чек) *pl*. **quote** *vt* цити́ровать *impf*, про~ *pf*; ссыла́ться *impf*, сосла́ться *pf* на+*acc*; (*price*) назнача́ть *impf*, назна́чить *pf*.

R

rabbi *n* равви́н.

rabbit *n* кро́лик.

rabble *n* сброд.

rabid *adj* бе́шеный. **rabies** *n* бе́шенство.

race[1] *n* (*ethnic* ~) ра́са; род.

race[2] *n* (*contest*) (*on foot*) бег; (*of cars etc.*; *fig*) го́нка, го́нки *f pl*; (*of horses*) ска́чки *f pl*; ~**track** трек; (*for horse* ~) скакова́я доро́жка; *vi* (*compete*) состяза́ться *impf* в ско́рости; (*rush*) мча́ться *impf*; *vt* бежа́ть *impf* наперегонки́ c+*instr*. **racecourse** *n* ипподро́м. **racehorse** *n* скакова́я ло́шадь.

racial *adj* ра́совый. **rac(ial)ism** *n* раси́зм. **rac(ial)ist** *n* раси́ст, ~ка; *adj* раси́стский.

racing *n* (*horses*) ска́чки *f pl*; (*cars*) го́нки *f pl*; ~ **car** го́ночный автомоби́ль *m*; ~ **driver** го́нщик.

rack *n* (*for hats etc.*) ве́шалка; (*for plates etc.*) стелла́ж; (*in train etc.*) се́тка; *vt*: ~ **one's brains** лома́ть *impf* себе́ го́лову.

racket[1] *n* (*bat*) раке́тка.

racket[2] *n* (*uproar*) шум; (*illegal activity*) раке́т. **racketeer** *n* рэкети́р.

racy *adj* колори́тный.

radar *n* (*system*) радиолока́ция; (*apparatus*) радиолока́тор, рада́р; *attrib* рада́рный.

radiance *n* сия́ние. **radiant** *adj* сия́ющий. **radiate** *vt* & *i* излуча́ть(ся) *impf*, излучи́ться *pf*. **radiation** *n* излуче́ние. **radiator** *n* батаре́я; (*in car*) радиа́тор.

radical *adj* радика́льный; *n* радика́л.

radio *n* ра́дио *neut indecl*; (*set*) радиоприёмник; *vt* ради́ровать *impf* & *pf* +*dat*.

radioactive *adj* радиоакти́вный. **radioactivity** *n* радиоакти́вность. **radiologist** *n* радио́лог; рентгено́лог. **radiotherapy** *n* радиотерапи́я.

radish *n* реди́ска.

radius *n* ра́диус.

raffle *n* лотере́я; *vt* разы́грывать *impf*, разыгра́ть *pf* в лотере́е.

raft *n* плот.

rafter *n* (*beam*) стропи́ло.

rag *n* тря́пка; *pl* (*clothes*) лохмо́тья (-ьев) *pl*.

rage *n* я́рость; **all the** ~ после́дний крик мо́ды; *vi* беси́ться *impf*; (*storm etc.*) бушева́ть *impf*.

ragged *adj* (*jagged*) зазу́бренный; (*of clothes*) рва́ный.

raid *n* налёт; (*by police*) обла́ва; *vt* де́лать *impf*, c~ *pf* налёт на+*acc*.

rail *n* пери́ла (-л) *pl*; (*rly*) рельс; **by** ~ по́ездом. **railing** *n* пери́ла (-л) *pl*.

railway *n* желе́зная доро́га; *attrib* железнодоро́жный. **railwayman** *n* железнодоро́жник.

rain *n* дождь *m*; *v impers*: **it is** (**was**) ~**ing** идёт (шёл) дождь; *vt* осыпа́ть *impf*, осы́пать *pf* +*instr* (**upon** +*acc*); *vi* осыпа́ться *impf*, осы́паться *pf*. **rainbow** *n* ра́дуга. **raincoat** *n* плащ. **raindrop** *n* дождева́я ка́пля. **rainfall** *n* (*amount of rain*) коли́чество оса́дков. **rainy** *adj* дождли́вый; ~ **day** чёрный день *m*.

raise *vt* (*lift*) поднима́ть *impf*, подня́ть *pf*; (*heighten*) повыша́ть *impf*, повы́сить *pf*; (*provoke*) вызыва́ть *impf*, вы́звать *pf*; (*money*) собира́ть *impf*, собра́ть *pf*; (*children*) расти́ть *impf*.

raisin *n* изю́минка; *pl* (*collect*) изю́м.

rake n (tool) гра́бли (-бель & -блей) pl; vt грести́ impf; (~ together, up) сгреба́ть impf, сгрести́ pf.

rally vt & i спла́чивать(ся) impf, сплоти́ть(ся) pf; vi (after illness etc.) оправля́ться impf, опра́виться pf; n (meeting) слёт; ми́тинг; (motoring ~) (авто)ра́лли neut indecl; (tennis) обме́н уда́рами.

ram n (sheep) бара́н; vt (beat down) трамбова́ть impf, y~ pf; (drive in) вбива́ть impf, вбить pf.

ramble vi (walk) прогу́ливаться impf, прогуля́ться pf; (speak) бубни́ть impf; n прогу́лка. **rambling** adj (incoherent) бессвя́зный.

ramification n (fig) после́дствие.

ramp n скат.

rampage vi бу́йствовать impf.

rampant adj (plant) бу́йный; (unchecked) безуде́ржный.

rampart n вал.

ramshackle adj ве́тхий.

ranch n ра́нчо neut indecl.

rancid adj прого́рклый.

rancour n зло́ба.

random adj случа́йный; at ~ науда́чу.

range n (of mountains) цепь; (artillery ~) полиго́н; (of voice) диапазо́н; (scope) круг, преде́лы m pl; (operating distance) да́льность; vi (vary) колеба́ться impf, по~ pf; (wander) броди́ть impf; ~ over (include) охва́тывать impf, охвати́ть pf.

rank[1] n (row) ряд; (taxi ~) такси́; (grade) зва́ние, чин, ранг; vt (classify) классифици́ровать impf & pf; (consider) счита́ть impf (as +instr); vi: ~ with быть в числе́+gen.

rank[2] adj (luxuriant) бу́йный; (in smell) злово́нный; (gross) я́вный.

rankle vi боле́ть impf.

ransack vt (search) обша́ривать impf, обша́рить pf; (plunder) гра́бить impf, o~ pf.

ransom n вы́куп; vt выкупа́ть impf, вы́купить pf.

rant vi вопи́ть impf.

rap n стук; vt (resko) ударя́ть impf, уда́рить pf; vi стуча́ть impf, сту́кнуть pf.

rape[1] vt наси́ловать impf, из~ pf; n изнаси́лование.

rape[2] n (plant) рапс.

rapid adj бы́стрый; n: pl поро́г, быстрина́. **rapidity** n быстрота́.

rapt adj восхищённый; (absorbed) поглощённый. **rapture** n восто́рг. **rapturous** adj восто́рженный.

rare[1] adj (of meat) недожа́ренный.

rare[2] adj ре́дкий. **rarity** n ре́дкость.

rascal n плут.

rash[1] n сыпь.

rash[2] adj опроме́тчивый.

rasher n ло́мтик (беко́на).

rasp n (file) ра́шпиль m; (sound) скре́жет; vt: ~ out га́ркнуть pf.

raspberry n мали́на (no pl; usu collect).

rasping adj (sound) скрипу́чий.

rat n кры́са; ~ race го́нка за успе́хом.

ratchet n храпови́к.

rate n но́рма, ста́вка; (speed) ско́рость; pl ме́стные нало́ги m pl; at any ~ во вся́ком слу́чае; vt оце́нивать impf, оцени́ть pf; (consider) счита́ть impf, vi счита́ться impf (as +instr).

rather adv скоре́е; (somewhat) дово́льно; he (she) had (would) ~ он (она́) предпочёл (-чла́) бы+inf.

ratification n ратифика́ция. **ratify** vt ратифици́ровать impf & pf.

rating n оце́нка.

ratio n пропо́рция.

ration n паёк, рацио́н; vt норми́ровать impf & pf; be ~ed выдава́ться impf, вы́даться pf по ка́рточкам.

rational adj разу́мный. **rationalism** n рационали́зм. **rationality** n разу́мность. **rationalize** vt обосно́вывать impf, обоснова́ть pf; (industry etc.) рационализи́ровать impf & pf.

rattle vi & t (sound) греме́ть impf (+instr); ~ along (move) грохота́ть impf; ~ off (utter) отбарабани́ть pf; n (sound) треск, гро́хот; (toy) погрему́шка. **rattlesnake** n грему́чая змея́.

raucous adj ре́зкий.

ravage vt опустоша́ть impf, опустоши́ть pf; n: pl разруши́тельное де́йствие.

rave vi бре́дить impf; ~ about быть в восто́рге от+gen.

raven n во́рон.

ravenous adj голо́дный как волк.

ravine n уще́лье.

ravishing adj восхити́тельный.

raw adj сыро́й; (*inexperienced*) нео́пытный; ~ **material(s)** сырьё (*no pl*).

ray n луч.

raze vt: ~ **to the ground** ровня́ть *impf*, с~ pf с землёй.

razor n бри́тва; ~**blade** ле́звие.

reach vt (*attain, extend to, arrive at*) достига́ть *impf*, дости́чь & дости́гнуть pf +gen, до+gen; доходи́ть *impf*, дойти́ pf до+gen; (*with hand*) дотя́гиваться *impf*, дотяну́ться pf до+gen; vi (*extend*) простира́ться *impf*; n досяга́емость; (*pl, of river*) тече́ние.

react vi реаги́ровать *impf*, от~, про~ pf (**to** на+acc). **reaction** n реа́кция. **reactionary** adj реакцио́нный; n реакционе́р. **reactor** n реа́ктор.

read vt чита́ть *impf*, про~, прочёсть pf; (*mus*) разбира́ть *impf*, разобра́ть pf; (~ **a meter etc.**) снима́ть *impf*, снять pf показа́ния +gen; (*univ*) изуча́ть *impf*; (*interpret*) толкова́ть *impf*. **readable** adj интере́сный. **reader** n чита́тель m, ~ница; (*book*) хрестома́тия.

readily adv (*willingly*) охо́тно; (*easily*) легко́. **readiness** n гото́вность. **reading** n чте́ние; (*on meter*) показа́ние.

ready adj гото́вый (**for** к+dat, на+acc); **get** ~ гото́виться *impf*; ~**made** гото́вый; ~ **money** нали́чные де́ньги (-ге́г, -ньга́м) pl.

real adj настоя́щий, реа́льный; ~ **estate** недви́жимость. **realism** n реали́зм. **realist** n реали́ст. **realistic** adj реалисти́чный, -и́ческий. **reality** n действи́тельность; **in** ~ действи́тельно. **realization** n (*of plan etc.*) осуществле́ние; (*of assets*) реализа́ция; (*understanding*) осозна́ние. **realize** vt (*plan etc.*) осуществля́ть *impf*, осуществи́ть pf; (*assets*) реализова́ть *impf* & pf; (*apprehend*) осозна́вать *impf*, осозна́ть pf. **really** adv действи́тельно, в са́мом де́ле.

realm n (*kingdom*) короле́вство; (*sphere*) о́бласть.

reap vt жать *impf*, сжать pf; (*fig*) пожина́ть *impf*, пожа́ть pf.

rear¹ vt (*lift*) поднима́ть *impf*, подня́ть pf; (*children*) воспи́тывать *impf*, воспита́ть pf; vi (*of horse*) станови́ться *impf*, стать pf на дыбы́.

rear² n за́дняя часть; (*mil*) тыл; **bring up the** ~ замыка́ть *impf*, замкну́ть pf ше́ствие; adj за́дний; (*also mil*) ты́льный. **rearguard** n арьерга́рд; ~ **action** арьерга́рдный бой.

rearmament n перевооруже́ние.

rearrange vt меня́ть *impf*.

reason n (*cause*) причи́на, основа́ние; (*intellect*) ра́зум, рассу́док; vi рассужда́ть *impf*; ~ **with** (*person*) угова́ривать *impf* +acc. **reasonable** adj разу́мный; (*inexpensive*) недорого́й.

reassurance n успока́ивание. **reassure** vt успока́ивать *impf*, успоко́ить pf.

rebate n ски́дка.

rebel n повста́нец; vi восстава́ть *impf*, восста́ть pf. **rebellion** n восста́ние. **rebellious** adj мяте́жный.

rebound vi отска́кивать *impf*, отскочи́ть pf; n рикоше́т.

rebuff n отпо́р; vt дава́ть *impf*, дать pf +dat отпо́р.

rebuild vt перестра́ивать *impf*, перестро́ить pf.

rebuke vt упрека́ть *impf*, упрекну́ть pf; n упрёк.

rebuttal n опроверже́ние.

recalcitrant adj непоко́рный.

recall vt (*an official*) отзыва́ть *impf*, отозва́ть pf; (*remember*) вспомина́ть *impf*, вспо́мнить pf; n о́тзыв; (*memory*) па́мять.

recant vi отрека́ться *impf*, отре́чься pf.

recapitulate vt резюми́ровать *impf* & pf.

recast vt переде́лывать *impf*, переде́лать pf.

recede vi отходи́ть *impf*, отойти́ pf.

receipt n (*receiving*) получе́ние; pl (*amount*) вы́ручка; (*written* ~) квита́нция. **receive** vt (*admit, entertain*) принима́ть *impf*, приня́ть pf; (*get, be given*) получа́ть *impf*, получи́ть pf. **receiver** n (*radio, television*) приёмник; (*tel*) тру́бка.

recent adj неда́вний; (*new*) но́вый. **recently** adv неда́вно.

receptacle n вмести́лище. **reception** n приём; ~ **room** приёмная sb. **receptionist** n секрета́рь m, -рша, в

приёмной. receptive *adj* воспри-
и́мчивый.
recess *n* (*parl*) кани́кулы (-л) *pl*;
(*niche*) ни́ша. **recession** *n* спад.
recipe *n* реце́пт.
recipient *n* получа́тель *m*.
reciprocal *adj* взаи́мный. **recipro-
cate** *vt* отвеча́ть *impf* (взаи́мно-
стью) на+*acc*.
recital *n* (со́льный) конце́рт. **recitation** *n* публи́чное чте́ние. **recite** *vt*
деклами́ровать *impf*, про~ *pf*; (*list*)
перечисля́ть *impf*, перечи́слить *pf*.
reckless *adj* (*rash*) опроме́тчивый;
(*careless*) неосторо́жный.
reckon *vt* подсчи́тывать *impf*, подс-
чита́ть *pf*; (*also regard as*) счита́ть
impf, счесть *pf* (*to be* +*instr*); *vi*:
on рассчи́тывать *impf*, рассчита́ть
pf на+*acc*; ~ **with** счита́ться *impf*
с+*instr*. **reckoning** *n* счёт; **day of** ~
час распла́ты.
reclaim *vt* тре́бовать *impf*, по~ *pf*
обра́тно; (*land*) осва́ивать *impf*,
осво́ить *pf*.
recline *vi* полулежа́ть *impf*.
recluse *n* затво́рник.
recognition *n* узнава́ние; (*acknowledgement*) призна́ние. **recognize** *vt*
узнава́ть *impf*, узна́ть *pf*; (*acknowledge*) признава́ть *impf*, призна́ть *pf*.
recoil *vi* отпря́дывать *impf*, отпря́-
нуть *pf*.
recollect *vt* вспомина́ть *impf*, вспо́м-
нить *pf*. **recollection** *n* воспомина́-
ние.
recommend *vt* рекомендова́ть *impf*
& *pf*. **recommendation** *n* рекоменда́-
ция.
recompense *n* вознагражде́ние; *vt*
вознагражда́ть *impf*, вознагради́ть
pf.
reconcile *vt* примиря́ть *impf*, прими-
ри́ть *pf*; ~ **o.s.** примиря́ться *impf*,
примири́ться *pf* (*to* с+*instr*). **reconciliation** *n* примире́ние.
reconnaissance *n* разве́дка. **reconnoitre** *vt* разве́дывать *impf*, разве́-
дать *pf*.
reconstruct *vt* перестра́ивать *impf*,
перестро́ить *pf*. **reconstruction** *n*
перестро́йка.
record *vt* запи́сывать *impf*, записа́ть
pf; *n* за́пись; (*minutes*) протоко́л;
(*gramophone* ~) грампласти́нка;

(*sport etc.*) реко́рд; **off the** ~ не-
официа́льно; *adj* реко́рдный; ~-
breaker, -holder рекордсме́н, ~ка;
~-**player** прои́грыватель *m*. **recorder** *n* (*mus*) блок-фле́йта. **recording** *n* за́пись.
recount[1] *vt* (*narrate*) переска́зывать
impf, пересказа́ть *pf*.
re-count[2] *vt* (*count again*) пересчи́-
тывать *impf*, пересчита́ть *pf*; *n*
пересчёт.
recoup *vt* возвраща́ть *impf*, верну́ть
pf (*losses* поте́рянное).
recourse *n*: **have** ~ **to** прибега́ть
impf, прибе́гнуть *pf* к+*dat*.
recover *vt* (*regain possession*) полу-
ча́ть *impf*, получи́ть *pf* обра́тно;
возвраща́ть *impf*, верну́ть *pf*; *vi* (~
health) поправля́ться *impf*, попра́-
виться *pf* (*from* по́сле+*gen*). **recovery** *n* возвраще́ние; выздоровле́-
ние.
recreate *vt* воссоздава́ть *impf*, вос-
созда́ть *pf*.
recreation *n* развлече́ние, о́тдых.
recrimination *n* взаи́мное обвине́-
ние.
recruit *n* новобра́нец; *vt* вербова́ть
impf, за~ *pf*. **recruitment** *n* вер-
бо́вка.
rectangle *n* прямоуго́льник. **rectangular** *adj* прямоуго́льный.
rectify *vt* исправля́ть *impf*, испра́-
вить *pf*.
rector *n* (*priest*) прихо́дский свяще́н-
ник; (*univ*) ре́ктор. **rectory** *n* дом
прихо́дского свяще́нника.
rectum *n* прямая́ кишка́.
recuperate *vi* поправля́ться *impf*,
попра́виться *pf*. **recuperation** *n*
выздоровле́ние.
recur *vi* повторя́ться *impf*, повто-
ри́ться *pf*. **recurrence** *n* повторе́-
ние. **recurrent** *adj* повторя́ющийся.
recycle *vt* перераба́тывать *impf*,
перерабо́тать *pf*.
red *adj* кра́сный; (*of hair*) ры́жий; *n*
кра́сный цвет; (*polit*) кра́сный *sb*;
in the ~ в долгу́; ~-**handed** с поли́-
чным; ~ **herring** ло́жный след;
~-**hot** раскалённый докрасна́; **R~
Indian** инде́ец, индиа́нка; ~ **tape**
волоки́та. **redcurrant** *n* кра́сная
сморо́дина (*no pl; usu collect*). **redden** *vt* окра́шивать *impf*, окра́сить

pf в кра́сный цвет; *vi* красне́ть *impf*, по~ *pf*. **reddish** *adj* краснова́тый; (*hair*) рыжева́тый.

redecorate *vt* отде́лывать *impf*, отде́лать *pf*.

redeem *vt* (*buy back*) выкупа́ть *impf*, вы́купить *pf*; (*from sin*) искупа́ть *impf*, искупи́ть *pf*. **redeemer** *n* искупи́тель *m*. **redemption** *n* вы́куп; искупле́ние.

redeploy *vt* передислоци́ровать *impf* & *pf*.

redo *vt* переде́лывать *impf*, переде́лать *pf*.

redouble *vt* удва́ивать *impf*, удво́ить *pf*.

redress *vt* исправля́ть *impf*, испра́вить *pf*; ~ **the balance** восстана́вливать *impf*, восстанови́ть *pf* равнове́сие; *n* возмеще́ние.

reduce *vt* (*decrease*) уменьша́ть *impf*, уме́ньшить *pf*; (*lower*) снижа́ть *impf*, сни́зить *pf*; (*shorten*) сокраща́ть *impf*, сократи́ть *pf*; (*bring to*) доводи́ть *impf*, довести́ *pf* (**to** в+*acc*). **reduction** *n* уменьше́ние, сниже́ние, сокраще́ние; (*discount*) ски́дка.

redundancy *n* (*dismissal*) увольне́ние. **redundant** *adj* изли́шний; **make** ~ увольня́ть *impf*, уво́лить *pf*.

reed *n* (*plant*) тростни́к; (*in oboe etc.*) язычо́к.

reef *n* риф.

reek *n* вонь; *vi*: ~ (**of**) воня́ть *impf* (+*instr*).

reel[1] *n* катушка; *vt*: ~ **off** (*story etc.*) отбараба́нить *pf*.

reel[2] *vi* (*stagger*) поша́тываться *impf*, пошатну́ться *pf*.

refectory *n* (*monastery*) тра́пезная *sb*; (*univ*) столо́вая *sb*.

refer *vt* (*direct*) отсыла́ть *impf*, отосла́ть *pf* (**to** к+*dat*); *vi*: ~ **to** (*cite*) ссыла́ться *impf*, сосла́ться *pf* на +*acc*; (*mention*) упомина́ть *impf*, упомяну́ть *pf* +*acc*. **referee** *n* судья́ *m*; *vt* суди́ть *impf*. **reference** *n* (*to book etc.*) ссы́лка; (*mention*) упомина́ние; (*testimonial*) характери́стика; ~ **book** спра́вочник. **referendum** *n* рефере́ндум.

refine *vt* очища́ть *impf*, очи́стить *pf*. **refined** *adj* (*in style etc.*) утончён-ный; (*in manners*) культу́рный. **re-**

finement *n* утончённость. **refinery** *n* (*oil* ~) нефтеочисти́тельный заво́д.

refit *vt* переобору́довать *impf* & *pf*.

reflect *vt* отража́ть *impf*, отрази́ть *pf*; *vi* размышля́ть *impf*, размы́слить *pf* (**on** о+*prep*). **reflection** *n* отраже́ние; размышле́ние; **on** ~ поду́мав. **reflective** *adj* (*thoughtful*) серьёзный. **reflector** *n* рефле́ктор. **reflex** *n* рефле́кс; *adj* рефле́ктор-ный. **reflexive** *adj* (*gram*) возвра́т-ный.

reform *vt* реформи́ровать *impf* & *pf*; *vt* & *i* (*of people*) исправля́ть(ся) *impf*, испра́вить(ся) *pf*; *n* рефо́рма; исправле́ние. **Reformation** *n* Рефо́рма́ция.

refract *vt* преломля́ть *impf*, преломи́ть *pf*.

refrain[1] *n* припе́в.

refrain[2] *vi* возде́рживаться *impf*, воздержа́ться *pf* (**from** от+*gen*).

refresh *vt* освежа́ть *impf*, освежи́ть *pf*. **refreshments** *n pl* напи́тки *m pl*.

refrigerate *vt* охлажда́ть *impf*, охлади́ть *pf*. **refrigeration** *n* охлажде́-ние. **refrigerator** *n* холоди́льник.

refuge *n* убе́жище; **take** ~ находи́ть *impf*, найти́ *pf* убе́жище. **refugee** *n* бе́женец, -нка.

refund *vt* возвраща́ть *impf*, возврати́ть *pf*; (*expenses*) возмеща́ть *impf*, возмести́ть *pf*; *n* возвраще́ние (де́нег); возмеще́ние.

refusal *n* отка́з. **refuse**[1] *vt* отка́зы-вать *impf*, отказа́ть *pf*.

refuse[2] *n* му́сор.

refute *vt* опроверга́ть *impf*, опрове́ргнуть *pf*.

regain *vt* возвраща́ть *impf*, верну́ть *pf*.

regal *adj* короле́вский.

regale *vt* угоща́ть *impf*, угости́ть *pf* (**with** +*instr*).

regalia *n pl* рега́лии *f pl*.

regard *vt* смотре́ть *impf*, по~ *pf* на+*acc*; (*take into account*) счи-та́ться *impf* с+*instr*; ~ **as** счита́ть *impf* +*instr*, за+*instr*; **as** ~**s** что каса́ется+*gen*; *n* (*esteem*) уваже́ние; (*attention*) внима́ние; *pl* приве́т. **re-garding** *prep* относи́тельно+*gen*. **regardless** *adv* не обраща́я внима́-ния; ~ **of** не счита́ясь с+*instr*.

regatta *n* регата.

regenerate *vt* перерождать *impf*, переродить *pf*. **regeneration** *n* перерождение.

regent *n* регент.

régime *n* режим.

regiment *n* полк. **regimental** *adj* полковой. **regimentation** *n* регламентация.

region *n* регион. **regional** *adj* региональный.

register *n* реестр; (*also mus*) регистр; *vt* регистрировать *impf*, за~ *pf*; (*a letter*) отправлять *impf*, отправить *pf* заказным. **registered** *adj* (*letter*) заказной. **registrar** *n* регистратор. **registration** *n* регистрация; ~ **number** номер машины. **registry** *n* регистратура; ~ **office** загс.

regression *n* регресс. **regressive** *adj* регрессивный.

regret *vt* сожалеть *impf* o+*prep*; *n* сожаление. **regretful** *adj* полный сожаления. **regrettable** *adj* прискорбный. **regrettably** *adv* к сожалению.

regular *adj* регулярный; (*also gram*) правильный; *n* (*coll*) завсегдатай. **regularity** *n* регулярность. **regulate** *vt* регулировать *impf*, y~ *pf*. **regulation** *n* регулирование; *pl* правила *neut pl*.

rehabilitate *vt* реабилитировать *impf* & *pf*. **rehabilitation** *n* реабилитация.

rehearsal *n* репетиция. **rehearse** *vt* репетировать *impf*, от~ *pf*.

reign *n* царствование; *vi* царствовать *impf*; (*fig*) царить *impf*.

reimburse *vt* возмещать *impf*, возместить *pf* (+*dat of person*). **reimbursement** *n* возмещение.

rein *n* повод.

reincarnation *n* перевоплощение.

reindeer *n* северный олень *m*.

reinforce *vt* подкреплять *impf*, подкрепить *pf*. **reinforcement** *n* (*also pl*) подкрепление.

reinstate *vt* восстанавливать *impf*, восстановить *pf*. **reinstatement** *n* восстановление.

reiterate *vt* повторять *impf*, повторить *pf*.

reject *vt* отвергать *impf*, отвергнуть *pf*; (*as defective*) браковать *impf*, за~ *pf*; *n* брак. **rejection** *n* отказ (**of** от+*gen*).

rejoice *vi* радоваться *impf*, об~ *pf* (**in, at** +*dat*). **rejoicing** *n* радость.

rejoin *vt* (**вновь**) присоединяться *impf*, присоединиться *pf* к+*dat*.

rejuvenate *vt* омолаживать *impf*, омолодить *pf*.

relapse *n* рецидив; *vi* снова впадать *impf*, впасть *pf* (**into** в+*acc*); (*into illness*) снова заболевать *impf*, заболеть *pf*.

relate *vt* (*tell*) рассказывать *impf*, рассказать *pf*; (*connect*) связывать *impf*, связать *pf*; *vi* относиться *impf* (**to** к+*dat*). **related** *adj* родственный.

relation *n* отношение; (*person*) родственник, -ица. **relationship** *n* (*connection; liaison*) связь; (*kinship*) родство. **relative** *adj* относительный; *n* родственник, -ица. **relativity** *n* относительность.

relax *vt* ослаблять *impf*, ослабить *pf*; *vi* (*rest*) расслабляться *impf*, расслабиться *pf*. **relaxation** *n* ослабление; (*rest*) отдых.

relay *n* (*shift*) смена; (*sport*) эстафета; (*electr*) реле *neut indecl*; *vt* передавать *impf*, передать *pf*.

release *vt* (*set free*) освобождать *impf*, освободить *pf*; (*unfasten, let go*) отпускать *impf*, отпустить *pf*; (*film etc.*) выпускать *impf*, выпустить *pf*; *n* освобождение; выпуск.

relegate *vt* переводить *impf*, перевести *pf* (в низшую группу). **relegation** *n* перевод (в низшую группу).

relent *vi* смягчаться *impf*, смягчиться *pf*. **relentless** *adj* непрестанный.

relevance *n* уместность. **relevant** *adj* относящийся к делу; уместный.

reliability *n* надёжность. **reliable** *adj* надёжный. **reliance** *n* доверие. **reliant** *adj*: **be** ~ **upon** зависеть *impf* от+*gen*.

relic *n* остаток, реликвия.

relief[1] *n* (*art, geol*) рельеф.

relief[2] *n* (*alleviation*) облегчение; (*assistance*) помощь; (*in duty*) смена. **relieve** *vt* (*alleviate*) облегчать *impf*, облегчить *pf*; (*replace*) сменять *impf*, сменить *pf*; (*unburden*) освобождать *impf*, освободить *pf* (**of** от+*gen*).

religion *n* рели́гия. **religious** *adj* религио́зный.

relinquish *vt* оставля́ть *impf*, оста́вить *pf*; (*right etc.*) отка́зываться *impf*, отказа́ться *pf* от+*gen*.

relish *n* (*enjoyment*) смак; (*cul*) припра́ва; *vt* смакова́ть *impf*.

relocate *vt* & *i* перемеща́ть(ся) *impf*, перемести́ть(ся) *pf*.

reluctance *n* неохо́та. **reluctant** *adj* неохо́тный; **be ~ to** не жела́ть *impf* +*inf*.

rely *vi* полага́ться *impf*, положи́ться *pf* (**on** на+*acc*).

remain *vi* остава́ться *impf*, оста́ться *pf*. **remainder** *n* оста́ток. **remains** *n pl* оста́тки *m pl*; (*human ~*) оста́нки (-ков) *pl*.

remand *vt* содержа́ть *impf* под стра́жей; **be on ~** содержа́ться *impf* под стра́жей.

remark *vt* замеча́ть *impf*, заме́тить *pf*; *n* замеча́ние. **remarkable** *adj* замеча́тельный.

remarry *vi* вступа́ть *impf*, вступи́ть *pf* в но́вый брак.

remedial *adj* лече́бный. **remedy** *n* сре́дство (**for** от, про́тив+*gen*); *vt* исправля́ть *impf*, испра́вить *pf*.

remember *vt* по́мнить *impf*, вспомина́ть *impf*, вспо́мнить *pf*; (*greet*) передава́ть *impf*, переда́ть *pf* приве́т от+*gen* (**to** +*dat*). **remembrance** *n* па́мять.

remind *vt* напомина́ть *impf*, напо́мнить *pf* +*dat* (**of** +*acc*, о+*prep*). **reminder** *n* напомина́ние.

reminiscence *n* воспомина́ние. **reminiscent** *adj* напомина́ющий.

remiss *predic* небре́жный. **remission** *n* (*pardon*) отпуще́ние; (*med*) реми́ссия. **remit** *vt* пересыла́ть *impf*, пересла́ть *pf*. **remittance** *n* перево́д де́нег; (*money*) де́нежный перево́д.

remnant *n* оста́ток.

remonstrate *vi*: **~ with** увещева́ть *impf* +*acc*.

remorse *n* угрызе́ния *neut pl* со́вести. **remorseful** *adj* по́лный раска́яния. **remorseless** *adj* безжа́лостный.

remote *adj* отдалённый; **~ control** дистанцио́нное управле́ние.

removal *n* (*taking away*) удале́ние;

(*of obstacles*) устране́ние. **remove** *vt* (*take away*) убира́ть *impf*, убра́ть *pf*; (*get rid of*) устраня́ть *impf*, устрани́ть *pf*.

remuneration *n* вознагражде́ние. **remunerative** *adj* вы́годный.

renaissance *n* возрожде́ние; **the R~** Возрожде́ние.

render *vt* воздава́ть *impf*, возда́ть *pf*; (*help etc.*) ока́зывать *impf*, оказа́ть *pf*; (*role etc.*) исполня́ть *impf*, испо́лнить *pf*; (*stone*) штукату́рить *impf*, о~, от~ *pf*. **rendering** *n* исполне́ние.

rendezvous *n* (*meeting*) свида́ние.

renegade *n* рене́гат, ~ка.

renew *vt* (*extend; continue*) возобновля́ть *impf*, возобнови́ть *pf*; (*replace*) обновля́ть *impf*, обнови́ть *pf*. **renewal** *n* (воз)обновле́ние.

renounce *vt* отверга́ть *impf*, отве́ргнуть *pf*; (*claim*) отка́зываться *impf*, отказа́ться *pf* от+*gen*.

renovate *vt* ремонти́ровать *impf*, от~ *pf*. **renovation** *n* ремо́нт.

renown *n* сла́ва. **renowned** *adj* изве́стный; **be ~ for** сла́виться *impf* +*instr*.

rent *n* (*for home*) квартпла́та; (*for premises*) (аре́ндная) пла́та; *vt* (*of tenant*) арендова́ть *impf* & *pf*; (*of owner*) сдава́ть *impf*, сдать *pf*.

renunciation *n* (*repudiation*) отрица́ние; (*of claim*) отка́з.

rep *n* (*comm*) аге́нт.

repair *vt* ремонти́ровать *impf*, от~ *pf*; *n* (*also pl*) ремо́нт (*only sg*); почи́нка; **in good/bad** ~ в хоро́шем/плохо́м состоя́нии.

reparations *n pl* репара́ции *f pl*.

repatriate *vt* репатрии́ровать *impf* & *pf*. **repatriation** *n* репатриа́ция.

repay *vt* отпла́чивать *impf*, отплати́ть *pf* (*person* +*dat*). **repayment** *n* отпла́та.

repeal *vt* отменя́ть *impf*, отмени́ть *pf*; *n* отме́на.

repeat *vt* & *i* повторя́ть(ся) *impf*, повтори́ть(ся) *pf*; *n* повторе́ние. **repeatedly** *adv* неоднокра́тно.

repel *vt* отта́лкивать *impf*, оттолкну́ть *pf*; (*enemy*) отража́ть *impf*, отрази́ть *pf*.

repent *vi* раска́иваться *impf*, раска́яться *pf*. **repentance** *n* раска́яние.

repentant *adj* раскаивающийся.

repercussion *n* последствие.

repertoire *n* репертуар. **repertory** *n* (*store*) запас; (*repertoire*) репертуар; ~ **company** постоянная труппа.

repetition *n* повторение. **repetitious, repetitive** *adj* повторяющийся.

replace *vt* (*put back*) класть *impf*, положить *pf* обратно; (*substitute*) заменять *impf*, заменить *pf* (**by** +*instr*). **replacement** *n* замена.

replay *n* переигровка.

replenish *vt* пополнять *impf*, пополнить *pf*.

replete *adj* насыщенный; (*sated*) сытый.

replica *n* копия.

reply *vt & i* отвечать *impf*, ответить *pf* (**to** на+*acc*); *n* ответ.

report *vt* сообщать *impf*, сообщить *pf*; *vi* докладывать *impf*, доложить *pf*; (*present o.s.*) являться *impf*, явиться *pf*; *n* сообщение; доклад; (*school*) табель *m*; (*sound*) звук взрыва, выстрела. **reporter** *n* корреспондент.

repose *n* (*rest*) отдых; (*peace*) покой.

repository *n* хранилище.

repossess *vt* изымать *impf*, изъять *pf* за неплатёж.

reprehensible *adj* предосудительный.

represent *vt* представлять *impf*; (*portray*) изображать *impf*, изобразить *pf*. **representation** *n* (*being represented*) представительство; (*statement of case*) представление; (*portrayal*) изображение. **representative** *adj* изображающий (**of** +*acc*); (*typical*) типичный; *n* представитель *m*.

repress *vt* подавлять *impf*, подавить *pf*. **repression** *n* подавление, репрессия. **repressive** *adj* репрессивный.

reprieve *vt* отсрочивать *impf*, отсрочить *pf* +*dat* приведение в исполнение (смертного) приговора; *n* отсрочка приведения в исполнение (смертного) приговора; (*fig*) передышка.

reprimand *n* выговор; *vt* делать *impf*, с~ *pf* выговор +*dat*.

reprint *vt* переиздавать *impf*, переиздать *pf*; *n* переиздание.

reprisal *n* ответная мера.

reproach *vt* упрекать *impf*, упрекнуть *pf* (**with** в+*prep*). **reproachful** *adj* укоризненный.

reproduce *vt* воспроизводить *impf*, воспроизвести *pf*; *vi* размножаться *impf*, размножиться *pf*. **reproduction** *n* (*action*) воспроизведение; (*object*) репродукция; (*of offspring*) размножение. **reproductive** *adj* воспроизводительный.

reproof *n* выговор. **reprove** *vt* делать *impf* с~ *pf* выговор +*dat*.

reptile *n* пресмыкающееся *sb*.

republic *n* республика. **republican** *adj* республиканский; *n* республиканец, -нка.

repudiate *vt* (*renounce*) отказываться *impf*, отказаться *pf* от+*gen*; (*reject*) отвергать *impf*, отвергнуть *pf*. **repudiation** *n* отказ (**of** от+*gen*).

repugnance *n* отвращение. **repugnant** *adj* противный.

repulse *vt* отражать *impf*, отразить *pf*. **repulsion** *n* отвращение. **repulsive** *adj* отвратительный.

reputable *adj* пользующийся хорошей репутацией. **reputation, repute** *n* репутация. **reputed** *adj* предполагаемый *impf*, отвергнуть. **reputedly** *adv* по общему мнению.

request *n* просьба; **by, on,** ~ по просьбе; *vt* просить *impf*, по~ *pf* +*acc*, +*gen* (*person* +*acc*).

requiem *n* реквием.

require *vt* (*demand; need*) требовать *impf*, по~ *pf* +*gen*; (*need*) нуждаться *impf* в+*prep*. **requirement** *n* требование; (*necessity*) потребность. **requisite** *adj* необходимый; *n* необходимая вещь. **requisition** *n* реквизиция; *vt* реквизировать *impf* & *pf*.

resale *n* перепродажа.

rescind *vt* отменять *impf*, отменить *pf*.

rescue *vt* спасать *impf*, спасти *pf*; *n* спасение. **rescuer** *n* спаситель *m*.

research *n* исследование (+*gen*); (*occupation*) исследовательская работа; *vi*: ~ **into** исследовать *impf* & *pf* +*acc*. **researcher** *n* исследователь *m*.

resemblance *n* сходство. **resemble**

vt походи́ть *impf* на+*acc*.

resent *vt* возмуща́ться *impf*, возмути́ться *pf*. **resentful** *adj* возмущённый. **resentment** *n* возмуще́ние.

reservation *n* (*doubt*) огово́рка; (*booking*) предвари́тельный зака́з; (*land*) резерва́ция. **reserve** *vt* (*keep*) резерви́ровать *impf & pf*; (*book*) зака́зывать *impf*, заказа́ть *pf*; *n* (*stock*; *mil*) запа́с, резе́рв; (*sport*) запасно́й игро́к; (*nature ~ etc.*) запове́дник; (*proviso*) огово́рка; (*self-restraint*) сде́ржанность; *attrib* запасно́й. **reserved** *adj* (*person*) сде́ржанный. **reservist** *n* резерви́ст.

reservoir *n* (*for water*) водохрани́лище; (*for other fluids*) резервуа́р.

resettle *vt* переселя́ть *impf*, переселить *pf*. **resettlement** *n* переселе́ние.

reshape *vt* видоизменя́ть *impf*, видоизмени́ть *pf*.

reshuffle *n* перестано́вка.

reside *vi* прожива́ть *impf*. **residence** *n* (*residing*) прожива́ние; (*abode*) местожи́тельство; (*official ~ etc.*) резиде́нция. **resident** *n* (*постоя́нный*) жи́тель *m*, ~ница; *adj* прожива́ющий; (*population*) постоя́нный. **residential** *adj* жило́й.

residual *adj* оста́точный. **residue** *n* оста́ток.

resign *vt* отка́зываться *impf*, отказа́ться *pf* от+*gen*; *vi* уходи́ть *impf*, уйти́ *pf* в отста́вку; ~ **o.s. to** покоря́ться *impf*, покори́ться *pf* +*dat*. **resignation** *n* отста́вка, заявле́ние об отста́вке; (*being resigned*) поко́рность. **resigned** *adj* поко́рный.

resilient *adj* выно́сливый.

resin *n* смола́.

resist *vt* сопротивля́ться *impf* +*dat*; (*temptation*) устоя́ть *pf* пе́ред+*instr*. **resistance** *n* сопротивле́ние. **resistant** *adj* сто́йкий.

resolute *adj* реши́тельный. **resolution** *n* (*character*) реши́тельность; (*vow*) заро́к; (*at meeting etc.*) резолю́ция; (*of problem*) разреше́ние. **resolve** *vt* (*decide*) реша́ть *impf*, реши́ть *pf*; (*settle*) разреша́ть *impf*, разреши́ть *pf*; *n* реши́тельность; (*decision*) реше́ние.

resonance *n* резона́нс. **resonant** *adj*

зву́чный.

resort *vi*: ~ **to** прибега́ть *impf*, прибе́гнуть *pf* к+*dat*; *n* (*place*) куро́рт; **in the last** ~ в кра́йнем слу́чае.

resound *vi* (*of sound etc.*) раздава́ться *impf*, разда́ться *pf*; (*of place*) оглаша́ться *impf*, огласи́ться *pf* (*with* +*instr*).

resource *n* (*usu pl*) ресу́рс. **resourceful** *adj* нахо́дчивый.

respect *n* (*relation*) отноше́ние; (*esteem*) уваже́ние; **with** ~ **to** что каса́ется+*gen*; *vt* уважа́ть *impf*. **respectability** *n* респекта́бельность. **respectable** *adj* прили́чный. **respectful** *adj* почти́тельный. **respective** *adj* свой. **respectively** *adv* соотве́тственно.

respiration *n* дыха́ние. **respirator** *n* респира́тор. **respiratory** *adj* дыха́тельный.

respite *n* переды́шка.

resplendent *adj* блиста́тельный.

respond *vi*: ~ **to** отвеча́ть *impf*, отве́тить *pf* на+*acc*; (*react*) реаги́ровать *impf*, про~, от~ *pf* на+*acc*. **response** *n* отве́т; (*reaction*) о́тклик. **responsibility** *n* отве́тственность; (*duty*) обя́занность. **responsible** *adj* отве́тственный (**to** пе́ред +*instr*; **for** за+*acc*); (*reliable*) надёжный. **responsive** *adj* отзы́вчивый.

rest[1] *vi* отдыха́ть *impf*, отдохну́ть *pf*; *vt* (*place*) класть *impf*, положи́ть *pf*; (*allow to* ~) дава́ть *impf*, дать *pf* о́тдых+*dat*; *n* (*repose*) о́тдых; (*peace*) поко́й; (*mus*) па́уза; (*support*) опо́ра.

rest[2] *n* (*remainder*) оста́ток; (*the others*) остальны́е *sb pl*.

restaurant *n* рестора́н.

restful *adj* успока́ивающий.

restitution *n* возвраще́ние.

restive *adj* беспоко́йный.

restless *adj* беспоко́йный.

restoration *n* реставра́ция; (*return*) восстановле́ние. **restore** *vt* реставри́ровать *impf & pf*; (*return*) восста́навливать *impf*, восстанови́ть *pf*.

restrain *vt* уде́рживать *impf*, удержа́ть *pf* (**from** от+*gen*). **restraint** *n* сде́ржанность.

restrict *vt* ограни́чивать *impf*, ограни́чить *pf*. **restriction** *n* ограниче́ние. **restrictive** *adj* ограничи́тельный.

result vi сле́довать impf; происходи́ть impf (**from** из+gen); ~ **in** конча́ться impf, ко́нчиться pf +instr; n результа́т; **as a** ~ в результа́те (**of** +gen).

resume vt & i возобновля́ть(ся) impf, возобнови́ть(ся) pf. **résumé** n резюме́ neut indecl. **resumption** n возобновле́ние.

resurrect vt (fig) воскреша́ть impf, воскреси́ть pf. **resurrection** n (of the dead) воскресе́ние; (fig) воскреше́ние.

resuscitate vt приводи́ть impf, привести́ pf в созна́ние.

retail n ро́зничная прода́жа; attrib ро́зничный; adv в ро́зницу; vt продава́ть impf, прода́ть pf в ро́зницу; vi продава́ться impf в ро́зницу. **retailer** n ро́зничный торго́вец.

retain vt уде́рживать impf, удержа́ть pf.

retaliate vi отпла́чивать impf, отплати́ть pf тем же. **retaliation** n отпла́та, возме́здие.

retard vt замедля́ть impf, заме́длить pf. **retarded** adj отста́лый.

retention n удержа́ние. **retentive** adj (memory) хоро́ший.

reticence n сде́ржанность. **reticent** adj сде́ржанный.

retina n сетча́тка.

retinue n сви́та.

retire vi (withdraw) удаля́ться impf, удали́ться pf; (from office etc.) уходи́ть impf, уйти́ pf в отста́вку. **retired** adj в отста́вке. **retirement** n отста́вка. **retiring** adj скро́мный.

retort[1] vt отвеча́ть impf, отве́тить pf ре́зко; n возраже́ние.

retort[2] n (vessel) рето́рта.

retrace vt: ~ **one's steps** возвраща́ться impf, возврати́ться pf.

retract vt (draw in) втя́гивать impf, втяну́ть pf; (take back) брать impf, взять pf наза́д.

retreat vi отступа́ть impf, отступи́ть pf; n отступле́ние; (withdrawal) уедине́ние; (place) убе́жище.

retrenchment n сокраще́ние расхо́дов.

retrial n повто́рное слу́шание де́ла.

retribution n возме́здие.

retrieval n возвраще́ние; (comput) по́иск (информа́ции); vt брать impf,

retrograde adj (fig) реакцио́нный.

retrospect n: **in** ~ ретроспекти́вно. **retrospective** adj (law) име́ющий обра́тную си́лу.

return vt & i (give back; come back) возвраща́ть(ся) impf, возврати́ть(ся) impf, верну́ть(ся) pf; vt (elect) избира́ть impf, избра́ть pf; n возвраще́ние; возвра́т; (profit) при́быль; **by** ~ обра́тной по́чтой; **in** ~ взаме́н (**for** +gen); **many happy** ~s! с днём рожде́ния!; ~ **match** отве́тный матч; ~ **ticket** обра́тный биле́т.

reunion n встре́ча (друзе́й и т. п.); **family** ~ сбор всей семьи́. **reunite** vt воссоединя́ть impf, воссоедини́ть pf.

reuse vt сно́ва испо́льзовать impf & pf.

rev n оборо́т; vt & i: ~ **up** рвану́ть(ся) pf.

reveal vt обнару́живать impf, обнару́жить pf. **revealing** adj показа́тельный.

revel vi пирова́ть impf; ~ **in** наслажда́ться impf +instr.

revelation n открове́ние.

revenge vt: ~ **o.s.** мстить impf, отомсти́ть pf (**for** за+acc; **on** +dat); n месть.

revenue n дохо́д.

reverberate vi отража́ться impf. **reverberation** n отраже́ние; (fig) о́тзвук.

revere vt почита́ть impf. **reverence** n почте́ние. **Reverend** adj (in title) (его́) преподо́бие. **reverent(ial)** adj почти́тельный.

reverie n мечта́ние.

reversal n (change) измене́ние; (of decision) отме́на. **reverse** adj обра́тный; ~ **gear** за́дний ход; vt (change) изменя́ть impf, измени́ть pf; (decision) отменя́ть impf, отмени́ть pf; vi дава́ть impf, дать pf за́дний ход; n (the ~) обра́тное sb; (~ **gear**) за́дний ход; (~ **side**) обра́тная сторона́. **reversible** adj обрати́мый; (cloth) двусторо́нний. **reversion** n возвраще́ние. **revert** vi возвраща́ться impf (**to** в+acc, к+dat); (law) переходи́ть impf, перейти́ pf (**to** к+dat).

review n (re-examination) пересмо́тр; (mil) пара́д; (survey) обзо́р;

(*criticism*) реце́нзия; *vt* (*re-examine*) пересма́тривать *impf*, пересмотре́ть *pf*; (*survey*) обозрева́ть *impf*, обозре́ть *pf*; (*troops etc.*) принима́ть *impf*, приня́ть *pf* пара́д+*gen*; (*book etc.*) рецензи́ровать *impf*, про~ *pf*. **reviewer** *n* реце́нзе́нт.

revise *vt* пересма́тривать *impf*, пересмотре́ть *pf*; исправля́ть *impf*, испра́вить *pf*; *vi* (*for exam*) гото́виться *impf* (for к+*dat*). **revision** *n* пересмо́тр, исправле́ние.

revival *n* возрожде́ние; (*to life etc.*) оживле́ние. **revive** *vt* возрожда́ть *impf*, возроди́ть *pf*; (*resuscitate*) оживля́ть *impf*, оживи́ть *pf*; *vi* ожива́ть *impf*, ожи́ть *pf*.

revoke *vt* отменя́ть *impf*, отмени́ть *pf*.

revolt *n* бунт; *vt* вызыва́ть *impf*, вы́звать *pf* отвраще́ние у+*gen*; *vi* бунтова́ть *impf*, взбунтова́ться *pf*. **revolting** *adj* отврати́тельный.

revolution *n* (*single turn*) оборо́т; (*polit*) револю́ция. **revolutionary** *adj* революцио́нный; *n* революционе́р. **revolutionize** *vt* революционизи́ровать *impf* & *pf*. **revolve** *vt* & *i* враща́ть(ся) *impf*. **revolver** *n* револьве́р.

revue *n* ревю́ *neut indecl*.

revulsion *n* отвраще́ние.

reward *n* вознагражде́ние; *vt* (воз)награжда́ть *impf*, (воз)награди́ть *pf*.

rewrite *vt* перепи́сывать *impf*, переписа́ть *pf*; (*recast*) переде́лывать *impf*, переде́лать *pf*.

rhapsody *n* рапсо́дия.

rhetoric *n* рито́рика. **rhetorical** *adj* ритори́ческий.

rheumatic *adj* ревмати́ческий. **rheumatism** *n* ревмати́зм.

rhinoceros *n* носоро́г.

rhododendron *n* рододе́ндрон.

rhubarb *n* реве́нь *m*.

rhyme *n* ри́фма; *pl* (*verse*) стихи́ *m pl*; *vt* & *i* рифмова́ть(ся) *impf*.

rhythm *n* ритм. **rhythmic(al)** *adj* ритми́ческий, -чный.

rib *n* ребро́.

ribald *adj* непристо́йный.

ribbon *n* ле́нта.

rice *n* рис.

rich *adj* бога́тый; (*soil*) ту́чный;

(*food*) жи́рный. **riches** *n pl* бога́тство. **richly** *adv* (*fully*) вполне́.

rickety *adj* (*shaky*) расша́танный.

ricochet *vi* рикошети́ровать *impf* & *pf*.

rid *vt* освобожда́ть *impf*, освободи́ть *pf* (of от+*gen*); get ~ of избавля́ться *impf*, изба́виться *pf* от+*gen*. **riddance** *n*: good ~! ска́тертью доро́га!

riddle *n* (*enigma*) зага́дка.

riddled *adj*: ~ with изрешечённый; (*fig*) прони́занный.

ride *vi* е́здить *indet*, е́хать *det*, по~ *pf* (on horseback верхо́м); *vt* е́здить *indet*, е́хать *det*, по~ *pf* на+*prep*; *n* пое́здка, езда́. **rider** *n* вса́дник, -ица; (*clause*) дополне́ние.

ridge *n* хребе́т; (on cloth) ру́бчик; (*of roof*) конёк.

ridicule *n* насме́шка; *vt* осме́ивать *impf*, осмея́ть *pf*. **ridiculous** *adj* смешно́й.

riding *n* (horse-~) (верхова́я) езда́.

rife *predic* распространённый.

riff-raff *n* подо́нки (-ков) *pl*.

rifle *n* винто́вка; *vt* (*search*) обы́скивать *impf*, обыска́ть *pf*.

rift *n* тре́щина (*also fig*).

rig *vt* оснаща́ть *impf*, оснасти́ть *pf*; ~ out наряжа́ть *impf*, наряди́ть *pf*; ~ up скола́чивать *impf*, сколоти́ть *pf*; *n* бурова́я устано́вка. **rigging** *n* такела́ж.

right *adj* (*position*; *justified*; *polit*) пра́вый; (*correct*) пра́вильный; (*the one wanted*) тот; (*suitable*) подходя́щий; ~ angle прямо́й у́гол; *vt* исправля́ть *impf*, испра́вить *pf*; *n* пра́во; (*what is just*) справедли́вость; (~ side) пра́вая сторона́; (the R~; *polit*) пра́вые *sb pl*; be in the ~ быть пра́вым; by ~s по пра́ву; ~ of way пра́во прохо́да, прое́зда; *adv* (*straight*) пря́мо; (*exactly*) то́чно, как раз; (*to the full*) соверше́нно; (*correctly*) пра́вильно; как сле́дует; (on the ~) спра́во (от пра́во); (to the ~) напра́во; ~ away сейча́с.

righteous *adj* (*person*) пра́ведный; (*action*) справедли́вый.

rightful *adj* зако́нный.

rigid *adj* жёсткий; (*strict*) стро́гий. **rigidity** *n* жёсткость; стро́гость.

rigmarole *n* каните́ль.

rigorous adj стро́гий. **rigour** n стро́гость.

rim n (of wheel) о́бод; (spectacles) опра́ва. **rimless** adj без опра́вы.

rind n кожура́.

ring¹ n кольцо́; (circle) круг; (boxing) ринг; (circus) (цирково́я) аре́на; ~ road кольцева́я доро́га; vt (encircle) окружа́ть impf, окружи́ть pf.

ring² vi (sound) звони́ть impf, по~ pf; (ring out, of shot etc.) раздава́ться impf, разда́ться pf; (of place) оглаша́ть impf, огласи́ть pf (with +instr); vt звони́ть impf, по~ pf в+acc; ~ back перезва́нивать impf, перезвони́ть pf; ~ off пове́сить pf тру́бку; ~ up звони́ть impf, по~ pf +dat; n звон, звоно́к.

ringleader n глава́рь m.

rink n като́к.

rinse n полоска́ть impf, вы́~ pf; n полоска́ние.

riot n бунт; **run** ~ бу́йствовать impf; (of plants) бу́йно разраста́ться impf, разрасти́сь pf; vi бунтова́ть impf, взбунтова́ться pf. **riotous** adj бу́йный.

rip vt & i рва́ть(ся) impf; разо~ pf; ~ up разрыва́ть impf, разорва́ть pf; n проре́ха, разре́з.

ripe adj зре́лый, спе́лый. **ripen** vt де́лать impf, c~ pf зре́лым; vi созрева́ть impf, созре́ть pf. **ripeness** n зре́лость.

ripple n рябь; vt & i покрыва́ть(ся) impf, покры́ть(ся) pf ря́бью.

rise vi поднима́ться impf, подня́ться pf; повыша́ться impf, повы́ситься pf; (get up) встава́ть impf, встать pf; (rebel) восстава́ть impf, восста́ть pf; (sun etc.) в(о)сходи́ть impf, взойти́; n подъём, возвыше́ние; (in pay) приба́вка; (of sun etc.) восхо́д. **riser** n: **he is an early** ~ он ра́но встаёт. **rising** n (revolt) восста́ние.

risk n риск; vt рискова́ть impf, рискну́ть pf +instr. **risky** adj риско́ванный.

risqué adj непристо́йный.

rite n обря́д. **ritual** n ритуа́л; adj ритуа́льный.

rival n сопе́рник, -ица; adj сопе́рничающий; vt сопе́рничать impf c+instr. **rivalry** n сопе́рничество.

river n река́. **riverside** attrib прибре́жный.

rivet n заклёпка; vt заклёпывать impf, заклепа́ть pf; (fig) прико́вывать impf, прикова́ть pf (on к+dat).

road n доро́га; (street) у́лица; ~block заграждёние на доро́ге; ~map (доро́жная) ка́рта; ~sign доро́жный знак. **roadside** n обо́чина; attrib придоро́жный. **roadway** n мостова́я sb.

roam vt & i броди́ть impf (по+dat).

roar n (animal's) рёв; vi реве́ть impf.

roast vt & i жа́рить(ся) impf, за~, из~ pf; adj жа́реный; ~ beef ро́стбиф; n жарко́е sb.

rob vt гра́бить impf, о~ pf; красть impf, y~ pf у+gen (of +acc); (deprive) лиша́ть impf, лиши́ть pf (of +gen). **robber** n граби́тель m. **robbery** n грабёж.

robe n (also pl) ма́нтия.

robin n мали́новка.

robot n ро́бот.

robust adj кре́пкий.

rock¹ n (geol) (го́рная) поро́да; (cliff etc.) скала́; (large stone) большо́й ка́мень m; **on the** ~s (in difficulty) на мели́; (drink) со льдом.

rock² vt & i кача́ть(ся) impf, качну́ть(ся) pf; n (mus) рок; ~ing-chair кача́лка; ~ and roll рок-н-ро́лл.

rockery n альпина́рий.

rocket n раке́та; vi подска́кивать impf, подскочи́ть pf.

rocky adj скали́стый; (shaky) ша́ткий.

rod n (stick) прут; (bar) сте́ржень m; (fishing-~) у́дочка.

rodent n грызу́н.

roe¹ n икра́; (soft) моло́ки (-о́к) pl.

roe² (-deer) n косу́ля.

rogue n плут.

role n роль.

roll¹ n (cylinder) руло́н; (register) рее́стр; (bread) бу́лочка; ~call перекли́чка.

roll² vt & i ката́ть(ся) indet, кати́ть(ся) det, по~ pf; (~ up) свёртывать(ся) impf, сверну́ть(ся) pf; vt (~ out) (dough) раска́тывать impf, раската́ть pf; vi (sound) греме́ть impf; ~ over перевора́чиваться impf, переверну́ться pf; n (of drums) бараба́нная дробь; (of thunder) раска́т.

roller n (small) ро́лик; (large) като́к;

(*for hair*) бигуди́ *neut indecl*; ~-
skates коньки́ *m pl* на ро́ликах.
rolling *adj* (*of land*) холми́стый; ~-
pin ска́лка. ~-stock подвижно́й со-
ста́в.
Roman *n* ри́млянин, -янка; *adj* ри́м-
ский; ~ **Catholic** (*n*) като́лик, -и́чка;
(*adj*) ри́мско-католи́ческий.
romance *n* (*tale; love affair*) рома́н;
(*quality*) рома́нтика.
Romanesque *adj* рома́нский.
Romania *n* Румы́ния. **Romanian** *n*
румы́н, ~ка; *adj* румы́нский.
romantic *adj* романти́чный, -ческий.
romanticism *n* романти́зм.
romp *vi* вози́ться *impf*.
roof *n* кры́ша; ~ **of the mouth** нёбо;
vt крыть *impf*, покры́ть *pf*.
rook[1] *n* (*chess*) ладья́.
rook[2] *n* (*bird*) грач.
room *n* ко́мната; (*in hotel*) но́мер;
(*space*) ме́сто. **roomy** *adj* просто́р-
ный.
roost *n* насе́ст.
root[1] *n* ко́рень *m*; **take** ~ укореня́ть-
ся *impf*, укорени́ться *pf*; *vi* пуска́ть
impf, пусти́ть *pf* ко́рни; ~ **out** вы-
рыва́ть *impf*, вы́рвать *pf* с ко́рнем; ~
rooted to the spot прико́ванный к
ме́сту.
root[2] *vi* (*rummage*) ры́ться *impf*; ~
for боле́ть *impf* за +*acc*.
rope *n* верёвка; ~-ladder верёвочная
ле́стница; *vt* ~ **in** (*enlist*) втя́гивать
impf, втяну́ть *pf*; ~ **off** о(т)гора́жи-
вать *impf*, о(т)городи́ть *pf* верёв-
кой.
rosary *n* чётки (-ток) *pl*.
rose *n* ро́за; (*nozzle*) се́тка.
rosemary *n* розмари́н.
rosette *n* розе́тка.
rosewood *n* ро́зовое де́рево.
roster *n* расписа́ние дежу́рств.
rostrum *n* трибу́на.
rosy *adj* ро́зовый; (*cheeks*) румя́ный.
rot *n* гниль; (*nonsense*) вздор; *vi* гнить
impf, с~ *pf*; *vt* гнои́ть *impf*, с~ *pf*.
rota *n* расписа́ние дежу́рств. **rotary**
adj враща́тельный, ротацио́нный.
rotate *vt* & *i* враща́ть(ся) *impf*. **rotation** *n* враще́ние; **in** ~ по о́череди.
rote *n*: **by** ~ наизу́сть.
rotten *adj* гнило́й; (*fig*) отврати́-
тельный.
rotund *adj* (*round*) кру́глый; (*plump*)

по́лный.
rouble *n* рубль *m*.
rough *adj* (*uneven*) неро́вный; (*coarse*)
гру́бый; (*sea*) бу́рный; (*approximate*) приблизи́тельный; ~ **copy**
черновик; *n*: **the** ~ тру́дности *f pl*;
vt: ~ **it** жить *impf* без удо́бств.
roughage *n* гру́бая пи́ща. **roughly**
adv гру́бо; (*approximately*) приблизи́-
тельно.
roulette *n* руле́тка.
round *adj* кру́глый; ~-shouldered
суту́лый; *n* (~ *object*) круг; (*circuit;
also pl*) обхо́д; (*sport*) тур, ра́унд;
(*series*) ряд; (*ammunition*) патро́н;
(*of applause*) взрыв; *adv* вокру́г; (*in
a circle*) по кру́гу; **all** ~ круго́м; **all
the year** ~ кру́глый год; *prep* вокру́г+*gen*; круго́м+*gen*; по+*dat*; ~
the corner (*motion*) за́ угол, (*posi-
tion*) за угло́м; *vt* (*go* ~) огиба́ть
impf, обогну́ть *pf*; ~ **off** (*complete*)
заверша́ть *impf*, заверши́ть *pf*; ~
up сгоня́ть *impf*, согна́ть *pf*; ~-up
заго́н; (*raid*) обла́ва. **roundabout** *n*
(*merry-go-round*) карусе́ль; (*road
junction*) кольцева́я тра́нспортная
развя́зка; *adj* око́льный.
rouse *vt* буди́ть *impf*, раз~ *pf*; (*to
action etc.*) побужда́ть *impf*, побу-
ди́ть *pf* (**to** к+*dat*). **rousing** *adj*
восто́рженный.
rout *n* (*defeat*) разгро́м.
route *n* маршру́т, путь *m*.
routine *n* заведённый поря́док, ре-
жи́м; *adj* устано́вленный; очеред-
но́й.
rove *vi* скита́ться *impf*.
row[1] *n* (*line*) ряд.
row[2] *vi* (*in boat*) грести́ *impf*.
row[3] *n* (*dispute*) ссо́ра; (*noise*) шум;
vi ссо́риться *impf*, по~ *pf*.
rowdy *adj* бу́йный.
royal *adj* короле́вский; (*majestic*)
великоле́пный. **royalist** *n* роялист;
adj рояли́стский. **royalty** *n* член,
чле́ны *pl*, короле́вской семьи́; (*fee*)
а́вторский гонора́р.
rub *vt* & *i* тере́ть(ся) *impf*; *vt* (*polish,
chafe*) натира́ть *impf*, натере́ть *pf*;
(~ *dry*) вытира́ть *impf*, вы́тереть
pf; ~ **in, on** втира́ть *impf*, втере́ть
pf; ~ **out** стира́ть *impf*, стере́ть *pf*;
~ **it in** растравля́ть *impf*, растра-
ви́ть *pf* ра́ну.

rubber n резина; (*eraser, also* ~ **band**) резинка; *attrib* резиновый; ~ **stamp** (*fig*) штамповать *impf*.

rubbish n мусор; (*nonsense*) чепуха.

rubble n щебень m.

rubella n краснуха.

ruby n рубин.

ruck vt (~ **up**) мять *impf*, из~, с~ *pf*.

rucksack n рюкзак.

rudder n руль m.

ruddy adj (*face*) румяный; (*damned*) проклятый.

rude adj грубый. **rudeness** n грубость.

rudimentary adj рудиментарный. **rudiments** n pl основы f pl.

rueful adj печальный.

ruff n (*frill*) брыжи (-жей) pl; (*of feathers, hair*) кольцо (перьев, шерсти) вокруг шеи.

ruffian n хулиган.

ruffle n оборка; vt (*hair*) ерошить *impf*, взъ~ *pf*; (*water*) рябить *impf*; (*person*) смущать *impf*, смутить *pf*.

rug n (*mat*) ковёр; (*wrap*) плед.

rugby n регби *neut indecl*.

rugged adj (*rocky*) скалистый.

ruin n (*downfall*) гибель; (*building, ruins*) развалины f pl, руины f pl; vt губить *impf*, по~ *pf*. **ruinous** adj губительный.

rule n правило; (*for measuring*) линейка; (*government*) правление; **as a** ~ как правило; vt & i править *impf* (+instr); (*decree*) постановлять *impf*, постановить *pf*; ~ **out** исключать *impf*, исключить *pf*. **ruled** adj линованный. **ruler** n (*person*) правитель m, ~ница; (*object*) линейка. **ruling** n (*of court etc.*) постановление.

rum n (*drink*) ром.

Rumania(n) *see* **Romania(n)**

rumble vi громыхать *impf*; n громыхание.

ruminant n жвачное (животное) sb.

ruminate vi (*fig*) размышлять *impf* (*over, on* o+prep).

rummage vi рыться *impf*.

rumour n слух; vt: **it is** ~**ed that** ходят слухи (pl), что.

rump n крестец; ~ **steak** ромштекс.

rumple vt мять *impf*, из~, с~ *pf*; (*hair*) ерошить *impf*, взъ~ *pf*.

run vi бегать *indet*, бежать *det*, по~ *pf*; (*work, of machines*) работать *impf*; (*ply, of bus etc.*) ходить *indet*, идти *det*; (*seek election*) выставлять *impf*, выставить *pf* свою кандидатуру; (*of play etc.*) идти *impf*; (*of ink, dye*) расплываться *impf*, расплыться *pf*; (*flow*) течь *impf*; (*of document*) гласить *impf*; vt (*manage, operate*) управлять *impf* +instr; (*a business etc.*) вести *impf*; ~ **dry, low** иссякать *impf*, иссякнуть *pf*; ~ **risks** рисковать *impf*; ~ **across, into** (*meet*) встречаться *impf*, встретиться *pf* c+instr; ~ **away** (*flee*) убегать *impf*, убежать *pf*; ~ **down** (*knock down*) задавить *pf*; (*disparage*) принижать *impf*, принизить *pf*; **be** ~ **down** (*of person*) переутомиться *pf* (*in past tense*); ~-**down** (*decayed*) запущенный; ~ **in** (*engine*) обкатывать *impf*, обкатать *pf*; ~ **into** *see* ~ **across**; ~ **out** кончаться *impf*, кончиться *pf*; ~ **out of** истощать *impf*, истощить *pf* свой запас +gen; ~ **over** (*glance over*) бегло просматривать *impf*, просмотреть *pf*; (*injure*) задавить *pf*; ~ **through** (*pierce*) прокалывать *impf*, проколоть *pf*; (*money*) проматывать *impf*, промотать *pf*; (*review*) повторять *impf*, повторить *pf*; ~ **to** (*reach*) (*of money*) хватать *impf*, хватить *pf* impers+gen+acc; **the money won't** ~ **to a car** этих денег не хватит на машину; ~ **up against** наталкиваться *impf*, натолкнуться *pf* на +acc; n бег; (*sport*) перебежка; (*journey*) поездка; (*period*) полоса; **at a** ~ бегом; **on the** ~ в бегах; **on** большой спрос на+acc; **in the long** ~ в конце концов.

rung n ступенька.

runner n (*also tech*) бегун; (*of sledge*) полоз; (*bot*) побег; ~ **bean** фасоль; ~-**up** участник, занявший второе место. **running** n бег; (*management*) управление (*of* +instr); **be in the** ~ иметь *impf* шансы; adj бегущий; (*of* ~) беговой; (*after pl n, in succession*) подряд; ~ **commentary** репортаж; ~ **water** водопровод. **runway** n взлётно-посадочная полоса.

rupee n рупия.

rupture n разрыв; vt & i проры-

ва́ть(ся) *impf*, прорва́ть(ся) *pf*.
rural *adj* се́льский.
ruse *n* уло́вка.
rush[1] *n* (*bot*) тростни́к.
rush[2] *vt & i* (*hurry*) торопи́ть(ся) *impf*, по~ *pf*; *vi* (*dash*) броса́ться *impf*, бро́ситься *pf*; (*of water*) нести́сь *impf*; по~ *pf*; *vt* (*to hospital etc.*) умча́ть *pf*; *n* (*of blood etc.*) прили́в; (*hurry*) спе́шка; **be in a** ~ торопи́ться *impf*; ~**-hour(s)** часы́ *m pl* пик.
Russia *n* Росси́я. **Russian** *n* ру́сский *sb*; *adj* (*of* ~ *nationality, culture*) ру́сский; (*of* ~ *State*) росси́йский.
rust *n* ржа́вчина; *vi* ржаве́ть *impf*, за~, по~ *pf*.
rustic *adj* дереве́нский.
rustle *n* ше́лест, шо́рох, шурша́ние; *vi & t* шелесте́ть *impf* (+*instr*); ~ **up** раздобыва́ть *impf*; раздобы́ть *pf*.
rusty *adj* ржа́вый.
rut *n* колея́.
ruthless *adj* безжа́лостный.
rye *n* рожь; *attrib* ржано́й.

S

Sabbath *n* (*Jewish*) суббо́та; (*Christian*) воскресе́нье. **sabbatical** *n* годи́чный о́тпуск.
sable *n* со́боль.
sabotage *n* диве́рсия; *vt* саботи́ровать *impf* & *pf*. **saboteur** *n* диверса́нт.
sabre *n* са́бля.
sachet *n* упако́вка.
sack[1] *vt* (*plunder*) разгра́бить *pf*.
sack[2] *n* мешо́к; (*dismissal*): **get the** ~ быть уво́ленным; *vt* увольня́ть *impf*, уво́лить *pf*. **sacking** *n* (*hessian*) мешкови́на.
sacrament *n* та́инство; (*Eucharist*) прича́стие. **sacred** *adj* свяще́нный, свято́й. **sacrifice** *n* же́ртва; *vt* же́ртвовать *impf*, по~ *pf* +*instr*. **sacrilege** *n* святота́тство. **sacrosanct** *adj* свяще́нный.
sad *adj* печа́льный, гру́стный. **sadden** *vt* печа́лить *impf*, о~ *pf*.
saddle *n* седло́; *vt* седла́ть *impf*, о~ *pf*; (*burden*) обременя́ть *impf*, обремени́ть *pf* (*with* +*instr*).
sadism *n* сади́зм. **sadist** *n* сади́ст.

sadistic *adj* сади́стский.
sadness *n* печа́ль, грусть.
safe *n* сейф; *adj* (*unharmed*) невреди́мый; (*out of danger*) в безопа́сности; (*secure*) безопа́сный; (*reliable*) надёжный; ~ **and sound** цел и невреди́м. **safeguard** *n* предохрани́тельная ме́ра; *vt* предохраня́ть *impf*, предохрани́ть *pf*. **safety** *n* безопа́сность; ~**-belt** реме́нь *m* безопа́сности; ~ **pin** англи́йская була́вка; ~**-valve** предохрани́тельный кла́пан.
sag *vi* (*of rope, curtain*) провиса́ть *impf*, прови́снуть *pf*; (*of ceiling*) прогиба́ться *impf*, прогну́ться *pf*.
saga *n* са́га.
sage[1] *n* (*herb*) шалфе́й.
sage[2] *n* (*person*) мудре́ц; *adj* му́дрый.
Sagittarius *n* Стреле́ц.
sail *n* па́рус; *vt* (*a ship*) управля́ть *impf* +*instr*; *vi* пла́вать *indet*, плыть *det*; (*depart*) отплыва́ть *impf*, отплы́ть *pf*. **sailing** *n* (*sport*) па́русный спорт; ~**-ship** па́русное су́дно. **sailor** *n* матро́с, моря́к.
saint *n* свято́й *sb*. **saintly** *adj* свято́й.
sake *n*: **for the** ~ **of** ра́ди+*gen*.
salad *n* сала́т; ~**-dressing** припра́ва к сала́ту.
salami *n* саля́ми *f indecl*.
salary *n* жа́лованье.
sale *n* прода́жа; (*also amount sold*) сбыт (*no pl*); (*with reduced prices*) распрода́жа; **be for** ~ продава́ться *impf*. **saleable** *adj* хо́дкий. **salesman** *n* продаве́ц. **saleswoman** *n* продавщи́ца.
salient *adj* основно́й.
saliva *n* слюна́.
sallow *adj* желтова́тый.
salmon *n* ло́сось *m*.
salon *n* сало́н. **saloon** *n* (*on ship*) сало́н; (*car*) седа́н; (*bar*) бар.
salt *n* соль; ~**-cellar** соло́нка; ~ **water** морска́я вода́; ~**-water** морско́й; *adj* солёный; *vt* соли́ть *impf*, по~ *pf*. **salty** *adj* солёный.
salutary *adj* благотво́рный. **salute** *n* отда́ча че́сти; (*with guns*) салю́т; *vt & i* отдава́ть *impf*, отда́ть *pf* честь (+*dat*).
salvage *n* спасе́ние; *vt* спаса́ть *impf*, спасти́ *pf*.

salvation n спасе́ние; S~ Army А́рмия спасе́ния.

salve n мазь; vt: ~ one's conscience успока́ивать impf, успоко́ить pf со́весть.

salvo n залп.

same adj: the ~ тот же (са́мый); (applying to both or all) оди́н; (identical) одина́ковый; pron: the ~ одно́ и то́ же, то же са́мое; adv: the ~ таки́м же о́бразом, так же; all the ~ всё-таки, тем не ме́нее. **sameness** n однообра́зие.

samovar n самова́р.

sample n образе́ц; vt про́бовать impf, по~ pf.

sanatorium n санато́рий.

sanctify vt освяща́ть impf, освяти́ть pf. **sanctimonious** adj ха́нжеский. **sanction** n са́нкция; vt санкциони́ровать impf & pf. **sanctity** n (holiness) свя́тость; (sacredness) свяще́нность. **sanctuary** n святи́лище; (refuge) убе́жище; (for wild life) запове́дник.

sand n песо́к; vt (~ down) шкури́ть impf, по~ pf; ~dune дю́на.

sandal n санда́лия.

sandalwood n санда́ловое де́рево.

sandbank n о́тмель.

sandpaper n шку́рка; vt шлифова́ть impf, от~ pf шку́ркой.

sandstone n песча́ник.

sandwich n бутербро́д; vt: ~ between вти́скивать impf, всти́снуть pf ме́жду+instr.

sandy adj (of sand) песча́ный; (like sand) песо́чный; (hair) рыжева́тый.

sane adj норма́льный; (sensible) разу́мный.

sang-froid n самооблада́ние.

sanguine adj оптимисти́ческий.

sanitary adj санита́рный; гигиени́ческий; ~ towel гигиени́ческая поду́шка. **sanitation** n (conditions) санита́рные усло́вия neut pl; (system) водопрово́д и канализа́ция. **sanity** n психи́ческое здоро́вье; (good sense) здра́вый смысл.

sap n (bot) сок; vt (exhaust) истоща́ть impf, истощи́ть pf.

sapling n са́женец.

sapphire n сапфи́р.

sarcasm n сарка́зм. **sarcastic** adj сарка́сти́ческий.

sardine n сарди́на.

sardonic adj сардони́ческий.

sash[1] n (scarf) куша́к.

sash[2] n (frame) скользя́щая ра́ма; ~-window подъёмное окно́.

satanic adj сатани́нский.

satchel n ра́нец, су́мка.

satellite n спу́тник, сателли́т (also fig); ~ dish параболи́ческая анте́нна; таре́лка (coll); ~ TV спу́тниковое телеви́дение.

satiate vt насыща́ть impf, насы́тить pf.

satin n атла́с.

satire n сати́ра. **satirical** adj сатири́ческий. **satirist** n сати́рик. **satirize** vt высме́ивать impf, вы́смеять pf.

satisfaction n удовлетворе́ние. **satisfactory** adj удовлетвори́тельный. **satisfy** vt удовлетворя́ть impf, удовлетвори́ть pf; (hunger, curiosity) утоля́ть impf, утоли́ть pf.

saturate vt насыща́ть impf, насы́тить pf; I got ~d (by rain) я промо́к до ни́тки. **saturation** n насыще́ние.

Saturday n суббо́та.

sauce n со́ус; (cheek) на́глость. **saucepan** n кастрю́ля. **saucer** n блю́дце. **saucy** adj на́глый.

Saudi n сау́довец, -вка; adj сау́довский. **Saudi Arabia** n Сау́довская Ара́вия.

sauna n фи́нская ба́ня.

saunter vi прогу́ливаться impf.

sausage n соси́ска; (salami-type) колбаса́.

savage adj ди́кий; (fierce) свире́пый; (cruel) жесто́кий; n дика́рь m; vt искуса́ть pf. **savagery** n ди́кость; жесто́кость.

save vt (rescue) спаса́ть impf, спасти́ pf; (money) копи́ть impf, на~ pf; (put aside, keep) бере́чь impf; (avoid using) эконо́мить impf, с~ pf; vi: ~ up копи́ть impf, на~ pf де́ньги. **savings** n pl сбереже́ния neut pl; ~ bank сберега́тельная ка́сса. **saviour** n спаси́тель m.

savour vt смакова́ть impf.

savoury adj пика́нтный; (fig) поря́дочный.

saw n пила́; vt пили́ть impf; ~ up распи́ливать impf, распили́ть pf. **sawdust** n опи́лки (-лок) pl.

saxophone n саксофо́н.

say vt говори́ть impf, сказа́ть pf; to ~ **nothing of** не говоря́ уже́ о+prep; **that is to** ~ то есть; (let us) ~ ска́жем; **it is said (that)** говоря́т (что); n (opinion) мне́ние; (influence) влия́ние; **have one's** ~ вы́сказаться pf. **saying** n погово́рка.

scab n (on wound) струп; (polit) штрейкбре́хер.

scabbard n но́жны (gen -жен) pl.

scaffold n эшафо́т. **scaffolding** n леса́ (-со́в) pl.

scald vt обва́ривать impf, обвари́ть pf.

scale n (ratio) масшта́б; (grading) шкала́; (mus) га́мма; vt (climb) взбира́ться impf, взобра́ться pf на+acc; ~ **down** понижа́ть impf, пони́зить pf.

scales[1] n pl (of fish) чешуя́ (collect).

scales[2] n pl весы́ (-со́в) pl.

scallop n гребешо́к; (decoration) фесто́н.

scalp n ко́жа головы́.

scalpel n ска́льпель m.

scaly adj чешу́йчатый; (of boiler etc.) покры́тый на́кипью.

scamper vi бы́стро бе́гать impf; (frolic) резви́ться impf.

scan vt & i (verse) сканди́ровать(ся) impf; vt (intently) рассма́тривать impf; (quickly) просма́тривать impf, просмотре́ть pf; (med) просве́чивать impf, просвети́ть pf; n просве́чивание.

scandal n сканда́л; (gossip) спле́тни (-тен) pl. **scandalize** vt шоки́ровать impf & pf. **scandalous** adj сканда́льный.

Scandinavia n Скандина́вия. **Scandinavian** adj скандина́вский.

scanty adj ску́дный.

scapegoat n козёл отпуще́ния.

scar n шрам; vt оставля́ть impf, оста́вить pf шрам на+prep.

scarce adj дефици́тный; (rare) ре́дкий. **scarcely** adv едва́. **scarcity** n дефици́т; ре́дкость.

scare vt пуга́ть impf, ис-, на~ pf; ~ **away, off** отпу́гивать impf, отпугну́ть pf; n па́ника. **scarecrow** n пу́гало.

scarf n шарф.

scarlet adj (n) а́лый (цвет).

scathing adj уничтожа́ющий.

scatter vt & i рассыпа́ть(ся) impf, рассы́пать(ся) pf; (disperse) рассе́ивать(ся) impf, рассе́ять(ся) pf; ~ **brained** ве́треный. **scattered** adj разбро́санный; (sporadic) отде́льный.

scavenge vi ры́ться impf в отбро́сах. **scavenger** n (person) мусо́рщик; (animal) живо́тное sb, пита́ющееся па́далью.

scenario n сцена́рий. **scene** n (place of disaster etc.) ме́сто; (place of action) ме́сто де́йствия; (view) вид, пейза́ж; (picture) карти́на; (theat) сце́на, явле́ние; (incident) сце́на; **behind the** ~s за кули́сами; **make a** ~ устра́ивать impf, устро́ить pf сце́ну. **scenery** n (theat) декора́ция; (landscape) пейза́ж. **scenic** adj живопи́сный.

scent n (smell) арома́т; (perfume) духи́ (-хо́в) pl; (trail) след. **scented** adj души́стый.

sceptic n ске́птик. **sceptical** adj скепти́ческий. **scepticism** n скептици́зм.

schedule n (timetable) расписа́ние; vt составля́ть impf, соста́вить pf расписа́ние +gen.

schematic adj схемати́ческий. **scheme** n (plan) прое́кт; (intrigue) махина́ция; vi интригова́ть impf.

schism n раско́л.

schizophrenia n шизофрени́я. **schizophrenic** adj шизофрени́ческий; n шизофре́ник.

scholar n учёный sb; **scholarly** adj учёный. **scholarship** n учёность; (payment) стипе́ндия.

school n шко́ла; attrib шко́льный; vt (train) приуча́ть impf, приучи́ть pf (to к+dat, +inf). **school-book** n уче́бник. **schoolboy** n шко́льник. **schoolgirl** n шко́льница. **schooling** n обуче́ние. **school-leaver** n вы́пускни́к, -и́ца. **school teacher** n учи́тель m, ~ница.

schooner n шху́на.

sciatica n и́шиас.

science n нау́ка; ~ **fiction** нау́чная фанта́стика. **scientific** adj нау́чный. **scientist** n учёный sb.

scintillating adj блиста́тельный.

scissors n pl но́жницы (-ц) pl.

scoff vi (mock) смея́ться impf (**at** над+instr).

scold *vt* брани́ть *impf*, вы́~ *pf*.

scoop *n* (*large*) черпа́к; (*ice-cream* ~) ло́жка для моро́женого; *vt* (~ *out*, *up*) выче́рпывать *impf*, вы́черпать *pf*.

scooter *n* (*motor* ~) мотороллер.

scope *n* (*range*) преде́лы *m pl*; (*chance*) возмо́жность.

scorch *vt* (*fingers*) обжига́ть *impf*, обже́чь *pf*; (*clothes*) сжига́ть *impf*, сжечь *pf*.

score *n* (*of points etc.*) счёт; (*mus*) партиту́ра; *pl* (*great numbers*) мно́жество; *vt* (*notch*) де́лать *impf*, с~ *pf* зару́бки на+*prep*; (*points etc.*) получа́ть *impf*, получи́ть *pf*; (*mus*) оркестрова́ть *impf* & *pf*; *vi* (*keep* ~) вести́ *impf*, с~ *pf* счёт. **scorer** *n* счётчик.

scorn *n* презре́ние; *vt* презира́ть *impf* презре́ть *pf*. **scornful** *adj* презри́тельный.

Scorpio *n* Скорпио́н.

scorpion *n* скорпио́н.

Scot *n* шотла́ндец, -дка. **Scotch** *n* (*whisky*) шотла́ндское ви́ски *neut indecl*. **Scotland** *n* Шотла́ндия. **Scots**, **Scottish** *adj* шотла́ндский.

scoundrel *n* подле́ц.

scour[1] *vt* (*cleanse*) отчища́ть *impf*, отчи́стить *pf*.

scour[2] *vt* & *i* (*rove*) ры́скать *impf* (по+*dat*).

scourge *n* бич.

scout *n* разве́дчик; (**S**~) бойска́ут; *vi*: ~ **about** разы́скивать *impf* (for +*acc*).

scowl *vi* хму́риться *impf*, на~ *pf*; *n* хму́рый взгляд.

scrabble *vi*: ~ **about** ры́ться *impf*.

scramble *vi* кара́бкаться *impf*, вс~ *pf*; (*struggle*) дра́ться *impf* (for за +*acc*); ~**d eggs** яи́чница-болту́нья.

scrap[1] *n* (*fragment etc.*) кусо́чек; *pl* оста́тки *m pl*; *pl* (*of food*) объе́дки (-ков) *pl*; ~ **metal** металло́м; *vt* сдава́ть *impf*, сдать *pf* в утиль.

scrap[2] *n* (*fight*) дра́ка; *vi* дра́ться *impf*.

scrape *vt* скрести́ *impf*; (*graze*) цара́пать *impf*, о~ *pf*; ~ **off** отскреба́ть *impf*, отскрести́ *pf*; ~ **through** (*exam*) с трудо́м вы́держивать *impf*, вы́держать *pf*; ~ **together** наскреба́ть *impf*, наскрести́ *pf*.

scratch *vt* цара́пать *impf*, о~ *pf*; *vt* & *i* (*when itching*) чеса́ть(ся) *impf*, по~ *pf*; *n* цара́пина.

scrawl *n* кара́кули *f pl*; *vt* писа́ть *impf*, на~ *pf* кара́кулями.

scrawny *adj* сухопа́рый.

scream *n* крик; *vi* крича́ть *impf*, кри́кнуть *pf*.

screech *n* визг; *vi* визжа́ть *impf*.

screen *n* ши́рма; (*cin*, *TV*) экра́н; ~**play** сцена́рий; *vt* (*protect*) защища́ть *impf*, защити́ть *pf*; (*hide*) укрыва́ть *impf*, укры́ть *pf*; (*show film etc.*) демонстри́ровать *impf* & *pf*; (*check on*) проверя́ть *impf*, прове́рить *pf*; ~ **off** отгора́живать *impf*, отгороди́ть *pf* ши́рмой.

screw *n* винт; *vt* (~ *on*) приви́нчивать *impf*, привинти́ть *pf*; (~ *up*) зави́нчивать *impf*, завинти́ть *pf*; (*crumple*) ко́мкать *impf*, с~ *pf*; ~ **up one's eyes** щу́риться *impf*, со~ *pf*. **screwdriver** *n* отвёртка.

scribble *vt* строчи́ть *impf*, на~ *pf*; *n* кара́кули *f pl*.

script *n* (*of film etc.*) сцена́рий; (*of speech etc.*) текст; (*writing system*) письмо́; ~**-writer** сценари́ст.

Scripture *n* свяще́нное писа́ние.

scroll *n* сви́ток; (*design*) завито́к.

scrounge *vt* (*cadge*) стреля́ть *impf*, стрельну́ть *pf*; *vi* попроша́йничать *impf*.

scrub[1] *n* (*brushwood*) куста́рник; (*area*) за́росли *f pl*.

scrub[2] *vt* мыть *impf*, вы́~ *pf* щёткой.

scruff *n*: **by the** ~ **of the neck** за ши́ворот.

scruffy *adj* обо́дранный.

scrum *n* схва́тка вокру́г мяча́.

scruple *n* (*also pl*) колеба́ния *neut pl*; угрызе́ния *neut pl* со́вести. **scrupulous** *adj* скрупулёзный.

scrutinize *vt* рассма́тривать *impf*. **scrutiny** *n* рассмотре́ние.

scuffed *adj* поцара́панный.

scuffle *n* пота́совка.

sculpt *vt* вая́ть *impf*, из~ *pf*. **sculptor** *n* ску́льптор. **sculpture** *n* скульпту́ра.

scum *n* на́кипь.

scurrilous *adj* непристо́йный.

scurry *vi* поспе́шно бе́гать *indet*, бежа́ть *det*.

scuttle[1] n (coal ~) ведёрко для у́гля.

scuttle[2] vi (run away) удира́ть impf, удра́ть pf.

scythe n коса́.

sea n мо́ре; attrib морско́й; ~ **front** на́бережная sb; **~-gull** ча́йка; ~-**level** у́ровень m мо́ря; **~-lion** морско́й лев; **~-shore** побере́жье. **seaboard** n побере́жье. **seafood** n проду́кты m pl мо́ря.

seal[1] n (on document etc.) печа́ть; vt скрепля́ть impf, скрепи́ть pf печа́тью; (close) запеча́тывать impf, запеча́тать pf; ~ **up** заде́лывать impf, заде́лать pf

seal[2] n (zool) тюле́нь m; (fur-~) ко́тик.

seam n шов; (geol) пласт.

seaman n моря́к, матро́с.

seamless adj без шва.

seamstress n швея́.

seance n спирити́ческий сеа́нс.

seaplane n гидросамолёт.

searing adj паля́щий.

search vt обы́скивать impf, обыска́ть pf; vi иска́ть impf (for +acc); n по́иски m pl; о́быск; **~-party** по́исковая гру́ппа. **searching** adj (look) испыту́ющий. **searchlight** n проже́ктор.

seasick adj: I was ~ меня́ укача́ло. **seaside** n бе́рег мо́ря.

season n сезо́н; (one of four) вре́мя neut го́да; ~ **ticket** сезо́нный биле́т; vt (flavour) приправля́ть impf, припра́вить pf. **seasonable** adj по сезо́ну; (timely) своевре́менный. **seasonal** adj сезо́нный. **seasoning** n припра́ва.

seat n (place) ме́сто; (of chair) сиде́нье; (chair) стул; (bench) скаме́йка; (of trousers) зад; ~ **belt** привязно́й реме́нь m; vt сажа́ть impf, посади́ть pf; (of room etc.) вмеща́ть impf, вмести́ть pf; be ~ed сади́ться impf, сесть pf.

seaweed n морска́я во́доросль.

secateurs n pl сека́тур.

secede vi отка́лываться impf, отколо́ться pf. **secession** n отко́л.

secluded adj укро́мный. **seclusion** n укро́мность.

second[1] adj второ́й; **~-class** второкла́ссный; **~-hand** поде́ржанный; (of information) из вторы́х рук; ~-

rate второразря́дный; ~ **sight** ясновиде́ние; on ~ **thoughts** взве́сив всё ещё раз; **have ~ thoughts** переду́мывать impf, переду́мать pf (about +acc); n второ́й sb; (date) второ́е (число́) sb; (time) секу́нда; pl (comm) това́р второ́го со́рта; ~ **hand** (of clock) секу́ндная стре́лка; vt (support) подде́рживать impf, поддержа́ть pf; (transfer) откомандиро́вывать impf откомандирова́ть pf. **secondary** adj втори́чный, второстепе́нный; (education) сре́дний.

secondly adv во-вторы́х.

secrecy n секре́тность. **secret** n та́йна, секре́т; adj та́йный, секре́тный; (hidden) потайно́й.

secretarial adj секрета́рский. **secretariat** n секретариа́т. **secretary** n секрета́рь m, -рша; (minister) мини́стр.

secrete vt (conceal) укрыва́ть impf, укры́ть pf; (med) выделя́ть impf, вы́делить pf. **secretion** n укрыва́ние; (med) выделе́ние.

secretive adj скры́тный.

sect n се́кта. **sectarian** adj секта́нтский.

section n се́кция; (of book) разде́л; (geom) сече́ние. **sector** n се́ктор.

secular adj све́тский. **secularization** n секуляриза́ция.

secure adj (safe) безопа́сный; (firm) надёжный; (emotionally) уве́ренный; vt (fasten) закрепля́ть impf, закрепи́ть pf; (guarantee) обеспе́чивать impf, обеспе́чить pf; (obtain) достава́ть impf, доста́ть pf. **security** n безопа́сность; (guarantee) зало́г; pl це́нные бума́ги f pl.

sedate adj степе́нный.

sedation n успокое́ние. **sedative** n успока́ивающее сре́дство.

sedentary adj сидя́чий.

sediment n оса́док.

seduce vt соблазня́ть impf, соблазни́ть pf. **seduction** n обольще́ние. **seductive** adj соблазни́тельный.

see vt & i ви́деть impf, y~ pf; vt (watch, look) смотре́ть impf, по~ pf; (find out) узнава́ть impf, узна́ть pf; (understand) понима́ть impf, поня́ть pf; (meet) ви́деться impf, y~ pf c+instr; (imagine) представля́ть impf, предста́вить pf себе́; (escort,

~ off) провожа́ть *impf*, проводи́ть *pf*; *about* (*attend to*) забо́титься *impf*, по~ *pf* o+*prep*; ~ **through** (*fig*) ви́деть *impf*, наскво́зь+*acc*.

seed *n* се́мя *neut*. **seedling** *n* сея́нец; *pl* расса́да. **seedy** *adj* (*shabby*) потрёпанный.

seeing (that) *conj* ввиду́ того́, что.

seek *vt* иска́ть *impf* +*acc, gen*.

seem *vi* каза́ться *impf*, по~ *pf* (+*instr*).

seemingly *adv* по-ви́димому.

seemly *adj* прили́чный.

seep *vi* проса́чиваться *impf*, просочи́ться *pf*.

seethe *vi* кипе́ть *impf*, вс~ *pf*.

segment *n* отре́зок; (*of orange etc.*) до́лька; (*geom*) сегме́нт.

segregate *vt* отделя́ть *impf*, отдели́ть *pf*. **segregation** *n* сегрега́ция.

seismic *adj* сейсми́ческий.

seize *vt* хвата́ть *impf*, схвати́ть *pf*; *vi*: ~ **up** заеда́ть *impf*, зае́сть *pf* *impers*+*acc*; ~ **upon** ухва́тываться *impf*, ухвати́ться *pf* за+*acc*. **seizure** *n* захва́т; (*med*) припа́док.

seldom *adv* ре́дко.

select *adj* и́збранный; *vt* отбира́ть *impf*, отобра́ть *pf*. **selection** *n* (*choice*) вы́бор. **selective** *adj* разбо́рчивый.

self *n* со́бственное «я» *neut indecl*.

self- *in comb* само-; ~**absorbed** эгоцентри́чный; ~**assured** самоуве́ренный; ~**catering** (**accommodation**) жильё с ку́хней; ~**centred** эгоцентри́чный; ~**confessed** открове́нный; ~**confidence** самоуве́ренность; ~**confident** самоуве́ренный; ~**conscious** засте́нчивый; ~**contained** (*person*) незави́симый; (*flat etc.*) отде́льный; ~**control** самооблада́ние; ~**defence** самозащи́та; ~**denial** самоотрече́ние; ~**determination** самоопределе́ние; ~**effacing** скро́мный; ~**employed** незави́симый предпринима́тель *m*; ~**esteem** самоуваже́ние; ~**evident** очеви́дный; ~**governing** самоуправля́ющий; ~**help** самопо́мощь; ~**importance** самомне́ние; ~**imposed** доброво́льный; ~**indulgent** изба́лованный; ~**interest** со́бственный интере́с; ~**pity** жа́лость к себе́; ~**portrait** автопортре́т; ~**preservation** самосохране́ние; ~**reliance** само-

стоя́тельность; ~**respect** самоуваже́ние; ~**righteous** *adj* ха́нжеский; ~**sacrifice** самопоже́ртвование; ~**satisfied** самодово́льный; ~**service** самообслу́живание (*attrib: in gen after n*); ~**styled** самозва́нный; ~**sufficient** самостоя́тельный.

selfish *adj* эгоисти́чный. **selfless** *adj* самоотве́рженный.

sell *vt & i* продава́ть(ся) *impf*, прода́ть(ся) *pf*; *vt* (*deal in*) торгова́ть *impf* +*instr*; ~ **out** распродава́ть *impf*, распрода́ть *pf*. **seller** *n* продаве́ц. **selling** *n* прода́жа. **sell-out** *n*: **the play was a** ~ пье́са прошла́ с аншла́гом.

Sellotape *n* (*propr*) ли́пкая ле́нта.

semantic *adj* семанти́ческий. **semantics** *n* сема́нтика.

semblance *n* ви́димость.

semen *n* се́мя *neut*.

semi- *in comb* полу-; ~**detached house** дом, разделённый о́бщей стено́й. **semibreve** *n* це́лая но́та. **semicircle** *n* полукру́г. **semicircular** *adj* полукру́глый. **semicolon** *n* то́чка с запято́й. **semiconductor** *n* полупроводни́к. **semifinal** *n* полуфина́л.

seminar *n* семина́р. **seminary** *n* семина́рия.

semiquaver *n* шестна́дцатая но́та.

semitone *n* полуто́н.

senate *n* сена́т; (*univ*) сове́т. **senator** *n* сена́тор.

send *vt* посыла́ть *impf*, посла́ть *pf* (**for** за+*instr*); ~ **off** отправля́ть *impf*, отпра́вить *pf*; ~**off** про́воды (-дов) *pl*. **sender** *n* отправи́тель *m*.

senile *adj* ста́рческий. **senility** *n* ста́рческое слабоу́мие.

senior *adj* (*n*) ста́рший (*sb*); ~ **citizen** стари́к, стару́ха. **seniority** *n* старшинство́.

sensation *n* сенса́ция; (*feeling*) ощуще́ние. **sensational** *adj* сенсацио́нный.

sense *n* чу́вство; (*good* ~) здра́вый смысл; (*meaning*) смысл; *pl* (*sanity*) ум; *vt* чу́вствовать *impf*. **senseless** *adj* бессмы́сленный.

sensibility *n* чувстви́тельность; *pl* самолю́бие. **sensible** *adj* благоразу́мный. **sensitive** *adj* чувстви́тельный; (*touchy*) оби́дчивый. **sensitiv-**

ity *n* чувстви́тельность.
sensory *adj* чувстви́тельный.
sensual, sensuous *adj* чу́вствен-
ный.
sentence *n* (*gram*) предложе́ние;
(*law*) пригово́р; *vt* пригова́ривать
impf, приговори́ть *pf* (to к+*dat*).
sentiment *n* (*feeling*) чу́вство; (*opinion*) мне́ние. **sentimental** *adj* сенти-
мента́льный. **sentimentality** *n* сен-
тимента́льность.
sentry *n* часово́й *sb*.
separable *adj* отдели́мый. **separate**
adj отде́льный; *vt & i* отделя́ть(ся)
impf, отдели́ть(ся) *pf*. **separation** *n*
отделе́ние. **separatism** *n* сепара-
ти́зм. **separatist** *n* сепарати́ст.
September *n* сентя́брь *m*; *adj* сен-
тя́брьский.
septic *adj* септи́ческий.
sepulchre *n* моги́ла.
sequel *n* (*result*) после́дствие; (*continuation*) продолже́ние. **sequence**
n после́довательность; ~ **of events**
ход собы́тий.
sequester *vt* секвестрова́ть *impf &
pf*.
sequin *n* блёстка.
Serb(ian) *adj* се́рбский; *n* серб, ~ка.
Serbia *n* Се́рбия. **Serbo-Croat(ian)**
adj сербскохорва́тский.
serenade *n* серена́да.
serene *adj* споко́йный. **serenity** *n*
споко́йствие.
serf *n* крепостно́й *sb*. **serfdom** *n*
крепостно́е пра́во.
sergeant *n* сержа́нт.
serial *adj*: ~ **number** сери́йный но́-
мер; *n* (*story*) рома́н с продолже́-
нием; (*broadcast*) сери́йная поста-
но́вка. **serialize** *vt* ста́вить *impf*,
по~ *pf* в не́скольких частя́х. **series** *n* (*succession*) ряд; (*broadcast*)
се́рия переда́ч.
serious *adj* серьёзный. **seriousness**
n серьёзность.
sermon *n* про́поведь.
serpent *n* змея́.
serrated *adj* зазу́бренный.
serum *n* сы́воротка.
servant *n* слуга́ *m*, служа́нка. **serve**
vt служи́ть *impf*, по~ *pf* +*dat* (as,
for +*instr*); (*attend to*) обслу́живать
impf, обслужи́ть *pf*; (*food; ball*) по-
дава́ть *impf*, пода́ть *pf*; (*sentence*)

отбыва́ть *impf*, отбы́ть *pf*; (*writ
etc.*) вруча́ть *impf*, вручи́ть *pf* (on
+*dat*); *vi* (*be suitable*) годи́ться (for
на+*acc*, для+*gen*); (*sport*) подава́ть
impf, пода́ть *pf* мяч; it ~s him right
поде́лом ему́ (*dat*). **service** *n* (*act
of serving*; *branch of public work*;
eccl) слу́жба; (*quality of* ~) обслу́-
живание; (*of car etc.*) техобслу́жи-
вание; (*set of dishes*) серви́з; (*sport*)
пода́ча; (*transport*) сообще́ние; **at
your** ~ к ва́шим услу́гам; *vt* (*car*)
проводи́ть *impf*, провести́ *pf* тех-
обслу́живание +*gen*; ~ **charge** пла́-
та за обслу́живание; ~ **station** ста́н-
ция обслу́живания. **serviceable** *n*
(*useful*) поле́зный; (*durable*) про́ч-
ный. **serviceman** *n* военнослужа́-
щий *sb*.
serviette *n* салфе́тка.
servile *adj* рабо́лепный.
session *n* заседа́ние, се́ссия.
set[1] *vt* (*put*; ~ *clock*, *trap*) ста́вить
impf, по- *pf*; (*table*) накрыва́ть *impf*,
накры́ть *pf*; (*bone*) вправля́ть *impf*,
впра́вить *pf*; (*hair*) укла́дывать
impf, уложи́ть *pf*; (*gem*) оправля́ть
impf, опра́вить *pf*; (*bring into state*)
приводи́ть *impf*, привести́ *pf* (in, to
в+*acc*); (*example*) подава́ть *impf*,
пода́ть *pf*; (*task*) задава́ть *impf*,
зада́ть *pf*; *vi* (*solidify*) тверде́ть
impf, за~ *pf*; засты́ва́ть *impf*,
засты́(ну)ть *pf*; (*sun etc.*) заходи́ть
impf, зайти́ *pf*; сади́ться *impf*, сесть
pf; ~ **about** (*begin*) начина́ть *impf*,
нача́ть *pf*; (*attack*) напада́ть *impf*,
напа́сть *pf* на+*acc*; ~ **back** (*impede*)
препя́тствовать *impf*, вос~ *pf* +*dat*;
~-**back** неуда́ча; ~ **in** наступа́ть
impf, наступи́ть *pf*.; ~ **off** (on *journey*) отправля́ться *impf*, отпра́вить-
ся *pf*; (*enhance*) оттеня́ть *impf*,
оттени́ть *pf*; ~ **out** (*state*) излага́ть
impf, изложи́ть *pf*; (*on journey*) see
~ **off**; ~ **up** (*business*) осно́вывать
impf, основа́ть *pf*.
set[2] *n* набо́р, компле́кт; (*of dishes*)
серви́з; (*radio*) приёмник; (*television*) телеви́зор; (*tennis*) сет; (*theat*)
декора́ция; (*cin*) съёмочная пло-
ща́дка.
set[3] *adj* (*established*) устано́влен-
ный.
settee *n* дива́н.

setting n (*frame*) опра́ва; (*surroundings*) обстано́вка; (*of mechanism etc.*) устано́вка; (*of sun etc.*) захо́д.
settle vt (*decide*) реша́ть *impf*, реши́ть *pf*; (*reconcile*) ула́живать *impf*, ула́дить *pf*; (*a bill etc.*) опла́чивать *impf*, оплати́ть *pf*; (*calm*) успока́ивать *impf*, успоко́ить *pf*; vi посели́ться *impf*, посели́ться *pf*; (*subside*) оседа́ть *impf*, осе́сть *pf*; ~ **down** уса́живаться *impf*, усе́сться *pf* (**to** за+*acc*). **settlement** n поселе́ние; (*agreement*) соглаше́ние; (*payment*) упла́та. **settler** n поселе́нец.
seven adj & n семь; (*number 7*) семёрка. **seventeen** adj & n семна́дцать. **seventeenth** adj & n семна́дцатый. **seventh** adj & n седьмо́й; (*fraction*) седьма́я sb. **seventieth** adj & n семидеся́тый. **seventy** adj & n се́мьдесят; pl (*decade*) семидеся́тые го́ды (-до́в) m pl.
sever vt (*cut off*) отреза́ть *impf*, отре́зать *pf*; (*relations*) разрыва́ть *impf*, разорва́ть *pf*.
several pron (*adj*) не́сколько (+gen).
severance n разры́в; ~ **pay** выходно́е посо́бие.
severe adj стро́гий, суро́вый; (*pain, frost*) си́льный; (*illness*) тяжёлый. **severity** n стро́гость, суро́вость.
sew vt шить *impf*, с~ *pf*; ~ **on** пришива́ть *impf*, приши́ть *pf*; ~ **up** зашива́ть *impf*, заши́ть *pf*.
sewage n сто́чные во́ды f pl; ~-**farm** поля́ neut pl ороше́ния. **sewer** n сто́чная труба́. **sewerage** n канализа́ция.
sewing n шитьё; ~-**machine** швейная маши́на.
sex n (*gender*) пол; (*sexual activity*) секс; **have** ~ име́ть *impf* сноше́ние. **sexual** adj полово́й, сексуа́льный; ~ **intercourse** полово́е сноше́ние. **sexuality** n сексуа́льность. **sexy** adj эроти́ческий.
sh int ти́ше!; тсс!
shabby adj ве́тхий.
shack n лачу́га.
shackles n pl око́вы (-в) pl.
shade n тень; (*of colour, meaning*) отте́нок; (*lamp-*~) абажу́р; **a** ~ чуть-чу́ть; vt затеня́ть *impf*, затени́ть *pf*; (*eyes etc.*) заслоня́ть *impf*, заслони́ть *pf*; (*drawing*) тушева́ть

impf, за~ *pf*. **shadow** n тень; vt (*follow*) та́йно следи́ть *impf* за+*instr*. **shadowy** adj тёмный. **shady** adj тени́стый; (*suspicious*) подозри́тельный.
shaft n (*of spear*) дре́вко; (*arrow; fig*) стрела́; (*of light*) луч; (*of cart*) огло́бля; (*axle*) вал; (*mine, lift*) ша́хта.
shaggy adj лохма́тый.
shake vt & i тряст́и(сь) *impf*; vi (*tremble*) дрожа́ть *impf*; vt (*weaken*) колеба́ть *impf*, по~ *pf*; (*shock*) потряса́ть *impf* потрясти́ *pf*; ~ **hands** пожима́ть *impf*, пожа́ть *pf* ру́ку (**with** +dat); ~ **one's head** покача́ть *pf* голово́й; ~ **off** стря́хивать *impf*, стряхну́ть *pf*; (*fig*) избавля́ться *impf*, изба́виться *pf* от+*gen*.
shaky adj ша́ткий.
shallow adj ме́лкий; (*fig*) пове́рхностный.
sham vt & i притворя́ться *impf*, притвори́ться *pf* +*instr*; n притво́рство; (*person*) притво́рщик, -ица; adj притво́рный.
shambles n ха́ос.
shame n (*guilt*) стыд; (*disgrace*) позо́р; **what a** ~! как жаль!; vt стыди́ть *impf*, при~ *pf*. **shameful** adj позо́рный. **shameless** adj бессты́дный.
shampoo n шампу́нь m.
shanty[1] n (*hut*) хиба́рка; ~ **town** трущо́ба.
shanty[2] n (*song*) матро́сская пе́сня.
shape n фо́рма; vt придава́ть *impf*, прида́ть *pf* фо́рму+*dat*; vi: ~ **up** скла́дываться *impf*, сложи́ться *pf*. **shapeless** adj бесфо́рменный. **shapely** adj стро́йный.
share n до́ля; (*econ*) а́кция; vt дели́ть *impf*, по~ *pf*; (*opinion etc.*) ~ **out** разделя́ть *impf*, раздели́ть *pf*. **shareholder** n акционе́р.
shark n аку́ла.
sharp adj о́стрый; (*steep*) круто́й; (*sudden; harsh*) ре́зкий; n (*mus*) дие́з; adv (*with time*) ро́вно; (*of angle*) кру́то. **sharpen** vt точи́ть *impf*, на~ *pf*.
shatter vt & i разбива́ть(ся) *impf*, разби́ть(ся) *pf* вдре́безги; vt (*hopes etc.*) разруша́ть *impf*, разру́шить *pf*.
shave vt & i бри́ть(ся) *impf*, по~ *pf* n бритьё. **shaver** n электри́ческая

бри́тва.

shawl n шаль.

she pron она́.

sheaf n сноп; (of papers) свя́зка.

shear vt стричь impf, o~ pf. **shears** n pl но́жницы (-ц) pl.

sheath n но́жны (gen -жен) pl.

shed[1] n сара́й.

shed[2] vt (tears, blood, light) пролива́ть impf, проли́ть pf; (skin, clothes) сбра́сывать impf, сбро́сить pf.

sheen n блеск.

sheep n овца́. **sheepish** adj скон-фу́женный. **sheepskin** n овчи́на; ~ **coat** дублёнка.

sheer adj (utter) су́щий; (textile) прозра́чный; (rock etc.) отве́сный.

sheet n (on bed) простыня́; (of glass, paper, etc.) лист.

sheikh n шейх.

shelf n по́лка.

shell n (of mollusc etc.) ра́ковина; (of tortoise) щит; (of egg, nut) скорлупа́; (of building etc.) о́стов; (explosive ~) снаря́д; vt (peas etc.) лущи́ть impf, об~ pf; (bombard) обстре́ливать impf, обстреля́ть pf. **shellfish** n (mollusc) моллю́ск; (crustacean) ракообра́зное sb.

shelter n убе́жище; vt (provide with refuge) приюти́ть pf; vt & i укрыва́ть(ся) impf, укры́ть(ся) pf.

shelve[1] vt (defer) откла́дывать impf, отложи́ть pf.

shelve[2] vi (slope) отло́го спуска́ться impf.

shelving n (shelves) стелла́ж.

shepherd n пасту́х; vt проводи́ть impf, провести́ pf.

sherry n хе́рес.

shield n щит; vt защища́ть impf, защити́ть pf.

shift vt & i (change position) переме-ща́ть(ся) impf, перемести́ть(ся) pf; (change) меня́ть(ся) impf; n переме-ще́ние; переме́на; (of workers) сме́-на; ~ **work** сме́нная рабо́та. **shifty** adj скользкий.

shimmer vi мерца́ть impf; n мерца́-ние.

shin n го́лень.

shine vi свети́ть(ся) impf; (glitter) блесте́ть impf; (excel) блиста́ть impf; (sun, eyes) сия́ть impf; vt (a light) освеща́ть impf, освети́ть pf

фонарём (on +acc); n гля́нец.

shingle n (pebbles) га́лька.

shingles n опоя́сывающий лиша́й.

shiny adj блестя́щий.

ship n кора́бль m; су́дно; vt (transport) перевози́ть impf, перевезти́ pf; (dispatch) отправля́ть impf, от-пра́вить pf. **shipbuilding** n судо-строе́ние. **shipment** n (dispatch) отпра́вка; (goods) па́ртия. **shipping** n суда́ (-до́в) pl. **ship-shape** adv в по́лном поря́дке. **ship-wreck** n кораблекруше́ние; be ~ed терпе́ть impf, по~ pf кораблекру-ше́ние. **shipyard** n верфь.

shirk vt увили́вать impf, увильну́ть pf от+gen.

shirt n руба́шка.

shit n (vulg) говно́; vi срать impf, по~ pf.

shiver vi (tremble) дрожа́ть impf; n дрожь.

shoal n (of fish) стая.

shock n (emotional) потрясе́ние; (impact) уда́р, толчо́к; (electr) уда́р то́ком; (med) шок; vt шоки́ровать impf. **shocking** adj (outrageous) сканда́льный; (awful) ужа́сный.

shoddy adj халту́рный.

shoe n ту́фля; vt подко́вывать impf, подкова́ть pf. **shoe-lace** n шнуро́к. **shoemaker** n сапо́жник. **shoe-string** n: on a ~ с небольши́ми сре́дст-вами.

shoo int кш!; vt прогоня́ть impf, прогна́ть pf.

shoot vt & i (discharge) стреля́ть impf (a gun из+gen; at в+acc, по +dat); (arrow) пуска́ть impf, пу-сти́ть pf; (kill) застре́ливать impf, застрели́ть pf; (execute) расстре́-ливать impf, расстреля́ть pf; (hunt) охо́титься impf на+acc; (football) бить impf (по воро́там); (cin) сни-ма́ть impf, снять pf (фильм); vi (go swiftly) проноси́ться impf, проне-сти́сь pf; ~ **down** (aircraft) сбива́ть impf, сбить pf; ~ **up** (grow) бы́стро расти́ impf, по~ pf; (prices) под-ска́кивать impf, подскочи́ть pf; n (branch) росто́к, побе́г; (hunt) охо́-та. **shooting** n стрельба́; (hunting) охо́та. **~-gallery** тир.

shop n магази́н; (workshop) мастер-ска́я sb, цех; ~ **assistant** продаве́ц,

-вщи́ца; ~-lifter магази́нный вор; ~-lifting воровство́ в магази́нах; ~ steward цехово́й ста́роста *m*; ~-window витри́на; *vi* де́лать *impf*, с~ *pf* поку́пки (*f pl*). **shopkeeper** *n* ла́вочник. **shopper** *n* покупа́тель *m*, ~ница. **shopping** *n* поку́пки *f pl*; **go, do one's** ~ де́лать *impf*, с~ *pf* поку́пки; ~ **centre** торго́вый центр.

shore[1] *n* бе́рег.

shore[2] *vt*: ~ **up** подпира́ть *impf*, подпере́ть *pf*.

short *adj* коро́ткий; (*not tall*) ни́зкого ро́ста; (*deficient*) недоста́точный; **be** ~ **of** испы́тывать *impf*, испыта́ть *pf* недоста́ток в+*prep*; (*curt*) ре́зкий; **in** ~ одни́м сло́вом; ~ **change** обсчи́тывать *impf*, обсчита́ть *pf*; ~ **circuit** коро́ткое замыка́ние; ~ **cut** коро́ткий путь *m*; ~ **list** оконча́тельный спи́сок; ~-**list** включа́ть *impf*, включи́ть *pf* в оконча́тельный спи́сок; ~-**lived** недолгове́чный; ~-**sighted** близору́кий; (*fig*) недальнови́дный; ~ **story** расска́з; **in** ~ **supply** дефици́тный; ~-**tempered** вспы́льчивый; ~-**term** краткосро́чный; ~-**wave** коротково́лновый. **shortage** *n* недоста́ток. **shortcoming** *n* недоста́ток. **shorten** *vt & i* укора́чивать(ся) *impf*, укороти́ть(ся) *pf*. **shortfall** *n* дефици́т. **shorthand** *n* стеногра́фия; ~ **typist** машини́стка-стенографи́стка. **shortly** *adv*: ~ **after** вско́ре (по́сле +*gen*); ~ **before** незадо́лго (до+*gen*). **shorts** *n pl* шо́рты (-т) *pl*.

shot *n* (*discharge of gun*) вы́стрел; (*pellets*) дробь; (*person*) стрело́к; (*attempt*) попы́тка; (*phot*) сни́мок; (*cin*) кадр; (*sport*) (*stroke*) уда́р; (*throw*) бросо́к; **like a** ~ неме́дленно; ~-**gun** дробови́к.

should *v aux* (*ought*) до́лжен (бы) +*inf*: **you** ~ **know that** вы должны́ э́то знать; **he** ~ **be here soon** он до́лжен бы быть тут ско́ро; (*conditional*) бы +*past*: **I** ~ **say** я бы сказа́л(а); **I** ~ **like** я бы хоте́л(а).

shoulder *n* плечо́; ~-**blade** лопа́тка; ~-**strap** брете́лька; взва́ливать *impf*, взвали́ть *pf* на пле́чи; (*fig*) брать *impf*, взять *pf* на себя́.

shout *n* крик; *vi* крича́ть *impf*, кри́кнуть *pf*; ~ **down** перекри́кивать

impf, перекрича́ть *pf*.

shove *n* толчо́к; *vt & i* толка́ть(ся) *impf*, толкну́ть *pf*; ~ **off** (*coll*) убира́ться *impf*, убра́ться *pf*.

shovel *n* лопа́та; *vt* (~ *up*) сгреба́ть *impf*, сгрести́ *pf*.

show *vt* пока́зывать *impf*, показа́ть *pf*; (*exhibit*) выставля́ть *impf*, вы́ставить *pf*; (*film etc.*) демонстри́ровать *impf*, про~ *pf*; *vi* (*also* ~ **up**) быть ви́дным, заме́тным; ~ **off** (*vi*) привлека́ть *impf*, привле́чь *pf* к себе́ внима́ние; ~ **up** see *vi*; (*appear*) появля́ться *impf*, появи́ться *pf*; *n* (*exhibition*) вы́ставка; (*theat*) спекта́кль *m*; (*effect*) ви́димость; ~ **of hands** голосова́ние подня́тием руки́; ~-**case** витри́на; ~-**jumping** соревнова́ние по ска́чкам; ~-**room** сало́н. **showdown** *n* развя́зка.

shower *n* (*rain*) до́ждик; (*hail; fig*) град; (~-*bath*) душ; *vt* осыпа́ть *impf*, осы́пать *pf* +*instr* (**on** +*acc*); *vi* принима́ть *impf*, приня́ть *pf* душ. **showery** *adj* дождли́вый.

showpiece *n* образе́ц. **showy** *adj* показно́й.

shrapnel *n* шрапне́ль.

shred *n* клочо́к; **not a** ~ ни ка́пли; *vt* мельчи́ть *impf*, из~ *pf*.

shrewd *adj* проница́тельный.

shriek *vi* визжа́ть *impf*; взви́гнуть *pf*.

shrill *adj* пронзи́тельный.

shrimp *n* креве́тка.

shrine *n* святы́ня.

shrink *vi* сади́ться *impf*, сесть *pf*; (*recoil*) отпря́нуть *pf*; *vt* осыпа́ть *impf*, вы́звать *pf* уса́дку у+*gen*; ~ **from** избега́ть *impf* +*gen*. **shrinkage** *n* уса́дка.

shrivel *vi* смо́рщиваться *impf*, смо́рщиться *pf*.

shroud *n* са́ван; *vt* (*fig*) оку́тывать *impf*, оку́тать *pf* (**in** +*instr*).

Shrove Tuesday вто́рник на ма́сленой неде́ле.

shrub *n* куст. **shrubbery** *n* куста́рник.

shrug *vt & i* пожима́ть *impf*, пожа́ть *pf* (плеча́ми).

shudder *n* содрога́ние; *vi* содрога́ться *impf*, содрогну́ться *pf*.

shuffle *vt & i* (*one's feet*) ша́ркать *impf* (нога́ми); *vt* (*cards*) тасова́ть *impf*, с~ *pf*; *n* тасо́вка.

shun vt избегать impf +gen.

shunt vi (rly) маневрировать impf, с~ pf; vt (rly) переводить impf, перевести pf на запасной путь.

shut vt & i (also ~ down) закрывать(ся) impf, закрыть(ся) pf; ~ out (exclude) исключать impf, исключить pf; (fence off) загораживать impf, загородить pf; (keep out) не пускать impf, пустить pf; ~ up (vi) замолчать pf; (imper) заткнись!

shutter n ставень m; (phot) затвор.

shuttle n челнок.

shy¹ adj застенчивый.

shy² vi (in alarm) отпрядывать impf, отпрянуть pf.

Siberia n Сибирь. **Siberian** adj сибирский; n сибиряк, -ячка.

sick adj больной; be ~ (vomit) рвать impf, вы~ pf impers +acc: he was ~ его вырвало; feel ~ тошнить impf impers +acc; be ~ of надоедать impf, надоесть pf +nom (object) & dat (subject): I'm ~ of her она мне надоела; ~-leave отпуск по болезни. **sicken** vi вызывать impf, вызвать pf тошноту, (disgust) отвращение, y+gen; vi заболевать impf, заболеть pf. **sickening** adj отвратительный.

sickle n серп.

sickly adj болезненный; (nauseating) тошнотворный. **sickness** n болезнь; (vomiting) тошнота.

side n сторона; (of body) бок; ~ by ~ рядом (with c+instr); on the ~ на стороне; vi: ~ with вставать impf, встать pf на сторону+gen; ~-effect побочное действие; ~-step (fig) уклоняться impf, уклониться pf от+gen; ~-track (distract) отвлекать impf, отвлечь pf. **sideboard** n буфет; pl баки (-к) pl. **sidelight** n боковой фонарь m. **sideline** n (work) побочная работа.

sidelong adj (glance) косой.

sideways adv боком.

siding n запасной путь m.

sidle vi: ~ up to подходить impf, подойти pf к (+dat) бочком.

siege n осада; lay ~ to осаждать impf, осадить pf; raise the ~ of снимать impf, снять pf осаду c+gen.

sieve n сито; vt просеивать impf, просеять pf.

sift vt просеивать impf, просеять pf; (fig) тщательно рассматривать impf, рассмотреть pf.

sigh vi вздыхать impf, вздохнуть pf; n вздох.

sight n (faculty) зрение; (view) вид; (spectacle) зрелище; pl достопримечательности f pl; (on gun) прицел; at first ~ с первого взгляда; catch ~ of увидеть impf; know by ~ знать impf в лицо; lose ~ of терять impf, по~ pf из виду; (fig) упускать impf, упустить pf из виду.

sign n знак; (indication) признак; (~board) вывеска; vt & abs подписывать(ся) impf, подписать(ся) pf; vi (give ~) подавать impf, подать pf знак; ~ on (as unemployed) записываться impf, записаться pf в списки безработных; (~ up) нанимать impf, наняться pf.

signal n сигнал; vt & i сигнализировать impf & pf. **signal-box** n сигнальная будка. **signalman** n сигнальщик.

signatory n подписавший sb; (of treaty) сторона, подписавшая договор.

signature n подпись.

significance n значение. **significant** adj значительный. **signify** vt означать impf.

signpost n указательный столб.

silage n силос.

silence n молчание, тишина; vt заставить pf замолчать. **silencer** n глушитель m. **silent** adj (not speaking) безмолвный; (of film) немой; (without noise) тихий; be ~ молчать impf.

silhouette n силуэт; vt: be ~d вырисовываться impf, вырисоваться pf (against на фоне+gen).

silicon n кремний. **silicone** n силикон.

silk n шёлк; attrib шёлковый. **silky** adj шелковистый.

sill n подоконник.

silly adj глупый.

silo n силос.

silt n ил.

silver n серебро; (cutlery) столовое серебро; adj (of ~) серебряный; (silvery) серебристый; ~-plated посеребрённый. **silversmith** n серебряных дел мастер. **silverware** n столо́вое серебро́. **silvery** adj серебри́стый.

similar adj подо́бный (to +dat). **similarity** n схо́дство. **similarly** adv подо́бным о́бразом.

simile n сравне́ние.

simmer vt кипяти́ть impf на ме́дленном огне́; vi кипе́ть impf на ме́дленном огне́; ~ **down** успока́иваться impf, успоко́иться pf.

simper vi жема́нно улыба́ться impf, улыбну́ться pf.

simple adj просто́й; ~**-minded** тупова́тый. **simplicity** n простота́. **simplify** vt упроща́ть impf, упрости́ть pf. **simply** adv про́сто.

simulate vt притворя́ться impf, притвори́ться pf (conditions etc.); модели́ровать impf & pf. **simulated** adj (pearls etc.) иску́сственный.

simultaneous adj одновреме́нный.

sin n грех; vi греши́ть impf, со~ pf.

since adv с тех пор; prep c+gen; conj с тех пор как; (reason) так как.

sincere adj и́скренний. **sincerely** adv с тех пор; **yours** ~ и́скренне Ваш. **sincerity** n и́скренность.

sinew n сухожи́лие.

sinful adj гре́шный.

sing vt & i петь impf, про~, с~ pf.

singe vt пали́ть impf, о~ pf.

singer n певе́ц, -ви́ца.

single adj оди́н; (unmarried) (of man) нежена́тый; (of woman) незаму́жняя; (bed) односпа́льный; ~**-handed** без посторо́нней по́мощи; ~**-minded** целеустремлённый; ~ **parent** мать/оте́ц-одино́чка; ~ **room** ко́мната на одного́; n (ticket) биле́т в оди́н коне́ц; pl (tennis etc.) одино́чная игра́ vt: ~ **out** выделя́ть impf, вы́делить pf. **singly** adv по-одному́.

singular n еди́нственное число́; adj еди́нственный; (unusual) необыча́йный. **singularly** adv необыча́йно.

sinister adj злове́щий.

sink vi (descend slowly) опуска́ться impf, опусти́ться pf; (in mud etc.) погружа́ться impf, погрузи́ться pf; (in water) тону́ть impf, по~ pf; vt (ship) топи́ть impf, по~ pf; (pipe, post) вка́пывать impf, вкопа́ть pf; n ра́ковина.

sinner n гре́шник, -ица.

sinus n па́зуха.

sip vt пить impf, ма́ленькими глотка́ми; n ма́ленький глото́к.

siphon n сифо́н; ~ **off** (also fig) перека́чивать impf, перекача́ть pf.

sir n сэр.

siren n сире́на.

sister n сестра́; ~**-in-law** (husband's sister) золо́вка; (wife's sister) своя́ченица; (brother's wife) неве́стка.

sit vi (be sitting) сиде́ть impf; (~ down) сади́ться impf, сесть pf; (parl, law) заседа́ть impf; vt уса́живать impf, усади́ть pf; (exam) сдава́ть impf; ~ **back** отки́дываться impf, откину́ться pf; ~ **down** сади́ться impf, сесть pf; ~ **up** приподнима́ться impf, приподня́ться pf; (not go to bed) не ложи́ться impf спать.

site n (where a thing takes place) ме́сто; (where a thing is) местоположе́ние.

sitting n (parl etc.) заседа́ние; (for meal) сме́на; ~**-room** гости́ная sb.

situated adj: **be** ~ находи́ться impf. **situation** n местоположе́ние; (circumstances) положе́ние; (job) ме́сто.

six adj & n шесть; (number 6) шестёрка. **sixteen** adj & n шестна́дцать. **sixteenth** adj & n шестна́дцатый. **sixth** adj & n шесто́й; (fraction) шеста́я sb. **sixtieth** adj & n шестидеся́тый. **sixty** adj & n шестьдеся́т; pl (decade) шестидеся́тые го́ды (-до́в) m pl.

size n разме́р; vt: ~ **up** оце́нивать impf, оцени́ть pf. **sizeable** adj значи́тельный.

sizzle vi шипе́ть impf.

skate[1] n (fish) скат.

skate[2] n (ice-~) конёк; (roller-~) конёк на ро́ликах; vi ката́ться impf на конька́х; **skating-rink** като́к.

skeleton n скеле́т.

sketch n зарисо́вка; (theat) скетч; vt & i зарисо́вывать impf, зарисова́ть pf. **sketchy** adj схемати́ческий; (superficial) пове́рхностный.

skew adj косо́й; **on the** ~ ко́со.

skewer n ве́ртел.

skin n лы́жа; ~**-jump** трампли́н; vi ходи́ть impf на лы́жах.

skid n зано́с; vi заноси́ть impf, занести́ pf impers+acc.

skier n лы́жник. **skiing** n лы́жный спорт.

skilful *adj* иску́сный. **skill** *n* мастерство́; (*countable*) поле́зный на́вык.
skilled *adj* иску́сный; (*trained*) квалифици́рованный.

skim *vt* снима́ть *impf*, снять *pf* (*cream* сли́вки *pl*, *scum* на́кипь) c+*gen*; *vi* скользи́ть *impf* (**over, along** по+*dat*); ~ **through** бе́гло просма́тривать *impf*, просмотре́ть *pf*; *adj*: ~ **milk** снято́е молоко́.
skimp *vt & i* скупи́ться *impf* (на+*acc*). **skimpy** *adj* ску́дный.

skin *n* ко́жа; (*hide*) шку́ра; (*of fruit etc.*) кожура́; (*on milk*) пе́нка; *vt* сдира́ть *impf*, содра́ть *pf* ко́жу, шку́ру, c+*gen*; (*fruit*) снима́ть *impf*, снять *pf* кожуру́ c+*gen*. **skinny** *adj* то́щий.

skip[1] *vi* скака́ть *impf*; (*with rope*) пры́гать *impf* че́рез скака́лку; *vt* (*omit*) пропуска́ть *impf*, пропусти́ть *pf*.
skip[2] *n* (*container*) скип.
skipper *n* (*naut*) шки́пер.
skirmish *n* схва́тка.
skirt *n* ю́бка; *vt* обходи́ть *impf*, обойти́ *pf* стороно́й; ~**ing-board** пли́нтус.
skittle *n* ке́гля; *pl* ке́гли *f pl*.
skulk *vi* (*hide*) скрыва́ться *impf*; (*creep*) кра́сться *impf*.
skull *n* че́реп.
skunk *n* скунс.
sky *n* не́бо. **skylark** *n* жа́воронок. **skylight** *n* окно́ в кры́ше. **skyline** *n* горизо́нт. **skyscraper** *n* небоскрёб.
slab *n* плита́; (*of cake etc.*) кусо́к.
slack *adj* (*loose*) сла́бый; (*sluggish*) вя́лый; (*negligent*) небре́жный; *n* (*of rope*) слабина́; *pl* брю́ки (-к) *pl*.
slacken *vt* ослабля́ть *impf*, осла́бить *pf*; *vt & i* (*slow down*) замедля́ть(ся) *impf*, заме́длить(ся) *pf*; *vi* ослабева́ть *impf*, ослабе́ть *pf*.
slag *n* шлак.
slam *vt & i* захло́пывать(ся) *impf*, захло́пнуть(ся) *pf*.
slander *n* клевета́; *vt* клевета́ть *impf*, на~ *pf* на+*acc*. **slanderous** *adj* клеветни́ческий.
slang *n* жарго́н. **slangy** *adj* жарго́нный.
slant *vt & i* наклоня́ть(ся) *impf*, наклони́ть(ся) *pf*; *n* укло́н. **slanting**

adj косо́й.
slap *vt* шлёпать *impf*, шлёпнуть *pf*; *n* шлепо́к; *adv* пря́мо. **slapdash** *adj* небре́жный. **slapstick** *n* фарс.
slash *vt* (*cut*) поро́ть *impf*, рас~ *pf*; (*fig*) уре́зывать *impf*, уре́зать *pf*; *n* разре́з; (*sign*) дробь.
slat *n* пла́нка.
slate[1] *n* сла́нец; (*for roofing*) кро́вельная пли́тка.
slate[2] *vt* (*criticize*) разноси́ть *impf*, разнести́ *pf*.
slaughter *n* (*of animals*) убо́й; (*massacre*) резня́; *vt* (*animals*) ре́зать *impf*, за~ *pf*; (*people*) убива́ть *impf*, уби́ть *pf*. **slaughterhouse** *n* бо́йня.
Slav *n* славяни́н, -я́нка; *adj* славя́нский.
slave *n* раб, рабы́ня; *vi* рабо́тать *impf* как раб. **slavery** *n* ра́бство.
Slavic *adj* славя́нский.
slavish *adj* ра́бский.
Slavonic *adj* славя́нский.
slay *vt* убива́ть *impf*, уби́ть *pf*.
sleazy *adj* убо́гий.
sledge *n* са́ни (-не́й) *pl*.
sledge-hammer *n* кува́лда.
sleek *adj* гла́дкий.
sleep *n* сон; **go to** ~ засыпа́ть *impf*, засну́ть *pf*; *vi* спать *impf*; (*spend the night*) ночева́ть *impf*, пере~ *pf*. **sleeper** *n* спя́щий *sb*; (*on track*) шпа́ла; (*sleeping-car*) спа́льный ваго́н. **sleeping** *adj* спя́щий; ~**-bag** спа́льный мешо́к; ~**-car** спа́льный ваго́н; ~**-pill** снотво́рная табле́тка. **sleepless** *adj* бессо́нный. **sleepy** *adj* со́нный.
sleet *n* мо́крый снег.
sleeve *n* рука́в; (*of record*) конве́рт.
sleigh *n* са́ни (-не́й) *pl*.
sleight-of-hand *n* ло́вкость рук.
slender *adj* (*slim*) то́нкий; (*meagre*) ску́дный; (*of hope etc.*) сла́бый.
sleuth *n* сы́щик.
slice *n* кусо́к; *vt* (~ **up**) нареза́ть *impf*, наре́зать *pf*.
slick *adj* (*dextrous*) ло́вкий; (*crafty*) хи́трый; *n* нефтяна́я плёнка.
slide *vi* скользи́ть *impf*; *vt* (*drawer etc.*) задвига́ть *impf*, задви́нуть *pf*; *n* (*children's* ~) го́рка; (*microscope* ~) предме́тное стекло́; (*phot*) диапозити́в, слайд; (*for hair*) зако́лка.
sliding *adj* (*door*) задвижно́й.

slight[1] *adj* (*slender*) тóнкий; (*inconsiderable*) небольшóй; (*light*) лёгкий; **not the ~est** ни малéйшего, -шей (*gen*); **not in the ~est** ничýть.

slight[2] *vt* пренебрегáть *impf*, пренебрéчь *pf* +*instr*; *n* обѝда.

slightly *adv* слегкá, немнóго.

slim *adj* тóнкий; (*chance etc.*) слáбый; *vi* худéть *impf*, по~ *pf*.

slime *n* слизь. **slimy** *adj* слѝзистый; (*person*) скóльзкий.

sling *vt* (*throw*) швырять *impf*, швырнýть *pf*; (*suspend*) подвéшивать *impf*, подвéсить *pf*; *n* (*med*) пéревязь.

slink *vi* крáсться *impf*.

slip *n* (*mistake*) ошѝбка; (*garment*) комбинáция; (*pillowcase*) нáволочка; (*paper*) листóчек; ~ **of the tongue** обмóлвка; **give the ~** ускользнýть *pf* от+*gen*; *vi* скользѝть *impf*, скользнýть *pf*; (*fall over*) поскользнýться *pf*; (*from hands etc.*) выскáльзывать *impf*, выскользнуть *pf*; *vt* (*insert*) совáть *impf*, сýнуть *pf*; ~ **off** (*depart*) ускользáть *impf*, ускользнýть *pf*; ~ **up** (*make mistake*) ошибáться *impf*, ошибѝться *pf*. **slipper** *n* тáпка. **slippery** *adj* скóльзкий.

slit *vt* разрезáть *impf*, разрéзать *pf*; (*throat*) перерéзать *pf*; *n* щель; (*cut*) разрéз.

slither *vi* скользѝть *impf*.

sliver *n* щéпка.

slob *n* неряха *m & f*.

slobber *vi* пускáть *impf*, пустѝть *pf* слюни.

slog *vt* (*hit*) сильно ударять *impf*, удáрить *pf*; (*work*) упóрно рабóтать *impf*.

slogan *n* лóзунг.

slop *n*: *pl* помóи (-óев) *pl*; *vt & i* выплёскивать(ся) *impf*, выплескать(ся) *pf*.

slope *n* (*artificial*) наклóн; (*geog*) склон; *vi* имéть *impf* наклóн. **sloping** *adj* наклóнный.

sloppy *adj* (*work*) неряшливый; (*sentimental*) сентиментáльный.

slot *n* отвéрстие; ~**-machine** автомáт; *vt*: ~ **in** вставлять *impf*, встáвить *pf*.

sloth *n* лень.

slouch *vi* (*stoop*) сутýлиться *impf*.

slovenly *adj* неряшливый.

slow *adj* мéдленный; (*tardy*) медлѝтельный; (*stupid*) тупóй; (*business*) вялый; **be ~** (*clock*) отставáть *impf*, отстáть *pf*; *adv* мéдленно; *vt & i* (~ **down**, **up**) замедлять(ся) *impf*, замéдлить(ся) *pf*.

sludge *n* (*mud*) грязь; (*sediment*) отстóй.

slug *n* (*zool*) слизняк.

sluggish *adj* вялый.

sluice *n* шлюз.

slum *n* трущóба.

slumber *n* сон; *vi* спать *impf*.

slump *n* спад; *vi* рéзко пáдать *impf*, (у)пáсть *pf*; (*of person*) свáливаться *impf*, свалѝться *pf*.

slur *vt* говорѝть *impf* невнятно; *n* (*stigma*) пятнó.

slush *n* слякоть.

slut *n* (*sloven*) неряха; (*trollop*) потаскýха.

sly *adj* хитрый; **on the ~** тайкóм.

smack[1] *vi*: ~ **of** пáхнуть *impf* +*instr*.

smack[2] *n* (*slap*) шлепóк; *vt* шлёпать *impf*, шлёпнуть *pf*.

small *adj* мáленький, небольшóй, мáлый; (*of agent, particles; petty*) мéлкий; ~ **change** мéлочь; ~**-scale** мелкомасштáбный; ~ **talk** свéтская бесéда.

smart[1] *vi* сáднить *impf impers*.

smart[2] *adj* элегáнтный; (*brisk*) быстрый; (*cunning*) лóвкий; (*sharp*) смекáлистый (*coll*).

smash *vt & i* разбивáть(ся) *impf*, разбѝть(ся) *pf*; *vi*: ~ **into** врезáться *impf*, врéзаться *pf* в+*acc*; *n* (*crash*) грóхот; (*collision*) столкновéние; (*blow*) сильный удáр.

smattering *n* повéрхностное знáние.

smear *vt* смáзывать *impf*, смáзать *pf*; (*dirty*) пáчкать *impf*, за~, ис~ *pf*; (*discredit*) порóчить *impf*, о~ *pf*; *n* (*spot*) пятнó; (*slander*) клеветá; (*med*) мазóк.

smell *n* (*sense*) обоняние; (*odour*) зáпах; *vt* чýвствовать *impf* зáпах+*gen*; (*sniff*) нюхать *impf*, по~ *pf*; *vi*: ~ **of** пáхнуть *impf* +*instr*. **smelly** *adj* вонючий.

smelt *vt* (*ore*) плáвить *impf*; (*metal*) выплавлять *impf*, выплавить *pf*.

smile *vi* улыбáться *impf*, улыбнýться *pf*; *n* улыбка.

smirk vi ухмыля́ться impf, ухмыль-
ну́ться pf; n ухмы́лка.

smith n кузне́ц.

smithereens n: (in)to ~ вдре́безги.

smithy n ку́зница.

smock n блу́за.

smog n тума́н (с ды́мом).

smoke n дым; ~-**screen** дымова́я за-
ве́са; vt & i (cigarette etc.) кури́ть
impf, по~ pf; vt (cure; colour) коп-
ти́ть impf, за~ pf; vi (abnormally)
дыми́ть impf; (of fire) дыми́ться
impf. **smoker** n кури́льщик, -ица,
куря́щий sb. **smoky** adj ды́мный.

smooth adj (surface etc.) гла́дкий;
(movement etc.) пла́вный; vt при-
гла́живать impf, пригла́дить pf; ~
over сгла́живать impf, сгла́дить pf.

smother vt (stifle, also fig) души́ть
impf, за~ pf; (cover) покрыва́ть
impf, покры́ть pf.

smoulder vi тлеть impf.

smudge n пятно́; vt сма́зывать impf,
сма́зать pf.

smug adj самодово́льный.

smuggle vt провози́ть impf, про-
везти́ pf контраба́ндой; (convey secretly) проноси́ть impf, пронести́ pf.
smuggler n контрабанди́ст. **smug-
gling** n контраба́нда.

smut n са́жа; (indecency) непристо́й-
ность; (within institution) буфе́т.

snack n заку́ска; ~ **bar** заку́сочная
sb, (within institution) буфе́т.

snag n (fig) загво́здка; vt зацепля́ть
impf, зацепи́ть pf.

snail n ули́тка.

snake n змея́.

snap vi (of dog or person) огрыза́ть-
ся impf, огрызну́ться pf (at на+acc);
vt & i (break) обрыва́ть(ся) impf,
оборва́ть(ся) pf; vt (make sound)
щёлкать impf, щёлкнуть pf +instr;
~ **up** (buy) расхва́тывать impf, рас-
хвата́ть pf; n (sound) щёлк; (photo)
сни́мок; adj (decision) скоропали́-
тельный. **snappy** adj (brisk) живо́й;
(stylish) шика́рный. **snapshot** n
сни́мок.

snare n лову́шка.

snarl vi рыча́ть impf, за~ pf; n ры-
ча́ние.

snatch vt хвата́ть impf, (с)хвати́ть
pf; vi: ~ **at** хвата́ться impf, (с)хва-

ти́ться pf за+acc; n (fragment)
обры́вок.

sneak vi (slink) кра́сться impf; vt
(steal) стащи́ть pf; n я́бедник, -ица
(coll). **sneaking** adj та́йный. **sneaky**
adj лука́вый.

sneer vi насмеха́ться impf (at над
+instr).

sneeze vi чиха́ть impf, чихну́ть pf;
n чиха́нье.

snide adj ехи́дный.

sniff vi шмы́гать impf, шмыгну́ть pf
но́сом; vt ню́хать impf, по~ pf.

snigger vi хихи́кать impf, хихи́кнуть
pf; n хихи́канье.

snip vt ре́зать impf (но́жницами); ~
off среза́ть impf, сре́зать pf.

snipe vi стреля́ть impf из укры́тия
(at в+acc); (fig) напада́ть impf, на-
па́сть pf на+acc. **sniper** n сна́йпер.

snippet n отре́зок; pl (of news etc.)
обры́вки m pl.

snivel vi (run at nose) распуска́ть
impf, распусти́ть pf со́пли; (whimper) хны́кать impf.

snob n сноб. **snobbery** n сноби́зм.
snobbish adj сноби́стский.

snoop vi шпио́нить impf; ~ **about**
разню́хивать impf, разню́хать pf.

snooty adj чва́нный.

snooze vi вздремну́ть pf; n коро́т-
кий сон.

snore vi храпе́ть impf.

snorkel n шно́ркель m.

snort vi фы́ркать impf, фы́ркнуть pf.

snot n со́пли (-ле́й) pl.

snout n ры́ло, мо́рда.

snow n снег; ~-**white** белосне́жный;
vi: **it is** ~**ing**, **it snows** идёт снег;
~**ed under** зава́ленный рабо́той; **we
were** ~**ed up, in** нас занесло́ сне́гом.
snowball n снежо́к. **snowdrop** n
подсне́жник. **snowflake** n снежи́нка.
snowman n сне́жная ба́ба. **snow-
storm** n мете́ль. **snowy** adj сне́ж-
ный; (snow-white) белосне́жный.

snub vt игнори́ровать impf & pf.

snuff[1] n (tobacco) ню́хательный
таба́к.

snuff[2] vt: ~ **out** туши́ть impf, по~
pf.

snuffle vi сопе́ть impf.

snug adj ую́тный.

snuggle vi: ~ **up to** прижима́ться
impf, прижа́ться pf к+dat.

so *adv* так; (*in this way*) так, таки́м о́бразом; (*thus, at beginning of sentence*) ита́к; (*also*) та́кже, то́же; *conj* (*therefore*) поэ́тому; **and ~ on** и так да́лее; **if** ~ в тако́м слу́чае; ~ ... **as** так(о́й)... как; ~ **as to** с тем что́бы; **~-called** так называ́емый; (**in**) ~ **far as** насто́лько; ~ **long!** пока́!; ~ **long as** поско́льку; ~ **much** насто́лько; ~ **much** до тако́й сте́пени; ~ **much the better** тем лу́чше; ~ **that** что́бы; ~... **that** так... что; ~ **to say, speak** так сказа́ть; ~ **what?** ну и что?

soak *vt* мочи́ть *impf*, на~ *pf*; (*drench*) прома́чивать *impf*, промочи́ть *pf*; ~ **up** впи́тывать *impf*, впита́ть *pf*; *vi*: ~ **through** проса́чиваться *impf*, просочи́ться *pf*; **get ~ed** промока́ть *impf*, промо́кнуть *pf*.

soap *n* мы́ло; *vt* мы́лить *impf*, на~ *pf*; ~ **opera** многосери́йная переда́ча; ~ **powder** стира́льный порошо́к. **soapy** *adj* мы́льный.

soar *vi* пари́ть *impf*; (*prices*) подска́кивать *impf*, подскочи́ть *pf*.

sob *vi* рыда́ть *impf*; *n* рыда́ние.

sober *adj* тре́звый; *vt & i:* ~ **up** отрезвля́ть(ся) *impf*, отрезви́ть(ся) *pf*. **sobriety** *n* тре́звость.

soccer *n* футбо́л.

sociable *adj* общи́тельный. **social** *adj* обще́ственный, социа́льный; **S~ Democrat** социа́л-демокра́т; ~ **sciences** обще́ственные нау́ки *f pl*; ~ **security** социа́льное обеспе́чение. **socialism** *n* социали́зм. **socialist** *n* социали́ст; *adj* социалисти́ческий. **socialize** *vt* обща́ться *impf*. **society** *n* о́бщество. **sociological** *adj* социологи́ческий. **sociologist** *n* социо́лог. **sociology** *n* социоло́гия.

sock *n* носо́к.

socket *n* (*eye*) впа́дина; (*electr*) штёпсель *m*; (*for bulb*) патро́н.

soda *n* со́да; ~-**water** со́довая вода́.

sodden *adj* промо́кший.

sodium *n* на́трий.

sodomy *n* педера́стия.

sofa *n* дива́н.

soft *adj* мя́гкий; (*sound*) ти́хий; (*colour*) нея́ркий; (*malleable*) ко́вкий; (*tender*) не́жный; ~ **drink** безалкого́льный напи́ток. **soften** *vt & i*

смягча́ть(ся) *impf*, смягчи́ть(ся) *pf*. **softness** *n* мя́гкость. **software** *n* програ́ммное обеспе́чение.

soggy *adj* сыро́й.

soil[1] *n* по́чва.

soil[2] *vt* па́чкать *impf*, за~, ис~ *pf*.

solace *n* утеше́ние.

solar *adj* со́лнечный.

solder *n* припо́й; *vt* пая́ть *impf*; (~ *together*) спа́ивать *impf*, спая́ть *pf*. **soldering iron** *n* пая́льник.

soldier *n* солда́т.

sole[1] *n* (*of foot, shoe*) подо́шва.

sole[2] *n* (*fish*) морско́й язы́к.

sole[3] *adj* еди́нственный.

solemn *adj* торже́ственный. **solemnity** *n* торже́ственность.

solicit *vt* проси́ть *impf*, по~ *pf* +*acc, gen*, о+*prep*; *vi* (*of prostitute*) пристава́ть *impf* к мужчи́нам. **solicitor** *n* адвока́т. **solicitous** *adj* забо́тливый.

solid *adj* (*not liquid*) твёрдый; (*not hollow; continuous*) сплошно́й; (*firm*) про́чный; (*pure*) чи́стый; *n* твёрдое те́ло; *pl* твёрдая пи́ща. **solidarity** *n* солида́рность. **solidify** *vi* затвердева́ть *impf*, затверде́ть *pf*. **solidity** *n* твёрдость; про́чность.

soliloquy *n* моноло́г.

solitary *adj* одино́кий, уединённый; ~ **confinement** одино́чное заключе́ние. **solitude** *n* одино́чество, уедине́ние.

solo *n* со́ло *neut indecl*; *adj* со́льный; *adv* со́ло. **soloist** *n* соли́ст, ~ка.

solstice *n* солнцестоя́ние.

soluble *adj* раствори́мый. **solution** *n* раство́р; (*of puzzle etc.*) реше́ние. **solve** *vt* реша́ть *impf*, реши́ть *pf*. **solvent** *adj* растворя́ющий; (*financially*) платёжеспосо́бный; *n* раствори́тель *m*.

sombre *adj* мра́чный.

some *adj & pron* (*any*) како́й-нибудь; (*a certain*) како́й-то; (*a certain amount or number of*) не́который, *or often expressed by noun in* (*partitive*) *gen*; (*several*) не́сколько+*gen*; (~ *people, things*) не́которые *pl*; ~ **day** когда́-нибудь; ~ **more** ещё; ~ ... **others** одни́... други́е. **somebody, someone** *n, pron* (*def*) кто́-то; (*indef*) кто́-нибудь. **somehow** *adv* ка́к-то; ка́к-нибудь; (*for* *some reason*) почему́-то; ~ **or other** так и́ли ина́че.

somersault *n* са́льто *neut indecl*; *vi* кувырка́ться *impf*, кувыр(к)ну́ться *pf*.

something *n & pron* (*def*) чтó-то; (*indef*) чтó-нибудь; ~ **like** (*approximately*) приблизи́тельно; (*a thing like*) чтó-то вро́де+*gen*. **sometime** *adv* не́когда; *adj* бы́вший. **sometimes** *adv* иногда́. **somewhat** *adv* не́сколько, дово́льно. **somewhere** *adv* (*position*) (*def*) гдé-то; (*indef*) гдé-нибудь; (*motion*) куда́-то; куда́-нибудь.

son *n* сын; ~**-in-law** зять *m*.

sonata *n* сона́та.

song *n* пе́сня.

sonic *adj* звуково́й.

sonnet *n* сонéт.

soon *adv* ско́ро; (*early*) ра́но; **as** ~ **as** как то́лько; **as** ~ **as possible** как мо́жно скоре́е; ~**er or later** ра́но и́ли по́здно; **the** ~**er the better** чем ра́ньше, тем лу́чше.

soot *n* са́жа, ко́поть.

soothe *vt* успока́ивать *impf*, успоко́ить *pf*; (*pain*) облегча́ть *impf*, облегчи́ть *pf*.

sophisticated *adj* (*person*) искушённый; (*equipment*) сло́жный.

soporific *adj* снотво́рный.

soprano *n* сопра́но (*voice*) *neut & (person*) *f indecl*.

sorcerer *n* колду́н. **sorcery** *n* колдо́вство.

sordid *adj* гря́зный.

sore *n* боля́чка; *adj* больно́й; **my throat is** ~ у меня́ боли́т го́рло.

sorrow *n* печа́ль. **sorrowful** *adj* печа́льный. **sorry** *adj* жа́лкий; *predic*: **be** ~ жале́ть *impf* (**about** о+*prep*); жаль *impers*+*dat* (**for** +*gen*); ~! извини́(те)!

sort *n* род, вид, сорт; *vt* (*also* ~ **out**) сортирова́ть *impf*, рас~ *pf*; (*also fig*) разбира́ть *impf*, разобра́ть *pf*.

sortie *n* вы́лазка.

SOS *n* (ра́дио)сигна́л бе́дствия.

soul *n* душа́.

sound[1] *adj* (*healthy, thorough*) здоро́вый; (*in good condition*) испра́вный; (*logical*) здра́вый, разу́мный; (*of sleep*) кре́пкий.

sound[2] *n* (*noise*) звук, шум; *attrib*

звуково́й; ~ **effects** звуковы́е эффе́кты *m pl*; *vi* звуча́ть *impf*, про~ *pf*.

sound[3] *vt* (*naut*) измеря́ть *impf*, изме́рить *pf* глубину́ +*gen*; ~ **out** (*fig*) зонди́ровать *impf*, по~ *pf*; *n* зонд.

sound[4] *n* (*strait*) проли́в.

soup *n* суп; *vt*: ~**ed up** форси́рованный.

sour *adj* ки́слый; ~ **cream** смета́на; *vt & i* (*fig*) озлобля́ть(ся) *impf*, озло́бить(ся) *pf*.

source *n* исто́чник; (*of river*) исто́к.

south *n* юг; (*naut*) зюйд; *adj* ю́жный; *adv* к ю́гу, на юг; ~**-east** ю́го-восто́к; ~**-west** ю́го-за́пад. **southerly** *adj* ю́жный. **southern** *adj* ю́жный. **southerner** *n* южа́нин, -а́нка. **southward(s)** *adv* на юг, к ю́гу.

souvenir *n* сувени́р.

sovereign *adj* сувере́нный; *n* мона́рх. **sovereignty** *n* суверените́т.

soviet *n* сове́т; S~ **Union** Сове́тский Сою́з; *adj* (S~) сове́тский.

sow[1] *n* свинья́.

sow[2] *vt* (*seed*) се́ять *impf*, по~ *pf*; (*field*) засева́ть *impf*, засе́ять *pf*.

soya *n*: ~ **bean** со́евый боб.

spa *n* куро́рт.

space *n* (*place, room*) ме́сто; (*expanse*) простра́нство; (*interval*) промежу́ток; (*outer* ~) ко́смос; *attrib* косми́ческий; *vt* расставля́ть *impf*, расста́вить *pf* с промежу́тками. **spacecraft, -ship** *n* косми́ческий кора́бль *m*. **spacious** *adj* просто́рный.

spade *n* (*tool*) лопа́та; *pl* (*cards*) пи́ки (пик) *pl*.

spaghetti *n* спагéтти *neut indecl*.

Spain *n* Испа́ния.

span *n* (*of bridge*) пролёт; (*aeron*) разма́х; *vt* (*of bridge*) соединя́ть *impf*, соедини́ть *pf* сто́роны +*gen*; (*river*) берега́ +*gen*; (*fig*) охва́тывать *impf*, охвати́ть *pf*.

Spaniard *n* испа́нец, -нка. **Spanish** *adj* испа́нский.

spank *vt* шлёпать *impf*, шлёпнуть *pf*.

spanner *n* га́ечный ключ.

spar[1] *n* (*aeron*) лонжеро́н.

spar[2] *vi* боксирова́ть *impf*; (*fig*) препира́ться *impf*.

spare *adj* (*in reserve*) запасно́й; (*extra, to* ~) ли́шний; (*of seat, time*) свобо́дный; ~ parts запасны́е ча́сти f pl; ~ room ко́мната для госте́й; n: pl запча́сти f pl; vt (grudge) жале́ть impf, по~ pf +acc, gen; he ~d no pains он не жале́л трудо́в; (do without) обходи́ться impf, обойти́сь pf без+gen; (time) уделя́ть impf, удели́ть pf; (show mercy towards) щади́ть impf, по~ pf; (save from) избавля́ть impf, изба́вить pf от+gen: ~ me the details изба́вьте меня́ от подро́бностей.

spark n и́скра; ~-plug запа́льная свеча́; vt (~ off) вызыва́ть impf, вы́звать pf.

sparkle vi сверка́ть impf.

sparrow n воробе́й.

sparse adj ре́дкий.

Spartan adj спарта́нский.

spasm n спазм. **spasmodic** adj спазмоди́ческий.

spastic n парали́тик.

spate n разли́в; (fig) пото́к.

spatial adj простра́нственный.

spatter, splatter vt (liquid) бры́згать impf +instr; (person etc.) забры́згивать impf, забры́згать pf (with +instr); vi плеска́ть(ся) impf, плесну́ть pf.

spatula n шпа́тель m.

spawn vt & i мета́ть impf (икру́); vt (fig) порожда́ть impf, породи́ть pf.

speak vt & i говори́ть impf, сказа́ть pf; vi (make speech) выступа́ть impf, вы́ступить pf (с ре́чью); (~ out) выска́зываться impf, вы́сказаться pf (for за+acc; against про́тив+gen). **speaker** n говоря́щий sb; (giving speech) выступа́ющий sb; (orator) ора́тор; (S~, parl) спи́кер; (loud-~) громкоговори́тель m.

spear n копьё; vt пронза́ть impf, пронзи́ть pf копьём. **spearhead** vt возглавля́ть impf, возгла́вить pf.

special adj осо́бый, специа́льный. **specialist** n специали́ст, ~ка. **speciality** n специа́льность f. **specialization** n специализа́ция. **specialize** vt & i специализи́ровать(ся) impf & pf. **specially** adv осо́бенно.

species n вид.

specific adj осо́бенный. **specification(s)** n специфика́ция. **specify** vt уточня́ть impf, уточни́ть pf.

specimen n образе́ц, экземпля́р.

speck n кра́пинка, пя́тнышко.

speckled adj кра́пчатый.

spectacle n зре́лище; pl очки́ (-ко́в) pl.

spectacular adj эффе́ктный; (amazing) потряса́ющий.

spectator n зри́тель m.

spectre n при́зрак.

spectrum n спектр.

speculate vi (meditate) размышля́ть impf, размы́слить pf (on o+prep); (conjecture) гада́ть impf; (comm) спекули́ровать impf. **speculation** n (conjecture) дога́дка; (comm) спекуля́ция. **speculative** adj гипотети́ческий; спекуляти́вный. **speculator** n спекуля́нт.

speech n речь. **speechless** adj (fig) онеме́вший.

speed n ско́рость; vi мча́ться impf, про~ pf; (illegally) превыша́ть impf, превы́сить pf ско́рость; vt: ~ up ускоря́ть impf, уско́рить pf. **speed-boat** n быстрохо́дный ка́тер. **speedometer** n спидо́метр. **speedy** adj бы́стрый, ско́рый.

spell[1] n (charm) загово́р.

spell[2] vt (say) произноси́ть impf, произнести́ pf по бу́квам; (write) пра́вильно писа́ть impf, на~ pf; **how do you ~ that word?** как пи́шется э́то сло́во?

spell[3] n (period) пери́од.

spellbound adj зачаро́ванный.

spelling n правописа́ние.

spend vt (money; effort) тра́тить impf, ис~, по~ pf; (time) проводи́ть impf, провести́ pf.

sperm n спе́рма.

sphere n сфе́ра; (ball) шар. **spherical** adj сфери́ческий.

spice n пря́ность; vt приправля́ть impf, припра́вить pf. **spicy** adj пря́ный; (fig) пика́нтный.

spider n пау́к.

spike n (point) острие́; (on fence) зубе́ц; (on shoes) шип.

spill vt & i (liquid) пролива́ть(ся) impf, проли́ть(ся) pf; (dry substance) рассыпа́ть(ся) impf, рассы́пать(ся) pf.

spin vt (thread etc.) прясть impf, с~ pf; (coin) подбра́сывать impf, подбро́сить pf; vt & i (turn) кружи́ть(ся) impf; ~ out (prolong) затяги́-

вать *impf*, затянуть *pf*.

spinach *n* шпинат.

spinal *adj* спинной; ~ **column** спинной хребет; ~ **cord** спинной мозг.

spindle *n* ось *m*. **spindly** *adj* длинный и тонкий.

spine *n* (*anat*) позвоночник, хребет; (*prickle*) игла; (*of book*) корешок.

spineless *adj* (*fig*) бесхарактерный.

spinning *n* прядение; ~**wheel** прялка.

spinster *n* незамужняя женщина.

spiral *adj* спиральный; (*staircase*) винтовой; *n* спираль; *vi* (*rise sharply*) резко возрастать *impf*, возрасти *pf*.

spire *n* шпиль *m*.

spirit *n* дух, душа; *pl* (*mood*) настроение; *pl* (*drinks*) спиртное *sb*; ~ **level** ватерпас; *vt*: ~ **away** тайно уносить *impf*, унести *pf*. **spirited** *adj* живой. **spiritual** *adj* духовный. **spiritualism** *n* спиритизм. **spiritualist** *n* спирит.

spit¹ *n* (*skewer*) вертел.

spit² *vi* плевать *impf*, плюнуть *pf*; (*of rain*) моросить *impf*; (*of fire*) разбрызгивать *impf*, разбрызгать *pf* искры; (*sizzle*) шипеть *impf*; *vt*: ~ **out** выплёвывать *impf*, выплюнуть *pf*; ~**ing image** точная копия; *n* слюна.

spite *n* злоба; **in** ~ **of** несмотря на +*acc*. **spiteful** *adj* злобный.

spittle *n* слюна.

splash *vt* (*person*) забрызгивать *impf*, забрызгать *pf*; (~ **with** +*instr*); (~ *liquid*) брызгать *impf* +*instr*; *vi* плескать(ся) *impf*, плеснуть *pf*; (*move*) шлёпать *impf*, шлёпнуть *pf* (**through** по+*dat*); *n* (*act, sound*) плеск; (*mark made*) пятно.

splatter *see* **spatter**

spleen *n* селезёнка.

splendid *adj* великолепный. **splendour** *n* великолепие.

splice *vt* (*ropes etc.*) сращивать *impf*, срастить *pf*; (*film, tape*) склеивать *impf*, склеить *pf* концы+*gen*.

splint *n* шина.

splinter *n* осколок; (*in skin*) заноза; *vt & i* расщеплять(ся) *impf*, расщепить(ся) *pf*.

split *n* расщелина, расщеп; (*schism*) раскол; *pl* шпагат; *vt & i* расщеплять(ся) *impf*, расщепить(ся) *pf*;

раскалывать(ся) *impf*, расколоть(ся) *pf*; *vt* (*divide*) делить *impf*, раз~ *pf*; ~ **second** мгновение ока; ~ **up** (*part company*) расходиться *impf*, разойтись *pf*.

splutter *vi* брызгать *impf* слюной; *vt* (*utter*) говорить *impf* захлёбываясь.

spoil *n* (*booty*) добыча; *vt & i* (*damage; decay*) портить(ся) *impf*, ис~ *pf*; *vt* (*indulge*) баловать *impf*, из~ *pf*.

spoke *n* спица.

spokesman, -woman *n* представитель *m*, ~ница.

sponge *n* губка; ~ **cake** бисквит; *vt* (*wash*) мыть *impf*, вы~; *no* ~ *pf* губкой; *vi*: ~ **on** жить *impf* на счёт+*gen*. **sponger** *n* приживальщик. **spongy** *adj* губчатый.

sponsor *n* спонсор; *vt* финансировать *impf & pf*.

spontaneity *n* спонтанность. **spontaneous** *adj* спонтанный.

spoof *n* пародия.

spooky *adj* жуткий.

spool *n* катушка.

spoon *n* ложка; *vt* черпать *impf*, черпнуть *pf* ложкой. **spoonful** *n* ложка.

sporadic *adj* спорадический.

sport *n* спорт; ~**s car** спортивный автомобиль *m*; *vt* щеголять *impf*, щегольнуть *pf* +*instr*. **sportsman** *n* спортсмен. **sporty** *adj* спортивный.

spot *n* (*place*) место; (*mark*) пятно; (*pimple*) прыщик; **on the** ~ на месте; (*at once*) сразу; ~ **check** выборочная проверка; *vt* (*notice*) замечать *impf*, заметить *pf*. **spotless** *adj* абсолютно чистый. **spotlight** *n* прожектор; (*flg*) внимание. **spotty** *adj* прыщеватый.

spouse *n* супруг, ~а.

spout *vi* бить *impf* струёй; хлынуть *pf*; (*pontificate*) ораторствовать *impf*; *vt* извергать *impf*, извергнуть *pf*; (*verses etc.*) декламировать *impf*, про~ *pf*; *n* (*tube*) носик; (*jet*) струя.

sprain *vt* растягивать *impf*, растянуть *pf*; *n* растяжение.

sprawl *vi* разваливаться *impf*, развалиться *pf*; (*of town*) раскидываться *impf*, раскинуться *pf*.

spray[1] n (flowers) вét(оч)ка.

spray[2] n брызги (-г) pl; (atomizer) пульвериза́тор; vt опры́скивать impf, опры́скать pf (with +instr); (cause to scatter) распыля́ть impf, распыли́ть pf.

spread vt & i (news, disease, etc.) распространя́ть(ся) impf, распространи́ть(ся) pf; vi (~ out) расстила́ть impf, разостла́ть pf; (unfurl, unroll) развёртывать impf, разверну́ть pf; (bread etc. +acc; butter etc. +instr) нама́зывать impf, нама́зать pf; n (expansion) распростране́ние; (span) разма́х; (feast) пир; (paste) па́ста.

spree n кутёж; **go on a ~** кути́ть impf, кутну́ть pf.

sprig n вéточка.

sprightly adj бо́дрый.

spring vi (jump) пры́гать impf, пры́гнуть pf; vt (tell unexpectedly) неожи́данно сообща́ть impf, сообщи́ть pf (on +dat); **~ a leak** дава́ть impf, дать pf течь; **~ from** (originate) происходи́ть impf, произойти́ pf из+gen; n (jump) прыжо́к; (season) весна́, attrib весéнний; (water) исто́чник; (elasticity) упру́гость; (coil) пружи́на; **~-clean** генера́льная убо́рка. **springboard** n трампли́н.

sprinkle vt (with liquid) опры́скивать impf, опры́скать pf (with +instr); (with solid) посыпа́ть impf, посы́пать pf (with +instr). **sprinkler** n разбры́згиватель m.

sprint vi бéжать impf на коро́ткую диста́нцию; (rush) рвану́ться pf; n спринт. **sprinter** n спри́нтер.

sprout vi пуска́ть impf, пусти́ть pf ростки́; n росто́к; pl брюссéльская капу́ста.

spruce[1] adj наря́дный, элега́нтный; vt: **~ o.s. up** приводи́ть impf, привести́ pf себя́ в поря́док.

spruce[2] n ель.

spur n шпо́ра; (fig) сти́мул; **on the ~ of the moment** под влия́нием мину́ты; vt: **~ on** подхлёстывать impf, подхлестну́ть pf.

spurious adj подде́льный.

spurn vt отверга́ть impf, отве́ргнуть pf.

spurt n (jet) струя́; (effort) рыво́к; vi бить impf струёй; (make an effort) дéлать impf, с~ pf рыво́к.

spy n шпио́н; vi шпио́нить impf (on за+instr). **spying** n шпиона́ж.

squabble n перебра́нка; vi вздо́рить impf, по~ pf.

squad n кома́нда, гру́ппа.

squadron n (mil) эскадро́н; (naut) эска́дра; (aeron) эскадри́лья.

squalid adj убо́гий.

squall n шквал.

squalor n убо́жество.

squander vt растра́чивать impf, растра́тить pf.

square n (shape) квадра́т; (in town) пло́щадь; (on paper, material) клéтка; (instrument) науго́льник; adj квадра́тный; (meal) пло́тный; **~ root** квадра́тный ко́рень m; vt (accounts) своди́ть impf, свести́ pf; (math) возводи́ть impf, возвести́ pf в квадра́т; vi (correspond) соотвéтствовать impf (with +dat).

squash n (crowd) толку́чка; (drink) сок; vt разда́вливать impf, раздави́ть pf; (suppress) подавля́ть impf, подави́ть pf; vi вти́скиваться impf, вти́снуться pf.

squat adj призéмистый; vi сидéть impf на ко́рточках; **~ down** сади́ться impf, сесть pf на ко́рточки.

squatter n незако́нный жилéц.

squawk n клёкот; vi клекота́ть impf.

squeak n писк; (of object) скрип; vi пища́ть impf, пи́скнуть pf; (of object) скрипéть impf, скри́пнуть pf. **squeaky** adj пискл*и́вый, скрипу́чий.

squeal n визг; vi визжа́ть impf, ви́згнуть pf.

squeamish adj брезгли́вый.

squeeze n (crush) да́вка; (pressure) сжа́тие; (hand) пожа́тие; vt дави́ть impf; сжима́ть impf, сжать pf; **~ in** впи́хивать(ся) impf, впихну́ть(ся) pf; вти́скивать(ся) impf, вти́снуть(ся) pf; **~ out** выжима́ть impf, вы́жать pf; **~ through** проти́скивать(ся) impf, проти́снуть(ся) pf.

squelch vi хлю́пать impf, хлю́пнуть pf.

squid n кальма́р.

squint n косогла́зие; vi коси́ть impf; (screw up eyes) щу́риться impf.

squire n сквайр, помéщик.

squirm vi (wriggle) извива́ться impf, изви́ться pf.

squirrel n бе́лка.

squirt n струя́; vi бить impf струёй; vt пуска́ть impf, пусти́ть pf струю́ (substance +gen; **at** на+acc).

St. abbr (of **Street**) ул., у́лица; (of **Saint**) св., Свято́й, -а́я.

stab n уда́р (ножо́м etc.); (pain) вне-за́пная о́страя боль; vt наноси́ть impf, нанести́ pf уда́р (ножо́м etc.) (person +dat).

stability n усто́йчивость, стаби́ль-ность. **stabilize** vt стабилизи́ровать impf & pf.

stable adj усто́йчивый, стаби́льный; (psych) уравнове́шенный; n коню́ш-ня.

staccato n стакка́то neut indecl; adv стакка́то; adj отры́вистый.

stack n ку́ча; vt скла́дывать impf, сложи́ть pf в ку́чу.

stadium n стадио́н.

staff n (personnel) штат, сотру́дники m pl; (stick) по́сох, жезл; adj штат-ный; (mil) штабно́й.

stag n саме́ц-оле́нь m.

stage n (theat) сце́на; (period) ста́-дия; vt (theat) ста́вить impf, по~ pf; (organize) организова́ть impf & pf; ~**-manager** режиссёр.

stagger vi шата́ться impf, шатну́ть-ся pf; vt (hours of work etc.) рас-пределя́ть impf, распредели́ть pf. **be staggered** vi поража́ться impf, порази́ться pf. **staggering** adj по-тряса́ющий.

stagnant adj (water) стоя́чий; (fig) засто́йный. **stagnate** vi заста́ивать-ся impf, застоя́ться pf; (fig) косне́ть impf, за~ pf.

staid adj степе́нный.

stain n пятно́; (dye) кра́ска; vt па́ч-кать impf, за~, ис~ pf; (dye) окра́-шивать impf, окра́сить pf; ~**ed glass** цветно́е стекло́. **stainless** adj: ~ **steel** нержаве́ющая сталь.

stair n ступе́нька. **staircase, stairs** n pl ле́стница.

stake n (stick) кол; (bet) ста́вка; (comm) до́ля; **be at** ~ быть поста́-вленным на ка́рту; vt (mark out) огора́живать impf, огороди́ть pf ко́льями; (support) укрепля́ть impf, укрепи́ть pf ко́лом; (risk) ста́вить impf, по~ pf на ка́рту.

stale adj несве́жий; (musty, damp)

за́тхлый; (hackneyed) изби́тый.

stalemate n пат; (fig) тупи́к.

stalk n сте́бель m; vt высле́живать impf; vi (& t) (stride) ше́ствовать impf (по+dat).

stall n сто́йло; (booth)ларёк; pl (theat) парте́р; vi (of engine) гло́х-нуть impf, за~ pf; (play for time) оття́гивать impf, оття́нуть pf вре́-мя; vt (engine) неча́янно заглуша́ть impf, заглуши́ть pf.

stallion n жеребе́ц.

stalwart adj сто́йкий; n сто́йкий при-ве́рженец.

stamina n выно́сливость.

stammer vi заика́ться impf; n заика́-ние.

stamp n печа́ть; (postage) (почто́-вая) ма́рка; vt штампова́ть impf; vi то́пать impf, то́пнуть pf (нога́ми); ~ **out** поборо́ть pf.

stampede n пани́ческое бе́гство; vi обраща́ться impf в пани́ческое бе́г-ство.

stance n пози́ция.

stand n (hat, coat) ве́шалка; (music) пюпи́тр; (umbrella, support) под-ста́вка; (booth) ларёк; (taxi) сто-я́нка; (at stadium) трибу́на; (pos-ition) пози́ция; (resistance) сопроти-вле́ние; vi стоя́ть impf; (~ up) встава́ть impf, встать pf; (remain in force) остава́ться impf, оста́ться в си́ле pf; (put) ста́вить impf, по~ pf; (endure) терпе́ть impf, по~ pf; ~ **back** отходи́ть impf, отойти́ pf (**from** от+gen); (not go forward) держа́ть-ся impf позади́; ~ **by** (vi) (not inter-fere) не вме́шиваться impf, вме-ша́ться pf; (be ready) быть impf на гото́ве; (vt) (support) подде́рживать impf, поддержа́ть pf; (stick to) приде́рживаться impf +gen; ~ **down** (resign) уходи́ть impf, уйти́ pf с по́ста (**as** +gen); ~ **for** (signify) оз-знача́ть impf; (tolerate): **I shall not** ~ **for it** я не потерплю́; ~**-in** замести́-тель m; ~ **in** (for) замеща́ть impf, замести́ть pf; ~ **out** выделя́ться impf, вы́делиться pf; ~ **up** встава́ть impf, встать pf; ~ **up for** (defend) отста́ивать impf, отстоя́ть pf; ~ **up to** (endure) выде́рживать impf, вы́-держать pf; (not give in to) противо-стоя́ть impf +dat.

standard n (norm) станда́рт, норм; (flag) зна́мя neut; ~ **of living** жи́зненный у́ровень m; adj норма́льный, станда́ртный. **standardization** n нормализа́ция, стандартиза́ция. **standardize** vt стандартизи́ровать impf & pf; нормализова́ть impf & pf.

standing n положе́ние; adj (upright) стоя́чий; (permanent) постоя́нный.

standpoint n то́чка зре́ния.

standstill n остано́вка, засто́й, па́уза; **be at a ~** стоя́ть impf на мёртвой то́чке; **bring (come) to a ~** остана́вливать(ся) impf, останови́ть(ся) pf.

stanza n строфа́.

staple[1] n (metal bar) скоба́; (for paper) скре́пка; vt скрепля́ть impf, скрепи́ть pf.

staple[2] n (product) гла́вный проду́кт; adj основно́й.

star n звезда́; (asterisk) звёздочка; vi игра́ть impf, сыгра́ть pf гла́вную роль. **starfish** n морска́я звезда́.

starboard n пра́вый борт.

starch n крахма́л; vt крахма́лить impf, на~ pf. **starchy** adj крахма́листый; (prim) чо́порный.

stare n при́стальный взгляд; vi при́стально смотре́ть impf (**at** на+acc).

stark adj (bare) го́лый; (desolate) пусты́нный; (sharp) ре́зкий; adv соверше́нно.

starling n скворе́ц.

starry adj звёздный.

start n нача́ло; (sport) старт; vi начина́ться impf, нача́ться pf; (engine) заводи́ться impf, завести́сь pf; (set out) отправля́ться impf, отпра́виться pf; (shudder) вздра́гивать impf, вздро́гнуть pf; (sport) стартова́ть impf & pf; vt начина́ть impf, нача́ть pf (gerund, inf, +inf by, +gerund с того́, что...; **with** +instr, с +gen); (car, engine) заводи́ть impf, завести́ pf; (fire, rumour) пуска́ть impf, пусти́ть pf; (found) осно́вывать impf, основа́ть pf. **starter** n (tech) ста́ртёр; (cul) заку́ска. **starting-point** n отправно́й пункт.

startle vt испуга́ть pf.

starvation n го́лод. **starve** vi голода́ть impf; (to death) умира́ть impf, умере́ть с го́лоду; vt мори́ть impf,

по~, у~ pf го́лодом. **starving** adj голода́ющий; (hungry) о́чень голо́дный.

state n (condition) состоя́ние; (polit) госуда́рство, штат; adj (ceremonial) торже́ственный; пара́дный; (polit) госуда́рственный; vt (announce) заявля́ть impf, заяви́ть pf; (expound) излага́ть impf, изложи́ть pf. **stateless** adj не име́ющий гражда́нства.

stately adj вели́чественный. **statement** n заявле́ние; (comm) отчёт.

statesman n госуда́рственный де́ятель m.

static adj неподви́жный.

station n (rly) вокза́л, ста́нция; (social) обще́ственное положе́ние; (meteorological, hydro-electric power, radio etc.) ста́нция; (post) пост; vt размеща́ть impf, размести́ть pf.

stationary adj неподви́жный.

stationery n канцеля́рские принадле́жности f pl; (writing-paper) почто́вая бума́га; ~ **shop** канцеля́рский магази́н.

statistic n статисти́ческое да́нное. **statistical** adj статисти́ческий. **statistician** n стати́стик. **statistics** n стати́стика.

statue n ста́туя. **statuette** n статуэ́тка.

stature n рост; (merit) кали́бр.

status n ста́тус. **status quo** n ста́тус-кво́ neut indecl.

statute n стату́т. **statutory** adj устано́вленный зако́ном.

staunch adj ве́рный.

stave vt: ~ **off** предотвраща́ть impf, предотврати́ть pf.

stay n (time spent) пребыва́ние; vi (remain) остава́ться impf, оста́ться pf (**to dinner** обе́дать); (put up) остана́вливаться impf, останови́ться pf (**at** place) у+gen; (live) жить; ~ **behind** остава́ться impf, оста́ться pf; ~ **in** остава́ться impf, оста́ться pf до́ма; ~ **up** не ложи́ться impf спать; (trousers) держа́ться impf. **staying-power** n вынос́ливость.

stead n: **stand s.o. in good ~** ока́зываться impf, оказа́ться pf поле́зным кому́-л.

steadfast adj сто́йкий, непоколеби́мый.

steady adj (firm) усто́йчивый; (continuous) непреры́вный; (wind, temperature) ро́вный; (speed) постоя́нный; (unshakeable) непоколеби́мый; vt (boat etc.) приводи́ть impf, привести́ pf в равнове́сие.

steak n бифште́кс.

steal vt & abs ворова́ть impf, c~ pf; красть impf, y~ pf; vi (creep) кра́сться impf; подкра́дываться impf, подкра́сться pf. **stealth** n: by ~ укра́дкой. **stealthy** adj ворова́тый, та́йный, скры́тый.

steam n пар; at full ~ на всех пара́х; let off ~ (fig) дава́ть impf, дать pf вы́ход свои́м чу́вствам; vt па́рить impf; vi па́риться impf, по~ pf; (vessel) ходи́ть indet, идти́ det на пара́х; ~ up (mist over) запотева́ть impf, запоте́ть pf; поте́ть impf, за~, от~ pf; ~ engine парова́я маши́на. **steamer**, **steamship** n парохо́д. **steamy** adj напо́лненный па́ром; (passionate) горя́чий.

steed n конь m.

steel n сталь; adj стально́й; vt: ~ o.s. ожесточа́ться impf, ожесточи́ться pf; ~ works сталелите́йный заво́д. **steely** adj стально́й.

steep[1] adj круто́й; (excessive) чрезме́рный.

steep[2] vt (immerse) погружа́ть impf, погрузи́ть pf (in в+acc); (saturate) пропи́тывать impf, пропита́ть pf (in +instr).

steeple n шпиль m. **steeplechase** n ска́чки f pl с препя́тствиями.

steer vt управля́ть impf, пра́вить impf +instr; v abs рули́ть impf; ~ clear of избега́ть impf, избежа́ть pf +gen. **steering-wheel** n руль m.

stem[1] n сте́бель m; (of wine-glass) но́жка; (ling) осно́ва; vi: ~ from происходи́ть impf, произойти́ pf от+gen. **stem**[2] vt (stop) остана́вливать impf, останови́ть pf.

stench n злово́ние.

stencil n трафаре́т; (tech) шабло́н; vt наноси́ть impf, нанести́ pf по трафаре́ту. **stencilled** adj трафаре́тный.

step n (pace, action) шаг; (dance) па neut indecl; (of stairs, ladder) ступе́нь; ~ by ~ шаг за ша́гом; in ~ в но́гу; out of ~ не в но́гу; take ~s

принима́ть impf, приня́ть pf ме́ры vi шага́ть impf, шагну́ть pf; ступа́ть impf, ступи́ть pf; ~ aside сторони́ться impf, по~ pf; ~ back отступа́ть impf, отступи́ть pf; ~ down (resign) уходи́ть impf, уйти́ pf в отста́вку; ~ forward выступа́ть impf, вы́ступить pf; ~ in (intervene) вме́шиваться impf, вмеша́ться pf; ~ on наступа́ть impf, наступи́ть pf на +acc (s.o.'s foot кому́-л. на́ ногу); ~ over перешаги́вать impf, перешагну́ть pf +acc, че́рез+acc; ~ up (increase) повыша́ть impf, повы́сить pf. **step-ladder** n стремя́нка. **stepping-stone** n ка́мень m для перехо́да; (fig) сре́дство. **steps** n pl ле́стница.

stepbrother n сво́дный брат. **stepdaughter** n па́дчерица. **stepfather** n о́тчим. **stepmother** n ма́чеха. **stepsister** n сво́дная сестра́. **stepson** n па́сынок.

steppe n степь.

stereo n (system) стереофони́ческая систе́ма; (stereophony) стереофони́я; adj (recorded in ~) сте́рео indecl. **stereophonic** adj стереофони́ческий. **stereotype** n стереоти́п. **stereotyped** adj стереоти́пный.

sterile adj стери́льный. **sterility** n стери́льность. **sterilization** n стерилиза́ция. **sterilize** vt стерилизова́ть impf & pf.

sterling n сте́рлинг; pound ~ фунт сте́рлингов; adj сте́рлинговый.

stern[1] n корма́.

stern[2] adj суро́вый, стро́гий.

stethoscope n стетоско́п.

stew n (cul) мя́со тушёное вме́сте с овоща́ми; vt & i (cul) туши́ть(ся) impf, c~ pf; (fig) томи́ть(ся) impf.

steward n бортпроводни́к. **stewardess** n стюарде́сса.

stick[1] n па́лка; (of chalk etc.) па́лочка; (hockey) клю́шка.

stick[2] vt (spear) зака́лывать impf, заколо́ть pf; (make adhere) прикле́ивать impf, прикле́ить pf (to к+dat); (coll) (put) ста́вить impf, по~ pf; (lay) класть impf, положи́ть pf; (endure) терпе́ть impf, вы́~ pf; vi (adhere) ли́пнуть impf (to к+dat); прилипа́ть impf, прили́пнуть pf (to к+dat); ~ in (thrust in) втыка́ть *impf*, воткну́ть *pf*; (*into opening*) всо́вывать *impf*, всу́нуть *pf*; ~ on (*glue on*) накле́ивать *impf*, накле́ить *pf*; ~ out (*thrust out*) высо́вывать *impf*, вы́сунуть *pf* (*from* из+*gen*); (*project*) торча́ть *impf*; ~ to (*keep to*) приде́рживаться *impf*, придержа́ться *pf* +*gen*; (*remain at*) не отвлека́ться *impf* от+*gen*; ~ together держа́ться *impf* вме́сте; ~ up for защища́ть *impf*, защити́ть *pf*; be, get, stuck застрева́ть *impf*, застря́ть *pf*. **sticker** *n* накле́йка.

sticky *adj* ли́пкий.

stiff *adj* жёсткий, неги́бкий; (*prim*) чо́порный; (*difficult*) тру́дный; (*penalty*) суро́вый; be ~ (*ache*) боле́ть *impf*. **stiffen** *vt* де́лать *impf*, с~ *pf* жёстким; *vi* станови́ться *impf*, стать *pf* жёстким. **stiffness** *n* жёсткость; (*primness*) чо́порность.

stifle *vt* души́ть *impf*, за~ *pf*; (*suppress*) подавля́ть *impf*, подави́ть *pf*; (*sound*) заглуша́ть *impf*, заглуши́ть *pf*; *vi* задыха́ться *impf*, задохну́ться *pf*. **stifling** *adj* уду́шливый.

stigma *n* клеймо́.

stile *n* перела́з (coll).

stilettos *n pl* ту́фли *f pl* на шпи́льках.

still *adv* (всё) ещё; (*nevertheless*) тем не ме́нее; (*motionless*) неподви́жно; stand ~ не дви́гаться *impf*, дви́нуться *pf*; *n* (*quiet*) тишина́; *adj* ти́хий; (*immobile*) неподви́жный. **still-born** *adj* мертворождённый. **still life** *n* натюрмо́рт. **stillness** *n* тишина́.

stilted *adj* ходу́льный.

stimulant *n* возбужда́ющее сре́дство. **stimulate** *vt* возбужда́ть *impf*, возбуди́ть *pf*. **stimulating** *adj* возбуди́тельный. **stimulation** *n* возбужде́ние. **stimulus** *n* сти́мул.

sting *n* (*wound*) уку́с; (*stinger*; *fig*) жа́ло; *vt* жа́лить *impf*, у~ *pf*; *vi* (*burn*) жечь *impf*. **stinging** *adj* (*caustic*) язви́тельный.

stingy *adj* скупо́й.

stink *n* вонь; *vi* воня́ть *impf* (*of* +*instr*). **stinking** *adj* воню́чий.

stint *n* срок; *vi*: ~on скупи́ться *impf*, по~ *pf* на+*acc*.

stipend *n* (*salary*) жа́лование; (*grant*) стипе́ндия.

stipulate *vt* обусло́вливать *impf*, обусло́вить *pf*. **stipulation** *n* усло́вие.

stir *n* (*commotion*) шум; *vt* (*mix*) меша́ть *impf*, по~ *pf*; (*excite*) волнова́ть *impf*, вз~ *pf*; *vi* (*move*) шевели́ться *impf*, шевельну́ться *pf*; ~ up возбужда́ть *impf*, возбуди́ть *pf*. **stirring** *adj* волну́ющий.

stirrup *n* стре́мя *neut*.

stitch *n* стежо́к; (*knitting*) пе́тля; (*med*) шов; (*pain*) ко́лики *f pl*; *vt* (*embroider*, make line of ~es) строчи́ть *impf*, про~ *pf*; (*join by sewing*, make, suture) сшива́ть *impf*, сшить *pf*; ~ up зашива́ть *impf*, заши́ть *pf*. **stitching** *n* (*stitches*) стро́чка.

stoat *n* горноста́й.

stock *n* (*store*) запа́с; (*of shop*) ассортиме́нт; (*live~*) скот; (*cul*) бульо́н; (*lineage*) семья́; (*fin*) а́кции *f pl*; in ~ в нали́чии; out of ~ распро́дан; take ~ of крити́чески оце́нивать *impf*, оцени́ть *pf*; *adj* станда́ртный; *vt* име́ть в нали́чии; ~ up запаса́ться *impf*, запасти́сь *pf* (*with* +*instr*). **stockbroker** *n* биржево́й ма́клер. **stock-exchange** *n* би́ржа. **stockpile** *n* запа́с; *vt* нака́пливать *impf*, накопи́ть *pf*. **stock-taking** *n* переучёт.

stocking *n* чуло́к.

stocky *adj* призе́мистый.

stodgy *adj* тяжёлый.

stoic(al) *adj* стои́ческий. **stoicism** *n* стоици́зм.

stoke *vt* топи́ть *impf*.

stolid *adj* флегмати́чный.

stomach *n* желу́док, (*also surface of body*) живо́т; *vt* терпе́ть *impf*, по~ *pf*. **stomach ache** *n* боль в животе́.

stone *n* ка́мень *m*; (*of fruit*) ко́сточка; *adj* ка́менный; *vt* побива́ть *impf*, поби́ть *pf* камня́ми; (*fruit*) вынима́ть *impf*, вы́нуть *pf* ко́сточки из+*gen*. **Stone Age** *n* ка́менный век. **stone-deaf** *adj* соверше́нно глухо́й. **stone-mason** *n* ка́менщик. **stonily** *adv* с ка́менным выраже́нием, хо́лодно. **stony** *adj* камени́стый; (*fig*) ка́менный.

stool *n* табуре́т, табуре́тка.

stoop *n* суту́лость; *vt* & *i* суту́лить(ся) *impf*, с~ *pf*; (bend (down)) наклоня́ть(ся) *impf*, наклони́ть(ся) *pf*; ~ **to** (*abase o.s.*) унижа́ться *impf*, уни́зиться *pf* до+*gen*; (*condescend*) снисходи́ть *impf*, снизойти́ *pf* до +*gen*. **stooped, stooping** *adj* суту́лый.

stop *n* остано́вка; **put a ~ to** положи́ть *pf* коне́ц +*dat*; *vt* остана́вливать *impf*, останови́ть *pf*; (*discontinue*) прекраща́ть *impf*, прекрати́ть *pf*; (*restrain*) уде́рживать *impf*, удержа́ть (**from** от+*gen*); *vi* остана́вливаться *impf*, останови́ться *pf*; (*discontinue*) прекраща́ться *impf*, прекрати́ться *pf*; (*cease*) перестава́ть *impf*, переста́ть *pf* (+*inf*); ~ **up** *vt* затыка́ть *impf*, заткну́ть *pf*. **stoppage** *n* остано́вка; (*strike*) забасто́вка. **stopper** *n* про́бка. **stoppress** *n* э́кстренное сообще́ние в газе́те. **stop-watch** *n* секундоме́р.

storage *n* хране́ние. **store** *n* запа́с; (*storehouse*) склад; (*shop*) магази́н: **set ~ by** цени́ть *impf*; **what is in ~ for me?** что ждёт меня́ впереди́?; *vt* запаса́ть *impf*, запасти́ *pf*; (*put into storage*) сдава́ть *impf*, сдать *pf* на хране́ние. **storehouse** *n* склад. **store-room** кладова́я *sb*.

storey *n* эта́ж.

stork *n* а́ист.

storm *n* бу́ря, (*thunder ~*) гроза́; *vt* (*mil*) штурмова́ть *impf*; *vi* бушева́ть *impf*. **stormy** *adj* бу́рный.

story *n* расска́з, по́весть; (*anecdote*) анекдо́т; (*plot*) фа́була; ~**teller** расска́зчик.

stout *adj* (*strong*) кре́пкий; (*staunch*) сто́йкий; (*portly*) доро́дный.

stove *n* (*with fire inside*) печь; (*cooker*) плита́.

stow *vt* укла́дывать *impf*, уложи́ть *pf*. **stowaway** *n* безбиле́тный пасса жи́р.

straddle *vt* (*sit astride*) сиде́ть *impf* верхо́м на+*prep*; (*stand astride*) стоя́ть *impf*, расста́вив но́ги над+*instr*.

straggle *vi* отстава́ть *impf*, отста́ть *pf*. **straggler** *n* отста́вший *sb*. **straggling** *adj* разбро́санный. **straggly** *adj* растрёпанный.

straight *adj* прямо́й; (*undiluted*) неразба́вленный; *predic* (*in order*) в поря́дке; *adv* пря́мо; ~ **away** сра́зу. **straighten** *vt* & *i* выпрямля́ть(ся) *impf*, вы́прямить(ся) *pf*; *vt* (*put in*

order) поправля́ть *impf*, попра́вить *pf*. **straightforward** *adj* прямо́й; (*simple*) просто́й.

strain[1] *n* (*tension*) натяже́ние; (*sprain*) растяже́ние; (*effort, exertion*) напряже́ние; (*tendency*) скло́нность; (*sound*) звук; *vt* (*stretch*) натя́гивать *impf*, натяну́ть *pf*; (*sprain*) растя́гивать *impf*, растяну́ть *pf*; (*exert*) напряга́ть *impf*, напря́чь *pf*; (*filter*) проце́живать *impf*, процеди́ть *pf*; *vi* (*also exert o.s.*) напряга́ться *impf*, напря́чься *pf*. **strained** *adj* натя́нутый. **strainer** *n* (*tea ~*) си́течко; (*sieve*) си́то.

strain[2] *n* (*breed*) поро́да.

strait(s) *n* (*geog*) проли́в. **straitjacket** *n* смири́тельная руба́шка. **straits** *n pl* (*difficulties*) затрудни́тельное положе́ние.

strand[1] *n* (*hair, rope*) прядь; (*thread, also fig*) нить.

strand[2] *vt* сажа́ть *impf*, посади́ть *pf* на мель. **stranded** *adj* на мели́.

strange *adj* стра́нный; (*unfamiliar*) незнако́мый; (*alien*) чужо́й. **strangely** *adv* стра́нно. **strangeness** *n* стра́нность. **stranger** *n* незнако́мец.

strangle *vt* души́ть *impf*, за~ *pf*. **stranglehold** *n* мёртвая хва́тка. **strangulation** *n* удуше́ние.

strap *n* реме́нь *m*; *vt* (*tie up*) стя́гивать *impf*, стяну́ть *pf* ремнём. **strapping** *adj* ро́слый.

stratagem *n* хи́трость. **strategic** *adj* стратеги́ческий. **strategist** *n* страте́г. **strategy** *n* страте́гия.

stratum *n* слой.

straw *n* соло́ма; (*drinking*) соло́минка; **the last ~** после́дняя ка́пля; *adj* соло́менный.

strawberry *n* клубни́ка (*no pl*; *usu collect*); (*wild ~*) земляни́ка (*no pl*; *usu collect*).

stray *vi* сбива́ться *impf*, сби́ться *pf*; (*digress*) отклоня́ться *impf*, отклони́ться *pf*; *adj* (*lost*) заблуди́вшийся; (*homeless*) бездо́мный; *n* (*from flock*) отби́вшееся от ста́да живо́тное *sb*; ~ **bullet** шальна́я пу́ля.

streak *n* полоса́ (*of luck* везе́ния); (*tendency*) жи́лка; *vi* (*rush*) проноси́ться *impf*, пронести́сь *pf*. **streaked** *adj* с полоса́ми (**with**

+gen). **streaky** adj полоса́тый; (meat) с просло́йками жи́ра.

stream n (brook, tears) руче́й; (brook, flood, tears, people etc.) пото́к; (current) тече́ние; up/down ~ вверх/вниз по тече́нию; vi течь impf; струи́ться impf; (rush) проноси́ться impf, пронести́сь pf; (blow) развева́ться impf. **streamer** n вы́мпел. **stream-lined** adj обтека́емый; (fig) хорошо́ нала́женный.

street n у́лица; adj у́личный; ~ lamp у́личный фона́рь m.

strength n си́ла; (numbers) чи́сленность; on the ~ of в си́лу+gen. **strengthen** vt уси́ливать impf, уси́лить pf.

strenuous adj (work) тру́дный; (effort) напряжённый.

stress n напряже́ние; (mental) стресс; (emphasis) ударе́ние; vt (accent) ста́вить impf, по~ pf ударе́ние на+acc; (emphasize) подчёркивать impf подчеркну́ть pf. **stressful** adj стре́ссовый.

stretch n (expanse) отре́зок; at a ~ (in succession) подря́д; vt & i (widen, spread out) растя́гивать(ся) impf, растяну́ть(ся) pf; (in length, ~ out limbs) вытя́гивать(ся) impf, вы́тянуть(ся) pf; (tauten) натя́гивать(ся) impf, натяну́ть(ся) pf; (extend, e.g. rope, ~ forth limbs) протя́гивать(ся) impf, протяну́ть(ся) pf; vi (material, land) тяну́ться impf; ~ one's legs (coll) размина́ть impf, размя́ть pf но́ги. **stretcher** n носи́лки (-лок) pl.

strew vt разбра́сывать impf, разбро́са́ть pf; ~ with посыпа́ть impf, посы́пать pf +instr.

stricken adj поражённый.

strict adj стро́гий. **stricture(s)** n (стро́гая) кри́тика.

stride n (большо́й) шаг; pl (fig) успе́хи m pl; to take sth in one's ~ преодолева́ть impf, преодоле́ть pf что-л. без уси́лий; vi шага́ть impf.

strident adj ре́зкий.

strife n раздо́р.

strike n (refusal to work) забасто́вка; (mil) уда́р; vi (be on ~) бастова́ть impf; (go on ~) забастова́ть pf; (attack) ударя́ть impf, уда́рить pf; (the hour) бить impf, про~ pf; vt (hit)

ударя́ть impf, уда́рить pf; (impress) поража́ть impf, порази́ть pf; (discover) открыва́ть impf, откры́ть pf; (match) зажига́ть impf, заже́чь pf; (the hour) бить impf, про~ pf; (occur to) приходи́ть impf, прийти́ pf в го́лову+dat; ~ off вычёркивать impf, вы́черкнуть pf; ~ up начина́ть impf, нача́ть pf. **striker** n забасто́вщик. **striking** adj порази́тельный.

string n бечёвка; (mus) струна́; (series) ряд; pl (mus) стру́нные инструме́нты m pl; ~ bag, ~ vest се́тка; vt (thread) низа́ть impf, на~ pf; ~ along (coll) води́ть impf за нос; ~ out (prolong) растя́гивать impf, растяну́ть pf; **strung up** (tense) напряжённый. **stringed** adj стру́нный. **stringy** adj (fibrous) волокни́стый; (meat) жи́листый.

stringent adj стро́гий.

strip[1] n полоса́, поло́ска.

strip[2] vt (undress) раздева́ть impf, разде́ть pf; (deprive) лиша́ть impf, лиши́ть pf (of+gen); ~ off (tear off) сдира́ть impf, содра́ть pf; vi раздева́ться impf, разде́ться pf. **strip-tease** n стрипти́з.

stripe n полоса́. **striped** adj полоса́тый.

strive vi (endeavour) стреми́ться impf (for к+dat); (struggle) боро́ться impf (for за+acc; against про́тив +gen).

stroke n (blow, med) уда́р; (of oar) взмах; (swimming) стиль m; (of pen etc.) штрих; (piston) ход; vt гла́дить impf, по~ pf.

stroll n прогу́лка; vi прогу́ливаться impf, прогуля́ться pf.

strong adj (blow; of drinks) кре́пкий; (healthy) здоро́вый; (opinion etc.) твёрдый. **stronghold** n кре́пость. **strong-minded, strong-willed** adj реши́тельный.

structural adj структу́рный. **structure** n структу́ра; (building) сооруже́ние; vt организова́ть impf & pf.

struggle n борьба́; vi боро́ться impf (for за+acc; against про́тив+gen); (writhe, ~ with (fig)) би́ться (with над+instr).

strum vi бренча́ть impf (on на +prep).

strut[1] n (vertical) сто́йка; (horizontal) распо́рка.

strut[2] vi ходи́ть indet, идти́ det го́голем.

stub n огры́зок; (cigarette) оку́рок; (counterfoil) корешо́к; vt: ~ one's toe ударя́ться impf, уда́риться pf ного́й (on на+acc); ~ out гаси́ть impf, по~ pf.

stubble n жнивьё; (hair) щети́на.

stubborn adj упря́мый. **stubbornness** n упря́мство.

stucco n штукату́рка.

stud[1] n (collar, cuff) за́понка; (nail) гвоздь m с большо́й шля́пкой; vt (bestrew) усе́ивать impf, усе́ять pf (with +instr).

stud[2] n (horses) ко́нный заво́д.

student n студе́нт, ~ка.

studied adj напускно́й.

studio n сту́дия.

studious adj лю́бящий нау́ку; (diligent) стара́тельный.

study n изуче́ние; pl заня́тия neut pl; (investigation) иссле́дование; (art, mus) этю́д; (room) кабине́т; vt изуча́ть impf, изучи́ть pf; учи́ться impf, об~ pf +dat; (scrutinize) рассма́тривать impf, рассмотре́ть pf; vi (take lessons) учи́ться impf, об~ pf; (do one's studies) занима́ться impf.

stuff n (material) материа́л; (things) ве́щи f pl; vt набива́ть impf, наби́ть pf; (cul) начиня́ть impf, начини́ть pf; (cram into) запи́хивать impf, запиха́ть pf (into в+acc); (shove into) сова́ть impf, су́нуть pf (into в+acc); vi (overeat) объеда́ться impf, объе́сться pf. **stuffiness** n духота́. **stuffing** n наби́вка; (cul) начи́нка. **stuffy** adj ду́шный.

stumble vi (also fig) спотыка́ться impf, споткну́ться pf (over о+acc); ~ upon натыка́ться impf, наткну́ться pf на+acc. **stumbling-block** n ка́мень m преткнове́ния.

stump n (tree) пень m; (pencil) огры́зок; (limb) культя́; vt (perplex) ста́вить impf, по~ pf в тупи́к.

stun vt (also fig) оглуша́ть impf, оглуши́ть pf. **stunning** adj потряса́ющий.

stunt[1] n трюк.

stunt[2] vt заде́рживать impf, задержа́ть pf рост+gen. **stunted** adj низ-

коро́слый.

stupefy vt оглуша́ть impf, оглуши́ть pf. **stupendous** adj колосса́льный.

stupid adj глу́пый. **stupidity** n глу́пость. **stupor** n оцепене́ние.

sturdy adj кре́пкий.

stutter n заика́ние; vi заика́ться impf.

sty[1] n (pig~) свина́рник.

sty[2] n (on eye) ячме́нь m.

style n стиль m; (taste) вкус; (fashion) мо́да; (sort) род; (of hair) причёска. **stylish** adj мо́дный. **stylist** n (of hair) парикма́хер. **stylistic** adj стилисти́ческий. **stylize** vt стилизова́ть impf & pf.

stylus n игла́ звукоснима́теля.

suave adj обходи́тельный.

subconscious adj подсозна́тельный; n подсозна́ние. **subcontract** vt дава́ть impf, дать pf подря́дчику. **subcontractor** n подря́дчик. **subdivide** vt подразделя́ть impf, подраздели́ть pf. **subdivision** n подразделе́ние. **subdue** vt покоря́ть impf, покори́ть pf. **subdued** adj (suppressed, dispirited) пода́вленный; (soft) мя́гкий; (indistinct) приглушённый. **sub-editor** n помо́щник реда́ктора.

subject n (theme) те́ма; (discipline, theme) предме́т; (question) вопро́с; (thing on to which action is directed) объе́кт; (gram) подлежа́щее sb; (national) по́дданный sb; adj: ~ to (susceptible to) подве́рженный+dat; (on condition that) при усло́вии, что...; е́сли; be ~ to (change etc.) подлежа́ть impf +dat; vt: ~ to подверга́ть impf, подве́ргнуть pf +dat. **subjection** n подчине́ние. **subjective** adj субъекти́вный. **subjectivity** n субъекти́вность. **subject-matter** n (of book, lecture) содержа́ние, те́ма; (of discussion) предме́т.

subjugate vt покоря́ть impf, покори́ть pf. **subjugation** n покоре́ние.

subjunctive (mood) n сослага́тельное наклоне́ние.

sublet vt передава́ть impf, переда́ть pf в суба́ренду.

sublimate vt сублими́ровать impf & pf. **sublimation** n сублима́ция. **sublime** adj возвы́шенный.

subliminal adj подсозна́тельный.

sub-machine-gun n автома́т. **submarine** n подво́дная ло́дка. **submerge** vt погружа́ть impf, погрузи́ть pf. **submission** n подчине́ние; (for inspection) представле́ние. **submissive** adj поко́рный. **submit** vi подчиня́ться impf, подчини́ться pf (to +dat); vt представля́ть impf, предста́вить pf. **subordinate** n подчинённый sb; adj подчинённый; (secondary) второстепе́нный; (gram) прида́точный; vt подчиня́ть impf, подчини́ть pf. **subscribe** vi подпи́сываться impf, подписа́ться pf (to на+acc); ~ to (opinion) присоединя́ться impf, присоедини́ться pf к+dat. **subscriber** n подпи́счик; абоне́нт. **subscription** n подпи́ска, абонеме́нт; (fee) взнос. **subsection** n подразде́л. **subsequent** adj после́дующий. **subsequently** adv впосле́дствии. **subservient** adj рабо́ле́пный. **subside** vi убыва́ть impf, убы́ть pf; (soil) оседа́ть impf, осе́сть pf. **subsidence** n (soil) оседа́ние. **subsidiary** adj вспомога́тельный; (secondary) второстепе́нный; n филиа́л. **subsidize** vt субси́дировать impf & pf. **subsidy** n субси́дия. **subsist** vi (live) жить impf (on +instr). **substance** n вещество́; (essence) су́щность, суть; (content) содержа́ние. **substantial** adj (durable) про́чный; (considerable) значи́тельный; (food) пло́тный. **substantially** adv (basically) в основно́м; (considerably) значи́тельно. **substantiate** vt обосно́вывать impf, обоснова́ть pf. **substitute** n (person) замести́тель m; (thing) заме́на; vt заменя́ть impf, замени́ть pf +instr (for +acc); I ~ water for milk заменя́ю молоко́ водо́й. **substitution** n заме́на. **subsume** vt относи́ть impf, отнести́ pf к како́й-л. катего́рии. **subterfuge** n уве́ртка. **subterranean** adj подзе́мный. **subtitle** n подзаголо́вок; (cin) субти́тр. **subtle** adj то́нкий. **subtlety** n то́нкость.

subtract vt вычита́ть impf, вы́честь pf. **subtraction** n вычита́ние. **suburb** n при́город. **suburban** adj при́городный. **subversion** n подрывна́я де́ятельность. **subversive** adj подрывно́й. **subway** n подзе́мный перехо́д.

succeed vi удава́ться impf, уда́ться pf; the plan will ~ план уда́стся; he ~ed in buying the book ему́ удало́сь купи́ть кни́гу; (be successful) преуспева́ть impf, преуспе́ть pf (in в+prep); (follow) сменя́ть impf, смени́ть pf; (be heir) насле́довать impf & pf (to +dat). **succeeding** adj после́дующий. **success** n успе́х. **successful** adj успе́шный. **succession** n (series) ряд; (to throne) престолонасле́дие; right of ~ пра́во насле́дования; in ~ подря́д, оди́н за други́м. **successive** (consecutive) последова́тельный. **successor** n прее́мник.

succinct adj сжа́тый.

succulent adj со́чный.

succumb vi (to pressure) уступа́ть impf, уступи́ть pf (to +dat); (to temptation) поддава́ться impf, подда́ться pf (to +dat).

such adj тако́й; ~ people таки́е лю́ди; ~ as (for example) так наприме́р; (of a kind as) тако́й как; ~ beauty as yours така́я красота́ как ва́ша; (that which) тот, кото́рый; I shall read ~ books as I like я бу́ду чита́ть те кни́ги, кото́рые мне нра́вятся; ~ as to тако́й, что́бы; his illness was not ~ as to cause anxiety его́ боле́знь была́ не тако́й (серьёзной), что́бы вы́звать беспоко́йство; ~ and ~ тако́й-то; pron тако́в; ~ was his character тако́в был его́ хара́ктер; as ~ сам по себе́; ~ is not the case э́то не так. **suchlike** pron (inanimate) тому́ подо́бное; (people) таки́е лю́ди pl.

suck vt соса́ть impf; ~ in вса́сывать impf, всоса́ть pf; (engulf) заса́сывать impf, засоса́ть pf; ~ out выса́сывать impf, вы́сосать pf; ~ up to (coll) подли́зываться impf, подлиза́ться pf к+dat. **sucker** n (biol, rubber device) присо́ска; (bot) корнево́й побе́г. **suckle** vt корми́ть impf, на~ pf гру́дью. **suction** n вса́сывание.

sudden adj внеза́пный. **suddenly** adv вдруг. **suddenness** n внеза́пность.

sue vt & i подава́ть impf, пода́ть pf

в суд (на+*acc*); ~ **s.o. for damages** предъявля́ть *impf*, предъяви́ть *pf* (к) кому́-л. иск о возмеще́нии уще́рба.

suede *n* за́мша; *adj* за́мшевый.

suet *n* нутряно́е са́ло.

suffer *vt* страда́ть *impf*, по~ *pf* +*instr*, от+*gen*; (*loss, defeat*) терпе́ть *impf*, по~ *pf*; (*tolerate*) терпе́ть *impf*; *vi* страда́ть *impf*, по~ *pf* (from +*instr*, от+*gen*). **sufferance** *n*: **he is here on** ~ его́ здесь те́рпят. **suffering** *n* страда́ние.

suffice *vi & t* быть доста́точным (для+*gen*); хвата́ть *impf*, хвати́ть *pf impers*+*gen* (+*dat*). **sufficient** *adj* доста́точный.

suffix *n* су́ффикс.

suffocate *vt* удуша́ть *impf*, удуши́ть *pf*; *vi* задыха́ться *impf*, задохну́ться *pf*. **suffocating** *adj* уду́шливый. **suffocation** *n* удуше́ние.

suffrage *n* избира́тельное пра́во.

suffuse *vt* залива́ть *impf*, зали́ть *pf* (with +*instr*).

sugar *n* са́хар; *adj* са́харный; *vt* подсла́щивать *impf*, подсласти́ть *pf*; ~ **basin** са́харница; ~ **beet** са́харная свёкла; ~ **cane** са́харный тро́стник. **sugary** *adj* са́харный; (*fig*) слаща́вый.

suggest *vt* предлага́ть *impf*, предложи́ть *pf*; (*evoke*) напомина́ть *impf*, напо́мнить *pf*; (*imply*) намека́ть *impf*, намекну́ть *pf* на+*acc*; (*indicate*) говори́ть *impf* о+*prep*. **suggestion** *n* предложе́ние; (*psych*) внуше́ние. **suggestive** *adj* вызыва́ющий мы́сли (of о+*prep*); (*indecent*) соблазни́тельный.

suicidal *adj* самоуби́йственный; (*fig*) губи́тельный. **suicide** *n* самоуби́йство; **commit** ~ соверша́ть *impf*, соверши́ть *pf* самоуби́йство.

suit *n* (*clothing*) костю́м; (*law*) иск; (*cards*) масть; **follow** ~ (*fig*) сле́довать *impf*, по~ *pf* приме́ру; *vt* (*be convenient for*) устра́ивать *impf*, устро́ить *pf*; (*adapt*) приспоса́бливать *impf*, приспосо́бить *pf*; (*be* ~*able for, match*) подходи́ть *impf*, подойти́ *pf* (+*dat*); (*look attractive on*) идти́ *impf* +*dat*. **suitability** *n* приго́дность. **suitable** *adj* (*fitting*) подходя́щий; (*convenient*) удо́бный.

suitably *adv* соотве́тственно. **suitcase** *n* чемода́н.

suite *n* (*retinue*) сви́та; (*furniture*) гарниту́р; (*rooms*) апарта́менты *m pl*; (*mus*) сюи́та.

suitor *n* покло́нник.

sulk *vi* ду́ться *impf*. **sulky** *adj* наду́тый.

sullen *adj* угрю́мый.

sully *vt* пятна́ть *impf*, за~ *pf*.

sulphur *n* се́ра. **sulphuric** *adj*: ~ **acid** се́рная кислота́.

sultana *n* (*raisin*) изю́минка; *pl* кишми́ш (*collect*).

sultry *adj* зно́йный.

sum *n* су́мма; (*arithmetical problem*) арифмети́ческая зада́ча; *pl* арифме́тика; *v*: ~ **up** (*summarize*) подводи́ть *impf*, подвести́ *pf* ито́ги (+*gen*); *vt* (*appraise*) оце́нивать *impf*, оцени́ть *pf*.

summarize *vt* сумми́ровать *impf & pf*. **summary** *n* резюме́ *neut indecl*, сво́дка; *adj* сумма́рный; (*dismissal*) бесцеремо́нный.

summer *n* ле́то; *attrib* ле́тний. **summer-house** *n* бесе́дка.

summit *n* верши́на; ~ **meeting** встре́ча на верха́х.

summon *vt* вызыва́ть *impf*, вы́звать *pf*; ~ **up one's courage** собира́ться *impf*, собра́ться *pf* с ду́хом. **summons** *n* вы́зов; (*law*) пове́стка в суд; *vt* вызыва́ть *impf*, вы́звать *pf* в суд.

sumptuous *adj* роско́шный.

sun *n* со́лнце; **in the** ~ на со́лнце. **sunbathe** *vi* загора́ть *impf*. **sunbeam** *n* со́лнечный луч. **sunburn** *n* зага́р; (*inflammation*) со́лнечный ожо́г. **sunburnt** *adj* загоре́лый; **become** ~ загора́ть *impf*, загоре́ть *pf*.

Sunday *n* воскресе́нье.

sundry *adj* ра́зный; **all and** ~ всё и вся.

sunflower *n* подсо́лнечник. **sunglasses** *n pl* очки́ (-ко́в) *pl* от со́лнца.

sunken *adj* (*cheeks, eyes*) впа́лый; (*submerged*) погружённый; (*ship*) зато́пленный; (*below certain level*) ни́же (како́го-л. у́ровня).

sunlight *n* со́лнечный свет. **sunny** *adj* со́лнечный. **sunrise** *n* восхо́д со́лнца. **sunset** *n* зака́т. **sunshade**

n (*parasol*) зо́нтик; (*awning*) наве́с.
sunshine n со́лнечный свет. **sun-stroke** n со́лнечный уда́р. **suntan** n зага́р. **sun-tanned** adj загоре́лый.
super adj замеча́тельный. **superb** adj превосхо́дный. **supercilious** adj высокоме́рный. **superficial** adj пове́рхностный. **superficiality** n пове́рхностность. **superfluous** adj ли́шний. **superhuman** adj сверхчелове́ческий. **superintendent** n заве́дующий sb (of +*instr*); (*police*) ста́рший полице́йский офице́р. **superior** n ста́рший sb; adj (*better*) превосхо́дный; (*in rank*) ста́рший; (*haughty*) высокоме́рный. **superiority** n превосхо́дство. **superlative** adj превосхо́дный; n (*gram*) превосхо́дная сте́пень. **superman** n сверхчелове́к. **supermarket** n универса́м. **supernatural** adj сверхъесте́ственный. **superpower** n сверхдержа́ва. **supersede** vt заменя́ть impf, замени́ть pf. **supersonic** adj сверхзвуково́й. **superstition** n суеве́рие. **superstitious** adj суеве́рный. **superstructure** n надстро́йка. **supervise** vt наблюда́ть impf за+*instr*. **supervision** n надзо́р. **supervisor** n нача́льник; (*of studies*) руководи́тель m.
supper n у́жин; have ~ у́жинать impf, по~ pf.
supple adj ги́бкий. **suppleness** n ги́бкость.
supplement n (*to book*) дополне́ние; (*to periodical*) приложе́ние; vt дополня́ть impf, допо́лнить pf. **supplementary** adj дополни́тельный.
supplier n поставщи́к. **supply** n (*stock*) запа́с; (*econ*) предложе́ние; pl (*mil*) припа́сы (-ов) pl, vt снабжа́ть impf, снабди́ть pf (with +*instr*).
support n подде́ржка; vt подде́рживать impf, поддержа́ть pf; (*family*) содержа́ть impf. **supporter** n сторо́нник; (*sport*) боле́льщик. **supportive** adj уча́стливый.
suppose vt (*think*) полага́ть impf; (*presuppose*) предполага́ть impf, предположи́ть pf; (*assume*) допуска́ть impf, допусти́ть pf. **supposed** adj (*assumed*) предполага́емый. **supposition** n предположе́ние.
suppress vt подавля́ть impf, пода-

ви́ть pf. **suppression** n подавле́ние.
supremacy n госпо́дство. **supreme** adj верхо́вный.
surcharge n наце́нка.
sure adj уве́ренный (of в+*prep*; that что); (*reliable*) ве́рный; ~ enough действи́тельно; he is ~ to come on обяза́тельно придёт; make ~ of (*convince o.s.*) убежда́ться impf, убеди́ться pf в+*prep*; make ~ that (*check up*) проверя́ть impf, прове́рить pf что. **surely** adv наверняка́.
surety n пору́ка; stand ~ for руча́ться impf, поручи́ться pf за+*acc*.
surf n прибо́й; vi занима́ться impf, заня́ться pf сёрфингом.
surface n пове́рхность; (*exterior*) вне́шность; on the ~ (*fig*) вне́шне; under the ~ (*fig*) по существу́; adj пове́рхностный; vi всплыва́ть impf, всплыть pf.
surfeit n (*surplus*) изли́шек.
surge n волна́; vi (*rise, heave*) взды-ма́ться impf; (*emotions*) нахлы́нуть pf; ~ forward ри́нуться pf вперёд.
surgeon n хиру́рг. **surgery** n (*treatment*) хирурги́я; (*place*) кабине́т; (~ hours*) приёмные часы́ m pl (врача́). **surgical** adj хирурги́ческий.
surly adj (*morose*) угрю́мый; (*rude*) грубый.
surmise vt & i предполага́ть impf, предположи́ть pf.
surmount vt преодолева́ть impf, преодоле́ть pf.
surname n фами́лия.
surpass vt превосходи́ть impf, превзойти́ pf.
surplus n изли́шек; adj изли́шний.
surprise n (*astonishment*) удивле́ние; (*surprising thing*) сюрпри́з; vt удивля́ть impf, удиви́ть pf; (*come upon suddenly*) застава́ть impf, заста́ть pf враспло́х; be ~d (*at*) удивля́ться impf, удиви́ться pf (+*dat*). **surprising** adj удиви́тельный.
surreal adj сюрреалисти́ческий. **surrealism** n сюрреали́зм. **surrealist** n сюрреали́ст; adj сюрреалисти́ческий.
surrender n сда́ча; (*renunciation*) отка́з; vt сдава́ть impf, сдать pf; (*give up*) отка́зываться impf, отказа́ться pf от+*gen*; vi сдава́ться impf, сда́ться pf; ~ o.s. to предава́ться impf,

преда́ться pf +dat.
surreptitious adj та́йный.
surrogate n замени́тель m.
surround vt окружа́ть impf, окружи́ть pf (with +instr). **surrounding** adj окружа́ющий. **surroundings** n (environs) окре́стности f pl; (milieu) среда́.
surveillance n надзо́р.
survey n (review) обзо́р; (inspection) инспе́кция; (poll) опро́с; vt (review) обозрева́ть impf, обозре́ть pf; (inspect) инспекти́ровать impf, про~ pf; (poll) опра́шивать impf, опроси́ть pf. **surveyor** n инспе́ктор.
survival n (surviving) выжива́ние; (relic) пережи́ток. **survive** vt пережива́ть impf, пережи́ть pf; vi выжива́ть impf, вы́жить pf. **survivor** n уцеле́вший sb; (fig) боре́ц.
susceptible adj подве́рженный (to влия́нию +gen); (sensitive) чувстви́тельный (to к+dat); (impressionable) впечатли́тельный.
suspect n подозрева́емый sb; adj подозри́тельный; vt подозрева́ть impf (of в+prep); (assume) полага́ть impf (that что).
suspend vt (hang up) подве́шивать impf, подве́сить pf; приостана́вливать impf, приостанови́ть pf; (debar temporarily) вре́менно отстраня́ть impf, отстрани́ть pf; ~ed sentence усло́вный пригово́р. **suspender** n (stocking) подвя́зка. **suspense** n неизве́стность. **suspension** n (halt) приостано́вка; (of car) рессо́ры f pl; ~ bridge вися́чий мост.
suspicion n подозре́ние; on ~ по подозре́нию (of в+loc); (trace) отте́нок. **suspicious** adj подозри́тельный.
sustain vt (support) подде́рживать impf, поддержа́ть pf; (suffer) потерпе́ть pf. **sustained** adj (uninterrupted) непреры́вный. **sustenance** n пи́ща.
swab n (mop) шва́бра; (med) тампо́н; (specimen) мазо́к.
swagger vi расха́живать impf с ва́жным ви́дом.
swallow[1] n глото́к; vt прогла́тывать impf, проглоти́ть pf; ~ up поглоща́ть impf, поглоти́ть pf.
swallow[2] n (bird) ла́сточка.

swamp n боло́та; vt залива́ть impf, зали́ть pf; (fig) зава́ливать impf, завали́ть pf (with +instr). **swampy** adj боло́тистый.
swan n ле́бедь m.
swap n обме́н; vt (for different thing) меня́ть impf, об~, по~ pf (for на +acc); (for similar thing) обме́ниваться impf, обменя́ться pf +instr.
swarm n рой; (crowd) толпа́; vi рои́ться impf; толпи́ться impf; (teem) кише́ть impf (with +instr).
swarthy adj сму́глый.
swastika n сва́стика.
swat vt прихло́пывать impf, прихло́пнуть pf.
swathe n (expanse) простра́нство; vt (wrap) заку́тывать impf, заку́тать pf.
sway n (influence) влия́ние; (power) власть m & i кача́ть(ся) impf, качну́ть(ся) pf; vt (influence) име́ть impf влия́ние на+acc.
swear vi (vow) кля́сться impf, по~ pf; (curse) руга́ться impf, ругну́ться pf; ~-word руга́тельство.
sweat n пот; vi поте́ть impf, вс~ pf. **sweater** n сви́тер. **sweaty** adj по́тный.
swede n брю́ква.
Swede n швед, ~дка. **Sweden** n Шве́ция. **Swedish** adj шве́дский.
sweep n (span) разма́х; (chimney-~) трубочи́ст; vt подмета́ть impf, подмести́ pf; vi (go majestically) ходи́ть indet, идти́ det, пойти́ pf велича́во; (move swiftly) мча́ться impf; ~ away смета́ть impf, смести́ pf. **sweeping** adj (changes) радика́льный; (statement) огу́льный.
sweet n (sweetmeat) конфе́та; (dessert) сла́дкое sb; adj сла́дкий; (fragrant) души́стый; (dear) ми́лый. **sweeten** vt подсла́щивать impf, подсласти́ть pf. **sweetheart** n возлю́бленный, -нная sb. **sweetness** n сла́дость.
swell vi (up) опуха́ть impf, опу́хнуть pf; vt & i (a sail) надува́ть(ся) impf, наду́ть(ся) pf; vt (increase) увели́чивать impf, увели́чить pf; n (of sea) зыбь. **swelling** n о́пухоль.
swelter vi изнемога́ть impf от жары́. **sweltering** adj зно́йный.
swerve vi ре́зко свёртывать, свора́чивать impf, сверну́ть pf.

swift adj бы́стрый.

swig n глото́к; vt хлеба́ть impf.

swill n по́йло; vt (rinse) полоска́ть impf, вы́~ pf.

swim vi пла́вать indet, плыть det; vt (across) переплыва́ть impf, переплы́ть pf +acc, че́рез+acc. **swimmer** n плове́ц, пловчи́ха. **swimming** n пла́вание. **swimming-pool** n бассе́йн для пла́вания. **swim-suit** n купа́льный костю́м.

swindle vt обма́нывать impf, обману́ть pf; n обма́н. **swindler** n моше́нник.

swine n свинья́.

swing vi кача́ться impf, качну́ться pf; vt кача́ть impf, качну́ть pf +acc, instr; (arms) разма́хивать impf +instr; n кача́ние; (shift) крен; (seat) каче́ли (-лей) pl; **in full ~** в по́лном разга́ре.

swingeing adj (huge) грома́дный; (forcible) си́льный.

swipe n си́льный уда́р; vt с си́лой ударя́ть impf, уда́рить pf.

swirl vi крути́ться impf; n (of snow) вихрь m.

swish vi (cut the air) рассека́ть impf, рассе́чь pf во́здух со сви́стом; (rustle) шелесте́ть impf; vt (tail) взма́хивать impf, взмахну́ть pf +instr; (brandish) разма́хивать impf +instr; n (of whip) свист; (rustle) ше́лест.

Swiss n швейца́рец, -ца́рка; adj швейца́рский.

switch n (electr) выключа́тель m; (change) измене́ние; vt & i (also ~ over) переключа́ть(ся) impf, переключи́ть(ся) pf; vt (swap) меня́ться impf, об~, по~ pf +instr; **~ off** выключа́ть impf, вы́ключить pf; **~ on** включа́ть impf, включи́ть pf. **switchboard** n коммута́тор.

Switzerland n Швейца́рия.

swivel vt & i враща́ть(ся) impf.

swollen adj взду́тый.

swoon n о́бморок; vi па́дать impf, упа́сть pf в о́бморок.

swoop vi: **~ down** налета́ть impf, налете́ть pf (on на+acc); n налёт; **at one fell ~** одни́м уда́ром.

sword n меч.

sycophantic adj льсти́вый.

syllable n слог.

syllabus n програ́мма.

symbol n си́мвол. **symbolic(al)** adj символи́ческий. **symbolism** n символи́зм. **symbolize** vt символизи́ровать impf.

symmetrical adj симметри́ческий. **symmetry** n симметри́я.

sympathetic adj сочу́вственный. **sympathize** vi сочу́вствовать impf (with +dat). **sympathizer** n сторо́нник. **sympathy** n сочу́вствие.

symphony n симфо́ния.

symposium n симпо́зиум.

symptom n симпто́м. **symptomatic** adj симтомати́чный.

synagogue n синаго́га.

synchronization n синхрониза́ция. **synchronize** vt синхронизи́ровать impf & pf.

syndicate n синдика́т.

syndrome n синдро́м.

synonym n сино́ним. **synonymous** adj синоними́ческий.

synopsis n конспе́кт.

syntax n си́нтаксис.

synthesis n си́нтез. **synthetic** adj синтети́ческий.

syphilis n си́филис.

Syria n Си́рия. **Syrian** n сири́ец, сири́йка; adj сири́йский.

syringe n шприц; vt спринцева́ть impf.

syrup n сиро́п; (treacle) па́тока.

system n систе́ма; (network) сеть; (organism) органи́зм. **systematic** adj системати́ческий. **systematize** vt систематизи́ровать impf & pf.

T

tab n (loop) пе́телька; (on uniform) петли́ца; (of boot) ушко́; **keep ~s on** следи́ть impf за+instr.

table n стол; (chart) табли́ца; **~cloth** ска́терть; **~spoon** столо́вая ло́жка; **~ tennis** насто́льный те́ннис; vt (for discussion) предлага́ть impf, предложи́ть pf на обсужде́ние.

tableau n жива́я карти́на.

tablet n (pill) табле́тка; (of stone) плита́; (memorial) мемориа́льная доска́; (name plate) доще́чка.

tabloid n (newspaper) малоформа́тная газе́та; (derog) бульва́рная газе́та.

taboo *n* табу́ *neut indecl*; *adj* за-прещённый.

tacit *adj* молчали́вый. **taciturn** *adj* неразгово́рчивый.

tack[1] *n* (*nail*) гво́здик; (*stitch*) намёт-ка; (*naut*) галс; (*fig*) курс; *vt* (*fasten*) прикрепля́ть *impf*, прикрепи́ть *pf* гво́здиками; (*stitch*) смётывать *impf*, смета́ть *pf* на живу́ю ни́тку; (*fig*) добавля́ть *impf*, доба́вить *pf* (*(on)to* +*dat*); *vi* (*naut*, *fig*) лави́ровать *impf*.

tack[2] *n* (*riding*) сбру́я (*collect*).

tackle *n* (*requisites*) снасть (*collect*); (*sport*) блокиро́вка; *vt* (*problem*) бра́ться *impf*, взя́ться *pf* за+*acc*; (*sport*) блоки́ровать *impf* & *pf*.

tacky *adj* ли́пкий.

tact *n* такт(и́чность). **tactful** *adj* такти́чный.

tactical *adj* такти́ческий. **tactics** *n pl* та́ктика.

tactless *adj* беста́ктный.

tadpole *n* голова́стик.

Tadzhikistan *n* Таджикиста́н.

tag *n* (*label*) ярлы́к; (*of lace*) нако-не́чник; *vt* (*label*) прикрепля́ть *impf*, прикрепи́ть *pf* ярлы́к на+*acc*; *vi*: ~ **along** (*follow*) тащи́ться *impf* сза́ди; **may I ~ along?** мо́жно с ва́ми?

tail *n* хвост; (*of shirt*) ни́жний коне́ц; (*of coat*) фа́лда; (*of coin*) обра́тная сторона́ моне́ты; **heads or ~s?** орёл и́ли ре́шка?; *pl* (*coat*) фрак; *vt* (*shadow*) высле́живать *impf*; *vi*: ~ **away, off** постепе́нно уменьша́ться *impf*; (*grow silent, abate*) затиха́ть *impf*. **tailback** *n* хвост.

tailcoat *n* фрак.

tailor *n* портно́й *sb*; ~-**made** сши́тый на зака́з; (*fig*) сде́ланный индиви-дуа́льно.

taint *vt* по́ртить *impf*, ис~ *pf*.

Taiwan *n* Тайва́нь *m*.

take *vt* (*various senses*) брать *impf*, взять *pf*; (*also seize, capture*) за-хва́тывать *impf*, захвати́ть *pf*; (*receive, accept*; ~ **breakfast**; ~ **medi-cine**; ~ **steps**) принима́ть *impf*, при-ня́ть *pf*; (*convey, escort*) провожа́ть *impf*, проводи́ть *pf*; (*public trans-port*) е́здить *impf*, е́хать *det*, по~ *pf* +*instr*, на+*prep*; (*photograph*) снима́ть *impf*, снять *pf*; (*occupy*; ~

time) занима́ть *impf*, заня́ть *pf*; (*impers*) **how long does it ~?** ско́лько вре́мени ну́жно?; (*size in clothing*) носи́ть *impf*; (*exam*) сда-ва́ть *impf*; *vi* (*be successful*) име́ть *impf* успе́х (*of injection*) приви-ва́ться *impf*, приви́ться *pf*; ~ **after** походи́ть *impf* на+*acc*; ~ **away** (*re-move*) убира́ть *impf*, убра́ть *pf*; (*subtract*) вычита́ть *impf*, вы́честь *pf*; ~-**away** магази́н, где продаю́т на вы́нос; ~ **back** (*return*) возвраща́ть *impf*, возврати́ть *pf*; (*retrieve, re-tract*) брать *impf*, взять *pf* наза́д; ~ **down** (*in writing*) запи́сывать *impf*, записа́ть *pf*; (*remove*) снима́ть *impf*, снять *pf*; ~ **s.o.**, **sth for**, **to be** принима́ть *impf*, приня́ть *pf* за+*acc*; ~ **from** отнима́ть *impf*, отня́ть *pf* у, от+*gen*; ~ **in** (*carry in*) вноси́ть *impf*, внести́ *pf*; (*lodgers*; *work*) брать *impf*, взять *pf*; (*clothing*) ушива́ть *impf*, уши́ть *pf*; (*under-stand*) понима́ть *impf*, поня́ть *pf*; (*deceive*) обма́нывать *impf*, обма-ну́ть *pf*; ~ **off** (*clothing*) снима́ть *impf*, снять *pf*; (*mimic*) передра́з-нивать *impf*, передразни́ть *pf*; (*aeroplane*) взлета́ть *impf*, взлете́ть *pf*; ~-**off** (*imitation*) подража́ние; (*aeron*) взлёт; ~ **on** (*undertake*; *hire*) брать *impf*, взять *pf* на себя́; (*ac-quire*) приобрета́ть *impf*, приобре-сти́ *pf*; (*at game*) сража́ться *impf*, срази́ться *pf* с+*instr* (*at* в+*acc*); ~ **out** вынима́ть *impf*, вы́нуть *pf*; (*dog*) выводи́ть *impf*, вы́вести *pf* (*for a walk* на прогу́лку); (*to theatre, restaurant etc.*) приглаша́ть *impf*, пригласи́ть *pf* (*to* в+*acc*); **we took them out every night** мы при-глаша́ли их куда́-нибудь ка́ждый ве́чер; ~ **it out on** срыва́ть *impf*, сорва́ть *pf* всё на+*prep*; ~ **over** при-нима́ть *impf*, приня́ть *pf* руково́д-ство +*instr*; ~ **to** (*thing*) пристра-сти́ться *pf* к+*dat*; (*person*) привя́-зываться *impf*, привяза́ться *pf* к +*dat*; (*begin*) станови́ться *impf*, стать *pf* +*inf*; ~ **up** (*interest oneself in*) занима́ться *impf*, заня́ться *pf*; (*with an official etc.*) обраща́ться *impf*, обрати́ться *pf* с+*instr*, к+*dat*; (*challenge*) принима́ть *impf*, при-ня́ть *pf*; (*time, space*) занима́ть *impf*, заня́ть *pf*; ~ **up with** (*person*) свя́зываться *impf*, связа́ться *pf* c+*instr*; *n* (*cin*) дубль *m*.

taking *adj* привлека́тельный.

takings *n pl* сбор.

talcum powder *n* тальк.

tale *n* расска́з.

talent *n* тала́нт. **talented** *adj* тала́нтливый.

talk *vi* разгова́ривать *impf* (**to, with** c+*instr*); (*gossip*) спле́тничать *impf*, на~ *pf*; *vt & i* говори́ть *impf*, по~ *pf*; ~ **down to** говори́ть *impf* свысока́ c+*instr*; ~ **into** угова́ривать *impf*, уговори́ть *pf* +*inf*; ~ **out of** отгова́ривать *impf*, отговори́ть *pf* +*inf*, от+*gen*; ~ **over** (*discuss*) обсужда́ть *impf*, обсуди́ть *pf*; ~ **round** (*persuade*) переубежда́ть *impf*, переубеди́ть *pf*; *n* (*conversation*) разгово́р; (*lecture*) бесе́да; *pl* перегово́ры (-ров) *pl*. **talkative** *adj* болтли́вый. (*derog*) болтли́вый. **talker** *n* говоря́щий *sb*; (*chatterer*) болту́н (*coll*); (*orator*) ора́тор. **talking-to** (*coll*) вы́говор.

tall *adj* высо́кий; (*in measurements*) ро́стом в+*acc*.

tally *n* (*score*) счёт; *vi* соотве́тствовать (**with** +*dat*).

talon *n* ко́готь *m*.

tambourine *n* бу́бен.

tame *adj* ручно́й; (*insipid*) пре́сный; *vt* прируча́ть *impf*, приручи́ть *pf*. **tamer** *n* укроти́тель *m*.

tamper *vi*: ~ **with** (*meddle*) тро́гать *impf*, тро́нуть *pf*; (*forge*) подде́лывать *impf*, подде́лать *pf*.

tampon *n* тампо́н.

tan *n* (*sun~*) зага́р; *adj* желтова́то-кори́чневый; *vt* (*hide*) дуби́ть *impf*, вы́~ *pf*; (*beat*) (*coll*) дуба́сить *impf*, от~ *pf*; *vi* загора́ть *impf*, загоре́ть *pf*; (*of sun*) **tanned** загоре́лый.

tang *n* (*taste*) ре́зкий при́вкус; (*smell*) о́стрый за́пах.

tangent *n* (*math*) каса́тельная *sb*; (*trigonometry*) та́нгенс; **go off at a** ~ отклоня́ться *impf*, отклони́ться *pf* от те́мы.

tangerine *n* мандари́н.

tangible *adj* осяза́емый.

tangle *vt & i* запу́тывать(ся) *impf*, запу́таться *pf*; *n* пу́таница.

tango *n* та́нго *neut indecl*.

tangy *adj* о́стрый; ре́зкий.

tank *n* бак; (*mil*) танк.

tankard *n* кру́жка.

tanker *n* (*sea*) та́нкер; (*road*) автоцисте́рна.

tantalize *vt* дразни́ть *impf*.

tantamount *predic* равноси́лен (-льна) (**to** +*dat*).

tantrum *n* при́ступ раздраже́ния.

tap[1] *n* кран; *vt* (*resources*) испо́льзовать *impf & pf*; (*telephone conversation*) подслу́шивать *impf*.

tap[2] *n* (*knock*) стук; *vt* стуча́ть *impf*, по~ *pf* в+*acc*, по+*dat*; **~-dance** (*vi*) отбива́ть *impf*, отби́ть *pf* чечётку; (*n*) чечётка; **~-dancer** чечёточник, -ица.

tape *n* (*cotton strip*) тесьма́; (*adhesive, magnetic, measuring, etc.*) ле́нта; **~-measure** руле́тка; ~ **recorder** магнитофо́н; ~ **recording** за́пись; *vt* (*seal*) закле́ивать *impf*, закле́ить *pf*; (*record*) запи́сывать *impf*, записа́ть *pf* на ле́нту.

taper *vt & i* су́живать(ся) *impf*, су́зить(ся) *pf*.

tapestry *n* гобеле́н.

tar *n* дёготь *m*.

tardy *adj* (*slow*) медли́тельный; (*late*) запозда́лый.

target *n* мише́нь, цель.

tariff *n* тари́ф.

tarmac *n* (*material*) гудро́н; (*road*) гудрони́рованное шоссе́ *neut indecl*; (*runway*) бетони́рованная площа́дка; *vt* гудрони́ровать *impf & pf*.

tarnish *vt* де́лать *impf*, с~ *pf* ту́склым; (*fig*) пятна́ть *impf*, за~ *pf*; *vi* тускне́ть *impf*, по~ *pf*.

tarpaulin *n* брезе́нт.

tarragon *n* эстраго́н.

tart[1] *adj* (*taste*) ки́слый; (*fig*) ко́лкий.

tart[2] *n* (*pie*) сла́дкий пиро́г.

tart[3] *n* (*prostitute*) шлю́ха.

tartan *n* шотла́ндка.

tartar *n* ви́нный ка́мень *m*.

task *n* зада́ча; **take to** ~ де́лать *impf*, с~ *pf* вы́говор+*dat*; ~ **force** операти́вная гру́ппа.

Tass *abbr* ТАСС, Телегра́фное аге́нтство Сове́тского Сою́за.

tassel *n* ки́сточка.

taste *n* (*also fig*) вкус; **take a** ~ **of** про́бовать *impf*, по~ *pf*; *vt* чу́вствовать *impf*, по~ *pf* вкус+*gen*;

(*sample*) пробовать *impf*, по~ *pf*; (*fig*) вкушать *impf*, вкусить *pf*; (*wine etc.*) дегустировать *impf* & *pf*; *vi* иметь вкус, привкус (**of** +*gen*). **tasteful** *adj* (сделанный) со вкусом. **tasteless** *adj* безвкусный. **tasting** *n* дегустация. **tasty** *adj* вкусный.

tatter *n* *pl* лохмотья (-ьев) *pl*. **tattered** *adj* оборванный.

tattoo *n* (*design*) татуировка; *vt* татуировать *impf* & *pf*.

taunt *n* насмешка; *vt* насмехаться *impf* над+*instr*.

Taurus *n* Телец.

taut *adj* туго натянутый; тугой.

tavern *n* таверна.

tawdry *adj* мишурный.

tawny *adj* рыжевато-коричневый.

tax *n* налог; ~**-free** освобождённый от налога; *vt* облагать *impf*, обложить *pf* налогом; (*strain*) напрягать *impf*, напрячь *pf*; (*patience*) испытывать *impf*, испытать *pf*. **taxable** *adj* подлежащий обложению налогом. **taxation** *n* обложение налогом. **taxing** *adj* утомительный. **taxpayer** *n* налогоплательщик.

taxi *n* такси *neut indecl*; ~**-driver** водитель *m* такси; ~ **rank** стоянка такси; *vi* (*aeron*) рулить *impf*.

tea *n* чай; ~ **bag** пакетик с сухим чаем; ~ **cloth**, ~ **towel** полотенце для посуды; ~ **cosy** чехольщик (для чайника); ~**cup** чайная чашка; ~**leaf** чайный лист; ~**pot** чайник; ~**spoon** чайная ложка; ~ **strainer** чайное ситечко.

teach *vt* учить *impf*, на~ *pf* (*person* +*acc*; *subject* +*dat*, *inf*); преподавать *impf* (*subject* +*acc*); (*coll*) проучивать *impf*, проучить *pf*. **teacher** *n* учитель *m*, ~ница; преподаватель *m*, ~ница; ~**-training college** педагогический институт. **teaching** *n* (*instruction*) обучение; (*doctrine*) учение.

teak *n* тик; *attrib* тиковый.

team *n* (*sport*) команда; (*of people*) бригада; (*of horses etc.*) упряжка; ~**-mate** член той же команды; ~**work** сотрудничество; *vi* (~ **up**) объединяться *impf*, объединиться *pf*.

tear^1 *n* (*rent*) прореха; *vt* (*also* ~ **up**) рвать *impf*; (*also* ~ **up**) разрывать

impf, разорвать *pf*; *vi* рваться *impf*; (*rush*) мчаться *impf*; ~ **down**, **off** срывать *impf*, сорвать *pf*; ~ **out** вырывать *impf*, вырвать *pf*.

tear^2 *n* (~*drop*) слеза; ~**-gas** слезоточивый газ. **tearful** *adj* слезливый.

tease *vt* дразнить *impf*.

teat *n* сосок.

technical *adj* технический; ~ **college** техническое училище. **technicality** *n* формальность. **technically** *adv* (*strictly*) формально. **technician** *n* техник. **technique** *n* техника; (*method*) метод. **technology** *n* технология, техника. **technological** *adj* технологический. **technologist** *n* технолог.

teddy-bear *n* медвежонок.

tedious *adj* скучный. **tedium** *n* скука.

teem^1 *vi* (*swarm*) кишеть *impf* (with +*instr*).

teem^2 *vi*: **it is** ~**ing** (**with rain**) дождь льёт как из ведра.

teenage *adj* юношеский. **teenager** *n* подросток. **teens** *n* *pl* возраст от тринадцати до девятнадцати лет.

teeter *vi* качаться *impf*, качнуться *pf*.

teethe *vi*: **the child is teething** у ребёнка прорезываются зубы; **teething troubles** (*fig*) начальные проблемы *f* *pl*.

teetotal *adj* трезвый. **teetotaller** *n* трезвенник.

telecommunication(s) *n* дальняя связь. **telegram** *n* телеграмма. **telegraph** *n* телеграф; ~ **pole** телеграфный столб. **telepathic** *adj* телепатический. **telepathy** *n* телепатия. **telephone** *n* телефон; *vt* (*message*) телефонировать *impf* & *pf* +*acc*, о+*prep*; (*person*) звонить *impf*, по~ *pf* (по телефону) +*dat*; ~ **box** телефонная будка; ~ **directory** телефонная книга; ~ **exchange** телефонная станция; ~ **number** номер телефона. **telephonist** *n* телефонист, ~ка. **telephoto lens** *n* телеобъектив. **telescope** *n* телескоп. **telescopic** *adj* телескопический. **televise** *vt* показывать *impf*, показать *pf* по телевидению. **television** *n* телевидение; (*set*) телевизор; *attrib* телевизионный. **telex** *n* телекс.

tell *vt* & *i* (*relate*) рассказывать *impf*,

рассказа́ть pf (thing told +acc, o+prep; person told +dat); vt (utter, inform) говори́ть impf, сказа́ть pf (thing uttered +acc; thing informed about o+prep; person informed +dat); (order) веле́ть impf & pf +dat; ~ one thing from another отлича́ть impf, отличи́ть pf +acc от+gen; vi (have an effect) сказа́ться pf (on на+prep); ~ off отчи́тывать impf, отчита́ть pf; ~ on, ~ tales about я́бедничать impf, на~ pf на+acc. teller n (of story) расска́зчик; (of votes) счётчик; (in bank) касси́р. telling adj (effective) эффекти́вный; (significant) многозначи́тельный. telltale n спле́тник; adj преда́тельский.

temerity n де́рзость.

temp n рабо́тающий sb вре́менно; vi рабо́тать impf вре́менно.

temper n (character) нрав; (mood) настрое́ние; (anger) гнев; lose one's ~ выходи́ть impf, вы́йти pf из себя́; vt (fig) смягча́ть impf, смягчи́ть pf. temperament n темпера́мент. temperamental adj темпера́ментный. temperance n (moderation) уме́ренность; (sobriety) тре́звенность. temperate adj уме́ренный. temperature n температу́ра; (high ~) повы́шенная температу́ра; take s.o.'s ~ измеря́ть impf, изме́рить pf температу́ру +dat.

tempest n бу́ря. tempestuous adj бу́рный.

template n шабло́н.

temple[1] n (religion) храм.

temple[2] n (anat) висо́к.

tempo n темп.

temporal adj (of time) временно́й; (secular) мирско́й.

temporary adj вре́менный.

tempt vt соблазня́ть impf, соблазни́ть pf; ~ fate испы́тывать impf, испыта́ть pf судьбу́. temptation n собла́зн. tempting adj соблазни́тельный.

ten adj & n де́сять; (number 10) деся́тка. tenth adj & n деся́тый.

tenable adj (logical) разу́мный.

tenacious adj це́пкий. tenacity n це́пкость.

tenancy n (renting) наём помеще́ния; (period) срок аре́нды. tenant

n аренда́тор.

tend[1] vi (be apt) име́ть скло́нность (to к+dat, +inf).

tend[2] vt (look after) уха́живать impf за+instr.

tendency n тенде́нция. tendentious adj тенденцио́зный.

tender[1] vt (offer) предлага́ть impf, предложи́ть pf; vi (make ~ for) подава́ть impf, пода́ть pf зая́вку (на торга́х); n предложе́ние; legal ~ зако́нное плате́жное сре́дство.

tender[2] adj (delicate, affectionate) не́жный. tenderness n не́жность.

tendon n сухожи́лие.

tendril n у́сик.

tenement n (dwelling-house) жило́й дом; ~-house многокварти́рный дом.

tenet n до́гмат, при́нцип.

tennis n те́ннис.

tenor n (direction) направле́ние; (purport) смысл; (mus) те́нор.

tense[1] n вре́мя neut.

tense[2] vt напряга́ть impf, напря́чь pf; adj напряжённый. tension n напряже́ние.

tent n пала́тка.

tentacle n щу́пальце.

tentative adj (experimental) про́бный; (preliminary) предвари́тельный.

tenterhooks n pl: be on ~ сиде́ть impf как на иго́лках.

tenth see ten

tenuous adj (fig) неубеди́тельный.

tenure n (of property) владе́ние; (of office) пребыва́ние в до́лжности; (period) срок; (guaranteed employment) несменя́емость.

tepid adj теплова́тый.

term n (period) срок; (univ) семе́стр; (school) че́тверть; (technical word) те́рмин; (expression) выраже́ние; pl (conditions) усло́вия neut pl; (relations) отноше́ния neut pl; on good ~s в хоро́ших отноше́ниях; come to ~s with (resign o.s. to) покоря́ться impf, покори́ться pf к+dat; vt называ́ть impf, назва́ть pf.

terminal adj коне́чный; (med) смерте́льный; n (electr) зажи́м; (computer, aeron) термина́л; (terminus) коне́чная остано́вка.

terminate vt & i конча́ть(ся) impf, ко́нчить(ся) pf (in +instr). termination n прекраще́ние.

terminology *n* терминоло́гия.

terminus *n* коне́чная остано́вка.

termite *n* терми́т.

terrace *n* терра́са; (*houses*) ряд домо́в.

terracotta *n* терракота.

terrain *n* ме́стность.

terrestrial *adj* земно́й.

terrible *adj* ужа́сный. **terribly** *adv* ужа́сно.

terrier *n* терье́р.

terrific *adj* (*huge*) огро́мный; (*splendid*) потряса́ющий. **terrify** *vt* ужаса́ть *impf*, ужасну́ть *pf*.

territorial *adj* территориа́льный. **territory** *n* террито́рия.

terror *n* у́жас; (*person*; *polit*) терро́р. **terrorism** *n* террори́зм. **terrorist** *n* террори́ст, ~ка. **terrorize** *vt* терроризи́ровать *impf* & *pf*.

terse *adj* кра́ткий.

tertiary *adj* трети́чный; (*education*) вы́сший.

test *n* испыта́ние, про́ба; (*exam*) экза́мен; контро́льная рабо́та; (*analysis*) ана́лиз; ~-tube проби́рка; *vt* (*try out*) испы́тывать *impf*, испыта́ть *pf*; (*check up on*) проверя́ть *impf*, прове́рить *pf*; (*give exam to*) экзаменова́ть *impf*, про~ *pf*.

testament *n* завеща́ние; Old, New T~ Ве́тхий, Но́вый заве́т.

testicle *n* яи́чко.

testify *vi* свиде́тельствовать *impf* (to в по́льзу+*gen*; against про́тив+*gen*); *vt* (*declare*) заявля́ть *impf*, заяви́ть *pf*; (*be evidence of*) свиде́тельствовать о+*prep*.

testimonial *n* рекоменда́ция, характери́стика. **testimony** *n* свиде́тельство.

tetanus *n* столбня́к.

tetchy *adj* раздражи́тельный.

tête-à-tête *n* & *adv* тет-а-те́т.

tether *n*: be at, come to the end of one's ~ дойти́ *pf* до то́чки; *vt* привя́зывать *impf*, привяза́ть *pf*.

text *n* текст. **textbook** *n* уче́бник.

textile *adj* тексти́льный; *n* ткань; *pl* тексти́ль *m* (*collect*).

textual *adj* тексто́вой.

texture *n* тексту́ра.

than *conj* (*comparison*) чем; other ~ (*except*) кро́ме+*gen*.

thank *vt* благодари́ть *impf*, по~ *pf* (for за+*acc*); ~ God сла́ва Бо́гу; ~

you спаси́бо; благодарю́ вас; *n pl* благода́рность; ~s to (*good result*) благодаря́ +*dat*; (*bad result*) из-за+*gen*. **thankful** *adj* благода́рный. **thankless** *adj* неблагода́рный. **thanksgiving** *n* благодаре́ние.

that *demonstrative adj* & *pron* тот; ~ which тот кото́рый; *rel pron* кото́рый; *conj* что; (*purpose*) что́бы; *adv* так, до тако́й сте́пени.

thatched *adj* соло́менный.

thaw *vt* раста́пливать *impf*, растопи́ть *pf*; *vi* та́ять *impf*, рас~ *pf*.

the *def article, not translated*; *adv* тем; the ... the ... чем...тем; ~ more ~ better чем бо́льше, тем лу́чше.

theatre *n* теа́тр; (*lecture* ~) аудито́рия; (*operating* ~) операцио́нная *sb*; ~-goer театра́л. **theatrical** *adj* театра́льный.

theft *n* кра́жа.

their, theirs *poss pron* их; свой.

theme *n* те́ма.

themselves *pron* (*emph*) (они́) са́ми; (*refl*) себя́; -ся (*suffixed to vt*).

then *adv* (*at that time*) тогда́; (*after that*) пото́м; now and ~ вре́мя от вре́мени; *conj* в тако́м слу́чае, тогда́; *adj* тогда́шний; by ~ к тому́ вре́мени; since ~ с тех пор.

thence *adv* отту́да. **thenceforth, -forward** *adv* с того́/э́того вре́мени.

theologian *n* тео́лог. **theological** *adj* теологи́ческий. **theology** *n* теоло́гия.

theorem *n* теоре́ма. **theoretical** *adj* теорети́ческий. **theorize** *vi* теоретизи́ровать *impf*. **theory** *n* тео́рия.

therapeutic *adj* терапевти́ческий. **therapist** *n* (*psychotherapist*) психотерапе́вт. **therapy** *n* терапи́я.

there *adv* (*place*) там; (*direction*) туда́; *int* вот!; ну!; ~ is, are есть, име́ется (-ются); ~ you are (*on giving sth*) пожа́луйста. **thereabouts** *adv* (*near*) побли́зости; (*approximately*) приблизи́тельно. **thereafter** *adv* по́сле э́того. **thereby** *adv* таки́м о́бразом. **therefore** *adv* поэ́тому. **therein** *adv* в э́том. **thereupon** *adv* зате́м.

thermal *adj* теплово́й, терми́ческий; (*underwear*) тёплый.

thermometer *n* термо́метр, гра́дусник. **thermos** *n* те́рмос. **thermostat**

n термоста́т.

thesis *n* (*proposition*) те́зис; (*dissertation*) диссерта́ция.

they *pron* они́.

thick *adj* то́лстый, (*in measurements*) толщино́й в+*acc*; (*dense*) густо́й; (*stupid*) тупо́й; ~-skinned толстоко́жий. **thicken** *vt & i* утолща́ть(ся) *impf*, утолсти́ть(ся) *pf* (*make, become denser*) сгуща́ть(ся) *impf*, сгусти́ть(ся) *pf*; *vi* (*become more intricate*) усложня́ться *impf*, усложни́ться *pf*. **thicket** *n* ча́ща. **thickness** *n* (*also dimension*) толщина́; (*density*) густота́; (*layer*) слой. **thickset** *adj* корена́стый.

thief *n* вор. **thieve** *vi* ворова́ть *impf*. **thievery** *n* воровство́.

thigh *n* бедро́.

thimble *n* напёрсток.

thin *adj* (*slender; not thick*) то́нкий; (*lean*) худо́й; (*too liquid*) жи́дкий; (*sparse*) ре́дкий; *vt & i* де́лать(ся) *impf*, с~ *pf* то́нким, жи́дким; *vi* (*also* ~ *out*) реде́ть *impf*, по~ *pf*; *vt*: ~ **out** проре́живать *impf*, проре́дить *pf*.

thing *n* вещь; (*object*) предме́т; (*matter*) де́ло.

think *vt & i* ду́мать *impf*, по~ *pf* (**about**, of o+*prep*); (*consider*) счита́ть *impf*, счесть *pf* (**to be** +*instr*, за+*acc*; **that** что); *vi* (*reflect, reason*) мы́слить *impf*; (*intend*) намерева́ться *impf* (*of doing* +*inf*); ~ **out** проду́мывать *impf*, проду́мать *pf*; ~ **over** обду́мывать *impf*, обду́мать *pf*; ~ **up, of** приду́мывать *impf*, приду́мать *pf*. **thinker** *n* мысли́тель *m*. **thinking** *adj* мы́слящий; *n* (*reflection*) размышле́ние; **to my way of** ~ по моему́ мне́нию.

third *adj & n* тре́тий; (*fraction*) треть; T~ **World** страны́ *f pl* тре́тьего ми́ра.

thirst *n* жа́жда (**for** +*gen* (*fig*)); *vi* (*fig*) жа́ждать *impf* (**for** +*gen*). **thirsty** *adj*: **be** ~ хоте́ть пить.

thirteen *adj & n* трина́дцать. **thirteenth** *adj & n* трина́дцатый.

thirtieth *adj & n* тридца́тый. **thirty** *adj & n* три́дцать; *pl* (*decade*) тридца́тые го́ды (-до́в) *m pl*.

this *demonstrative adj & pron* э́тот; **like** ~ вот так; ~ **morning** сего́дня у́тром.

thistle *n* чертополо́х.

thither *adv* туда́.

thorn *n* шип. **thorny** *adj* колю́чий; (*fig*) терни́стый.

thorough *adj* основа́тельный; (*complete*) соверше́нный. **thoroughbred** *adj* чистокро́вный. **thoroughfare** *n* прое́зд; (*walking*) прохо́д. **thoroughgoing** *adj* радика́льный. **thoroughly** *adv* (*completely*) соверше́нно. **thoroughness** *n* основа́тельность.

though *conj* хотя́; несмотря́ на то, что; **as** ~ как бу́дто; *adv* одна́ко.

thought *n* мысль; (*meditation*) размышле́ние; (*intention*) наме́рение; *pl* (*opinion*) мне́ние. **thoughtful** *adj* заду́мчивый; (*considerate*) внима́тельный. **thoughtless** *adj* необду́манный; (*inconsiderate*) невнима́тельный.

thousand *adj & n* ты́сяча. **thousandth** *adj & n* ты́сячный.

thrash *vt* бить *impf*, по~ *pf*; ~ **out** (*discuss*) обстоя́тельно обсужда́ть *impf*, обсуди́ть *pf*; *vi*: ~ **about** мета́ться *impf*. **thrashing** *n* (*beating*) взбу́чка (coll).

thread *n* ни́тка, нить (*also fig*); (*of screw etc.*) резьба́; *vt* (*needle*) продева́ть *impf*, проде́ть *pf* ни́тку в +*acc*; (*beads*) нани́зывать *impf*, низа́ть *pf*; ~ **one's way** пробира́ться *impf*, пробра́ться *pf* (**through** че́рез+*acc*). **threadbare** *adj* потёртый.

threat *n* угро́за. **threaten** *vt* угрожа́ть *impf*, грози́ть *impf*, при~ *pf* (*person* +*dat*; **with** +*instr*; **to do** +*inf*).

three *adj & n* три; (*number 3*) тро́йка; ~-**dimensional** трёхме́рный; ~-**quarters** три че́тверти. **threefold** *adj* тройно́й; *adv* втройне́. **threesome** *n* тро́йка.

thresh *vt* молоти́ть *impf*.

threshold *n* поро́г.

thrice *adv* три́жды.

thrift *n* бережли́вость. **thrifty** *adj* бережли́вый.

thrill *n* тре́пет; *vt* восхища́ть *impf*, восхити́ть *pf*; **be thrilled** быть в восто́рге. **thriller** *n* приключе́нческий, детекти́вный (*novel*) рома́н, (*film*) фильм. **thrilling** *adj* захва́тывающий.

thrive *vi* процвета́ть *impf*.

throat n го́рло.

throb vi (heart) си́льно би́ться impf; пульси́ровать impf; n бие́ние; пульса́ция.

throes n pl: **in the ~** в мучи́тельных попы́тках.

thrombosis n тромбо́з.

throne n трон, престо́л; **come to the ~** вступа́ть impf, вступи́ть pf на престо́л.

throng n толпа́; vi толпи́ться impf; vt заполня́ть impf, запо́лнить pf.

throttle n (tech) дро́ссель m; vt (strangle) души́ть impf, за~ pf; (tech) дроссели́ровать impf & pf; ~ **down** сбавля́ть impf, сба́вить pf газ.

through prep (across, via, ~ opening) че́рез+acc; (esp ~ thick of) сквозь+acc; (air, streets etc.) по+dat; (agency) посре́дством+gen; (reason) из-за+gen; adv наскво́зь; (from beginning to end) до конца́; **be ~ with** (sth) ока́нчивать impf, око́нчить pf; (s.o.) порыва́ть impf, порва́ть pf с+instr; **put ~** (on telephone) соединя́ть impf, соедини́ть pf; ~ **and ~** совершенно; adj (train) прямо́й; (traffic) сквозно́й. **throughout** adv повсю́ду, во всех отноше́ниях; prep по всему́ (всей, всему́); pl всем+dat; (from beginning to end) с нача́ла до конца́+gen.

throw n бросо́к; vt броса́ть impf, бро́сить pf; (confuse) смуща́ть impf, смути́ть pf; (rider) сбра́сывать impf, сбро́сить pf; (party) устра́ивать impf, устро́ить pf; ~ **o.s. into** броса́ться impf, бро́ситься pf в+acc; ~ **away, out** выбра́сывать impf, вы́бросить pf; ~ **down** сбра́сывать impf, сбро́сить pf; ~ **in** (add) доба́влять impf, доба́вить pf; (sport) вбра́сывать impf, вбро́сить pf; ~ **in** вбра́сывание мяча́; ~ **off** сбра́сывать impf, сбро́сить pf; ~ **open** распа́хивать impf, распахну́ть pf; ~ **out** (see also ~ away) (expel) выгоня́ть impf, вы́гнать pf; (reject) отверга́ть impf, отве́ргнуть pf; ~ **over, ~ up** (abandon) броса́ть impf, бро́сить pf; ~ **up** подбра́сывать impf, подбро́сить pf; (vomit) рвать impf, вы́~ pf impers; **he threw up** его́ вы́рвало.

thrush n (bird) дрозд.

thrust n (shove) толчо́к; (tech) тя́га; vt (shove) толка́ть impf, толкну́ть pf; (~ into, out of; give quickly, carelessly) со́вать impf, су́нуть pf.

thud n глухо́й звук; vi па́дать impf, pf с глухи́м сту́ком.

thug n головоре́з (coll).

thumb n большо́й па́лец; **under the ~ of** под башмако́м у+gen; vt: ~ **through** перели́стывать impf, перелиста́ть pf; ~ **a lift** голосова́ть impf, про~ pf.

thump n (blow) тяжёлый уда́р; (thud) глухо́й звук, стук; vt колоти́ть impf, по~ pf в+acc, по+dat; vi колоти́ться impf.

thunder n гром; vi греме́ть impf; **it thunders** гром греми́т. **thunderbolt** n уда́р мо́лнии. **thunderous** adj громово́й. **thunderstorm** n гроза́. **thundery** adj грозово́й.

Thursday n четве́рг.

thus adv так, таки́м о́бразом.

thwart vt меша́ть impf, по~ pf +dat; (plans) расстра́ивать impf, расстро́ить pf.

thyme n тимья́н.

thyroid n (~ gland) щитови́дная железа́.

tiara n тиа́ра.

tick n (noise) ти́канье; (mark) пти́чка; vi ти́кать impf, ти́кнуть pf; vt отмеча́ть impf, отме́тить pf пти́чкой; ~ **off** (scold) отде́лывать impf, отде́лать pf.

ticket n биле́т; (label) ярлы́к; (season ~) ка́рточка; (cloakroom ~) номеро́к; (receipt) квита́нция; ~ **collector** контролёр; ~ **office** (биле́тная) ка́сса.

tickle n щеко́тка; vt щекота́ть impf, по~ pf; (amuse) весели́ть impf, по~, раз~ pf; vi щекота́ть impf, по~ pf impers; **my throat ~s** у меня́ щеко́чет в го́рле. **ticklish** adj (fig) щекотли́вый; **to be ~** боя́ться impf щеко́тки.

tidal adj прили́во-отли́вный; ~ **wave** прили́вная волна́.

tide n прили́в и отли́в; **high ~** прили́в; **low ~** отли́в; (current, tendency) тече́ние; **the ~ turns** (fig) собы́тия принима́ют друго́й оборо́т; vt: ~ **over** помога́ть impf, помо́чь pf +dat of person спра́виться (*difficulty* c+*instr*); **will this money ~ you over?** вы протя́нете с э́тими деньга́ми?

tidiness *n* аккура́тность. **tidy** *adj* аккура́тный; (*considerable*) поря́дочный; *vt* убира́ть, убра́ть *pf*; приводи́ть *impf*, привести́ *pf* в поря́док.

tie *n* (*garment*) га́лстук; (*cord*) завя́зка; (*link*; *tech*) связь; (*equal points etc.*) ра́вный счёт; **end in a ~** зака́нчиваться ничье́й, зако́нчиться *pf* вничью́; (*burden*) обу́за; *pl* (*bonds*) у́зы (уз) *pl*; *vt* свя́зывать *impf*, связа́ть *pf* (*also fig*); (**~ up**) завя́зывать *impf*, завяза́ть *pf*; (*restrict*) ограни́чивать *impf*, ограни́чить *pf*; **~ down** (*fasten*) привя́зывать *impf*, привяза́ть *pf*; **~ up** (*tether*) привя́зывать *impf*, привяза́ть *pf*; (*parcel*) перевя́зывать *impf*, перевяза́ть *pf*; *vi* (*be ~d*) завя́зываться *impf*, завяза́ться *pf*; (*sport*) сыгра́ть *pf* вничью́; **~ in, up, with** совпада́ть *impf*, совпа́сть *pf* c+*instr*.

tier *n* ряд, я́рус.

tiff *n* размо́лвка.

tiger *n* тигр.

tight *adj* (*cramped*) те́сный; у́зкий; (*strict*) стро́гий; (*taut*) туго́й; **~ corner** (*fig*) тру́дное положе́ние. **tighten** *vt & i* натя́гиваться *impf*, натяну́ться *pf*; (*clench, contract*) сжима́ть(ся) *impf*, сжа́ться *pf*; **~ one's belt** поту́же затяги́вать *impf*, затяну́ть *pf* по́яс (*also fig*), затяну́ть *pf* по́яс (*also fig*), затяну́ть *pf* по́яс (*discipline etc.*) подтя́гивать *impf*, подтяну́ть *pf* (*coll*). **tightly** *adv* (*strongly*) про́чно; (*closely, cramped*) те́сно. **tightrope** *n* натя́нутый кана́т. **tights** *n pl* колго́тки (-ток) *pl*.

tile *n* (*roof*) черепи́ца (*also collect*); (*decorative*) ка́фель *m* (*also collect*); *vt* крыть *impf*, по~ *pf* черепи́цей, ка́фелем. **tiled** *adj* (*roof*) черепи́чный; (*floor*) ка́фельный.

till¹ *prep* до+*gen*; **not ~** то́лько (**Friday** в пя́тницу; **the next day** на сле́дующий день); *conj* пока́ не; **not ~ то́лько когда́.

till² *n* ка́сса.

till³ *vt* возде́лывать *impf*, возде́лать *pf*.

tiller *n* (*naut*) ру́мпель *m*.

tilt *n* накло́н; **at full ~** по́лным хо́дом;

vt & i наклоня́ть(ся) *impf*, наклони́ть(ся) *pf*; (*heel (over)*) крени́ть(ся) *impf*, на~ *pf*.

timber *n* лесоматериа́л.

time *n* вре́мя *neut*; (*occasion*) раз; (*mus*) такт; (*sport*) тайм; *pl* (*period*) времена́ *pl*; (*in comparison*) раз; **five ~s as big** в пять раз бо́льше; (*multiplication*) **four ~s** четы́режды; **~ and ~ again, ~ after ~** не раз, ты́сячу раз; **at a ~** ра́зом, одновреме́нно; **at the ~** в э́то вре́мя; **at ~s** времена́ми; **at the same ~** в то же вре́мя; **before my ~** до меня́; **for a long ~** до́лго; (*up to now*) давно́; **for the ~ being** пока́; **from ~ to ~** вре́мя от вре́мени; **in ~** (*early enough*) во́-время; (*with ~*) со вре́менем; **in good ~** заблаговре́менно; **in ~ with** в такт +*dat*; **in no ~** момента́льно; **on ~** во́-время; **one at a ~** по одному́; **be in ~** успева́ть *impf*, успе́ть *pf* (**for** к+*dat*, **на**+*acc*); **have ~ to** (*manage*) успева́ть *impf*, успе́ть *pf* +*inf*; **have a good ~** хорошо́ проводи́ть *impf*, провести́ *pf* вре́мя; **it is ~** пора́ (**to** +*inf*); **what is the ~?** кото́рый час?; **~ bomb** бо́мба заме́дленного де́йствия; **~-consuming** отнима́ющий мно́го вре́мени; **~ difference** ра́зница во вре́мени; **~-lag** отстава́ние во вре́мени; **~ zone** часово́й по́яс; *vt* (*choose*) выбира́ть *impf*, вы́брать *pf* вре́мя +*gen*; (*ascertain ~ of*) измеря́ть *impf*, изме́рить *pf* вре́мя +*gen*. **timeless** *adj* ве́чный. **timely** *adj* своевре́менный. **timetable** *n* расписа́ние; гра́фик.

timid *adj* ро́бкий.

tin *n* (*metal*) о́лово; (*container*) ба́нка; (*cake-~*) фо́рма; (*baking ~*) про́тивень *m*; **~ foil** оловя́нная фольга́; **~-opener** консе́рвный нож; **~ned food** консе́рвы (-вов) *pl*.

tinge *n* отте́нок; *vt* (*also fig*) слегка́ окра́шивать *impf*, окра́сить *pf*.

tingle *vi* (*sting*) коло́ть *impf impers*; **my fingers ~** у меня́ ко́лет па́льцы; **his nose ~d with the cold** моро́з пощи́пывал ему́ нос; (*burn*) горе́ть *impf*.

tinker *vi*: **~ with** вози́ться *impf* c+*instr*.

tinkle *n* звон, звя́канье; *vi* (*& t*) звене́ть *impf* (+*instr*).

tinsel *n* мишура́.

tint *n* отте́нок; *vt* подкра́шивать *impf*, подкра́сить *pf*.

tiny *adj* кро́шечный.

tip[1] *n* (*end*) ко́нчик.

tip[2] *n* (*money*) чаевы́е (-ы́х) *pl*; (*advice*) сове́т; (*dump*) сва́лка; *vt & i* (*tilt*) наклоня́ть(ся) *impf*, наклони́ть(ся) *pf*; (*give* ~) дава́ть *impf*, дать *pf* (*person +dat*; *money* де́ньги на чай, *information* ча́стную информа́цию); ~ **out** выва́ливать *impf*, вы́валить *pf*; ~ **over, up** (*vt & i*) опроки́дывать(ся) *impf*, опроки́нуть(ся) *pf*.

Tippex *n* (*propr*) бели́ла.

tipple *n* напи́ток.

tipsy *adj* подвы́пивший.

tiptoe *n*: **on** ~ на цы́почках.

tip-top *adj* превосхо́дный.

tirade *n* тира́да.

tire *vt* (*weary*) утомля́ть *impf*, утоми́ть *pf*; *vi* утомля́ться *impf*, утоми́ться *pf*. **tired** *adj* уста́лый; **be** ~ **of**: **I am** ~ **of him** он мне надое́л; **I am** ~ **of playing** мне надое́ло игра́ть; ~ **out** изму́ченный. **tiredness** *n* уста́лость. **tireless** *adj* неутоми́мый. **tiresome** *adj* надое́дливый. **tiring** *adj* утоми́тельный.

tissue *n* ткань; (*handkerchief*) бума́жная салфе́тка. **tissue-paper** *n* папиро́сная бума́га.

tit[1] *n* (*bird*) сини́ца.

tit[2] *n*: ~ **for tat** зуб за́ зуб.

titbit *n* ла́комый кусо́к; (*news*) пика́нтная но́вость.

titillate *vt* щекота́ть *impf*, по~ *pf*.

title *n* (*of book etc.*) загла́вие; (*rank*) зва́ние; (*sport*) зва́ние чемпио́на; ~**holder** чемпио́н; ~**page** ти́тульный лист; ~ **role** загла́вная роль. **titled** *adj* титуло́ванный.

titter *n* хихи́канье; *vi* хихи́кать *impf*, хихи́кнуть *pf*.

to *prep* (*town, a country, theatre, school, etc.*) в+*acc*; (*the sea, the moon, the ground, post-office, meeting, concert, north, etc.*) на+*acc*; (*the doctor; towards; up* ~; *one's surprise etc.*) к+*dat*; (*with accompaniment of*) под+*acc*; (*in toast*) за+*acc*; (*time*) **ten minutes** ~ **three** без десяти́ три; (*compared with*) в сравне́нии с+*instr*; **it is ten** ~ **one that**

де́вять из десяти́ за то, что; ~ **the left** (*right*) нале́во (напра́во); (*in order to*) чтобы+*inf*; *adv*: **shut the door** ~ закро́йте дверь; **come** ~ приходи́ть *impf*, прийти́ *pf* в созна́ние; ~ **and fro** взад и вперёд.

toad *n* жа́ба. **toadstool** *n* пога́нка.

toast *n* (*bread*) поджа́ренный хлеб; (*drink*) тост; *vt* (*bread*) поджа́ривать *impf*, поджа́рить *pf*; (*drink*) пить *impf*, вы́~ *pf* за здоро́вье +*gen*. **toaster** *n* то́стер.

tobacco *n* таба́к. **tobacconist's** *n* (*shop*) таба́чный магази́н.

toboggan *n* са́ни (-не́й) *pl*; *vi* ката́ться *impf* на саня́х.

today *adv* сего́дня; (*nowadays*) в на́ши дни; *n* сего́дняшний день *m*; ~**'s newspaper** сего́дняшняя газе́та.

toddler *n* малы́ш.

toe *n* па́лец ноги́: (*of sock etc.*) носо́к; *vt*: ~ **the line** (*fig*) ходи́ть *indet* по стру́нке.

toffee *n* (*substance*) ири́с; (*a single* ~) ири́ска.

together *adv* вме́сте; (*simultaneously*) одновре́менно.

toil *n* тяжёлый труд; *vi* труди́ться *impf*.

toilet *n* туале́т; ~ **paper** туале́тная бума́га. **toiletries** *n pl* туале́тные принадле́жности *f pl*.

token *n* (*sign*) знак; (*coin substitute*) жето́н; **as a** ~ **of** в знак +*gen*; *attrib* символи́ческий.

tolerable *adj* терпи́мый; (*satisfactory*) удовлетвори́тельный. **tolerance** *n* терпи́мость. **tolerant** *adj* терпи́мый. **tolerate** *vt* терпе́ть *impf*, по~ *pf*; (*allow*) допуска́ть *impf*, допусти́ть *pf*. **toleration** *n* терпи́мость.

toll[1] *n* (*duty*) по́шлина; **take its** ~ ска́зываться *impf*, сказа́ться *pf* (**on** на+*prep*).

toll[2] *vi* звони́ть *impf*, по~ *pf*.

tom(-cat) *n* кот.

tomato *n* помидо́р; *attrib* тома́тный.

tomb *n* моги́ла. **tombstone** *n* надгро́бный ка́мень *m*.

tomboy *n* сорване́ц.

tome *n* том.

tomorrow *adv* за́втра; *n* за́втрашний день *m*; ~ **morning** за́втра у́тром; **the day after** ~ послеза́втра; **see you**

~ до за́втра.

ton n то́нна; (pl, lots) ма́сса.

tone n тон; vt: ~ **down** смягча́ть impf, смягчи́ть pf; ~ **up** тонизи́ровать impf & pf.

tongs n щипцы́ (-цо́в) pl.

tongue n язы́к; ~-**in-cheek** с насме́шкой, ирони́чески; ~-**tied** косноязы́чный; ~-**twister** скорогово́рка.

tonic n (med) тонизи́рующее сре́дство; (mus) то́ника; (drink) напи́ток «то́ник».

tonight adv сего́дня ве́чером.

tonnage n тонна́ж.

tonsil n минда́лина. **tonsillitis** n тонзилли́т.

too adv сли́шком; (also) та́кже, то́же; (very) о́чень; (moreover) к тому́ же; **none** ~ не сли́шком.

tool n инструме́нт; (fig) ору́дие.

toot n гудо́к; vi гуде́ть impf.

tooth n зуб; (tech) зубе́ц; attrib зубно́й; ~-**brush** зубна́я щётка. **toothache** n зубна́я боль. **toothless** adj беззу́бый. **toothpaste** n зубна́я па́ста. **toothpick** n зубочи́стка. **toothy** adj зуба́стый (coll).

top[1] n (toy) волчо́к.

top[2] n (of object; fig) верх; (of hill etc.) верши́на; (of tree) верху́шка; (of head) маку́шка; (lid) кры́шка; (upper part) ве́рхняя часть; ~ **hat** цили́ндр; ~-**heavy** переве́шивающий в свое́й ве́рхней ча́сти; ~-**secret** соверше́нно секре́тный; on ~ **of** (position) на+prep, сверх+gen; (on to) на+acc; on ~ **of everything** сверх всего́; from ~ **to bottom** све́рху до́низу; **at the** ~ **of one's voice** во весь го́лос; **at** ~ **speed** во весь опо́р; (foremost) са́мый высо́кий; (foremost) пе́рвый; vt (cover) покрыва́ть impf, покры́ть pf; (exceed) превосходи́ть impf, превзойти́ pf; (cut ~ off) обреза́ть impf, обре́зать pf верху́шку +gen; ~ **up** (with liquid) долива́ть impf, доли́ть pf.

topic n те́ма, предме́т. **topical** adj актуа́льный.

topless adj с обнажённой гру́дью.

topmost adj са́мый ве́рхний; са́мый ва́жный.

topographical adj топографи́че-

ский. **topography** n топогра́фия.

topple vt & i опроки́дывать(ся) impf, опроки́нуть(ся) pf.

topsy-turvy adj повёрнутый вверх дном; (disorderly) беспоря́дочный; adv вверх дном.

torch n электри́ческий фона́рь m; (flaming) фа́кел.

torment n муче́ние, му́ка; vt му́чить impf, за~, из~ pf.

tornado n торна́до neut indecl.

torpedo n торпе́да; vt торпеди́ровать impf & pf.

torrent n пото́к. **torrential** adj (rain) проливно́й.

torso n ту́ловище; (art) торс.

tortoise n черепа́ха. **tortoise-shell** n черепа́ха.

tortuous adj изви́листый.

torture n пы́тка; (fig) му́ка; vt пыта́ть impf; (torment) му́чить impf, за~, из~ pf.

toss n бросо́к; **win (lose) the** ~ (не) выпада́ть impf, вы́пасть pf жре́бий impers (**I won the** ~ мне вы́пал жре́бий); vt броса́ть impf, бро́сить pf; (coin) подбра́сывать impf, подбро́сить pf; (head) вски́дывать impf, вски́нуть pf; (salad) переме́шивать impf, перемеша́ть pf; vi (in bed) мета́ться impf; ~ **aside, away** отбра́сывать impf, отбро́сить pf; ~ **up** броса́ть impf, бро́сить pf жре́бий.

tot[1] n (child) малы́ш; (of liquor) глото́к.

tot[2]: ~ **up** (vt) скла́дывать impf, сложи́ть pf; (vi) равня́ться impf (**to** +dat).

total n ито́г, су́мма; adj о́бщий; (complete) по́лный; **in** ~ в це́лом, вме́сте; vt подсчи́тывать impf, подсчита́ть pf; vi равня́ться impf +dat. **totalitarian** adj тоталита́рный. **totality** n вся су́мма целико́м; **the** ~ **of** весь. **totally** adv соверше́нно.

totter vi шата́ться impf.

touch n прикоснове́ние; (sense) осяза́ние; (shade) отте́нок; (taste) при́вкус; (small amount) чу́точка; (of illness) лёгкий при́ступ; **get in** ~ **with** свя́зываться impf, связа́ться pf c+instr; **keep in (lose)** ~ **with** подде́рживать impf, поддержа́ть pf (теря́ть impf, по~ pf) связь, конта́кт c+instr; **put the finishing**

~es to отде́лывать *impf*, отде́лать *pf*; *vt* (*lightly*) прикаса́ться *impf*, прикосну́ться *pf* к+*dat*; каса́ться *impf*, косну́ться *pf* +*gen*; (*also disturb*; *affect*) тро́гать *impf*, тро́нуть *pf*; (*be comparable with*) идти́ *impf* в сравне́нии с+*instr*; *vi* (*be contiguous*; *come into contact*) соприкаса́ться *impf*, соприкосну́ться *pf*; ~ **down** приземля́ться *impf*, приземли́ться *pf*; ~**down** поса́дка; ~ **(up)on** (*fig*) каса́ться *impf*, косну́ться *pf* +*gen*; ~ **up** поправля́ть *impf*, попра́вить *pf*. **touched** *adj* тро́нутый. **touchiness** *n* оби́дчивость. **touching** *adj* тро́гательный. **touchstone** *n* про́бный ка́мень *m*. **touchy** *adj* оби́дчивый.

tough *adj* жёсткий; (*durable*) про́чный; (*difficult*) тру́дный; (*hardy*) выно́сливый. **toughen** *vt* & *i* де́лать(ся) *impf*, с~ *pf* жёстким.

tour *n* (*journey*) путеше́ствие, пое́здка; (*excursion*) экску́рсия; (*of artistes*) гастро́ли *f pl*; (*of duty*) объе́зд; *vi* (& *t*) путеше́ствовать *impf* (по+*dat*); (*theat*) гастроли́ровать *impf*. **tourism** *n* тури́зм. **tourist** *n* тури́ст, ~ка.

tournament *n* турни́р.

tousle *vt* взъеро́шивать *impf*, взъеро́шить *pf* (*coll*).

tout *n* зазыва́ла *m*; (*ticket* ~) жучо́к.

tow *vt* букси́ровать *impf*; *n*: **on** ~ на букси́ре.

towards *prep* к+*dat*.

towel *n* полоте́нце.

tower *n* ба́шня; *vi* вы́ситься *impf*, возвыша́ться *impf* (**above** над+*instr*).

town *n* го́род; *attrib* городско́й; ~ **hall** ра́туша. **townsman** *n* горожа́нин.

toxic *adj* токси́ческий.

toy *n* игру́шка; *vi*: ~ **with** (*sth in hands*) верте́ть *impf* в рука́х; (*trifle with*) игра́ть *impf* (с)+*instr*.

trace *n* след; *vt* (*track* (*down*)) высле́живать *impf*, вы́следить *pf*; (*copy*) кальки́ровать *impf*, с~ *pf*; ~ **out** (*plan*) набра́сывать *impf*, наброса́ть *pf*; (*map, diagram*) черти́ть *impf*, на~ *pf*.

tracing-paper *n* ка́лька.

track *n* (*path*) доро́жка; (*mark*) след; (*rly*) путь *m*, (*sport, on tape*) доро́ж-

ка; (*on record*) за́пись; ~ **suit** трениро́вочный костю́м; **off the beaten** ~ в глуши́; **go off the** ~ (*fig*) отклоня́ться *impf*, отклони́ться *pf* от те́мы; **keep** ~ **of** следи́ть *impf* за +*instr*; **lose** ~ **of** теря́ть *impf*, по~ *pf* след+*gen*; *vt* просле́живать *impf*, проследи́ть *pf*; ~ **down** высле́живать *impf*, вы́следить *pf*.

tract[1] *n* (*land*) простра́нство.

tract[2] *n* (*pamphlet*) брошю́ра.

tractor *n* тра́ктор.

trade *n* торго́вля; (*occupation*) профе́ссия, ремесло́; ~ **mark** фабри́чная ма́рка; ~ **union** профсою́з; ~**unionist** член профсою́за; *vi* торгова́ть *impf* (**in** +*instr*); *vt* (*swap like things*) обме́ниваться *impf*, обменя́ться *pf* +*instr*; (~ **for sth different**) обме́нивать *impf*, обменя́ть *pf* (**for** на+*acc*); ~ **in** сдава́ть *impf*, сдать *pf* в счёт поку́пки но́вого. **trader, tradesman** *n* торго́вец. **trading** *n* торго́вля.

tradition *n* тради́ция. **traditional** *adj* традицио́нный. **traditionally** *adv* по тради́ции.

traffic *n* движе́ние; (*trade*) торго́вля; ~ **jam** про́бка; *vi* торгова́ть *impf* (**in** +*instr*). **trafficker** *n* торго́вец (**in** +*instr*). **traffic-lights** *n pl* светофо́р.

tragedy *n* траге́дия. **tragic** *adj* траги́ческий.

trail *n* (*trace, track*) след; (*path*) тропи́нка; *vt* (*track*) высле́живать *impf*, вы́следить *pf*; *vt* & *i* (*drag*) таска́ть(ся) *indet*, тащи́ть(ся) *det*. **trailer** *n* (*on vehicle*) прице́п; (*cin*) (кино)-ро́лик.

train *n* по́езд; (*of dress*) шлейф; *vt* (*instruct*) обуча́ть *impf*, обучи́ть *pf* (**in** +*dat*); (*prepare*) гото́вить *impf* (**for** к+*dat*); (*sport*) трениро́вать *impf*, на~ *pf*; (*animals*) дрессирова́ть *impf*, вы́~ *pf*; (*aim*) наводи́ть *impf*, навести́ *pf*; (*plant*) направля́ть *impf*, напра́вить *pf* рост+*gen*; *vi* приготавливаться *impf*, пригото́виться *pf* (**for** к+*dat*); (*sport*) трениро́ваться *impf*, на~ *pf*. **trainee** *n* стажёр, практика́нт. **trainer** *n* (*sport*) тре́нер; (*of animals*) дрессиро́вщик; (*shoe*) кроссо́вка. **training** *n* обуче́ние; (*sport*) трениро́вка; (*of animals*) дрессиро́вка; ~-**college** (*teachers'*) педагоги́ческий институ́т.

traipse vi таска́ться indet, тащи́ться det.

trait n черта́.

traitor n преда́тель m, ~ница.

trajectory n траекто́рия.

tram n трамва́й.

tramp n (vagrant) бродя́га m; vi (walk heavily) то́пать impf. **trample** vt топта́ть impf, по~, ис~ pf; ~ down выта́птывать impf, вы́топтать pf; ~ on (fig) попира́ть impf, попра́ть pf.

trampoline n бату́т.

trance n транс.

tranquil adj споко́йный. **tranquillity** n споко́йствие. **tranquillize** vt успока́ивать impf, успоко́ить pf. **tranquillizer** n транквилиза́тор.

transact vt (business) вести́ impf; (a deal) заключа́ть impf, заключи́ть pf. **transaction** n де́ло, сде́лка; pl (publications) труды́ m pl.

transatlantic adj трансатланти́ческий.

transcend vt превосходи́ть impf, превзойти́ pf. **transcendental** adj (philos.) трансцендента́льный.

transcribe vt (copy out) перепи́сывать impf, переписа́ть pf. **transcript** n ко́пия. **transcription** n (copy) ко́пия.

transfer n (of objects) перено́с, переме́щение; (of money; of people) перево́д; (of property) переда́ча; (design) переводна́я карти́нка; vt (objects) переноси́ть impf, перенести́ pf; перемеща́ть impf, перемести́ть pf; (money; people; design) переводи́ть impf, перевести́ pf; (property) передава́ть impf, переда́ть pf; vi (to different job) переходи́ть impf, перейти́ pf; (change trains etc.) переса́живаться impf, пересе́сть pf. **transferable** adj допуска́ющий переда́чу.

transfix vt (fig) прико́вывать impf, прикова́ть pf к ме́сту.

transform vt & i преобразо́вывать(ся) impf, преобразова́ть(ся) pf; ~ into vt & i превраща́ть(ся) impf, преврати́ть(ся) pf в+acc. **transformation** n преобразова́ние; превраще́ние. **transformer** n трансформа́тор.

transfusion n перелива́ние (кро́ви).

transgress vt наруша́ть impf, нару́шить pf; vi (sin) греши́ть impf, за~ pf. **transgression** n наруше́ние; (sin) грех.

transience n мимолётность. **transient** adj мимолётный.

transistor n транзи́стор; ~ radio транзи́сторный приёмник.

transit n транзи́т; in ~ (goods) при перево́зке; (person) по пути́; ~ camp транзи́тный ла́герь m. **transition** n перехо́д. **transitional** adj перехо́дный. **transitive** adj перехо́дный. **transitory** adj мимолётный.

translate vt переводи́ть impf, перевести́ pf. **translation** n перево́д. **translator** n перево́дчик.

translucent adj полупрозра́чный.

transmission n переда́ча. **transmit** vt передава́ть impf, переда́ть pf. **transmitter** n (радио)переда́тчик.

transparency n (phot) диапозити́в. **transparent** adj прозра́чный.

transpire vi (become known) обнару́живаться impf, обнару́житься pf; (occur) случа́ться impf, случи́ться pf.

transplant vt переса́живать impf, пересади́ть pf; (med) де́лать impf, с~ pf переса́дку+gen; n (med) переса́дка.

transport n (various senses) тра́нспорт; (conveyance) перево́зка; attrib тра́нспортный; vt перевози́ть impf, перевезти́ pf. **transportation** n тра́нспорт, перево́зка.

transpose vt переставля́ть impf, переста́вить pf; (mus) транспони́ровать impf & pf. **transposition** n переста́новка; (mus) транспони́ро́вка.

transverse adj попере́чный.

transvestite n трансвести́т.

trap n ловушка (also fig), западня́; vt (catch) лови́ть impf, пойма́ть pf (в лову́шку); (jam) защемля́ть impf, защеми́ть pf. **trapdoor** n люк.

trapeze n трапе́ция.

trapper n звероло́в.

trappings n pl (fig) (exterior attributes) вне́шние атрибу́ты m pl; (adornments) украше́ния neut pl.

trash n дрянь (coll). **trashy** adj дрянно́й.

trauma n тра́вма. **traumatic** adj травмати́ческий.

travel n путеше́ствие; ~ **agency** бюро́ neut indecl путеше́ствий; ~ **sick: be** ~**-sick** ука́чивать impf; укача́ть pf impers +acc; **I am** ~**-sick in cars** меня́ в маши́не ука́чивает; vi путеше́ствовать impf; vt объезжа́ть impf, объе́хать pf. **traveller** n путеше́ственник; (salesman) коммивояжёр; ~**'s cheque** тури́стский чек.

traverse vt пересека́ть impf, пересе́чь pf.

travesty n паро́дия.

trawler n тра́улер.

tray n подно́с; **in-** (**out-**)~ корзи́нка для входя́щих (исходя́щих) бума́г.

treacherous adj преда́тельский; (unsafe) ненадёжный. **treachery** n преда́тельство.

treacle n па́тока.

tread n похо́дка; (stair) ступе́нька; (of tyre) проте́ктор; vi ступа́ть impf, ступи́ть pf; ~ **on** наступа́ть impf, наступи́ть pf на+acc; vt топта́ть impf.

treason n изме́на.

treasure n сокро́вище; vt высоко́ цени́ть impf. **treasurer** n казначе́й. **treasury** n (also fig) сокро́вищница; **the T~** госуда́рственное казначе́йство.

treat n (pleasure) удово́льствие; (entertainment) угоще́ние; vt (have as guest) угоща́ть impf, угости́ть pf (to +instr); (med) лечи́ть impf (for от +gen; with +instr); (behave towards) обраща́ться impf с+instr; (process) обраба́тывать impf, обрабо́тать pf (with +instr); (discuss) трактова́ть impf о+prep; (regard) относи́ться impf, отнести́сь pf к+dat (as как к+dat). **treatise** n тракта́т. **treatment** n (behaviour) обраще́ние; (med) лече́ние; (processing) обрабо́тка; (discussion) тракто́вка. **treaty** n догово́р.

treble adj тройно́й; (trebled) утро́енный; adv втро́е; n (mus) дискáнт; vt & i утра́ивать(ся) impf, утро́ить(ся) pf.

tree n де́рево.

trek n (migration) переселе́ние; (journey) путеше́ствие; vi (migrate) переселя́ться impf, пересели́ться pf;

(journey) путеше́ствовать impf.

trellis n шпале́ра; (for creepers) решётка.

tremble vi дрожа́ть impf (with от +gen). **trembling** n дрожь; **in fear and** ~ трепеща́.

tremendous adj (huge) огро́мный; (excellent) потряса́ющий.

tremor n дрожь; (earthquake) толчо́к. **tremulous** adj дрожа́щий.

trench n кана́ва, ров; (mil) око́п.

trend n направле́ние, тенде́нция. **trendy** adj мо́дный.

trepidation n тре́пет.

trespass n (on property) наруше́ние грани́ц; vi наруша́ть impf, нару-ши́ть pf грани́цу (on +gen); (fig) вторга́ться impf, вто́ргнуться pf (on в+acc). **trespasser** n наруши́тель m.

trestle n ко́злы (-зел, -злам) pl; ~ **table** стол на ко́злах.

trial n (test) испыта́ние (also ordeal), про́ба; (law) проце́сс, суд; (sport) попы́тка; **on** ~ (probation) на испыта́нии; (of objects) взя́тый на про́бу; (law) под судо́м; ~ **and error** ме́тод проб и оши́бок.

triangle n треуго́льник. **triangular** adj треуго́льный.

tribal adj племенно́й. **tribe** n пле́мя neut.

tribulation n го́ре, несча́стье.

tribunal n трибуна́л.

tributary n прито́к. **tribute** n дань; **pay** ~ (fig) отдава́ть impf, отда́ть pf дань (уваже́ния) (to +dat).

trice n: **in a** ~ мгнове́нно.

trick n (ruse) хи́трость; (deception) обма́н; (conjuring ~) фо́кус; (stunt) трюк; (joke) шу́тка; (habit) привы́чка; (cards) взя́тка; **play a** ~ **on** игра́ть impf, сыгра́ть pf шу́тку с +instr; vt обма́нывать impf, обману́ть pf. **trickery** n обма́н.

trickle vi сочи́ться impf.

trickster n обма́нщик. **tricky** adj сло́жный.

tricycle n трёхколёсный велосипе́д.

trifle n пустя́к; a ~ (adv) немно́го +gen; vi шути́ть impf, по- (with с+instr). **trifling** adj пустяко́вый.

trigger n (of gun) куро́к; vt: ~ **off** вызыва́ть impf, вы́звать pf.

trill n трель.

trilogy n трило́гия.

trim n поря́док, гото́вность; **in fighting** ~ в боево́й гото́вности; **in good** ~ (sport) в хоро́шей фо́рме; (haircut) подстри́жка; adj опря́тный; vt (cut, clip, cut off) подреза́ть impf, подре́зать pf; (hair) подстрига́ть impf, подстри́чь pf; (a dress etc.) отде́лывать impf, отде́лать pf. **trimming** n (on dress) отде́лка; (to food) гарни́р.

Trinity n Тро́ица.

trinket n безделу́шка.

trio n три́о neut indecl; (of people) тро́йка.

trip n пое́здка, путеше́ствие, экску́рсия; (business ~) командиро́вка; vi (stumble) спотыка́ться impf, споткну́ться pf (over o+acc); vt (also ~ up) подставля́ть impf, подста́вить pf но́жку +dat (also fig); (confuse) запу́тывать impf, запу́тать pf.

triple adj тройно́й; (tripled) утро́енный; vt & i утра́ивать(ся) impf, утро́ить(ся) pf. **triplet** n (mus) трио́ль; (one of ~s) близне́ц (из тро́йни); pl тро́йня.

tripod n трено́жник.

trite adj бана́льный.

triumph n торжество́, побе́да; vi торжествова́ть impf, вос~ pf (over над+instr). **triumphal** adj триумфа́льный. **triumphant** adj (exultant) торжеству́ющий; (victorious) победоно́сный.

trivia n pl ме́лочи (-че́й) pl. **trivial** adj незначи́тельный. **triviality** n тривиа́льность. **trivialize** vt опошля́ть impf, опо́шлить pf.

trolley n теле́жка; (table on wheels) сто́лик на колёсиках. **trolley-bus** n тролле́йбус.

trombone n тромбо́н.

troop n гру́ппа, отря́д; pl (mil) войска́ neut pl; vi идти́ impf, по~ pf стро́ем.

trophy n трофе́й; (prize) приз.

tropic n тро́пик. **tropical** adj тропи́ческий.

trot n рысь; vi рыси́ть impf; (rider) е́здить indet, е́хать det, по~ pf ры́сью; (horse) ходи́ть indet, идти́ det, пойти́ pf ры́сью.

trouble n (worry) беспоко́йство, трево́га; (misfortune) беда́; (unpleasantness) неприя́тности f pl; (effort, pains) труд; (care) забо́та; (disrepair) неиспра́вность (with в+prep); (illness) боле́знь; **heart** ~ больно́е се́рдце; ~**maker** наруши́тель m, ~ница споко́йствия; **ask for** ~ напра́шиваться impf, напроси́ться pf на неприя́тности; **be in** ~ име́ть impf неприя́тности; **get into** ~ попа́сть pf в беду́; **take** ~ стара́ться impf, по~ pf (to +inf); **take the** ~ труди́ться impf, по~ pf (to +inf); **the** ~ **is (that)** беда́ в том, что; vt (make anxious, disturb, give pain) беспоко́ить impf; **may I** ~ **you for ...?** мо́жно попроси́ть у вас +acc?; vi (take the ~) труди́ться impf. **troubled** adj беспоко́йный. **troublesome** adj (restless, fidgety) беспоко́йный; (capricious) капри́зный; (difficult) тру́дный.

trough n (for food) корму́шка.

trounce vt (beat) поро́ть impf, вы́~ pf; (defeat) разбива́ть impf, разби́ть pf.

troupe n тру́ппа.

trouser-leg n штани́на (coll). **trousers** n pl брю́ки (-к) pl, штаны́ (-но́в) pl.

trout n форе́ль.

trowel n (for building) мастеро́к; (garden ~) садо́вый сово́к.

truancy n прогу́л. **truant** n прогу́льщик; **play** ~ прогу́ливать impf, прогуля́ть pf.

truce n переми́рие.

truck[1] n: **have no** ~ **with** не име́ть impf никаки́х дел с+instr.

truck[2] n (lorry) грузови́к; (rly) ваго́н-платфо́рма.

truculent adj свире́пый.

trudge vi уста́ло тащи́ться impf.

true adj (faithful, correct) ве́рный; (correct) пра́вильный; (story) правди́вый; (real) настоя́щий; **come** ~ сбыва́ться impf, сбы́ться pf.

truism n трюи́зм. **truly** adv (sincerely) и́скренне; (really, indeed) действи́тельно; **yours** ~ пре́данный Вам.

trump n ко́зырь m; vt бить impf, по~ pf ко́зырем; ~ **up** фабрикова́ть impf, с~ pf.

trumpet n труба́; vt (proclaim) труби́ть impf o+prep. **trumpeter** n труба́ч.

truncate vt усека́ть impf, усе́чь pf.

truncheon n дуби́нка.

trundle vt & i ката́ть(ся) indet, кати́ть(ся) det, по~ pf.

trunk n (stem) ствол; (anat) ту́ловище; (elephant's) хо́бот; (box) сунду́к; pl (swimming) пла́вки (-вок) pl; (boxing etc.) трусы́ (-со́в) pl; ~ **call** вы́зов по междугоро́дному телефо́ну; ~ **road** магистра́льная доро́га.

truss n (girder) фе́рма; (med) грыжево́й банда́ж; vt (tie (up), bird) свя́зывать impf, связа́ть pf; (reinforce) укрепля́ть impf, укрепи́ть pf.

trust n дове́рие; (body of trustees) опе́ка; (property held in ~) дове́рительная со́бственность; (econ) трест; **take on** ~ принима́ть impf, приня́ть pf на ве́ру; vt доверя́ть impf, дове́рить pf +dat (with +acc; to +inf); vi (hope) наде́яться impf, по~ pf. **trustee** n опеку́н. **trustful, trusting** adj дове́рчивый. **trustworthy, trusty** adj надёжный, ве́рный.

truth n пра́вда; **tell the** ~ говори́ть impf, сказа́ть pf пра́вду: **to tell you the** ~ по пра́вде говоря́. **truthful** adj правди́вый.

try n (attempt) попы́тка; (test, trial) испыта́ние, про́ба; vt (taste; sample) про́бовать impf, по~ pf; (patience) испы́тывать impf, испыта́ть pf; (law) суди́ть impf (for за+acc); vi (endeavour) стара́ться impf, по~ pf; ~ **on** (clothes) примеря́ть impf, приме́рить pf. **trying** adj тру́дный.

tsar n царь m. **tsarina** n цари́ца.

tub n ка́дка; (bath) ва́нна; (of margarine etc.) упако́вка.

tubby adj то́лстенький.

tube n тру́бка, труба́; (toothpaste etc.) тю́бик; (underground) метро́ neut indecl.

tuber n клу́бень m. **tuberculosis** n туберкулёз.

tubing n тру́бы m pl. **tubular** adj тру́бчатый.

tuck n (in garment) скла́дка; vt (thrust into, ~ away) засо́вывать impf, засу́нуть pf; (hide away) пря́тать impf, с~ pf; ~ **in** (shirt etc.) заправля́ть impf, запра́вить pf; ~ **in, up** (blanket, skirt) подтыка́ть impf, подоткну́ть pf; ~ **up** (sleeves) засу́чивать impf, засучи́ть pf; (in bed) укры-

ва́ть impf, укры́ть pf.

Tuesday n вто́рник.

tuft n пучо́к.

tug vt тяну́ть impf, по~ pf; vi (sharply) дёргать impf, дёрнуть pf (at за+acc); n рыво́к; (tugboat) букси́р.

tuition n обуче́ние (in +dat).

tulip n тюльпа́н.

tumble vi (fall) па́дать impf, (у)па́сть pf; n паде́ние. **tumbledown** adj полуразру́шенный. **tumbler** n стака́н.

tumour n о́пухоль.

tumult n (uproar) сумато́ха; (agitation) волне́ние. **tumultuous** adj шу́мный.

tuna n туне́ц.

tundra n ту́ндра.

tune n мело́дия; **in** ~ в тон, (of instrument) настро́енный; **out of** ~ не в тон, фальши́вый, (of instrument) расстро́енный; **change one's** ~ (пере)меня́ть impf, перемени́ть pf тон; vt (instrument; radio) настра́ивать impf, настро́ить pf; (engine etc.) регули́ровать impf, от~ pf; ~ **in** настра́ивать impf, настро́ить pf (radio) ра́дио (to на+acc); vi: ~ **up** настра́ивать impf, настро́ить pf инструме́нт(ы). **tuneful** adj мелоди́чный. **tuner** n (mus) настро́йщик; (receiver) приёмник.

tunic n туни́ка; (of uniform) ки́тель m.

tuning n настро́йка; (of engine) регулиро́вка; ~-**fork** камерто́н.

tunnel n тунне́ль m; vi прокла́дывать impf, проложи́ть pf тунне́ль m.

turban n тюрба́н.

turbine n турби́на.

turbulence n бу́рность; (aeron) турбуле́нтность. **turbulent** adj бу́рный.

tureen n су́пник.

turf n дёрн.

turgid adj (pompous) напы́щенный.

Turk n ту́рок, турча́нка. **Turkey** n Ту́рция.

turkey n индю́к, f инде́йка; (dish) индю́шка.

Turkish adj туре́цкий. **Turkmenistan** n Туркмениста́н.

turmoil n (disorder) беспоря́док; (uproar) сумато́ха.

turn n (change of direction) поворо́т;

(*revolution*) оборо́т; (*service*) услу́-
га; (*change*) измене́ние; (*one's* ~ *to
do sth*) о́чередь; (*theat*) но́мер; ~ **of
phrase** оборо́т ре́чи; **at every** ~ на
ка́ждом шагу́; **by**, **in turn(s)** по
о́череди; *vt* (*handle, key, car around,
etc*.) повора́чивать *impf*, поверну́ть
pf; (*revolve, rotate*) враща́ть *impf*;
(*page; on its face*) перевёртывать
impf, переверну́ть *pf*; (*direct*) на-
правля́ть *impf*, напра́вить *pf*; (*cause
to become*) де́лать *impf*, с~ *pf* +*instr*;
(*on lathe*) точи́ть *impf*; *vi* (*change
direction*) повора́чивать *impf*, повер-
ну́ть *pf* (*rotate*) враща́ть *impf*; (~
round) повора́чиваться *impf*, повер-
ну́ться *pf*; (*become*) станови́ться
impf, стать *pf* +*instr*; ~ **against**
ополча́ть *impf*, ополчи́ться *pf* на
+*acc*, про́тив+*gen*; ~ **around** *see* ~
round; ~ **away** (*vt & i*) отвора́чи-
вать(ся) *impf*, отверну́ть(ся) *pf*;
(*refuse admittance*) прогоня́ть *impf*,
прогна́ть *pf*; ~ **back** (*vi*) повора́-
чивать *impf*, поверну́ть *pf* наза́д;
(*vt*) (*bend back*) отгиба́ть *impf*, ото-
гну́ть *pf*; ~ **down** (*refuse*) отклоня́ть
impf, отклони́ть *pf*; (*collar*) отгиба́ть
impf, отогну́ть *pf*; (*make quieter*)
де́лать *impf*, с~ *pf* ти́ше; ~ **grey** (*vi*)
седе́ть *impf*, по~ *pf*; ~ **in** (*so as to
face inwards*) повора́чивать *impf*,
поверну́ть *pf* внутрь; ~ **inside out**
вывора́чивать *impf*, вы́вернуть *pf*
наизна́нку; ~ **into** (*change into*) (*vt
& i*) превраща́ть(ся) *impf*, пре-
врати́ть(ся) *pf* в+*acc*; (*street*)
свора́чивать *impf*, сверну́ть *pf* на
+*acc*; ~ **off** (*light, radio etc*.) вы-
ключа́ть *impf*, вы́ключить *pf*; (*vi*)
(*branch off*) свора́чивать *impf*,
сверну́ть *pf*; ~ **on** (*light, radio etc*.)
включа́ть *impf*, включи́ть *pf*; (*tap*)
открыва́ть *impf*, откры́ть *pf*; (*attack*) напада́ть *impf*, напа́сть *pf* на
+*acc*; ~ **out** (*light etc*.): *see* ~ **off**;
(*prove to be*) ока́зываться *impf*,
оказа́ться *pf* (**to be** +*instr*); (*drive
out*) выгоня́ть *impf*, вы́гнать *pf*;
(*pockets*) вывёртывать *impf*, вы́-
вернуть *pf*; (*be present*) приходи́ть
impf, прийти́ *pf*; (*product*) выпу-
ска́ть *impf*, вы́пустить *pf*; ~ **over**
(*page, on its face, roll over*) (*vt & i*)

перевёртывать(ся) *impf*, переверт-
ну́ть(ся) *pf*; (*hand over*) передава́ть
impf, переда́ть *pf*; (*think about*)
обду́мывать *impf*, обду́мать *pf*;
(*overturn*) (*vt & i*) опроки́дывать-
(ся) *impf*, опроки́нуть(ся) *pf*; ~ **pale**
бледне́ть *impf*, по~ *pf*; ~ **red**
красне́ть *impf*, по~ *pf*; ~ **round** (*vi*)
(*rotate*) повёртываться *impf*, повер-
ну́ться *pf*; (~ *one's back*; ~ *to face sth*)
повёртываться *impf*, поверну́ться
pf; (~ *to face*) обора́чиваться *impf*,
оберну́ться *pf*; (*vt*) повёртывать
impf, поверну́ть *pf*; ~ **sour** скиса́ть
impf, ски́снуть *pf*; ~ **to** обраща́ться
impf, обрати́ться *pf* к+*dat* (**for a**
+*instr*); ~ **up** (*appear*) появля́ться
impf, появи́ться *pf*; (*be found*) на-
ходи́ться *impf*, найти́сь *pf*; (*shorten
garment*) подшива́ть *impf*, подши́ть
pf; (*crop up*) подвёртываться *impf*,
подверну́ться *pf*; (*bend up; stick up*)
(*vt & i*) загиба́ть(ся) *impf*, загну́ть-
(ся) *pf*; (*make louder*) де́лать *impf*,
с~ *pf* гро́мче; ~ **up one's nose** во-
роти́ть *impf* нос (**at** от+*gen*) (*coll*);
~ **upside down** перевора́чивать
impf, переверну́ть *pf* вверх дном.
turn-out *n* коли́чество приходя́щих.
turn-up *n* (*on trousers*) обшла́г.

turner *n* то́карь *m*.
turning *n* (*road*) поворо́т. **turning-
point** *n* поворо́тный пункт.
turnip *n* ре́па.
turnover *n* (*econ*) оборо́т; (*of staff*)
теку́честь рабо́чей си́лы.
turnpike *n* доро́жная заста́ва.
turnstile *n* турнике́т.
turntable *n* (*rly*) поворо́тный круг;
(*gramophone*) диск.
turpentine *n* скипида́р.
turquoise *n* (*material, stone*) бирюза́;
adj бирюзо́вый.
turret *n* ба́шенка.
turtle *n* черепа́ха.
turtle-dove *n* го́рлица.
tusk *n* би́вень *m*, клык.
tussle *n* дра́ка; *vi* дра́ться *impf* (**for**
за+*acc*).
tutor *n* (*private teacher*) ча́стный до-
ма́шний учи́тель *m*, ~ница; (*univ*)
преподава́тель *m*, ~ница; (*primer*)
уче́бник; *vt* (*instruct*) обуча́ть *impf*,
обучи́ть *pf* (**in** +*dat*); (*give lessons
to*) дава́ть *impf*, дать *pf* уро́ки+*dat*;
(*guide*) руководи́ть *impf* +*instr*.

tutorial *n* консультáция.

tutu *n* (*ballet*) пáчка.

TV *abbr* (*of* **television**) ТВ, телеви́дение; (*set*) телеви́зор.

twang *n* (*of string*) рéзкий звук (натя́нутой струны); (*voice*) гнусáвый гóлос.

tweak *n* щипóк; *vt* щипáть *impf*, (у)щипнýть *pf*.

tweed *n* твид.

tweezers *n pl* пинцéт.

twelfth *adj & n* двенáдцатый. **twelve** *adj & n* двенáдцать.

twentieth *adj & n* двадцáтый. **twenty** *adj & n* двáдцать; *pl* (*decade*) двадцáтые гóды (-дóв) *m pl*.

twice *adv* двáжды; ~ **as** вдвóе, в два рáза +*comp*.

twiddle *vt* (*turn*) вертéть *impf* +*acc*, *instr*; (*toy with*) игрáть *impf* +*instr*; ~ **one's thumbs** (*fig*) бездéльничать *impf*.

twig *n* вéточка, прут.

twilight *n* сýмерки (-рек) *pl*.

twin *n* близнéц; *pl* (*Gemini*) Близнецы́ *m pl*; ~ **beds** пáра односпáльных кровáтей; ~ **brother** брат-близнéц; ~ **town** гóрод-побратúм.

twine *n* бечёвка, шпагáт; *vt* (*twist*, *weave*) вить *impf*, с~ *pf*; *vt & i* (~ *round*) обвивáть(ся) *impf*, обви́ть(ся) *pf*.

twinge *n* при́ступ (бóли); (*of conscience*) угрызéние.

twinkle *n* мерцáние; (*of eyes*) огонёк; *vi* мерцáть *impf*, сверкáть *impf*. **twinkling** *n* мерцáние; **in the** ~ **of an eye** в мгновéние óка.

twirl *vt & i* (*twist, turn*) вертéть(ся) *impf*; (*whirl, spin*) кружи́ть(ся) *impf*.

twist *n* (*bend*) изги́б, поворóт; (~*ing*) кручéние; (*in story*) поворóт фáбулы; *vt* скру́чивать *impf*, крути́ть *impf*, с~ *pf*; (*distort*) искажáть *impf*, искази́ть *pf*; (*sprain*) подвёртывать *impf*, подвернýть *pf*; *vi* (*climb*, *meander, twine*) ви́ться *impf*. **twisted** *adj* искривлённый (*also fig*).

twit *n* дурáк.

twitch *n* подёргивание; *vt & i* дёргать(ся) *impf*, дёрнуть(ся) *pf* (**at** за +*acc*).

twitter *n* щéбет; *vi* щебетáть *impf*, чири́кать *impf*.

two *adj & n* два, две (*f*); (*collect; 2*

pairs) двóе; (*number 2*) двóйка; **in** ~ (*in half*) нáдвое, пополáм; ~**seater** двухмéстный (автомоби́ль); ~**way** двустóронний. **twofold** *adj* двойнóй; *adv* вдвóйне. **twosome** *n* пáра.

tycoon *n* магнáт.

type *n* тип, род; (*printing*) шрифт; *vt* писáть *impf*, на~ *pf* на маши́нке. **typescript** *n* маши́нопись. **typewriter** *n* пи́шущая маши́нка. **typewritten** *adj* маши́нопи́сный.

typhoid *n* брюшнóй тиф.

typical *adj* типи́чный. **typify** *vt* служи́ть *impf*, по~ *pf* типи́чным примéром +*gen*.

typist *n* машини́стка.

typography *n* книгопечáтание; (*style*) оформлéние.

tyrannical *adj* тирани́ческий. **tyrant** *n* тирáн.

tyre *n* ши́на.

U

ubiquitous *adj* вездесýщий.

udder *n* вы́мя *neut*.

UFO *abbr* (*of* **unidentified flying object**) НЛО, неопóзнанный летáющий объéкт.

ugh *int* тьфу!

ugliness *n* урóдство. **ugly** *adj* некраси́вый, урóдливый; (*unpleasant*) неприя́тный.

UK *abbr* (*of* **United Kingdom**) Соединённое Королéвство.

Ukraine *n* Украи́на. **Ukrainian** *n* украи́нец, -нка; *adj* украи́нский.

ulcer *n* я́зва.

ulterior *adj* скры́тый.

ultimate *adj* (*final*) послéдний, окончáтельный; (*purpose*) конéчный. **ultimately** *adv* в конéчном счёте, в концé концóв. **ultimatum** *n* ультимáтум.

ultrasound *n* ультразвýк. **ultra-violet** *adj* ультрафиолéтовый.

umbilical *adj:* ~ **cord** пупови́на.

umbrella *n* зóнтик, зонт.

umpire *n* судья́ *m*; *vt & i* суди́ть *impf*.

umpteenth *adj:* **for the** ~ **time** в котóрый раз.

unabashed *adj* без всякого смущéния. **unabated** *adj* неослáбленный.

unable *adj*: be ~ to не мочь *impf*, с~ *pf*; быть не в состоянии; (*not know how to*) не уметь *impf*, с~ *pf*. **unabridged** *adj* несокращённый. **unaccompanied** *adj* без сопровождения; (*mus*) без аккомпанемента. **unaccountable** *adj* необъяснимый. **unaccustomed** *adj* (*not accustomed*) непривыкший (to к+*dat*); (*unusual*) непривычный. **unadulterated** *adj* настоящий; (*utter*) чистейший. **unaffected** *adj* непринуждённый. **unaided** *adj* без помощи, самостоятельный. **unambiguous** *adj* недвусмысленный. **unanimity** *n* единодушие. **unanimous** *adj* единодушный. **unanswerable** *adj* (*irrefutable*) неопровержимый. **unarmed** *adj* невооружённый. **unashamed** *adj* бессовестный. **unassailable** *adj* неприступный; (*irrefutable*) неопровержимый. **unassuming** *adj* скромный. **unattainable** *adj* недосягаемый. **unattended** *adj* без присмотра. **unattractive** *adj* непривлекательный. **unauthorized** *adj* неразрешённый. **unavailable** *adj* не имеющийся в наличии, недоступный. **unavoidable** *adj* неизбежный. **unaware** *predic*: be ~ of не сознавать *impf* +acc; не знать *impf* o+*prep*. **unawares** *adv* врасплох.

unbalanced *adj* (*psych*) неуравновешенный. **unbearable** *adj* невыносимый. **unbeatable** *adj* (*unsurpassable*) не могущий быть превзойдённым; (*invincible*) непобедимый. **unbeaten** *adj* (*undefeated*) непокорённый; (*unsurpassed*) непревзойдённый. **unbelief** *n* неверие. **unbelievable** *adj* невероятный. **unbeliever** *n* неверующий *sb*. **unbiased** *adj* беспристрастный. **unblemished** *adj* незапятнанный. **unblock** *vt* прочищать *impf*, прочистить *pf*. **unbolt** *vt* отпирать *impf*, отпереть *pf*. **unborn** *adj* ещё не рождённый. **unbounded** *adj* неограниченный. **unbreakable** *adj* небьющийся. **unbridled** *adj* разнузданный. **unbroken** *adj* (*intact*) неразбитый, целый; (*continuous*) непрерывный; (*unsurpassed*) непобитый; (*horse*) необъезженный. **unbuckle** *vt* расстёгивать *impf*, расстегнуть *pf*. **unburden** *vt*:

~ o.s. отводить *impf*, отвести *pf* душу. **unbutton** *vt* расстёгивать *impf*, расстегнуть *pf*.

uncalled-for *adj* неуместный. **uncanny** *adj* жуткий, сверхъестественный. **unceasing** *adj* непрерывный. **unceremonious** *adj* бесцеремонный. **uncertain** *adj* (*not sure, hesitating*) неуверенный; (*indeterminate*) неопределённый, неясный; be ~ (*not know for certain*) точно не знать *impf*; in no ~ terms недвусмысленно. **uncertainty** *n* неизвестность; неопределённость. **unchallenged** *adj* не вызывающий возражений. **unchanged** *adj* неизменившийся. **unchanging** *adj* неизменяющийся. **uncharacteristic** *adj* нетипичный. **uncharitable** *adj* немилосердный, жестокий. **uncharted** *adj* неисследованный. **unchecked** *adj* (*unrestrained*) необузданный. **uncivilized** *adj* нецивилизованный. **unclaimed** *adj* невостребованный. **uncle** *n* дядя *m*.

unclean *adj* нечистый. **unclear** *adj* неясный. **uncomfortable** *adj* неудобный. **uncommon** *adj* необыкновенный; (*rare*) редкий. **uncommunicative** *adj* неразговорчивый, сдержанный. **uncomplaining** *adj* безропотный. **uncomplicated** *adj* несложный. **uncompromising** *adj* бескомпромиссный. **unconcealed** *adj* нескрываемый. **unconcerned** *adj* (*unworried*) беззаботный; (*indifferent*) равнодушный. **unconditional** *adj* безоговорочный, безусловный. **unconfirmed** *adj* неподтверждённый. **unconnected** *adj* ~ with не связанный c+*instr*. **unconscious** *adj* (*also unintentional*) бессознательный; (*predic*) без сознания; be ~ of не сознавать *impf* +*gen*; *n* подсознательное *sb*. **unconsciousness** *n* бессознательное состояние. **unconstitutional** *adj* неконституционный. **uncontrollable** *adj* неудержимый. **uncontrolled** *adj* бесконтрольный. **unconventional** *adj* необычный; оригинальный. **unconvincing** *adj* неубедительный. **uncooked** *adj* сырой. **uncooperative** *adj* неотзывчивый. **uncouth** *adj* грубый. **uncover** *vt* раскрывать *impf*, раскры́ть *pf*. **uncritical** *adj* некрити́чный.

unctuous *adj* еле́йный.

uncut *adj* неразре́занный; (*unabridged*) несокращённый.

undamaged *adj* неповреждённый.

undaunted *adj* бесстра́шный. **undecided** *adj* (*not settled*) нерешённый; (*irresolute*) нереши́тельный. **undefeated** *adj* непокорённый. **undemanding** *adj* нетре́бовательный. **undemocratic** *adj* недемократи́ческий. **undeniable** *adj* неоспори́мый.

under *prep* (*position*) под+*instr*; (*direction*) под+*acc*; (*fig*) под +*instr*; (*less than*) ме́ньше+*gen*; (*in view of, in the reign, time of*) при+*prep*; ~-**age** несовершенноле́тний; ~**way** на ходу́; *adv* (*position*) внизу́; (*direction*) вниз; (*less*) ме́ньше.

undercarriage *n* шасси́ *neut indecl*. **underclothes** *n pl* ни́жнее бельё. **undercoat** *n* (*of paint*) грунто́вка. **undercover** *adj* та́йный. **undercurrent** *n* подво́дное тече́ние; (*fig*) скры́тая тенде́нция. **undercut** *vt* (*price*) назнача́ть *impf*, назна́чить *pf* бо́лее ни́зкую це́ну чем+*nom*. **underdeveloped** *adj* слабора́звитый. **underdog** *n* неуда́чник.

underdone *adj* недожа́ренный. **underemployment** *n* непо́лная за́нятость. **underestimate** *vt* недооце́нивать *impf*, недооцени́ть *pf*; *n* недооце́нка. **underfoot** *adv* под нога́ми.

undergo *vt* подверга́ться *impf*, подве́ргнуться *pf* +*dat*; (*endure*) переноси́ть *impf*, перенести́ *pf*. **undergraduate** *n* студе́нт, ~ка. **underground** *n* (*rly*) метро́ *neut indecl*; (*fig*) подпо́лье; *adj* подзе́мный; (*fig*) подпо́льный; *adv* под землёй; (*fig*) подпо́льно. **undergrowth** *n* подле́сок. **underhand** *adj* закули́сный. **underlie** *vt* (*fig*) лежа́ть *impf* в осно́ве +*gen*. **underline** *vt* подчёркивать *impf*, подчеркну́ть *pf*. **underlying** *adj* лежа́щий в осно́ве. **underling** *n* подчинённый *sb*.

undermine *vt* (*authority*) подрыва́ть *impf*, подорва́ть *pf*; (*health*) разруша́ть *impf*, разру́шить *pf*.

underneath *adv* (*position*) внизу́; (*direction*) вниз; *prep* (*position*) под

+*instr*; (*direction*) под+*acc*; *n* ни́жняя часть; *adj* ни́жний.

undernourished *adj* исхуда́лый; **be ~** недоеда́ть *impf*.

underpaid *adj* низкоопла́чиваемый. **underpants** *n pl* трусы́ (-со́в) *pl*. **underpass** *n* прое́зд под полотно́м доро́ги; тонне́ль *m*. **underpin** *vt* подводи́ть *impf*, подвести́ *pf* фунда́мент под+*acc*; (*fig*) подде́рживать *impf*, поддержа́ть *pf*. **underprivileged** *adj* обделённый; (*poor*) бе́дный. **underrate** *vt* недооце́нивать *impf*, недооцени́ть *pf*.

underscore *vt* подчёркивать *impf*, подчеркну́ть *pf*. **under-secretary** *n* замести́тель *m* мини́стра. **underside** *n* ни́жняя сторона́, низ. **undersized** *adj* малоро́слый. **understaffed** *adj* неукомплекто́ванный.

understand *vt* понима́ть *impf*, поня́ть *pf*; (*have heard say*) слы́шать *impf*. **understandable** *adj* поня́тный. **understanding** *n* понима́ние; (*agreement*) соглаше́ние; *adj* (*sympathetic*) отзы́вчивый.

understate *vt* преуменьша́ть *impf*, преуме́ньшить *pf*. **understatement** *n* преуменьше́ние.

understudy *n* дублёр.

undertake *vt* (*enter upon*) предпринима́ть *impf*, предприня́ть *pf*; (*responsibility*) брать *impf*, взять *pf* на себя́; (+*inf*) обя́зываться *impf*, обяза́ться *pf*. **undertaker** *n* гробовщи́к. **undertaking** *n* предприя́тие; (*pledge*) гара́нтия.

undertone *n* (*fig*) подте́кст; **in an ~** вполго́лоса. **underwater** *adj* подво́дный. **underwear** *n* ни́жнее бельё. **underweight** *adj* исхуда́лый. **underworld** *n* (*mythology*) преиспо́дняя *sb*; (*criminals*) престу́пный мир. **underwrite** *vt* (*guarantee*) гаранти́ровать *impf* & *pf*. **underwriter** *n* страхо́вщик.

undeserved *adj* незаслу́женный. **undesirable** *adj* нежела́тельный; *n* нежела́тельное лицо́. **undeveloped** *adj* нера́звитый; (*land*) незастро́енный. **undignified** *adj* недосто́йный. **undiluted** *adj* неразба́вленный. **undisciplined** *adj* недисциплини́рованный. **undiscovered** *adj* неоткры́тый. **undisguised** *adj* я́вный.

undisputed *adj* бесспо́рный. **undistinguished** *adj* зауря́дный. **undisturbed** *adj* (*untouched*) нетро́нутый; (*peaceful*) споко́йный. **undivided** *adj*: ~ **attention** по́лное внима́ние **undo** *vt* (*open*) открыва́ть *impf*, откры́ть *pf*; (*untie*) развя́зывать *impf*, развяза́ть *pf*; (*unbutton, unhook, unbuckle*) расстёгивать *impf*, расстегну́ть *pf*; (*destroy, cancel*) уничтожа́ть *impf*, уничто́жить *pf*. **undoubted** *adj* несомне́нный. **undoubtedly** *adv* несомне́нно. **undress** *vt & i* раздева́ть(ся) *impf*, разде́ть(ся) *pf*. **undue** *adj* чрезме́рный. **unduly** *adv* чрезме́рно.

undulating *adj* волни́стый; (*landscape*) холми́стый.

undying *adj* (*eternal*) ве́чный.

unearth *vt* (*dig up*) выка́пывать *impf*, вы́копать *pf* из земли́; (*fig*) раска́пывать *impf*, раскопа́ть *pf*. **uneasiness** *n* (*anxiety*) беспоко́йство; (*awkwardness*) нело́вкость. **uneasy** *adj* беспоко́йный; нело́вкий. **uneconomic** *adj* нерента́бельный. **uneconomical** *adj* (*car etc.*) неэкономи́чный; (*person*) неэконо́мный. **uneducated** *adj* необразо́ванный. **unemployed** *adj* безрабо́тный. **unemployment** *n* безрабо́тица; ~ **benefit** посо́бие по безрабо́тице. **unending** *adj* бесконе́чный. **unenviable** *adj* незави́дный. **unequal** *adj* нера́вный. **unequalled** *adj* непревзойдённый. **unequivocal** *adj* недвусмы́сленный. **unerring** *adj* безоши́бочный.

uneven *adj* неро́вный. **uneventful** *adj* непримеча́тельный. **unexceptional** *adj* обы́чный. **unexpected** *adj* неожи́данный. **unexplored** *adj* неиссле́дованный.

unfailing *adj* неизме́нный; (*inexhaustible*) неисчерпа́емый. **unfair** *adj* несправедли́вый. **unfaithful** *adj* неве́рный. **unfamiliar** *adj* незнако́мый; (*unknown*) неве́домый. **unfashionable** *adj* немо́дный. **unfasten** *vt* (*detach, untie*) открепля́ть *impf*, открепи́ть *pf*; (*undo, unbutton, unhook*) расстёгивать *impf*, расстегну́ть *pf*; (*open*) открыва́ть *impf*, откры́ть *pf*. **unfavourable** *adj* неблагоприя́тный. **unfeeling** *adj*

бесчу́вственный. **unfinished** *adj* незако́нченный. **unfit** *adj* него́дный; (*unhealthy*) нездоро́вый. **unflagging** *adj* неослабева́ющий. **unflattering** *adj* неле́стный. **unflinching** *adj* непоколеби́мый. **unfold** *vt & i* развёртывать(ся) *impf*, разверну́ть(ся) *pf*; *vi* (*fig*) раскрыва́ться *impf*, раскры́ться *pf*. **unforeseen** *adj* непредви́денный. **unforgettable** *adj* незабыва́емый. **unforgivable** *adj* непрости́тельный. **unforgiving** *adj* непроща́ющий. **unfortunate** *adj* несча́стный; (*regrettable*) неуда́чный; *n* неуда́чник. **unfortunately** *adv* к сожале́нию. **unfounded** *adj* необоснова́нный. **unfriendly** *adj* недружелю́бный. **unfulfilled** *adj* (*hopes etc.*) неосуществлённый; (*person*) неудовлетворённый. **unfurl** *vt & i* развёртывать(ся) *impf*, разверну́ть(ся) *pf*. **unfurnished** *adj* немеблиро́ванный.

ungainly *adj* неуклю́жий. **ungovernable** *adj* неуправля́емый. **ungracious** *adj* нелюбе́зный. **ungrateful** *adj* неблагода́рный. **unguarded** *adj* (*incautious*) неосторо́жный.

unhappiness *n* несча́стье. **unhappy** *adj* несчастли́вый. **unharmed** *adj* невреди́мый. **unhealthy** *adj* нездоро́вый; (*harmful*) вре́дный. **unheard-of** *adj* неслы́ханный. **unheeded** *adj* незаме́ченный. **unheeding** *adj* невнима́тельный. **unhelpful** *adj* бесполе́зный; (*person*) неотзы́вчивый. **unhesitating** *adj* реши́тельный. **unhesitatingly** *adv* без колеба́ния. **unhindered** *adj* беспрепя́тственный. **unhinge** *vt* (*fig*) расстра́ивать *impf*, расстро́ить *pf*. **unholy** *adj* (*impious*) нечести́вый; (*awful*) ужа́сный. **unhook** *vt* (*undo hooks of*) расстёгивать *impf*, расстегну́ть *pf*; (*uncouple*) расцепля́ть *impf*, расцепи́ть *pf*. **unhurt** *adj* невреди́мый.

unicorn *n* единоро́г.

unification *n* объедине́ние.

uniform *n* фо́рма; *adj* единообра́зный; (*unchanging*) постоя́нный. **uniformity** *n* единообра́зие.

unify *vt* объединя́ть *impf*, объедини́ть *pf*.

unilateral *adj* односторо́нний.

unimaginable adj невообрази́мый. **unimaginative** adj лишённый воображе́ния, прозаи́чный. **unimportant** adj нева́жный. **uninformed** adj (ignorant) несве́дущий (about в +prep); (ill-informed) неосведомлённый. **uninhabited** adj необита́емый. **uninhibited** adj нестеснённый. **uninspired** adj бана́льный. **unintelligible** adj непоня́тный. **unintentional** adj неча́янный. **unintentionally** adv неча́янно. **uninterested** adj незаинтересо́ванный. **uninteresting** adj неинтере́сный. **uninterrupted** adj непреры́вный.

union n (alliance) сою́з; (joining together, alliance) объедине́ние; (trade ~) профсою́з. **unionist** n член профсою́за; (polit) униони́ст.

unique adj уника́льный.

unison n: in ~ (mus) в унисо́н; (fig) в согла́сии.

unit n едини́ца; (mil) часть.

unite vt & i соединя́ть(ся) impf, соедини́ть(ся) pf; объединя́ть(ся) impf, объедини́ть(ся) pf. **united** adj соединённый, объединённый; U~ **Kingdom** Соединённое Короле́вство; U~ **Nations** Организа́ция Объединённых На́ций; U~ **States** Соединённые Шта́ты m pl Аме́рики. **unity** n еди́нство.

universal adj всео́бщий; (many-sided) универса́льный. **universe** n вселе́нная sb; (world) мир.

university n университе́т; attrib университе́тский.

unjust adj несправедли́вый. **unjustifiable** adj непрости́тельный. **unjustified** adj неопра́вданный.

unkempt adj неча́саный. **unkind** adj недо́брый, злой. **unknown** adj неизве́стный.

unlawful adj незако́нный. **unleaded** adj неэтили́рованный. **unleash** vt (also fig) развя́зывать impf, развяза́ть pf.

unless conj е́сли... не.

unlike adj непохо́жий (на+acc); (in contradistinction to) в отли́чие от +gen. **unlikely** adj маловероя́тный; it is ~ that вряд ли. **unlimited** adj неограни́ченный. **unlit** adj неосвещённый. **unload** vt (vehicle etc.) разгружа́ть impf, разгрузи́ть pf;

(goods etc.) выгружа́ть impf, вы́грузить pf. **unlock** vt отпира́ть impf, отпере́ть pf; открыва́ть impf, откры́ть pf. **unlucky** adj (number etc.) несчастли́вый; (unsuccessful) неуда́чный.

unmanageable adj тру́дный, непоко́рный. **unmanned** adj автомати́ческий. **unmarried** adj холосто́й; (of man) нежена́тый; (of woman) незаму́жняя. **unmask** vt (fig) разоблача́ть impf, разоблачи́ть pf. **unmentionable** adj неупомина́емый. **unmistakable** adj несомне́нный, я́сный. **unmitigated** adj (thorough) отъя́вленный. **unmoved** adj: be ~ остава́ться impf, оста́ться pf равноду́шен, -шна.

unnatural adj неесте́ственный. **unnecessary** adj нену́жный. **unnerve** vt лиша́ть impf, лиши́ть pf му́жества; (upset) расстра́ивать impf, расстро́ить pf. **unnoticed** adj незаме́ченный.

unobserved adj незаме́ченный. **unobtainable** adj недосту́пный. **unobtrusive** adj скро́мный, ненавя́зчивый. **unoccupied** adj незаня́тый, свобо́дный; (house) пусто́й. **unofficial** adj неофициа́льный. **unopposed** adj не встре́тивший сопротивле́ния. **unorthodox** adj неортодокса́льный.

unpack vt распако́вывать impf, распакова́ть pf. **unpaid** adj (bill) неупла́ченный; (person) не получа́ющий пла́ты; (work) беспла́тный. **unpalatable** adj невку́сный; (unpleasant) неприя́тный. **unparalleled** adj несравни́мый. **unpleasant** adj неприя́тный. **unpleasantness** n неприя́тность. **unpopular** adj непопуля́рный. **unprecedented** adj беспрецеде́нтный. **unpredictable** adj непредсказу́емый. **unprejudiced** adj беспристра́стный. **unprepared** adj неподгото́вленный, него́товый. **unprepossessing** adj непривлека́тельный. **unpretentious** adj просто́й, без прете́нзий. **unprincipled** adj беспринци́пный. **unproductive** adj непродукти́вный. **unprofitable** adj невы́годный. **unpromising** adj малообеща́ющий. **unprotected** adj незащищённый. **unproven** adj недока́занный. **unprovoked** adj непровоци́рованный. **unpublished** adj неопублико́ванный, неи́зданный. **unpunished** adj безнака́занный.

unqualified adj неквалифици́рованный; (unconditional) безогово́рочный. **unquestionable** adj несомне́нный, неоспори́мый. **unquestionably** adv несомне́нно, бесспо́рно.

unravel vt & i распу́тывать(ся) impf, распу́тать(ся) pf; vt (solve) разга́дывать impf, разгада́ть pf. **unread** adj (book etc.) непрочи́танный. **unreadable** adj (illegible) неразбо́рчивый; (boring) неудобочита́емый. **unreal** adj нереа́льный. **unrealistic** adj нереа́льный. **unreasonable** adj (person) неразу́мный; (behaviour, demand, price) необосно́ванный. **unrecognizable** adj неузнава́емый. **unrecognized** adj непри́знанный. **unrefined** adj неочи́щенный; (manners etc.) гру́бый. **unrelated** adj не име́ющий отноше́ния (to к+dat), несвя́занный (to c+instr); we are ~ мы не ро́дственники. **unrelenting** adj (ruthless) безжа́лостный; (unremitting) неосла́бный. **unreliable** adj ненадёжный. **unremarkable** adj невыдаю́щийся. **unremitting** adj неосла́бный; (incessant) беспреста́нный. **unrepentant** adj нераска́явшийся. **unrepresentative** adj нетипи́чный. **unrequited** adj: ~ love неразделённая любо́вь. **unreserved** adj (full) по́лный; (open) откре́нний; (unconditional) безогово́рочный; (seat) незаброни́рованный. **unresolved** adj нерешённый. **unrest** n беспоко́йство; (polit) волне́ния neut pl. **unrestrained** adj несде́ржанный. **unrestricted** adj неограни́ченный. **unripe** adj незре́лый. **unrivalled** adj бесподо́бный. **unroll** vt & i развёртывать(ся) impf, разверну́ть(ся) pf. **unruffled** adj (smooth) гла́дкий; (calm) споко́йный. **unruly** adj непоко́рный.

unsafe adj опа́сный; (insecure) ненадёжный. **unsaid** adj: leave ~ молча́ть impf o+prep. **unsaleable** adj нехо́дкий. **unsalted** adj несолёный. **unsatisfactory** adj неудовлетвори́тельный. **unsatisfied** adj неудовлетворённый. **unsavoury** adj

(unpleasant) неприя́тный; (disreputable) сомни́тельный. **unscathed** adj невреди́мый; (predic) цел и невреди́м. **unscheduled** adj (transport) внеочередно́й; (event) незаплани́рованный. **unscientific** adj ненау́чный. **unscrew** vt & i отви́нчивать(ся) impf, отвинти́ть(ся) pf. **unscrupulous** adj беспринци́пный. **unseat** vt (of horse) сбра́сывать impf, сбро́сить pf с седла́; (parl) лиша́ть impf, лиши́ть pf парла́ментского мандата.

unseemly adj неподоба́ющий. **unseen** adj неви́данный. **unselfconscious** adj непосре́дственный. **unselfish** adj бескоры́стный. **unsettle** vt выбива́ть impf, вы́бить pf из колеи́; (upset) расстра́ивать impf, расстро́ить pf. **unsettled** adj (weather) неусто́йчивый; (unresolved) нерешённый. **unsettling** adj волну́ющий. **unshakeable** adj непоколеби́мый. **unshaven** adj небри́тый. **unsightly** adj непригля́дный, уро́дливый. **unsigned** adj неподпи́санный. **unskilful** adj неуме́лый. **unskilled** adj неквалифици́рованный. **unsociable** adj необщи́тельный. **unsold** adj непро́данный. **unsolicited** adj непро́шенный. **unsolved** adj нерешённый. **unsophisticated** adj просто́й. **unsound** adj (unhealthy, unwholesome) нездоро́вый; (not solid) непро́чный; (unfounded) необосно́ванный; of ~ mind душевнобольно́й. **unspeakable** adj (inexpressible) невырази́мый; (very bad) отврати́тельный. **unspecified** adj то́чно не ука́занный, неопределённый. **unspoilt** adj неиспо́рченный. **unspoken** adj невы́сказанный. **unstable** adj неусто́йчивый; (mentally) неуравнове́шенный. **unsteady** adj неусто́йчивый. **unstuck** adj: come ~ откле́иваться impf, откле́иться pf; (fig) прова́ливаться impf, провали́ться pf. **unsuccessful** adj неуда́чный, безуспе́шный. **unsuitable** adj неподходя́щий. **unsuited** adj неприго́дный. **unsung** adj невоспе́тый. **unsupported** adj неподдержа́нный. **unsure** adj неуве́ренный (of o.s. в себе́). **unsurpassed** adj непревзойдённый. **unsurprising** adj неудивительный. **unsuspected** *adj* (*unforeseen*) непредви́денный. **unsuspecting** *adj* неподозрева́ющий. **unsweetened** *adj* неподсла́щенный. **unswerving** *adj* непоколеби́мый. **unsympathetic** *adj* несочу́вствующий. **unsystematic** *adj* несистемати́чный.

untainted *adj* неиспо́рченный. **untangle** *vt* распу́тывать *impf*, распута́ть *pf*. **untapped** *adj*: ~ **resources** неиспо́льзованные ресу́рсы *m pl*. **untenable** *adj* несостоя́тельный. **untested** *adj* неиспы́танный. **unthinkable** *adj* невообрази́мый. **unthinking** *adj* безду́мный. **untidiness** *n* неопря́тность; (*disorder*) беспоря́док. **untidy** *adj* неопря́тный; (*in disorder*) в беспоря́дке. **untie** *vt* развя́зывать *impf*, развяза́ть *pf*; (*set free*) освобожда́ть *impf*, освободи́ть *pf*.

until *prep* до+*gen*; **not** ~ не ра́ньше +*gen*; ~ **then** до тех пор; *conj* пока́, пока́... не; **not** ~ то́лько когда́.

untimely *adj* (*premature*) безвре́менный; (*inappropriate*) неуме́стный. **untiring** *adj* неутоми́мый. **untold** *adj* (*incalculable*) бессчётный, несмётный; (*inexpressible*) невырази́мый. **untouched** *adj* нетро́нутый; (*indifferent*) равноду́шный. **untoward** *adj* неблагоприя́тный. **untrained** *adj* необу́ченный. **untried** *adj* неиспы́танный. **untroubled** *adj* споко́йный. **untrue** *adj* неве́рный. **untrustworthy** *adj* ненадёжный. **untruth** *n* непра́вда, ложь. **untruthful** *adj* лжи́вый.

unusable *adj* неприго́дный. **unused** *adj* неиспо́льзованный; (*unaccustomed*) непривы́кший (**to** к+*dat*); **I am** ~ **to this** я к э́тому не привы́к. **unusual** *adj* необыкнове́нный, необы́чный. **unusually** *adv* необыкнове́нно. **unutterable** *adj* невырази́мый.

unveil *vt* (*statue*) торже́ственно открыва́ть *impf*, откры́ть *pf*; (*disclose*) обнаро́довать *impf* & *pf*.

unwanted *adj* нежела́нный. **unwarranted** *adj* неопра́вданный. **unwary** *adj* неосторо́жный. **unwavering** *adj* непоколеби́мый. **unwelcome** *adj* нежела́тельный; (*unpleasant*) неприя́тный. **unwell** *adj* нездоро́вый. **unwieldy** *adj* громо́здкий. **unwilling**

adj несклóнный; **be** ~ не хотéть *impf*, за~ *pf* (**to** +*inf*). **unwillingly** *adv* неохóтно. **unwillingness** *n* неохóта. **unwind** *vt* & *i* разма́тывать(ся) *impf*, размота́ть(ся) *pf*; (*rest*) отдыха́ть *impf*, отдохну́ть *pf*. **unwise** *adj* не(благо)разу́мный. **unwitting** *adj* нево́льный. **unwittingly** *adv* нево́льно. **unworkable** *adj* непримен
и́мый. **unworldly** *adj* не от ми́ра сего́. **unworthy** *adj* недостóйный. **unwrap** *vt* развёртывать *impf*, разверну́ть *pf*. **unwritten** *adj*: ~ **law** непи́саный закóн.

unyielding *adj* упóрный, неподáтливый.

unzip *vt* расстёгивать *impf*, расстегну́ть *pf* (мóлнию+*gen*).

up *adv* (*motion*) наве́рх, вверх; (*position*) наверху́, вверху́; ~ **and down** вверх и вниз; (*back and forth*) взад и вперёд; ~ **to** (*towards*) к+*dat*; (*as far as, until*) до+*gen*; ~ **to now** до сих пор; **be** ~ **against** имéть *impf* дéло с+*instr*; **be** ~ **to** **you**+*inf*, э́то вам+*inf*, вы должны́+*inf*; **what's** ~? что случи́лось?; в чём дéло?; **your time is** ~ вáше врéмя истеклó; ~ **and about** на ногáх; **he isn't** ~ **yet** он ещё не встал; **he isn't** ~ **to this job** он не годи́тся для э́той рабóты; *prep* вверх по+*dat*; (*along*) (вдоль) по+*dat*; *vt* повышáть *impf*, повы́сить; *vi* (*leap up*) взять *pf*; *adj*: ~-**to-date** совремéнный; (*fashionable*) мóдный; ~-**and-coming** многообещáющий; *n*: ~**s and downs** (*fig*) преврáтности *f pl* судьбы́.

upbringing *n* воспитáние.

update *vt* модернизи́ровать *impf* & *pf*; (*a book etc.*) дополня́ть *impf*, допóлнить *pf*.

upgrade *vt* повышáть *impf*, повы́сить *pf* (по слýжбе).

upheaval *n* потрясéние.

uphill *adj* (*fig*) тяжёлый; *adv* в гóру.

uphold *vt* поддéрживать *impf*, поддержáть *pf*.

upholster *vt* обивáть *impf*, оби́ть *pf*. **upholsterer** *n* обóйщик. **upholstery** *n* оби́вка.

upkeep *n* содержáние.

upland *n* гори́стая часть страны́; *adj* нагóрный.

uplift *vt* поднимáть *impf*, подня́ть *pf*.

up-market *adj* дорогой.

upon *prep* (*position*) на+*prep*, (*motion*) на+*acc*; *see* **on**

upper *adj* верхний; (*socially, in rank*) высший; **gain the ~ hand** одерживать *impf*, одержать *pf* верх (**over** над+*instr*); *n* передок. **uppermost** *adj* самый верхний, высший; **be ~ in person's mind** больше всего занимать *impf*, занять *pf* мысли кого-л.

upright *n* стойка; *adj* вертикальный; (*honest*) честный; **~ piano** пианино *neut indecl*.

uprising *n* восстание.

uproar *n* шум, гам.

uproot *vt* вырывать *impf*, вырвать *pf* с корнем; (*people*) выселять *impf*, выселить *pf*.

upset *n* расстройство; *vt* расстраивать *impf*, расстроить *pf*; (*overturn*) опрокидывать *impf*, опрокинуть *pf*; *adj* (*miserable*) расстроенный; **~ stomach** расстройство желудка.

upshot *n* развязка, результат.

upside-down *adj* перевёрнутый вверх дном; *adv* вверх дном; (*in disorder*) в беспорядке.

upstairs *adv* (*position*) наверху; (*motion*) наверх; *n* верхний этаж; *adj* находящийся в верхнем этаже.

upstart *n* выскочка *m & f*.

upstream *adv* против течения; (*situation*) вверх по течению.

upsurge *n* подъём, волна.

uptake *n*: **be quick on the ~** быстро соображать *impf*, сообразить *pf*.

upturn *n* (*fig*) улучшение. **upturned** *adj* (*face etc.*) поднятый кверху; (*inverted*) перевёрнутый.

upward *adj* направленный вверх. **upwards** *adv* вверх; **~ of** свыше +*gen*.

uranium *n* уран.

urban *adj* городской.

urbane *adj* вежливый.

urchin *n* мальчишка *m*.

urge *n* (*incitement*) побуждение; (*desire*) желание; *vt* (*impel*, **~ on**) подгонять *impf*, подогнать *pf*; (*warn*) предупреждать *impf*, предупредить *pf*; (*try to persuade*) убеждать *impf*. **urgency** *n* срочность, важность; **a matter of great ~** срочное дело. **urgent** *adj* срочный; (*insistent*) настоятельный. **urgently** *adv* срочно.

urinate *vi* мочиться *impf*, по~ *pf*. **urine** *n* моча.

urn *n* урна.

US(A) *abbr* (*of United States of America*) США, Соединённые Штаты Америки.

usable *adj* годный к употреблению. **usage** *n* употребление; (*treatment*) обращение. **use** *n* (*utilization*) употребление, пользование; (*benefit*) польза; (*application*) применение; **it is no ~ (-ing)** бесполезно (+*inf*); **make ~ of** использовать *impf & pf*; пользоваться *impf* +*instr*; *vt* употреблять *impf*, употребить *pf*; пользоваться *impf* +*instr*; (*apply*) применять *impf*, применить *pf*; (*treat*) обращаться *impf* с+*instr*; **he often ~d to** привыкать *impf*, привыкнуть *pf* (**to** к+*dat*); **~ up** расходовать *impf*, из~ *pf*. **used** *adj* (*second-hand*) старый. **useful** *adj* полезный; **come in ~, prove ~** пригодиться *pf* (**to** +*dat*). **useless** *adj* бесполезный. **user** *n* потребитель *m*.

usher *n* (*theat*) билетёр; *vt* (*lead in*) вводить *impf*, ввести *pf*; (*proclaim*, **~ in**) возвещать *impf*, возвестить *pf*. **usherette** *n* билетёрша.

USSR *abbr* (*of Union of Soviet Socialist Republics*) СССР, Союз Советских Социалистических Республик.

usual *adj* обыкновенный, обычный; **as ~** как обычно. **usually** *adv* обыкновенно, обычно.

usurp *vt* узурпировать *impf & pf*. **usurper** *n* узурпатор.

usury *n* ростовщичество.

utensil *n* инструмент; *pl* утварь, посуда.

uterus *n* матка.

utilitarian *adj* утилитарный. **utilitarianism** *n* утилитаризм. **utility** *n* полезность; *pl*: **public utilities** коммунальные услуги *f pl*. **utilize** *vt* использовать *impf & pf*.

utmost *adj* (*extreme*) крайний; **this is of the ~ importance to me** это для меня крайне важно; *n*: **do one's ~** делать *impf*, с~ *pf* всё возможное.

Utopia *n* утопия. **utopian** *adj* утопический.

utter *attrib* по́лный, абсолю́тный; (*out-and-out*) отъя́вленный (*coll*); *vt* произноси́ть *impf*, произнести́ *pf*; (*let out*) издава́ть *impf*, изда́ть *pf*. **utterance** *n* (*uttering*) произнесе́ние; (*pronouncement*) выска́зывание. **utterly** *adv* соверше́нно.

Uzbek *n* узбе́к, -е́чка. **Uzbekistan** *n* Узбекиста́н.

V

vacancy *n* (*for job*) вака́нсия, свобо́дное ме́сто; (*at hotel*) свобо́дный но́мер. **vacant** *adj* (*post*) вака́нтный; (*post; not engaged, free*) свобо́дный; (*empty*) пусто́й; (*look*) отсу́тствующий. **vacate** *vt* освобожда́ть *impf*, освободи́ть *pf*. **vacation** *n* кани́кулы (-л) *pl*; (*leave*) о́тпуск.

vaccinate *vt* вакцини́ровать *impf* & *pf*. **vaccination** *n* приви́вка (**against** от, про́тив+*gen*). **vaccine** *n* вакци́на.

vacillate *vi* колеба́ться *impf*. **vacillation** *n* колеба́ние.

vacuous *adj* пусто́й. **vacuum** *n* ва́куум; (*fig*) пустота́; ~**-clean** чи́стить *impf*, вы́~, по~ *pf* пылесо́сом; ~ **cleaner** пылесо́с; ~ **flask** те́рмос.

vagabond *n* бродя́га *m*.

vagary *n* капри́з.

vagina *n* влага́лище.

vagrant *n* бродя́га *m*.

vague *adj* (*indeterminate, uncertain*) неопределённый; (*unclear*) нея́сный; (*dim*) сму́тный; (*absent-minded*) рассе́янный. **vagueness** *n* неопределённость, нея́сность; (*absent-mindedness*) рассе́янность.

vain *adj* (*futile*) тще́тный, напра́сный; (*empty*) пусто́й; (*conceited*) тщесла́вный; **in** ~ напра́сно.

vale *n* дол, доли́на.

valentine *n* (*card*) поздрави́тельная ка́рточка с днём свято́го Валенти́на.

valet *n* камерди́нер.

valiant *adj* хра́брый.

valid *adj* действи́тельный; (*weighty*) ве́ский. **validate** *vt* (*ratify*) утвержда́ть *impf*, утверди́ть *pf*. **validity** *n* действи́тельность; (*weightiness*)

ве́скость.

valley *n* доли́на.

valour *n* до́блесть.

valuable *adj* це́нный; *n pl* це́нности *f pl*. **valuation** *n* оце́нка. **value** *n* це́нность; (*math*) величина́; *pl* це́нности *f pl*; ~**added tax** нало́г на доба́вленную сто́имость; ~ **judgement** субъекти́вная оце́нка; *vt* (*estimate*) оце́нивать *impf*, оцени́ть *pf*; (*hold dear*) цени́ть *impf*.

valve *n* (*tech, med, mus*) кла́пан; (*tech*) ве́нтиль *m*; (*radio*) электро́нная ла́мпа.

vampire *n* вампи́р.

van *n* фурго́н.

vandal *n* ванда́л. **vandalism** *n* вандали́зм. **vandalize** *vt* разруша́ть *impf*, разру́шить *pf*.

vanguard *n* аванга́рд.

vanilla *n* вани́ль.

vanish *vi* исчеза́ть *impf*, исче́знуть *pf*.

vanity *n* (*futility*) тщета́; (*conceit*) тщесла́вие.

vanquish *vt* побежда́ть *impf*, победи́ть *pf*.

vantage-point *n* (*mil*) наблюда́тельный пункт; (*fig*) вы́годная пози́ция.

vapour *n* пар.

variable *adj* изме́нчивый; (*weather*) неусто́йчивый, переме́нный; *n* (*math*) переме́нная (величина́).

variance *n*: **be at** ~ **with** (*contradict*) противоре́чить *impf* +*dat*; (*disagree*) расходи́ться *impf*, разойти́сь *pf* во мне́ниях с+*instr*. **variant** *n* вариа́нт. **variation** *n* (*varying*) измене́ние; (*variant*) вариа́нт; (*variety*) разнови́дность; (*mus*) вариа́ция.

varicose *adj*: ~ **veins** расшире́ние вен.

varied *adj* разнообра́зный. **variegated** *adj* разноцве́тный. **variety** *n* разнообра́зие; (*sort*) разнови́дность; (*a number*) ряд; ~ **show** варьете́ *neut indecl*. **various** *adj* ра́зный.

varnish *n* лак; *vt* лакирова́ть *impf*, от~ *pf*.

vary *vt* разнообра́зить *impf*, меня́ть *impf*; *vi* (*change*) меня́ться *impf*; (*differ*) ра́зниться *impf*.

vase *n* ва́за.

Vaseline *n* (*propr*) вазели́н.

vast adj грома́дный. **vastly** adv значи́тельно.

VAT abbr (of **value-added tax**) нало́г на доба́вленную сто́имость.

vat n чан, бак.

vaudeville n водеви́ль m.

vault[1] n (leap) прыжо́к; vt перепры́гивать impf, перепры́гнуть pf; vi пры́гать impf, пры́гнуть pf.

vault[2] n (arch, covering) свод; (cellar) по́греб; (tomb) склеп. **vaulted** adj сво́дчатый.

VDU abbr (of **visual display unit**) монито́р.

veal n теля́тина.

vector n (math) ве́ктор.

veer vi (change direction) изменя́ть impf, измени́ть pf направле́ние; (turn) повора́чивать impf, повороти́ть pf.

vegetable n о́вощ; adj овощно́й. **vegetarian** n вегетариа́нец, -нка; attrib вегетариа́нский. **vegetate** vi (fig) прозяба́ть impf. **vegetation** n расти́тельность.

vehemence n (force) си́ла; (passion) стра́стность. **vehement** adj (forceful) си́льный; (passionate) стра́стный.

vehicle n тра́нспортное сре́дство; (motor ~) автомоби́ль m; (medium) сре́дство.

veil n вуа́ль; (fig) заве́са. **veiled** adj скры́тый.

vein n (of leaf; streak) жи́лка; in the same ~ в том же ду́хе.

velocity n ско́рость.

velvet n ба́рхат; adj ба́рхатный. **velvety** adj бархати́стый.

vending-machine n торго́вый автома́т. **vendor** n продаве́ц, -вщи́ца.

vendetta n венде́тта.

veneer n фане́ра; (fig) лоск.

venerable adj почте́нный. **venerate** vt благогове́ть impf пе́ред+instr. **veneration** n благогове́ние.

venereal adj венери́ческий.

venetian blind n жалюзи́ neut indecl.

vengeance n месть; **take** ~ мстить impf, ото~ pf (**on** +dat; **for** за+acc); **with a** ~ вовсю́. **vengeful** adj мсти́тельный.

venison n оле́нина.

venom n яд. **venomous** adj ядови́тый.

vent[1] n (opening) вы́ход (also fig), отве́рстие; vt (feelings) дава́ть impf, дать pf вы́ход+dat; излива́ть impf, изли́ть pf (**on** на+acc).

vent[2] n (slit) разре́з.

ventilate vt прове́тривать impf, прове́трить pf. **ventilation** n вентиля́ция. **ventilator** n вентиля́тор.

ventriloquist n чревовеща́тель m.

venture n предприя́тие; vi (dare) осме́ливаться impf, осме́литься pf; vt (risk) рискова́ть impf +instr.

venue n ме́сто.

veranda n вера́нда.

verb n глаго́л. **verbal** adj (oral) у́стный; (relating to words) слове́сный; (gram) отглаго́льный. **verbatim** adj досло́вный; adv досло́вно. **verbose** adj многосло́вный.

verdict n пригово́р.

verge n (also fig) край; (of road) обо́чина; (fig) грань; **on the** ~ of на гра́ни+gen; **he was on the** ~ **of telling all** он чуть не рассказа́л всё; vi: ~ **on** грани́чить impf c+instr.

verification n прове́рка; (confirmation) подтвержде́ние. **verify** vt проверя́ть impf, прове́рить pf; (confirm) подтвержда́ть impf, подтверди́ть pf.

vermin n вреди́тели m pl.

vernacular n родно́й язы́к; ме́стный диале́кт; (homely language) разгово́рный язы́к.

versatile adj многосторо́нний.

verse n (also bibl) стих; (stanza) строфа́; (poetry) стихи́ m pl. **versed** adj о́пытный, све́дущий (**in** в+prep).

version n (variant) вариа́нт; (interpretation) ве́рсия; (text) текст.

versus prep про́тив+gen.

vertebra n позвоно́к; pl позвоно́чник. **vertebrate** n позвоно́чное живо́тное sb.

vertical adj вертика́льный; n вертика́ль.

vertigo n головокруже́ние.

verve n жи́вость, энтузиа́зм.

very adj (that ~ same) тот са́мый; (this ~ same) э́тот са́мый; **at that** ~ **moment** в тот са́мый моме́нт; (precisely) как раз; **you are the** ~ **person I was looking for** как раз вас я иска́л; **the** ~ (even the) да́же, оди́н; **the** ~ **thought frightens me** одна́, да́же, мысль об э́том меня́ пуга́ет; (the extreme) са́мый; at the ~ end в са́мом конце́; adv о́чень; ~ much о́чень; ~ much +comp гора́здо +comp; ~+superl, superl; ~ first са́мый пе́рвый; ~ well (agreement) хорошо́, ла́дно; not ~ не о́чень, дово́льно +neg.

vessel n сосу́д; (ship) су́дно.

vest¹ n ма́йка; (waistcoat) жиле́т.

vest² n (prep+power) облека́ть impf, обле́чь pf (with +instr). **vested** adj: ~ **interest** ли́чная заинтересо́ванность; ~ **interests** (entrepreneurs) кру́пные предпринима́тели m pl.

vestibule n вестибю́ль m.

vestige n (trace) след; (sign) при́знак.

vestments n pl (eccl) облаче́ние.

vestry n ри́зница.

vet n ветерина́р; vt (fig) проверя́ть impf, прове́рить pf.

veteran n ветера́н; adj ста́рый.

veterinary adj ветерина́рный; n ветерина́р.

veto n ве́то neut indecl; vt налага́ть impf, наложи́ть pf ве́то на+acc.

vex vt досажда́ть impf, досади́ть pf +dat. **vexation** n доса́да. **vexed** adj (annoyed) серди́тый; (question) спо́рный. **vexatious, vexing** adj доса́дный.

via prep че́рез+acc.

viable adj (able to survive) жизнеспосо́бный; (feasible) осуществи́мый.

viaduct n виаду́к.

vibrant adj (lively) живо́й. **vibrate** vi вибри́ровать impf; vt (make ~) заставля́ть impf, заста́вить pf вибри́ровать. **vibration** n вибра́ция. **vibrato** n вибра́то neut indecl.

vicar n прихо́дский свяще́нник. **vicarage** n дом свяще́нника.

vicarious adj чужо́й.

vice¹ n (evil) поро́к.

vice² n (tech) тиски́ (-ко́в) pl.

vice- in comb вице-, замести́тель m; ~**chairman** замести́тель m председа́теля; ~**chancellor** (univ) проре́ктор; ~**president** вице-президе́нт.

viceroy n вице-коро́ль m.

vice versa adv наоборо́т.

vicinity n окре́стность; in the ~ побли́зости (of от+gen).

vicious adj зло́бный; ~ **circle** поро́чный круг.

vicissitude n превра́тность.

victim n же́ртва; (of accident) пострада́вший sb. **victimization** n пресле́дование. **victimize** vt пресле́довать impf.

victor n победи́тель m, ~ница.

Victorian adj викториа́нский.

victorious adj победоно́сный. **victory** n побе́да.

video n (~ recorder, ~ cassette, ~ film) ви́део neut indecl; ~ **camera** видеока́мера; ~ **cassette** видеокассе́та; ~ (**cassette**) **recorder** видеомагнитофо́н; ~ **game** видеоигра́; vt запи́сывать impf, записа́ть pf на ви́део.

vie vi сопе́рничать impf (with с+instr; for в+prep).

Vietnam n Вьетна́м. **Vietnamese** n вьетна́мец, -мка; adj вьетна́мский.

view n (prospect, picture) вид; (opinion) взгляд; (viewing) просмо́тр; (inspection) осмо́тр; in ~ of ввиду́ +gen; on ~ вы́ставленный на обозре́ния; with a ~ to с це́лью+gen, +inf; vt (pictures etc.) рассма́тривать impf; (inspect) осма́тривать impf, осмотре́ть pf; (mentally) смотре́ть impf на+acc. **viewer** n зри́тель m, ~ница. **viewfinder** n видоиска́тель m. **viewpoint** n то́чка зре́ния.

vigil n бо́дрствование; **keep** ~ бо́дрствовать impf, дежу́рить impf. **vigilance** n бди́тельность. **vigilant** adj бди́тельный. **vigilante** n дружи́нник.

vigorous adj си́льный, энерги́чный. **vigour** n си́ла, эне́ргия.

vile adj гну́сный. **vilify** vt черни́ть impf, о~ pf.

villa n ви́лла.

village n дере́вня; attrib дереве́нский. **villager** n жи́тель m дере́вни.

villain n злоде́й.

vinaigrette n припра́ва из у́ксуса и оли́вкового ма́сла.

vindicate vt опра́вдывать impf, оправда́ть pf. **vindication** n оправда́ние.

vindictive adj мсти́тельный.

vine n виногра́дная лоза́.

vinegar n у́ксус.

vineyard n виногра́дник.

vintage n (year) год; (fig) вы́пуск; attrib (wine) ма́рочный; (car) архаи́ческий.

viola n (mus) альт.

violate vt (treaty, privacy) нарушать impf, нарушить pf; (grave) осквернять impf, осквернить pf. **violation** n нарушение; осквернение.

violence n (physical coercion, force) насилие; (strength, force) сила. **violent** adj (person, storm, argument) свирепый; (pain) сильный; (death) насильственный. **violently** adv сильно, очень.

violet n (bot) фиалка; (colour) фиолетовый цвет; adj фиолетовый.

violin n скрипка. **violinist** n скрипач, ~ка.

VIP abbr (of very important person) очень важное лицо.

viper n гадюка.

virgin n девственница, (male) девственник; V~ **Mary** дева Мария. **virginal** adj девственный. **virginity** n девственность. **Virgo** n Дева.

virile adj мужественный. **virility** n мужество.

virtual adj фактический. **virtually** adv фактически. **virtue** n (excellence) добродетель; (merit) достоинство; **by ~ of** на основании+gen. **virtuosity** n виртуозность. **virtuoso** n виртуоз. **virtuous** adj добродетельный.

virulent adj (med) вирулентный; (fig) злобный.

virus n вирус.

visa n виза.

vis-à-vis prep (with regard to) по отношению к+dat.

viscount n виконт. **viscountess** n виконтесса.

viscous adj вязкий.

visibility n видимость. **visible** adj видимый. **visibly** adv явно, заметно.

vision n (sense) зрение; (apparition) видение; (dream) мечта; (insight) проницательность. **visionary** adj (unreal) призрачный; (impracticable) неосуществимый; (insightful) проницательный; n (dreamer) мечтатель m.

visit n посещение, визит; vt посещать impf, посетить pf; (call on) заходить impf, зайти pf к+dat. **visitation** n официальное посещение. **visitor** n гость m, посетитель m.

visor n (of cap) козырёк; (in car) солнцезащитный щиток; (of helmet) забрало.

vista n перспектива, вид.

visual adj (of vision) зрительный; (graphic) наглядный; ~ **aids** наглядные пособия neut pl. **visualize** vt представлять impf, представить pf себе.

vital adj абсолютно необходимый (**to, for** для+gen); (essential to life) жизненный; **of ~ importance** первостепенной важности. **vitality** n (liveliness) энергия. **vitally** adv жизненно.

vitamin n витамин.

vitreous adj стеклянный.

vitriolic adj (fig) едкий.

vivacious adj живой. **vivacity** n живость.

viva (voce) n устный экзамен.

vivid adj (bright) яркий; (lively) живой. **vividness** n яркость; живость.

vivisection n вивисекция.

vixen n лисица-самка.

viz. adv то есть, а именно.

vocabulary n (range, list, of words) словарь m; (range of words) запас слов; (of a language) словарный состав.

vocal adj голосовой; (mus) вокальный; (noisy) шумный; ~ **chord** голосовая связка. **vocalist** n певец, -вица.

vocation n призвание. **vocational** adj профессиональный.

vociferous adj шумный.

vodka n водка.

vogue n мода; **in ~** в моде.

voice n голос; vt выражать impf, выразить pf.

void n пустота; adj пустой; (invalid) недействительный; ~ **of** лишённый +gen.

volatile adj (chem) летучий; (person) непостоянный, неустойчивый.

volcanic adj вулканический. **volcano** n вулкан.

vole n (zool) полёвка.

volition n воля; **by one's own ~** по своей воле.

volley n (missiles) залп; (fig) град; (sport) удар с лёта; vt (sport) ударять impf, ударить pf с лёта. **volleyball** n волейбол.

volt n вольт. **voltage** n напряжение.

voluble *adj* говорли́вый.

volume *n* (*book*) том; (*capacity, size*) объём; (*loudness*) гро́мкость. **voluminous** *adj* обши́рный.

voluntary *adj* доброво́льный. **volunteer** *n* доброво́лец; *vt* предлага́ть *impf*, предложи́ть *pf*; *vi* (*offer*) вызыва́ться *impf*, вы́зваться *pf* (*inf*, +*inf*; **for** в+*acc*); (*mil*) идти́ *impf*, пойти́ *pf* доброво́льцем.

voluptuous *adj* сластолюби́вый.

vomit *n* рво́та; *vt* (& *i*) рвать *impf*, вы́рвать *pf impers* (+*instr*); **he was ~ing blood** его́ рва́ло кро́вью.

voracious *adj* прожо́рливый; (*fig*) ненасы́тный.

vortex *n* (*also fig*) водоворо́т, вихрь *m*.

vote *n* (*poll*) голосова́ние; (*individual* ~) го́лос; **the ~** (*suffrage*) пра́во го́лоса; (*resolution*) во́тум *no pl*; ~ **of no confidence** во́тум недове́рия (**in** +*dat*); ~ **of thanks** выраже́ние благода́рности; *vi* голосова́ть *impf*, про~ *pf* (**for** за+*acc*; **against** про́тив+*gen*); *vt* (*allocate by* ~) ассигнова́ть *impf* & *pf*; (*deem*) признава́ть *impf*, призна́ть *pf*; **the film was ~d a failure** фильм был при́знан неуда́чным; ~ **in** избира́ть *impf*, избра́ть *pf* голосова́нием. **voter** *n* избира́тель *m*.

vouch *vi*: ~ **for** руча́ться *impf*, поручи́ться *pf* за+*acc*. **voucher** *n* (*receipt*) распи́ска; (*coupon*) тало́н.

vow *n* обе́т; *vt* кля́сться *impf*, по~ *pf* в+*prep*.

vowel *n* гла́сный *sb*.

voyage *n* путеше́ствие.

vulgar *adj* вульга́рный, гру́бый, по́шлый. **vulgarity** *n* вульга́рность, по́шлость.

vulnerable *adj* уязви́мый.

vulture *n* гриф; (*fig*) хи́щник.

W

wad *n* комо́к; (*bundle*) па́чка. **wadding** *n* (*padding*) наби́вка.

waddle *vi* ходи́ть *indet*, идти́ *det*, пойти́ *pf* вперева́лку (*coll*).

wade *vt* & *i* (*river*) переходи́ть *impf*, перейти́ *pf* вброд; *vi*: ~ **through** (*mud etc.*) пробира́ться *impf*, про-

бра́ться *pf* по+*dat*; (*sth boring etc.*) одолева́ть *impf*, одоле́ть *pf*.

wafer *n* ва́фля.

waffle[1] *n* (*dish*) ва́фля.

waffle[2] *vi* трепа́ться *impf*.

waft *vt* & *i* нести́(сь) *impf*, по~ *pf*.

wag *vt* & *i* (*tail*) виля́ть *impf*, вильну́ть *pf* (+*instr*); *vt* (*finger*) грози́ть *impf*, по~ *pf* +*instr*.

wage[1] *n* (*pay*) *see* **wages**

wage[2] *vt*: ~ **war** вести́ *impf*, про~ *pf* войну́.

wager *n* пари́ *neut indecl*; *vi* держа́ть *impf* пари́ (**that** что); *vt* ста́вить *impf* по~ *pf*.

wages *n pl* за́работная пла́та.

waggle *vt* & *i* пома́хивать *impf*, пома́хать *pf* (+*instr*).

wag(g)on *n* (*carriage*) пово́зка; (*cart*) теле́га; (*rly*) ваго́н-платфо́рма.

wail *n* вопль *m*; *vi* вопи́ть *impf*.

waist *n* та́лия; (*level of* ~) по́яс; ~**deep, high** (*adv*) по по́яс. **waistband** *n* по́яс. **waistcoat** *n* жиле́т. **waistline** *n* та́лия.

wait *n* ожида́ние; **lie in** ~ (**for**) подстерега́ть *impf*, подстере́чь *pf*; *vi* (& *t*) (*also* ~ **for**) ждать *impf* (+*gen*); *vi* (*be a waiter, waitress*) быть официа́нтом, -ткой; ~ **on** обслу́живать *impf*, обслужи́ть *pf*. **waiter** *n* официа́нт. **waiting** *n*: ~**list** спи́сок; ~**room** приёмная *sb*; (*rly*) зал ожида́ния. **waitress** *n* официа́нтка.

waive *vt* отка́зываться *impf*, отказа́ться *pf* от+*gen*.

wake[1] *n* (*at funeral*) поми́нки (-нок) *pl*.

wake[2] *n* (*naut*) кильва́тер; **in the ~ of** по сле́ду +*gen*, за+*instr*.

wake[3] *vt* (*also* ~ **up**) буди́ть *impf*, раз~ *pf*; *vi* (*also* ~ **up**) просыпа́ться *impf*, просну́ться *pf*.

Wales *n* Уэ́льс.

walk *n* (*walking*) ходьба́; (*gait*) похо́дка; (*stroll*) прогу́лка; (*path*) тропа́; ~**out** (*strike*) забасто́вка; (*as protest*) демонстрати́вный ухо́д; ~**over** лёгкая побе́да; **ten minutes' ~ from here** де́сять мину́т ходьбы́ отсю́да; **go for a** ~ идти́ *impf*, пойти́ *pf* гуля́ть; **from all ~s of life** всех слоёв о́бщества; *vi* ходи́ть *indet*, идти́ *det*, пойти́ *pf*; гуля́ть *impf*, по~ *pf*; ~ **away, off** уходи́ть *impf*, уйти́ *pf*; ~ **in** входи́ть *impf*, войти́ *pf*; ~ **out** выходи́ть *impf*, вы́йти *pf*; ~ **out on** броса́ть *impf*, бро́сить *pf*; *vt* (*traverse*) обходи́ть *impf*, обойти́ *pf*; (*take for* ~) выводи́ть *impf*, вы́вести *pf* гуля́ть. **walker** *n* ходо́к. **walkie-talkie** *n* ра́ция. **walking** *n* ходьба́; ~-**stick** трость.

Walkman *n* (*propr*) во́кмен.

wall *n* стена́; *vt* обноси́ть *impf*, обнести́ *pf* стено́й; ~ **up** (*door, window*) заде́лывать *impf*, заде́лать *pf*; (*brick up*) замуро́вывать *impf*, замурова́ть *pf*.

wallet *n* бума́жник.

wallflower *n* желтофио́ль.

wallop *n* (*lack*) си́льный уда́р; *vt* си́льно ударя́ть *impf*, уда́рить *pf*.

wallow *vi* валя́ться *impf*; ~ **in** (*give o.s. up to*) погружа́ться *impf*, погрузи́ться *pf* в+*асс*.

wallpaper *n* обо́и (обо́ев) *pl*.

walnut *n* гре́цкий оре́х; (*wood, tree*) оре́ховое де́рево, оре́х.

walrus *n* морж.

waltz *n* вальс; *vi* вальси́ровать *impf*.

wan *adj* бле́дный.

wand *n* па́лочка.

wander *vi* броди́ть *impf*; (*also of thoughts etc.*) блужда́ть *impf*; ~ **from the point** отклоня́ться *impf*, отклони́ться *pf* от те́мы. **wanderer** *n* стра́нник.

wane *n*: **be on the** ~ убыва́ть *impf*; *vi* убыва́ть *impf*, убы́ть *pf*; (*weaken*) ослабева́ть *impf*, ослабе́ть *pf*.

wangle *vt* заполуча́ть *impf*, заполучи́ть *pf*.

want *n* (*lack*) недоста́ток; (*requirement*) потре́бность; (*desire*) жела́ние; **for** ~ **of** за недоста́тком +*gen*; *vt* хоте́ть *impf*, за~ *pf* +*gen*, *асс*; (*need*) нужда́ться *impf* в+*prep*; **I** ~ **you to come at six** я хочу́, чтобы ты пришёл в шесть. **wanting** *adj*: **be** ~ недостава́ть *impf* (*impers* +*gen*); **experience is** ~ недостаёт о́пыта.

wanton *adj* (*licentious*) распу́тный; (*senseless*) бессмы́сленный.

war *n* война́; (*attrib*) вое́нный; **at** ~ в состоя́нии войны́; ~ **memorial** па́мятник па́вшим в войне́.

ward *n* (*hospital*) пала́та; (*child etc.*) подопе́чный *sb*; (*district*) райо́н; *vt*:

~ **off** отража́ть *impf*, отрази́ть *pf*.

warden *n* (*prison*) нача́льник; (*college*) ре́ктор; (*hostel*) коменда́нт.

warder *n* тюре́мщик.

wardrobe *n* гардеро́б.

warehouse *n* склад. **wares** *n pl* изде́лия *neut pl*, това́ры *m pl*.

warfare *n* война́.

warhead *n* боева́я голо́вка.

warily *adv* осторо́жно.

warlike *adj* вои́нственный.

warm *n* тепло́; *adj* (*also fig*) тёплый; ~-**hearted** серде́чный; *vt & i* греть(ся) *impf*; согрева́ть(ся) *impf*, согре́ть(ся) *pf*; ~ **up** (*food etc.*) подогрева́ть(ся) *impf*, подогре́ть(ся) *pf*; (*liven up*) оживля́ть(ся) *impf*, оживи́ть(ся) *pf*; (*sport*) размина́ться *impf*, размя́ться *pf*; (*mus*) разы́грываться *impf*, разыгра́ться *pf*. **warmth** *n* тепло́; (*cordiality*) серде́чность.

warn *vt* предупрежда́ть *impf*, предупреди́ть *pf* (*about* о+*prep*). **warning** *n* предупрежде́ние.

warp *vt & i* (*wood*) коро́бить(ся) *impf*, по~, с~ *pf*; *vt* (*pervert*) извраща́ть *impf*, изврати́ть *pf*.

warrant *n* (*for arrest etc.*) о́рдер; *vt* (*justify*) опра́вдывать *impf*, оправда́ть *pf*; (*guarantee*) гаранти́ровать *impf & pf*. **warranty** *n* гара́нтия.

warrior *n* во́ин.

warship *n* вое́нный кора́бль *m*.

wart *n* борода́вка.

wartime *n*: **in** ~ во вре́мя войны́.

wary *adj* осторо́жный.

wash *n* мытьё; (*thin layer*) то́нкий слой; (*lotion*) примо́чка; (*surf*) прибо́й; (*backwash*) попу́тная волна́; **at the** ~ в сти́рке; **have a** ~ мы́ться *impf*, по~ *pf*; ~-**basin** умыва́льник; ~-**out** (*fiasco*) прова́л; ~-**room** умыва́льная *sb*; *vt & i* мы́ть(ся) *impf*, вы́~, по~ *pf*; *vt* (*clothes*) стира́ть *impf*, вы́~ *pf*; (*of sea*) омыва́ть *impf*; ~ **away, off, out** смыва́ть(ся) *impf*, смы́ть(ся) *pf*; (*carry away*) сноси́ть *impf*, снести́ *pf*; ~ **out** (*rinse*) спола́скивать *impf*, сполосну́ть *pf*; ~ **up** (*dishes*) мыть *impf*, вы́~, по~ *pf* (посу́ду); ~ **one's hands (of it)** умыва́ть *impf*, умы́ть *pf* ру́ки. **washed-out** *adj* (*exhausted*) утомлённый. **washer** *n* (*tech*) ша́йба.

washing n (of clothes) стúрка; (clothes) бельё; ~-machine стирáльная машúна; ~-powder стирáльный порошóк; ~-up (action) мытьё посýды; (dishes) грязная посýда; ~-up liquid жúдкое мы́ло для мытья́ посýды.

wasp n осá.

wastage n утéчка. waste n (desert) пустыня́; (refuse) отбрóсы m pl; (of time, money, etc.) растрáта; go to ~ пропадáть impf, пропáсть pf дáром; adj (desert) пустынный; (superfluous) ненýжный; (uncultivated) невозделанный; lay ~ опустошáть impf, опустошúть pf; ~ land пустырь m; ~ paper ненýжные бумáги f pl; (for recycling) макулатýра; ~ products отхóды (-дов) pl; ~ paper basket корзúна для бумáги; vt трáтить impf, по~, ис~ pf; (time) теря́ть impf, по~ pf; vi: ~ away чáхнуть impf, за~ pf. wasteful adj расточúтельный.

watch n (timepiece) часы́ (-сóв) pl; (duty) дежýрство; (naut) вáхта; keep ~ over наблюдáть impf за+instr; ~-dog сторожевóй пёс; ~-tower сторожевáя бáшня; vt (observe) наблюдáть impf; (keep an eye on) следúть impf за+instr; (look after) смотрéть impf, по~ pf за+instr; ~ television, a film смотрéть impf, по~ pf телевúзор, фильм; vi смотрéть impf; ~ out (be careful) беречься impf (for +gen); ~ out for ждать impf +gen; ~ out! осторóжно! watchful adj бдúтельный. watchman n (ночнóй) стóрож. watchword n лóзунг.

water n водá; ~-colour акварéль; ~-heater кипятúльник; ~-main водопровóдная магистрáль; ~ melon арбýз; ~-pipe водопровóдная трубá; ~-ski (n) вóдная лы́жа; ~-skiing водолы́жный спорт; ~-supply водоснабжéние; ~-way вóдный путь m; vt (flowers etc.) поливáть impf, полúть pf; (animals) поúть impf, на~ pf; (irrigate) орошáть impf, оросúть pf; vi (eyes) слезúться impf; (mouth): my mouth ~s у меня́ слю́нки текýт; ~ down разбавля́ть impf, разбáвить pf. watercourse n рýсло. watercress n кресс водянóй.

waterfall n водопáд. waterfront n часть гóрода примыкáющая к бéрегу. watering-can n лéйка. waterlogged adj заболóченный. watermark n водянóй знак. waterproof adj непромокáемый; n непромокáемый плащ. watershed n водораздéл. waterside n бéрег. watertight adj водонепроницáемый; (fig) неопровержúмый. waterworks n pl водопровóдные сооружéния neut pl. watery adj водянúстый.

watt n ватт.

wave vt (hand etc.) махáть impf, махнýть pf +instr; (flag) размáхивать impf +instr; vi (~ hand) махáть impf, по~ pf (at +dat); (flutter) развевáться impf; ~ aside отмáхиваться impf, отмахнýться pf от+gen; ~ down останáвливать impf, остановúть pf; n (in various senses) волнá; (of hand) взмах; (in hair) завúвка. wavelength n длинá волны́. waver vi колебáться impf. wavy adj волнúстый.

wax n воск; (in ear) сéра; vt вощúть impf, на~ pf. waxwork n восковáя фигýра; pl музéй восковы́х фигýр.

way n (road, path, route; fig) дорóга, путь m; (direction) сторонá; (manner) óбраз; (method) спóсоб; (respect) отношéние; (habit) привы́чка; by the ~ (fig) кстáти, мéжду прóчим; on the ~ по дорóге, по путú; this ~ (direction) сюдá; (in this ~) такúм óбразом; the other ~ round наоборóт; under ~ на ходý; be in the ~ мешáть impf; get out of the ~ уходúть impf, уйтú pf с дорóги; give ~ (yield) поддавáться impf, поддáться pf (to +dat); (collapse) обрýшиваться impf, обрýшиться pf; go out of one's ~ стáраться impf, по~ pf изо всех сил +inf; get, have, one's own ~ добивáться impf, добúться pf своегó; make ~ уступáть impf, уступúть pf дорóгу (for +dat). waylay vt (lie in wait for) подстерегáть impf, подстерéчь pf; (stop) перехвáтывать impf, перехватúть pf по путú. wayside adj придорóжный; n: fall by the ~ выбывáть impf, вы́быть pf из строя́.

wayward adj своенрáвый.

WC *abbr* (*of* water-closet) убо́рная *sb.*
we *pron* мы.

weak *adj* сла́бый. **weaken** *vt* ослаб-
ля́ть *impf*, осла́бить *pf*; *vi* слабе́ть
impf, o~ *pf*. **weakling** *n* (*person*)
сла́бый челове́к; (*plant*) сла́бое рас-
те́ние. **weakness** *n* сла́бость.
weal *n* (*mark*) рубе́ц.
wealth *n* бога́тство; (*abundance*) изо-
би́лие. **wealthy** *adj* бога́тый.
wean *vt* отнима́ть *impf*, отня́ть *pf*
от груди́; (*fig*) отуча́ть *impf*, оту-
чи́ть *pf* (*of, from* от+*gen*).
weapon *n* ору́жие. **weaponry** *n* во-
оруже́ние.
wear *n* (*wearing*) но́ска; (*clothing*)
оде́жда; (~ *and tear*) изно́с; *vt* но-
си́ть *impf*, быть в+*prep*; **what shall
I ~?** что мне наде́ть?; *vi* носи́ться
impf; ~ **off** (*pain, novelty*) прохо-
ди́ть *impf*, пройти́ *pf*; (*cease to have
effect*) перестава́ть *impf*, переста́ть
pf де́йствовать; ~ **out** (*clothes*) из-
на́шивать(ся) *impf*, износи́ть(ся) *pf*;
(*exhaust*) измучивать *impf*, изму́-
чить *pf*.
weariness *n* уста́лость. **wearing,
wearisome** *adj* утоми́тельный. **weary**
adj уста́лый; *vt & i* утомля́ть(ся)
impf, утоми́ть(ся) *pf*.
weasel *n* ла́ска.
weather *n* пого́да; **be under the ~**
нева́жно себя́ чу́вствовать *impf*; ~-
beaten обве́тренный; ~ **forecast**
прогно́з пого́ды; *vt* (*storm etc.*) вы-
де́рживать *impf*, вы́держать *pf*; (*expose to atmosphere*) подверга́ть
impf, подве́ргнуть *pf* атмосфе́рным
влия́ниям. **weather-cock, weather-
vane** *n* флю́гер. **weatherman** *n* ме-
теоро́лог.
weave¹ *vt & i* (*fabric*) ткать *impf*,
co~ *pf*; *vt* (*fig; also wreath etc.*)
плести́ *impf*, c~ *pf*. **weaver** *n* ткач,
~и́ха.
weave² *vi* (*wind*) ви́ться *impf*.
web *n* (*cobweb; fig*) паути́на; (*fig*)
сплете́ние. **webbed** *adj* перепо́н-
чатый. **webbing** *n* тка́ная ле́нта.
wed *vt* (*of man*) жени́ться *impf & pf*
на+*prep*; (*of woman*) выходи́ть *impf*,
вы́йти *pf* за́муж за+*acc*; (*unite*) co-
чета́ть *impf & pf*; *vi* пожени́ться *pf*.
wedded *adj* супру́жеский; ~ **to** (*fig*)
пре́данный +*dat*. **wedding** *n* сва́дьба;

~-**cake** сва́дебный
торт; ~-**day** день *m* сва́дьбы; ~-**dress**
подвене́чное пла́тье; ~-**ring** обру-
ча́льное кольцо́.
wedge *n* клин; *vt* (~ *open*) закли́ни-
вать *impf*, закли́нить *pf*; *vt & i*: ~
in(to) вкли́нивать(ся) *impf*, вкли́-
нить(ся) *pf* (в+*acc*).
wedlock *n* брак; **born out of** ~ рождённый вне бра́ка, внебра́чный.
Wednesday *n* среда́.
weed *n* сорня́к; ~-**killer** гербици́д; *vt*
поло́ть *impf*, вы́~ *pf*; ~ **out** удаля́ть
impf, удали́ть *pf*. **weedy** *adj* (*person*) то́щий.
week *n* неде́ля; ~-**end** суббо́та и вос-
кресе́нье, выходны́е *sb pl*. **weekday** *n*
бу́дний день *m*. **weekly** *adj* еже-
неде́льный; (*wage*) неде́льный; *adv*
еженеде́льно; *n* еженеде́льник.
weep *vi* пла́кать *impf*. **weeping willow** *n* плаку́чая и́ва.
weigh *vt* (*also fig*) взве́шивать *impf*,
взве́сить *pf*; (*consider*) обду́мывать
impf, обду́мать *pf*; *vt & i* (*so much*)
ве́сить *impf*; ~ **down** отягоща́ть
impf, отяготи́ть *pf*; ~ **on** тяготи́ть
impf; ~ **out** отве́шивать *impf*, отве́-
сить *pf*; ~ **up** (*appraise*) оце́нивать
impf, оцени́ть *pf*. **weight** *n* (*also authority*) вес; (*load, also fig*) тя́жесть;
(*sport*) шта́нга; (*influence*) влия́ние;
lose ~ худе́ть *impf*, по~ *pf*; **put on**
~ толсте́ть *impf*, по~ *pf*; ~-**lifter**
штанги́ст; ~-**lifting** подня́тие тя́жо-
стей; *vt* (*make heavier*) утяжеля́ть
impf, утяжели́ть *pf*. **weightless** *adj*
невесо́мый. **weighty** *adj* ве́ский.
weir *n* плоти́на.
weird *adj* (*strange*) стра́нный.
welcome *n* приём; *adj* жела́нный;
(*pleasant*) прия́тный; **you are** ~
(*don't mention it*) пожа́луйста; **you
are** ~ **to use my bicycle** мой вело-
сипе́д к ва́шим услу́гам; **you are**
to stay the night вы мо́жете пере-
ночева́ть у меня́/нас; *vt* приве́тст-
вовать *impf* (& *pf* in *past tense*); *int*
добро́ пожа́ловать!
weld *vt* сва́ривать *impf*, свари́ть *pf*.
welder *n* сва́рщик.
welfare *n* благосостоя́ние; **W~ State**
госуда́рство всео́бщего благосостоя́-
ния.
well¹ *n* коло́дец; (*for stairs*) ле́стнич-

ная кле́тка.

well² *vi*: ~ **up** (*anger etc.*) вскипа́ть *impf*, вскипе́ть *pf*; **tears** ~**ed up** глаза́ напо́лнились слеза́ми.

well³ *adj* (*healthy*) здоро́вый; **feel** ~ чу́вствовать *impf*, по~ *pf* себя́ хорошо́, здоро́вым; **get** ~ поправля́ться *impf*, попра́виться *pf*; **look** ~ хорошо́ вы́глядеть *impf*; **all is** ~ всё в поря́дке; *int* ну(!); *adv* хорошо́; (*very much*) о́чень; **as** ~ то́же; **as** ~ **as** (*in addition to*) кро́ме+*gen*; **it may** ~ **be true** вполне́ возмо́жно, что э́то так; **very** ~! хорошо́!; ~ **done!** молоде́ц!; ~**balanced** уравнове́шенный; ~**behaved** (благо)воспи́танный; ~**being** благополу́чие; ~**bred** благовоспи́танный; ~**built** кре́пкий; ~**defined** чёткий; ~**disposed** благоскло́нный; ~ **done** (*cooked*) (хорошо́) прожа́ренный; ~**fed** отко́рмленный; ~**founded** обосно́ванный; ~**groomed** (*person*) хо́леный; ~**heeled** состоя́тельный; ~**informed** (хорошо́) осведомлённый (**about** в+*prep*); ~**known** изве́стный; ~**meaning** де́йствующий из лу́чших побужде́ний; ~**nigh** почти́; ~**off** состоя́тельный; ~**paid** хорошо́ опла́чиваемый; ~**preserved** хорошо́ сохрани́вшийся; ~**to-do** состоя́тельный; ~**wisher** доброжела́тель *m*.

wellington (boot) *n* рези́новый сапо́г.

Welsh *adj* уэ́льский. **Welshman** *n* валли́ец. **Welshwoman** *n* валли́йка.

welter *n* пу́таница.

wend *vt*: ~ **one's way** держа́ть *impf* путь.

west *n* за́пад; (*naut*) вест; *adj* за́падный; *adv* на за́пад, к за́паду. **westerly** *adj* за́падный. **western** *adj* за́падный; *n* (*film*) ве́стерн. **westward(s)** *adv* на за́пад, к за́паду.

wet *adj* мо́крый; (*paint*) непросо́хший; (*rainy*) дождли́вый; ~ **through** промо́кший до ни́тки; *n* (*dampness*) вла́жность; (*rain*) дождь *m*; *vt* мочи́ть *impf*, на~ *pf*.

whack *n* (*blow*) уда́р; *vt* колоти́ть *impf*, по~ *pf*. **whacked** *adj* разби́тый.

whale *n* кит.

wharf *n* при́стань.

what *pron* (*interrog*, *int*) что; (*how much*) ско́лько; (*rel*) (то,) что; ~ (...)

for заче́м; ~ **if** а что е́сли; ~ **is your name** как вас зову́т?; *adj* (*interrog*, *int*) како́й; ~ **kind of** како́й. **whatever**, **whatsoever** *pron* что бы ни +*past* (~ **you think** что бы вы ни ду́мали); всё, что (**take** ~ **you want** возьми́те всё, что хоти́те); *adj* како́й бы ни+*past* (~ **books he read(s)** каки́е бы кни́ги он ни прочита́л); (*at all*): **there is no chance** ~ нет никако́й возмо́жности; **is there any chance** ~? есть ли хоть кака́я-нибу́дь возмо́жность?

wheat *n* пшени́ца.

wheedle *vt* (*coax into doing*) угова́ривать *impf*, уговори́ть *pf* с по́мощью ле́сти; ~ **out of** выма́нивать *impf*, вы́манить *pf* у+*gen*.

wheel *n* колесо́; (*steering* ~, *helm*) руль *m*; (*potter's*) гонча́рный круг; *vt* (*push*) ката́ть *indet*, кати́ть *det*, по~ *pf*; *vt* & *i* (*turn*) повёртывать(ся) *impf*, поверну́ть(ся) *pf*; *vi* (*circle*) кружи́ться *impf*. **wheelbarrow** *n* та́чка. **wheelchair** *n* инвали́дное кре́сло.

wheeze *vi* сопе́ть *impf*.

when *adv* когда́; *conj* когда́, в то вре́мя как; (*whereas*) тогда́ как; (*if*) е́сли; (*although*) хотя́. **whence** *adv* отку́да. **whenever** *adv* когда́ же; *conj* (*every time*) вся́кий раз когда́; (*at any time*) когда́; (*no matter when*) когда́ бы ни+*past*; **we shall have dinner** ~ **you arrive** во ско́лько бы вы ни прие́хали, мы пообе́даем.

where *adv* & *conj* (*place*) где; (*whither*) куда́; **from** ~ отку́да. **whereabouts** *adv* где; *n* местонахожде́ние. **whereas** *conj* тогда́ как; хотя́. **whereby** *adv* & *conj* посре́дством чего́. **wherein** *adv* & *conj* в чём. **wherever** *adv* & *conj* (*place*) где бы ни+*past*; (*whither*) куда́ бы ни+*past*; ~ **he goes** куда́ бы он ни пошёл; ~ **you like** где/куда́ хоти́те. **wherewithal** *n* сре́дства *neut pl*.

whet *vt* точи́ть *impf*, на~ *pf*; (*fig*) возбужда́ть *impf*, возбуди́ть *pf*.

whether *conj* ли; **I don't know** ~ **he will come** я не зна́ю, придёт ли он; ~ **he comes or not** придёт (ли) он и́ли нет.

which *adj* (*interrog*, *rel*) како́й; *pron* (*interrog*) како́й; (*person*) кто; (*rel*) кото́рый; (rel to whole statement) что; ~ **is** ~? (persons) кто из них кто?; (things) что-что? **whichever** adj & pron како́й бы ни+past (~ **book you choose** каку́ю бы кни́гу ты ни вы́брал); любо́й (take ~ **book you want** возьми́те любу́ю кни́гу).

whiff n за́пах.

while n вре́мя neut; **a little** ~ недо́лго; **a long** ~ до́лго; **for a long** ~ (up to now) давно́; **for a** ~ на вре́мя; **in a little** ~ ско́ро; **it is worth** ~ сто́ит э́то сде́лать; vt: ~ **away** проводи́ть impf, провести́ pf; conj пока́; в то вре́мя как; (although) хотя́; (contrast) a; **we went to the cinema** ~ **they went to the theatre** мы ходи́ли в кино́, а они́ в теа́тр. **whilst** see **while**

whim n при́хоть, капри́з.

whimper vi хны́кать impf; (dog) скули́ть impf.

whimsical adj капри́зный; (odd) причудли́вый.

whine n (wail) вой; (whimper) хны́канье; vi (dog) скули́ть impf; (wail) выть; (whimper) хны́кать impf.

whinny vi ти́хо ржать impf.

whip n кнут, хлыст; vt (lash) хлеста́ть impf, хлестну́ть pf; (cream) сбива́ть impf, сбить pf; ~ **off** ски́дывать impf, ски́нуть pf; ~ **out** выха́тывать impf, вы́хватить pf; ~ **round** бы́стро поверну́ться impf, поверну́ться pf; ~-**round** сбор де́нег; ~ **up** (stir up) разжига́ть impf, разже́чь pf.

whirl n круже́ние; (of dust, fig) вихрь m; (turmoil) сумато́ха; vt & i кружи́ть(ся) impf, за~ pf. **whirlpool** n водоворо́т. **whirlwind** n вихрь m.

whirr vi жужжа́ть impf.

whisk n (of twigs etc.) ве́ничек; (utensil) муто́вка; (movement) пома́хивание; vt (cream etc.) сбива́ть impf, сбить pf; ~ **away**, **off** (brush off) сма́хивать impf, смахну́ть pf; (take away) бы́стро уноси́ть impf, унести́ pf.

whisker n (human) во́лос на лице́; (animal) ус; pl (human) бакенба́рды f pl.

whisky n ви́ски neut indecl.

whisper n шёпот; vt & i шепта́ть impf, шепну́ть pf.

whistle n (sound) свист; (instrument) свисто́к; vi свисте́ть impf, свист-

нуть pf; vt насви́стывать impf.

white adj бе́лый; (hair) седо́й; (pale) бле́дный; (with milk) с молоко́м; **paint** ~ кра́сить impf, по~ pf в бе́лый свет; ~-**collar worker** слу́жащий sb; ~ **lie** неви́нная ложь; n (colour) бе́лый цвет; (egg, eye) бело́к; (~ person) бе́лый sb. **whiten** vt бели́ть impf, на~, по~, вы́~ pf; vi беле́ть impf, по~ pf. **whiteness** n белизна́. **whitewash** n побе́лка; vt бели́ть impf, по~ pf; (fig) обеля́ть impf, обели́ть pf.

whither adv & conj куда́.

Whitsun n Тро́ица.

whittle vt: ~ **down** уменьша́ть impf, уме́ньшить pf.

whiz(z) vi: ~ **past** просвисте́ть pf.

who pron (interrog) кто; (rel) кото́рый.

whoever pron кто бы ни+past; (he who) тот, кто.

whole adj (entire) весь, це́лый; (intact, of number) це́лый; n (thing complete) це́лое sb; (all there is) весь sb; (sum) су́мма; **on the** ~ в о́бщем. **wholehearted** adj безаве́тный. **whole-heartedly** adv от всего́ се́рдца. **wholemeal** adj из непросе́янной муки́. **wholesale** adj опто́вый; (fig) ма́ссовый; adv о́птом. **wholesaler** n опто́вый торго́вец. **wholesome** adj здоро́вый. **wholly** adv по́лностью.

whom pron (interrog) кого́ etc.; (rel) кото́рого etc.

whoop n крик; vi крича́ть impf, кри́кнуть pf; ~ **it up** бу́рно весели́ться impf; ~-**ing cough** коклю́ш.

whore n проститу́тка.

whose pron (interrog, rel) чей; (rel) кото́рого.

why adv почему́; int да ведь!

wick n фити́ль m.

wicked adj ди́кий. **wickedness** n ди́кость.

wicker attrib плетёный.

wicket n (cricket) воро́тца.

wide adj широ́кий; (extensive) обши́рный; (in measurements) в+acc ширино́й; ~ **awake** по́лный внима́ния; ~ **open** широко́ откры́тый (off target) ми́мо це́ли. **widely** adv широко́. **widen** vt & i расширя́ть(ся) impf, расши́рить(ся) pf. **widespread** adj распространённый.

widow n вдова́. **widowed** adj овдовёвший. **widower** n вдовéц.

width n ширинá; (fig) широтá; (of cloth) полотнище.

wield vt (brandish) размáхивать impf +instr; (power) пóльзоваться impf +instr.

wife n женá.

wig n парик.

wiggle vt & i (move) шевелить(ся) impf, по~, шевельнуть(ся) pf (+instr).

wigwam n вигвáм.

wild adj дикий; (flower) полевóй; (uncultivated) невозделанный; (tempestuous) буйный; (furious) нейстовый; (ill-considered) необдуманный; be ~ about быть без умá от+gen; ~-**goose chase** сумасбрóдная затéя; n: pl дéбри (-рей) pl **wildcat** adj (unofficial) неофициáльный. **wilderness** n пустыня. **wildfire** n: **spread like** ~ распространяться impf, распространиться pf с молниенóсной быстротóй. **wildlife** n живáя прирóда. **wildness** n дикость.

wile n хитрость.

wilful adj (obstinate) упрямый; (deliberate) преднамéренный.

will n вóля; (~-power) сила вóли; (at death) завещáние; **against one's** ~ прóтив вóли; **of one's own free** ~ добровóльно; **with a** ~ с энтузиáзмом; **good** ~ дóбрая вóля; **make one's** ~ писáть impf, на~ pf завещáние; vt (want) хотéть impf, за~ pf +gen, acc; v aux: **he** ~ **be president** он бýдет президéнтом; **he** ~ **return tomorrow** он вернётся зáвтра; ~, **you open the window?** открóйте окнó, пожáлуйста. **willing** adj готóвый; (eager) стáрательный. **willingly** adv охóтно. **willingness** n готóвность.

willow n ива.

willy-nilly adv вóлей-невóлей.

wilt vi поникáть impf, поникнуть pf.

wily adj хитрый.

win n побéда; vt & i выигрывать impf, выиграть pf; vt (obtain) добивáться impf, добиться pf +gen; ~ **over** угова́ривать impf, уговорить pf; (charm) располагáть impf, расположить pf к себé.

wince vi вздрáгивать impf, вздрóгнуть pf.

winch n лебёдка; поднимáть impf, поднять pf с пóмощью лебёдки.

wind[1] n (air) вéтер; (breath) дыхáние; (flatulence) вéтры m pl; ~ **instrument** духовóй инструмéнт; ~**swept** открытый ветрáм; **get** ~ **of** пронюхивать impf, пронюхать pf; vt (make gasp) заставля́ть impf, застáвить pf задохнýться.

wind[2] vi (meander) виться impf; извивáться impf; vt (coil) намáтывать impf, намотáть pf; (watch) заводить impf, завести pf; (wrap) укýтывать impf, укýтать pf; ~ **up** (vt) (reel) смáтывать impf, смотáть pf; (watch) see **wind**[2]; (vt & i) (end) кончáть(ся) impf, кóнчить(ся) pf. **winding** adj (meandering) извилистый; (staircase) винтовóй.

windfall n пáдалица; (fig) золотóй дождь.

windmill n ветряná мéльница.

window n окнó; (of shop) витрина; ~-**box** нарýжный ящик для цветóв; ~-**cleaner** мóйщик óкон; ~-**dressing** оформлéние витрин; (fig) показýха; ~-**frame** окóнная рáма; ~-**ledge** подокóнник; ~-**pane** окóнное стеклó; ~-**shopping** рассмáтривание витрин; ~-**sill** подокóнник.

windpipe n дыхáтельное гóрло. **windscreen** n ветровóе стеклó; ~ **wiper** двóрник. **windsurfer** n виндсéрфингист. **windsurfing** n виндсéрфинг. **windward** adj навéтренный. **windy** adj вéтреный.

wine n винó; ~ **bar** винный погребóк; ~ **bottle** винная бутылка; ~ **list** кáрта вин; ~-**tasting** дегустáция вин. **wineglass** n рюмка. **winery** n винный завóд. **winy** adj винный.

wing n (also polit) крылó; (archit) флигель m; (sport) фланг; pl (theat) кулисы f pl. **winged** adj крылáтый.

wink n (blink) моргáние; (as sign) подмигивание; vi мигáть impf, мигнýть pf; ~ **at** подмигивать impf, подмигнýть pf +dat; (fig) смотрéть impf, по~ pf сквозь пáльцы на+acc.

winkle vt: ~ **out** выкóвыривать impf, выковырять pf.

winner n победитель m, ~ница. **winning** adj (victorious) выигравший; (shot etc.) решáющий; (charming) обаятельный; n: pl выигрыш; ~-**post** финишный столб.

winter n зимá; attrib зимний. **wintry**

adj зи́мний; (*cold*) холо́дный.

wipe *vt* (*also* ~ *out inside of*) вытира́ть *impf*, вы́тереть *pf*; ~ **away**, **off** стира́ть *impf*, стере́ть *pf*; ~ **out** (*exterminate*) уничтожа́ть *impf*, уничто́жить *pf*; (*cancel*) смыва́ть *impf*, смыть *pf*.

wire *n* про́волока; (*carrying current*) про́вод; ~ **netting** про́волочная се́тка. **wireless** *n* ра́дио *neut indecl*. **wiring** *n* электропрово́дка. **wiry** *adj* жи́листый.

wisdom *n* му́дрость; ~ **tooth** зуб му́дрости. **wise** *adj* му́дрый; (*prudent*) благоразу́мный.

wish *n* жела́ние; **with best** ~**es** всего́ хоро́шего, с наилу́чшими пожела́ниями; *vt* хоте́ть *impf*, за~ *pf* (I ~ I **could see him** мне хоте́лось бы его́ ви́деть; I ~ **to go** я хочу́ пойти́; I ~ **you to come early** я хочу́, что́бы вы ра́но пришли́; I ~ **the day were over** хорошо́ бы день уже́ ко́нчился); жела́ть *impf* +*gen* (I ~ **you luck** жела́ю вам уда́чи); (*congratulate on*) поздравля́ть *impf*, поздра́вить *pf* (I ~ **you a happy birthday** поздравля́ю тебя́ с днём рожде́ния); *vi*: ~ **for** жела́ть *impf* +*gen*; мечта́ть *impf* o+*prep*. **wishful** *adj*: ~ **thinking** самообольще́ние; приня́тие жела́емого за действи́тельное.

wisp *n* (*of straw*) пучо́к; (*hair*) клочо́к; (*smoke*) стру́йка.

wisteria *n* глици́ния.

wistful *adj* тоскли́вый.

wit *n* (*mind*) ум; (*wittiness*) остроу́мие; (*person*) остря́к; **be at one's** ~**'s end** не знать *impf* что де́лать.

witch *n* ве́дьма; ~-**hunt** охо́та за ве́дьмами. **witchcraft** *n* колдовство́.

with *prep* (*in company of, together* ~) (вме́сте) c+*instr*; (*as a result of*) от+*gen*; (*at house of, in keeping of*) y+*gen*; (*by means of*) +*instr*; (*in spite of*) несмотря́ на+*acc*; (*including*) включа́я+*acc*; ~ **each/one another** друг с дру́гом.

withdraw *vt* (*retract*) брать *impf*, взять *pf* наза́д; (*hand*) отдёргивать *impf*, отдёрнуть *pf*; (*cancel*) снима́ть *impf*, снять *pf*; (*mil*) выводи́ть *impf*, вы́вести *pf*; (*money from circulation*) изыма́ть *impf*, изъя́ть из обраще́ния; (*diplomat etc.*) отзы-

ва́ть *impf*, отозва́ть *pf*; (*from bank*) брать *impf*, взять *pf*; *vi* удаля́ться *impf*, удали́ться *pf*; (*drop out*) выбыва́ть *impf*, вы́быть *pf*; (*mil*) отходи́ть *impf*, отойти́ *pf*. **withdrawal** *n* (*retraction*) взя́тие наза́д; (*cancellation*) сня́тие; (*mil*) отхо́д; (*money from circulation*) изъя́тие; (*departure*) ухо́д. **withdrawn** *adj* за́мкнутый.

wither *vi* вя́нуть *impf*, за~ *pf*. **withering** *adj* (*fig*) уничтожа́ющий.

withhold *vt* (*refuse to grant*) не дава́ть *impf*, дать *pf* +*gen*; (*payment*) уде́рживать *impf*, удержа́ть *pf*; (*information*) ута́ивать *impf*, утаи́ть *pf*.

within *prep* (*inside*) внутри́+*gen*, в+*prep*; (~ *the limits of*) в преде́лах +*gen*; (*time*) в тече́ние +*gen*; *adv* внутри́; **from** ~ изнутри́.

without *prep* без+*gen*; ~ **saying goodbye** не проща́ясь; **do** ~ обходи́ться *impf*, обойти́сь *pf* без+*gen*.

withstand *vt* выде́рживать *impf*, вы́держать *pf*.

witness *n* (*person*) свиде́тель *m*; (*eye*~) очеви́дец; (*to signature etc.*) завери́тель *m*; **bear** ~ **to** свиде́тельствовать *impf*, за~ *pf*; ~-**box** ме́сто для свиде́тельских показа́ний; *vt* быть свиде́телем+*gen*; (*document etc.*) заверя́ть *impf*, заве́рить *pf*.

witticism *n* остро́та. **witty** *adj* остроу́мный.

wizard *n* волше́бник, колду́н.

wizened *adj* морщи́нистый.

wobble *vt & i* шата́ть(ся) *impf*, шатну́ть(ся) *pf*; *vi* (*voice*) дрожа́ть *impf*. **wobbly** *adj* ша́ткий.

woe *n* го́ре; ~ **is me!** го́ре мне! **woeful** *adj* жа́лкий.

wolf *n* волк; *vt* пожира́ть *impf*, пожра́ть *pf*.

woman *n* же́нщина. **womanizer** *n* воло́кита. **womanly** *adj* же́нственный. **womb** *n* ма́тка.

wonder *n* чу́до; (*amazement*) изумле́ние; (**it's) no** ~ неудиви́тельно; *vt* интересова́ться *impf* (I ~ **who will come** интере́сно, кто придёт); *vi*: I **shouldn't** ~ **if** неудиви́тельно бу́дет, е́сли; I ~ **if you could help me** не могли́ бы вы мне помо́чь? ~ **at** удивля́ться *impf*, удиви́ться *pf* +*dat*. **wonderful, wondrous** *adj* замеча́тельный.

wont *n*: **as is his** ~ по своему обыкновению; *predic*: **be** ~ **to** иметь привычку+*inf*.

woo *vt* ухаживать *impf* за+*instr*.

wood *n* (*forest*) лес; (*material*) дерево; (*firewood*) дрова *pl*. **woodcut** *n* гравюра на дереве. **wooded** *adj* лесистый. **wooden** *adj* (*also fig*) деревянный. **woodland** *n* лесистая местность; *attrib* лесной. **woodpecker** *n* дятел. **woodwind** *n* деревянные духовые инструменты *m pl*. **woodwork** *n* столярная работа; (*wooden parts*) деревянные части (-тей) *pl*. **woodworm** *n* жучок. **woody** *adj* (*plant etc*) (с) деревянистый; (*wooded*) лесистый.

wool *n* шерсть. **woollen** *adj* шерстяной. **woolly** *adj* шерстистый; (*indistinct*) неясный.

word *n* слово; (*news*) известие; **by** ~ **of mouth** устно; **have a** ~ **with** поговорить *pf* с+*instr*; **in a** ~ одним словом; **in other** ~s другими словами; ~ **for** слово в слово; ~ **processor** компьютер(-издатель) *m*; *vt* выражать *impf*, выразить *pf*; формулировать *impf*, с~ *pf*. **wording** *n* формулировка.

work *n* работа; (*labour; toil; scholarly* ~) труд; (*occupation*) занятие; (*studies*) занятия neut pl; (*of art*) произведение; (*book*) сочинение; *pl* (*factory*) завод; (*mechanism*) механизм; **at** ~(*doing*~) за работой; (*at place of* ~) на работе; **out of** ~безработный; ~**force** рабочая сила; ~**load** нагрузка; *vi* (*also function*) работать *impf* (**at, on** над+*instr*); (*study*) заниматься *impf*, заняться *pf*; (*also toil, labour*) трудиться *impf*; (*have effect, function*) действовать *impf*; (*succeed*) удаваться *impf*, удаться *pf*; *vt* (*operate*) управлять *impf* +*instr*; обращаться *impf* с+*instr*; (*wonders*) творить *impf*, со~ *pf*; (*soil*) обрабатывать *impf*, обработать *pf*; (*compel to* ~) заставлять *impf*, заставить *pf* работать; ~ **in**вставлять *impf*, вставить *pf*; ~ **off** (*debt*) отрабатывать *impf*, отработать *pf*; (*weight*) сгонять *impf*, согнать *pf*; (*energy*) давать *impf*, дать *pf* выход +*dat*; ~ **out** (*solve*) находить *impf*, найти *pf* решение +*gen*; (*plans etc*.)

разрабатывать *impf*, разработать *pf*; (*sport*) тренироваться *impf*; **everything** ~**ed out well** всё кончилось хорошо; ~ **out at** (*amount to*) составлять *impf*, составить *pf*; ~ **up** (*perfect*) вырабатывать *impf*, выработать *pf*; (*excite*) возбуждать *impf*, возбудить *pf*; (*appetite*) нагуливать *impf*, нагулять *pf*. **workable** *adj* осуществимый, реальный. **workaday** *adj* будничный. **workaholic** *n* труженик. **worker** *n* работник; (*manual*) рабочий *sb*. **working** *adj*: ~ **class** рабочий класс; ~ **hours** рабочее время neut; ~ **party** комиссия. **workman** *n* работник. **workmanlike** *adj* искусный. **workmanship** *n* искусство, мастерство. **workshop** *n* мастерская *sb*.

world *n* мир, свет; *attrib* мировой; ~**-famous** всемирно известный; ~**war** мировая война; ~**-wide** всемирный. **worldly** *adj* мирской; (*person*) опытный.

worm *n* червь *m*; (*intestinal*) глист; *vt*: ~ **o.s. into** вкрадываться *impf*, вкрасться *pf* в+*acc*; ~ **out** выведывать *impf*, выведать *pf* (**of** y+*gen*); ~ **one's way** пробираться *impf*, пробраться *pf*.

worry *n* (*anxiety*) беспокойство; (*care*) забота; *vt* беспокоить *impf*, о~ *pf* (**about** o+*prep*); *vi* беспокоиться *impf*, о~ *pf* (**about** o+*prep*).

worse *adj* худший; *adv* хуже; *n*: **from bad to** ~всё хуже и хуже. **worsen** *vt & i* ухудшать(ся) *impf*, ухудшить(ся) *pf*.

worship *n* поклонение (**of**+*dat*); (*service*) богослужение; *vt* поклоняться *impf* +*dat*; (*adore*) обожать *impf*. **worshipper** *n* поклонник, -ица.

worst *adj* наихудший, самый плохой; *adv* хуже всего; *n* самое плохое.

worth *n* (*value*) цена, ценность; (*merit*) достоинство; **give me a pound's** ~ **of petrol** дайте мне бензина на фунт; *adj*: **be** ~ (*of equal value to*) стоить *impf* (**what is it** ~? сколько это стоит?); (*deserve*) стоить *impf* +*gen* (**is this film** ~ **seeing?** стоит посмотреть этот фильм?). **worthless** *adj* ничего не стоящий; (*useless*) бесполезный. **worthwhile** *adj* стоящий. **worthy** *adj* достойный.

would v aux (conditional): he ~ be angry if he found out он бы рассердился, если бы узнал; (expressing wish) she ~ like to know она бы хотела знать; I ~ rather я бы предпочёл; (expressing indirect speech): he said he ~ be late он сказал, что придёт поздно.

would-be adj: ~ actor человек мечтающий стать актёром.

wound n рана; vt ранить impf & pf.
wounded adj раненый.

wrangle n пререкание; vi пререкаться impf.

wrap n (shawl) шаль; vt (also ~ up) завёртывать impf, завернуть pf; ~ up (in wraps) закутывать(ся) impf, закутать(ся) pf; ~ped up in (fig) поглощённый +instr. **wrapper** n обёртка. **wrapping** n обёртка; ~ paper обёрточная бумага.

wrath n гнев.

wreak vt: ~ havoc on разорять impf, разорить pf.

wreath n венок.

wreck n (ship) останки (-ов) корабля; (vehicle, person, building, etc.) развалина; vt (destroy, also fig) разрушать impf, разрушить pf; be ~ed терпеть impf, по~ pf крушение; (of plans etc.) рухнуть pf. **wreckage** n обломки m pl крушения.

wren n крапивник.

wrench n (jerk) дёрганье; (tech) гаечный ключ; (fig) боль; vt (snatch, pull out) вырывать impf, вырвать pf (from y+gen); ~ open взламывать impf, взломать pf.

wrest vt (wrench) вырывать impf, вырвать pf (from y+gen).

wrestle vi бороться impf. **wrestler** n борец. **wrestling** n борьба.

wretch n несчастный sb; (scoundrel) негодяй. **wretched** adj жалкий; (unpleasant) скверный.

wriggle vi извиваться impf, извиться pf; (fidget) ёрзать impf; ~ out of увиливать impf, увильнуть от+gen.

wring vt (also ~ out) выжимать impf, выжать pf; (extort) исторгать impf, исторгнуть pf (from y+gen); (neck) свёртывать impf, свернуть pf (+dat); ~ one's hands ломать impf, с~ pf руки.

wrinkle n морщина; vt & i морщить-

(ся) impf, с~ pf.

wrist n запястье; ~-watch наручные часы (-сов) pl.

writ n повестка.

write vt & i писать impf, на~ pf; ~ down записывать impf, записать pf; ~ off (cancel) списывать impf, списать pf; the car was a ~-off машина была совершенно испорчена; ~ out выписывать impf, выписать pf (in full полностью); ~ up (account of) подробно описывать impf, описать pf; (notes) переписывать impf, переписать pf; ~-up (report) отчёт. **writer** n писатель m, ~ница.

writhe vi корчиться impf, с~ pf.

writing n (handwriting) почерк; (work) произведение; in ~ в письменной форме; ~-paper почтовая бумага.

wrong adj (incorrect) неправильный, неверный; (the wrong …) не тот (I have bought the ~ book я купил не ту книгу; you've got the ~ number (tel) вы не туда попали); (mistaken) неправый (you are ~ ты неправ); (unjust) несправедливый; (sinful) дурной; (out of order) неладный; (side of cloth) левый; ~ side out наизнанку; ~ way round наоборот; n зло; (injustice) несправедливость; be in the ~ быть неправым; do ~ грешить impf, со~ pf; adv неправильно, неверно; go ~ не получаться impf, получиться pf; vt обижать impf, обидеть pf; (be unjust to) быть несправедливым к+dat. **wrongdoer** n преступник, грешник, -ица. **wrongful** adj несправедливый. **wrongly** adv неправильно; (unjustly) несправедливо.

wrought adj: ~ iron сварочное железо.

wry adj (smile) кривой; (humour) сухой, иронический.

X

xenophobia n ксенофобия.

X-ray n (picture) рентген(овский снимок); pl (radiation) рентгеновы лучи m pl; vt (photograph) делать impf, с~ pf рентген +gen.

Y

yacht n я́хта. **yachting** n па́русный спорт. **yachtsman** n яхтсме́н.

yank vt рвану́ть pf.

yap vi тя́вкать impf, тя́вкнуть pf.

yard[1] n (piece of ground) двор.

yard[2] n (measure) ярд. **yardstick** n (fig) мери́ло.

yarn n пря́жа; (story) расска́з.

yawn n зево́к; vi зева́ть impf, зевну́ть pf; (chasm etc.) зия́ть impf.

year n год; ~ **in**, ~ **out** из го́да в год.

yearbook n ежего́дник. **yearly** adj ежего́дный, годово́й; adv ежего́дно.

yearn vi тоскова́ть impf (for по+dat). **yearning** n тоска́ (for по+dat).

yeast n дро́жжи (-же́й) pl.

yell n крик; vi крича́ть impf, кри́кнуть pf.

yellow adj жёлтый; n жёлтый цвет. **yellowish** adj желтова́тый.

yelp n визг; vi визжа́ть impf, ви́згнуть pf.

yes adv да; n утвержде́ние, согла́сие; (in vote) го́лос «за».

yesterday adv вчера́; n вчера́шний день m; ~ **morning** вчера́ у́тром; **the day before** ~ позавчера́; ~'s **newspaper** вчера́шняя газе́та.

yet adv (still) ещё; (so far) до сих пор; (in questions) уже́; (nevertheless) тем не ме́нее; **as** ~ пока́, до сих пор; **not** ~ ещё не; conj одна́ко, но.

yew n тис.

Yiddish n и́диш.

yield n (harvest) урожа́й; (econ) дохо́д; vt (fruit, revenue, etc.) приноси́ть impf, принести́ pf; дава́ть impf, дать pf; (give up) сдава́ть impf, сдать pf; vi (give in) (to enemy etc.) уступа́ть impf, уступи́ть pf (to +dat); (give way) поддава́ться impf, подда́ться pf (to +dat).

yoga n йо́га.

yoghurt n кефи́р.

yoke n (also fig) ярмо́; (fig) и́го; (of dress) коке́тка; vt впряга́ть impf, впрячь pf в ярмо́.

yolk n желто́к.

yonder adv вон там; adj вон тот.

you pron (familiar sg) ты; (familiar pl, polite sg & pl) вы; (one) not usu translated; v translated in 2nd pers sg or by impers construction; ~ **never know** никогда́ не зна́ешь.

young adj молодо́й; **the** ~ молодёжь; n (collect) детёныши m pl.

youngster n ма́льчик, де́вочка.

your(s) poss pron (familiar sg; also in letter) твой; (familiar pl, polite sg & pl; also in letter) ваш; свой. **yourself** pron (emph) (familiar sg) (ты) сам (m), сама́ (f); (familiar pl, polite sg & pl) (вы) са́ми; (refl) себя́; -ся (suffixed to vt); **by** ~ (independently) самостоя́тельно, сам; (alone) оди́н.

youth n (age) мо́лодость; (young man) ю́ноша m; (collect, as pl) молодёжь; ~ **club** молодёжный клуб; ~ **hostel** молодёжная турба́за. **youthful** adj ю́ношеский.

Yugoslavia n Югосла́вия.

Z

zany adj смешно́й.

zeal n рве́ние, усе́рдие. **zealot** n фана́тик. **zealous** adj ре́вностный, усе́рдный.

zebra n зе́бра.

zenith n зени́т.

zero n нуль m, ноль m.

zest n (piquancy) пика́нтность; (ardour) энтузиа́зм; ~ **for life** жизнера́достность.

zigzag n зигза́г; adj зигзагообра́зный; vi де́лать impf, с~ pf зигза́ги; идти́ det зигза́гами.

zinc n цинк.

Zionism n сиони́зм. **Zionist** n сиони́ст.

zip n (~ fastener) (застёжка-)мо́лния; vt & i: ~ **up** застёгивать(ся) impf, застегну́ть(ся) pf на мо́лнию.

zodiac n зодиа́к; **sign of the** ~ знак зодиа́ка.

zombie n челове́к спя́щий на ходу́.

zone n зо́на; (geog) по́яс.

zoo n зоопа́рк. **zoological** adj зоологи́ческий; ~ **garden(s)** зоологи́ческий сад. **zoologist** n зоо́лог. **zoology** n зооло́гия.

zoom vi (rush) мча́ться impf; ~ **in** (phot) де́лать impf, с~ pf наплы́в; ~ **lens** объекти́в с переме́нным фо́кусным расстоя́нием.

Zulu adj зулу́сский; n зулу́с, ~ка.

Appendix I **Spelling Rules**

It is assumed that the user is acquainted with the following spelling rules which affect Russian declension and conjugation.

1. **ы, ю,** and **я** do not follow **г, к, х, ж, ч, ш,** and **щ;** instead, **и, у,** and **а** are used, e.g. **ма́льчики, кричу́, лежа́т, ноча́ми;** similarly, **ю** and **я** do not follow **ц;** instead, **у** or **а** are used.

2. Unstressed **о** does not follow **ж, ц, ч, ш,** or **щ;** instead, **е** is used, e.g. **му́жем, ме́сяцев, хоро́шее.**

Appendix II **Declension of Russian Nouns**

The following patterns are regarded as regular and are not shown in the dictionary entries. Forms marked * should be particularly noted.

1 *Masculine*

Singular	nom	acc	gen	dat	instr	prep
	обе́д	~	~а	~у	~ом	~е
	слу́ча|й	~й	~я	~ю	~ем	~е
	марш	~	~а	~у	~ем	~е
	каранда́ш	~	~а́	~у́	~о́м*	~е́
	сцена́ри|й	~й	~я	~ю	~ем	~и*
	портфе́л|ь	~ь	~я	~ю	~ем	~е

Plural	nom	acc	gen	dat	instr	prep
	обе́д|ы	~ы	~ов	~ам	~ами	~ах
	слу́ча|и	~и	~ев	~ям	~ями	~ях
	ма́рш|и	~и	~ей*	~ам	~ами	~ах
	карандаш|и́	~и́	~е́й*	~а́м	~а́ми	~а́х
	сцена́ри|и	~и	~ев*	~ям	~ями	~ях
	портфе́л|и	~и	~ей*	~ям	~ями	~ях

2 *Feminine*

Singular	nom	acc	gen	dat	instr	prep
	газе́т|а	~у	~ы	~е	~ой	~е
	ба́н|я	~ю	~и	~е	~ей	~е
	ли́ни|я	~ю	~и	~и*	~ей	~и*
	ста́ту|я	~ю	~и	~е*	~ей	~е*
	бол|ь	~ь	~и	~и*	~ью*	~и*

Plural	nom	acc	gen	dat	instr	prep
газе́т|ы		~ы	~	~ам	~ами	~ах
ба́н|и		~и	~ь*	~ям	~ями	~ях
ли́ни|и		~и	~й*	~ям	~ями	~ях
ста́ту|и		~и	~й*	~ям	~ями	~ях
бо́л|и		~и	~ей*	~ям	~ями	~ях

3 Neuter

Singular	nom	acc	gen	dat	instr	prep
чу́вств|о		~о	~а	~у	~ом	~е
учи́лищ|е		~е	~а	~у	~ем	~е
зда́ни|е		~е	~я	~ю	~ем	~и*
ущел|ье		~ье	~ья	~ью	~ьем	~ье

Plural	nom	acc	gen	dat	instr	prep
чу́вств|а		~а	~	~ам	~ами	~ах
учи́лищ|а		~а	~	~ам	~ами	~ах
зда́ни|я		~я	~й*	~ям	~ями	~ях
ущел|ья		~ья	~ий*	~ьям	~ьями	~ьях

Appendix III Declension of Russian Adjectives

The following patterns are regarded as regular and are not shown in the dictionary entries.

Singular	nom	acc	gen	dat	instr	prep
Masculine тёпл|ый		~ый	~ого	~ому	~ым	~ом
Feminine тёпл|ая		~ую	~ой	~ой	~ой	~ой
Neuter тёпл|ое		~ое	~ого	~ому	~ым	~ом

Plural	nom	acc	gen	dat	instr	prep
Masculine тёпл|ые		~ые	~ых	~ым	~ыми	~ых
Feminine тёпл|ые		~ые	~ых	~ым	~ыми	~ых
Neuter тёпл|ые		~ые	~ых	~ым	~ыми	~ых

Appendix IV Conjugation of Russian Verbs

The following patterns are regarded as regular and are not shown in the dictionary entries.

1. **-e-** conjugation

(a) **чита́|ть**	~ю	~ешь	~ет	~ем	~ете	~ют
(b) **сия́|ть**	~ю	~ешь	~ет	~ем	~ете	~ют
(c) **про́б|овать**	~ую	~уешь	~ует	~уем	~уете	~уют
(d) **рис|ова́ть**	~у́ю	~у́ешь	~у́ет	~у́ем	~у́ете	~у́ют

2. **-и-** conjugation

(a) **говор|и́ть**	~ю́	~и́шь	~и́т	~и́м	~и́те	~я́т
(b) **стро́|ить**	~ю	~ишь	~ит	~им	~ите	~ят

Notes

1. Also belonging to the **-e-** conjugation are:

i) most other verbs in **-ать** (but see Note 2(v) below), e.g. **жа́ждать** (жа́жду, -ждешь); **пря́тать** (пря́чу, -чешь), **колеба́ть** (коле́блю, -блешь).

ii) verbs in **-еть** for which the 1st pers sing **-ею** is given, e.g. **жале́ть.**

iii) verbs in **-нуть** for which the 1st pers sing **-ну** is given (e.g. **вя́нуть**), ю becoming у in the 1st pers sing and 3rd pers pl.

iv) verbs in **-ять** which drop the я in conjugation, e.g. **ла́ять** (ла́ю, ла́ешь); **се́ять** (се́ю, се́ешь).

2. Also belonging to the **-и-** conjugation are:

i) verbs in consonant + **-ить** which change the consonant in the first person singular, e.g. **досади́ть** (-ажу́, -ади́шь), or insert an **-л-**, e.g. **доба́вить** (доба́влю, -вишь).

ii) other verbs in vowel + **-ить**, e.g. **затаи́ть, кле́ить** (as 2b above).

iii) verbs in **-еть** for which the 1st pers sing is given as consonant + **ю** or **у**, e.g. **звене́ть** (-ню́, -ни́шь), **ви́деть** (ви́жу, ви́дишь).

iv) two verbs in **-ять (стоя́ть, боя́ться).**

v) verbs in **-ать** whose stem ends in **ч, ж, щ,** or **ш,** not changing between the infinitive and conjugation, e.g. **крича́ть** (-чу́, -чи́шь). Cf. Note 1(i).

Key to the Russian Alphabet

Capital	Lower-case	Approximate English Sound
А	а	a
Б	б	b
В	в	v
Г	г	g
Д	д	d
Е	е	ye
Ё	ё	yo
Ж	ж	zh (as in mea*s*ure)
З	з	z
И	и	i
Й	й	y
К	к	k
Л	л	l
М	м	m
Н	н	n
О	о	o
П	п	p
Р	р	r
С	с	s
Т	т	t
У	у	oo
Ф	ф	f
Х	х	kh (as in lo*ch*)
Ц	ц	ts
Ч	ч	ch
Ш	ш	sh
Щ	щ	shch
Ъ	ъ	˝ ("hard sign"; not pronounced as separate sound)
Ы	ы	y
Ь	ь	´ ("soft sign"; not pronounced as separate sound)
Э	э	e
Ю	ю	yu
Я	я	ya